Facts at your Fingertips

Facts
Finger

PUBLISHED BY
THE READER'S DIGEST ASSOCIATION LIMITED
LONDON · NEW YORK · SYDNEY · MONTREAL

at your tips

Contents

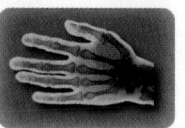

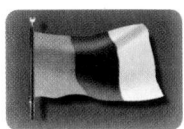

Contents

The modern world is awash with information. Some of this information is false, some of it mistaken, much of it useless or ephemeral. So how can anybody know what is worth knowing? And if there is some fact about the world you need to find out in a hurry, how can you be sure that the source is sound and the facts correct?

maps

infographics

Facts at your Fingertips is the answer. It is a distillation of all the most asked and most useful facts about the world. It is a book that smelts the pure gold of real knowledge from mountains of informational slag. It is the sensible first port of call before you turn on your computer or go down to the library, because nine times out of ten it will save you the trouble.

What is a fact? There is more than one kind of fact in the world, and this is reflected in the book. Some facts are measurable, like the height of Everest (page 50); some are grounded in historical evidence, like the dates of office of Robert Walpole (page 596); some are scientifically provable, like the formula for calculating the volume of a cylinder (page 519); some are matters of accepted scholarship, like the reasons for the fall of the Roman Empire (page 175).

timelines

Tannenberg
Two Russian armies are routed by a small German force.

First Marne
German forces are driven back from Paris.

Masurian Lakes
The Russians are heavily defeated.

First Ypres
British troops hold off the German advance in Flanders.

Second Ypres
Germany uses poison gas.

Isonzo Front
Italy's offensives against Austria-Hungary make minimal gains.

Verdun
Germany attempts to 'bleed France white' in a battle of attrition.

1914

30 AUG 1914

5-12 SEP 1914

15 SEP 1914

30 OCT 1914

1915

22 APR 1915

23 JUN 1915

1916

21 FEB 1916

June 28 Archduke Franz Ferdinand is assassinated; Austria-Hungary declares war on Serbia.

Aug 1 Germany declares war on Russia;
Aug 3 Germany declares war on France;
Aug 4 Germany invades Belgium; Great Britain declares war on Germany.

Feb 19 The first Zeppelin raid hits England.

April 25 Allied troops land at Gallipoli.

May 7 *Lusitania* is sunk by a U-boat off Ireland.

Dec 7 Turks trap British at Kut in Mesopotamia.
Dec 19 Allied troops evacuate the Dardanelles.

April 29 The Anglo-Indian garrison surrenders at Kut.

diagrams

In **Facts at your Fingertips**, you will often find a mix of all the different species of fact on the same page. Take the Second World War on pages 214-15. Here you will find a chronology of events, biographies of the war leaders, an explanation of the key theatres of war, and figures which give the mournful death toll of the Holocaust.

Most pages are heavily illustrated, because maps, diagrams, timelines, drawings and photographs are often the best way of presenting facts. A picture of DNA's double helix (pages 150-1) means more than words; a 'wealth map' of the world gets the point across more effectively than a list of rich and poor

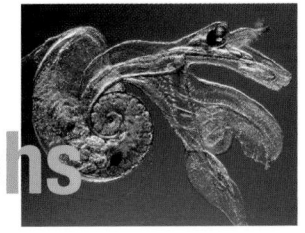

photographs

countries (pages 462-3); and a contemporary portrait of Louis XIV (page 199) tells you not only what he looked like, but also about how he saw himself and his place in history.

There are other pages in **Facts at your Fingertips** which consist entirely of lists, because sometimes the bare statistics are all you need to know: American presidents with their dates of office (page 602), all the laureates of the Nobel prize for literature (page 584), all the happy winners of the Eurovision Song Contest (page 583).

statistics

1936	Harold L. Davis, *Honey in the Horn*
1937	Margaret Mitchell, *Gone With the Wind*
1938	John Phillips Marqu[...], *The Late George*
1939	Marjorie Kinnan Ra[...], *The Yearling*
1940	John Steinbeck, *The Grapes of Wra[...]*
1941	No award
1942	Ellen Glasgow, *In T[...]*

Understanding the structure of **Facts at your Fingertips** is the first step to getting the most out of it. There are nine chapters, each of which covers a different area of knowledge.

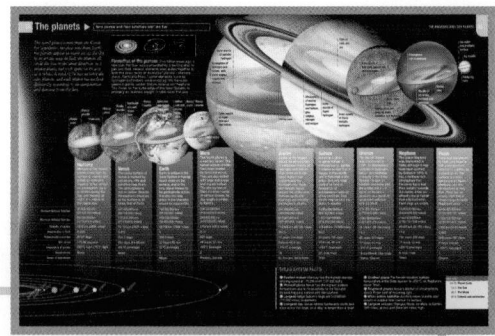

The Universe and our planet looks at the birth and growth of the Cosmos, the formation of the Earth and its geographical character.

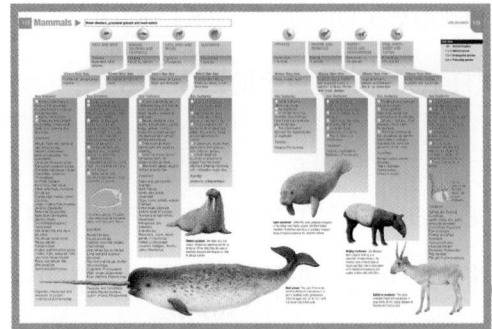

Life on Earth focuses on the origins of plants and animals. It traces the development of life and looks at the vast variety of modern life forms and their classification.

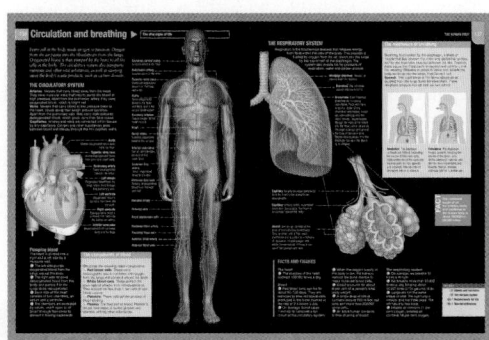

The human body focuses on our own highly successful species, and examines in detail how our bodies function, how they can go wrong, what they are physically capable of.

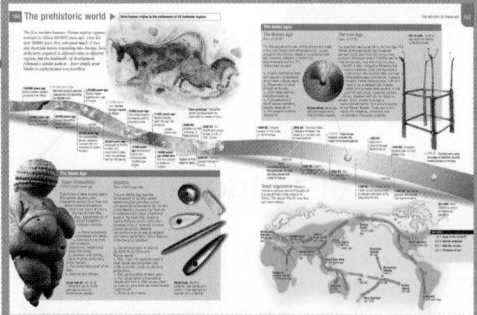

The history of mankind chronicles what we know about our own past, from the first glimmer of recorded history to the most recent historic events.

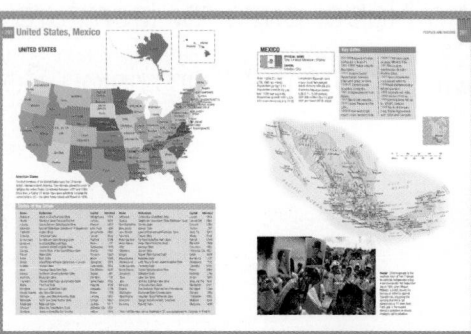

Peoples and nations is an inventory of the present-day geopolitical scene: there are facts and figures for every country in the world, along with an overview of global and international bodies.

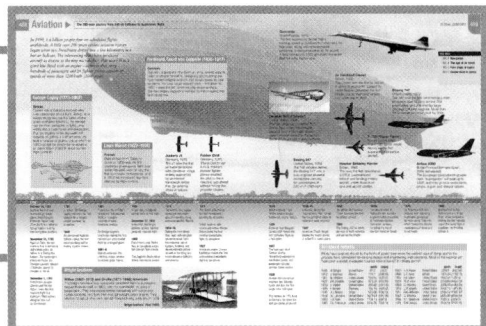

The global economy looks at the world's natural resources, finance, trade, agriculture, transport, communications.

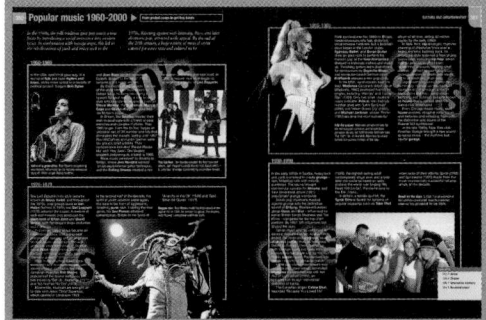

Culture and entertainment deals with all the achievements of the human spirit and intellect: religion, philosophy, psychology, literature, art, music, sport, cinema.

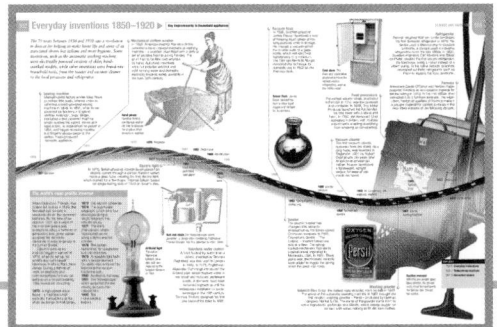

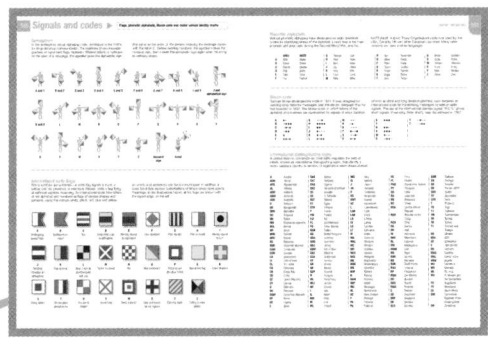

Science and invention gives the facts about technology, medicine and the pure sciences.

Ready reference provides useful lists, statistics and conversion tables.

Cross-referencing panels on the right-hand edge of the page tell you about the pages connected to the one you are looking at, and let you explore the factual network which lies beneath the surface of the book.

Go to **Facts at your Fingertips** whenever you have a factual question of any kind. Once you have picked it off the shelf, the answer is already within your grasp.

The Universe and our planet

The Universe and our planet

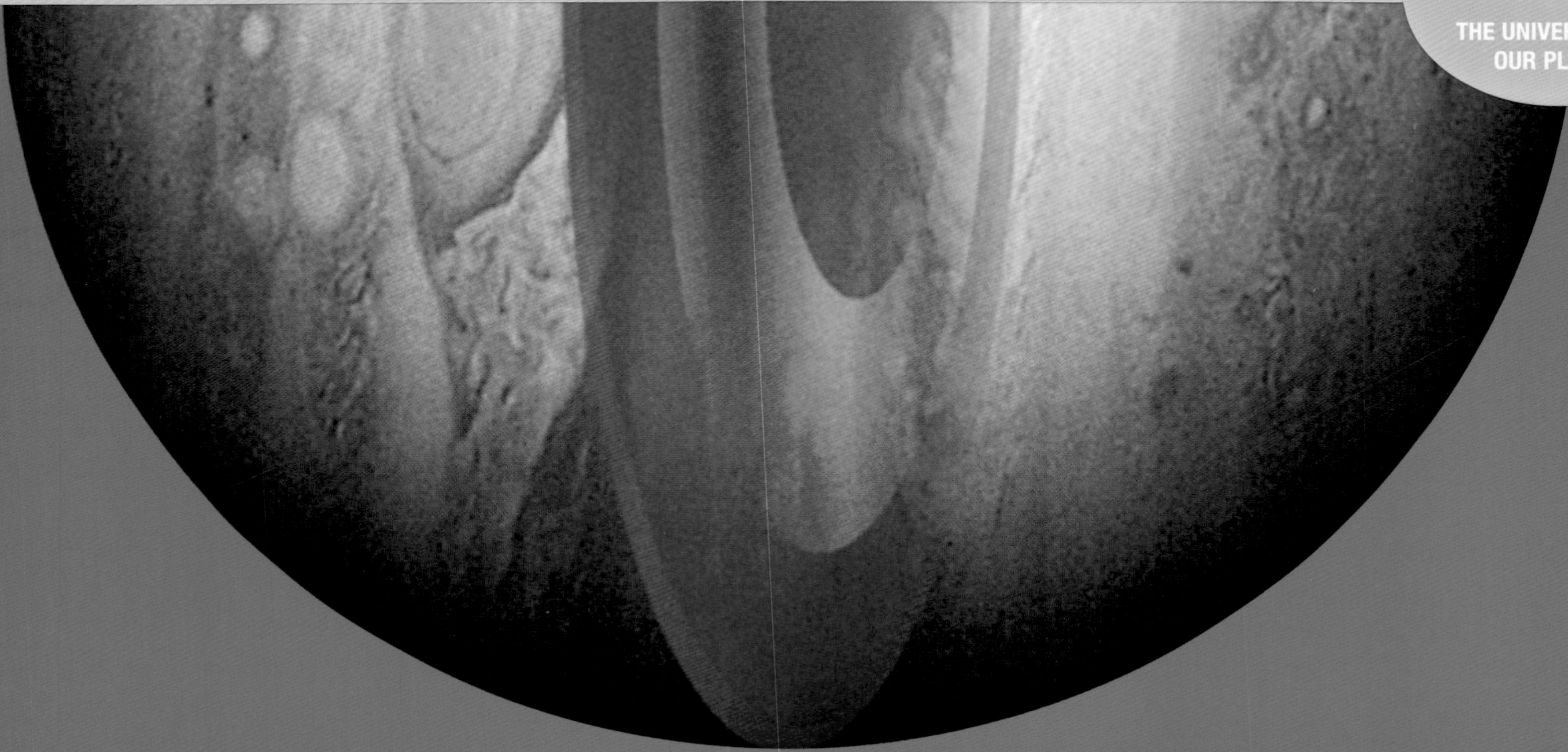

THE UNIVERSE AND
OUR PLANET

The universe
and our planet

Planet Earth ▶

The Earth was created from an immense cloud of dust particles and gas circling a newly formed star – our Sun. It became the fifth-largest planet in the Solar System and, as far as we know, the only body in the Solar System to support life. The Earth orbits the Sun and rotates on its own tilted axis, producing the cycles of seasons and day and night.

THE FORMATION OF OUR WORLD

The Earth was formed in stages over billions of years. Since its creation it has been in a constant state of flux. Its temperature, atmosphere and geography have all altered dramatically, and it continues to change.

1 A cold, dark beginning The Earth and other planets were created 4.6 billion years ago from a cloud of gas and dust swirling around the embryonic Sun. The Earth formed as particles of the dust collided and merged. The Sun was much smaller and dimmer than it is today, and the early Solar System was dark and cold.

Earth statistics

Total surface area	509 600 000 km^2 (197 000 000 sq miles)
Land area	29 per cent, 148 000 000 km^2 (57 000 000 sq miles)
Speed of rotation	1674 km/h (1040 mph)
Orbit speed around the Sun	107 180 km/h (66 600 mph)
Inclination of axis	23.44 degrees

2 Melting pot From 4.6 to 4.2 billion years ago, gravity compacted the Earth's interior, and decomposing radioactive elements caused it to melt. Iron sank to form the core, leaving lighter materials to make up the mantle.

EFFECTS OF THE EARTH'S POSITION, TILT AND ROTATION

The most obvious effect of the Earth's movements is the cycle of day and night, but its tilt and position also account for day length and seasons.

The seasons Earth's axis of rotation tilts at about 23 degrees from the vertical. This means that during the northern summer (southern winter), the Northern Hemisphere is tilted towards the Sun and the Southern Hemisphere away from it. This is enough to account for the temperature differences we see between summer and winter. In the northern winter (southern summer) the position is reversed. During summer, the Sun rises higher in the sky than in winter and the time from sunrise to sunset (a solar day) is longer.

Day and night The Earth rotates on its axis roughly once every 24 hours as it orbits the Sun. Because it tilts as it orbits, days and nights are unequal in length, except at the spring and autumn equinoxes.

Equinoxes There are two days each year when the Earth's axis passes through the upright position and neither the Northern nor Southern Hemispheres are inclined towards the Sun. On these days, night and day are of equal length all over the world. They occur around March 21 (vernal equinox) and September 22 (autumnal equinox).

Solstices These are the longest and shortest days in the year, that is, the day with the greatest amount of daylight and the day with the least daylight. In the Northern Hemisphere the summer solstice is on or around June 21 and the winter solstice is on or around December 21. The opposite is true in the Southern Hemisphere.

Climate zones Latitudes round the Equator are at roughly the same distance from the Sun throughout the year and therefore experience little temperature variation. Because the Earth tilts, variation in temperature increases with latitude, and the poles experience the greatest contrast, having 24 hours of sunlight daily at the height of summer and 24 hours of darkness in midwinter. This is a major determining factor of climatic zones. Tropical and subtropical climates round the Equator are uniformly warm; the temperate climates of higher latitudes have greater seasonal variation, and the far north and south experience extreme winter cold.

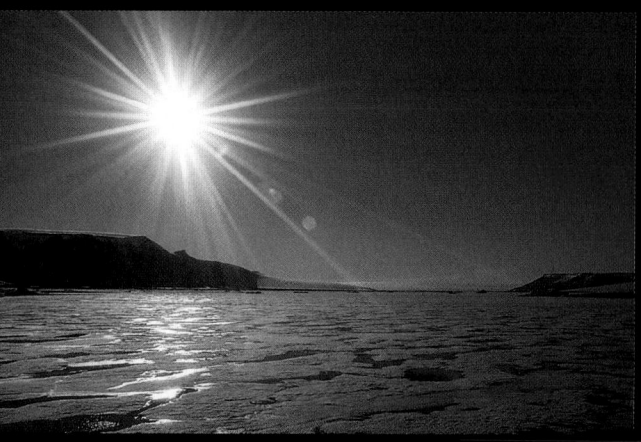

Midnight sun The Sun does not dip below the horizon in midsummer at the poles so there is daylight throughout the night.

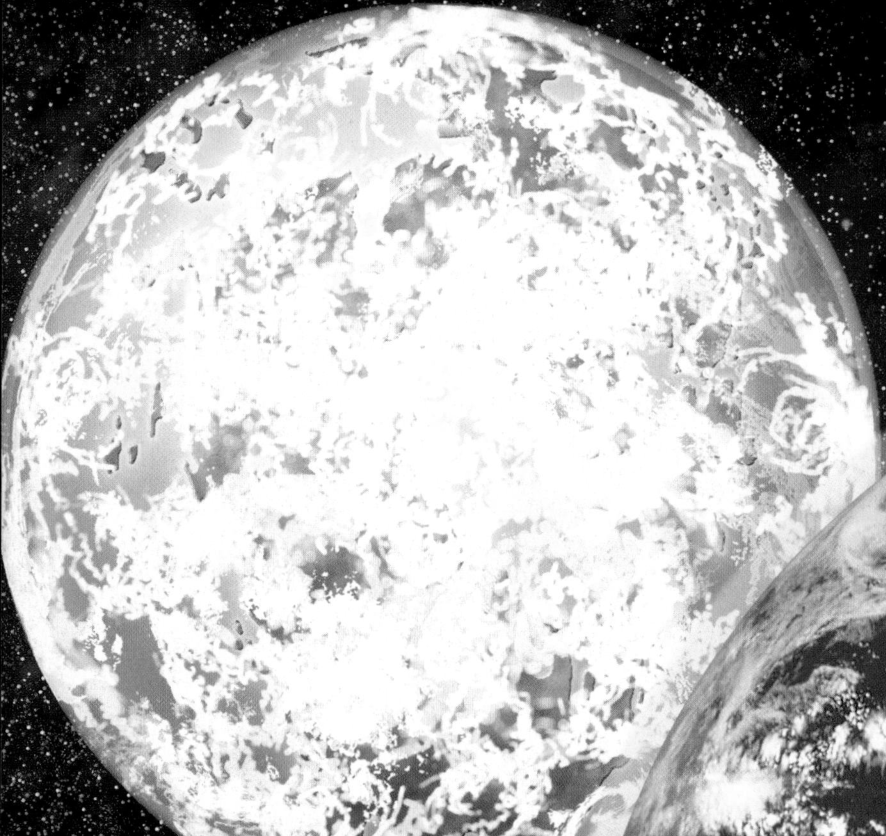

4 Towards the modern world As the oxygen in the atmosphere built up, a protective layer of ozone formed, blocking ultraviolet radiation from the Sun and making the surface waters of the oceans safe for complex organisms to evolve. By 400 million years ago, the colonisation of land by plants and animals was well under way and the planet was beginning to resemble the Earth we know today.

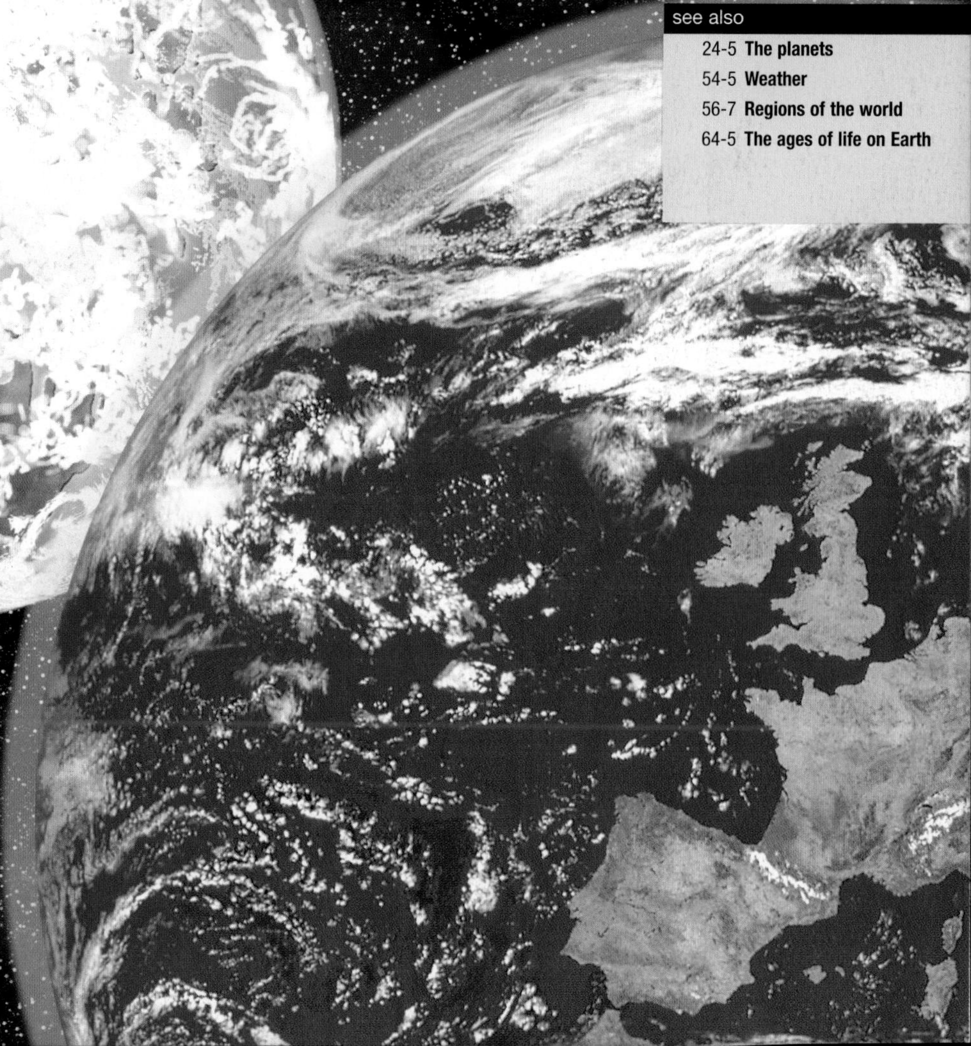

see also
24-5 **The planets**
54-5 **Weather**
56-7 **Regions of the world**
64-5 **The ages of life on Earth**

3 The surface cools Between 4.2 and 3.8 billion years ago, the Earth's surface cooled and the crust formed. Bombardment by icy comets provided water which, supplemented by water vapour that billowed out from volcanoes, slowly filled the seas. As this period ended, bombardment ceased and the first life appeared in the seas. Cyanobacteria used the Sun's energy and carbon dioxide to produce food and expelled oxygen as a waste product, which gradually accumulated in the young atmosphere.

Fifteen billion years ago our Universe did not exist. It came into being in a cosmic explosion, the Big Bang, expanding from nothing to 2 billion billion km (1.25 billion billion miles) wide in a single second, and it is still expanding today. At present, scientists can only speculate about why the Big Bang occurred, but we are beginning to understand what happened in the first few moments.

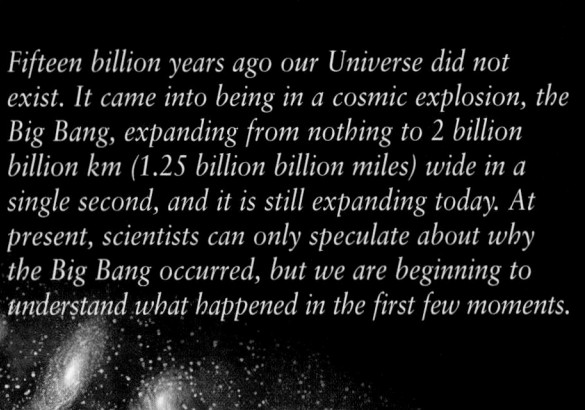

1 **The Local Group** There are billions of galaxies in the Universe, each containing billions of stars. Typically, galaxies cluster together. Our Galaxy is one of about 30 in a cluster known as the Local Group. One of the nearest galaxies to ours is Andromeda, 2.2 light years away.

EARLY EVOLUTION OF THE UNIVERSE

Within a second after the Big Bang, the building blocks of all matter were created, but it took a further 2 billion years before the first stars and galaxies started to form.

After 1 millionth of a trillionth of a trillionth of a second (10^{-43} secs) The temperature of the infant Universe is 100 000 billion billion billion°C. The Universe expands rapidly and fills with radiation, mostly in the form of light and heat. Gravity appears as a distinct force.

After 10 000 trillionths of a trillionth of a second (10^{-32} seconds) Expansion slows down. Quarks, the smallest known particles, appear and start to combine to create larger subatomic particles.

After 10 millionths of a second (10^{-5} seconds) Subatomic particles combine to form protons and neutrons, the two components of the nuclei of atoms.

After 100 seconds The temperature drops to 1 billion°C. Space is now filled with protons, neutrons and electrons; the three particles that make up atoms. Over the next 32 000 years, protons and neutrons react with background radiation to combine and form nuclei of hydrogen and helium – the two simplest chemical elements.

After 1 billion years The Universe becomes transparent and its temperature drops to around 4000°C, low enough for complete atoms to form. These become pulled together by gravity, creating clumps of matter.

After 2 billion years The first stars and galaxies begin to condense from clouds of gaseous hydrogen and helium.

Measuring space

Distances in space are so vast that kilometres and miles are too small to express them. Instead, units such as the light year, astronomical unit and parsec are used.

● **Light year** This is the distance travelled by light in a year (9461 billion km/5880 billion miles). Light from Proxima Centauri, our closest star after the Sun, takes 4.2 years to reach Earth, so Proxima Centauri is 4.2 light years away.

● **Astronomical unit** This smaller unit of measurement is the average distance of the Earth from the Sun (153 million km/95 million miles).

● **Parsec** 3.26 light years. It is used for measuring star distances.

2 Earth's Galaxy Our Galaxy is a rotating spiral of billions of stars. The Sun is situated in the Orion Arm of the spiral, 24 000 light years from the centre. What we see in the night sky is a plane view of our Galaxy's densely packed centre.

FACT The Universe has no edge and nothing exists beyond it, not even space.

3 The Solar System This is composed of nine planets and their moons, as well as around 10 000 asteroids, orbiting the Sun. Pluto, usually the farthest known planet from the Sun, has an average distance from the Sun of 5900 million km (3666 million miles).

4 The Earth Our planet and its moon orbit the Sun at an average distance of 150 million km (93 million miles). The Earth is the third planet from the Sun.

LOOKING BACK IN TIME

How do we know what happened billions of years ago? Put simply, we can see it. Looking across the vast distances to stars, space and time become impossible to separate. We can only see objects when the light from them reaches us. The farther away an object is, the longer it takes. For instance, it takes eight years for the light from the brightest star, Sirius, to travel to Earth, so we are actually looking at it as it was eight years ago. With more distant objects we are looking even farther back in time. It takes the light from the Virgo Cluster, for example, 50 million years to reach us. So we are looking at it as it was long before human beings even existed.

As well as light, stellar objects emit other types of radiation, such as radio waves. These can be detected by specialised telescopes, and the data they provide helps to build up a fuller picture of the Universe.

At the moment, the farthest galaxies that we can perceive are 13 billion light years away, only 2 billion years after the Big Bang. In theory, if we could see far enough we should be able to see right to the beginning of the Universe.

Big Bang

The term Big Bang was facetiously coined by the astronomer Fred Hoyle, who did not believe in the theory. He considered it a return to an almost Biblical version of creation.

Stars are not distributed evenly throughout the Universe; they clump together in galaxies. In their turn, galaxies group together in clusters and superclusters. Although stars appear closely packed in galaxies, they are separated by vast distances. If our Sun were the size of a grain of sand, its nearest star neighbour would be 6 km (4 miles) away.

Measuring magnitude

There are two methods for measuring the magnitude, or brightness, of a star.

Apparent, or visual, magnitude is the brightness of a star as it appears from Earth. A very bright star is magnitude one and a barely visible one is magnitude six. Apparent magnitude does not take a star's distance from Earth into account. As something farther way looks fainter than something closer, it is not appropriate for making comparisons between stars.

Absolute magnitude is defined as the apparent magnitude that a star would have if viewed from a standard distance of 32.6 light years (10 parsecs). This standardised measurement allows the true brightness of stars to be compared.

GALAXY TYPES

Galaxies are classified by shape. There are three main types:

Spiral About 30 per cent of galaxies are believed to be spiral. There are two kinds. **Normal spirals** are pinwheel-shaped with a central bulge and spiral arms. **Barred spirals** (left) have an elongated central region and protruding arms.

Elliptical Most galaxies are thought to be this shape, a stretched sphere. They range from the virtually spherical to almost flattened. M87 in Virgo is an example

Irregular Many galaxies have an ill-defined structure with no definite outline. The Magellanic Cloud in our Local Cluster is an example of an irregular galaxy.

The Milky Way

Our Galaxy consists of at least 200 billion stars and their planets, grouped into a flattened disc with spiral arms and a bulge at its centre. Looking up from Earth along the plane of this disc, the Galaxy appears as a luminous band of stars and glowing gas – the Milky Way – spanning the sky. The whole Galaxy is sometimes referred to as the Milky Way Galaxy, but strictly speaking the term refers to the luminous band of stars visible from Earth.

FACT Using the Hubble Space Telescope, researchers have found 600 stars adrift in space between the Virgo Cluster galaxies.

Neighbour The Andromeda galaxy, photographed here from Earth, is our nearest galaxy neighbour. There are no external images of our own galaxy as nothing manmade has ever travelled beyond it.

EARTH'S GALAXY FACTS

● It rotates around its centre, and the Sun takes 225 million years to complete one circuit.
● It is 100 000 light years in diameter.
● The central bulge is 10 000 light years across and 20 000 light years thick. It contains only old stars.
● The disc formed by the spiral arms is 3000 light years thick.
● The Sun lies 30 000 light years from the centre of the Galaxy, in the Orion Arm.
● The centre of the Galaxy is Sagittarius A – a source of powerful radio waves that could be a black hole.

GALAXY FEATURES

Black holes The name given to immeasurably dense collapsed stars with such a strong gravitational pull that nothing, not even light, can escape from them. The size of black holes is dependent upon the mass of the collapsed star. Because they are invisible no black hole has been detected directly. Their existence can only be inferred from the effect they have on other objects.

Quasars These are cores of very active distant galaxies, possibly with black holes at their centres. They are point sources of

radio waves. Because they are so distant, light from them has taken a long time to reach us. When we look at a quasar, we are looking at a galaxy in a very early stage of its evolution.

Colliding galaxies If galaxies move close enough for their gravitational fields to affect each other, the structure of one or both galaxies can alter radically. They may collide and even merge. The closest colliding galaxies to us are NGC 4038 and 4039, known as the Antennae. They are just 80 light years apart and streams of material from

them are already converging. Eventually the two systems will merge.

Dark matter Also known as missing mass, this is matter that cannot be seen directly, because it emits little or no radiation. Its presence can be inferred from the effect it has on other bodies. Its gravitational force explains the rotation speeds of galaxies and the fact that they tend to group together into clusters. It has been estimated that as much as 90 per cent of the matter in the Universe is dark matter, in the form of particles left over from the Big Bang.

It is impossible to estimate how many stars there are in the Universe. There are thought to be around 200 billion stars in our Galaxy alone, although only about 6000 of these are visible with the naked eye from Earth. Stars are fuelled by the nuclear fusion of hydrogen atoms. They display a great range of sizes, brightness, colour and stages of development, from red giants to white dwarfs, nebulae to supernovae.

LIFE CYCLE OF A STAR

Stars are created in swirling clouds of cosmic dust and gas called nebulae. Within the nebulae strong gravitational forces are at work pulling particles together to form clumps called Bok globules. As gravity pulls the particles closer and closer together temperatures in these spinning masses soar to around 10 000 000°C. Under such extreme conditions, hydrogen nuclei combine creating helium atoms in a process called nuclear fusion. Energy is released and a protostar is born.

Star birth

Protostars condense in clouds of gas and dust called nebulae. They then follow one of four possible life cycles, depending on their original mass.

1 Small (a mass less than one-tenth that of the Sun) Called **red dwarfs**, these small stars glow feebly for a long period, gradually losing energy. The red colour indicates a relatively low surface temperature. Red dwarfs are the most common type of star.

4 Supergiant (a mass 100 times that of the Sun) Stars in this category have a life span of only a few million years. They eventually collapse in on themselves under the weight of their own gravity to become **black holes**.

3 Large (a mass greater than 1.4 times that of the Sun) Large stars have a period of maturity of only a few million years because they burn their fuel quickly, before becoming **red supergiants**. The core then cools and contracts suddenly, causing an explosion, called a **supernova**, that blows away the star's outer layers. If the core survives the explosion it cools and contracts further into a small, dense **neutron star** or **pulsar**.

2 Medium (a mass 0.1–1.4 times that of the Sun) After about 10 billion years these stars use up most of their hydrogen fuel and begin to cool. As the outer layers fall inwards they heat up again, and the star expands to become a **red giant**. Meanwhile the hot, dense core burns elements such as carbon and helium. Eventually, the outer gaseous layers begin to dissipate, creating a **planetary nebula**. Once the outer gases have completely dispersed, only the dense core remains, which cools and shrinks to become a **white dwarf**.

Why stars shine

Stars shine as a consequence of the nuclear fusion of hydrogen into helium which is constantly taking place in their cores. These reactions release energy in the form of heat and light. The Sun converts 600 million tonnes of hydrogen into helium every second, with a resultant loss of 4 million tonnes in mass.

Stellar variations

Variable and double stars are notable star types.
Double stars are either:
a. two stars in close proximity moving around a common centre (also called binary stars), e.g. Mizar; or
b. two stars far away from each other, but which appear close because they lie in the same direction when viewed from Earth.
Variable stars appear to vary in brightness over time.

CLASSIFYING THE STARS

To tell a star's type and life-cycle stage, astronomers use a graph called a Hertzsprung-Russell diagram. A star's position is worked out by plotting its brightness against its temperature, deduced from the colour of the light that the star emits. Young, hot stars tend to be blue, and older, cooler stars are usually red or orange. The star is classified according to the area of the graph in which it falls.

Red supergiants Largest and among the brightest of stars, having a large mass but a low density (e.g. Betelgeuse)

Brightness On this diagram, 1 equals 1 unit of the Sun's luminosity, but luminosity can be expressed in other ways.

Red giants Large stars in the latter stages of stellar evolution with diameters 10-100 times that of the Sun.

Surface temperature

Hotter stars 50 000°C   Cooler stars 3500°C

Brighter stars 1 000 000
100 000
10 000
1000
100
10
1
0.1
0.10
0.001
Dimmer stars 0.0001

Hot subdwarfs Stars at the centre of planetary nebulae.

Main sequence A narrow band into which most stars cluster, including the Sun at the present time. It runs from hot, bright stars in the top left to cooler, dimmer stars at bottom right.

White dwarfs Small, dense stars near the end of their life cycle, which are slowly cooling down (e.g. Sirius B).

Red dwarfs Stars of a small mass and low temperature, which glow feebly.

FACT Stars over 120 times more massive than the Sun cannot exist. They would be blown apart by their own radiation

KEY TERMS

● **Neutron star** A dim star of high density at the end of its life cycle composed predominantly or entirely of neutrons.
● **Pulsars** Probably rotating neutron stars, emitting intermittent radio signals.
● **Light year** The distance travelled by light in one year (9460 billion km/5900 billion miles).
● **Black hole** A collapsed star with such high gravity that not even light can escape from it.

STARS CLOSEST TO EARTH

Star	Distance
Sun	149 600 000 km (93 000 000 miles)
Proxima Centauri	4.24 light years
Alpha Centauri A	4.34
Alpha Centauri B	4.34
Barnard's Star	5.97
Wolf 359	7.8
Lalande 21185	8.19
UV Ceti A	8.55
UV Ceti B	8.55
Sirius A	8.68

BRIGHTEST STARS SEEN FROM EARTH

A star's brightness is affected by distance. A close dim star might appear brighter than a distant bright star. The lower the figure, the brighter the star.

Star	Constellation	Brightness (apparent magnitude)
Sirius	Canis Major	-1.46
Canopus	Carina	-0.72
Arcturus	Boötes	-0.04
Rigil Kentaurus	Orion	0.02
Vega	Lyra	0.03
Capella	Auriga	0.08
Rigel	Orion	0.12
Procyon	Canis Minor	0.38
Betelgeuse	Orion	0.50

The Sun is a mature, medium-sized star that formed from a collapsing cloud of gas about 4.6 billion years ago. It burns 700 million tonnes of hydrogen in its core every second, and converts about 5 million tonnes a second into pure energy. In about 5 billion years, when this fuel begins to run low, the Sun will expand into a red giant, and engulf the inner planets – including the Earth.

SUN STATISTICS

Age	4. 6 billion years +
Life span	About 13 billion years
Diameter	1 392 000 km (865 000 miles)
Composition by mass	71% hydrogen 27% helium 2% heavier gases
Temperature at core	15 million °C
Surface temperature	5500 °C
Rotation period	25–36 days
Distance from Earth	149 597 893 km (92 970 000 miles) 1 astronomical unit
Time for sunlight to reach Earth	8.3 minutes
Surface gravity	38 times that of Earth

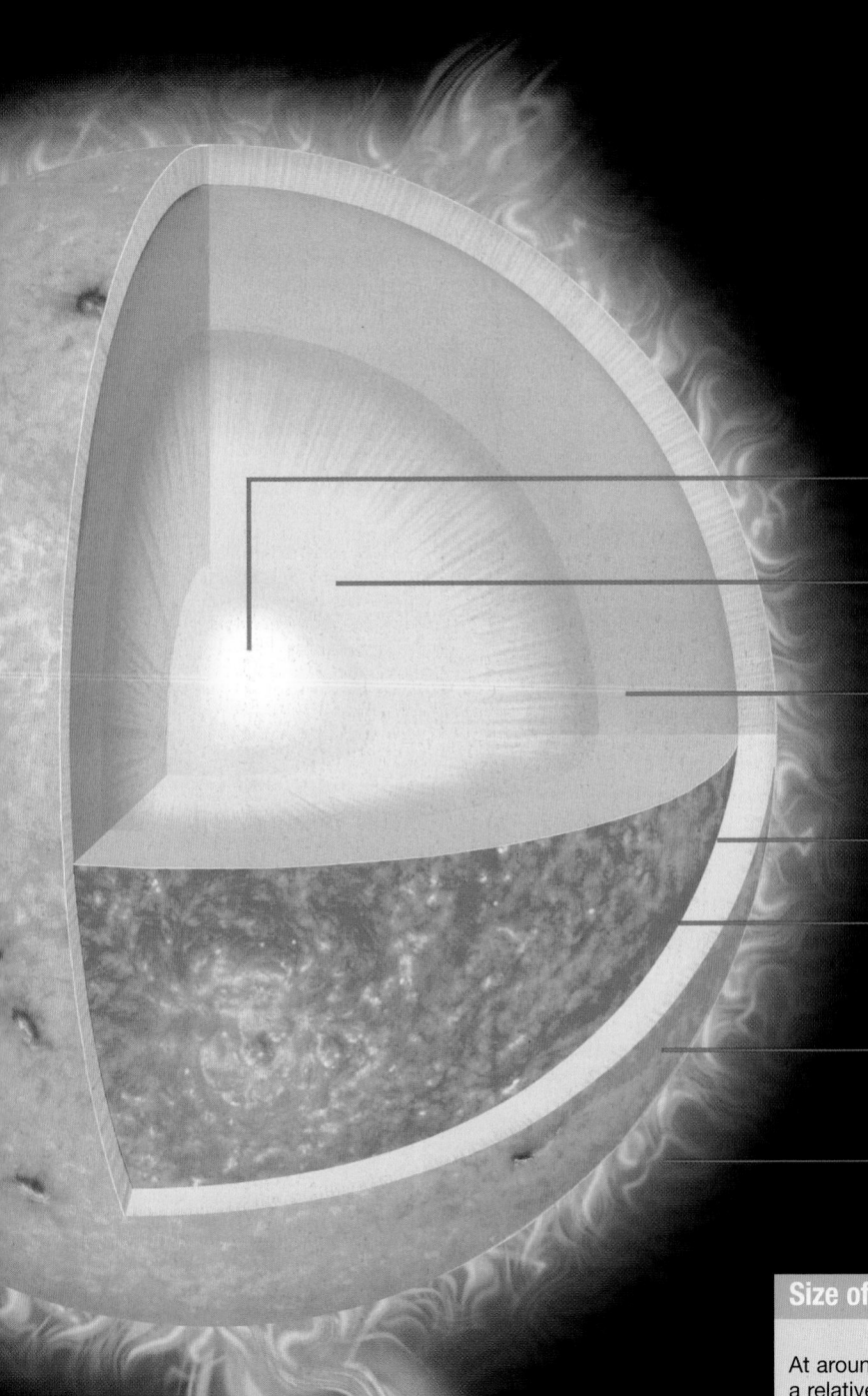

SOLAR STRUCTURE

Interior

Core Diameter 450 000 km (280 000 miles). Temperature 15 million °C. Here the thermonuclear fusion of hydrogen to form helium produces the Sun's energy.

Radiative layer Extends to 70 per cent of the Sun's radius. Temperature ranges from 2 million to 7 million °C. Heat energy generated by the core is carried outwards by radiation.

Convective layer 200 000 km (125 000 miles) deep. Temperature ranges from 2 million to 5500 °C. Heat energy is carried upwards by streams of gas.

Atmosphere

Photosphere 300–500 km (200–300 miles) deep. Temperature 4500–7600°C. Bright surface of the Sun which emits most of its energy as light and heat.

Chromosphere 2000–3000 km (1200–1900 miles) deep. Temperature 4000-50 000°C. Visible as a distinct pink layer during solar eclipses. Characterised by flame-like protrusions of gas.

Corona Constantly changing halo of plumes and loops of very hot gases up to 1.6 million km (1 million miles) thick. Temperature 2 million °C. Visible to the naked eye only during total eclipses.

Solar wind Continuous stream of X-rays, gamma rays, protons and electrons flowing into space at 3 million km/h (2 million mph). Higher speed streams emanate from holes in the corona.

Size of the Sun

At around 1.4 million km (864 000 miles) in diameter the Sun is a relatively small star. The red giant Betelgeuse is hundreds of times larger. Even so, the Sun dwarfs the other objects in the Solar System. It is 109 times wider than the Earth, and more than 1 million Earth-sized planets could fit inside it.

SURFACE ACTIVITY

Sunspots

- Dark patches that often appear as pairs or groups on the Sun's surface, usually around the Sun's equator.
- They are regions where the magnetic field of the Sun is stonger.
- Sunspots last from one hour to six months, depending on size, with larger ones being longer-lived.
- Diameters vary from 300 km (186 miles) to 100 000 km (62 150 miles).

Solar flares

- Violent, short-lived bursts of magnetic energy that emit radiation and charged particles into space.
- Flares occur in the chromosphere and lower corona.
- Typically, they last 20 minutes, but the longest observed was 13 hours on August 16, 1989.

Prominences

- Cool, dense, flame-like clouds in the upper chromosphere and lower corona, forming massive arches or loops.
- They are supported by magnetic fields, which gives them their characteristic arched appearance.
- Prominences are most common during the peak of the solar cycle.
- Quiescent prominences are usually arch-shaped and change little. They are concentrated at the poles, can be tens of thousands of kilometres high and tend to be long-lived, lasting several months.
- Active prominences display rapid motion and are usually concentrated near the equator. They are associated with sunspots, and last a few days.

Faculae

- Temporary bright patches on the surface of the Sun.
- They are sites of strong magnetic

Prominences An arch of relatively cool, charged gases erupts from the Sun's surface. Sometimes the gases escape into space

fields and are slightly hotter than the Sun's normal surface temperature.
- Faculae often appear before the formation of sunspots and persist for several days after the sunspots have disappeared.
- They also occur near the Sun's poles.

Solar cycles

The level of the Sun's activity varies, following a fairly regular cycle of about 11 years, thought to be caused by magnetic fields slowing the flow of heat from the Sun's core to the surface. The most obvious indicator of solar cycles is the number of sunspots, cooler areas visible as dark depressions in the photosphere (right), that are visible on the Sun's surface. During a cycle sunspots appear, grow in number, then gradually die away. Solar cycles also see an increase in flares and a stronger solar wind.

Solar cycles have a marked effect on the Earth. The increase in flares and the solar wind means that more charged particles from the Sun reach the Earth at these times. They intensify the effects of the northern and southern lights (aurora borealis and aurora australis). Charged solar particles can also interfere with radio signals and cause surges in power lines, sometimes resulting in blackouts.

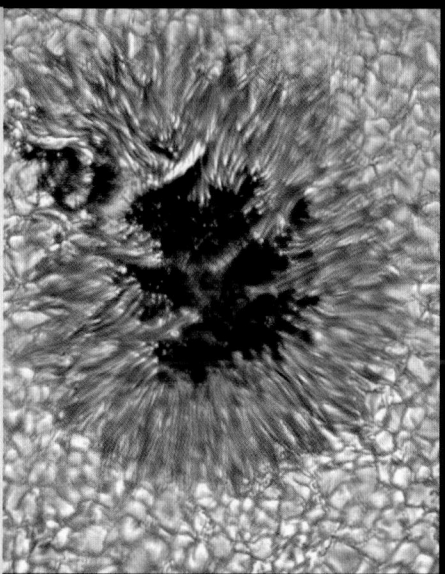

FACT It takes 10 million years for heat generated in the Sun's core to reach its outer layer, the photosphere.

The word planet comes from the Greek for 'wanderer', because seen from Earth the planets appear to move across the sky in an erratic way. In fact, the planets all circle the Sun in the same direction, in a similar plane, and each spins on its axis as it orbits. A total of 76 moons orbit the nine planets, and each planet has evolved differently, according to its composition and distance from the Sun.

Formation of the planets Five billion years ago, a new star, the Sun, was surrounded by a swirling disc of gas and dust. Heavier elements were pulled together to form the inner, rocky or 'terrestrial' planets – Mercury, Venus, Earth and Mars. Lighter elements, such as hydrogen and helium, were swept up into the outer gaseous giants Jupiter, Saturn, Uranus and Neptune. Tiny Pluto, on the outer edge of the Solar System, is probably an asteroid, caught in orbit round the Sun.

Inner mantle of metallic hydrogen

Atmosphere of hydrogen and helium, with some sulphur, oxygen and nitrogen

Outer mantle of liquid hydrogen and helium

Solid rocky core

Rocky crust — Rocky mantle — Iron core

Rocky crust — Rocky mantle

Rocky mantle — Semisolid iron and nickel core

Rocky mantle — Solid iron and nickel inner core — Molten iron and nickel outer core

Rocky crust — Rocky mantle

Mercury
Mercury is the closest planet to the Sun. Its surface is scarred and pitted by meteorite impacts. It has almost no atmosphere, so is scorched during the day and freezing at night. It is visible to the naked eye.

Venus
The rocky surface of Venus is marked by volcanoes, rifts and solidified lava flows. The atmosphere is rich in carbon dioxide. Atmospheric pressure at the surface is 90 times that of Earth.

Earth
Earth is unique in the Solar System in having liquid water on the surface, and is the only planet known to be geologically active. It is also the only place in the Universe known to support life.

Mars
The fourth planet is a vast red desert. The barren wastes of Mars have been eroded by ferocious winds. They are also dotted with large volcanoes and impact craters. The atmosphere of Mars consists mainly of carbon dioxide. Its day length is similar to Earth's.

	Mercury	Venus	Earth	Mars
Minimum distance from Sun	45 900 000 km (28 520 000 miles)	107 400 000 km (66 740 000 miles)	147 000 000 km (91 340 000 miles)	206 700 000 km (128 440 000 miles)
Maximum distance from Sun	69 700 000 km (43 300 000 miles)	109 000 000 km (67 730 000 miles)	152 000 000 km (94 450 000 miles)	249 000 000 km (154 730 000 miles)
Diameter at equator	4878 km (3031 miles)	12 104 km (7521 miles)	12 756 km (7926 miles)	6794 km (4222 miles)
Mass relative to Earth	0.055	0.815	1	0.11
Period of orbit round Sun	87.97 days	224.7 days	365.3 days	687 days
Spin period	175.94 daysmin	243 days 3 h 50 min	23 hours 56 min	24 hours 37 min
Temperature at surface	350°C day/–170°C night	480°C (average)	22°C (average)	–63°C (average)
Known moons	None	None	1	2
Names of main moons			Moon	Phobos, Deimos

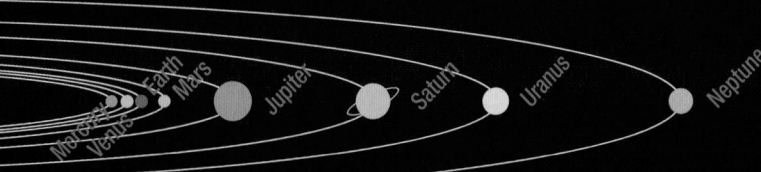

Mercury Venus Earth Mars Jupiter Saturn Uranus Neptune Pluto

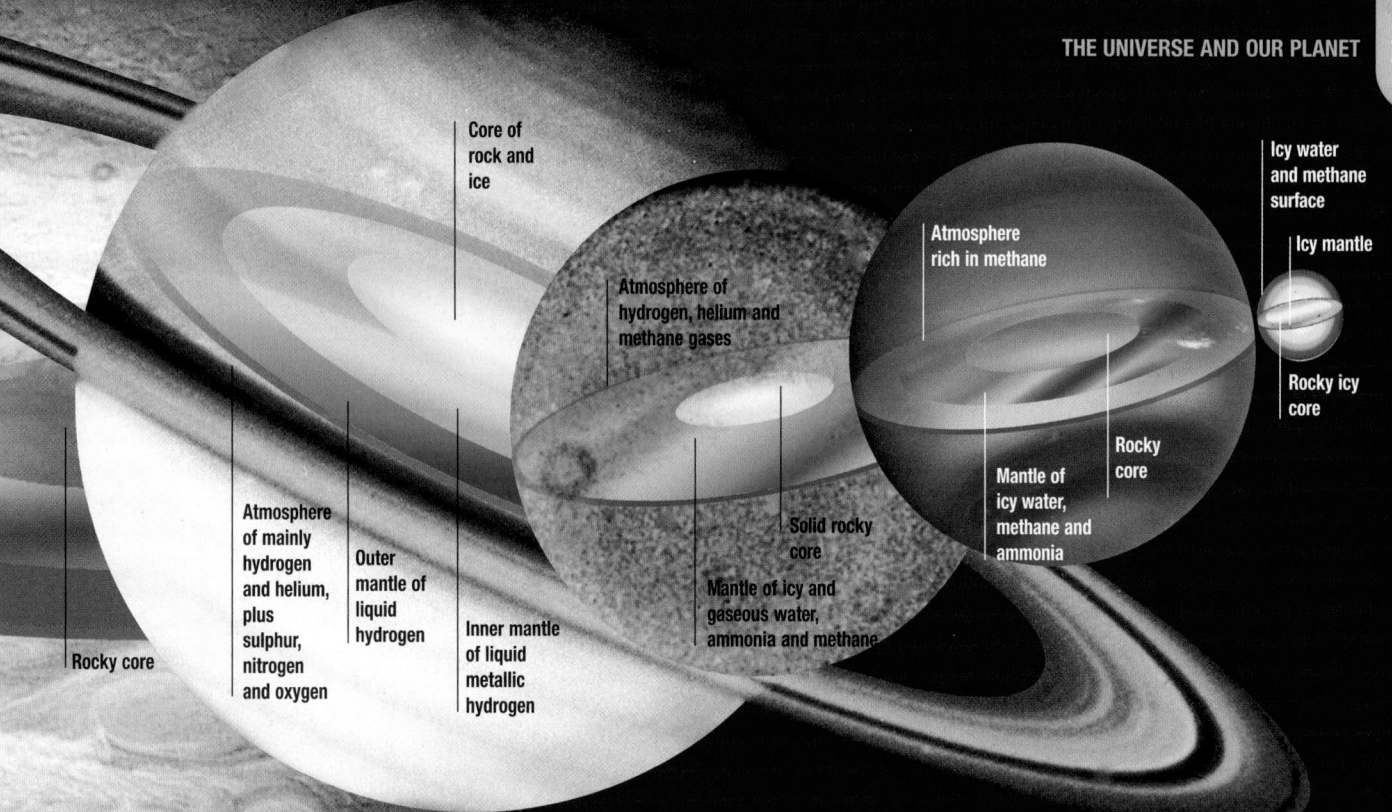

Core of
rock and
ice

Icy water
and methane
surface

Icy mantle

Atmosphere
rich in methane

Atmosphere of
hydrogen, helium and
methane gases

Rocky icy
core

Rocky
core

Atmosphere
of mainly
hydrogen
and helium,
plus
sulphur,
nitrogen
and oxygen

Outer
mantle of
liquid
hydrogen

Inner mantle
of liquid
metallic
hydrogen

Solid rocky
core

Mantle of icy and
gaseous water,
ammonia and methane

Mantle of
icy water,
methane and
ammonia

Rocky core

Jupiter	Saturn	Uranus	Neptune	Pluto
Jupiter is the largest planet. Its atmosphere is composed mainly of hydrogen and helium. High pressure in the lower regions has compressed the hydrogen into liquid and metallic layers around the rocky core. Surface spots and markings are actually atmospheric storms.	Saturn is a globe of gases similar in composition to Jupiter. It rotates so fast that it bulges in the middle and is flattened at the poles. Saturn's rings consist of tens of thousands of subdivisions made up of ice particles. Fast winds whip around the planet's equator.	The planet Uranus was discovered in 1781. Its atmosphere consists of hydrogen, helium and methane. Uniquely in the Solar System, its axis of rotation coincides with the orbital plane – it spins on its side – possibly as a result of an ancient collision with a comet.	The planet Neptune was discovered in 1846, although it may have been spotted by Galileo in 1613. It has a methane-rich atmosphere that becomes liquid and then metallic towards the centre. It has an almost circular (rather than elliptical) orbit. Faint rings are visible.	Pluto was discovered in 1930, and there is still some question whether it qualifies as a planet at all. The surface is a solid landscape of frozen methane, and the atmosphere is very thin. Pluto has an erratic orbit that at times brings it inside Neptune's orbit.
741 000 000 km (460 000 000 miles)	1 3352 600 000 km (840 505 640 miles)	2 74 300 000 km (1 703 443 820 miles)	4 545 670 000 km (2 824 679 338 miles)	4 434 990 000 km (2 755 902 786 miles)
816 000 000 km (507 000 000 miles)	1 507 000 000 km (936 000 000 miles)	3 004 000 000 km (1867 000 000 miles)	4 444 450 000 km (2 761 781 230 miles)	7 304 330 000 km (4538 910 662 miles)
142 800 km (88 736 miles)	119 900 km (74 506 miles)	51 108 km (31 764 miles)	49 493 km (30 755 miles)	2390 km (1485 miles)
317.9	95.2	14.5	17.2	0.002
11 years 314 days	29 years 168 days	83 years 273 days	164 years 292 days	248 years 197 days
9 hours 55.5 min	10 hours 40 min	17 hours 14 min	17 hours 15 min	6 days 9 hours
–150°C (average)	–180°C (average)	–214°C (average)	–220°C (average)	–230°C (average)
16	30, plus rings	18 confirmed, plus rings	8, plus rings	1
Io, Europa, Ganymede	Titan	Titania, Oberon	Triton	Charon

SOLAR SYSTEM FACTS

Fastest mover Mercury has the highest average orbiting speed at 172 248 km/h (107 030 mph).

Hottest place Venus has the highest surface temperature due to its proximity to the Sun and its heat-trapping, carbon-rich atmosphere.

Largest rings Saturn's rings are 270 000 km (170 000 miles) in diameter.

Longest day Venus rotates backwards on its axis once every 243 days, so a 'day' is longer than a 'year'.

Coldest place The lowest recorded surface temperature in the Solar System is –235°C, on Neptune's moon Triton.

Brightest planet Venus's blanket of cloud reflects about 79 per cent of incoming light.

Most active satellite Jupiter's moon Io emits vast clouds of sulphur from vents in its surface.

Largest volcano Olympus Mons, on Mars, is 600 km (375 miles) across and 25 km (15 miles) high.

Most of the planets in the Solar System have natural satellites, or moons. Our Moon was probably formed 4.6 billion years ago when debris from a collision between the Earth and a passing asteroid fused together. The Moon's gravity exerts a strong influence on the Earth, causing the tides and, over millions of years, slowing the spin of the Earth, lengthening the day.

THE FACE OF THE MOON

Unlike the Earth, the Moon is not tectonically active; there are no volcanoes nor violent earthquakes, just the occasional tremor. Nor is there any running water, rain, snow or wind to erode the landscape. The surface features of the Moon are mainly the result of meteorite impacts.

Two main landscape areas have been identified: the cratered, older highlands and the younger 'maria', or 'seas'. These areas are characterised by a number of features.

Maria Medieval astronomers described the smooth, dark areas visible on the Moon's surface as 'seas'. They were later given romantic names such as Mare Tranquillitatis (Sea of Tranquillity)

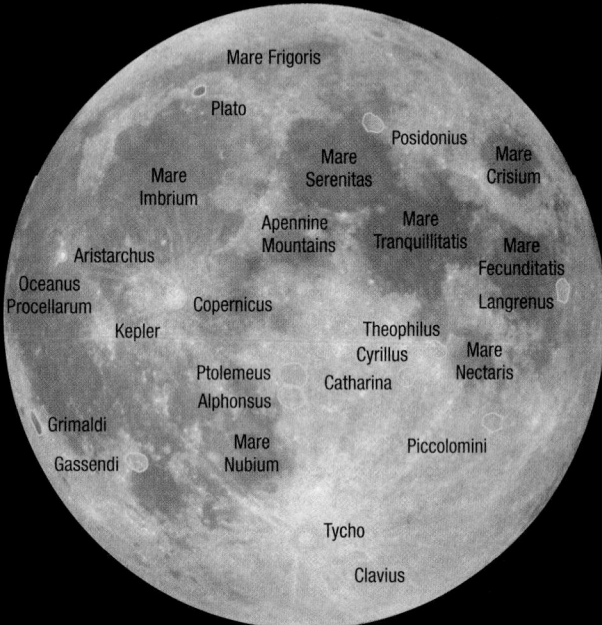

Mare Frigoris
Plato
Posidonius
Mare Serenitas
Mare Crisium
Mare Imbrium
Apennine Mountains
Mare Tranquillitatis
Aristarchus
Mare Fecunditatis
Oceanus Procellarum
Copernicus
Langrenus
Kepler
Theophilus
Cyrillus
Mare Nectaris
Ptolemeus
Catharina
Alphonsus
Grimaldi
Mare Nubium
Piccolomini
Gassendi
Tycho
Clavius

Moon statistics

Average distance from Earth (centre to centre)	384 400 km (238 828 miles)
Time to orbit Earth	27.32 days
Time to spin once on axis	27.32 days
Interval between new moons	29 days 12 hrs 44 mins 3 secs
Average orbital velocity	3680 km/h (2286 mph)
Average diameter	3476.6 km (2160 miles)
Density (water=1)	3.34
Volume (Earth=1)	0.02
Surface gravity (Earth=1)	0.165

and Mare Imbrium (Sea of Showers). We now know that they do not contain water. These areas, which cover 16 per cent of the Moon's surface, are the result of meteorite impacts on its surface soon after its formation. The force of the impacts cracked the surface, causing lava to flood out. The cooled and solidified lava flows formed the smooth areas.

Craters Found all over the surface of the Moon, craters are the result of bombardment by meteorites, mainly between 500 and 700 million years after the Moon's formation.

Mountains At the same time as the maria were being formed, the meteorite bombardment also threw up mountain ranges, such as the lunar Apennines that border the Mare Imbrium.

Domes These circular, shallow-sided raised areas, often with a central pit, are associated with maria. They are thought to be extinct volcanic vents, similar to shield volcanoes found on Earth.

Rays Formed by material ejected from impact craters.

Moon dust A steady rain of minor debris from space has eroded the surface, leaving the Moon covered in a light layer of dust.

DARK SIDE OF THE MOON

Gravitational forces between the Earth and the Moon keep them in synchronous rotation. That is, the time the Moon takes to spin once on its axis is the same as it takes to orbit the Earth, so the same side of the Moon always faces us. The far or 'dark' side was a mystery until October 1959, when the Soviet spacecraft *Luna 3* sent back images of it. These revealed that it is more cratered than the near side and has only one mare. The lack of maria is probably due to the crust being thicker on the far side and therefore not cracking and releasing lava when hit by meteorites.

Moon composition

More than 2000 samples of Moon rock have been collected and brought back to Earth. These indicate that there are many rock types on the Moon, but they can be broadly divided into two categories: basaltic volcanic rocks associated with the maria, and aluminium and calcium-rich rocks, relics of the Moon's earlier history.

Recent probes indicate that there may be frozen water at the Moon's poles. If it could be melted, it could help to support life on a permanent lunar space station.

FACT
The Moon is moving away from the Earth at a rate of about 4 cm (1¹/₂ in) a year.

THE TIDES

The twice daily rise and fall of the oceans results from the interplay of the gravitational forces of Earth, Moon and Sun.
The Moon pulls on the oceans on the side of the Earth facing it, causing a bulge – high tide. The solid Earth on the opposite side is also pulled towards the Moon, and away from the oceans, which are also flung outwards by the Earth's spin, causing an equivalent high tide on the other side. Low tides occur where water has been drawn away.
The Sun also has a gravitational effect on the Earth. When it is in line with the Moon, at the time of the new and full moons, they act together to create particularly high tides (spring tides). When the Moon and Sun lie at right angles, at the time of the half moon, they work against each other, resulting in low tides (neap tides).

The tidal range in any place is also affected by the shape of the coastline and depth of water. The height between high and low tides along open coastline can be as much as 61 m (20 ft), and in restricted narrow bays, up to 15 m (50 ft). In the open ocean it is rarely more than 60 m (2 ft).

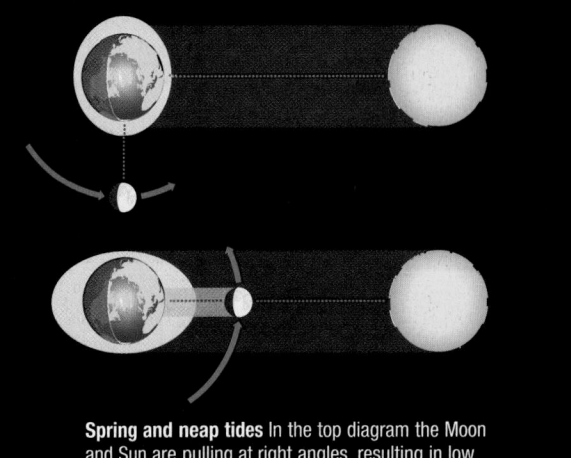

Spring and neap tides In the top diagram the Moon and Sun are pulling at right angles, resulting in low (neap) tides. Below, the Sun and Moon are in line, their combined gravity creating high (spring) tides.

Earthrise as first seen on the Apollo 8 mission in 1968. From the Moon the Earth is seen to rise and set just as we can see the Moon rising and setting from the Earth.

PHASES OF THE MOON

From Earth we only see the side of the Moon that is reflecting light from the Sun. As the Moon circles the Earth each month, we see different amounts of its illuminated face, which gives the impression that the Moon changes shape. These phases range from the new moon, when none of it is visible from Earth, to the full moon, when the entire face is lit. In this diagram the small moons show how the Sun's light shines onto the Moon and the large moons show how it appears from the Earth throughout the month.

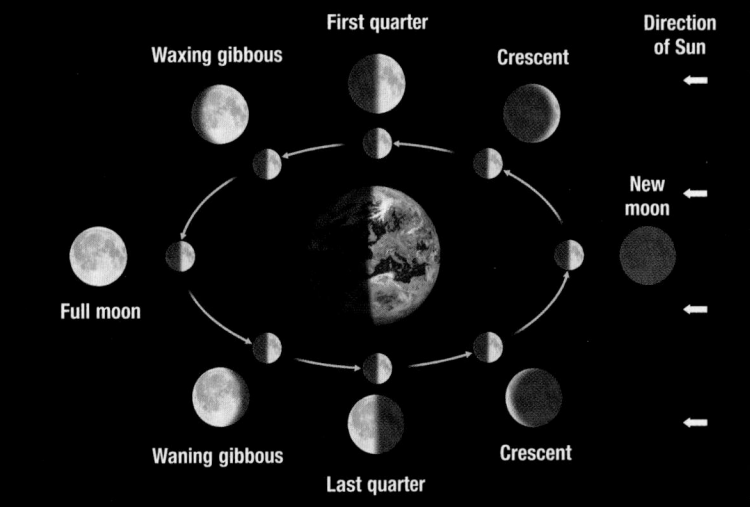

First quarter

Waxing gibbous

Crescent

Direction of Sun

New moon

Full moon

Waning gibbous

Last quarter

Crescent

The Solar System is littered with solid debris left over from the formation of the planets. Comets and asteroids orbit the Sun, while meteors are fragments that enter Earth's atmosphere and burn up. Large fragments that hit the ground are called meteorites.

COMETS

Comets are like large, dirty snowballs, a few kilometres in diameter, made up of rocks and dust held together by ice and frozen gas. They originate in distant regions of the Solar System beyond Pluto. Occasionally, the gravity of a passing star nudges a comet from these outer reaches into the inner Solar System, leaving it in elliptical orbit around the Sun.

A comet emits no light of its own, so for most of its orbit it is invisible. When it passes close to the Sun, and its crust begins to melt, it produces a glowing cloud of gas and dust, the coma. In most comets a luminous gas tail can also be seen, pointing away from the Sun because it is deflected by the solar wind.

Some comets have orbits that frequently bring them close to the Sun and visible from Earth. Halley's comet is one such, with a return period of about 76 years. Each time they pass close to the Sun comets lose material, until eventually they disappear.

Well-known comets

Name	Discovered	Return period (years)
Halley	239 BC	76
Tycho	1577	Not known
Kirch (Newton)	1680	8814
Encke	1786	3.3
Tuttle	1790	13.7
Great Comet	1843	512.6
Donati	1858	1950
Swift-Tuttle	1872	125
Wolf	1884	8.4
Daylight Comet	1910	Not known
Schwassmann-Wachmann 1	1908	15
Arend-Roland	1957	Not known
Seki-Lines	1962	Not known
Kohoutek	1973	75 000
West	1975	500 000
Shoemaker-Levy	1992	None – crashed into Jupiter in 1992
Hale-Bopp	1995	18 000

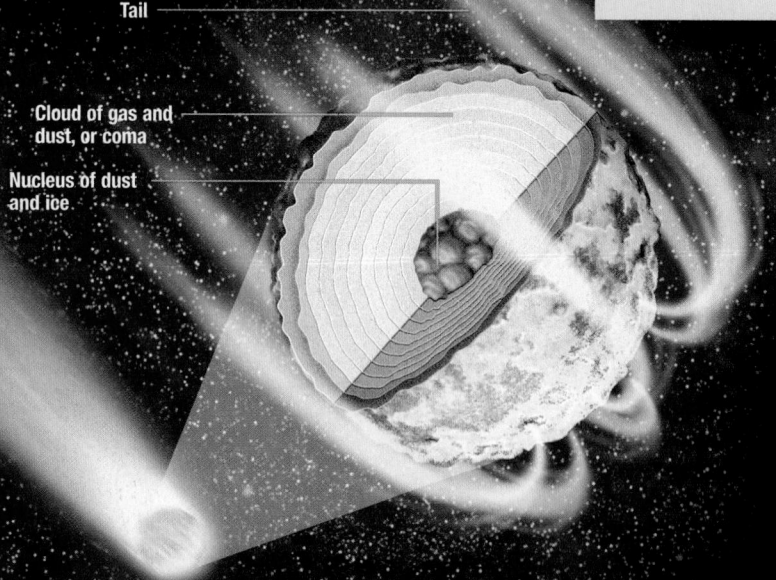

Tail

Cloud of gas and dust, or coma

Nucleus of dust and ice

COMET FACTS

● 900 comets are currently known.
● About 25 comets are seen from Earth through telescopes every year.
● The tail of a comet can be up to 300 million km (200 million miles) long.
● Comets travel at speeds of up to 20 km/s (12 miles/s).
● The coma of a comet can be larger than the Sun.

ASTEROIDS

Asteroids, or minor planets, are rocky or metallic bodies found unevenly distributed in the Asteroid Belt between Mars and Jupiter, shown here as a blue band. They are thought to be material that failed to form a planet because of the gravitational pull of Jupiter. There are at least 1 million asteroids in the Solar System. They range in size from 10 m (35 ft) to about 900 km (560 miles) in diameter. The largest are roughly spherical and have a similar structure to planets. One, Ida, has a satellite.

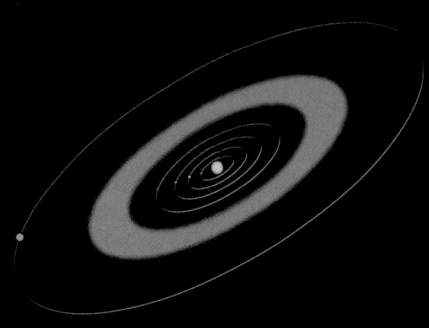

Major asteroids
The ten largest known asteroids (with their diameters) are:

Ceres	940 km (584 miles)
Pallas	580 km (360 miles)
Vesta	576 km (358 miles)
Hygeia	430 km (267 miles)
Interamnia	338 km (210 miles)
Juno	288 km (180 miles)
Psyche	248 km (154 miles)
Thule	130 km (80 miles)
Astraea	120 km (75 miles)
Feronia	96 km (60 miles)

METEOR SHOWERS

When small fragments of natural space debris (meteoroids) enter the Earth's atmosphere, they burn up. The result is a bright streak of light in the sky, known as a meteor, or shooting star. Meteoroids are about the size of a grain of sand and an estimated 100 million a day zip through the thin air at up to 209 200 km/h (130 000 mph), 65 km (40 miles) above the Earth's surface. Dust trails from comets cause regular meteor showers.

Shooting star A meteor arches through the sky, its gas tail deflected away from the Sun by the solar wind.

Regular meteor showers caused by the Earth passing through comet trail debris.

Quadrantids	(1-6 Jan)
Lyrids	(19-25 April)
Alpha-Scorpiids	(20 April-19 May)
Eta Aquariids	(1-8 May)
Delta Aquariids	(15 July-20 Aug)
Perseids	(27 July-17 Aug)
Orionids 1	(5-25 Oct)
Taurids	(25 Oct-25 Nov)
Leonids	(14-20 Nov)
Geminids	(8-14 Dec)
Ursids	(19-24 Dec)

METEORITES

Meteorites are pieces of rocky or metallic space debris that actually collide with the Earth. There are three recognised types:

● **Stony meteorites**: rocky with small amounts of nickel and iron. Most meteorites are of this type, but as they are difficult to tell from terrestrial rocks, they often go unnoticed.

● **Iron meteorites**: mainly iron and nickel, thought to originate in the cores of asteroids. They account for about 4 per cent of known meteorite falls. The largest known meteorites are of this type.

● **Stony-iron meteorites**: approximately 50 per cent nickel and iron and 50 per cent rock. Also thought to originate in asteroids. They account for about 1 per cent of known meteorite falls.

TEN HEAVIEST METEORITES

The heaviest known meteorites were found at:

Hoba West, Namibia	(60 tonnes)
Ahnighito, West Greenland	(34 tonnes)
Bacuberito, Mexico	(27 tonnes)
Mbosi, Tanzania	(26 tonnes)
Agpalik, W. Greenland	(21 tonnes)
Armanty, Outer Mongolia	(20 tonnes)
Chupaderos, Mexico	(14 tonnes)
Willamette, Oregon, USA	(14 tonnes)
Campo del Cielo, Argentina	(13 tonnes)
Mundrabilla, Western Australia	(12 tonnes)

METEORITE FACTS

● About 1 tonne of meteorites hits the Earth every day; most of them are very small and go unnoticed.
● Meteorites hurtle through the atmosphere at speeds of 32-95 km/s (20-60 miles/s)
● No person is known to have been killed by a meteorite fall.

Wolf Creek Crater A meteorite weighing more than 50 000 tonnes formed this crater in Australia.

Meteorite craters

Most meteorites are destroyed on impact, but large meteorites may leave behind a crater, which gives some idea of their size.

Name	Discovered	Diameter
Meteor Crater, Arizona, USA	1871	1265 m (4150 ft)
Wolf Creek, Australia	1947	675 m (2200 ft)
Boxhole, Australia	1937	175 m (574 ft)
Odessa, Texas, USA	1921	170 m (558 ft)
Oesal, Estonia	1927	100 m (328 ft)
Waqer, Arabia	1932	100 m (328 ft)

see also
14-15 **Planet Earth**
24-5 **The planets**
52-3 **Earth's atmosphere**

The Earth is made up of concentric layers, the core, mantle and crust, each with its own distinctive physical and chemical characteristics. These layers are not homogeneous; the variations within them explain the existence of such phenomena as continental drift, volcanoes, earthquakes and the Earth's magnetic field.

INSIDE THE EARTH

Our deepest drills have failed to penetrate beyond the Earth's crust so information about our planet's internal structure has to be gleaned from a variety of other sources. These include the behaviour of earthquake waves as they pass through the Earth, the composition of meteorites, which are remnants of other planetary material, and the chemistry of rare mantle rocks occasionally found at the surface. This evidence combines to give us a picture of an Earth composed of four distinct concentric layers.

Crust Solid outer layer ranges in thickness from a minimum of 5 km (3 miles) beneath the oceans to a maximum of 80 km (50 miles) under the highest mountain ranges. Two types of crust exist: young, thin, dense basaltic oceanic crust comprising 65 per cent of the Earth's surface; and older, thicker, less dense continental crust, comprising 35 per cent of the Earth's surface.

Mantle A mainly solid layer 2900 km (1800 miles) thick. Average density 3–4.5 times that of water. Temperature 700–1800°C (1300–3300°F). Composed largely of a dense rock called garnet peridotite. Convection currents in a partially melted zone at the top of the mantle provide the driving force for continental drift. Although solid, the rest of the mantle also moves in slow currents.

Core Begins at a depth of 2900 km (1800 miles). Total diameter 6900 km (4300 miles). Composed predominantly of iron with some nickel and a small amount of a lighter element – probably sulphur.
The core is divided into:

Outer core A liquid layer 2100 km (1300 miles) thick.

Inner core A solid layer 2700 km (1700 miles) in diameter, thought to rotate at a different speed from the rest of the Earth. Temperature in the centre is estimated at 4000–5000°C (7200–9000°F).

Earth's magnetic field

The Earth has a powerful magnetic field, as if there were a giant bar magnet at its centre. The field is created by interactions between movements in the liquid outer core and the rotation of the Earth, which together act like a natural dynamo, generating electricity and creating a magnetic field as a consequence.

The Earth's magnetic field is not fixed. At present it is angled at around 11 degrees from the axis on which the planet spins, so that the Earth's magnetic poles do not coincide exactly with its geographical poles. The magnetic north pole is about 850 km (530 miles) from the geographical pole. But this position changes slightly over time; it is currently moving towards the geographical pole at a rate of about 11 km (7 miles) a year. The polarity of the field also reverses at intervals of approximately 1 million years so that magnetic north becomes south and vice versa. These reversals are probably due to changes in the liquid movements of the outer core.

FACT New ocean floor is being created at mid-ocean ridges at a rate of 3.5 km² (1.3 sq miles) a year.

PLATE TECTONICS

The Earth's crust and upper mantle (together called the lithosphere) are divided into rigid interlocking segments, or plates, which are in constant motion in relation to each other. Their movement is driven by convection currents in the mantle. The plates carry the continents and underlie the oceans, although their boundaries do not necessarily coincide with continent margins. Plates are created or destroyed along constructive and convergent boundaries.

Constructive boundaries These occur at mid-ocean ridges. Upwelling magma drives the plates apart, adding new material along their edges in the process. The Mid Atlantic Ridge is a major example. Plates at mid-ocean ridges can move apart at a rate of 15 cm (6 in) a year.

Conservative boundaries Two plates slide past each other along a transform fault, being neither created nor destroyed. They are characterised by earthquake activity. California's San Andreas Fault is an example of a conservative plate boundary.

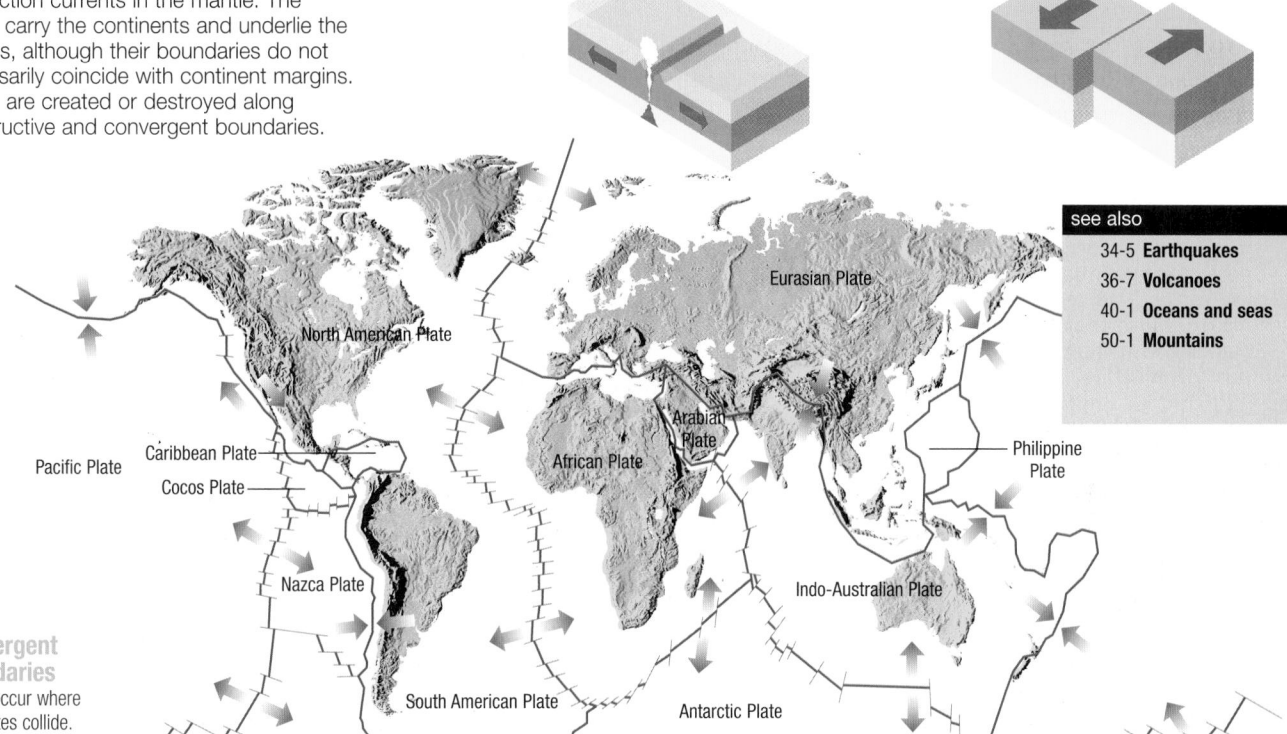

Convergent boundaries
These occur where two plates collide. There are three recognised types:

Oceanic/continental Dense oceanic crust sinks beneath continental crust and into the mantle, where it melts causing volcanoes and earthquakes. Sediments on the edge of the plates are folded and thrust up. The Andes are an example of this type of boundary.

Continental/continental Plates carrying continents or islands collide. The margins of both plates are forced upwards causing earthquakes, volcanism and major fold-mountain regions. The Himalayas are the result of a collision between plates carrying Asia and India.

Oceanic/oceanic One oceanic plate is forced under the other. Rising magma from melting of the descending plate creates a volcanic island arc, such as Japan or the Aleutians.

A shifting world

The position of continents is not fixed. Over geological time they have been created and destroyed; come together and moved apart. The maps below show how the present continents have come into being, and how they might be positioned in the future.

250 million years ago The continents were joined together into one large landmass called Pangaea, from the Greek meaning 'all lands'.

135 million years ago Pangaea split into Laurasia in the north (North America and Eurasia) and Gondwana in the south (Africa, South America, Australia, India and Antarctica).

Today The Atlantic is widening, and a new constructive plate boundary appears to be forming along Africa's Rift Valley, but this might fail.

The future If current movements continue, the Atlantic will widen, Africa will collide with Europe, Australia will collide with South-east Asia, and California will slide north to Alaska.

From the formation of the planet right up to the present day the Earth's long history is recorded in its rocks. Geology can reveal a range of information about past environments, for instance where deserts, volcanoes, seas and forests once existed. It can also tell us about the position of past continents and how old they are. Rocks are constantly being created and destroyed by erosion, deposition, volcanism and mountain building.

Quantities of main elements in the Earth's crust

Element	%	Element	%
Oxygen (O)	45.0	Magnesium (Mg)	2.8
Silicon (Si)	27.0	Sodium (Na)	2.3
Aluminium (Al)	8.0	Potassium (K)	1.7
Iron (Fe)	5.8	Hydrogen (H)	1.5
Calcium (Ca)	4.7	Titanium (Ti)	0.6

CATEGORIES OF ROCK

Rocks are aggregates of minerals or organic matter, either consolidated or loose. Thus, in geological terms, sand and gravel are technically rocks, along with more familiar examples such as marble, sandstone and granite. Minerals are naturally occurring inorganic substances such as quartz and calcite.

Geologists divide rock into categories related to how the rock was formed. The three main categories are:

- Igneous
- Sedimentary
- Metamorphic

Sedimentary rocks are formed by the accumulation and cementation of mud, silt or sand derived from the breakdown of pre-existing rocks, and from organic material such as trees or shells. Deposits precipitated from water, for instance rock salt, are also included. Sedimentary rocks represent less than 5 per cent of the Earth's crust, but 75 per cent of the Earth's land surface.
Appearance Usually fragments cemented together by calcite, quartz or other minerals. Sedimentary rock outcrops often have a layered appearance; the layers represent successive periods of sediment deposition. Many sedimentary rocks contain fossils – preserved organic remains. Some limestones are composed entirely of cemented shell fragments.
Examples Sandstone, limestone, rock salt, peat.

Ironstone (Hamersley Range, Pilbara Region, Western Australia) This sedimentary rock clearly shows depositional layering. It is cemented by iron compounds which gives it its distinctive red colour.

Igneous rocks were once molten; they include lavas, such as basalts, erupted by volcanoes, and rocks such as granites which originated as hot liquids deep in the Earth's crust. The first surface rocks created after the formation of the Earth were igneous. Today igneous rocks represent 95 per cent of the Earth's crust.
Appearance Igneous rocks are usually very hard. They are made up of crystals of different minerals such as quartz and feldspar. In some rocks, for example granite, the crystals are very large and can be clearly seen. By contrast, the crystals in lavas tend to be small and are difficult to see with the naked eye. Igneous rock faces are very uniform in appearance. They are not normally layered, although they may be cracked or have a patchy coloration.
Examples Granite, basalt, andesite, obsidian.

Granite outcrop (Joshua Tree National Park, California) This outcrop shows the characteristic manner in which igneous granite weathers and erodes into rounded blocks and boulders.

Sill Magma intrudes into horizontal fractures in the rock, then cools and hardens.

Magma chamber Molten rock store deep underground.

A marble quarry (Greece) Marble is metamorphosed limestone which has recrystallised under heat and pressure.

see also

30-1 **Structure of the Earth**

36-7 **Volcanoes**

38-9 **Earth's treasures**

Heat Volcanic activity and magma alter surrounding rock.

Faulting and folding Existing rock layers are crushed and compressed.

Metamorphic rocks are igneous or sedimentary rocks that have been altered by heat and/or pressure, either because they have been buried and folded deep in the crust, or because they have come into contact with molten igneous rock. Metamorphism can result in the formation of completely new minerals. It can also destroy original structures such as sedimentary layering or fossils. Intense pressure can cause the realignment of minerals, forming new layers. About 1 per cent of rocks in the crust are metamorphic.

Appearance Metamorphic rocks are usually crystalline and often show layering.

Examples Marble, gneiss, schist, slate, coal.

Sedimentary environment Deposits build up in coastal waters.

Layering Older layers of sediment become compressed by the build-up of new layers overlying them.

The oldest rocks on Earth

The oldest known rocks date back to the early formation of the Earth's crust. Originally igneous, they have been changed over time into metamorphic rocks.

● **Gneisses** at Isua in Greenland dated at 3824 million years old.

● **Eclogites** from Roberts Victor Mine in South Africa dated at 4000 million years.

● **Zircon** (a mineral), found in Australia, eroded from its original rock, dated at 4200 million years.

THE ROCK CYCLE

The rocks of the Earth's crust are constantly being created, worn down and redeposited in a slow cycle.

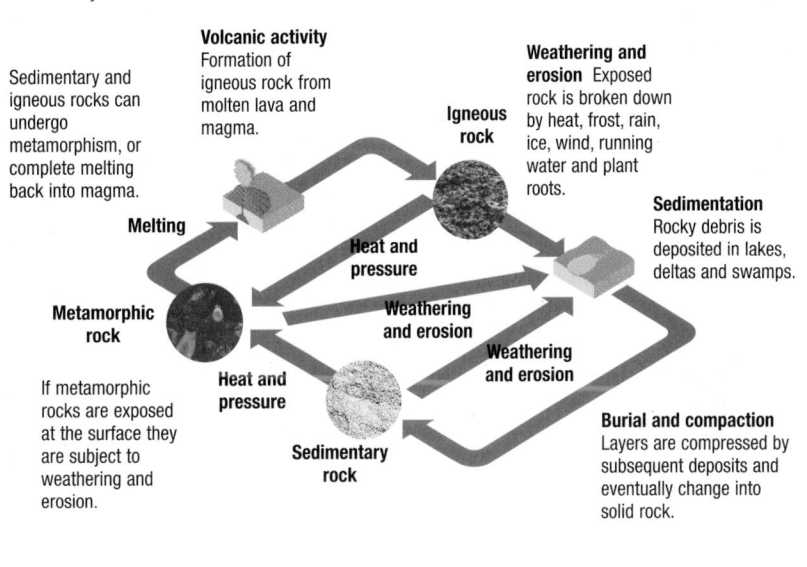

Sedimentary and igneous rocks can undergo metamorphism, or complete melting back into magma.

Melting

Volcanic activity Formation of igneous rock from molten lava and magma.

Igneous rock

Weathering and erosion Exposed rock is broken down by heat, frost, rain, ice, wind, running water and plant roots.

Sedimentation Rocky debris is deposited in lakes, deltas and swamps.

Heat and pressure

Weathering and erosion

Metamorphic rock

If metamorphic rocks are exposed at the surface they are subject to weathering and erosion.

Heat and pressure

Weathering and erosion

Sedimentary rock

Burial and compaction Layers are compressed by subsequent deposits and eventually change into solid rock.

Earthquakes are natural phenomena caused by sudden movements within the Earth's crust. These movements release stresses that have built up in rock due to movement of the interlocking tectonic plates that make up the Earth's crust. Most earthquakes are so small, or occur at such depth (greater than 300 km/200 miles), that they are not felt at the surface.

HOW EARTHQUAKES HAPPEN

Rocks do not bend or break easily and tend to absorb strains and stresses. But there comes a point when they will give way, breaking or moving along fault lines (pre-existing cracks) and releasing energy in the form of seismic waves, which vibrate through the surrounding rock and any structures, such as buildings, on the surface. Most earthquakes occur at boundaries between the plates of the Earth's crust. Here, friction is produced as the plates move relative to each other, and strain builds up prior to its release as an earthquake.

Earthquakes can also be initiated by volcanoes, meteorite impacts, and by human activities such as bomb explosions, the filling of reservoirs, and the injection of fluids into wells for oil recovery. Unlike earthquakes that occur at faults, these are the result of the sudden input of energy, which imposes an immediate stress on the rocks.

Earthquakes are classified by their depth of origin:

- **Shallow** – less than 70 km (40 miles)
- **Intermediate** – 70–300 km (40–186 miles)
- **Deep** – greater than 300 km (186 miles)

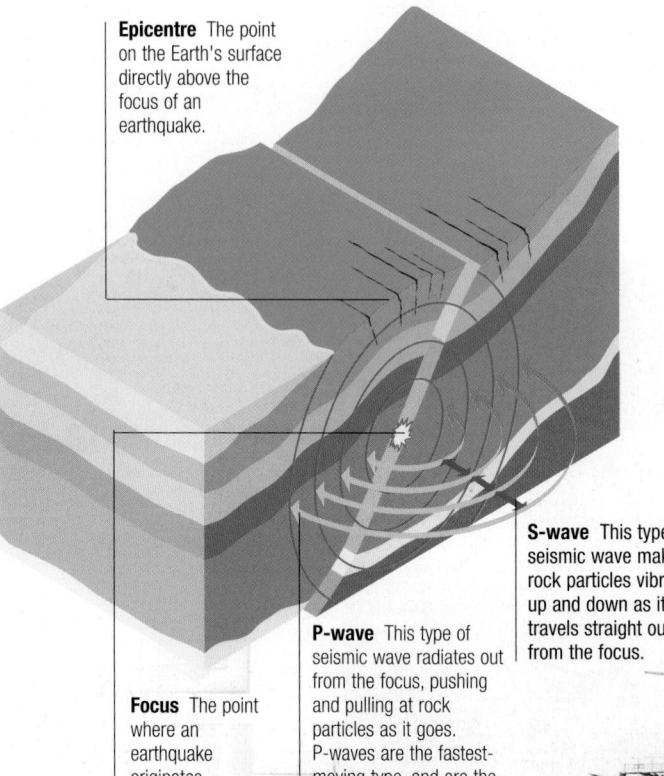

Epicentre The point on the Earth's surface directly above the focus of an earthquake.

S-wave This type of seismic wave makes rock particles vibrate up and down as it travels straight out from the focus.

P-wave This type of seismic wave radiates out from the focus, pushing and pulling at rock particles as it goes. P-waves are the fastest-moving type, and are the first to be picked up by earthquake monitoring stations.

Focus The point where an earthquake originates.

MEASURING EARTHQUAKES

There are two ways to measure earthquake size: **magnitude**, based on instrumental readings of the amount of energy an earthquake releases; and **intensity**, based on the effect an earthquake has. These are measured on different scales.

The **Richter scale** was developed in 1935 by Charles F. Richter as a way to compare the magnitude of earthquakes.

Magnitude is obtained from recordings of earth movements during earthquakes, made on machines called seismographs.
Each whole number on the Richter scale represents a release of energy 31 times greater than the previous whole number point. The scale has no upper limit, but the greatest earthquake ever recorded measured 9.5.

The **Modified Mercalli scale**, developed in the 1930s, is used to assess intensity. It grades earthquakes on a scale of I–XII depending on their effects.

I–II	Barely felt, generally not recognised as an earthquake.
III–IV	Often felt, no damage.
V–VI	Felt widely, objects moved, slight damage.
VII	Damage to poorly constructed buildings.
VIII	Damage to well-constructed buildings.
IX–X	Landslides, wholesale destruction.
XI	Total damage, visible ground movement.
XII	Total damage over large area, objects thrown into air.

Earthquake damage A stretch of elevated highway is tipped on its side by the Kobe earthquake, Japan, in 1995. The quake measured 7.5 on the Richter scale.

Major earthquakes since 1900

Location	Magnitude
Chile 1960	9.5
Alaska 1964	9.2
Aleutian Islands 1957	9.1
Kamchatka 1952	9.0
Ecuador 1906	8.8
Kuril Islands 1958	8.7
Aleutian Islands 1965	8.7
India 1950	8.6
Chile 1922	8.5
Indonesia 1938	8.5

TSUNAMIS

Tsunamis are giant ocean waves. The most common causes are submarine earthquakes that shift a significant area of sea floor upwards or downwards, displacing millions of cubic tonnes of water. Travelling outwards from the displacement, the water builds into a large, destructive wave when it reaches shallow coastal waters. The sudden introduction of a large amount of material into the ocean by an erupting submarine volcano, or the sudden slide downslope of ocean-floor sediments, or a landslide into water from a cliff or collapsing volcano, has a similar effect. Tsunamis are relatively common in the earthquake-prone region around Japan, and the word 'tsunami' is Japanese for 'port wave'.

Sometimes called tidal waves, tsunamis have nothing to do with tides, although they can be exacerbated by local tidal conditions.

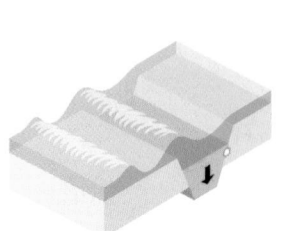

Underwater earthquake Movement of the seabed causes the displacement of a large block of water.

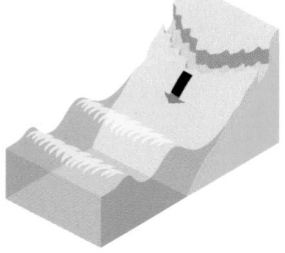

Landslide The sudden collapse of a cliff into the sea triggers a wave.

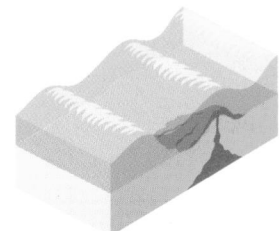

Underwater volcano An extensive lava flow from a submarine eruption displaces a large water volume.

FACTS

- Between 200 and 300 earthquakes occur annually in the UK and surrounding continental shelf.
- Ninety per cent of earthquakes occur along plate boundaries.
- There are about 8000 micro-earthquakes every day. These have a magnitude of 2 or less and are not commonly felt, although they are recorded by sensitive seismographs.
- About 7000 shocks a year of magnitude 4 or greater are recorded worldwide.
- On average, one earthquake of magnitude 8 or higher occurs somewhere in the world in every 12 months.

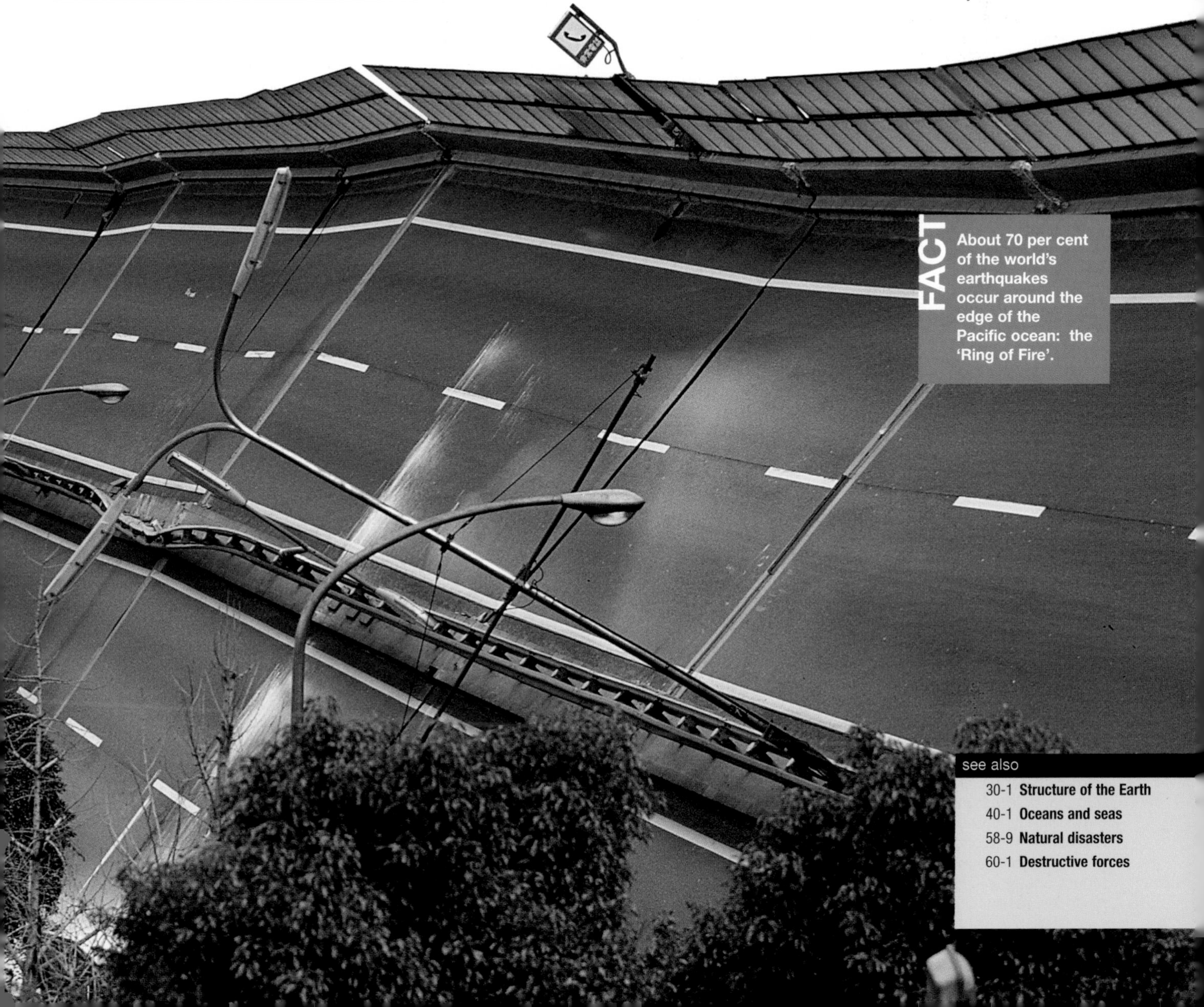

FACT About 70 per cent of the world's earthquakes occur around the edge of the Pacific ocean: the 'Ring of Fire'.

see also
30-1 **Structure of the Earth**
40-1 **Oceans and seas**
58-9 **Natural disasters**
60-1 **Destructive forces**

Volcanoes are naturally occurring vents or fissures in the Earth's surface through which molten, gaseous or solid material is ejected. They occur mainly along plate boundaries and there are more than 1500 active volcanoes in the world today. Volcanic ash, circulating in the upper atmosphere, can cause temporary changes in global weather.

TYPES OF VOLCANO

Most volcanoes are one of four major shapes. The shape depends on factors that include age and type of eruption.

Lava domes Form by the slow release of extremely thick lava. Domes can be solitary, form in clusters, grow in existing craters or appear along the flanks of volcanic cones. A dome has been growing slowly within the crater of Mount St Helens since its eruption in 1980.

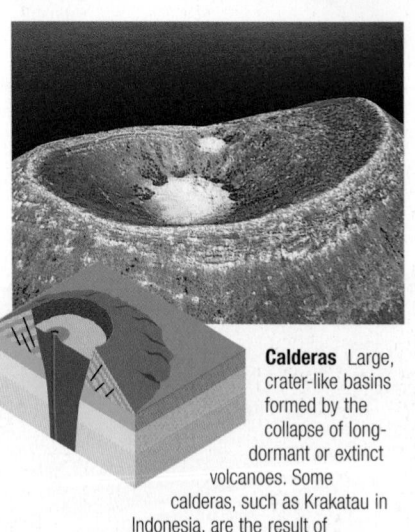

Calderas Large, crater-like basins formed by the collapse of long-dormant or extinct volcanoes. Some calderas, such as Krakatau in Indonesia, are the result of cataclysmic explosions that destroy the erupting volcano. Others result from the collapse of the cone once the magma chamber below has emptied and can no longer support it.

Shield volcanoes Large with broad summit areas and gently sloping sides, formed from very runny basaltic lava flows. Some of the largest volcanoes in the world are shield volcanoes – the island of Hawaii is made up of five coalesced shield volcanoes of successively younger ages.

Composite or stratovolcanic cones The classic volcanic cone is built up by multiple eruptions of lava and ash over hundreds or thousands of years. Composite cones can grow to great heights, and comprise 60 per cent of the Earth's individual volcanoes. Examples include Mount Fuji in Japan and Mount Rainier in the USA.

Life history of a volcano

⬤ **Eruptive stage** Violent phase with continuous or periodic eruption of lavas, gases or solid material. This may be short or long-lived. Paricutin, Mexico, was in eruption for nine years. Stromboli, Italy, has been in eruption for over 2000 years.

⬤ **Fumarolic stage** For a long period after it has ceased to erupt, a volcano continues to emit acid gases and vapour.

⬤ **Cooling stage** The ground still contains latent heat, which can heat ground water to form hot springs. Examples include the geysers and hot springs of Yellowstone National Park, USA, and North Island, New Zealand.

⬤ **Dormancy and extinction** The last traces of volcanic heat disappear and the volcano gradually reduces through erosion. As the magma beneath the volcano cools and contracts, the cone might collapse, forming a caldera. Finally, erosion might completely eradicate the volcano, or leave only the harder rock in the vent, now called a volcanic pipe. Examples of volcanoes that have become inactive in recent geological time include Mount Shasta in California and Mount Hood in Oregon, USA.

Inside a volcano

The diagram below shows the major features of a composite volcano.

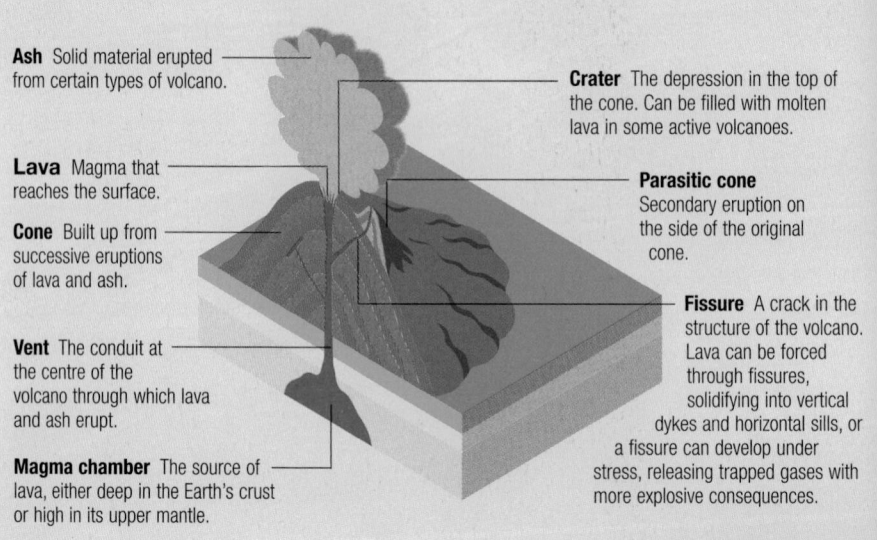

Ash Solid material erupted from certain types of volcano.

Lava Magma that reaches the surface.

Cone Built up from successive eruptions of lava and ash.

Vent The conduit at the centre of the volcano through which lava and ash erupt.

Magma chamber The source of lava, either deep in the Earth's crust or high in its upper mantle.

Crater The depression in the top of the cone. Can be filled with molten lava in some active volcanoes.

Parasitic cone Secondary eruption on the side of the original cone.

Fissure A crack in the structure of the volcano. Lava can be forced through fissures, solidifying into vertical dykes and horizontal sills, or a fissure can develop under stress, releasing trapped gases with more explosive consequences.

Volcanic Explosivity Index

The Volcanic Explosivity Index (VEI) is used to judge the size of an eruption. It is based on a number of observations, including the volume and height of material erupted. In the geological past there have been infrequent supervolcanoes, much larger than anything witnessed in the historic past. The most recent was in North America (Yellowstone National Park area) some 2 million years ago.

VEI	Eruption type	Plume height	Volume	Occurrence
0	non-explosive	100 m	1000 m²	Every day
1	gentle	100-1000 m	10 000 m²	Every day
2	explosive	1-5 km	1 million m²	Every week or so
3	severe	3-15 km	10 million m²	Every year or so
4	cataclysmic	10-25 km	100 million m²	Every few decades
5	paroxysmal	25 km	1 km²	About once a century
6	colossal	25 km	10 km²	Every few centuries
7	supercolossal	25 km	100 km²	Every few 1000 years
8	megacolossal	25 km	1000 km²	Every few 100 000 years

Where volcanoes occur

The great majority of volcanoes are concentrated along the boundaries of tectonic plates.

At constructive boundaries, such as mid-ocean ridges, where plates are moving apart, lava is erupted from the upper mantle.

At convergent boundaries, where one plate plunges beneath the other, material on the upper surface of the sinking plate is dragged down until it reaches a depth where it becomes molten. Being less dense than the surrounding solid rock it rises up to be erupted at the surface.

Volcanoes also occur above 'hot spots' created by uprising plumes of hot material in the mantle. As the plate moves slowly over a hot spot, a chain – or arc – of volcanic islands, such as Hawaii, is produced.

Mount Hekla, Iceland Iceland straddles the Mid Atlantic Ridge, an active constructive plate margin, and was created by the build-up of basalt eruptions from submarine volcanoes.

From flint tools to uranium nuclear fuel, the Earth's crust has always provided resources for mankind. Today, for instance, fossil fuels – coal, oil and natural gas – account for more than 75 per cent of the world's energy needs. Metals, minerals, clays and rocks are exploited to provide us with everything from pottery to construction materials, medicines to jewellery.

COAL

Coal is a carbon-rich mineral deposit formed by the fossilisation of plants growing in swampy or deltaic conditions. Coal is ranked by its carbon content, which is dependent on its stage of formation. As peat becomes more deeply buried, pressure from overlying layers of rock forces out water and gases, and the percentage of carbon left in the remaining layer increases. Peat is 50 per cent carbon, lignite 72 per cent, bituminous coal 85 per cent and anthracite 93 per cent.

OIL AND GAS

Oil is a liquid fossil fuel formed by the decomposition, without oxygen, of microscopic animals and plants and their subsequent heating. Organic deposits that can give rise to oil are laid down in brackish or marine conditions in deltas and seas, where they are rapidly buried in mud.

Oil is rarely found in its place of origin as it tends to migrate with water through pervious rocks, such as sandstone. Oil reservoirs form where oil and water collect in a layer of pervious rock (known as the reservoir rock) beneath a layer of impervious rock — the cap rock. This combination, called a trap, can occur in a variety of rock structures. Subsidence can create a space where oil and gas collect.

High temperatures within the crust cause natural gas dissolved in the oil to boil off, forming a layer above the oil.

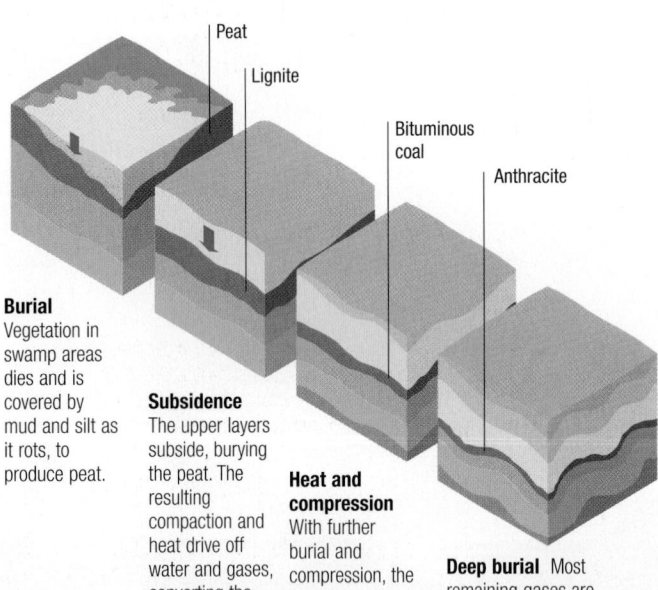

Peat

Lignite

Bituminous coal

Anthracite

Burial
Vegetation in swamp areas dies and is covered by mud and silt as it rots, to produce peat.

Subsidence
The upper layers subside, burying the peat. The resulting compaction and heat drive off water and gases, converting the peat into brown coal (lignite).

Heat and compression
With further burial and compression, the lignite turns into bituminous coal.

Deep burial Most remaining gases are driven off, turning the bituminous layer into anthracite.

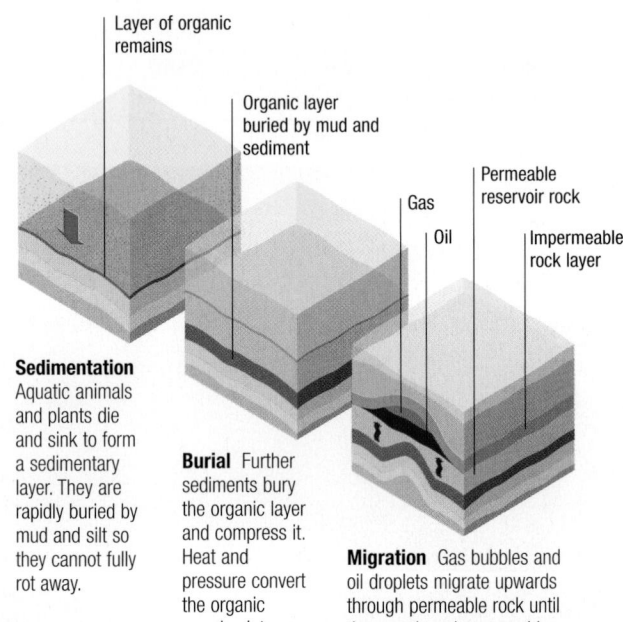

Layer of organic remains

Organic layer buried by mud and sediment

Gas

Oil

Permeable reservoir rock

Impermeable rock layer

Sedimentation
Aquatic animals and plants die and sink to form a sedimentary layer. They are rapidly buried by mud and silt so they cannot fully rot away.

Burial Further sediments bury the organic layer and compress it. Heat and pressure convert the organic remains into gas and oil.

Migration Gas bubbles and oil droplets migrate upwards through permeable rock until they reach an impermeable layer. Earth movements fold or fault the rocks, creating trap structures that hold the oil and gas.

WHAT ARE MINERALS?

Minerals are naturally occurring inorganic substances. Some are composed of just one element; diamonds, for example, are composed of carbon. More commonly, minerals are composed of two or more elements: quartz is a combination of silicon and oxygen, and iron pyrite is a combination of iron and sulphur. Rocks are made up of combinations of minerals. Those that are exploited for their constituent mineral elements are known as ores.

The majority of minerals form in the Earth's crust. They crystallise out from molten rock (magma) as it cools in chambers deep within the crust. Water that has been superheated by magma deposits minerals in veins and cavities. And metamorphism creates new minerals.

Some minerals, such as salt and gypsum, form from water evaporation at the Earth's surface. They may subsequently be buried by layers of sediments, such as sand, forming shallow or deep-buried deposits.

In lakes and seas, mineral deposits form from minerals that were dissolved in water precipitating out and falling to the bottom, where they are eventually buried.

Diamond A lump of diamond has formed in a conglomerate of rock.

Gemstones Some minerals are cut or faceted and artificially polished for use as gemstones. Gems can be transparent, translucent or opaque, and are classified as either precious (P) or semiprecious (S). The transparent stones are the mostly highly valued.

see also
30-1 **Structure of the Earth**
32-3 **Geology of the Earth**
500-1 **Fossil fuels**
508-9 **Mineral resources**

Mineral	P/S	Hardness	Colour/Pattern
Agate	S	7	Bands of varying colour
Amethyst	S	7	Purple/violet often banded with white
Aquamarine	S	7.5-8	Pale blue/green
Cairngorm	S	7	Brown
Diamond	P	10	Colourless; also yellow, blue, pink. Star pattern
Emerald	P	7.5-8	Green
Garnet	S	7-7.5	Red to brown
Opal	S	7	Many colours, milky to black. Brightly coloured flecks
Ruby	P	9	Red
Sapphire	P	9	Blue to colourless
Topaz	S	8	Yellow, blue or pink
Tourmaline	S	7–7.5	Pink to green
Zircon	S	7.5	Light brown, grey, yellow, green, colourless

Agate This gemstone forms in old lava flows.

Emeralds These transparent stones have a diamond-like lustre.

Metals All metals occur naturally in the Earth's crust. A few are found in pure form, but most metals occur in combination with other elements in rocks and minerals, which are known as ores. Metals are extracted from their ores by various physical and chemical methods, including crushing, flotation, gravity separation and smelting. The table lists some important metals and their ores.

Gold nugget Gold is often found in a relatively pure form.

Iron pyrite Iron is often found combined with other elements.

Metal	Common ores	Characteristics
Aluminium	Bauxite	Silvery white, very light
Arsenic	Arsenopyrite	Silvery white, hardness 6, poisonous
Copper	Chalcopyrite, chalcocite	Copper red, hardness 3, malleable
Gold	Native (pure) metal	Yellow, hardness 3, malleable
Iron	Haematite, iron pyrite, limonite, magnetite	Grey, hardness 5, malleable, magnetisable
Lead	Galena	Blue/white, hardness 2, malleable, soft
Mercury	Cinnabar	Silvery white, liquid, poisonous
Platinum	Occurs with other metals, eg iridium, osmium, gold	Silvery grey, hard, malleable
Silver	Native (pure) metal and argentite	Silver, hardness 3, malleable
Tin	Cassiterite	Silvery white, corrosion-resistant, malleable
Titanium	Occurs in igneous rocks	White, corrosion-resistant, high strength
Uranium	Pitchblende (uraninite)	Silvery white, radioactive, heavy
Zinc	Sphalerite	Bluish white, brittle

Oceans are large, deep, open expanses of water, while seas are shallower and partly encircled by land. Both oceans and seas are comprised of salt water. Taken together, the five oceans (Pacific, Atlantic, Indian, Southern and Arctic) contain 97 per cent of all the water on the Earth and cover about 71 per cent of its surface.

OCEAN PROFILES

The oceans form one vast, continuous area of water dotted with continents and islands. They are in a state of slow but unremitting change, expanding or contracting as the relative positions of the continents change. The longest mountain range on the planet is the mid-ocean ridge beneath the Atlantic, stretching 50 000 km (30 000 miles) from the Arctic to the South Atlantic, where it divides, one branch extending into the Pacific, the other stretching across the Indian Ocean.

On the ocean floor

The ocean floor is divided into the **continental shelf**, the gently sloping margin extending seawards from the shore; the **continental slope**, where the shelf ends and plunges steeply to the **ocean basin floor** where can be found:
- **Abyssal plains** Flat, featureless expanses of ocean floor at depths of 4000-6000 m (13 000-19 500 ft).
- **Spreading ridges** Places where two plates of the Earth's crust are moving apart. New crust forms in these regions.
- **Fracture zones** Cracks in the oceanic crust at right angles to spreading ridges.
- **Seamounts** Volcanic cone-shaped or flat-topped underwater mountains.
- **Trenches** Deep valleys where one crustal plate slides under another.

Pacific Ocean
The Pacific is by far the largest ocean, being twice the size of the Atlantic. It covers about a third of the Earth's surface, and contains more than half the water on the planet.

Atlantic Ocean
The second-largest ocean, the Atlantic is widening at a rate of 2-4 cm (3/4-1 1/2 in) per year along the Mid Atlantic Ridge.

	Pacific Ocean	Atlantic Ocean
Area	180 000 000 km² (70 000 000 sq miles)	106 000 000 km² (40 000 000 sq miles)
Volume	724 000 000 km³ (173 000 000 cu miles)	354 000 000 km³ (85 000 000 cu miles)
Average depth	3940 m (12 930 ft)	3310 m (10 860 ft)
Deepest point	Mariana Trench, 10 920 m (35 826 ft)	8648 m (28 374 ft)
Widest point	17 700 km (11 000 miles)	9600 km (5965 miles)
Features	**East Pacific Rise** A range of underwater mountains along a spreading ridge; 2000-3000 m (6500-9800 ft) high, they lie 3300 m (10 800 ft) below the surface. **Volcanic islands** Hundreds of volcanic islands are scattered across the Pacific, many are inhabited. **Great Barrier Reef** The world's largest living structure is situated in the Pacific, off the coast of Australia.	**Mid Atlantic Ridge** A spine of submarine volcanic features running roughly north to south marking a constructive plate boundary. The ridge is up to 4000 m (13 123 ft) high. **Sargasso Sea** An area of calm water in the western North Atlantic. The water surface is covered by green-brown *Sargassum* seaweed.

FACTS AND FIGURES

- **Total length of world's coastlines** 504 000 km (312 000 miles)
- **Warmest sea** Persian Gulf
- **Saltiest sea** Red Sea
- **Deepest trench** Mariana Trench (Pacific Ocean) 10 920 m (35 826 ft) below sea level. At 8863 m (29 029 ft)

Mount Everest could be completely sunk in the Mariana Trench.
- **Longest trench** Aleutian Trench (Pacific Ocean) 1700 km (1055 miles)
- **Highest seamount** Great Meteor Tablemount (North Atlantic) 4000 m (13 123 ft) high

SEAS

Seas are subdivisions of the oceans, especially where oceans are partly bounded by land. Seas are always salt water. Large landlocked bodies of salt water such as the Dead and Caspian seas are properly classified as lakes.

- **Coral Sea** 4 791 000 km² (1 850 000 sq miles. Part of the Pacific Ocean, lying between Australia and New Caledonia.
- **China Sea** Part of the Pacific Ocean, it has two areas: the East China Sea, 13 248 000 km² (481 850 sq miles); and the South China Sea, 2 318 000 km² (894 980 sq miles).
- **Caribbean Sea** 2 640 000 km² (1 019 000 sq miles) Part of the Atlantic Ocean containing many islands.

- **Mediterranean Sea** 2 516 999 km² (971 000 sq miles) An almost landlocked and tideless body of water. In 50 million years, if present plate motions continue to force Africa northwards, the Mediterranean will probably close up altogether.
- **Bering Sea** 2 270 000 km² (880 000 sq miles) Part of the northern North Pacific, lying between Alaska and Kamchatka, the Bering Sea is often frozen for several months each winter.

- **Sea of Okhotsk** 1 528 000 km² (589 961 sq miles) An extension of the north-west North Pacific, off the eastern coast of Russia.
- **Sea of Japan** 1 008 8000 km² (389 200 sq miles) Part of the North Pacific, between Japan, Korea and Russia.
- **Andaman Sea** 777 000 km² (297 572 sq miles) Part of the Indian Ocean, lying between the Andaman Islands and Thailand.

Indian Ocean

The Indian Ocean comprises about a fifth of the total area covered by seawater. It is the third-largest ocean.

75 000 000 km² (29 000 000 sq miles)

292 000 000 km³ (70 000 000 cu miles)

3840 m (12 600 ft)

Java Trench, 7450 m (24 442 ft)

Not applicable

Mid-Indian Ocean Ridge
This stretches from the Red Sea in the north almost to the southern limit of the Indian Ocean.

Ninety East Ridge
A major feature stretching 2735 km (1700 miles).

Red Sea
453 000 km² (175 000 sq miles) Lies over a spreading ridge and has been widening for the last 25 million years.

Southern Ocean

Includes all water lying south of latitude 55°S, and is the fourth-largest ocean. In winter, more than half the surface is covered by ice.

35 000 000 km² (13 500 000 sq miles)

Unknown

Unknown

4500 m (14 765 ft)

Not applicable

Information about the remote Southern Ocean is incomplete since Antarctic ice extends seawards hundreds of kilometres from the continent and observations from the ice-covered regions are sparse.

Arctic Ocean

The smallest and shallowest ocean, containing just 1 per cent of the Earth's salt water. A thick sheet of ice covers it for most of the year.

14 090 000 km² (5 440 000 sq miles)

17 000 km³ (4100 cu miles)

1205 m (3950 ft)

Pole Abyssal Plain, 5450 m (17 880 ft)

Not applicable

Arctic Mid-Ocean Ridge
An extension of the Mid Atlantic Ridge; actively spreading.

see also

26-7 **The Moon**
30-1 **Structure of the Earth**
46-7 **Islands in the sea**
472-3 **Harvesting the seas**

OCEAN CURRENTS

Ocean currents can be divided into surface (warm) and deep water (cold).
Surface currents Driven by the wind, surface currents can be up to 80 km (50 miles) wide, and move at speeds of up to 220 km (136 miles) per day in roughly circular patterns, called gyres. There are two gyres in the Northern Hemisphere (clockwise) and three in the Southern Hemisphere (anti-clockwise). Water is warmed at the Equator, and this heat is transported by the currents towards the poles.
Deep-water currents Changes in water density create deep-water currents. The colder and saltier the water, the greater its density. Water is at its coldest and saltiest near the poles, where it sinks down to the ocean floor. It spreads slowly towards the Equator at a rate of a few metres a day, and warmer water flows in to take its place.

■ **Surface currents** **1** West Australia Current; **2** North Pacific Current; **3** North Equatorial Current; **4** Equatorial Counter Current; **5** South Equatorial Current; **6** East Australia Current; **7** Florida Current; **8** Gulf Stream; **9** North Atlantic Drift; **10** North Equatorial Current; **11** Guinea Current; **12** Brazil Current; **13** Agulhas Current; **14** Somali Current.

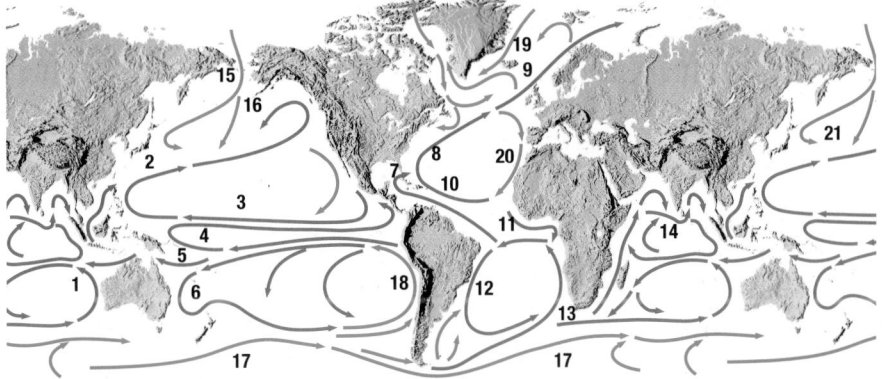

■ **Deep-water currents** **15** Kamchatka Current; **16** Aleutian Current; **17** Antarctic Circumpolar Current; **18** Peru (Humboldt) Current; **19** East Greenland Current; **20** Canaries Current; **21** Japan Current.

Rivers are a vital element in the Earth's water cycle, transporting water that falls as rain or snow back to the sea. In the process, rivers irrigate the land and provide a rich habitat for wildlife. With the exception of the frozen polar regions, rivers occur right across the Earth's land surface. They can even be found in the driest deserts, although their flow may be intermittent.

RIVER FORMATION

Water finds its own level, and surface water will tend to channel along depressions and hollows and make its way, under the influence of gravity, downhill to the sea. Rivers are formed when small channels combine to become a major feature. Rivers have their origin in high ground, and tend to be small but fast-flowing near their source, gradually growing larger, wider and slower-flowing farther down their length as tributaries join them and they approach the sea.

Rivers have three main stages. In the first stage, young rivers carve downwards, forming characteristic V-shaped valleys and picking up rocky debris in the process. Waterfalls and rapids are common features of young rivers. In the second stage, rivers slow and begin to deposit material at the same time as eroding the river channel. Flood plains develop along second-stage rivers, and they begin to meander. In the final stage they flow sluggishly, and meanders become more pronounced. Remaining sediment is deposited in an estuary or delta.

Deltas

Some rivers form deltas where they meet the sea. As water enters the sea, it suddenly loses speed and deposits any suspended particles of sand or mud (sediment) that it was carrying. Over time, these particles may build up until they block the river. The river then divides and flows to either side of the blockage, each new stream forming its own banks. As division continues, a delta is formed. There are two types of delta:
Fan-shaped deltas are called arcuate deltas – eg the Nile.
Lobe-shaped deltas are called bird-foot deltas – eg the Mississippi.

Fan delta The Nile delta is a classic fan shape. The Nile splits into several channels far inland, and these deposit the sediment in the delta area. Strong wave action in the Mediterranean redistributes the sediment along the delta front.

Lobe delta The Mississippi has a lobe or bird-foot delta. A small number of major channels carry sediment out to sea, extending the delta in a characteristic tongue shape.

Sediment deposit

Sediment deposit

Distributary channels

THE WORLD'S LONGEST RIVERS

1 Nile

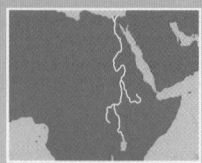

The Nile is the world's longest river; it has the third-largest drainage basin (area of land drained). Its volume of water is relatively small because much of the area it drains is so dry.

Location: NE Africa
Length: 6700 km (4100 miles)
Drainage basin: 3.3 million km^2 (1.3 million sq miles)
Source: East African Rift Valley (White Nile); Ethiopian Highlands (Blue Nile)
Major tributaries: None
Flows into: Mediterranean

2 Amazon

The world's second-longest river; and arguably the longest, depending on which channel in its delta it is measured from. It has the largest drainage basin.

Location: South America
Length: 6400 km (4000 miles)
Drainage basin: 7 million km^2 (2.7 million sq miles)
Source: Eastern flanks of the Andes mountain range
Major tributaries: Negro, Japura, Putumayo, Napo, Ucayali, Jurua, and Purus
Flows into: Atlantic Ocean

3 Chiang Jiang

The Chiang Jiang begins in Tibet, where it is fed by melting snow. It is Asia's largest river, and the world's deepest. In places, floods have caused the river to rise by up to 50 m (170 ft).

Location: East Asia
Length: 6300 km (4000 miles)
Drainage basin: 1.8 million km^2 (0.7 million sq miles)
Source: Tibetan plateau
Major tributaries: Gan, Han, Jialing, Litang
Flows into: East China Sea

4 Mississippi

The Mississippi divides the USA in two. The word Mississippi derives from Algonquin, a Native Indian language, meaning 'father of waters'.

Location: North America
Length: 6000 km (3700 miles)
Drainage basin: 3.2 million km^2 (1.2 million sq miles)
Source: Lake Itasca, Minnesota, USA
Major tributaries: Missouri and the Arkansas
Flows into: Gulf of Mexico

5 Yenisei

The Yenisei drains an area of Siberia almost as large as that drained by the Mississippi. In places it reaches a width of 40 km (25 miles). It is frozen throughout winter.

Location: Russia
Length: 5540 km (3442 miles)
Drainage basin: 2.5 million km^2 (1 million sq miles)
Source: Lake Baikal
Major tributaries: Angara, Nizhnaya Tunguska
Flows into: Kara Sea (Arctic Ocean)

WATERFALLS

Within a river's lifetime a waterfall is a temporary feature that is eventually worn away. Waterfalls are divided into three types:

Cataract A high fall over which large volumes pass.

Cascade Low in height and less steep than cataracts. The term also describes a series of small falls along a river.

Rapids An increase in channel steepness causes turbulent flow and white water.

Waterfalls form for one of four main reasons:

Change in rock type When a river passes from harder to softer rock, it erodes the softer rock more quickly, creating a drop.

Change in topography Raised blocks such as lava flows and land uplifted by faults create platforms.

Glaciation Waterfalls drop from hanging valleys left high on a valley side after the glacier ice has melted.

Drop in sea level The river has to cut down along its channel, causing a sharp change of gradient.

The world's highest waterfall Angel Falls drops 807 m (2650 ft) in total.

FACTS

Waterfall with the largest volume: Stanley (Boyoma) Congo, 17 000 m^3 (600 900 cu ft) a second.

Widest waterfall: Chutes de Khone (Khone Falls), Mekong River in Laos 10.8 km (6^3/$_4$ miles) wide. The volume of water passing over it has been estimated at 11 600 m^3 (410 000 cu ft) a second, although its height is only 70 m (230 ft).

Highest waterfall in Europe: Utigård, Nesdale, Norway 800 m (2625 ft).

see also
44-5 **Lakes**
48-9 **Glaciers**
50-1 **Mountains**

Other major rivers

Murray (Australia) 3800 km (2300 miles) Australia's longest river.

Volga (Russia) 3700 km (2300 miles) The longest river in Europe.

Danube (Europe) 2800 km (1800 miles) The only east-flowing river in Europe.

Rhine (Europe) 1300 k (800 miles) The longest river in western Europe.

6 Huang He

The Huang He (Yellow River) runs eastwards from Tibet, over the North China Plain. It deposits an estimated 1.4 billion tonnes of sediment at its mouth each year, making its delta the fastest growing in the world, increasing by 2 km (1 mile) each year.

Location: China
Length: 5464 km (3400 miles)
Drainage basin: 750 000 km^2 (300 000 sq miles)
Source: Tibetan plateau
Major tributaries: Wei, Fen
Flows into: Yellow Sea

7 Ob

The Ob originates in the Altai mountains, where Russia, Mongolia and China meet. It snakes through western Siberia before meeting the Irtysh about 500 km (300 miles) east of the Ural mountains.

Location: Russia
Length: 5410 km (3362 miles)
Drainage basin: 2.9 million km^2 (1.1 million sq miles)
Source: Altai mountains
Major tributaries: Irtysh, Chulym, Biya, Katun
Flows into: Arctic Ocean

8 Zaire

The Zaire (formerly the Congo) drains west Central Africa's rain forests, and is the world's second-largest river by volume of water after the Amazon. It flows north then west in an arc.

Location: W/Central Africa
Length: 4700 km (2900 miles)
Drainage basin: 3.5 million km^2 (1.3 million sq miles)
Source: Hills of northern Zambia
Major tributaries: Lualaba, Lomami, Aruwimi
Flows into: Atlantic Ocean

9 Amur

The Amur is one of Asia's principal waterways. It rises along the border of Siberia and Manchuria. For about 1600 km (1000 miles) it forms the border between Russia and China, where it is known as the Heilong.

Location: Russia/China
Length: 4400 km (2734 miles)
Drainage basin: Unknown
Source: Yablonovy Mountains, southern Siberia
Major tributaries: Shilka, Songhu, Argun
Flows into: Sea of Okhotsk

10 Lena

The Lena starts life close to the source of the Yenisei. But while the Yenisei heads north-east, the Lena flows north-west, ending in a 400 km (250 mile) wide delta.

Location: Russia
Length: 4400 km (2734 miles)
Drainage basin: Unknown
Source: Mountains around Lake Baikal
Major tributaries: Vilyui, Vitim, Chara
Flows into: Laptev Sea (Arctic Ocean)

A lake is any large body of water, either fresh or salt water, that is completely surrounded by land. Many so-called seas, such as Galilee and the Dead Sea, are technically lakes. Lakes become more common at higher latitudes as evaporation is less in these colder climes.

LAKE FORMATION

Lake basins are formed by a variety of Earth's processes.

⬤ Tectonic forces in the Earth's crust cause rock-folding, subsidence and faulting, creating large depressions where water collects.
⬤ Landslides, mud flows, lava flows and glacial debris block valleys, which slowly fill with water.
⬤ Glaciers scour depressions out of the bedrock.
⬤ Violent volcanic eruptions and collapsed cones produce volcanic craters deep enough for a lake to form.
⬤ River meanders are cut off to form oxbow lakes.

Rift lakes Blocks of land sink along faults. Faulting produces some of the deepest lakes. Lakes Tanganyika, Malawi, Albert and Edward are examples of rift valley lakes in East Africa's Great Rift Valley.

Folds Downfolded rocks create depressions in which lake water can collect.

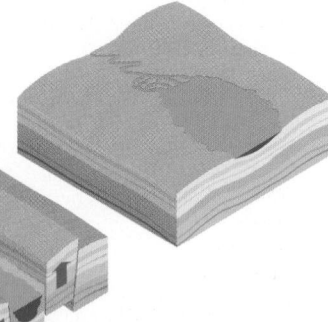

Crater lakes High-rimmed lakes form in the collapsed cones (calderas) of extinct or dormant volcanoes.

THE WORLD'S LARGEST LAKES

1 Caspian Sea

The Caspian Sea is fed by the Volga River. It is linked to the Baltic, White and Black seas. The Caspian Sea has no outlets and, over the millennia, has become salty. It lies 28 m (92 ft) below sea level.

Location: South-eastern Europe/south-western Asia
Area: 370 998 km²
(143 243 sq miles)
Maximum depth: 995 m
(3264 ft)
Length: 1200 km (746 miles)

2 Lake Superior

Lake Superior is the biggest and westernmost of North America's Great Lakes. Much of its northern shoreline is in Ontario, Canada. The rest is shared between the three states of Michigan, Wisconsin and Minnesota in the USA.

Location: North America
Area: 82 100 km²
(31 700 sq miles)
Maximum depth: 405 m
(1330 ft)
Length: 560 km (350 miles)

3 Lake Victoria

Lake Victoria is Africa's largest lake. Its surface is 130 m (3720 ft) above sea level. The main river running into Lake Victoria is the Kagera. At its northern end Lake Victoria drains into the River Nile.

Location: East Central Africa
Area: 69 490 km²
(26 830 sq miles)
Maximum depth: 823 m
(270 ft)
Length: 337 km (209 miles)

4 Lake Huron

The second-largest of the Great Lakes, Lake Huron receives the waters of Lake Superior and Lake Michigan, and drains into Lake Erie. Like Lake Superior, it has shores in both Canada and the USA.

Location: North America
Area: (including arms such as Georgian Bay and Saginaw Bay) 59 600 km²
(23 000 sq miles)
Maximum depth: 229 m
(750 ft)
Length: 332 km (206 miles)

5 Lake Michigan

Lake Michigan is North America's third-largest lake. It is contained entirely within the USA, but is shared between the states of Wisconsin, Michigan, Indiana and Illinois.

Location: North Central United States
Area: 57 800 km²
(22 300 sq miles)
Maximum depth: 281 m
(923 ft)
Length: 494 km (307 miles)

Lake life cycles Lakes are fed by rain, meltwater and ground water via springs, streams and rivers. Some lakes are permanent features, others are more short-lived. They may evaporate as the climate becomes more arid, or fill up with sediment leaving a bog or swamp in their place. In arid regions lakes rise and fall with the seasons and sometimes dry up for long periods. In some lakes where there is no outflow, substances dissolved in the water become concentrated. These salt or soda lakes can be rich in salts, sulphates and carbonates. If there is a lot of water evaporation, these minerals can form solid deposits.

Salt lake Talah Lake in Chile's Atacama Desert is rich in dissolved solids, and a salt rim forms where the lake waters have evaporated under the arid conditions.

OTHER LARGE LAKES

South America	Km²	Sq miles
Maracaibo, Venezuela	13 300	5150
Titicaca, Peru-Bolivia	8300	3200
Poopó, Bolivia	2600	1000
Buenos Aires, Chile-Argentina	2240	865
Chiquita, Argentina	1850	714
Europe		
Vänern, Sweden	5585	2156
Iso Saimaa, Finland	4377	1690
Vättern, Sweden	1912	738
Sevan, Armenia	1360	525
Mälaren, Sweden	1140	440
Inari, Finland	1102	425
Australasia		
Eyre, South Australia*	9300	3600
Torrens, South Australia*	5776	2230
Gairdner, South Australia*	4780	1845
Frome, South Australia*	2400	900
Amadeus, NT, Australia*	880	340
Taupo, North Island, NZ	606	234

* Usually dry

Alpine glacial lakes

There are 11 major lakes fringing the Alps: Geneva, Maggiore, Lugano, Como, Garda, Neuchâtel, Luzern, Zürich, Constance, Attersee and Chiemsee.

During the last Ice Age glaciers carved a way through the mountains, deepening valleys and depositing debris.

At the end of the Ice Age the glaciers melted. Water filled the valleys and was dammed by rocky debris.

Artificial lakes

Many of the world's lakes have been created artificially by the damming of rivers. Lake Nasser, behind the Aswan dam on the River Nile, is an example. It is 480 km (300 miles) long and about 14 per cent of its water evaporates, reducing the volume of the Nile downstream. The area was the site of the ancient temples of Abu Simbel, which were moved to preserve them.

FACTS

Greatest volume of fresh water Lake Baikal holds a fifth of the Earth's fresh surface water, approximately 22 995 km³ (5517 cu miles)

Unique ecology Lake Baikal contains 1000 unique species.

Highest navigable Lake Titicaca (south-eastern Peru and western Bolivia) is 3810 m (12 500 ft) above sea level. It is also 196 km (122 miles) long, and has an average width of 56 km (35 miles).

6 Lake Tanganyika

Lake Tanganyika is Africa's second-largest lake by area, and the second-deepest in the world. It is drained by the Lukunga River, which flows into the Zaire.

Location: East Central Africa
Area: 32 900 km²
(12 700 sq miles)
Maximum depth: 1435 m
(4702 ft)
Length: 680 km (420 miles)

7 Aral Sea

The Aral Sea is the second-largest saltwater lake on the planet. In 1960, it was the world's fourth-largest lake overall, but diversion of its feeder rivers for crop irrigation has since caused it to shrink dramatically. Today, its volume is less than a fifth what it once was.

Location: Central Asia, in south-western Kazakhstan and north-western Uzbekistan
Area: 32 370 km²
(12 500 sq miles)
Maximum depth: 54 m
(177 ft)
Length: 270 km (168 miles)

8 Great Bear Lake

Great Bear Lake is the largest lake entirely within Canada. It lies near the northern coast and straddles the Arctic Circle, making it one of the world's most northerly lakes.

Location: Northwest Territories, north-western Canada
Area: 31 790 km²
(12 270 sq miles)
Maximum depth: 396 m
(1299 ft)
Length: 300 km (186 miles)

9 Lake Baikal

Lake Baikal is by far the deepest lake in the world. Its waters reach depths of over 1.5 km (1 mile) in places. It is fed by the Selenga, Barguzin and Verkhnaya Angara rivers and more than 300 mountain streams.

Location: Southern Siberia
Area: 31 500 km²
(12 200 sq miles)
Maximum depth: 1620 m
(5315 ft)
Length: 636 km (395 miles)

10 Lake Malawi

Lake Malawi, also known as Lake Nyasa, lies south-east of Lake Tanganyika along eastern Africa's Great Rift Valley.

Location: Malawi-Mozambique-Tanzania
Area: 29 604 km²
(11 430 sq miles)
Maximum depth: 695 m
(2280 ft)
Length: 627 km (390 miles)

Crater Lake, Oregon, USA, formed in a caldera created by the collapse of Mount Mazama volcano over 6000 years ago.

Glacial lake Loch Coruisk in the Scottish Highlands fills a valley scoured out by a glacier during the last glaciation.

Islands in the sea

The life of the Earth's sea-locked regions

Islands form in various ways. Chunks can shear off the continents and be carried into the sea on oceanic plates: these fragments are what constitute the world's biggest islands. Submarine volcanism creates islands and island chains such as Iceland and Hawaii, and coral grows in shallow waters and can eventually make dry land. Islands are constantly born and destroyed as sea level fluctuates.

FACT

The isle of Surtsey near Iceland was born violently in 1963, when a volcanic eruption broke the surface of the North Sea.

The world's largest islands

The biggest islands are not volcanic: they are all tracts of land that have broken away from a continental landmass. One, Australia, is so large that it is not classified as an island at all – it is a continent in its own right. These satellite images show the world's ten largest islands to scale.

1 Charles Darwin, in 1835, was the first to guess that the round coral atolls of tropical waters had built up on the remnants of once live volcanoes.

2 As a volcano sinks, a coral reef grows on its submerged sides, just beneath the surface. This is called a fringing reef. What is left of the volcano is colonised by vegetation.

3 The dead volcano all but disappears, but the shape of the new coral islands reflects the conical form of the sunken mountain.

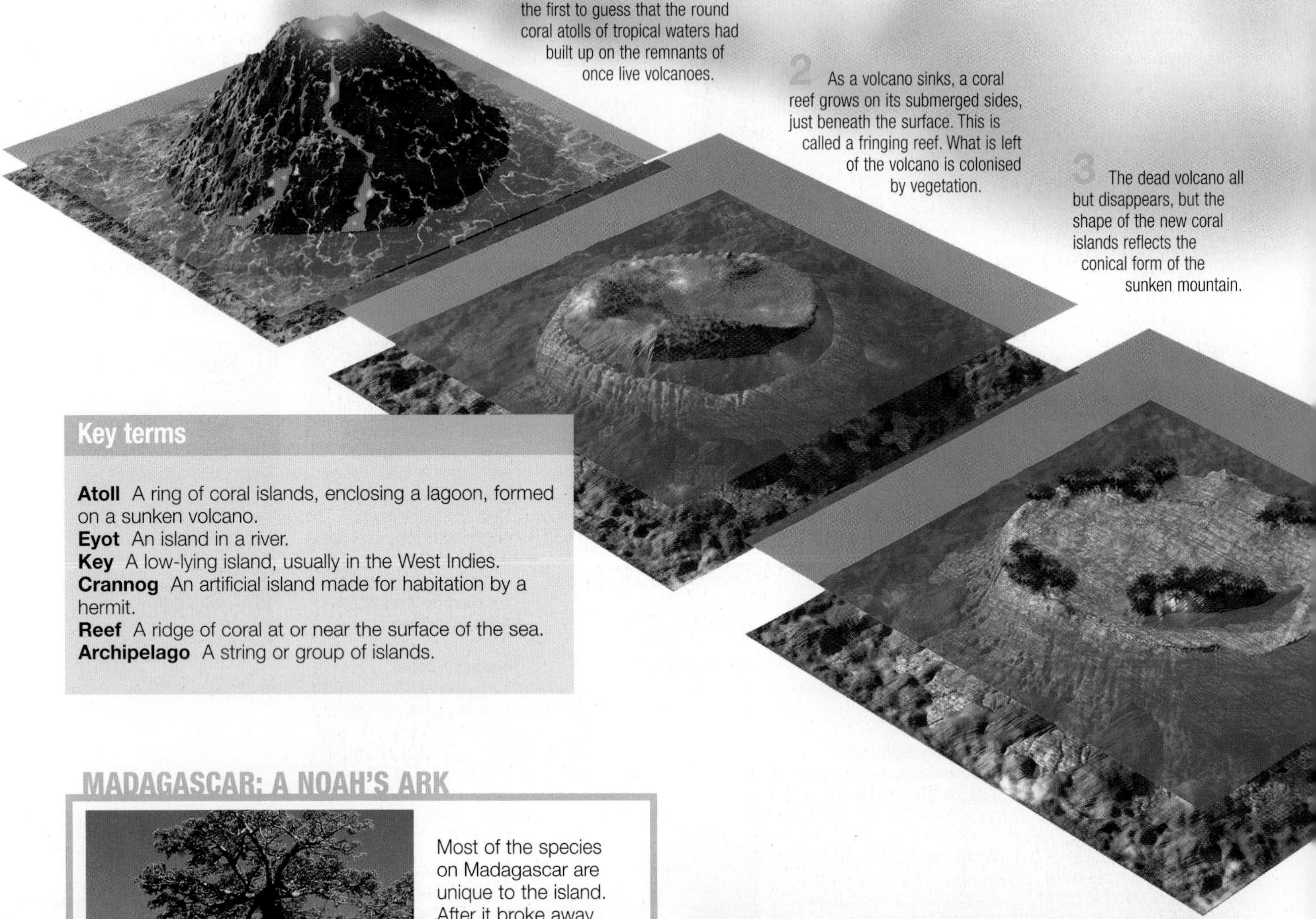

Key terms

Atoll A ring of coral islands, enclosing a lagoon, formed on a sunken volcano.
Eyot An island in a river.
Key A low-lying island, usually in the West Indies.
Crannog An artificial island made for habitation by a hermit.
Reef A ridge of coral at or near the surface of the sea.
Archipelago A string or group of islands.

MADAGASCAR: A NOAH'S ARK

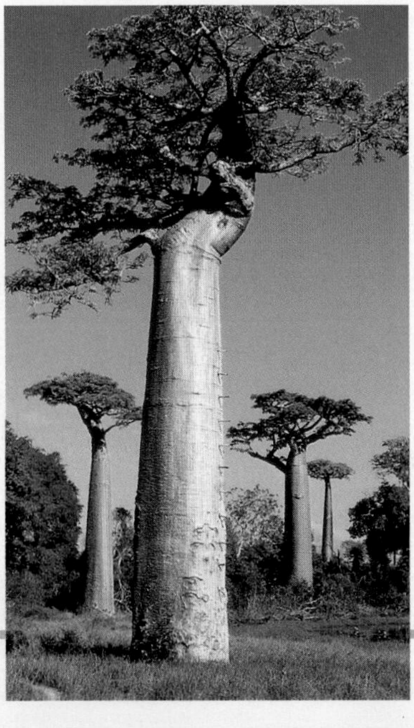

Most of the species on Madagascar are unique to the island. After it broke away from the African mainland, the animals on the island took their own evolutionary path. One of the strangest living things on Madagascar is the baobab (left), a giant water-filled sponge of a tree which deflates like a balloon when toppled.

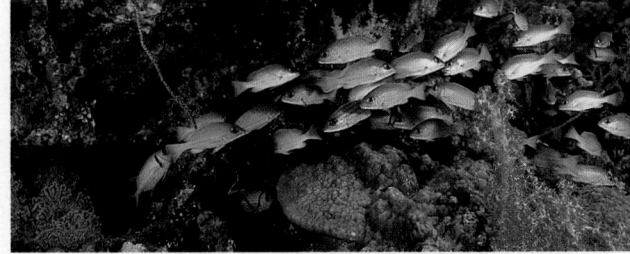

Cities of coral The Great Barrier Reef in Australia, the world's longest coral structure, stretches 2027 km (1260 miles) and has built up over the millennia to more than 300 m (984 ft) high. Some coral islands grow up from the sea floor, without being anchored on a dead volcano or submerged mountain. Corals can only survive in shallow waters so these high islands have built up as the sea level has risen.

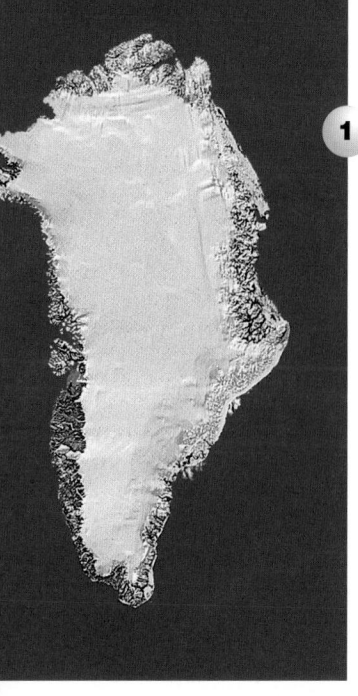

1 Greenland **North Atlantic.**
Area: 2 175 600 km² (839 780
sq miles). Around 85 per cent of
Greenland is covered by ice. The
ice is 3 km (2 miles) thick in places,
and accounts for 10 per cent of the
world's fresh water.

2 New Guinea **Australasia.** Area: 808 510 km² (312 085
sq miles). Natural extremes make New Guinea one of the most
dangerous islands on Earth. Volcanoes dot its mountain backbone,
and tsunamis are a common occurrence along its coast.

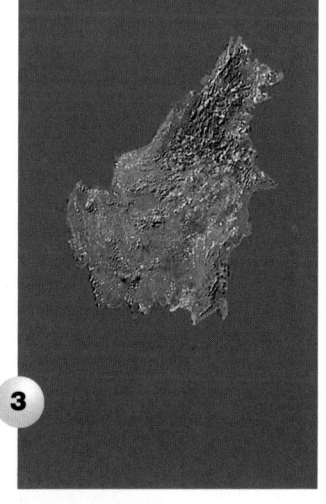

4 Madagascar
Indian Ocean.
Area: 594 100 km²
(229 322 sq miles).
Madagascar has
evolved unique flora and
fauna in isolation from
the African mainland.

3 Borneo **South China Sea.**
Area: 757 050 km² (292 220 sq miles).
It has the world's largest cave, the
Sarawak Chamber, at 300 m (990 ft).

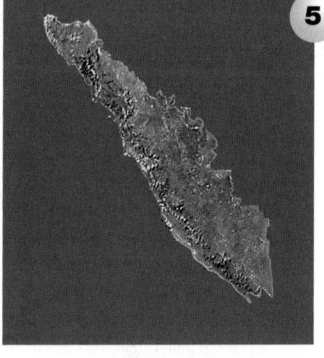

5 Sumatra
Indian Ocean.
Area: 524 100 km²
(202 300 sq miles).
Its Lake Toba is
a vast crater of
1166 km² (450
sq miles), formed
when a volcano
exploded around
60 000 years ago.

6 Baffin Island
Canadian Arctic.
Area: 476 070 km²
(183 760 sq miles).
Baffin is the largest
island of the Canadian
Arctic archipelago.

7 Honshu **Sea of Japan.**
Area: 230 455 km² (88 955
sq miles). Contains the
world's largest urban
mass, Tokyo-Yokohama.

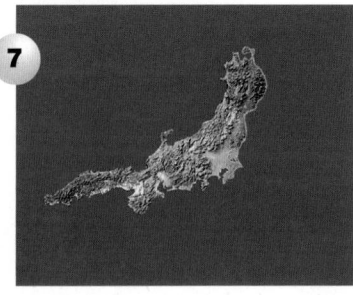

8 Great Britain **North Atlantic.**
Area: 229 870 km²
(88 730 sq miles). Britain
occupies 1/1000 of the Earth's
surface, but has 1/100 of
its population.

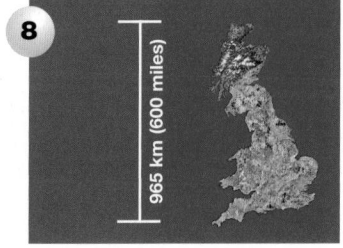

965 km (600 miles)

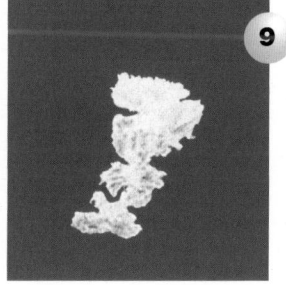

9 Ellesmere Island
Canadian Arctic.
Area: 212 690 km²
(82 100 sq miles). An
ice shelf on the
northern coast
produces raft-like ice
islands, which have
been used as floating
research stations.

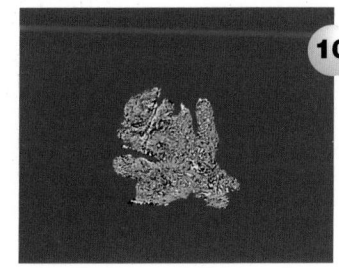

10 Victoria Island
Canadian Arctic.
Area: 212 200 km²
(81 910 sq miles). The
third-largest island of the
Canadian Arctic
archipelago, it was not
explored by Europeans
until 1851.

see also
30-1 **Structure of the Earth**
36-7 **Volcanoes**
40-1 **Oceans and seas**

Glaciers are made up of fallen snow that compresses into large, thickened ice masses. Eventually they become so heavy that they move very slowly downhill. Some glaciers are as small as football pitches, while others grow to be over 160 km (100 miles) long. They occur where snowfall in winter exceeds melting in summer, conditions that presently prevail only in high mountain areas and polar regions.

LONGEST GLACIERS

The lengths of the world's largest glaciers are represented on this diagram by the blue blocks.

Lambert-Fisher 515 km (320 miles)
Arctic Institute 418 km (260 miles)
Nimrod-Lennox-King 290 km (180 miles)
Denman 241 km (150 miles)
Beardmore 225 km (140 miles)
Recovery 225 km (140 miles)
Slessor 185 km (115 miles)
Petermanns 200 km (124 miles)
Humboldt 114 km (71 miles)
Novaya Zemlya 418 km (260 miles)
Siachen 70 km (44 miles)
Tasman 27 km (17 miles)
Franz Joseph 11 km (7 miles)
Bering (Alaska) 204 km (126 miles)
Hubbard (Alaska) 146 km (91 miles)
Aletsch 35 km (22 miles)
Fedchenko 77 km (48 miles)
Langiökull 64 km (40 miles)
Jostedals 75 km (45 miles)

Antarctica   Greenland   Russia   India/Pakistan   New Zealand   USA   Switzerland   Tajikistan   Iceland   Norway

HOW AND WHY GLACIERS FORM

- Glaciers form when snow remains in one location long enough to transform into ice.
- Each year, new layers of snow bury and compress the previous layers.
- Glaciers are constantly added to by snowfall along their upper reaches. Once the compressed ice reaches a critical thickness, around 8 m (25 ft), it becomes so heavy that it starts to move under the influence of gravity.

- The ends (snouts) of glaciers periodically retreat or advance, depending on the balance between snow accumulation and ice melting and evaporation.
- Glacier retreats and advances are usually very slow occurrences, noticeable only over long periods of time. However, glaciers can retreat rapidly with movement visible over a few months. Alternatively, they may surge forward several metres a day for weeks or even months.

Features of a glacier Glaciers originate in high mountain snowfields and move down valleys. Rocks and other debris from the valley sides and floor become frozen into the glacier and are carried along by it.

Accumulation zone Snow builds up in the upper reaches of a mountain and becomes frozen and compressed.

Lateral moraine An accumulation of rock debris and dirty ice forms along each side of the glacier as it picks up rock fragments from the valley sides.

Medial moraine When two glaciers meet, their lateral moraines combine to form a medial moraine down the middle of the merged glacier.

Crevasses Giant cracks form as a result of stresses that build up within the moving mass of ice.

Valley floor Where the glacier meets the ground, large amounts of rock and soil are ground up by the tremendous weight of the glacier and by the rocks that become embedded in its lower surface.

Snout the leading edge of the glacier.

Terminal moraine Debris deposited at the snout marks the stages in a glacier's retreat.

Meltwater

Key terms

Arete A jagged, narrow ridge between two glaciers.

Cirque A bowl-shaped hollow that is caused by a glacier eroding into a mountainside.

Drumlin A teardrop-shaped hill formed from till deposited by a receding glacier. Drumlins run parallel to a glacier's flow.

Erratic block A large rock picked up by a glacier and deposited, often a great distance away, when the glacier finally melted.

Fjord A long, deep, narrow coastal valley, originally carved out by a glacier, that filled with sea water after the glacier had melted.

Glaciated valley A trough-shaped, often steep-sided valley formed by glacial action. Examples can be seen in the English Lake District and Yosemite National Park, USA.

Till or boulder clay The material – ranging from house-sized boulders to clay particles – laid down as an unsorted deposit when a glacier melts.

A mountain is any landmass that stands significantly above its surroundings. The distinction between a mountain and a hill is arbitrary, not being defined by any internationally accepted measurement, but in Britain a mountain is usually defined as a hill that reaches at least 600 m (2000 ft) above sea level.

MOUNTAIN FORMATION

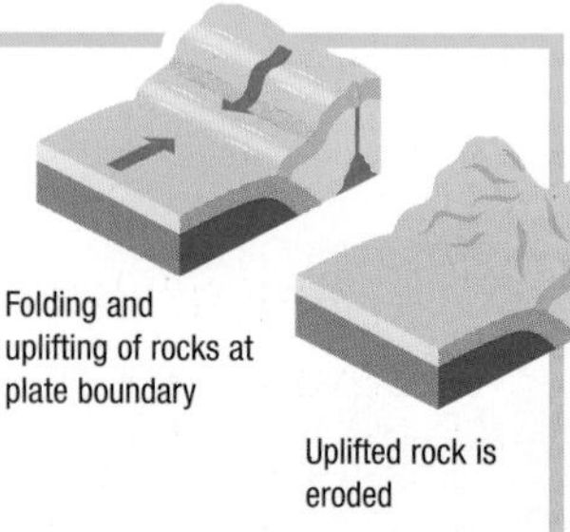

Mountains are categorised according to how they formed.

⬤ **Fold mountains** The majority of mountains are created when tectonic plates collide, causing folding and uplifting of rocks along the plate boundaries, a process called orogenesis. The uplifted land is then eroded into peaks and valleys. Examples: Himalayas, Andes and Alps.

⬤ **Volcanoes** Many volcanoes create a cone of erupted material; ash, lava or both. Such cones can reach great heights. Mount Erebus, an active volcano in Antarctica, is 4032 m (13 200 ft) high. Examples: Kilimanjaro, Mt St Helens.

⬤ **Erosional mountains** These form from high ground that has been deeply eroded, for instance by rivers. Examples: Blue Mountains, Australia; Table Mountain, Cape Town, South Africa.

⬤ **Island mountains** These are isolated hills that remain after erosion has worn away the surrounding land. Examples: Uluru (Ayers Rock), Australia; the pinnacles of the Metéora, Spain.

Folding and uplifting of rocks at plate boundary

Uplifted rock is eroded

Highest mountains on each continent

Mountains occur on all the world's continents, but some continents are flatter than others. No new mountain ranges have been created in Australia for millions of years, and its surface has undergone much erosion, whereas the Alps and the Himalayas formed as recently as 10 million years ago.

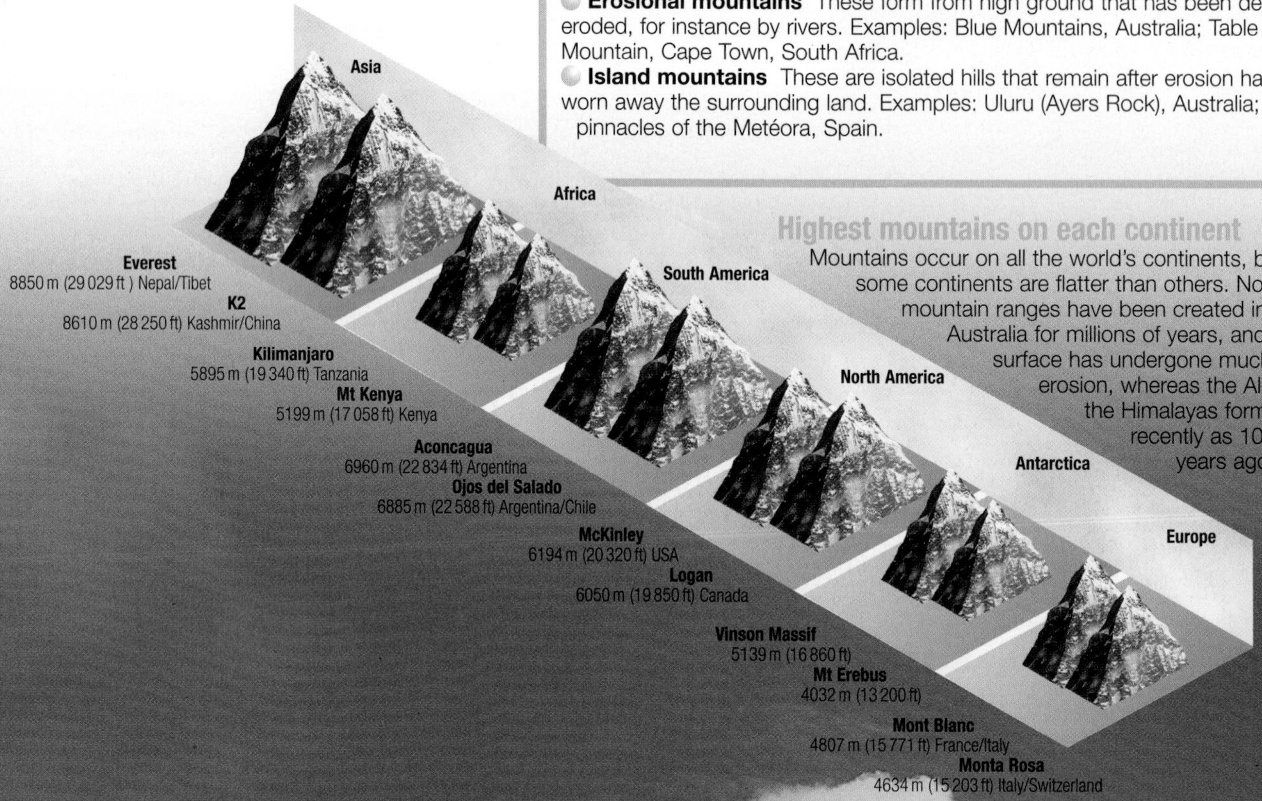

Asia

Everest
8850 m (29 029 ft) Nepal/Tibet
K2
8610 m (28 250 ft) Kashmir/China

Africa

Kilimanjaro
5895 m (19 340 ft) Tanzania
Mt Kenya
5199 m (17 058 ft) Kenya

South America

Aconcagua
6960 m (22 834 ft) Argentina
Ojos del Salado
6885 m (22 588 ft) Argentina/Chile

North America

McKinley
6194 m (20 320 ft) USA
Logan
6050 m (19 850 ft) Canada

Antarctica

Vinson Massif
5139 m (16 860 ft)
Mt Erebus
4032 m (13 200 ft)

Europe

Mont Blanc
4807 m (15 771 ft) France/Italy
Monta Rosa
4634 m (15 203 ft) Italy/Switzerland

Mount Everest The world's highest mountain above sea level dominates the Himalayas, a range of young fold mountains created when India collided with Asia. Everest's pyramidal shape is the result of erosion by glaciers.

FACT
The Himalayas (including the Karakorams) contain 96 of the world's 100 tallest mountains.

Mountains and ranges of the world

LONGEST MOUNTAIN RANGES
1. **Andes** South America 7242 km (4500 miles)
2. **Rockies** North America 6035 km (3750 miles)
3. **Himalaya/Karakoram/Hindu Kush** Asia 3862 km (2400 miles)
4. **Great Dividing Range** Australia 3651 km (2250 miles)
5. **Brazilian East Coast Range** Brazil 3058 km (1900 miles)
6. **Sumatran Range** Java 2897 km (1800 miles)
7. **Tien Shan** China 2253 km (1400 miles)
8. **Eastern Ghats** India 2092 km (1300 miles)

HIGHEST RANGES (Maximum height above sea level)
Himalaya/Karakoram/Hindu Kush 8848 m (29 028 ft)
Andes up to 6959 m (22 864 ft)
Alaska Range up to 6194 m (20 321 ft)

OTHER MOUNTAINS AND RANGES
Alps Europe 1207 km (750 miles) long.
Ben Nevis Scotland 1343 m (4406 ft). Highest UK peak.
Mauna Kea Hawaii 10 206 m (33 484 ft) from seabed.
Mount Fuji Japan 3798 m (12 460 ft). A young volcano.

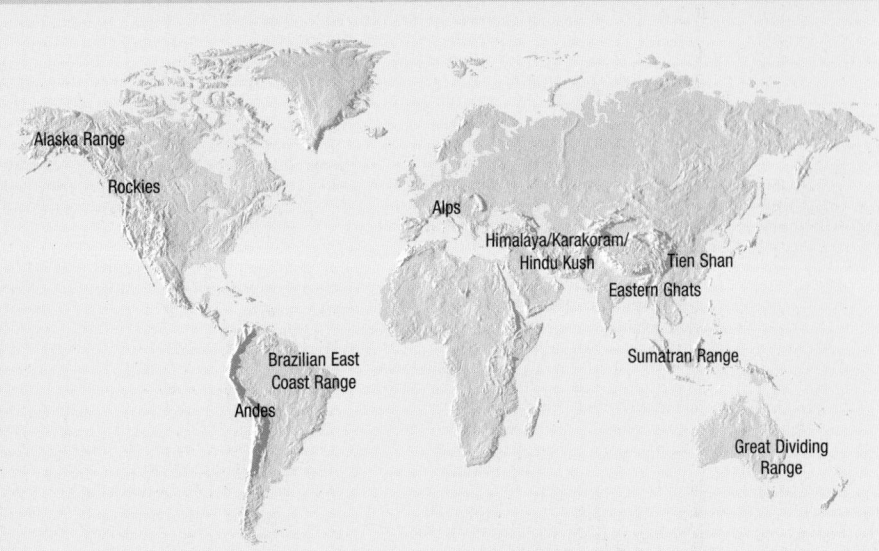

Alaska Range
Rockies
Alps
Himalaya/Karakoram/Hindu Kush
Tien Shan
Eastern Ghats
Sumatran Range
Brazilian East Coast Range
Andes
Great Dividing Range

Erosion

With the exception of recently formed volcanoes, the appearance of a mountain or range is due almost entirely to the effects of erosion. The jagged ridges and pointed peaks that we commonly associate with mountain ranges have been formed by the powerful erosive action of glaciers. Even near the equator, high mountains are snow-capped and susceptible to glaciation. Mounts Kenya and Kilimanjaro in east Africa are old volcanoes whose peaks have been sculpted by ice. Other mountains, such as Australia's Blue Mountains, are formed when horizontal rocks forming high ground are cut through by rivers.

Rock type is another factor in determining the shape of mountains. The soft mudstone of Italy's Dolomites, for example, erodes more easily than the overlying limestone layers. The undercut limestone eventually collapses forming steep cliffs.

The French Alps Glacial action has produced jagged peaks and ridges.

The Dolomites, Italy The magnesium-rich limestone (called dolomite) typical of the area has eroded into pinnacles and cliffs.

see also
30-1 **Structure of the Earth**
36-7 **Volcanoes**
42-3 **Rivers**
48-9 **Glaciers**

The atmosphere is an envelope of air held near to the Earth by gravity. It absorbs energy from the Sun, recycles water and other chemicals, and works with electrical and magnetic forces to provide a moderate climate, and so support life on Earth. It also shields us from high-energy radiation and the vacuum of space.

LAYERS OF THE ATMOSPHERE

The atmosphere extends over about 600 km (370 miles) out from the Earth's surface. Four distinct main layers have been identified, and each layer has particular chemical, physical and temperature characteristics. At the edge of the atmosphere is a boundary layer, the exosphere, a region of hydrogen and helium that gradually merges into space.

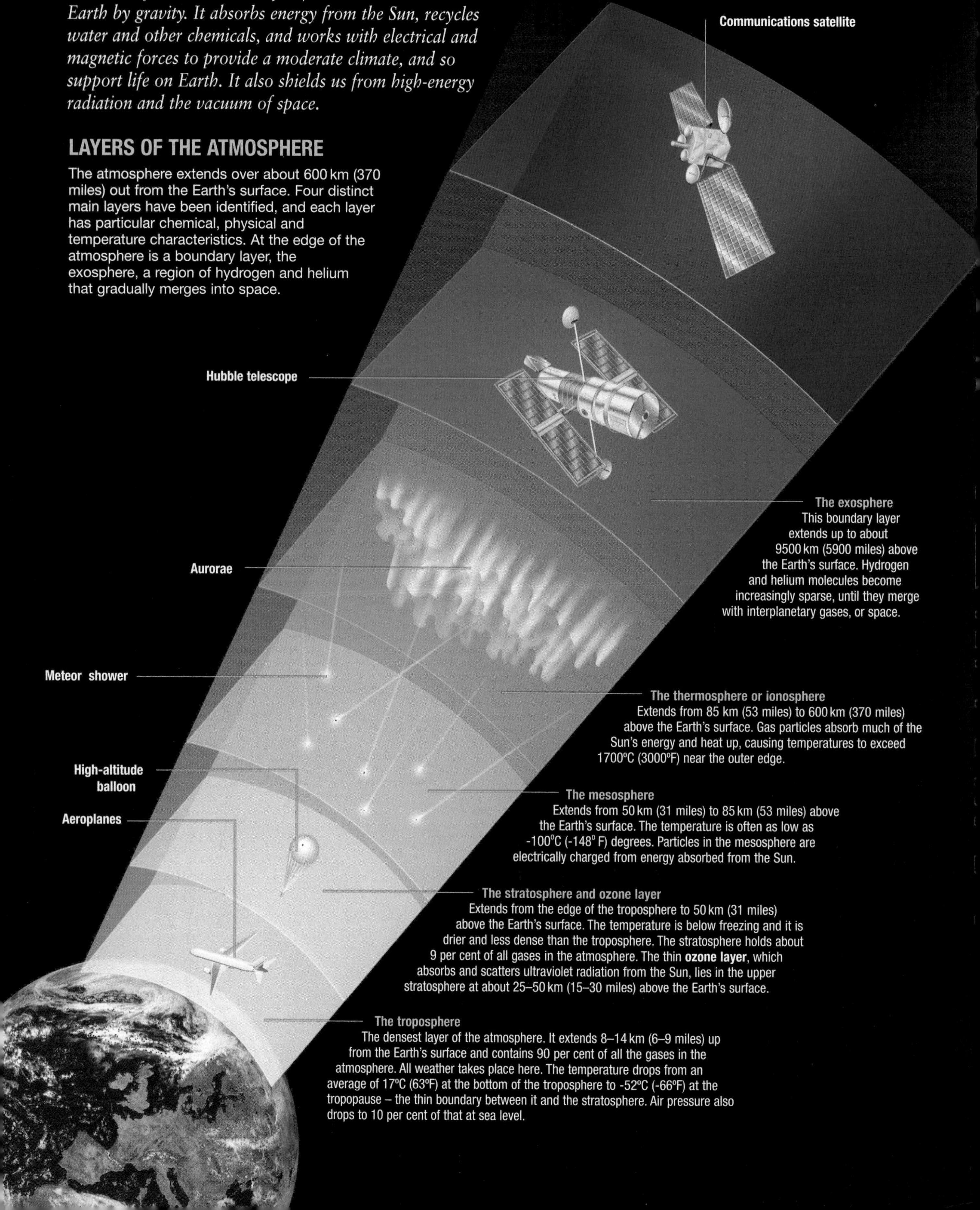

Communications satellite

Hubble telescope

Aurorae

Meteor shower

High-altitude balloon

Aeroplanes

The exosphere
This boundary layer extends up to about 9500 km (5900 miles) above the Earth's surface. Hydrogen and helium molecules become increasingly sparse, until they merge with interplanetary gases, or space.

The thermosphere or ionosphere
Extends from 85 km (53 miles) to 600 km (370 miles) above the Earth's surface. Gas particles absorb much of the Sun's energy and heat up, causing temperatures to exceed 1700°C (3000°F) near the outer edge.

The mesosphere
Extends from 50 km (31 miles) to 85 km (53 miles) above the Earth's surface. The temperature is often as low as -100°C (-148° F) degrees. Particles in the mesosphere are electrically charged from energy absorbed from the Sun.

The stratosphere and ozone layer
Extends from the edge of the troposphere to 50 km (31 miles) above the Earth's surface. The temperature is below freezing and it is drier and less dense than the troposphere. The stratosphere holds about 9 per cent of all gases in the atmosphere. The thin **ozone layer**, which absorbs and scatters ultraviolet radiation from the Sun, lies in the upper stratosphere at about 25–50 km (15–30 miles) above the Earth's surface.

The troposphere
The densest layer of the atmosphere. It extends 8–14 km (6–9 miles) up from the Earth's surface and contains 90 per cent of all the gases in the atmosphere. All weather takes place here. The temperature drops from an average of 17°C (63°F) at the bottom of the troposphere to -52°C (-66°F) at the tropopause – the thin boundary between it and the stratosphere. Air pressure also drops to 10 per cent of that at sea level.

Atmospheric effects visible from Earth

The Aurorae The aurora borealis in the Northern Hemisphere and the aurora australis in the Southern Hemisphere are light phenomena visible in the night sky at higher latitudes. They occur when high-speed particles emitted by the Sun enter the Earth's thermosphere and are channelled around the magnetic poles. Here they excite air molecules, causing them to release light – usually green or red. Spectacular arcs, curtains and streamers are created by the movements of the excited air molecules along lines of the Earth's magnetic field. Aurorae are more common during sunspot activity as more solar particles are released at these times.

Rainbows Rainbows are produced when sunlight is refracted through raindrops, splitting it into the seven component colours of white light. All rainbows are part of a perfect circle. Entire circular rainbows are visible only from aircraft and are called 'glories'.

Solar and lunar haloes These are created by light from the Sun or Moon passing through ice crystals high in the sky.

Parhelia Also called sundogs or mock suns, parhelia are partial haloes or bright spots that appear on either side of the Sun from light reflecting off ice crystals in high, cirrostratus clouds.

Sun pillars These are streaks of light rising from the Sun at sunrise or sunset, caused by the reflection of light by ice crystals in high cloud.

Aurora effect The aurora borealis lights up the Northern Hemisphere night sky.

GREENHOUSE EFFECT AND GLOBAL WARMING

The greenhouse effect is a natural phenomenon that helps to heat the Earth's surface. The process is so named because it is very much like the warming effect found in greenhouses. The Earth's atmosphere acts like the greenhouse glass, which the Sun's rays penetrate to warm the Earth's surface. Some heat is reflected back from the surface and much of it escapes into space. However, some is absorbed by naturally occurring atmospheric gases, such as carbon dioxide and methane. An increase in these greenhouse gases in the atmosphere means an increase in the amount of heat trapped, resulting in a rise in the Earth's temperature – the phenomenon known as global warming. Scientists fear that human activities such as the burning of fossil fuels are increasing the level of greenhouse gases and therefore global warming. There is speculation that this will lead to sudden changes in weather patterns and rising sea levels as the polar ice caps start to melt.

Normal conditions Earth's surface reflects heat from the Sun, and some of this escapes through the atmosphere into space.

Global warming When greenhouse gases build up in the atmosphere they absorb reflected heat, stopping its escape back into space.

The ozone layer

Ozone (O_3) is a gas composed of three atoms of oxygen combined. It is created when ultraviolet radiation (part of sunlight) strikes the stratosphere, splitting oxygen molecules (O_2) into two atoms of oxygen (O). These oxygen atoms quickly combine with ordinary oxygen molecules to form ozone. The ozone layer absorbs ultraviolet radiation, shielding the Earth from its harmful effects, which include inducing skin cancer. **What is the ozone hole?** An area of the ozone layer centred over Antarctica has thinned to around 30 per cent of normal levels, allowing more ultraviolet radiation to reach the surface of the Earth. Seasonal fluctuations in ozone levels are natural, but manmade chemicals such as chlorofluorocarbons (CFCs) have made the hole bigger as they react with ozone and destroy it. These reactions occur in stratospheric clouds, found only in polar regions, where the effect is concentrated. Depletion is greater over the South Pole where there are more stratospheric clouds.

FACT The atmosphere is composed mainly of nitrogen – 78 per cent. Only 21 per cent is oxygen.

Ozone hole The hole in the ozone layer over the Antarctic shows up as a blue circle in this image created from data collected from space.

Weather occurs in the troposphere, the layer of the atmosphere next to the Earth. It is the sum total of several physical conditions, including temperature, wind speed and direction, atmospheric pressure, precipitation and humidity, as they occur in any one place or region at any one time. The Earth's weather is a highly unpredictable system in constant flux.

WHAT MAKES WEATHER HAPPEN?

Atmospheric pressure is the key to explaining overall weather conditions. It can be defined as the downward force exerted by the atmosphere at any given point on the Earth, and it is extremely variable. Low atmospheric pressure gives rise to unsettled weather. In a low-pressure region, air rises and cools. Water vapour in the air condenses and clouds form – in the same way that warm air forms condensation on a cold window – and rain often results. High atmospheric pressure brings settled weather. Air is compressed by the high pressure and warms up, no clouds form and there are often clear skies. Wind is also controlled by air pressure because air tends to flow from a high-pressure area into a low-pressure area.

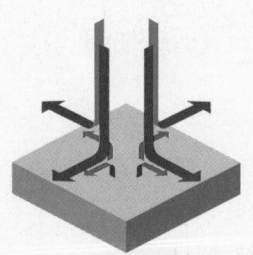 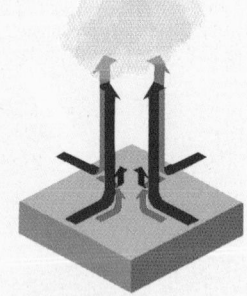

High atmospheric pressure Cold air slowly descends. As it falls, it is compressed and warms up, and generally brings warm, settled weather.

Low atmospheric pressure Air slowly rises and cools. Water in the air condenses, creating clouds and unsettled weather.

Wind Wind blows from areas of high pressure to areas of low pressure. When the Sun warms an area of air at the Earth's surface, that air expands, gets lighter and rises. Rising air exerts less pressure than static or falling air so this is an area of low pressure. Cooler, heavier air from a high-pressure area flows in to fill the void left by the warmer air, creating wind. The nearer the high-pressure area to the low-pressure area, or the greater the difference in pressure or temperature between the two areas, the faster the wind blows.

Prevailing wind patterns
Trade winds, Westerlies and Easterlies, blow in bands across the globe.

Rain Rising warm air carries water vapour high into the sky, where it cools, forming water droplets around dust particles in the air. These drops freeze into ice crystals and when they become heavy enough, they begin to fall. On meeting warmer air on the way down, the ice crystals melt to form raindrops.

Snow Snowflakes form when water vapour freezes into ice crystals in cold clouds. The ice crystals attract cooled water droplets and grow in size. Eventually they become heavy enough to fall, and if the air is cold enough they fall all the way to the earth as snow, without melting.
 Snowflake shape This depends on the temperature of the air. When water freezes, its molecules, each made up of two hydrogen atoms and one oxygen atom, join together in hexagonal patterns, which is why snowflakes are always six-sided. In colder air, several may join up and freeze together to form snowflakes that are needle or rod shaped.

Thunder and lightning When cold air and warm air meet, the cold air sinks and moves under the warm air, forcing it to rise rapidly. The rising air takes water vapour with it, which quickly cools and condenses, forming cumulonimbus clouds, sometimes called thunderheads. As the water vapour condenses, heat is released, which pushes the air even higher. Water droplets and ice particles crash together, resulting in a separation of electrical charges in the cloud: positively charged particles move to the top and negatively charged ones to the bottom. The difference between the two builds up until an electrical discharge – lightning – takes place between the negative charge in the cloud and the positively charged ground, or prominent objects such as tall trees or buildings. This is followed by a return discharge from the ground back up to the cloud. The second discharge is visible as a lightning flash. Thunder is a side effect of lightning. The lightning flash superheats the air around it, causing it to expand faster than the speed of sound, 1238 km/h (769 mph), causing a loud sonic boom, or thunder.

Beaufort scale

Wind strength can be estimated by comparing the wind's effects against the internationally agreed Beaufort scale.

Force	Effects
0	Smoke rises straight up, no motion.
1	Smoke drifts slowly, leaves barely move.
2	Drifting smoke clearly indicates wind direction.
3	Gentle winds. Leaves rustle, wind felt on face.
4	Moderate winds. Leaves in constant motion, dust blows.
5	Small trees sway, paper blows away.
6	Strong winds. Large branches sway.
7	Whole trees sway.
8	Gales. Tree twigs break, hard to walk.
9	Branches break, roof tiles blown down.
10	Small trees uprooted, roofs damaged.
11	Violent storms. Widespread building damage.
12	Hurricane winds. Severe destruction.

Background: Tornado at Caldwell, Kansas, USA, on March 13, 1990.

Hurricanes

Revolving storms in areas of extreme low pressure with winds that exceed 119 km/h (74 mph or 64 knots) are called hurricanes. They rotate anticlockwise in the Northern Hemisphere and clockwise in the Southern Hemisphere. Hurricanes are called by different names in different parts of the world: cyclones around the Indian Ocean, south-east Pacific and Australia; typhoons in the north-east Pacific and on the Asian mainland; and hurricanes in the USA and Caribbean. There are on average over 120 of these tropical cyclonic storms around the world every year.

Tornadoes

These are small-scale but very strong whirlwinds, or twisters, common in the United States. Tornadoes can develop in low-pressure weather systems. In the strongest thunderstorms, the lower part of a thunder cloud may start spinning. If this spinning air reaches down to the ground it becomes a tornado. Tornadoes are normally no more than 400 m (1/4 mile) across, but they can be very destructive. They travel at between 30-60 km/h (20-40 mph) and winds at the centre can rotate at almost 300 km/h (200 mph). Heavy rain and thunder usually accompany tornadoes.

El Niño

The phenomenon known as El Niño is a periodic reversal of Pacific Ocean currents that affects global weather conditions.

In a normal year warm water in the Pacific flows west towards Australia and Indonesia. There, it evaporates quickly, creating storm clouds over Australia. Warm water off the South American coast is replaced by cold, nutrient-rich water coming up the coast from Antarctica, creating good fishing grounds.

In an El Niño year the winds and currents that hold warm water in place off Australia weaken. The warm water flows back eastwards towards Peru, and spreads out along the coast of the Americas. Here it evaporates and creates rain clouds and thunderstorms. Rain fails to materialise in Australia, causing drought. The thunderstorms drive warm humid air high into the atmosphere, where it interferes with the normal currents of air circulation, causing extreme and unpredictable weather conditions as far away as Europe.

A normal year Warm surface currents in the Pacific Ocean flow westwards and bring rain to Australia.

An El Niño year Warm surface currents in the Pacific reverse, causing storms in America and drought in Australia.

Cirrus High wispy clouds consisting of ice occurring in fair weather.

Cumulus Puffy mid-level white clouds consisting of water and ice, usually associated with fair weather.

Cumulonimbus (thunderheads) Dark, puffy clouds consisting of water. They often produce thunderstorms.

Clouds

Clouds form when air rises and the water vapour contained within it cools and condenses, turning into water or ice. The following factors can cause air to rise:

● Heating from areas of ground warmed by the Sun.

● Interaction between weather fronts: the boundaries between large air masses. A cold front brings in cold air behind it and pushes beneath warm air, forcing it to rise; a warm front brings in warm air which slides over cold air.

● Mountains: when winds blow against mountains, air is forced upwards.

Stratus Flat, low clouds consisting of water droplets. They sometimes produce light rain or drizzle. Fog is very low-lying stratus cloud.

Nimbostratus Thick, dark, low-level clouds consisting of water droplets. They can produce rain or drizzle.

see also

14-15 **Planet Earth**

52-3 **Earth's atmosphere**

60-1 **Destructive forces**

The Earth's land surface can be split up into six major vegetation zones; desert, coniferous forest, temperate forest, tropical forest, grassland, and tundra and poles. Each zone has its own particular characteristics, determined by climate, topography and latitude. Native species are adapted to the conditions of each region.

Deserts Deserts are areas where evaporation exceeds rainfall. They occur over a wide range of latitudes, between 15 and 35 degrees on either side of the Equator.
⬤ One-quarter of the Earth's land surface is classified as desert or semidesert (semidesert supports scrubby vegetation).
⬤ Deserts form where clouds are prevented from developing by barrier mountains, wind patterns or other factors. Barrier mountains force up air carried by the prevailing wind. Water vapour in the air condenses and falls as rain or snow, so when the air reaches the far side of the mountain it is dry. Some deserts, such as the Gobi, are so far from the sea that moist air never reaches them.
⬤ Deserts often have large temperature swings between day and night. The Sahara can reach 55°C (131°F) by day and drop below freezing at night.

Key

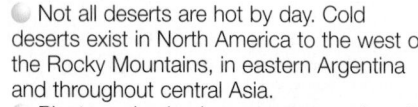

▨ **Deserts**

▨ **Coniferous forest**

▨ **Temperate forest**

▨ **Tropical forest**

▨ **Grasslands**

▨ **Tundra and poles**

⬤ Not all deserts are hot by day. Cold deserts exist in North America to the west of the Rocky Mountains, in eastern Argentina and throughout central Asia.
⬤ Plants and animals are scarce or absent from deserts. Those that are present are adapted to arid conditions.

Coniferous forest Also called taiga, boreal forest or northern evergreen forest, coniferous forest extends in a thick belt across Canada, Russia and Scandinavia in the Northern Hemisphere.
⬤ There is strong seasonal variation with long, cold winters, when temperatures rarely

Sea of sand Dunes, such as these in the Namib Desert, are slow-moving waves of sand driven by the wind. They can be more than 400 m (1300 ft) high.

Prairies

Amazon basin

Pampas

rise above freezing, and brief, warm summers: between summer and winter, temperatures can fluctuate by 56°C (133°F).
⬤ Coniferous forests are far less diverse than other forest types. Insects occur in some variety, but birds and mammals are uncommon. Some forests contain no more than eight species of tree.
⬤ Coniferous forest trees, such as pines and spruces, are evergreen, keeping their leaves, or needles, all through the year.

Temperate forest Temperate forest occurs mainly between latitudes of 30 and 60 degrees on either side of the Equator.
⬤ In the Northern Hemisphere, temperate forest is dominated by deciduous (leaf-shedding) trees such as oak, ash, beech and hickory.
⬤ In the Southern Hemisphere, temperate forest trees are evergreen.
⬤ Temperate forests experience a mild, seasonal climate with no great extremes in temperature (average 10°C/50°F) or rainfall. They support a wide range of plant and animal species.

Tropical forest Tropical forests, commonly described as jungle, occur within 23.5 degrees either side of the Equator, where they experience very little seasonal variation in temperature and daylength – conditions ideal for optimum plant growth.
⬤ The majority of the planet's plant species and a huge proportion of its animal species live in the lowland tropical rain forests,

The world's largest deserts

Desert	Location	Approximate area
Sahara	N Africa	9 000 000 km² (3 500 000 sq miles)
Australian	Australia	3 800 000 km² (1 470 000 sq miles)
Arabian	SW Asia	1 300 000 km² (502 000 sq miles)
Takla Makan	China	1 245 000 km² (327 000 sq miles)
Gobi	Central Asia	1 040 000 km² (401 000 sq miles)
Kalahari	Southern Africa	520 000 km² (201 000 sq miles)
Turkestan	Central Asia	450 000 km² (174 000 sq miles)
Namib	SW Africa	310 000 km² (120 000 sq miles)
Sonoran	USA/Mexico	260 000 km² (100 000 sq miles)
Somali	Somalia	120 000 km² (310 000 sq miles)
Thar	India/Pakistan	100 000 km² (260 000 sq miles)

Great plains Temperate grassland is known by different names around the world, including steppe, pampas and veldt. This is mid grass prairie in Oklahoma, USA.

Temperate grasslands are found in the interior areas of continents, where winters are cold and summers are hot and dry. Rainfall is moderate, ranging between 250-500 cm (10-20 in) a year.

Tundra and poles Tundra is found between the Arctic ice cap and the northern edge of the coniferous forests. It also occurs at high altitudes farther south (alpine tundra).

Tundra is defined by the presence of permafrost, a layer of permanently frozen ground. It is characterised by low-growing plants adapted to survival in the cold.

Tundra covers about a fifth of the world's land surface. It gives way to coniferous forest wherever the average temperature of the warmest month exceeds 10°C (50°F).

The Arctic ice cap covers most of the Arctic Ocean and Greenland. It expands in winter to cover the most northerly parts of Alaska, Canada, Scandinavia and Russia, as well as the far north of the Atlantic and Pacific oceans.

The Antarctic ice cap covers virtually the entire continent of Antarctica all year round. In winter it expands over most of the sea up to 60 degrees north of the South Pole.

Deforestation

Forests across the world are threatened by logging and clearance for agriculture. This problem is particularly acute in the tropics, where human population growth is greatest and many of the most economically valuable trees occur. Tropical forest once covered more than 16 per cent of the Earth's land surface, but now that figure is less than 6 per cent. The immediate effects of deforestation are habitat loss, native species extinction, soil erosion and, in areas of high rainfall, catastrophic flooding. Longer-term consequences may include exacerbation of the greenhouse effect as carbon dioxide, a greenhouse gas normally removed by trees, builds up in the atmosphere.

Life in the balance Lowland tropical rain forest, such as this in Borneo, is both the most productive and most threatened of Earth's natural habitats.

where rain falls almost daily and trees fruit all year round.

Tropical cloud forest, at higher altitudes, and monsoon and subtropical forests, at higher latitudes, support slightly less diverse flora and fauna, but are still more species rich than most temperate forests.

Grasslands Grasslands divide into two distinct types, savannah in the tropics and temperate grasslands at midlatitudes.

Savannahs exist in Africa, India, Australia and the northern part of South America. Although they occur in tropical latitudes, they are semiarid. Temperatures are always high, averaging around 17°C (63°F). Rainfall is typically 50-150 cm (20-60 in) a year. Most rain falls in a short annual rainy, or wet, season during which low-lying areas may flood. Wet seasons are characterised by rapid plant growth but are followed by long periods of drought (dry seasons).

Ice store More than 98 per cent of the world's fresh water is frozen in the polar ice caps. The Antarctic ice cap is more than 3 km (2 miles) thick in places. The Arctic ice cap is thinner due to the warming effect of ocean currents.

see also
14-15 **Planet Earth**
54-5 **Weather**

Natural disasters ▶

Earthquakes and volcanoes are among the most violent and unpredictable of all nature's forces. High-risk areas are along plate margins and coastlines. Some of today's largest cities, including Tokyo, Los Angeles and Mexico City, have been built in these dangerous zones.

The deadliest earthquakes on record

Date	Location	Estimated deaths	Magnitude	Comments
July 1201	Eastern Mediterranean	1.1 million	Unknown	
January 23, 1556	Shansi, China	830 000	Unknown	Death toll from floods, famine and disease as high as 1 million.
July 27, 1976	Tangshan, China	655 000	8.0	Official estimated death toll.
August 9, 1138	Aleppo, Syria	230 000	Unknown	
December 22, 856	Damghan, Iran	200 000	Unknown	Major fissures, landslides.
December 16, 1920	Gansu, China	200 000	8.6	
May 22, 1927	Xining, China	200 000	8.3	Large fissures in the ground.
March 23, 893	Ardabil, Iran	150 000	Unknown	
September 1, 1923	Kwanto, Japan	143 000	8.3	Cause of the Great Fire of Tokyo.
October 5, 1948	Ashkhabad, Turkmenistan	110 000	7.3	
December 28, 1908	Messina, Italy	70 000 to 100 000	7.5	Deaths from earthquake and (estimated) tsunami.
September, 1290	Chihli, China	100 000	Unknown	
November, 1667	Shemakha, Azerbaijan	80 000	Unknown	
November 18, 1727	Tabriz, Iran	77 000	Unknown	
November 1, 1755	Lisbon, Portugal	70 000	8.7	
December 25, 1932	Gansu, China	70 000	7.6	
May 31, 1970	Yungay, Peru	66 800	7.8	
1268	Silicia, Asia Minor	60 000	Unknown	
January 11, 1693	Sicily, Italy	60 000	Unknown	
May 30, 1935	Quetta, Pakistan	30 000 to 60 000	7.5	
December 7, 1988	Armenia, USSR	Over 55 000	6.9	
February 4, 1783	Calabria, Italy	50 000	Unknown	
June 20, 1990	Iran	50 000	7.7	

Worldwide danger zones

FACTS AND FIGURES

● The largest earthquake ever was recorded off the coast of Chile on May 22, 1960. It measured 9.5 on the Richter scale.
● The Montagua earthquake in Guatemala in 1976 made more than 1 million people homeless. It also caused US$1.25 billion worth of damage.
● The largest volcanic eruption ever recorded was Krakatau in Indonesia in 1883. The blast was heard 4635 km (2800 miles) away and the collapse of the volcano caused 150 m (500 ft) waves in the nearby Sunda Strait. Ash from the eruption hung in the upper atmosphere causing global temperatures to drop by an average of 1.2°C (2.1°F) over the next 12 months.
● The largest volcanic eruption of the 20th century in the USA was Novarupta in Alaska in 1912. The eruption produced 21 km² of volcanic material – 30 times the amount ejected by Mount St Helens in 1980.
● The largest death toll from a tsunami was on the west coast of Japan in 1896. About 27 000 people died.

The worst volcanic eruptions of the 20th century

Date	Location	Estimated deaths	Comments
May 8, 1902	Mt Pelée, Martinique	Over 40 000	Pelée had been dormant for centuries. Its explosive eruption killed everyone in the town of St Pierre with the exception of a prisoner, in a poorly ventilated cell in the local prison who escaped the suffocating cloud of ash, and one other man who somehow made his way safely through the burning city.
November 1985	Armero, Nevado del Ruiz, Colombia	25 000	The town of Armero was overrun by mud flows in 1595, and again in 1845, killing hundreds of people in each instance. During the ensuing 140-year period of inactivity, people forgot about the danger and the town was rebuilt on the same site. Mud flows triggered by the 1985 eruption completely destroyed the town again.
May 19, 1919	Keluit, Indonesia	5110	Water pouring from the crater lake that had capped the volcano before the eruption drowned many people on the lower slopes.
October 24, 1902	Santa Maria, Guatemala	4500	500 were killed by the eruption itself. The remainder died from starvation and disease that resulted from the destruction of the surrounding area.
January 21, 1951	Mt Lamington, New Guinea	2942	Erupted without warning. The explosion was heard 320 km (200 miles) away.
March 29, 1982	El Chichón, Mexico	1879	Few of the dead were ever found.
August 21, 1986	Lake Nyos, Cameroon	Over 1700	An eruption beneath the lake released a cloud of poisonous gas that killed people in the surrounding area.
May 7-8, 1902	La Soufrière, St Vincent	1565	Eruption began the day before the Mt Pelée cataclysm. Most deaths were caused by ash flows.
December 18, 1931	Merapi, Java	1369	
January 30, 1911	Taal, Philippines	1335	The worst of several eruptions of this volcano in the 20th century.

Deadliest volcanic eruptions on record

Year	Eruption	Estimated deaths	Cause of death
1815	Tambora, Indonesia	92 000	Starvation
1883	Krakatau, Indonesia	36 000	Tsunami
1902	Mont Pelée, Martinique	30 000	Lava flows
1985	Nevado del Ruiz, Colombia	25 000	Mud flows
1792	Unzen, Japan	15 000	Volcano collapse
1586	Keluit, Indonesia	10 000	Unknown
1783	Lakagigar (Laki), Iceland	9000	Starvation
1919	Keluit, Java	5110	Drowning
1902	Santa Maria, Guatemala	4500	Starvation
79	Mt Vesuvius, Italy	3360	Lava flows

Worldwide danger zones Nine out of ten volcanoes occur along the boundaries between the plates of the Earth's crust. The zone of plate boundaries that encircle the Pacific Ocean has been called the 'Ring of Fire'. The majority of the remaining volcanoes appear where liquid magma from deep in the mantle forces its way through the crust. These areas are known as hot spots. One such hot spot gave rise to the Hawaiian Islands.

Avalanches, landslides, giant waves and violent weather have all been the cause of terrible catastrophes. As our understanding of these and other dangerous natural phenomena improves, so does our ability to predict them and take measures to minimise the destruction they cause.

Guarding against earthquakes and volcanoes

● **Earth movements** are monitored globally using instruments called seismometers. These pick up the minor vibrations which often precede major earthquakes.

● **Volcanoes often 'bulge'** before an eruption as magma slowly rises into them. Tiltmeters placed on a volcano can measure this and warn of an impending eruption.

● **Modern buildings** are designed to withstand shocks in locations that are susceptible to earthquakes.

● **Emergency evacuation plans** have been put in place by countries most at risk, particularly in Europe, the USA and Japan.

TSUNAMI

The devastation tsunamis can cause is legendary. Tsunami monitoring stations have been established in the Pacific since 1949. Although these provide an early-warning system, there is little defensive action that can be taken other than evacuation.

Worst tsunamis of the 20th century

Date	Location	Est. deaths
1960	Agadir, Morocco*	12 000
1960	Chile/Pacific Islands/Japan	5000
1976	Philippines	5000
1933	Japan/Hawaii	3000
1946	Japan*	1088
1944	Japan	998
1979	Lomblem Islands, Indonesia	700
1979	Colombia	500
1946	Hawaii/Aleutians/California	173
1964	Alaska/Aleutians/California*	122

* Combined effect of tsunami and earthquake

AVALANCHES AND LANDSLIDES

Avalanches and landslides are the rapid mass movement of either snow and ice or earth under gravity. They are triggered by a number of factors.

● **Weight** A heavy snowfall can provide enough extra weight to destabilise a sloping snowfield causing it to slide downhill, often taking rocks and trees with it.

● **Water** Excessive rainfall or seeping ground water can destabilise and lubricate soil on a slope causing it to slide.

● **Earthquakes** The vibrations from earthquakes can destabilise both earth and snow causing landslides and avalanches.

● **Noise** Vibrations caused by loud noises can trigger avalanches. Gunfire in the Alps during the First World War is known to have caused several avalanches.

● **Explosions** Avalanches can also be started by explosions. In many places where avalanches are a threat, they are set off artificially by using controlled explosions.

● **Volcanoes** Volcanic eruptions are often associated with landslides and lahars. Lahars are mud flows caused when water from a crater lake, or melted snow from the summit and sides of an erupting volcano, mixes with ash and slides downhill.

The worst avalanches and landslides of the 20th century

Date	Location	Est. deaths	Comments
Dec 16, 1920	Gansu, China	180 000	Landslide
May 31, 1970	Yungay, Peru	17 500	Landslide
Dec 13, 1916	Italian Alps	10 000	Avalanche
Dec 13, 1941	Huarás, Peru	5000	Avalanche
Jan 10, 1962	Nevada Huascaran, Peru	3500	Avalanche
Sep 27,1987	Medellin, Columbia	683	Landslide
March 19, 1971	Chungar, Peru	600	Avalanche
Jan 11, 1966	Rio de Janeiro, Brazil	550	Landslide
Feb 15, 1949	Northern Assam, India	500	Landslide
Nov 13-14, 1963	Grand Riviere du Nord, Haiti	500	Landslide
Jan 11, 1954	Blons, Austria	411	Avalanche

Wave of destruction Boats have been carried inland and dumped on a railway line by a tsunami that hit Alaska.

STORMS

A storm is any violent disturbance in the atmosphere with wind speeds of 90 km/h (55 mph) or higher – force 10 or above on the Beaufort scale. There are about 1600 storms taking place around the world at any one time.

The most destructive storms on record

Date	Location	Est. deaths	Name
1970	Bangladesh	300 000–500 000	Cyclone
1731	Calcutta, India	300 000	Cyclone
1881	China	300 000	Typhoon
1876	Bakargani, Bangladesh	215 000	Cyclone
1991	Bangladesh	200 000	Cyclone
1882	Bombay, India	100 000	Cyclone
1942	Bangladesh	61 000	Cyclone
1822	Bangladesh	50 000	Cyclone
1864	Calcutta, India	50 000	Cyclone
1912	China	50 000	Typhoon
1922	Shantou, China	28 000	Typhoon
1780	West Indies	24 000	Hurricane
Other storms			
1588	UK	20 000	Winter storm
1985	Bangladesh	11 000	Cyclone
1906	Hong Kong	10 000	Typhoon
1974	Honduras	10 000	Hurricane Fifi
1985	Philippines	1363	Typhoon Ike
1989	Shaturia, Bangladesh	1300	Cyclone

Worldwide danger zones Severe storms occur most frequently around Antarctica and the North Pole. However, because of their remoteness these are rarely a danger to large numbers of people. The majority of truly devastating storms occur in the tropics, within about 23 degrees either side of the Equator. This area includes many densely populated cities and countries. Storms have different names, depending on their location.

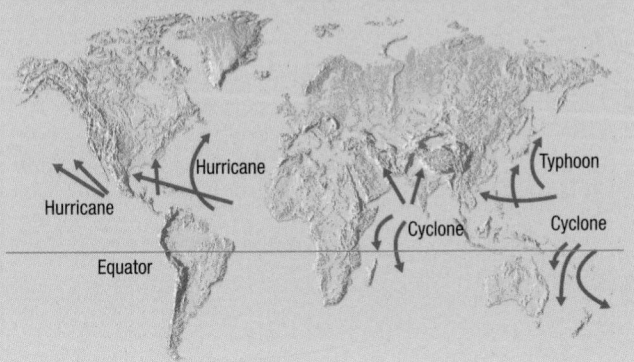

FLOODS

Floods can be caused by high tides, tsunamis or heavy rainfall. River floods can be exacerbated by deforestation upstream – this is the principal cause of the floods that have devastated Bangladesh in recent decades.

Worst floods of the 20th century

Date	Location	Est. deaths
1931	Huang He, China	3 700 000
1970	Bangladesh	300 000–500 000
1939	Henan, China	200 000
1911	Chang Jiang, China	100 000
1942	Bengal, India	40 000
1965	Bangladesh	30 000
1963	Bangladesh	22 000
1965	Bangladesh	17 000
1979	Morvi, India	5000–15 000
1906	Hong Kong	10 000

Bad El Niño years

The El Niño that occurred in the winter of 1982-3 led to drought and bush fires in Australia, Africa and Indonesia, hurricanes in Hawaii and flooding in Peru. The death toll attributed to El Niño was more than 1300. The costs from loss of property and livelihood have been estimated at US$13 billion. The worst El Niño of the 20th century occurred in 1997-8 and played havoc with the world's weather for a year. California, Mexico, Peru and Ecuador experienced heavy rains, with floods and mud slides that killed hundreds of people. Indonesia and Malaysia suffered severe droughts and extensive forest fires.

FACTS AND FIGURES

◐ The most rain recorded over 24 hours was 187 cm (73.6 in) on the island of Réunion in the Indian Ocean in March 1952.
◐ A 762 m (2500 ft) waterspout (a whirlwind that sucks up water) was recorded off the English coast in 1987.
◐ The longest lightning flash on record measured 30 km (19 miles).

◐ The most people killed by a single lightning flash was 81 passengers of a jet that crashed after being struck on December 8, 1963, above Maryland, USA.
◐ The most people killed by hailstones was 246 in a storm in the city of Moradabad, India, on April 20, 1888.
◐ Australian meteorologist Clement L. Wragg introduced naming of hurricanes in 1887.

FACT In freak weather on November 23, 1981, 58 whirlwinds were recorded across central England and North Wales.

Life on Earth

Life on Earth

Geologists break down the 4.6 billion years of the Earth's history into a hierarchy of time intervals, based on major changes in rock formation. The largest intervals – the Palaeozoic, Mesozoic and Cenozoic – are called eras. These are sub-divided into periods, such as the Jurassic. Periods are further divided into epochs, such as the Oligocene.

Precambrian

4.6 billion years ago
The **Earth is formed**.

4.5 billion years ago
The **Moon is formed**.

3.8 billion years ago
First life appears. It consists of primitive single-celled organisms.

Fossil bacteria

3.3 billion years ago
Cyanobacteria, or blue-green algae, appear. These are single-celled organisms able to harness energy from sunlight by photosynthesis.

Fossil cyanobacteria

2.1 billion years ago
The **first single-celled organisms with a nucleus** appear.

720 million years ago
The **first multicellular animals** appear.

Palaeozoic

Mesozoic

Cenozoic

Palaeozoic

Cambrian
550–505 million years ago

Trilobites and other marine animals with hard shells appear. Cambrian rocks are the first to contain an abundance of fossils.

Ordovician
505–438 million years ago

The **first fishes** appear, along with the first corals. The fishes are the first vertebrates.

Jawless fish, *Drepanaspis*

Silurian
438–408 million years ago

The **first land plants and first jawed fishes** appear.

Devonian
408–360 million years ago

Land plants and fishes diversify. The **first insects and amphibians** appear.

Carboniferous
360–286 million years ago

Amphibians and fishes diversify. **The first reptiles** appear. Dominant land plants include club mosses.

Club mosses

Permian
286–245 million years ago

Reptiles diversify. Seed-bearing plants establish themselves. At the end of the Permian, the trilobites become extinct.

Mesozoic

Coelophysis dinosaur

Triassic
245–208 million years ago

Early dinosaurs appear.

Jurassic
208–144 million years ago

Dinosaurs flourish. Primitive mammals and birds appear.

Quetzalcoatlus

Cretaceous
144–65 million years ago

Flowering plants develop. **First placental mammals** appear. Flying reptiles include the giant *Quetzalcoatlus*.

At the end of the Cretaceous, **a mass extinction includes the disappearance of the dinosaurs.**

Divisions of geological time

Precambrian
4.6 billion–550 million years ago

Palaeozoic (ancient life)
550–245 million years ago

Mesozoic (middle life)
245–65 million years ago

Cenozoic (recent life)
65 million years ago to present

Tertiary

Palaeocene
65–57 million
years ago

Cenozoic:
Tertiary period
65–1.8 million years ago

The **first large mammals emerge**.

Tertiary

Early horses, camels, rodents, elephants and monkeys appear, along with the first bats and whales. The 33 tonne leaf-browsing *Indricotherium* is the largest land mammal ever.

Birds and flowering plants diversify.

Eocene
57–34 million
years ago

Indricotherium

TIMESCALE OF LIFE

If the 4.6 billion years since the Earth's formation were crammed into the thousand years from AD 1000 to the eve of 2000, it would yield the following dates:
1000 Formation of the Earth.
1173 First life appears.
1543 First single-celled organisms with a nucleus appear.
1843 Multicellular animals appear.
1891 The first land plants appear.
1950s to mid 80s The age of the dinosaurs.
Mid-December 1999 Early modern man, *Homo sapiens*, appears.
Around December 22, 1999 The emergence of modern man, *Homo sapiens sapiens*.

FOSSILS

The story of life's evolution on Earth is written in the fossil evidence. Fossils are the remains or traces of living organisms preserved in rock. They include footprints and chemical remains as well as petrified bones and shells. The oldest-known fossils date back 3.5 billion years; they are of bacteria and were discovered in the Barberton Greenstone Belt, southern Africa, in 1996.

Conditions conducive to fossilisation are very specific and the majority of living things do not become fossilised after death. The fossil record is not complete; it gives only an occasional glimpse of the life forms that existed in the past.

How fossils form

To become fossilised, organic remains need to be buried quickly by sediment to prevent them from decaying or

Preserved in rock Buried plant or animal remains, such as these 40 million-year-old *Knightia alta* fish, leave an impression in the rock, or even become rock themselves.

being destroyed. So fossilisation is most likely in an environment where rapid sedimentation is taking place, such as a sea, lake or swamp.

Once buried, the remains may dissolve, leaving a mould of the original form in the surrounding sediment. In some cases, new minerals crystallise in the space, creating a 'cast' of the organism.

Alternatively, hard parts, such as shell or bone, may become mineralised, or petrified, that is replaced, molecule by molecule, by mineral-rich solutions in the sediment: they become rock.

Sometimes, soft parts of animals or plants are preserved in very fine sediment or by carbonisation. This happens when the oxygen and hydrogen in organic remains dissolve leaving only a carbon film on the rock in the shape of the original animal or plant.

Tertiary

Aegyptopithecus, a cat-sized primate, is believed to be **an ancestor of modern man**.

Oligocene
34–23 million
years ago

Tertiary

Amebelodon

Early apes, dogs and bears appear. **Large browsing mammals flourish**. These include *Amebelodon*, equipped with huge tusks for gouging out water plants.

Miocene
23–5 million
years ago

The **australopithecines, upright-walking hominids,** appear and diversify.

Homo habilis, *Homo erectus* and finally ***Homo sapiens*, early modern man,** emerge in Africa.

'Upright man',
Homo erectus

Pliocene
5–1.8 million years ago

Pleistocene
1.8 million–10 000 years ago

Cenozoic:
Quaternary period
1.8 million years ago to present

Quaternary

Holocene
10 000 years ago
to present

Evolution is the idea that living things change from generation to generation, with features that favour survival tending to be passed down. Over millennia, inherited features amplify and diverge, creating the huge variety of species alive today. Evolutionary theory, as first postulated by Charles Darwin and others in the 1850s, has had an influence far beyond the bounds of science.

EVOLUTION – A BIOLOGICAL ARMS RACE

To understand how evolution works, imagine a bird that eats nothing but one species of beetle; imagine also that this beetle lives in burrows that it digs deep into the ground.

To eat, the bird must stick its beak down the long, thin burrows. So birds with the longest, thinnest beaks are more likely to survive and breed than birds with shorter, fatter beaks. Therefore most birds in the next generation will have the genes for a long thin beak.

Meanwhile, beetles with a natural predisposition to burrow deep are less likely to be eaten. Consequently, the genes that bestow this ability are more likely to be found in the next generation of beetles.

Passing on the improvement The result – over hundreds of generations – is that the birds' beaks will become longer and thinner, while the beetles tunnel even farther from their reach. It might look like the bird's beak is designed to catch beetles, and that the beetles have a strategy to avoid the birds. But this is an illusion, created by natural weighting in favour of one feature in both animals.

This bias is what Darwin called 'natural selection'. Nature 'selects' the birds with longer beaks, and the deep-digging beetles, and so ensures that the biological arms race goes on.

Divergent evolution Divergent evolution (also known as adaptive radiation) is the process by which several species evolve from a single common ancestral species.

Divergent evolution at work The many species of finch living on the Galápagos Islands off Ecuador in South America are a famous

NATURAL SELECTION AT WORK

Although evolution is usually a long-term process, it can sometimes be observed in action. Britain's peppered moth, for example, altered its appearance over a relatively short period in response to changing environmental conditions caused by the Industrial Revolution.

Before industrialisation, all peppered moths were a mottled grey, camouflaging them against the lichen-covered trees on which they lived. But in the 1850s, a darker variety was found in Manchester, where pollution had been killing tree lichens and blackening the tree bark. Under these circumstances, the darker moth was better camouflaged than the mottled one, and it soon spread widely throughout industrial England.

Both types exist today and are still the same species, but one or other does better in different areas.

Changing with the times In an environment blackened by soot, the darker form of peppered moth (above) was better adapted to survive.

example of divergent evolution – Darwin's study of these birds contributed to his formulation of a theory of evolution. The original population consisted of a few birds of one species blown in from mainland South America. These birds strayed and spread across the islands, where new populations adapted to the different types of food and different types of environment. Gradually distinct new species of finch evolved, displaying the different beak shapes favoured for each food type.

Changing shape Galápagos finches evolved different beak shapes exploiting different food sources. A heavily built beak is best for cracking open seeds, while a slender beak makes it easier to catch insects.

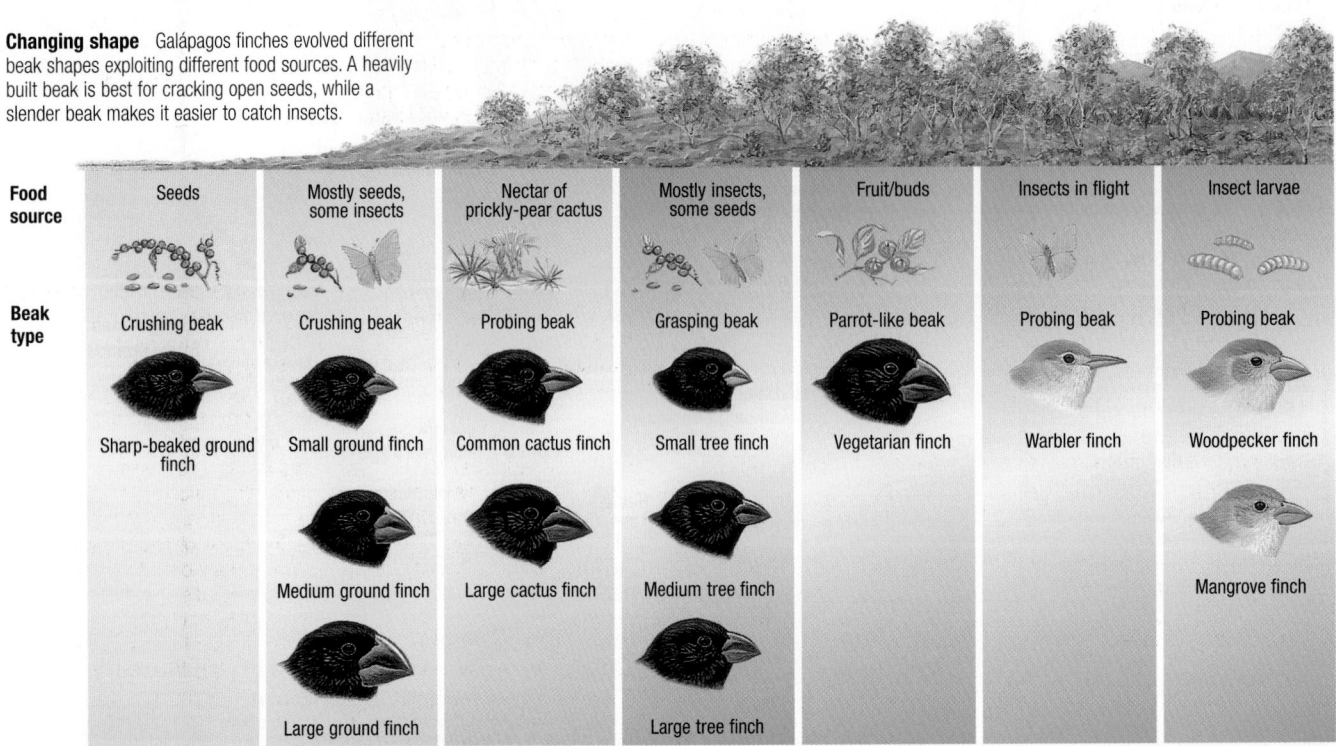

Food source	Seeds	Mostly seeds, some insects	Nectar of prickly-pear cactus	Mostly insects, some seeds	Fruit/buds	Insects in flight	Insect larvae
Beak type	Crushing beak	Crushing beak	Probing beak	Grasping beak	Parrot-like beak	Probing beak	Probing beak
	Sharp-beaked ground finch	Small ground finch	Common cactus finch	Small tree finch	Vegetarian finch	Warbler finch	Woodpecker finch
	Medium ground finch	Large cactus finch	Medium tree finch				Mangrove finch
	Large ground finch		Large tree finch				

Main extinctions: the big five

Sudden environmental change in the past has led to mass extinctions. Scientists have identified five major events:

1 End of the Ordovician
(438 million years ago)
Global cooling led to the extinction of 70 per cent of marine life.

2 Late Devonian
(365 million years ago)
A sharp drop in sea level led to the extinction of many marine invertebrates and most fishes.

3 End of the Permian
(245 million years ago)
Formation of the Pangaea supercontinent, and a drop in sea level, caused a 96 per cent extinction of marine species.

4 End of the Triassic
(208 million years ago)
Sea level drop led to the extinction of 40 per cent of all species.

5 Cretaceous-Tertiary
(65 million years ago)
A meteorite impact and high volcanic activity resulted in the extinction of 70 per cent of animal species, including the dinosaurs.

We may be experiencing a mass extinction now, as a result of human activities. If current rates of extinction continue, we can expect half of the world's known species to have disappeared by the end of the 21st century.

Taking to the air Wings have evolved more than once in the history of life on Earth, but not always in the same way. The skeletal structure supporting the wings of birds and bats, for instance, is completely different.

Convergent evolution Sometimes similar features evolve in completely unrelated species. This convergent evolution happens when the two species evolve a solution to the same problem of lifestyle or environment. More often than not, the anatomy underlying these features is different in each species.

Convergent evolution at work The wings of bats and birds are an example of convergent evolution. They are superficially similar – because any flying animal will need to be equipped with something resembling a set of wings – but the underlying structure is very different: bats' wings are supported by elongated finger bones, birds' are not. Another example is the shape of sharks and dolphins. Although completely unrelated, both have fins and gently curving, streamlined bodies adapted for an aquatic lifestyle.

see also
64-5 **Ages of life on Earth**
86-7 **Dinosaurs**
350-1 **Scientific thinkers**
542-7 **Biology**

How new species emerge

Members of the same species can mate and produce fertile offspring together. If part of a population becomes isolated in a way that prevents it from breeding with the rest, and the two groups then experience different living conditions, they will be driven by natural selection to evolve in different ways. Eventually, the genetic differences between the two groups will become so great that even if they come together again, they will not be able to interbreed – two distinct species will have evolved.

KEY TERMS

Darwinism The theory that natural selection is the mechanism of evolution.
Evolution A change in the genetic composition of a population over time.
Fitness The ability of an organism to survive and reproduce; it is a measure of reproductive success.
Natural selection The tendency for useful variations to be preserved down the generations.
Neo-Darwinism The application of modern genetic knowledge to Darwin's theory.
Population A group of interbreeding individuals that occupies a defined geographical region – such as a particular species of fish in a lake.
Speciation The development of new species, which occurs when different populations of the same species evolve along different lines and under the influence of different environmental conditions.
Survival of the fittest A term coined by the 19th-century English philosopher Herbert Spencer to describe the survival of those organisms that are best fitted to exist in their environment.

The recipe for the origins of life is unknown, but likely ingredients were methane, carbon dioxide, ammonia and water in the atmosphere and seas of the young Earth. The action of ultraviolet radiation or lightning could have combined these chemicals into amino acids, the building blocks of protein – and so of all living things.

WHAT IS LIFE?

Anything alive, rather than dead or inanimate, will:
- **metabolise**, carry out chemical processes involved in, for example, producing energy or eliminating waste.
- **grow** and develop.
- **respond to stimuli** such as light or heat.
- **reproduce** either sexually or asexually.

The simplest forms of life are single cells, which have:
- **cell membranes** to insulate them from the environment and to allow the selective flow of chemicals into and out of each cell.
- **the ability to harness** or produce energy.
- **genetic material** to allow them to reproduce.

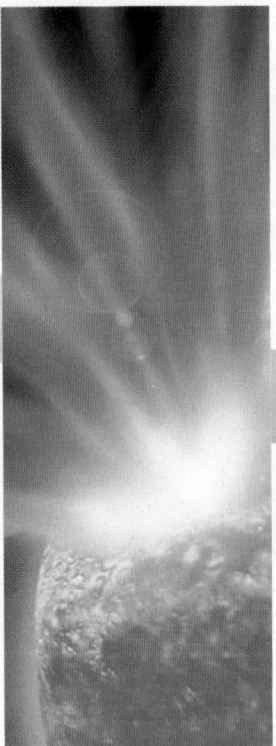

Over 4.5 billion years ago
The Earth's thin surface crust is hot and unstable. It is wracked by volcanoes and earthquakes and bombarded by meteorites. The atmosphere contains no oxygen. It is composed mainly of hydrogen and small amounts of the gases helium, krypton and xenon.

4.5 billion years ago
According to one theory a large rocky body collides with the Earth, stripping away the first-generation atmosphere and triggering further volcanism. The Moon is formed from debris from the collision.

4.35 billion years ago
Volcanic gases and water vapour released by the collision create a new, hydrogen-rich atmosphere.

3.8 billion years ago
The first life forms appear, probably around volcanic vents on the ocean bed and in hydrothermal pools, where there is a good supply of minerals and warmth. They consist of single-celled archaebacteria. These have a very simple cell structure, with no nucleus, and can exist without oxygen. These organisms may have used hydrogen sulphide from the volcanic vents as their energy source.

Life in a test tube

Life may have been formed in conditions of either extreme heat or extreme cold. Laboratory experiments have provided evidence for both theories.

Extreme heat In 1953, American scientists Stanley Miller and Harold Urey passed an electrical current to simulate lightning through a cocktail of compounds thought to be present in the early Earth's atmosphere and seas. Amino acids, the basis of protein, were among the new substances formed.
Extreme cold In the 1960s, another American, Leslie Orville, froze a similar mix of chemicals. A constituent compound of DNA was created, suggesting that life might have evolved during one of several ice ages that occurred in the millions of years of Earth's early history.

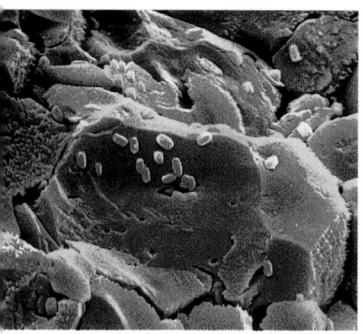

Earliest fossils The evolution of living forms from organic chemicals occurred remarkably soon after the formation of the Earth. Among the oldest evidence of life on Earth are 3.5 billion-year-old bacteria fossils (shown on the left in a computer-enhanced image). Evidence suggests that life began a mere 700 million years after the planet's formation.

The coming of the nucleus

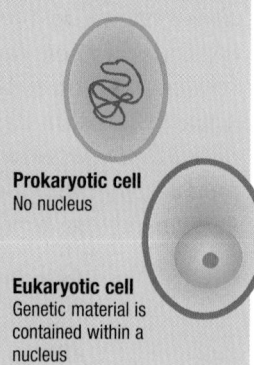

The earliest life forms were single cells, with no nucleus, known as prokaryotes. As life evolved, different parts of the cell took on specific, specialised functions – for instance, respiration – with genetic material becoming focused in one area called the nucleus, bound by a membrane. Cells with a nucleus are described as eukaryotic. They are more organised than prokaryotic cells, which gave them the potential to evolve into more complex life forms. All multicellular life is eukaryotic, while all bacteria are prokaryotic.

Prokaryotic cell
No nucleus

Eukaryotic cell
Genetic material is contained within a nucleus

3.5 billion years ago
Some organisms can now produce chlorophyll, which allows them to create energy by photosynthesis. These cyanobacteria – or blue-green algae – spread in watery environments across the surface of the Earth. Over time, excess oxygen released by the cyanobacteria starts to accumulate in the Earth's atmosphere.

2.1 billion years ago
Amounts of atmospheric oxygen are about 1 per cent of current levels, enough to support the development of organisms that respire – that is, use oxygen to fuel their metabolic processes. A layer of ozone, created by the combination of oxygen molecules, starts to form in the upper atmosphere. Cells with a nucleus – called eukaryotes – appear.

720 million years ago
Some eukaryotic cells begin to live in groups. Over time, cells in these colonies take on specialised roles for the colony, such as respiration, until they become inter-dependent and can no longer exist singly. They are now part of a multicellular organism. New species are evolving, including by 600 million years ago the first to have hard exoskeletal parts.

420 million years ago
Oxygen in the atmosphere has increased to about 10 per cent of current levels, and continues to rise over the next 100 million years. The ozone layer thickens, acting as a filter of ultraviolet rays from the Sun, which are harmful to life. This makes the land surface of the Earth habitable. The first land plants appear.

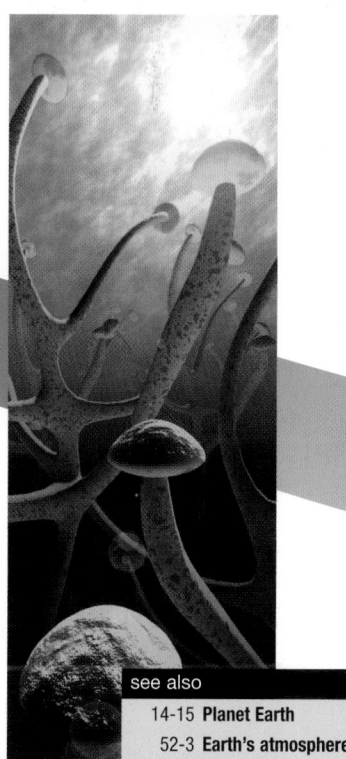

Stromatolites Rounded structures formed by mats of cyanobacteria (blue-green algae) are the most common fossil evidence of early life. These modern stromatolites (left) were found in Australia.

see also
14-15 **Planet Earth**
52-3 **Earth's atmosphere**
70-1 **Evolution of plants**

Plants and their precursors were the first life forms to colonise the early Earth. They evolved from simple single-celled organisms into the great variety of plants we know today, including, mosses, ferns, conifers and flowering plants. It is vegetation that supports all other life on Earth, by providing food and by creating and maintaining our atmosphere.

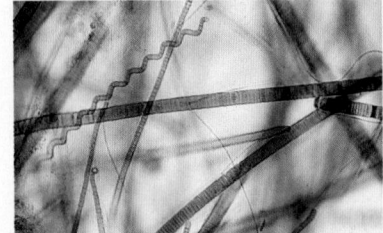

Green algae A simple, early plant form that still thrives today.

WHAT IS A PLANT?

Plants share some characteristics with all living things. Like animals they:
- are composed of cells with a **nucleus**.
- can **respire**, making use of oxygen in the atmosphere to fuel their metabolism.
- can **reproduce**.

Plants differ from animals in that they:
- lack **mobility**, usually being rooted in one place.
- create their own food by **photosynthesis** (see page 74).
- have rigid **cellulose cell walls**, giving them structure and support.
- lack specialised **sensory organs** and a **nervous system**.

PRECAMBRIAN

1 billion years ago
Photosynthesising green algae appear.

3.5 billion years ago
Cyanobacteria (blue-green algae) photosynthesising bacteria evolve.

550

550–505 million years ago
Larger, multicellular green algae and seaweeds appear, as well as some red and brown algae.

CAMBRIAN

505

500 million years ago
First land plants begin to colonise marshland.

ORDOVICIAN

438

408 million years ago
Seed-bearing plants first appear that no longer need water to reproduce.

SILURIAN

408

433 million years ago
First vascular plants evolve.

DEVONIAN

360

Ancient lineage Together with mosses, liverworts (left) are the most direct living descendants of the earliest land plants.

Club mosses

Simple, small-leaved, club mosses are vascular plants, that flourished in the warm, swamp-like conditions of the Carboniferous period. By then, some had changed from their earlier creeping forms into large, branching trees. These larger club mosses – up to 45 m (150 ft) tall – had specially thickened trunks with a central woody core, and shallow rooting systems which spread out to anchor them in the mud. However, these giants were too specialised, and when the swamps dried up at the end of the Carboniferous period, many became extinct. The few club mosses that survive are smaller than their ancient ancestors.

Stag's horn club moss An American example of the small club mosses that survive today.

Learning to live on land: vascular plants

It is likely that the first land plants evolved from seaweeds and other green algae that were swept ashore by the tide, then gradually adapted to life in the challenging environment outside the water. These pioneering land-dwellers, however, still could not survive in completely dry conditions and initially lived in and around bogs and ponds. They were small and lacked roots, relying on surrounding water for moisture.

To survive on dry land, plants had to develop ways to prevent themselves from drying out. They did this by gradually acquiring extra cellulose thickening in their cell walls and an internal tubular transport system, along which water and nutrients could move around the plant. To draw water and minerals from the ground into this system, plants also developed roots, which held them firmly in one place. Such plants are known as **vascular plants**. These early plants reproduced via specialist reproductive cells called spores.

Ferns

Ferns thrived in the Carboniferous swamps, usually in the slightly drier areas. Size varied greatly, some being less than 1 m (3 ft) high, while others grew up to 18 m (60 ft). Ferns have extensive root systems and specialised leaves – known as fronds – which produce spores on their underside. Ferns produce copious amounts of spores, and some species can also reproduce vegetatively. This flexibility has made them one of the Earth's most successful types of plant.

Modern ferns In the Carboniferous period ferns dominated the Earth's vegetation. They are still widespread today with 100 000 known species.

FUNGI

Neither plants nor animals, fungi are grouped into their own separate kingdom. There are about 100 000 species of fungus in existence today.

Although many species appear to grow like plants, they cannot photosynthesise their own food. Some live as parasites, others break down dead matter into nutrients, which they then absorb. Along with bacteria, fungi are responsible for the decay of dead material, which helps to clean the planet, recycling the constituent

Modern fungi Fungi appeared on land around 400 million years ago.

chemicals. The only part of a fungus we usually see is its fruiting body, where microscopic spores are produced. The main part, a mass of slender tubes or hyphae, known as the mycelium, remains underground.

A mycelium can cover a huge area. One spread over 15 ha (37 acres) was discovered in a North American forest. Some fungi, such as yeasts, are microscopic – each consisting of just a single cell.

Flowering plants

Flowering plants, or angiosperms, first appeared at the end of the Jurassic period, and they now dominate the plant world. The key to their success is their ability to use different methods of reproduction (see page 75) and to colonise almost every environment found on Earth. Four out of every five plants living today are angiosperms.

South African protea The earliest flowers appeared during the age of the dinosaurs.

Timeline

360–286 million years ago
Club mosses and ferns dominate the vegetation.

285 million years ago
First conifers appear.

CARBONIFEROUS

286–245 million years ago
Horsetails are now the dominant land plants, with many varieties evolving.

286

PERMIAN

245–208 million years ago
First modern ferns appear, although horsetails still dominate.

245

TRIASSIC

208

208–144 million years ago
Forests of ferns and conifers are becoming established.

JURASSIC

144

144–65 million years ago
Flowering plants come to dominate every type of environment.

CRETACEOUS

65

Horsetails

Giant, tree-like horsetails first appeared in the swamps of the Carboniferous period. From these, smaller varieties evolved, and went on to dominate the plant world well into the Triassic. Characterised by small, narrow leaves and jointed, hollow stems with a ribbed texture, they grew tall, so could compete successfully for sunlight with which to photosynthesise food. But eventually most proved too specialised to adapt readily to change, and they became extinct.

Last horsetail *Equisetum* is the only surviving horsetail genus.

Spores or seeds?

The earliest vascular plants reproduced via spores, which require damp external conditions to fertilise. The first plants to reproduce by seeds, which do not need water for fertilisation, appeared during the Devonian. Seed cases also protect the dormant plant embryo, which can then survive until conditions are suitable for germination. These advantages meant that seed-bearing plants could colonise a far greater variety of habitats.

see also
74-5 **How plants live**
542-7 **Biology**

Plant life is enormously varied. It ranges from single, microscopic cells to the largest living things on Earth – California's giant sequoias. Vegetation can be found in almost all Earth's environments and it is this immense diversity that is the key to its success. Plants can also live to a great age – there are 4600-year-old bristlecone pines in the Rocky Mountains of North America.

Early blossom
Magnolias were some of the first flowering plants to evolve.

GREEN ALGAE

Chlorophytes
40 000 species

Key features:

- Range from single-cell to multicellular species.
- Contain chlorophyll, so can carry out photosynthesis (see page 74).
- Produce 70 per cent of all oxygen released into the atmosphere by photosynthesis.
- Live in water or a moist environment.
- Reproduce both asexually and sexually (see page 75).

LIVERWORTS, HORNWORTS AND MOSSES

Bryophytes
29 000 species

Key features:

- The simplest land plants.
- Do not possess vascular tissue (see page 74).
- Lack proper roots and leaves.
- Small and low to the ground, with some growing on other plants.
- Rely for water on surrounding moisture.
- Can live only in damp places.
- Reproduce via spores (see page 71).

FERNS, CLUB MOSSES AND HORSETAILS

Pteridophytes
13 000 species

Key features:

- Descended directly from the simplest land plants.
- Are vascular plants (see page 70).
- Possess roots.
- Ferns have special leaves called fronds.
- Require damp conditions for reproduction but not as reliant on surface water as liverworts and mosses.
- Reproduce via spores (see page 71).

CONE-BEARING PLANTS

Gymnosperms
936 species

Key features:

- Possess a complex vascular system (see page 74).
- Have an extensive root system.
- Pollinated by the wind (see page 75).
- Reproduce via seeds (see page 71).
- Seeds usually produced in a cone-like structure.
- Do not produce flowers or fruits.

FLOWERING PLANTS

Angiosperms
250 000 species

Key features:

- Are the most successful group of plants ever.
- Are found in almost any kind of environment.
- Possess great variation in size, form and structure.
- Have a complex vascular system (see page 74).
- Produce flowers.
- Pollinated by animals, wind and water (see page 75).
- Reproduce via seeds (see page 71).
- Seeds grow inside an ovary, which swells to become a fruit.

Cones

Conifers produce cones which develop from the female sexual organs after pollination in the same way as fruits, nuts and seed heads develop from the flowers of flowering plants. Cones protect the pollinated (fertilised) female sex cells while they develop into seeds. When the seeds are mature and conditions are right for their dispersal, the cone opens to release them. Cone-bearing plants are an ancient group, and cones themselves have changed little in the hundreds of millions of years since they first made their appearance – a tribute to their successful design.

Wide open This Scots pine (*Pinus silvestris*) cone has shed its seeds.

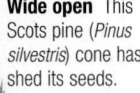

Ancient design
The cone of the monkey puzzle tree (*Araucaria araucaria*) has remained unchanged since the Jurassic period.

Shut tight This giant fir (*Abies grandis*) cone is closed with its seeds held inside.

Flowering plants are divided into two groups depending on how many seed leaves (*cotyledons*) they produce. The seed leaf is a structure in the plant's embryo, which in many species acts as a food store for the embryo and often appears above ground as the sprouting seed's first leaves.

ONE SEED LEAF

Monocotyledons
About 50 000 species

- Seeds produce one seed leaf on germination.
- Leaves have veins running in parallel along their length.
- Vascular tissue is scattered randomly throughout the stem.
- Includes lilies, grasses and many related cereal crops, and among trees, the fruit-bearing palms.

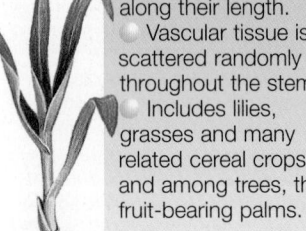

Narrow leaf Monocotyledons have blade-shaped leaves.

TWO SEED LEAVES

Dicotyledons
About 200 000 species

- Seeds produce two seed leaves on germination.
- Generally more complex than monocotyledons.
- Veins spread net-like across their leaves.
- Vascular tissue is arranged in an orderly ring around the stem.
- Includes most flowering plants, and many hardwood trees, such as oaks, limes and beeches.

Broad leaf The leaves of dicotyledons (right) are wide with rounded edges.

Longest seaweed

Pacific giant kelp (*Macrocystis pyrifera*) is the world's biggest seaweed. It has fronds that can grow up to 60 m (196 ft) long. They can reach this length in just one year, making this plant of coastal waters the fastest-growing form of marine life.

Largest seed

The rare coco de mer palm (*Lodoicea maldivica*), produces the biggest seeds of any living plant. Each one weighs up to 20 kg (44 lb) and takes about ten years to ripen. In the past, sailors thought that such seeds grew at the bottom of the sea. In fact, the palm grows in the Seychelles in the Indian Ocean.

Widest flower

The widest single flowers grow on the Rafflesia plant (*Rafflesia arnoldii*), which lives in the rain forests of South-east Asia. They are about 91 cm (3 ft) across and weigh up to 15 kg (7 lb). To attract flies — as pollinators — they give off a foul smell, reminiscent of rotting meat.

Tallest flower

The tallest single flower belongs to the Titan arum (*Amorphophallus titanum*) from Sumatra. Up to 2.6 m (9 ft) high, it stinks of rotting fish, which attracts the insects that help to pollinate it. The flower grows at a rate of several centimetres a day and collapses just two days after reaching its full size.

Tallest flowerhead

The flowers of some plants grow in clusters called flowerheads. The tallest flowerhead is found on the giant puya (*Puya raimondii*) from Bolivia. It can be over 10 m (33 ft) tall and contain up to 8000 separate flowers. Puya plants live for about 150 years before growing this flowerhead, and then they die.

see also

70-1 **Evolution of plants**

74-5 **How plants live**

542-7 **Biology**

Plants need light, water and the right soil and temperature conditions to thrive. Light and warmth are provided by the Sun, whose energy is also utilised to make food by photosynthesis. Water, along with essential nutrients and minerals such as nitrogen, potassium and magnesium, is obtained from the soil through the roots. Water is also used in photosynthesis, and creates a build-up of pressure within a plant's cells, called turgor pressure. Without this, the cell walls would collapse, and the plant would wilt and eventually die.

Leaves
Leaves contain most of the chlorophyll used in photosynthesis. They also regulate water loss through openings called stomata, found mainly on the underside of the leaf. Stomata open and close in response to the need to release or retain water.

PHOTOSYNTHESIS

Photosynthesis is the process by which plants use the Sun's energy to combine simple substances, present all around them, into food.

The key to this process is the green pigment chlorophyll. This substance is found in chloroplasts – tiny structures in a plant's leaves. It absorbs the light energy from the Sun, which is then used to combine water from the soil and carbon dioxide from the air to produce a sugary food called glucose. Oxygen is released into the atmosphere as a by-product. Nearly all atmospheric oxygen – upon which most life on Earth depends – is created by photosynthesis.

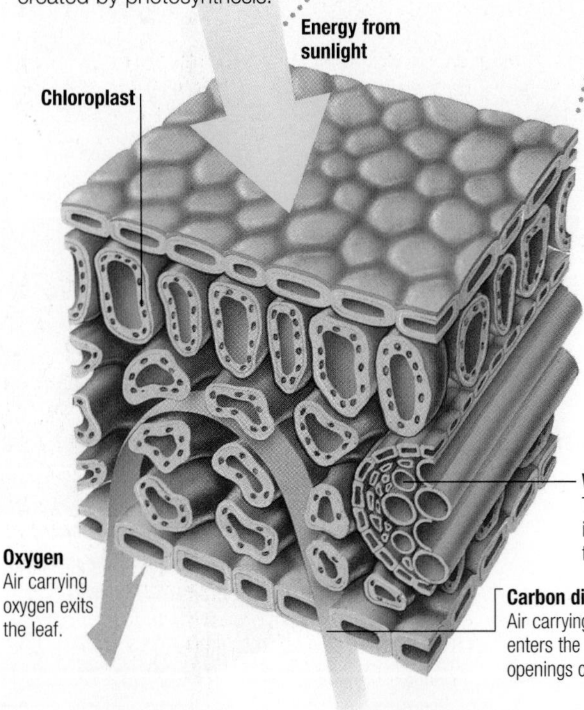

Xylem tubes
Water and dissolved minerals are transported from the roots to the leaves along the hollow xylem tubes. A material called lignin reinforces the tubes, making them strong and waterproof.

Phloem tubes
Food and amino acids, which are made in the leaves, travel up and down the stems and roots along phloem tubes.

Stem
All but the most primitive plants have a system of tubes, known as vascular tissue, that carries water and nutrients around the plant. There are two separate sets of tubes – xylem tubes and phloem tubes.

Energy from sunlight

Chloroplast

Oxygen
Air carrying oxygen exits the leaf.

Water
This is drawn into the leaf through its veins.

Carbon dioxide
Air carrying carbon dioxide enters the leaf through openings called stomata.

Nodules
Some plants have knot-like protuberances on their roots, containing bacteria that can absorb and convert (fix) atmospheric nitrogen into ammonia (NH_3), which the plant then uses to make nitrates and amino acids.

Roots
A network of roots anchors the plant in the ground. Roots also absorb water and essential minerals from the soil and can store nutrients. They vary greatly in size and number, depending on the size of a plant and the conditions under which it grows.

Flower
A flower is the sexual reproductive unit that produces and houses the plant's sex cells (gametes). Some flowers produce both male and female sex cells; other plants have separate male and female flowers, either on the same or different plants.

Anthers
Upper part of the stamen, produces pollen.

Pollen
Male gametes or sex cells are found in pollen grains.

Style
Stalk supporting the stigma. The stigma, style and ovary together are called the carpel.

Ovary
Female gametes or egg cells are found in the ovary.

Stigma
Pollen grains falling on the stigma release male gametes which travel down the stigma to the ovary where they fertilise the eggs.

SEED DISPERSAL

Once fertilisation has taken place, seeds are produced. These new seeds need to move away from the parent plant both to find space to germinate and grow and to help to colonise new areas. A number of agents help to achieve this:

Wind   Light seeds with feathery parachutes, such as dandelion, catch the wind and can be carried long distances. Seeds with 'wings' and aerofoils, such as sycamore (right) and lime, rotate in the air and ride the wind like tiny aircraft.

Animals   Seeds with hooks, such as burdock (right), cling to animals' coats and get carried off. The seeds in fruits eaten by animals usually pass unharmed through their gut. By the time they emerge, they will usually have travelled some distance from the parent plant.

Explosive mechanisms   Some seedpods are designed to explode when mature, scattering the seeds far and wide. Broom (right) sheds its seeds in this way.

'Pepper pot' mechanisms
Plants, such as the poppy, have seedpods that are perforated like a pepper pot. Seeds sprinkle from them as they sway in the wind.

Water   Plants living by water can use currents or tides to distribute seeds. Such seeds must float and be waterproof. Coconuts, for instance, are carried from beach to beach by the sea.

POLLINATION

When pollen is transferred from the anthers to the stigma an outgrowth from the pollen grain passes down through the style to the ovary. Male gametes travel down the tube to fertilise the egg cells within the ovary. Self-pollination occurs when the pollen is from the same plant; cross-pollination when the pollen is from a different plant.

Species which have male and female flowers on separate plants can only ever be cross-pollinated. Some flowers having both male and female parts can be self or cross-pollinated while others have mechanisms that prevent self-pollination.

Pollen is usually carried by the wind or by animals, such as bees.

By wind   Wind-blown pollen tends to be very smooth and light to aid buoyancy in the air. Most grasses rely on the wind to transport their pollen, as do many trees.

By animals   This is a more reliable and targeted method. It also encourages cross-fertilisation, which helps to increase the genetic variety of a species. Animal pollinators are usually invertebrates or small mammals. This pollen is commonly large with a rough surface to help it cling to the pollinator's body. Pollen is picked up and deposited as the animal visits successive flowers. Flowers attract potential pollinators by colour, shape, scent and the promise of nectar.

Windblown   The male flowers, or catkins, of hazel bushes use the wind to spread their pollen.

see also
56-7 **Regions of the world**
542-7 **Biology**

Plants of arid areas

Plants that live in dry places often develop long roots to reach water deep in the ground. They also need to conserve water once they have it. Water vapour is lost through microscopic pores in the leaves called stomata, which open and close to control this loss, a process called transpiration. To limit transpiration, plants in arid conditions often have one or more of the following features:

● **fewer stomata**, which limits the amount of water that can be lost.
● **stomata that close** during the day and open at night, when there is no drying effect from the Sun.
● **a waxy cuticle** on the leaf surface, which helps to reduce water loss.
● **no leaves** – leafless plants such as cacti have a smaller surface area from which transpiration can take place.
● **fleshy stems and leaves** – cacti and succulents store water in this way.

Dry area plants with leathery, hard or spiny leaves, adaptations to low-nutrient soils, include Australian Banksias, eucalypts and acacias. They are slow-growing and often resistant to fire.

Desert beauty The prickly pear has a whole range of water-retaining features.

Both the largest and the oldest living things on Earth are trees. Vital to the Earth's ecology, trees also offer food and shelter to a wide variety of animals and other organisms such as fungi and other plants. Their large, deep roots help to conserve water and prevent soil erosion. In addition, like all green plants, trees clean the air by taking in carbon dioxide and releasing oxygen during photosynthesis.

WHAT IS A TREE?

A tree is a difficult thing to define precisely. Under different circumstances the same plant may be described as either a tree or a shrub. Generally, a tree:

◗ must be **a woody perennial** (a plant that renews its growth every year)
◗ must be **at least 3 m (10 ft) tall**
◗ must have **a single stem**, known as a trunk, which is self-supporting.

Deciduous trees In temperate climates, many trees lose all their leaves in autumn at the end of the growing season. This is a way of conserving moisture and energy through the cold, dark months. In spring, they will grow a new set of leaves and start photosynthesising food again.

Evergreen trees These trees lose only a few leaves at a time, but do so all year round. They conserve water during winter by having specially adapted leaves. These are often spiky (needles), having a small surface area and a waxy coating with few stomata (see page 74) to limit water loss. In extremes of climate, such as severe frost or drought, evergreens may lose all their leaves for a while.

INSIDE A TREE

Trees grow by adding cells in concentric layers just underneath the bark. These growth layers give the ringed appearance of wood in cross-section, each ring representing a single year's growth. New cells are made by a thin layer of specialist tissue called the cambium which lies a short distance beneath the bark. It produces different types of cell on its inner and outer surfaces:

◗ **Xylem cells,** which transport water, are produced on the **inside** surface and build up annually to form the internal bulk of the tree.

◗ **Phloem cells,** which transport nutrients, are produced on its **outside** surface, to form a thin layer immediately under the bark.

As the tree grows due to the addition of xylem layers, the bark – made up of old, dead cambium and phloem cells – cracks or flakes off to accommodate the tree's expansion.

Xylem lives only for a few years, dying off as its function is taken over by successive newer layers. Once dead it no longer transports water and becomes dry, dense heartwood which strengthens and supports the trunk.

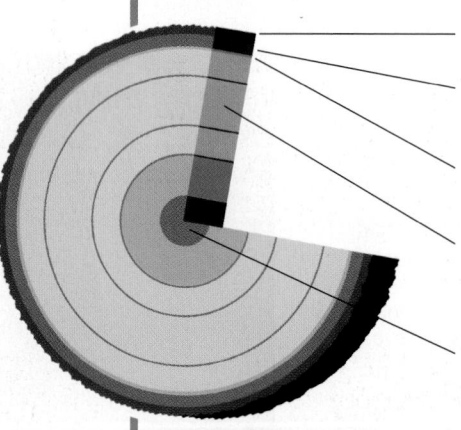

Bark Protective hard or flaky outer layer of dead phloem and cambium.

Phloem Spongy cells directly beneath the bark that carry nutrient-rich sap around the tree.

Cambium Thin layer of cells that manufactures xylem on its inner surface and phloem on its outer.

Xylem (sapwood) Tube-like transport cells on the inside of the tree that take water and minerals from the roots to the leaves.

Heartwood Dead xylem of previous years, which strengthens the tree and acts as a sink for waste matter.

TREE FERNS

Pteridophytes
About 300 species

Key features:
◗ The largest representatives of the pteridophytes.
◗ Tree ferns are one of the oldest forms of vascular plants.
◗ They are found in humid, mountainous regions of the tropics, and in warmer parts of the Southern Hemisphere.
◗ Tall, pillar-like trunks are topped by a crown of huge lacy leaves, known as fronds.
◗ Most are 6-9 m (20-30 ft) tall; some grow up to 24 m (80 ft). The fronds can be up to 4.6 m (15 ft) long.
◗ Tree ferns reproduce by means of spores (see page 71), that are carried by the wind.

CYCADS, GINKGOES AND CONIFERS

Gymnosperms
About 600 species

Key features:
Cycads (about 100 species)
◗ Primitive seed plants, that grow in the tropics.
◗ Resemble squat palms.
◗ Male and female cones occur on separate trees.
Ginkgo (1 species)
◗ Flourished in the Jurassic.
◗ Grow wild only in China, but are cultivated worldwide.
◗ Tall and graceful with delicate, pale green leaves.
Conifers (about 500 species)
◗ Most varied group of cone-bearing trees.
◗ Range from giant redwoods to dwarf arctic pines.
◗ Most are hardy evergreens.
◗ Male and female cones are found on the same tree.

PALM TREES

Angiosperms
(Monocotyledons)
About 2500 species

Key features:
◗ Found throughout the tropics, where they are often important economically – dates, coconuts, bananas and various oils all come from palm trees.
◗ Like many more primitive trees, such as ferns and cycads, palms have a fibrous trunk that grows upright without thickening, lacks bark and does not generally divide into branches.
◗ Most are tall. Coconut palms, for example, can grow up to 30 m (100 ft) tall.
◗ Long trunk is topped by a crown of very large, long leaves, divided up into thin, finger-like leaflets.

BROAD-LEAVED TREES

Angiosperms
(Dicotyledons)
More than 4000 species

Key features:
◗ Are the most familiar and varied group of trees.
◗ Most are slow-growing; their trunks become thicker as they grow taller and divide into a network of branches and twigs
◗ Have a large canopy of relatively small leaves.
◗ Tend to form a wide-spreading network of deep, branching roots, which aids stability.
◗ Most are deciduous, although their ancestors may have been evergreens. Some species that grow in tropical regions, where there is plenty of water and light all year round, are still evergreen.

Deepest roots
Fig trees (*Ficus spp.*), can have very long roots. One growing in South Africa has roots 120 m (390 ft) deep. They are the longest ever found.

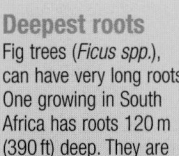

Tallest living tree
The 112 m (368 ft) Mendocino Tree, a Pacific coast redwood (*Sequoia sempervirens*) in Montgomery State Reserve, California, is the tallest tree in the world.

Tallest ever
Measured in 1872 at 133 m (435 ft) high, that's taller than St Paul's Cathedral in London, an Australian mountain ash (*Eucalyptus regnans*) is the tallest ever recorded tree. It grew by the Watts River, Victoria, Australia.

Oldest trees
The oldest living plants are thought to be bristlecone pines (*Pinus longaeva*) growing in the Rockies of North America. Some are at least 4600 years old.

FACT As a rough guide to a tree's age, measure the girth of its trunk about 1.5 m (5 ft) up from the ground. Each 2.5 cm (1 in) of girth represents approximately one year.

Fastest growing
A white albizia (*Albizia falcata*) tree in Borneo grew 10.7 m (35 ft) in 13 months, or about 2.5 cm (1 in) a day. The speed with which this species can grow makes it an important timber crop.

Widest ever
In the late 18th century a European chestnut (*Castanea sativa*), on Mount Etna in Sicily, was recorded as having a girth of 58 m (190 ft). No other tree has ever been known to equal this.

Widest living tree
'El Tule', a swamp cypress (*Taxodium mucronatum*) growing in Oaxaca, Mexico, has a trunk with a girth of 46 m (150 ft). This is the largest in any living plant.

Giant leaves
Many palms have large leaves, but the raffia palm (*Raphia ruffia*), which grows around the the Indian Ocean, has the largest leaves found on any plant. The central stalk alone can reach a length of 3.7 m (12 ft), with the leaf blade itself being over 18 m (60 ft) long.

Heaviest living thing
'General Sherman', a giant sequoia (*Sequoiadendron giganteum*), growing in California is the heaviest living thing on Earth. It weighs about 2500 tonnes, the equivalent of 19 fully grown blue whales. It stands 84 m (275 ft) tall with a girth of 25 m (83 ft).

see also
70-5 **Plants**
542-7 **Biology**

The first organised life, simple bacteria consisting of single cells without a nucleus, would eventually give rise to all life on Earth. But it was only with the evolution of eukaryotes – cells with a nucleus – around 2.1 billion years ago, that the evolution of multicellular life finally became possible.

One cell engulfs another

As multicellular life evolved from the first eukaryotic cells, the cells themselves became increasingly complex. Larger eukaryotic cells developed mutually beneficial relationships with other, smaller ones, eventually incorporating them. The smaller cells could now perform useful functions, such as respiration or photosynthesis, for their hosts. Over time, the engulfed cells lost their autonomy and became specialised parts of the host cell – its organelles. Chloroplasts (see page 74) and mitochondria are cell organelles.

The origin of sexual reproduction

Without the emergence of eukaryotic cells, there would have been no sex. Packaging genetic information into one specialised part of a cell – the nucleus – made sexual reproduction possible. Unlike asexual reproduction, which creates only offspring that are genetically identical to the parent, sexual reproduction combines genetic material from two individuals, allowing for an infinite number of combinations. Genetically varied populations can evolve much faster than those that are not. The rapid evolution of life forms after the arrival of eukaryotes illustrates this. During the 1.5 billion years or so when only prokaryotic cells existed, the most developed life forms were bacteria. But in the 1 billion years since eukaryotic cells appeared there has been an explosion of multicellular life.

800 million years ago
Single-celled animals (protozoans) first appear in the fossil record.

680 million years ago
The **earliest fossil evidence of multicellular animals** dates from this time. Examples are impressions of soft-bodied animals found in the Ediacara Hills of South Australia in the 1940s. Some are unrelated to modern life, but some resemble the worms and arthropods of today.

PRECAMBRIAN

2.1 billion years ago
Eukaryotes, cells with a nucleus containing their genetic information, first appear.

THE CAMBRIAN EXPLOSION

What happened?

- 550 million years ago, life on Earth underwent a huge expansion.
- 70 new animal phyla appeared, including 30 that still exist.
- 470 new animal families appeared.
- A wide range of animal forms was created.
- Basic forms of all animals alive today were established. Only improvements and variations have occurred since.

Why did it happen?

Scientists have put forward a number of possible explanations. The truth may be a combination of them:

Continental break-up At the end of the Precambrian, a giant supercontinent called Rodinia began to break up. This involved underwater volcanic activity, which pumped minerals into the sea and raised sea levels. Higher sea levels drowned most of the land, creating shallow, mineral-rich seas separated by deep ocean troughs: new environments for rapidly evolving life forms to exploit. Never before or since in the history of the Earth has such an unbounded ecological opportunity been available.

After the freeze The creation of the supercontinent Rodinia in the Precambrian was accompanied by a severe ice age, causing a mass extinction of primitive life. Explosions of new life tend to follow mass extinctions, and the eventual warming of the Earth at the end of the Precambrian heralded the appearance, around 720 million years ago, of the first multicellular animals. Because multicellular life allows for the development of diversity, the rapid evolution of new species was inevitable. Competition for mates, living space and food fuelled the evolution of new species through natural selection.

720 million years ago
Multicellular animals (metazoans) are thought to have evolved, although there is no fossil evidence from this date. Scientists using the molecular clock theory (see box opposite) estimate that they would have originated around this time.

Spriggina, **an early animal fossil** from the Ediacara Hills. Scientists are unsure what kind of animal *Spriggina* was. Some believe that it was an ancestral arthropod, others think that it was part of a group that led to segmented worms.

Slow, fast, slow When life first moves into a new environment, population growth is usually slow because only a small number of individuals is reproducing. As numbers increase, so the rate of growth increases until the available space is full. Further expansion is then impossible and the rate of growth slows down until the population reaches a sustainable level. Any colonisation of a new environment, if unrestrained by external factors, will conform to this pattern. Some scientists argue that this model is true of the Cambrian explosion. The evolution of multicellular life in a world full of ecological niches waiting to be filled would inevitably show a slow initial increase, followed by an explosion of new life forms. The only explanation needed for the Cambrian explosion is the existence of an empty environment to fill, and life forms with the evolutionary potential to fill it.

THE TRILOBITES

Trilobites are one of the largest and most diverse group of extinct animals to appear during the Cambrian explosion of life. Some 15 000 species are known. Trilobites were arthropods, like today's crabs, insects and spiders. They scavenged along the seabed and evolved a variety of shapes and sizes. Tiny *Agnostus*, for example, was just 7 mm (¼ in) long, while later species, such as *Isotelus*, grew to up to 70 cm (28 in).

Trilobite means 'three lobes' because the bodies of many species had a threefold division, with a raised central portion down the back flanked by a flatter portion on either side. They had a hard outer casing or exoskeleton and many pairs of legs. The exoskeleton was vital to the development of multicellular life. It provided a protective framework on which an animal could grow and allowed for an increase in cell number and type. Cell specialisation made adaptation to a wide range of conditions possible.

The trilobites were highly successful and thrived until the end of the Permian, when they succumbed to a mass extinction that wiped out 96 per cent of all marine life.

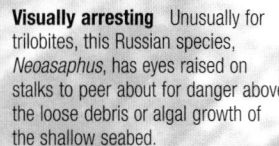

Visually arresting   Unusually for trilobites, this Russian species, *Neoasaphus*, has eyes raised on stalks to peer about for danger above the loose debris or algal growth of the shallow seabed.

The Burgess Shale – a fossil portrait

In 1909, Charles Doolittle Walcott, discovered some extremely well-preserved fossils in a formation called the Burgess Shale in British Columbia, Canada. Doolittle, an American palaeontologist, found 140 different species which he estimated to be about 530 million years old. They included some of the first creatures known to have had hard body parts and 20 species for which no earlier evidence has ever been found.

The Burgess Shale fossils are a scientific treasure trove. The fossilising conditions were so good that even internal organs and soft-bodied animals were preserved, offering unique clues about the nature of animal evolution.

The fossils also give a snapshot of a marine community just after the Cambrian explosion of new life and provide the oldest evidence of a group of interacting species.

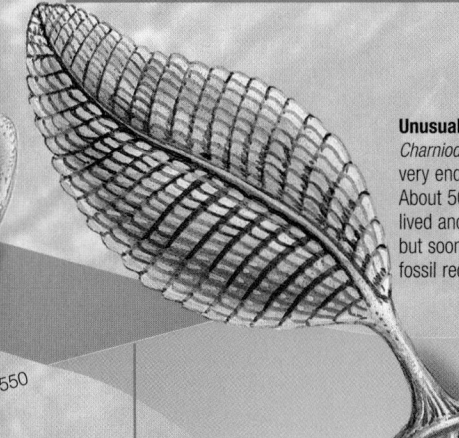

Unusual life forms
Charniodiscus appeared at the very end of the Precambrian. About 50 cm (20 in) long, it lived anchored to the seabed, but soon disappears from the fossil record.

Ancient arthropod   This well-preserved fossil of a lobster-like creature is from the Burgess Shale.

550

CAMBRIAN

550 million years ago
Cambrian explosion
All known phyla emerge at this time including arthropods, flatworms, molluscs, chordates and sponges.

Molecular clocks

The fossil record is often incomplete, so scientists have devised other ways of ascertaining when particular species are likely to have first appeared on Earth. One of these is to use molecular evidence from the study of proteins, organic compounds found in all living species.

Proteins are made up of amino acids. In the 1960s, it was found that different species have different amino acid sequences for the same protein. It was concluded that the number of differences was proportional to the time since those different species evolved from a common ancestor. So the longer a species has existed, the more differences, or mutations, there will have been. Mutation rates are then used to estimate when species evolved.

see also
32-3 **Geology of the Earth**
64-5 **Ages of life on Earth**
66-7 **Evolution explained**

Fishes hold a crucial place in the history of animal evolution. They evolved from chordates, animals with a stiffened rod running along their bodies, to become the first true vertebrates – animals with backbones. All other vertebrate groups – amphibians, reptiles, birds and mammals, including humans – would ultimately emerge from fishes.

500 million years ago
The first true fishes, Agnathans, appear. The jawless Agnathans, show great diversity and colonise both salt water and fresh. Their descendants – the hagfish and lampreys – still exist. Other key features of Agnathans:

● They had a cartilage skeleton.

● They had bony external plates.

● They were filter feeders that combined their gills as a breathing and filter-feeding mechanism.

● They did not have fins.

440–400 million years ago
First jawed fishes emerge. The earliest forms are Acanthodians, which probably evolve in the sea, but soon colonise fresh water too. Having jaws lets them become active predators – see the box 'The benefit of jaws'. Other key features of Acanthodians:

● They had fins.

● They used their gills to breathe but no longer used them for filter feeding.

● They had an enlarged gut to digest larger food.

CAMBRIAN

505

Over 515 million years ago
Conodonts, small eel-like chordates, emerge. They have fish-like muscles and are possible ancestors of the fishes.

530–525 million years ago
The earliest known chordate appears. At 4 cm (1½ in) long, *Pikaia gracilens* has a head, notochord (primitive backbone) and fish-like muscles. *Pikaia*'s relationship to the similar conodonts is uncertain.

First forerunner *Pikaia* is the earliest creature known to have possessed a spinal rod.

ORDOVICIAN

435

SILURIAN

Filter feeder
Arandaspis fed by hoovering up silt from the seabed and sifting out detritus and microorganisms.

The evolution of gills

Gills are the organs that most aquatic animals use to obtain oxygen from the surrounding water. The first gills appeared in sea-living invertebrates. Below a certain size, these creatures got enough oxygen from the water by simple exchange through their body surfaces. But as they became bigger, they had to increase their surface areas by infolding areas of the body: in this way they could absorb more oxygen. Over millions of years of evolution these folded areas developed an increased blood supply and became gills. By the time fishes appeared, gills were already complex internal organs. Later, their efficiency was improved by the fish pumping water over them (left), much as we pump air over our lungs when we breathe. The total surface area of the gills of any fish far exceeds that of its outer body surface.

Aqua lungs
A fish pumps water through its mouth over its gills to extract oxygen.

HAVING A BACKBONE

All animals with a flexible spinal rod along their bodies during some stage of their development are known as chordates. Scientists place them in a large group, or phylum, called the Chordata. In vertebrates, this spinal rod has evolved into a true backbone made up of distinct bones, called vertebrae, that are linked together. Exactly how the spinal rod, or notochord, originated, is still unknown but its appearance along with attached muscles down the back, was a major step in animal evolution. It has a number of advantages:

● It makes movement more efficient.

● It provides support for the shoulder and pelvic girdles – the attachment sites of various limbs and appendages.

● It protects the dorsal (spinal) nerve cord, allowing the nervous system to develop and become more sophisticated.

Jawed fishes

Acanthodians
Earliest jawed fishes

- Resembled modern sharks.

- Evolved in the sea at the beginning of the Silurian.

- Later moved into fresh water.

Placoderms
Heavily armoured marine fishes

- Emerged in the early Devonian.

- Short-lived group, died out in the early Carboniferous.

Lobe-finned fishes (*Sarcopterygians*)
Seven species survive today: six lungfish and the coelacanth

- Fleshy, lobe-shaped fins, supported by bones and rays. Muscles in the fins.

- Amphibians evolved from this group.

Osteichthyans
Include the majority of modern fishes

- Emerged in the early Devonian.

- Skeletons made of bone.

- 20 000 modern species (half of all vertebrates).

Ray-finned fishes (*Actinopterygians*)
Earliest group of bony fishes to appear

- Bony spines, known as rays, support the fins. No muscles in the fins.

- Evolved into the huge range of modern freshwater and sea fishes, from salmon to sea horses, sturgeon to plaice.

Chondrichthyans
Include sharks, skates and rays

- Emerged in the early Devonian.

- Skeletons made of cartilage.

- Teeth and body scales replaced throughout life.

390 million years ago (early Devonian)
New groups of jawed fishes emerge, including sharks, skates and rays. Early kinds of bony fishes, the group that includes most modern fishes, appear.

380 million years ago
Lobe-finned fishes appear. These are the forebears of the amphibians and hence of the reptiles, birds and mammals.

Fearsome hunter
Placoderm *Dunkleosteus* reached 6 m (20 ft) long.

SILURIAN

408

DEVONIAN

360

Armour plated
Drepanaspis was a jawless fish well protected from attack.

420 million years ago
Life starts to move from salt water into fresh water. Giant invertebrates called Eurypterids, or sea scorpions, often nearly 2 m (7 ft) long, were the first predators to venture into fresh water. They were soon followed by jawed fishes that competed with them for food.

THE BENEFIT OF JAWS

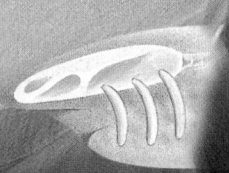 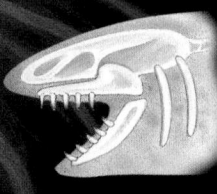

Jaws probably evolved from the first pair of gill supports, located in jawless fishes just behind the mouth (above), while teeth developed from skin lining the mouth. It was a crucial development. Jaws enabled fish to move up a level in the food chain from passive filter feeding on detritus to actively pursuing and seizing prey. As a result, jawed fishes soon diversified in diet and lifestyle. Part of the gut enlarged to digest the larger food being eaten, and the fish themselves grew bigger.

Devonian survivor Background: A coloured X-ray of a mako shark skull. With skates and rays, sharks have survived relatively little changed since the Devonian.

see also

64-5 **Ages of life on Earth**

66-7 **Evolution explained**

96-9 **Fishes**

The first animals to colonise dry land were not air-breathing fish or early amphibians but myriapods, the ancestors of centipedes and millipedes. The oldest-known tracks of these ancient arthropods were found in fossilised sediments in northern England. They suggest that the earliest dry-land pioneers did not come from the sea, but from fresh water. The first tetrapods (vertebrates with four limbs), including amphibians and reptiles, did not evolve until nearly 100 million years later.

Coelacanth

The coelacanth belongs to a group of lobe-finned fishes that had been presumed extinct since the end of the Cretaceous period, about 65 million years ago. Then, a living specimen caught in the Indian Ocean in 1938, was identified by a South African scientist. Local fishermen were astounded at the interest in this find.

The coelacanth belongs to the same group of fishes that evolved into amphibians.

They had apparently been catching it for years, but discarding it as it was not good to eat. Since this first identification about 200 specimens have been caught off the Comoros Islands. To ensure the species' survival fisherman are now urged to release any coelacanths they catch.

500 million years ago
Plants begin to colonise the land.
505

460–440 million years ago
Invertebrates move from fresh water onto land. Myriapods and spiders are the earliest types found in the fossil record.

ORDOVICIAN

377 million years ago
***Panderichthys* appears, a likely precursor of true amphibians.** It was a fish with an amphibian-like skull and ribs, and paired muscular fins, which could have been the starting point for the evolution of legs.

438

SILURIAN

408

DEVONIAN

KEY TERMS

● **Amphibians**
Tetrapods that require water for part of their life cycle. They lay eggs in water and their larvae are aquatic and breathe using gills. The larvae metamorphose into land-dwelling adults that breathe using lungs. Amphibians were the first land-dwelling vertebrates.
● **Arthropods**
Invertebrates with jointed limbs and a hard protective and supportive outer skeleton. Crustaceans, insects, arachnids and millipedes and centipedes (myriapods) are all examples of arthropods.
● **Lobe-finned fish**
A group of fish with fleshy fins that gave rise to tetrapods. Lungfish and coelacanths are living examples.
● **Reptiles**
The first vertebrates to live entirely on land. Adaptations to land-dwelling include a watertight skin and air-breathing lungs.
● **Tetrapods**
Vertebrates with four limbs. All amphibians, reptiles, birds and mammals are tetrapods. Their limbs are all based on the same five-digit pattern – pentadactyl limbs (Greek for five fingers).

First steps These 460 million-year-old fossilised tracks from England's Lake District are the earliest evidence of animal life on land.

363 million years ago
Invertebrates diversify. Flightless insects evolve.

The first amphibians evolve from a group of lobe-finned freshwater fishes called the Rhipidistians. They include *Acanthostega*, which was 60 cm (2 ft) long and had limbs adapted for scrabbling through dense swamp vegetation.

ADAPTING TO LIFE ON LAND

The land was an untapped source of food but in order to exploit this the first land colonisers had to overcome a number of problems and dangers including:

● **Water loss**, amphibians need to keep their skins moist to avoid drying out.
● **Reproduction** – fish and amphibians need an aquatic environment to lay eggs and to support their young.
● The **full force of gravity** – in water, animals do not have to carry their whole weight; in air they do.

The first land-dwellers developed different strategies to cope with these factors. Arthropods developed a hard exoskeleton that protected them from drying out and supported their weight.
Amphibians evolved lungs and limbs so that they could breathe and move on land. But they still returned to water to breed. Reptiles' scales and self-contained eggs, that provided a sealed aquatic environment for the developing foetus, allowed them to become the first entirely terrestrial vertebrates.

FACT

The first areas of land to be colonised by plants were flood plains along the edges of rivers.

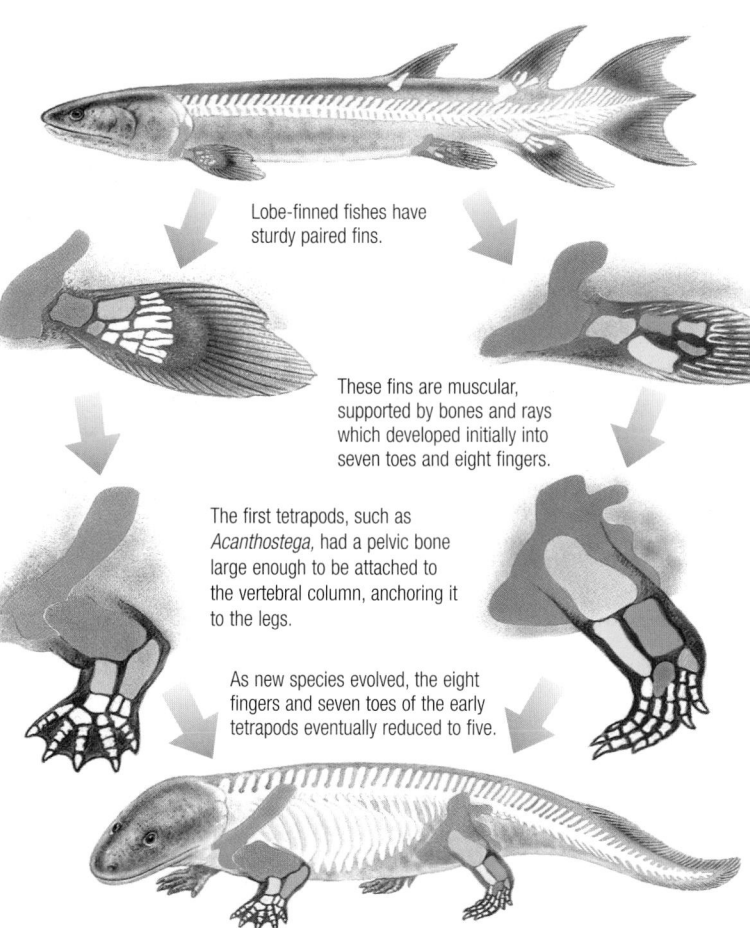

Lobe-finned fishes have sturdy paired fins.

These fins are muscular, supported by bones and rays which developed initially into seven toes and eight fingers.

The first tetrapods, such as *Acanthostega,* had a pelvic bone large enough to be attached to the vertebral column, anchoring it to the legs.

As new species evolved, the eight fingers and seven toes of the early tetrapods eventually reduced to five.

Legs eventually became strong enough for true walking.

WHY DID LEGS EVOLVE?

Recent work on Devonian *Acanthostega*, one of the very earliest tetrapods, indicates that the development of four limbs was not initially an adaptation for walking on land. These creatures were still better adapted for life in water than for life on dry land. They lived in bayou-like swamps and breathed like fish. Their spine and ribs could not support their gut, and their four limbs were, in any case, too weak to walk with.

So, what purpose did the four protolimbs serve? It is thought that they were initially simply a specialised fin, which helped the animal to manœuvre under water in search of food through the dead vegetation of the swamps. From these beginnings, their descendants may have started to use their limbs to move briefly onto land, either for breeding or as an escape route from predators.

The narrow-based fins of the lobe-finned fishes were ideal precursors of limbs. The paired fins of *Panderichthys*, for example, were supported by a single bone which joined the shoulder and hip girdles. At the other end were two wrist bones and then the rays that supported the fin. This was a much stronger arrangement than that of the ray-finned fish.

Main structural differences between fish and tetrapods.

Fish	Tetrapod
Flexible backbone	More rigid backbone
Thin ribs	Sturdy ribs
Shoulder girdle poorly developed and attached to skull, unable to bear weight.	Well-developed shoulder girdle, separate from skull, weight-bearing.
Pelvic girdle poorly developed, unable to bear weight.	Pelvic girdle well developed, weight-bearing. Pelvis fused to vertebrae.
Limb bones short	Limb bones longer, joints stronger and more flexible.
No digits	Toed and fingered limbs modified for walking, jumping, climbing, flying, grasping.

360 million years ago
Winged insects, including giant dragonflies, appear, as do scorpions, worms and snails. Amphibians diversify into about 20 families.

310 million years ago
The lizard-like *Hylonomus* – found in Nova Scotia – is one of the earliest reptiles. Just 20 cm (8 in) long, it is an active land animal with strong jaws. Remains of it were discovered in hollow trunks where it may have sheltered or looked for food.

360

CARBONIFEROUS

345 million years ago
The amniotic egg frees tetrapods from reliance on water for reproduction. Another major step is the evolution of scales, which decrease water loss through the skin.

334 million years ago
The amphibian *Proterogyrinus* appears. It is large – 1 m (3 ft) long – and walks competently on land. It feeds on fish and land invertebrates, and is a reptile ancestor.

Living at the same time, the 25 cm (10 in) *Eucritta melanolimnites* (literally 'the creature from the black lagoon') combines amphibian and reptilian features. It may be capable of walking.

286

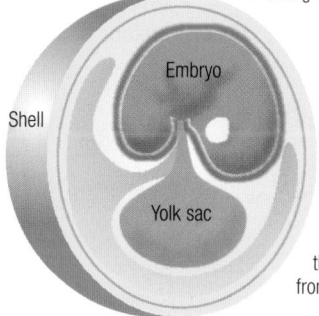

Shell

Embryo

Yolk sac

Life preserver
An amniotic egg has an impervious shell, which protects the embryo inside from the environment.

New kind of hunter
Early reptile *Hylonomus* fed on land invertebrates.

The first dinosaurs were small two-legged carnivores living around 228 million years ago. They later evolved into many different groups including the herbivorous giants such as Apatosaurus. In all, the dinosaurs dominated the Earth for 155 million years, making them an extremely successful animal group. If that reign had been a month, then by comparison, the time that modern humans have existed would be just 1 minute.

Nesting and hatching

Dinosaurs, like most reptiles, laid eggs, although a few species with wide pelvises may have given birth to live young. The largest eggs known would have weighed about 10 kg (22 lb); while the smallest weighed just 400 g (14 oz). Some dinosaurs, such as the 3.6 m (12 ft) long *Troodon*, nested in colonies. Some protected their eggs until they hatched, and a few may have fed and cared for their young as they grew. Most hatchlings would have been mobile almost from birth and not stayed in the nest for any appreciable time.

Eggs in stone
Fossilised eggs of the dinosaur *Oviraptor* found in the Gobi Desert.

1 CHASMATOSAURUS
Dinosaur precursor
Chasmatosaurus was one of the first known archosaurs. Resembling a long-legged crocodile, *Chasmatosaurus* was a carnivorous, predominantly water-dwelling creature, although it could walk on land with a lizard-like gait.
Size: 2 m (7 ft) long
Where found: South Africa and China

3 PETEINOSAURUS
This small pterosaur (flying reptile) was one of the first vertebrates to fly, rather than simply glide. Its skeleton was very light and its wings stretched from an elongated finger to its foot. *Peteinosaurus* had small sharp teeth and was probably insectivorous, catching its prey on the wing.
Wingspan: 60 cm (2 ft)
Where found: Cene, northern Italy

4 COELOPHYSIS
This dinosaur was a small, slender hunter. Fossil finds have shown evidence of herding and cannibalism.
Size: 0.6-3 m (2-10 ft) long
Where found: Arizona and New Mexico, USA

Permian

245

human figure
for scale only

Triassic

End of the Permian, 245 million years ago
Over 70 per cent of vertebrates disappear in the **Earth's most catastrophic mass extinction**.

235 million years ago
Several distinct **reptile groups have evolved**, including the archosaurs ('ruling reptiles').

228 million years ago
The earliest-known dinosaurs, *Eoraptor* and *Herrerasaurus*, **have appeared**.

2 PLATEOSAURUS
The oldest-known herbivorous dinosaur, and the first to walk on four legs, although capable of rearing up on two. It was also the first dinosaur to weigh over a tonne, and (with *Coelophysis*) the first known to live in herds.
Size: Up to 11 m (35 ft) long
Where found: Europe

Late Triassic
The **first mammals evolve** from mammal-like reptiles.

208

Jurassic

Walking tall

The key to the dinosaurs' success lay in an efficient new way of walking. Their immediate ancestors were the meat-eating archosaurs, some of which developed a semisprawling stance. They were able to run for short distances with almost straight legs, much as crocodiles do today. These gave rise to small, two-legged archosaurs, such as *Lagosuchus*; it was from these that the dinosaurs evolved.

Upright advantage   The oldest-known dinosaurs, *Eoraptor* and *Herrerasaurus*, were small carnivores, living about 228 million years ago. Like *Lagosuchus* they walked on two legs. They had a more upright stance, however, with straight legs tucked under their bodies. This freed the front legs for other uses such as grasping and clawing. Thus the early dinosaurs had a huge advantage over other reptile groups: the

improved stance meant they were quicker, and their legs could support more weight, allowing them to grow bigger.

Back to four legs   Later, many of the biggest dinosaurs, such as the sauropods, moved around on four legs, because they needed the extra support for their enormous bulk. They were plant eaters, so did not need to chase after prey or to use their front limbs to grasp and tear it up. Some, such as *Plateosaurus*, could rear up on their hind legs to reach food in the treetops or escape quickly if in danger.

Sprawling stance
Hylonomus first reptile

Semisprawling stance
Chasmatosaurus archosaur precursor to dinosaurs

Erect stance
Deinonychus dinosaur predator

Vertebrate family tree

From their origins as amphibians in the late Devonian, land-living vertebrates diversified into many different groups. Some, such as the dinosaurs and plesiosaurs, appeared and after many million years, finally became extinct. Others, such as mammals, birds, crocodiles and snakes, still survive.

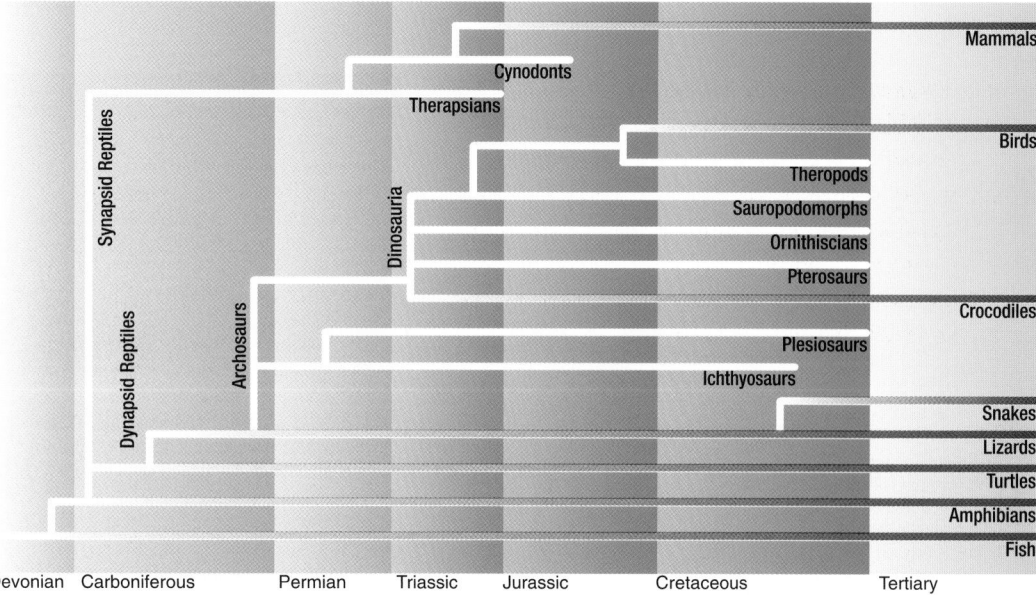

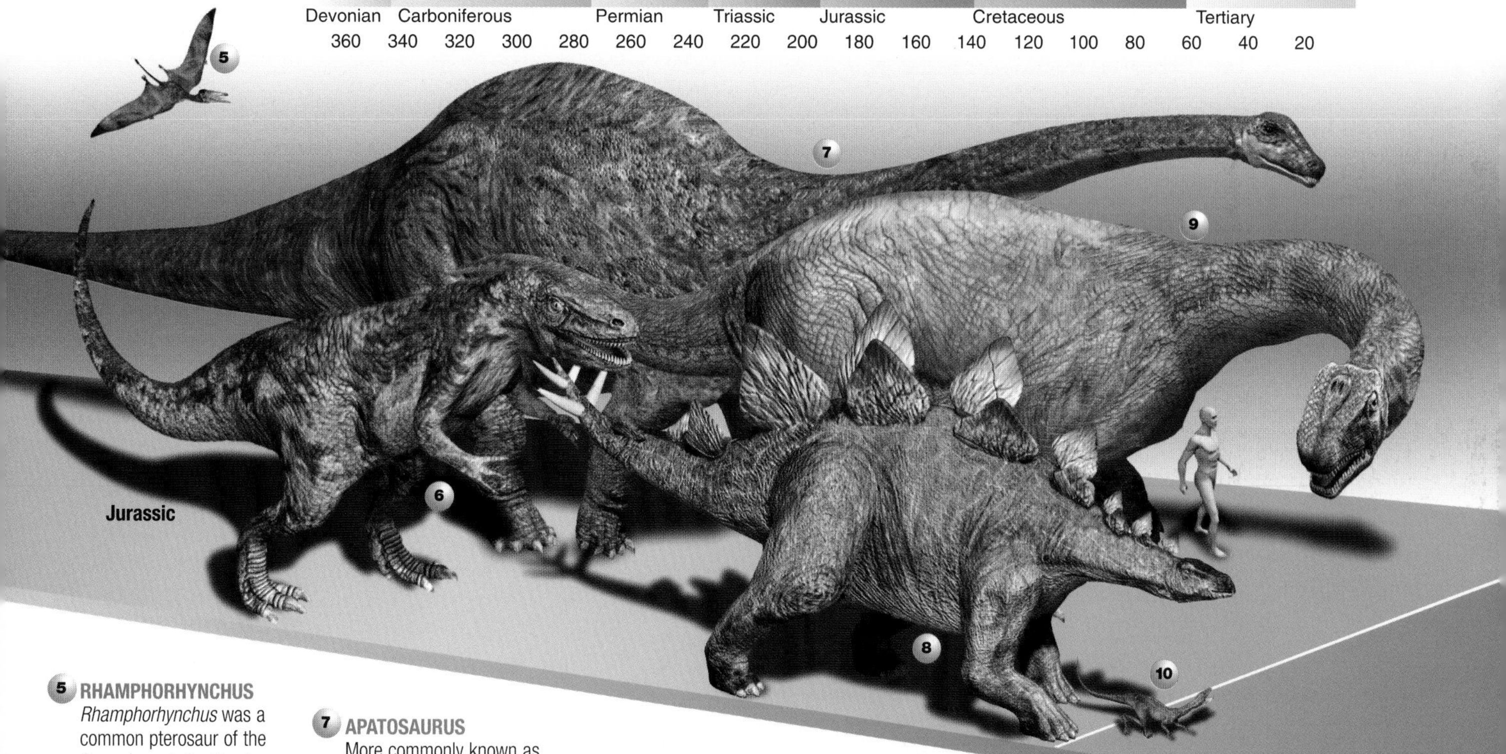

Jurassic

Compsognathus (shown here at actual size)

5 RHAMPHORHYNCHUS
Rhamphorhynchus was a common pterosaur of the Jurassic period with a long tail ending in a diamond-shaped rudder. A fish-eater, it dragged its lower jaw through the water to catch its prey on its sharp teeth.
Wingspan: Up to 1.8 m (6 ft)
Where found: UK, Germany and Tanzania

6 MEGALOSAURUS
This large carnivore was one of the top predators in Europe during the Jurassic.
Size: 12 m (40 ft) long
Where found: UK

7 APATOSAURUS
More commonly known as *Brontosaurus*, meaning 'thunder lizard', *Apatosaurus* was a giant herbivore. It 'raked' leaves off trees with its gappy, peg-like teeth, and, despite its huge bulk, could rise up on its hind legs to reach the highest vegetation. It may also have used this ability to crash down on predators such as *Allosaurus*.
Size: Up to 21 m (70 ft) long and weighing up to 33 tonnes.
Where found: North America

8 STEGOSAURUS
The diamond-shaped plates arranged alternately in two rows down *Stegosaurus*' back present something of a mystery. What was their function? They could have been for protection, signalling or temperature regulation. *Stegosaurus* had one of the smallest brains in relation to body size of any dinosaur.
Size: Up to 9 m (30 ft) long.
Where found: USA

9 CAMARASAURUS
A large herbivore that roamed in herds, possibly making long migrations in search of food. Piles of polished stones preserved in the same rocks as *Camarasaurus* fossil remains suggest that, like some modern birds, *Camarasaurus* swallowed stones to aid the grinding up of tough vegetable foods in the stomach. Prominent nasal openings on the top of the head may also have acted as a cooling device for the brain.
Size: Up to 18 m (59 ft) long
Where found: North America

10 COMPSOGNATHUS
The smallest of the dinosaurs *Compsognathus* was a swift, two-legged hunter. It had hollow bones and probably weighed only about 3.6 kg (8 lb). Its long tail would have aided balance while running.
Size: 60 cm (2 ft) long
Where found: Germany and France

The Cretaceous period saw the emergence of new types of dinosaur, such as the three-horned Triceratops. By the late Cretaceous, however, the dinosaurs' supremacy was waning, and their fate was finally sealed when an ecological disaster culminated in their mass extinction.

Taking to the air

The ability to glide was evolved by reptiles five separate times between the Permian and the Jurassic. But only one group, the pterosaurs, were capable of sustained flight achieved by flapping their wings.

Pterosaur aeronautics   Pterosaurs flew on wings formed from flaps of flexible skin, like those of bats. Like dinosaurs, the pterosaurs evolved into a wide range of sizes. The smallest were no bigger than pigeons, whereas the largest, the giant *Quetzalcoatlus* of the late Cretaceous period, had a wingspan equal to that of a Spitfire: approximately 12 m (40 ft). Also like the dinosaurs, pterosaurs declined during the late Cretaceous and none survived the mass extinction of 65 million years ago.

Last link   Birds did not arise from the earlier flying or gliding reptiles. The fossil record strongly points towards them evolving from small carnivorous dinosaurs in the late Jurassic and coexisting with pterosaurs for 70 million years. Most scientists believe that modern birds are the closest living link to the dinosaurs.

14

ARCHAEOPTERYX
Fossils of *Archaeopteryx*, the world's first bird, were found preserved in exceptional detail in the limestone of Solnhofen, Germany. They show an animal the size of a crow having both dinosaur and bird features and provide the clearest evidence that birds evolved from dinosaurs. *Archaeopteryx* – meaning 'ancient wing' – had teeth, a bony tail and claws on its wings (dinosaur features), as well as a wishbone and feathers (bird-like features).

12 IGUANODON
Iguanodon was bipedal but probably also walked on all fours. One of its characteristic features was a thumb spike, which it may have used as a weapon in self-defence or in mating disputes.
Size: Up to 10 m (33 ft) long
Where found: UK, Europe and the USA

13 DEINONYCHUS
A fast and agile predator, *Deinonychus* was built to hunt and kill. It was two-legged and lightweight with shearing teeth that curved backwards. Its powerful hind legs were each armed with a large, sharp, slashing claw on its second toe – *Deinonychus* means 'terrible claw'. Its long tail, stiffened with bony rods, helped it to maintain its balance when attacking its prey.
Size: 3-4 m (10-13 ft) long
Where found: North America

14 PTERODACTYLUS
With its long neck, short tail and much elongated fourth finger, which supported its wing, *Pterodactylus* was a typical Cretaceous pterosaur. It preyed predominantly on fish and had long, narrow jaws and sharp teeth.
Wingspan: up to 75 cm (2 ft 5 in)
Where found: Africa, Europe, UK

11 POLACANTHUS
Polacanthus was a squat, armoured herbivore related to the ankylosaurs and stegosaurs, and characterised by bony spikes on its flanks. It has been difficult to reconstruct the appearance of *Polacanthus* as only its hind legs and some body armour have ever been found. Some experts believe it is actually the same animal as *Hylaeosaurus*.
Size: 4 m (13 ft) long
Where found: UK

12

13

15 ICHTHYOSAUR
Ichthyosaurs were the reptile equivalent of dolphins. They hunted fish and free-swimming molluscs, such as ammonites and belemnites. Ichthyosaurs gave birth to live young.
Size: Up to 9 m (30 ft) long
Where found: UK, Europe, North and South America.

11

CRETACEOUS
144-65 million years ago

15

16

Marine reptiles

While dinosaurs ruled the land, other reptiles dominated the seas. The nothosaurs were efficient swimmers with paddle-like limbs. They were extinct by the late Triassic, but their relatives, the plesiosaurs, survived until the end of the Cretaceous.

Sea monsters   The dominant carnivores, however, were the pliosaurs, heavily built creatures up to 12 m (40 ft) long, with a short neck and large head. They ate other marine reptiles, as well as fish. The dolphin-like ichthyosaurs thrived throughout the Jurassic, but had died out by the mid Cretaceous. Other sea reptiles included the Triassic placodonts, which fed on molluscs, and early forms of crocodile and marine turtle.

16 PLESIOSAUR
Plesiosaurs were marine reptiles that lived along coasts much like modern seals. They used their long necks to sweep their heads through shoals of fish, which they caught with jaws edged with needle-like teeth.
Size: Up to 15 m (50 ft) long
Where found: UK, Europe, Africa and the USA

WHY DID THE DINOSAURS DIE OUT?

The dinosaurs were one group among many that perished in a mass extinction 65 million years ago. The cause of this extinction has been the subject of much debate.

Two theories are currently favoured:

Meteorite impact   There is strong evidence that a large meteorite hit the Earth near what today is the Yucatán Peninsula of Mexico. Geologists estimate that the meteorite was about 10 km (6 miles) across and that it shattered and melted the Earth's crust to a depth of almost 30 km (20 miles).

The effects of the impact would have been catastrophic, throwing up millions of tonnes of dust into the atmosphere, blocking out the sun and drastically reducing temperatures around the globe. Another consequence would have been the release of sulphur into the atmosphere. This would have combined with water vapour to create corrosive acid rain, turning the world's seas and oceans into acid baths.

Volcanic activity   The effect of the meteorite impact was compounded by a simultaneous event happening on the other side of the world in what is now India. For 2–3 million years at the end of the Cretaceous and the beginning of the Tertiary, this large area was subject to violent volcanic activity. Carbon dioxide and volcanic dust released by the volcanism would also have caused acid rain and adversely affected the climate. In addition, there is a theory that the element selenium, released by the volcanoes, was poisonous to dinosaurs.

Who survived, and why?   There seems to be little pattern to the species that died out and those that survived. Dinosaurs succumbed, but crocodiles and many other reptiles survived; birds and marsupial mammals suffered, but placental mammals escaped; simple plants coped better than flowering plants.

One factor is noticeable, however: all land creatures weighing more than about 25 kg (55 lb) were wiped out. The reasons for this are unclear but the currently favoured theory is that the warm-blooded, nocturnal and often burrow-dwelling mammals – which also happened to be small – were better equipped for survival in the cooled climatic conditions of the time than many other groups, particularly large, possibly cold-blooded dinosaurs, who could not control their body temperature as effectively as the mammals.

21 QUETZALCOATLUS
The largest flying creature of all time, *Quetzalcoatlus* was one of the last pterosaurs, becoming extinct at the end of the Cretaceous. *Quetzalcoatlus* probably used its vast wings to glide long distances on rising thermals. Some scientists believe it ate carrion, using its long neck and toothless jaws to probe deep inside carcasses. Others think it fed on fish or shellfish.
Wingspan: 12 m (40 ft)
Where found: USA

19 SAUROLOPHUS
One of the larger duck-billed dinosaurs, *Saurolophus* had a bony crest, and an inflatable bag of skin on its snout, which it used to produce bellowing sounds. A communal herbivore, *Saurolophus* may have used alarm calls to alert the herd to the presence of predators.
Size: 9-12 m (30-40 ft) long
Where found: North America and Asia

20 TYRANNOSAURUS REX
One of the largest known carnivorous dinosaurs, and by far the biggest still in existence at the end of the Cretaceous period. *Tyrannosaurus rex* means 'king of the tyrant reptiles', an apt description of a beast with a 1.5 m (5 ft) long head and a mouth filled with 15 cm (6 in) long serrated teeth. *T. rex* also had a powerful tail and hind limbs, but its forelimbs were tiny.
Size: 13 m (43 ft) long
Where found: USA

17 TRICERATOPS
The herbivorous *Triceratops* was one of the last dinosaurs to live on Earth. It had a bony frill on the skull to intimidate predators and protect its neck region, and three facial horns – the name *Triceratops* means 'three-horn face'.
Size: Up to 9 m (30 ft) long
Where found: USA

18 STEGOCERAS
Stegoceras had a thick, domed skull suggesting that head-butting was an important part of its lifestyle, either as defence or more likely as a mating display ritual. This herbivore probably lived in herds.
Size: 2 m (6 ft 6 in) long
Where found: North America

see also

28-9 **Comets and meteorites**

36-7 **Volcanoes**

104-11 **Birds**

It is hard to pinpoint when mammals evolved, because mammalian characteristics, such as fur and lactation, are not easily fossilised so are lost to the fossil record. But mammalian teeth patterns have been found in some reptile fossils from the late Permian. Called mammal-like reptiles, it is likely that these were the ancestors of true mammals. When the dinosaurs became extinct, mammals moved into the niches they had left vacant.

WHY DID MAMMALS FLOURISH?

Tens of thousands of mammal species evolved in the 65 million years after the Cretaceous/Tertiary mass extinction. A large number of these were herbivores, which grazed on the flowering plants, particularly grasses, which were also spreading and diversifying. Warm-bloodedness gave the mammals a particular advantage: they could regulate their own body temperature and therefore thrive in a wide range of temperatures and environments. They also had the intelligence to survive and flourish in rapidly changing conditions. The mammals did not displace the dinosaurs, they simply diversified to fill the niches left empty after their extinction.

280–245 million years ago
Mammal-like reptiles appear. They have mammalian features, such as incisor, canine and cheek teeth.

230 million years ago
Cynodonts, such as *Thrinaxodon*, **appear**.

First true mammals appear. All known forms at this time are shrew-sized insectivores.

208–144 million years ago
Mammals remain small, nocturnal creatures throughout the Jurassic, evolving such attributes as warm-bloodedness, giving birth to live young and feeding their young on milk.

100–75 million years ago
Marsupial mammals appear in South America, then radiate across the entire supercontinent of Gondwana, consisting of Australia, Antarctica, India, Africa and South America.

PERMIAN

245

TRIASSIC

100 million years ago
Monotreme mammals appear in Australia.

MEGAZOSTRODON
This tiny creature, one of the earliest-known mammals, was just 13 cm (5 in) long. It fed on insects and was probably nocturnal. *Megazostrodon* may have laid eggs, like today's platypuses and echidnas. It lived from the late Triassic until the early Jurassic.

208

JURASSIC

Late Jurassic
Multituberculate mammals appear.

144

CRETACEOUS

Returning to the sea

Whales, dolphins and porpoises are the only mammals completely adapted to living their entire lives in the sea, yet they evolved from land-dwelling forebears.

There is evidence, based on its teeth, that the earliest-known whale, the 54-million-year-old *Pakicetus*, descended from a flesh-eating ancestor of hoofed mammals, such as *Pachyaena*. The early whales were not well adapted to aquatic living and probably spent a lot of time on land, moving around on paddle-shaped limbs. Today's whales, including the baleen whales, evolved from the primitive toothed whales, such as *Pakicetus*.

Another group of mammals that took to life in the sea was the sirenians, or sea cows. Unlike whales, the sirenians are herbivores. DNA studies indicate that they share an ancestor with elephants.

The four kinds of mammal

By the end of the Cretaceous, four mammal groups existed:

1 **Placentals** Mammals that produce fully developed live young nurtured on milk. Currently the largest group.

2 **Marsupials** Mammals that produce immature young, generally nurtured in a pouch after birth.

3 **Monotremes** Egg-laying mammals that probably evolved completely separately from other mammals. They were mostly confined to Australia, although some fossils have also been found in South America. The duck-billed platypus and the echidna are modern examples.

4 **Multituberculates** Rodent-like herbivores so called because their teeth had ridges (tubercles) on their biting surface. Like marsupials, they produced immature young.

Pachyaena

Ambulocetus

Pakicetus

INDRICOTHERIUM

Indricotherium was the largest land mammal that ever lived. At 8 m (26 ft) long it dwarfed even the greatest mammoths. It is an ancestor of the rhinoceros and weighed an estimated 33.5 tonnes. It had a flexible upper lip that enabled it to browse on leaves much like a modern giraffe.

How elephants evolved

Today there are two varieties of elephant, the African and Indian, but since elephants first appeared more than 160 species have existed. They originated in North Africa in the Eocene. The earliest types, such as *Moeritherium*, were pig-sized and looked very little like their modern counterparts, with no trunk or tusks. These features evolved in the Miocene as adaptations to help the animals to reach food, and later became important in communication. Elephants became larger through the Miocene and Pliocene, probably as a protection from predators. By the start of the Pleistocene, some had surpassed even today's African elephant in size. The steppe mammoth (*Mammathus trogontherii*) was 4.6 m (15 ft) tall at the shoulder. Elephants existed in Europe, and the Americas, as well as Africa and Asia.

African elephant

Indian elephant

AMEBELODON

Standing 3 m (10 ft) tall, *Amebelodon* had two adjacent flattened tusks projecting 1 m (3 ft) beyond its lower jaw, forming a shovel-like cutting edge. It probably used this, along with its trunk, to gouge out and grab hold of water plants, its main food, from river bottoms. It lived in North America.

SMILODON

The archetypal 'sabre-toothed' cat, *Smilodon* was a powerfully built predator with 18 cm (7 in) long serrated canine teeth. *Smilodon*'s jaw could open 120 degrees to accommodate the driving of these dagger-like teeth into its prey. It lived in North and South America.

70 million years ago
Placental mammals evolve in Asia.

65 million years ago
Mass extinction brings the end of the dinosaurs and many other animal groups.

57–34 million years ago
Whales, sea cows, horses, camels, primates, ruminants, rodents and elephants appear. Australia and South America evolve many new marsupial forms.

65–57 million years ago
Multituberculate mammals are dominant. Most herbivorous mammals are small, but the first large mammals do emerge. These include the hippo-like *Coryphodon*, found in North America, Europe and Asia, and the South American astraphotheres, herbivores with tusks and small trunks, some of which reach the size of a modern rhinoceros.

The supercontinent of Gondwana begins to break up.

34–23 million years ago
Multituberculates become extinct, replaced in most niches by placental rodents. At sea, baleen whales appear. Early pigs, cats and rhinos appear.

23–5 million years ago
North and South America join, leading to an influx of placental mammals to the south, where they begin to displace marsupials. **Marsupials become extinct in Europe and North America.**

Worldwide, grasslands spread, leading to the evolution of new, faster-running species in many mammal families.

5 million years ago
The first hominids appear in Africa.

1.8 million years ago
Homo habilis the first known member of genus *Homo* appears.

120 000 years ago
Modern humans emerge.

PALEOCENE

65

57

EOCENE

34

OLIGOCENE

23

MIOCENE

PLIOCENE

5

1.8

PLEISTOCENE

Minke whale
(*Balaenoptera acutorostrata*)

Aetiocetus

With more than 1.5 million named species the animal kingdom is the largest and most diverse group of living things on Earth. More than a million of these are insects. Only multicellular organisms are now defined as belonging to the animal kingdom, but there is also a host of one-celled organisms, the protozoa, that share many animal features.

WHAT IS AN ANIMAL?

All animals, like all plants, have cells with a nucleus. Animals generally differ from plants in that they:

● **are mobile** during some part of their life cycle.
● **cannot manufacture their own food**, but need to consume organic matter produced by other living things.
● **have cells** without rigid cell walls.
● **have sensory organs** and some sort of nervous system with a central coordinating point (the brain) to control movements and body functions.
● **do not have** specific growing points; growth takes place throughout the body and generally ceases at adulthood.

All creatures great and small
Animals have colonised virtually every environment on Earth, from mountain peaks to the depths of the oceans. This has led to the evolution of an incredible variety of body shapes and life strategies to cope with the conditions those environments impose.

How cells arrange themselves

The simplest multicellular animals – the sponges – are little more than collections of individual cells joined randomly together. Liquidise a sponge and eventually it will recover, as its cells simply rearrange themselves. Sponges do have specialised cells, but these do not combine to form specific organised structures. In all other animals, cells arrange themselves in more complex ways to form tissues and organs.

Double bud
Jellyfishes, hydras and sea anemones are some of the simplest animals with specialised structures. As embryos they consist of two layers: an outer layer from which the outer body wall forms, and an inner layer from which specific organs, such as the gut, develop. This development from two layers has led to them being called diploblastic animals (from the Greek, meaning 'double bud').

Triple bud
All other animals, from flatworms to humans, are triploblastic ('triple bud'), having three layers as embryos. The additional middle layer develops into complex organs and organ systems.

Simplest structure Sponges have no organs

FACT The longest-known worm is the boot-lace worm (*Lineus longissimus*). A specimen found in 1864 was more than 55 m (180 ft) long.

Tallest mammal
The giraffe grows up to 6 m (20 ft) tall.

Largest moth
The atlas moth has a wingspan of 30 cm (12 in).

Largest invertebrate
The Atlantic giant squid can weigh up to 2 tonnes.

Classification of animal life Taxonomists classify all living things by placing them into a hierarchy of groups based on shared characteristics such as the possession of a backbone, or the suckling of young. This diagram takes you through the classification of a tiger from the largest group, Phylum, down to the smallest, Species.

see also
112-3 **Animal records**
122-3 **Endangered species**
124-5 **Protecting species**
542-7 **Biology**

KEY

Phylum
Order
Class
Family

Path through classification

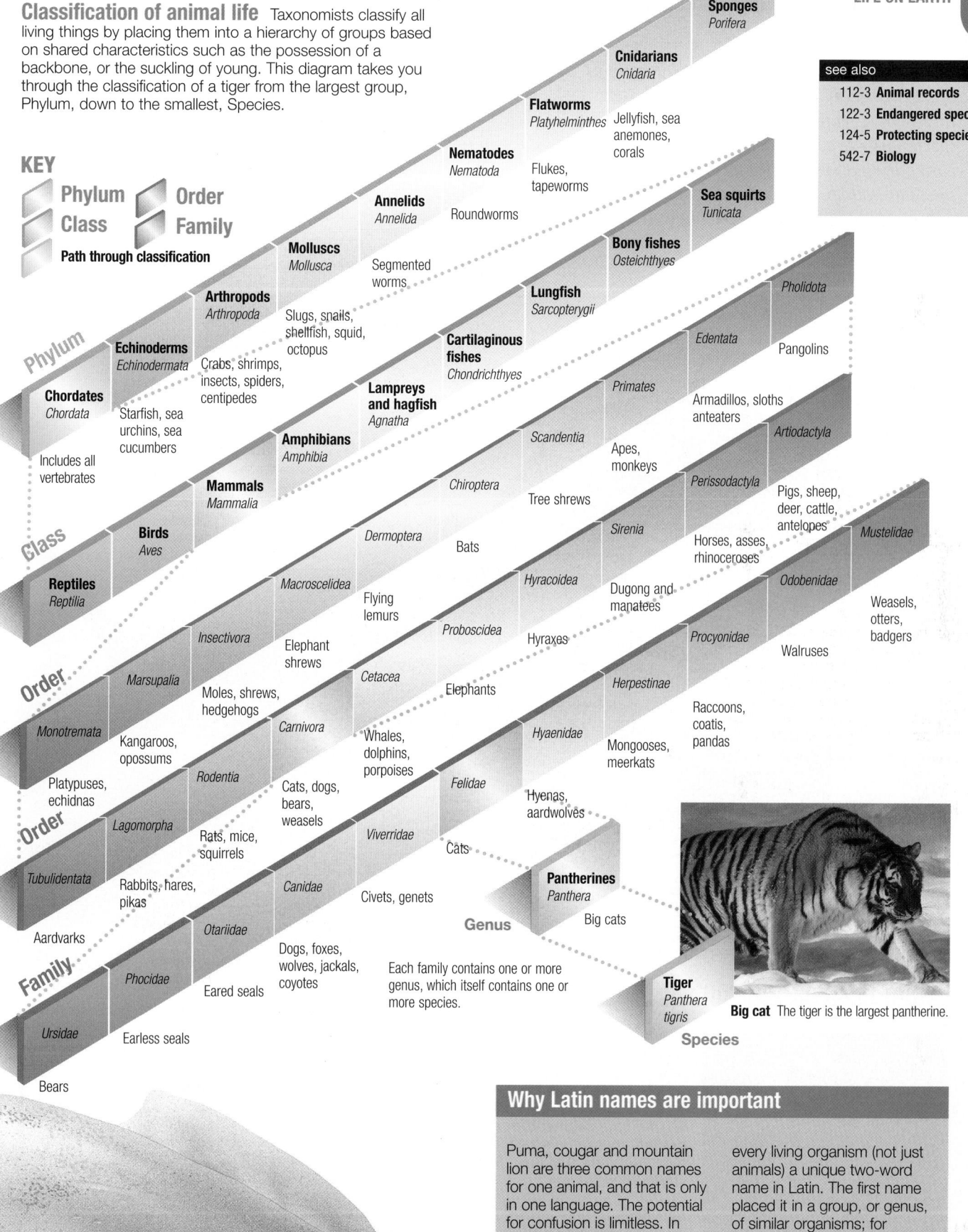

Phylum

Sponges
Porifera

Cnidarians
Cnidaria
Jellyfish, sea anemones, corals

Flatworms
Platyhelminthes
Flukes, tapeworms

Nematodes
Nematoda
Roundworms

Annelids
Annelida
Segmented worms

Molluscs
Mollusca
Slugs, snails, shellfish, squid, octopus

Arthropods
Arthropoda
Crabs, shrimps, insects, spiders, centipedes

Echinoderms
Echinodermata
Starfish, sea urchins, sea cucumbers

Chordates
Chordata
Includes all vertebrates

Sea squirts
Tunicata

Bony fishes
Osteichthyes

Lungfish
Sarcopterygii

Cartilaginous fishes
Chondrichthyes

Lampreys and hagfish
Agnatha

Amphibians
Amphibia

Mammals
Mammalia

Birds
Aves

Reptiles
Reptilia

Class

Pholidota
Pangolins

Edentata
Armadillos, sloths anteaters

Primates
Apes, monkeys

Scandentia
Tree shrews

Chiroptera
Bats

Dermoptera
Flying lemurs

Macroscelidea
Elephant shrews

Insectivora
Moles, shrews, hedgehogs

Marsupalia
Kangaroos, opossums

Monotremata
Platypuses, echidnas

Artiodactyla
Pigs, sheep, deer, cattle, antelopes

Perissodactyla
Horses, asses, rhinoceroses

Sirenia
Dugong and manatees

Hyracoidea
Hyraxes

Proboscidea
Elephants

Cetacea
Whales, dolphins, porpoises

Carnivora
Cats, dogs, bears, weasels

Rodentia
Rats, mice, squirrels

Lagomorpha
Rabbits, hares, pikas

Tubulidentata
Aardvarks

Order

Order

Mustelidae
Weasels, otters, badgers

Odobenidae
Walruses

Procyonidae
Raccoons, coatis, pandas

Herpestinae
Mongooses, meerkats

Hyaenidae
Hyenas, aardwolves

Felidae
Cats

Viverridae
Civets, genets

Canidae
Dogs, foxes, wolves, jackals, coyotes

Otariidae
Eared seals

Phocidae
Earless seals

Ursidae
Bears

Family

Pantherines
Panthera
Big cats

Genus

Each family contains one or more genus, which itself contains one or more species.

Tiger
Panthera tigris

Species

Big cat The tiger is the largest pantherine.

Why Latin names are important

Puma, cougar and mountain lion are three common names for one animal, and that is only in one language. The potential for confusion is limitless. In the 18th century, a Swedish doctor and naturalist, Carolus Linnaeus, established a naming system to avoid such confusion. His system gives every living organism (not just animals) a unique two-word name in Latin. The first name placed it in a group, or genus, of similar organisms; for example, *Homo*. The second designated its species, for example, *sapiens*. More than 200 years on, Linnaeus's naming system is still in use.

Molluscs and arthropods ▶

Molluscs and arthropods are two major groups of invertebrates, animals without a backbone. Invertebrates comprise 95 per cent of all animal species. All are soft-bodied but some have a hard outer skeleton, called an exoskeleton, which serves as both an anchor point for muscles and as protection for the rest of the body.

Insects
(class Insecta – see pages 94–95)

Arthropods
(phylum Arthropoda)

Arachnids
(class Arachnida – see pages 94–95)

Crustaceans
(class Crustacea – see opposite)

Slugs and snails
(class Gastropoda – see opposite)

Molluscs
(phylum Mollusca)

Bivalves
(class Pelecypoda – see opposite)

Squids and octopuses
(class Cephalopoda – see opposite)

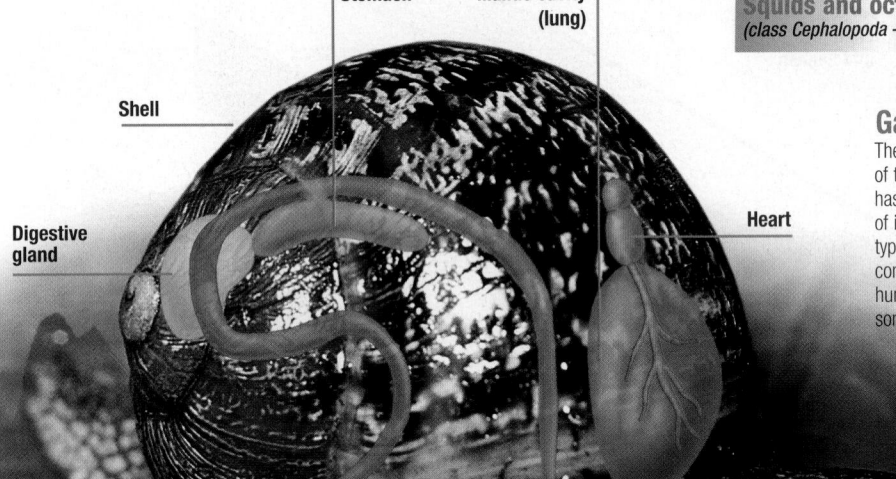

Stomach

Mantle cavity (lung)

Shell

Heart

Digestive gland

Anus

Mouth

Gastropod body plan
The European garden snail (*Helix aspersa*) is one of the most familiar gastropods. Like all snails, it has an asymmetrical body caused by the twisting of its shell. The garden snail's internal anatomy is typical of gastropods. Most of the elements it contains are also found in vertebrates, including humans, although the shapes of the organs are somewhat different.

Eye

Intestine

Brain

WHAT IS AN ARTHROPOD?

Body shell All arthropods have a hard, jointed outer skeleton usually made of chitin – a fibrous organic compound.

● Arthropod means 'jointed foot'. Arthropods have multiple pairs of flexible, **jointed legs**.

● They have **segmented bodies**, encased in a hard outer skeleton called the cuticle or exoskeleton.

● In order to grow, they **periodically shed and replace their exoskeletons**. This process is called ecdysis.

WHAT IS A MOLLUSC?

● Molluscs are **soft-bodied invertebrates**, but many are covered by a hard shell generated by a fold of skin called the mantle. Squids, octopuses and cuttlefish have some hard internal structures, such as cuttlebone.

● Molluscs are **cold-blooded and produce eggs**.

● The body of a mollusc is made of **three parts**: the head; the central mass containing the vital organs, such as the stomach; and a muscular foot or other means of locomotion.

● Most molluscs **live in the sea**, but a few live in fresh water, and the majority of slugs and snails live on land.

SLUGS AND SNAILS

Gastropods
About 50 000 species

Where they live:
Sea water; fresh water; also damp environments on land

Key features:
● Land snails and slugs have a flat, muscular foot on which they glide across the ground – the name gastropod means 'belly-footed'. In sea-living gastropods, the foot is often smaller.
● Snails have a single shell, in a spiral or semi-spiral form. Slugs and sea slugs (or nudibranchs) have no shell.
● Most land snails and some freshwater ones have eyes on stalks.

Species:
Common limpet
(Patella vulgata)
Common periwinkle
(Littorina littorea)
Grey slug (Lireak maximus)
Four-coloured sea slug
(Chromodoris quadricolor)

BIVALVES

Pelecypods
About 8000 species

Where they live:
Salt and fresh water

Key features:
● Their bodies are encased by two hinged shells (or valves).
● They feed and breathe by drawing water between the valves and over large gills, which extract both oxygen and food particles.
● Most have separate sexes, but some can be both male and female, alternating between sexes according to surrounding water temperature.
● They have a 'foot' that can be pushed out and pulled in to help them to move around.
● Some are free swimming; others burrow in sand, mud or rock.

Species:
Blue mussel
(Mytilus edulis)
Common cockle
(Cardium edule)
Common European oyster
(Ostrea edulis)
Common fingernail clam
(Pisidium casertanum)
Pilgrim's scallop
(Pecten jacobaeus)
Shipworm (Teredo navalis)
Small razor shell
(Ensis ensis)
Swan mussel
(Anodonta cygnaea)
Varied scallop
(Chlamys varius)

SQUIDS AND OCTOPUSES

Cephalopods
About 750 species

Where they live:
Temperate and tropical seas

Key features:
● Have soft bodies with no shell, and either eight arms (octopuses) or ten (cuttlefish and squids), each equipped with rows of suckers.
● Two of the arms of squids and cuttlefish are long, retractile tentacles, used to catch prey. Octopuses use all their arms for this purpose.
● All can move at speed by using a siphon effect to produce a jet of water.
● When frightened, most species release clouds of ink to cover their escape.

Species:
Atlantic giant squid
(Architeuthis dux)
Chambered nautilus
(Nautilus pompilius)
Common cuttlefish
(Sepia officinalis)
Common octopus
(Octopus vulgaris)
Common squid
(Loligo loligo)
Dwarf squid
(Alloteuthis subulata)
Giant octopus
(Octopus apollyon)
Jewelled squid
(Lycoteuthis diadema)
North American squid
(Loligo pealei)
Short-finned squid
(Illex illecebrosus)

CRABS, SHRIMPS, PRAWNS AND LOBSTERS

Crustaceans
About 30 000 species

Where they live:
Salt and fresh water; moist places on land

Key features:
● Heads have two pairs of antennae.
● Protected by hard exoskeletons, made of protein and a horny substance called chitin.
● Appendages on each section of exoskeleton, modified to act as feelers, mouthparts, legs and paddle-like swimmerets.
● Pass through a larval stage before growing into their adult form.

Species:
American spiny lobster
(Panulirus argus)
Brine shrimp
(Artemia sacina)
Common prawn
(Palaemon serratus)
Dromid crab
(Dromia vulgaris)
Edible crab
(Cancer pagurus)
Goose barnacle
(Lepas anatifera)
King lobster
(Nephrops norvegicus)
Krill (Euphausia superba)
Mantis shrimp
(Squilla empusa)
Robber crab (Birgus latro)
Rock barnacle
(Balanus balanoides)
Sapphire shrimp
(Sapphirina fulgens)
Slipper lobster
(Scyllarus arctus)

see also
90-1 **Animal kingdom**
112-3 **Animal records**
122-3 **Endangered species**
124-5 **Protecting species**

FACTS AND FIGURES

● The giant clam (Tridacna gigas) is the largest bivalve on Earth. Found in coral reefs in the Indian and Pacific oceans, its shell grows up to 1.4 m (4 ft 6 in) across.

● The sea snail Bitium, found off China, is one of the smallest molluscs, measuring less than 1 mm (1/32 in) long.

● The heaviest crustacean is the North Atlantic lobster (Homarus americanus). One specimen caught in 1977 weighed over 20 kg (44 lb).

● The Pacific giant octopus (Octopus dofleini) is the world's largest, with an average armspan of 2.5 m (8 ft 2 in).

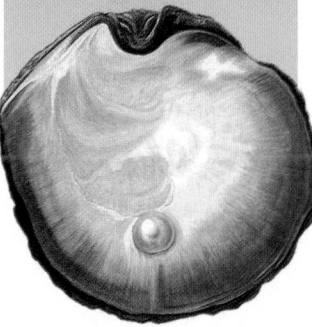

How pearls form
Oysters and some other molluscs create pearls in response to their body tissue being irritated by a grain of sand or other foreign object. The animal isolates the offending object by covering it with a smooth substance called nacre, creating the pearl.

Atypical crustacean
Unlike other lobsters, the American spiny lobster (Panulirus argus) has no claws.

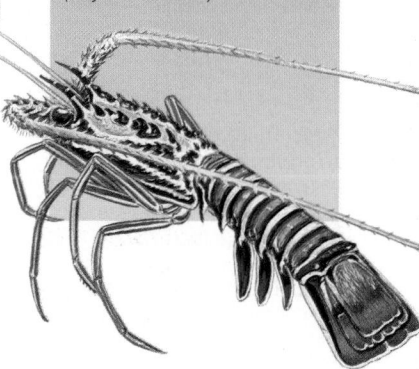

Arachnids and insects are arthropods. Like all arthropods, they have bodies that are symmetrical, segmented and covered with a hard exoskeleton. All arachnids and insects breathe air, even those that spend most of their lives under water. Arachnids breathe by means of simple lungs, insects by using a system of air sacs and tubules connected to holes in the exoskeleton.

Sting in the tail
Scorpions catch most of their prey using their pincers alone. The poisonous sting that they carry on their tail is used almost exclusively in self-defence.

WHAT IS AN ARACHNID?

● **Arachnids** include spiders, scorpions, harvestmen, ticks and mites.
● Their bodies are divided into **two sections**: a fused head and thorax (prosoma) and an abdomen.
● They have **four pairs of jointed legs** attached to the prosoma.
● **Two further pairs of appendages** are attached to the prosoma: the chelicerae, which hold the fangs and are generally adapted for grasping, and the pedipalps, sometimes used as feelers, sometimes equipped (as in a scorpion) with pincers.
● Unlike insects, **arachnids lack antennae and wings**.
● Arachnids are **carnivorous** apart from some plant-eating mites.

SPIDERS

Aranae
About 30 000 species

Where they live:

On land worldwide except the poles; some freshwater habitats

Key features:

● Eight legs and up to eight eyes.
● They have special silk-producing glands. The silk is forced through structures called spinnerets.
● The female is always larger than the male.

Species:

Ant spider
(*Myrmarchne formicaria*)
Black widow
(*Latrodectus mactans*)
Cardinal spider
(*Tegenaria parietina*)
Common garden spider
(*Araneus diadematus*)
European tarantula
(*Lycosa tarentula*)

Garden spider
(*Araneus diadmatus*)
Goliath bird-eating spider
(*Theraphosa leblondi*)
House spider
(*Tegenaria domestica*)
Money spider
   (genus *Dismodicus*,
   several species)
      Sydney funnel-
      web spider
         (*Atrax*
         robustus)
Wasp
spider
(*Ariope*
bruennichi)
Water spider
(*Argyroneta aquatica*)
Wolf spider
(*Lycosa narbonensis*)
Zebra spider
(*Salticus scenicus*)

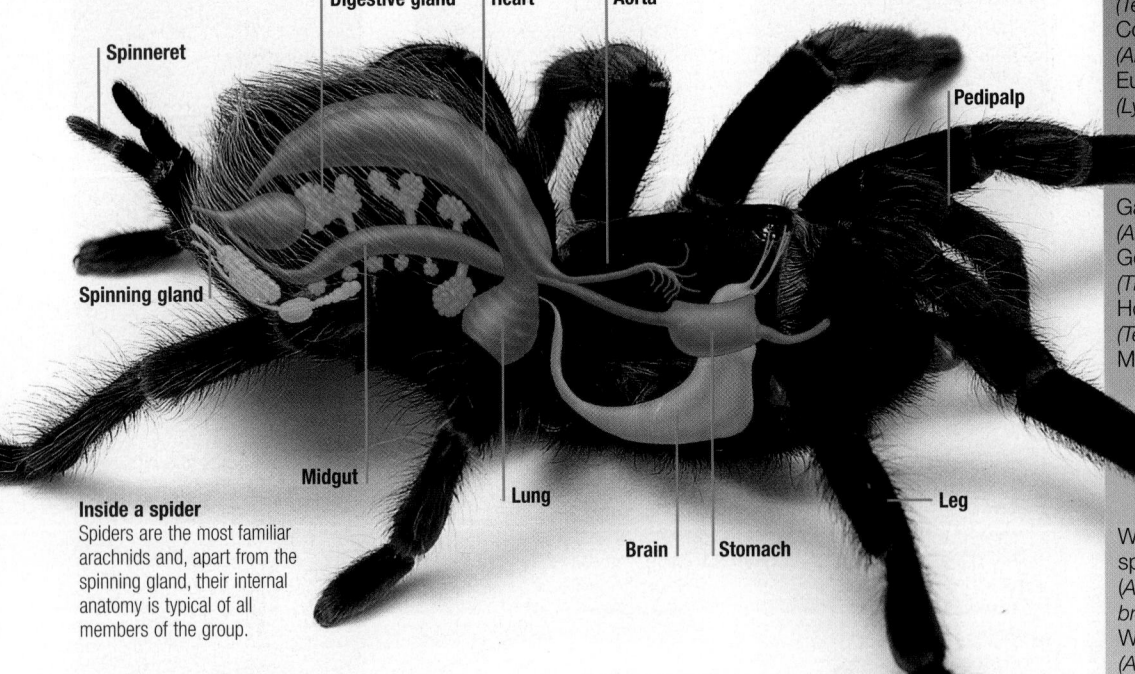

Spinneret

Digestive gland   Heart   Aorta

Pedipalp

Spinning gland

Midgut

Lung

Leg

Brain   Stomach

Inside a spider
Spiders are the most familiar arachnids and, apart from the spinning gland, their internal anatomy is typical of all members of the group.

FACTS AND FIGURES

● The largest spider is the goliath bird-eating spider (*Theraphosa leblondi*) from South America. Its legs can span more than 28 cm (11 in).

● The insect with the longest recorded life span is the splendour beetle (*Buprestis aurulenta*) at 47 years.

● The venom of the North American black widow spider (*Latrodectus mactans*) is 15 times more potent than that of a rattlesnake.

● Spider silk is stronger than any other known fibre of equivalent thickness, natural or artificial.

● The smallest winged insect is the Tanzanian parasitic wasp (*Caraphractus cinctus*). It has a wingspan of just 0.2 mm (0.008 in).

● The loudest insect is the African cicada (*Brevisana brevis*). At 107 decibels, it is almost as loud as a road drill.

FACT
More than a million species of insect are known. Thousands more are discovered every year.

see also
90-1 **Animal kingdom**
112-3 **Animal records**
122-3 **Endangered species**
124-5 **Protecting species**

BEETLES AND WEEVILS

Coleoptera
More than 370 000 species

Where they live:
Land and freshwater habitats worldwide except the poles

Key features:
● Beetles and weevils form the largest insect order and account for more than a quarter of all the species in the animal kingdom.
● They have hard, leathery forewings called elytra, which fold down to protect the hind wings.

Species:
Cockchafer
(Melolontha melolontha)
Colorado beetle
(Leptinotarsa decemlineata)
Deathwatch beetle
(Xestobium rufouillosum)
Glow-worm
(Lampyris noctiluca)
Grain weevil
(Sitophilus granarius)
Goliath beetle
(Goliathus giganteus)
Great diving beetle
(Dystiscus marginalis)
Two-spot ladybird
(Adalia bipunctata)

FLIES

Diptera
About 90 000 species

Where they live:
On land and in the air worldwide except the poles

Key features:
● Flies have one pair of wings, antennae and compound eyes.
● They have a pair of modified wings, called halteres, used for balance.
● They produce legless larvae called maggots.
● They are the main insect carriers of human diseases, including malaria, sleeping sickness and yellow fever.

Species:
Bluebottle
(Calliphora vomitoria)
Crane fly (daddy longlegs)
(Tipula maxima)
Horse fly (Tabanus bromius)
House fly
(Musca domestica)
Mosquito (family Culicidae, many genera and species)
Robber fly
(Asilus crabroniformis)
Tsetse fly (genus Glossina, many species)

BEES, WASPS AND ANTS

Hymenoptera
More than 120 000 species

Where they live:
On land and in the air worldwide except the poles

Key features:
● Bees and wasps possess two pairs of wings.
● The first segment of the abdomen is constricted to form a waist.
● Bees and wasps have a poisonous sting.
● Many species have complex social structures.

Species:
Army ant (genus Eciton, several species)
Common wasp
(Vespula vulgaris)
Garden bumblebee
(Bombus hortorum)
Giant hornet (Vespa crabo)
Honey bee (Apis mellifera)
Leafcutter ant (genus Atta, several species)
Leafcutter bee
(Megachile centuncularis)
Oak apple wasp
(Biorrhiza pallida)
Tawny mining bee
(Andrena fulva)
Wood ant (Formica rufa)

BUTTERFLIES AND MOTHS

Lepidoptera
About 150 000 species

Where they live:
On land and in the air worldwide except the poles

Key features:
● They pass through a four-stage life cycle: egg, larva (caterpillar), pupa or chrysalis, adult.
● Butterflies are active by day and most moths by night.
● Butterfly antennae are shaped like clubs; moths' antennae are plumed or feathery.
● The adults have long, coiled tongues, which they use to feed on nectar.

Species:
Atlas moth (Attacus atlas)
Clothes moth
(Tineola bisselliella)
Common snout butterfly
(Libytheana bachmanii)
Death's-head hawkmoth
(Acherontia atropos)
Garden tiger moth
(Arctia caja)
Gypsy moth
(Porthetria dispar)
Hummingbird Hawkmoth
(Macroglossum stellatarum)
Large cabbage white
(Pieris brassicae)
Monarch butterfly
(Danaus plexippus)
Painted lady
(Cynthia cardui)
Queen Alexandra's birdwing butterfly
(Ornithoptera alexandrae)
Red admiral
(Vanessa atalanta)

WHAT IS AN INSECT?

● Adult insects' bodies are divided into **three sections**: the head, the thorax and the abdomen.
● They have **antennae or 'feelers'** attached to their heads.
● They have **three pairs of legs** attached to the thorax and (usually) two pairs of wings.
● They almost all lay eggs and **go through one or more larval stages** before becoming adults. As larvae, they often look very different from the adults.

Egg

Caterpillar

Chrysalis

Adult butterfly

Gaining their wings
Butterflies and moths go through a complete metamorphosis from caterpillar to adult, with their bodies undergoing a total change of form.

Fish have evolved and adapted to virtually all the fresh and saltwater habitats of the world. They range in size from the marine dwarf goby found in the Chagos Archipelago of the Indian Ocean, measuring less than 10 mm (¹/₂ in) from tip to tail, to the whale shark, which reaches lengths of nearly 20 m (65 ft). Fish make up the largest group of vertebrates, with about 25 000 known species.

WHAT IS A FISH?

⬤ Fish are **cold-blooded vertebrates** found in seas, oceans and fresh waters.
⬤ All fish, apart from lungfish, breathe using **gills**.
⬤ They move through water with the aid of **fins**.
⬤ In most cases, their skins are covered with **scales**.

CLASSIFYING FISH

Modern fish can be broadly grouped into four divisions:

Lampreys and hagfish These belong to the superclass Agnatha, meaning 'without jaws'. They are primitive, eel-like creatures (see right) having rounded mouths which are not articulated into jaws. They do have teeth, however. Other characteristics include smooth, scaleless, slimy skin and single, or unpaired, fins.

Dorsal fin

Pelvic fin

Pectoral fin

Swim bladder

Kidney

Heart

Brain

Anal fin

Intestine

Pelvic fin

Liver

Primitive bony fish Most fish of the subclass Sarcopterygii have become extinct, but a few, such as the coelacanth (above), remain. Strictly speaking, they are not bony fish at all, as many parts of the skeleton are made of cartilage. The head is, however, usually formed from a mosaic of tiny bones. The flexible spine has no vertebrae.

Cartilaginous fish The class Chondrichthyes includes sharks (below), rays, skates and dogfish. They have skeletons made entirely of cartilage. They have jaws (and teeth) and their skin is covered in scales. Once fully grown, the teeth and scales cease to develop but are replaced as they wear out.

Modern bony fish Fish of the subclass Actinopterygii are distinguished by their bony skeletons. Features typical of this class include thin scales on the skin, paired pelvic and pectoral fins, a simple, flap-like covering over the gills, and a swim bladder – a variable-buoyancy device which allows the fish to float at different depths.

Sensitive snout

Brain

Spleen

Backbone

Rectal gland

Kidney

Successful body design
The basic shark body plan has been around since before the dinosaurs. Its streamlined shape is perfectly adapted to an aquatic lifestyle. Sharks are never still, they have to keep moving to ensure a constant flow of water over their gills.

Heart

Gill

Liver

Stomach

Pancreas

Cloaca (anus and reproductive duct)

SHARKS

Pleurotremata
More than 350
species

Where they live:

Seas and oceans
worldwide; some rivers

Key features:

- Cartilaginous fish with streamlined bodies and muscular tails, which they use to propel themselves through water.
- Greyish skins, a high dorsal fin and five to seven pairs of gill slits.
- Excellent sense of smell and specialist cells on their head for short-range detection of electricity produced by the muscles of prey.
- Remained virtually unchanged for 400 million years.
- Mostly saltwater fish, although a few spend much of their lives in fresh water.

Species:

Basking shark
(Cerorhinus maximus)
Bull shark
(Carcharhinus leucas)
Common hammerhead shark (Sphyrna Zygaena)
Fierce shark
(Carcharias ferox)
Frilled shark
(Chlamydoselachus anguineus)
Great white shark
(Carcharodon carcharias)
Lesser spotted dogfish
(Scyliorhinus canicula)
Mako shark
(Isurus oxyrinchus)
Nurse shark
(Gingkymostoma cirratum)
Thresher shark
(Alopias vulpinus)
Tiger shark
(Galeocardo cuvieri)
Whale shark
(Rhincodon typus)
Wobbegong shark
(Orectolobus maculatus)
Zebra shark
(Stegotoma fasciatum)

SKATES, RAYS AND RABBITFISH

Rajiformes
More than 400
species

Where they live:

Temperate and tropical
seas; some rivers

Key features:

- Cartilaginous fish with flattened bodies, enlarged wing-like pectoral fins and long, tapering tails.
- Mostly bottom-dwellers, feeding with blunt, crushing teeth on invertebrates and other fish. Some open-water species eat plankton – tiny plants and animals in the upper layers of the sea.
- The gill openings are on the underside of the body, as is the mouth in bottom-feeders.

Water wings The manta ray
(Manta birostris) 'flies' through its
native tropical waters by flapping
its large pectoral fins. With a
maximum length of 5 m (16 ft),
it is the biggest of the rays.

Species:

Common skate (Raja batis)
Common stingray
(Dasyatis pastinaca)
Eyed electric ray
(Torpedo torpedo)
Great toothed sawfish
(Pristis microdon)
Guitar fish
(Rhinosatos productus)
Manta ray (Manta birostris)
Rabbitfish
(Chimaera monstrosa)

Hidden hunter
Moray eels are found in temperate
waters but are most common on coral
reefs in the tropics. They hide in crevices
and seize fish that swim into reach.

EELS

Anguilliformes
More than 500
species

Where they live:

From coral reefs to
the deep sea; also
fresh waters

Key features:

- Snake-like bony fish with elongated dorsal and anal fins, and no scales.
- Feeds on fish and invertebrates.
- Freshwater eels (Anguilla) breed at sea, often migrating long distances from their home waters. European and North American freshwater eels, for example, breed in the Sargasso Sea of the North Atlantic.

Species:

American eel
(Anguilla rostrata)
Armed spiny eel
(Mastacembalus armatus)
Bicoloured false moray eel
(Chlopsis bicolor)
Conger eel (Conger conger)
Deepwater eel
(Cyema atrum)
European eel
(Anguilla anguilla)
Giant moray eel
(Gymnothorax javanicus)
Gray's cutthroat eel
(Synaphobranchus pinnatus)
Gulper eel
(Eurypharynx pelecanoides)
Japanese eel
(Anguilla japonica)
Moray eel (Muraena helena)
Pelican-fish eel
(Saccopharynx ampullaceus)
Snake eel
(Ophichthys gomesii)
Yellow garden eel
(Heteroconger luteolus)
Zebra moray eel
(Echidna zebra)

HERRING AND PILCHARDS

Clupeiformes
More than 400
species

Where they live:

Shallow waters of seas
worldwide; some lakes
and rivers

Key features:

- Silvered greenish blue coloured fish.
- Swim close to the surface of the water to feed on plankton.
- Herring travel in schools, which can be several miles in length and width.
- They include many species that are important to humans for food.

Species:

Anchovy
(Engraulis encrasiolus)
Atlantic herring
(Clupea harengus)
Atlantic menhaden
(Brevoorta tyrannus)
Australian sardine
(Sardinops neo-pilcharus)
Denticiptoid herring
(Denticeps clupeoides)
Japanese sardine
(Sardinops melanosticta)
Pacific herring
(Clupea pallasii)
Pilchard (Sardina pilchardus)
Shad (Alosa alosa)
South African sardine
(Sardinops ocellata)
South American sardine
(Sardinops sagax)
Sprat (Sprattus sprattus)

SALMON, TROUT, PIKE AND SMELT

Salmoniformes
About 1000 species

Where they live:
Northern Hemisphere; open ocean, coastal waters, rivers and lakes

Key features:
● Salmon and trout have wide mouths and powerful teeth. Pike and smelt have narrow, pointed heads with sharp teeth.
● All are born in fresh water; salmon migrate to the sea when two years old.
● In the wild, salmon, trout and smelt return to their place of birth to spawn (spawning season runs from September to January).

Species:
Arctic char
(Salvelinus alpinus)
Atlantic salmon (Salmo salar)
Dog salmon
(Oncorhynchus keta)
European brown trout
(Salmo trutta)
European smelt
(Osmerus eperlanus)
Grayling
(Thymallus thymallus)
Longnose lancet fish
(Alepisaurus ferox)
Pacific lancet fish
(Alepisaurus borealis)
Pike (Esox lucius)
Pink salmon
(Oncorhynchus gorbuscha)
Rainbow trout
(Salmo gairdneri)
River trout
(Salmo trutta fario)
Silver salmon
(Oncorhynchus kitsutch)
Sockeye salmon
(Oncorhynsus nerka)

Deep-sea monster
The bizarre-looking Pacific lancet fish grows to 1.8 m (6 ft) long. Like many deep-water fish, it has long, fang-like teeth to catch the smaller fish on which it feeds.

CARP AND CHARACHINS

Cypriniformes
About 3500 species

Where they live:
Worldwide in fresh water, except Australia and Antarctica

Key features:
● Omnivorous and carnivorous freshwater fish with elongated bodies.
● Long dorsal fins.
● Some species hibernate in the mud at the bottom of rivers and streams.

Piranha!
South America's red piranha is known as a dangerous meat-eater, but many of the 50 piranha species eat seeds and fruit which have fallen into the water.

Species:
Bitterling (Rhodeus sericeus)
Clown loach
(Botia macracantha)
Common carp
(Cyprinus carpio)
Goldfish (Carassius auratus)
Minnow (Phoxinus phoxinus)
Neon tetra
(Pracherodon innesi)
Red piranha
(Serrasalmus naterreri)
Roach (Rutilus rutilus)

CATFISH

Siluriformes
More than 2500 species

Where they live:
Lakes and rivers worldwide; also tropical coastal waters

Key features:
● Secretive, bottom-dwelling scavengers and hunters. Mostly nocturnal.
● Their bodies are scaleless or covered in bony plates arranged in rows.
● Broad, flat heads; thick bodies, and long, sensitive barbels (feelers).
● The upper jaw functions mostly as a point for the attachment of barbels.

Species:
Brown bullhead catfish
(Ictalurus nebolosus)
Channel catfish
(Ictalurus punctatus)
Crucifix catfish (Arius proops)
East European giant catfish
(Silurus glanic)
Electric eel
(Electrophorus electricus)
European wels
(Silurus glanis)
Giant catfish
(Pangasianodon gigas)
Glass catfish
(Kryptopterus bicirrhis)
Striped dwarf catfish
(Mystus vittatus)
Sucking catfish
(Bagarius bagarius)
Upside-down catfish
(Synodontis multipunctatus)

COD

Gadiformes
About 800 species

Where they live:
Northern Hemisphere; mostly cold sea water but also lakes and rivers

Key features:
● Two anal fins, three dorsal fins, and at least one barbel (feeler) on the lower jaw.
● Spotted brown to grey in colour, white underneath.
● They are carnivorous.
● They grow to 1.8 m (6 ft) long.
● They include several species that are important to humans as food.

Species:
Arctic Greenland cod
(Arctogadus glacialis)
Atlantic cod (Gadus morhua)
Atlantic tomcod
(Microgadus tomcod)
Burbot (Lota lota)
Common ling (Molva molva)
East Siberia cod
(Arctogadus borisovi)
Greenland cod (Gadus ogac)
Haddock
(Melanogramus aeglifinus)
Hake (Merluccius merluccius)
Pacific cod
(Gadus macrophalus)
Pacific tomcod
(Microgadus proxismus)
Whiting
(Merlangius merlangus)

Fish whiskers
Catfish are named after their whisker-like barbels, which they use to detect food on the bottoms of rivers and lakes.

SILVERSIDES

Atheriniformes
About 200 species

Where they live:

Fresh, coastal and ocean waters of warm and temperate regions

Key features:

- Small fish with slim bodies and a silver band on each side.
- Two pectoral fins.
- Live in large schools.
- Most lay eggs inside aquatic plants.

Fish out of water
Flying fish escape predators by bursting out of the water and gliding through the air on their wing-like pectoral (shoulder) fins.

Species:

Atlantic flying fish
(*Cypselurus melanurus*)
California grunion
(*Leuresthes tenuis*)
Guppy (*Lebistes reticulatus*)
Houndfish
(*Tylosurus crocodilus*)
Jacksmelt silverside
(*Atherinopsis californiensis*)
Sardine silverside
(*Hubbsiella sardina*)

STICKLEBACKS, PIPEFISH AND SEA HORSES

Gasterosteiformes
About 220 species

Where they live:

Coastal waters, lakes and rivers in temperate and tropical regions

Key features:

- Sticklebacks have a row of spines along their backs in place of a dorsal fin.
- Pipefish and sea horses have a horse-like head. Sea horses swim in a vertical position with the aid of an undulating dorsal fin. Most pipefish swim in a horizontal position.
- Males of all species are closely involved in the rearing of young. Male pipefish and sea horses have a brood pouch in which the young hatch.

Species:

Black-spotted stickleback
(*Gasterosteus wheatlandi*)
Common Atlantic pipefish
(*Syngnathus fuscus*)
Common sea horse
(*Hippocampus guttulatus*)
Dwarf sea horse
(*Hippocampus zosterae*)
Leafy seadragon
(*Phycodurus eques*)
Nine-spined stickleback
(*Pungitius pungitius*)
North American freshwater stickleback
(*Culaea inconstans*)
Spotted sea horse
(*Hippocampus kuda*)
Three-spined stickleback
(*Gasterosteus aculeatus*)
Tiger pipefish
(*Filicampus tigris*)

Gripping tail
Sea horses have prehensile tails, which allow them to grip onto vegetation in their shallow-water habitat. From this anchorage they feed on tiny animals by sucking them into their mouths.

PERCH AND PERCH-LIKE FISHES

Perciformes
More than 6000 species

Where they live:

Worldwide, in fresh water, seas and oceans

Key features:

- Most have spines on the dorsal, anal and pelvic fins.
- By far the largest group of fishes, with about 150 different families in all.
- They include many food and game fishes, such as tuna, mackerel, marlin, swordfish and sea bass.

Popular pets Angelfishes, and other members of this group, are prized for their colourful appearance.

Families:

Angelfishes
(Pomacanthidae)
Barracudas (Sphyraenidae)
Blennies (Blennioidei, several families)
Cichlids (Cichlidae)
Gobies (Gobiidae)
Icefishes (Chaenichthyidae)
Marlins (Istiophoridae)
Mudskippers
(Periophthalmidae)
Mullets (Mugilidae)
Parrotfishes (Scaridae)
Perches (Percidae)
Sea bass (Serranidae)
Tunas, mackerels
(Scombridae)
Wrasses (Labridae)

Level-headed
The strangely distorted head of the flatfish shows that it evolved from a round-bodied ancestor.

FLATFISH

Pleuronectiformes
About 500 species

Where they live:

All seas, especially those in warm and temperate regions

Key features:

- Flatfish have a flattened body, fringed with dorsal and anal fins.
- During the larval stage, one eye moves to join the other on the same side of the head.
- They lurk on the bottom of sandy or muddy coastal waters with their upper surfaces coloured to blend with the surroundings.
- Carnivorous and bony. Most lie in wait for prey.

Species:

Atlantic halibut
(*Hippoglossus hippoglossus*)
Black-sea turbot
(*Scophthalmus maeoticus*)
Brill turbot
(*Scophthalmus rhombus*)
California halibut
(*Parlichthys californicus*)
Common sole (*Solea solea*)
Dab (*Limanda limanda*)
Hogchoker
(*Trinectes maculatus*)
Norwegian topknot
(*Phrynorhombus norvegicus*)
Peacock flounder
(*Bothus lunatus*)
Plaice
(*Pleuronectes platessa*)
Smallmouth flounder
(*Paralichthys dentatus*)
Summer flounder
(*Paralichtys dentatus*)
Turbot
(*Scophthalmus maximus*)
Winter flounder
(*Pseudopleuronectes americanus*)

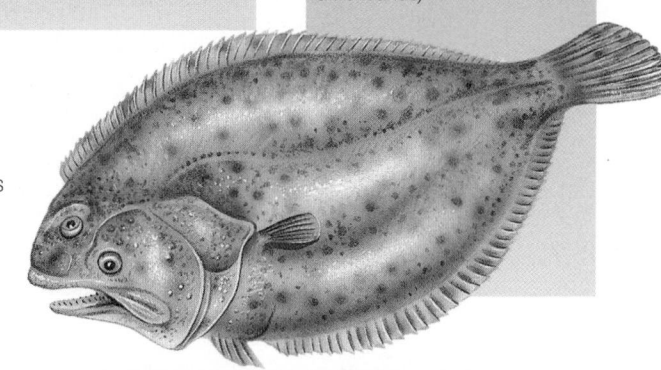

Most amphibians have two distinct phases to their lives. They start off as water-dwellers, then pass through a complete change in their physical form as they are transformed into land-dwelling adults. During this metamorphosis, they slowly change shape, growing legs and replacing their gills with air-breathing lungs.

WHAT IS AN AMPHIBIAN ?

● Adult amphibians are **air-breathing, egg-laying, cold-blooded** vertebrates.
● **Born in water**, most spend the majority of their adult lives on land.
● Many amphibians **hibernate** during the winter months.
● Most are **nocturnal**.

3 Feathery, external gills are clearly visible

2 After two weeks, tadpoles emerge.

4 Hind legs appear about three weeks after hatching.

5 Front limbs develop at about four to five weeks old.

1 Eggs are laid in water in early spring

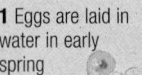

LIFE CYCLE OF A FROG

Frogs spend most of their adult life on dry land, but nearly all species return to the water to breed:
● The male approaches the female from behind, holding her around the body while she releases her eggs, called spawn, into the water.
● Protective jelly surrounding the eggs swells on contact with the water and the eggs, often in groups of several thousand, float just below the surface, where they are fertilised by sperm released into the water by the male.
● After around two weeks the eggs hatch into tadpoles, which feed on algae and weeds in the water. They breathe for the next few weeks by means of external gills.
● Gradually, the frog's limbs begin to take shape and the tail shrinks.
● By the time it is six weeks old, the young frog is fully formed and ready to leave the water. Its gills have been replaced by internal lungs and its tail has disappeared. At this stage it will switch from a vegetarian diet to a diet of insects and will live out the rest of its life near the water's edge.

6 By five to six weeks, lungs have replaced gills. Soon the tail will disappear.

heart

stomach

lung

intestine

cloaca

Typical amphibian   Most amphibians have a life cycle similar to that of the common frog (*Rana temporaria*, left), with nearly all species, regardless of their final adult form, starting out in life as legless, fish-like tadpoles. Common frogs are found all over Europe and Asia. Their coloration and markings are very variable.

Poisonous frogs

The tropical forests of Central and South America are home to tiny frogs, barely 5 cm (2 in) long. The skin glands of these colourful creatures produce a poison so toxic that the indigenous tribes of Colombia use it to coat their arrowheads – hence the name, arrow-poison frogs.
    Unlike most frogs, the 100-odd arrow-poison species are active during the day. They can afford to be obvious because their gaudy skins warn any would-be attacker to leave well alone or risk being poisoned. Safe from most aggressors, they move around the forest floor, looking for ants, their staple diet. Some also possess sticky pads on their fingers and toes, which help them to climb plants and trees in search of food.

Pretty deadly   Even touching Costa Rica's strawberry arrow-poison frog (*Dendrobates pumilio*) can prove fatal.

FACTS AND FIGURES

⬤ The largest amphibian is the Chinese giant salamander (*Andrias davidianus*), which grows to around 1.8 m (6 ft) in length and weighs about 60 kg (9 stone).

⬤ The smallest amphibian is the Cuban frog (*Sminthillus limbatus*), which is just 8.5 mm (³/₈ in) long.

⬤ The rarest amphibian is the painted frog (*Discoglossus nigriventer*), a native of Israel. Only five of them have been sighted since it was first discovered in 1940.

NEWTS AND SALAMANDERS

Urodela
About 360 species

Where they live:
Temperate regions, mostly north of the Equator.

Key features:
⬤ Short legs and long bodies.
⬤ They feed off small worms and insects.
⬤ Skins are smooth or warty, but are never covered in scales.
⬤ They move by wriggling from side to side in an S-shaped pattern.
⬤ They tend to stay hidden in damp places.

Species:
Alpine newt (*Triturus alpestris*)
Axolotl (*Ambystoma mexicanum*)
Congo eel (*Amphiuma tridactylum*)
European fire salamander (*Salamandra salamandra*)
Hellbender (*Cryptobranchus alleganiensis*)
Japanese giant salamander (*Megalobatrachus japonicus*)
Marbled newt (*Triturus marmoratus*)
Mudpuppy (*Necturus maculosis*)
Siren (*genus Sirenidae, three species*)

FROGS AND TOADS

Anura
About 3500 species

Where they live:
Most temperate and some tropical regions.

Key features:
⬤ Bodies tend to be squat and short.
⬤ Powerful rear legs are well adapted for jumping.
⬤ Skins are moist and feet webbed.
⬤ Long, extensible tongues are used for catching prey.

Species:
Asiatic climbing toad (*Pedostibes hosii*)
Bullfrog (*Rana catesbeiana*)
Common frog (*Rana temporaria*)
Edible frog (*Rana esculenta*)
Eurasian midwife toad (*Alytes obstetricians*)
Giant aquatic frog (*Telematobius culeus*)
Grass frog (*Limonaoedus ocularis*)
Leopard toad (*Bufo pardalis*)
Ornate horned toad (*Ceratophrys ornata*)

CAECILIANS

Gymnophiona
About 200 species

Where they live:
Tropical and subtropical regions.

Key features:
⬤ Entirely without limbs.
⬤ They spend most of their time underground.
⬤ Much of their time is spent burrowing for their staple diet of termites and earthworms.
⬤ Skins are grooved, giving the impression of being segmented.
⬤ Rarely observed, so that many have no common name.

Species:
Basilan caecilian (*Icythyophis gladulosus*)
Cameroon caecilian (*Geotrypetes seraphini*)
Ceylonese caecilian (*Icythyophis glutinosus*)
Koatao caecilian (*Icythyophis kohtaonsis*)
Lafrentz caecilian (*Dermophis oaxacae*)
Dermophis mexicanus
Icythyophis kohtaoensis
Typhlonectes natans

see also
82-3 **The move to land**
90-1 **Animal kingdom**
112-3 **Animal records**

Giant tadpole The pale pink axolotl (*Ambystoma mexicanum*) never really grows up. It acquires four legs and can breed, but remains water-based, never losing its gills. Few survive in the wild today. Their only natural habitat is in lakes around Mexico City.

Secretive lifestyle The South American caecilian (*Siphonops annulatus*), spends most of its time burrowing underground, looking for food.

Breathable skin

The largest family of salamanders, the lungless salamanders, breathe through their skin rather than through lungs. A thin, moist membrane, the epithelium, covers their skin surface and lines their mouths. Just below it is a network of tiny blood vessels. Oxygen dissolves in the moisture of the epithelium and passes through the thin membrane into the blood. At the same time, waste gases, such as carbon dioxide, pass out in the opposite direction. This process requires continuous moisture, so animals with breathable skin tend to live in damp places.

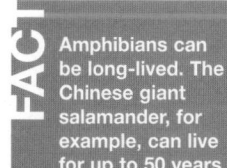

FACT Amphibians can be long-lived. The Chinese giant salamander, for example, can live for up to 50 years.

Reptiles live in most warm and temperate regions. They thrive in the tropics, where their greatest variety and abundance is found. As cold-blooded creatures, reptiles are entirely dependent on heat transferred from the surrounding air in order to maintain bodily functions. Many species are excellent climbers, aided by claws – or scales equipped with minute hooks – and strong tails that can be used to cling onto branches.

Flexible jaws A snake can devour prey up to three times its size in one gulp. Highly elastic joints in its jaws and even between skull bones allow it to open its mouth remarkably wide. The maxillary bone, which holds the top fangs, swings forward when the mouth opens. Once in the stomach the victim's body is rapidly broken down by powerful enzymes that can dissolve hair, feathers and even bone.

WHAT IS A REPTILE?

- Reptiles are **cold-blooded, air-breathing** vertebrates.
- Reptiles **lay yolk-filled eggs with hard shells**, enabling reproduction to take place on land.
- They have **scales** rather than feathers or hair.
- Their **skin is dry**, with few, if any, glands.
- With the exception of snakes, they **move around on four legs**, which project from the side of the body.
- Members of the order Squamata, **lizards and snakes, shed their skins** at intervals.

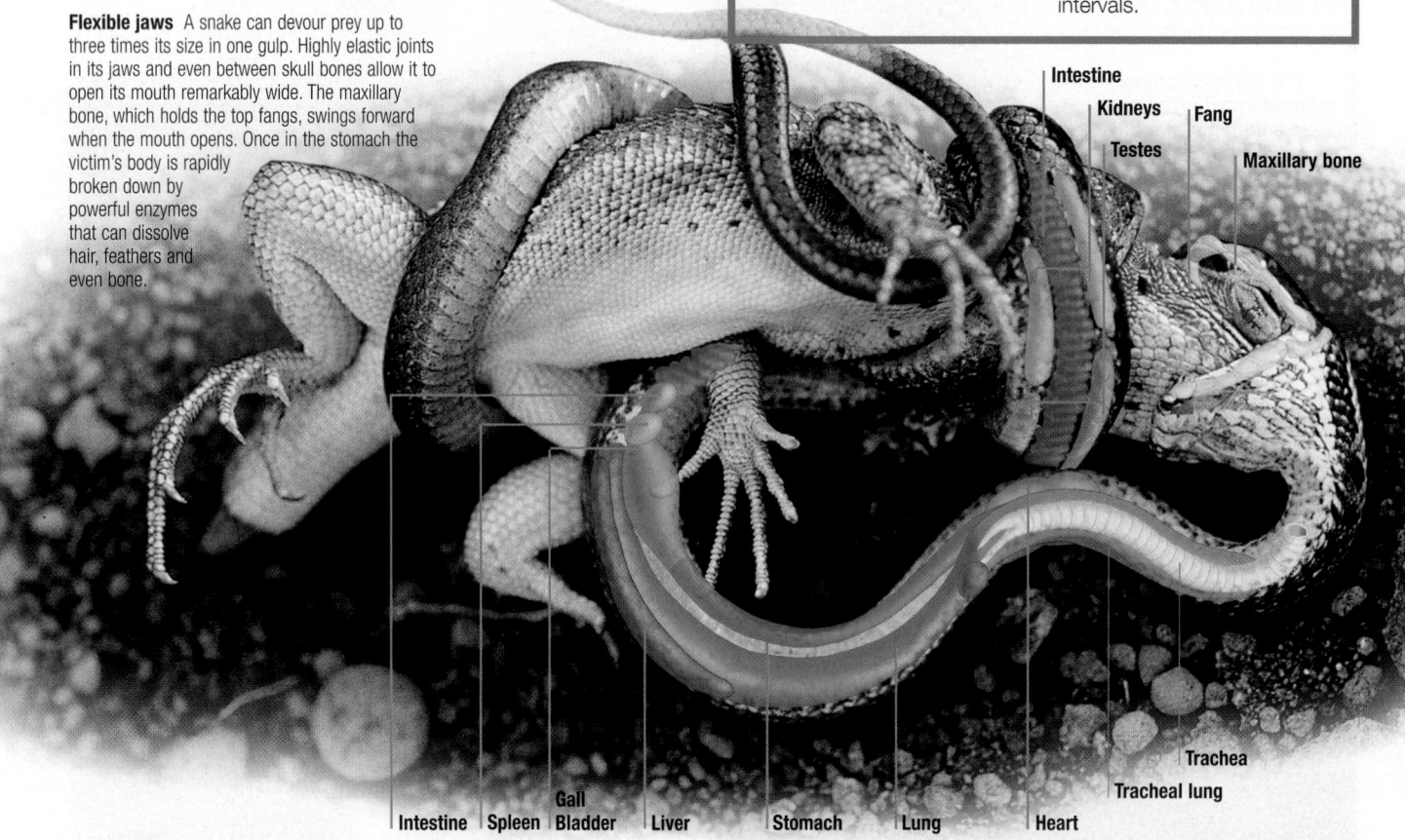

Intestine

Kidneys   Fang

Testes   Maxillary bone

Intestine | Spleen | Gall Bladder | Liver | Stomach | Lung | Heart

Trachea
Tracheal lung

FACTS AND FIGURES

- Reptiles come in a great variety of sizes. They range in length from a 3 cm (1¼ in) gecko (*Sphaerodactylus parthenopion*), found in the British Virgin Islands, to the anaconda (*Eunectes murinus*), a snake native to South America, which can grow to 9 m (29 ft) or longer.

- The heaviest reptile is the marine leatherback turtle (*Dermochelys coriacea*). It can weigh over 700 kg (0.7 tonnes).

- Dinosaurs, pterosaurs and ichthyosaurs were all reptiles.

- Mammals and birds are both descended from reptiles.

A living fossil?

The tuatara is the sole survivor of the sphenodontid group of reptiles, which appeared about 225 million years ago. It is found only on a few islets in Cook Strait, New Zealand. About 70 cm (28 in) long, tuataras outwardly resemble lizards but their skulls and teeth show marked differences. They are nocturnal, emerging at dusk to feed on insects, small animals and birds' eggs. Some live to be 100 years old.

The world's most dangerous snakes

The most dangerous snakes, when attacking their victims, inject venom through grooves or hollows in their fangs. The fangs act like hypodermic needles, which puncture the flesh of the victim when the snake strikes, introducing the poison into the prey's bloodstream.

Mambas These snakes are common in the countries of sub-Saharan Africa. They are among the fastest and most aggressive of all snakes. Their speed of attack is so great that they can pluck a bird out of the sky and kill it with an injection of venom almost before it has hit the ground.

Cobras These are found in Asia and Africa. The spitting cobra has the most fearsome reputation because it can spit blinding venom into the eyes of its victim from a range of nearly 3 m (10 ft).

Coral snakes The toxic venom of the relatively small coral snakes of the Americas is very powerful. Would-be predators are warned of the potential danger by the snakes' distinctive colouring of red, black, yellow and white bands.

see also
82-3 **The move to land**
84-7 **Dinosaurs**
90-1 **Animal kingdom**
112-3 **Animal records**

SNAKES

Serpentes
More than 2300
species

Where they live:

Most tropical and
temperate zones

Key features:

- Vision is limited, but attuned to movement.
- Hearing is restricted to ground vibrations, but sense of touch is acute.
- Have a sense of smell and can pick up airborne particles for analysis using the tongue.
- Some species have a pit between eye and nostril that is sensitive to infrared radiation so they can detect warm-blooded creatures in the dark.

Species:

Anaconda (Eunectes murinus)
Common king snake (Lampropeltis getulus)
King cobra (Ophiophagus hannah)
Madagascar boa constrictor (Sanzinia madagascariensis)
Reticulate python (Python reticulatus)
Rock python (Python sebae)
Royal python (Python regius)
Sidewinder (Crotalus cerastes)
Spitting cobra (Naja nigricollis)
Western diamond-back rattlesnake (Crotalus adamanteus)

LIZARDS

Lacertilia
More than 3700
species

Where they live:

Worldwide, but mostly
in the tropics

Key features:

- Have ear drums and movable eyelids.
- Lay leathery-shelled eggs in a nest.
- Most are small to medium-sized. Exceptions include monitor lizards, such as the Komodo dragon, which can be over 2 m (7 ft) long.
- Chiefly eat insects or vegetation.
- Most have four legs, but some, such as the European slow-worm, have none, like snakes.
- Many can shed their tail if attacked; it regrows.

Species:

Common lizard (Lacerta vivipara)
Emerald lizard (Lacerta viridis)
Frilled lizard (Chlamydosaurus kingi)
Fringe-toed lizard (Acanthodactylus erythrurus)
Jewelled lizard (Lacerta lepida)
Komodo dragon (Varanus komodoensis)
Sand lizard (Lacerta agilis)
Schreiber's lizard (Lacerta schreiberi)
Slow-worm (Anguis fragilis)
Stehlin's lizard (Lacerta stehlinii)
Wall lizard (Lacerta muralis)

TURTLES AND TORTOISES

Chelonia
About 270 species

Where they live:

South-east Europe, west
Asia, North Africa, South
and Central America

Key features:

- Body is protected by a hard shell.
- Head and limbs can be withdrawn into the shell when under attack.
- Shell of a turtle is lighter and more streamlined than that of a land tortoise.
- Land tortoises are herbivores.
- Marine turtles are herbivores; freshwater turtles are carnivores.
- Turtles can lay up to 200 eggs at a time.

Deep-sea diver Like all marine turtles, the green turtle (Chelonia mydas) spends most of its life under water, where it can hold its breath for over 30 minutes. Flat legs act like flippers, pushing it along.

Species:

African spurred tortoise (Testudo sulcata)
Giant leathery turtle (Dermochelys coriacea)
Green turtle (Chelonia mydas)
Hawksbill turtle (Eretmochelys imbricata)
Loggerhead turtle (Caretta caretta)
Red-legged tortoise (Testudo denticulata)
Snapping turtle (Chelydra serpentina)
Spur-thighed tortoise (Testudo graeca)
Starred tortoise (Testudo elegans)
Stinkpot (Sternotherus odoratus)

CROCODILES AND ALLIGATORS

Crocodylia
22 species

Where they live:

Near freshwater shores
in warmer regions

Key features:

- Lizard-like shape, with armoured skin made from large, strong, partially ossified (bony) plates.
- Teeth are situated in deep hollows (known as alveoli) in the jaw.
- Move through the water by swishing their tails in a side-to-side motion.
- Adults feed on fish and turtles; young feed on insects, worms and tiny fish.
- They are the largest modern reptiles. Male saltwater crocodiles, from tropical Asia and the Pacific, grow to about 3.2 m (10 ft 6 in) long – and in some cases to more than twice that length.

Species:

American alligator (Alligator mississippiensis)
Australian crocodile (Crocodylus johnsoni)
Cuban crocodile (Crocodylus rhombifer)
Gavial (Gavialis gangeticus)
Mugger crocodile (Crocodylus palustris)
Nile crocodile (Crocodylus niloticus)
Saltwater crocodile (Crocodylus porosus)
Spectacled caiman (Caiman crocodilus)

Crocodile – teeth visible on both jaws

Alligator – only upper teeth visible

Walking on water
The broad feet and long, scale-fringed toes of the basilisk lizard (Basiliscus plumiformes) mean it can sprint on the surface of water to escape from predators. This ability has led to it acquiring a further name – the Jesus Christ lizard.

Feathers are the one characteristic that separates birds from all other creatures. Feathers serve the dual function of aiding flight and helping to regulate body temperature. Birds have the most acute colour vision in the animal kingdom and are capable of distinguishing far more hues than humans can. Most birds restrict their activities to the hours of daylight, when this sense can be fully exploited.

WHAT IS A BIRD?

- A bird has **feathers and a bill**, but no teeth.
- Birds are **warm-blooded, air-breathing, two-legged** vertebrates.
- They communicate by means of **visual display or sound**.
- Birds' **eyesight is usually acute**, but their sense of smell is poor.
- **Almost all birds can fly.** They have streamlined bodies, highly adapted forelimbs (wings) and hollow bones.

Primary flight feather

Secondary flight feather

Lung

Kidney

Large intestine

Cloaca

Crop

Chest muscles

Sternum

Gizzard

Tail feather

Down feather

Every flight feather has a central shaft with a series of barbs sprouting from it. These barbs are linked by tiny hooks, giving the feather its solid appearance. The flight feathers give the wing an unbroken surface to push against the air in flight. Down feathers, which insulate the bird, are distinguished by their lack of interlocking hooks.

How birds fly

Birds can fly because air provides resistance to their flapping wings in much the same way as water provides resistance against a rowing boat's oars. The down-stroke of the wings provides lift. For every downward and back-ward movement of the wings, there is a corresponding upward and forward movement of the bird itself. The whole wing surface pushes against the air just as the blade of an oar pushes against the water. On the return stroke, the wing is tilted so that its thin leading edge can slice through the air with least resistance. Birds require strong chest muscles, anchored to a large sternum, to power their wings.

FACTS AND FIGURES

- There are nearly 9000 species of bird alive today.

- The bird with the largest wingspan is the wandering albatross (*Diomedea exulans*), measuring 3.2 m (10 ft 6 in) from wing tip to wing tip.

- The bee hummingbird (*Mellisuga helenae*) has the smallest wingspan of any bird at 5.5 cm (2¼ in).

- Birds exist on every continent. The emperor penguin (*Aptenodytes forsteri*) spends the winter in Antarctica, the only vertebrate to do so.

- More than 1000 extinct species of bird have been identified from fossils.

OSTRICH

Struthioniformes
1 species

RHEAS

Rheiformes
2 species

EMUS AND CASSOWARIES

Casuariiformes
4 species

KIWIS

Apterygiformes
3 species

see also
86-7 **Last days of the dinosaurs**
90-1 **Animal kingdom**
112-3 **Animal records**

Where it lives:
Open grasslands and semidesert regions in Africa

Where they live:
The open plains of South America

Where they live:
Deserts, plains and forests in Australia and New Guinea

Where they live:
Forests in New Zealand

Key features:
- It is flightless.
- It has a long, flexible neck, small head and duck-like bill.
- It is a fast runner, capable of sprinting at up to 65 km/h (40 mph).
- It has long, powerful legs with two toes on each foot.
- The male is black and white with a large, white plume of tail feathers. The female is a drab brown.

Species:
Ostrich (Struthio camelus)

Giant egg The ostrich has the largest egg (below) of any living bird, weighing an average 1.7 kg (3 lb 12 oz), the equivalent of about two dozen hen's eggs. Its shell, although only 1.5 mm (1/16 in) thick, is strong enough to support a 127 kg (20 stone) man.

Key features:
- They are flightless.
- They are smaller than the ostrich or emu.
- Their heads and necks are feathered.
- They have three toes on each foot.

Species:
Common rhea
(Rhea americana)
Lesser rhea (Pterocnemia pennata)

On the run
The common rhea (above) – like its African and Australian counterparts, the ostrich and emu – can reach impressive speeds. Its long legs double as a defensive weapon – they can deliver a powerful kick.

Key features:
- They are flightless.
- They reach 2 m (7 ft) tall.
- The emu has dark brown plumage, with naked blue spots on each side of the neck.
- The female emu has a sac in her throat, enabling her to emit a loud booming note.
- Cassowaries have bare heads with a horny helmet-like casque on top. Their plumage is black.
- Both the emu and cassowaries have three toes on each foot.

Species:
Emu
(Dromaius novaehollandiae)
Common cassowary
(Casuarius casuarius)
Dwarf cassowary
(Casuarius bennetti)
Single-wattled cassowary
(Casuarius unappendiculatus)

Key features:
- Kiwis are flightless.
- They have long, hair-like brown plumage.
- They are nocturnal.
- They have weak eyes, but well-developed senses of hearing and smell.
- They have a long bill, which they use to probe the soil for worms and insects.
- They lay the largest eggs in proportion to body size of any bird, equal to a quarter of the female's total weight.

Species:
Common kiwi
(Apteryx australis)
Little grey kiwi
(Apteryx owenii)
Rotaroa kiwi (Apteryx hastii)

Why birds have different bills

The shape of birds' bills are directly related to their main food type. Birds of prey have hooked bills, which are ideal for tearing apart the flesh of their victims. By contrast, the long, straight bills of many wading birds are fitted for finding and removing food from mud and wet sand; the curved end of the avocet's bill is an adaptation from this shape for snapping up tiny creatures from shallow water. One of the strangest bills of any bird is that of the skimmer. This fish-eater hunts by flying low over water with the bottom half of its bill trawling through the surface. As soon as it makes contact with prey, the bill snaps shut.

Other features of birds' bills can be explained by different factors. Colour, for instance, helps in species recognition and in some cases as an indicator of fitness as a mate. The bills of puffins are bright only during the breeding season; in autumn and winter they become dull and grey. Other factors affect colour too. The red spot on a herring gull's bill prompts their chicks to peck at it, which in turn stimulates the parent to regurgitate food for them.

Avocet

Skimmer

Puffin

Herring gull

PENGUINS
Sphenisciformes
18 species

Where they live:
Coastal and open ocean waters in the Southern Hemisphere

Key features:
- Penguins are flightless; their wings are modified to serve as flippers.
- They have short, stiff, closely packed feathers.
- They feed on fish, squid and free-swimming crustaceans, such as krill.
- They breed on coasts from Antarctica to the Galapagos Islands, often in colonies numbering thousands of pairs.

Species:
Adelie penguin
(Pygoscelis adeliae)
Chinstrap penguin
(Pygoscelis antarctica)
Crested penguin
(Eudyptes pachyrhynchus)
Emperor penguin
(Aptenodytes forsteri)
Gentoo penguin
(Pygoscelis papua)
Jackass penguin
(Speniscus demersus)
King penguin
(Aptenodytes patagonica)
Little penguin
(Eudyptula minor)
Magellanic penguin
(Speniscus magellanicus)
Rockhopper penguin
(Eudyptes crestatus)

Special adaptations Along with all other penguins, the feet of the crested penguin are positioned at the rear of their bodies to aid swimming. On land, this leads them to walk upright. Their wings have become adapted as paddles for swimming; the wing bones have fused together to help to stiffen these flippers.

DIVERS
Gaviiformes
4 species

Where they live:
Cold lakes and coastal waters in the Northern Hemisphere

Key features:
- Divers feed on fish, crustaceans and insects.
- Their legs are set far back on their bodies.
- They have webbed feet.
- Their bodies are streamlined for diving.
- They are able to dive to depths of 60 m (200 ft).
- They are also known as loons.

Species:
Black-throated diver
(Gavia arctica)
Great northern diver or common loon
(Gavia immer)
Red-throated diver
(Gavia stellata)
White-billed diver
(Gavia adamsii)

Born water dwellers
Divers, like this red-throated diver, are so well adapted to life in the water that they actually have great difficulty moving about on land. Their feet are so far back on their bodies that they can only toboggan along on their bellies. As a consequence, all nest very close to the water.

GREBES
Podicipediformes
About 20 species

Where they live:
Lakes, rivers and coastal waters in temperate regions

Key features:
- Grebes are weak fliers.
- They do not have webbed feet but instead have horny flaps on their toes to increase their surface areas for swimming.
- They feed on small fish and other aquatic animals.
- Many perform elaborate courtship 'dances'.
- Grebes build floating nests on open water or among reeds.

Species:
Black-throated grebe
(Podiceps novaehollandiae)
Great crested grebe
(Podiceps cristatus)
Great grebe
(Podiceps major)
Hoary-headed grebe
(Podiceps poliocephalus)
Least grebe
(Podiceps dominicus)
Little grebe
(Podiceps ruficollis)
Pied-billed grebe
(Podilymbus podiceps)
Red-necked grebe
(Podiceps griseigena)
Silver grebe
(Podiceps occipitalis)
Western grebe
(Aechmophorus occidentalis)

Dressed to impress In common with all grebes, the great crested grebe is more colourful in the breeding season than during the rest of the year. Once autumn arrives, and nesting is over, it moults its bright headdress.

ALBATROSSES, PETRELS AND FULMARS
Procellariiformes
More than 100 species

Where they live:
Oceans and coastlines worldwide

Ocean glider
The northern fulmar looks superficially like a seagull but is distinguished by its long, straight wings and single tubular nostril. It nests on cliffs across the Northern Hemisphere.

Key features:
- All have hooked bills with a single tubular nostril running along the top and opening near the end.
- They have webbed feet.
- They visit land only to breed.
- They feed on fish, squid or carrion from on or near the water's surface.

Species:
Black-footed albatross
(Diomedea nigripes)
Fulmar prion
(Pacyptila crassirostris)
Northern fulmar
(Fulmarus glacialis)
Royal albatross
(Diomedea epomophora)
Short-tailed albatross
(Diomedea albatrus)
Short-tailed shearwater
(Puffinus tenuirostris)
Shy albatross
(Diomedea cauta)
Southern fulmar
(Fulmarus glacialoides)
Southern giant petrel
(Macronectes gigantus)
Steller's albatross
(Diomedea albatrus)
Wandering albatross
(Diomedea exulans)
Waved albatross
(Diomedea irrorata)

PELICANS AND GANNETS

Pelecaniformes
About 60 species

Where they live:

Worldwide, except the interiors of continents and the poles

Key features:

● All of its members have webbing between all four toes of their feet – not just three toes, as in other birds with webbed feet.
● They are all fish-eaters. Some obtain their food by diving from the air, some by diving from the water's surface. Frigate birds steal food from other sea birds.
● This group also includes cormorants, boobies, frigate birds, tropic birds and darters (or snakebirds).

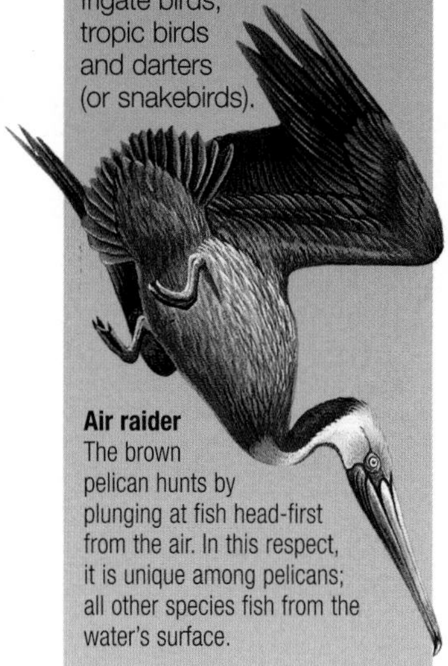

Air raider
The brown pelican hunts by plunging at fish head-first from the air. In this respect, it is unique among pelicans; all other species fish from the water's surface.

Species:

American darter or snakebird (*Anhinga anhinga*)
Blue-footed booby (*Sula nebouxii*)
Great cormorant (*Phalacrocorax carbo*)
Great white pelican (*Pelecanus onocrotalus*)
Magnificent frigate bird (*Fregata magnificens*)
Northern gannet (*Morus bassanus*)
Red-billed tropic bird (*Phaeton aethereus*)
Spot-billed pelican (*Pelecanus philippensis*)

HERONS, STORKS AND FLAMINGOES

Ciconiiformes
About 120 species

Where they live:

Freshwater and coastal habitats worldwide, except the poles

Key features:

● They are water birds with long legs and necks.
● Most feed on fish and other small aquatic creatures. Some storks prefer drier environments, and feed on small land animals, such as frogs and insects.
● This group also includes ibises, spoonbills, egrets and bitterns.

Species:

African open-billed stork (*Anastromus lamelligerus*)
Cattle egret (*Bubulcus ibis*)
Eurasian bittern (*Botaurus stellaris*)
Goliath heron (*Ardea goliath*)
Greater flamingo (*Phoenicopterus ruber*)
Grey heron (*Ardea cinerea*)
Marabou stork (*Leptoptilos crumeniferus*)
Painted stork (*Mycteria leucocephala*)
Scarlet ibis (*Eudocimus ruber*)
Snowy egret (*Egretta thula*)
White spoonbill (*Platalea leucorodia*)
White stork (*Ciconia ciconia*)
Wood stork (*Mycteria americana*)

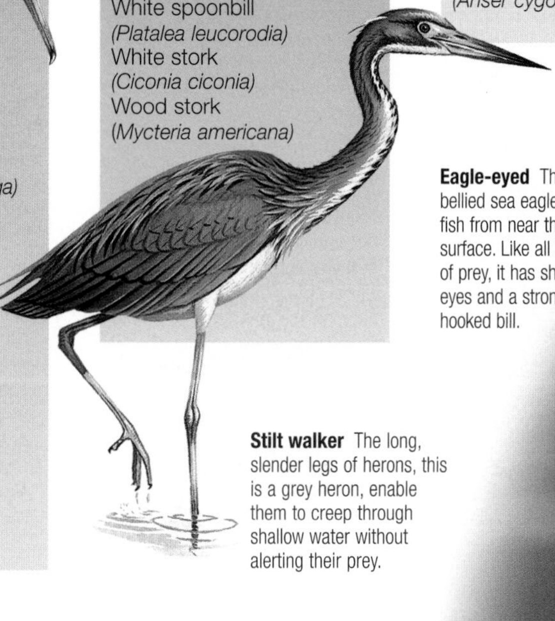

Stilt walker The long, slender legs of herons, this is a grey heron, enable them to creep through shallow water without alerting their prey.

DUCKS, GEESE AND SWANS

Anseriformes
More than 150 species

Where they live:

Worldwide, except for the Antarctic

Key features:

● They have plump bodies, short legs and webbed feet.
● They have an oil gland near the base of the tail. The bird pecks at the gland, then transfers the oil to its feathers to waterproof them.
● They line their nests with down. Almost all nest on the ground.
● The members of this group are commonly known as waterfowl.

Species:

Bean goose (*Anser fabalis*)
Black swan (*Cygnus atratus*)
Canada goose (*Branta canadensis*)
Common eider duck (*Somateria mollissima*)
Mallard duck (*Anas platyrhynchos*)
Mandarin duck (*Aix galericulata*)
Mute swan (*Cygnus olor*)
Red-breasted merganser (*Mergus serrator*)
Snow goose (*Anser coerulescens*)
Swan goose (*Anser cygonides*)

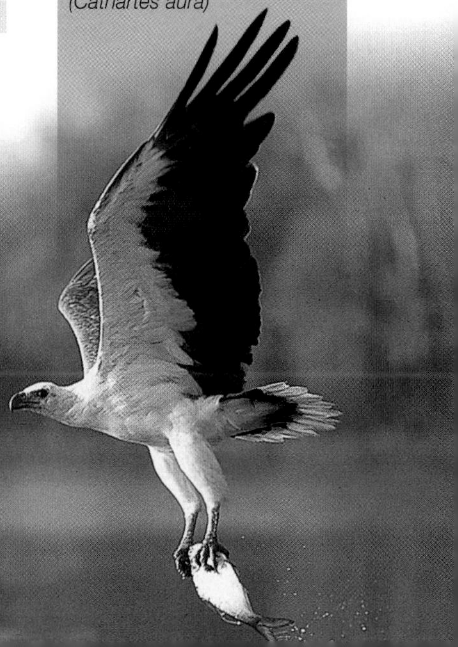

Eagle-eyed The white-bellied sea eagle grabs fish from near the surface. Like all birds of prey, it has sharp eyes and a strongly hooked bill.

BIRDS OF PREY

Falconiformes
About 280 species

Where they live:

Worldwide, except for the Antarctic

Key features:

● All are carnivorous and have hooked beaks and powerful claws.
● They have extremely sharp eyesight and are active during the day.
● They have long wings in relation to their body size.
● This group includes eagles, buzzards, harriers, condors, falcons, kestrels, hawks, kites and vultures.

Species:

Andean condor (*Vultur gryphus*)
Bald eagle (*Haliaeetus leucocephalus*)
Black kite (*Milvus migrans*)
Common kestrel (*Falco tinnunculus*)
Crested caracara (*Polyborus plancus*)
Eurasian buzzard (*Buteo buteo*)
Hen harrier (*Circus cyaneus*)
Osprey (*Pandion haliaetus*)
Peregrine falcon (*Falco peregrinus*)
Secretary bird (*Sagittarius serpentarius*)
Turkey vulture (*Cathartes aura*)

PHEASANTS, GROUSE AND TURKEYS

Galliformes
More than 230 species

CRANES, RAILS AND BUSTARDS

Gruiformes
About 200 species

WADERS, AUKS, SKUAS AND GULLS

Charadriiformes
More than 300 species

PIGEONS AND DOVES

Columbiformes
About 300 species

Where they live:
Worldwide, except for Antarctica

Where they live:
Worldwide, except the poles

Where they live:
Worldwide, in freshwater and saltwater habitats

Where they live:
Worldwide, except the poles

Key features:
- They are heavy-bodied and weak fliers.
- They spend most of their time on the ground where they forage for seeds, worms and insects.
- The red jungle fowl is the ancestor of the domestic chicken.
- This group includes quails, peacocks, guinea fowl, partridges and currasows. Its members are often called game birds or fowl.

Species:
Black grouse (Lyrurus tetrix)
California quail (Callipepla californica)
Capercaillie (Petrao urogallus)
Common pheasant (Phasianus colchicus)
Common quail (Coturnix coturnix)
Great argus pheasant (Argusianus argus)
Great currasow (Crax rubra)
Greater prairie chicken (Tympanuchus cupido)
Grey partridge (Perdix perdix)
Helmeted guinea fowl (Numidia meleagris)
Himalayan snowcock (Tetroagallus himalayensis)
Mallee fowl (Leipoa ocellata)
Peacock (Pavo cristatus)
Red grouse (Lagopus scoticus)
Red jungle fowl (Gallus gallus)
Wild turkey (Meleagris gallopavo)

Prepared for winter The willow grouse is adapted to survive in the frozen north. Its plump body and feathered feet help it to retain heat, and, in winter, it turns almost completely white.

Key features:
- These birds live in a range of habitats, from wetlands to dry plains.
- They are all omnivores that nest on the ground.
- Cranes and bustards have long necks and legs. Rails are more round-bodied with shorter necks and legs.
- Cranes fly with their necks straight out and legs trailing behind them. Rails are weak fliers. Bustards, although strong fliers, prefer to run from danger.

Weighty flier
At weights of up to 18 kg (40 lb), the great bustard is one of the world's heaviest flying birds.

Species:
Black-necked crane (Grus nigricollis)
Common coot (Fulica atra)
Common crane (Grus grus)
Common moorhen (Gallinula chloropus)
Great bustard (Otis tarda)
Hooded crane (Grus monacha)
Little bustard (Otis tetrax)
Sandhill crane (Grus canadensis)
Takahe (Porpyrio mantelli)
Water rail (Rallus aquaticus)
Whooping crane (Grus americana)

Key features:
- Gulls, terns, skuas and auks (including guillemots, puffins and razorbills) have webbed feet; waders do not.
- Gulls, terns, skuas and auks all eat fish. Waders feed on invertebrates.
- Most waders have long legs and long, narrow bills for probing mud or sand in search of food.
- Almost all species are migratory.
- Waders include avocets, oystercatchers, jacanas, plovers, sandpipers, stilts and turnstones.

Species:
Arctic skua (Stercorarius parasiticus)
Arctic tern (Sterna paradisea)
Atlantic puffin (Fratercula arctica)
Black skimmer (Rhyncops niger)
Black-winged stilt (Himantopus himantopus)
Comb-crested jacana (Irediparra gallinacea)
Common guillemot (Uria aalge)
Common gull (Larus canus)
Common snipe (Gallinago gallinago)
Eurasian curlew (Numenius araquata)
Eurasian oystercatcher (Haematopus ostralegus)
Herring gull (Larus argentatus)
Killdeer (Charadrius vociferus)
Kittiwake (Rissa tridactyla)
Little auk (Alle alle)
Northern lapwing (Vanellus vanellus)
Pacific gull (Larus pacificus)
Pied avocet (Recurvirostra avosetta)
Razorbill (Alca torda)
Red-necked phalarope (Phalaropus lobatus)
Ruff (Philomachus pugnax)

Key features:
- Pigeons and doves are plump-bodied birds, with short necks, small heads and slim, rounded bills.
- They eat fruit and seeds.
- They are strong fliers.
- The eggs are incubated by both parents.
- They produce a nutritive liquid (pigeon's milk) from the lining of the crop to feed the young. Flamingoes are the only other birds known to do this.
- This group contains many island species, including the now-extinct dodo (Raphus cucullatus) of Mauritius.

Fabulous feathers Doves from temperate zones tend to have fairly dull plumage but those from the tropics can have brilliant colours.

Species:
Collared dove (Streptopelia decaocto)
Dusky dove (Streptopelia lugens)
Red-necked pigeon (Columba squamosa)
Spotted pigeon (Columba maculosa)
Superb fruit dove (Ptilinopus superbus)
Turtle dove (Streptopelia turtur)
Victoria crowned pigeon (Goura victoria)
Wood pigeon (Columba palumbus)

PARROTS

Psittaciformes
About 300 species

CUCKOOS AND TURACOS

Cuculiformes
About 150 species

OWLS

Strigiformes
About 130 species

NIGHTJARS

Caprimulgiformes
More than 80 species

see also
90-1 **Animal kingdom**
112-3 **Animal records**
122-3 **Endangered species**
124-5 **Protecting species**

Where they live

The tropics and some temperate areas of the Southern Hemisphere

Where they live:

Temperate and tropical regions worldwide

Where they live:

Worldwide, except for Antarctica

Where they live:

Worldwide, except the poles

Key features:

Pretty polly The scarlet macaw is one of the most familiar parrots, but, like many members of this family, is threatened by demand from the pet trade.

● This group includes some of the world's most brightly coloured birds.
● They have powerful, hooked bills, the top half of which is connected to the skull by a hinge-like joint.
● Two of their toes point forwards and two point backwards.
● They feed primarily on fruit, seeds and nuts.
● Many species fly in large flocks, calling noisily to one another.
● All but a few species nest in holes in trees.

Species:

African grey parrot
(*Psittacus erithacus*)
Budgerigar
(*Melopsittacus undulatus*)
Galah (*Cactua rosicapilla*)
Kakapo
(*Strigops habroptilus*)
Kea (*Nestor notabilis*)
Rainbow lorikeet
(*Trichoglossus haematodus*)
Sulphur-crested cockatoo
(*Cacatua galerita*)

Key features:

● All members of this group have slim bodies, strong legs and long tails.
● Cuckoos are generally grey or brown. Turacos are very brightly coloured.
● Cuckoos are famous for laying their eggs in other birds' nests but in fact, less than half of all cuckoo species do this.
● Most cuckoos are insectivores but roadrunners also feed on lizards and snakes. Turacos are fruit-eaters.

Species:

Black and white cuckoo
(*Clamator jacobinus*)
Common cuckoo
(*Cuculus canorus*)
Drongo cuckoo
(*Surniculus lugubris*)
Great blue turaco
(*Corythaeola cristata*)
Greater roadrunner
(*Geococcyx californiana*)
Great spotted cuckoo
(*Clamator glandarius*)
Hoatzin
(*Opisthocomus hoatzin*)
Knysa turaco
(*Tauraco corythaix*)
Lesser roadrunner
(*Geococcyx velox*)
Squirrel cuckoo
(*Piaya cayana*)
Striped cuckoo
(*Tapera naevia*)

Key features:

● Owls are nocturnal and carnivorous.
● They have hooked beaks and powerful feet, equipped with sharp talons.
● Their plumage is soft to muffle the sound of their flight from prey.
● They have sharp hearing and large, forward-facing eyes to pinpoint prey in almost total darkness.
● They can turn their heads right around to look behind themselves without moving their bodies.

Species:

Barn owl (*Tyto alba*)
Buffy fish owl
(*Ketupa ketupa*)
Burrowing owl
(*Athene cunicularia*)
Dusky eagle owl
(*Bubo coromandus*)
Elf owl (*Micrathene whitneyi*)
Great grey owl
(*Strix nebulosa*)
Snowy owl
(*Nyctea scandiaca*)
Tawny owl (*Strix aluco*)
White-fronted scops owl
(*Otus sagittatus*)

Down to earth The greater roadrunner is a cuckoo that has taken to life on the ground. It uses its long tail as a counterweight to make sharp turns as it sprints after prey.

Key features:

● Nightjars are nocturnal or active during twilight.
● They feed on insects caught while in flight.
● They have long, pointed wings and tiny feet.
● They are all extremely well camouflaged.
● This group also contains the frogmouths of South-east Asia and Australia. Frogmouths look similar to nightjars. They are also nocturnal but catch their food on the ground.

Vanishing act
Nightjars spend the daylight hours resting perfectly still. Their camouflage is so good that they are rarely seen.

Species:

Common nighthawk
(*Chordeiles minor*)
Dusky nightjar
(*Veles binotatus*)
European nightjar
(*Caprimulgus europaeus*)
Greater eared nightjar
(*Eurostopodus macrotis*)
Oilbird (*Steatornis caripensis*)
Sickle-winged nightjar
(*Eleothreptus anomalus*)
Spotted nightjar
(*Eurostopodus guttatus*)
Tawny frogmouth
(*Podargus strigoides*)

SWIFTS AND HUMMINGBIRDS

Apodiformes
About 440 species

Where they live:
Tropical and temperate regions worldwide

Key features:
● All of these birds are small. Hummingbirds include the smallest birds on Earth.
● Swifts hunt flying insects and spend more time in the air than any other kind of bird. They even sleep on the wing.
● Hummingbirds' fast wing-beat enables them to hover in front of the flowers on whose nectar they feed.

Species:
Alpine swifts (*Apus melba*)
Bee hummingbird (*Calypte helenae*)
Blue-fronted lancebill (*Doryfera johanne*)
Eurasian swift (*Apus apus*)
Giant hummingbird (*Patagonia gigas*)
Great dusky swift (*Cypseloides senex*)
Hairy hermit (*Glaucis hirsuta*)
Pallid swift (*Apus pallidus*)
Sooty barbthroat (*Threnetes niger*)
Spot-fronted swift (*Cypseloides cherriei*)
Tooth-billed hummingbird (*Androdon aequatorialis*)

TROGONS

Trogoniformes
About 35 species

Where they live:
Tropical forests of Africa, Asia and the Americas

Key features:
● Most trogons eat insects caught in flight but some are fruit-eaters.
● They have brilliantly coloured plumage.
● Two of their four toes point backwards.

Species:
Mountain trogon (*Trogon mexicanus*)
Resplendent quetzal (*Pharomachrus mocinno*)

Telling tails Male resplendent quetzals use their tails to attract females. The length of the tail is a measure of an individual's fitness and his quality as a mate.

Making a splash The common kingfisher (right) dives from a perch above the water to catch its prey.

Controlled flight The ability to hold their position in the air and fly backwards has enabled hummingbirds, such as this rufous hummingbird of North America, to exploit a food source few other vertebrates can access – nectar. Different species feed from different flowers.

KINGFISHERS AND HORNBILLS

Coraciiformes
About 190 species

Where they live:
Worldwide in temperate and tropical regions

Key features:
● This group also includes bee-eaters, rollers, hoopoes and todies.
● Most members have brightly coloured plumage.
● They are all carnivorous apart from hornbills, which also eat fruit.
● Kingfishers have big heads and dagger-like bills.
● Hornbills have massive, curved bills.

Species:
Abyssinian roller (*Coracias abyssinica*)
Amazon kingfisher (*Chloroceryle amazona*)
Belted kingfisher (*Megaceryle alcyon*)
Common bee-eater (*Merops apiaster*)

Common kingfisher (*Alcedo atthis*)
Great Indian hornbill (*Buceros bicornis*)
Green kingfisher (*Chloroceryle americana*)
Helmeted hornbill (*Rhinoplax vigil*)
Hoopoe (*Upupa epops*)
Jamaican tody (*Todus todus*)
Kookaburra (*Dacelo novaeguineae*)
Little kingfisher (*Ceyx pusillus*)
Malachite kingfisher (*Alcedo cristata*)

WOODPECKERS AND TOUCANS

Piciformes
About 400 species

Where they live:
Worldwide, except Australia and Antarctica

Key features:
● All of this group, which includes honey guides, jacamars, barbets and puffbirds, are tree-dwellers that spend most of their lives alone.
● They all have two toes that point forwards and two that point backwards.
● Woodpeckers hammer at trees for grubs to eat, using straight, pointed bills.
● Toucans eat mostly fruit, and have large, brightly coloured bills to reach for their food.

Firm grip A woodpecker grips with its strong, clawed feet and uses its stiff tail for support. It uses its beak to enlarge natural holes in trees to make its nest.

Species:
Black-spotted barbet (*Capito niger*)
Black woodpecker (*Dryocopus martius*)
Collared puffbird (*Bucco capensis*)
Greater honey guide (*Indicator indicator*)
Green aracari (*Pteroglossus viridis*)
Green woodpecker (*Picus viridis*)
Lettered toucan (*Pteroglossus inscriptus*)
Northern flicker (*Colaptes auratus*)
Paradise jacamar (*Galbula dea*)
Toco toucan (*Rhamphastos toco*)
Wryneck (*Jynx torquilla*)

PERCHING BIRDS

Passeriformes
About 5400
species

Where they live:

Worldwide, except
the poles

Key features:

● This group includes
about 60 per cent of all
living bird species.
● The vast majority are
small birds, less than
25 cm (10 in) long.
● They have toes
adapted for grasping
twigs or branches. The
toes can lock into place,
enabling these birds to
sleep while perching.
● They are all land birds,
although some species fly
over seas and oceans
during migration.

Families:

Perching birds divide into
more than 50 families:
Accentors (Prunellidae)
American orioles
(Icteridae)
Ant pipits
(Conopophagidae)
Antbirds (Formicariidae)
Australian tree creepers
(Climacteridae)
Birds of paradise
(Pardisaeidae)
Bowerbirds and catbirds
(Ptilonorhynchidae)
Broadbills (Eurylaimidae)
Bulbuls (Pycnonotidae)
Cotingas (Cotingidae)
Crows, magpies and jays
(Corvidae)
Cuckoo-shrikes
(Campephagidae)
Dippers (Cinclidae)
Drongos (Dicruridae)
Finches (Fringillidae)
Flowerpeckers (Dicaeidae)
Flycatchers, thrushes
and warblers
(Muscicapidae)
Hawaiian honeycreepers
(Drepanididae)
Honeyeaters
(Meliphagidae)
Larks (Alaudidae)
Leafbirds (Irenidae)

Lyrebirds (Menuridae)
Manakins (Pipridae)
Mockingbirds (Mimidae)
New Zealand wrens
(Xenticidae)
Nuthatches (Sittidae)
Orioles (Orioidae)
Ovenbirds (Furnaridae)
Pittas (Pittidae)
Plantcutters (Phytotomidae)
Scrub birds
(Atrichornithidae)
Sharpbills (Oxyruncidae)
Shrikes (Laniidae)
Song-shrikes
(Cracticidae)
Sparrows and
weavers (Ploceidae)
Starlings (Sturnidae)
Sunbirds
(Nectariniidae)
Swallows and martins
(Hirundinidae)
Tanagers, cardinals,
sugar birds and
buntings (Emberizidae)
Tapaculos
(Rhinocryptidae)
Tits and chickadees
(Paridae)
Tree-creepers (Certhiidae)
Tyrant flycatchers
(Tyrannidae)
Vireos (Vireonidae)

Wagtails and pipits
(Motacillidae)
Wattlebirds
(Callaeidae)
Waxwings and palmchats
(Bombycillidae)
Weaver-finches (Estrildidae)
White-eyes (Zosteropidae)
Woodcreepers
(Dendrocoplapidae)
Wood swallows (Artamidae)
Wood warblers (Parulidae)
Wrens (Troglodytidae)

THE ASCENDANCY OF PERCHING BIRDS

Perching birds make up the great majority of the birds on the planet. They include all of the so-called 'songbirds', such as finches, starlings and warblers, as well as the crows, swallows and more exotic species such as birds of paradise.

Perching birds are considered to be the most highly evolved of all the birds. They have three toes that point forwards and one that points backwards, enabling them to grip onto twigs and so exploit scrubland and wooded habitats. Their generally small size has led to their success in many grassland habitats as well, particularly reed beds and marshes.

Even where perches are totally unavailable, perching birds still prosper. From the snow buntings of the Arctic to the sand larks and trumpeter finches of the Sahara desert, they survive on amounts of food too small or widely scattered to sustain larger or less mobile species.

Of all the perching birds alive today, more than three-quarters are songbirds, or 'oscines'. They are separated from the more primitive 'suboscine' perching birds by their more highly developed vocal organ, or syrinx, which can produce the uninterrupted stream of song characteristic of this group.

The earliest-known fossils of perching birds date from around 40 million years ago, although scientists believe that the group has existed since the Cretaceous period. Their global domination is more recent. In the early Miocene, 25 million years ago, the group underwent an adaptive explosion which paralleled the spread of grasslands caused by global climatic change.

Around 3 million years ago, a second adaptive explosion began, leading to a huge increase in the numbers of species. The trigger for this is unclear, although environmental change may again be a factor as it occurred during a period of four major cycles of glaciation.

see also
90-1 **Animal kingdom**
112-3 **Animal records**
122-3 **Endangered species**
124-5 **Protecting species**

Hanging around Grasping feet enable perching birds to exploit a range of food sources that would otherwise be unreachable. Sunbirds for example, probe into flowers for nectar from their vantage points of twigs and stems which they grip with their opposing claws.

Common coloniser
House sparrows have exploited human settlements across the globe for food and nesting sites. However, this successful little bird is becoming less common in the UK.

Animal records ▶

Animals have developed abilities that allow them to live even in the most extreme conditions. The emperor penguin (Aptenodytes forsteri), for example, can breed in the severe Antarctic winter. Males are able to incubate their single egg with external temperatures as low as –60°C (–76°F), surviving solely on fat reserves in the body for 62 to 67 days without a break.

ACUTE SENSES

Most complicated song
Male humpback whales (*Megaptera novaeangliae*) have the world's longest, most complicated songs. Each can last over 30 minutes, and can be heard by other whales up to 160 km (100 miles) away.

Loudest sound
The low-frequency pulses that fin whales (*Balaenoptera physalus*) and blue whales (*Balaenoptera musculus*) make in order to communicate with each other have been measured at up to 188 decibels – the loudest sound emitted from a living source.

Best sense of smell
Sharks have more highly developed scent organs and a better sense of smell than any other fish. They can detect as little as one part of mammalian blood in 100 million parts of water.

Sharpest hearing
Ultrasonic echolocation gives bats the most acute hearing of any terrestrial animal. Most species can hear frequencies up to about 80 kHz, although some are able to detect sound at 250 kHz. The human limit is only around 20 kHz.

LARGEST

Land animal
The largest land animal is the African bush elephant (*Loxodonta africana africana*). The biggest recorded specimen is thought to have weighed 12 tonnes.

Land carnivore
The Kodiak bear, from Alaska, is the largest land carnivore. Members of this race of brown bear (*Ursus arctos*) can weigh over half a tonne and stand 3.7 m (12 ft) tall.

Carnivore
The largest animal that actively hunts prey is the sperm whale (*Physeter macrocephalus*). It can be 26 m (85 ft) long and weigh up to 50 tonnes.

Fish
The whale shark (*Rhincodon typus*) reaches lengths of 12 m (40 ft). It is a filter feeder, using its gills to strain crustaceans and fish out of the water.

Reptile
The saltwater crocodile (*Crocodylus porosus*, below), from Asia and the Pacific, is the largest living reptile, at around 6 m (20 ft) long and weighing up to 1.5 tonnes. The longest is South-east Asia's reticulated python (*Python reticulatus*), which can be 10 m (33 ft) long.

Bird
The largest living bird is the ostrich (*Struthio camelus*), which can grow to 2.7 m (8 ft 10 in) tall.

Mammal
The blue whale (*Balaenoptera musculus*) is the biggest living mammal and probably the largest animal ever. The heaviest specimen ever recorded weighed 190 tonnes, while the longest measured 33.5 m (110 ft).

SMALLEST

Bird
The world's smallest bird is the bee hummingbird (*Mellisuga helenae*, shown life-size

Fish
The smallest fish, and the smallest known vertebrate, is the dwarf goby (*Trimmatom*

Mammal
The smallest mammal is the bumblebee bat (*Craseonycteris thonglongyai*) from

Most shocking animal
The electric eel or paroque (*Electrophorus electricus*), from northern South America, can release a shock of up to 650 volts to immobilise and kill prey – strong enough to stun an adult human.

Fastest insect runners
Cockroaches can run at up to 5 km/h (3 mph), the fastest land speed in the insect world. This is amazingly fast. Scaled up to human size, it would be like running at 320 km/h (200 mph).

Fastest land animal
The cheetah (*Acinonyx jubatus*) can move faster than any other creature on dry land. In three seconds, from a standing start, it can reach a speed of around 96 km/h (60 mph).

Most fertile animal
With no predators and unlimited food, one cabbage aphid (*Brevicoryne brassicae*) could create an 822 million tonne mass of offspring every year – three times the weight of the human population.

Longest hibernation

Marmots can hibernate for nine months a year, so may spend 75 per cent of their lives in deep sleep. Sloths, opossums and armadillos spend up to 80 per cent of their lives asleep or dozing.

Longest insect

The world's longest insect is *Pharnacia kirbyi*, a stick insect from Borneo. Its body is up to 33 cm (13 in) long, and its 54.6 cm (21$^{1}/_{2}$ in) legs are so long that they can get tangled when it sheds its skin.

Longest-lived animal

Giant tortoises can live longer than any other land animal. One on Tonga was said to be 193 when it died in 1966. The oldest authenticated age is 152, for a specimen that died in Mauritius in 1918.

Longest pregnancy

Gestation periods of up to 38 months have been recorded among Alpine salamanders (*Salamandra atra*) in southern Europe. One or two young are born, within a few hours of each other.

Longest migration

Every year the Arctic tern (*Sterna paradisaea*) flies 40 000 km (25 000 miles) from the Southern Ocean to its Arctic breeding ground and back. In 25 years, this equals a return-trip to the Moon.

Most legs

Centipedes and millipedes have more legs than any other animal. The record number of legs counted on a centipede is 354; millipedes have been recorded with around 700 legs each.

Greediest animal

The larva of the polyphemus moth (*Antheraea polyphemus*) consumes 86 000 times its birthweight in its first 56 days. This is equal to a 3.17 kg (7 lb) human baby taking in 273 tonnes of food.

Most poisonous animal

Arrow-poison frogs, like the yellow-banded one (*Dendrobates leucomelas*, above), secrete some of the deadliest biological toxins in the world. The most lethal poisons are found in the skin of the golden arrow-poison frog (*Phyllobates terribilis*), native to the jungles of South and Central America.

There are three groups of living mammals: placentals, marsupials and monotremes. In placental mammals, such as humans, the young develop inside the mother's body. Marsupials – kangaroos, koalas and the like – give birth to immature young who develop further in the mother's pouch. Monotremes, such as the platypus, are the oldest and most primitive mammals, giving birth to young who hatch from eggs outside the mother's body.

WHAT IS A MAMMAL?

- Mammals are **warm-blooded** vertebrates.
- They have **mammary glands** that produce milk so that the newly born have an immediate food supply.
- With the exception of mature whales, dolphins and porpoises, they have **hair** on their bodies, which helps to maintain a stable body temperature.
- They have a **middle ear**, containing three small bones which modify and transmit sound waves to the inner ear.
- They have **seven vertebrae in the neck**.

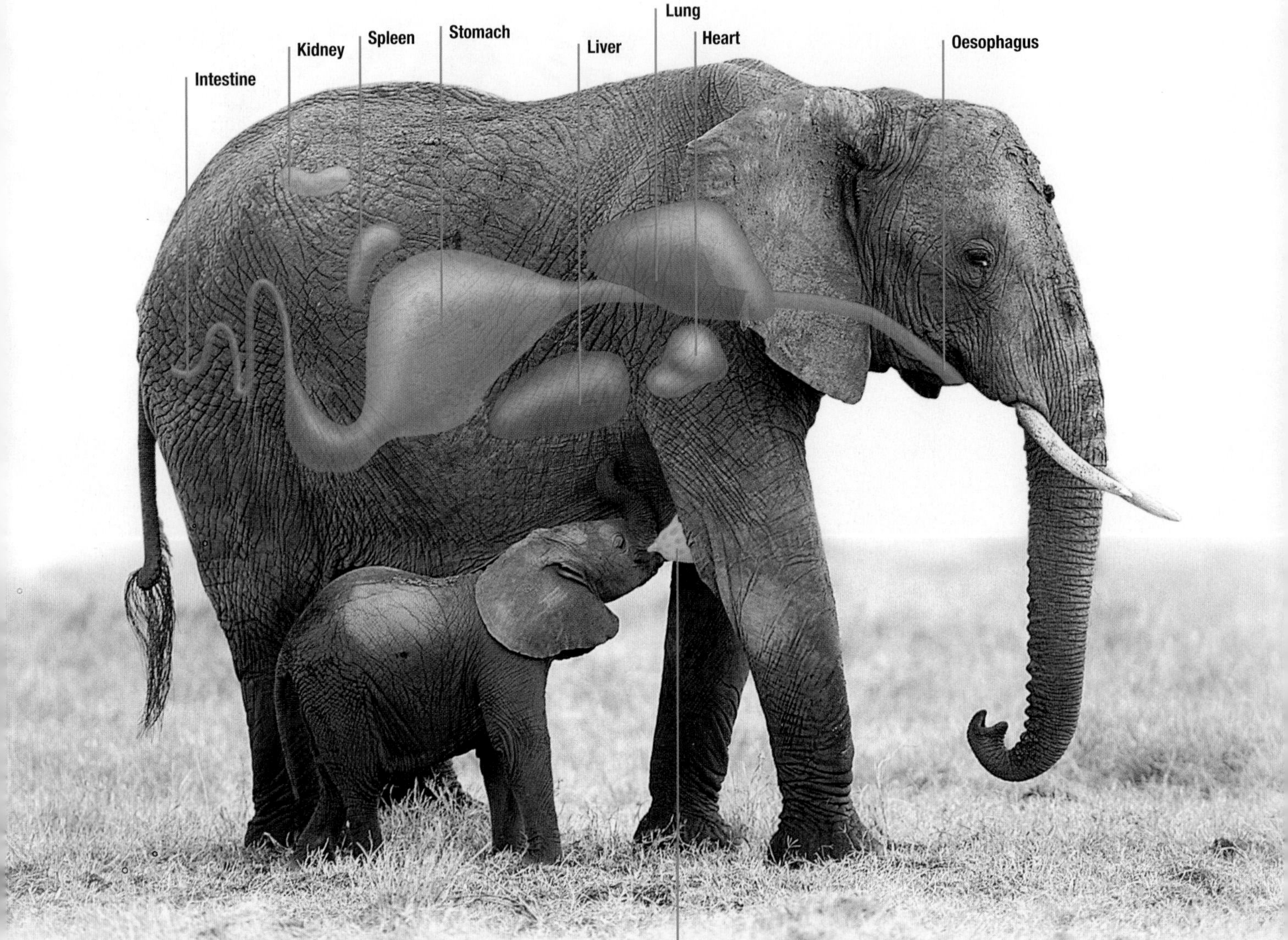

Intestine   Kidney   Spleen   Stomach   Liver   Lung   Heart   Oesophagus

Mammary gland

FACTS AND FIGURES

- There are more than 4000 species of mammal.

- The smallest land mammal is the pygmy or Savi's shrew (*Suncus etruscus*). Its body is just 4-5 cm (1½-2 in) long. It can creep into holes made by large earthworms.

- Nearly a quarter of all mammals can fly. Bats make up 23 per cent of known mammal species.

- No two zebras have exactly the same pattern of stripes and no two giraffes have the same pattern of spots.

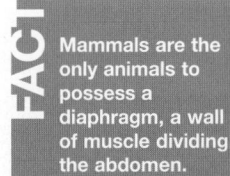

FACT

Mammals are the only animals to possess a diaphragm, a wall of muscle dividing the abdomen.

PLATYPUSES AND ECHIDNAS

Monotremata
3 species

KANGAROOS, OPOSSUMS AND KOALAS

Marsupialia.
About 250 species

SHREWS, MOLES AND HEDGEHOGS

Insectivora
Nearly 400 species

ELEPHANT SHREWS

Macroscelidea
12 species

see also

88-9 **Rise of the mammals**
90-1 **Animal kingdom**
122-3 **Endangered species**
124-5 **Protecting species**

Where they live:

Australia and New Guinea

Where they live:

Australia, New Guinea and the Americas

Where they live:

Worldwide, except poles and Australasia

Where they live:

Africa

Key features:

- Monotremes are the most primitive mammals.
- They are the only mammals that lay eggs. But, like other mammals, they have mammary glands and hair.
- There are three living species, two echidnas and the platypus.
- Echidnas have long, sticky tongues and powerful, short limbs fitted with claws for catching and eating ants.

Families:

Echidnas (Tachyglossidae)
Platypus (Ornithorhynchidae)

Spineless A baby short-nose echidna (*Tachyglossus aculeatus*) lacks the distinctive spiny coat that will help to protect it as an adult.

Key features:

- Marsupials have relatively small brains.
- The young are born tiny and immature. In most species, females carry their young in a pouch for several weeks after their birth.
- Marsupial mothers can nurture three generations of young at once, one in utero, one in the pouch and one approaching independence.

Families:

Bandicoots (Peramelidae)
Kangaroos and wallabies (Macropodidae)
Marsupial anteaters (Myrmecobiidae)
Marsupial cats and mice (Dasyuridae)
Marsupial moles (Notorycidae)
Opossums (Didelphidae)
Phalangers and possums (Phalangeridae)
Rat opossums (Caenolestidae)
Wombats (Vombatidae)

Key features:

- They are insect-eaters – hence their name, insectivores.
- They are small, with narrow snouts and sharp, simple teeth.
- Have poor eyesight, but a good sense of smell.
- Many are nocturnal.

Families:

Golden moles (Chrysochloridae)
Hedgehogs (Erinaceidae)
Moles (Talpidae)
Otter shrews (Potamogalidae)
Shrews (Soricidae)
Solenodons (Solenodonitdae)
Tenrecs (Tenrecidae)

Key features:

- They are rat-like, with long sensitive snouts.
- They eat insects, eggs and small mammals.
- They used to be included in the Insectivora, but are no longer believed to be closely related to 'true' shrews.

Family:

Elephant shrews (Macroscelididae)

Leaps and bounds Although they usually scuttle around on all fours at the first sign of danger, elephant shrews can rear up on their long, slender hind limbs and bound off at great speed. When doing this, they resemble miniature kangaroos.

Placentals versus marsupials

During the Cretaceous marsupials were the dominant mammal and coexisted with placentals by exploiting different food sources. However, where placental mammals have been introduced into marsupial populations, the marsupials have tended to lose out. This is not always the case. Despite competition from placentals, many Australian marsupial species still flourish.

Placentals	Marsupials
Generally have larger brains	Generally have smaller brains
Can regulate temperature well	Can become torpid in extreme cold
Large placenta – uses up a lot of energy	Small placenta – conserves energy
Mature young at birth	Immature young at birth
Birth can be difficult – mother and offspring vulnerable	Birth easy – young then protected in pouch until sufficiently mature

Reaching safety The sole aim of a newly born kangaroo, known as a joey, is to crawl into the security of its mother's pouch, where it latches on to one of her teats and suckles.

FLYING LEMURS

Dermoptera
2 species

BATS

Chiroptera
Nearly 1000 species

TREE SHREWS

Scandentia
About 20 species

PROSIMIANS, MONKEYS AND APES

Primates
About 230 species

Where they live:
South-east Asia

Where they live:
Most temperate and tropical regions

Where they live:
Tropical forests of Asia

Where they live:
Mostly in tropical and subtropical regions. Man lives everywhere.

Key features:
- They can glide more than 120 m (400 ft) at a time on flaps of skin that extend along each side of the body from neck to forelimb to hind limb and tail.
- They hang upside down when resting.
- They feed on buds and leaves.

Family:
Flying lemurs or colugos (Dermopteridea)

Key features:
- Nocturnal.
- They eat fruit or insects – also nectar, small animals and blood.
- Insectivorous bats use echolocation to find prey.
- They are the only true fliers (as opposed to gliders) among mammals.
- Their wings are an extension of the skin, supported between forelimb, hind limb and tail.

Families:
Bulldog bats (Noctilionidae)
Disk-winged bats (Thyropteridae)
Free-tailed bats (Molossidae)
Fruit bats (Pteropidae)
Funnel-eared bats (Natalidae)
Harpy fruit bats (Harpyionycteridae)
Horseshoe bats (Rhinolophidae)
Leaf-nosed bats (Phyllostomidae)
Long-tongued bats (Macroglossidae)
New Zealand short-tailed bats (Mystacindae)
Old World leaf-nosed bats (Hipposideridae)

Key features:
- Squirrel-like, with long noses.
- They eat insects, fruit and seeds.
- Good hearing and vision.
- Around 45 cm (18 in) long, including their tails.
- They are sometimes classed as small, primitive primates.

Family:
Tree shrews (Tupaiidae)

Key features:
- Eyes that face forward.
- Grasping hands and feet, some with opposable thumbs.
- Flat nails, rather than claws.
- They are adapted for climbing.
- Two mammary glands on the chest.
- Increased brain size in advanced species.
- In more advanced primates, the face is naked or bearded, and the snout tends to be shorter than in prosimians – such as lemurs, lorises and tarsiers.

Getting a grip Most primates, such as the chimpanzee (*Pan troglodytes*), have feet and hands with an opposable thumb, which can be placed opposite the other digits. This allows primates to get a firm grip on the branches of the trees in which they live. The increased dexterity that an opposable thumb brings has allowed man to evolve complex tool-making skills.

Annual migration The large mouse-eared bat (*Myotis myotis*) migrates between its summer and winter homes, frequently covering distances of over 260 km (160 miles). It is rarely seen in the colder months, when it hibernates in caves.

Rat-tailed bats (Rhinopomatidae)
Sac-winged bats (Emballonuridae)
Slit-faced bats (Nycteridae)
Smokey bats (Furipteridae)
Sucker-footed bats (Myzopodidae)
Vampire bats (Desmontidae)
Vespertilionid bats (Vespertilionidae)

Families:
Aye-ayes (Daubentoniidae)
Gibbons (Hylobatidae)
Great apes (Pongidae)
Indri and sifakas (Indriidae)
Lemurs (Lemuridae)
Lorises, pottos and bushbabies (Lorisidae)
Man (Hominidae)
New World monkeys and marmosets (Cebidae)
Old World monkeys (Cercopithecidae)
Spider monkeys, howler monkeys and sakis (Atelidae)
Tarsiers (Tarsiidae)

ARMADILLOS, SLOTHS AND ANTEATERS

Edentata
30 species

PANGOLINS

Pholidota
7 species

AARDVARKS

Tubulidentata
1 species

RABBITS, HARES AND PIKAS

Lagomorpha
About 65 species

Where they live:
South America

Where they live:
Africa and South-east Asia

Where they live:
Central and Southern Africa

Where they live:
All continents, except Antarctica

Key features:
- Long snouts and long, sticky tongues.
- Teeth small or absent.
- Their backbones are reinforced, making them strong diggers when they excavate ant hills for food.
- Well-developed sense of smell.
- The most primitive brains of any New World mammals.

Families:
Anteaters (Myrmecophagidae)
Armadillos (Dasyodidae)
Sloths (Bradypodidae)

Key features:
- Long, prehensile tail.
- Nocturnal.
- They are covered with overlapping horny scales.
- They feed on ants and termites.
- Toothless, but with long, sticky tongue and strong claws.

Family:
Pangolins (Manidae)

Key features:
- Long snout, large ears and thick tail.
- They feed entirely on termites and ants.
- They use strong claws to break open mounds of termites, which they lap up with a long, sticky tongue.
- They live on grasslands and in open forests.
- Nocturnal, sleeping in deep burrows by day.

Family:
Aardvark (Orycteropidae)

Key features:
- Ground-dwelling herbivores.
- At the front of the mouth they have an extra pair of chisel-shaped upper and lower incisor teeth for cutting through plant stems.
- Sharp eyesight and hearing, which enable them to escape in good time from potential predators.

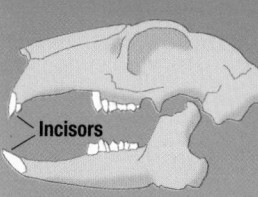

→ Incisors

Families:
Rabbits and hares (Leporidae)
Pikas (Ochotonidae)

Slow mover By day the three-toed sloth (*Bradypus tridactylus*) hangs from a branch by its long, curved claws. Even after sunset, it shifts only a few metres in search of food.

Suit of armour Thick, overlapping scales cover almost the entire body of the tree pangolin (*Manis tricuspis*). If attacked, it curls up, leaving the cutting edge of its scales to inflict damage on the attacker.

Mountain-dweller The northern pika (*Ochotona princeps*), a relative of rabbits and hares, lives in large colonies, mostly high up in remote, rocky parts of north-western North America.

Feeding machine Having ripped open its prey's home with its long front claws, the giant anteater (*Myrmecophaga tridactyla*), sweeps the insects into its mouth with its sticky tongue.

RATS AND MICE

Rodentia
More than 1800 species

WHALES, DOLPHINS AND PORPOISES

Cetacea
About 80 species

CATS, DOGS AND BEARS

Carnivora
270 species

ELEPHANTS

Proboscidea
2 species

Where they live:
Worldwide, except polar regions

Where they live:
All oceans and some rivers

Where they live:
Worldwide, including Arctic and Antarctic

Where they live:
Sub-Saharan Africa, India, Sri Lanka, South-east Asia

Key features:

● Known collectively as rodents, the group also includes beavers, squirrels and guinea pigs.
● Mostly herbivorous.
● Chisel-like incisor teeth for gnawing. These teeth never stop growing and stay sharp.

Families:

African mole rats, bamboo rats (Rhizomyidae)
Beavers (Castoridae)
Birch and jumping mice (Zapodidae)
Cane rats (Thryonomyidae)
Capybaras (Hydrochoeridae)
Chinchilla rats (Abrocomidae)
Chinchillas, viscachas (Chinchillidae)
Dormice (Gliridae)
Field mice, deer mice, voles, lemmings, muskrats (Cricetidae)
Guinea pigs, cavies, maras (Caviidae)
Hutias, coypus (Capromyidae)
Jerboas (Dipodidae)
Mole rats (Spalacidae)
New World porcupines (Erethizontidae)
Old World porcupines (Hystricidae)
Old World rats and mice (Muridae)
Pacaranas (Dinomyidae)
Pacas, agoutis (Dasyproctidae)
Pocket gophers (Geomyidae)
Pocket mice, kangaroo rats and mice (Heteromydae)
Rock rats, dassie rats (Petromuridae)
Spiny rats (Echimyidae)

Squirrels, chipmunks and marmots (Sciuridae)
Tuco-tucos (Ctenomyidae)

Key features:

● Marine mammals.
● Known collectively as cetaceans, they divide into two groups: toothed whales and baleen whales.
● Baleen whales (grey, humpback, right and rorqual whales) have no teeth. Instead, they have plates of stiff, hair-like material (whalebone) that sieve out plankton.
● Toothed whales, plus dolphins and porpoises, hunt down their prey.
● Nasal openings (blowholes) at the top of the head. No external ears and almost no hair.
● Highly social, they communicate using a large repertoire of noises.

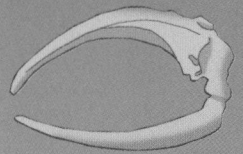

The arched upper jaw of a baleen whale allows space for the baleen plates, which hang down from it.

Families:

Beaked whales (Hyperoodontidae)
Dolphins and killer whales (Delphinidae)
Grey whale (Eschrichtiidae)
Long-snouted dolphins (Stenidae)
Narwhal and beluga whales (Monodontidae)
Porpoises (Phocoenidae)
Right whales (Balaenidae)
River dolphins (Platanistidae)

Rorquals and humpback whales (Balaenopteridae)
Sperm whales (Physeteridae)

Key features:

● Known collectively as carnivores, they also include foxes, wolves, hyenas, otters, skunks, seals and walruses.
● Mostly predatory meat-eaters, though many canids (dogs, jackals, wolves, foxes) are omnivorous and the giant panda is almost entirely herbivorous.
● Their large, pointed canine teeth are good for stabbing.
● Many have specialised carnassial teeth, for shearing through meat.
● Brains are usually large in relation to body size.

Families:

Bears and giant panda (Ursidae)
Cats (Felidae)
Civets and genets (Viverridae)
Dogs, foxes, jackals, wolves (Canidae)
Eared seals (Otariidae)
Earless seals (Phocidae)
Hyenas and aardwolves (Hyaenidae)
Mongooses and meerkats (Herpestinae)
Raccoons, coatis, lesser panda (Procyonidae)
Walrus (Odobenidae)
Weasels, badgers, skunks, otters (Mustelidae)

Key features:

● Largest of living land mammals, adults weigh 6 tonnes and more.
● Herbivores. An adult male eats up to 180 kg (400 lb) of herbage a day.
● Long boneless trunk – a combination of upper lips, palate and nostrils. Tusks are elongated upper incisors.
● In prehistoric times, there were some 300 species; now only two survive.
● African elephant (*Loxodonta africana*) is bigger than the Asian elephant (*Elephas maximus*), with noticeably larger ears.

Family:

Elephants (Elephantidae)

Status symbols The tusks of a bull walrus (*Odobenus rosmarus*) can be up to 90 cm (35 in) long. They are used in courtship disputes and displays to help to attract a mate.

HYRAXES

Hyracoidea
7 species

DUGONG AND MANATEES

Sirenia
4 species

HORSES, ASSES AND RHINOCEROSES

Perissodactyla
15 species

PIGS, GOATS, SHEEP AND CATTLE

Artiodactyla
150 species

see also
90-1 **Animal kingdom**
112-3 **Animal records**
122-3 **Endangered species**
124-5 **Protecting species**

Where they live:
Africa, Arabia, Syria

Where they live:
Tropical coastal waters and adjacent rivers of western Atlantic, Pacific and Indian oceans

Where they live:
Tropical America, eastern and Southern Africa, southern Asia

Where they live:
All continents, except Australia and Antarctica

Key features:
- Small, compact, rabbit-sized body.
- No visible tail.
- Front feet have four hoof-like toes; hind feet have three toes and one grooming claw.
- Two-chambered stomach for digesting diet of vegetation.

Family:
Hyraxes (Procaviidae)

Key features:
- Marine mammals, which live almost continuously submerged.
- Known collectively as sirenians.
- Herbivores, browsing on marine plant life.
- Complex three-chambered stomachs.
- Placid, slow and defenceless.

Families:
Dugong (Dugongidae)
Manatees (Trichechidae)

Key features:
- The group also includes zebras and tapirs.
- They are large herbivores. Grass is an important part of their diet.
- On each hind foot, they possess one or three hoofed toes.
- The most primitive of the perissodactyls are the tapirs, which probably resemble the common ancestor of the order.

Families:
Horses, asses, zebras (Equidae)
Tapirs (Tapiridae)
Rhinoceroses (Rhinocerotidae)

Key features:
- The group also includes giraffes, deer and camels.
- They are frequently described as 'cloven-hoofed' because hoofs are divided in two. In fact, each cloven hoof consists of two hoofed toes.
- Herbivores, often grazing in large herds on grasslands.
- Stomachs and intestines are specially adapted for digesting the large quantities of cellulose found in plants.
- Many have horns or antlers.

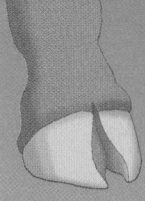

The two surviving toes form the 'cloven hoof' of many artiodactyls.

Families:
Camels and lamoids (Camelidae)
Cattle, sheep and goats, antelopes (Bovidae)
Chevrotains (Tragulidae)
Deer (Cervidae)
Giraffes and okapi (Giraffidae)
Hippopotamuses (Hippopotamidae)
Peccaries (Tayassuidae)
Pigs (Suidae)
Pronghorn (Antilocapridae)

Lone swimmer Unlike the more gregarious dugong of the Indian and Pacific oceans, the West Indian manatee (*Trichechus manatus*) is a solitary creature, living in tropical waters of the western Atlantic.

Hidden herbivore The Malayan tapir (*Tapirus indicus*) is a nocturnal creature living in the densest parts of the forests of South-east Asia. Man's destruction of its habitat is threatening this elusive species with extinction.

Well armed The tusk of the Arctic narwhal (*Monodon monoceros*) is in fact a modified tooth, growing out from the upper jaw. Up to 3 m (10 ft), it is found only in the male.

Safety in numbers The saiga antelope (*Saiga tatarica*) grazes in large herds on the grassy steppes of Russian and Central Asia.

While plants can manufacture their food using photosynthesis, animals have no such ability. They need to find their food and ingest it. They have developed a wide range of methods for doing this. A few are parasites: they obtain their food by attaching themselves to the body of another animal from which they draw vital nutrients. Most, however, take in solid or liquid organic material, which they have to digest in order to break it down into soluble nutrients that their bodies can absorb and use. This kind of feeding is known as holozoic.

THREE KINDS OF FEEDING

There are three major types of holozoic feeder: **fluid-feeders**, **microphagous feeders**, which feed on microscopic food particles, and **macrophagous feeders**, which feed on larger food particles.

1 Fluid-feeders Organic liquids, such as nectar, blood and sap, are food sources for fluid-feeders. Most are insects with piercing and sucking mouth-parts, such as mosquitoes, or long tongues, such as butterflies. Hummingbirds and vampire bats are among the few vertebrate fluid-feeders.

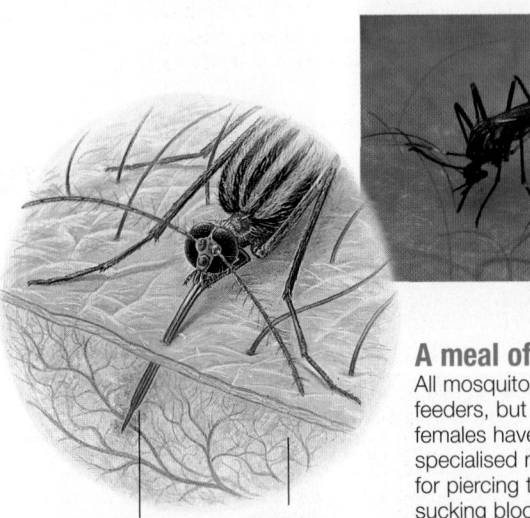

A meal of blood

All mosquitoes are fluid-feeders, but only the females have the specialised mouth-parts for piercing the skin and sucking blood. They need the blood to mature their eggs. Both male and female mosquitoes feed on plant nectar for its energy-giving nutrients.

Human skin

Piercing mouth-parts

Living off the host animal

Some parasites, such as tapeworms and roundworms, live in the host's gut. External parasites, such as fleas, lice, mites and ticks, live on the host's skin, finding their food either on the surface of the skin or by piercing it, usually to suck the host's blood.

Specialised life The human head louse has specialised feet for gripping firmly onto hair shafts. It draws its nutrients from sucking blood.

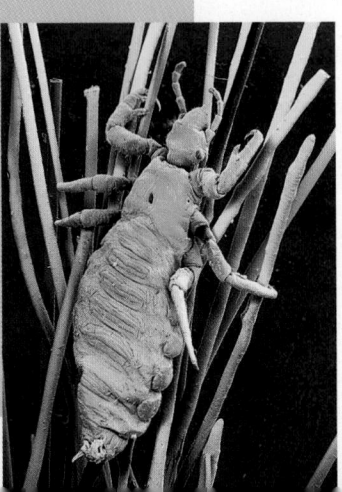

2 Microphagous feeders Because their food consists of tiny particles, which they need a lot of, **microphagous feeders** feed almost continuously. There are two types:
● **Filter-feeders** These range from small, sedentary invertebrate animals like barnacles to baleen whales, the largest creatures on Earth.

Filter-feeders sift their food from water. Barnacles use microscopic hair-like projections called cilia to do this. Baleen whales have plates of a horny substance known as baleen or whalebone on each side of the upper jaw. They use their huge tongues to force water through the plates, which strain out the food particles in the water.

Most filter-feeders live in the water that they feed from, but some, such as flamingoes, are essentially land-living animals.
● **Deposit-feeders** These feed on organic matter within sediments, such as soil, or eat detritus that they scoop or suck off the sea bottom. Starfishes, sea urchins and many molluscs and worms are deposit-feeders. Most do not have specialised feeding structures.

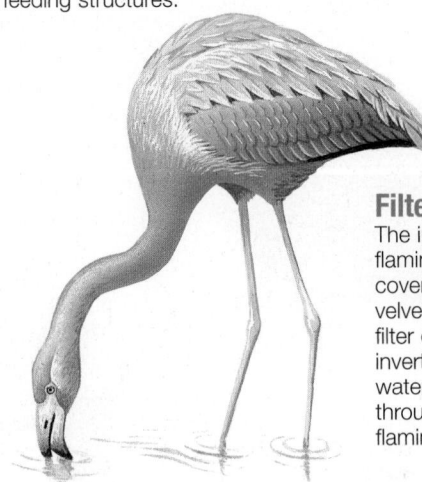

Filtering for food

The inside of a flamingo's bill is covered with tiny, velvet-like hairs. These filter out algae and invertebrates from the water squeezed through them by the flamingo's tongue.

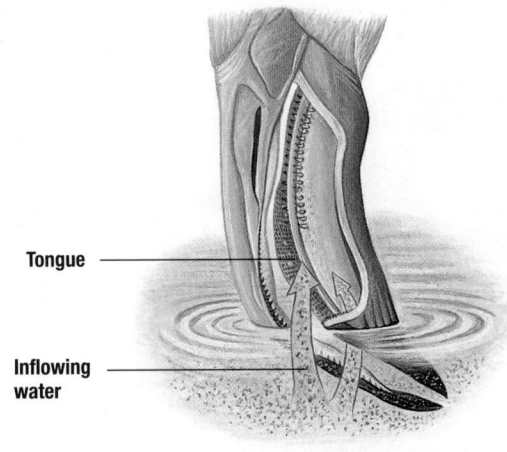

Tongue

Inflowing water

Carnivorous snails

Unlike land-dwelling slugs and snails, the ocean-dwelling gastropod molluscs known as heteropods are all voracious meat-eaters. Heteropods have a swimming fin and locate their prey by sight. They actively hunt other sea creatures, including small fish. Some species grow up to 30 cm (12 in) long.

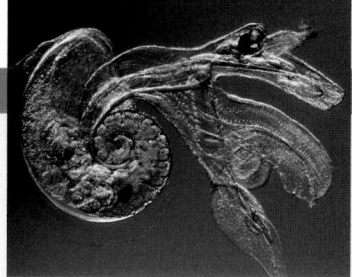

Sharp eyes   Like other heteropods, *Atlanta peronii* has large, projecting eyes (visible here at the top) for locating its prey.

3 Macrophagous feeders

By feeding on large food particles, **macrophagous feeders** are able to be quite selective about what they eat and when they eat it. They include:

🌑 **Carnivores**   Meat-eating animals, such as dogs, cats and crocodiles, either catch prey or scavenge. Their teeth are adapted for piercing, cutting and tearing.

🌑 **Omnivores**   Omnivores, such as humans, eat a mixture of meat and plant material. This is reflected in the structure of their teeth – some are adapted for cutting and others for grinding.

🌑 **Herbivores**   Herbivores live entirely on plant material. Some herbivores, such as rabbits, cows and sheep, crop off grass and other plants at ground level, and are known as grazers. Others, such as giraffes and goats, pluck their food from bushes and trees, and are called browsers.

Specialised food-finding

Of necessity, carnivores have to hunt for their food. Most rely on sight, sound or smell to track down their prey, but some use more sophisticated techniques:

🌑 **Heat**   Two families of snake, the boas and the pit vipers, have developed heat detectors so sensitive that they can effectively see their prey in the dark. Pit vipers can detect changes in temperature as small as 0.0003°C.

🌑 **Electricity**   Some fish such as sharks and rays have specialised organs in their heads which detect the tiny electric currents generated by living creatures. This can help them to hunt in murky waters. The duck-billed platypus also has electricity detectors.

🌑 **Echolocation**   The echolocation used by insectivorous bats is so accurate that they can hunt insects with deadly precision in complete darkness, locating insects as small as midges up to 20 m (70 ft) away. They emit pulses (about ten per second) of very high frequency sounds (up to 200 000 hertz) produced in their larynx. Much of the bat's brain is dedicated to interpreting the reflections of these sounds back to them.

Chewing the cud   Plant matter is difficult to digest. Plant cell walls are composed of a complex sugar called cellulose which is tough and fibrous. To cope with this, herbivores have a longer digestive tract than carnivores. The ruminants, such as cows, have a four-chambered stomach which splits the digestive process into several stages.

see also
74-5 **How plants live**
542-7 **Biology**

4   Next the cud is passed into the third chamber, the omasum, where water is absorbed.

5   Lastly, the residue enters the abomasum, or stomach proper, where the final digestion and absorption of nutrients takes place.

Intestine

Oesophagus

Rumen

Omasum

Reticulum

Abomasum

Diaphragm

1   Food enters the first two chambers, the rumen and the reticulum, where it is partially digested by the enzyme cellulase, secreted by specialised bacteria that live in the gut. Some nutrients are absorbed at this stage.

2   The cow regurgitates the partially digested food, or cud, for further chewing

3   The cud is swallowed back into the reticulum for further digestion.

Extinction is a natural process: 95 per cent of all species that have ever lived, from Tyrannosaurus rex to Neanderthal man, are long since dead and gone. But hundreds of species disappeared in the 20th century because of humankind's unprecedented gift for destruction. These are some of the species which are unlikely to live long into the third millennium.

Shrinking home The golden bamboo lemur was only discovered in 1987. Its habitat is a single small patch of rain forest in the east of Madagascar which has been eroded by slash-and-burn agriculture. Its total population is estimated at 1000. There are currently five golden bamboo lemurs in captivity.

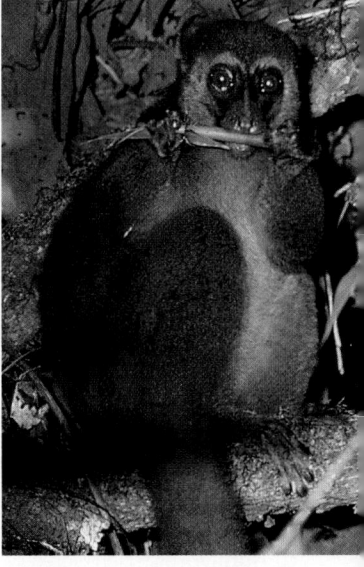

Quantifying the dangers

The factors affecting an animal's chances of survival are varied and complex. They include many immeasurable things such as its 'cuddly' appeal. Any league table of endangered species is therefore misleading. It is impossible to say when one near-extinct species is closer to oblivion than another.

It is not unknown for species to recover unexpectedly, and some benefit from captive breeding programmes that replenish their numbers.

Dying breed This thylacine, or Tasmanian wolf (left), was shot dead in 1930. Although there have been sightings since, and a male thylacine was accidentally killed in 1961, it is now feared that the species is extinct. Thousands of species die out every year – most of them in the rain forests, where we are losing species new to science before they have even been named.

WHY SPECIES DIE OUT

The golden toad (right, pictured in captivity) is one of many species threatened by loss of habitat. No one has seen five in the same place for decades, and it has not been seen at all since 1989. Some species are in natural decline. But the three main threats to species are all the result of human activity: they are hunting, pollution and the destruction of habitat, in particular rain forest, which is exploited for timber or cleared for farm land.

Biting the bullet

The main cause of the decline of the Californian condor is lead poisoning, the result of eating shotgun pellets in carrion. It became extinct in the wild in 1987, when the last one was captured. Since then, captive-bred condors have been released into the wild. They were carefully numbered (see right) and seven are known to have survived.

Passenger pigeon

THE RISING TIDE OF EXTINCTION

Man annihilated 30 or so species in the 17th century and about the same number again in the 18th. Around 100 were destroyed in the 19th century, and hundreds more in the 20th. This list names a few of the animals which are now gone with the exact year of extinction, where it is known.

1600s

Aurochs (1627)

Malagasy elephant bird

Malagasy giant lemur

Dodo (1662)

1700s

Blue antelope (1799)

Leguat's waterhen

Mauritian giant tortoise

Steller's sea cow (1768)

1800s

Great auk (1844)

Burchell's zebra (1883)

Spectacled cormorant (c.1850)

Labrador duck (1875)

Oregon bison (c.1800)

Rat kangaroo

Hare-lipped suckerfish (1893)

Falklands fox (1876)

1900s

Passenger pigeon (1914)

Palestinian painted frog (1956)

Golden bandicoot

Mount Glorious torrent frog

Lesser bilby

Syrian wild ass (1928)

Bali tiger (1937)

Japanese wolf (1905)

Barbary lion (1922)

Pig-footed bandicoot (1925)

Schomburgk's deer

Platypus frog

Martinique muskrat (1902)

Texas red wolf (1970)

Badlands bighorn sheep (1905)

Dodo

Japanese wolf

Among the rarest of all

Fish and amphibians

Chinese paddle fish

Baltic sturgeon

Barnard's rock catfish

Red-finned blue-eye

Aruba Island Ellinopygosteos

Asprete

Dwarf pygmy goby

Ganges shark

Large-tooth sawfish

Golden toad

Mammals

Mediterranean monk seal

Changjiang dolphin

Scimitar-horned oryx

Northern hairy-nosed
  wombat

Ethiopian wolf

Pygmy hog

Kouprey

Javan rhinoceros

Golden bamboo lemur

Birds

Spix's macaw

Californian condor

Kauai oo

Bali starling

Eskimo curlew

Madagascar fish-eagle

Amsterdam albatross

Mauritius parakeet

Mauritius kestrel

Pink pigeon

Insects

Pygmy hog-sucking louse

Delta green ground beetle

Cromwell chafer

St Helena earwig

Queen Alexandra's
  birdwing butterfly

Sri Lankan relict ant

Frey's damselfly

Torreya pygmy grasshopper

Reptiles

Chinese alligator

Orinoco crocodile

Jamaican iguana

Cayman Island ground
  iguana

Aruba Island rattlesnake

Kemp's Ridley sea turtle

Painted terrapin

St Vincent blacksnake

Dahl's toad-headed turtle

Drowned out Kemp's Ridley sea turtle nests only at Ranch Nuevo on the Gulf of Mexico. Fifty years ago 42 000 females were counted in a single day, now only a few hundred remain. The turtles are at risk from fishermen, because they drown when they become entangled in fishing nets.

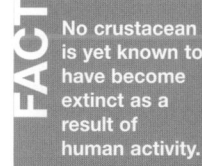

FACT

No crustacean is yet known to have become extinct as a result of human activity.

Fragile beauty Every autumn, monarch butterflies migrate from their breeding grounds in north-eastern North America to forests in the mountains of central Mexico. Logging, however, is threatening these overwintering sites which are vital to their survival. Migrating monarch butterflies are now recognised as an endangered species.

Dying by numbers

At the most recent count, the number of species officially listed as endangered was 5205. Indonesia, China and Brazil have the greatest number of endangered species. This list shows the percentage of threatened animals worldwide:

11 per cent of birds

20 per cent of reptiles

25 per cent of mammals

25 per cent of amphibians

34 per cent of fishes

see also

90-1 **Animal kingdom**

112-3 **Animal records**

124-5 **Protecting species**

Protecting species ▶ | Preserving Earth's biodiversity |

A hundred years ago, overhunting and the introduction of alien species were the causes of most extinctions. Today, the biggest threat is habitat loss. Demands for timber and for land to feed expanding human populations mean that forests and other natural habitats are disappearing faster than ever.

CONSERVATION

The first major steps towards nature conservation were taken in North America in the second half of the 19th century. In 1871, in response to reports of incredible natural wonders, a US government expedition was mounted to investigate a place called Yellowstone in the Rocky Mountains. Their report led President Ulysses S. Grant to declare the area in 1872 the world's first ever national park.

Protecting habitats Since that time, national parks have been set up all over the world. Together with other kinds of sanctuary, such as wildlife refuges and nature reserves, they protect many of the planet's most biologically important and vulnerable habitats from human settlement and agriculture.

Hunting bans At the time that the first national parks were being established, some animals were being hunted to extinction. Protecting individual species by imposing hunting restrictions was the next step, and one of the first creatures to benefit was the northern fur seal (*Callorhinus ursinus*). In 1911, Japan, Russia, Canada and the United States signed a joint treaty to curb hunting, so that populations might increase.

Success story Since the curb on hunting imposed in 1911, the northern fur seal (*Callorhinus ursinus*) has bounced back to repopulate north Pacific coastlines.

Captive breeding and reintroduction
For some creatures, protection in the wild is not enough and the only way of saving the species is to breed from captive populations. The goal of all captive breeding programmes is to establish a large enough bank of animals to make reintroduction into the wild possible. In order for this to be successful, the species' natural habitat has itself to be protected and the risk of hunting removed. Successful captive breeding and reintroduction programmes include that for the Arabian oryx. In 1972, this antelope became extinct in the wild. Today, its wild population numbers 1500, all derived from reintroduced individuals.

North America

Great Plains
Gone for good
Two hundred years ago, the natural grassland known as prairie stretched right across the Great Plains. Today, just a fraction remains and much of that is threatened by overgrazing.

Everglades
Drying out
Canals, floodgates, and levees divert water for fields and towns. Pollution is also a problem.

Shrinking home Loss of habitat threatens the Florida Key deer (*Odocoileus virginianus clavium*).

Amazon Basin
Felled for furniture
The world's largest rain forest is being cleared at a rate of 61 000 km² (24 000 sq miles) a year. Much timber is shipped to developed countries to be used in furniture or building products.

South America

Pampas
Ranch land
Large swathes of these South American grasslands have been turned over to farming, and a lot of what remains is threatened.

Key

■ Forest	■ Deserts
■ Grassland	■ Islands
■ Wetlands	■ Oceans

Restoring degraded habitats

The restoration of habitats degraded by human activity is a relatively new conservation idea, but in areas such as the Mascarene islands of the Indian Ocean, it is already proving a workable option.

Following the arrival of Europeans in Mauritius in the 16th century these islands suffered from the destruction of natural vegetation, hunting of native animals and introduction of alien species. Since the 1980s the creation of protected areas, reintroduction of native species from breeding programmes, and the eradication of alien invaders such as goats and rabbits have met with considerable success.

FACT  One 55 km² (21 sq mile) area of rain forest in Peru was found to be home to no fewer than 1200 species of butterfly.

Spanish forests
Attacked from all sides
Acid rain, intentional forest fires and clearance by farmers degrade the unique Spanish forests.

Aral Sea
Evaporating into the air
The area of the Aral Sea has been reduced by 57 per cent by the damming and the diversion of tributaries for irrigation.

Russia
Indifferent government
Many of Russia's habitats were badly damaged during the Communist era. Prospects for the future look little better as the government elected in 1999 begins to dismantle environmental laws.

China
Tide of humanity
Like its neighbour India, China has a vast population putting enormous demands on its land and pressure on its natural habitats.

Asia

Europe

India
Trodden underfoot
With a human population of almost a billion and rising, all of India's natural habitats are severely threatened.

South-east Asia
Population pressures
Logged for profit and burned to make way for farm land, less than a quarter of the original forest remains.

Sahel
Sea of sand
Overgrazed by livestock and cleared of timber for firewood, the semiarid Sahel is rapidly becoming desert proper.

Africa

Ethiopian highlands
Delicate issue
Overgrazing and loss of grasslands to crops threaten this area's fragile natural balance.

Up in the branches The lar gibbon (*Hylobates concolor*) is just one creature threatened by deforestation in South-east Asia.

Zaire Basin
Chipping away
Although less heavily logged than other rain forests, the Zaire Basin is losing almost 1 per cent of its tree cover every year.

Rodriguez Island
Eaten away
Deforestation and grazing by sheep, cattle and goats, all introduced species, have obliterated almost all natural island habitats.

Philippine reefs
Blown up and poisoned
Fishing with dynamite and cyanide have destroyed huge areas of coral reef, and still continue illegally.

Australasia

Malagasy forests
Almost gone
If current felling rates continue, Madagascar will have lost all of its forest by 2006.

Mauritius
Lost with the dodo
Just 3 per cent of the forest that once covered these islands remains, although work is under way to repair the damage (see box: *Restoring degraded habitats*).

Tasmanian forests
Under pressure
Although better protected than it once was, Tasmania's temperate rain forest continues to be logged and clear-felled for new plantations.

Nowhere to hide Its number already reduced by hunting, the unique aye-aye (*Daubentonia madagascariensis*) may soon be homeless too.

What is biodiversity?

Biodiversity is an expression of the variety of life in a certain area. This can mean the number of species (species richness) and their abundance, or the range of types of organism (species diversity) or a combination of the two. Different habitats have different natural levels of biodiversity. Rain forests, for example, with their great range and number of species have a higher biodiversity than deserts.

Maintaining biodiversity is important because species that share a habitat are interdependent – if one becomes extinct it has a knock-on effect on the rest. In extreme cases, the loss of one species may lead to the extinction of others dependent upon it.

From a human perspective, if we lose species, we risk losing sources of lifesaving drugs – most modern medicines are ultimately derived from wild plants.

see also
90-1 **Animal kingdom**
112-3 **Animal records**
122-3 **Endangered species**

Homo sapiens is the only representative of the hominid family alive today. But around 1–2 million years ago, several hominid species coexisted. Because the study of early man has been made largely through the fossil record which is incomplete, it is not clear how these species were related. Much of what has been inferred is conjectural, although recent techniques, such as comparative biochemistry, have helped to fill the gaps.

WHAT IS A HOMINID?

● A hominid is **a primate**. The other primates are prosimians, monkeys, gorillas, chimpanzees and orang-utans.
● It is **bipedal**, that is, two-footed, and consequently will **walk upright**.
● It has a relatively **large brain**.
　There are two confirmed genera of hominids: *Australopithecus* and *Homo*. The genus *Ardipithecus* may eventually be classified as the earliest-known hominid.

① 30 million years ago
Aegyptopithecus, perhaps the first man-like ape or hominoid, is living in what is now Egypt.

4.2–3.9 million years ago
Australopithecus anamensis appears in East Africa. It is the earliest-known member of the australopithecines – a group of true hominids (see box above), as distinct from man-like apes or hominoids. Although this species has a rather ape-like jaw, its leg bones clearly show that it walked upright.

③ 4–3 million years ago
Australopithecus afarensis is living in various parts of Africa. This is the last common ancestor to all the known species of hominid that emerge later. On average less than 1.5 m (5 ft) tall, with a small brain, long arms and short legs, evidence also suggests that there is a marked difference in size between the sexes. 'Lucy', the first fossil of this species ever found, appears to have been just 1.1 m (3 ft 8 in) tall.

10 million years ago
Afropithecus appears in East Africa, Asia and Europe. They have teeth with thickened tooth enamel, probably as a result of changing to a diet of hard fruit, roots and nuts. Heavily enamelled teeth last longer, enabling the animal that has them to feed efficiently to a greater age. This eventually leads to an increase in the average life span.

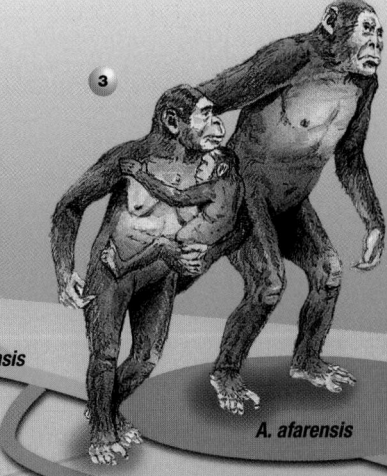

A. anamensis

10–5 million years ago
Gap in the fossil record

A. ramidus

A. afarensis

② 20–16 million years ago
Proconsul, a small ape that is believed to be a common ancestor of both modern apes and humans, lives in the tropical rain forests of Africa. It clambers along the branches of the trees on all fours.

4.4 million years ago
The ape-like **Ardipithecus ramidus** lives in the area now known as Ethiopia. It probably walks upright on two legs, leading some experts to class it as the first true hominid.

A. bahrelghazali

3.5–3 million years ago
Australopithecus bahrelghazali appears in Africa. It is similar to *Australopithecus afarensis*, but with a less ape-like jaw.

Two legs good . . .

Becoming bipedal – walking upright on two legs – played a key role in the evolution of human intelligence. There are two major reasons for this. First, bipedalism requires greater coordination, leading to a more developed nervous system and larger brain. Secondly, it frees the hands for carrying and manipulation. The consequent development of manipulative skills, such as those required for toolmaking, also encourages brain development.
　Being upright confers other advantages. It increases height, which is useful for spying prey and predators in the open savannah. It also helps to keep the body cool, by raising it up, away from the hot ground and closer to cooling air currents above. It also minimises the body area being exposed to the heating effect of strong sunlight.

Standing tall Humans are not alone in walking upright. Occasionally, apes do too, but less efficiently. Their anatomy is not so well adapted as that of humans to being bipedal. There are disadvantages to being upright. Bipeds cannot run as fast as quadrupeds, and the extra wear and tear bipedalism places on the hips, back and knees can lead to disabilities.

Gorilla
Centre of gravity in front of hips

Leg swings forward

Human
Centre of gravity between hips

Knee locks to support the body's weight

Feet are directly under hips and knees

The invention of human society

All primates lead complex social lives, so being socially adept is often more important than appearance or physical prowess. Developing the necessary social skills makes intense intellectual demands, which has helped to develop primate, and particularly human, intelligence.

Features of the development of human social organisation
◗ Larger brains and changes in the voice box lead to greater manipulative abilities and the development of speech.
◗ Use of fire allows groups to stay in one place, at least temporarily, as it provides warmth and protection.
◗ Manufacture and use of tools increases food-gathering efficiency.
◗ Complex communication skills, both verbal and visual, allow for cooperation to find food.
◗ Sharing of food leads to communal living and social organisation.
◗ Division of labour: the males hunt together; the females educate the children.
◗ Immature young and a long infancy and childhood create the need for parental supervision and encourages the formation of groups to share childrearing.
◗ Communal living, increased security and complex communication skills lead to the emergence of culture, such as art, spiritual belief and ritual.
◗ Long childhood allows time for individuals to acquire the culture of their social group.

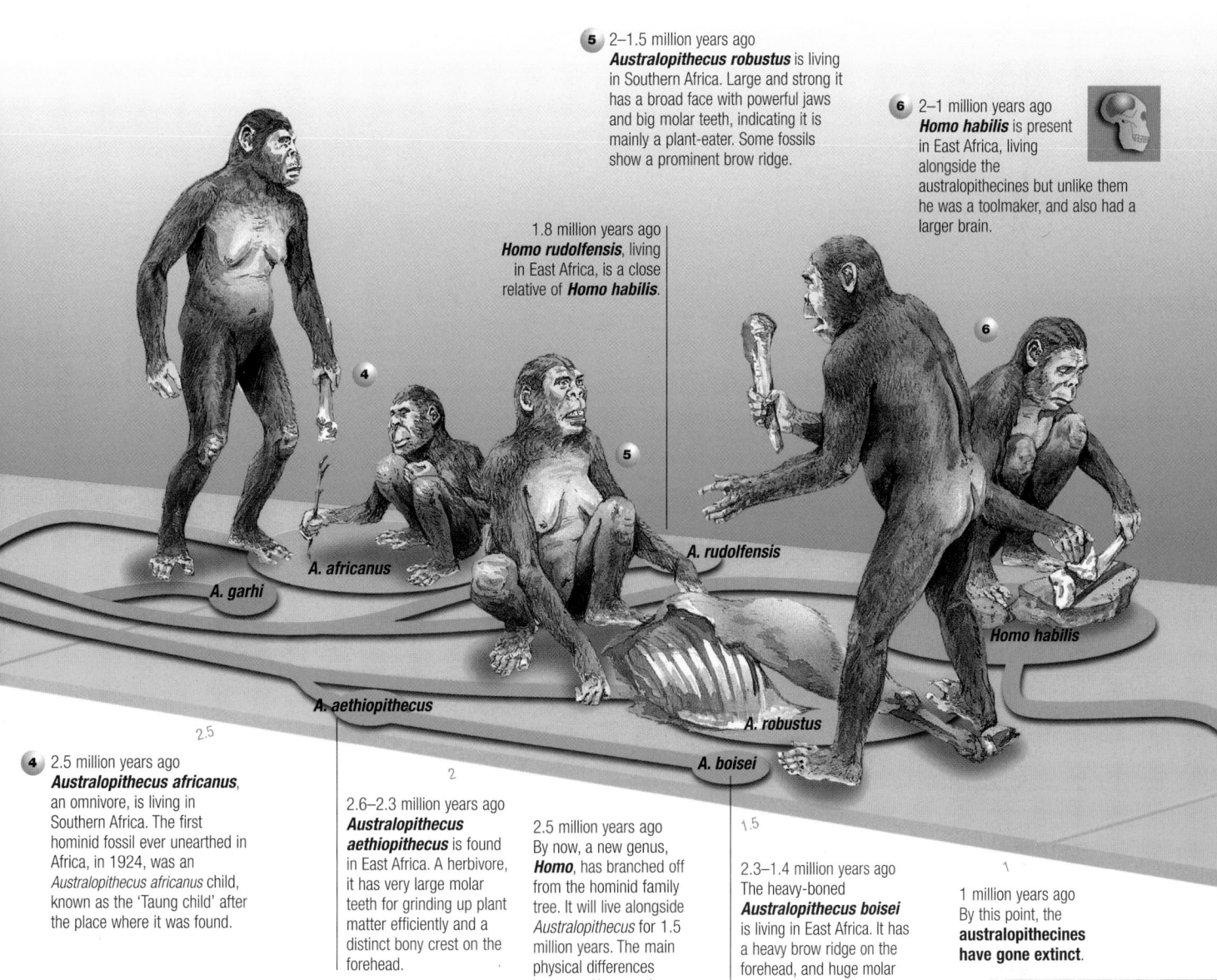

5 2–1.5 million years ago
Australopithecus robustus is living in Southern Africa. Large and strong it has a broad face with powerful jaws and big molar teeth, indicating it is mainly a plant-eater. Some fossils show a prominent brow ridge.

6 2–1 million years ago
Homo habilis is present in East Africa, living alongside the australopithecines but unlike them he was a toolmaker, and also had a larger brain.

1.8 million years ago
Homo rudolfensis, living in East Africa, is a close relative of *Homo habilis*.

A. garhi

A. africanus

A. rudolfensis

A. aethiopithecus

A. robustus

A. boisei

Homo habilis

4 2.5 million years ago
Australopithecus africanus, an omnivore, is living in Southern Africa. The first hominid fossil ever unearthed in Africa, in 1924, was an *Australopithecus africanus* child, known as the 'Taung child' after the place where it was found.

2.6–2.3 million years ago
Australopithecus aethiopithecus is found in East Africa. A herbivore, it has very large molar teeth for grinding up plant matter efficiently and a distinct bony crest on the forehead.

2.5 million years ago
By now, a new genus, *Homo*, has branched off from the hominid family tree. It will live alongside *Australopithecus* for 1.5 million years. The main physical differences between *Homo* and *Australopithecus* are *Homo*'s
◗ increased brain size
◗ finer jaw with smaller teeth
◗ new position of the voice box, which will eventually make speech possible.

2.3–1.4 million years ago
The heavy-boned *Australopithecus boisei* is living in East Africa. It has a heavy brow ridge on the forehead, and huge molar teeth, which suggest that it is predominantly a plant-eater. Males are much larger and heavier set than females.

1 million years ago
By this point, the **australopithecines have gone extinct**.

see also
66-7 **Evolution explained**
88-9 **Rise of the mammals**
128-9 **Emergence of man**

For 200 000 years, the dominant human species in Europe and Asia was Homo neanderthalensis. *The Neanderthals were short and stocky, they lived in sophisticated social groups and had larger brains than modern man. Yet around 30 000 years ago they were ousted from their dominant position and driven to extinction by new arrivals from Africa –* Homo sapiens.

NEANDERTHAL MAN

Neanderthals appeared in Europe about 250 000 years ago – the name comes from the Neander Valley, near Dusseldorf, Germany, where remains were first found in 1856. There is ample evidence to suggest that the Neanderthals were cultural beings. Skilfully wrought stone tools and jewellery have been found. Graves show that they buried

9 200 000–140 000 years ago
Homo sapiens evolves in sub-Saharan Africa. He is lighter-built than *Homo neanderthalensis*, but his level of culture and technology is similar.
Other key features:
◔ He is capable of complex speech.
◔ He uses fire for cooking, as well as for smoking and drying meat to preserve it.
◔ He wears a wide range of clothing.

700 000 years ago
Homo heidelbergensis evolves from *Homo erectus* populations in Africa and Europe. He is tall – over 1.8 m (6 ft) – with a powerful anatomy and a large brain. Other key features:
◔ He can control fire.
◔ He is capable of more competent speech than *Homo erectus*.
◔ He makes a wider range of stone tools than *Homo erectus*, including hand axes, cleavers and butchering tools.

600 000 years ago
The Earth's climate starts to fluctuate dramatically, resulting in a **series of ice ages**. Surviving these climatic extremes requires flexible and resourceful behaviour. Thus natural selection will favour the more intelligent, resourceful larger-brained individuals.

c.120 000 years ago
Homo sapiens sapiens (modern man) evolves.

100 000 years ago
Homo sapiens sapiens starts to spread from Africa into Europe and Asia, where he lives alongside *Homo neanderthalensis*.

7

8

9

10

H. erectus

H. heidelbergensis

H. neanderthalensis

H. sapiens

H. sapiens sapiens

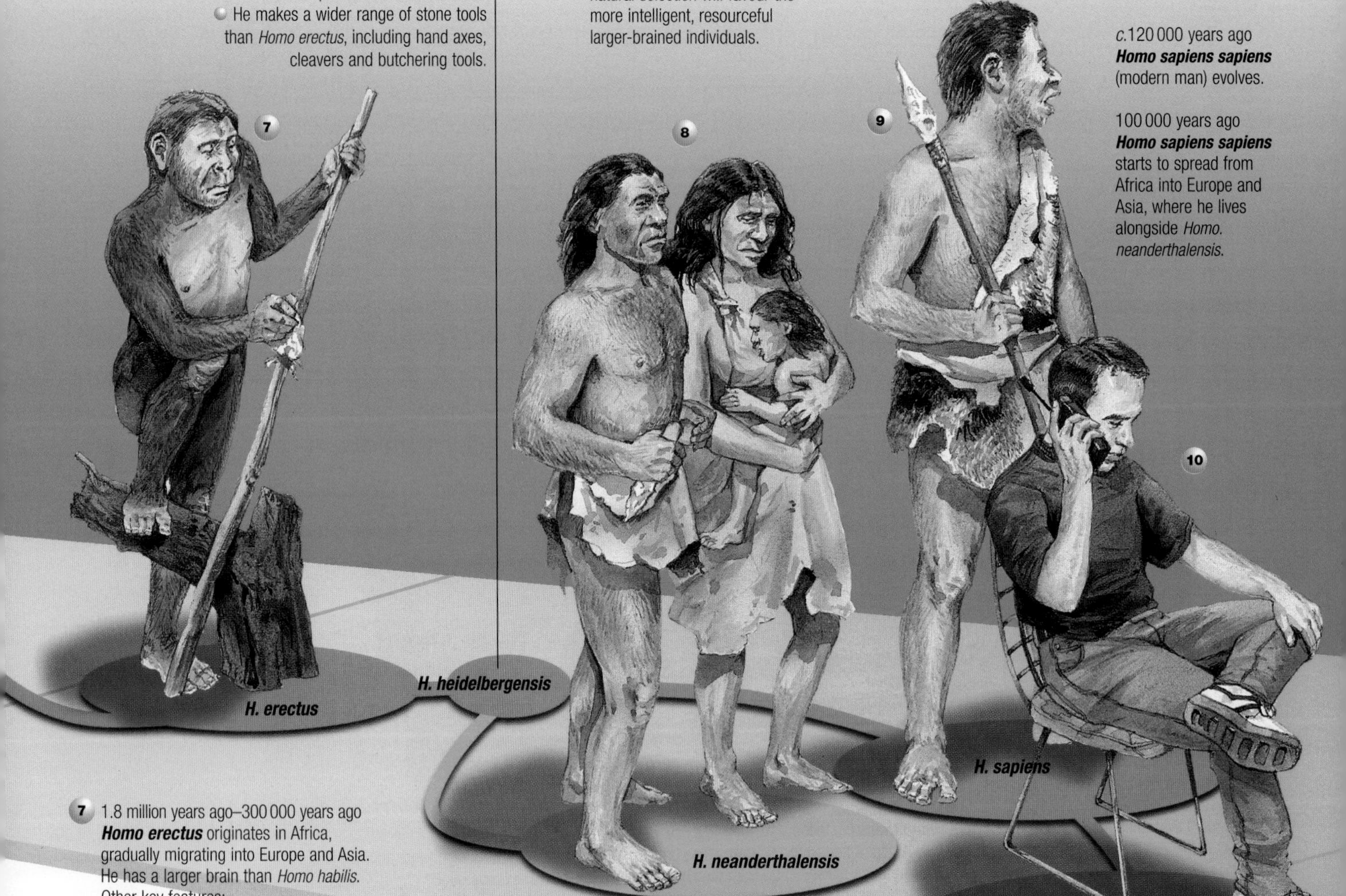

7 1.8 million years ago–300 000 years ago
Homo erectus originates in Africa, gradually migrating into Europe and Asia. He has a larger brain than *Homo habilis*.
Other key features:
◔ He is a toolmaker, producing scrapers, axes and cleavers.
◔ He is a meat-eater, so probably has a more nutritious diet than earlier hominids, which helps brain development.
◔ Remains suggest he was capable of rudimentary speech.
◔ There is some evidence that he used fire.
◔ He is well adapted to cope with big variations in climate.

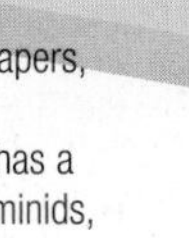

8 250 000–30 000 years ago
Homo neanderthalensis is living in Europe and Asia. He is stockier and shorter than modern humans – about 1.68 m (5 ft 6 in) tall – but has a bigger brain.
Other key features:
◔ His anatomy implies that he uses complex speech.
◔ He shows evidence of cultural development in terms of art and spiritual belief.
◔ He uses fire for heating, and possibly cooking.
◔ He wears clothes made from hide and fur, and also uses jewellery.

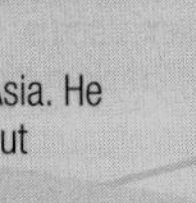

10 30 000 years ago
Homo sapiens sapiens is now the only species of the genus *Homo*. The rapid cultural and technological development from primitive man to modern man in just 30 000 years has made *Homo sapiens sapiens* the dominant species on Earth.

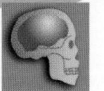

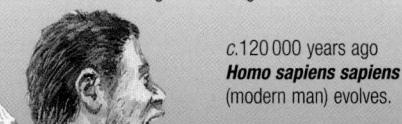

their dead with some ceremony. Skeletons with serious, but healed injuries and advanced arthritis indicate that they cared for their old and infirm. They also used fire – vital for survival in the cold climate of the period.

So why did these strong, intelligent hominids die out about 30 000 years ago? The most likely theory is that they were simply outclassed by the more adaptable *Homo sapiens sapiens* – also known as 'Cro-Magnon man', named after the place in the Dordogne, France, where they were first found.

Beneath the skin A marked brow ridge, low forehead and receding lower jaw distinguish the Neanderthal skull (above left) from the Cro-Magnon (above, right).

The rise of *Homo sapiens* Cro-Magnon

man started moving into Europe from Africa about 100 000 years ago, initially living alongside the Neanderthals. Then, around 40 000 years ago, Cro-Magnon culture advanced rapidly, enabling them eventually to displace their less adaptable Neanderthal neighbours.

Two main theories have been put forward to explain the evolution of *Homo sapiens*. The 'Candelabra' – a reference to different branches of *Homo* evolution – theory says that they developed simultaneously from populations of different *Homo* species in Asia, Europe and Africa. The more favoured 'Out of Africa' theory postulates that they evolved from a single, African stock, and began to spread to the rest of the world just 100 000 years ago.

DNA analysis of Neanderthal remains shows that they cannot be the ancestors of modern man. Other DNA research (see Mitochondrial Eve, right) indicates that everyone alive today is descended from a human population living in Africa 140 000 to 200 000 years ago.

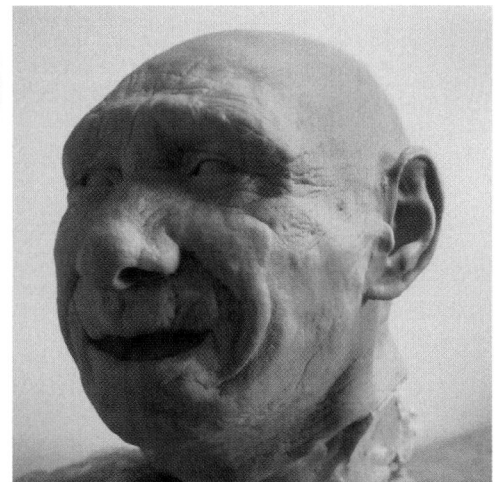

Face from the past This reconstruction, based on a skull found at Monte Circeo in Italy, shows that the Neanderthal face was not so dissimilar from ours.

Mitochondrial Eve

In 1986 researchers at the University of California concluded that all humans were descended from a single woman who lived in Africa some 200 000 years ago. They based this on analysis of DNA taken from the mitochondria, specific parts of the human cell. This DNA differs from DNA in the cell nucleus and it passes only through the female line. It mutates at a very rapid but steady rate. By comparing the mitochondrial DNA of women from various ethnic groups, they could estimate how long it took for each group to diverge from a common ancestor. In effect, they constructed a family tree for mankind, at the base of which was the Mitochondrial Eve, everyone's 10 000th great grandmother. This doesn't mean that she was the only woman in existence, but that it is her lineage that has survived to the present day.

see also
66-7 **Evolution explained**
88-9 **Rise of the mammals**

Origins of race

Despite physical differences between the ethnic groups that make up the species *Homo sapiens*, all modern humans are remarkably similar genetically.

Several theories have been proposed to explain the origin of race. The Candelabra theory of evolution proposed that Asians, Australian Aborigines and modern Africans among others, emerged from *Homo* *erectus* populations, while white people evolved from European Neanderthals. Recent research has disproved this theory.

The categorisation of humans by race is now seen as having little meaning. The physical differences on which we base 'race' are essentially minor adaptations to environmental conditions. Narrow, prominent noses, for example, are advantageous in a cold climate, because they are better at warming chilly air as it enters the body. Skin colour corresponds largely to latitude. In hot, tropical regions, high levels of the dark pigment melanin protect the skin from the harmful effects of strong sunlight. Skin colour is no more significant genetically than the difference between a black cat and a tabby.

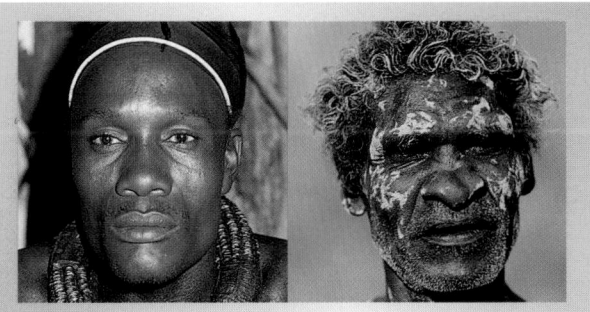

The human body

The Beauty of the Human Body

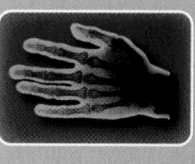

The adult skeleton provides the body's internal scaffolding; it is made up of 206 bones and accounts for one-fifth of the body's total weight. Muscles control movement throughout the body, including automatic actions such as heartbeat, movement of the gut and blinking. Muscles make up over half the body's total weight.

THE SKELETON

The skeleton supports the body, protects internal organs, and allows a wide variety of movement. Most bones are connected together by ligaments to form flexible joints.

Cartilage A type of connective tissue, cartilage forms shock-absorbing discs between vertebrae, gives elasticity and strength to the knee joint, and surrounds the end of every long bone where it meets other bones to form a joint. It also joins the ribs to the breastbone.

MUSCLES

There are three kinds of muscle. Striped muscle, so called because of its striated appearance under the microscope, makes up the majority. It contracts in response to messages from the brain. Smooth muscle is not under conscious control. It controls the digestive, urinary, reproductive and circulatory systems, and such unconscious responses as adjusting the iris in the eye. Cardiac muscle is found only in the heart, and is unique in being able to contract rhythmically and continuously.

THE SPINE

An adult's spine consists of 26 bones called vertebrae. It is divided into four sections.

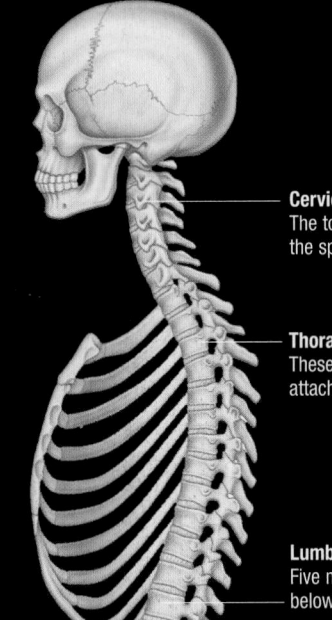

Cervical vertebrae
The top seven bones of the spine in the neck.

Thoracic vertebrae
These 12 vertebrae are attached to the ribs.

Lumbar vertebrae
Five more vertebrae are below the ribs.

Sacrum and coccyx
The sacrum is made of five vertebrae and the coccyx of four. In adults the vertebrae are fused together.

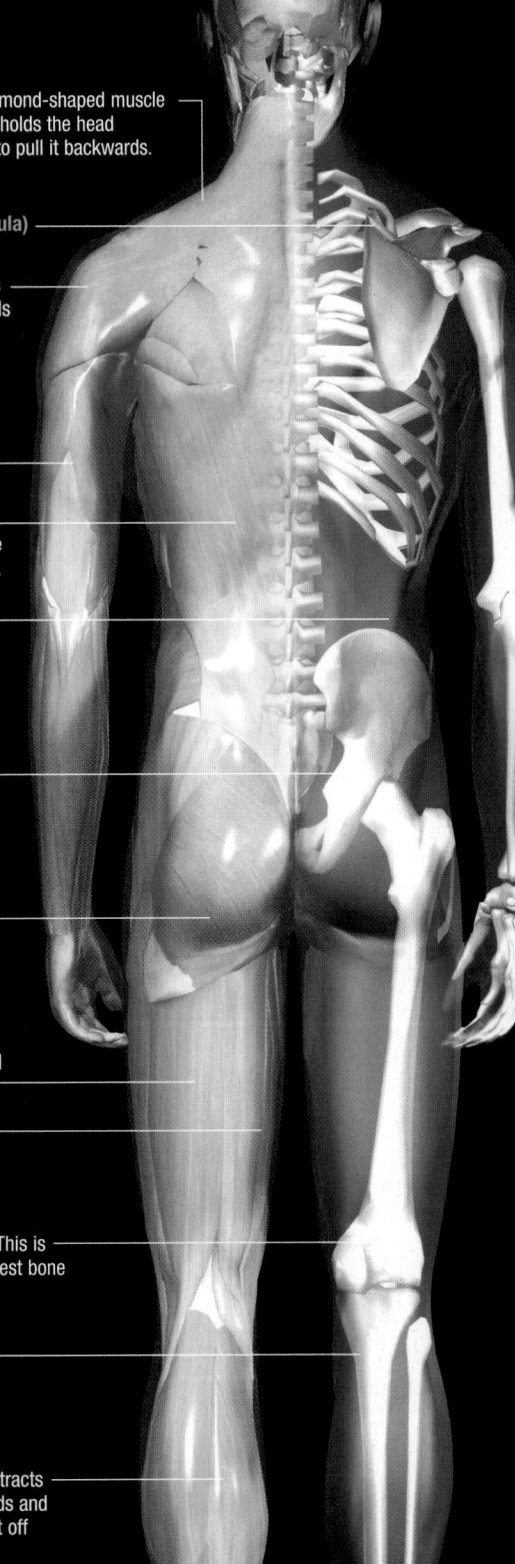

Trapezius A large, diamond-shaped muscle in the upper back, this holds the head straight and contracts to pull it backwards.

Shoulder blade (scapula)

Shoulder deltoid This raises the arm outwards from the body.

Triceps This contracts to straighten the arm.

Latissimus dorsi This large back muscle holds the body upright.

Ribs These protect internal organs and the chest cavity.

Hip (ilium) Outer part of the pelvic girdle.

Gluteus maximus This is the largest muscle in the body.

Hamstring muscles These contract to bend the leg at the knee.

Adductor muscles These contract to pull the leg inwards.

Thigh bone (femur) This is the longest and strongest bone in the body.

Shinbone (tibia) This is the major load-bearing bone of the lower leg.

Calf muscle This contracts to pull the heel upwards and lift the back of the foot off the ground.

Fibula The smaller of the two lower leg bones.

Achilles' tendon This tough cord links the bottom of the calf muscle to the heel and pulls the heel upwards when the calf muscle contracts.

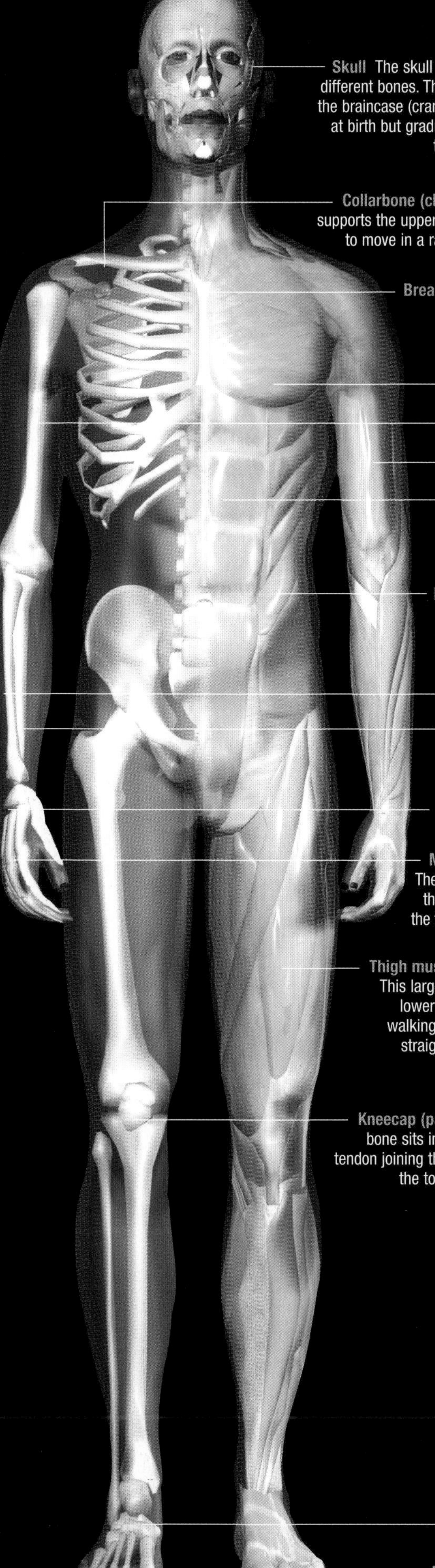

Skull The skull is formed from 22 different bones. The bones that form the braincase (cranium) are separate at birth but gradually fuse together through childhood.
Collarbone (clavicle) This bone supports the upper arm and allows it to move in a range of directions.
Breastbone (sternum) This bony plate connects the ribs.
Pectoral muscle
Humerus
Biceps
Trunk deltoids These muscles contract to bend the body forward.
External obliques These muscles contract to twist the torso.
Radius
Ulna
Wrist bones (carpals) There are eight of these in each wrist.
Metacarpal bones The five long bones of the hand that lead to the fingers and thumb.
Thigh muscle (quadriceps) This large muscle pulls the lower leg forward when walking and holds the leg straight when standing.
Kneecap (patella) This small bone sits inside the cord-like tendon joining the thigh muscle to the top of the shinbone.
Heel bones

HOW DO MUSCLES WORK?

Muscles produce movement by contracting, and are arranged in opposing pairs or groups. The illustration shows one of these pairs. To raise the forearm, the biceps at the front of the upper arm contract and shorten while the triceps at the back relax and lengthen. To lower the forearm, the actions of these muscles are reversed. The biceps are stronger than the triceps because raising the arm works against the pull of gravity.

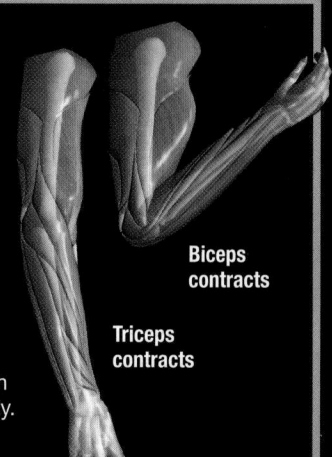

Biceps contracts
Triceps contracts

Joints between bones

There are two categories of joint:
Fixed joints Places where bones become fused together and there is little or no movement, such as in the skull.
Synovial joints Lubricated joints that allow free movement.

The six types of synovial joint

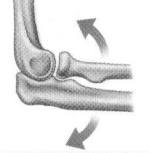

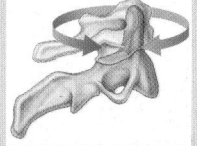

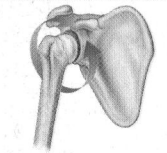

Hinge Movement in one plane only, as at the elbow. Round end of one bone fits the scooped end of other.

Pivot A projection from one bone turns within a ring-shaped socket on another, as in vertebrae.

Ball and socket Circular movement as at the hip. Close fit of ball-ended bone into rounded socket.

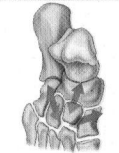

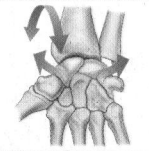

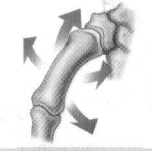

Gliding A joint where the flat surfaces of bones slide over each other. Gliding joints occur in the foot.

Ellipsoidal The egg-shaped end of one bone fits into the elliptical cavity of another, as at the wrist.

Saddle This kind of joint occurs at the base of the thumb. It allows for limited movement in two planes.

All the bones in the body

There are four classes of bone: long bones (limbs); short bones (wrist and ankles); flat bones (skull); and irregular bones (face, vertebrae). The bones of the hands and feet constitute half the total number of bones in the body.

Skull	22	Pectoral girdle	4
Ears	6	Hip bones	2
Vertebrae	26	Arms (2 x 30)	60
Vertebral ribs	24	Legs (2 x 29)	58
Sternum	3		
Throat	1	**Total**	**206**

see also
134-5 **The brain and nerves**
138 **Glands and hormones**
154-5 **Human capacity**
160-1 **Disorders/diseases**

The brain and nerves ▶

The brain and nervous system control our perceptions, thoughts and voluntary actions, and also most of the body's internal processes. The brain is contained within the hard bones of the skull and cushioned against injury by surrounding membranes, while the spinal cord – the central pathway of the nervous system – runs through a channel within the tough vertebrae of the spine.

THE BRAIN

There are three major areas in the brain: the cerebrum, the cerebellum and the brain stem.

The cerebrum is the largest part of the brain, and is associated with conscious activities and intelligence. It is divided into two hemispheres, and consists of grey matter (neuron cells) and white matter (nerve fibres).

The brain is wrapped in three separate membranes. The space between these membranes contains fluid, which allows the brain to float and thus insulates it from knocks to the head. The same membranes extend over the spinal cord.

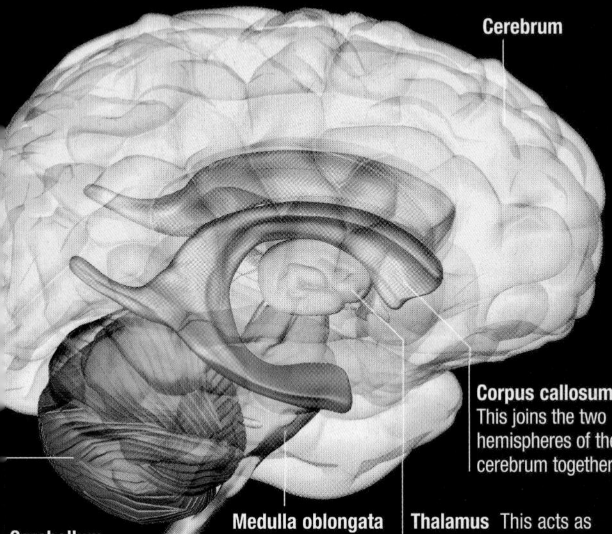

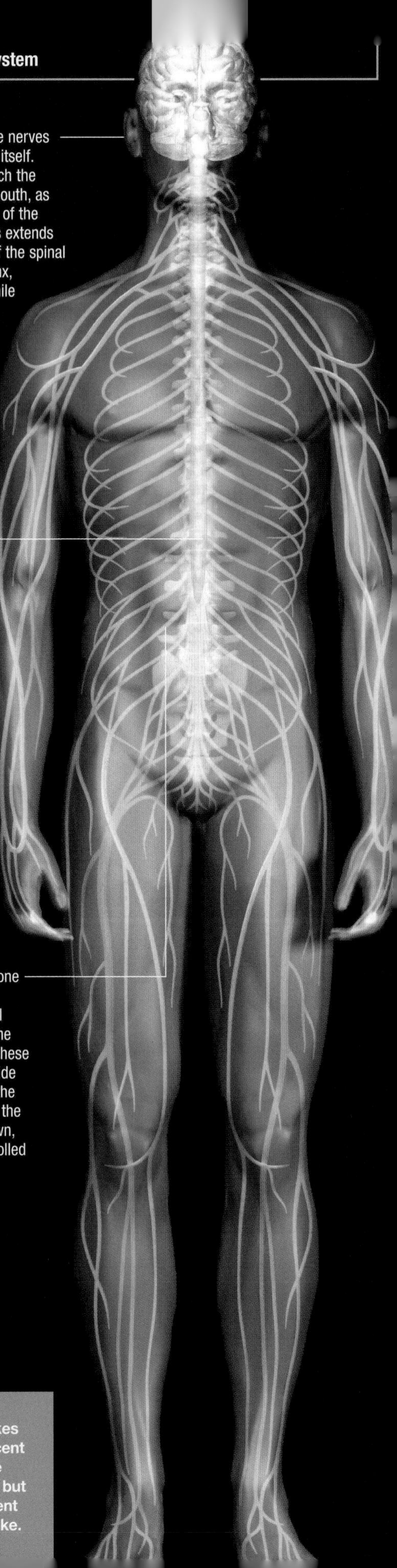

Cranial nerves Twelve nerves emerge from the brain itself. These subdivide to reach the eyes, nose, ears and mouth, as well as all the muscles of the face. One of the nerves extends down, independently of the spinal cord, to the heart, larynx, lungs and stomach, while another goes to muscles in the neck, where it helps to control the vocal apparatus.

Spinal cord This runs from the brain stem down through the vertebrae to just below the 12th rib in the lumbar region of the back. It varies in length from 37 to 45 cm (15 to 18 in) depending on the height of the person, and is about as thick as a little finger.

Spinal nerves Thirty-one pairs of large nerves emerge from the spinal cord through gaps at the rear of the vertebrae. These then divide and subdivide to reach every part of the body, from the back of the head and the neck down, apart from those controlled by the cranial nerves.

Cerebrum

Corpus callosum This joins the two hemispheres of the cerebrum together.

Cerebellum This part of the brain coordinates movement and balance.

Medulla oblongata This controls heart rate and breathing.

Brain stem This connects the brain to the spinal cord.

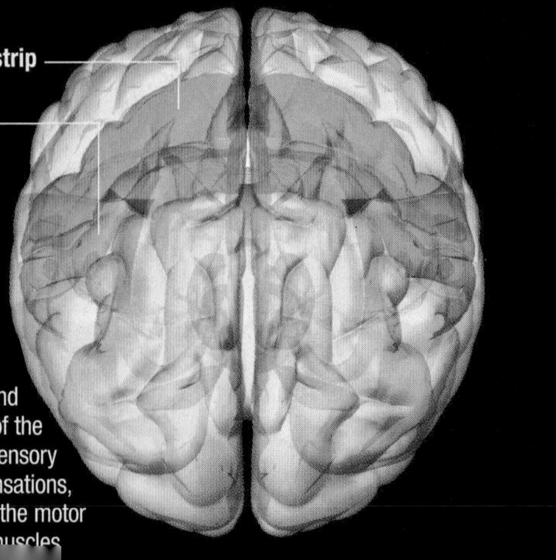

Thalamus This acts as a sort of junction box, sending incoming nerve impulses to different areas of the brain.

Somatosensory strip

Motor strip

Cerebral cortex Different parts of the cerebral cortex (the outer surface of the cerebrum, seen here from above) process information from and for different parts of the body. The somatosensory strip processes sensations, for instance, while the motor strip controls the muscles.

FACT The brain makes up just 2 per cent of the average adult's weight but uses 20 per cent of oxygen intake.

THE NERVOUS SYSTEM

A network of nerves extends throughout our bodies, carrying sensory information to the brain and instructions from it. The brain and the spinal cord together form the central nervous system (CNS); the rest of the network is known as the peripheral nervous system (PNS).

The spinal cord

The spinal cord is an extension of the brain and is formed from the same grey and white matter, although it is organised differently from that in the brain, with the grey matter on the inside and the white matter on the outside.

The spinal cord channels nerve signals from every part of the body to the brain and carries messages back again. It is more than just a connecting cable, however. Many nerve signals are processed in the spinal cord itself, including most reflex actions. By bypassing the brain in this way, response times become much faster, enabling the body to react to potential danger extremely quickly. The knee-jerk reaction is the best-known reflex, but others include the instant removal of a hand from a hot object. It is only after the hand has been removed that the brain registers what has happened and we feel pain.

Nerve root Several nerve roots combine to form each spinal nerve. Roots entering the back of the spinal cord bring messages from the muscles and skin. Those leaving from the front (not shown) carry instructions to them.

Tracts These bundles of nerve fibres run through the spinal cord to and from the brain

Spinal nerve Thirty-one spinal nerves emerge from each side of the spinal cord. Only the bases of the nerves are shown in this illustration.

Protective membranes As in the brain, the nerve tissue of the spinal cord is encased by three separate fluid-filled membranes.

Vertebra The spinal cord is encased by the bones of the spine, or vertebrae, which protect it from damage. The rear of one vertebra is shown here.

NERVE STRUCTURE

The nerve cell or neuron is the fundamental unit in the nervous system. Each neuron has a cell body with a nucleus and the metabolic structures found in other kinds of cell. Extending from the cell body is a nerve cell fibre, or axon, which carries signals to other cells. Axons are microscopically thin but some can be up to 1 m (39 in) long, for example the ones that extend from the spinal cord to the fingertips. They are encased in sheaths of the protein myelin, which insulate them and help to increase the speed at which they carry nerve impulses.

Neurons do not connect with each other directly. Information is passed from one to another at an interface, called a synapse. Here, a chemical substance called a neurotransmitter is released, which carries the impulses across the gap to a branching dendrite from another neuron. Each axon may end in several synapses, enabling it to link with more than one other neuron.

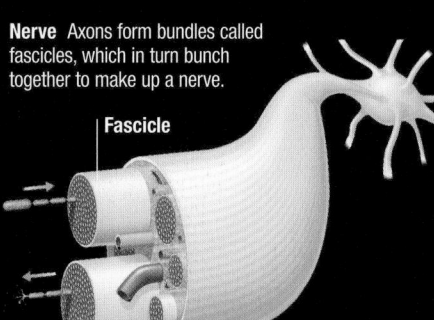

Nerve Axons form bundles called fascicles, which in turn bunch together to make up a nerve.

Fascicle

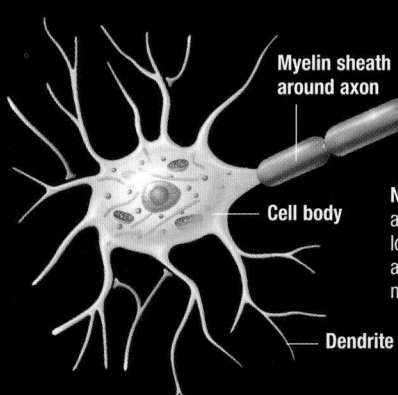

Myelin sheath around axon

Cell body

Neuron With their far-reaching axons, neurons are by far the longest cells in the body. There are more than 1000 billion neurons in the brain alone.

Synapse

Dendrite

Different types of nerve cell

There are three types of nerve cell or neuron:
Sensory neurons Carry information from sensory receptors to the central nervous system (CNS).
Motor neurons Carry information from the CNS to the organs and muscles.
Association neurons Found only in the CNS, these link sensory and motor nerves, and transport incoming messages to the brain, where they are interpreted, and the appropriate instructions sent out.

FACTS AND FIGURES

● The brain has about 1000 billion nerve cells.
● Signals travel along nerves at up to 360 km/h (225 mph): a message sent from head to toe arrives in about 1/50 of a second.
● The left hemisphere of the brain controls the right side of the body and vice-versa. Some 90 per cent of the human population is right-handed, which means that the left hemispheres of their brains are dominant.
● The average adult male brain weighs 1.4 kg (3 lb); the average adult female brain 1.25 kg (2 3/4 lb).
● The mass of brain tissue reaches a maximum at the age of 20 years, and thereafter decreases.
● The spinal cord stops growing when a child reaches four years old. After that, only the spinal nerves continue to grow

Circulation and breathing ▶

Every cell in the body needs oxygen to function. Oxygen from the air passes into the bloodstream from the lungs. Oxygenated blood is then pumped by the heart to all the cells in the body. The circulatory system also transports nutrients and other vital substances, as well as carrying away the body's waste products, such as carbon dioxide.

THE CIRCULATORY SYSTEM

Arteries Vessels that carry blood away from the heart. They have muscular walls that help to pump the blood at high pressure. Apart from the pulmonary artery, they carry oxygenated blood, which is bright red.

Veins Vessels that carry blood at low pressure back to the heart. Valves along their length prevent backflow. Apart from the pulmonary vein, they carry dark-coloured deoxygenated blood, which gives veins their blue colour.

Capillaries Arteries and veins are connected within tissues by tiny capillaries. Oxygen and other substances pass between blood and tissues through the thin capillary walls.

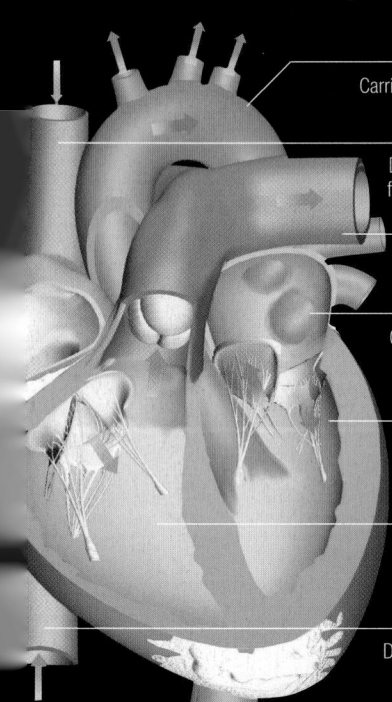

Aorta
Carries oxygenated blood away from the heart

Superior vena cava
Drains deoxygenated blood from arms and upper body.

Pulmonary artery
Takes deoxygenated blood to the lungs.

Left atrium
Oxygenated blood from the lungs enters here through the pulmonary vein.

Left ventricle
Oxygenated blood is pumped from here into the aorta.

Right ventricle
Deoxygenated blood is pumped from here into the pulmonary artery.

Inferior vena cava
Drains blood from the lower body and the legs.

Pumping blood

The heart is divided into a right and a left side by a muscular wall.

● The left side pumps oxygenated blood from the lungs around the body.

● The right side receives deoxygenated blood from the body and pumps it to the lungs to be reoxygenated.

● Each side of the heart consists of two chambers, an atrium and a ventricle.

● The chambers are separated by valves, which open to let blood through then close to prevent it flowing backwards.

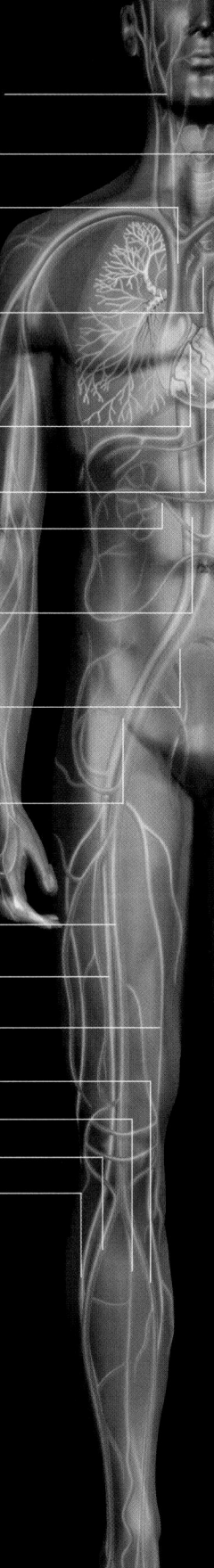

Common carotid artery
Supplies blood to the head.

Subclavian artery
Supplies blood to the arms.

Superior vena cava
Carries deoxygenated blood from the head and arms.

Aorta
Takes oxygenated blood to the head and body, and is the largest blood vessel.

Coronary arteries
Supply oxygen to the heart muscle.

Heart

Renal artery
Supplies oxygenated blood to the kidneys.

Inferior vena cava
Carries deoxygenated blood from the lower body.

Common iliac artery
Takes oxygenated blood to the legs.

Common iliac vein
Returns deoxygenated blood from the legs and feet.

Femoral artery

Femoral vein

Great saphenous vein

Posterior tibial artery

Posterior tibial vein

Anterior tibial artery

Anterior tibial vein

The components of blood

Blood has the following major components:
● **Red blood cells** These carry haemoglobin, which combines with oxygen from the lungs and carries it around the body.
● **White blood cells** These protect the body against attacks from microorganisms. They account for less than 1 per cent of total blood volume.
● **Platelets** These cells aid the process of blood clotting.
● **Plasma** The fluid part of blood. Plasma is 90 per cent water, it carries glucose and vitamins, among other substances.

THE RESPIRATORY SYSTEM

Respiration is the biochemical process that releases energy from food within the cells of the body. This process is fuelled by oxygen from the air, drawn into the lungs by the movement of the diaphragm. The system also expels the by-products of respiration, water and carbon dioxide.

Windpipe (trachea) Inhaled air passes down the trachea.

Bronchus The windpipe divides into two bronchi.

Bronchiole Each bronchus branches into numerous bronchioles. Each bronchiole ends in a cluster of tiny chambers called alveoli, which are surrounded by very fine blood vessels. Oxygen passes through the walls of the alveoli into the blood, which returns to the heart to be pumped around the body. At the same time, carbon dioxide passes from the blood into the air in the alveoli to be exhaled.

Capillary carrying deoxygenated blood from the heart to the alveoli to be reoxygenated.

Capillary carrying newly oxygenated blood from the lungs to the heart to be pumped around the body.

Alveoli are tiny air pockets at the ends of the branching bronchioles. They are lined with a thin, moist membrane and supplied by a network of capillaries. Inhaled oxygen and waste carbon dioxide diffuses in and out of the bloodstream here.

The mechanics of breathing

Breathing is controlled by the diaphragm, a sheet of muscle that lies between the chest and abdominal cavities, and by the intercostal muscles between the ribs. Together, these cause the chest cavity to expand and contract, and the resulting difference in pressure inside and outside the body sucks air into the lungs, then forces it out.

Speech The vocal cords of the larynx vibrate as air expelled from the lungs flows between them. These vibrations produce sounds that we can control.

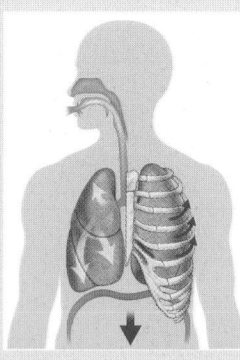

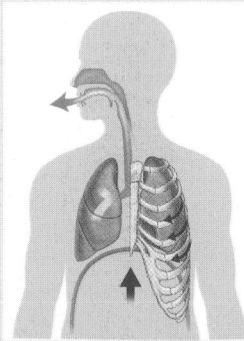

Inhalation The diaphragm contracts and flattens, increasing the volume of the chest cavity, while contraction of the intercostal muscles pulls the ribs upwards and outwards. Internal pressure decreases and air is drawn in.

Exhalation The diaphragm relaxes upwards, reducing the volume of the chest cavity. As the intercostal muscles relax, the ribs move downwards and inwards. Internal pressure increases and air is pushed out.

FACT The combined length of all the arteries, veins and capillaries in the human body is about 150 000 km (93 000 miles).

FACTS AND FIGURES

The heart
● The muscles of the heart contract 100 000 times a day.

Blood
● Red blood cells survive for about 80–120 days. They are replaced by new red blood cells produced in the bone marrow at the rate of 2.5 billion a day.
● On average, blood takes 1 minute to complete a full circuit of the circulatory system.

● When the oxygen supply in the body is low, the kidneys instruct the bone marrow to make more red blood cells.
● Blood accounts for about 8 per cent of a person's total body weight.
● A single drop of blood contains around 250 million red cells and more than 300 000 white cells.
● An adult human contains 5 litres (9 pints) of blood.

The respiratory system
● On average, we breathe 18 times a minute.
● We breathe more than 25 000 times a day, inhaling about 14 200 litres (3124 gallons) of air.
● Lungs are not the same shape or size. The right lung is broader and has three lobes. The left has only two lobes.
● Inhaled air contains 21 per cent oxygen; exhaled air contains 16 per cent oxygen.

Glands and hormones ▶

Glands are groups of cells, and some, known as endocrine glands, produce chemicals called hormones. They are scattered around the body and together make up the endocrine system. Each hormone acts on a specific target: some trigger other glands; others regulate the way organs work. Unlike the nervous system, which sends instant messages demanding immediate action, most hormones take effect slowly.

THE ENDOCRINE SYSTEM

Most endocrine glands work by secreting hormones into the blood, which transports them to their target. Others secrete hormones via a duct directly into their target. Endocrine glands are controlled by an area of the brain called the hypothalamus. Hormones are very specific; they affect only their own target cells. They are broken down slowly after release.

Major endocrine glands and hormones

Hormone	Target	Functions
Pituitary gland		
Adrenocorticotropic	Adrenal glands	Influences body's response to stress; controls use of nutrients.
Antidiuretic	Kidneys	Regulates production of urine; helps to constrict small arteries.
Thyroid–stimulating hormone	Thyroid gland	Stimulates thyroid gland; influences metabolism, circulation and growth.
Growth hormone	Muscle and bone	Stimulates growth and metabolism.
Pineal gland		
Melatonin	Hypothalamus	Affects body temperature, sleep and appetite.
Thyroid gland		
Thyroid hormones	Most cells	Increase metabolic rate; control growth.
Adrenal glands		
Adrenaline and noradrenaline	Circulatory system and muscles	Increases metabolic rate, heart rate and blood flow to muscles.
Pancreas		
Insulin and glucagon	Liver, fatty tissue and muscles	Regulates level of glucose in blood.
Ovaries		
Oestrogen and progesterone	Sex organs and other tissues	Influences development of female sex organs and sexual characteristics; controls the menstrual cycle.
Testes		
Testosterone	Sex organs and other tissues	Influences development of male sex organs and sexual characteristics.

Control system Hormone secretion works through a feedback system that ensures the right amount of a hormone is available when it is needed. The system works in two ways.
● **Negative feedback** If the concentration of a hormone is too high, the excess in the blood acts as an indicator to the secreting gland to reduce production.
● **Positive feedback** Some glands are stimulated to further production of a hormone when the level in the blood is already high. Oxytocin, which is released by the pituitary gland to stimulate uterine contractions during childbirth, works in this way.

Pituitary gland The pituitary is the intermediary between the hypothalamus and the rest of the endocrine system. The hormones that it secretes influence all the other endocrine glands. It also secretes hormones that affect tissues and organs.

Pineal gland (Not shown) The function of this small gland at the back of the brain is not known.

Thyroid gland Larger in women than in men, this gland sometimes increases in size during menstruation.

Adrenal gland The body has two adrenal glands, one above each kidney.

Pancreas This is the largest gland in the body and has two vital functions: the formation of pancreatic juice, which is the most important of the digestive juices, and the production of insulin and glucagon, which control blood sugar levels. Insufficient production of insulin leads to diabetes.

Testes In men, these two glands begin producing testosterone at between 9 and 14 years old, leading to the onset of puberty.

Ovaries In women, the ovaries sit slightly above and on either side of the bladder. They start to form eggs and produce sex hormones between 8 and 13 years old.

FACT Overproduction of the human growth hormone by the pituitary gland in childhood can lead to gigantism.

The body's first lines of defence against infection and disease are physical and chemical barriers such as the skin and digestive juices of the stomach. If these are breached, the immune system comes into play. This includes the deployment of specialist blood cells which engulf and destroy invading pathogens. The lymphatic system creates these cells and also removes infectious microbes from the fluid that bathes the body's tissues.

THE LYMPHATIC SYSTEM

The lymphatic system is a network of vessels and nodes that extends throughout the body. It makes lymphocytes, which remove harmful organisms from the fluid that leaks into the body's tissues from blood capillaries. This fluid, once it enters the lymph vessels, is known as lymph. As lymph passes through the lymph nodes (swellings along the lymphatic vessels), lymphocytes destroy any harmful microorganisms; the purified lymph is then returned to the bloodstream via the veins entering the heart.

Fighting infection The body's first level of defence includes physical barriers such as the skin, and chemical barriers such as antibacterial enzymes in tears and mucus. If microbes get past these, they are attacked by defensive cells called leucocytes produced by the spleen, lymph system and bone marrow. There are several different types but they attack microbes in two main ways. Phagocytes engulf and digest pathogens. Lymphocytes produce, and release into the blood, protein molecules called antibodies which attach themselves to foreign microorganisms.

Defence by phagocytes
Phagocytes, whether in the body's tissues or circulating in the blood, protect the body by engulfing invading microbes, then digesting them.

Phagocyte

Invading microbes

How antibodies work Protein molecules released by lymphocytes attach themselves to pathogens. The antibodies slow down the invaders and act like a beacon to nearby phagocytes, which come and engulf them.

Lymphocyte

Protein molecule

Invading pathogen

FACTS AND FIGURES

● The human body produces more than 200 different hormones.
● A single lymphocyte can make 1 million antibodies an hour.
● The 'swollen glands' that sometimes accompany illness are actually swollen lymph nodes. Lymph nodes expand as they become more active in fighting off infection and disease.

Lymph nodes

Right lymphatic duct
Drains lymph from the right upper body into the right subclavian vein.

Subclavian veins

Thymus Produces lymphocytes and distributes them to the lymphatic system.

Thoracic duct
Drains lymph from the left side of the head and upper body, and from the lower body, into the left subclavian vein.

Spleen Produces and stores lymphocytes.

Left and right lumbar trunks
Drain lymph from the abdomen and legs into the thoracic duct.

Lymph vessels
Drain fluid from body tissues.

As soon as food passes our lips, the digestive system begins converting it into essential nutrients. The digestion and absorption of food takes place in the gut, a tube extending from the mouth to the anus. Muscle action and enzymes break it down into molecules that are absorbed into the bloodstream. The whole process takes about 24 hours.

Structure of teeth

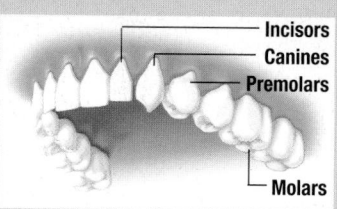

- Incisors
- Canines
- Premolars
- Molars

Teeth are embedded in the jawbone, and appear as tooth buds by the sixth week of gestation. Humans have two sets of teeth, a temporary (milk) set, and a permanent adult set. The 20 milk teeth begin to appear at around six months old. From six years the already formed adult teeth push out the milk teeth. Most adults have 8 incisors, 4 canines, 8 premolars and 12 molars.

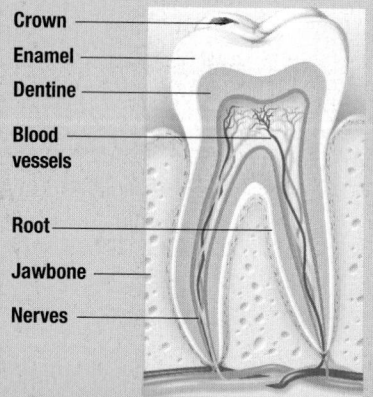

- Crown
- Enamel
- Dentine
- Blood vessels
- Root
- Jawbone
- Nerves

1 Teeth, salivary glands and tongue Teeth grind the food. Saliva softens and lubricates food and enzymes in it begin the digestion of carbohydrates. The tongue rises and pushes the food to the back of the mouth and down the throat.

2 Oesophagus Transports food from the throat to the stomach by means of rhythmic wave-like muscular contractions.

3 Stomach Produces hydrochloric acid and the enzyme pepsin, which break down proteins. The enzyme lipase breaks down fats. The action of the muscular walls blends the food and gastric juices into a watery paste.

4 Liver Produces bile, a thick, green solution that breaks down fats.

5 Gall bladder Bile is stored in this sac. When food is eaten, the amount of bile entering the small intestine increases.

6 Pancreas Secretes enzymes that break down proteins, carbohydrates and fats, and sodium bicarbonate, which neutralises stomach acid.

7 Small Intestine Secretes enzymes, which, together with bile and pancreatic juice, complete digestion. Most of the nutrients and water needed by the body are absorbed here. Glucose and amino acids are absorbed into the bloodstream. Fatty acids and glycerol enter the lymph stream and are taken to the liver.

8 Colon Muscular movement converts the residue from the small intestine into faeces. The progress of waste is slow, to allow the reabsorption of water.

9 Rectum Waste triggers reflex contractions that propel the faeces along the anal canal and out of the anus.

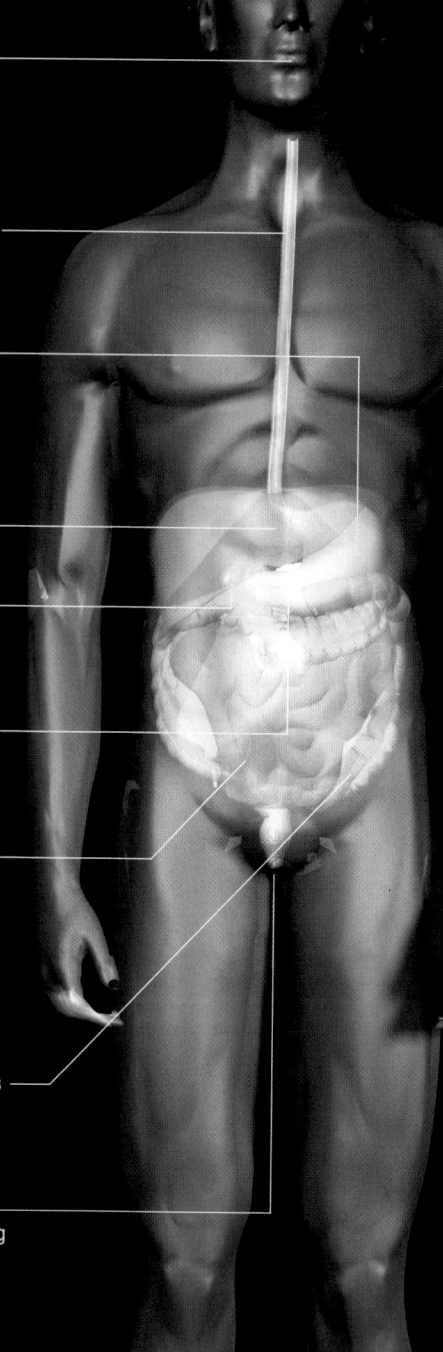

FUNCTIONS OF THE LIVER

The liver is the largest gland in the body. It is a chemical processing plant with several functions.

- **Making bile** Some liver cells make bile, which empties into the small intestine, where it helps to break down fats.
- **Storing fuel** Blood contains dissolved glucose, a sugar the body uses as fuel. The liver controls the glucose level by converting surplus into glycogen, which it stores. If the blood glucose level falls, the liver converts glycogen back to glucose.

- **Processing fats** Fats from food are sent to the liver for processing. The liver turns them into a form that the body can use, and it also acts as a fat store.
- **Processing proteins** The liver processes amino acids – chemical units that make up proteins. When amino acids are broken down they create ammonia, a substance that is poisonous. The liver turns this into urea, which is safely disposed of in urine and sweat.
- **Making blood** In foetuses, the liver makes red blood cells. In children and

adults it stores copper and iron, which are needed to make blood's oxygen-carrying substance, haemoglobin.
- **Cleaning blood** Cells in the liver remove old white blood cells, and engulf bacteria and viruses.
- **Storing vitamins** The liver is a major vitamin storage depot, storing vitamins A, B12, D, E and K.
- **Neutralising toxins** The liver removes substances such as alcohol and drugs from the blood and turns them into safer chemicals.

The urinary system's main functions are to remove waste products from the body, to maintain its water balance and to adjust the concentration of fluids in the blood. The major organs are the two kidneys, which filter waste products out of the blood and reabsorb useful ones. Waste products pass into the bladder, and out of the body through the urethra.

Male and female urinary tract
In the male, the bottom of the bladder lies beside the prostate gland. The urethra passes along the penis. In the female, the bladder lies above the uterus and vagina. The urethra exits the body in front of the vagina, within the labial folds.

THE KIDNEY IN CLOSE-UP

Each kidney contains about 1 million tiny blood filtration units, called nephrons, which remove waste products and excess water from the blood to make urine. Tubules carry urine into the renal pelvis, from where it flows to the bladder, where it collects before being expelled.

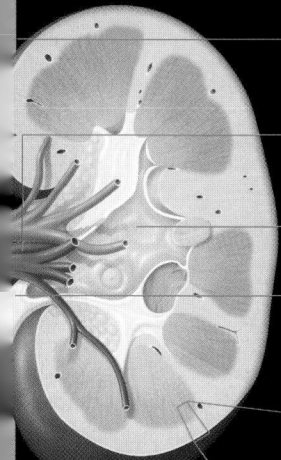

Renal artery Feeds blood to the kidney from the main artery of the body, the aorta.

Renal vein Carries blood from the kidney to the main vein of the body, the vena cava.

Renal pelvis Urine collects here.

Ureter Transports urine from the kidney to the bladder.

Collecting tubule Collects the urine, which consists of waste substances and the remaining water.

Proximal convoluted tubule Wrapped by capillaries, which reabsorb water, glucose and other vital substances through their walls into the blood.

Bowman's capsule Blood plasma is forced through the thin walls of the tiny capillaries clustered inside this sac. This plasma then passes into the proximal convoluted tubule.

Kidney Filters out urea, uric acid and excess water from the blood.

Ureter Carries urine from the kidney to the bladder.

Bladder A large muscular bag that stores urine. At the exit to the bladder is a circular sphincter muscle that acts as a valve, releasing urine into the urethra when the bladder is full.

Urethra Tube leading from the bladder, down which urine passes to exit the body.

The importance of water

Water is essential to the body's well-being. As it passes through the kidneys, it dilutes toxins and allows sufficient urine to be produced to keep the body's chemical balance in order. Water is the medium in which all chemical processes occur within the body's metabolism. It is mostly stored in muscle, blood and skin, and accounts for 60 per cent of an adult's weight.

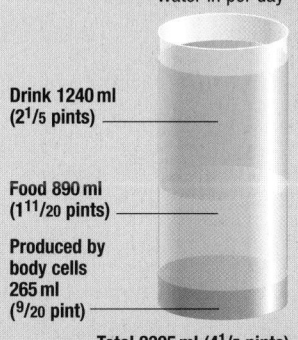

Water in per day

Drink 1240 ml
($2^{1}/_{5}$ pints)

Food 890 ml
($1^{11}/_{20}$ pints)

Produced by body cells
265 ml
($9/_{20}$ pint)

Total 2395 ml ($4^{1}/_{5}$ pints)

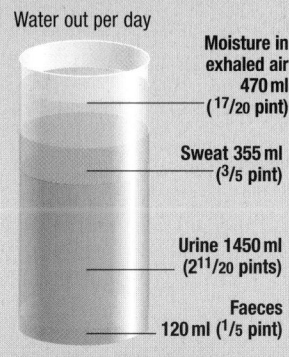

Water out per day

Moisture in exhaled air
470 ml
($^{17}/_{20}$ pint)

Sweat 355 ml
($3/_{5}$ pint)

Urine 1450 ml
($2^{11}/_{20}$ pints)

Faeces
120 ml ($1/_{5}$ pint)

Total 2395 ml ($4^{1}/_{5}$ pints)

The skin is the largest organ in the body. An adult's skin has a surface area of about 2 m² (21 sq ft). It forms a protective layer, helps temperature regulation, synthesises vitamin D and contains the nerves that transmit the sensations of touch, pain, heat and cold. Nails and hair are both formed by the skin, and are largely made up of dead cells. Nails protect the sensitive fingertips and make it easier to pick up small objects. Hair plays an important role in regulating body temperature.

SKIN STRUCTURE

Skin is made up of two main layers, a thin outer layer or epidermis, and a thicker foundation layer, or dermis.

● **The epidermis** varies in thickness according to the part of the body it covers (the thickest areas are on the back, the hands and the soles of the feet) and contains no blood vessels. It is constantly regenerated as dead cells on the surface are worn away and replaced by new cells moving up from below.

● **The dermis,** made of fibrous, elastic tissue, contains the touch, pressure and temperature sensory nerves, blood vessels and sweat and sebaceous glands. It also contains 3 million or so hair follicles. The dermis includes the many permanent folds that appear on the skin's surface as fingerprint patterns. Beneath the dermis is a layer of fatty tissue, the hypodermis, which provides insulation.

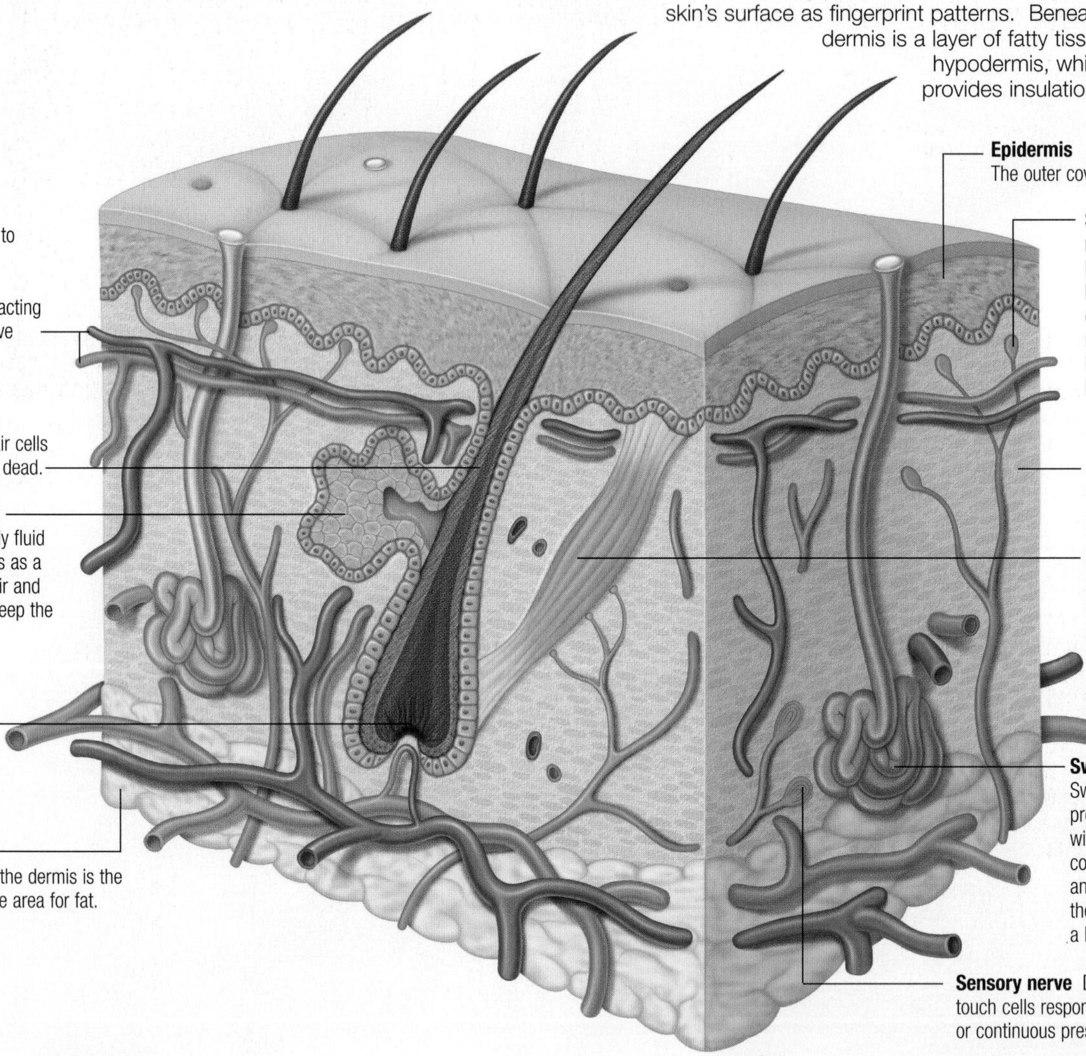

Blood vessels
Blood vessels help to regulate body temperature by expanding or contracting to dispel or conserve body heat.

Hair shaft
New hair growth is constant, but all hair cells above the bulb are dead.

Sebaceous gland
This secretes an oily fluid (sebum), which acts as a lubricant for the hair and skin and helps to keep the skin supple.

Hair bulb
The sac around the bulb and shaft is called the hair follicle.

Hypodermis
This layer beneath the dermis is the body's main storage area for fat.

Epidermis
The outer covering.

Sensory nerve
Nerve cells beneath the epidermis respond to light touch, heat or pain.

Dermis
The inner layer.

Hair-erector muscle
Contracts in response to cold or fear, making hair stand on end.

Sweat gland
Sweat is produced within the coiled tubule and reaches the surface via a long duct.

Sensory nerve Deep-set touch cells respond to heavy or continuous pressure.

DAMAGE LIMITATION

When skin is broken, a scab forms to provide a protective cap over the damaged area while it heals. Scabs form from a sticky, fibrous substance called fibrin, which is produced in the blood whenever and wherever a blood vessel is broken. Fibrin meshes together and traps escaping blood cells in a clot, which then dries to become a scab. As a cut or scratch heals from the inside outwards, the scab moves nearer the surface. Once the damage to the skin has been completely repaired, the scab falls away.

Flaky surface An electron micrograph of the surface of human skin, magnified about 200 times, shows how layers of dead cells peel back and become flakes, which then fall away. Household dust consists largely of these flakes, which are shed at a rate of 4 kg (9 lb) a person a year.

Controlling body temperature

The skin helps to control body temperature in three ways:

● **Perspiration** The evaporation of sweat helps to cool the body to maintain a skin temperature of 36.1–37.8°C (97–100°F). This evaporation occurs constantly and imperceptibly. However, body temperature can rise rapidly, through muscular activity or as a result of an increase in the surrounding temperature. When this occurs, the sweat glands can secrete up to 3 litres (5¼ pints) of perspiration an hour over a short period.

● **Blood circulation** When body temperature rises, capillaries in the skin widen and the increased blood flow allows more heat to escape. When body temperature drops, the capillaries contract, retaining warmth inside the body.

● **Goose bumps** Hair erector muscles contract and form goose bumps in response to cold. The pits between the bumps hold heat and the erect hairs trap a layer of warmer air against the skin.

SWEAT GLANDS AND PERSPIRATION

Perspiration reaches the surface of the skin through tiny openings (pores) in the epidermis leading from the sweat glands. There are two kinds of sweat gland:

● **Normal sweat glands** Normal (eccrine) sweat glands occur all over the body, but are concentrated in large numbers on the soles of the feet and palms of the hands. They secrete a slightly acidic, watery, salty sweat that helps both to regulate body temperature by cooling the skin when it evaporates and to expel small amounts of waste substances.

● **Sexual sweat glands** The sexual (apocrine) glands begin to function at puberty, producing viscous, protein-rich sweat in response to emotional stimuli such as sexual excitement and feelings of fear or anger. They are larger than ordinary sweat glands and occur in the eyelids, in the areola and nipple of the breast, in the armpits and around the anus and external genitalia. The sweat produced by these glands is odourless but the action of bacteria on it can give it a distinctive smell.

SKIN COLOUR

Human skin colour ranges from pale pink to dark brown. The variation in colour is caused by different amounts of pigments in the cells between the dermis and epidermis. The dark layers in the picture on the right are melanin cells, which give skin a dark colour.

Natural sunblock Ultraviolet (UV) light is potentially very damaging to skin, and is present at high levels in strong sunlight. The dark pigment melanin blocks the passage of UV light. This picture was shot under UV light. From left to right, the three women are of European, African and Asian origin. The African skin appears the most violet because it is reflecting the most UV light.

FINGERPRINTS

Patterns of ridges occur in the skin on the inner surfaces of the fingers, thumbs and palms, and also on the soles and the lower surface of the toes. Their function is to aid grip. On the fingers and thumbs, these unchanging patterns are known as fingerprints. Each ridge is 0.2–0.4 mm (0.008–0.016 in) wide, and the patterns are classified by their major features: arches, loops and whorls. Fingerprints are unique to each individual, except for identical twins, who have matching fingerprints.

Arch   Loop

Whorl   Composite

FACTS AND FIGURES

● The average person has around 2.5 million sweat glands.

● The palms of the hands have the largest concentration of sweat glands, with up to 500 per cm² of skin (3225 per sq in).

● The body produces more than 1 litre (1¾ pints) of sweat every day, even when almost totally inactive.

● The epidermis is 0.1 mm (0.004 in) thick on the face and 1 mm (0.04 in) on the soles of the feet.

● There are up to 1 million hairs on the top of the head. Each grows about 0.3 mm (0.01 in) a day.

● Hair gets its colour from the pigments melanin and carotene. Greying is caused by a gradual loss of these pigments and a build-up of air bubbles in the shaft of the hair.

● The average person sheds about 80 hairs a day.

● In one year fingernails grow by 2.5 cm (1 in). They grow faster in summer than in winter.

● A tan is the result of a build-up of the pigment melanin in response to exposure to ultraviolet light.

● The pigment carotene gives skin a yellowish colour.

Nails

Nails develop from the epidermis, and are formed from a fibrous protein called keratin. Growth occurs in the nail root beneath the skin of the cuticle. As with hair, only the nail root consists of live cells: most of it consists of dead cells. The apparent perception of touch in the nails is due to the large number of nerves in the nail bed and surrounding skin.

see also

136-7 **Circulation/breathing**

138 **Glands and hormones**

146-7 **Smell/taste/touch**

160-1 **Disorders/diseases**

The eyes contain more than 70 per cent of the body's sensory receptors. Changing patterns of light are detected by the eyes and fed as nervous impulses to the brain, which interprets, assesses and reacts to the images it receives. The human eye can operate in a wide range of conditions, rapidly accommodating to low light levels, for instance, as the eye and brain coordinate to make the most of the available information.

ADJUSTING FOR LIGHT

We can see in a wide range of light conditions because the iris contracts or expands to vary the size of the hole (the pupil) at its centre. In low light, the pupil widens to allow in as much light as possible; in bright light, it shrinks to prevent excess light damaging the eye.

Focusing Muscles adjust the lens as light passes through it to focus incoming light rays onto the retina, forming an image.

Shortsightedness (myopia) The image is focused slightly in front of the retina, and is corrected by glasses with concave lenses.

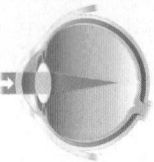

Longsightedness (hypermetropia) The image is focused slightly behind the retina, and is corrected by glasses with convex lenses.

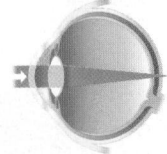

Astigmatism The eyeball is not quite spherical and the eye muscles cannot bring things into sharp focus. It particularly affects close vision, and is corrected by glasses with a cylindrical curvature.

Are you colour-blind?

Normal colour vision needs red, blue and green cone cells to be working perfectly in order to detect all the colours of the spectrum. Some individuals are unable to distinguish between particular colours because certain cone cells are absent or malfunctioning. This condition, called colour blindness, is more common among men than women because the genes that lead to it are carried on the X chromosome. Among Europeans, 8 per cent of males suffer from colour blindness, compared with just 0.5 per cent of females.

Test yourself
If you cannot make out a number from this pattern of dots, then you are probably colour-blind.

THE EYE: OUR WINDOW ON THE WORLD

Each eye sits within a bony socket, and is anchored by muscles. Light enters the eye through the transparent cornea, where it is roughly focused, and passes via the pupil to a lens. This focuses the light more precisely, through the transparent fluid (vitreous humour) that fills the eyeball. It forms an image on a curved screen called the retina at the back of the eye. The retina contains light-sensitive cells called rods and cones. The cones, which respond to particular colours, are clustered in the middle of the retina; the rods, which respond to black and white, are on the periphery. In response to stimulation, the rods and cones produce nervous impulses that are transmitted via the optic nerve to the brain.

Lens This sits directly behind the pupil and provides fine adjustment to focus.

Iris This pigmented muscle controls the size (aperture) of the pupil.

Pupil The hole through which light enters the eye.

Cornea This strongly curved window provides most of the eye's focusing power.

Retina The layer at the back of the eye where rods and cones are concentrated.

Optic nerve This is a bundle of about 1 million separate nerve fibres.

Vitreous humour This jelly-like, transparent fluid fills the eyeball and helps it to maintain its spherical shape.

Sclera This tough, fibrous layer makes up the white of the eye.

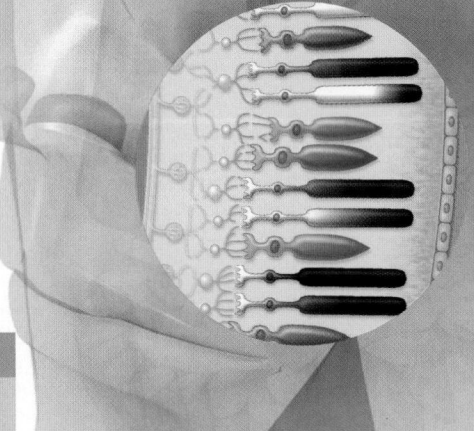

Rods and cones Rods (the longer, darker cells) distinguish between black and white, and are the only receptors active in low light levels. Cones enable us to see colours but require intense light (daylight) to do so.

Protection and mobility

Eyelids and conjunctiva The eyelids protect the eye externally. Inside them, and extending over the eyeball, a transparent membrane known as the conjunctiva provides extra protection.

Tears The cornea must be kept clear for light to enter the eye. Tear fluid (which contains nutrients and protects the eye from bacteria) is washed over the eye by the blinking movements of the eyelids.

Eye muscles The eyeball sits in a sling of six muscles suspended in the bony eye socket. These enable the eyeball to swivel in several directions.

FACTS AND FIGURES

● For the cells in the retina to function properly, the pattern of light falling on them must keep changing (without change, the cells' nerves cease to fire). The eye makes about 50 tiny flickering movements every second in order for this to happen.

● There are about 125 million rod cells in the retina, and about 7 million cone cells.

● Colour blindness is experienced by people with normal vision when the light fails. As evening draws on, we lose first the ability to see red, then orange, yellow and green. Blue is the last colour to disappear, and the first to re-emerge in the morning light.

The ear both detects sound and governs our senses of balance and movement. The eardrum vibrates in response to sound waves in the air and passes these vibrations to the inner ear, where they are converted into nerve impulses. The slightly different wave patterns detected by each ear allow us to sense the direction of sounds. The inner ear's fluid-filled canals are highly sensitive to movement, providing the brain with an instantaneous signal of any change in the head's position.

HOW SOUND REACHES THE BRAIN

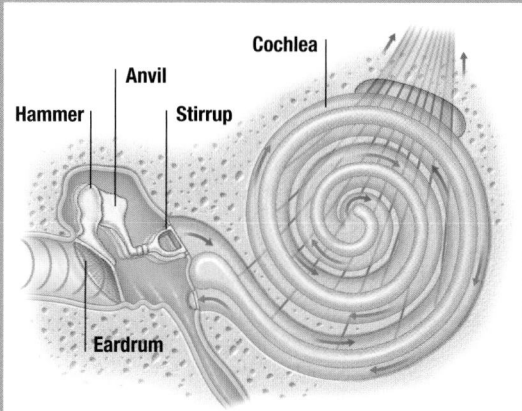

Hammer | Anvil | Stirrup | Cochlea | Eardrum

1 Sound waves strike the eardrum and vibrate the hammer, anvil and stirrup bones, which together modify and transfer the vibrations to the inner ear.
2 The fluid-filled chambers within the cochlea carry these vibrations to the corti, a set of membranes spiralling inside it.
3 Tiny hairs along the corti are stimulated by vibrations of different frequencies, converting each into a nervous impulse.
4 These impulses are carried by the vestibulo-cochlear nerve to the temporal lobe of the brain, where they are interpreted as sounds.

Maintaining balance

The fluid-filled semicircular canals of the inner ear are fixed at right angles to each other, which means that movement in any direction causes fluid to move in one or more canals. Receptor-hair cells in each canal detect this movement and send information to the brain. Hair cells in the utricle and saccule chambers press on one set of receptors when the head is held upright, and on others when the head is tilted. Information from these organs helps the brain to control eye movements so that an object can be held in view even when the head is moving.

Sixth sense
Balance is the sense we consider least often.

THE EAR: AN ORGAN IN THREE PARTS

The ear is divided into three sections; the outer, middle and inner ear. The outer ear consists of the auricle or pinna (made of skin and cartilage), and the curved auditory canal. The pinna is shaped to guide sound waves into the ear. The outer part of the auditory canal is lined with fine hairs and glands that secrete wax. The middle ear includes the eardrum (tympanic membrane) stretched across the inner end of the auditory canal. Inside the drum lie three small bones, the hammer (malleus), anvil (incus) and stirrup (stapes), which transmit vibrations to the inner ear. This consists of the spiral cochlea, which converts vibrations into electronic impulses, and the vestibular apparatus, which controls balance. The latter consists of three fluid-filled semicircular canals, which detect movement, and the utricle and saccule, which respond to gravity.

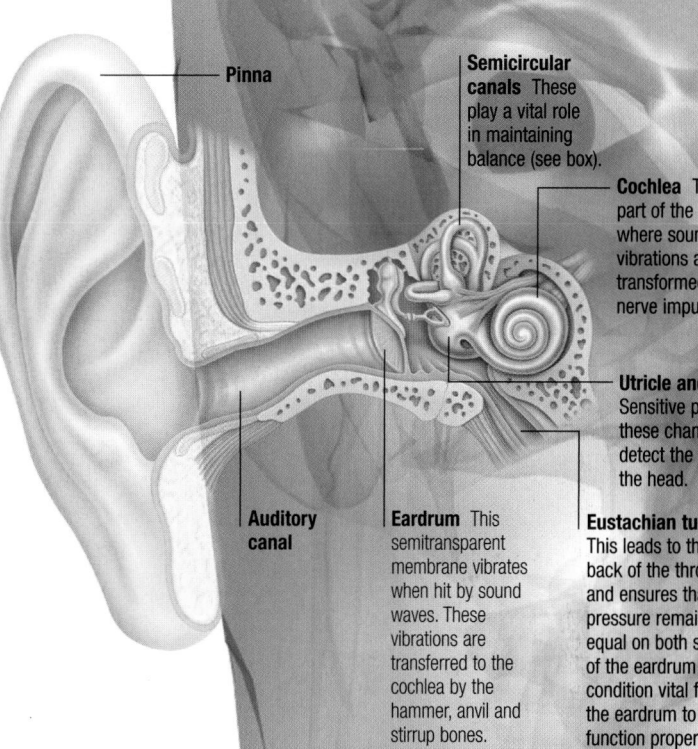

Pinna

Semicircular canals These play a vital role in maintaining balance (see box).

Cochlea The part of the ear where sound vibrations are transformed into nerve impulses.

Utricle and saccule Sensitive patches in these chambers detect the position of the head.

Auditory canal

Eardrum This semitransparent membrane vibrates when hit by sound waves. These vibrations are transferred to the cochlea by the hammer, anvil and stirrup bones.

Eustachian tube This leads to the back of the throat and ensures that air pressure remains equal on both sides of the eardrum – a condition vital for the eardrum to function properly.

FACTS AND FIGURES

◉ Most humans can detect sounds pitched between 20 and 20 000 hertz. A rumbling juggernaut produces some sounds lower than 20 hertz, while screeching brakes may exceed 20 000 hertz.
◉ Permanent damage to the ears can be caused by sounds louder than 100 decibels. A jet aeroplane taking off creates noise ranging upwards from 120 decibels in volume.
◉ The hammer, anvil and stirrup are the smallest bones in the human body.
◉ The eardrum measures about 8 mm (3/8 in) across.

see also
134-5 **The brain and nerves**
154-5 **Human capacity**
160-1 **Disorders/diseases**

Odour molecules from myriad sources float freely in the air and our sense of smell lets us detect the more pungent of these from a distance. Smell also works in tandem with our taste buds to distinguish differences in flavour between foods. The sense of touch provides information that the brain needs to work out other properties of objects, such as their temperature, texture, hardness and weight.

SMELL

Nerve endings inside the nose contain receptor cells that detect chemical molecules in the air. These cells are concentrated in an area about the size of a postage stamp in the nasal cavity on each side of the nose. The receptor cells respond to specific molecules and the nerves send messages via the olfactory bulbs to the brain.

What is a smell?

Chemicals that evaporate easily into the air, called volatile chemicals, are detected by receptor cells in the nose. Volatile chemicals are produced in different quantities by different substances. Those that produce the largest quantities are the easiest to smell. One of the smelliest substances on Earth is vanilla. It is 1000 times more potent than garlic oil and 15 000 times more potent than lemon peel.

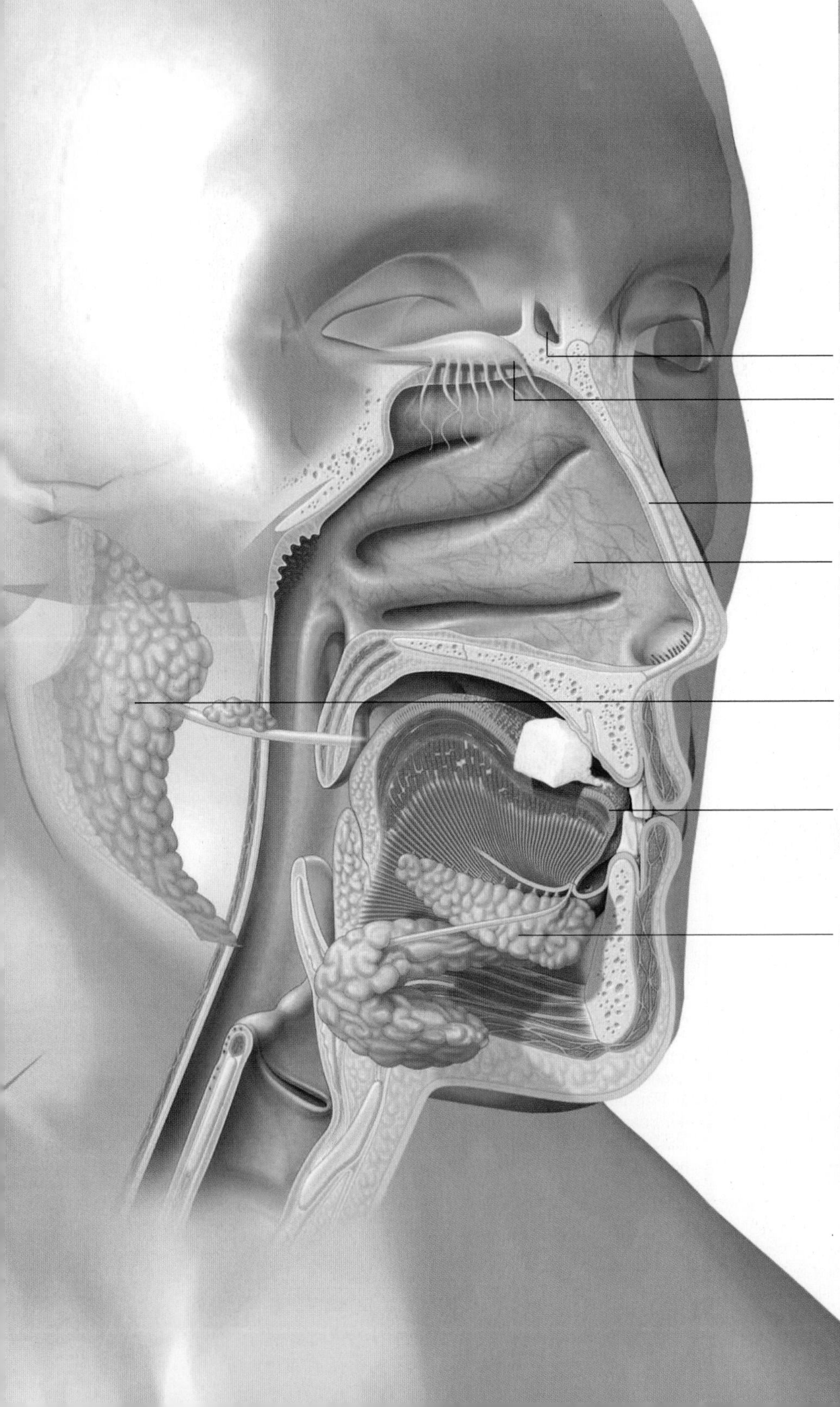

Frontal sinus

Olfactory bulb There are two of these bundles of nervous tissue, one beneath each eye. Nerves project down through the bone of the skull from each into the nasal cavity.

Nasal cartilage The bridge of the nose. It is this cartilage that is damaged if the nose is broken.

Nasal cavity There are two of these large spaces, corresponding to each nostril, lying between the eye sockets and the roof of the mouth. They are separated by a thin layer of cartilage and bone. Beneath a layer of protective mucus the lining of the nasal cavity is packed with blood vessels to warm incoming air.

Salivary gland Saliva dissolves food chemicals, keeps the mouth moist and lubricates the passage of food down the throat.

Tongue The taste buds are concentrated on the surface of the tongue, which also serves to push food to the back of the mouth for swallowing.

Salivary gland

FACT The tongue is the only muscle in the human body that is attached at just one end.

TASTE

Taste buds are small sense organs concentrated on the tongue but they also exist in the throat and on the palate. On the tongue, they are found in small projections called papillae, which vary in shape and location. Taste buds are sensitive to four different sensations: bitter, sour, salty and sweet; all the different flavours we recognise are made up of combinations of these four plus odours detected by the nose. Taste receptor cells are stimulated by chemicals in food after it has been dissolved by saliva, and transmit signals to the brain for interpretation.

Taste areas Rounded (vallate) papillae are situated near the rear of the tongue, ridged (foliate) papillae along the sides, mushroom-shaped (fungiform) papillae on the top surface, and hair-like (filiform) papillae around the tip. Taste buds that respond to the four categories of flavour are concentrated on different parts of the tongue, although some can be stimulated to a lesser degree by one or more of the other main taste categories.

● Bitter
● Sour
● Salty
● Sweet

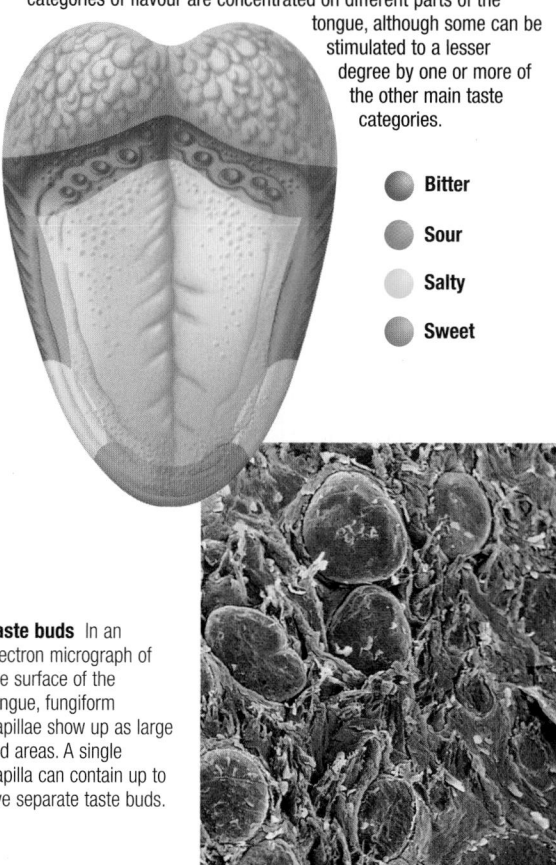

Taste buds In an electron micrograph of the surface of the tongue, fungiform papillae show up as large red areas. A single papilla can contain up to five separate taste buds.

FACTS AND FIGURES

● The 10 000 taste buds on the tongue survive only a few days each, and are constantly being replaced.
● Democritus, the Greek philosopher who first suggested the presence of atoms, thought that sharp odours were produced by pointed atoms and sweet odours by rounded ones.
● Humans can detect 10 000 different odours. Children can recognise more odours than adults, as the olfactory receptors begin to waste away from birth.
● The nose contains around 50 million smell receptor cells.
● The human foetus has a sense of 'smell' and 'taste'. Odours from the mother's food and drink pass to the foetus via the amniotic fluid. At 12 weeks the foetus begins to swallow amniotic fluid, and monitoring has shown that there is a preference for sweet flavours.

TOUCH

Human skin is packed with sensory receptors that give the body its sense of touch. Sensory nerves vary in structure, but all react immediately to physical sensations, converting them into nerve impulses to be transmitted via the central nervous system to the area of the brain called the thalamus. Here the impulses are sorted and passed on to the sensory regions of the brain.

Some receptor cells lie close to the surface of the skin and are sensitive to a light touch and heat; others are found at deeper levels and respond to heavy pressure.

Touch receptors are not distributed evenly around the body. The hands, feet and lips have far more than anywhere else. This reflects the importance of touch in these areas, which spend more time in contact with other objects than any other parts of the body.

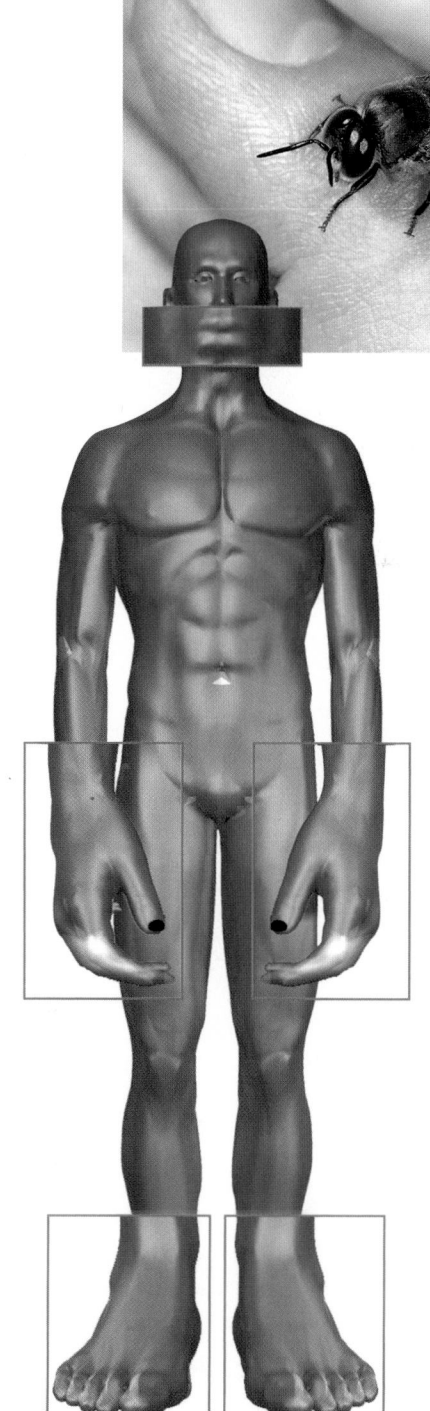

Tiny steps Touch sensors are so concentrated on our hands that we can feel the minute changes in pressure caused by an insect walking over them. By contrast the same amount of pressure on our back will elicit almost no response at all. Among other things, touch sensors in our hands enable the brain to tell how hard or soft objects are, and how much pressure to exert when holding them or picking them up.

Touch sensitive Our ability to feel objects by touch is amplified in our mouth, hands and feet, which have a greater concentration of touch receptors. This diagram illustrates the proportionately greater sensitivity in these areas.

see also

134-5 **The brain and nerves**
140 **The digestive system**
148-9 **Pregnancy and birth**
160-1 **Disorders/diseases**

During the first eight weeks of a human pregnancy the fertilised egg develops into an embryo. Its cells divide at extraordinary speed, producing clusters that form the emerging organs. Blood vessels begin to form 17 days after conception. Limbs appear as buds by the third week. By the eighth week, the foetus, although only 2.5 cm (1 in) long, is clearly recognisable as a human being.

THE FIRST DAYS AFTER FERTILISATION

The rapid development of the fertilised egg into an embryo occurs mainly within the lining of the uterus – but it actually begins while the egg is still travelling down the Fallopian tube. As well as cells that develop into the embryo (embryoblast cells), the fertilised egg produces trophoblast cells that develop into the placenta – which will supply oxygen and nutrients to the baby from its mother through the umbilical cord, and carry away waste products.

Fighting to fertilise
Human sperm cells writhe on the surface of an egg cell (ovum), which dwarfs them. Although only one sperm will gain entry to the egg and fertilise it, it takes many to break down the egg cell's outer coating (by releasing protein-dissolving enzymes) before this can happen.

Moment of conception High in the Fallopian tube a single tadpole-shaped sperm cell penetrates the outer membrane of the ovum, then sheds its body and tail. The head, containing the sperm's nucleus and genetic material, travels to the nucleus of the ovum.

Ovary Eggs at different stages of development ripen within the ovary.

Fallopian tube (oviduct) The egg passes down the oviduct to the womb.

0–30 hours The nuclei of the ovum and sperm, which each contain 23 chromosomes, fuse together to form a single zygote cell, which has 46 chromosomes – all the genetic information required to make a new person. The zygote travels down the Fallopian tube towards the uterus, or womb, and begins to divide, first into two new cells (at 30 hours old), then four, then eight and so on.

Womb (uterus) The outer wall of the womb is thick and muscular. It is the strongest muscle in the body.

30 hours–6 days The process of cell division occurs many times before the womb is reached.

6–8 days The cluster of cells, now called a blastocyst, has developed a hollow interior filled with fluid (this will become the amniotic sac in which the embryo will later float). It has reached the womb and implants itself in the lining. At this point pregnancy begins.

Cells become specialised
The blastocyst's outer layer penetrates the womb's lining, forming what will become the placenta. The cells within the blastocyst are grouped into three layers, the ectoderm, mesoderm and endoderm. Taking instructions from the genes: the brain and spinal cord, nerves and skin will develop from the ectoderm; muscles, bones, blood vessels and kidneys will develop from the mesoderm; and the oesophagus, stomach, intestine, bladder, pancreas, liver and lining of the lungs will develop from the endoderm.

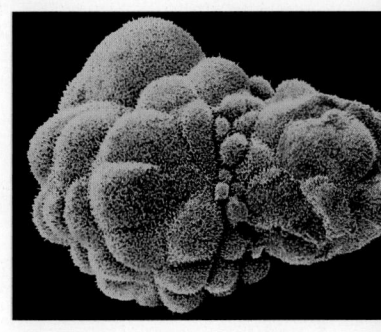

STAGES OF PREGNANCY

Between eight days and four weeks the cells of the blastocyst diversify and the organs gradually begin to develop. At four weeks the blastocyst still does not look recognisably human but is already 80 000 times bigger than the original egg. By the time it is born, the baby will be about a million times bigger again.

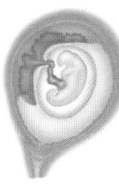

4 weeks The heart has begun to beat. At this point, the embryo is just 5 mm (1/4 in) long.

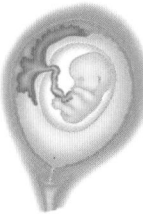

6 weeks The embryo obtains all of its nourishment and oxygen from the placenta and umbilical cord. It now has a simple brain.

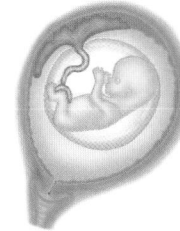

8 weeks Now called a foetus, it has recognisable limbs and measures 2.5 cm (1 in) long. It starts to move, but this is not yet felt by the mother.

THE REPRODUCTIVE ORGANS

The female reproductive (sex) organs are inside the body. Every month, one of the ovaries releases an egg (ovum), which travels to the womb (uterus), where an enriched blood supply has developed ready to nourish it. If the egg is not fertilised, it is expelled with the uterine blood, in the menstrual flow (period).

The male sex organs are both inside and outside the body. Sperm formed by the testes mature in about two weeks, and are stored in tubes above them. When the penis erects, sperm moves from these to the urethra, mixing with fluid on the way to form semen. This flows into the penis to be ejected during intercourse.

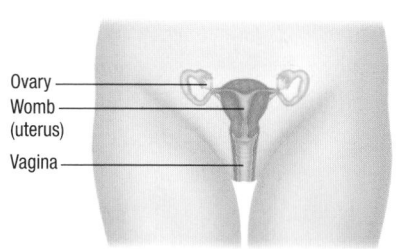

Ovary
Womb (uterus)
Vagina

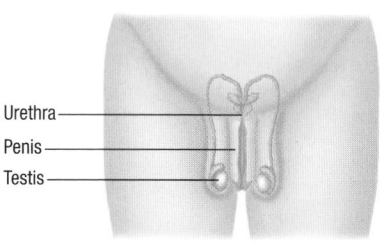

Urethra
Penis
Testis

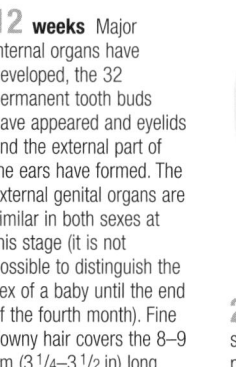

12 weeks Major internal organs have developed, the 32 permanent tooth buds have appeared and eyelids and the external part of the ears have formed. The external genital organs are similar in both sexes at this stage (it is not possible to distinguish the sex of a baby until the end of the fourth month). Fine downy hair covers the 8–9 cm (3 1/4–3 1/2 in) long foetus, which is now able to swallow.

22 weeks All the body systems are established. If born prematurely now the 15–25 cm (6–10 in) long baby could survive with medical support.

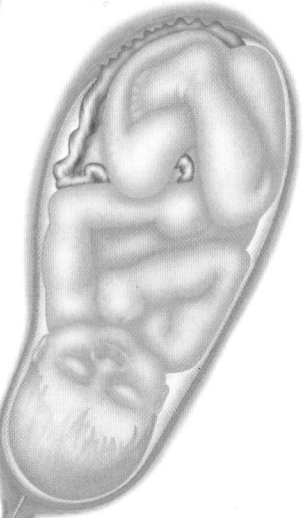

38 weeks The baby is fully formed with its head engaged (positioned downwards facing the pelvis), ready to be born.

Giving birth

Delivery occurs in three stages.

● **First stage** The amniotic sac around the foetus ruptures and the fluid drains away (the waters break). The muscles of the womb begin to contract and the neck of the cervix relaxes and widens (dilates). This stage can take up to 10 hours.
● **Second stage** Contractions occur more frequently. The baby moves down the birth canal (cervix and vagina), emerging head first. The mother pushes with her abdominal muscles to help the baby to be born. This stage may take 2 hours for a first baby.
● **Third stage** The placenta (afterbirth) is expelled. Hormones released during the birth cause the mother's breasts to begin producing colostrum, a rich precursor to milk, almost immediately.

Birth problems

● **Premature baby** A baby born before 37 weeks of pregnancy is not fully developed. It must spend time in an incubator, which helps with breathing and maintains body temperature.
● **Breach baby** The baby is born feet or buttocks first, having failed to turn during pregnancy in order for the head to face the pelvis.
● **Caesarean section** If mother or baby are at risk through natural delivery, an incision is made in the mother's abdomen and the baby is lifted out.

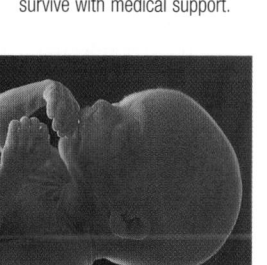

Just over halfway At five months, the foetus looks fully formed. Before birth, however, it will more than double in length and put on thick layers of fat.

Cells are the smallest structural units in the body, and are grouped into different types of tissue. All types of cell have a similar internal structure regardless of their function, and most cells have a nucleus that contains a substance called

DNA, which carries the genetic information that is passed from parent to child. DNA controls not only the distinguishing features of each person, but also the way in which individual cells function.

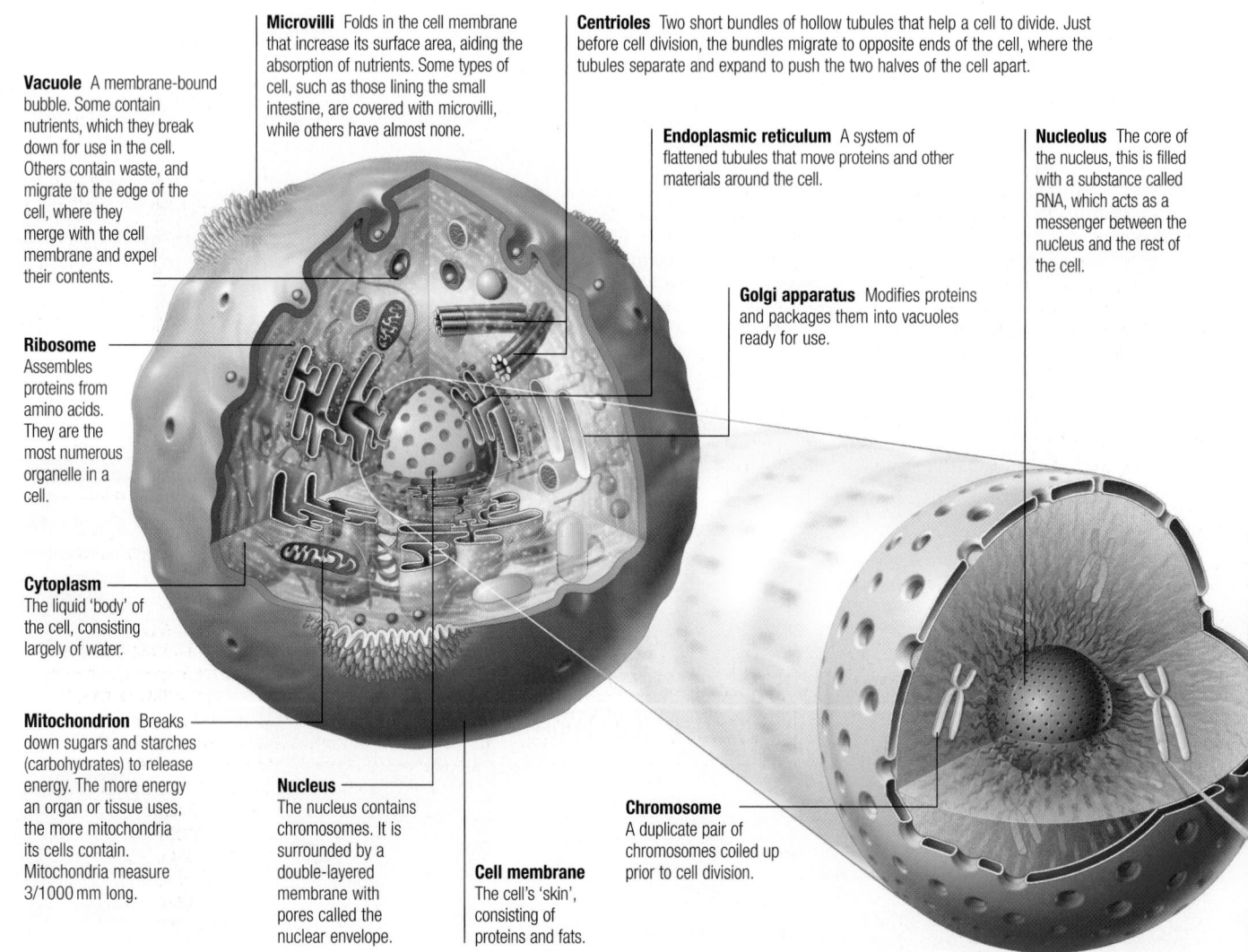

Microvilli Folds in the cell membrane that increase its surface area, aiding the absorption of nutrients. Some types of cell, such as those lining the small intestine, are covered with microvilli, while others have almost none.

Centrioles Two short bundles of hollow tubules that help a cell to divide. Just before cell division, the bundles migrate to opposite ends of the cell, where the tubules separate and expand to push the two halves of the cell apart.

Vacuole A membrane-bound bubble. Some contain nutrients, which they break down for use in the cell. Others contain waste, and migrate to the edge of the cell, where they merge with the cell membrane and expel their contents.

Endoplasmic reticulum A system of flattened tubules that move proteins and other materials around the cell.

Nucleolus The core of the nucleus, this is filled with a substance called RNA, which acts as a messenger between the nucleus and the rest of the cell.

Golgi apparatus Modifies proteins and packages them into vacuoles ready for use.

Ribosome Assembles proteins from amino acids. They are the most numerous organelle in a cell.

Cytoplasm The liquid 'body' of the cell, consisting largely of water.

Mitochondrion Breaks down sugars and starches (carbohydrates) to release energy. The more energy an organ or tissue uses, the more mitochondria its cells contain. Mitochondria measure 3/1000 mm long.

Nucleus The nucleus contains chromosomes. It is surrounded by a double-layered membrane with pores called the nuclear envelope.

Cell membrane The cell's 'skin', consisting of proteins and fats.

Chromosome A duplicate pair of chromosomes coiled up prior to cell division.

CELL STRUCTURE AND FUNCTION

All cells consist of an outer membrane enclosing fluid called cytoplasm. Within this are specialised structures, called organelles, that carry out the cell's tasks. At the centre of the cell is the nucleus, which contains genetic material (DNA) in the form of chromosomes and acts as the cell's control centre. Most cells contain a complete set of genetic instructions, but within each cell only those needed for its particular function are activated. For example, instructions for making the hormone insulin are present in the DNA of every cell, but are only used in cells in the pancreas.

Although most cells contain the same types of organelle, cells are a different shape and size, and have differing life spans, depending on their function. Fat cells are globular and contain a droplet of fat, while nerve cells have long, branching axions for transmitting messages. Some cells are able to change shape. White blood cells, for example, can become long and thin to squeeze through tiny capillaries, or send out 'arms' to grab and engulf microorganisms.

CHROMOSOMES

Chromosomes are threadlike structures found in the cell nucleus. Each consists of a giant molecule of DNA coiled round a protein core.

For most of the time chromosomes are unravelled so that their DNA can be easily accessed. Just before a cell divides, they coil up into bundles fat enough to be seen under a microscope. Each bundle replicates itself, forming two identical versions that link up in an X shape. As the cell divides, each pair of chromosomes splits apart and one copy is drawn into each new cell. Not long after the new cells separate, the bundled chromosomes unravel again.

All human cells with a nucleus have 46 chromosomes, apart from sperm and egg cells, which each have 23. The 46 chromosomes in nonsex cells are copies of the 23 from the mother's egg and the 23 from the father's sperm. The chromosomes in every sex cell are unique (see page 547), so brothers or sisters are never completely alike. Identical twins are the same because they develop from one egg that splits in two after fertilisation, the point at which the two sets of parental chromosomes amalgamate in one nucleus.

DNA: WHAT IS IT?

The term DNA stands for deoxyribonucleic acid, a chemical that exists in all living organisms (and can survive in their remains for thousands of years after death). It carries all the information a cell requires to make the proteins that it needs in order to function. DNA molecules are made up of a series of smaller units consisting of pairs of chemical bases. There are four bases: adenine (A), thymine (T), guanine (G) and cytosine (C). They always pair in the same combinations – adenine to thymine and guanine to cytosine. The order in which the four chemical bases occur along the length of the molecule provides the genetic code. In order to duplicate itself prior to cell division, a DNA molecule splits along its length and each side reproduces the missing half, replicating the entire sequence for use in the new cell.

Genes
A gene is a segment of DNA containing the instructions for the formation of one particular protein. The term is also used to describe a section of DNA that determines a specific physical characteristic, such as the gene for blue eyes, or function, such as insulin production.

In order to put the genetic instructions into operation, a substance called RNA (ribonucleic acid) unzips the section of the DNA molecule carrying the gene needed by the cell, and makes a copy of one side of it. This RNA copy then travels to the cell's protein-building ribosomes. Amino acids in the ribosomes have chemical markers that enable them to recognise the chemical bases on the RNA copies that arrive from the nucleus, and the appropriate amino acids line up alongside each other. They then bond together to form the protein.

The repeating base-pair units in DNA appear in various different sequences. The order of the base pairs in one molecule of DNA (one chromosome) is known as its genetic code. The combined order in all 46 chromosomes (a complete set of DNA) is known as the genome.

The Human Genome Project

The Human Genome Project was begun in 1990 – its aims are to determine the sequence of all 3 billion base pairs in human DNA and identify every one of our genes. In February 2001, the first of these objectives was achieved, at least in working draft form. Nine-tenths of the sequence has now been determined; a final version should be ready in 2004.

Understanding the human genome could mean an end to hereditary diseases. By comparing the sequence of a healthy person with that of one suffering from a hereditary disease, the mutations responsible could be identified. With that information, gene replacement therapy could not only cure symptoms but prevent the condition from ever being passed on.

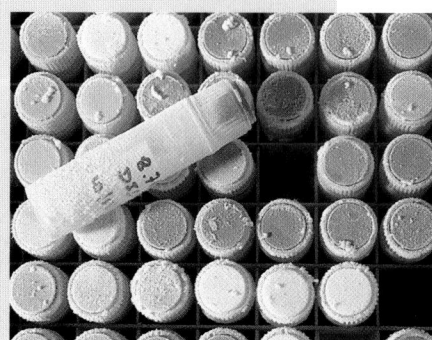

On ice DNA from people with hereditary diseases is stored at a gene bank in France.

FACTS AND FIGURES

- The human body is made up of about 100 000 billion cells.
- The largest cell in the human body is the egg cell, or ovum, which can measure up to 0.035 mm in diameter.
- Cells lining the mouth usually last for less than three days, so must be replaced at this rate.
- Humans have around 30 000 genes, yet they make up only 3 per cent of our DNA; the remaining 97 per cent, known as 'junk' DNA, apparently does nothing.
- There are no standard genetic differences between people of different races. Indeed, there is often greater variation between individuals of the same race than of different races.
- An undamaged tooth can retain stable DNA for thousands of years.
- Bacteria share 20 per cent of our genes, mice 90 per cent and chimpanzees 99 per cent.

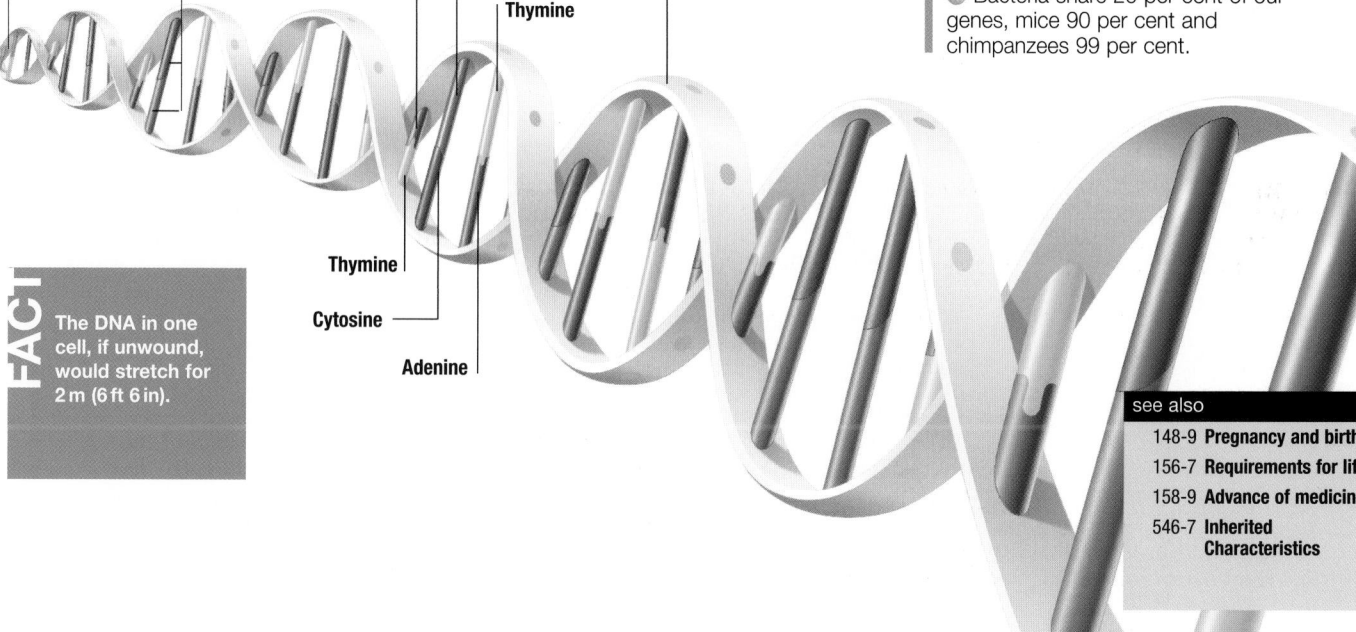

DNA unravelled DNA is structured like a spiral ladder (double helix). This illustration shows a molecule of DNA stretched out.

Base pair Chemical bases pair up to form the rungs of the ladder. The order in which the base pairs occur provides the genetic instructions, or code.

Triplet Each triplet of base pairs provides the code for one amino acid, from which proteins are assembled.

Sugar string Each chemical base is attached to a molecule of sugar called deoxyribose. The deoxyribose molecules bond together to form the 'supports' of the DNA ladder.

Adenine
Guanine
Thymine
Thymine
Cytosine
Adenine

FACT The DNA in one cell, if unwound, would stretch for 2 m (6 ft 6 in).

see also
148-9 **Pregnancy and birth**
156-7 **Requirements for life**
158-9 **Advance of medicine**
546-7 **Inherited Characteristics**

It was William Shakespeare who first recognised seven ages of man, from birth through to death. What he wrote still holds true, but several intervening milestones have since been added to his list. The greatest amount of change in our brains occurs between birth and the age of seven. In that time we develop from having simple, almost instinctive, behaviour patterns to a rounded and conscious understanding of the world. Our bodies undergo constant change but alter most noticeably during puberty and as we start to age.

Young achievers

- **Fu Mingxia** of China was just 12 years 141 days old when she became the women's world platform diving champion.
- **Michael Kearney** became the world's youngest graduate in 1994 at the age of 10 years and 4 months, when he obtained a degree in anthropology from the University of Alabama, USA.

Birth A newborn baby can see (although not focus clearly), hear and has primitive reflexes, such as sucking and finger grasping. It can recognise the shape of a human face, and, by three days old, can tell its mother's voice from those of others.

2-6 months During this time, different emotions begin to emerge and become clearly defined. Fear and anger separate and the first signs of satisfaction become apparent. At four months, babies start to recognise objects and by six months have begun to explore the shapes and sizes of things using their mouths.

1-2 years Babies become toddlers and learn to walk. By the time they are two they can run and kick a ball without overbalancing; they can also string two words (noun and adjective) together. Emotionally, they begin to feel jealousy and guilt. Fear of imaginary monsters and darkness begins.

3-4 years Children move from being able to copy lines and circles to complete letters. Speech becomes more grammatical and sentences longer. The sense of balance improves, enabling climbing, hopping and running on tiptoe.

Birth	2 months	6 months	9 months	1 year	2 years	3 years	4 years

Up to 2 months Babies learn to focus their eyes and smile. The first smiles are just mimicry of adult faces but babies soon learn that smiling elicits positive responses from others and the process becomes linked with pleasure. During the first eight weeks of life, memory of the existence of objects is limited to 15 seconds.

6-9 months Babies start to focus on facial expressions rather than just facial features, and depth perception improves. During this period, babies realise that hidden objects continue to exist. They learn to sit up and to crawl. The foundations of speech are laid as they go from cooing through babbling to increasingly accurate imitation of adult noises.

9-12 months Most babies utter their first recognisable words, and begin to imitate their mother's actions, such as combing hair. Babies can walk with assistance.

2-3 years Children begin to understand the concept of sharing and start to play with others. They increasingly link images of objects with thoughts about them, and improve in their ability to classify things.

4-5 years Peers become important to children and they start to make closer friends. Coordination improves and they become able to write some letters without needing to copy them. During this period, identification with the parent of the same sex as the child is at its strongest. By five years old, the brain has reached three quarters of its adult size.

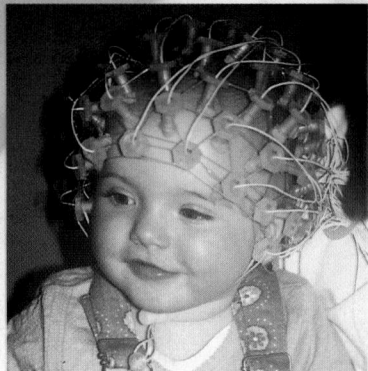

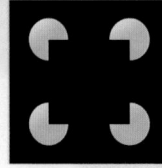

Shape recognition Research into the age at which babies begin to recognise shapes has revealed that at eight months they show more interest in a square shape (top) than a random collection of elements. At six months they are no more interested in one than the other.

PUBERTY

At puberty, hormones trigger changes in growth and in development of the sex organs, and prepare the body to reproduce. Rapid growth and weight increase occurs, as do psychological and emotional changes. These changes start in girls at some point between 9 and 13 years, and in boys between 10 and 15.

- **Boys** The testes secrete the male hormone testosterone, which is responsible for the growth of facial, body and pubic hair, an increase in muscle bulk, a deepening of the voice, growth of the genital organs, and the development of sperm in the testes.

- **Girls** The ovaries secrete the female hormones oestrogen and progesterone. These cause breasts to develop, the hips to broaden, and pubic and underarm hair to appear; menstruation begins at about the same time.

Older mum A combination of improved nutrition and health, advances in fertility treatment and medical knowledge is extending the age at which women give birth well into middle age.

Golden oldies

- **Jenny Wood-Allen** completed the 1999 London marathon at 87.
- **William Baldwin** tightrope-walked across Boulder Canyon in Colorado, USA, when he was 82.
- **Jack MacKenzie** skied 100 miles to the North Pole, aged 77.
- **Oscar Swahn** won an Olympic silver medal for shooting, aged 72.
- **Wong Yui Hoi** took up snowboarding in 1995, when he was 75.

5-7 years Children can increasingly distinguish between letters. For the first time, their world is dominated by other children rather than adults, and they learn social roles and their own limits by play. At five, thought is centred on the present, but by seven concepts of past and future have started to form.

15-20 years The body reaches its maximum height and the brain its full size.

30-40 years Testosterone levels in men begin to fall (from mid 30s).

40-60 years Physiological processes start to decline. By their late 50s many men have enlarged prostate glands. Thinning of hair occurs in both sexes as cells that normally produce hair follicle nourishment die. Greying, and baldness in men, either begin or accelerate during this period. Menstruation ceases, usually between the ages of 45 and 50, and the female menopause begins.

80 years onwards Physiological processes decline further, and the incidence of osteoarthritis greatly increases. The structure of the brain deteriorates, although this is not always accompanied by a reduction in mental ability.

| 5 years | 10 years | 20 years | 30 years | 40 years | 50 years | 60 years | 70 years | 80 years |

9-15 years Puberty begins, starting with a sudden growth spurt and other physical changes. Girls begin to menstruate about two and a half years after puberty begins.

20-30 years The body increases in bulk with extra muscle and fat.

60-80 years Vision and hearing deteriorate, skin begins to sag and wrinkles appear. The gradual loss of the protein collagen causes muscles to waste away. The lungs cannot fully inflate or deflate as they lose their elasticity, and bones become less dense and more brittle. The walls of arteries thicken and harden, raising blood pressure, and the risk of heart disease increases.

FACTS AND FIGURES

- Jeanne Calment of Arles, France, lived to be 122: the longest human life ever documented. She died in 1997.
- Genes can influence life span. Some citizens of Limone in Italy have inherited a gene mutation that produces increased beneficial cholesterol, reducing the risk of heart disease.
- Gene mutations can quicken the ageing process. People suffering from Werner's syndrome carry a mutation that causes them to age prematurely. By their teens they have the wrinkled skin and grey hair of extreme old age; they succumb to cancers or heart disease, and die young.

Up and over Age need be no barrier to an active life, as Californian Carol Johnston proves. At 85 years old, he still competes in pole-vaulting tournaments and holds the world record for his age.

see also

132-3 **Skeleton and muscles**

138 **Glands and hormones**

154-5 **Human capacity**

160-1 **Disorders/diseases**

Human capacity ▶ | The body's strengths and weaknesses

Compared with those of the rest of the animal kingdom, human physical attributes seem rather meagre. Nevertheless, people have achieved some incredible feats of speed, strength and endurance, which continue to be exceeded almost every year. Our greatest human strengths come in our intellectual and manufacturing abilities, which have allowed us to modify our environment rather than adapt to it.

SPEED COMPARISONS

Human beings seem to be getting faster all the time, but there are some animals that we will never catch up with. Whereas performance in our species is improved by physical training, performance in theirs has been honed through thousands of years of evolutionary pressure.

PHYSIOLOGICAL DIFFERENCES

Humans differ from other animals in life processes and systems. Examples of the most important differences are:

Number of brain cells
Sea snail: 20 000
Fruit fly: 100 000
Mouse: 5 million
Monkey: 10 billion
Human: 1000 billion

Body temperature
Shark: 25°C (77°F)
Snake: 31°C (88°F)
Human: 37°C (99°F)
Elephant: 38°C (100°F)
Duck: 44°C (111°F)

Heartbeats per minute
Elephant: 25–28
Human: 70–80
Dog: 90-100
Mouse: 500-600
Hummingbird: 1000

Typical life span
Snakes and lizards: 25–30
Chimpanzee: 35–40
Mussel: 50–100
Human: 70–85
Giant tortoise: 100–150

Fastest land snake:
Black mamba (*Dendroaspis polylepis*) 16–19 km/h (10–12 mph).

Fastest human male:
Maurice Greene, USA, ran 100 m at 36.77 km/h (22.85 mph), June 16, 1999, in Athens, Greece.

Fastest long-distance animal:
The pronghorn antelope (*Antilocapra americana*) 1.6 km (1 mile) at 67 km/h (42 mph), or 6 km (4 miles) at 56 km/h (35 mph). The fastest animal on land over a sustained distance.

Fastest-flying bird:
Peregrine falcon (*Falco peregrinus*) 200 km/h (124 mph) when 'stooping' or 'plunge-diving' from a height, the fastest speed reached by any living animal.

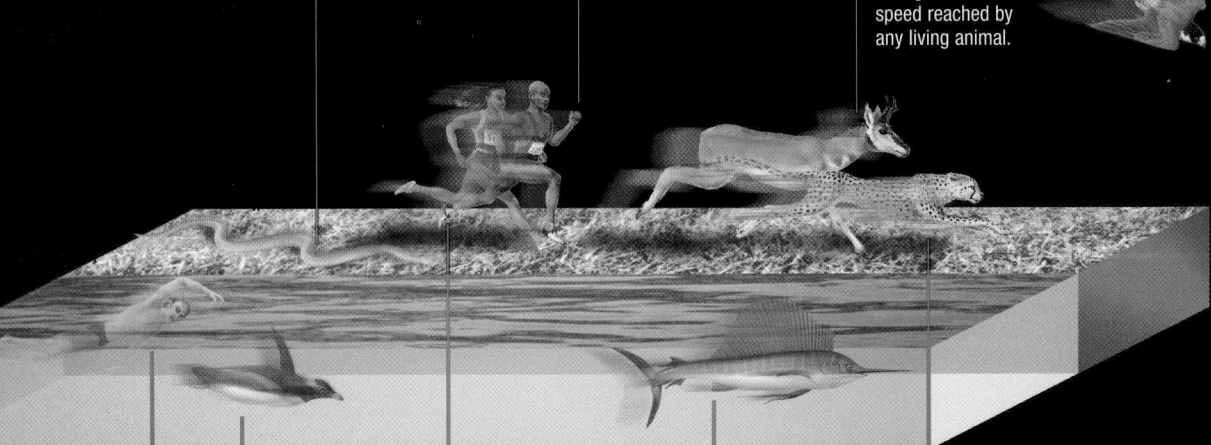

Fastest-swimming human:
Anthony Ervin, USA, 50 m at 8.49 km/h (5.28 mph), March 23, 2000, in Minneapolis, USA.

Fastest-swimming bird:
Gentoo penguin (*Pygoscelis papua*) 27 km/h (17 mph).

Fastest human female:
Florence Griffith-Joyner, USA, ran 100 m at 34.32 km/h (1.33 mph), July 16, 1988, in Indianapolis, USA.

Fastest fish:
Cosmopolitan sailfish (*Istiophorus platypterus*) 109 km/h (68 mph).

Fastest short-distance land animal:
Cheetah (*Acinonyx jubatus*) 96–101 km/h (60–63 mph); capable of reaching 96 km/h (60 mph) in 3 seconds from a standing start. The fastest land animal.

Areas in which humans surpass other animals

Intelligence Humans not only have extremely large brains for their size but also the most highly developed frontal lobes of any species (the frontal lobes are where planning, forethought and other 'intellectual' functions take place).

Communication Speech is unique to humans. It lets us communicate complex thoughts, ideas and knowledge. Written language enables us to pass these on without being present.

Handiness The human hand is capable of a range of grips, and combines strength with sensitivity. This enables us to make and use all kinds of objects, tools, weapons and machinery.

Parental care We are supremely careful parents; our young have a far higher chance of survival than those of other species.

Areas in which humans trail other animals

Smell We are able to smell most objects only when they are right under our noses. Many other animals can pick up and interpret odours from miles away.

Hearing Our hearing is moderately good, but the range of frequencies we can hear is narrower than that of many animals. Dogs, bats, whales and dolphins, for example, can hear much higher frequencies.

Visual acuity Although we are good at understanding what we see, our eyes are not particularly good at registering fine detail, especially after dark.

Thermoregulation Our bodies' lack of insulation makes us poor at coping with sudden changes in temperature.

Speeding up In 1999 Maurice Greene set a world 100 m record with a time of 9.79 seconds, a one-second improvement on the record in 1900 of 10.8 seconds. There will come a time when factors such as the human heart rate will limit further improvements in athletic performance.

FACTS AND FIGURES

● In February 2001, Joe Decker from the USA was officially crowned the world's fittest man. In 24 hours he cycled 161 km (100 miles), ran 16 km (10 miles), powerwalked 8 km (5 miles), kayaked 9.5 km (6 miles) and swam 3 km (2 miles) before going on to complete 3000 abdominal crunches, 1100 jumping jacks, 1100 push-ups, 1000 leg-lifts, 16 km (10 miles) on a skiing machine, 16 km (10 miles) on a rowing machine and a three-hour gym session in which he lifted 126 371 kg (278 540 lb) in weights.

● On June 1, 1998, Susie Maroney became the first person to swim nonstop from Mexico to Cuba. The Australian completed the journey in 38 hours and 33 minutes, setting the record for the longest swim in the open sea without flippers by anyone.

● Italian Reinhold Messner has scaled all 14 of the world's mountains over 8000 m (26 250 ft) high without the assistance of oxygen. He is the only person ever to have achieved this feat.

Global human life expectancy

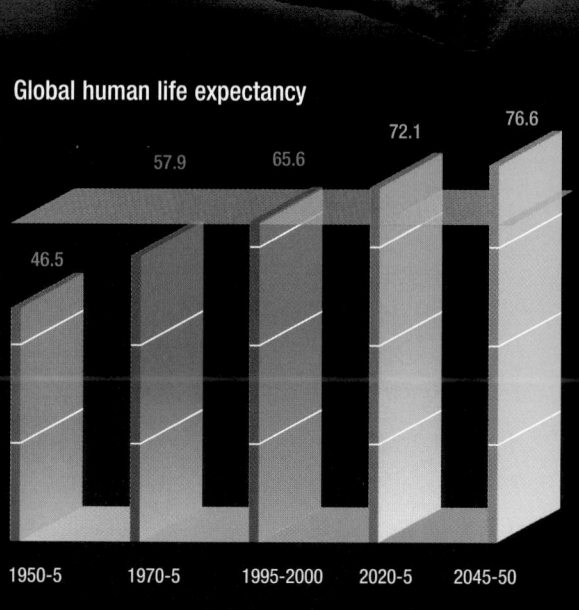

	46.5	57.9	65.6	72.1	76.6
	1950-5	1970-5	1995-2000	2020-5	2045-50

65
60
40
20

Old world Between 1950 and 2000, life expectancy at birth increased by almost 20 years. Scientists expect the rate of increase to tail off, but still predict that people born in 2050 will live for 11 years longer, on average, than those born in 2000.

Without a wide range of nutrients, the human body would rapidly sicken and die. Some provide it with the energy it needs to function, others are important for growth or maintaining organs or tissues. The body also requires exercise to keep the muscles, heart and lungs in shape, and – for unknown reasons – adequate sleep.

Components of food

Food provides the body with four main components:

● **Macronutrients** Fats, carbohydrates and proteins.
● **Micronutrients** Vitamins and minerals.
● **Fibre** Roughage found in plant foods. It is essential for efficient digestion.
● **Water** Found in all types of food. The body needs a minimum of 1.5 litres daily.

FOOD BALANCE

For optimum health, the body requires a diet with the following proportions of fats, proteins and carbohydrates:

● **Carbohydrates** 58 per cent.
● **Unsaturated and polyunsaturated fats** 20 per cent.
● **Proteins** 12 per cent.
● **Saturated fats** 10 per cent.

ENERGY AND FOOD

Even when at rest, the human body requires energy to maintain body temperature and to build and repair cells. The main sources of energy are glucose and fatty acids obtained from food. The energy is released by a complex series of chemical reactions, known as the Krebs cycle, that takes place when oxygen is also present. The process is known as respiration.

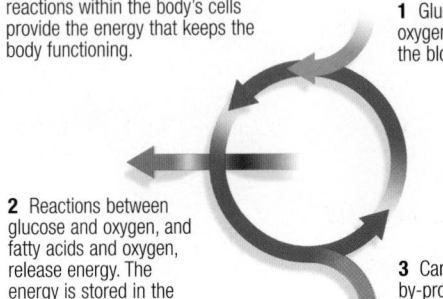

Cellular respiration Chemical reactions within the body's cells provide the energy that keeps the body functioning.

1 Glucose, fatty acids and oxygen are delivered to a cell by the bloodstream.

2 Reactions between glucose and oxygen, and fatty acids and oxygen, release energy. The energy is stored in the cell in a chemical called ATP until it is needed, and then released again.

3 Carbon dioxide and water are by-products of the process, and are transported away from the cell.

Vitamins and minerals
Vitamins are organic (carbon-based) substances essential to health. With the exceptions of vitamin D and niacin the body cannot manufacture vitamins for itself, so they have to be obtained from food. Fat-soluble vitamins can be stored by the body but water-soluble vitamins cannot. Water-soluble vitamins are therefore required daily. Minerals are inorganic substances, such as iron, fluorine, sulphur, zinc and calcium, that cannot be produced in the body, but are also essential to health. Minerals needed only in minute amounts are known as trace minerals. In the following tables, RDA stands for recommended daily amount.

Fat-soluble vitamins

Vitamin	RDA	Sources	Functions
A (retinol or carotene)	0.8–1 mg	Fish liver oils, liver, egg yolk, dairy products, fortified margarine, green, orange and yellow vegetables, orange and yellow fruits	Growth, vision, formation of bones and teeth, protects against infections of digestive, respiratory and urinary systems
D	0.005–0.01 mg	Produced in the skin when exposed to sunlight, fortified dairy products and margarine, cod liver oil, oily fish, liver, egg yolk	Ensures blood clotting, healthy nerve and muscle function, strong bones and teeth
E	8–10 mg	Green vegetables, beans, vegetable oils, whole-grain cereals, nuts, eggs	Helps to produce and protect red blood cells, protects cell membranes
K_1 and K_2	0.06–0.09 mg	Leafy green vegetables, potatoes, wheat germ, egg yolk, cheese, pork, liver; K_2 is produced in the gut by bacteria	Produce substances in the liver that promote blood clotting

Water-soluble vitamins

Vitamin	RDA	Sources	Functions
B_1 (thiamine)	1–1.4 mg	Liver, fish, milk, eggs, nuts, beans, wholemeal bread	Helps nerves and muscles to function
B_2 (riboflavin)	1.2–1.6 mg	Leafy vegetables, peas and beans, liver, meat, eggs, milk, cheese	Maintains healthy mucous membranes and skin
B_2 (niacin)	13–18 mg	Fruits, liver, meat, eggs, fish, nuts, peas and beans	Sex hormone production; maintenance of nerves and digestive system
B_2 (pantothenic acid)	4–7 mg	Most foods, particularly green vegetables, peanuts, liver, whole-grain cereals; also produced by bacteria in gut	Sex hormone production; maintenance of skin and nervous system
B_6 (pyridoxine)	2 mg	Most foods, particularly bananas, potatoes, beans, liver, meat, whole-grain cereals, wheat germ; also produced by bacteria in gut	Production of antibodies, red blood cell production, healthy skin
B_6 (biotin)	0.03–0.2 mg	Most foods, particularly nuts, beans, liver, eggs, oats, wheat germ	Excretion of waste, and excretion from protein breakdown
B_6 (folic acid)	0.4 mg	Green vegetables, fruits, nuts, beans, liver, eggs, wholemeal bread	Helps in DNA and red blood cell production; healthy nervous system
B_{12}	0.003 mg	Meat, liver, fish, eggs, dairy products (except butter)	Helps red blood cell production, maintenance of nervous system
C	60 mg (100 mg for smokers)	Raw fruits and vegetables, particularly peppers, potatoes, broccoli, citrus fruits, tomatoes, blackcurrants	Builds resistance to infection, promotes growth and healthy blood vessels, bones, teeth and gums

Minerals

Mineral	RDA	Sources	Functions
Calcium	0.8–1.2 g	Fish, eggs, dairy products, pulses, nuts, green vegetables, soya bean products, hard water	Normal heart action, blood clotting, muscle contraction, transmission of nerve impulses, growth and maintenance of bones and teeth
Chlorine	2–3 g	All foods, salt	Constituent of blood and other body fluids
Magnesium	0.3–0.35 g	Green vegetables, meat, milk, fish, nuts, pulses, whole-grain cereals	Healthy bones and teeth, normal muscle and nerve activity
Phosphorus	0.8–1.2 g	Dairy products, eggs, fish, meat, poultry, pulses, nuts, bread, whole-grain cereals	Healthy bones and teeth, production of DNA, conversion and storage of energy in cells, healthy nerve and muscle function
Potassium	2.5 g	All foods	Muscle contraction, transmission of nerve impulses
Sodium	2.5 g	Most foods, salt	Muscle contraction, transmission of nerve impulses
Sulphur	1.2 g	Foods rich in protein, such as eggs, milk, meat and pulses	Constituent of some proteins, such as insulin

Trace minerals (microminerals)

Mineral	RDA	Sources	Functions
Chromium	50–200 mg	Meat, liver, yeast, fruits, nuts, wholemeal bread, whole-grain cereals	Helps in the breakdown of carbohydrates
Cobalt	–	Liver, kidney, meat, eggs	Formation of red blood cells
Copper	2–3 mg	Shellfish, meat, fish, liver, nuts, wholemeal bread, pulses	Formation of red blood cells, normal function for some enzymes
Fluorine	1.5–4 mg	Sardines, tea, fluoridated water	Promotes healthy bones and teeth and prevents tooth decay
Iron	10–18 mg	Shellfish, meat, liver, eggs, nuts, pulses, fruits, wholemeal bread	Constituent of oxygen-carrying molecules in red blood cells
Molybdenum	0.15–0.5 g	Liver, pulses, barley, buckwheat	Important constituent of many enzymes
Zinc	15 mg	Seafood, eggs, milk, meat, liver, yeast, pulses, wholemeal bread	Healing, growth, sperm production; constituent of many enzymes

Sleep We know a lot about what happens during sleep but we still don't really know why we need it. Metabolic functions slow down during sleep but brain activity doesn't, it simply changes. The brain stem controls our falling asleep and awakening and regulates cycles of dreaming and non-dreaming sleep. Most dreams occur during rapid eye movement (REM) sleep. When the body is in non-rapid eye movement (NREM) sleep, temperature, blood pressure and heart rate fall. Sleep patterns vary depending on age, fitness and levels of physical activity, but follow the general cycle illustrated below. Extreme sleep deprivation can cause personality changes and memory loss.

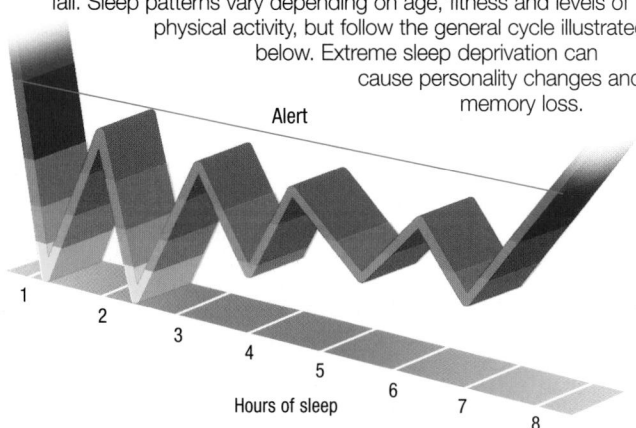

Hours of sleep

NREM Stage 1: The lightest sleep.

NREM Stage 2: Breathing deepens.

NREM Stage 3: Growth hormone produced; duration of this stage is reduced in adult life.

NREM Stage 4: The deepest kind of sleep; very little brain activity. This stage diminishes after a person passes 60 years of age.

REM: Rapid eye movement; dreaming occurs.

Burning the calories

The table below shows the energy expended per hour by an adult of average size and fitness undergoing different activities:

Badminton	340 kcal (1428 kJ)	**Jogging**	630 kcal (2646 kJ)
Climbing stairs	620 kcal (2604 kJ)	**Lying in bed**	60 kcal (252 kJ)
Cycling	660 kcal (2772 kJ)	**Squash**	600 kcal (2520 kJ)
Football	540 kcal (2268 kJ)	**Standing**	120 kcal (504 kJ)
Gardening, heavy	420 kcal (1764 kJ)	**Swimming**	720 kcal (3024 kJ)
Gardening, light	270 kcal (1134 kJ)	**Tennis**	480 kcal (2016 kJ)
Gymnastics	420 kcal (1764 kJ)	**Walking briskly**	300 kcal (1260 kJ)
Housework	270 kcal (1134 kJ)	**Walking slowly**	180 kcal (756 kJ)

FACTS AND FIGURES

The average person spends a third of his or her life asleep.

Per day, a typical 1-year-old sleeps for 14 hours, a 5-year-old sleeps for 12 hours, and 90 per cent of adults sleep for 6-9 hours.

The average person consumes about 40 tonnes of food in a lifetime.

The past five centuries have seen huge leaps in our understanding of how the human body works and in the causes, prevention and cure of disease. Five hundred years ago, for instance, not even the circulation of the blood was understood, nor was the existence of disease-causing microbes realised. Today, we have decoded the entire human genetic blueprint, can create life in a test tube, and have an arsenal of drugs with which to combat disease.

Single earpiece Early stethoscopes looked little like they do today. To use this 19th-century example, the doctor would put the rounded end to a patient's chest and the pointed end, which channelled the sound, to his ear.

UNDERSTANDING THE BODY

1500

1600

1700

1800

1628 William Harvey theorises that blood, pumped by the heart, circulates around the body.

1661 Marcello Malpighi confirms Harvey's circulation theory.

1761 B.G. Morgagni writes *On the Causes of Diseases*, the beginning of scientific anatomical study using cadavers.

1815 René Laënnec invents the stethoscope.

1858 German pathologist Rudolf Virchow proposes that the body's cells develop from one cell, the fertilised ovum, which itself has developed from cells of the two parents.

1543 Anatomical drawings published for the first time in *The Seven Books on the Structure of the Human Body* by Andries Vesalius.

1726 Stephen Hales measures blood pressure.

1796 Edward Jenner introduces vaccination against smallpox.

1882 Walther Fleming discovers chromosomes, the carriers of genetic information.

Contraception

1220 BC Condom use recorded in ancient Egypt.
1844 Rubber condoms are mass-produced after Charles Goodyear patents rubber vulcanisation.
1909 The contraceptive intrauterine device (IUD) for women is invented by Richard Richter.

1916 The first birth-control clinic is opened, by Margaret Sanger in the USA.
1959 The female contraceptive pill is developed by Gregory Pincus. A year later, it becomes available in the USA.

Advent of the coil This IUD from the early 20th century was one of the first internal contraceptive devices.

Louis Pasteur French microbiologist.

1870-80s Louis Pasteur shows that microorganisms are responsible for infectious diseases. Pasteur develops vaccines against rabies and anthrax. He also pioneers pasteurisation, in which heat is used to kill disease-carrying organisms in foods.

Medical milestones

*c.***400 BC** Hippocrates observes that malaria is associated with a certain locality and climate and so lays the foundations of epidemiology – the study of the causes and distribution of diseases.
1666 Thomas Sydenham publishes a study on epidemics, *Observationes Medicae*, establishing principles of medical examination and epidemiology. Sydenham is also the first to use quinine in treating malaria, and iron in treating anaemia.
1780s Digitalis is used by British physician William Withering to treat oedema (dropsy).
1796 Edward Jenner inoculates a boy with the mild disease cowpox as protection

against the deadly disease smallpox. Vaccination becomes standard practice in treating smallpox.
1805 German pharmacist Friedrich Sertürner extracts morphine from opium.
1842 US surgeon Crawford Long first uses ether as an anaesthetic, in an operation to remove a tumour.
1899 Aspirin, derived from plant extracts, is developed by the German chemist Heinrich Dreser.
1910 German chemist Paul Ehrlich develops salvarsan – the first synthetic antibacterial drug capable of fighting a specific disease – to treat syphilis.

1928 Penicillin, the world's first antibiotic, is discovered by British bacteriologist Alexander Fleming. It is developed as a commercial drug by Howard Florey and Ernst Chain in 1940.
1953 US doctor Jonas Salk produces a polio vaccine.
1980 The global eradication of smallpox due to mass vaccination is announced.
2001 DNA vaccination is being developed. This technique, of injecting DNA from a disease-causing microbe into muscle, induces a robust and long-lasting immunity and has the potential to protect us against all diseases.

LOOKING INSIDE LIVING PEOPLE

In 1895, while investigating the properties of cathode rays, Austrian physicist Wilhelm Röntgen recorded a new form of radiation that penetrated flesh and cloth. He named his discovery 'X-rays', and produced photographs of hands that showed the bones. X-rays were the beginnings of non-invasive imaging as a diagnostic tool. Since then, techniques that reveal the structure and chemistry of the body have added to our knowledge of how it works.

1895 X-rays are first used to show two-dimensional images of bones. They can detect fractures, bone diseases and foreign bodies.

1950 Ultrasound – two-dimensional images of soft internal tissue are produced by echoes from high-frequency sound waves.

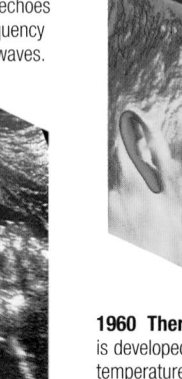

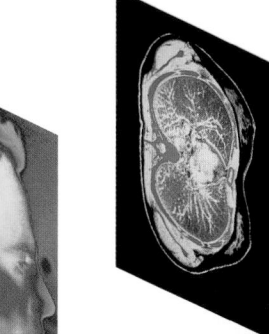

1960 Thermography is developed to record temperature differences on the body. It detects inflammation and rapid cell division, indicating possible cancer growth.

1972 Computerised axial tomography (CAT) scanning is developed. It uses a computer to convert cross-section X-rays into 3-D images of organs and body cavities to show tumours and other signs of disease or injury.

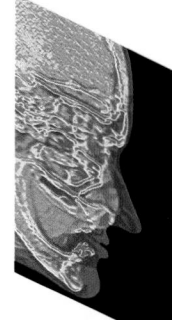

1980 Magnetic resonance imaging (MRI), in which the body is surrounded by a strong magnetic field and scanned with radio waves, is used to create cross-sectional 3-D images. It can reveal the entire fabric of the body from soft tissues, such as those in the brain, to tooth enamel.

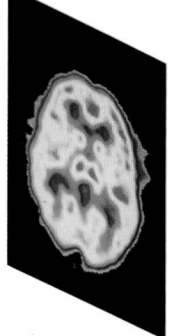

1987 The positron emission tomography (PET) scan, which introduces short-life radioactive elements into the body to reveal the body's chemistry, is developed to show abnormalities in the brain, such as those caused by strokes.

1900 Karl Landsteiner identifies blood groups, ensuring safe blood transfusions.

1900

1929 Hans Berger discovers electrical activity in the brain and invents the electroencephalograph (EEG), which uses electrodes to monitor it.

1944 Oswald Avery, Maclyn McCarty and Colin MacLeod discover that DNA carries genetic information.

1952 Amniocentesis (examination of amniotic fluid from the womb, using a hollow needle) is developed by British geneticist Douglas Bevis.

1950

1984 Genetically engineered human insulin is produced. The AIDS virus (later called HIV) is discovered by French immunologist Luc Montaigner.

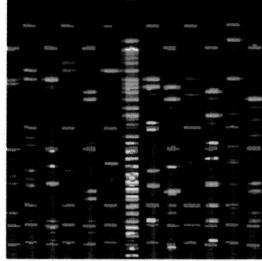

Colour coded A DNA sequence is shown on a computer screen. Each coloured band represents one of the four nucleotides that make up DNA.

2000

1921 Frederick Banting and Charles Best isolate the hormone insulin, and use it successfully in the treatment of diabetes.

Frederick Banting and Charles Best

1953 The double helix structure of DNA is identified by James Watson and Francis Crick.

1973 Stanley Cohen and Herbert Boyer introduce new genes into bacterial cells, the first step towards genetic engineering.

2000 A draft of the complete human genome is released by two rival teams of scientists, one from the international non-profit Human Genome Project consortium, the other from a private American company Celera Genomics.

Early stage human embryo The cells of a fertilised egg change into stem cells a few days after conception.

Using cloning to treat disease

Cloning of human embryos is a controversial area of medical research, but this technology could have major medical benefits such as the treatment of Parkinson's disease and spinal-cord injuries. Embryos contain specialist cells called stem cells that can develop into any form of tissue. Transplanting stem cells from cloned embryos under 14 days old into patients suffering from incurable injuries or diseases stimulates the growth of healthy organ and tissue cells.

Apart from physical injury and natural wear and tear, there are three main causes of illness. They are: invasion by microorganisms such as viruses; errors in our genetic makeup; or exposure to external factors such as pollution, pollens, poor diet or drug abuse.

How viruses multiply

Viruses are the most simple living things. Some scientists do not even consider them alive at all since they cannot reproduce without the help of other organisms.

All viruses are parasitic. They reproduce by invading a host cell, shedding their protective outer coats, and using the host cell's DNA to replicate their own genetic material many times over. Each replicated strand of genetic material acquires an outer protein coat to form a new virus.

INFECTIOUS DISEASES

Infectious diseases are caused by microorganisms. Symptoms of disease appear when these microbes begin to multiply. There are four main categories of disease-inducing microbes:

Viruses Consisting only of genetic material surrounded by a protective coat, viruses are totally dependent on the living cells of other organisms to reproduce. In the process, they cause a wide range of diseases from the common cold and influenza to AIDS and smallpox, and they are not treatable with antibiotics.

Bacteria Simple single-celled organisms. Bacteria live in a range of habitats, including the surface of the body and intestines. Most are harmless, but some cause disease. Illnesses caused by bacteria are generally treatable by antibiotics.

Protists Single-celled organisms that are larger and much more complex than bacteria. Most are non-parasitic and harmless, but parasitic types cause diseases such as sleeping sickness.

Fungi Single-celled or multicellular organisms that feed on living matter or dead remains. Most are non-parasitic, but some parasitic types can cause disease if they become established on or in the body. Fungi are responsible for thrush and athlete's foot.

The seven most deadly infectious diseases According to the World Health Organization statistics, the following diseases currently account for the highest number of deaths around the world:

Disease	Infective agent	Method of transmission	Incubation	Symptoms	Treatment	Deaths annually (est.)
Pneumonia	Various viruses	Airborne	Variable	Cough, fever	Relief of symptoms	3 500 000
HIV/AIDS	Virus	Sexual contact, mother to baby, blood transfusion	Variable, about seven years	Weight loss, diarrhoea, lethargy, fever, shortness of breath, infections	Plenty of fluids, antibiotics if severe	2 285 000
Diarrhoeal diseases	Bacteria	Direct contact with infected person, food	One to two days	Severe diarrhoea and dehydration	Treatment of infections, but incurable	2 219 000
Tuberculosis (TB)	Bacterium	Infected cows' milk, airborne	Several weeks to several years	Cough with bloodstained mucous secretions, chest pain	Antibiotics	1 498 000
Malaria	Protist	Bites by mosquitoes	Ten to fourteen days	Sweating, fatigue, severe episodic fever and chills	Antimalarial drugs	1 110 000
Measles	Virus	Airborne	Seven to fourteen days	Red skin rash, fever, severe cold	Relief of symptoms	888 000
Whooping cough	Bacterium	Droplets from infected person	Twelve to twenty days	Sneezing, sore throat, fever, prolonged fits of coughing followed by vomiting	Antibiotics	346 000

Other common infectious diseases

Disease	Infective agent	Method of transmission	Incubation	Symptoms	Treatment
Chickenpox	Virus	Direct contact with infected person, airborne	Eleven to twenty-one days	Skin rash, sore throat, headaches, fever, lethargy	Relief of symptoms
Cholera	Bacterium	Contaminated food or water	One to five days	Severe diarrhoea and dehydration	Fluids, antibiotics
Common cold	Various viruses	Hand to hand contact, airborne	One to three days	Sneezing, blocked or runny nose, sore throat, aching muscles	Relief of symptoms
Diphtheria	Bacterium	Contact with infected person, airborne	Four to six days	Fever, grey membrane in throat, occasionally damage to heart	Antibiotics and antitoxin
Influenza (flu)	Virus	Airborne	One to three days	Alternating sweats and chills, headaches, sore throat, fever	Relief of symptoms
Typhoid	Bacterium	Contaminated food or water	Seven to fourteen days	Abdominal discomfort, diarrhoea, headaches, fever	Antibiotics

COMMON MEDICAL PROBLEMS

The human body is subject to many ailments and conditions.

Skeleton and muscles

Osteoarthritis Degeneration of the cartilage at the ends of bones leads to swelling, stiffness and pain in the joints.

Rheumatoid arthritis The body's immune system attacks its own tissues, causing severe inflammation of the lining of the soft tissue that encloses joints. It affects hips, feet, wrist and finger joints, causing painful swelling and stiffness. Finger joints may become deformed.

Rheumatism Covers all mild forms of inflammatory arthritis.

Senses

Anosmia The sense of smell is lost due to a brain injury.

Cataract The lens of the eye clouds over, causing blurred vision.

Glaucoma High pressure of fluids within the eye damage the optic nerve and nerve fibres in the retina, causing loss of vision.

Retinitis pigmentosa Degeneration of the retina produces poor night vision, and occasionally blindness.

Heart and blood circulation system

Angina Thickening of the coronary arteries reduces the blood supply to the heart, causing intense chest pains. Blood clots in the clogged arteries (coronary thromboses) cause heart attacks. Stress, smoking, high blood pressure, high blood cholesterol, obesity and lack of exercise can all lead to the onset of angina. Genetic factors and diabetes may also contribute.

High blood pressure (hypertension) Higher than normal pressure within the arteries affects the pumping force of the heart. The heart muscle thickens to compensate for this, and eventually there is an enlargement of the whole heart.

Anaemia This condition results from low levels of oxygen-carrying red blood cells in the blood. It is characterised by pale skin colour and extreme tiredness.

Sickle-cell anaemia Red blood cells become 'sickle-shaped' and cause obstructions within the blood vessels, affecting organs such as the brain and kidneys. It is a hereditary disease.

Respiratory system

Bronchitis Inflammation of the tubes linking the lungs and windpipe causes a productive cough.

Emphysema Irreversible damage to the lungs' air sacs causes breathlessness.

Digestive and urinary systems

Cystitis Bacterial infection in the bladder creates a frequent need to pass water. Cystitis is more common in women than men.

Diarrhoea Faeces become watery due to food poisoning, viral, bacterial or fungal infection. Diarrhoea can also be related to chronic bowel conditions such as irritable bowel syndrome and Crohn's disease.

Pernicious anaemia In this form of anaemia the intestine is unable to absorb vitamin B12, causing a shortage of red blood cells.

Ulcers Weakening of the gut's protective mucous layer causes sores in the stomach or duodenum.

Kidney stones (calculi) Solid lumps form inside the kidney from urinal chemicals, causing pain and difficulty in passing water.

Renal failure The kidneys are unable to filter blood properly, producing a build-up of waste products in the body.

Skin and hair

Skin inflammations Some of the more common conditions include eczema (itching and blisters), also called dermatitis, which can be either inherited or caused by an allergy; psoriasis (painful skin inflammation with silvery scales), which is usually inherited; and urticaria (itchy inflamed weals, also known as hives or nettle rash), which is caused by an allergy.

Vitiligo (leucoderma) Impairment of the melanin-producing cells causes loss of colour from patches of the skin.

Glands and hormones

Diabetes melitus Excessively high blood sugar leads to insufficient production of insulin by the pancreas. It can be genetic or caused by obesity.

Hyperthyroidism Overproduction or underproduction of thyroid hormones produces a range of effects. Overproduction increases the body's metabolic rate and leads to excessive sweating, weight loss and irregular heartbeat; underproduction causes weight gain, hair loss and tiredness.

Pituitary dwarfism or gigantism Underproduction or overproduction of the pituitary growth hormone during childhood causes, respectively, stunted or excessive growth.

Immune disorders

When our immune systems go wrong, the specialised cells that normally attack foreign particles begin to attack the body's own cells. This can lead to auto-immune disorders such as insulin-dependent diabetes, multiple sclerosis and arthritis. Insulin-dependent diabetes, for instance, results from the destruction of the cells in the pancreas that produce insulin.

Allergies are also immune disorders. Harmless substances that we breathe in, swallow or which enter our bodies through the skin, are wrongly identified by our immune system as dangerous and are attacked. This causes inflammation at the point of contact and symptoms such as nausea, itching and sneezing. In extreme cases anaphylactic shock, a potentially fatal drop in blood pressure, results. Common allergens include house dust, pollen and various foods.

Disorders of the brain and nervous system

Most illnesses of the brain and nervous system are the result of chemical imbalances or damage to the brain or nerves.

Alzheimer's disease Progressive degeneration of brain tissue leads to diminishing intellectual ability.

Epilepsy Sudden, local electrical activity of nerve cells in the brain produces recurrent fits or fleeting periods of loss of consciousness. Epilepsy can have many causes, including injury to the brain, high fever and tumours.

Motor neurone disease (MND) Degeneration of spinal cord and brain cells causes weakness and muscle wastage.

Multiple sclerosis (MS) Progressive destruction by the body's immune system of the protective coating of nerve fibres causes the brain and nervous system to break down.

Parkinson's disease Caused by a deficiency in the brain of a chemical called dopamine, which assists the nerves in carrying messages, it produces tremor, rigidity and loss of spontaneous movements.

Schizophrenia A group of disabling disorders that are characterised by an inability to acknowledge reality.

Stroke The rupture or blocking of a blood vessel causes damage to the brain. Affected brain cells die, which can result in loss of function in the body areas controlled by them.

see also

139 **The immune system**

156-7 **Requirements for life**

158-9 **Advance of medicine**

568-71 **Practising medicine**

The history of mankind

The history of mankind

From the earliest civilisations to today's world

2500 BC | 2000 BC | 1500 BC | 1000 BC | 500 BC

Ancient Middle East

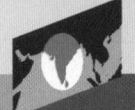

- **3500-2500** Sumerian city states founded
- **2000** Hittites invade Anatolia (Turkey)
- **1750** Babylonian Empire founded
- ***c*.1200** Hebrews settle Israel
- **740-612** Assyrian empires dominate Middle East
- **521** Persian Empire extends from Nile to Indus

Ancient Egypt

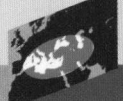

- ***c*.2800-2160** Old Kingdom
- **2050-1780** Middle Kingdom
- **1720** Hyksos rule begins
- **1560** New Kingdom founded
- **671-651** Assyrians invade Egypt
- **525** Persians conquer Egypt

India

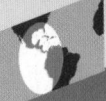

- ***c*.2500** Indus Valley civilisation develops
- ***c*.1550** Aryans invade Northern India
- **1000-600** Hindu states established
- ***c*.525** Buddha begins teaching

Ancient Greece

- ***c*.2000** Minoan civilisation emerges in Crete
- ***c*.1900** Mycenaeans settle in Greece
- ***c*.1500** Minoan civilisation collapses
- ***c*.1125** Dorians invade Greece
- ***c*.750** First Greek colonies founded

Ancient America

- ***c*.2600** Neolithic culture first emerges in Central America
- ***c*.1200-*c*.400** Olmec culture in Mexico
- ***c*.900-*c*.400** Chavin culture in Peru

China

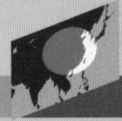

- ***c*.1600-1050** First Chinese civilisation
- ***c*.1000-256** 'Classical Age'
- ***c*.604-531** Life of Lao-Tzu'
- **551-479** Life of Confucius

Africa

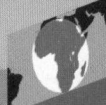

- ***c*.1000** First Kushite civilisation

Rome

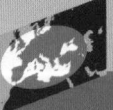

- ***c*.900** Etruscans settle in Italy
- **753** Rome founded

Byzantium

Japan

Medieval and early modern Europe

Isiamic Middle East

Russia

Modern Western civilisation

2500 BC | 2000 BC | 1500 BC | 1000 BC | 500 BC

500 BC   **0**   **AD 500**   **AD 1000**   **AD 1500**   **AD 2000**

334-326 Alexander conquers the Middle East

332-330 Alexander conquers Egypt   **30 BC** Romans annex Egypt

322-185 Mauryan Empire   **320-480** Gupta Empire of Northern India   **1206-1526** Delhi Sultanate   **1526-1707** Mughal Empire   **1612-1858** British conquest   **1947** Indian independence

469-429 'Golden Age' of Athens   **334-146** Hellenistic age   **146** Romans conquer Greece

AD100-300 Moche and Nazca cultures in Peru   **300-500** Teotihuacan culture in Mexico   **1000-1400** Chimu kingdom in Peru   **1325-1530** Aztec Empire in Mexico   **c.1438-1533** Inca Empire in Peru   **1530-96** Spanish conquest

221-210 Reign of Qin Shi Huangdi   **304** Hun invasions   **477** Buddhism becomes state religion   **850-900** Rule by warlords   **960-1279** Cultural flowering under Song Dynasty   **1275** Marco Polo reaches Beijing   **1557** Portuguese at Macao   **1839-60** Opium Wars   **1900-1** Boxer rebellion   **1949** People's Republic

500 BC-AD 200 Nok civilisation in Nigeria   **146** Roman Africa founded   **AD 50-400** Empire of Axum   **c.700** Empire of Ghana emerges   **c.700-1000** Spread of Islam   **c.1100-1250** Zimbabwe civilisation   **c.1500** Slave trade begins   **1878** 'Scramble for Africa'   **1945** Colonial independence begins to spread

510 Roman Republic founded   **264-146** Punic Wars   **27 BC** Augustus becomes first emperor   **476** Last Western emperor deposed

330 Constantinople founded   **636-838** Arab threat   **867** Orthodox Church breaks with Rome   **1453** Ottomans take Constantinople

c.300 Yamato clan unifies Japan   **794-1185** Heian period   **1192-1333** Kamakura Shogunate   **1338-1586** Ashikaga Shogunate   **1598-1868** Tokugawa Shogunate   **1941-45** Second World War

500 Barbarian kingdoms   **756** Moorish state in Spain   **1095-1272** Crusades   **c.1300-1600** Renaissance   **c.1530-1650** Reformation   **c.1700-1789** Enlightenment

630-60 Arab conquests   **909-1171** Fatimid Caliphate in Egypt   **c.1300-1920** Ottoman Empire   **1923** Turkish Republic founded

988 Kievan Rus adopts Byzantine Christianity   **1480** Unification of Russia around Muscovy   **1917** Russian Revolution

1492 Columbus reaches New World   **1760s** James Watt perfects steam engine   **1776** American Revolution   **1789** French Revolution   **1959** Silicon chip invented

500 BC   **0**   **AD 500**   **AD 1000**   **AD 1500**   **AD 2000**

The first modern humans (Homo sapiens sapiens) emerged in Africa 100 000 years ago. Over the next 50 000 years they colonised much of Asia and Australia before expanding into Europe. New skills were acquired at different rates in different regions, but the landmarks of development followed a similar pattern – from simple stone blades to sophisticated iron jewellery.

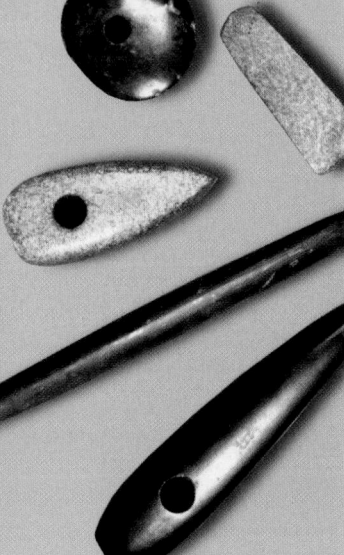

100 000 years ago *Homo sapiens sapiens* emerges from Africa.

45 000 years ago The first modern humans migrate into Europe from the Middle East.

c.25 000 years ago Female 'Venus' figurines are made in Europe.

18 000 years ago The last Ice Age reaches its height.

15 000 years ago The climate begins to improve and the ice sheets melt.

11 000 years ago Hunters spread south through the Americas.

Cave paintings Palaeolithic animal paintings adorn the cave walls at Lascaux, France.

50 000 years ago The first humans arrive in Australia.

40 000 years ago Upper Palaeolithic tools begin to appear in Europe.

6000 BC Irrigation is first practised, in Mesopotamia.

4500 BC The world's first-known temple is built, at Eridu, Sumer.

30 000 years ago The Neanderthals die out, unable to compete with the ancestors of modern humans.

20 000 years ago Art begins to flourish in Africa and south-west Europe, with rock paintings and carved objects.

12 000 years ago Animals and plants are domesticated; Neolithic Age begins.

10 000 years ago (8000 BC) The first images of gods are created.

7000 BC Copper is first used for tools.

5200 BC Farming spreads throughout Europe.

25 000 ya · *20 000 years ago* · *15 000 ya* · *10 000 years ago* · *4500 BC*

The Stone Age

Upper Palaeolithic
40 000-10 000 years ago

Early humans were already expert flint workers by the Upper Palaeolithic period. More than 100 distinct tools and weapons have been found at sites in Europe and the Near East. Typical features of Upper Palaeolithic cultures included:

- Stone spearheads, arrowheads and blades.
- Bone and ivory tools and weapons (fish-hooks, needles and spear-throwers).
- Jewellery and clothing, made of skins sewn using bone needles.
- The ceremonial burial of the dead.
- Cave art and statues.

Stone-age art The 'Venus of Willendorf', carved 25 000 years ago, is one of the earliest known sculptures.

Neolithic
From 12 000 years ago

The later Stone Age saw the development of farming, which replaced hunter-gathering as the primary mode of existence. By the end of the Neolithic, humans had learned to cultivate many crops: wheat and barley in the Near East, maize in Central America, rice in China and potatoes in South America. Farming created surpluses, allowing populations to grow and to establish permanent settlements. Other features of the Neolithic included:

- The domestication of animals (by 6000 BC in China and Mesopotamia).
- New tools – for example, axes to clear forests and bring new land under cultivation, hoes, sickles and grindstones.
- The use of pottery to store grain.
- The construction of the earliest villages and towns, often surrounded by walls to corral livestock (Jericho and Catal Hüyük).
- Tombs built of stone.

Stone tools Neolithic craftsmen were expert stone-workers. These hammers and axes date from *c.*5000 BC.

The metal ages

The Bronze Age
From 3000 BC

The first experiments with metalworking were made in Iran and Turkey some 9000 years ago. Copper and gold were the first metals to be used for tools and weapons, followed by bronze (an alloy of copper and tin). The Bronze Age featured:

● Copper and bronze tools and weapons (spearheads, arrowheads, chisels, saws).
● The practice of trade throughout Europe.
● Early mines and ore extraction methods.
● High standards of craftsmanship (jewellery, statues, decoration).
● The creation of stone alignments.

Bronze shield Bronze Age craftsmen created many finely decorated weapons.

The Iron Age
From 1200 BC

Iron was first used long before the Iron Age. The Hittites of Anatolia made iron weapons between 2000 and 1200 BC. Ironworking spread to Greece in about 1000 BC, and to northern Europe, Asia and Africa by about 750 BC. It was brought to Britain by the Celts – members of an Iron Age culture originating in the Austrian Alps. Iron had three advantages over bronze: it gave a sharper, harder-wearing edge, it did not need to be combined with another metal, and supplies were plentiful. It was used for nails, tools, weapons, cooking utensils, jewellery and also for religious articles. The European Iron Age is conventionally said to end with the spread of the Roman Empire. There was no Iron Age in the Americas, where iron was introduced by European colonists.

Iron brazier This Iron Age piece has stylised ox-head terminals.

4000 BC Amazon pottery is first made, in the Americas.

3000 BC The Indus Valley civilisation emerges. The wheel is in use here and in Mesopotamia.

2100 BC Stonehenge, England, reaches the height of its development.

1200 BC Agriculture spreads through North America.

1100 BC European peoples start to build hilltop forts.

800 BC The first iron-using societies at Hallstatt, Austria, herald Europe's Iron Age.

3000 BC

3500 BC Early city-states thrive in Mesopotamia; the first standing stones are raised in Europe.

2686 BC Egypt's Old Kingdom begins (to 2181 BC).

2000 BC The first palaces are built in Crete.

1500 BC

1000 BC

100 BC

Great migrations Modern humans spread slowly throughout the world from their origins in Africa. The South Pacific was the last area settled.

1300 BC The settlers of the Pacific Ocean islands begin to migrate eastwards to Fiji, Tonga and Samoa.

1000 BC Agriculture spreads into Central and South America.

AD 1000 New Zealand is settled by Polynesian seafarers.

North-west Europe 40 000 years ago

Middle East 90 000 years ago

Central Asia 25,000 years ago

Japan 30 000 years ago

Bering Strait 15 000 years ago

North America 12,000 years ago

Indus Valley 40 000 years ago

South-east Asia 40 000 years ago

Hawaiian Islands AD 400

Marquesas Islands 200 BC

Southern/ eastern Africa 200 000 years ago

Fiji 1300 BC

Tahiti 200 BC

Easter Island AD 300

Australia 40 000 years ago

New Zealand AD 1000

Patagonia 11 000 years ago

Civilisation is closely linked to the rise of cities. Urban life emerged as agriculture started to support artisans, traders, government and organised religion as well as people living on the land. From about 3000 BC, cities grew up on the banks of the Tigris and Euphrates rivers in Mesopotamia ('Between the Rivers'), part of the 'Fertile Crescent'. They were independent city-states at first, then part of empires. At the same time Egypt grew in power, and the eastern Mediterranean became a crossroads for traders and empire-builders.

Back to Canaan After the flight from Egypt the Jews returned to the ancestral land of Canaan, establishing the kingdoms of Israel and Judah.

Landmarks of civilisation

Many of the major developments that we associate with Western civilisation first emerged in the Fertile Crescent after 10 000 BC.

● **Cities** Some of the world's oldest cities are found in the Middle East, such as Jericho, founded c.8350 BC. Çatal Hüyük, in Anatolia, was the largest city in the world; it flourished 6250-5400 BC.

● **Wheel** The wheel started off in Mesopotamia c.3500 BC as a potter's tool. It was used for vehicles after c.3200 BC.

● **Legal systems** Hammurabi (c.1792-1750 BC), king of Babylon, codified the oldest known laws. The Jewish Torah dates from the 4th century BC.

● **Writing** Around 3300 BC, the Sumerians developed one of the earliest writing systems, a picture-based script called cuneiform, impressed on clay tablets. In about 1100 BC, the Phoenicians created a sound-based alphabet, later the basis of all modern European scripts.

● **Astronomy** The city of Ur was the birthpace of astronomy. By c.1000 BC the Babylonians were predicting lunar eclipses and tracking planets.

● **Mathematics** The number system of Mesopotamia gave us the 60 minute hour and 360 degree circle.

● **Monotheism** Belief in a single all-powerful god was a key feature of Judaism, and later of both Christianity and Islam.

FACT The Philistines settled around Gaza in the 12th or 11th century BC, perhaps from Crete. The region is still named after them: Palestine.

Homeland of empires The 'Fertile Crescent' of well-watered lands in the Middle East allowed the development of a succession of empires, whose core areas are shown here.

Hittite deity Judaism forbade such representations.

Bible Lands

The historical story of the Bible begins with Abraham, the first patriarch. The Hebrews, or Israelites, claimed descent from his grandson Jacob. After slavery in Egypt and nomadic wandering, they settled in Canaan, clashing with the Philistines. With the decline of the rival Egyptian and Hittite empires, the Israelites became a powerful kingdom under David. They later suffered defeat by the Assyrians (721 BC), captivity in Babylon (c.586-538 BC), and conquest by Alexander (333 BC). By the time of Jesus, Palestine was part of the Roman province of Judaea.

Great leaders of the Israelites include:
● **Abraham** (c.1800 BC) Founding father of the Hebrew nation, Abraham is said to have migrated to Canaan from Ur about 1800 BC.
● **Moses** (c.1200s BC) According to the Bible story Moses led the Hebrews from Egypt and received the Ten Commandments on Mount Sinai.
● **David** (reigned c.1000-961 BC) David founded the Israelite royal dynasty. He became king of Judah, then of Israel, uniting the Israelites. He made Jerusalem his capital.
● **Solomon** (reigned c.973-922 BC) Son of David, Solomon was the greatest king of Israel, famed for his wisdom. He built up Israel's military and trading strength, and constructed the first Temple of Jerusalem.

c.10 000 BC The earliest farming occurs, in the north and north-east of the Fertile Crescent.

c.8500 BC Sheep are domesticated in the Fertile Crescent.

c.6500 BC Çatal Hüyük, Turkey, becomes one of the largest towns of the late Stone Age.

c.3000 BC Major urban centres develop in Mesopotamia.

c.2350 BC Sumer is united as an empire under Sargon of Akkad.

c.1800 BC Abraham and his family leave Ur for Canaan, as described in the Old Testament.

1285 BC The Egyptians and Hittites clash at Kadesh, near the Sea of Galilee.

c.9000 BC Jericho grows into a town of about 2000 people.

c.7000 BC Copper is first used in toolmaking.

c.6000 BC The development of irrigation permits agriculture to spread beyond river banks.

c.3300 BC The earliest cuneiform writing is used in Mesopotamia.

c.2200 BC Rise of Ur, which flourishes as the main city of Sumer for the next two centuries.

c.1300 - 1250 BC The Hebrews leave Egypt (the Exodus).

The Phoenicians

For several thousand years from about 3000 BC, the Phoenicians were expert ship-builders and sailors. They traded around the Mediterranean from their city-states Byblos, Tyre, Sidon and Beirut (in modern Lebanon), and set up coastal colonies including Carthage in North Africa. They were famous for glassware, ivory work and purple dye. Their cities were sacked by Alexander.

Phoenician glassware
An incense bottle from the 3rd-1st centuries BC.

The Assyrians

Once a subject people of Babylon, the Assyrians emerged as a power in their own right in about 1350 BC. After 740 BC, under a succession of strong kings, Assyria won control of most of the area between Egypt and the Persian Gulf. **Ashurbanipal** (reigned c.668-627 BC), who conquered Egypt, created the largest empire the world had known. The Assyrian Empire was ended by the Medes and Chaldeans in 612 BC.

Assyrian warriors
A basalt relief showing charioteers, from the 8th century BC.

The Persians

Originally a nomadic tribe, the Persians settled in the Assyrian Empire in about 850 BC. Under **Cyrus the Great** (d.529 BC) they conquered Babylon and created the Achaemenid Empire, stretching from Egypt to Afghanistan. **Darius I** ('the Great', reigned 521-486 BC) consolidated the empire, but was defeated by the Greeks at Marathon in 490 BC. The Persian Empire was conquered by Alexander in 330 BC.

Sacrificial scene
A gold statuette c.1150 BC from Susa, Iran, representing a devotee with a goat.

Çatal Hüyük
Harran
Carchemish
Tigris
Ugarit
Euphrates
Nimrud • Nineveh
ASSYRIA • Ashur
MEDEA
Mediterranean Sea
Mari •
Samarra •
AKKAD
• Eshnun
Babylon • Kish
BABYLONIA • Nippur
ELAM
• Isin
SUMER • Lagash
Uruk • • Susa
Eridu • Ur
Arabian Desert
CHALDEA
PERSIA
• Persepolis
Mt Sinai
The Gulf
Red Sea

The Hittites

From about 1700 to 1200 BC, the north-eastern Mediterranean was dominated by the Hittites, based in Hattusas (modern Bogazköy). They had expanded as far as Babylon by 1595 BC. War with Egypt culminated in the celebrated Battle of **Kadesh** in 1285 BC, and a treaty sealed by marriage between a Hittite princess and Pharaoh Ramesses II. After 1200 BC, the Hittites were overrun by the Sea Peoples from Greece and the central Mediterranean.

The Babylonians

Babylon was a leading power by 1750 BC. The lawmaker **Hammurabi** came to power in 1792 BC, expanded the empire and brought all Mesopotamia under one rule. Babylon came under Assyrian domination in 721 BC, but then re-emerged as the Chaldean, or neo-Babylonian Empire under **Nebuchadnezzar II** (reigned c.604-562 BC) – who built the famous Hanging Gardens. The empire fell to Cyrus II of Persia in 539 BC, and to Alexander in 331 BC.

The Sumerians

The Sumerians established the world's first real civilisation. Their city-states such as Ur, Uruk, Eridu and Kish flourished in southern Mesopotamia (now Iraq) in about 5000 BC. **Sargon** (c.2370-2315 BC) brought all the cities of southern Mesopotamia under his control to create the Sumerian Empire. It was conquered by the Elamites in about 2000 BC, then by the Babylonians and Assyrians.

c.1000-961 BC David extends Israel as far as Palestine and Syria.

c.922 Israel and Judah split after the death of King Solomon.

c.668-627 BC The Assyrian Empire reaches its greatest extent but starts to lose military superiority, beginning a period of decline.

586 BC Jerusalem is destroyed, and 5000 Jews deported to Babylon (the 'Babylonian Captivity').

537 BC Jews return from Babylon and rebuild the Temple in Jerusalem.

331 BC Alexander captures Babylon, ensuring the conquest of the Persian Empire.

1000 BC

500 BC

c.1200 BC The Sea Peoples spread through the Middle East; the Philistines settle in Canaan.

922 BC Jerusalem is sacked by the Egyptians.

605 BC Nebuchadnezzar II of Babylon defeats the Egyptians and Assyrians at Carchemish.

539 BC Cyrus the Great of Persia captures Babylon.

333 BC Alexander the Great defeats Darius III of Persia at the Battle of the Issus.

323 BC Alexander dies.

Egypt's civilisation flourished on the Nile for 3000 years. Many of its great monuments remain, of which the best known are the pyramids and the sphinx. Egyptian society was broadly constant over that period: it was itself pyramid-shaped, with the lone figure of the pharaoh at the top and the mass of peasant farmers at the bottom. Society was highly organised, a feat made possible by the invention of writing. It also had a sophisticated theology based on a pantheon of gods and a highly developed mythology.

DEATH AND MUMMIES

It was not only pharaohs who were mummified. The preservation of the body was an important religious ritual for people at all levels of society, as it was believed that the soul returned to the body to take nourishment. The process of mummification took about 70 days, after which the body was released to relatives for burial. The body would be interred with spells from the *Book of the Dead*, which were inscribed on papyri, and with *shabti* (funerary statuettes) to accompany it in the afterlife.

The Sphinx Sculpted from an outcrop of rock, the Great Sphinx is a portrait of the pharaoh Khafre, and stands in front of his pyramid at Giza.

Rulers of the world beyond

Osiris The god of the underworld, Osiris is swaddled like a mummy and carries a sceptre and a ceremonial whip.
Horus Horus is the hawk-headed god of the sky, source of royal authority.
Seth God of storms and chaos, Seth hacked Osiris to death and scattered the body parts.
Isis The sister-wife of Osiris, Isis used magic to revive her husband after Seth had murdered him.
Taweret Protectress of pregnant women, Taweret has the body of a hippopotamus, with a lion's paws and a crocodile's tail.
Bes Bes is a dwarfish god of the household.
Thoth God of the Moon and of knowledge, Thoth is shown as an ibis or a baboon.
Anubis Anubis is the jackal-headed god of mummification.
Ra The sun-god Ra (right) is often shown with a hawk's head.

The great pharaohs

Djoser (2668-2649 BC) Egypt's first pyramid-builder, Djoser commissioned the step pyramid at Saqqara.
Khufu (2589-2566 BC) Khufu built the Great Pyramid of Cheops at Giza.
Hatshepsut (2551-2528 BC) For 20 years Hatshepsut ruled as a female king (Egypt did not then recognise queens). She wore the ritual false beard to defuse antifemale criticism of her reign, and is often portrayed in art as a man.
Pepi II (2278-2184 BC) Ascending the throne at six, and ruling until he was 100, Pepi had the longest reign known to history.
Tuthmosis III (1504-1483 BC) The soldier-pharaoh Tuthmosis extended Egyptian territory to its greatest extent.
Akhenaten (1350-1334 BC) With his wife Nefertiti, Akhenaten banned the worship of all gods but Aten, the sun-disc. He built the huge temples at Karnak and Luxor.

Tutankhamun (1334-1325 BC) A very minor pharaoh who died in his teens, Tutankhamun is known mainly for his tomb and its fabulous treasures, discovered by Howard Carter in 1922.
Ramesses II (1279-1212 BC) Ramesses built the rock temple at Abu Simbel, and raised more monuments than any other pharaoh in his 66-year reign.
Cleopatra (51-30 BC) Cleopatra was the lover of Julius Caesar and Mark Antony. Her Egypt was conquered by Rome in 30 BC, bringing the age of the pharaohs to an end.

Abu Simbel The four colossal seated statues of Ramesses II are 20 m (70 ft) high. In the 1960s they were moved to higher ground to preserve them from the rising waters of Lake Nasser. Abu Simbel is about 250 km (155 miles) south of Philae.

Philae

c.5000 BC Cattle herders occupy the fertile Sahara.

c.2630 BC The Step Pyramid of Djoser is built at Saqqara.

c.2584-2565 BC The Great Pyramid of Khufu (Cheops) is built at Giza.

2498 BC The 5th Dynasty kings (to 2345) adopt the cult of Ra at Heliopolis.

2181-2040 BC The First Intermediate Period brings political chaos to Egypt.

1782 BC The decline of royal authority results in the Second Intermediate Period (to 1555 BC).

c.3100 BC Egypt is first unified, by King Menes of Upper Egypt.

c.2600 BC The Old Kingdom reaches its zenith, with the 4th Dynasty kings (2613-2498).

c.2558-2532 BC The Pyramid of Khafre (Chephren) and the Sphinx are built at Giza.

2040 BC The 11th Dynasty kings reunite Egypt as the Middle Kingdom (to 1782 BC).

5000 BC | 2500 BC | 2000 BC

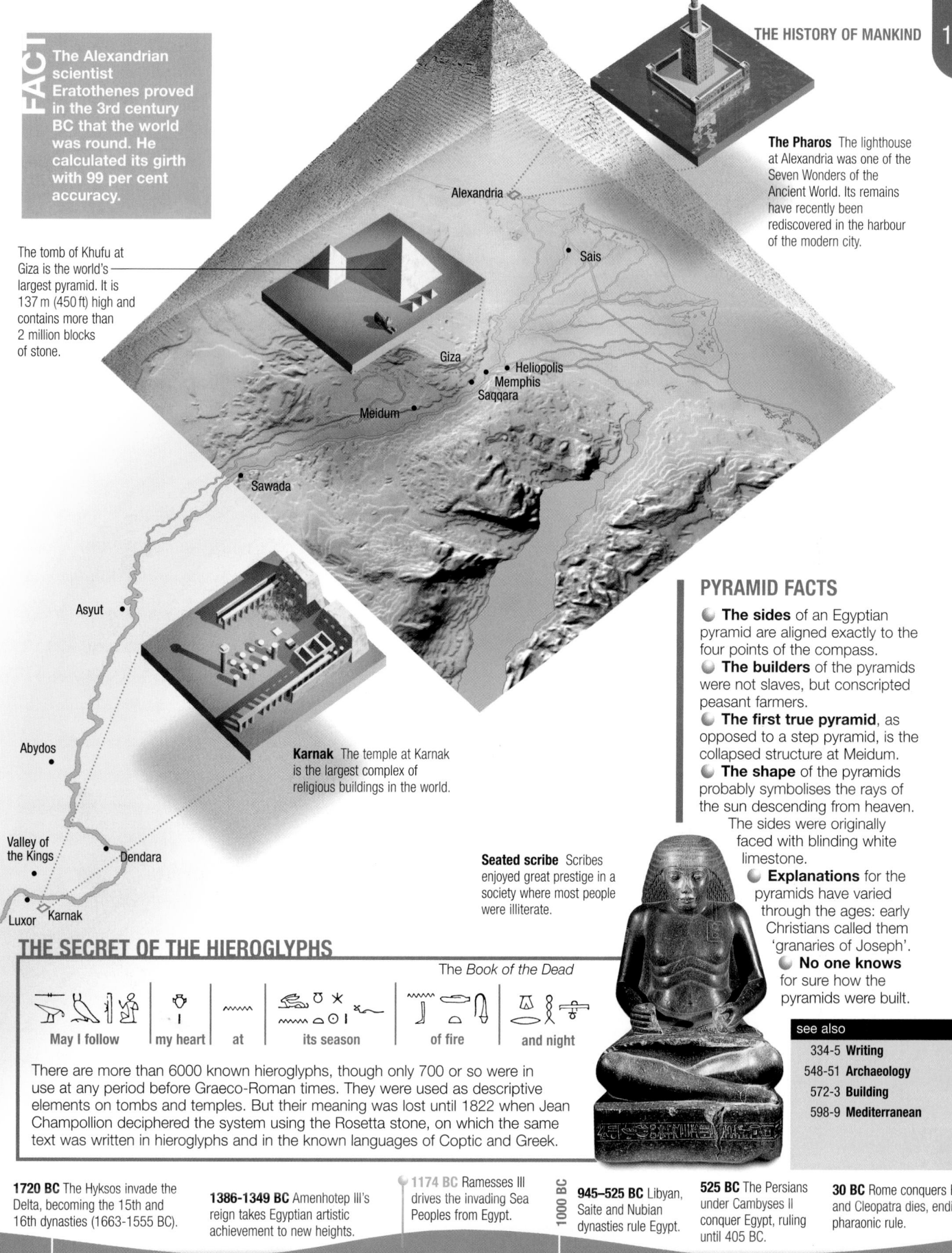

The Pharos The lighthouse at Alexandria was one of the Seven Wonders of the Ancient World. Its remains have recently been rediscovered in the harbour of the modern city.

The tomb of Khufu at Giza is the world's largest pyramid. It is 137 m (450 ft) high and contains more than 2 million blocks of stone.

Alexandria

Sais

Giza • Heliopolis
Memphis
Saqqara
Meidum

Sawada

Asyut

Abydos

Valley of the Kings
Dendara
Luxor Karnak

Karnak The temple at Karnak is the largest complex of religious buildings in the world.

PYRAMID FACTS

● **The sides** of an Egyptian pyramid are aligned exactly to the four points of the compass.

● **The builders** of the pyramids were not slaves, but conscripted peasant farmers.

● **The first true pyramid**, as opposed to a step pyramid, is the collapsed structure at Meidum.

● **The shape** of the pyramids probably symbolises the rays of the sun descending from heaven. The sides were originally faced with blinding white limestone.

● **Explanations** for the pyramids have varied through the ages: early Christians called them 'granaries of Joseph'.

● **No one knows** for sure how the pyramids were built.

Seated scribe Scribes enjoyed great prestige in a society where most people were illiterate.

THE SECRET OF THE HIEROGLYPHS

The *Book of the Dead*

| May I follow | my heart | at | its season | of fire | and night |

There are more than 6000 known hieroglyphs, though only 700 or so were in use at any period before Graeco-Roman times. They were used as descriptive elements on tombs and temples. But their meaning was lost until 1822 when Jean Champollion deciphered the system using the Rosetta stone, on which the same text was written in hieroglyphs and in the known languages of Coptic and Greek.

1720 BC The Hyksos invade the Delta, becoming the 15th and 16th dynasties (1663-1555 BC).

1386-1349 BC Amenhotep III's reign takes Egyptian artistic achievement to new heights.

1174 BC Ramesses III drives the invading Sea Peoples from Egypt.

945–525 BC Libyan, Saite and Nubian dynasties rule Egypt.

525 BC The Persians under Cambyses II conquer Egypt, ruling until 405 BC.

30 BC Rome conquers Egypt and Cleopatra dies, ending pharaonic rule.

1000 BC

1500 BC

1570 BC Ahmose drives the Hyksos out of Egypt and creates the New Kingdom (to 1070 BC).

1291-1278 BC Seti I builds the great Temple of Amun at Karnak and the Temple of Seti at Abydos.

1069 BC Egypt's Third Intermediate Period begins as the high priests of Thebes usurp royal power.

500 BC

323 BC Alexander the Great conquers Egypt; his Ptolemaic successors rule as Egypt's last dynasty.

Many of the essential characteristics of European culture and civilisation were forged in ancient Greece, including a new sense of individual identity in relation to society, the world and the gods. Following the Minoan and Mycenaean civilisations, Greece became a dominant force in the Mediterranean for 400 years, before Alexander the Great briefly created one of the largest empires of the ancient world, spreading Greek (Hellenistic) culture to Egypt and deep into Asia.

Dolphin fresco from Knossos
One of the first Greek cultures to emerge was at Knossos on Crete.

2000 BC Minoan palace culture begins on Crete.

1500 BC (or earlier) A huge eruption of Santorini (Thera) destroys Minoan towns and islands.

*c.***1125-1025 BC** Dorians settle in northern Greece.

*c.***800 BC** The poet Homer composes the epics *Iliad* and *Odyssey*.

730 BC Sparta becomes a leading power after defeating the Messenians.

*c.***508 BC** Democracy begins to appear in Greek cities.

2000 BC

1000 BC

500 BC

1600-1400 BC The palace of Minos is built at Knossos.

*c.*1250 BC The Greeks destroy Troy, in Asia Minor.

*c.***1000 BC** Greeks begin to colonise Asia Minor.

776 BC The first Olympic Games are held.

*c.***735 BC** The first Greek colony is founded in Sicily, at Naxos.

483 BC Themistocles builds the Athenian fleet.

480 BC The Persians are defeated by the Athenian fleet at Salamis.

Great Greek leaders

● **Solon** *c.***640-560 BC** The Athenian statesman Solon created a code of moderate laws that became the basis of all Greek and Roman law.
● **Aristides** *c.***530-c.467 BC** The Athenian general Aristides defeated the Persians at Marathon, Salamis and Plataea. Known as 'the Just',

he was influential in Athenian politics and in the Delian League against the Persians.
● **Themistocles** *c.***525-c.460 BC** After the Battle of Marathon Themistocles encouraged the Athenians to build a navy to ward off Persian invasions. It crushed the Persian fleet at Salamis.

● **Pericles** *c.***495-429 BC** Pericles led Athens *c.*460-429 BC, presiding over the city's golden age of art and culture and its imperial expansion.
● **Lysander d.395 BC** Lysander was a Spartan naval commander whose victory at Aegospotami in 405 BC led to Sparta's defeat of Athens.

490 BC The Athenians defeat the Persians under Darius at Marathon, a turning point in the Persian Wars.

Empire builder Pericles spread democracy throughout the Athenian Empire.

The Greek world
Greek civilisation extended across the Aegean to Ionia in the Persian Empire.

The Mycenaeans
The first mainland Greek civilisation was based around Mycenae, from 1580 to 1100 BC.

MACEDONIA
Vergina
Mt Olympus
EPIRUS
THESSALY
THRACE
CHALCIDICE
Lemnos
Troy
Delphi
Elis
ACHAEA
BOEOTIA
EUBOEA
Lesbos
AEOLIS
Olympia
Mycenae
Thebes
Pergamum
ARCADIA
Corinth
Athens
Aegean Sea
MESSENIA
ATTICA
Chios
Phocaea
PERSIAN
Argos
Sardis
EMPIRE
Pylos
Sparta
Andros
LACONIA
IONIA
Delos
Samos
Ephesus
Kythera
Naxos
Advance of the
Dorians
Thera
Kos
Halicarnassus
Crete
Knossos
Mallia
Rhodes
Phaestos
Gournia
Karpathos

The city-states
The city-state (*polis*) emerged in the 8th century BC. The political unit was a walled town; Athens, Sparta and Thebes were among the leading city-states, but there were many others. Their independence was curtailed by the Macedonian conquest.

The Minoans
The Minoans developed one of the earliest Mediterranean civilisations. Their trade-based culture flourished from 2000 to 1450 BC.

The Dorians
The Dorians were Greek-speaking invaders from the north who spread through Greece, Crete and western Asia Minor (Turkey) from 1125 to 1025 BC. Their Iron Age technology supplanted the Mycenaean Bronze age.

The legacy of Greece

● **Democracy** Rule (*kratos*) by the people (*demos*) was introduced in Athens under Cleisthenes (early 6th century BC), replacing the rule of 'tyrants'. All male citizens had the right to speak and vote at the Assembly.

● **Philosophy and science** Greek thought combined belief in reason with enquiry into the world and how people should live. Socrates (*c.*470-399 BC), Plato (*c.*428-348) and Aristotle (384-322 BC) laid the foundations of Western philosophy. Pythagoras (*c.*582-*c.*507 BC), Euclid (lived *c.*300 BC) and Archimedes (*c.*287-212 BC) made significant advances in mathematics, science and astronomy.

● **Athletics and sport** Greek sport featured formal competition in running, discus and javelin throwing, wrestling and boxing. There were four large regular meetings, including the Panhellenic Games at Olympia (from 776 BC).

● **Theatre** Songs and dances at religious festivals were developed from about 530 BC into plays. Tragedies, notably by Aeschylus (*c.*525-455 BC), Sophocles (*c.*496-405 BC) and Euripides (*c.*485-406 BC) dealt with fate; comedies, like those by Aristophanes (*c.*448-*c.*380 BC), offered knock-about humour.

● **Art and architecture** Greek sculpture was influential in Western art until the 19th century, while the calm elegance of Greek architecture is still seen an ideal by some modern architects.

● **Medicine** Hippocrates (*c.*460-377 BC), the 'Father of Medicine', from Kos, developed the first theories of illness and healing based on observation rather than religion.

● **History** Greek authors founded the Western tradition of separating historical events from myth, and using evidence from eyewitnesses and visits to historical sites. The great Greek historians were Herodotus (*c.*484-420 BC), Thucydides (*c.*460-396 BC) and Xenophon (*c.*430-354 BC).

Greek achievement
(Above) An Athenian doctor at work.
(Left) Drunkenness held up for ridicule in figures from Greek comedy.

478 BC Athens forms the Delian League, a Greek alliance against Persia.

447 BC Work begins on the Parthenon.

385 BC Plato founds the Academy in Athens.

334-326 BC Alexander the Great creates an empire stretching from Greece to India.

*c.***276 BC** Alexander's empire is split into Antigonid Macedon, Seleucid Asia, and Ptolemaic Egypt.

197 BC Philip V of Macedon is defeated by the Romans and loses control of Greece.

479 BC The Greek states led by Sparta and Athens defeat the Persians at Plataea, ending the Persian threat.

431-404 BC The Peloponnesian War takes place between Athens and Sparta; Sparta finally prevails.

338 BC Philip II of Macedon becomes ruler of Greece after defeating the Hellenic League at Chaeronea.

300 BC

323 BC Alexander dies in Babylon.

292-280 BC The Colossus of Rhodes is built.

146 BC The Romans sack Corinth and make Greece a Roman province.

Alexander the Great

Alexander (b.356 BC), son of Philip II and a pupil of **Aristotle**, became king of Macedon in 336 BC. By the time he died, little more than a decade later, he had conquered virtually the whole of the known world east of Greece.

Alexander's campaigns began in 334, when he invaded the Persian Empire with the largest army ever to leave Greece. He defeated Darius III the following year, and was made Pharaoh in Egypt, where he founded the city of **Alexandria**.

Darius raised a huge new army against Alexander. The climactic battle at **Gaugamela** (in modern Iraq) in 331 was an overwhelming Greek victory. Alexander occupied Babylon and the Persian capitals of **Susa** and **Persepolis**.

In 330, Alexander's army marched through eastern Persia, founding the cities of **Herat** and **Kandahar** (in modern Afghanistan). They advanced into Sogdiana, where they fought a two-year campaign against King Oxyartes (whose daughter, **Roxana**, Alexander married). Crossing the Hindu Kush mountains, Alexander invaded the Indus Valley in 327, defeating the powerful rajah **Porus** at the **Hydaspes**. His army finally refused to march farther into India, and Alexander was forced to return to Persia via the southern coast. He died of a fever at Babylon in 323 BC, aged 32. By 304 BC the empire had been divided among his squabbling generals.

Warrior king Alexander fights alongside his troops.

Alexander's route

In a series of whirlwind campaigns Alexander's army swept through Central Asia.

➤ Alexander's empire
➤ Alexander's route

Rome flourished for about 800 years, developing a technically advanced and sophisticated society not seen again in the Western world until the 16th century. The early Roman state was a republic, ruled by a senate of leading citizens with elected magistrates or consuls. However, the highly efficient Roman army had carved out a vast territory by the 1st century BC, and the conquered dominions required the authority of an emperor. Despite frequent mismanagement, Rome sustained the empire for 400 years.

Growth of empire Rome gained its first territories outside Italy after the first Punic War against Carthage. The Roman Empire reached its greatest extent in 117, under Emperor Trajan.

Roman territory 201 BC

Roman provinces AD 117

THE LEGACY OF ROME

● **Law** The Roman legal system was codified in 450 BC, and was regularly modified as the empire grew. Much modern Western law is based on principles established by the Romans.

● **Building and engineering** Roman building was unsurpassed for 1000 years. Architects and engineers extended Greek ideas by developing the arch and the dome (as in the Pantheon, Rome), and the use of concrete. Roman engineers also created a network of roads throughout the empire. Many of the routes are still in use today.

● **Towns and cities** Many modern European cities (including London, Paris, Cologne and Toledo) were founded by the Romans.

● **Preservation of ancient cultures** The Romans adopted and preserved much of the best of the cultures they conquered, including Greek traditions of sculpture, learning and literature.

● **Language and literature** Latin remained the universal language of the Christian world until after the Renaissance. It also formed the basis of the Romance languages, such as Italian, French, Spanish, Portuguese and Romanian. The great works of Roman literature and history, by writers such as Virgil, Livy, Horace, Ovid, Pliny and Juvenal, provided a major inspiration to the Renaissance.

● **Christianity** Although originally opposed to Christianity, the Roman Empire was mainly Christian at its close. Through its network of churches and monasteries, and the universal use of Latin, the Church preserved the traditions of internationalism and learning in Europe long after the collapse of Roman political power.

Roman engineering The Pont du Gard, the finest surviving Roman aqueduct.

HIBERNIA

Deva (Chester)
Eboracum (York)
BRITANNIA
Londinium (London)
GERMANIA INFERIOR
Colonia Agrippina (Cologne)
BELGICA
Durocortorum (Reims)
GALLIA LUGDUNENSIS
Lutetia (Paris)
Augusta Treverorum (Trier)
Augustodunum (Autun)
GERMANIA SUPERIOR
RHAETIA
NORICUM
AQUITANIA
Lugdunum (Lyon)
Mediolanum (Milan)
PANNONIA
Burdigala (Bordeaux)
GALLIA NARBONENSIS
ALPES GRAIAE
ALPES COTTIAE
ALPES MARITIMAE
Ravenna
ITALIA
ILLYRICUM
HISPANIA TARRACONENSIS
Baeterrae (Béziers)
Arelate (Arles)
Forum Iulii (Fréjus)
Segovia
Massilia (Marseille)
Roma (Rome)
LUSITANIA
Toletum (Toledo)
Tarraco (Tarragona)
CORSICA
Ostia
Emerita Augusta (Mérida)
BAETICA
SARDINIA
Pompeii
Hispalis (Seville)
Carthago Nova (Cartagena)
Caesarea (Cherchell)
SICILIA
MAURETANIA TINGITANA
MAURETANIA CAESARIENSIS
Thamugadi (Timgad)
Carthago (Carthage)
Syracusae
NUMIDIA
AFRICA
Leptis Magna

Imperial coins Two gold aureus coins, with the heads of Caligula, emperor AD 37-41 (left), and Constantine the Great.

753 BC Traditional date for the founding of Rome.

451-450 BC Codification of Roman law, known as the 'Twelve Tables'.

264-241 BC First Punic War between Rome and Carthage, won by Rome.

202 BC Hannibal is finally defeated at Zama, near Carthage, ending the second Punic War.

130-120 BC Rome annexes part of Gaul (southern France), Asia Minor (Turkey) and North Africa.

58-51 BC Caesar conquers Gaul and raids Britain (55 BC).

500 BC
300 BC
100 BC

510 BC Last Etruscan king, Lucius Tarquin, is expelled from Rome.

390 BC Rome is sacked by the Gauls.

218 BC Second Punic War begins; Carthaginians under Hannibal invade northern Italy.

149-146 BC Third Punic War: Rome destroys Carthage.

72 BC Spartacus's slave revolt is crushed by Pompey and Crassus.

44 BC Caesar is assassinated by the republican senators Brutus and Cassius.

Five reasons why Rome flourished

1 Efficient, disciplined, professional army Rome's well-organised army, with superior weapons technology, outclassed all enemies. Colonies of ex-soldiers also helped to maintain security in all the imperial territories.

2 Excellent communications Roman ports, roads and aqueducts ensured efficient transport and supply.

3 Good administration A single language, an empire-wide legal code and an effective system of territorial governors made it possible to maintain control over large and diverse territories.

4 Peace and stability Long periods of relative peace and stability within the empire (the Pax Romana) allowed trade to flourish and a confident, inclusive imperial culture to develop. After AD 212, Roman citizenship was granted to all free men in the empire, to increase their sense of belonging to the Roman world.

5 Economic order The empire's huge and efficient trading network encouraged economic activity, generating tax revenue and both private and civic wealth.

Five reasons why Rome fell

1 Overstretched defences After the crisis of the the 3rd century, the empire lost its ability to dominate beyond its borders.

2 Oppressive rule Rather than ruling in cooperation with local rulers, the later emperors attempted to maintain Roman power through force alone.

3 Internal division After the splitting of the empire in AD 330, the wealthy Eastern Empire increasingly refused to pay for defence of the West.

4 Taxation The senatorial class was exempt from taxation, and the centralised tax collection system became oppressive and inefficient.

5 Barbarian armies From the 3rd century the Roman army relied on barbarian soldiers. Germanic tribes were attracted to the empire and settled there in large numbers, eventually becoming a threat to Rome.

Roman rulers

Julius Caesar c.100-44 BC A general, politician and writer, Caesar won military victories in Gaul in 58-49 BC, and made two expeditions to Britain. In 49 BC, his troops occupied Rome. Ruling as a dictator, he was assassinated by the republican senators Brutus and Cassius.

Augustus 63 BC-AD 14 The adopted son of Julius Caesar, Augustus was the first emperor. After Caesar's death, he defeated Brutus and Cassius in 42 BC, then Mark Antony in 31 BC. A ruthless politician, he brought peace, security and prosperity after decades of civil war.

Caligula AD 12-41 The third emperor (from AD 37), Caligula was a mentally unstable and tyrannical ruler. He was killed by the Praetorian Guard (imperial bodyguards).

Claudius 10 BC-AD 54 Claudius, the fourth emperor (AD 41-54), was scholarly and intelligent. He repaired much of Caligula's damage, and added Britain to the empire.

Nero c.AD 37-68 Emperor AD 54-68, Nero was a murderous tyrant. He persecuted the Christians, whom he blamed for the fire that ravaged Rome in AD 64.

Trajan c.AD 53-117 Trajan ruled AD 98-117, bringing the empire to its greatest extent.

Hadrian AD 76-138 Hadrian ruled AD 117-138, Rome's golden age. He consolidated the empire behind defensible frontiers, such as Hadrian's Wall.

Diocletian AD 245-31 Diocletian restored order after a period of short-lived emperors. He ruled from AD 284 to 305.

Constantine the Great c.AD 274-337 Emperor from AD 306 to 337, Constantine divided the empire, founded a new capital at Byzantium, renamed Constantinople (now Istanbul). His Edict of Milan (AD 313) proclaimed tolerance of Christianity.

see also

336-7 **Mythology**
366-7 **Architecture**
384-5 **Western literature**
598-9 **Mediterranean**

30 BC Octavian becomes the first emperor, taking the name Augustus.

AD 64 Rome burns; Nero blames the Christians and begins persecuting them.

AD 80 The Colosseum is completed in Rome. It seats 50 000 spectators.

AD 192-7 Civil war in the Roman Empire.

AD 312-37 After years of fragmentation, the empire is reorganised by Constantine.

AD 410 Rome is sacked by the Visigoths.

AD 43 Rome begins the conquest of Britain.

AD 79 Vesuvius erupts, engulfing Pompeii and Herculaneum.

AD 98-117 Trajan builds roads, bridges and aqueducts across a vast empire.

AD 251 Pressure from Goths forces Rome to withdraw from outlying provinces.

AD 392 Pagan worship is prohibited in the empire, in favour of Christianity.

AD 406 The Vandals, Alans and Sueves invade the Roman Empire.

The collapse of the Roman world left a mosaic of competing successor kingdoms in Europe. But many of the Germanic tribes were highly Romanised, had fought for the Romans as mercenaries and had adopted their Christian religion. The changes they brought about were often more evolutionary than sudden. It was a time of turmoil, but out of the turmoil emerged new peoples and powers – and a new stage of European history.

East Anglian kingdom
A helmet found at Sutton Hoo is one of many artefacts displaying the wealth of East Anglia in the early 7th century.

Peoples of the Dark Ages Barbarian tribes helped to bring down Rome but they also preserved and spread many aspects of Roman civilisation including Christianity and the Latin language. As Rome fell apart local Barbarian rulers increasingly replaced Imperial authority, redrawing the map of Europe. The 'Barbarians' included:

🔵 **Angles and Saxons** Pagan tribes from Denmark, including the Angles and Saxons, came to Britain from the 5th century, driving local Celtic peoples west. They developed a vernacular literature and their tongue, Anglo-Saxon, was the forerunner of English. St Augustine converted them to Christianity in the 7th century.

🔵 **Franks** The Franks were a Germanic people who in the 5th century created a kingdom which included large parts of modern France and Germany. By the 8th century they ruled northern Germany as well.

🔵 **Huns** In the 4th century nomadic tribes called Huns began to terrorise central and south-eastern Europe, forcing migrations and destabilising Rome. They reached a peak under Attila (434-53) but after 451 fell into factionalism.

🔵 **Lombards** The Lombards came from the Danube area to occupy much of Italy until defeated by the Franks in 774.

🔵 **Ostrogoths** The 'Eastern Goths' settled in the Ukraine but were driven westwards by the Huns in 370. In the 5th century, under Theodoric, they came to dominate Italy.

🔵 **Slavs** The Slavs originated south of the Baltic Sea. They were subjugated by the Goths and Huns, and spread to the Ukraine, Germany and the Balkans, becoming the ancestors of today's Russians, Ukrainians, Poles and Serbs.

🔵 **Vandals** The Vandals' name is still a byword for destruction. They devastated Spain in 409, and the Spanish province Andalusia is named after them. In 429 they invaded North Africa, establishing a capital at Carthage from where they sacked Rome in 455.

🔵 **Visigoths** The 'Western Goths' settled within the Roman Empire, contributing to its fall and sacking Rome. They made a kingdom in France and Spain, holding Spanish lands until conquered by the Arabs in 711.

Barbarian migrations
Germanic peoples began to migrate towards western Europe in the 1st century BC. In AD 376, the Visigoths crossed the Danube in force, opening the way for a flood of other tribes into Roman lands, from the Balkans to Britain to North Africa.

c.450 ANGLES, SAXONS
486
FRANKS
Trier
Toulouse
412
Milan
406-9
VANDALS
SLAVS AND AVARS
c.450-75
488-9
Ravenna
OSTROGOTHS
VISIGOTHS
370-8
HUNS AND ALANS
c.375
Cartagena
429-32
Rome
408-10
Carthage
455
Constantinople

402 The Western Empire moves its court from Milan to Ravenna.

◀ **410** Alaric becomes king of the Visigoths and sacks Rome.

🔵 *c.*450 The Angles and Saxons begin their conquest of Britain.

493 The Ostrogoth Theodoric the Great becomes king of Italy.

507 The Franks defeat the Visigoths, uniting most of France.

*c.*550 Bubonic plague ravages Europe.

406-7 Vandals invade the Roman Empire.

435 St Patrick takes Christianity to Ireland.

476 The last Roman emperor, Romulus Augustulus, is deposed.

496 Clovis, king of the Franks, converts to Christianity.

533 The Byzantines begin to restore Roman power in Italy.

597 St Augustine begins mission to Christianise England.

VIKINGS

The Vikings were sailors and traders. They emerged from **Norway**, **Denmark** and **Sweden** around the end of the 8th century AD, and terrorised Europe for more than 200 years. Their first major recorded raid was in 793 on the monastery at **Lindisfarne** in northern England. Their shallow-draft longships could travel far inland on rivers to loot monasteries and capture cattle and slaves. From the mid 9th century they occupied large areas of England (the **'Danelaw'**), eastern Ireland, western Scotland and Normandy.

Swedish Vikings travelled along the rivers of eastern Europe to the Black Sea, trading with the Arabs and Byzantines. They established ruling dynasties around Kiev and Novgorod. The Norwegian Vikings settled in **Iceland** after 870 and **Greenland** after 982. In c.1000 they set up a short-lived colony in North America. King **Cnut** ('Canute') of Denmark (c.994-1035) was simultaneously king of Denmark, England and Norway. In the course of the 10th century, the Vikings gradually converted to Christianity.

Viking Europe, c.900

Viking raids of the 8th-10th centuries broke up the Frankish Empire, assisted by Magyar invasions in the east.

← **Viking raids**

← **Magyar raids**

▮ **Frankish kingdoms**

▮ **Areas settled by Vikings**

▮ **Arab and Moorish states**

Atlantic Ocean

DANELAW · NORWAY · SWEDEN · DENMARK

UMAYYAD CALIPHATE · WEST FRANKIA · EAST FRANKIA · Magyars · Balts

VENICE · ITALY · BULGAR KHANATE

Atlantic Ocean

Norse · Swedes · Danes · Balts · Sorbs · Avars · Magyars

CELTIC AND ANGLO-SAXON KINGDOMS

ASTURIAS

UMAYYAD CALIPHATE

NDRISID CALIPHATE

Quierzy · Aachen · Regensburg · Rome · VENICE · LOMBARD DUCHIES · Vlachs · Bulgars · Khazars

Constantinople · Black Sea

Viking longboat Built for speed, flat-bottomed longboats were ideal for raiding parties.

see also

338-9 **World mythology**
598-9 **Mediterranean**

Europe in 800

Charlemagne's Europe was dominated by the two great Christian empires of the Byzantines and the Franks.

▮ **Frankish Empire**

▮ **Byzantine Empire**

▮ **Arab and Moorish states**

Empire builder Charlemagne doubled the Frankish lands and ruthlessly imposed Christianity.

Charlemagne

Charles I 'the Great' (742-814), known as Charlemagne, was the greatest of the Germanic rulers who dominated Europe after the Roman Empire. He became king of the **Franks** in succession to his father Pepin III 'the Short' in 768, and aggressively expanded Frankish authority over all the German kingdoms outside England and Scandinavia. On Christmas Day, 800, Pope **Leo III** confirmed Charles' supremacy in Europe by crowning him emperor – the first western emperor since Roman times, and the first ruler of the **'Holy Roman Empire'**. Charles fought ceaselessly against the empire's enemies, including Arab, Magyar and Viking raiders. He maintained diplomatic relations with Byzantium, Baghdad and the English kingdoms, and presided over a revival of learning known as the **Carolingian Renaissance**. His successors failed to maintain the empire's strong central authority, directly contributing to the rise of **feudalism** in Europe.

c.700 Lindisfarne Gospels: magnificent Anglo-Saxon illuminated manuscript.

751 Pepin III becomes the first Carolingian king of the Franks.

800 Charlemagne, king of the Franks, is crowned Emperor of the West in Rome.

865 The Viking 'Great Army' invades England.

965 King Harald Bluetooth is baptised, and the Danish Vikings convert to Christianity.

1000 Christianity is introduced to Sweden, led by King Olaf.

1054 The Eastern Orthodox Church splits from the Roman Church (the 'Great Schism').

700

900

1000

732 The Franks defeat an Arab invasion near Poitiers, France.

793 Viking raids begin with an attack on Lindisfarne, England.

860 The Kiev Vikings (Rus) attack Constantinople.

878 Wessex, led by King Alfred, repulses Danish Vikings at Edington.

987 Hugh Capet's accession in France marks the end of Carolingian rule.

1016 The Normans begin their conquest of southern Italy.

1066 Duke William of Normandy defeats Harold of England at Hastings.

Within a few years of his crucifixion, Jesus's message spread beyond the Jews and grew into a cult stretching across the Roman Empire. When the empire collapsed, the Western Church preserved much of the learning and traditions of Rome, eventually becoming the dominant force of the medieval world.

ROME'S CHRISTIAN LEGACY

As Roman rule began to fail in Western Europe, the Christian Church took on a political and cultural role as well as a spiritual one. By 600 much of Europe was Christian (see map) owing to the activities of early **missionaries** (see below). The Church was now the only major institution to preserve its authority from Roman times, and almost the only unifying and civilising influence in Europe. From the 9th century its prestige and power were enhanced by association with the **Holy Roman Empire** of Charlemagne and his succesors.

Relations between the popes and Holy Roman emperors deteriorated during the Middle Ages, and the existence of an alternative Roman tradition in the Byzantine east led to the separation of Catholic and **Orthodox** Churches. The split was worsened by the intervention of the **Crusaders** against the Byzantines' Muslim enemies. Factional strife in Rome led to the removal of the papacy to Avignon (1309-77), and then to the **Great Schism** (1378-1417), when there were rival popes in Rome and Avignon.

The authority of the pope was restored in the Renaissance, but marred by family ambitions, decadence and corruption that helped to fuel the **Reformation**.

Christian areas by 350
Christian areas by 600
† Early monastic sites
⇨ Later spread of Christianity

Iona
Armagh
Clonard
Whithorn
Whitby
Canterbury
Rotomagus (Rouen)
Augusta Treverorum (Trier)
Marmoutier
Turones (Tours)
Vesontio (Besançon)
Lugdunum (Lyon)
Vercelli
Aquilea
Mediolanum (Milan)
Sirmium
Ravenna
Salonae (Split)
Bracara (Braga)
Caesaraugusta (Zaragosa)
Narbonnensis (Narbonne)
Massilia
Nursia
Monte Cassino
Rome
Nola
Toletum (Toledo)
Carales (Cagliari)
Hispalis (Seville)
Hippo Regius
Thagaste
Carthage
Nicopolis
to Scandinavia and Eastern Europe
Ptolem
Ptolem

Celtic Church

The Christian church of Ireland owed its origins to **St Patrick** (*c*.390-460). It survived the Dark Ages isolated from the upheavals in continental Europe and developed a strong monastic tradition. The Celtic Church sent missionaries to Scotland, northern England and the Franks. In England, Celtic Christianity rivalled Roman Christianity until the **Synod of Whitby** in 664.

Who's who among the missionaries of Europe

● **St Paul** (d. *c*.67) Paul had the privileges of a Roman citizen. He travelled widely, taking the Christian message to the Aegean islands, Asia Minor, Greece, Italy and possibly Spain.
● **St Columba** (*c*.521-97) Columba was abbot of Iona, which became a centre of Celtic Christianity.

● **St Columban** (*c*.540-615) The Irish missionary monk Columban took Christianity to the pagan Franks and established monastic centres of noted asceticism in France and northern Italy.
● **St Augustine of Canterbury** (d. 605) A Benedictine prior, Augustine was sent by

Pope Gregory I to re-evangelise Britain in 597. He became the first archbishop of Canterbury.
● **St Boniface** (675-754). The English-born monk Boniface was called the 'Apostle of Germany'. Appointed as archbishop of Mainz in 751, he was killed preaching in Friesland.

The Roman Catholic Church

The Roman Catholic Church was originally geographically equivalent to the Roman Empire of the West. Its leader, the pope, claimed direct succession from **St Peter**, and the right of jurisdiction over the entire Christian world. The organisation of the Church, its preservation of the **Latin** language and much Roman learning, its massive cathedral-building programme, its sponsorship of the Crusades, its monastic orders and its power and wealth defined the Middle Ages.

*c.***4-6 BC** Jesus of Nazareth is born in Palestine.

*c.***26-34** Jesus is crucified.

*c.***46-57** St Paul travels across the Mediterranean on his missionary journeys.

100

*c.***200** Church leaders assemble Christian writings into the New Testament.

313 The Edict of Milan makes Christianity formally tolerated within the Roman Empire.

325 The Council of Nicaea rejects Arianism as a heresy.

380 Emperor Theodosius makes Christianity Rome's official religion.

*c.***AD 23-30** Jesus begins to preach his message publicly.

*c.***36** The 'Christian' message of Jesus begins to spread to non-Jews.

*c.***64** St Peter is executed in Rome; the persecution of Christians begins.

*c.***300** The popular Arian doctrine leads to divisions among Christians.

354-430 St Augustine of Hippo creates a coherent Christian theology.

Monastic orders

Withdrawal from society in pursuit of a truly spiritual life was formalised by the creation of monastic communities within the Christian Church. The originators of this formal ('regular') monasticism were St Basil the Great (c.330-79) in the East and St Benedict of Nursia (c.480-547) in the West. The monastic orders exerted great influence in medieval Europe.

● **Benedictines** St Benedict's order of monks spread rapidly from its first house at Monte Cassino, Italy (525), to several thousand houses by the 11th century. The Order of **Cluny** (early 10th century onwards) resulted from the first major reform of the Benedictine order.

● **Carthusians** The austere Carthusian order was founded in 1084 at La Chartreuse by St Bruno of Cologne.

● **Cistercians** Founded in 1098 by Robert of Molesme at Cîteaux, France, the Cistercian order was based on a strict interpretation of St Benedict's Rule. It was a prosperous order with large agricultural estates.

● **Franciscans** The Franciscans (Friars Minor) were the first order of friars (mendicant or begging monks), founded in 1209 by St Francis of Assisi (1182-1226).

● **Dominicans** The Dominican order (Friars Preachers), founded in 1215 by St Dominic (1170-1221), emphasised public preaching.

● **Augustinians** Augustinian canons flourished from around 1100. Their Rules were based on that of St Augustine of Hippo.

Franciscan The Grey Friars adopted poverty as a sign of spirituality.

Dominican Many influential scholars and teachers were Black Friars.

Benedictine The Black Monks were the most numerous of all monastic orders.

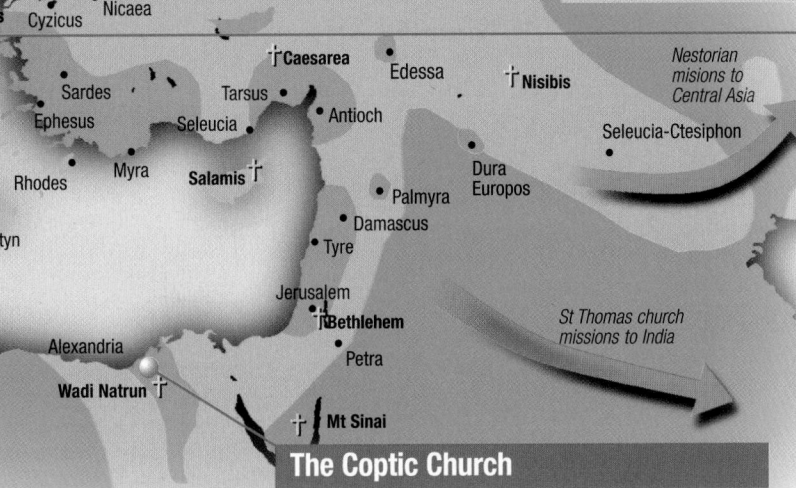

The Eastern Orthodox Church

The Orthodox tradition encompasses a group of Churches centred on the Patriarch of **Constantinople** and rejecting the supremacy of the pope. Early self-governing subdivisions include the **Russian** Orthodox Church (founded 998).

see also
180-1 **The rise of Islam**
340-1 **Religions**
352-3 **Western art**
598-9 **Mediterranean**

The Nestorian Church

The Nestorian church was created by the followers of **Nestorius** (d. 451), bishop of Constantinople. Its basic belief was that Jesus combined distinct human and divine natures. The Nestorians were expelled by the Orthodox Church in 489, and resettled in **Persia**; their missionaries spread to India, Sri Lanka and China.

(Map labels)

to Russia
Chersonesus
Marcianopolis
Adrianople
Constantinople
Thessalonica
✝Chalcedon
✝Mt Athos   Cyzicus   Nicaea
Artashat
Amasia
✝Caesarea
Edessa
✝Nisibis
Sardes
Tarsus
Antioch
Seleucia-Ctesiphon
Corinth
Ephesus
Seleucia
Myra
Salamis✝
Dura Europos
Rhodes
Palmyra
Gortyn
Damascus
Tyre
Jerusalem
✝Bethlehem
Alexandria
Petra
Wadi Natrun ✝
✝ Mt Sinai

Nestorian missions to Central Asia

St Thomas church missions to India

The Coptic Church

Traditionally founded by **St Mark** the Evangelist, the Coptic Church developed in **Egypt** (particularly Alexandria) after the 2nd century. It split from the rest of the Church over the definition of Christ's nature, and was associated with early Christian **monasticism**. The Church still exists in Egypt, and is strong in Ethiopia.

The East-West Schism

Bitter disputes over doctrine and papal authority began to divide the Western and Eastern Churches from the 9th century. Mutual excommunications were pronounced by Rome and Constantinople in 1054 (lifted only in 1965). This marked the first great formal separation of the Christian Church – into Roman Catholic in the West and Orthodox in the East.

(Timeline)

451 The Copts split from the rest of the Church.

525 St Benedict of Nursia founds the first major Western monastery at Monte Cassino, Italy.

800 Charlemagne is crowned Emperor of the West by the pope.

1076-7 Pope Gregory VII excommunicates the Holy Roman Emperor Henry IV.

1202-4 The Fourth Crusade sacks the Byzantine capital, Constantinople.

1291 Acre, the last Crusader state, falls to the Muslims.

500

1500

496 Clovis, king of the Franks, converts to Christianity.

596 Pope Gregory the Great sends St Augustine to England.

1000

1054 The Eastern Orthodox Church formally parts with the Church of Rome.

1095 First Crusade: Christians conquer the Holy Land.

1225-74 Life of St Thomas Aquinas, the greatest theologian of the Middle Ages.

1453 Constantinople falls to the Ottomans.

In AD 610, after a series of divine revelations, the Prophet Muhammad founded a religion based on faith in a single god, clear social rules and the promise of an afterlife. Arab conquests quickly spread Islam though south-west Asia, the Middle East and North Africa. Christian Europe was hostile to Islam, but later benefited from the preservation of Greek culture and the scientific and medical knowledge of Arab Muslims.

The Middle East

Islam's expansion beyond Arabia began with the Muslim conquest of Sasanian (Persian) Iraq and Byzantine Syria in 633-41. **Jerusalem** was captured in 638, and became the third city of Islam. In 637 Muslim forces defeated the Sasanians at Qadisiya, and by 650 all of Persia was under Islamic rule. The First **Crusade** (1099) established Christian territories in the Middle East, but these were mostly reconquered by Saladin, the **Ayyubid** sultan of Egypt, in 1187. The Middle East was dominated by the Ottoman Empire after 1516.

Spain & Portugal

Visigothic Spain and Portugal were conquered in 711-19 by an Arab and Berber (Moorish) army from North Africa. The Moors took Córdoba, Seville, Malaga, Toledo, Zaragoza and Granada, but were defeated at Poitiers, France, in 732 by the Franks. The **Umayyad Caliphate of Córdoba** ruled Spain until 1031, followed by the **Almoravids** (1090-1145), then the **Almohads** (1145-1212). Northern Spain remained Christian, and gradually reconquered the south. The last Moorish kingdom, Granada, fell in 1492.

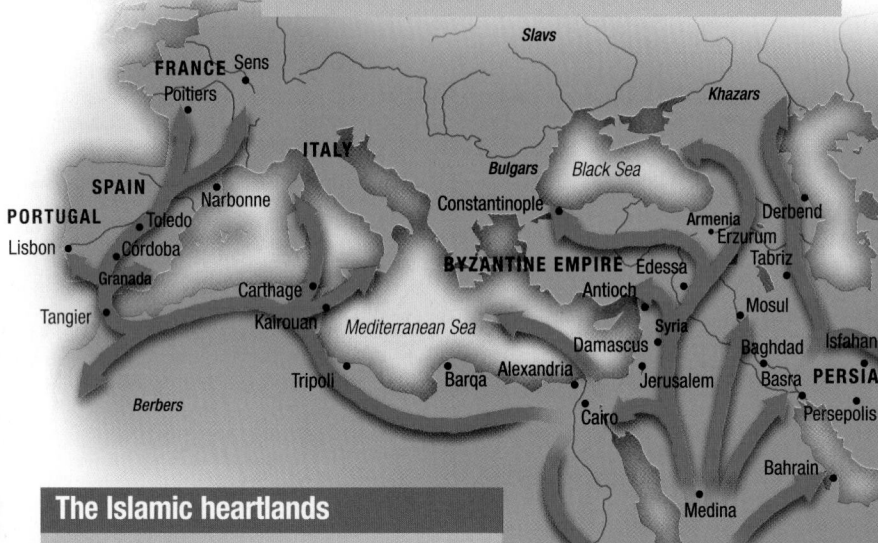

Moorish stronghold A view of the Alhambra, the greatest palace-fortress of Islamic Spain.

The Islamic heartlands

Muhammad's death (632) was followed at first by an ordered succession, the so-called **Orthodox Caliphate**. The first caliph, Muhammad's father-in-law Abu Bakr, is considered the founder of the **Sunni** tradition, and the last, Ali, of the **Shiite**. In 681, civil war brought the **Umayyad** caliphate to power, but feuding between Sunnis and Shiites continued. A rebellion by the **Abbasids** in 750 ended Umayyad rule everywhere except Spain, beginning the political fragmentation of the Islamic world. The Abbasids presided over the greatest age of Islamic culture (including the reign of **Harun ar-Rashid**, from 786 to 809, immortalised by the *Arabian Nights*). However, Persia rebelled under the **Safarids** and **Samanids** from 874, and in 914 Egypt fell to the **Fatimid** caliphate. The authority of the Abbasid caliphs became largely symbolic after Baghdad was captured by the Shiite **Buwayhids** in 950. The Abbasids were finally swept away by the Mongols in 1258.

North Africa

Muslim Arab forces under Amr conquered Byzantine Egypt in 639-40, then advanced westward. By 710 all of North Africa was in Muslim hands. The Berber **Almoravid** dynasty gained control of Morocco and Algeria in 1054 and Spain in 1090, to create an empire spanning the Strait of Gibraltar. In 1147-72 the **Almohad** dynasty supplanted the Almoravids, ruling from Marrakech until 1269.

Advance of Islam Islam spread rapidly across the Middle East, North Africa and Persia in the 7th century, as Arab armies overran the Byzantine and Persian empires. Its advance through India and South-east Asia was much more gradual.

AD 570 Muhammad is born in Mecca.

622 Muhammad withdraws to Medina (the Hijra), beginning the Islamic era.

634-644 Under Omar, Muslims take Jerusalem, and invade Mesopotamia, Asia Minor, Persia and Egypt.

670 Islam advances across North Africa.

732 Arab armies are heavily defeated by the Franks at Poitiers.

750 The Abbassids defeat the Umayyads and rule the Islamic world until 1258.

909 The Shiite Fatimids establish an empire in North Africa (to 1171).

600

610 Muhammad experiences revelations of the word of God.

632 Muhammad dies. Abu Bakr becomes his successor (caliph).

661 The Umayyad dynasty becomes established in Damascus; it rules until 750.

700

711 Muslim Arab forces from North Africa invade Spain.

762 The Abbasids make Baghdad the Islamic capital.

AD 900

Asia Minor and the Balkans

Asia Minor (Turkey) remained the centre of Byzantine power during Islam's initial rise; Arab sieges of Constantinople in 670-7 and 716-17 ended in heavy defeats. After 1038 the Muslim **Seljuk Turks** overran much of western Asia and Asia Minor, defeating the Byzantines at Manzikert (1071) and resisting the Crusaders. The Seljuk empire was destroyed by the Mongols in 1243. Its successor, the **Ottoman Empire**, expanded rapidly at the expense of the Byzantines (Constantinople fell in 1453, becoming the Ottoman capital). Ottoman forces overran the Middle East, the Balkans and most of North Africa in the 16th century.

Central and southern Asia

The Arab hold on Persia after 650 was brief. From 977 to 1186, the entire region from eastern Persia to north India fell to the **Ghaznavids** of Afghanistan. The Ghaznavids lost part of their empire to the Seljuks in 1040, and the rest to the **Ghurids** in 1186. In 1206, the Muslim **Sultanate of Delhi** emerged, dominating the Indian subcontinent under the Khalji dynasty by 1321. It was crushed by Tamerlane in 1398, and later destroyed by his descendants the **Mughals**.

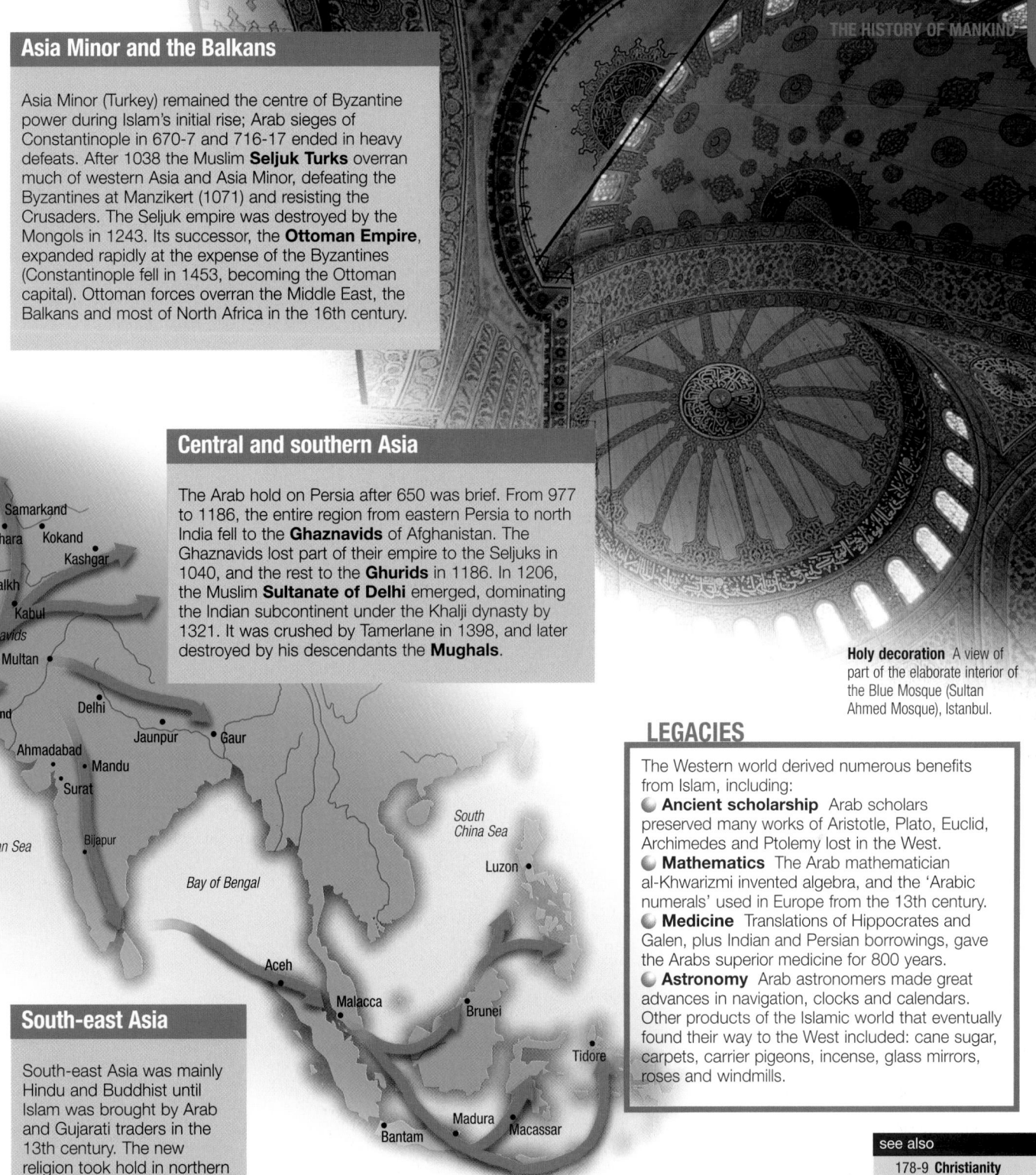

Holy decoration A view of part of the elaborate interior of the Blue Mosque (Sultan Ahmed Mosque), Istanbul.

South-east Asia

South-east Asia was mainly Hindu and Buddhist until Islam was brought by Arab and Gujarati traders in the 13th century. The new religion took hold in northern Sumatra, Java, the southern Philippines, the Malay peninsula and the Moluccas.

Map labels: Samarkand, Bukhara, Kokand, Kashgar, Merv, Balkh, Kabul, *Ghaznavids*, Multan, Sind, Delhi, Ahmadabad, Jaunpur, Gaur, Mandu, Surat, *Arabian Sea*, Bijapur, *Bay of Bengal*, *South China Sea*, Luzon, Aceh, Malacca, Brunei, Tidore, Bantam, Madura, Macassar

LEGACIES

The Western world derived numerous benefits from Islam, including:

- **Ancient scholarship** Arab scholars preserved many works of Aristotle, Plato, Euclid, Archimedes and Ptolemy lost in the West.
- **Mathematics** The Arab mathematician al-Khwarizmi invented algebra, and the 'Arabic numerals' used in Europe from the 13th century.
- **Medicine** Translations of Hippocrates and Galen, plus Indian and Persian borrowings, gave the Arabs superior medicine for 800 years.
- **Astronomy** Arab astronomers made great advances in navigation, clocks and calendars. Other products of the Islamic world that eventually found their way to the West included: cane sugar, carpets, carrier pigeons, incense, glass mirrors, roses and windmills.

1055 The Abbassids are defeated by the Seljuks of Asia Minor.

1085 The Almoravids invade Spain.

1147 The Almohads take Marrakech and make it their capital.

1172 The Almohads extend their power through Spain.

1212 The Almohads begin to retreat from Spain; by 1248 Granada is the only Muslim kingdom in Spain.

1258 The Mongols sack Baghdad, ending Abbassid rule, but in 1260 are heavily defeated at Ain Jalut.

1492 Islam is driven out of Europe with the capture of Granada

1000 — 1200 — 1400

1054 The Almoravids begin the conquest of Morocco and Algeria.

1095 First Crusade: Christians attack the Holy Land, taking Jerusalem in 1099.

1187 The Muslim reconquest of Jerusalem prompts the Third Crusade.

1206 The Sultanate of Delhi is founded (to 1526).

1299 The Ottoman empire is founded by Osman I, in succession to the Seljuk empire.

1453 The Ottomans capture Constantinople.

Around AD 1000 Europe was divided among many monarchs and regional lords whose authority over their territories varied greatly. Trade expanded, towns grew and won autonomy, craftsmen formed guilds, and universities were founded. Writers such as Dante and Chaucer produced masterpieces, and massive cathedrals were built to assert belief in the power of the divine order.

Medieval Europe

Europe's states began to achieve something like their modern forms by the late 13th century, as shown here. The Church, trade and education networks, and a common aristocratic culture united Europe.

English territories

Aragonese territories

Venetian territories

Genoese territories

Holy Roman Empire

Major castles
Lords built castles in order to control their local territory.

Cathedrals
Cathedrals were the most ambitious architectural works of their age.

Trade fairs
Huge annual trade fairs attracted merchants from all over Europe.

Universities
During the 12th century, universities formed and supplanted monasteries as centres of learning.

Hanseatic League
The Hansa was an alliance of north German cities, formed in 1241 to protect and promote trading interests abroad. Centring on the Baltic, it included over 70 towns in the late 14th century. The Hansa commanded its own army and navy and had outposts in London, Bruges, Novgorod and Bergen.

FEUDAL EUROPE

Power in medieval Europe lay with kings and great aristocrats. In many areas – England, for example – all land was said to be held from the king. Layers of nobility held **fiefs** (large estates) from the king and aristocrats in return for military service (feudalism). Peasants were sometimes free, but normally owed a range of rents and services to landholders. Political power was often unstable, and during the chaotic 11th century, the Church drew commoners into 'Peace of God' movements which coerced knights and nobles into regional truces.

St Andrews
Edinburgh
Carrickfergus
Newcastle
Dublin
York
Limerick
Caernarvon
ENGLAND
Lynn
Norwich
Cambridge
Bristol   Oxford   London   Antwerp
Cologne
Canterbury   Bruges
Portchester   Lille   Louvain   Liege
Tournai   Mainz
Arras   Worms
Bayeaux   Rouen   Heidel
Mont-St-Michel   Paris   Reims
Provins
Chartres   Troyes   Strasbourg
Angers   Bourges   Vézelay
Poitiers   Besançon
FRANCE   Cluny   Geneva
Bordeaux   Lyon
Cahors   Milan
NAVARRE   Toulouse
Medina del   Foix   Avignon   Genoa
Campo   Carcassonne   Beaucaire   GENOA
Burgos   Zaragoza   Marseille
Santiago de
Compostela
PORTUGAL   Salamanca   ARAGON
Lisbon   Toledo   Barcelona
CASTILE   Valencia   Cors
Cordoba
Seville
Cadiz   EMIRATE OF   Sardinia
GRANADA   Granada

1066 William of Normandy defeats Harold II of England at Hastings.

AD 1000

1150 The first paper is made in Europe, using an Arab technique.

1215 Magna Carta establishes customary limits to royal power in England.

1241 The Mongols invade Poland, Hungary and Bohemia, reaching Vienna before withdrawing.

1299 The Ottoman Empire is founded, by Osman I.

1307 Dante begins to write *The Divine Comedy*.

1311 Reims cathedral, a masterpiece of Gothic architecture, is completed.

1130 The Normans, led by Roger II, establish a Kingdom of Sicily.

1170 Thomas Becket is murdered in Canterbury Cathedral.

1236 Ferdinand III of Castile and León captures Córdoba from the Moors.

1289 The first use of spectacles is recorded.

1300

***c*.1300** Gunpowder is manufactured in Europe for the first time.

1309 Pope Clement V moves the papacy to Avignon, France (until 1377).

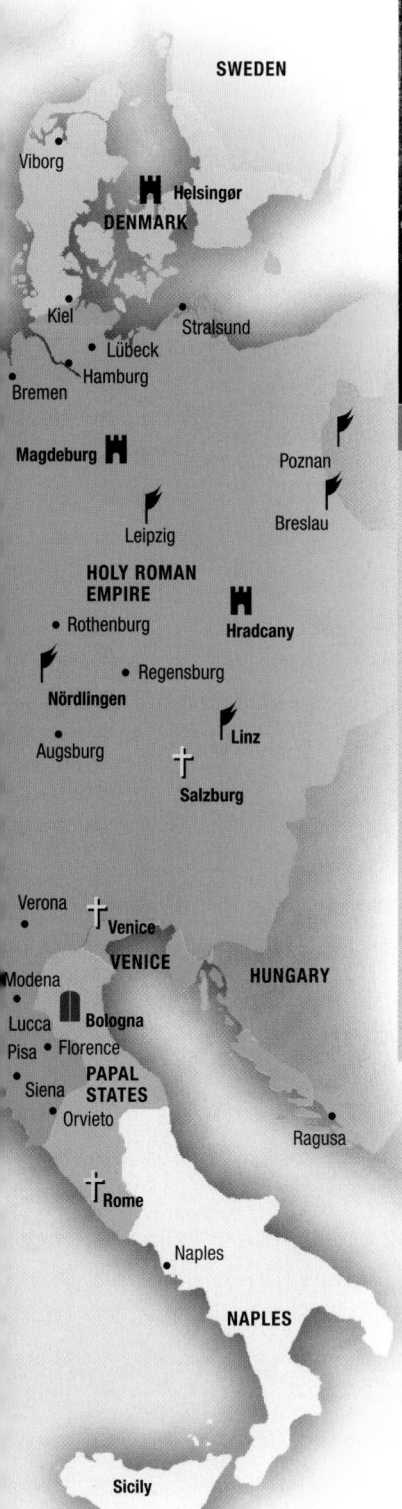

The Hundred Years' War (1338-1453)

The Hundred Years' War was in fact a series of wars between England and France conducted over 115 years. The main cause was contested territories in France, including Guyenne, Aquitaine, Normandy and Anjou. The war began when Edward III of England asserted a claim to the French throne, and the French king retaliated by confiscating Aquitaine, Edward's hereditary fiefdom. English victories followed at **Crécy** (1346) and **Poitiers** (1356), and in 1415 Henry V of England took Normandy after victory at **Agincourt**. Under the Treaty of Troyes (1420) Henry's infant son Henry VI was proclaimed king of France on the death of Charles VI in 1422. **Joan of Arc** persuaded the French heir to claim the crown as Charles VII. Charles's troops gradually evicted English forces from France. The war ended with the French capture of Bordeaux in 1453, leaving Calais as the only English territory in France.

see also
178-9 **Christianity**
180-1 **The rise of Islam**
576-7 **Weapons of war**
598-601 **Ready Reference**

The Black Death

Bubonic plague struck Europe in 1347, probably brought from central Asia by black rats and their fleas. By 1351, the total death toll was about 25 million – over a third of the entire European population. At its height in Paris, the 'Black Death' claimed about 800 people a day. Medical understanding was limited: the pope's doctor believed it was possible to catch the disease by looking at a victim. The plague caused labour shortages and violent discontent, hastening the end of feudalism. In some areas, population levels did not fully recover until the 16th century.

Piety and plunder
A 12th-century Crusader knight seeks a blessing ahead of his campaign.

THE CRUSADES

The Crusades were a series of wars waged by Christian Europeans against the Muslim states in the Middle East. Ostensibly the purpose was to secure access to pilgrimage sites in the Holy Land but political and economic motives were at least as important. The **First Crusade** (1095-9) was launched after an appeal from Pope Urban II; an army of 30 000 advanced through Asia Minor (Turkey), taking Jerusalem (1099) and massacring its 40 000 inhabitants. The Crusaders founded the Christian Kingdom of Jerusalem and other Crusader states. These states were almost completely overrun by the Muslim warrior Saladin after the failure of a **Second Crusade** (1147-9). The **Third Crusade** (1188-92), led by Holy Roman Emperor Frederick Barbarossa, Richard I (the Lionheart) of England and Philip II of France, failed to recover Jerusalem from Saladin. The **Fourth Crusade** (1202-4) was diverted by the Venetians, and the Crusaders then went on to sack Constantinople, capital of the Byzantine Empire. Crusades continued throughout the 13th century but were largely failures as the Islamic world was becoming stronger and more united. Jerusalem was briefly recovered in the Sixth Crusade (1228-9) but lost again in 1244. Acre, the last Christian stronghold in the Middle East, was captured by the Muslims in 1291.

1314 Robert Bruce secures Scottish independence by defeating the English at Bannockburn.

1337 Philip VI of France confiscates Guienne, sparking off the Hundred Years' War.

1353 The English poet Geoffrey Chaucer begins *The Canterbury Tales.*

1389 The Ottomans overrun the Balkans after the Battle of Kosovo.

1429 French forces under Joan of Arc raise the English siege of Orleans.

1455-85 The York and Lancaster dynasties contest the English throne (the 'Wars of the Roses').

1315-19 Famine, floods and a cattle plague devastate much of Western Europe.

1348 The Black Death reaches Florence, Paris and London.

1378-1417 The Church is divided between rival popes in Rome and Avignon.

1415 Henry V of England defeats the French at Agincourt.

1453 The Ottoman Turks capture Constantinople, ending the Byzantine Empire.

1485 Henry Tudor defeats Richard III of England at Bosworth.

There was a flourishing civilisation in the Indus Valley by 2500 BC. Repeated invasions of India from central Asia brought a succession of empires, influenced at first by Hinduism and Buddhism and then by Islam. The last of these was the Mughal (or Mogul) Empire. But India's wealth and sophisticated economy continued to attract both trade and military invasion from the east as well as the west – most spectacularly in the form of the British Raj.

The Gupta Empire

The Gupta kings presided over a golden age in which science, philosophy and the arts flourished. Their empire along the Ganges reached its greatest size under **Chandra Gupta II** (reigned 376-401), but was destroyed at the end of the 5th century by the White Huns.

Indus — Gandhara
Barbaricum
Panchala
Mathura
Arabian Sea — Ujjain — Kosala
Ganges
Varanasi — Pataliputra
Nalanda
Machilipatnam — Kalinga — Utkala — Vanga — Pundra
Simhapura
Bay of Bengal

c.5000 BC Farmers in the flood plains of the Indus Valley settle into villages.

c.1500 BC Indus Valley civilisation dies out, for unknown reasons.

563-483 BC Siddharta Gautama, (the Buddha) lives and teaches in India.

c.500 BC Parts of the epic *Ramayana* are written.

321 BC Chandragupta Maurya founds the Mauryan Dynasty.

c.185 BC The Mauryans are replaced by the Sunga dynasty.

c.AD 78-102 The Kushans occupy the Indus Valley and Punjab.

319 Chandragupta I founds the Gupta Empire on the Ganges.

c.2500 BC The Indus Valley civilisation includes at least five major cities.

c.1500 BC Aryans spread from the Indus Valley into the Ganges region, founding Hinduism.

500 BC

518 BC Darius I, king of Persia, conquers the Indus Valley.

326-325 BC Alexander the Great occupies the Indus Valley.

c.269-238 BC Mauryan control spreads across India under Asoka.

c.135-58 BC The nomadic Sakas invade northern India.

0

c.200 The epics *Ramayana* and *Mahabharata* take on their final form.

The Mauryan Empire

The first great empire of the Indian subcontinent, developed after the withdrawal of Alexander the Great's armies from the Indus Valley in 325 BC. Named after **Chandragupta Maurya** (reigned c.321-297 BC), the Mauryan Empire extended across northern India, and included modern Pakistan and Afghanistan. It reached its greatest extent and cultural peak under King **Asoka** (reigned c.269-238 BC). Asoka's first experience of military conquest so horrified him that in about 263 BC he converted to Buddhism and renounced war. He developed a system of government based on Buddhist principles: rulers were to be responsible for the people's welfare, and to behave with respect, tolerance, honesty and compassion – precepts he had inscribed in stone. The empire fragmented after Asoka's death. The last Mauryan emperor was killed in 185 BC, and replaced by the Hindu Sunga dynasty.

Bodhi tree Buddhist motifs from a shrine of Asoka.

Uttarapatha — Indus
Avanti
Junagadh — Mathura
Ujjain — Sanchi — Magadha
Arabian Sea — Sarnath — Ganges
Dakshinapatha — Pataliputra
Suvarnagiri — Tosali — Vanga
Bay of Bengal

TOP TEMPLES

Ajanta caves The 29 Ajanta caves in northern Maharashtra were carved from solid rock between the 1st century BC and the 7th century AD. They were dwellings and shrines for Buddhist monks, and were decorated with fresco paintings and carvings.

Khajuraho The site of 50 Hindu and Jain temples dating mainly from AD 950 to 1050, Khajuraho is near Kanpur, in north-central India. The 22 surviving temples are famed for their erotic sculpture.

Mahabalipuram A Hindu religious complex south of Madras, Mahabalipuram was built under the Pallava dynasty in the 7th century AD. The site includes the remains of the 'Seven Pagodas' made of single huge blocks of stone.

Taj Mahal The great masterpiece of Mughal architecture, the Taj Mahal was built on the River Jumna at Agra in 1632-48. It commemorates the wife of emperor Shah Jahan, Mumtaz-i-Mahal, who died in childbirth in 1629. Designed by a Turkish architect, it is built of white marble and semiprecious stones.

The Cholas and South-east Asia

Indian influence spread well beyond the subcontinent. Hinduism and Buddhism permeated South-east Asia from India in the 2nd and 3rd centuries AD. The Buddhist temple of Borobudur, Java, was built by the Sailendra Empire (c.750-850), while the Hindu-Buddhist Khmers dominated mainland South-east Asia from about 900 to 1431. The Cholas, a sea-going Tamil civilisation (Tamils are an ethnically distinct south Indian Hindu population), spread Indian influence in a series of expeditions in the 10th and 11th centuries. **Rajaraja I** (reigned AD 985-1016) conquered Kerala and northern Ceylon (Sri Lanka); his son **Rajendra** (reigned 1016-44) took Malacca and the Malay Peninsula.

Ghaznavids

Arabian Sea

Gurjara-Pratiharas

Chandellas

Rashtrakutas

Hoysalas *Pallavas* **KALINGA** **ORISSA**

Madurai • Kanchipuram

Pandyas • Gangaikondacholapuram

Tanjore

SAYLAN

Bay of Bengal

Siva as Lord of the Dance
A Chola bronze from Tamil Nadu in southern India.

*c.***335-76** Samudra extends the Gupta Empire to the Indus Valley.

*c.***480** The White Huns destroy the Gupta Empire.

1081 The Cholas conquer Ceylon (Sri Lanka).

1206 The Muslim Sultanate of Delhi is founded (to 1526).

1398 The Sultanate of Delhi is crushed by Tamerlane.

1526 Babur defeats the Sultanate of Delhi at Panipat, founding the Mughal Empire.

1700 The British East India Company controls many Indian trading ports.

1500

500

1000

1803 The Mughal capital Delhi falls to the British East India Company.

*c.***350** The erotic classic *Kamasutra* is written.

*c.***711** Muslim forces from Iraq enter north India.

1186 The Ghaznavids lose Lahore to the Afghan Ghurids.

*c.***1321** The Sultanate of Delhi expands to southern India.

1498 The Portuguese navigator Vasco da Gama reaches India.

1565 The Mughals defeat the Vijayanagar empire of south-east India.

1632 Shah Jahan begins construction of the Taj Mahal.

1857 The last Mughal emperor is exiled by the British.

1746-61 Britain and France compete for control of India.

The Mughal Empire

Mughal miniature
Shah Jahan with one of his sons, painted in 1615 by Manohar.

The Mughals were a Muslim dynasty of mixed Turkic and Mongol descent, founded by the Timurid conqueror **Babur** 'the Tiger' (1483-1530). Babur captured Delhi in 1526 and his forces overran most of northern India. The golden age of the Mughal Empire (see map) was under **Akbar** (reigned 1556-1605), whose enlightened court at Fatehpur Sikri promoted religious tolerance and oversaw the greatest achievements of Mughal art and architecture, **Jehangir** (reigned 1605-27) and **Shah Jahan** (1628-58). **Aurangzeb** (1659-1707) extended the empire almost to the southern tip of India, but persecuted Sikhs and Hindus, causing widespread internal friction. Religious strife and court rivalries after his reign left the empire vulnerable to British and French aggression. The empire was kept alive in name only by the British until 1857.

Kabul

Lahore •

• Panipat

Fatehpur Sikri • Delhi

Surat • • Agra

Arabian Sea

Allahabad •

AHMADNAGAR

BIJAPUR **GOLCONDA** **GONDWANA** • Gaur

VIJAYANAGAR

Bay of Bengal

see also

268-9 **India**

340-3 **Religions**

For much of world history, China was the richest and most powerful nation on earth. Until the 19th century, it remained almost entirely self-sufficient, amassing huge national wealth by exporting silk, spices and (later) porcelain. Japan remained culturally in the shadow of its powerful neighbour for many centuries, but was equally insular and self-reliant.

China's ruling dynasties

Political power in China was held by a succession of major dynasties; central control of such a huge nation was possible only because the vast, sophisticated and largely meritocratic Chinese civil service was maintained throughout changes of rule. The chaos that swept China in the 'Three Kingdoms' and the 'Five Dynasties and Ten Kingdoms' periods emphasised the value of this continuity.

Qin (Ch'in) 221-206 BC
The Ch'in gave their name to China. Qin Shi Huangdi, the 'First Emperor' (reigned 221-210 BC), created a strong centralised state with a standardised written language, and built much of the Great Wall.

Images of life and afterlife (Above) Life size terracotta warriors, each face unique, from the tomb of emperor Qin Shi Huangdi, *c.*210 BC. (Below) An earthenware tomb guardian figure from the Tang dynasty, AD 618-907.

● **Shang** *c.*1600-1050 BC
The Shang rulers controlled most of northern China. Their achievements included writing, a calendar, social classes, bureaucracy, cast bronze, jade carving and pottery.

● **Zhou** *c.*1000-256 BC
The Zhou presided over China's 'Classical Age', the era of Confucius (*c.*551-479 BC), Lao-Zi (*c.*604-531 BC), iron and the ox-drawn plough.

● **Han** 206 BC-AD 220 The Han maintained a strong centralised government run on Confucian principles of moderation. They oversaw a period of prosperity and cultural flowering, trading silk with the Roman Empire via the 'Silk Route'.

● **Tang** AD 618-907
The Tang gained control of China from the Sui dynasty, after nearly 400 years of turmoil in the 'Three Kingdoms' period. Stability and a cosmopolitan culture stimulated trade, printing developed, and Buddhism spread; poetry hit a golden age, around AD 70.

*c.*6000 BC Pottery and domesticated animals and plants first appear in China.

*c.*551-479 BC Life of Confucius.

*c.*353 BC Work begins on the Great Wall.

*c.*AD 50 Buddhism reaches China.

220-80 The 'Three Kingdoms' period of turmoil ends Han rule.

304 The Huns (Xiongnu) invade China.

850-900 Peasant revolts bring local warlord rule to most of China.

979 The Song Dynasty reunites China.

5000 BC

1000 BC

250 BC

0

250

1000

China

Japan

*c.*5000-250 BC The Neolithic Jomon culture produces pottery and jewellery in Japan.

660 BC The nation of Japan is founded, according to legend.

250 BC-AD 250 Japanese Yayoi culture produces iron and bronze, textiles, and rice cultivation.

405 The Yamato court at Nara unifies Japan.

*c.*550 Buddhism is introduced to Japan.

900-1100 A purely Japanese culture, script and language emerge.

Japan's turbulent history

The first recognisable states in Japan began to emerge around AD 300, within the **Yayoi** culture. Attempts to create a unified and centralised state, however, began in the **Yamato** period (AD 300-710). The court was moved from Nara to **Heian** (Kyoto) in 794 to escape growing Buddhist influence over the shogun (emperor). The Heian period lasted until 1185, dominated by the powerful **Fujiwara** family. The decline of central authority at the end of the period allowed the rise of **feudalism**.

The **Kamakura** shoguns (1185-1333) were effectively dominated by the Minamoto and Hojo families, and Japan repelled two Mongol invasions (1274 and 1281). From 1336 to 1568 Japan was ruled by the **Ashikaga** (or Muromachi) shoguns, but suffered from political instability, peasant unrest and civil war, exacerbated by militant 'Pure Land' Buddhist monks. In 1467-77 this instability resulted in the **Onin War**, and the century-long Warring States period.

Reunification was effected by **Oda Nobunaga**, **Hideyoshi Toyotomi** and **Tokugawa Ieyasu** between 1568 and 1600. The resulting Tokugawa Shogunate lasted until 1868. Political conservatism was matched by growing **isolationism**, with European traders excluded and Japanese Christians persecuted. Japan's anti-foreign policy was finally dropped only in the **Meiji** period (1868-1912).

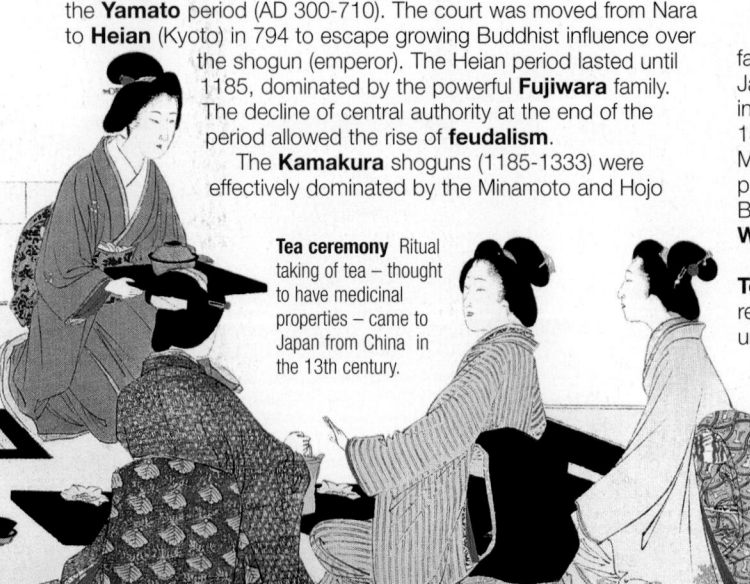

Tea ceremony Ritual taking of tea – thought to have medicinal properties – came to Japan from China in the 13th century.

FACT The indigenous religion of Japan, Shinto, goes back to prehistoric times. It has no founder or sacred text but many modern Japanese still worship at Shinto shrines.

Artistic achievements in China

Jade Green, white, grey – even blue, red and yellow – jade was imported into China in prehistoric times, mainly from central Asia. It was carved into fine jewellery and ornaments – much sought after because the stone was thought to have powers of healing or even of conferring immortality.

Lacquerware The hard, black resin of the rhus lacquer tree was used for decoration before 400 BC. Layers of lacquer were applied to a base, and then incised and carved to create elaborate scenes and designs. Boxes, dishes, food containers, even whole thrones, were lacquered.

Metalwork Cast bronze dates back to c.2000 BC, often in the form of large ritual vessels used for offerings of food and wine in sacrificial ceremonies.

Painting Exquisite brush and ink painting developed in the Tang period, far outstripping Western art in observation, technique and delicacy. Landscape painting was fully established by the 900s.

Pottery Neolithic earthenware pots show flair for design, and very early use of the wheel. Fine modelling is seen, for example, in ceramic horses of the Tang period, decorated with characteristic three-colour glaze.

CHINESE FIRSTS

Abacus The abacus was used in China around 500 BC.

Cast iron The Chinese developed cast iron in about 600 BC.

Gunpowder Explosives were used in fireworks and signals in the Tang period, and in weapons during the Song.

Magnetic compass The magnetised needle was first used by Chinese navigators in about AD 1000.

Paper China produced the world's first paper c.AD 105.

Porcelain Hard, fine, white pottery was made in China from about 50 BC.

Printing The Chinese pioneered printing methods from the 2nd century AD. Woodblock printing was introduced in the 6th century.

Silk Legend says that silk-weaving began in 2640 BC.

Song (Sung) 960-1279 The Song oversaw a period of cultural achievement and growing prosperity through expanding trade. Paper currency was developed and widely used; printing helped to spread literacy; and painting, sculpture and philosophy all made important advances.

1126 Jurzhen tribes invade northern China and establish Ch'in Empire.

1211 The Mongols overrun the Ch'in Empire.

Yuan (Mongols) 1280-1368 Genghis Khan (c.1167-1227) united Mongolia, seizing Beijing in 1215 and destroying the Ch'in Empire in north China by 1234. His successor Kublai Khan overran the surviving Southern Song Empire in 1268-79, and founded the Yuan dynasty with a capital at Beijing. Popular uprisings drove out the Yuan in 1335-68.

1275 Marco Polo reaches Beijing.

1300

Ming 1368-1644 The Ming dynasty was established by the rebel Zhu Yuanzhang, who reconquered Mongol China in 1368-88. Chinese rule was extended to Korea, Mongolia, Turkestan, Vietnam and Burma. China remained at peace for most of the 15th and 16th centuries.

Ming artistry Flower-motif vase, 16th century.

1405-33 Admiral Zheng He sails to India, the Persian Gulf and East Africa.

1514 The first Portuguese traders reach China.

1500

1542-50 Ming forces defeat two Mongol invasions.

1644 The Manchus (Qing) overthrow the Ming dynasty.

Qing (Manchu) 1644-1912 The Manchus gained control of China in 1616-52 and created the largest of all Chinese empires. China resisted European influence until the 19th century, when Manchu power began to decline. The last emperor, six-year-old Pu Yi, abdicated in 1912.

1899-1901 The anti-Western Boxer Rising is defeated.

c.1800 Britain begins to export Indian opium to China.

1912 The Qing are overthrown and a republic is declared.

1900

c.1100 The *daimyo* (feudal barons) rise to power in Japan.

1274 and 1281 Mongol invasions of Japan are prevented by typhoons.

1467-77 The Onin War ushers in the 'Warring States' period in Japan.

1542 The first European traders arrive in Japan.

1582 Hideyoshi Toyotomi begins to unify Japan.

1639 Japan adopts isolationist policies towards the West.

1853 Japan is forced to open its ports to trade.

1905 Japan becomes the dominant power in East Asia.

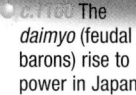

Samurai

Also known in Japanese as *bushi*, the samurai (literally meaning 'one who serves') emerged as a warrior class in the late Heian period (11th-12th centuries). The rise of the samurai occurred in parallel with the rise of the *sengoku daimyo*, the feudal barons who were their employers.

The samurai was a highly trained professional warrior, bound to his lord by a strict code of loyalty, in much the same way as a medieval European knight. For 700 years samurai dominated Japan as a military elite, their monopoly only coming to an end with the creation of a modern imperial army in the 19th century.

The vast scale and natural wealth of Africa are matched by a diversity and richness of culture. From the 1000-year Kingdom of Meroë in southern Egypt to the fabulous wealth of the West African Gold Coast to the mysterious builders of great Zimbabwe, African peoples traded, worshipped and built empires across a vast continent. Arabs arrived from the 7th century, and Europeans from the 15th – first in search of trade, then as settlers, farmers and adventurers drawn by tales of minerals, gems and gold.

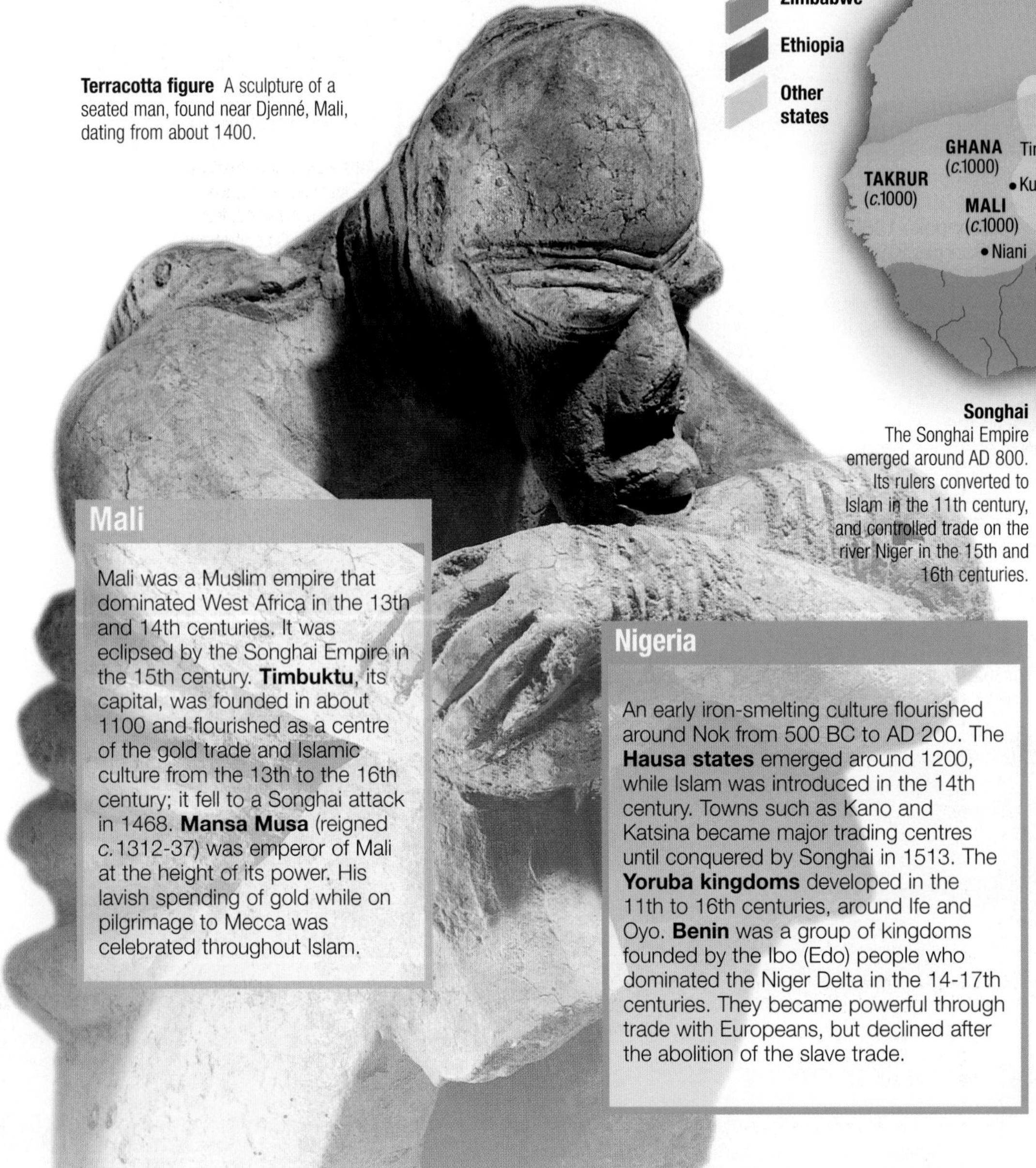

African empires

Pre-colonial Africa saw the rise and fall of a number of states, whose homelands are shown here. Their power was largely based on trade.

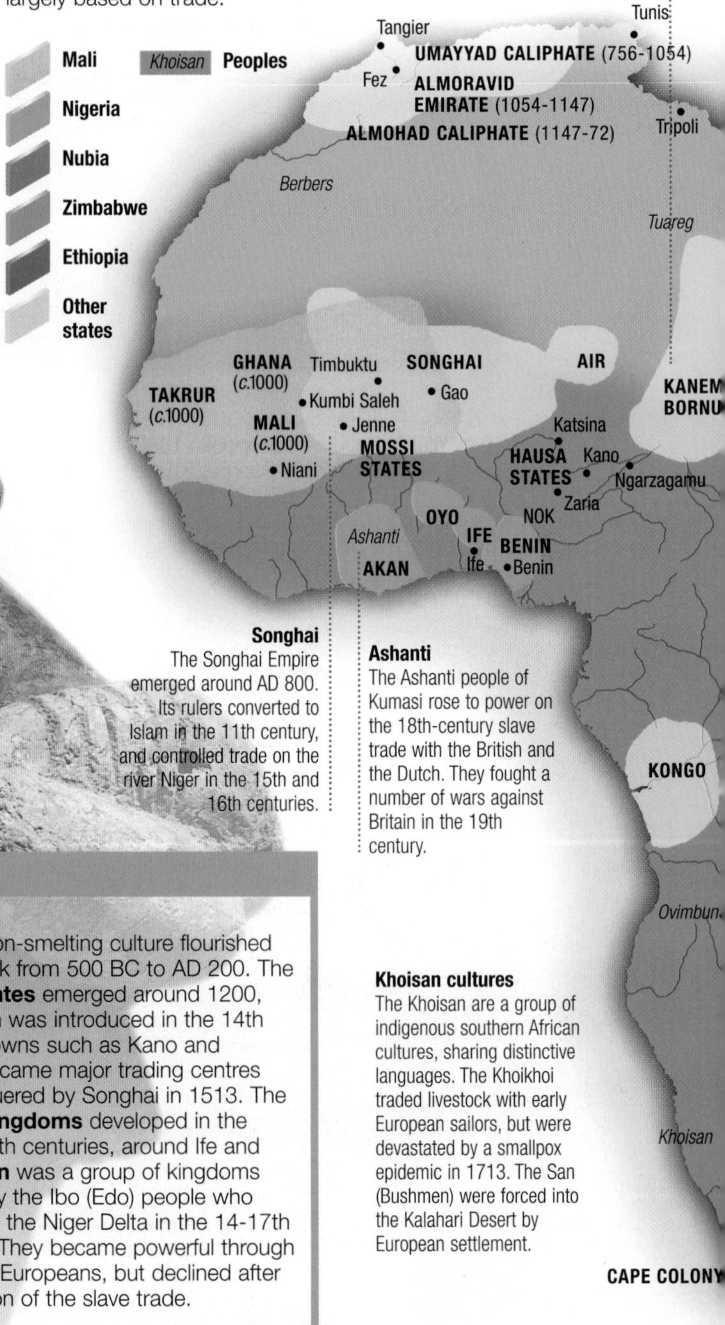

Mali
Nigeria
Nubia
Zimbabwe
Ethiopia
Other states

Khoisan **Peoples**

Empire of Kanem-Bornu
Around 1070, Kanem-Bornu became the first sub-Saharan state to convert to Islam. It dominated Saharan trade in the 13th century, but collapsed in the 19th.

UMAYYAD CALIPHATE (756-1054)
ALMORAVID EMIRATE (1054-1147)
ALMOHAD CALIPHATE (1147-72)

Tangier · Tunis · Fez · Tripoli · Berbers · Tuareg

GHANA (c.1000) · Timbuktu · SONGHAI · AIR · KANEM-BORNU
TAKRUR (c.1000) · Kumbi Saleh · Gao · Katsina
MALI (c.1000) · Jenne · HAUSA STATES · Kano · Ngarzagamu
MOSSI STATES · Zaria
Niani · OYO · NOK
Ashanti · IFE · BENIN
AKAN · Ife · Benin
KONGO
Ovimbun
Khoisan
CAPE COLONY

Terracotta figure A sculpture of a seated man, found near Djenné, Mali, dating from about 1400.

Mali

Mali was a Muslim empire that dominated West Africa in the 13th and 14th centuries. It was eclipsed by the Songhai Empire in the 15th century. **Timbuktu**, its capital, was founded in about 1100 and flourished as a centre of the gold trade and Islamic culture from the 13th to the 16th century; it fell to a Songhai attack in 1468. **Mansa Musa** (reigned c.1312-37) was emperor of Mali at the height of its power. His lavish spending of gold while on pilgrimage to Mecca was celebrated throughout Islam.

Nigeria

An early iron-smelting culture flourished around Nok from 500 BC to AD 200. The **Hausa states** emerged around 1200, while Islam was introduced in the 14th century. Towns such as Kano and Katsina became major trading centres until conquered by Songhai in 1513. The **Yoruba kingdoms** developed in the 11th to 16th centuries, around Ife and Oyo. **Benin** was a group of kingdoms founded by the Ibo (Edo) people who dominated the Niger Delta in the 14-17th centuries. They became powerful through trade with Europeans, but declined after the abolition of the slave trade.

Songhai
The Songhai Empire emerged around AD 800. Its rulers converted to Islam in the 11th century, and controlled trade on the river Niger in the 15th and 16th centuries.

Ashanti
The Ashanti people of Kumasi rose to power on the 18th-century slave trade with the British and the Dutch. They fought a number of wars against Britain in the 19th century.

Khoisan cultures
The Khoisan are a group of indigenous southern African cultures, sharing distinctive languages. The Khoikhoi traded livestock with early European sailors, but were devastated by a smallpox epidemic in 1713. The San (Bushmen) were forced into the Kalahari Desert by European settlement.

c.7000 BC Pastoral farmers inhabit Libya and Algeria.

c.3100 BC Egypt is first unified, by King Menes.

1567-1320 BC The 'New Kingdom' in Egypt; Napata (Nubia) becomes a major centre.

c.500 BC-AD 200 The Nok civilisation develops in Nigeria.

AD 300-400 The kingdom of Axum reaches its height.

c.500 Bantu farmers and herders reach South Africa.

c.700 Empire of ancient Ghana emerges.

c.5000 BC Cattle herders occupy the fertile Sahara.

c.2584-2465 BC The pyramids are built at Giza.

590 BC The Egyptians sack Napata; Meroë becomes the Nubian capital.

146 BC The Roman province of Africa is established.

c.400 The first towns develop in sub-Saharan Africa.

AD 642 The Arabs conquer Egypt.

Nubia

Nubia was known as **Kush** to the ancient Egyptians. King Piye of Kush conquered the entire Nile Valley around 732 BC, founding Egypt's 25th dynasty. The Kingdom of **Meroë** emerged in the 6th century BC and survived for almost 1000 years, developing a culture and religion that combined local and Egyptian elements. Nubia became Christian c.AD 540, but the north was conquered by Egypt in 652 and the south became part of the Islamic Funj kingdom of Sudan in the 16th century.

Mythical eagle A carving from Great Zimbabwe (c.AD 1200-1400), thought to represent a messenger of the gods.

Ethiopia

Known to ancient Egyptians as **Punt**, Ethiopia was home to the powerful kingdom of **Axum** from the 2nd to 8th centuries AD. It was the first African kingdom to adopt Christianity (in 321), and became a great stronghold of the Coptic Church – but was isolated by neighbouring hostile Islamic states for some 300 years from 702. The **Solomonid** dynasty came to power in 1270. In the 16th century, the reduced kingdom enlisted Portuguese help against Muslim attacks. The last Solomonid emperor, Hailie Selassie, died in 1975.

Ethiopian illumination Christ between Heaven, Hell and the world, from a 10th-century Ethiopian manuscript.

East African Trading States

Traders from Arabia visited East Africa as early as the 8th century AD. They created coastal settlements such as **Malindi**, **Mombasa** and **Kilwa**, which attracted Arab and Persian migrants from the 12th century and became wealthy and independent Islamic city-states. These states traded tools and weapons, textiles, Indian glass beads, Islamic pottery and Chinese porcelain for African ivory, ambergris (for perfumes), tortoiseshell and gold. In 1498 the Portuguese arrived and forced the city-states to pay tribute; they imposed colonial rule after Ottoman attacks in the late 16th century. The **Sultanate of Oman** ousted the Portuguese in the 17th century, and took control of much of the coast, overseeing an escalation in the slave trade after 1780. Britain and Germany took colonial control of most of East Africa from the 1880s.

FATIMID CALIPHATE
MAMLUKE SULTANATE (from 1250)
OTTOMAN EMPIRE (16th-19th centuries)
Alexandria
Cairo

WADAI
NUBIA
Dongola • MEROE
DARFUR Soba • ALWA
FUNJ EMPIRE
AXUM
• Axum
ETHIOPIA (from 1100) ADAL • Berbera

BUNYORO
BUGANDA
• Mogadishu

Buganda A major trader in slaves and ivory, Buganda became a British protectorate in 1900.

Kikuyu
• Malindi
• Mombasa
• Pemba
• Zanzibar

• Kilwa Kisiwani

Shona

Great Zimbabwe • Sofala
MWENE MUTAPA • Chibuene

Zimbabwe

South-eastern Africa was occupied by Bantu-speaking farmers in the 5th to 10th centuries AD; they exported gold and copper to Arab traders on the coast after about 900. The Shona kingdom of the Mwene Mutapa rose to form an empire based on **Great Zimbabwe**, a walled palace complex that flourished from about 1250 to 1450. By the late 15th century, the palace complex was in decline (perhaps because of a shift in the gold trade) but the Mwene Mutapa Empire extended over much of south-eastern Africa. Its decline was triggered by Portuguese incursions in the 17th century.

see also
180-1 **The rise of Islam**
206-7 **New nations**
216-7 **End of empire**
306-25 **Africa**

c.700-1000 Islam spreads through north-west Africa.

900 Arab merchants settle in East Africa.

c.1300 The empire of Benin develops.

1488 Bartholomeu Dias rounds the Cape of Good Hope.

c.1500 The European trade in African slaves begins.

1652 The Dutch found a colony at the Cape.

1698 Omani Arabs evict the Portuguese from East Africa.

1835-9 The Boers trek north from Britain's Cape Colony.

c.850 Kanem-Bornu develops as a major trading empire.

c.1250 The Mali Empire reaches its height.

c.1400 Great Zimbabwe is completed.

1505 The Portuguese sack Kilwa.

1546 Songhai destroys the Mali Empire.

c.1700 Ashanti power rises on the Gold Coast (to 1901).

1875-1914 European nations divide the continent in the 'Scramble for Africa'.

The people of ancient America developed distinctive civilisations in almost total isolation from the rest of the world. In Mexico, Central America and the Andes, farming peoples created complex urban societies centred on religious cults. Their cultures spread to the hunting and farming societies of North America. All these cultures were destroyed after the arrival of Europeans in 1492.

Olmecs

The first American civilisation emerged in about 1200 BC on the shores of eastern Mexico. Olmec cities centred on temple platforms and pyramid mounds. Sculptors worked in jade, obsidian, serpentine and – on a monumental scale – basalt. Trading and political influence extended throughout Central America, and Olmec culture formed the basis of most later civilisations of the region, the Aztecs, for instance, adopting Olmec gods. By 400 BC the culture had disappeared and the cities were destroyed and abandoned.

Basalt head The Olmecs made massive stone heads, perhaps of gods, weighing up to 20 tonnes.

Aztecs

The Aztec Empire was founded by the Mexica people in about 1325. They established a capital at **Tenochtitlán** on Lake Texcoco (Mexico City was later built over the site). The Aztecs conquered much of Central America, enforcing huge tribute payments that included human sacrificial victims. Hernán Cortés reached Tenochtitlán in 1519, and Aztec power was destroyed within 20 years by the conquistadores, supported by rebel subject peoples of the empire.

Tenochtitlán The temple was the centre of Aztec life, religious ritual shaping every aspect of existence.

Toltec warriors Feathered headdresses show that these men were nobles of high rank.

Toltecs

Toltec invaders from the north created an empire across much of Central America after about AD 900, based around **Tula** (Tollán). The former Maya lands of the Yucatán became the centre of a combined Toltec-Maya culture, including the cities **Chichén Itzá** (with its Temple of the Warriors and Castillo pyramid) and **Mayapán**. Toltec influence declined in central Mexico after 1200; the highland regions were taken over by the Mixtecs.

Mayan skill A late-period incense burner.

Maya

Early Mayan culture dates from about 2600 BC. From around 200 BC, a temple-based society was organised into city-states (such as **Tikal**). The Maya developed hieroglyphic writing, and had an advanced astronomical calendar. Political and trading links were forged with cities of south and central Mexico, and an empire established with wide influence. The civilisation collapsed in about AD 750-900 for unknown reasons. 'Post-Classic' Maya culture was revived in Yucatán with Toltec support, after AD 1200 but slid into civil war within 300 years.

---

*c.*5000 BC Maize farming begins in the highlands of Central America.

*c.*1200 BC Olmec culture emerges on the Gulf Coast of Mexico (to *c.*400 BC).

*c.*700 BC The Adena people of the eastern woodlands of North America begin mound-building.

*c.*AD 100 The Moche culture rises in coastal Peru (to *c.*AD 600).

*c.*400-800 The bow and arrow begin to replace the spear thrower in North America.

*c.*750-900 The Maya 'Classic' culture collapses; its cities are abandoned.

*c.*2500 BC The early Inuit (Eskimo) peoples spread along the ice-bound coasts of North America.

*c.*900 BC Chavín culture emerges in Peru (to *c.*400 BC).

*c.*100 BC The Hopewell culture replaces the Adena in eastern North America.

*c.*AD 150 Teotihuacán, Mexico, becomes Central America's first true city.

*c.*650 Teotihuacán declines for unknown reasons, and falls into ruin.

*c.*900 The Anasazi of south-west North America develop the first Pueblo settlements.

American empires

The pre-Conquest Americas were home to a range of cultures including the Aztecs of Mexico and the Incas of Peru.

Key religious sites

Palenque, Mexico Mayan temples with carvings and inscriptions, 7-8th century.

Tikal, Guatemala Monumental pyramids built by Mayan kings, c.8th century.

Teotihuacan, Mexico Huge sacred pyramid erected c.1st century.

Tenochtitlán, Mexico Aztec temple complex dating from the 14th century.

Machu Picchu, Peru Inca site c.1300s, housing the stone Intihuatana, probably devoted to sun-worship.

Map labels

Onoeta
Anasazi
Canyon de Chelly • Mesa Verde
• Pueblo Bonito
Hohokam
Mogollon
Cahokia •
Adena •
• Hopewell
Mississippian
Emerald
• Mound
• Lake Jackson

Quito •

Chan Chan • Chavín de Huántar
Moche •
Pachacamac • • Huari
• Machu Picchu
• Cuzco
Incas • Tiahuanaco

Santiago •

North America

Few North American cultures were urban, so little remains of key sites apart from earthworks. The **Adena** and **Hopewell** peoples dominated the Midwest for over 1000 years from 700 BC, building extensive ritual and burial mounds such as Serpent Mound, Ohio. The **Mississippians** succeeded the Hopewell around AD 600, farming maize and beans in the Mississippi valley; their city of Cahokia had a population of 30 000 by 1050, and they developed the bow and arrow as weapons. The **Anasazi** and **Pueblo** maize-growing cultures emerged in the south-west after 600, building their distinctive villages of adobe and stone. European settlers destroyed all the native cultures by 1900.

Inca figurine A gold statuette representing a concubine, buried with an Inca emperor.

Incas

Inca civilisation emerged in 13th-14th century Peru, tracing its origins to the semi-legendary god-king ('Inca') **Manco Capac**. A series of expansionist campaigns by **Pachacuti Inca Yupanqui** (reigned 1438-71) and his successors created an empire that dominated the Andes from Equador to Chile. The Incas developed a strong, centralised administration and imposed the use of their language. A network of roads led to the religious and political capital, **Cuzco**, the 'Navel [of the World]', whose massive walls of polygonal cut stone were assembled without mortar. The spectacular **Machu Picchu** was a town and ceremonial centre high in the Andes. Inca religion was based on worship of the Sun and past Inca rulers held to be descended from the Sun. The Inca Empire was made vulnerable by a succession dispute after the death of Inca Huayna Capac in 1525. It disintegrated with the invasion of a small force of Spanish conquistadores led by **Francisco Pizarro** in 1532-3. Pizarro executed the Inca claimant **Atahualpa** after helping him to depose his half-brother Huáscar. The last Inca dynasty died out in 1572 with the beheading by the Spanish of **Tupac Amaru** at Cuzco.

see also
192-3 **The age of exploration**
286-305 **The Americas**
338-9 **World mythology**

Timeline

*c.*950 The Toltecs emerge as a major military power in Central America.

*c.*1050 The mound city of Cahokia flourishes in Illinois.

*c.*1200 Toltec culture collapses and is replaced by the Mixtecs. The world's largest pyramid is built at Cholula.

1492 Christopher Columbus, in search of Asia, lands in the Bahamas.

1607 The first permanent European settlement in North America is set up at Jamestown, Virginia.

1625 The native population of Central America falls to 1.25 million, one-tenth of the figure for 1500.

1890 The massacre of the Sioux at Wounded Knee, South Dakota, marks the final subjugation of the native peoples of the Americas.

1000

*c.*1000 The Vikings set up a short-lived colony at L'Anse aux Meadows, Newfoundland.

*c.*1325 Tenochtitlán, capital of the Aztecs, is founded.

1472 The Inca Empire reaches its zenith in Peru.

1519 Hernán Cortés lands in Mexico. In 1521 he captures Tenochtitlán after a 93 day siege.

1531-3 Francisco Pizarro vanquishes the Incas. Spain rules Peru.

1500

1700 The number of European settlers in North America exceeds 250 000.

1900

In the 15th century, improvements in shipping and a demand for Far Eastern silks and spices led European navigators to explore new waters. The Portuguese worked around Africa to India and beyond, while Columbus crossed the Atlantic. The whole world was now open to European exploration, trade and settlement.

The great voyages Over a period of 300 years, from Columbus in 1492 to Cook in 1768, European maritime explorers opened up the entire world. Trade empires and then European colonists followed in their wake.

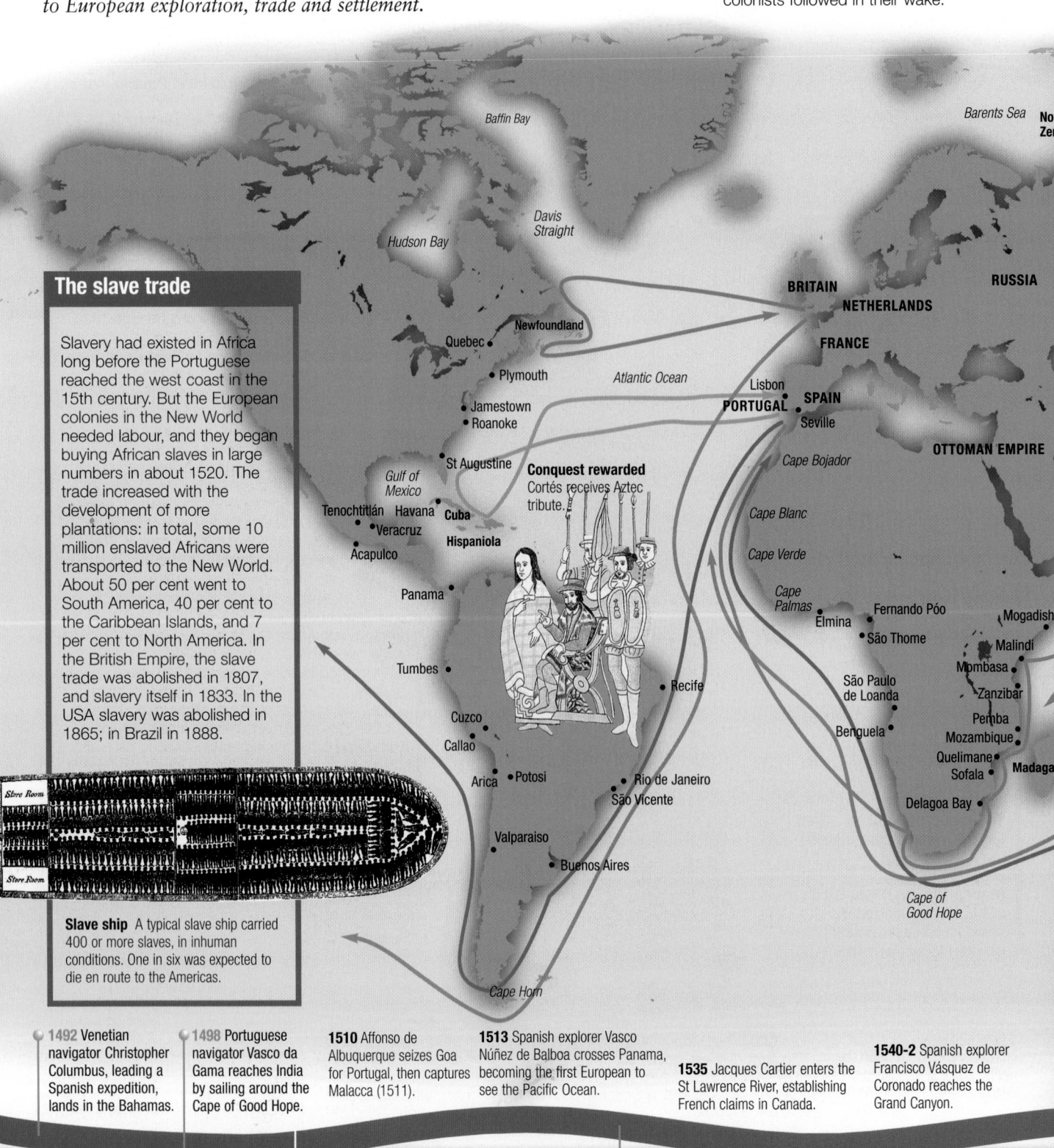

The slave trade

Slavery had existed in Africa long before the Portuguese reached the west coast in the 15th century. But the European colonies in the New World needed labour, and they began buying African slaves in large numbers in about 1520. The trade increased with the development of more plantations: in total, some 10 million enslaved Africans were transported to the New World. About 50 per cent went to South America, 40 per cent to the Caribbean Islands, and 7 per cent to North America. In the British Empire, the slave trade was abolished in 1807, and slavery itself in 1833. In the USA slavery was abolished in 1865; in Brazil in 1888.

Slave ship A typical slave ship carried 400 or more slaves, in inhuman conditions. One in six was expected to die en route to the Americas.

Conquest rewarded
Cortés receives Aztec tribute.

1492 Venetian navigator Christopher Columbus, leading a Spanish expedition, lands in the Bahamas.

1498 Portuguese navigator Vasco da Gama reaches India by sailing around the Cape of Good Hope.

1510 Affonso de Albuquerque seizes Goa for Portugal, then captures Malacca (1511).

1513 Spanish explorer Vasco Núñez de Balboa crosses Panama, becoming the first European to see the Pacific Ocean.

1535 Jacques Cartier enters the St Lawrence River, establishing French claims in Canada.

1540-2 Spanish explorer Francisco Vásquez de Coronado reaches the Grand Canyon.

1497 Genoese navigator John Cabot, leading an English expedition, reaches Newfoundland.

1500 Pedro Álvares Cabral lands in Brazil. He claims it for Portugal.

1512 Portuguese navigator Francisco Serrão explores the Spice Islands (Moluccas).

1519 Portuguese navigator Ferdinand Magellan's exedition circumnavigates the world.

1538-42 Spanish conquistador Hernando de Soto explores Florida and the North American south-east.

Spice and potatoes

One of the aims of European explorers was to gain trading access to spices. These were used in large quantities in Europe to preserve and flavour food, and were highly profitable trade items. The explorers found suppliers of cinnamon in Ceylon (Sri Lanka), pepper in South-east Asia, nutmeg and cloves in the Moluccas (the 'Spice Islands') and ginger in China. They also encountered new foods in the Americas: potatoes, maize, tomatoes, turkey, pumpkin, chillies, chocolate. Another profitable new product from the Americas was tobacco.

Cocoa plant A watercolour from a French album, dated 1686, depicts plants of the West Indies.

FACT The accurate calculation of longitude became possible only in the 1760s. Before this, navigation had been uncertain for any ship out of sight of land.

JAPAN
Nagasaki
Kagoshima
CHINA
MOGHUL INDIA
Macau
Bay of Bengal
Madras
Colombo
Manila
Ladrones Islands
Pacific Ocean
Philippines
Malacca
Brunei
Spice Islands (Moluccas)
Tidore
Sumatra
Batavia
Java
New Guinea
Indian Ocean
New Holland (Australia)
Fiji Islands
Van Diemen's Land (Tasmania)
New Zealand

Vasco da Gama The Portuguese navigator, from a contemporary illustration.

Columbus 1492-3
da Gama 1497-8
Cabot 1497-8
Magellan/Elcano 1519-22
Cook 1768-71

NEW IMPERIAL POWERS

Several European states saw the potential of exploration to increase their economic and political power. The trading empires they created ultimately became the great territorial empires of the 19th century.

Portugal Under the royal patronage of Prince Henry 'the Navigator' (1394-1460), Portugal was the pioneer of European maritime exploration. Portuguese navigators opened the sea route to the riches of the Far East, setting up a chain of trading stations including Luanda, Mozambique, Goa, Malacca and Macau. Brazil was at first thought unpromising but later became Portugal's most important colonial possession.

Spain The voyages of Christopher Columbus, sponsored by Spain, failed to reach the Far East, but led to a huge Spanish Empire in the Americas. Vast quantities of silver from the Potosi mines in Peru were shipped annually to Spain, financing both Spain's political domination of Europe and a boom in Europe's trade with Asia. The Spanish Empire in the Americas and the Philippines proved more durable than Spain's own power.

Netherlands A long war against Spain (1567-1648) encouraged Dutch mariners to attack Spanish and Portuguese colonial possessions. They were outstandingly successful in South-east Asia, led by the Netherlands East India Company (founded 1602). For most of the 17th century, the Dutch ran the greatest trading empire the world had ever seen, extending from Amsterdam to Cape Town to Japan.

England English colonial expansion began with the settlement of the east coast of North America from 1607, but gathered pace only in the 18th century, after a series of wars with the Netherlands. The East India Company (1600-1873) oversaw huge territorial expansion in India, the French were driven out of North America, the Dutch from Africa, and the voyages of James Cook opened up the South Pacific. Only in North America was British expansion checked – and there by the American colonists themselves.

France After the decline of the Dutch Empire, Britain's only serious colonial rival was France. French explorers had created an empire in the interior of North America, and in the early 18th century French influence in India matched that of Britain. In the Seven Years' War (1756-63), however, Britain systematically overran the French colonial empire.

1540-3 Spanish conquistador Francisco de Orellana crosses the Andes and sails down the Amazon.

1577-80 English navigator Francis Drake makes the second circumnavigation of the globe

1608 Samuel de Champlain founds a French colony at Quebec, Canada.

1610 English navigator Henry Hudson explores Hudson Bay and the Hudson River.

1620 The Pilgrim Fathers set up a colony at New Plymouth, Massachusetts.

1679-82 Robert de la Salle claims the entire Mississippi river valley for France.

1768-79 James Cook makes three expeditions to the Pacific, claiming Australia for Britain.

1545-52 Spanish missionary Francis Xavier travels to Goa, Sri Lanka, Japan and China.

1596-7 Dutch navigator Willem Barents dies while seeking a route to Asia via the north of Russia.

The Dutch found a colony at Batavia (Jakarta), as capital of their East Indies possessions.

1642-4 Dutch navigator Abel Tasman visits Tasmania, New Zealand, New Guinea and Australia.

In the 14th century, a new mood of enquiry stirred in Italy, and spread across Europe. Inspired by the rediscovery of classical learning, scholars and artists began to reappraise the world. This led to a new confidence in human capabilities, and a flowering of the arts. This change was known as the Renaissance, or 'Rebirth'. It took about 200 years, and represents the transition from the medieval world to a modern one.

NORTHERN RENAISSANCE

From about the 14th century a new outlook, known as **humanism**, emerged in northern Europe, inspired by classical authors and developed by scholars such as Erasmus and Thomas More. Humanism was a secular philosophy, not incompatible with Christianity but rejecting dogma and unquestioning obedience to authority. Its spirit of enquiry turned Europe into the crucible of modern **science** by the 17th century. Technology flowered too. In the mid 15th century Johann Gutenberg invented movable type, revolutionising **printing** and the dissemination of knowledge. Jan van Eyck (1390-1441) developed **oil paints**, increasing the detail, light effects and colours available to artists. Paintings became a commodity, sought after by a new class of wealthy private patron. Classical themes became increasingly prominent in **architecture**. Sceptical questioning also gave rise to criticism of the Church – but most Renaissance thinkers wanted reform, not the turmoil of the Reformation that followed.

Family snapshot The human scale and jewel-bright colours mark out van Eyck's *Arnolfini Portrait* (1434) as a Renaissance work.

SOUTHERN RENAISSANCE

Architects such as Filippo Brunelleschi began studying Roman ruins in the early 15th century, using them as the basis for a **new architecture** which was also championed by artists (classical architecture began to feature in paintings). The architect Andrea **Palladio** (1508-80) created temple-like palaces and villas characterised by classical symmetry. From Giotto (c.1267-1337) onwards, **painting** was increasingly **naturalistic**, concerned with accurate portrayal of reality rather than with symbolic meaning. Subject matter became more secular in the 15th century, reflecting a new attitude towards the place of mankind in the cosmos. **Sculpture** was strongly influenced by surviving Roman works, and sculptors such as **Donatello** and **Michelangelo** aspired to match classical creativity. Discoveries of key Roman pieces, such as Laocoon in 1506, provided renewed inspiration.

Prosperous and competitive **city-states** (including Florence, Milan and Venice), ruled by a sophisticated nobility, cultivated scholars, musicians, painters and architects. Artists were no longer considered simply as craftsmen: the anonymity of medieval guilds was slowly replaced by a new **individualism**. In addition, patrons permitted artists (notably Leonardo da Vinci) to indulge in other interests, such as science, engineering, poetry and music. Major advances in **medicine** were permitted by the progressive attitudes of Italian universities, especially regarding human dissection. The Flemish physician Andreas **Versalius** (1514-64) published his ground-breaking *On the Structure of the Human Body* (1543) in Italy; it was the first major advance in medical knowledge since Roman times.

Engineering feat The dome of Florence cathedral – largest in the world – was the first ever built without a wooden supporting frame.

*c.*1305-6 Giotto paints the Arena Chapel frescoes.

*c.*1345-1438 The Doges' Palace is built in Venice.

*c.*1415 Jan van Eyck masters the use of oil paints.

1430-2 Brunelleschi and Donatello study the ruins of ancient Rome.

1450 Gutenberg revolutionises printing by using movable type

1479 The Spanish Inquisition is created.

1495-7 Leonardo da Vinci paints *The Last Supper*.

1504 Michelangelo completes his sculpture *David*.

*c.*1340 Petrarch writes his epic poem *Africa* in the style of the Roman poet Virgil.

1420-36 Florence cathedral's dome is built, to a design by Brunelleschi.

Medici rule begins in Florence.

1472 Sheet music is first printed in Bologna, Italy.

1480 Botticelli paints *The Birth of Venus*.

1503 Leonardo da Vinci paints the *Mona Lisa*.

AD 1300 · AD 1400 · AD 1450 · AD 1500

A new style of painting Ideas about art were transformed in the Renaissance. New methods were developed, new subjects explored and the laws of perspective discovered. Technical mastery attained undreamed-of heights. Religious painting began to measure itself by the standards of flesh and blood existence.

The Flagellation Painted in about 1458 for the sacristy of the cathedral of Urbino, Italy, *The Flagellation* by Piero della Francesca (*c*.1420-92) is one of the most mysterious of his paintings. The indifference of the three contemporary figures to the scourging of Christ behind them is a striking departure from convention.

The static attitudes of the figures, their careful poses and the space that separates them are all devices used by the artist to create an effect of calm and grandeur, deliberately recalling the sculpture of the classical past.

Christ is placed in a realistic, believable world, with ordinary human beings around him. This reflects the Renaissance reassessment of the Christian story, and was a way of making the Christian message more immediate to viewers.

The composition is complex, with two centres of focus that appear almost unrelated – but the viewer's eye is led by the architectural setting from one to the other. Painting in the Middle Ages tended to have far simpler, centralised compositions.

The depiction of Classical architecture (columns and capitals) reflects Renaissance interest in the Greek and Roman past. The Classical setting also expresses the historical nature of the scene.

The use of perspective and foreshortening creates the illusion of depth. This effect distinguishes paintings of the Renaissance from medieval work, but in this painting it is undermined by the exaggerated and overprecise architecture.

The artist's observation of detail is very thorough, as seen here in the fall of cloth, rendered by careful shading. The use of light and shade makes an important contribution to the illusion of depth.

The figures reflect the artist's close observation of anatomy. Painters and sculptors wanted to depict the world naturalistically. With later developments in painting, figures would gradually become more emotional and expressive.

1505 Erasmus publishes *In Praise of Folly*.

1510-12 Raphael paints *The School of Athens*.

1517 Luther initiates the Reformation, at Wittenberg, Germany.

AD 1550

1551 Palladio designs the Villa Rotunda.

1562 The Wars of Religion break out in France (to 1598).

*c.***1590** The first microscope is made, by Hans and Zacharias Jansen.

1633 The Inquisition condemns Galileo's belief that the Earth orbits the Sun.

Michelangelo paints the Sistine Chapel

1513 Machiavelli completes *The Prince*.

1543 Copernicus argues that the Sun is the centre of the planetary system.

Elizabeth I accedes to the throne of England.

1582 The Gregorian calendar is introduced in Catholic countries.

AD 1600

1600-8 The Flemish painter Rubens works in Italy.

Until about 1500 all Christians in Europe belonged to the Roman Catholic Church. But within 50 years, the continent was divided between Catholics and Protestants (who rejected the religious authority of Rome). Hundreds of thousands of people were caught up in the struggle between the two faiths.

Key reformers Pressure for religious change was articulated by a wide range of religious thinkers after Martin Luther. Some, like Luther himself or Henry VIII, sought specific reforms. Others, like Zwingli or Calvin, advocated a radically new spirituality that meant a complete break with the Roman Catholic Church.

⚫ **Ulrich Zwingli (1484-1531)** Zwingli was a Swiss reformer and priest. From about 1517, he started to argue that scripture was the only religious authority. He converted the people of Zürich to Protestantism, and his 67 theses on reformation were adopted by Zürich's canton government. He died in battle against the Catholic cantons.

⚫ **Henry VIII (1491-1547)** Henry was king of England from 1509 to 1547. When the pope refused his request for a divorce from Catherine of Aragon, Henry split with Rome and created the (Protestant) Church of England, with himself at its head (1534). He also dissolved England's monasteries (1536-40) and appropriated their property. The resulting religious conflict lasted over 100 years.

⚫ **John Calvin (1509-64)** A French lawyer and theologian, Calvin advocated a strict form of Protestantism, based on the idea that every event is planned by God (predestination). He led the city of Geneva from 1536, making it a haven for Europe's Protestants.

⚫ **John Knox (c.1513-72)** Knox was a founder of the (Protestant) Church of Scotland (1560). He converted to Protestantism in the 1540s and, after being imprisoned by the French for an anti-Catholic conspiracy, became chaplain to

Zwingli Ulrich Zwingli made the Swiss canton of Zürich a Protestant centre.

Edward VI of England. At the accession of the Catholic Mary I, he fled to Frankfurt, then Geneva, where he met Calvin. In 1559 he returned to Scotland to lead the reform movement.

⚫ **Henry IV (1553-1610)** Henry was the Huguenot leader and king of France from 1589 to 1610. To protect himself he twice professed Catholicism, but promulgated the Edict of Nantes (1598), granting religious freedoms and bringing peace after the Wars of Religion.

1415 The Bohemian John Hus is burnt for heresy, triggering the Hussite Wars (1419-34).

1517 Martin Luther pins his 95 theses to the door of the castle church at Wittenberg.

1528 Henry VIII dismisses Cardinal Wolsey for failing to secure the pope's permission for his divorce.

1534 The Society of Jesus (Jesuits) is founded by Ignatius Loyola. Henry VIII becomes head of the English Church.

1525

1500

1514 The Fuggers, a German banking family, are licensed by Pope Leo X to sell indulgences.

1521 Luther excommunicated after writing tracts attacking the papacy and Catholic dogma.

1523 Two Protestants are burnt as heretics in the Spanish Netherlands – the start of 30 years of persecution.

1535 Thomas More is executed for refusing to accept Henry VIII as head of the Church of England.

1536-40 Henry VIII closes 800 Catholic monasteries in England.

1541 John Calvin founds a Reformed Church at Geneva.

Martin Luther

Martin Luther (1483-1546) was an Augustinian friar of humble origins. From 1512, he was professor of theology at the University of Wittenberg in Germany. Infuriated by the sale of indulgences (the remission of punishment for a sin), he challenged the Roman Catholic Church to respond to his 95 theses (propositions about the state of the Church) by pinning them to the door of a church in the town in 1517. He sought to restore purity of faith to the Church, based on the Gospels, and called upon Germany's ruling princes to take up this Protestant cause. However, he was alarmed by democratic interpretations of his doctrine of the 'priesthood of all believers', and therefore emphasised order and obedience within the Church.

Excommunicated in 1521, Luther was summoned to the Diet (parliament) of Worms by Emperor Charles V, but refused to retract his beliefs. He married an ex-nun in 1525, and spent the remainder of his life pursuing his cause and creating a translation of the Bible that helped both to spread his ideas and to unify the German language.

St Bartholomew's Day Massacre French Huguenots (Protestants) are slaughtered in 1572 by Catholic troops after rumours of a Protestant plot.

Reformation criticism of the Church

As the Reformation proceeded, political issues became as important as religious arguments in determining Europe's alliances. Nonetheless, Protestantism was rooted in a series of profound criticisms of the Church.

Church corruption Many Christians felt that the opulence of the Renaissance Church was counter to the teaching of the Gospels.

Lack of Biblical authority Renaissance Humanism fostered a questioning attitude and drew attention to the gap between practices such as selling indulges and the teachings of Jesus.

Low calibre of the priesthood Many Christians began to question the calibre and training of priests, the value of their rule of enforced celibacy, and ultimately the claim of the pope to be 'Christ's Vicar on Earth'.

Reliance on unbiblical doctrines Protestants rejected the Church's insistence on the high status and intercessionary powers of Mary, mother of Jesus, and the saints; they also questioned the value of pilgrimages and relics.

Church control of access to the Bible Protestants demanded that the Bible and church services should be made available in languages people spoke. The use of Latin, combined with the Roman Catholic Church's hold on education, gave the Church a monopoly on Biblical interpretation and prevented people hearing the Christian message except through the filter of the Church itself.

The responses of the Counter Reformation

The Papacy's response to Protestant criticisms was a combination of reform and vigorous defence, spearheaded by the Council of Trent. This 'Counter Reformation' prevented the disintegration of the Church, and led to a stricter, reformed Catholicism.

Baroque style An even grander artistic style developed in the late 16th century, expressing the Church's renewed confidence.

New institutions The Society of Jesus (Jesuits), founded in 1534, incorporated Humanist views into Catholic teaching, making it more appealing to influential lay Christians.

New religious orders The Council of Trent established a new, dynamic preaching order, the Capuchins, to meet the laity's demands for religious instruction. It also set up a programme of improved education for priests.

A precise exposition of Catholic doctrine The Council of Trent's greatest achievement was the clearest definition to date of the beliefs required of all Catholics, including an insistence on all the established sacraments.

Increased Church control The reactivation of the Inquisition and the creation of the first 'Index of Prohibited Books' tightened the Church's control over the education of its members. A Catholic wishing to read the works of any of the reformers (or of certain lay authors like Machiavelli) was required to obtain specific permission from the Church before doing so.

1545-63 The Council of Trent initiates the Counter Reformation.

1550

1555 The Peace of Augsburg: Emperor Charles V permits the German princes to choose the religion of their subjects.

1563 French Protestants (Huguenots) are granted limited toleration.

1572 Some 30 000 Huguenots are massacred, on St Bartholomew's Day.

1593 Henry IV of France converts back to Catholicism.

1600

1618 The Thirty Years' War begins, pitting Protestants against the Catholic Habsburgs (to 1648).

1542 The Inquisition is re-established by Pope Paul III to check the growth of Protestantism.

1558 The Protestant Elizabeth I accedes to the throne of England.

1562 The Wars of Religion break out in France (to 1598).

1575

1566 The Low Countries revolt against their Spanish rulers (to 1609).

1598 The Edict of Nantes grants freedom of worship to French Protestants.

1642-6 Civil wars break out in Britain, partly over religious disputes.

Wars of Religion

The religious turmoil of the Reformation boiled over into outright war on numerous occasions in the 16th and early 17th centuries. Among the major conflicts were:

French Wars of Religion Religious differences gave rise to a series of wars in 1562-98 between the French houses of Bourbon and Guise. The Catholic Guise faction repeatedly attempted to destroy the Protestant Huguenots, many of whom fled to England, the Netherlands and Switzerland to escape.

The Dutch Revolt The Protestant Dutch waged a long war against Spanish rule of the Low Countries (1566-1609).

Spanish Armada Philip II of Spain attempted in 1588 to conquer and reconvert Protestant England. His large fleet (Armada) was driven into the North Sea and destroyed by storms off Scotland and Ireland.

Thirty Years' War A series of religious wars devastated Germany from 1618 to 1648. The Catholic side was led by the Habsburg emperors and their Spanish supporters; the Protestants were sustained by interventions from Christian IV of Denmark, Gustavus II Adolphus of Sweden and the Catholic Cardinal Richelieu of France, who feared the power of the Habsburgs and the Holy Roman Empire.

see also
194-5 **The Renaissance**
340-1 **Religions**
412-3 **Printing**

Louis XIV's declaration 'L'état, c'est moi' *(I am the State)* expressed all the arrogance of an absolute king. But such power also gave some monarchs the confidence to grant certain liberties, and to allow a new intellectual movement – the Enlightenment – to blossom. They prided themselves on their tolerant patronage of intellectual and cultural developments, yet were ruthless when free thinking began to look like revolutionary discontent.

Sun King Louis XIV's nickname reflected his absolute power, his sumptuous court (at Versailles from 1682), and his era of dazzling cultural achievements.

Anglo-Dutch Wars

Three wars were fought between Britain and the United Provinces of the Netherlands. The first hostilities were in 1652-4, when Britain closed its possessions to Dutch ships. The Dutch took control of the English Channel, but the English blockaded the Dutch coast and enforced a peace treaty. Continuing trade rivalry and the British seizure of New York provoked a second conflict in 1665-7. The Plague and Fire in London weakened British efforts, and the Dutch won trade concessions. War again broke out in 1672-4, after Charles II assisted Louis XIV against the Dutch, before being repulsed at Texel (1673).

War of the Spanish Succession

Charles II of Spain died in 1700 with no heir; Philip of Anjou (Louis XIV's grandson) succeeded him. England, Austria, and others feared French ambitions and made an alliance. Philip gave the Spanish Netherlands to Louis, but in 1704-9 the Allies defeated France at **Blenheim** and in other battles. Then Charles of Austria (Philip's rival for the Spanish throne) became Holy Roman Emperor, giving him a claim to both Austria and Spain. The compromise **Treaty of Utrecht** (1713) confirmed Philip as king of Spain in return for renouncing claims to France; the Spanish Netherlands became Austrian. Charles refused at first but signed in 1714, establishing a balance of power in Europe.

1643 Louis XIV accedes to the throne of France, aged 5.

1648 The Thirty Years' War ends; the Dutch win complete independence from Spain.

1652 The first Anglo-Dutch War breaks out.

1666 Much of London is destroyed in the Great Fire.

1685 Huguenots (French Protestants) are persecuted by Catholics and flee from France.

1697 Eugène of Savoy ends Austria's war with the Turks by a victory at Zenta: the Habsburgs recover Hungary.

1701 The War of the Spanish Succession begins (to 1714).

1704 Allied victory at Blenheim curbs French expansion in Europe.

1649 Charles I of England is beheaded, and the Commonwealth (republic) is established (to 1653).

1660 The monarchy is restored in England, with the accession of Charles II.

1684 Isaac Newton proposes his theory of gravitation.

1688-9 William III (of Orange) and Mary II (daughter of James II) accede to the throne of England in the 'Glorious Revolution'.

1700 Start of the Great Northern War between Sweden and Russia (to 1721).

1703 Peter the Great founds St Petersburg; it becomes the Russian capital in 1712.

NEW IDEAS BLOSSOM

The Enlightenment was an intellectual movement driven by scientific discovery and sceptical inquiry. It freed thinking from Renaissance loyalty to classical wisdom, and deeply questioned religion, society and politics. Enlightenment thinkers believed that a scientific approach could reveal a universal order, upon which to base government, morality and religion. This 'Age of Reason' held out new prospects of equality and human progress. Key figures included:

● **Francis Bacon (1561-1626)** Bacon was an English lawyer, politician and thinker. He was an early advocate of the scientific approach to inquiry, and a precursor of the Enlightenment.

● **Thomas Hobbes (1588-1679)** Hobbes was an English mathematician and philosopher, who maintained that natural life is 'nasty, brutish and short'.

● **René Descartes (1596-1650)** A French philosopher and mathematician, Descartes founded Rationalism – the idea that all knowledge is derived from pure reason.

● **Benedict de Spinoza (1632-77)** The Dutch philosopher Spinoza identified God with nature, and believed that humans were subject to natural law. Overcoming personal desire was the basis of a good society.

● **John Locke (1632-1704)** A champion of freedom, the English philosopher Locke argued that governments exist only by consent of the governed.

● **Baron de Montesquieu (1689-1755)** The French philosopher Montesquieu proposed the separation of government powers (legislative, executive and judicial) to ensure freedom of the individual.

● **David Hume (1711-76)** The Scottish anti-Rationalist philosopher Hume held that knowledge comes from a kind of instinct, based on perception, not from pure reason.

● **Jean-Jacques Rousseau (1712-78)** Rousseau's book *The Social Contract* argues that government exists to uphold justice, equality and freedom.

● **Denis Diderot (1713-84)** The French philosopher and writer Diderot edited (with Jean d'Alembert) the 35-volume *Encyclopédie ou Dictionnaire Raisonné* (1751-80), the first general encyclopedia.

● **Adam Smith (1723-90)** The Scottish philosopher Smith invented 'laissez-faire' economics, arguing that free markets promoted prosperity throughout society.

● **Immanuel Kant (1724-1804)** The German philosopher Kant argued that universal moral laws could be founded on reason rather than dogma and faith.

Outspoken radical In works such as *Candide* (1759), Voltaire (1694-1778) openly ridiculed the pretensions of philosophers, clergy, monarchy and nobility. He championed justice, tolerance and liberty, providing an intellectual foundation for the French Revolution.

Europe's empires, 1715

Austrian Habsburgs

Spanish Habsburgs

France

Great Britain

Russia

Ottoman Empire

Non-aligned states

Papal States

Poland

Sweden

Dutch Republic

Prussia

Louis XIV (1638-1715) Louis acceded to the throne at the age of five, and was king of France from 1643 to 1715. He took full control of the state on the death of Cardinal Mazarin in 1661, and ruled with a firm belief in his own absolute power and the divine right of kings. He built up France's army, and waged expansionist campaigns until checked by the War of the Grand Alliance (1688-97) and the War of the Spanish Succession (1701-14).

Charles XII (1682-1718) King of Sweden from 1697 to 1718, Charles early in the Great Northern War (1700-21) defended Sweden from attack by Russia, Poland, Denmark and Saxony. He crushed the Russians at Narva (1700) and invaded Russia in 1709, but was defeated at Poltava. He resumed the war five years later, but was killed invading Norway. The war cost Sweden its position as a leading power.

★ **Battles**

Stockholm

London · Texel

Narva ★ · St Petersburg

Paris · Amsterdam · Berlin · Riga

Lisbon

Dettingen ★ · Prague

Moscow

Madrid · Milan **Blenheim** · Warsaw

Vienna · Buda · Kiev

Venice

Rome

Naples · Belgrade

Poltava ★

Istanbul

Maria Theresa (1717-80) Daughter of Charles VI, Maria became the Habsburg ruler when just 23 (see *War of the Austrian Succession*). She ruled as an 'enlightened despot', supporting the arts, introducing some reforms and reorganising institutions such as the military. Her reign was fundamentally conservative, and more radical change was accomplished only under her son Joseph II.

Frederick II 'the Great' (1712-86) King of Prussia 1740-86, Frederick made his country a major power, winning Silesia from the Habsburgs in the War of the Austrian Succession. He made an alliance with Russia to partition Poland (1772), and acquired Brandenburg and Pomerania. A brilliant soldier, he was a reformer and the patron of Voltaire, but an absolute ruler.

Peter I 'the Great' (1672-1725) Peter ruled Russia from 1682 to 1725. He fought for Russian access to the Black Sea (Russo-Turkish Wars) and Baltic (Great Northern War), building up Russian military and naval strength beyond anything seen before. He founded St Petersburg in 1703 and made it his capital. A tour of Europe in 1697-8 led to the modernisation of Russian industry, society and bureaucracy. As emperor, his methods were often brutal, but he laid the foundations of modern Russia, making it a major power.

1707 The Act of Union unites England and Scotland.

1720 J.S. Bach writes the Brandenburg Concertos.

1740 Frederick II ('the Great') accedes to the throne of Prussia.

1745 A second Jacobite rebellion, ended at Culloden (1746), fails to restore the Stuarts to the English throne.

1757 Robert Clive captures Calcutta to establish British dominance of India.

1761 The Peace of Paris: Britain's supremacy in India and North America is recognised.

1772 Poland is partitioned by Prussia, Russia and Austria.

1709 The Swedes are routed by the Russians at Poltava.

1739 War between England and Spain over South American trade ('The War of Jenkins' Ear') begins (to 1748).

1740

1750

1756

1740 The War of the Austrian Succession begins (to 1748).

1755 An earthquake in Lisbon kills 60 000 people.

1756 The Seven Years' War begins (to 1763). Birth of Wolfgang Amadeus Mozart.

1759 British forces under James Wolfe capture Quebec from the French.

1762 Catherine II 'the Great' becomes sole ruler of Russia after the murder of her husband Peter III.

War of the Austrian Succession

A dispute over Austrian succession led to a war on three continents, involving six major powers and precipitating long-term shifts in European relations. Charles VI of Austria died in 1740 without an heir. He wanted the succession to pass via his daughter Maria Theresa, whose husband Francis would become Holy Roman Emperor. But Francis was opposed by Bavaria, Prussia and France. Spain contested Maria Theresa's claim to Italian land, and Britain challenged France over Indian and American territory. Austria lost Silesia to Prussia, and Spain was given three duchies in northern Italy.

Charles Albert of Bavaria became Holy Roman Emperor in 1743. Britain and Austria defeated France at Dettingen (1743) but France took British Madras (1746). Charles Albert died in 1745 and Francis became Holy Roman Emperor, as originally planned. The war ended with the signing of peace at Aix la Chapelle (1748). Prussia was now a great power and the Anglo-French struggle over colonies had begun.

Seven Years' War

The Seven Years' War followed the War of the Austrian Succession. Austria, France, Russia, Saxony, Sweden and Spain fought against Prussia, Britain and Hanover; France and Britain also fought in North America and India. The war began when Prussia invaded Saxony (1756); Prussia faced defeat until Russia withdrew. Britain defeated France in 1759 at home and overseas. The war ended with Prussian possession of Silesia, and Britain gaining most French territory in eastern North America, control of India, and several Caribbean islands.

see also

344-5 **Western thought**

598-601 **European leaders**

The violent contrast between gross social injustice and Enlightenment ideals of freedom and equality precipitated increasing instability in 18th-century France. As belief in the old order and absolute monarchy crumbled, calls for reform turned to riots, then rebellion, then a revolution. Out of the chaos emerged one of modern history's most controversial giants, Napoleon Bonaparte.

CAUSES OF THE FRENCH REVOLUTION

1. **Government bankruptcy** The cost of wars meant Louis XVI had to summon the States-General (parliament) for the first time since 1614 to request funds. It demanded reforms in return.
2. **The Enlightenment** French intellectuals proposed new, egalitarian forms of government, leading to widespread discontent with existing social and political structures.
3. **Social inequality** The peasantry and urban poor had to pay the bulk of taxation, while the aristocracy were largely exempt.
4. **Revolution in America** French participants in the American Revolution (1775-83) saw liberty and a democracy triumph. They returned with a passion for reform and change at home.
5. **Harvest failure** Failure of the 1788 harvest caused price rises, of bread especially. These added to the hardships of the poor, who still paid feudal dues and taxes to the state.
6. **Louis XVI's weakness** Louis was popular but indecisive and made repeated concessions that undermined royal prestige. His frivolous wife Marie-Antoinette was detested.

1775-83 The American Revolution brings independence to the USA, largely on Enlightenment principles.

1789 Widespread riots in Paris lead to the storming of the Bastille prison on July 14 – the start of the Revolution.

1791 Louis XVI tries to flee Paris. He is forced to approve a new constitution ending the absolute monarchy in France.

1793 French forces occupy the Austrian Netherlands (Belgium). Louis XVI is guillotined.

1793-6 A counter-revolution in the Vendée region of western France is suppressed.

1799 A coup makes Napoleon First Consul, ending the Revolution.

1796-7 French forces (led by Napoleon) defeat the Austrians in Italy.

1787 Attempts to reform the French finances and tax system fail.

1790

1790 A new National Assembly abolishes the nobility in France.

1792 The French Republic is declared. The Revolutionary Wars begin as foreign powers intervene (to 1802).

1793-4 Moderate deputies are expelled from the Convention, and the Reign of Terror begins, led by Robespierre.

1795-9 Revolutionary rule in France is formalised under the 'Directory'.

1798 Napoleon attempts to conquer Egypt, but is defeated by Nelson at the Battle of the Nile.

Great leveller The guillotine was introduced in 1792 as a quick, merciful and 'democratic' instrument of execution.

Key figures of the Revolution

Georges Danton (1759-94) A lawyer and militant anti-Royalist, Danton was a member of the radical Jacobin group. He demanded the trial of Louis XVI and the creation of a republic. He was exiled in 1791-2 but returned as minister of justice, only to resign over the revolutionary council's harsh judgments. Danton led the government from April 1793, but opposed the Terror. Conflict with Robespierre led to his execution a year later.

Jean-Paul Marat (1743-93) A doctor and journalist, Marat joined the National Assembly in 1792. His popularity with the *sans-culottes* (the poor) alarmed the Girondins who saw him as a dangerous

Bold leader Danton called for 'boldness, ever more boldness', and did more than any other to create the Republic.

demagogue. He was murdered in the bath by Charlotte Corday, a Girondin supporter.

Comte de Mirabeau (1749-91) Mirabeau took part as a commoner (member of the 'Third Estate') in the 1789 States-General. After Third Estate delegates defiantly renamed it the National Assembly, Mirabeau helped to force Louis to accept it as the legitimate voice of government. But he failed to persuade Louis to form a constitutional monarchy.

Maximilien de Robespierre (1758-94) Robespierre led the revolutionary Jacobins and engineered the overthrow of the Girondins, who drew support from the provinces and tried to curb the powers of the Paris Assembly. He was elected to the Committee of Public Safety and led it after Danton. He was famed for incorruptibility, and helped to orchestrate the Terror. Robespierre was arrested and executed after a coup in 1794.

Louis de Saint-Just (1767-94) An administrator early in the Revolution, Saint-Just supported Robespierre. He was instrumental in the downfall of Danton and advocated the Terror. He was arrested and guillotined in the same coup as Robespierre.

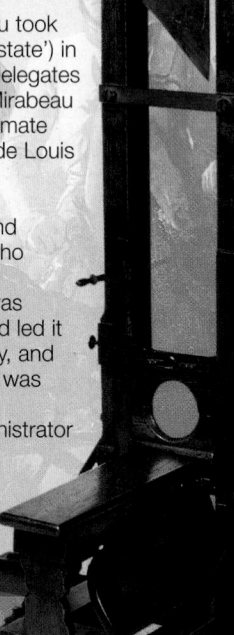

Napoleon's Europe
At the height of his power, Napoleon directly or indirectly controlled half of Europe. He waged war from Spain to the outskirts of Moscow.

French empire, 1812

States dependent on France, 1812

★ French victories

★ French defeats

Atlantic Ocean

North Sea

GREAT BRITAIN
London

SWEDEN

NETHERLANDS

Coruña 1809

Waterloo 1815

CONFEDERATION OF THE RHINE

PRUSSIA
Berlin

Friedland 1807

RUSSIAN EMPIRE

FRANCE
Paris

Leipzig 1813

Eylau 1807

PORTUGAL

Vitoria 1813

Jena 1805

GRAND DUCHY OF WARSAW

Moscow

Toulouse 1814

HELVETIA

Ulm 1805

Austerlitz 1805

Borodino 1812

Albuera 1811   Madrid

Marengo 1800

Wagram 1809

Trafalgar 1805

SPAIN

ITALY

AUSTRIAN EMPIRE   Vienna

CORSICA

PAPAL STATES

ILLYRIAN PROVINCES

Mediterranean Sea

Rome

NAPLES

OTTOMAN EMPIRE

Black Sea

Constantinople

1800 Napoleon leads French forces to complete victory in Italy.

1804 Napoleon becomes Emperor of France.

1805 Britain defeats the French and Spanish fleet at Trafalgar, while Napoleon defeats Austria and Russia at Ulm and Austerlitz.

1807 Napoleon tries to blockade British trade, and invades Portugal through Spain.

1812 Napoleon invades Russia, but is finally forced to retreat in winter with huge losses.

1810

1815 'The Hundred Days': Napoleon seizes power again in France, but is defeated at Waterloo (Belgium). The Congress of Vienna restores the European monarchies.

1802 Peace is agreed between France and Britain in the Treaty of Amiens, but Britain resumes war in 1803.

1805 Britain organises a new coalition against France (with Austria, Sweden, Russia, Naples).

1806 Prussia joins war against France, but is defeated at Jena.

1808-14 The Peninsular War: Britain fights France in Spain and Portugal.

1813 French armies are defeated at Vitoria in Spain (June) and at Leipzig in Germany (October).

1814 Allied troops invade France; Napoleon is exiled.

CONSEQUENCES OF THE FRENCH REVOLUTION

1 **Abolition of feudalism** The abolition of the last of the 'feudal' ties binding peasants to their landlords brought France into line with Europe's most progresive states.

2 **Recognition of the Rights of Man** The Revolutionary concept of essential rights guaranteeing individual liberty is the foundation of modern human rights legislation.

3 **Destruction of the Church's power** The ending of the political power of the Church in France paved the way to a more secular society and liberated education.

4 **Two decades of war** The Revolution brought economic and political turmoil to Europe. French Revolutionary armies were often greeted as liberators, but disillusion generally followed.

5 **A symbolic message** The Revolution sent shock waves through Europe's ruling classes. After the fall of Napoleon, many governments introduced repressive measures to quash liberalism and reform.

6 **Inspiration** As the first modern revolution, attempting to transform the entire social and political fabric of a nation, the Revolution served as a model for liberation struggles in South America and Europe in the 19th and 20th centuries.

The 'Little Corporal'

Napoleon Bonaparte (1769-1821), born in Corsica, rose rapidly to the rank of general in the Revolutionary Army. He was a leader of the 1799 coup and became First Consul. He crowned himself Emperor in 1804, and introduced popular reforms in government, the law and education. His wars were highly successful at first, and by 1812 he had created the largest European empire since Roman times. But the Peninsular War (1807-13) ended in defeat and in 1812 he decided to invade Russia. After defeat at Leipzig (1813), he was deposed. He lost at Waterloo (1815).

see also
198-9 **Age of kings**
202-3 **Creation of the US**
344-5 **Western thought**
600-1 **European leaders**

Britain's prosperous North American colonies found their wealth attracting ever more taxation and control. Resentment against the distant ruler grew, finally spilling over into rebellion. The American Revolution brought freedom and an enlightened and democratic constitution. Over the following decades the United States expanded across the entire continent, sparking the Indian Wars. But North and South were deeply divided, and the price of eventual unity was the bitter and costly Civil War.

Boston Tea Party Citizens dressed as Mohawks board British ships and throw hated taxed tea into the Charles River.

Causes of the American Revolution

1 **Taxation** Britain tried to recoup the cost of the Seven Years' War from the colonies but denied them a place in parliament. This 'taxation without representation' was deeply resented.

2 **Colonial trade** Britain tried to restrict commerce between the North American states and other trading partners.

3 **A ban on expansion** The colonists resented a British prohibition on expanding into the West.

4 **Religious differences** Many colonists were dissenters who came to America to find religious freedom. The established position of the Anglican Church was seen as a threat.

5 **Propaganda** Patriot (pro-independence) propagandists deliberately inflamed public opinion against British rule.

1607 The first permanent English settlement is established at Jamestown, Virginia.

1664 England seizes New Amsterdam from the Dutch, and renames it New York.

1764-5 The Sugar and Stamp Acts impose new taxes on the colonies, dividing the colonists into Loyalists and separatist 'Patriots'.

1620 The Pilgrim Fathers found the Plymouth settlement in Massachusetts.

1700

1763 France cedes North American territories to Britain after the Seven Years' War.

1770 The 'Boston Massacre': a mob provokes British soldiers, and five colonists are killed.

1775 British forces skirmish with colonial militias at Lexington and Concord.

1777 British forces under Burgoyne surrender at Saratoga. France offers military help to the colonists.

Call to arms A statue to the 'Minutemen' who fired on the British at Concord.

1773 The 'Boston Tea Party' – protest at import taxes. The colonies agree a provisional government at the First Continental Congress.

1776 A Declaration of Independence is approved by the Second Continental Congress (July 4).

1781 British forces under Cornwallis surrender at Yorktown, ending the war.

1783 Britain recognises American independence by the Treaty of Paris.

Key figures of the American Revolution

● **John Adams (1735-1826)** Adams was influential in drafting the Declaration of Independence and the Constitution. He later helped to negotiate the Treaty of Paris, and served as the second US president (1797-1801).

● **Marquis of Cornwallis (1738-1805)** Cornwallis was the British commander in South Carolina. After initial successes, he moved north and was isolated and defeated at Yorktown in 1781.

● **Benjamin Franklin (1706-90)** A printer, publisher, scientist and statesman, Franklin helped to draft the Declaration of Independence. He enlisted French help for the colonists and negotiated the Treaty of Paris.

● **Thomas Jefferson (1743-1826)** A wealthy Virginia planter and statesman, Jefferson was the main author of the Declaration of Independence. He was third president of the USA (1801-9).

● **Lord North (1732-92)** North was British prime minister 1770-82. He tried to appease the colonists, but George III prevented him from compromising during the war.

● **Thomas Paine (1737-1809)** Paine's pamphlet *Common Sense* (1776) turned American opinion towards independence. His *The Rights of Man* (1791) was a seminal text for revolutionaries.

● **Paul Revere (1735-1818)** A Boston silversmith and printer, Revere warned of the British approach to Lexington and Concord in April 1775.

● **George Washington (1732-99)** Washington commanded the Continental Armies, driving the British from Boston in 1776 and forcing their final surrender at Yorktown. He was elected first US president in 1789.

Consequences of the American Revolution

1 **A new Constitution** The colonists drafted a Constitution based on Enlightenment principles. By 1790, the United States was the most democratic nation in the world.

2 **Liberalisation** The Anglican Church in America was separated from the state, and freedom of worship was guaranteed. Slavery was gradually abolished in the Northern states. Hereditary titles were forbidden.

3 **Expansion of the USA** US settlements gradually pushed west into Indian territory.

4 **Revolutionary ideas** The American experience showed for the first time in modern history that revolt against the old order could be successful – ideas that inspired revolutions in France (1789) and later in South America.

Growth of the USA

The modern USA grew out of 13 British colonies on the east coast that declared independence in 1776. Over the following 100 years they expanded south and west by conquest, purchase and settlement. There are now 50 states, the last to join being Hawaii in 1959.

- **pre-1750** (the 13 original British colonies)
- **1790** (including territories gained by Treaty of Paris)
- **1820** (including the Louisiana Purchase)
- **1855** (including territories won from Mexico 1846-8)
- **post-1850** (including territories settled after the Indian Wars)

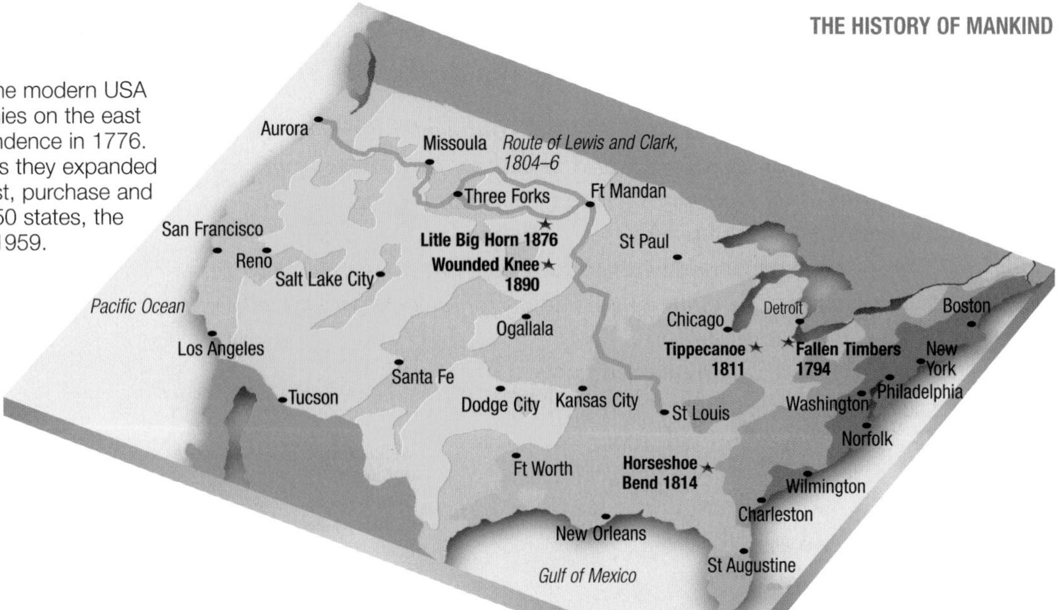

Aurora

Missoula *Route of Lewis and Clark, 1804–6*

Three Forks   Ft Mandan

San Francisco

Little Big Horn 1876 St Paul
Wounded Knee ★
1890

Reno   Salt Lake City

Pacific Ocean

Los Angeles

Ogallala   Chicago   Detroit   Boston

Tippecanoe ★   **Fallen Timbers**   New
1811   1794   York

Santa Fe   Philadelphia

Tucson   Dodge City   Kansas City   Washington

St Louis   Norfolk

Ft Worth   **Horseshoe** ★
Bend 1814   Wilmington

Charleston

New Orleans

Gulf of Mexico   St Augustine

1787 The US Constitution is ratified by the states.

1804-6 Lewis and Clark pioneer an overland route to the West Coast.

1846-8 The Mexican-American War; the USA gains Texas, New Mexico and California.

1861 Southern states secede, forming the Confederate States of America. The resulting Civil War (to 1865) begins badly for the North.

1863 The Civil War turns against the South with Northern victories at Gettysburg and Vicksburg.

1867 The USA buys Alaska from Russia for $7.2 million.

1869 The Union Pacific Railroad links the US Atlantic and Pacific coasts.

1890 A massacre of the Sioux peoples at Wounded Knee ends the Indian Wars.

1800

1850

1789 George Washington becomes the first president (to 1797).

1803 The USA buys the huge Louisiana territory from France.

1812-15 'War of 1812' with Britain ends inconclusively.

1848-9 The California gold rush encourages settlers to head West.

1863 President Lincoln declares all slaves in rebel territory to be free.

1865 The main Confederate Army surrenders at Appomatox, Virginia. Lincoln is assassinated.

1876 A US Cavalry detatchment under General Custer is wiped out by the Sioux at Little Bighorn.

A house divided: the American Civil War

As the USA expanded in the 1800s, rivalries and divisions became increasingly apparent. There were tensions between state and federal governments, and between the interests of the industrialising and more populous North and the still agricultural South.

Slavery, though widely detested in the North, was the basis of Southern landowners' prosperity. A carefully contrived balance in Congress was threatened every time a new state joined the Union, and debate raged over whether to allow slavery in new states such as Kansas.

Hostility between North and South was exacerbated by two events. In 1859, **John Brown**, a militant abolitionist, staged a violent antislavery raid and was captured and hanged in Virginia. The following year, **Abraham Lincoln** was elected president. His pro-Union and antislavery views aroused Southern fears of a loss of power to the North.

In 1861 seven Southern ('Confederate') states withdrew from the Union and war with the North soon followed.

Jefferson Davis (1808-89) Davis became president of the Confederacy (South) in 1861. He tried to continue fighting after Lee's surrender at Appomattox, but was captured and imprisoned.

Ulysses S. Grant (1822-85) In 1862 Grant became commander in chief of the Union armies; he won a series of victories, including Vicksburg (1863), and brought about Lee's surrender in 1865 after a prolonged campaign at Richmond. He was later twice elected president (1869-77).

Thomas 'Stonewall' Jackson (1824-63) One of the Confederacy's most gifted generals, Jackson won his nickname after a heroic stand at Bull Run (1861). He was accidentally killed by his own men at Chancellorsville.

Robert E. Lee (1807-70) A brilliant, popular general, Lee commanded the Confederate Army of Northern Virginia and won victories at Fredericksburg and Chancellorsville. He was defeated at Gettysburg (1863) and surrendered at Appomattox in 1865.

Abraham Lincoln (1809-65) A self-taught lawyer and a congressman, Lincoln was elected president in 1860. His opposition to slavery provoked the secession of the Confederate states. The resulting Civil War brought four years of suffering and turmoil, but saved the Union and put an end to slavery. After the war, Lincoln was assassinated by a Confederate sympathiser.

William T. Sherman (1820-91) Under Sherman's command in 1864 Union forces took Atlanta and laid waste the Georgia countryside – brutal but decisive inroads into Confederate heartlands.

Siege mortar The 13 in (32 cm) Union mortar 'Dictator', used at the siege of the Confederate city of Petersburg, Virginia.

see also
200-1 **Europe in turmoil**
288-9 **United States**
602-3 **Worldwide**

Largely spared from the wars and revolutions of continental Europe, Britain in the 18th and 19th centuries led the world in making the change from agriculture to an industrial economy. Demand for goods boomed, fuelling mechanisation and new ways of using water, coal and steam to drive production. The ripples spread outwards to Europe, North America and eventually to every part of the globe as innovation followed upon innovation.

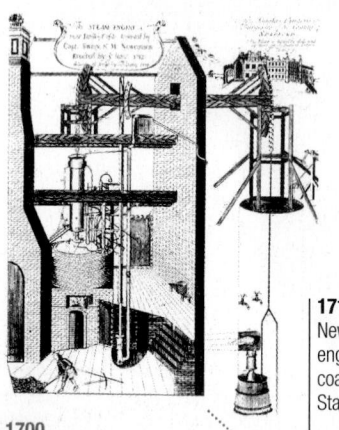

Revolutionary power
Thomas Newcomen built the world's first successful steam engine in 1712. It was used to pump water from a coal mine.

Water-driven Richard Arkwright invented his spinning machine – powered by a water wheel and named a 'water frame' – in about 1768. It made a firm yarn for woven cloth.

1712 Thomas Newcomen's steam engine is installed at a coal mine in Staffordshire.

1761 The Bridgewater Canal, Britain's first entirely artificial waterway, is completed.

1771 Richard Arkwright's textile mill at Cromford, Derbyshire, establishes the factory system.

1779 The world's first cast-iron bridge is completed by Abraham Darby at Ironbridge, Shropshire.

1793 The cotton gin is introduced in Georgia, USA, by Eli Whitney

1807 Gas street lighting is installed in Pall Mall, London.

1700

1712

1701 The first practicable mechanical seed drill is invented by Jethro Tull of Berkshire, England.

1709 Abraham Darby of Coalbrookdale, Shropshire, uses coked coal to produce cheaper iron.

1750

1733 John Kay's flying shuttle speeds the process of weaving.

1768

1765 James Watt's condenser makes steam engines much more efficient.

1767 James Hargreaves invents the spinning jenny.

1785 The first power loom is patented by Edmund Cartwright of Leicestershire.

1800

1793

1800 The first electric battery is built by Alessandro Volta in Italy.

1808 Richard Trevithick demonstrates a railway locomotive in London.

WHY THE INDUSTRIAL REVOLUTION HAPPENED

1 **Wealth and resources** In the 18th century, Britain was the wealthiest country in Europe, with the most productive agriculture. It had the economic base, capital and market demand to shift from farming to manufactured products, and had the energy resources – in coal – to achieve this.

2 **Rapid population growth** In Britain, then elsewhere, the population increased steeply in the 18th century, creating the need for more efficient farming. Agricultural mechanisation improved the speed of production, reducing labour costs and making products cheaper – and increasing demand yet further.

3 **Increased demand** The growing need for cloth in particular could not be met by traditional production, and inspired mechanical inventions such as the spinning jenny to speed the processing of imported American cotton. This set a precedent for the mechanisation of industry.

4 **New energy sources** First water wheels, then coal and steam provided power to drive machinery and replace the need for physical labour.

5 **New markets** The acquisition of foreign colonies and the growth of towns and cities at home opened up new opportunities for trade.

6 **Improved transport** New transport systems allowed the efficient movement of raw materials and distribution of manufactured goods, at first using canals (from the 1760s) and then railways (from the 1830s).

7 **Political and economic changes** Land was no longer the sole source of wealth and power. Social change meant entrepreneurs could profit from their work, and provided incentives to invest.

Mechanical separator Eli Whitney's 1793 cotton gin vastly speeded up the separation of seeds from cotton fibres, and helped to make the USA the world's leading cotton producer.

FACT The term 'industrial revolution' was coined by French observers of the revolutionary changes taking place in 18th-century Britain.

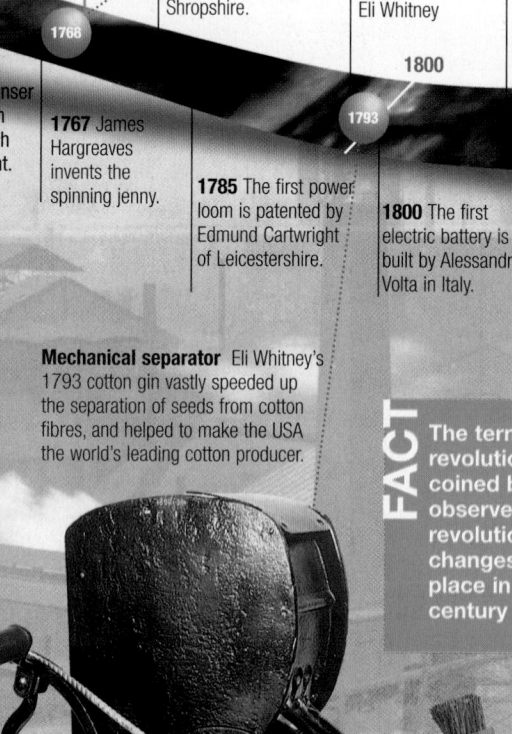

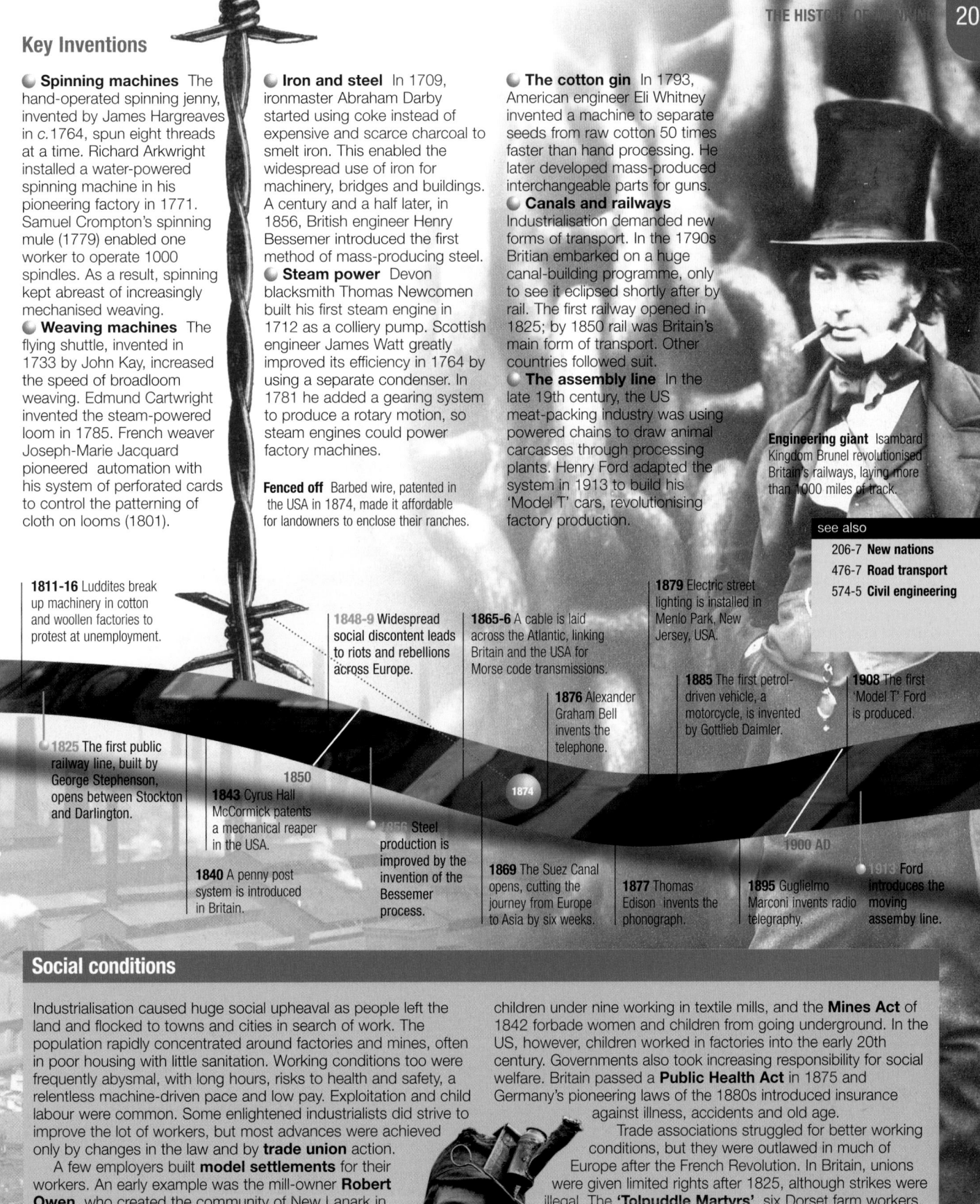

Key Inventions

● **Spinning machines** The hand-operated spinning jenny, invented by James Hargreaves in c.1764, spun eight threads at a time. Richard Arkwright installed a water-powered spinning machine in his pioneering factory in 1771. Samuel Crompton's spinning mule (1779) enabled one worker to operate 1000 spindles. As a result, spinning kept abreast of increasingly mechanised weaving.

● **Weaving machines** The flying shuttle, invented in 1733 by John Kay, increased the speed of broadloom weaving. Edmund Cartwright invented the steam-powered loom in 1785. French weaver Joseph-Marie Jacquard pioneered automation with his system of perforated cards to control the patterning of cloth on looms (1801).

● **Iron and steel** In 1709, ironmaster Abraham Darby started using coke instead of expensive and scarce charcoal to smelt iron. This enabled the widespread use of iron for machinery, bridges and buildings. A century and a half later, in 1856, British engineer Henry Bessemer introduced the first method of mass-producing steel.

● **Steam power** Devon blacksmith Thomas Newcomen built his first steam engine in 1712 as a colliery pump. Scottish engineer James Watt greatly improved its efficiency in 1764 by using a separate condenser. In 1781 he added a gearing system to produce a rotary motion, so steam engines could power factory machines.

Fenced off Barbed wire, patented in the USA in 1874, made it affordable for landowners to enclose their ranches.

● **The cotton gin** In 1793, American engineer Eli Whitney invented a machine to separate seeds from raw cotton 50 times faster than hand processing. He later developed mass-produced interchangeable parts for guns.

● **Canals and railways** Industrialisation demanded new forms of transport. In the 1790s Britain embarked on a huge canal-building programme, only to see it eclipsed shortly after by rail. The first railway opened in 1825; by 1850 rail was Britain's main form of transport. Other countries followed suit.

● **The assembly line** In the late 19th century, the US meat-packing industry was using powered chains to draw animal carcasses through processing plants. Henry Ford adapted the system in 1913 to build his 'Model T' cars, revolutionising factory production.

Engineering giant Isambard Kingdom Brunel revolutionised Britain's railways, laying more than 1000 miles of track.

see also
206-7 **New nations**
476-7 **Road transport**
574-5 **Civil engineering**

1811-16 Luddites break up machinery in cotton and woollen factories to protest at unemployment.

1848-9 Widespread social discontent leads to riots and rebellions across Europe.

1865-6 A cable is laid across the Atlantic, linking Britain and the USA for Morse code transmissions.

1879 Electric street lighting is installed in Menlo Park, New Jersey, USA.

1876 Alexander Graham Bell invents the telephone.

1885 The first petrol-driven vehicle, a motorcycle, is invented by Gottlieb Daimler.

1908 The first 'Model T' Ford is produced.

1825 The first public railway line, built by George Stephenson, opens between Stockton and Darlington.

1850

1843 Cyrus Hall McCormick patents a mechanical reaper in the USA.

1840 A penny post system is introduced in Britain.

1856 Steel production is improved by the invention of the Bessemer process.

1869 The Suez Canal opens, cutting the journey from Europe to Asia by six weeks.

1874

1877 Thomas Edison invents the phonograph.

1895 Guglielmo Marconi invents radio telegraphy.

1900 AD

1913 Ford introduces the moving assembly line.

Social conditions

Industrialisation caused huge social upheaval as people left the land and flocked to towns and cities in search of work. The population rapidly concentrated around factories and mines, often in poor housing with little sanitation. Working conditions too were frequently abysmal, with long hours, risks to health and safety, a relentless machine-driven pace and low pay. Exploitation and child labour were common. Some enlightened industrialists did strive to improve the lot of workers, but most advances were achieved only by changes in the law and by **trade union** action.

A few employers built **model settlements** for their workers. An early example was the mill-owner **Robert Owen**, who created the community of New Lanark in Scotland in 1783. Others included Cadbury's garden city, **Bournville**, and the communities established by the manufacturer **Krupp** in Essen, Germany.

Slowly governments began to take action to improve working and living conditions and eradicate the worst abuses. Britain's **Factory Act** of 1833 stopped

children under nine working in textile mills, and the **Mines Act** of 1842 forbade women and children from going underground. In the US, however, children worked in factories into the early 20th century. Governments also took increasing responsibility for social welfare. Britain passed a **Public Health Act** in 1875 and Germany's pioneering laws of the 1880s introduced insurance against illness, accidents and old age.

Trade associations struggled for better working conditions, but they were outlawed in much of Europe after the French Revolution. In Britain, unions were given limited rights after 1825, although strikes were illegal. The **'Tolpuddle Martyrs'**, six Dorset farm workers, were transported to Australia in 1834 for union activity, provoking a public outcry. Unions gradually won more rights and membership grew steadily through the 19th century.

Child labour Boys as young as 13 and 14 were still working in mines in the United States into the early 20th century.

The French Revolution and the Napoleonic Wars reshaped Europe and changed the balance of power. The mighty Spanish and Ottoman empires faded while Germany and Italy began a process of unification that turned them into world powers. Advanced nation-states such as Britain and France vied with one another to seize new territory, culminating in the 1880s 'Scramble for Africa' that carved up a whole continent.

The drive for colonies
By 1900, European colonial powers were racing to acquire territory across the globe.

Germany
Italy
Spain
France
Portugal
Belgium
Netherlands
USA
Gt Britain

Explorers who opened the world

● **Heinrich Barth (1821-65)** Barth was a German scholar who crossed the Sahara to West Africa in an 1849-55 British government expedition.
● **Sir Richard Burton (1821-90)** Burton travelled in Arabia in 1853-4, disguised as a Muslim, and reached Mecca. In 1857-9, he explored East Africa from Zanzibar, looking for the source of the Nile.
● **René Caillié (1799-1838)** In 1826-7 the French explorer Caillé became the first European to reach the fabled city of Timbuktu.
● **David Livingstone (1813-73)** Livingstone was a British doctor and missionary who became the first European to cross Africa from the Atlantic coast to the Indian Ocean in 1853-6.

Sir Richard Burton

● **Mungo Park (1771-1806)** Park was the first European to explore the River Niger in West Africa. He made a first expedition in 1795-6 and a second in 1805-6.
● **John Hanning Speke (1827-64)** Speke travelled in search of the source of the Nile with Burton in 1857-9. He continued on his own to Lake Victoria, making a reutrn journey in 1860-2.
● **Henry Morton Stanley (1841-1904)** Stanley was a British-American journalist who found the missing David Livingstone when he was lost in 1871. Stanley showed that Lake Victoria was the source of the Nile, and crossed Africa via the Congo to the Atlantic coast.

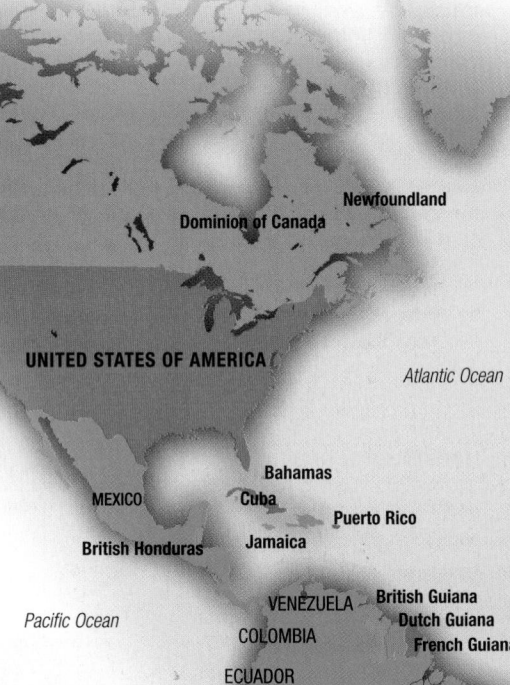

Newfoundland
Dominion of Canada
UNITED STATES OF AMERICA
Atlantic Ocean
Bahamas
Cuba
MEXICO
Puerto Rico
British Honduras
Jamaica
Pacific Ocean
VENEZUELA
British Guiana
Dutch Guiana
COLOMBIA
French Guiana
ECUADOR
BRAZIL
BOLIVIA
PARAGUAY
URUGUAY
ARGENTINA

BRITAIN'S COLONIAL WARS

Resistance by local populations led empire-building Britain into frequent conflicts.
● **Afghan Wars** Britain went to war in 1838-42, 1878-80 and 1919 to gain control of Afghanistan and secure the north-west frontier of India. From 1880 to 1919 Britain controlled the Khyber Pass and influenced Afghan foreign policy.
● **Opium Wars** Britain fought in 1839-42 and 1856-60 to protect its illegal trade in opium in China. The trade was damaging to Chinese society but British victories increased access to markets and brought possession of Hong Kong.
● **Indian Mutiny** In 1857-8 widespread rebellion broke out against British rule, led by Indian soldiers of the East India Company. After The mutiny was crushed the British government took over the rule of India.
● **Zulu War** Britain attempted to annex Zululand in January 1879, but was resisted by the Zulus under King Cetshwayo, who almost wiped out a British column of 1700 troops at Isandhlwana. The British triumphed after a renewed campaign in March.
● **South African (Boer) Wars** Britain attempted to annex the Boer (Afrikaner) republics in 1877. War followed in 1880-1, resulting in a Boer victory and an uneasy peace. War broke out again in 1899-1902. After initial defeats Britain imposed colonial rule.
● **Ashanti Wars** Britain fought a series of wars in the Gold Coast (Ghana), finally achieving the dissolution of the Ashanti confederation in 1896, and the seizure of their territories as a British protectorate.

Fighting spirit Ragtag Boers proved a match for the British army.

1788 The first British convict ships arrive at Botany Bay, Australia.

1804 A slave revolt makes Haiti the first independent country in Latin America.

1800

1819-26 Simón Bolívar leads South America to independence, but fails to unite the new republics.

1831-6 Charles Darwin makes his round-the-world voyage in HMS *Beagle*.

1850

1853-6 Britain, France, Turkey and Piedmont defeat Russia in the Crimean War.

1783 Britain loses its American colonies at the end of the War of American Independence.

1796-9 The British take control of Ceylon and southern India.

1806 The British occupy Cape Province of South Africa.

1821 Britain takes over the Gold Coast and The Gambia in West Africa.

1826 Britain annexes Lower Burma and Assam.

1830 France conquers Algeria.

1840 Britain annexes New Zealand, but colonisation precipitates the first New Zealand ('Maori') War (1843-8).

THE MAKING OF MODERN GERMANY

Unlike France and England, the Holy Roman Empire failed in medieval times to develop a strong central power under a single strong monarchy. Until the 17th century, Germany remained a mosaic of many states ruled by minor princes, each with its own borders, laws, customs duties and political structures. In the aftermath of the Thirty Years' War (1618-48) Prussia rose to prominence as the most powerful but moves towards integration did not begin until the 19th century. Napoleon forcibly unified all the German-speaking states except Prussia and Austria in the **Confederation of the Rhine** (1806-13). In 1814-15 at the Congress of Vienna the conservative Prince **Clemens von Metternich** masterminded a 39-state **German Confederation** that included Austria and Prussia. Economic ties soon followed in the form of a **Zollverein** (Customs Union) led by Prussia. Political unification was pursued by the Prussian 'Iron Chancellor' **Otto von Bismarck**. He established the **North German Confederation** after the Austro-Prussian War of 1866 and extended it after the Franco-Prussian War of 1870-1 to include southern Germany – a union known as the **Second Reich**. The king of Prussia, **Wilhelm I** (1797-1888), became the first Kaiser (Emperor) in 1871. Bismarck introduced social welfare legislation and a common currency, but was dismissed by Kaiser **Wilhelm II** (reigned 1888-1918) in 1890. A period of colonial expansion then began under Bismarck's successor Leo von Caprivi (1890-4) and Wilhelm II.

Otto von Bismarck

THE UNIFICATION OF ITALY

For more than 1000 years after the fall of Rome, Italy was a patchwork of city-states and small kingdoms, often under foreign rule. Hopes for unification grew after Napoleon's invasion of 1796-7 and a short-lived partial union followed. But by 1815 the country was again split into many states. Led by the radical nationalist, **Giuseppe Mazzini**, the **Risorgimento** ('resurrection') movement rapidly won support. In 1859, Italian and French forces drove the Austrians from Lombardy and then in 1861 **Giuseppe Garibaldi**'s volunteer 'Red Shirts' toppled the Naples monarchy. **Victor Emmanuel II** of Piedmont-Sardinia became king of Italy. Full unification followed in 1870, when Venice and Papal Rome were annexed, and Rome was made the national capital.

Australia: from penal colony to Commonwealth

The eastern part of Australia was claimed for Britain by **James Cook** in 1770, and named New South Wales. Britain used the new territory to settle transported convicts: the first **penal colony** was established in 1778. British government-assisted free settlement of Australia began in the 1830s, once the rich grasslands west of the Blue Mountains were opened to **sheep and wheat farming**.

Five further colonies were founded: Tasmania in 1825; Western Australia 1829; South Australia 1836; Victoria 1851; Queensland 1859. **Goldrushes** in the 1850s and 1860s encouraged new waves of immigration from Europe, particularly to New South Wales and Victoria. The colonies were largely self-governing from the 1850s, and were federated as the Commonwealth of Australia in 1901.

1857-8 The Indian Mutiny breaks out against British rule in India.

1867 Eastern Canada becomes a self-governing Dominion within the British Empire.

1877 Queen Victoria becomes Empress of India.

1883 Tunisia becomes a French protectorate.

1885 Leopold II of Belgium acquires the Congo as a personal fief.

1899-1902 Britain eventually defeats the Boers in the South African War ('Boer War').

1860-70 The Second New Zealand War pits Maoris against European settlers.

1862 France creates a protectorate in Indo-China (Vietnam, Cambodia).

1870-1 The Franco-Prussian War leads to the siege of Paris and the Commune. Germany is united under Prussia.

1882 The British occupy Egypt to protect their interests in the Suez Canal.

1898 The USA seizes Cuba, Puerto Rico, Guam and the Philippines in the Spanish-American War.

1901 Australia becomes a self-governing Commonwealth.

The assassination in Sarajevo of Archduke Franz Ferdinand of Austria-Hungary plunged Europe into war. Mass armies were mobilised in the hope of a decisive victory, but the war turned into a bloody and horrific stalemate that lasted four years and destroyed three empires.

Western Front 1914-18

Front line 1914-15
Front line Nov 1918
★ Major battles

Ypres
Messines
Passchendaele
Loos
Arras
Somme
Albert
Cambrai
Mons
St Quentin
Le Cateau
Verdun
St Mihiel
FRANCE
BELGIUM
LUXEMBOURG
NETHERLANDS
Brussels
Paris

FIVE CAUSES OF THE WAR

1 German ambition Germany's quest for world-power status led to clashes of interest with Britain, France and Russia.

2 A naval arms race The German attempt to build a world-class navy caused paranoia in Britain, the world's greatest sea power.

3 The alliance system Europe's system of alliances meant that any crisis could drag the whole continent into war.

4 Mass mobilisation Germany's Schlieffen Plan made mobilisation unstoppable and required the invasion of neutral Belgium, making a limited conflict impossible.

5 Jingoistic nationalism Powerful elements in several European governments sought a decisive war to focus patriotism and repress political discontent at home.

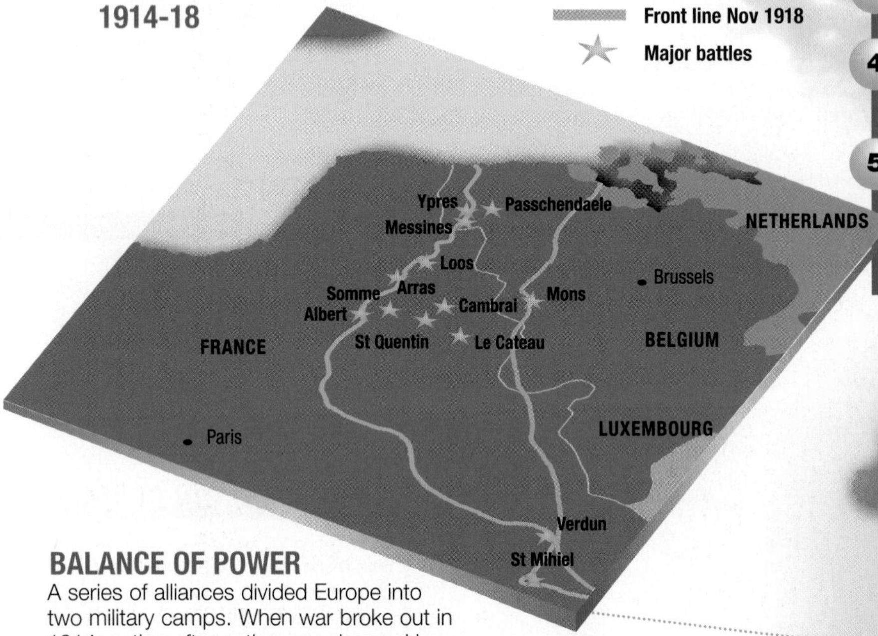

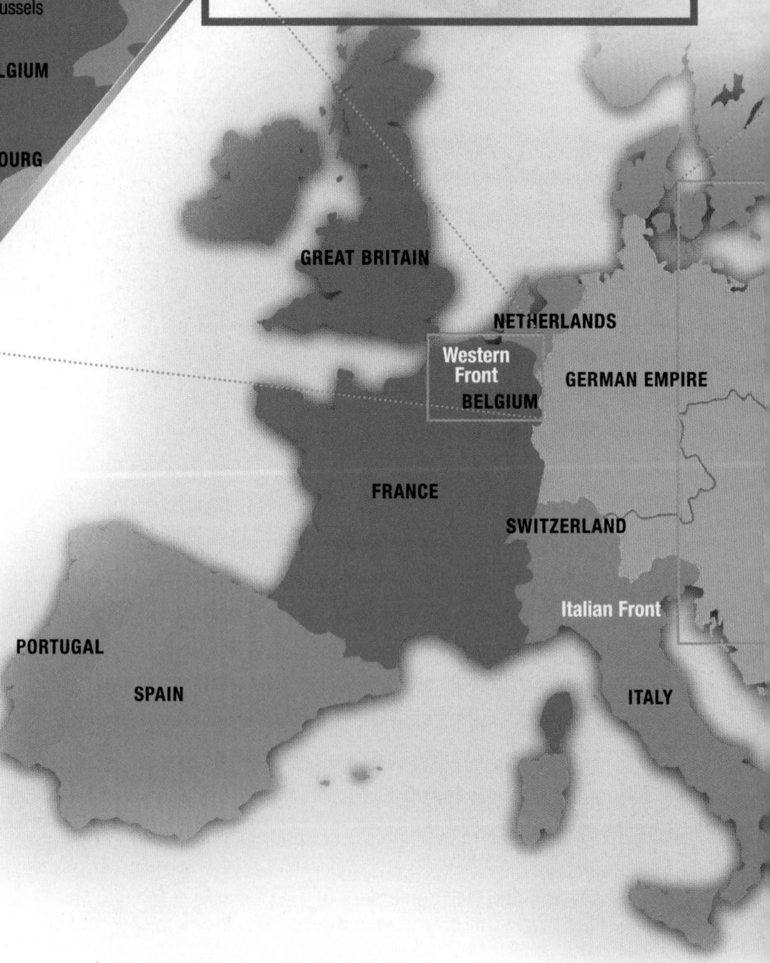

BALANCE OF POWER

A series of alliances divided Europe into two military camps. When war broke out in 1914, nation after nation was dragged in.

Central Powers
Germany, Austria-Hungary and Italy (Triple Alliance), plus Ottoman Empire and Bulgaria.

Allied Powers
France, Russia and Great Britain (Triple Entente), plus Serbia, Belgium, Japan, Italy (in 1915), Portugal, Romania, Greece and USA.

Neutral states

GREAT BRITAIN
NETHERLANDS
Western Front
BELGIUM
GERMAN EMPIRE
FRANCE
SWITZERLAND
Italian Front
PORTUGAL
SPAIN
ITALY

Manpower under arms	
7 710 000	11 330 000

Battleships	
48	97

Submarines	
37	37

Tannenberg
Two Russian armies are routed by a small German force.

First Marne
German forces are driven back from Paris.

First Ypres
British troops hold off the German advance in Flanders.

Masurian Lakes
The Russians are heavily defeated.

Second Ypres
Germany uses poison gas.

Isonzo Front
Italy's offensives against Austria-Hungary make minimal gains.

Verdun
Germany attempts to 'bleed France white' in a battle of attrition.

1914

30 AUG 1914
5-12 SEP 1914
30 OCT 1914
1915
15 SEP 1914
22 APR 1915
23 JUN 1915
1916
21 FEB 1916

June 28 Archduke Franz Ferdinand is assassinated; Austria-Hungary declares war on Serbia.

Aug 1 Germany declares war on Russia;
Aug 3 Germany declares war on France;
Aug 4 Germany invades Belgium; Great Britain declares war on Germany.

Feb 19 The first Zeppelin raid hits England.

April 25 Allied troops land at Gallipoli.

May 7 *Lusitania* is sunk by a U-boat off Ireland.

Dec 7 Turks trap British at Kut in Mesopotamia.
Dec 19 Allied troops evacuate the Dardanelles.

April 29 The Anglo-Indian garrison surrenders at Kut.

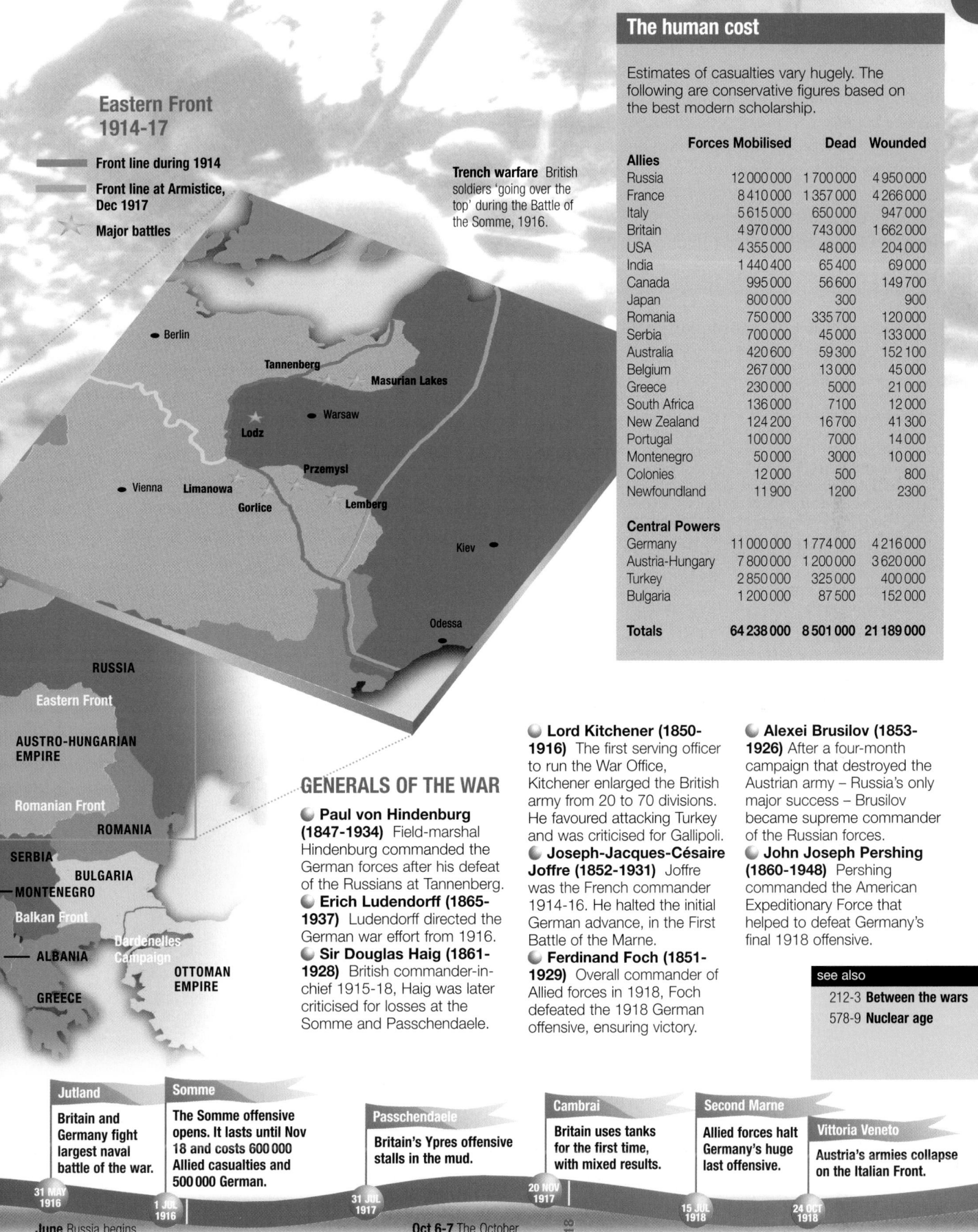

Eastern Front 1914-17

▬▬ Front line during 1914

▬▬ Front line at Armistice, Dec 1917

★ Major battles

Trench warfare British soldiers 'going over the top' during the Battle of the Somme, 1916.

Berlin
Tannenberg
Masurian Lakes
Warsaw
Lodz
Przemysl
Vienna • Limanowa
Gorlice
Lemberg
Kiev
Odessa

RUSSIA
Eastern Front
AUSTRO-HUNGARIAN EMPIRE
Romanian Front
ROMANIA
SERBIA
BULGARIA
MONTENEGRO
Balkan Front
Dardanelles Campaign
ALBANIA
OTTOMAN EMPIRE
GREECE

The human cost

Estimates of casualties vary hugely. The following are conservative figures based on the best modern scholarship.

	Forces Mobilised	Dead	Wounded
Allies			
Russia	12 000 000	1 700 000	4 950 000
France	8 410 000	1 357 000	4 266 000
Italy	5 615 000	650 000	947 000
Britain	4 970 000	743 000	1 662 000
USA	4 355 000	48 000	204 000
India	1 440 400	65 400	69 000
Canada	995 000	56 600	149 700
Japan	800 000	300	900
Romania	750 000	335 700	120 000
Serbia	700 000	45 000	133 000
Australia	420 600	59 300	152 100
Belgium	267 000	13 000	45 000
Greece	230 000	5 000	21 000
South Africa	136 000	7 100	12 000
New Zealand	124 200	16 700	41 300
Portugal	100 000	7 000	14 000
Montenegro	50 000	3 000	10 000
Colonies	12 000	500	800
Newfoundland	11 900	1 200	2 300
Central Powers			
Germany	11 000 000	1 774 000	4 216 000
Austria-Hungary	7 800 000	1 200 000	3 620 000
Turkey	2 850 000	325 000	400 000
Bulgaria	1 200 000	87 500	152 000
Totals	**64 238 000**	**8 501 000**	**21 189 000**

GENERALS OF THE WAR

Paul von Hindenburg (1847-1934) Field-marshal Hindenburg commanded the German forces after his defeat of the Russians at Tannenberg.

Erich Ludendorff (1865-1937) Ludendorff directed the German war effort from 1916.

Sir Douglas Haig (1861-1928) British commander-in-chief 1915-18, Haig was later criticised for losses at the Somme and Passchendaele.

Lord Kitchener (1850-1916) The first serving officer to run the War Office, Kitchener enlarged the British army from 20 to 70 divisions. He favoured attacking Turkey and was criticised for Gallipoli.

Joseph-Jacques-Césaire Joffre (1852-1931) Joffre was the French commander 1914-16. He halted the initial German advance, in the First Battle of the Marne.

Ferdinand Foch (1851-1929) Overall commander of Allied forces in 1918, Foch defeated the 1918 German offensive, ensuring victory.

Alexei Brusilov (1853-1926) After a four-month campaign that destroyed the Austrian army – Russia's only major success – Brusilov became supreme commander of the Russian forces.

John Joseph Pershing (1860-1948) Pershing commanded the American Expeditionary Force that helped to defeat Germany's final 1918 offensive.

see also
212-3 **Between the wars**
578-9 **Nuclear age**

Jutland
Britain and Germany fight largest naval battle of the war.

Somme
The Somme offensive opens. It lasts until Nov 18 and costs 600 000 Allied casualties and 500 000 German.

Passchendaele
Britain's Ypres offensive stalls in the mud.

Cambrai
Britain uses tanks for the first time, with mixed results.

Second Marne
Allied forces halt Germany's huge last offensive.

Vittoria Veneto
Austria's armies collapse on the Italian Front.

31 MAY 1916
1 JUL 1916
31 JUL 1917
20 NOV 1917
15 JUL 1918
24 OCT 1918

June Russia begins offensive under Brusilov that smashes the Austrian Front.

1917 **Jan 8** Germany begins submarine warfare.

Apr 6 The USA declares war on Germany.

Oct 6-7 The October Revolution takes Russia out of the war, freeing German troops for the West.

1918 **Mar 3** Germany and Russia sign the Treaty of Brest-Litovsk.

Oct 4 Germany requests an armistice.

Nov 11 (11am) An armistice halts all fighting on the Western Front.

Russia entered the 20th century an absolute monarchy ruled by Romanov tsars who had been in power for 300 years. Alongside the immense wealth of a few, millions lived in extreme poverty. Discontent was mounting but calls for reform went unheeded, fuelling radical movements and ideas of social change. Revolution in 1905 forced Nicholas II to establish a parliament and in 1917 installed the world's first socialist government. By 1922 the USSR had come into being with Vladimir Ilych Lenin at its head.

FACT
Germany helped Lenin return to Russia in 1917. He was thought so dangerous his train was sealed until it crossed the border.

MAIN CAUSES OF THE REVOLUTION

1 **Liberal opposition** Liberals and intellectuals had long opposed tsarist autocracy. As early as 1825, moderates in the military tried to seize power and enforce reforms (the Decembrist revolt).

2 **Rapid economic change** Industrialisation created an oppressed urban proletariat that became increasingly politicised.

3 **Repressive government** Harsh measures introduced by rulers such as Alexander III in the 1880s alienated public support and created a fertile breeding ground for revolutionary ideas.

4 **Weakness of Nicholas II** Nicholas II ignored calls for reform of the political system, and his reluctant creation of a powerless Duma (parliament) in 1905 did nothing to restore confidence in his reign. The influence of Rasputin on the tsarina seemed to many to symbolise the court's terminal degeneracy.

5 **Military defeat** Russia's defeat by Japan in 1904-5 and disastrous failures in the First World War (costing 7 million casualties) led to increasingly hostile public opinion.

6 **Food shortages** Inflation and food shortages caused by the war created suffering and hardship, especially in Russian cities.

Fiery orator Lenin addresses Russian troops in 1920.

1861 Alexander II emancipates Russia's serfs.

1894 Nicholas II accedes to the Russian throne.

1903 The Russian Social Democratic Workers' Party splits into Bolshevik and Menshevik factions.

1905 Revolution follows the massacre of protestors in St Petersburg. Nicholas agrees to an elected Duma.

Mar 12, 1917 (OS Feb 27) The Petrograd garrison mutinies, turning a revolt into the Menshevik-led 'February Revolution'.

Mar 15, 1917 Nicholas II abdicates; the Duma establishes a moderate, multiparty Provisional Government.

May 3-4, 1917 (OS Apr 20-21) The 'April Days' demonstrations occur against the government's failure to end Russia's part in the war.

1881 Alexander II is assassinated by revolutionaries, and is succeeded by his son Alexander III.

1900

1902-3 Strikes and civil unrest occur in Russian industrial centres.

1904-5 Russia is humiliated by defeat in the Russo-Japanese War.

1915

1914 Russia enters the First World War against the Central Powers.

Mar 8, 1917 (OS Feb 23) Bread riots in Petrograd (St Petersburg).

Mar 13-15, 1917 Soviets (councils) of workers, soldiers and peasants are set up across Russia.

April 16, 1917 Lenin returns from Switzerland to Petrograd and calls for revolution against the Provisional Government.

The 1905 Revolution: the 'dress rehearsal'

Strikes, heavy taxation and disgust with inept handling of the **Russo-Japanese War** boiled over in 1905. A demonstration in St Petersburg on January 22 (OS January 9), petitioned Tsar Nicholas II for reform; but Cossack troops opened fire on the unarmed crowds converging on the Winter Palace, killing between 50 and 1000 (estimates vary). Deep resentment at this **'Bloody Sunday'** resulted in strikes, assassinations and revolts in Poland, Latvia, Georgia and Finland. Nicholas ruled for 12 more years but his people's devotion was fatally undermined. He was forced to introduce reforms, creating an elected parliament, the Duma. A general strike led by Leon Trotsky and a mutiny on the battleship *Potemkin* won more concessions, including freedoms of conscience, speech and association. The moderates were satisfied and revolt died out; 15 000 had died.

THE RUSSIAN CIVIL WAR (1918-20)

Many groups including nationalists, republicans, democrats and even radical Socialist Revolutionaries opposed the Bolsheviks after they seized power in 1917. A loose alliance – the **'White Army'** – was formed in opposition to the Bolshevik **'Red Army'** created by Trotsky in late 1917. Whites were united in opposing Lenin and the peace treaty with Germany, but failed to coordinate. Fighting was widespread, from northern Russia to the Caucasus and Ukraine. Foreign powers including Britain, France, Japan and the USA aided the Whites but failed to hold territory against the Reds. White resistance weakened, crippled by internal divisions and the failure to develop a popular alternative to Bolshevism. In 1920 the White Army was defeated in the Crimea and later anti-Bolshevik uprisings were put down. Transcaucasian republics were crushed in 1922, followed by the creation of the USSR. The post-revolutionary turmoil was over, having cost some 13 million lives.

Key figures

🔲 **Alexander Kerensky (1881-1970)** Kerensky headed the Provisional Government of July-October 1917. He failed to withdraw Russia from the First World War or to introduce reforms.

🔲 **Vladimir Ilych Lenin (1870-1924)** A political theorist and revolutionary Marxist, Lenin devoted his life to establishing a Communist Russian state. He led the Bolshevik revolution of 1917, founded the Communist Party and became the first head of state of the USSR. A pragmatic leader, he permitted some capitalist reforms in his 1921 New Economic Policy.

🔲 **Nicholas II (1868-1918)** Nicholas was the last tsar, reigning 1894-1917. He abdicated after the February Revolution and was executed.

🔲 **Rasputin (1872-1916)** Grigori Rasputin, a Siberian holy man, claimed to be able to alleviate the haemophilia of the tsar's son Alexei. He briefly dominated state affairs through his influence over the tsarina but was murdered by monarchists.

🔲 **Joseph Stalin (1879-1953)** Stalin played a minor role in the October Revolution, and led the Communist Party from 1922. He succeeded Lenin as head of state and turned the USSR into a world power. Stalin ruled as a dictator, eliminating rivals in a series of murderous 'purges'. His reign of terror and policy of forced collectivisation cost an estimated 25 million lives.

🔲 **Pyotr Stolypin (1862-1911)** Prime minister of Russia after the 1905 revolution, Stolypin introduced reforms – notably in land ownership – but not fast enough to satisfy radicals. As a result, he was unpopular with both left and right. He resigned in March 1911, and was assassinated six months later.

🔲 **Leon Trotsky (1879-1940)** A Communist theorist, Trotsky met Lenin in London in 1902. He returned to Russia in 1905 and led the St Petersburg Soviet (workers' council) in a strike that won major reforms. In 1917 he founded the Red Army, leading it throughout the Civil War. Trotsky was the obvious successor to Lenin, but lost out to Stalin and was exiled in 1929. He continued to write and promote the cause of 'world revolution' until murdered in Mexico on Stalin's orders.

Trotsky (1879-1940)

Political forces in Russia

Narodniki ('Populists') The Narodniki were socialists who in the 1860s and 70s favoured republican, liberal government and Western technology. Some formed the People's Will terrorist movement that assassinated Alexander II in 1881.

Octobrists Political moderates, the Octobrists were satisfied with the tsar's concessions of October 1905.

Kadets (Constitutional Democrats) The Kadets considered the 1905 changes inadequate. They wanted further reforms, including a limited monarchy. They dominated the first Duma, but then declined in influence.

Black Hundreds (League of the Russian People) After the 1905 revolution, nationalists calling themselves Black Hundreds carried out attacks on revolutionaries and Jews.

Socialist Revolutionary Party Heirs to the Narodniki movement, the Socialist Revolutionaries sought revolution by mobilising the peasantry, using terrorism if necessary. They formed a majority in the Provisional Government, but were disbanded after the Civil War.

Social Democratic Workers' Party A Marxist party founded by Georgi Plekhanov in 1898, the Social Democratic Workers' Party sought revolution led by industrial workers. In 1903 it split into Bolshevik and Menshevik factions.

Bolsheviks ('Majority') Led by Lenin, the Bolsheviks saw themselves as the vanguard of a popular socialist revolution. They supported the use of violence to overthrow the state and establish a 'dictatorship of the proletariat'.

Mensheviks ('Minority') The Mensheviks were moderate socialists who favoured peaceful action through the Duma.

Sept 8-12, 1917 An attempted counter-revolutionary coup by army commander General Kornilov fails.

Sept 1917 Bolsheviks gain control of the Petrograd and Moscow Soviets.

Nov 6-7, 1917 (OS Oct 24-25) The Bolsheviks overthrow the Provisional Government in the 'October Revolution'.

July 1918 The royal family are executed.

1920 The Whites fail to capture Moscow, and the Red Army defeats a Polish invasion. **1920**

1924 Lenin dies; by 1929, Stalin has outmanoeuvred Trotsky and become leader of the USSR.

July 1917 The Bolshevik party is outlawed after mass armed demonstrations (the 'July Days'); its leaders are arrested or go into hiding.

Oct 20, 1917 Lenin returns from hiding in Finland and urges armed revolution.

Dec 1917 The Bolsheviks abolish private property, redistribute land, nationalise banks and put workers in control of industry.

Mar 3, 1918 The Bolshevik government signs a humiliating peace treaty with Germany. Civil war breaks out (to 1920).

Aug 1918 An attempt to assassinate Lenin leads to the 'Red Terror' – an attempt to crush all opposition to Bolshevism.

1921 Lenin introduces the New Economic Policy.

1922 Lenin proclaims the foundation of the Union of Soviet Socialist Republics (USSR).

Fallen idol Children contemplate a dismantled statue of Alexander III in 1918. After the Revolution many tsarist monuments were destroyed.

NOTE: Russia abandoned the 'Old Style' Julian calendar in February 1918. Old Style (OS) dates are given here where they are significant.

Aftershocks from the First World War continued to rock Europe for two decades. The world economy cycled between boom and bust in the 1920s, and voters were tempted by radical ideas, particularly those of militaristic right-wing parties. In the late 1930s, the aggressive Nazi regime in Germany was mirrored in Japan and Italy, pushing the world towards another major war.

GERMANY'S FLASHPOINTS

The Treaty of Versailles (signed June 28, 1919) not only burdened Germany with guilt for the First World War and with heavy reparations payments, but also redrew parts of the map of Europe. Austria-Hungary and the Russian and Ottoman Empires ceased to exist, while Germany lost territories, as shown on the map. Many of these areas had long-established German populations and industrial centres; their occupation or seizure by other states caused bitter resentment in Germany, and this sense of injustice was exploited by the Nazis.

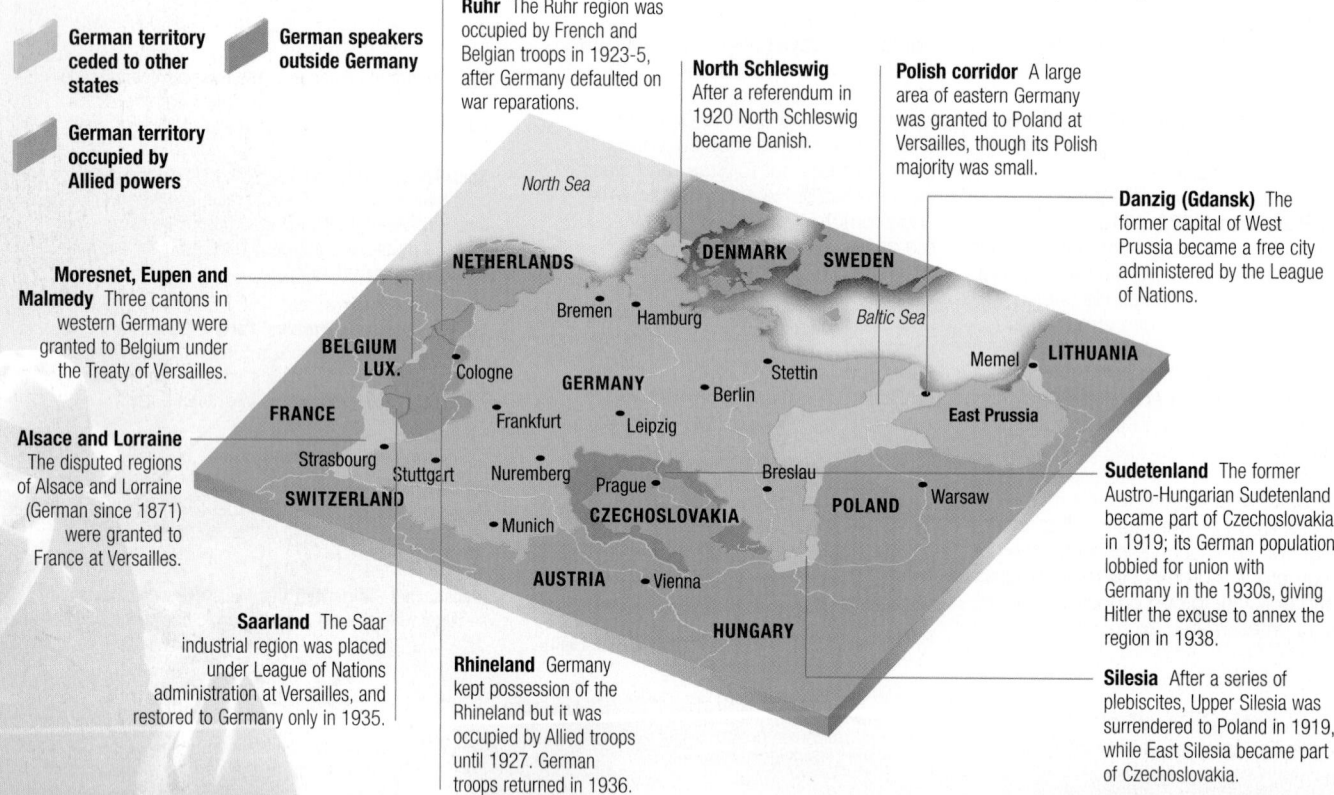

German territory ceded to other states

German speakers outside Germany

German territory occupied by Allied powers

Ruhr The Ruhr region was occupied by French and Belgian troops in 1923-5, after Germany defaulted on war reparations.

North Schleswig After a referendum in 1920 North Schleswig became Danish.

Polish corridor A large area of eastern Germany was granted to Poland at Versailles, though its Polish majority was small.

Danzig (Gdansk) The former capital of West Prussia became a free city administered by the League of Nations.

Moresnet, Eupen and Malmedy Three cantons in western Germany were granted to Belgium under the Treaty of Versailles.

Alsace and Lorraine The disputed regions of Alsace and Lorraine (German since 1871) were granted to France at Versailles.

Saarland The Saar industrial region was placed under League of Nations administration at Versailles, and restored to Germany only in 1935.

Rhineland Germany kept possession of the Rhineland but it was occupied by Allied troops until 1927. German troops returned in 1936.

Sudetenland The former Austro-Hungarian Sudetenland became part of Czechoslovakia in 1919; its German population lobbied for union with Germany in the 1930s, giving Hitler the excuse to annex the region in 1938.

Silesia After a series of plebiscites, Upper Silesia was surrendered to Poland in 1919, while East Silesia became part of Czechoslovakia.

North Sea, NETHERLANDS, DENMARK, SWEDEN, Bremen, Hamburg, *Baltic Sea*, BELGIUM, LUX., Cologne, GERMANY, Stettin, Memel, LITHUANIA, FRANCE, Frankfurt, Berlin, East Prussia, Strasbourg, Leipzig, Stuttgart, Nuremberg, Breslau, Prague, POLAND, Warsaw, SWITZERLAND, Munich, CZECHOSLOVAKIA, AUSTRIA, Vienna, HUNGARY

ECONOMIC CRISIS

The First World War had a major impact on the world economy. Many economies had expanded artificially during the war, leading to a collapse in demand once the war was over. Most countries had also borrowed heavily, and were unable to back their borrowings by gold reserves, causing a collapse of the **Gold Standard** and **devaluation**. In the USA, banks became overexposed in the speculative stockmarket boom of the late 1920s. The USA also suffered agricultural blight (the **'Dust Bowl'**) in the 1930s, caused by inflated farm prices and overworked land.

When the US stockmarket began to fall on **October 24, 1929**, panicked speculators tried to sell stocks at any price, leading to a collapse that quickly spread around the world. By 1931 there were 8 million unemployed in the USA, 5 million in Germany and 2.75 million in Britain.

Apart from increasing support for extremist politics, the Depression also prompted the US president, Roosevelt, to introduce his **New Deal**, a largely successful programme of massive public works intended to create jobs. In Hitler's Germany, a huge **rearmament** programme provided a similar boost to the economy (and those of Germany's rivals) – but the price was an arms race that hastened the drift towards war.

Dustbowl farmers Real hardship hit US farms in the Depression.

1918 The First World War ends; a Peace Conference in Paris excludes Germany.

1920 League of Nations meets for the first time; The USA refuses to join.

1922 Mussolini forms a Fascist government in Italy.

1925 Hitler publishes *Mein Kampf* (*My Struggle*).

1929 The Wall Street Crash sets off worldwide economic depression.

1919 The left-wing 'Spartacist' uprising fails in Germany.

1921 German war reparations are set at 269 billion Marks (£6.5 billion).

1923 France and Belgium occupy the Ruhr. The German currency collapses.

1926 A General Strike in Britain lasts just nine days, though miners strike for six months.

1928 Trading volume on the New York Stock Exchange hits an all-time record.

The rise of the dictators

The period between the wars saw one-party dictatorships established across Europe. In the USSR, Stalin began a policy of systematically eliminating critics and rivals. In Germany, Hitler succeeded the Weimar Republic via the ballot box, but then used his Nazi thugs to destroy political opponents. Mussolini dismantled Italy's democracy and used the Fascist Blackshirt militia to intimidate other politicians. Elsewhere too the 1920s and 30s saw the rise of authoritarian strongmen, from Horthy in Hungary (1920) and Salazar in Portugal (1928) to King Alexander in Yugoslavia (1929) and Franco in Spain (1939).

Benito Mussolini (1883-1945)

Mussolini was a journalist before he founded the National Fascist Party. He ruled Italy from 1922, establishing himself as a dictator by 1926. He was initially widely supported for his economic reforms and for his annexation of Ethiopia in 1936 and Albania in 1939. But once war broke out Italy suffered a series of disastrous defeats. Mussolini was deposed in 1943 and executed by partisans in 1945.

Joseph Stalin (1879-1953)

Born Joseph Dzhugashvili in Georgia, Stalin ('man of steel') became secretary-general of the Communist Party Central Committee in the USSR in 1922. He became head of state in 1927, presiding over a reign of terror in the 1930s that included show trials, purges, prison camps and the execution of some 10 million people. From 1941, he led the Soviet Union's titanic struggle against Nazi Germany and dominated the Allied settlement postwar, imposing Soviet rule over Eastern Europe.

see also
208-9 **First World War**
214-5 **Second World War**
462-3 **Principles of economics**

Adolf Hitler (1889-1945)

Hitler was born in Austria, and served with distinction in the First World War. He joined the National Socialist German Workers' Party (Nazis) in 1919, and became its leader in 1921. A failed coup in 1923 led to two years' imprisonment, during which he wrote his manifesto *Mein Kampf*. Hitler rallied militaristic support around the call to eliminate the Jews, to create a Greater Germany through eastern expansion, and to refute the Versailles Treaty. By 1933 the Nazis were the largest party in government, and Hitler became chancellor, then dictator (*Führer*). Under his autocratic leadership in the Second World War, Germany suffered catastrophic defeat.

The Spanish Civil War (1936-9)

In 1931 a republic was declared in Spain, sparking a political crisis that became a testing ground for a wider European conflict between left and right. The **Republicans** included socialists, communists, anarchists and regional separatists. They were opposed by the **Nationalists** – monarchists, conservative Catholics and the fascist Falange Party. In 1936 a pro-Nationalist army uprising led by General Francisco Franco plunged Spain into civil war. Germany and Italy aided the Nationalists and the USSR the Republicans. Britain and France did not intervene, though many volunteers joined the pro-Republican **International Brigades**. The Republicans gradually lost ground and in April 1939 Madrid fell. The Falange became the sole legal party and Franco the head of a fascist state until his death in 1975.

Francisco Franco

1930 The Nazis win 100 seats in German elections.

1932 The Nazi Party becomes the largest political party in Germany after elections.

1934 Hitler arrests his SA rivals and other political opponents in the 'Night of the Long Knives'.

1936 Italy and Germany form a 'Rome-Berlin Axis'.

1936-9 Civil war devastates Spain.

1938 Germany occupies Austria and the Sudetenland. The Nazis attack Jews on the night of Nov. 9 – 'Kristallnacht'.

1930

1931 Spain is declared a republic.

1933 **Hitler becomes chancellor of Germany.**

1935

1935 German Jews are stripped of their rights, and anti-Semitism is given legal sanction.

1936 Britain's King Edward VIII abdicates.

1937 German bombers destroy the Republican Spanish town of Guernica.

1939 German invasions of Czechoslovakia and Poland provoke world war.

The costliest war in history engulfed more than three-quarters of the world's people. Entire populations were targeted by aerial bombing, scorched-earth policies, concentration camps and genocide – many of which were justified by creeds of racial superiority. At its close – marked by the first, devastating use of atomic weapons – the Allied victors had to face a new world order, which included the demise of their old colonial empires and a hugely enhanced Soviet power.

FIVE CAUSES OF THE WAR

1 **Resentment at Versailles** The Versailles Treaty humiliated Germany, which had to forfeit territory and suffered prolonged economic hardship. Deep-felt resentment fuelled extremist nationalist politics.

2 **Preoccupation with anti-Communism** Western powers tolerated extreme right-wing parties as a counterweight to Communism, not acknowledging the full implication of their dictatorial ambitions.

3 **Territorial ambitions** The three Axis powers all sought new territories: Germany in Eastern Europe, Italy in Africa and the eastern Mediterranean, Japan in South-east Asia.

4 **An arms race** Rearmament stimulated the depressed 1930s economies, but it also created an arms race and growing mistrust among the European powers.

5 **The failure of internationalism** The League of Nations failed to check aggression. Western leaders, haunted by the horror of the First World War, preferred compromise and appeasement to confronting the aggressors.

August 23 The Nazi-Soviet non-aggression pact frees Hitler to invade Poland.

September 3 Britain and France, Canada, Australia and New Zealand declare war on Germany.

April 9 German troops invade Denmark and Norway.

May 10-14 Germany invades the Netherlands, Belgium, Luxembourg and France.

Versailles avenged Adolf Hitler at the Eiffel Tower in Paris, 1940.

April 17 Yugoslavia surrenders to German forces.

December 7 Japan launches a surprise attack on the US naval base at Pearl Harbor, Hawaii.

1939

March 31 Britain and France promise to support Poland.

September 1 Germany invades Poland.

1940

May 28-June 4 338 000 British and French troops are evacuated from Dunkirk, northern France.

July 10-August Battle of Britain: British fighter planes resist German air attacks.

1941

June 22 Germany launches its invasion of the USSR (Operation Barbarossa).

1942

February 15 Singapore falls to Japanese forces, with 70 000 British and Commonwealth prisoners.

THEATRES OF WAR

Europe Germany's victory over Poland (1939) was followed in summer 1940 by the occupation of Denmark, Norway, the Netherlands, Belgium and much of France. In early 1941, conquest of Yugoslavia and Greece completed German domination. The Allied counterattack began in Italy in 1943, followed by the D-Day landings in France in 1944. The Allied advance into Germany in 1944-5 was held up only at Arnhem (September 1944) and in the Ardennes.

North Africa Italian forces in North Africa suffered heavy defeats before the arrival of Rommel's Afrika Korps (February 1941). The Allies overcame Rommel only in late 1942, after defeating him at El Alamein and landing troops in French North Africa.

The Russian Front The war against Germany was won in the east by the Soviet Union. Despite initial victories, Germany found its forces drawn into an unwinnable war with a front at times 2700 km (1700 miles) long and an enemy who refused to surrender. Defeat at Stalingrad (1943) was a turning point, and the failure of the 1943 Kursk offensive the beginning of the end.

The Pacific Japan needed to defeat the USA in the Pacific quickly, before US industrial production proved decisive. But a stunning blow at Pearl Harbor (December 1941) was followed by the loss of the key Japanese aircraft carriers at Midway (June 1942) and a US counteroffensive at Guadalcanal, Solomon Islands (August 1942). The remnants of the Japanese navy were destroyed at Leyte Gulf (October 1944), leaving Japan itself open to attack.

The Far East Coinciding with their attack on Pearl Harbor, the Japanese stormed European colonial possessions in the Far East and South-east Asia: Hong Kong and Malaya (December 1941); the Dutch East Indies (January 1942) and the Philippines (December 1941). Japan occupied British-held Burma (January-March 1942), and threatened India. Their advance was finally halted at Imphal and Kohima, India (April 1944). Allied advances in Burma, China and Borneo in early 1945 ended Japan's Asian empire.

Pearl Harbor The surprise attack on the US fleet in 1941 was a tactical triumph but a political disaster for Japan. The US immediately entered the war with all its industrial might, and the battle for the Pacific began.

The war leaders

Winston Churchill 1874-1965 Churchill was a seasoned British politician, aged 64 at the outbreak of war. A long-term opponent of appeasement, he became prime minister of a coalition government in 1940. He inspired determined resistance to Hitler through stirring speeches, political resolve, a solid grasp of strategy and skilled diplomacy.

Douglas MacArthur 1880-1964 MacArthur was a retired US general who was recalled to defend the Philippines in 1941. Appointed Supreme Allied Commander in the South-west Pacific, he oversaw the island-to-island campaign that led to Japan's defeat.

Franklin Delano Roosevelt 1882-1945 Roosevelt was in his third presidential term when the USA entered the war. He prepared the country for an

Bulldog spirit Winston Churchill's uncompromising stand against the Nazis united Britons through six years of war.

anti-Japanese war from 1937, and led the national war effort, dying 26 days before the German surrender.

Tojo Hideki 1884-1948 Tojo was a professional soldier of samurai descent, who rose to become the Japanese war minister (1940-4) and then prime minister (1941-4). He initiated the attack on Pearl Harbor and oversaw Japanese conquests in the Pacific, before military losses forced his resignation. He was hanged as a war criminal.

Bernard Montgomery 1887-1976 Commander of Britain's 8th Army in North Africa and Italy, Montgomery defeated Rommel in 1942 at El Alamein. He commanded Allied ground forces on D-Day.

Charles de Gaulle 1890-1970 A professional soldier with a distinguished record in the First World War, de Gaulle led the French government in exile (Free French) during the war and inspired anti-German resistance in occupied France.

Dwight D. Eisenhower 1890-1969 Eisenhower was Supreme Commander of Allied forces in Europe (1942-5); he led the Allied 'Torch' landings in North Africa in 1942 and in Italy in 1943, then directed the 1944 D-Day landings.

Erwin Rommel 1891-1944 Rommel was a professional soldier with an outstanding record in the First World War. He led a division in the German invasion of France. In 1941, he became commander of the

Afrika Korps, and won a series of victories, until El Alamein. Implicated in a plot against Hitler in 1944, he committed suicide.

Hermann Göring 1893-1946 A First World War pilot, Göring became Minister of Interior and Air Minister in 1933. He rebuilt the Luftwaffe (air force), but was discredited after the Battle of Britain. Condemned in 1946 as a war criminal, he took poison before his execution.

Georgi Zhukov 1895-1974 Zhukov was a Tsarist conscript before joining the Red Army in 1918. He became the greatest Russian commander of the war. After the German invasion of the USSR, he supervised the defence of Leningrad and Moscow, and was appointed commander-in-chief of Soviet troops. He won decisive victories at Stalingrad and Kursk in 1943, and led the Soviet advance on Berlin.

June 4-5 US planes sink four Japanese aircraft carriers in the Battle of Midway.

November 4 British and Commonwealth forces finally defeat Rommel's Afrika Korps at El Alamein, Egypt.

July 5-17 The Kursk offensive leads to Germany's decisive defeat on the Russian Front.

September 3 Italy surrenders as Allied forces advance north from Sicily.

October 17-25 US forces destroy the remaining Japanese fleet at Leyte Gulf, the largest naval battle in history.

May 8 VE Day (Victory in Europe): Germany surrenders unconditionally.

August 14 Japan surrenders unconditionally, following the destruction of Hiroshima (August 6) and Nagasaki (August 9) by US atomic bombs.

1943

1944

September 13 The Germans attack Stalingrad.

January 31 Over 80 000 troops of the German Sixth Army surrender at Stalingrad.

July 10 British and US troops land in Sicily.

1945

June 6 (D-Day) Allied forces land successfully in north-west France.

D-Day landing Allied troops land in Normandy, France (June 6, 1944) to open the 'Second Front' against Germany.

Decisive weapon The atom bomb dropped on Hiroshima had more destructive power than all other armaments used up to that time put together.

see also

212-3 **Between the wars**
576-9 **Weapons of war**

The Holocaust

The term 'holocaust' refers specifically to Nazi persecution of the Jews, although many others fell victim to the creed of racial purity, including gypsies, homosexuals and the mentally ill. State-sponsored persecution in the 1930s turned to outright genocide during the war and some 6 million Jews died in the so-called 'final solution'.

Jewish Holocaust deaths (1939-45)

Austria	65 000	Italy	9000
Belgium	50 000	Latvia	8000
Czech.	277 000	Lithuania	135 000
France	83 000	Netherlands	106 000
Germany	180 000	Poland	3 000 000
Greece	71 000	Romania	370 000
Hungary	450 000	USSR	1 000 000

The world map altered dramatically after the Second World War, as European colonial empires fell apart. Nationalist leaders emerged from local educated elites and African soldiers returned from the war with raised expectations. The colonial powers, weakened by war, failed to reassert authority, and Russia and China offered alternative political visions. India won its freedom in 1947, setting a precedent for much of Asia and Africa.

Algeria

Algeria had been ruled by France since 1848. The Front de Libération Nationale (**FLN**) began a violent independence campaign in 1954, provoking a harsh French response. Settlers rioted to keep Algeria French, causing a political crisis in France and a new government (1958) under **de Gaulle**. Fighting in Algeria continued, and in April 1961 the anti-independence **OAS** group attempted a coup in France. Independence was granted on March 18, 1962, and the colonists were evacuated.

Coming of age Large areas of Africa and Asia became independent of their former colonial rulers after 1945. In the majority of cases, independence was granted peacefully, as shown.

■ Independence war, with dates

■ Independence granted peacefully, since 1945

Independence day Algeria celebrated when eight years of bloody conflict ended with independence from France in 1962.

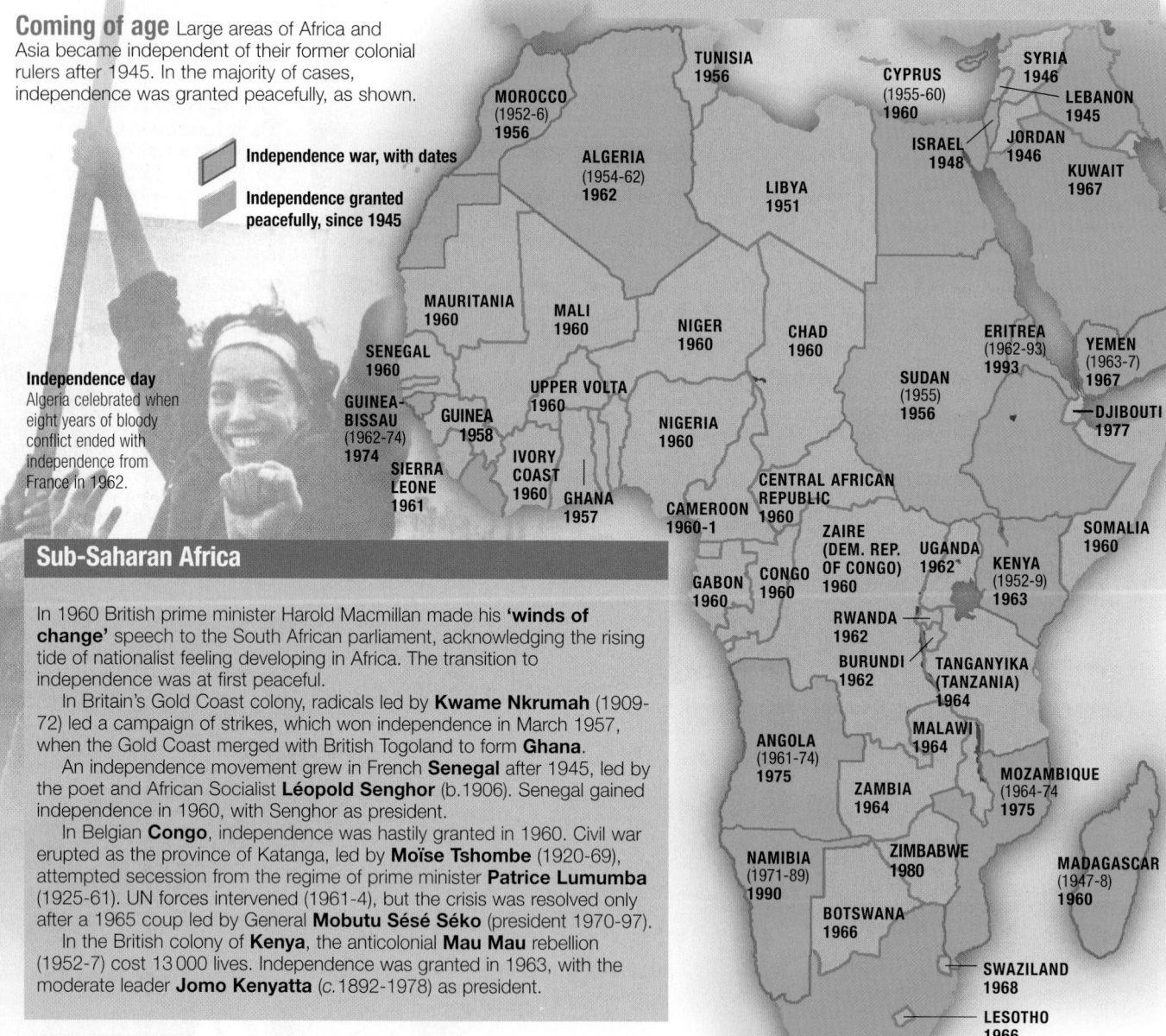

Sub-Saharan Africa

In 1960 British prime minister Harold Macmillan made his **'winds of change'** speech to the South African parliament, acknowledging the rising tide of nationalist feeling developing in Africa. The transition to independence was at first peaceful.

In Britain's Gold Coast colony, radicals led by **Kwame Nkrumah** (1909-72) led a campaign of strikes, which won independence in March 1957, when the Gold Coast merged with British Togoland to form **Ghana**.

An independence movement grew in French **Senegal** after 1945, led by the poet and African Socialist **Léopold Senghor** (b.1906). Senegal gained independence in 1960, with Senghor as president.

In Belgian **Congo**, independence was hastily granted in 1960. Civil war erupted as the province of Katanga, led by **Moïse Tshombe** (1920-69), attempted secession from the regime of prime minister **Patrice Lumumba** (1925-61). UN forces intervened (1961-4), but the crisis was resolved only after a 1965 coup led by General **Mobutu Sésé Séko** (president 1970-97).

In the British colony of **Kenya**, the anticolonial **Mau Mau** rebellion (1952-7) cost 13 000 lives. Independence was granted in 1963, with the moderate leader **Jomo Kenyatta** (c.1892-1978) as president.

Map labels

MOROCCO (1952-6) 1956
TUNISIA 1956
CYPRUS (1955-60) 1960
SYRIA 1946
LEBANON 1945
ISRAEL 1948
JORDAN 1946
KUWAIT 1967
ALGERIA (1954-62) 1962
LIBYA 1951
MAURITANIA 1960
MALI 1960
NIGER 1960
CHAD 1960
ERITREA (1962-93) 1993
YEMEN (1963-7) 1967
SENEGAL 1960
SUDAN (1955) 1956
DJIBOUTI 1977
GUINEA-BISSAU (1962-74) 1974
GUINEA 1958
UPPER VOLTA 1960
NIGERIA 1960
SIERRA LEONE 1961
IVORY COAST 1960
GHANA 1957
CAMEROON 1960-1
CENTRAL AFRICAN REPUBLIC 1960
SOMALIA 1960
GABON 1960
CONGO 1960
ZAIRE (DEM. REP. OF CONGO) 1960
UGANDA 1962
KENYA (1952-9) 1963
RWANDA 1962
BURUNDI 1962
TANGANYIKA (TANZANIA) 1964
ANGOLA (1961-74) 1975
MALAWI 1964
MOZAMBIQUE (1964-74) 1975
ZAMBIA 1964
NAMIBIA (1971-89) 1990
ZIMBABWE 1980
MADAGASCAR (1947-8) 1960
BOTSWANA 1966
SWAZILAND 1968
LESOTHO 1966

Timeline

1940-1 Italy gives up Eritrea, Somalia and Ethiopia.

1945 Japan abandons its East Asian conquests.

1946 The Philippines become independent from the USA.

1947 India and Pakistan become independent of Britain (August 15).

1948 Burma becomes independent from Britain.

1948-60 Malayan communists wage guerrilla war against Britain.

1949 Indonesia becomes independent of the Netherlands.

1952-7 Mau Mau rebels in Kenya battle British colonial forces.

1954 Vietnamese forces defeat France at Dien Bien Phu.

1954-62 The Algerian war for independence brings France close to civil war.

1955-9 The EOKA pro-Greek terrorist campaign divides Cyprus.

1956 Britain and France intervene unsuccessfully in Egypt's Suez Crisis.

1957 Malaya and Ghana gain independence from Britain.

Israel

Jewish immigration to Palestine began in the Ottoman period (to 1918), inspired by **Zionism**, the political movement for a Jewish homeland. Immigration increased under the **British Mandate** (from 1923), leading to unrest between Jews and Palestinian Arabs. In 1947, after a Jewish **terrorist campaign**, the UN devised a plan to partition Palestine into separate Jewish and Arab states. The state of Israel was proclaimed on May 14, 1948, under **David Ben-Gurion** (1886-1973), and survived immediate attack by the **Arab League** (Egypt, Transjordan, Syria, Iraq and Lebanon). Israel won further wars in 1967 (the **Six Day War**) and in 1973 (the **Yom Kippur War**).

Lost leader For a time Sukarno was revered by the Indonesian people, but his adoption of Maoist ideas led to his downfall.

Indonesia

The Netherlands ruled the 'East Indies' from the early 17th century. The Partai Nasional Indonesia (PNI) was formed in 1927 by **Sukarno** (1901-70), under whom Indonesia gained quasi-independence in 1942, during the Japanese occupation. Sukarno declared full independence on the Japanese surrender in 1945. The returning Dutch faced a guerrilla war (1945-9) and granted independence to Indonesia in 1949, though they retained **Ambon** (to 1950) and **Western New Guinea** (until 1963). Sukarno's autocratic rule provoked a military coup in 1965 that effectively removed him from power.

East Timor was ruled by Portugal from 1702. After the Portuguese revolution in 1974, the **Fretilin** movement proclaimed independence, but East Timor was invaded by **Indonesia**. UN intervention in 1999 finally brought independence.

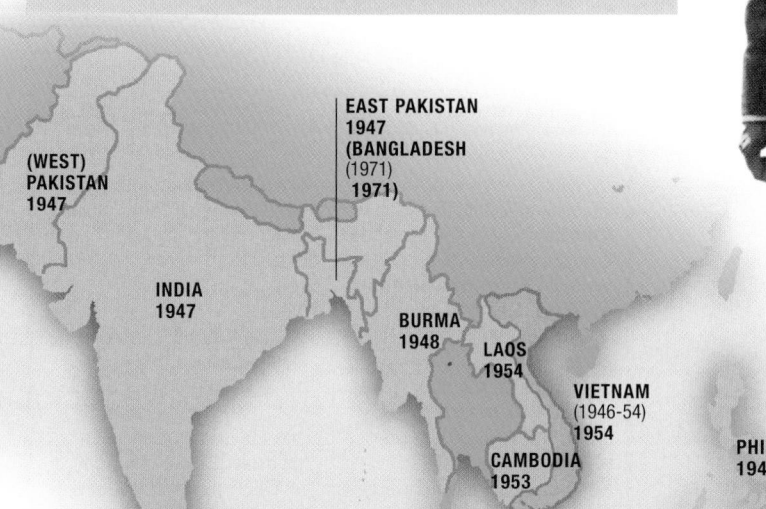

(WEST) PAKISTAN 1947

EAST PAKISTAN 1947 (BANGLADESH (1971) 1971)

INDIA 1947

BURMA 1948

LAOS 1954

VIETNAM (1946-54) 1954

CAMBODIA 1953

PHILIPPINES 1946

BRUNEI 1984

MALAYSIA (1948-66) 1957-63

INDONESIA (1945-9) 1949-63

EAST TIMOR (1975-99) 1975, 1999

PAPUA NEW GUINEA 1975

see also

214-5 **Second World War**
218-9 **The Cold War**
220-1 **New world order**

India and Pakistan

India had been controlled by Britain since the 18th century. The **Indian National Congress** was founded in 1885 and in the 1920s and 1930s pressed for independence under the leadership of **Jawaharlal Nehru** (1880-1964) and **Mohandas Gandhi** (1869-1948). Meanwhile, the **Muslim League** (founded 1905) demanded a separate Muslim state (**Pakistan**). Amid escalating violence after 1945, Britain proposed two separate states; independence came into effect on August 15, 1947.

Malaysia

Malaya had been ruled by Britain since the early 19th century. In 1946, control was offered to the Malay sultans but unrest and guerrilla war followed, led by the Communist Party (the **Malayan Emergency**, 1948-60). Independence was granted on August 31, 1957, but the war continued. **Malaysia** was formed in 1963 by Malaya, Sarawak, Sabah and Singapore (ejected 1965).

Malayan Emergency Every peasant became a communist suspect.

1960 Cyprus gains independence from Britain.

1963 Indonesia seizes Western New Guinea (Irian Jaya) from the Dutch.

1965 Singapore becomes independent of Malaya.

1967 Britain withdraws from Aden, a major strategic base.

1971 East Pakistan (Bangladesh) wins independence from Pakistan.

1975 Indonesia seizes Portuguese East Timor.

1997 Britain returns Hong Kong to China.

1961 Indian forces seize Portugal's colonies of Goa, Daman and Diu.

1964 Malta gains independence from Britain.

1965-75 The USA is drawn into the Vietnam War.

1968 Britain announces the withdrawal of all forces east of Suez.

1974 A left-wing revolution in Portugal ends Portuguese colonialism.

1980 Southern Rhodesia becomes independent as Zimbabwe

1999 Portugal returns Macau to China.

The USA and the USSR emerged from the Second World War as the planet's superpowers. Their opposing ideologies shaped international politics for 45 years. The threat of nuclear destruction held both sides back from war; instead they maintained a nervous and uneasy truce, a 'cold war' characterised by political posturing, spying and small proxy wars fought in other territories.

Behind the Iron Curtain

Winston Churchill used the term 'Iron Curtain' at Fulton, USA, in 1946 to refer to the divide between the Soviet bloc (USSR and its East European satellites) and the West. It became a physical reality as the East retreated behind closely guarded borders.

The **Berlin Airlift** was an early Cold War confrontation. Berlin consisted of four Allied zones, but the whole city lay within the Soviet bloc. In retaliation for currency reforms in West Germany, the USSR cut off all land links to West Berlin (June 1948). The Western Allies kept West Berlin supplied by an airlift, until the blockade was lifted in May 1949.

On the death of Stalin, some countries in Eastern Europe sought a more liberal communist policy.

In October 1956, the **Hungarian Uprising** occurred in support of the reformist government of **Imre Nagy** (1896-1958), who announced Hungary's withdrawal from the Warsaw Pact. Soviet troops invaded on November 4 and crushed the revolt.

In 1968, Czechoslovakia saw a period of liberalisation (the **Prague Spring**) under premier **Alexander Dubcek**, who attempted to introduce 'socialism with a human face'. The USSR invaded on August 20 to crush the revolt. Dubcek was replaced in April 1969.

The military balance in the early 1960s

NATO
Founder members (1949): Belgium, Canada, Denmark, France (withdrew forces 1966), Iceland, Italy, Luxembourg, Netherlands, Norway, Portugal, UK, USA; plus Greece (1952), Turkey (1952), West Germany (1955), Spain (1982)

Warsaw Treaty
(created 1955, disbanded 1991) USSR, Bulgaria, East Germany, Czechoslovakia, Hungary, Poland, Albania (to 1968), Romania

Ground forces
8 million | 7.7 million

Battleships and aircraft carriers
76 |

Submarines
nuclear 32 conventional 260 | nuclear 12 conventional 495

Tanks
16 000 | 38 000

Bomber aircraft
2260 | 1600

Intercontinental and medium-range ballistic missiles
700 | 776

Korea

The former Japanese-occupied territory of Korea was divided in 1946 into (pro-Soviet) North Korea and (pro-Western) South Korea. In June 1950, South Korea was invaded by the North, leading to the intervention of a largely US **United Nations** force. A massive **Chinese** counteroffensive in support of the North (January 1951) resulted in a stalemate along the border. An **armistice** was signed in 1953, and the two Koreas remain strictly divided by a Demilitarised Zone (DMZ).

Cuba and the missile crisis

In 1959 a left-wing revolution led by **Fidel Castro** (1927-) ousted the corrupt regime of the dictator **Fulgencio Batista** in Cuba. Castro was a lawyer who had previously been exiled to the USA and Mexico. The revolution was initially welcomed by the USA, but relations soured as Castro nationalised American-owned property and declared himself a Marxist. His revolutionary comrade **Ernesto 'Che' Guevara** (1928-67) began to transfer Cuba's economic ties from the USA to the USSR.

After US-backed Cuban exiles mounted a failed invasion at the **Bay of Pigs** (1961), Castro turned increasingly to the USSR for political support. In 1962 he permitted the USSR to build **missile bases** in Cuba; these were detected by US aerial surveys (see right) on October 14. The USA saw this as a direct threat and blockaded Cuba: President **John F. Kennedy** told the Soviet leader **Nikita**

Khrushchev to withdraw the missiles or face nuclear attack. The world appeared to be on the brink of all-out conflict, but the USSR backed down (October 26) and removed the missiles. This was the most dangerous moment of the Cold War: thereafter USA and USSR began to seek **'peaceful coexistence'**.

Castro's regime had a major influence on left-wing liberation movements in South America and Africa. Che Guevara was killed in Bolivia attempting to incite communist revolt. But the collapse of the USSR in 1990 has left Cuba isolated.

1946-9 Communist governments take over in Bulgaria, Hungary, Romania and Poland.

1948-9 The Soviet blockade of Berlin is broken by the 'Berlin Airlift'.

1950 China supports North Korea against UN forces in the Korean War (to 1953).

1956 Soviet troops crush a popular uprising in Hungary.

1962 The USA and USSR come close to nuclear war in the Cuban Missile Crisis.

1945

1950

1960

1945 The Allied summit at Yalta divides Europe into postwar spheres of influence.

1948 Communists seize power in Czechoslovakia.

1949 Communists win the Chinese civil war; the USSR explodes its first atomic bomb.

1955 The Warsaw Pact treaty is signed by the USSR and its allies.

1959 Fidel Castro's leftist forces seize power in Cuba.

1964 The USA intervenes militarily in Vietnam against communist forces.

Africa

Much of Africa was granted independence in the 1960s. The main theatres of conflict were the Portuguese colonies, which were denied independence until 1975.

Civil war occurred in **Angola** from 1974 between the leftist MPLA (backed by the USSR and Cuba) and UNITA (backed by South Africa and the USA). The MPLA took power in 1975, but sporadic fighting continues. **Mozambique**'s Marxist independence movement FRELIMO took power in 1975.

South Africa supported the RENAMO guerrillas in a 16-year civil war (to 1992).

The socialist regime of **Gamal Abdul Nasser** (1918-70) of **Egypt** accepted Soviet aid after the Suez Crisis (1956). Nasser's successor **Anwar Sadat** (1918-81) cultivated US links from 1972.

Emperor Haile Selassie of **Ethiopia** was overthrown in a socialist coup in 1974, by Colonel **Haile Mariam Mengistu** with Soviet backing. Mengistu's repressive rule lasted until 1991.

Indochina

Vietnam, Cambodia and Laos (**French Indochina**) were occupied by the **Japanese** in the Second World War. Each produced communist independence movements that resisted the return of French colonial rule after the war.

The communist **Vietnamese Republic** led by **Ho Chi Minh** (1890-1969) defeated the French at **Dien Bien Phu** (1954). The country was then divided into communist North Vietnam and non-communist South Vietnam.

US intervention to prevent reunification led to the full-scale **Vietnam War** (1964-73). North Vietnam overran South Vietnam in 1975.

In the parallel civil war in **Laos**, victory for the communist **Pathet Lao** also came in 1975.

In **Cambodia**, the victory of the communist **Khmer Rouge** in 1975 led to a regime of extreme brutality under which 2 million people died. Vietnam invaded in 1979 to depose the Khmer Rouge, finally withdrawing in 1989.

Latin America

Under the Monroe Doctrine of 1823, the USA opposed all outside intervention in the Americas. After 1945, the doctrine came to mean resistance to communist regimes, even where they were supported by the local people.

Leftist reforms in **Guatemala** provoked a US-inspired military coup in 1954. The resulting guerrilla war (1960-96) saw the unleashing of right-wing death squads and terrorism.

A civil war (1980-92) in **El Salvador** between the US-backed government and the leftist FMLN guerrillas claimed 75 000 lives.

In **Nicaragua**, the corrupt, US-backed Somoza regime was overthrown in 1979. The USA then supported 'Contra' rebels in a brutal ten-year civil war.

A communist government under **Salvador Allende** was elected in 1970 in **Chile**. A US-sponsored military coup under **Augusto Pinochet** led to repression and systematic elimination of political opponents.

Face of resistance A young Sandinista guerrilla wears a mask to hide his identity. The popular left-wing movement took power in Nicaragua in 1979, provoking a violent US-financed backlash.

see also
214–5 **Second World War**
216-7 **End of empire**
220-1 **New world order**
578-9 **Weapons of war**

China

The Chinese communists led by **Mao Ze-dong** (1893-1976) emerged victorious from the civil war of 1946-9; the US-backed Nationalists retreated to **Taiwan**. The communists then began a series of campaigns, led by the **People's Liberation Army** (PLA) to purge China of 'class enemies'. These included the **Great Leap Forward** of 1958-60 (a programme of land collectivisation) and the disastrous **Cultural Revolution** (1965-76), which brought the country close to anarchy. China split with the USSR in the late 1950s over ideological and territorial disputes. A thaw in relations with the USA followed a visit by President **Richard Nixon** in 1972. Communist ideology softened after Mao's death, leading to a slow movement towards a **market economy**.

Mao Ze-dong

1972 The USA launches a policy of détente towards the USSR and China.

1979 Soviet troops invade Afghanistan.

1983 The USA announces its 'Star Wars' satellite-based Strategic Defense Initiative.

1987 The USA and USSR remove intermediate-range nuclear weapons from Europe.

1989 Chinese troops crush a student protest in Tiananmen Square, Beijing.

1970   1980   1990

1968 The USSR crushes a reformist government in Czechoslovakia.

1975 Communist forces finally defeat the US-backed regime in South Vietnam.

1981 Martial law is imposed in Poland to curb the Solidarity trade union.

1985 The reformist Mikhail Gorbachev comes to power in the USSR.

1989 The communist regimes of Eastern Europe are overthrown.

1990 The Cold War is declared ended.

In the final decades of the 20th century the Cold War was replaced by an era of glasnost and perestroika (openness and reform) in the USSR followed by the collapse of Communism in Eastern Europe. Tensions eased and a 'new world order' of cooperation seemed to beckon. But as the dust settled a more complex picture emerged. New nations struggled for stability, Islam became a political force and the USA sought a new role. A world of power blocs gave way to a mosaic of competing perspectives and ambitions.

Afghanistan

In 1973 Afghanistan's monarchy was overturned by the left-leaning general **Mohammed Daud Khan** in a military coup. Five years later Daud was assassinated and a Marxist regime installed. In 1979, fearful that Islamic opposition would topple a client government, the USSR occupied the country.

Soviet troops faced a guerrilla war against US-supplied Islamic fighters (**mujaheddin**). Some 14 000 Soviets died before Mikhail Gorbachev, under political pressure at home and hoping for economic aid from the West, finally withdrew his troops in 1988-9. Civil war ensued, effectively won when the **Taliban** took Kabul in 1996.

Middle East

Civil war between Christian and Muslim militias erupted in **Lebanon** in 1975-6. Israel invaded in 1978 and in 1982. Terrorist groups such as **Islamic Jihad** and **Hezbollah** organised the kidnapping of Western hostages in the late 1980s, and Israel finally withdrew from southern Lebanon in 2000.

Palestinian resentment within **Israel** erupted in December 1987 in open rebellion. The 1993 **Oslo Accords** established limited Palestinian self-rule, but extremist violence continued. In 1995, Israel's prime minister **Yitzhak Rabin** was assassinated by a Jewish radical. **Ehud Barak** (elected 1999) offered Palestinians a generous settlement, but popular revolts continued and even intensified, provoking the election of the hardline **Ariel Sharon** as Israel's leader in 2001.

1980 The trade union Solidarity is founded in Poland.

1980

1982 Argentina invades the Falkland Islands, triggering war with Britain.

1983 The USA's 'Star Wars' initiative puts huge pressure on Soviet defence spending.

1985

1987 The USA and USSR agree to cut intermediate nuclear missiles in Europe.

1988 The USSR begins troop withdrawals from Afghanistan (completed 1989).

1990

1991 Boris Yeltsin becomes the first elected leader of the Russian Republic.

The shah of Iran flees, ceding power to Ayatollah Khomeini's Islamic revolution.

1981 Ronald Reagan becomes US president (to 1988).

1985 Mikhail Gorbachev becomes leader of the USSR.

1986 An explosion at the Chernobyl nuclear reactor in the USSR accelerates demands for government openness.

1989 The Communist regimes in Eastern Europe are successively overthrown by their own citizens.

GULF WAR

Iran and Iraq

From the 1960s **Muhammad Reza Shah Pahlavi** began a programme of reform aimed at creating a modern secular state in Iran. However, inflation, corruption and the brutal suppression of opposition led to riots in 1977-8.

The shah fled in January 1979, and a fundamentalist Islamic republic headed by **Ayatollah Ruholla Khomeini** was set up. Hostility to the West led to the seizure of the US embassy in Tehran in 1979. In 1989 the moderate **Hashemi Rafsanjani** became secular president.

In 1980, President **Saddam Hussein** of Iraq took advantage of the turmoil in Iran to invade the country in retaliation for Iran's assistance to rebel Kurds in Iraq. This triggered the **Iran-Iraq War** (1980-8), fought mainly around the **Shatt al'Arab** waterway.

Although Iraq was supported by arms supplied by the West and the USSR, Iran held firm. There were over 1 million casualties before peace was re-established in 1988. Just two years later, Iraq invaded Kuwait and was again at war (see *Gulf War*).

By the end of the Iran-Iraq War, Iraq had amassed foreign debts of about $80 billion. Kuwait's refusal to give aid was the pretext for another war. In August 1990, Iraq invaded Kuwait and claimed it as an Iraqi province. A UN-sponsored international coalition, led by the USA, assembled forces in Saudi Arabia to liberate Kuwait (above). 'Operation Desert Storm', a 39 day campaign of aerial bombardment, was followed by a ground campaign that lasted four days before Kuwait was liberated and Iraq capitulated (February 1991). Iraqi casualties exceeded 200 000, while the allied forces lost fewer than 300 troops.

PERESTROIKA & GLASNOST

Mikhail **Gorbachev** became leader of the USSR in 1985, after a succession of ageing, unreforming Soviet leaders had brought the country to a state of **economic stagnation**.

Gorbachev tried to modernise Soviet communism under the banners of **perestroika** (economic and social restructuring) and **glasnost** (government openness and accountability). But the introduction of limited democracy, press freedoms and free enterprise, and the release of dissidents, led to an unstoppable drive to overturn Communist rule. As the USSR liberalised, so the satellite states of East and Central Europe one by one voted in free elections for non-Communist governments (1989-90). Then Soviet states began to break away from the Union. By 1991 the USSR had ceased to exist, and instead a nominal '**Commonwealth of Independent States**' (CIS), came into being.

Mikhail Gorbachev
Gorbachev unleashed forces that led to the USSR's demise.

see also
216–7 **End of empire**
218-9 **The Cold War**

1991 The USSR is disbanded and Gorbachev resigns.

1992 Bosnia-Herzegovina declares independence from Yugoslavia; the resulting civil war lasts to 1995.

1994 Nelson Mandela becomes president of South Africa (to 1999). The UN fails to stop massacres in Rwanda.

1995 UN troops fail to end a civil war in Somalia.

1995

1996 Yasser Arafat becomes president of Palestine. The Taliban (Sunni fundamentalists) take over Afghanistan.

1997 President Mobutu of Zaire is ousted by opposition forces led by Laurent Kabila.

1998 Indonesia's President Suharto is forced from office, after 30 years in power.

1999 Serb troops are driven out of Kosovo by a NATO bombing campaign.

2000

2000 Vladimir Putin is elected president of Russia; Israeli troops withdraw from Lebanon.

2001 George W. Bush takes office as president of the USA; Ariel Sharon is elected prime minister of Israel.

The collapse of Communism in Eastern Europe

Discontent with Communist rule flared up in the early 1980s in **Poland**, centred on the Gdansk shipyard where the **Solidarity** trade union was active. Solidarity was banned in 1982, but the ban was lifted in April 1989, leading to a Solidarity victory in free elections in June, and the first non-Communist government in the Soviet bloc. In September **Hungary** opened its border with Austria and a mass exodus began of East Germans heading for the West. The Hungarian government declared a new republic, promising multiparty elections (held in 1990) and disbanding the Communist Party. Soon the spark of reform had become a blaze. By the end of 1989 **Erich Honecker** had resigned in East Germany and the **Berlin Wall** was down (below). In 1990 Czechoslovakia, Romania and some Yugoslav republics acquired non-Communist governments. States of the Soviet Union, starting with **Lithuania** and **Latvia**, pushed for independence, and in 1991 after an unsuccessful Communist coup the USSR was dissolved. The new governments of Eastern Europe faced many problems. Centralised economies had to be restructured and new political institutions established. Germany battled with the massive task of reunification, and regional tensions revived in many places, spilling over into war in the Balkans and Chechnya.

South Africa

International pressure on South Africa to abandon its policy of **apartheid** (racial segregation weighted in favour of the white minority) increased in the 1980s. Trade sanctions and cultural and sporting bans were imposed by many countries, creating a sense of isolation and damaging the economy. In 1989 **P.W. Botha** resigned as leader of the ruling National Party, to be replaced by moderate and reforming **F.W. de Klerk**. In 1990, de Klerk lifted the ban on the **African National Congress** (ANC) – the main black political party – and released the ANC leader **Nelson Mandela** after 27 years of imprisonment. The remaining apartheid legislation was removed in July 1991. Nonracial **free elections** were held for the first time in South Africa in April 1994, giving an overwhelming victory to the ANC, and Nelson Mandela became president.

Peoples and nations

Peoples and nations

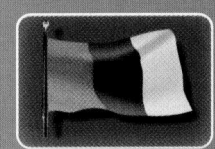

A century ago much of the world was divided up between empires; today it is dominated by sovereign states. With a total land area of 148 million km² (57 million sq miles), Earth is now home to 6 billion people – more than three times the number in 1900 and twice as many as in 1960.

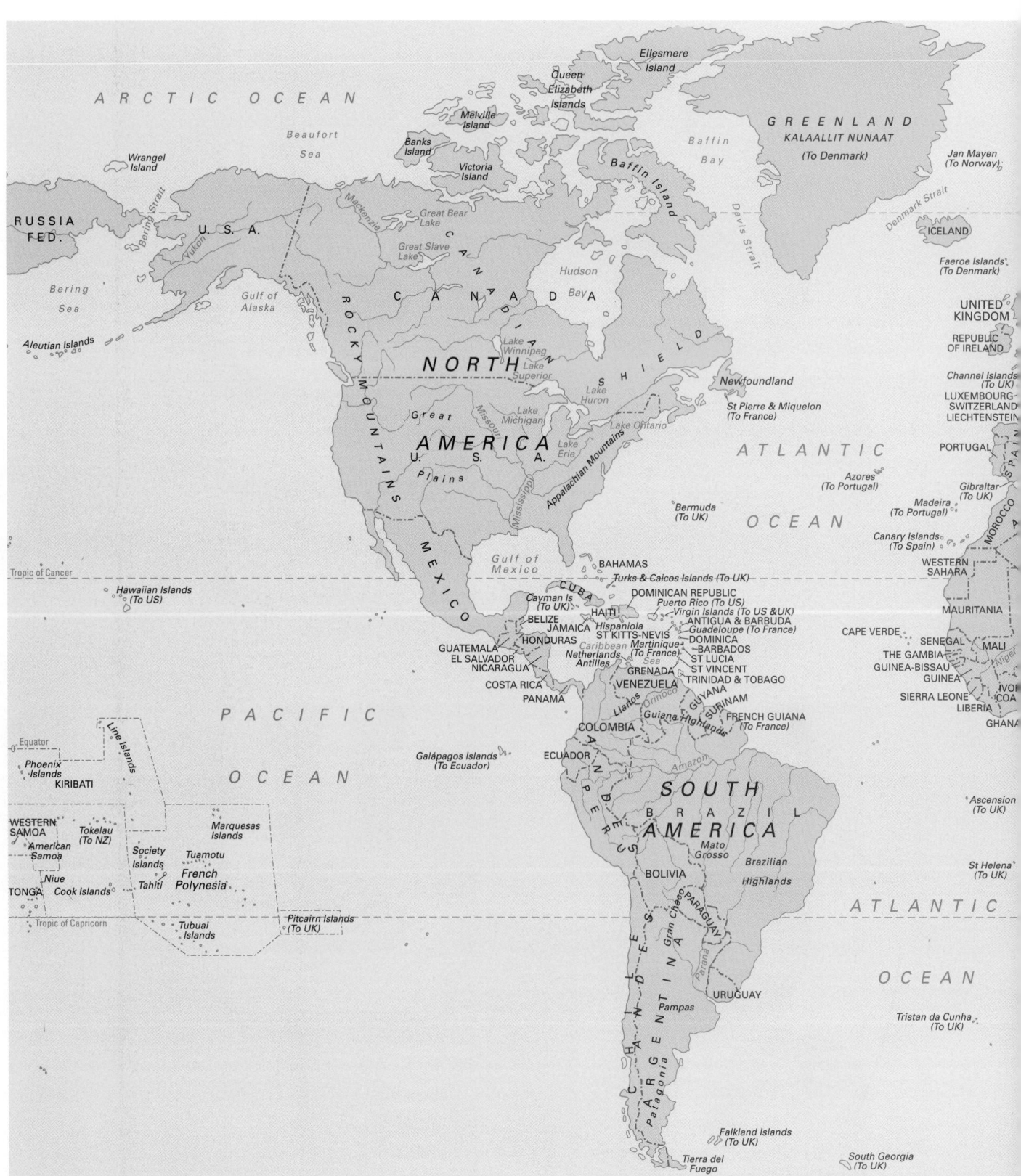

1 SLOVENIA
2 CROATIA
3 BOSNIA & HERZEGOVINA
4 YUGOSLAVIA
5 MACEDONIA
6 ALBANIA

ARCTIC OCEAN

Zemlya Frantsa Iosifa

Severnaya
Zemlya

Novosibirskiye
Ostrova

Svalbard
(To Norway)

Barents
Sea

Novaya
Zemlya

Kara
Sea

Laptev
Sea

East Siberian
Sea

Wrangel
Island

Arctic
Circle

Norwegian
Sea

RUSSIAN

Central
Siberian
Plateau

Bering
Sea

Sea of
Okhotsk

NORWAY
SWEDEN
FINLAND

Lake
Onega

URALS

FEDERATION

Ob

SIBERIA

Yenisey

Lena

Amur

ESTONIA
Lake
Ladoga

West
Siberian
Plain

Sakhalin

DENMARK
NETHERLANDS
BELGIUM
GERMANY
RUS.
LITHUANIA
LATVIA
BELARUS
POLAND

Baltic Sea

Central
Russian
Uplands

Volga

KAZAKHSTAN

Lake
Balkhash

MONGOLIA

Lake
Baykal

Altai

ASIA

Kuril Islands

Hokkaido

EUROPE
UKRAINE

Aral
Sea

Gobi Desert

Sea of
Japan

FRANCE
CZECH
REP.
SLOVAKIA
AUSTRIA
HUNGARY
MOLDOVA
ROMANIA

Black Sea

GEORGIA

Caspian Sea

UZBEKISTAN

KYRGYZSTAN

Tien Shan

Huang
He

NORTH
KOREA

Honshu

JAPAN

ITALY
SAN
MARINO
MONACO
ANDORRA
VATICAN
CITY

Kara
Kum

TURKMENISTAN

TAJIKISTAN

Taklimakan

CHINA

SOUTH
KOREA

Yellow
Sea

BULGARIA

ARMENIA

Caucasus

AZERBAIJAN

Elburz Mts

Kunlun Shan

Chang Jiang

East
China
Sea

PACIFIC

GREECE
TURKEY

CYPRUS
LEBANON
SYRIA
ISRAEL
JORDAN

IRAQ

IRAN

Zagros Mts

AFGHANISTAN

PAKISTAN

HIMALAYA

Xizang
(Tibet)

Brahmaputra

Okinawa
(To Japan)

Bonin Islands
(To Japan)

OCEAN

Mediterranean Sea

TUNISIA
MALTA

NEPAL

BHUTAN

TAIWAN

Northern
Marianas
(To US)

LIBYA
EGYPT

KUWAIT

BAHRAIN
QATAR
SAUDI
ARABIA

U.A.E.

The Gulf

Gulf of Oman

OMAN

INDIA

Ganges

Hong Kong
Macau

MARSHALL
ISLANDS

SAHARA

Nile

Red Sea

Rub al-Khali

Arabian
Sea

Deccan

Bay of
Bengal

MYANMAR
(BURMA)

LAOS

VIETNAM

Luzon

Guam
(To US)

ALGERIA

NIGER
CHAD
SUDAN

ERITREA

YEMEN

Gulf of Aden

DJIBOUTI

Lakshadweep
(To India)

Andaman
Islands
(To India)

THAILAND

South
China
Sea

PHILIPPINES

Caroline Islands

MICRONESIA

AFRICA

Ethiopian
Plateau
ETHIOPIA

CAMBODIA

Mindanao

NIGERIA
BURKINA
CAMEROON
C.A.R.
GREAT
RIFT
VALLEY

SRI
LANKA

Nicobar
Islands
(To India)

BRUNEI

PALAU

CONGO
GABON
EQUAT.
GUINEA
Gulf of
Guinea
SÃO
TOMÉ
& PRÍNCIPE

UGANDA

KENYA

SOMALIA

MALDIVES

MALAYSIA

Celebes
Sea

NAURU

KIRIBATI

DEM. REP.
OF THE
CONGO

Lake
Victoria

RWANDA
BURUNDI

SINGAPORE

Borneo

Sulawesi

Moluccas

GREAT RIFT VALLEY

TANZANIA

Lake
Tanganyika

SEYCHELLES

British Indian
Ocean Territory
(Chagos Archipelago)

Sumatra

INDONESIA

Java sea

Banda
Sea

New
Guinea

PAPUA
NEW GUINEA

Bougainville

SOLOMON
ISLANDS

Lake
Malawi

Java

Arafura
Sea

New
Britain

TUVALU

ANGOLA

COMOROS

Cocos Islands
(To Australia)

Christmas
Island
(To Australia)

Timor
Sea

Coral
Sea

ZAMBIA

Zambezi

MALAWI

INDIAN

VANUATU

FIJI

ZIMBABWE

MADAGASCAR

Mozambique Channel

MAURITIUS

OCEAN

Great
Sandy
Desert

Great
Artesian

Great Dividing Range

New
Caledonia
(To France)

Norfolk
Island
(To Australia)

NAMIBIA

BOTSWANA

MOZAMBIQUE

Réunion
(To France)

AUSTRALIA

Basin

Kalahari
Desert

Orange

SWAZILAND

Great
Victoria
Desert

SOUTH
AFRICA
LESOTHO

Drakensberg

Great
Australian
Bight

Darling

Murray

Tasman
Sea

NEW
ZEALAND

Tasmania

Kerguelen
(To France)

Heard Island
(To Australia)

World statistics

Land area The world's largest nation, Russia, accounts for more than 11 per cent of the total global land area, and is bigger than either Europe or Antarctica. The smallest, the Vatican City, covers just 44 hectares (109 acres). The figures include inland lakes and other waterways.

10 biggest countries

	Country	Area (km²)	(sq miles)
1.	Russia	17 075 400	6 592 850
2.	Canada	9 958 319	3 844 928
3.	United States	9 809 155	3 787 319
4.	China	9 571 300	3 695 500
5.	Brazil	8 511 996	3 286 500
6.	Australia	7 682 300	2 966 153
7.	India	3 287 263	1 269 219
8.	Argentina	2 766 889	1 068 302
9.	Kazakhstan	2 717 300	1 049 150
10.	Sudan	2 505 813	967 500

10 smallest countries

	Country	Area (km²)	(sq miles)
1.	Vatican City	0.44	0.17
2.	Monaco	1.95	0.75
3.	Nauru	21.3	8
4.	Tuvalu	26	10
5.	San Marino	61	24
6.	Liechtenstein	160	61.8
7.	Marshall Islands	180	70
8.	St Kitts & Nevis	261	101
9.	Maldives	298	115
10.	Malta	316	122

Population The world's most populous countries include many – but by no means all – of those that are the largest in area. Unsurprisingly, the smallest populations live correspondingly in some of the smallest island and landlocked nations. The figures are estimates for the year 2000.

10 largest populations

	Country	Population
1.	China	1 274 115 000
2.	India	1 030 000 000
3.	United States	281 421 906
4.	Indonesia	207 437 000
5.	Brazil	165 371 000
6.	Russia	145 943 000
7.	Pakistan	134 510 000
8.	Bangladesh	126 947 000
9.	Japan	126 505 000
10.	Nigeria	108 945 000

10 smallest populations

	Country	Population
1.	Vatican City	870
2.	Nauru	11 000
	Tuvalu	11 000
4.	Palau	18 000
5.	San Marino	26 000
6.	Liechtenstein	32 000
7.	Monaco	33 000
8.	St Kitts & Nevis	41 000
9.	Marshall Islands	61 000
10.	Antigua and Barbuda	67 000

Population density This is a better indicator of national social character than land area or population alone. Some of the world's smallest countries are the most crowded, and some of the largest are among the least densely peopled.

10 most densely populated countries

	Country	People per km²	per sq mile
1.	Monaco	16 410	42 667
2.	Singapore	5991	15 511
3.	Vatican City	1977	5118
4.	Malta	1203	3115
5.	Bahrain	921	2384
6.	Maldives	916	2374
7.	Bangladesh	845	2190
8.	Taiwan	604	1564
9.	Mauritius	569	1472
10.	Nauru	516	1341

10 least densely populated countries

	Country	People per km²	per sq mile
1.	Mongolia	1.53	3.96
2.	Namibia	2.01	5.21
3.	Australia	2.44	6.32
4.	Mauritania	2.45	6.35
5.	Surinam	2.51	6.5
6.	Iceland	2.63	6.81
7.	Botswana	2.7	6.99
8.	Libya	3.01	7.8
9.	Canada	3.04	7.87
10.	Guyana	3.95	10.23

Population growth rate Taken on its own, the rate of population growth says very little about a country. A high rate may be linked with high prosperity or go hand-in-hand with severe economic problems. Similarly, while many wealthy nations have a low or negative birth rate, so do those suffering from war or famine. The figures are for the five years up to 1999, for nations with populations of over 15 million.

10 fastest-growing populations

	Country	Growth rate (%)
1.	Egypt	3.4
2.	Tanzania	3.3
3.	Congo (Democratic Republic)	3.0
4.	Ethiopia	2.9
	Kenya	2.9
	Yemen	2.9
7.	Uganda	2.8
8.	Saudi Arabia	2.7
9.	Madagascar	2.6
10.	Syria	2.5

10 slowest-growing populations

	Country	Growth rate (%)
1.	Kazakhstan	−1.5
2.	Ukraine	−0.6
3.	Romania	−0.2
4.	Russia	−0.1
5.	Sudan	0.1
	Spain	0.1
	Italy	0.1
	Germany	0.1
	Japan	0.1
10.	United Kingdom	0.2

National wealth In terms of gross domestic product (GDP) – the total value of all the goods and services produced each year within a country – the major industrial nations dominate. The low GDP of Vatican City is due to its small size and to the fact that it has very little industry.

10 wealthiest countries

	Country	GDP (US million $)
1.	United States	9 178 000
2.	Japan	4 368 300
3.	Germany	2 149 600
4.	United Kingdom	1 463 800
5.	France	1 445 000
6.	Italy	1 176 400
7.	China	993 500
8.	Canada	638 900
9.	Spain	588 300
10.	Brazil	518 900

10 poorest countries

	Country	GDP (US million $)
1.	Tuvalu	9
2.	Vatican City	19
3.	São Tomé & Príncipe	35
4.	Kiribati	51
5.	Marshall Islands	91
6.	Palau	109
7.	Samoa	179
8.	Guinea-Bissau	205
9.	Comoros	207
10.	Dominica	244

Wealth per head This is a far better indicator of prosperity than overall GDP figures. However, it is not a satisfactory way of comparing relative living standards since it does not take into account differences in the cost of living. Most of the ten wealthiest nations are advanced industrial or 'post-industrial' societies, but Nauru has a small population enriched by huge mineral royalties.

10 wealthiest populations

	Country	GDP per head (US $)
1.	Luxembourg	45 348
2.	Liechtenstein	42 416
3.	Switzerland	37 428
4.	Japan	34 556
5.	Norway	34 356
6.	Denmark	33 981
7.	United States	33 922
8.	Nauru	33 476
9.	Iceland	30 627
10.	Sweden	27 536

10 poorest populations

	Country	GDP per head (US $)
1.	Democratic Republic of the Congo	18
2.	Ethiopia	94
3.	Myanmar (Burma)	122
4.	Bhutan	147
5.	Burundi	152
6.	Sierra Leone	153
7.	Tajikistan	163
8.	Malawi	173
9.	Guinea-Bissau	176
10.	North Korea	187

Life expectancy This is linked to prosperity, but also to lifestyle, availability of food and medical services, and other factors. In much of sub-Saharan Africa the spread of HIV/AIDS has had an effect in recent years. The figures are estimates for 2000 of life expectancy at birth; in most 'bottom ten' countries many children die in infancy, so the life expectancy for adults is significantly higher than these figures imply.

10 highest life expectancy

	Country	Life expectancy (years) (average of male and female)
1.	Japan	79.5
2.	Andorra	79
3.	Sweden	78.5
	Switzerland	78.5
5.	Iceland	78
	Monaco	78
7.	Australia	77.5
	Canada	77.5
	Greece	77.5
	Iraq	77.5

10 lowest life expectancy

	Country	Life expectancy (years) (average of male and female)
1.	Sierra Leone	34
2.	Uganda	41
3.	Guinea-Bisau	42.5
4.	Afghanistan	43.5
5.	Burundi	44.5
	Guinea	44.5
	Malawi	44.5
8.	The Gambia	45
9.	Ethiopia	45.5
	Mozambique	45.5

Literacy Poor education is another common result of low national and/or indvidual wealth – and is one of the major factors in holding back economic improvement. The figures are from UNESCO for the years 1996-8.

10 lowest literacy rates

	Country	Adult literacy rate (%)
1.	Niger	13.6
2.	Burkina	19.2
3.	Eritrea	20
4.	Somalia	24.1
5.	Nepal	27.5
6.	Mali	31
7.	Sierra Leone	31.4
8.	Afghanistan	31.5
9.	Senegal	33.1
10.	Cambodia	35

see also
454-5 **Wealth map of world**

ICELAND

OFFICIAL NAME
The Republic of Iceland

CAPITAL
Reykjavik

Area 103 000 km²
(39 769 sq miles)
Population 279 000
Population density 3 per km²
(7 per sq mile)
Population growth rate 1.1%
Life expectancy 76 (m); 80 (f)

Language Icelandic
Adult literacy rate 99%
Currency Icelandic krona
(US $1 = 93 krona)
GDP (US million $) 8300
GDP per head (US $) 30 627

Key dates

*c.*870 First Viking
settlements.
930 Establishes Althing,
world's first parliament.
1262 Althing accepts
rule by king of Norway.
1380 Comes under
Danish rule.
Late 18thC Famine after
volcanic eruptions
destroy farmland.
1918 Independence
under Danish crown.
1940-5 British and
American garrison to
prevent German invasion
in Second World War.
1944 Declares fully
independent republic.
1976 'Cod war' with UK
over fishing rights.

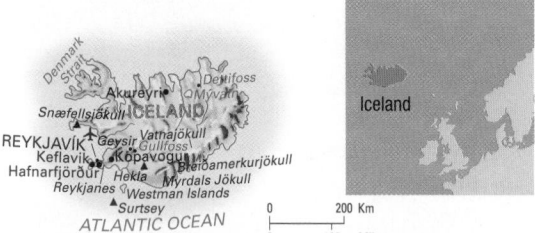

Centrally heated Iceland's capital Reykjavik is
entirely heated by geothermal energy – which also
provides much of the country's electric power.

IRELAND

OFFICIAL NAME
The Republic of Ireland

CAPITAL
Dublin

Area 70 285 km²
(27 137 sq miles)
Population 3 745 000
Population density 53 per km² (136 per sq mile)
Population growth rate 0.6%
Life expectancy 72 (m); 78 (f)
Languages Irish, English
Adult literacy rate 99%
Currency Irish pound (punt)
(US $1 = 0.87 Irish pound)
GDP (US million $) 86 900
GDP per head (US $) 23 486

FACT
The Irish adopted
the harp as their
symbol after the
occupying English
banned them from
playing bagpipes.

Key dates

1601 Battle of Kinsale
establishes English rule.
1695 Battle of the
Boyne leads to
Protestant supremacy.
1801 All Ireland becomes
part of United Kingdom.
1846-51 Famine kills
1 million; more than
1 million emigrate.
1916 British suppress
Easter Rising in Dublin;
15 leaders executed.
1919 Nationalists form
parliament (Dail) and
Irish Republican Army.
1921 Anglo-Irish Treaty
establishes Irish Free
State (dominion under
British crown); Northern
Ireland remains British.
1937 Independent Eire
established.
1949 Becomes republic.
1969-94 'Troubles' over
Northern Ireland.
1973 Joins European
Community.
1998 Good Friday
peace agreement
comes into force.

UNITED KINGDOM

OFFICIAL NAME
The United Kingdom of
Great Britain and Northern
Ireland

CAPITAL
London

Area 241 752 km²
(93 341 sq miles)
Population 59 200 000
Population density 245 per
km² (634 per sq mile)
Population growth rate 0.2%
Life expectancy 74 (m); 79 (f)
Languages English, Welsh
Adult literacy rate 99%
Currency pound sterling (£)
(US $1 = £0.69)
GDP (US million $) 1 463 800
GDP per head (US $) 24 726

Key dates

AD 43 Roman invasion.
*c.*410 Last Roman
troops leave Britain.
1066 Norman invasion.
1215 Magna Carta limits
power of king.
1337-1453 Hundred
Years' War in France.
1588 Defeat of Spanish
Armada.
1603 Union of English
and Scottish kingdoms
under James I and VI.
1642-51 English Civil
Wars; king deposed.
1660 Crown restored.
1688 Parliament
deposes James II in
'Glorious Revolution'.
1707 Act of Union joins
England and Scotland
as United Kingdom of
Great Britain.
1801 Ireland made part
of United Kingdom.
1815 Battle of Waterloo
ends Napoleonic Wars.
1914-18 First World War.
1939-45 Second World
War.
1945-51 'Welfare state'
created.
1960 Founder-member
of European Free Trade
Association.
1973 Joins European
Community.
1982 Falklands War.
1999 Scottish
parliament and Welsh
assembly established.

Cape Wrath · Dounreay · Pentland Firth · John o'Groats · Scrabster · Muckle Flugga · Shetland Islands · SHETLAND · Lerwick · Jarlshof · Fair Isle · Callanish (Calanais) · Stornoway (Steornabhagh) · Lewis (Leodhas) · Hebrides · The Minch · St Kilda · Tarbert (Tairbeart) · Ullapool · The · Moray Firth · Culbin Sands · Lochmaddy · North Uist · Uig · Inverness · Culloden · Sands of Forvie · Outer · South Uist · Lochboisdale · Skye · Loch Ness · Falls of Glomach · Aviemore · Cairngorm Mts · Aberdeen · Orkney Islands · ORKNEY · Skara Brae · Stromness · Kirkwall · Old Man of Hoy · Scapa Flow · Pentland Firth · Dounreay · Scrabster · John o'Groats · Barra · Castlebay · Rùm · Sound of Sleat · Mallaig · Fort William · Ben Nevis 1344m · Balmoral Castle · HIGHLANDS · NORTH SEA · Coll · Arinagour · Scarinish · Tiree · Staffa · Iona · Mull · Craignure · Oban · Achnacroish · Glen Coe · Bannoch Moor · Dundee · Perth · Tay Bridges · St Andrews · Colonsay · Scalasaig · Jura · The Trossachs · Stirling · Forth Bridges · Bass Rock · ATLANTIC OCEAN · Port Askaig · Islay · Greenock · Loch Lomond · Antonine Wall · Glasgow · Edinburgh · Traprain Law · Berwick-upon-Tweed · Port Ellen · Whitehouse · New Lanark · Arran · Kintyre · Ardrossan · Melrose · Tweed · Holy Island · Ayr · Giant's Causeway · Rathlin Island · Ailsa Craig · Cheviot Hills · Whin Sill · Newcastle upon Tyne · Coleraine · Dumfries · Gretna Green · Hadrian's Wall · Londonderry · Ballymena · North Channel · Cairnryan · Stranraer · Carlisle · Sunderland · Durham · Peterlee · NORTHERN · ULSTER · Lough Neagh · Antrim · Bangor · Carrickfergus · Dungannon · Lurgan · Belfast · Solway Firth · Lake District · Ullswater · Stockton-on-Tees · Middlesbrough · Cleveland Hills · Whitby · IRELAND · Lisburn · Sellafield · Windermere · Enniskillen · Armagh · DOWN · Scafell Pike 978m · Windermere · Scarborough · Newry · Mourne Mts · Douglas · Barrow-in-Furness · Lancaster · Ripon · Fountains Abbey · The Wolds · Flamborough Head · REPUBLIC OF IRELAND · IRISH SEA · Heysham · Harrogate · York · Fleetwood · Haworth · Leeds · Ouse · Kingston upon Hull · Spurn Head · Blackpool · Preston · Bradford · Blackburn · Wakefield · Doncaster · Grimsby · Liverpool Bay · Rochdale · Huddersfield · Peak · Rotherham · The Wolds · Holyhead · Anglesey · Llandudno · Bolton · Wigan · Manchester · Stockport · Sheffield · Lincoln · Warrington · Macclesfield · Trent · Menai Strait · Caernarfon · Chester · Crewe · Stoke-on-Trent · Nottingham · Boston · The Wash · Snowdonia · Wrexham · The Potteries · Derby · Vale of Belvoir · Lleyn Peninsula · Llangollen · ENGLAND · The Broads · Tremadog Bay · Mountains · Shrewsbury · Stafford · The Black Country · Rutland · Stamford · Norwich · Great Yarmouth · Cardigan Bay · Aberystwyth · 752m Plynlimon · Walsall · West Bromwich · Leicester · Corby · Peterborough · Fens · Breckland · East Anglia · Birmingham · Coventry · Rugby · Ely · Bury St Edmunds · WALES · Ludlow · Worcester · Stratford-upon-Avon · Northampton · Cambridge · Lavenham · Ipswich · Aldeburgh · Fishguard · Hereford · Midlands · Bedford · Milton Keynes · Harwich · Felixstowe · St David's · Mynydd Preseli · Black Mts · Ledbury · Gloucester · Cheltenham · Oxford · Luton · Stevenage · Colchester · Milford Haven · Swansea · Gower · Brecon Beacons · Forest of Dean · Cotswold Hills · Chiltern Hills · Harlow · Welwyn Garden City · Pembroke Dock · Caerleon · Vale of White Horse · St Albans · LONDON · Epping Forest · Southend-on-Sea · Cardiff · Bristol · Bath · Avebury · Reading · Windsor · Thames · Rochester · Sheerness · Ramsgate · Bristol Channel · Mendip Hills · Stonehenge · Guildford · Runnymede · Chatham · Gillingham · Canterbury · Goodwin Sands · Lundy · Exmoor · Glastonbury · Salisbury · North Downs · The Weald · Dover · St George's Channel · Taunton · Winchester · South Downs · Battle · Dungeness · Strait of Dover · Channel Tunnel · New Forest · Chichester · Brighton · Hastings · Eastbourne · Tintagel · Bodmin Moor · Dartmoor · Torquay · Lyme Bay · Chesil Beach · Portland Bill · Bournemouth · Poole · Dorchester · Weymouth · The Needles · Ryde · Spithead · The Solent · Newhaven · Beachy Head · Channel Islands · Exeter · Plymouth · Tor Bay · Penzance · Lands End · Truro · Falmouth · St Michael's Mount · Mount's Bay · Lizard Point · Isles of Scilly · United Kingdom · Km 0 50 100 · Miles 0 50

At the outbreak of the Second World War, the United Kingdom was the centre of the biggest empire in history. Over the following decades the British Empire evolved into the Commonwealth, a unique association of self-governing nations in which Britain is one among more than 50 equals. It is still in partnership with 13 overseas territories and two crown dependencies (which are ruled by the British monarchy but are self-governing).

UK DEVOLUTION

The United Kingdom became a little less united in 1997 when Scottish and Welsh voters approved proposals for greater self-government. A year later the people of Northern Ireland did the same by approving the 'Good Friday Agreement'.

Scotland gained a law making Parliament able to set some taxes. When the 129 newly elected members assembled on May 12, 1999, Scotland had its first independent government since the union with England in 1707.

The less powerful Welsh Assembly assumed only the duties of the UK government's Welsh Office. The 60 members can make decisions about the economy and public services, but cannot make laws or raise taxes. The Northern Ireland Assembly met in 1999 to resume home rule, suspended in 1986 because of terrorist violence.

Independent commonwealth members

Country	Date joined	Country	Date joined	Country	Date joined	Country	Date joined
Antigua and Barbuda	1981	Gambia, The	1965	Mozambique	1995	Singapore	1965
Australia	1931	Ghana	1957	Namibia	1990	Solomon Islands	1978
Bahamas	1973	Grenada	1974	Nauru	1968	South Africa	1931 (-1961);
Bangladesh	1972	Guyana	1966	New Zealand	1931		rejoined 1994
Barbados	1966	India	1947	Nigeria	1960	Sri Lanka	1948
Belize	1981	Jamaica	1962	Pakistan	1947	Swaziland	1968
Botswana	1966	Kenya	1963	Papua New Guinea	1975	Tanzania	1961
Britain	1931	Kiribati	1979	St Kitts and Nevis	1983	Tonga	1970
Brunei	1984	Lesotho	1966	St Lucia	1979	Trinidad and Tobago	1962
Cameroon	1995	Malawi	1964	St Vincent and		Tuvalu	1978
Canada	1931	Malaysia	1957	the Grenadines	1979	Uganda	1962
Cyprus	1961	Maldives	1982	Samoa	1970	Vanuatu	1980
Dominica	1978	Malta	1964	Seychelles	1976	Zambia	1964
Fiji Islands	1970	Mauritius	1968	Sierra Leone	1961	Zimbabwe	1980

UK crown dependences

	Date first came under British control
Channel Islands	1066
Isle of Man	1765

UK overseas territories

	Date first came under British administration
Anguilla	1650
Bermuda	1684
British Antarctic Territory	1908
British Indian Ocean Territory	1965
British Virgin Islands	1672
Cayman Islands	1670
Falkland Islands	1765/1833
Gibraltar	1704
Montserrat	1632
Pitcairn Islands	1790
St Helena and Dependencies	1659
South Georgia and South Sandwich Islands	1775
Turks and Caicos Islands	1765

UK Government expenditure 2000-1

Total spending by the British central government for the financial year 2000-1 amounted to around £365 billion. The chart on the right shows how the spending was divided up.

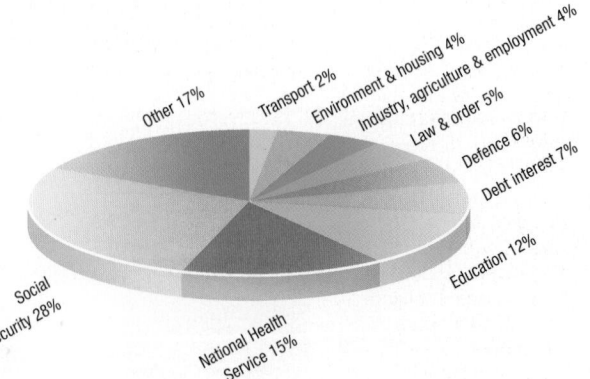

Other 17%
Transport 2%
Environment & housing 4%
Industry, agriculture & employment 4%
Law & order 5%
Defence 6%
Debt interest 7%
Education 12%
Social security 28%
National Health Service 15%

Population growth during the 20th century

Since 1900, the number of people in the UK has increased by more than half.

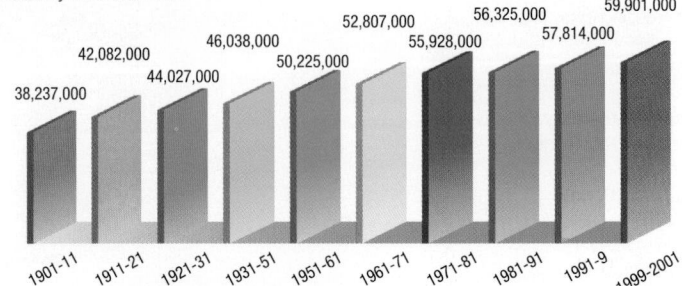

38,237,000
42,082,000
44,027,000
46,038,000
50,225,000
52,807,000
55,928,000
56,325,000
57,814,000
59,901,000

1901-11 1911-21 1921-31 1931-51 1951-61 1961-71 1971-81 1981-91 1991-9 1999-2001

Population at start of period

UK local goverment

The map shows the main British local government areas: English counties, unitary authorities and metropolitan districts, Scottish and Welsh unitary authorities, and Northern Ireland districts. Those not named on the map are keyed below.

1 Inverclyde
2 West Dunbartonshire
3 Renfrewshire
4 East Renfrewshire
5 Glasgow
6 East Dunbartonshire
7 North Lanarkshire
8 Falkirk
9 Clackmannanshire
10 West Lothian
11 Edinburgh
12 Newtownabbey
13 Carrickfergus
14 Belfast
15 Castlereagh
16 North Down
17 Stockton-on-Tees
18 Middlesbrough
19 Knowsley
20 Halton
21 St Helens
22 Wigan
23 Warrington
24 Trafford
25 Salford
26 Bolton
27 Blackburn with Darwen
28 Bury
29 Manchester
30 Stockport
31 Tameside
32 Oldham
33 Rochdale
34 Wolverhampton
35 Dudley
36 Walsall
37 Sandwell
38 Birmingham
39 Solihull
40 Reading
41 Wokingham
42 Bracknell Forest
43 Windsor & Maidenhead
44 Slough
45 Thurrock
46 Medway
47 Southend on Sea
48 Poole
49 Bournemouth
50 Southampton

51 Portsmouth
52 Neath Port Talbot
53 Rhondda, Cynon, Taff
54 Merthyr Tydfil
55 Caerphilly
56 Blaenau Gwent
57 Torfaen
58 Newport
59 South Gloucestershire
60 Bristol
61 Bath and North-east Somerset
62 North Somerset

London boroughs
(not keyed on map)

Barking & Dagenham
Barnet
Bexley
Brent
Bromley
Camden
City of London
City of Westminster
Croydon
Ealing
Enfield
Greenwich
Hackney
Hammersmith & Fulham
Haringey
Harrow
Havering
Hillingdon
Hounslow
Islington
Kensington & Chelsea
Kingston upon Thames
Lambeth
Lewisham
Merton
Newham
Redbridge
Richmond upon Thames
Southwark
Sutton
Tower Hamlets
Waltham Forest
Wandsworth

NORWAY

OFFICIAL NAME
The Kingdom of Norway

CAPITAL
Oslo

Area 323 877 km²
(125 050 sq miles)
Population 4 462 000
Population density 14 per
km² (35 per sq mile)
Population growth rate 0.4%
Life expectancy 74 (m); 80 (f)

Languages Norwegian,
Lapp
Adult literacy rate 99%
Currency Norwegian krone
(US $1 = 9.02 krone)
GDP (US million $) 152 200
GDP per head (US $) 34 356

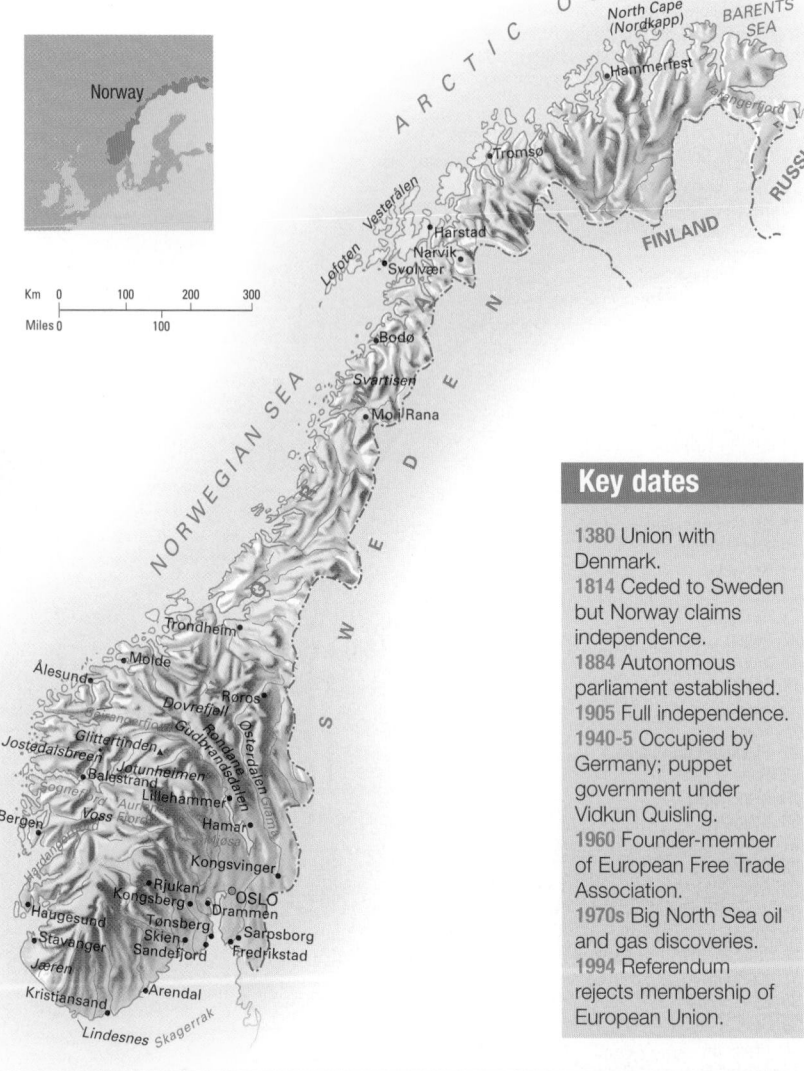

Nomads of the midnight sun

Life is changing for the Lapps living in the 'Land of the Midnight Sun' in northern Norway, Sweden, Finland and Russia. They have long wandered the highlands with their reindeer herds, but about half are now settled in communities, farming, fishing, hunting, trapping and foresting. The outside world has also had an impact: the Chernobyl nuclear disaster in 1986 contaminated their reindeer, and mining and hydroelectric schemes are changing their lands.

The Lapps (or Lapplanders), who call themselves 'Saami', are among Europe's oldest peoples. They migrated from central Asia shortly after the last ice age. Today about 60 000 Lapps live on some 388 500 km² (150 000 sq miles), mostly within the Arctic Circle and half of them in Norway. The various governments are keen to 'normalise' Lapp society, but the Lapps remain independent, and have their own parliaments in Norway, Finland and Sweden.

Key dates

1380 Union with Denmark.
1814 Ceded to Sweden but Norway claims independence.
1884 Autonomous parliament established.
1905 Full independence.
1940-5 Occupied by Germany; puppet government under Vidkun Quisling.
1960 Founder-member of European Free Trade Association.
1970s Big North Sea oil and gas discoveries.
1994 Referendum rejects membership of European Union.

DENMARK

OFFICIAL NAME
The Kingdom of Denmark

CAPITAL
Copenhagen

Area 43 094 km²
(16 639 sq miles)
Population 5 327 000
Population density 123 per
km² (319 per sq mile)
Population growth rate 0.1%
Life expectancy 72 (m); 77 (f)
Language Danish
Adult literacy rate 99%
Currency Danish krone
(US $1 = 8.28 krone)
GDP (US million $) 180 100
GDP per head (US $) 33 981

Key dates

*c.*950 Denmark united.
1387 Union with Norway.
1397 Union with Sweden.
1523 Cedes Sweden.
1814 Loses Norway.
1849 First democratic constitution.
1940-5 Neutral but occupied by Germany.
1960 Founder-member of European Free Trade Association.
1973 Joins European Community.

SWEDEN

OFFICIAL NAME
The Kingdom of Sweden

CAPITAL
Stockholm

Area 449 964 km²
(173 732 sq miles)
Population 8 861 000
Population density 20 per
km² (51 per sq mile)
Population growth rate 0.1%
Life expectancy 76 (m); 81 (f)
Languages Swedish,
Finnish, Lapp
Adult literacy rate 99%
Currency Swedish krona
(US $1 = 10.09 krona)
GDP (US million $) 243 700
GDP per head (US $) 27 536

Key dates

1397 Union of Sweden,
Denmark and Norway.
1523 Independence
from Denmark gained.
1809 Loses Finland to
Russia.
1814 Acquires Norway
in Napoleonic Wars.
1860-1900 Almost a
million Swedes emigrate,
most to North America.
1905 Loses Norway.
1914-18 Neutral in War.
1939-45 Neutral in War.
1960 Founder-member
of European Free Trade
Association.
1995 Joins EU.

Neighbours bridged Just over
600 years after the kingdoms of
Sweden and Denmark were first
politically united (and almost
500 years since they split apart
again), a huge new bridge spans
the Øresund Strait between the
Swedish city of Malmo and the
Danish capital Copenhagen.
The bridge, opened in July
2000, carries road traffic on the
upper deck, and trains on the
lower. It stretches for 7.7 km
(4.8 miles), and has a main
span of 490 m (1608 ft).

Germany and the Netherlands

GERMANY

OFFICIAL NAME
The Federal Republic
of Germany

CAPITAL
Berlin

Area 356 974 km²
(137 828 sq miles)
Population 82 087 000
Population density 230 per
km² (595 per sq mile)
Population growth rate
0.1%
Life expectancy 72 (m); 79 (f)

Language German
Adult literacy rate 99%
Currency deutschmark
(US $1 =
2.17 deutschmarks)
GDP (US million $)
2 149 600
GDP per head (US $) 26 208

FACT
The Ruhr region
has the world's
longest tram line;
it connects eight
cities along its
120 km (74 miles).

Key dates

800-43 Charlemagne's
empire spans Germany.
942 Otto I crowned
emperor; birth of Holy
Roman Empire.
1438 Habsburgs begin
rule as Emperors.
1806 Napoleon ends
Holy Roman Empire.
1815 Establishment of
German Confederation.
1870-1 Franco-Prussian
War; German Empire
founded, with Wilhelm I
as Kaiser; Bismarck
becomes chancellor.
1914-18 First World War
fought and lost.
1919 Weimar Republic
established.
1933 Adolf Hitler
becomes chancellor.
1934 Hitler declares
himself Führer;
establishes Third Reich.
1939-45 Second World
War fought and lost;
Germany divided into
four occupation zones.
1948-9 Russians
blockade Berlin.
1949 West Germany and
East Germany formed.
1957 West Germany
becomes founder-
member of European
Economic Community.
1961 Berlin Wall built.
1989 Berlin Wall falls.
1990 East and West
Germany reunified.
1999 Seat of
government transferred
from Bonn to Berlin.

Germany

0   40   80
0 20 40 60

DENMARK   BALTIC SEA

NORTH
SEA

Flensburg
Helgoland   Fehmarn
                                          Rügen
German   Kiel   Wagrien   Kühlungsborn Heiligendamm   Stralsund
Bight   SCHLESWIG-   Bad Doberan   Greifswald
East Friesian Islands   HOLSTEIN   Rostock
(Ostfriesische Inseln) Lübeck   Wismar
          Cuxhaven   Güstrow
Wilhelmshaven   BREMEN   HAMBURG   Schwerin   Neubrandenburg   MECKLENBURG-VORPOMMERN
  Emden   Bremerhaven   Hamburg
        Oldenburg   Lauenburg   Mecklenburg
                BREMEN   Lüneburg   Ravensbrück   Schwedt
          Bremen   an der Oder
                    Lüneburg Heath
                    (Lüneburger Heide)   Elbe
  NETHERLANDS Dortmund-Ems   LOWER SAXONY   Oranienburg   BRANDENBURG
          Canal   Celle   Stendal   Spandau   BERLIN
        Steinhuder   Wolfsburg   Brandenburg   Potsdam   Frankfurt
        Meer   Hannover   Brunswick SAXONY   Königs   an der Oder
  Osnabrück Minden Mittellandkanal (Braunschweig) Helmstedt (SACHSEN- Wusterhausen
        Rhine   Hameln   Hildesheim Salzgitter Magdeburg ANHALT)   Eisenhüttenstadt
    Münster d   Bielefeld   Goslar   Wernigerode Stassfurt Fläming   Spreewald
            Teutoburger Wald Detmold   Harz Quedlinburg Dessau   Wittenburg Cottbus
      NORTH RHINE-WESTPHALIA Paderborn   Eisleben Bitterfeld   Neider Lausitz
  Xanten Hamm   Göttingen   Halle Merseburg Leipzig   Hoyerswerda
  Gelsenkirchen Ruhr Dortmund Möhnestausee   Leuna Weissenfels   Reisa (SACHSEN) Ober Lausitz
  Oberhausen Bochum   Kassel   THÜRINGEN Naumburg   SAXONY (SACHSEN) Görlitz
  Duisburg Essen Hagen   Edersee Saarland   Buchenwald   Colditz   Dresden   Bautzen
  Krefeld Mülheim an der Ruhr   Eisenach   Weimar Altenburg Meissen   Zittau
  Düsseldorf Wuppertal   GERMANY Wartburg Gotha Erfurt Jena Gera Glauchau Augustusburg Saxon
        Solingen   Marburg   Oberhof Rudolstadt   Chemnitz Frieberg Switzerland
  Mönchengladbach Cologne Siegen an der Lahn   Zella-   Saalfeld Zwickau (Karl-Marx-Stadt)
        (Köln) Siegerland   Mehlis Suhl Schneeberg Aue Oberwiesenthal
      Bonn Westerwald   Giessen Vogelsberg Fulda Thüringer Plauen Erzgeb.
                          Wald Hohe Coburg   Hof   CZECH
        Eifel Koblenz HESSEN   Rhön   REPUBLIC
              Bad   Spessart   Schweinfurt Bamberg   Bayreuth Fichtelgebirge
        RHINELAND- Homburg Taunus Frankfurt am Main
        PALATINATE Hunsrück Wiesbaden Offenbach   Würzburg   Jura
  LUXEMBOURG   Bernkastel-Kues Mainz Darmstadt Aschaffenburg   Erlangen
      Trier   Worms   Odenwald   F r a n c o n i a Nuremburg
        SAARLAND Ludwigshafen Mannheim   Rothenburg (Nürnburg)
          Kaiserslautern Speyer Heidelberg   ob der Tauber   BAVARIA
  FRANCE Saarbrücken   Heilbronn   Regensburg Altmühl Franconian
              Karlsruhe   Ludwigsburg Nördlingen Jura
            Pforzheim BADEN- Stuttgart Schwäbisch Gmünd   Ingolstadt Blenheim
              Baden-Baden Esslingen am Neckar   Landshut   Passau
              Tübingen   Jura Swabian   Augsburg Dachau
            Kaiserstuhl Reutlingen Ulm   Munich Altötting AUSTRIA
            567m Freiburg   Swabian Swabia   (München)
            im Breisgau WÜRTTEMBURG   Ammersee
                Constance Mainau   Starnberger Chiemsee
          Lake Constance Friedrichshafen   See
          (Bodensee) Lindau Neuschwanstein Oberammergau
  SWITZERLAND   Allgäu Zugspitze Garmisch-
                    2963m Partenkirchen

POLAND

GDR – the other Germany

In 1949, both the Western Allies and the USSR declared a state in their zones of German occupation. In the west of the country, the Federal Republic came into being, and in the Soviet east, the German Democratic Republic.

The leadership of the new East German state was ultra-loyal to the USSR, aware that it was in the front line of the ideological confrontation with the West. The concrete barrier, hurriedly constructed around the western-controlled enclave of West Berlin in 1961, was officially called the 'antifascist protection wall'.

But the people of East Germany were never enthusiastic about Soviet socialism. In 1953 an uprising against Stalinism had been brutally suppressed, and a drain of qualified workers to the West had brought the economy close to collapse by 1960. This was the real purpose of the Wall: to stop valuable people leaving.

The government strove to make life inside the country comfortable. By the 1970s, the standard of living was much higher than in most socialist countries. But the mass of people compared their lives with those of West Germans – whose affluence they experienced vicariously, through television. Most GDR citizens were delighted when in 1989 the reforming Soviet leader Mikhail Gorbachev ended support for their hardline regime. Within weeks, popular pressure in both Germanies brought down the Wall, and reunification soon followed.

NETHERLANDS

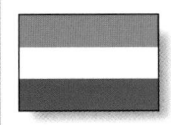

OFFICIAL NAME
The Kingdom of the Netherlands

CAPITAL
Amsterdam (govt at The Hague)

Area 33 939 km² (13 104 sq miles)
Population 15 810 000
Population density 463 per km² (1199 per sq mile)
Population growth rate 0.7%
Life expectancy 74 (m); 80 (f)

Language Dutch
Adult literacy rate 99%
Currency guilder
(US $1 = 2.44 guilders)
GDP (US million $) 384 100
GDP per head (US $) 24 449

Key dates

14th-15thC Dukes of Burgundy unite the Low Countries.
1516 Ruled by the Spanish monarchy.
1581 Dutch declare independence; recognised in 1648.
1652-74 Three naval wars against England.
1795-1813 French rule.
1815 Independent kingdom (with Belgium).
1830 Belgium breaks away to declare itself independent.
1940-5 Occupied by Germany despite neutrality.
1948 Joins Belgium and Luxembourg in Benelux customs union.
1949 Indonesia, its biggest colony, gains independence.
1957 Becomes founder-member of European Economic Community.
1992 Hosts Maastricht conference that creates closer European union.

Wind against water This wind farm in the Polders is just the latest example of Dutch use of wind power. Almost half the Netherlands lies below sea level, and wind-driven pumps have been used to drain it for more than 500 years.

FRANCE

OFFICIAL NAME
The French Republic

CAPITAL
Paris

Area 543 965 km²
(210 026 sq miles)
Population 59 099 000
Population density 108 per
km² (280 per sq mile)
Population growth rate 0.5%
Life expectancy 73 (m); 81 (f)
Languages French, Breton,
Basque and several
regional dialects
Adult literacy rate 95%
Currency French franc
(US $1 = 7.27 francs)
GDP (US million $)
1 445 000
GDP per head (US $) 24 553

Nuclear nation Around 77
per cent of the electricity
generated in France is
produced by nuclear power.

Bar chart values: 77, 47, 44, 38, 32, 29, 28, 19, 13, 13, 10

France, Sweden, Ukraine, Korea, Japan, Germany, United Kingdom, United States, Canada, Russia, Rest of the world*

Percentage of electricity produced by nuclear power, by country. *Denotes
countries that have nuclear production facilities.

Key dates

486 Frankish king Clovis
defeats the Romans.
1302 First Estates-
General (parliament).
1337-1453 Hundred
Years' War with England.
1789-99 Revolution
establishes republic.
1799 Napoleon seizes
power as emperor.
1815 Napoleon defeated;
monarchy is restored.
1848 Second Republic.
1852 Second Empire
under Louis Napoleon.
1870-1 Defeated in
Franco-Prussian War.
1871 Third Republic.
1914-18 First World War
fought mostly on French
territory; 1.4 million
French are killed.

1940-4 Defeat and
occupation by Germany.
1946 Fourth Republic.
1946-54 Revolution in
French Indochina.
1956 Independence for
Morocco and Tunisia.
1957 Becomes founder-
member of European
Economic Community.
1958 Fifth Republic; de
Gaulle president.
1962 Independence for
Algeria.
1966 French troops
withdrawn from NATO.
1968 Demonstrations
for educational and
political reforms.
1969 De Gaulle resigns.
1995-6 Renewed nuclear
testing in the Pacific.

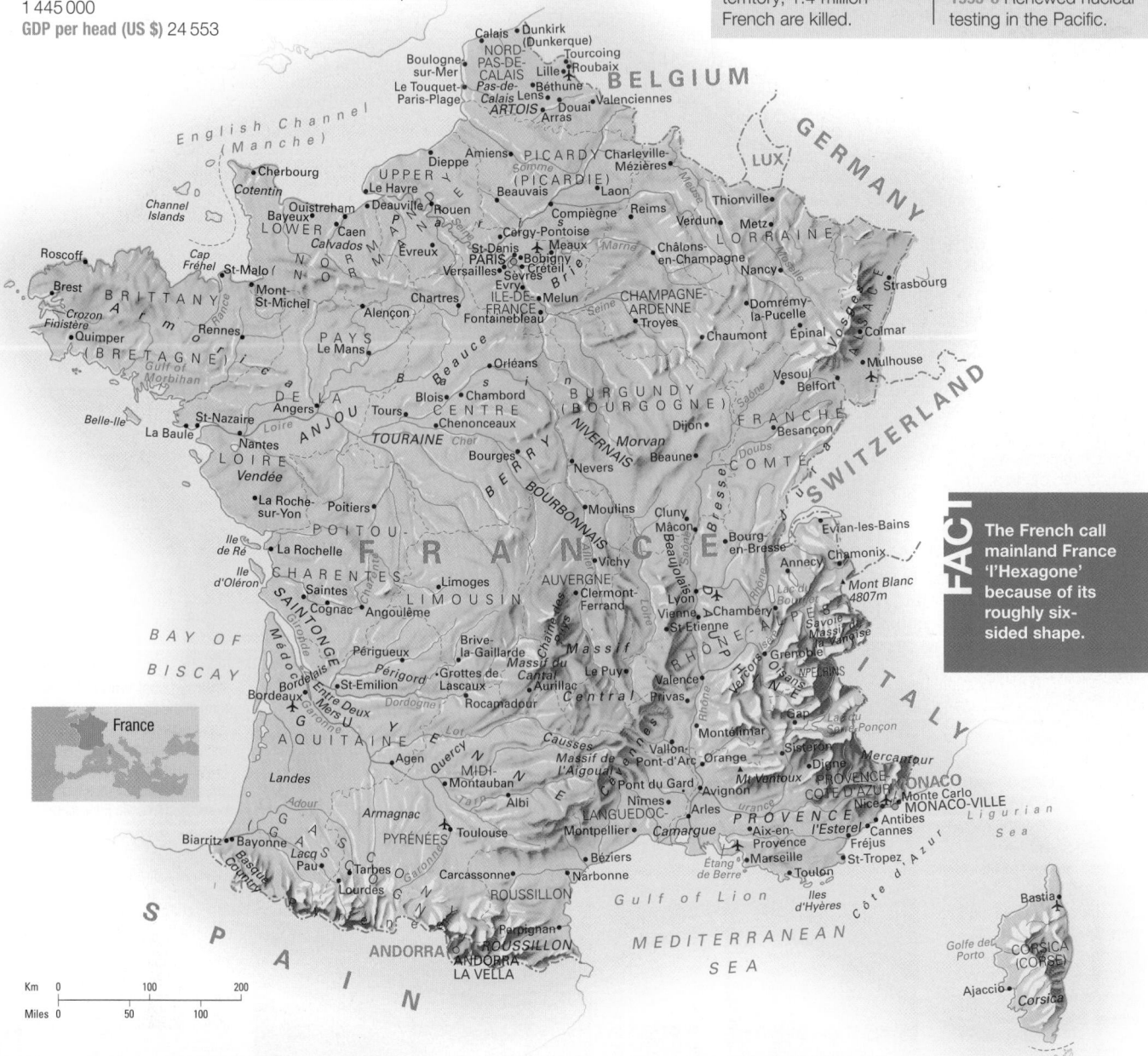

France

FACT
The French call
mainland France
'l'Hexagone'
because of its
roughly six-
sided shape.

Km 0 100 200
Miles 0 50 100

Alsace and Lorraine

For centuries, control of the provinces of Alsace and its larger western neighbour Lorraine swung to and fro between the rulers of France and Germany. The two nations contended for the region's rich iron, coal and potash resources. Alsace and Lorraine remain industrial, but traditional heavy industries are giving way to chemicals, textiles and electronics. And the fertile land still supports the vineyards of Alsace and the orchards and grain fields of Lorraine.

Alsace and Lorraine were part of Roman Gaul and later of the medieval Holy Roman Empire. France acquired the territory during the 17th and 18th centuries. Germany annexed Alsace and part of Lorraine in 1871, after winning the Franco-Prussian War.

They were restored to France in 1919 at the end of the First World War, and a movement began for autonomy. After Germany again annexed them during the Second World War – and around 20 000 of their citizens died in the German army on the Eastern Front – the two provinces were content to become French once again.

Today, Alsace and Lorraine have become a symbol of European unity. Their turbulent history has created a region where the two languages are spoken more or less equally and whose traditions, culture and architecture reflect both French and German influences.

As a gesture of reconciliation after the end of the Second World War, the Alsatian capital Strasbourg became the seat first of the Council of Europe and then of the European Parliament.

BELGIUM

OFFICIAL NAME
The Kingdom of Belgium

CAPITAL
Brussels

Area 30 528 km² (11 787 sq miles)
Population 10 152 000
Population density 334 per km² (866 per sq mile)
Population growth rate 0.2%
Life expectancy 72 (m); 79 (f)
Languages Flemish, French, German
Adult literacy rate 99%
Currency Belgian franc (US $1 = 44.7 Belgian francs)
GDP (US million $) 244 200
GDP per head (US $) 23 917

Key dates

1830 Independence from the Netherlands.
1914-18 Neutral but occupied by Germany.
1940-5 Neutral but occupied by Germany.
1948 Joins Netherlands and Luxembourg in Benelux union.
1957 Becomes founder-member of European Economic Community.
1993 Devolves power to three regions: Brussels, Flanders and Wallonia.

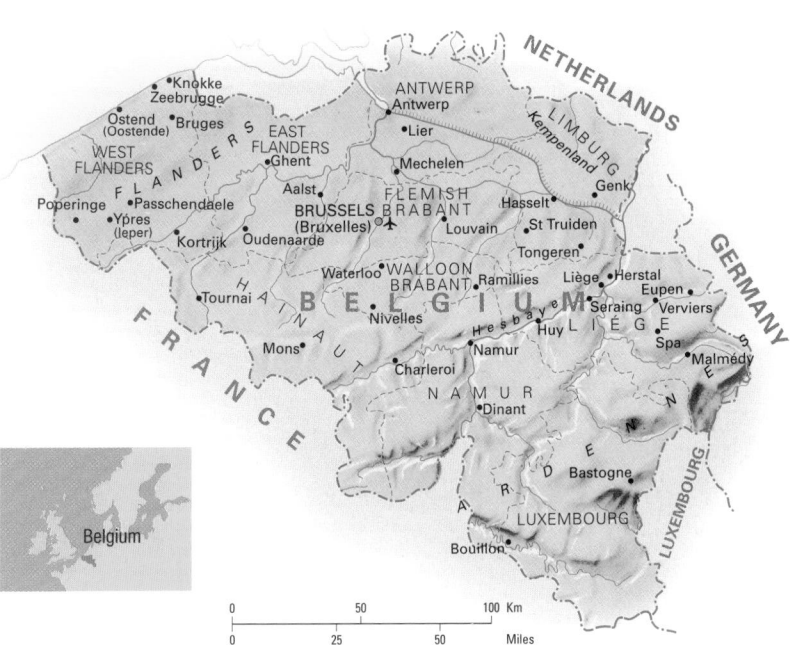

Belgium

LUXEMBOURG

OFFICIAL NAME
The Grand Duchy of Luxembourg

CAPITAL
Luxembourg

Area 2587 km² (999 sq miles)
Population 429 000
Population density 166 per km² (430 per sq mile)
Population growth rate 1.5%
Life expectancy 70 (m); 77 (f)
Languages Letzeburgish (German-Moselle-Frankish dialect), French, German
Adult literacy rate 99%
Currency Luxembourg franc (US $1 = 44.7 Luxembourg francs)
GDP (US million $) 19 500
GDP per head (US $) 45 348

Key dates

1815 Grand Duchy under Dutch king.
1890 Independence from the Netherlands.
1914-18 Neutral but occupied by Germany.
1940-5 Neutral but occupied by Germany.
1948 Joins Belgium and Netherlands in Benelux customs union.
1952 Headquarters for European Coal and Steel Community.
1957 Becomes founder-member of European Economic Community.

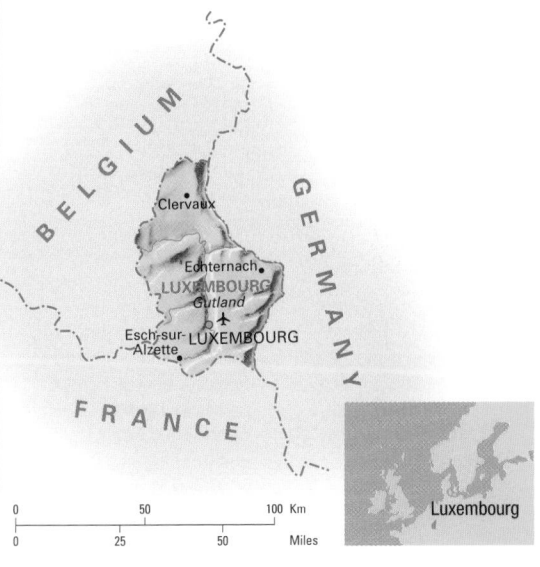

Luxembourg

SPAIN

OFFICIAL NAME
The Kingdom of Spain

CAPITAL
Madrid

Area 504 782 km²
(194 897 sq miles)
Population 39 418 000
Population density 78 per
km² (202 per sq mile)
Population growth rate 0.1%
Life expectancy 73 (m); 80 (f)
Languages Spanish

(Castilian), Catalan,
Galician, Basque
Adult literacy rate 95.8%
Currency peseta
(US $1 = 184 pesetas)
GDP (US million $) 588 300
GDP per head (US $) 14 942

Building a new Spain The
Guggenheim Museum in Bilbao,
designed by the American architect
Frank Gehry and opened in 1997,
symbolises the post-Franco
regeneration of Spanish culture.

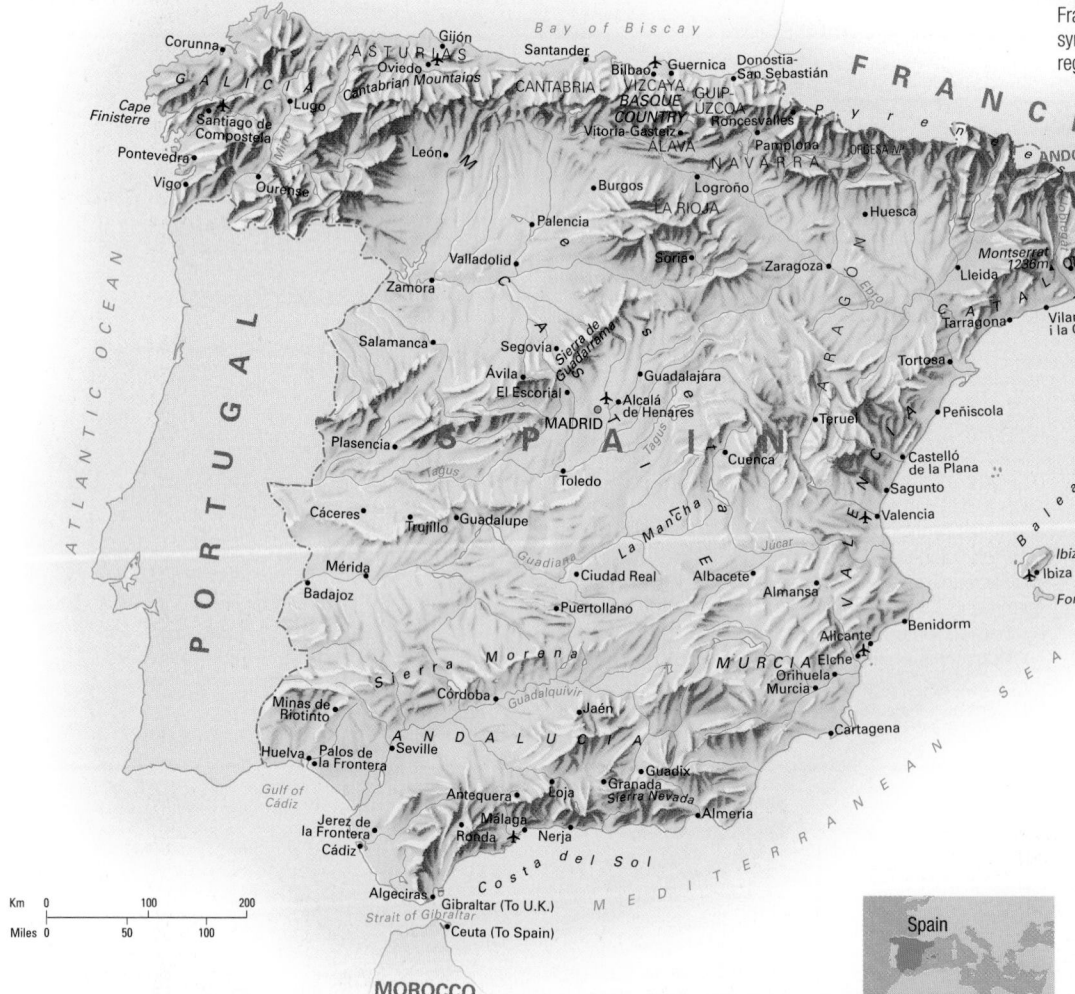

Key dates

711-18 Islamic Moors
conquer most of Spain.
11thC Christian kings
rise up against Moors.
1492 Moors defeated at
Granada; Spain unified.
16thC Spain establishes
empire in Americas.
1588 Armada against
England defeated.
1898 Spanish-American
War; Cuba, Puerto Rico
and the Philippines lost.
1936-9 Spanish Civil
War; General Franco
becomes dictator.
1968 Basque terrorist
campaign begins.
1975 Franco dies;
monarchy restored.
1980 Limited autonomy
for Catalonia and
Basque provinces.
1981 Military coup fails.
1986 Joins European
Community.

Spain's restless nationalities

Spain's two main ethnic
minorities – the Basque
and Catalan peoples –
have long sought
autonomy. Both were
repressed during Franco's
dictatorship, but in 1980
they gained regional
autonomy, each with their

own parliament. The
Basque country straddles
the western Pyrenees into
France, its three Spanish
provinces having 620 000
people. The Basques
speak a language
unrelated to any other.
A terrorist group, ETA

(*Euzkadi ta Azkatasuna* –
'Basque Homeland and
Liberty'), has killed more
than 800 people since
1968, with brief truces in
1989 and 1998–9.
   The four north-eastern
provinces of Catalonia are
home to 6 million people,

many speaking Catalan,
a distinct Romance
language. Catalonia was
independent from 1932
to 1939. Today it is
Spain's main industrial
area, and Barcelona, its
capital, is one of Spain's
most vibrant cities.

PORTUGAL

OFFICIAL NAME
The Portuguese Republic
CAPITAL
Lisbon

Area 92 270 km²
(35 626 sq miles)
Population 9 989 000
Population density 108 per
km² (280 per sq mile)
Population growth rate 0.1%
Life expectancy 71 (m); 78 (f)
Language Portuguese
Adult literacy rate 85%
Currency escudo
(US $1 = 222 escudos)
GDP (US million $) 108 900
GDP per head (US $) 10 922

Km 0 — 100
Miles 0 — 50

Portugal

Key dates

1143 Independent
kingdom established.
1419 Overseas
expansion begins.
1580 Spanish rule starts.
1640 Independence
regained from Spain.
1822 Brazil declares
independence.
1910 King deposed;
republic proclaimed.
1916-18 Fights alongside
Allies in First World War.
1926 Military coup
begins dictatorship.
1928 Antonio Salazar
becomes dictator.
1974 Military coup
restores civil rights.
1974-6 Gives up most
remaining colonies.
1976 Free elections.
1986 Joins European
Community.

ANDORRA

OFFICIAL NAME
The Principality of Andorra
CAPITAL
Andorra la Vella

Area 468 km²
(181 sq miles)
Population 80 000
Population density 158 per
km² (409 per sq mile)
Population growth rate 3.3%
Life expectancy 79 (m); 79 (f)

Languages Catalan,
French, Spanish
Adult literacy rate 99%
Currency French franc;
Spanish peseta
GDP (US million $) 1200
GDP per head (US $) 15 000

Key dates

819 Granted to Bishop
of Urgel from Louis the
Pious of Charlemagne.
1278-88 Joint rule by the
(Spanish) bishop and
French count (later king,
then president) begins.
1970 Women gain vote.
1993 Parliamentary
government begins.
1993 Joins UN.

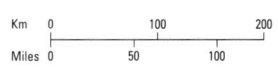

Km 0 — 100 — 200
Miles 0 — 50 — 100

Andorra

MALTA

OFFICIAL NAME
The Republic of Malta
CAPITAL
Valletta

Area 316 km²
(122 sq miles)
Population 386 000
Population density 1203 per
km² (3115 per sq mile)
Population growth rate 1.1%
Life expectancy 75 (m); 79 (f)
Languages Maltese,
English, Italian
Adult literacy rate 87.9%
Currency Maltese lira
(US $1 = 0.45 Maltese lira)
GDP (US million $) 3400
GDP per head (US $) 8947

Key dates

1520 Becomes fiefdom
of Order of St John.
1798 Seized by France.
1800 Becomes British
protectorate.
1814 Becomes British
crown colony.
1947 New constitution
gives self-government.
1956 Referendum in
favour of full integration
with Britain, but
negotiations stall.
1964 Full independence
under British crown.
1974 Establishes
Republic of Malta.
1990 Applies for
membership of
European Community.

FACT
Malta was given
the George Cross
in 1942 for its
people's courage
under German
bombardment.

Km 0 — 10
Miles 0 — 5

Malta

ITALY

OFFICIAL NAME
The Italian Republic

CAPITAL
Rome

Area 301 323 km²
(116 341 sq miles)
Population 57 343 000
Population density 191 per
km² (495 per sq mile)
Population growth rate 0.1%
Life expectancy 74 (m); 80 (f)
Languages Italian, German,
French, others
Adult literacy rate 97.1%
Currency Italian lira
(US $1 = 2148 lire)
GDP (US million $) 1 176 400
GDP per head (US $) 20 427

Key dates

From *c.*1000 City-states
rise to power.
16th-18thC Most Italian
states under Spanish
then Austrian control.
1796-1815 Most of Italy
ruled by France.
1848 Revolutions in
major Italian cities.
1861 Most of Italy
united as kingdom.
1866 Acquires Mantua
and Venetia after
Austro-Prussian War.
1870 Rome is made the
capital city.
1915-18 Joins with Allies
in First World War.
1922 Fascist Mussolini
named prime minister.
1925 Mussolini
becomes dictator.
1929 Independence
agreed for Vatican City.
1936 Seizes Ethiopia.
1939 Invades Albania.
1940-3 Joins with Axis
in Second World War.
1943 New government
joins Allies and declares
war on Germany.
1946 Republic declared.
1957 Becomes founder-
member of European
Economic Community.
1997 Leads peace-
keeping in Albania.

FACT Italy had 34
prime ministers
between 1946 and
2000, most lasting
only months.

VATICAN CITY

OFFICIAL NAME
The State of the Vatican City

CAPITAL
Vatican City

Area 0.44 km²
(0.17 sq mile)
Population 870
Population density 1977 per
km² (5118 per sq mile)
Population growth rate 0%

Life expectancy 74 (m); 80 (f)
Languages Italian, Latin
Adult literacy rate 100%
Currency Italian lira
GDP (US million $) 19
GDP per head (US $) 19 121

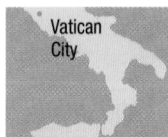

Tiny centre of the Catholic world

Vatican City (Stato della Citta del Vaticano) is the world's smallest nation. The absolute ruler is the pope, who is elected for life; the population is fewer than 1000; Latin is an official language; it has a birthrate of zero; and there is no income tax. The city-state is less than a quarter the size of London's Hyde Park, yet it has its own diplomatic corps, flag, bank, broadcasting station and postage stamps. The country is protected by the Swiss Guard, a corps of papal bodyguards founded during the Renaissance.

Vatican City is the surviving remnant of the Papal States that once dominated much of central Italy; in 1859, just before Italian unification, papal territory covered about 44 000 km² (17 000 sq miles). The Papal States were abolished in 1870, but the Vatican's independence was guaranteed by the Italian dictator Benito Mussolini in 1929. Located in the heart of Rome, on Vatican Hill near the bank of the Tiber, the state now covers only 44 ha (109 acres). Its buildings include St Peter's basilica, the world's largest church; and the Vatican palace, the home of popes since 1377 and the world's largest residential palace. Its art masterpieces include Michelangelo's ceiling frescoes in the Sistine Chapel. Other buildings house art, manuscripts, maps, coins and medals.

Christian soldiers The papal Swiss Guards, founded in 1505, parade in uniforms said to have been designed by Michelangelo.

SAN MARINO

OFFICIAL NAME
The Republic of San Marino

CAPITAL
San Marino

Area 61 km² (24 sq miles)
Population 26 000
Population density 492 per
km² (1250 per sq mile)
Population growth rate 1.5%
Life expectancy 73 (m); 79 (f)

Language Italian
Adult literacy rate 98.4%
Currency Italian lira
(US $1 = 2148 lire)
GDP (US million $) 500
GDP per head (US $) 19 230

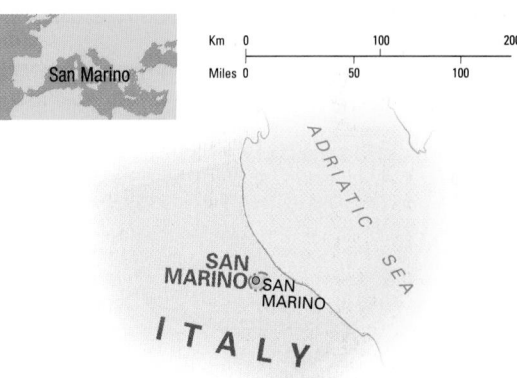

MONACO

OFFICIAL NAME
The Principality of Monaco

CAPITAL
Monaco

Area 1.95 km²
(0.75 sq mile)
Population 33 000
Population density 16 410
per km² (42 667 per sq
mile)
Population growth rate 0%
Life expectancy 78 (m); 78 (f)

Languages French,
Monegasque, Italian,
English
Adult literacy rate 99%
Currency French franc
(US $1 = 7.27 francs)
GDP (US million $) 847
GDP per head (US $) 26 470

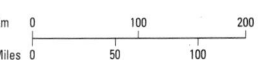

The Baltic Countries

ESTONIA

OFFICIAL NAME
The Republic of Estonia

CAPITAL
Tallinn

Km 0 50 100
Miles 0 50

Estonia

Area 45 227 km²
(17 462 sq miles)
Population 1 370 500
Population density 32 per km² (83 per sq mile)
Population growth rate 0.6%
Life expectancy 62 (m); 73 (f)

Languages Estonian, Russian
Adult literacy rate 99.7%
Currency kroon
(US $1 = 17.36 kroons)
GDP (US million $) 5400
GDP per head (US $) 3703

Key dates

1625 Swedish rule.
1721 Russian control.
1918 Independence proclaimed.
1940 Annexed to USSR.
1941-4 German occupation.
1990 Declares itself 'occupied' by USSR.
1991 Independence declared; recognised by USSR. Joins UN.
1993 Soviet troops leave.

LATVIA

OFFICIAL NAME
The Republic of Latvia

CAPITAL
Riga

Area 64 589 km²
(24 938 sq miles)
Population 2 432 000
Population density 38 per km² (98 per sq mile)
Population growth rate 0.1%
Life expectancy 60 (m); 73 (f)

Languages Latvian, Russian
Adult literacy rate 98%
Currency lats
(US $1 = 0.62 lats)
GDP (US million $) 6568
GDP per head (US $) 2680

Key dates

1800 Russian control.
1918 Independence proclaimed.
1940 Annexed to USSR.
1941-4 German occupation.
1990 Claims independence from USSR.
1991 Independence recognised by USSR. Joins UN.
1993 Soviet troops leave.

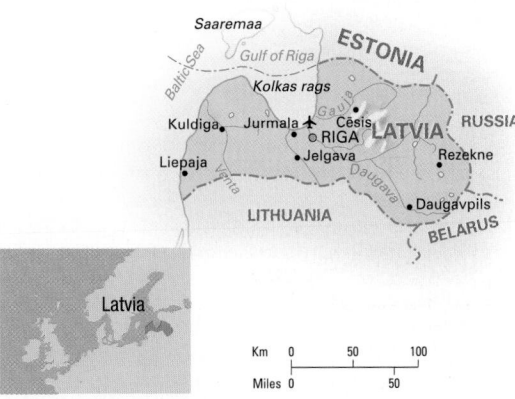

Latvia

Km 0 50 100
Miles 0 50

The long struggle for Baltic independence

Estonia, Latvia and Lithuania were the last states to join the USSR, and the first to leave it. They were always unwilling members of the Soviet club. Independent between the world wars, all three were assigned to the Soviet sphere of influence under the terms of the secret protocol of the 1939 Nazi-Soviet non-aggression treaty. They were annexed in 1940, and subjected to a vicious purge of anti-Stalinists.

During the 50 years of Soviet rule millions of ethnic Russians settled in the Baltic States. Few learnt the local languages or integrated with the culture of the Baltic peoples, and this Russocentric insensitivity caused deep resentment. But throughout their Soviet years, the Baltic States served as a kind of ersatz-West: life in well-kept cities such as Vilnius and Tallinn was comfortable,

civilised, and always a few degrees more liberal than in the Russian heartland.

Independence movements sprung up in the Baltic States almost as soon as Gorbachev's policy of glasnost came into being. When Moscow allowed communist regimes in eastern Europe to collapse, independence campaigners claimed that their peoples had as much right to self-determination as the Czechs or Poles, since they were also victims of Stalin's wartime land-grab. The logic was impeccable, but Gorbachev objected to the idea that a republic of the USSR might secede. In January 1991, independence demonstrators were attacked by Russian troops and five were killed.

Independence came in spite of Gorbachev later that year. The Russians in the Baltic States now found themselves unwelcome

foreigners, and were widely discriminated against. But the new authorities saw contentious measures (such as a language qualification for citizenship) as vital to the salvation of their native culture. They also pressed ahead with the reconstruction of a free market economy. Estonia in particular was helped by Finland, its neighbour and ethnic cousin.

All three benefited from the fact that their peoples' entrepreneurial spark had not been entirely extinguished by Soviet economic planning, and that the democratic interwar years were still well within living memory.

All three of the Baltic States have expressed a desire to join the European Union and the NATO defence alliance. Joining either would strengthen countries which, over the past eight centuries, have seen far more of occupation than of independence.

Estonia and Latvia were overrun in the 13th century by the Teutonic knights and the Livonian Brothers of the Sword, whose rule was later replaced by that of the Swedes and the Poles. In the 18th century, both countries fell under the dominion of Tsarist Russia. The collapse of Russia and Germany at the end of the First World War opened their way to independence in 1918, but freedom did not last long: the Nazi-Soviet pact of 1939 placed all three Baltic countries under Soviet control. Lithuania, to protect itself against inroads by Teutonic knights and the Brothers of the Sword, formed alliances which grew into the Grand Duchy of Lithuania, an empire which, in the Middle Ages, stretched across Europe from the Baltic to the Black Sea. In the 18th century, Lithuania, as well as Estonia and Latvia, disappeared into the Tsarist embrace.

LITHUANIA

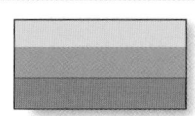

OFFICIAL NAME
The Republic of Lithuania

CAPITAL
Vilnius

Lithuania

Area 65 300 km²
(25 212 sq miles)
Population 3 699 000
Population density 57 per
km² (147 per sq mile)
Population growth rate 0.1%
Life expectancy 63 (m); 75 (f)
Languages Lithuanian,
Russian, Polish
Adult literacy rate 98.4%
Currency litas
(US $1 = 4 litas)
GDP (US million $) 10 472
GDP per head (US $) 2825

Flame of freedom A young
Lithuanian conscript shows his
distaste for the USSR by burning his
Soviet military passport during 1990
independence demonstrations.

Key dates

*c.*1200 Lithuania united
as kingdom.
14thC Great expansion.
1385 Union with Poland.
1795 Russian rule.
1919-20 Independence
after war with Russia.
1926 Military coup.
1940 Annexed to USSR.
1941-4 German
occupation.
1972 Anti-Soviet
demonstrations.
1990 Declares formal
independence.
1991 Independence
recognised by USSR.
Joins UN.
1993 Soviet troops leave.

FINLAND

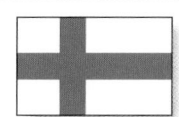

OFFICIAL NAME
The Republic of Finland

CAPITAL
Helsinki

Finland

Area 338 144 km²
(130 558 sq miles)
Population 5 165 000
Population density 15 per
km² (39 per sq mile)
Population growth rate 0.4%
Life expectancy 72 (m); 80 (f)

Languages Finnish,
Swedish, Lapp
Adult literacy rate 99%
Currency markka
(US $1 = 6.5 markka)
GDP (US million $) 129 000
GDP per head (US $) 25 048

Key dates

13thC Swedish rule.
1809 Russian rule after
prolonged wars.
1917 Declares
independence following
the Russian Revolution.
1918 Civil war.
1919 Republic
established.
1939-40 'Winter War'
against USSR: defeat
and loss of territory.
1941-4 Allied with
Germany against USSR.
1944 Defeated;
armistice with USSR.
1946 Declares neutrality.
1948 Signs treaty with
USSR.
1955 Joins UN.
1992 New treaty with
Russia.
1995 Joins European
Union.

Russian influence Finland
was ruled by Russia for most of
the 19th century. Even today,
their shared history is reflected
in Finnish architecture.

POLAND

OFFICIAL NAME
The Republic of Poland

CAPITAL
Warsaw

Area 312 685 km²
(120 728 sq miles)
Population 38 654 000
Population density 124 per
km² (320 per sq mile)
Population growth rate 0.3%
Life expectancy 67 (m); 76 (f)
Languages Polish, German
Adult literacy rate 99%
Currency zloty
(US $1 = 4 zlotys)
GDP (US million $) 155 400
GDP per head (US $) 4018

Key dates

966 Poland founded
under King Mieszko I.
1385 Lithuanian union.
1772-95 Partitioned by
Russia, Prussia, Austria.
1918 Independence
gained.
1939 Germany invades.
1947 Communist
government established.
1980 Solidarity trade
union established.
1981 Martial law;
Solidarity suspended.
1989 Open elections.
1990 Communist Party
dissolved.
1997 New constitution.
1999 Joins NATO.

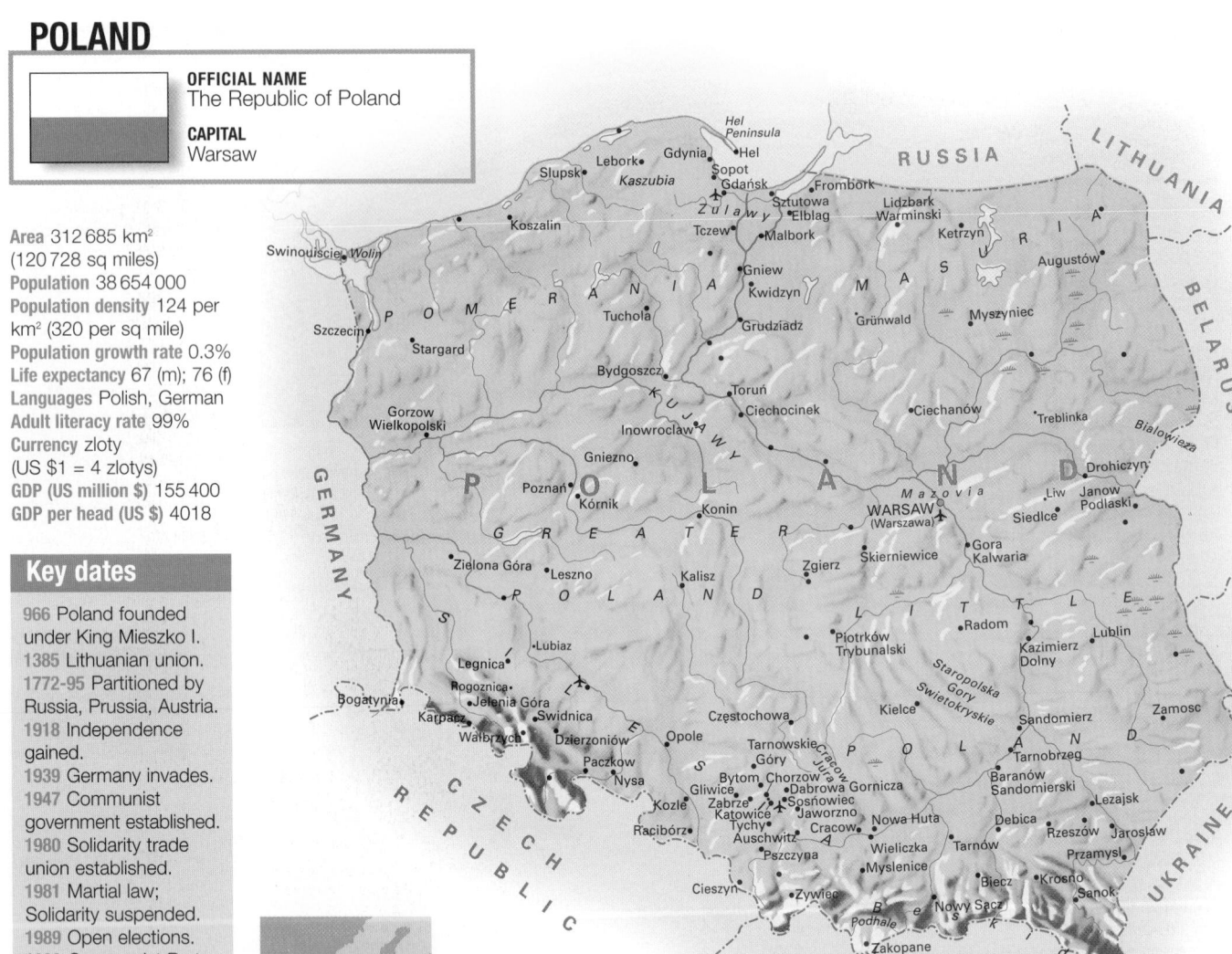

Poland's shifting history

Poland's frontiers have frequently shifted as its territories have been fought over by other nations. Yet a sense of national identity remained and Poland has always succeeded in reconstituting itself.

Territorially, the height of Poland's success came in the Middle Ages. Under the Jagiello dynasty the Polish-Lithuanian empire stretched to the Black Sea. But most of that land was lost to Russia in later centuries. At the end of the 18th century, Poland was partitioned between Russia, Prussia and Austria, and disappeared from the map.

An independent Polish state, with new boundaries, was re-established at the end of the First World War. In 1920 a dispute with

Soviet Russia over their border led to war, from which Poland emerged with a new swathe of land in the east. But this, and more besides, was lost in 1939. Germany invaded Poland from the west and the Soviet Union from the east. In 1941, with the German attack on the USSR, all Poland came under Nazi control. Under occupation, the country was known by the bureaucratic formula 'the General Government'.

At the end of the war, the USSR reclaimed the lands it had seized in 1939. These were absorbed into the Soviet republics of Byelorussia and the Ukraine. Poland was awarded a band of German territory. In effect, the whole country was transposed

240 km (150 miles) to the west. After the Iron Curtain came down, the newly democratic Polish republic found itself at the heart of a Europe reborn.

Poland's shifting frontiers
During and after the Second World War the boundaries of Poland shifted westwards.

■ Grand Duchy of Warsaw 1815
■ National boundaries 1921-39
■ National boundaries 1945-present

CZECH REPUBLIC

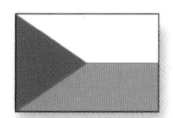

OFFICIAL NAME
The Czech Republic

CAPITAL
Prague

Area 78 864 km²
(30 450 sq miles)
Population 10 283 000
Population density 130 per
km² (338 per sq mile)
Population growth rate 0.1%
Life expectancy 70 (m); 77 (f)
Languages Czech, German

and others
Adult literacy rate 99%
Currency Czech koruna
(US $1 = 38 koruna)
GDP (US million $) 53 800
GDP per head (US $) 5228

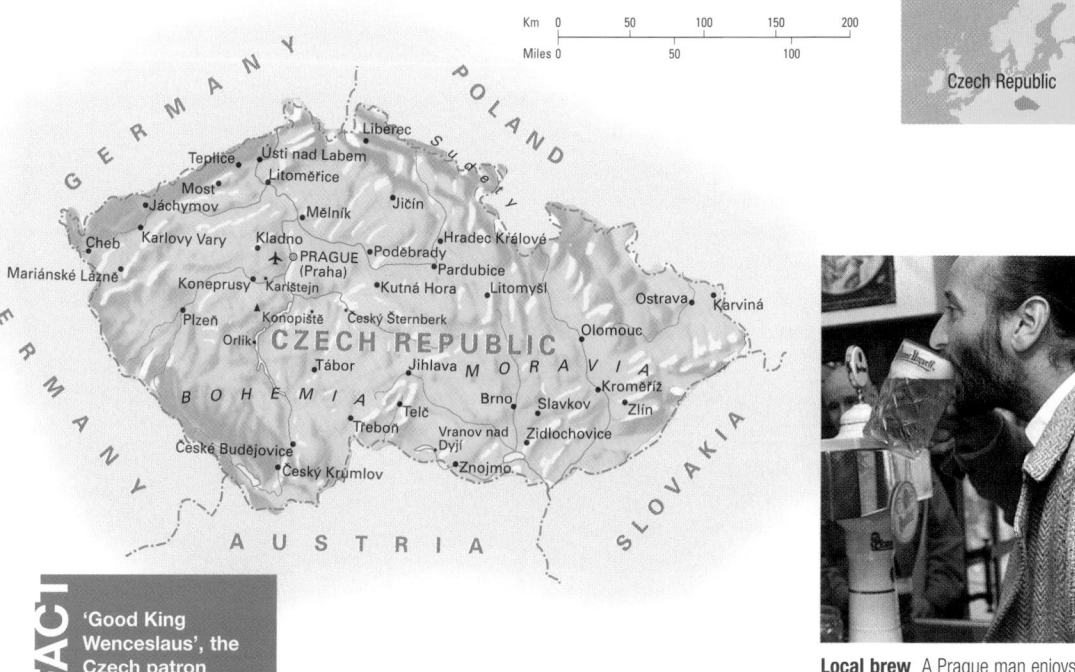

FACT 'Good King Wenceslaus', the Czech patron saint, was Duke of Bohemia from AD 925 to 929.

Local brew A Prague man enjoys his pilsner beer. A strong, pale lager, pilsner, or pils, takes its name from the Czech town of Pilsen (Plzen), where it was originally brewed.

Key dates

10thC Independent kingdom of Bohemia.
1212 Semi-independent kingdom within Holy Roman Empire.
1526 Habsburg rule.
1867 Becomes part of Austro-Hungarian Empire.
1918 Independence; unites with Slovakia as Czechoslovakia.
1938 Nazi Germany annexes Sudetenland.
1939 German invasion. Czechoslovakia split.
1945 Reunion as Czechoslovakia.
1948 Communists seize power.
1968 'Prague Spring' liberalisation is suppressed by a Soviet-led invasion.
1989 Prodemocracy demonstrations and strikes; Communist leaders resign.
1990 Multiparty elections; country officially renamed Czech and Slovak Federal Republic.
1993 Czech Republic peacefully divides from Slovakia. Joins UN.
1999 Joins NATO.

SLOVAKIA

OFFICIAL NAME
The Slovak Republic

CAPITAL
Bratislava

Area 49,036 km²
(18 933 sq miles)
Population 5 395 000
Population density 110 per
km² (285 per sq mile)
Population growth rate 0.4%
Life expectancy 68 (m); 76 (f)
Languages Slovak,
Hungarian, Czech and
others
Adult literacy rate 93%
Currency Slovak koruna
(US $1 = 48 koruna)
GDP (US million $) 19 500
GDP per head (US $) 3617

Key dates

907-1867 Under Hungarian rule.
1867-1918 Exists as part of the Austro-Hungarian Empire.
1918 Establishment of Czechoslovakia.
1939-45 Independence from Czechoslovakia under Nazi control.
1945 Reunion as Czechoslovakia.
1992 Slovakia declares independence.
1993 Slovakia peacefully divides from Czech Republic. Joins UN.

AUSTRIA

OFFICIAL NAME
The Republic of Austria

CAPITAL
Vienna

Area 83 858 km²
(32 378 sq miles)
Population 8 177 000
Population density 96 per
km² (250 per sq mile)
Population growth rate 0.5%
Life expectancy 73 (m); 80 (f)
Language German
Adult literacy rate 99%
Currency schilling
(US $1 = 15.2 schillings)
GDP (US million $) 215 300
GDP per head (US $) 26 646

FACT
In 1998 the Vienna Boys' Choir had its 500th anniversary. Both Schubert and Haydn once sang with the choir.

Key dates

955 German king Otto's rule begins.
962 Otto crowned Holy Roman Emperor.
1278 First Habsburg emperor.
1806 Austrian Empire.
1867 Dual monarchy of Austria-Hungary set up.
1914 Invades Serbia, starting First World War; one of Central Powers.
1918 Defeat; empire ends; republic founded.
1938 Nazi occupation: union with Germany.
1939-45 Fights the Second World War as part of Axis.
1945 Allied occupation.
1955 Independence recognised; occupation forces leave. Joins UN.
1995 Joins the European Union.

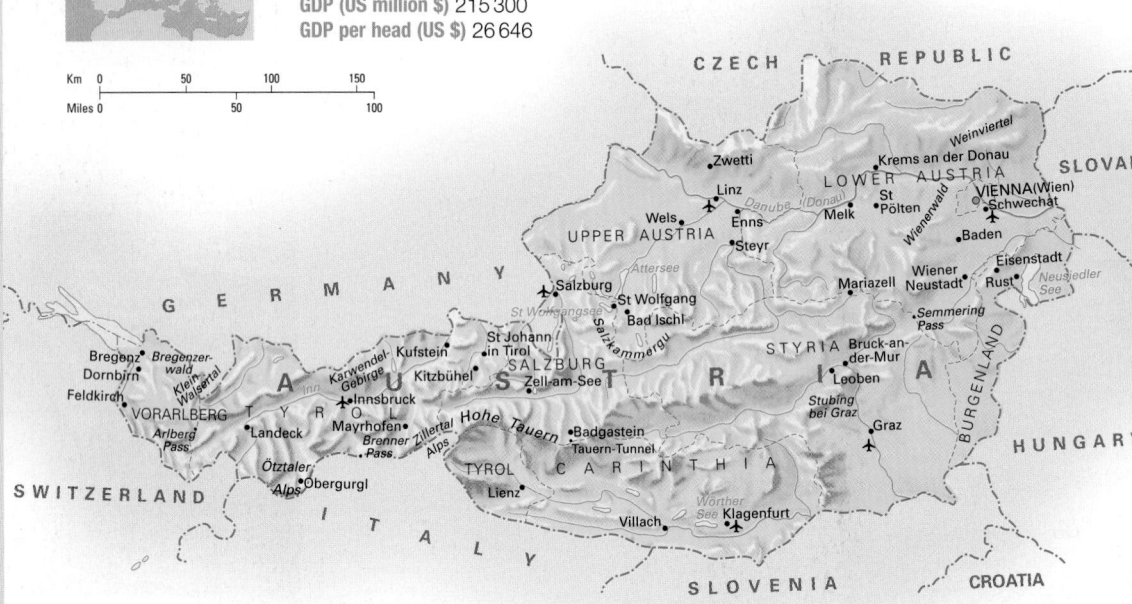

HUNGARY

OFFICIAL NAME
The Republic of Hungary

CAPITAL
Budapest

Area 93 030 km²
(35 919 sq miles)
Population 10 068 000
Population density 109 per
km² (281 per sq mile)
Population growth rate
0.4%
Life expectancy 65 (m); 74 (f)
Language Hungarian
Adult literacy rate 99%
Currency forint
(US $1 = 296 forints)
GDP (US million $) 48 500
GDP per head (US $) 4797

Key dates

9thC Magyar invasion.
1000 Stephen becomes first king of Hungary.
1526 Ottoman rule.
c.1700 Habsburg rule.
1867 Dual monarchy of Austria-Hungary set up.
1914-18 Fights First World War as one of Central Powers; republic proclaimed after defeat.
1919 Admiral Horthy takes power as regent.
1941-4 Second World War on the side of Axis.
1944 Soviet occupation.
1947-9 Communists take power.
1956 Soviet troops crush government-backed anti-Soviet protests.
1968 Economic reforms.
1989 New constitution.
1990 Free elections.
1991 Soviet troops leave. Association pact with European Community.

SWITZERLAND

OFFICIAL NAME
The Swiss Confederation

CAPITAL
Bern

Area 41 284 km²
(15 940 sq miles)
Population 7 140 000
Population density 172 per
km² (446 per sq mile)
Population growth rate 0.3%
Life expectancy 75 (m); 82 (f)

Languages German,
French, Italian and others
Adult literacy rate 99%
Currency Swiss franc (US
$1 = 1.69 Swiss francs)
GDP (US million $) 261 400
GDP per head (US $) 37 428

Key dates

962 Becomes part of
Holy Roman Empire.
1291 Founding of Swiss
Confederation.
1499 Full independence.
1798-1815 French rule.
1848 New federal
constitution.
1914-18 Neutral in War.
1920 League of Nations
founded in Geneva.
1939-45 Neutral in War.
1960 Founder-member
of European Free Trade
Association.
1963 Joins Council of
Europe.
1971 Women gain vote.
1986 Voters reject UN
membership.
1992 Voters reject closer
ties to European
Community.

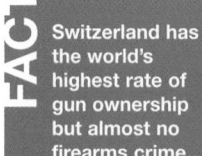

FACT Switzerland has
the world's
highest rate of
gun ownership
but almost no
firearms crime.

Switzerland's armed neutrality

About the only evidence of Switzerland's armed forces visible to the outside world has been the Swiss Army knife. The country's famed neutrality – proclaimed first in the 16th century – has been maintained by a countrywide militia. The militia keep arms, ammunition and uniforms at home, ready for speedy mobilisation.

The army was strengthened during the two World Wars to guard the borders, and it remained on alert during the Cold War. Today, military spending accounts for as much as a third of the national budget. That pays for such hardware as the 400 modern jet aircraft flown by the Swiss Air Force, as well as equipment for the militia.

Switzerland's federal constitution says simply that 'every Swiss male is liable for military service' and can be conscripted from the age of 20 to 42. Anyone unfit for military service must pay a military tax, but a civil service option is granted. Women can join up, but not for combat duties. The cantons – the constituent regions of the Swiss Confederation – provide their local soldiers with physical training under federal government supervision; the defence department then gives regular military training.

All military personnel do regular target practice while off duty. They also perform 'civil protection' duties in catastrophes or other emergencies.

At the beginning of the 21st century, Switzerland was preparing to ease its policy of 'security through autonomy' and replace it with 'security through cooperation' – prompted partly by events in the Balkans, less than an hour's flight away. It planned to cooperate with friendly nations in military training exercises and peace-support operations, and would expand its participation in international security organisations.

Part-time soldiers Swiss reservists cycle off on military exercises. Switzerland strongly defends its neutral status.

LIECHTENSTEIN

OFFICIAL NAME
The Principality of
Liechtenstein

CAPITAL
Vaduz

Area 160 km² (61.8 sq miles)
Population 32 000
Population density 200 per km² (518 per sq mile)
Population growth rate 0%
Life expectancy 66 (m); 73 (f)
Language German (Alemannic dialect)
Adult literacy rate 95%
Currency Swiss franc (US $1 = 1.69 Swiss francs)
GDP (US million $) 1315
GDP per head (US $) 42 416

Key dates

Until 1719 Part of Holy Roman Empire.
1719 Full independence.
1815-66 Member of German Confederation.
1924 Economic union with Switzerland.
1984 Women gain vote.
1990 Joins UN.
1991 Joins European Free Trade Association.

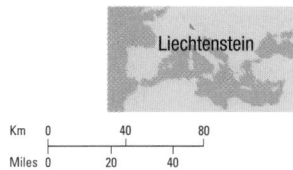

The Balkans

YUGOSLAVIA

OFFICIAL NAME
The Federal Republic of Yugoslavia

CAPITAL
Belgrade

Yugoslavia

Area 102 173 km²
(39 449 sq miles)
Population 10 637 000
Population density 104 per km² (269 per sq mile)
Population growth rate 0.1%
Life expectancy 68 (m); 74 (f)
Language Serbo-Croat
(Cyrillic script)
Adult literacy rate 89%
Currency Yugoslav new dinar (US $1 = 66.94 new dinars)
GDP (US million $) 15 243
GDP per head (US $) 1435

Key dates

1389 Ottoman rule.
1914 Austria-Hungary declares war on Serbia; start of First World War.
1918 Kingdom of Serbs, Croats and Slovenes established (renamed Yugoslavia in 1929).
1941-4 Nazi occupation.
1943 Belgrade liberated by Tito's partisans.
1945 Communist rule.
1980 Tito dies.

1990 Kosovo government dissolved.
1991 Slovenia, Croatia declare independence; war in Croatia.
1992 Macedonia and Bosnia & Herzegovina declare independence; war in Bosnia.
1995 Peace agreement.
1997-9 Kosovo war.
2000 Elections displace President Milosevic.

CROATIA

OFFICIAL NAME
The Republic of Croatia

CAPITAL
Zagreb

Area 56 610 km²
(21 857 sq miles)
Population 4 554 000
Population density 81 per km² (209 per sq mile)
Population growth rate 0.7%
Life expectancy 68 (m); 76 (f)
Language Serbo-Croat
(Roman script)
Adult literacy rate 93%
Currency kuna (US $1 = 8.39 kuna)
GDP (US million $) 20 100
GDP per head (US $) 4396

Key dates

1102 Hungarian rule.
1526-1699 Partial Ottoman rule.
1918 Kingdom of Serbs, Croats and Slovenes (later Yugoslavia).
1990 Elections won by nationalist, Tudjman.
1991-2 Independence declared; civil war.
1992 Peace agreed; UN troops deployed.
1993-4 New fighting.
1996 Joins Council of Europe.
1998 Last Serb-held enclave retaken.

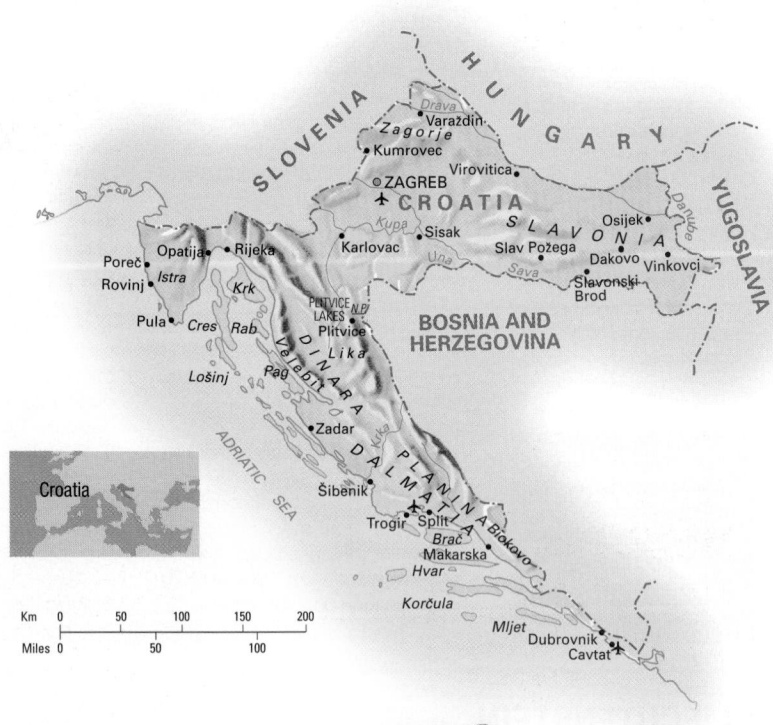

Croatia

YUGOSLAVIA IN PIECES

Postwar Yugoslavia was a federation of six republics. Serbs were traditionally Orthodox, Croats and Slovenes Catholic, and large Muslim communities lived in Macedonia, Montenegro and Bosnia. It was this religious and ethnic mix that led to the Balkan conflict of the 1990s. In 1991,

Croatia and Slovenia declared independence, leading to war between Croats and the Serb-dominated Yugoslav army. In 1992, the war shifted to Bosnia, which had also declared independence. Two million Muslims were 'ethnically cleansed'. Meanwhile, Serb President Milosevic

proclaimed a new Serb state. In 1995, NATO bombed Serb positions in Bosnia to force a peace. In 1998, conflict in Kosovo again brought NATO bombers into the fray. In 2000, the Serb people voted Milosevic out. But the Balkan tragedy is far from over.

Former Yugoslav republics

SLOVENIA

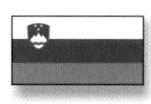

OFFICIAL NAME
The Republic of Slovenia

CAPITAL
Ljubljana

Area 20 253 km²
(7820 sq miles)
Population 1 986 000
Population density 98 per
km² (254 per sq mile)
Population growth rate 0.1%
Life expectancy 70 (m); 77 (f)
Languages Slovene, Serbo-
Croat (Roman script),
Hungarian, Italian

Adult literacy rate 99%
Currency tolar (US $1 =
240 tolars)
GDP (US million $) 19 700
GDP per head (US $) 9914

Key dates

1278 Habsburg rule.
1809-15 French control.
1867 Part of Austro-
Hungarian Empire.
1918 Becomes part of
Kingdom of Serbs,
Croats and Slovenes
(later Yugoslavia).
1990 Nationalist
coalition wins elections;
vote for independence.
1991 Independence
declared; fighting with
Serb-dominated
Yugoslav army ends
with ceasefire.
1992 Joins UN.
1996 Applies to join
European Union.

BOSNIA & HERZEGOVINA

OFFICIAL NAME
Bosnia and Herzegovina

CAPITAL
Sarajevo

Area 51 129 km²
(19 741 sq miles)
Population 3 839 000
Population density 82 per
km² (213 per sq mile)
Population growth rate 1.1%
Life expectancy 69 (m); 75 (f)
Languages Serbo-Croat
(Muslims and Croats use

Roman script; Serbs use
Cyrillic)
Adult literacy rate 93%
Currency marka
(US $1 = 2.17 marka)
GDP (US million $) 4200
GDP per head (US $) 997

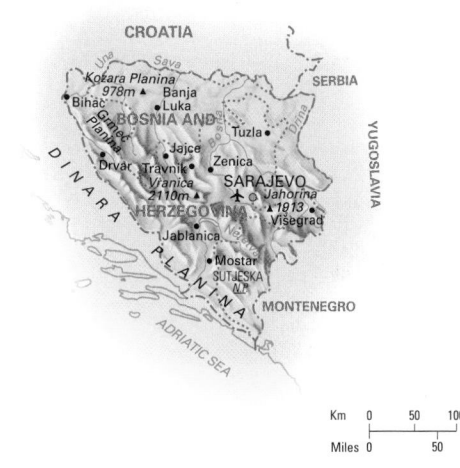

Key dates

1463 Ottoman rule.
1878 Austro-Hungarian
control.
1918 Becomes part of
Kingdom of Serbs,
Croats and Slovenes
(later Yugoslavia).
1992 Croats and
Muslims vote for
independence; Serbs
boycott vote. Civil war
starts; Serbs use
'ethnic cleansing'.
1995 NATO air strikes.
Peace accord sets up
two states with central
government; policed by
UN troops.
1996 Full relations with
Yugoslavia.

MACEDONIA

OFFICIAL NAME
The Former Yugoslav Republic
of Macedonia

CAPITAL
Skopje

Area 25 713 km²
(9928 sq miles)
Population 2 011 000
Population density 78 per
km² (201 per sq mile)
Population growth rate 1.5%
Life expectancy 69 (m); 73 (f)
Languages Macedonian,
Albanian, Serbo-Croat
(Cyrillic script)

Adult literacy rate 93%
Currency Macedonian
denar (US $1 = 64.04
denars)
GDP (US million $) 3200
GDP per head (US $) 1600

Key dates

1371 Ottoman rule.
1912-13 Balkan Wars
fought over Macedonia.
1918 Becomes part of
Kingdom of Serbs,
Croats and Slovenes
(later Yugoslavia).
1991 Declares
independence; dispute
with Greece delays
recognition.
1994 Continuing dispute
leads to Greek trade
embargo.
1995 New agreement
with Greece; trade
embargo lifted.
2000 Conflict with ethnic
Albanian population.

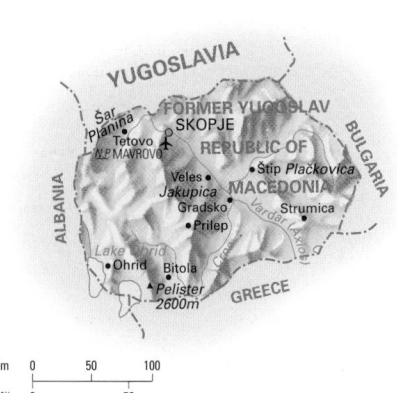

GREECE

OFFICIAL NAME
The Hellenic Republic

CAPITAL
Athens

Area 131 957 km²
(50 949 sq miles)
Population 10 626 000
Population density 80 per
km² (207 per sq mile)
Population growth rate 0.5%
Life expectancy 75 (m); 80 (f)

Language Greek (Demotiki,
or modern Greek)
Adult literacy rate 95.2%
Currency drachma
(US $1 = 378 drachmas)
GDP (US million $) 123 400
GDP per head (US $) 11 727

Olympic origins
The temple of Hera at Olympia (left), 2600 years old, is the most ancient temple of the religious complex where the original Olympic games were held. The games were staged every four years from the 8th century BC to the end of the 4th century AD

Key dates

5thC BC 'Golden Age' of ancient Greece.
146 BC Roman rule begins.
1453 Conquest by Ottoman Empire.
1829 Independence.
1912-13 Balkan Wars: victory over Turkey and Bulgaria.
1924 Becomes republic.
1941-4 Occupied by Germany.
1946-9 Civil war: rebel communists defeated.
1949 Monarchy returns.
1967 Military coup; martial law imposed.
1973 Republic declared.
1974 Martial law ends; civilian government and free elections.
1981 Joins European Community.
1995 Normal relations with Macedonia.

FACT

Greece has about 2000 islands and almost 15 000 km (9300 miles) of coastline.

TURKEY

OFFICIAL NAME
The Republic of Turkey

CAPITAL
Ankara

Area 779 452 km²
(300 948 sq miles)
Population 64 385 000
Population density 81 per
km² (211 per sq mile)
Population growth rate 1.2%
Life expectancy 63 (m); 66 (f)
Languages Turkish, Kurdish

Adult literacy rate 82.3%
Currency Turkish lira
(US $1 = 1 240 000 liras)
GDP (US million $) 209 200
GDP per head (US $) 3297

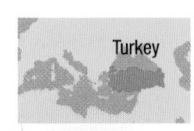
Turkey

Key dates

1299 Birth of Ottoman
Empire.
1912 First Balkan War
against Greece: defeat
and loss of territory.
1914-18 First World War
fought alongside
Germany; defeated.
1923 Atatürk proclaims
Republic of Turkey;
starts modernisation.
1960-1 Military rule.
1974 Invades northern
Cyprus.
1980 Military coup.
1983 Civilian rule.
1984 Kurdish terrorist
campaign begins.
1999 Kurdish leader
Abdullah Ocalan
sentenced to death.

CYPRUS

OFFICIAL NAME
The Republic of Cyprus

CAPITAL
Nicosia

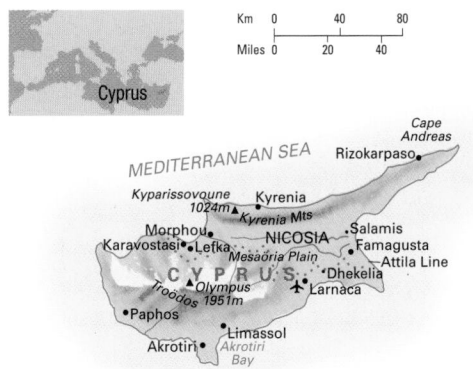
Cyprus

Area 9251 km²
(3572 sq miles)
Population 753 000
Population density 81 per
km² (210 per sq mile)
Population growth rate 1.1%
Life expectancy 75 (m); 79 (f)

Languages Greek, Turkish
Adult literacy rate 94%
Currency Cyprus pound
(US $1 = 0.64 Cyprus
pound)
GDP (US million $) 9200
GDP per head (US $) 12 266

Key dates

1489 Venetian rule.
1570 Ottoman rule.
1878 British rule.
1950s Terrorist attacks
on Britain, and between
Greeks and Turks.
1960 Independence.
1963 Fighting between
Greeks and Turks.
1964 UN peace-keeping
force arrives.
1974 Greek army coup;
Turkey invades north.
1983 Turks proclaim
Republic of Northern
Cyprus (unrecognised).

TENTATIVE CONTACTS ACROSS THE AEGEAN

It took violent earth tremors to bring about better relations between Turkey and Greece after centuries of enmity. When the suburbs of both Istanbul and Athens suffered serious damage in 1999, the shared human tragedy led to increased contact between the two nations.

Only two years before, they had agreed to find peaceful resolutions to future conflicts, and in 2000 signed a series of accords pledging peace. These developments were warmly welcomed by the two nations' NATO allies, since Turkey and Greece have a long history as uneasy neighbours.

The Ottoman Turks overthrew the Byzantine Empire in the 14th and 15th centuries, and ruled all of Greece by 1460. A Greek national revival began in the late 18th century, but it was not until 1821 that a successful revolt occurred. Fighting back, the Turks massacred 25 000 people and sold 45 000 into slavery, provoking the British, Russians and French to help Greece finally to win its War of Independence in 1829.

Greece failed to gain disputed border areas in a disastrous war against the Ottomans in 1897, but victory in the Balkan Wars of 1912-13 led to Greek seizure of Crete and parts of Macedonia. In the First World War, Greece reluctantly joined the Allies, while Turkey took the side of Germany. As a result, Greece gained Thrace from the final collapse of the Ottoman Empire. In 1919, Greek forces invaded Izmir in Asia Minor, but were driven out by troops led by Kemal Atatürk, the founder of modern Turkey, in 1922.

The last major conflict between the two countries was in Greek-dominated Cyprus in 1974, when Turkish forces invaded the north in response to a Greek-inspired military coup. The Turkish Cypriots declared their part of the island – making up about 40 per cent of the total – independent in 1983. If the Greek–Turkish thaw continues, Cyprus too may find stability.

BULGARIA

OFFICIAL NAME
The Republic of Bulgaria

CAPITAL
Sofia

Area 110 994 km²
(42 855 sq miles)
Population 8 208 000
Population density 74 per
km² (193 per sq mile)
Population growth rate 0.2%
Life expectancy 67 (m); 74 (f)

Languages Bulgarian,
Turkish
Adult literacy rate 92%
Currency lev (US $1 = 2.16
levs)
GDP (US million $) 11 900
GDP per head (US $) 1442

Regulars and new arrivals The Black Sea coast of
Bulgaria was a favourite destination for holidaymakers
from all over Eastern Europe in the Communist era. It
strove, with some success, to widen its appeal in the
1990s, and today is known for having perhaps the
best-run tourist industry in the former Soviet bloc.

Key dates

1018-1186 Part of
Byzantine Empire.
1396 Ottoman rule.
1908 Full independence
from Turkish rule.
1912-13 Balkan Wars.
1914-18 First World War
as German ally.
1939-44 Second World
War as German ally.
1944 Soviet occupation
after failure to make
separate peace with
Britain and USA.
1946 Monarchy is
abolished; government
headed by Communists.
1948 Full Communist
control.
1980s Ethnic Turks
suppressed; many flee.
1990 Ethnic suppression
reversed by reformist
government.
1990 Free elections.
1991 New constitution;
parliamentary republic.

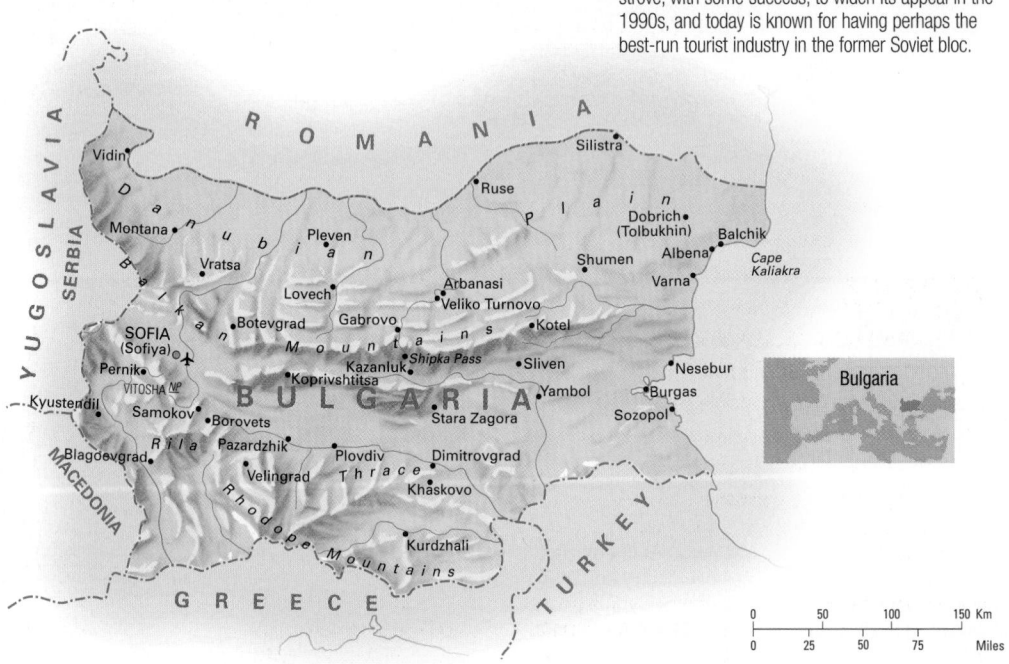

MOLDOVA

OFFICIAL NAME
The Republic of Moldova

CAPITAL
Chisinau

Area 33 700 km²
(13 010 sq miles)
Population 4 380 000
Population density 108 per
km² (281 per sq mile)
Population growth rate 0.5%
Life expectancy 62 (m); 69 (f)
Languages Moldovan,
Russian

Adult literacy rate 96.4%
Currency Moldovan leu
(US $1 = 12.89 Moldovan
leus)
GDP (US million $) 1049
GDP per head (US $) 287

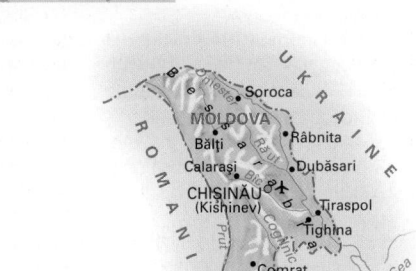

Key dates

16thC Turkish rule.
1812 Russian control.
1918-40 Part of
Romania.
1940 Becomes part of
Soviet Union.
1990 Declares self-
government; renamed
Republic of Moldova.
1991 Full independence;
joins Commonwealth of
Independent States.
1992 Joins UN.
1992-3 Ethnic unrest.
1994 Free elections.

ROMANIA

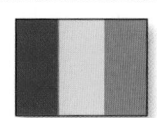

OFFICIAL NAME
Romania

CAPITAL
Bucharest

Area 238 391 km²
(92 043 sq miles)
Population 22 458 000
Population density 94 per
km² (244 per sq mile)
Population growth rate -0.2%
Life expectancy 65 (m); 73 (f)
Languages Romanian,
Hungarian, German and
others
Adult literacy rate 96.7%
Currency Romanian leu
(US $1 = 28 005 Romanian
leus)
GDP (US million $) 32 400
GDP per head (US $) 1440

Key dates

15thC Ottoman rule.
1829 Russian control.
1861 Romania united.
1878 Full independence.
1916-18 Ally of Britain in
First World War; gains
Transylvania.
1941-4 Ally of Germany
in Second World War.
1944 Joins Allies; Soviet
occupation begins.
1947 Communist rule.
1989 President Nicolae
Ceausescu overthrown.
1990 Free elections.

ALBANIA

OFFICIAL NAME
The Republic of Albania

CAPITAL
Tirana

Area 28 748 km²
(11 100 sq miles)
Population 3 113 000
Population density 132 per
km² (341 per sq mile)
Population growth rate
1.6%
Life expectancy 69 (m); 75 (f)
Languages Albanian

(dialects: Gheg in north,
Tosk in south)
Adult literacy rate 95%
Currency lek
(US $1 = 144 leks)
GDP (US million $) 3555
GDP per head (US $) 937

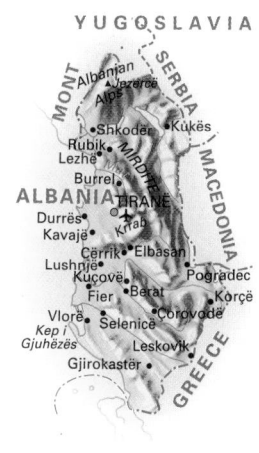

FACT Albania has
Europe's highest
infant mortality
rate; 37 babies in
every 1000 survive
less than a month.

Key dates

15thC Ottoman rule.
1912 First Balkan War:
gains independence.
1914-20 Occupied by
Italy in First World War.
1925 Becomes republic.
1928 President Zogu
proclaimed King Zog.
1939-44 Occupied by
Italy then Germany.
1944 Communist
partisans seize power.
1961 Splits with USSR.
1991 Open elections.
1992 Reforms begin.
1997 Riots follow crash
of investment funds.
1999 Influx of refugees
from Kosovo.

Albania's long isolation

While most of Europe made rapid economic
and social progress towards the end of the
20th century, Albania, the smallest Balkan state,
seemed to stand still. This was a legacy of its
extreme Stalinist regime of 45 years, the
longest-surviving in Europe. Today, with tight
government controls, political instability and a
weak infrastructure, Albania remains Europe's
poorest and least developed country, although
it has moved part-way towards democracy.

After Second World War occupation by Italy
and then (when Italy surrendered) Germany,
Albania began independence in 1945 under the
communism of former partisan leader Enver

Hoxha. He headed a repressive government
from 1945 to 1985 that imprisoned 200 000
people and executed some 5000. His regime
also banned all religions – and beards. Although
he had been close to Stalin, Hoxha broke with
the USSR in 1961 after Soviet leader Nikita
Khrushchev denounced his predecessor.
Hoxha switched allegiance to China, but that
relationship failed in 1978 when China's post-
Mao leadership introduced reforms.

After Hoxha died in 1985, his successor
Ramiz Alia relaxed Albania's isolationism by
establishing diplomatic relations with several
countries. The regime also became less harsh,

allowing religions and opposition parties in
1990; two years later, the Socialists
(Communists) were defeated at the polls.

Economic reforms bore some fruits – there
were more than 50 000 private businesses by
1993 – but troubles soon returned. Violence
followed the collapse of pyramid investment
schemes in 1997, and thousands fled to Italy. A
year later, the Kosovo crisis saw thousands of
ethnic Albanians stream into the country.

Albania remains unstable and is plagued by
widespread gangsterism. But its decades in the
political wilderness are over. Its future looks set
as a part of Europe rather than apart from it.

RUSSIA

OFFICIAL NAME
The Russian Federation

CAPITAL
Moscow

Area 17 075 400 km²
(6 592 850 sq miles)
Population 145 943 000
Population density 9 per km²
(22 per sq mile)
Population growth rate -0.1%
Life expectancy 58 (m); 71 (f)
Languages Russian, Tatar,
Yakut, Chuvash, Bashkir
and others
Adult literacy rate 99%
Currency rouble
(US $1 = 28 roubles)
GDP (US million $) 190 600
GDP per head (US $) 1300

Mighty empire
The Soviet Union consisted of 15
republics totalling 22 402 194 km²
(8 649 496 sq miles), with a total
population in 1985 of nearly 300
million.

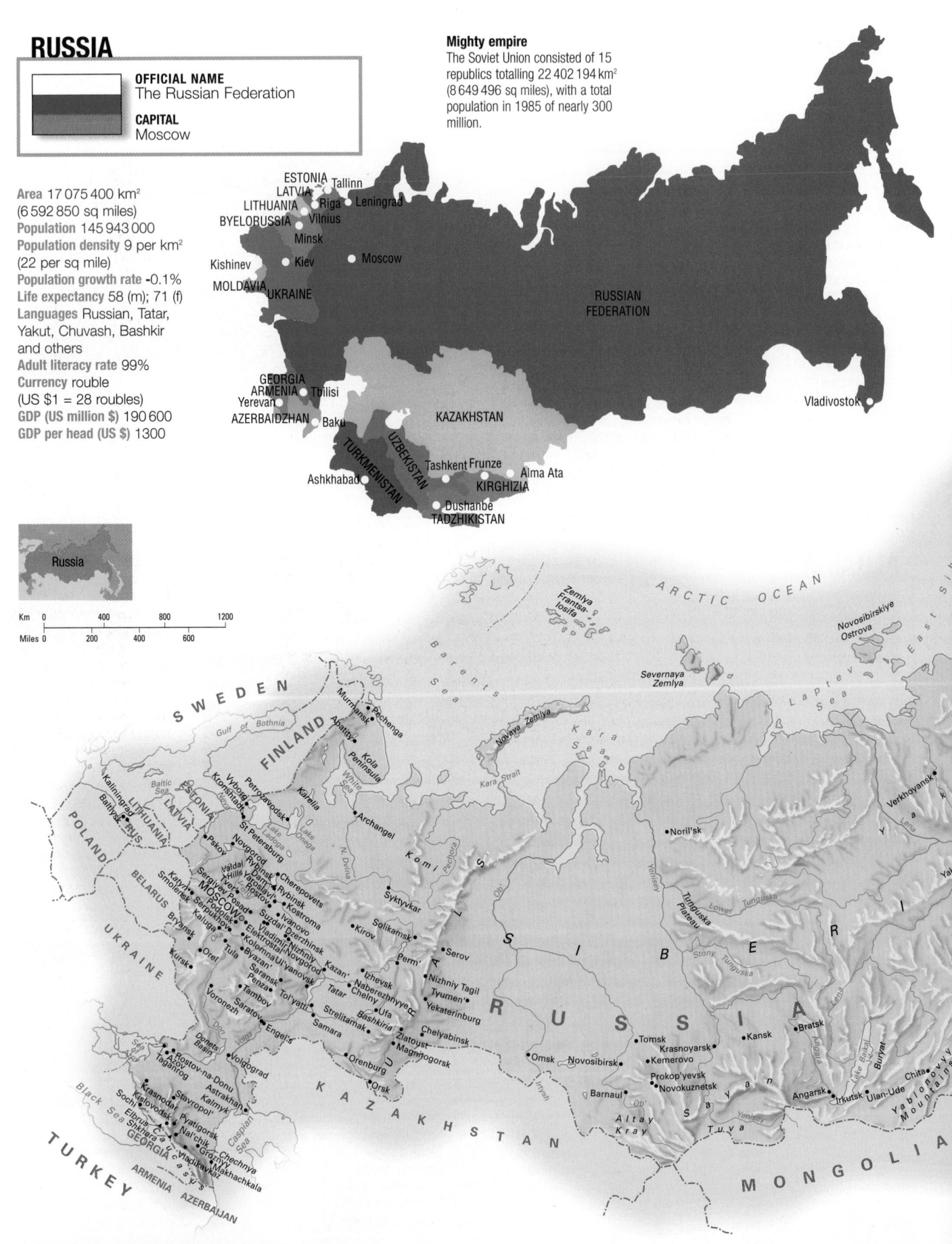

Russia

Russia's great upheaval

At the height of its success, between 1945 and 1985, Russia enjoyed enormous influence in the world. Moscow, the ancient heart of the Russian lands, was the capital of the largest country in the world. That country comprised 15 republics (of which the biggest was Russia itself, with about half the total Soviet population), and it commanded immense natural and industrial resources.

Russian influence extended beyond its borders into the hub of Europe. The Soviet Union also had three seats at the UN (one for the Ukraine, one for Belorussia and a third for Russia and the remaining republics) and a vast military capacity. Russia, in its 20th-century Soviet incarnation, was stronger than at any time in its history, feared or respected by the whole world. But Communist totalitarianism had frozen Russia's empire into one great ideological iceberg, and a long cold war with the West had almost bankrupted it.

Mikhail Gorbachev, appointed general secretary of the ruling Communist Party in 1985, introduced perestroika (restructuring) and glasnost (openness) to the USSR. These concessions encouraged the Soviet satellites and republics to demand independence, and drift away like ice floes: first the countries of eastern Europe, then the Baltic states, then the other 14 Soviet republics. Small-scale ethnic wars flared in several corners of the old Soviet state. The bloodiest was in Chechnya, in the Caucasus.

With the loss of the republics, Russia's stake in Europe was reduced to something less than it had been at the time of Catherine the Great in the 18th century. The Russian economy, exposed to the free market, went into steep decline, and Russia became dependent on Western aid. Millions of ordinary citizens were left bitter, destitute and nostalgic for the certainties of the Soviet past.

Since the collapse of the Communist empire in the early 1990s, Russia has been beset by violent crime and corruption, as well as by economic problems. The bewildering loss of empire and prestige came about in the space of one short decade. It will take Russia much longer to recover from the trauma.

Tough fighters Chechen rebels (above) fought ferociously for independence from Russia in the 1990s. They held out against a far more powerful Russian army even after the Chechen capital Grozny was virtually destroyed.

Market economy When Communism collapsed in Russia, so did many state-run industries and shops. People were forced to trade at private-enterprise markets (right) or barter for goods.

FACT The Trans-Siberian Railway, the world's longest, stretches 9438 km (5864 miles) eastwards from Moscow.

UKRAINE

OFFICIAL NAME
The Republic of Ukraine

CAPITAL
Kiev

Area 603 700 km²
(233 090 sq miles)
Population 50 106 000
Population density 84 per
km² (217 per sq mile)
Population growth rate -0.6%
Life expectancy 62 (m); 73 (f)
Languages Ukrainian,
Russian, Romanian,
Hungarian, Polish
Adult literacy rate 96%
Currency hryvnya
(US $1 = 5.41 hryvnyas)
GDP (US million $) 30 800
GDP per head (US $) 609

Key dates

9thC State of Kievan
Rus founded at Kiev.
14thC Polish and
Lithuanian rule.
1667-1790s Russia
gains control.
1918 Ukraine proclaims
independence.
1920 Russia invade.
1922 Founder-republic
of Soviet Union.
1941-4 Second World
War: occupied by
Germany. Resistance to
Germany and USSR.
1945 Becomes founder-
member of UN.
1954 Crimea transferred
from Russia to Ukraine.
1986 Chernobyl nuclear
disaster.
1990 Sovereignty over
Soviet laws declared.
1991 Independence;
joins Commonwealth of
Independent States.
1992 Dispute starts over
Crimean autonomy.
1995 Transfers nuclear
warheads to Russia for
destruction.

BELARUS

OFFICIAL NAME
The Republic of Belarus

CAPITAL
Minsk

Area 207 595 km²
(80 153 sq miles)
Population 10 159 000
Population density 49 per
km² (127 per sq mile)
Population growth rate 0.2%
Life expectancy 62 (m); 74 (f)
Languages Belarussian,
Russian
Adult literacy rate 97.9%
Currency Belarussian rouble
(US $1 = 1345.00
Belarussian roubles)
GDP (US million $) 11 991
GDP per head (US $) 1180

Key dates

13thC Part of Lithuania.
1569 Part of Poland.
1772-95 Comes under
Russian rule.
1918-19 Independence.
1919 Divided between
Poland and Russia.
1922 Founder-republic
of Soviet Union.
1939 Polish-occupied
areas retaken.
1941-4 Occupied by
Germany.
1945 Becomes founder-
member of UN.
1990 Sovereignty over
Soviet laws declared.
1991 Independence;
joins Commonwealth of
Independent States.
1996 Agrees economic
union with Russia.

GEORGIA

OFFICIAL NAME
Georgia

CAPITAL
Tbilisi

Area 69 700 km²
(26 911 sq miles)
Population 5 399 000
Population density 73 per
km² (188 per sq mile)
Population growth rate 1.3%
Life expectancy 68 (m); 76 (f)
Language Georgian
Adult literacy rate 99%
Currency lari
(US $1 = 1.97 lari)

GDP (US million $) 4400
GDP per head (US $) 869

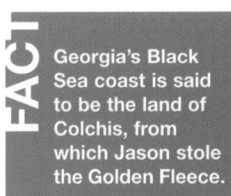

FACT
Georgia's Black
Sea coast is said
to be the land of
Colchis, from
which Jason stole
the Golden Fleece.

Georgia

Key dates

*c.*1800 Russian rule.
1918 Independence.
1921 Russia invades.
1922 Merged into USSR.
1936 Becomes separate
republic within USSR.
1990 Open elections.
1991 Independence.
mid 1990s Ethnic civil
wars after South
Ossetia and Abkhazia
declare independence.
1992 Joins UN.
1993 Joins
Commonwealth of
Independent States.
1994 Military pact with
Russia.

ARMENIA

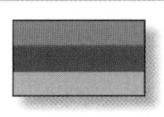

OFFICIAL NAME
The Republic of Armenia

CAPITAL
Yerevan

Area 29 800 km²
(11 500 sq miles)
Population 3 795 000
Population density 119 per
km² (308 per sq mile)
Population growth rate 1.1%
Life expectancy 67 (m); 74 (f)
Languages Armenian,
Kurdish
Adult literacy rate 98.8%
Currency dram (US $1 =
548 drams)
GDP (US million $) 1880
GDP per head (US $) 531

FACT
In the 4th century
Armenia was the
first country in the
world to adopt
Christianity as its
state religion.

Key dates

*c.*100 Armenian empire.
1514 Ottoman control.
1639 Persians invade
eastern Armenia.
1828 Russia annexes
eastern Armenia.
1915 Turkey deports
western Armenians;
many massacred.
1918 Independence.
1920 Russia invades.
1922 Merged into USSR.
1936 Becomes separate
republic within USSR.
1989-94 Wars with
Azerbaijan over enclave
of Nagorno-Karabakh.
1991 Independence;
joins Commonwealth of
Independent States.

Armenia

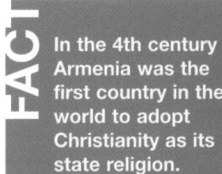

AZERBAIJAN

OFFICIAL NAME
The Azerbaijani Republic

CAPITAL
Baku

Area 86 600 km²
(33 400 sq miles)
Population 7 983 000
Population density 88 per
km² (229 per sq mile)
Population growth rate 0.4%
Life expectancy 65 (m); 74 (f)
Language Azerbaijani (Azeri)
Adult literacy rate 97.3%

Currency manat
(US $1 = 4579 manats)
GDP (US million $) 3600
GDP per head (US $) 471

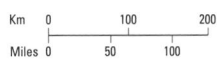

Azerbaijan

Key dates

16th-19thC Alternate
Persian and Ottoman
Turkish control.
1813 Russian control
begins.
1918 Independent state.
1920 Russia invades.
1922 Merged into USSR.
1936 Becomes separate
republic within USSR.
1989-94 Wars with
Armenia over enclave
of Nagorno-Karabakh.
1991 Independence;
joins Commonwealth of
Independent States.
1992 Joins UN.
1994 Ceasefire in
Nagorno-Karabakh.

SYRIA

OFFICIAL NAME
The Syrian Arab Republic

CAPITAL
Damascus

Area 185 180 km²
(71 498 sq miles)
Population 16 110 000
Population density 87 per
km² (225 per sq mile)
Population growth rate 2.5%
Life expectancy 64 (m); 68 (f)
Languages Arabic, Kurdish
Adult literacy rate 79.4%

Currency Syrian pound
(US $1 = 52.5 Syrian
pounds)
GDP (US million $) 16 500
GDP per head (US $) 1024

FACT The Syrian capital Damascus is one of the world's oldest cities, founded about 5000 years ago.

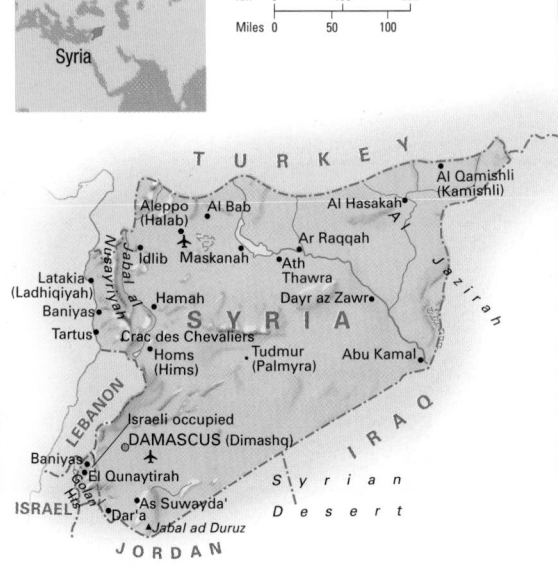

Key dates

1516 Ottoman rule.
1920 League of Nations gives France control.
1946 Independence after French and British control in Second World War.
1958-61 Joins Egypt in United Arab Republic.
1967 Golan Heights lost after defeat by Israel in Six-Day War.
1970 Military coup led by General Assad.
1971 Assad president.
1973 Yom Kippur War against Israel fails to regain Golan Heights.
1976 Peace-keeping force in Lebanon.
2000 Assad dies.

ISRAEL

OFFICIAL NAME
The State of Israel

CAPITAL
Jerusalem

Area 21 946 km²
(8473 sq miles)
Population 6 125 000
Population density 272 per
km² (705 per sq mile)
Population growth rate 2.1%
Life expectancy 75 (m); 79 (f)
Languages Hebrew, Russian,
Arabic, European languages

Adult literacy rate 95.6%
Currency new shekel (US
$1 = 4.15 new shekels)
GDP (US million $) 95 400
GDP per head (US $) 15 979

Key dates

1517 Ottoman rule.
1920 League of Nations gives Britain control of Palestine (Israel and West Bank).
1948 Independent state declared; Arab allies invade unsuccessfully.
1956 Suez War: briefly occupies Sinai.
1967 Six-Day War: victory over Arab allies; occupies Gaza Strip, West Bank, Sinai, Golan Heights and Jerusalem.
1973 Yom Kippur War: attack by Egypt and Syria fails.
1978 Attacks PLO bases in Lebanon. Camp David Accords with Egypt.
1979 Israeli-Egyptian peace agreement.
1980 Capital moved to Jerusalem from Tel Aviv.
1982 Sinai withdrawal. Invades southern Lebanon to attack PLO.
1987 Arab uprising in Gaza and West Bank.
1993 Oslo accord: Israel recognised; some Palestinian self-rule.
1994 Peace accord with Jordan. Palestinian self-rule for Gaza Strip and Jericho; Arafat heads Palestinian government.
2000 Withdrawal from southern Lebanon; new intifada.

Blustery frontier Wind generators built by an enterprising Jewish settler tower over abandoned Israeli trenches on the Golan Heights. United Nations troops man a border crossing between Israel and Syria a few hundred metres below.

CONFLICT IN THE BIBLE LANDS

Conflict between the Israelis and Palestinian Arabs is one of the modern world's most intractable problems. Both peoples claim that much of modern Israeli territory was theirs in ancient times, and both demand jurisdiction in Jerusalem, where their holiest shrines are located.

Their modern conflict began with the UN's decision in 1947 to divide Palestine between Jewish and Arab territory. Palestine had been put under British supervision in 1920, and hundreds of thousands of Jews had migrated there, following Britain's 1917 'Balfour declaration' in favour of a Jewish 'national home' in Palestine. Israel declared independence on May 14, 1948, and Arab forces invaded the next day in the first of several wars against the new state. The

Palestine Liberation Organisation (PLO) was formed in 1964 to re-establish independence for the Palestinian Arabs, and Yasser Arafat became its leader in 1969. In 1987, after Palestinians rioted in the Israeli-occupied Gaza Strip and West Bank, the PLO declared an independent Palestinian state. Two years later, Palestinians began a general uprising known as the intifada.

In 1993, after secret talks in Oslo, Norway, an accord was signed by Israel and the PLO, formally recognising each other's right to exist. Limited Palestinian self-rule was agreed, and a phased withdrawal of Israeli troops from the two Palestinian territories. Further agreements were signed, but extremists on both sides have extended the conflict into the 21st century.

LEBANON

OFFICIAL NAME
The Lebanese Republic

CAPITAL
Beirut

Area 10 452 km² (4036 sq miles)
Population 3 236 000
Population density 305 per km² (790 per sq mile)
Population growth rate 1.8%
Life expectancy 66 (m); 70 (f)
Languages Arabic, French, Kurdish, Armenian
Adult literacy rate 92.4%
Currency Lebanese pound (US $1 = 1514 Lebanese pounds)
GDP (US million $) 17 476
GDP per head (US $) 5478

Key dates

1516 Ottoman rule.
1920 League of Nations gives France control.
1943 Independence.
1975-6 Civil war.
1976 Syrian occupation.
1978 Israel invades to attack PLO bases; UN peace-keeping force.
1982 Israel again invades south.
1985-92 Shi'ite Muslim groups hold Western hostages.
1993 Israel attacks Hezbollah terrorists in south.
2000 Israel withdraws.

JORDAN

OFFICIAL NAME
The Hashemite Kingdom of Jordan

CAPITAL
Amman

Area 97 740 km² (37 738 sq miles)
Population 6 482 000
Population density 64 per km² (167 per sq mile)
Population growth rate 2.8%
Life expectancy 66 (m); 69 (f)
Language Arabic
Adult literacy rate 86.6%
Currency dinar (US $1 = 0.71 dinar)
GDP (US million $) 7500
GDP per head (US $) 1190

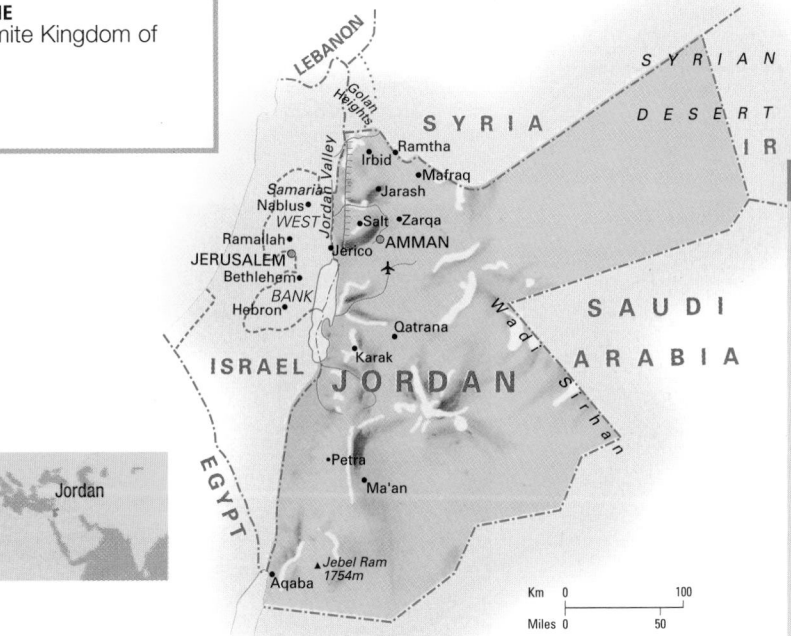

Key dates

1517 Ottoman rule.
1921 Partial self-rule (as Transjordan) under British control.
1946 Independence.
1948 War with Israel: Gains West Bank and East Jerusalem.
1967 Six-Day War: loses West Bank and East Jerusalem to Israel.
1988 Cedes West Bank responsibility to PLO.
1994 Peace accord with Israel.
1999 King Hussein dies after reigning 46 years.

IRAQ

OFFICIAL NAME
The Republic of Iraq

CAPITAL
Baghdad

Area 438 317 km²
(169 235 sq miles)
Population 22 450 000
Population density 50 per
km² (129 per sq mile)
Population growth rate 2.1%
Life expectancy 77 (m); 78 (f)
Languages Arabic, Kurdish,
Turkoman
Adult literacy rate 58%
Currency Iraqi dinar
(US $1 = 0.312 dinars)
GDP (US million $) 26 700
GDP per head (US $) 1189

FACT
Several ancient
civilisations grew
up in present-day
Iraq: Assyria,
Sumer, Babylonia
and Mesopotamia.

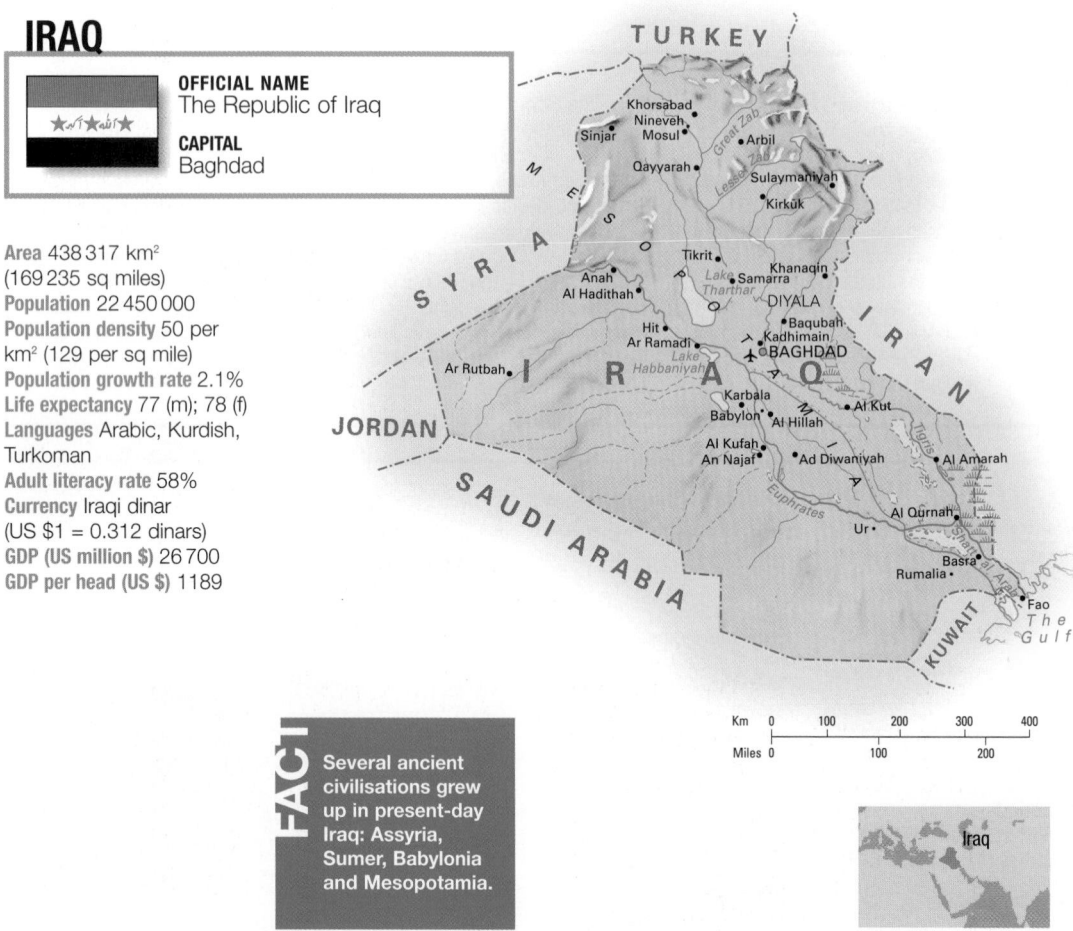

Km 0 100 200 300 400
Miles 0 100 200

Iraq

Key dates

539 BC Beginning of
Persian rule.
AD 637 Arab conquest.
1534 Beginning of
Ottoman rule.
1920 British control.
1932 Independence.
1945 Founder-member
of Arab League.
1958 Monarchy
overthrown; republic.
1961-75 Kurdish revolt;
intermittent fighting.
1979 Saddam Hussein
becomes president.
1980-8 Inconclusive war
after invading Iran.
1987-8 Poison gas used
against Kurds.
1990 Invades Kuwait.
1991 Gulf War lost to
US-led coalition. UN
imposes sanctions and
'safe zone' for Kurds.
1992 Allies impose no-
fly zone in south to
protect Shi'ite minority.
1996 US bombs military
targets after Iraqi troops
enter Kurdish territory.
1997 Dispute with UN
over obstruction of
weapons inspectors.

KUWAIT

OFFICIAL NAME
The State of Kuwait

CAPITAL
Kuwait City

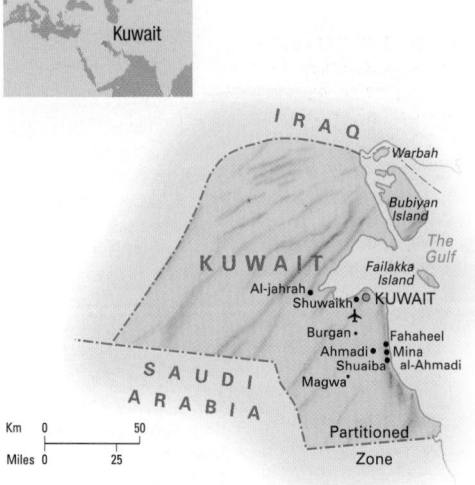

Km 0 50
Miles 0 25

Area 17 818 km²
(6880 sq miles)
Population 2 107 000
Population density 114 per
km² (295 per sq mile)
Population growth rate 5%
Life expectancy 71 (m); 73 (f)
Languages Arabic, English
Adult literacy rate 78.6%
Currency Kuwaiti dinar
(US $1 = 0.30 dinar)

GDP (US million $) 28 600
GDP per head (US $) 14 088

Legacy of war The Gulf War
left Kuwait littered with wrecked
and abandoned military
hardware, such as this Iraqi
tank. Around 600 oil wells were
set alight by Iraqi troops before
the conflict ended.

Key dates

1710 First Arab settlers.
1775 British mail depot.
1899 Self-governing
British protectorate.
1934 Oil discovered.
1961 Full independence.
1973-4 Embargoes oil
supplies to countries
supporting Israel in
Yom Kippur War.
1976-81, 1986 National
assembly suspended.
1980s Supports Iraq
during its war with Iran.
1981 Founder-member
of Gulf Cooperation
Council.
1990 Invaded by Iraq;
government goes into
exile in Saudi Arabia.
1991 Gulf War: US-led
coalition drives out Iraqi
forces, who sabotage
oil wells during retreat.
1992 National assembly
revived; elections held.
1993 US-led air strikes
repel Iraqi incursion.

SAUDI ARABIA

OFFICIAL NAME
The Kingdom of Saudi Arabia

CAPITAL
Riyadh

Area 2 240 000 km²
(864 869 sq miles)
Population 19 895 000
Population density 9 per km²
(23 per sq mile)
Population growth rate 2.7%
Life expectancy 68 (m); 71 (f)
Language Arabic

Adult literacy rate 63%
Currency riyal
(US $1 = 3.75 riyals)
GDP (US million $) 132 900
GDP per head (US $) 6585

Key dates

1906-32 Ibn Saud unites
Saudi Arabian kingdom.
1933 Oil discovered.
1945 Founder-member
of Arab League.
1948 War against Israel.
1973-4 Embargoes oil
supplies to countries
supporting Israel.
1975 King assassinated.
1981 Founder-member
of Gulf Cooperation
Council.
1987 Breaks diplomatic
relations with Iran.
1991 Joins US-led
coalition in Gulf War.
1992 King establishes
consultative council.
1996 Bomb kills 19 US
troops at military base.

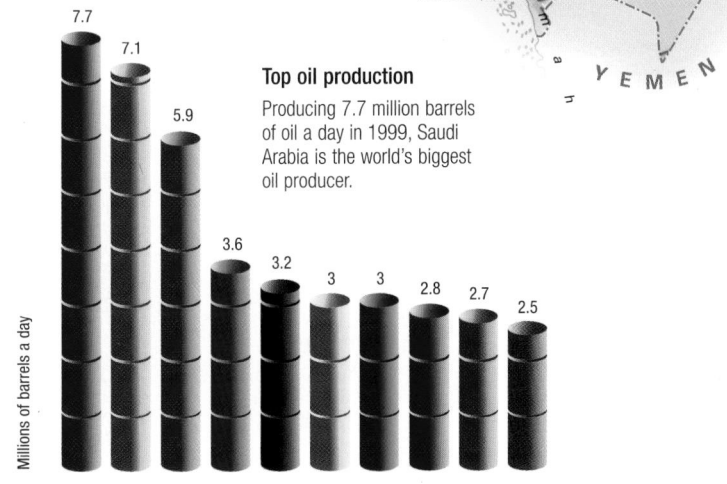

Largest oil-producing countries, 1999

Top oil production

Producing 7.7 million barrels
of oil a day in 1999, Saudi
Arabia is the world's biggest
oil producer.

FACT Saudi Arabia has
about 300 000
chauffeurs.
Women are not
allowed to drive
cars.

THE POLITICS OF OIL

Oil became both a source of conflict and a weapon in the 20th century. With the largest oil reserves located in the Middle East, that region became the focus of global economic and military rivalry.

The first oil to be discovered in the Middle East was in Persia (Iran) in 1908, followed by Iraq in 1927, then Bahrain, Kuwait, Saudi Arabia and Qatar in the 1930s. These nations were at first simply content to share in the profits of Western companies that had found and developed their vast resources. But they soon realised the advantages of ownership: Iran nationalised its oil industry in 1951, Iraq in 1972. Saudi Arabia and its neighbours were

becoming influential nations, and the final step was to turn oil into power as well as money.

The political power of oil was most clearly shown during five months in 1973-4, when the Arab-dominated Organisation of Petroleum Exporting Countries (OPEC) created an oil crisis by banning exports to Western nations supporting Israel in the Yom Kippur War. Oil's strategic importance was also evident when Iraq invaded Kuwait in 1990, drawing a quick Western military response. The defeated Iraqis set some 600 Kuwaiti oil wells on fire as they retreated. The subsequent international embargo on Iraqi oil exports showed that oil power can also be reversed.

The Middle East does not have a monopoly of crude oil supplies. After the OPEC crisis, the major Western nations accelerated their search for petroleum closer to home. Britain began to tap its North Sea oil fields in 1976. The USA discovered extensive reserves in Alaska, and it boosted the development of offshore wells in the Gulf of Mexico. A desire for energy self-reliance, and worries over the environmental impact of oil consumption, have prompted a search for alternative energy. Even so, in 2000, a jump in oil prices after producers reduced output showed how powerful the oil weapon still is.

BAHRAIN

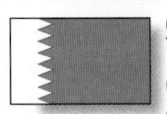

OFFICIAL NAME
The State of Bahrain

CAPITAL
Al Manamah

Area 695 km² (268 sq miles)
Population 666 000
Population density 921 per
km² (2384 per sq mile)
Population growth rate 3.1%
Life expectancy 66 (m); 69 (f)
Languages Arabic, English
Adult literacy rate 85.2%
Currency Bahraini dinar
(US $1 = 0.37 dinar)
GDP (US million $) 6800
GDP per head (US $) 10 625

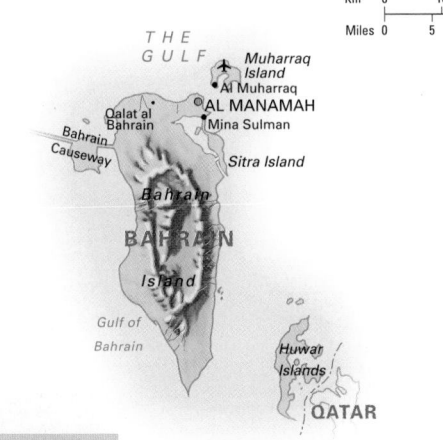

Key dates

17thC Persian rule.
1782 Arab Al Khalifah clan displaces Persians.
1861 Becomes British protectorate.
1931 Oil discovered.
1971 Independence.
1973 National assembly elected.
1975 National assembly dissolved by emir. Buys controlling interest in oil companies.
1981 Founder-member of Gulf Cooperation Council.
1991 Joins US-led coalition in Gulf War against Iraq.

QATAR

OFFICIAL NAME
The State of Qatar

CAPITAL
Doha

Area 11 437 km²
(4416 sq miles)
Population 589 000
Population density 47 per
km² (122 per sq mile)
Population growth rate 1.6%
Life expectancy 68 (m); 74 (f)
Languages Arabic, English
Adult literacy rate 79%

Currency Qatari rial
(US $1 = 3.64 rials)
GDP (US million $) 10 100
GDP per head (US $) 18 703

Key dates

1872 Beginning of Ottoman rule.
1916 Becomes British protectorate.
1939 Oil discovered.
1971 Independence.
1972 Bloodless coup: Sheik Khalifa deposes cousin, Sheik Ahmad.
mid-1970s Oil industry nationalised.
1981 Founder-member of Gulf Cooperation Council.
1991 Gulf War: joins US-led coalition against Iraq; provides air base.

UNITED ARAB EMIRATES

OFFICIAL NAME
The United Arab Emirates

CAPITAL
Abu Dhabi

Area 77 700 km²
(30 000 sq miles)
Population 2 938 000
Population density 35 per
km² (91 per sq mile)
Population growth rate 5.1%
Life expectancy 72 (m); 75 (f)
Languages Arabic, English
Adult literacy rate 79.2%

Currency dirham
(US $1 = 3.67 dirhams)
GDP (US million $) 50 200
GDP per head (US $) 18 455

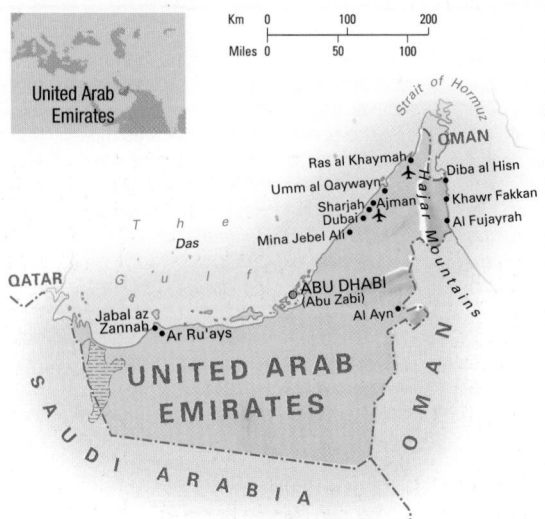

Key dates

7thC Islamic Arab control established.
1820 Britain enforces truces between warring (Trucial) states. Becomes British protectorate.
1958 Oil discovered.
1971 Independence; six of Trucial States, including Abu Dhabi and Dubai, form United Arab Emirates.
1972 Ras al Khaymah joins UAE.
1981 Founder-member of Gulf Cooperation Council.
1991 Joins US-led coalition in Gulf War.

OMAN

OFFICIAL NAME
The Sultanate of Oman

CAPITAL
Muscat

Area 309 500 km²
(119 500 sq miles)
Population 2 460 000
Population density 7 per km²
(19 per sq mile)
Population growth rate 2.3%
Life expectancy 67 (m); 71 (f)
Languages Arabic, English
Adult literacy rate 41%

Currency Omani rial
(US $1 = 0.38 rials)
GDP (US million $) 14 500
GDP per head (US $) 6782

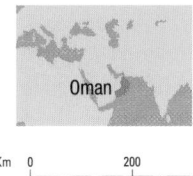

Oman

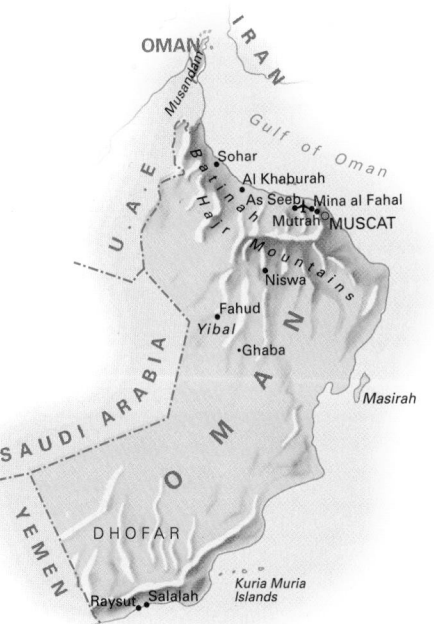

Km 0   200   400
Miles 0   100   200

Key dates

7thC Islamic conversion.
1507-1650 Portuguese control.
late 17thC Sets up east African slaving posts.
1957 Britain helps to defeat religious revolt.
1970 Modernisation begins; name changed to Oman (from Muscat and Oman).
1981 Founder-member of Gulf Cooperation Council.
1991 Joins US-led coalition in Gulf War against Iraq.
1992 Ends long border dispute with Yemen.

YEMEN

OFFICIAL NAME
The Republic of Yemen

CAPITAL
San'a

Area 527 968 km²
(203 850 sq miles)
Population 17 676 000
Population density 32 per km² (82 per sq mile)
Population growth rate 2.9%
Life expectancy 55 (m); 56 (f)
Language Arabic
Adult literacy rate 38%
Currency Yemeni rial
(US $1 = 166.4 rials)
GDP (US million $) 5200
GDP per head (US $) 304

Key dates

1839 UK takes Aden.
1918 North Yemen independent.
1968 Aden and South Yemen independent.
1971-2 War between North and South.
1978-9 War renewed.
1990 Union of North and South Yemen.
1994 Secession of South suppressed.

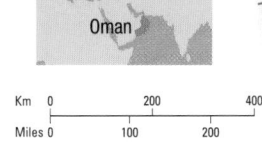

Yemen

Km 0   200
Miles 0   100

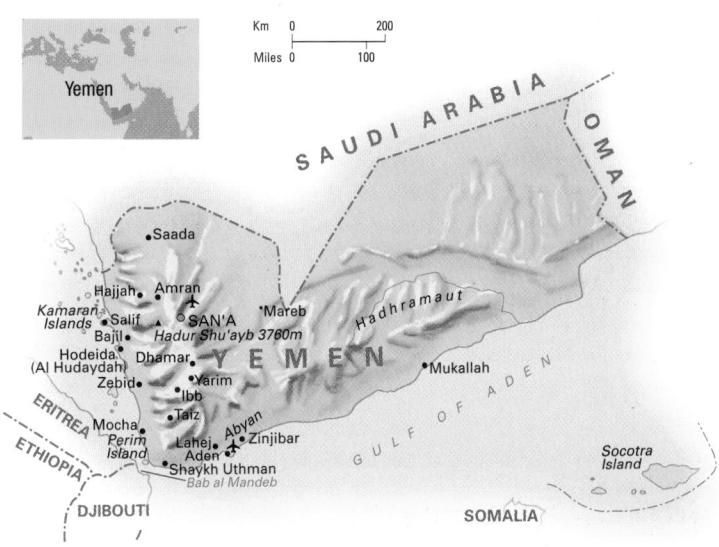

Desert capital San'a, the capital of unified Yemen at the edge of the 'Empty Quarter', grew to importance in the Middle Ages as a trading post on the route through the Arabian peninsula to the port of Aden.

IRAN

OFFICIAL NAME
The Islamic Republic of Iran

CAPITAL
Tehran (Teheran)

Area 1 648 000 km²
(636 296 sq miles)
Population 62 746 000
Population density 38 per
km² (97 per sq mile)
Population growth rate 1.2%
Life expectancy 58 (m); 59 (f)
Languages Farsi (Iranian),
Turkic and other local
languages
Adult literacy rate 72.3%
Currency Iranian rial
(US $1 = 1747 rials)
GDP (US million $) 54 700
GDP per head (US $) 1207

Key dates

*c.*550 BC Persian
empire established.
7thC AD Arab conquest.
1220 Mongol invasion.
1501 Savafid rule.
1826 Russian invasion.
1906 First constitution
and parliament.
1908 Oil discovered.
1925 Army officer Reza
Khan becomes shah.
1935 Renamed Iran
(formerly Persia).
1941-5 British and
Soviet occupation.
1951 Nationalises oil
industry.

1953 Boycott of Iranian
oil. Shah briefly exiled.
1961 'White Revolution'
starts modernisation.
1979 Shah flees; Islamic
republic set up, led by
Ayatollah Khomeini.
US hostages seized.
1980-8 Iraq invades;
inconclusive war.
1981 Hostages freed.
1989 Khomeini dies.
1991 Kurdish refugees
enter from Iraq.
1997 Moderate
Khatami elected
president.

Iran

Km	0		400		800
Miles	0	200		400	

The Kurds and Kurdistan

The 20 million Kurds, who claim descent from Noah, are the world's largest distinct ethnic group with no state of their own. Most have turned from a traditional life of nomadic herding to become farmers, but are fiercely loyal to their 3000-year-old culture and language. Kurdistan has never existed as a distinct state, yet the Kurds have played an important part in the history of western Asia from at least the 7th century.

After the First World War, the Allies proposed a separate Kurdish state, but Turkey refused to cede territory. A Kurdish terrorist campaign against the Turkish government began in the 1980s. A Kurdish republic had been established within Iran in 1946, but was abolished by the shah. Kurds in Iraq were victims of genocide in 1988-9.

After the 1991 Gulf War, Iraqi forces again assaulted Kurdish centres, and about 1.4 million refugees fled to Turkey and Iran. The UN has established Kurdish 'safe havens' in northern Iraq, but today the Kurds remain isolated in pockets of their traditional territories, still without a recognised homeland.

Nowhere to go Kurdish refugees, having fled from ruthless attacks by Saddam Hussein's Iraqi army, gather in Siranbar refugee camp (left) in neighbouring Iran in 1996. UN 'safe havens' were not enough to give permanent protection.

Ghost homeland The area the Kurds want as their national home (above) extends over the territories of six countries. Despite widespread international support for the Kurds, not one of the six is prepared to yield land.

PAKISTAN

OFFICIAL NAME
The Islamic Republic of
Pakistan

CAPITAL
Islamabad

Area 796 095 km²
(307 374 sq miles)
Population 134 510 000
Population density 164 per
km² (425 per sq mile)
Population growth rate 0.6%
Life expectancy 59 (m); 59 (f)
Languages Urdu, Punjabi,
Pushto, Sindhi, Saraiki,
English
Adult literacy rate 37.8%
Currency Pakistani rupee
(US $1 = 61 rupees)
GDP (US million $) 66 000
GDP per head (US $) 500

Pakistan

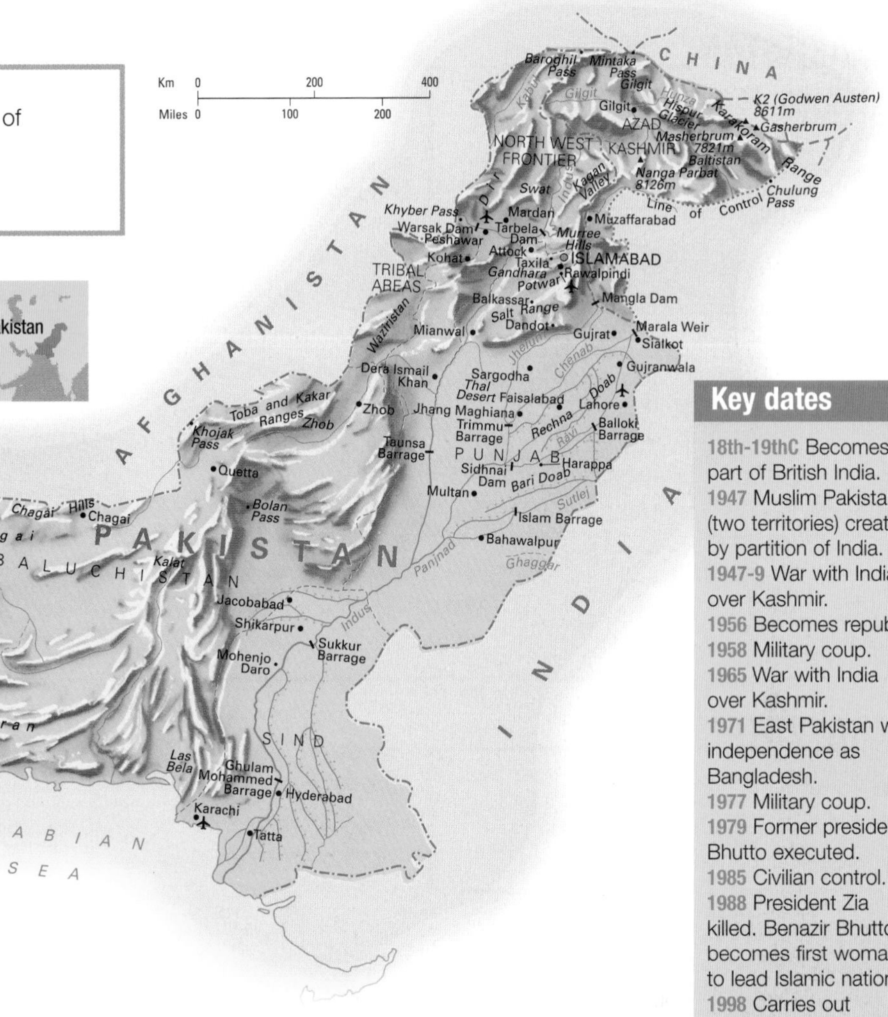

Key dates

18th–19thC Becomes
part of British India.
1947 Muslim Pakistan
(two territories) created
by partition of India.
1947-9 War with India
over Kashmir.
1956 Becomes republic.
1958 Military coup.
1965 War with India
over Kashmir.
1971 East Pakistan wins
independence as
Bangladesh.
1977 Military coup.
1979 Former president
Bhutto executed.
1985 Civilian control.
1988 President Zia
killed. Benazir Bhutto
becomes first woman
to lead Islamic nation.
1998 Carries out
nuclear weapons tests.

AFGHANISTAN

OFFICIAL NAME
The Islamic State of
Afghanistan

CAPITAL
Kabul

Afghanistan

Area 652 225 km²
(251 773 sq miles)
Population 18 800 000
Population density 29 per
km² (75 per sq mile)
Population growth rate 1%
Life expectancy 43 (m); 44 (f)
Languages Pashto, Dari

(dialect of Farsi or Iranian)
and many local languages
Adult literacy rate 31.5%
Currency afghani
(US $1 = 4750 afghanis)
GDP (US million $) 20 000
GDP per head (US $) 937

FACT
Afghanistan has
the world's
highest proportion
of disabled people
– more than 17
per cent.

Key dates

19thC Russia and UK
struggle for control.
1880 UK protectorate.
1919 Independence.
1973 Military coup
deposes monarchy.
1978 Pro-Soviet coup;
war with Islamic rebels.
1979 Soviet invasion to
shore up government.
1989 Soviet withdrawal.
1992 Rebels take power
and adopt Islamic law;
fighting continues.
1996 Fundamentalist
Taliban faction in power.

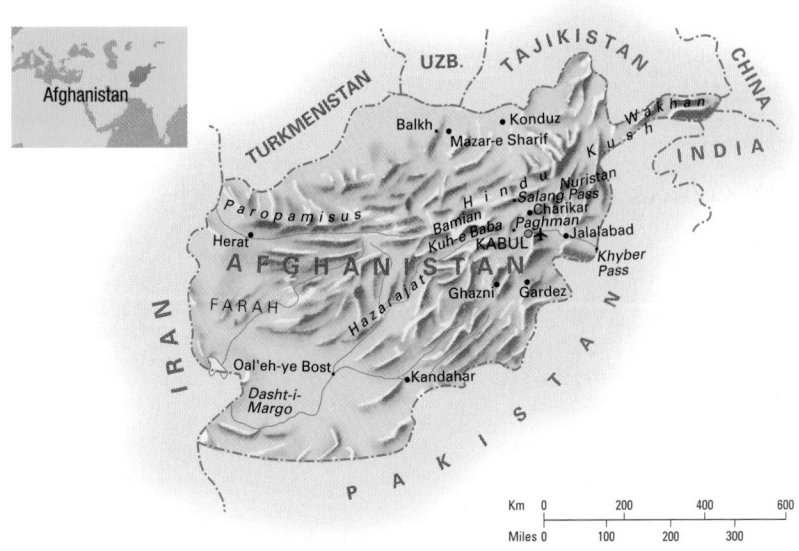

KAZAKHSTAN

OFFICIAL NAME
The Republic of Kazakhstan

CAPITAL
Astana

Area 2 717 300 km²
(1 049 150 sq miles)
Population 14 942 000
Population density 6 per km²
(14 per sq mile)
Population growth rate 1.5%
Life expectancy 64 (m); 73 (f)

Languages Kazakh,
Russian
Adult literacy rate 97.5%
Currency tenge
(US $1 = 145 tenge)
GDP (US million $) 15 900
GDP per head (US $) 1055

Kazakhstan

FACT
Dennis Tito, the world's first space tourist, took off from Kazakhstan's Baikonur launch pad in April 2001.

Key dates

13thC Mongol control.
1731 Russian protectorate.
1920 Autonomous Communist republic.
1936 Becomes republic of Soviet Union.
1950s 'Virgin Lands' project to cultivate the steppes.
1991 Independence; joins Commonwealth of Independent States.
1992 Joins UN.
1993 Approves Nuclear Non-Proliferation Treaty.
1998 Astana (formerly Akmola) declared capital in place of Almaty (Alma Ata).

KYRGYZSTAN

OFFICIAL NAME
The Kyrgyz Republic

CAPITAL
Bishkek

Kyrgyzstan

Area 198 500 km²
(76 600 sq miles)
Population 4 822 938
Population density 24 per km² (61 per sq mile)
Population growth rate 1%
Life expectancy 61 (m); 70 (f)
Languages Kyrgyz (Cyrillic

script; Latin script to be reintroduced), Russian
Adult literacy rate 97%
Currency som
(US $1 = 49 soms)
GDP (US million $) 1200
GDP per head (US $) 255

Key dates

13thC Mongol rule.
17thC Islam introduced.
1758 Chinese control begins.
1864 Russia replaces China as ruler.
1922 Merged into USSR.
1936 Becomes separate republic within USSR.
1990-5 Territorial dispute with Uzbeks.
1991 Independence; joins Commonwealth of Independent States.
1992 Joins UN.

TAJIKISTAN

OFFICIAL NAME
The Republic of Tajikistan

CAPITAL
Dushanbe

Area 143 100 km²
(55 251 sq miles)
Population 6 237 000
Population density 43 per km² (110 per sq mile)
Population growth rate 1.2%
Life expectancy 65 (m); 71 (f)
Languages Tajik (Cyrillic script), Russian

Adult literacy rate 97.7%
Currency Tajik rouble
(US $1 = 1260 Tajik roubles)
GDP (US million $) 1000
GDP per head (US $) 163

Key dates

13thC Mongol rule.
14th-19thC Uzbek rule.
late 19thC Partly under Russian control.
1922 Merged into USSR.
1929 Becomes separate republic within USSR.
1991 Independence declared; joins Commonwealth of Independent States.
1992 Joins UN. Islamic rebels start civil war.
1997 Government achieves peace agreement with rebels.

Tajikistan

TURKMENISTAN

OFFICIAL NAME
The Republic of Turkmenistan

CAPITAL
Ashgabat

Area 488 100 km²
(188 456 sq miles)
Population 4 384 000
Population density 10 per
km² (26 per sq mile)
Population growth rate 2.5%
Life expectancy 62 (m); 68 (f)
Languages Turkmen (Latin-
based script), Russian,
Uzbek, Kazakh

Adult literacy rate 98%
Currency manat
(US $1 = 5275 manats)
GDP (US million $) 3600
GDP per head (US $) 740

Km 0 400
Miles 0 200

Key dates

10thC Turkic settlement.
13thC Mongol rule.
14thC Islam introduced.
1885 Russian control.
1922 Becomes part of
USSR.
1925 Becomes separate
republic within USSR.
1991 Independence;
joins Commonwealth of
Independent States.
1992 Joins UN and
Muslim Economic
Cooperation
Organisation. New
constitution; elections.
1997 Approves private
ownership of land.

UZBEKISTAN

OFFICIAL NAME
The Republic of Uzbekistan

CAPITAL
Tashkent

Area 447 400 km²
(172 740 sq miles)
Population 23 954 000
Population density 54 per
km² (139 per sq mile)
Population growth rate 1.6%
Life expectancy 66 (m); 72 (f)
Languages Uzbek (Cyrillic
script; reverting to Latin
script), Russian, Kazakh

Adult literacy rate 97%
Currency som
(US $1 = 337 som)
GDP (US million $) 11 400
GDP per head (US $) 474

Key dates

7thC Arab conquest.
13thC Mongol rule.
14thC Tamerlane founds
Mongol Empire's capital
at Samarkand.
15thC Uzbek invasion.
19thC Russian control.
1924 Separate republic
of Soviet Union.
1991 Independence;
joins Commonwealth of
Independent States.
1992 Joins UN.
1997 Law bars political
parties representing
ethnic or religious
groups.

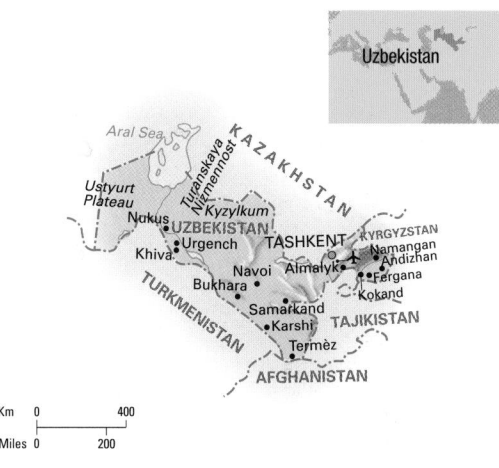

Km 0 400
Miles 0 200

MONGOLIA

OFFICIAL NAME
Mongolia

CAPITAL
Ulan Bator

Area 1 566 500 km²
(604 829 sq miles)
Population 2 382 525
Population density 2 per km²
(4 per sq mile)
Population growth rate 2.8%
Life expectancy 62 (m); 65 (f)
Languages Khalkha
Mongolian, Kazakh
Adult literacy rate 82.9%

Currency tugrik
(US $1 = 1094 tugrik)
GDP (US million $) 953
GDP per head (US $) 397

Key dates

13thC Genghis Khan
creates Mongol Empire.
1680s Chinese rule.
1911 Chinese forces
driven out.
1913 Self-rule by priest-
king ('Living Buddha')
under Russian control.
1924 'Living Buddha'
dies; Communist
republic established.
1961 Joins UN.
1966 Treaty with USSR;
60 000 Soviet troops
stationed in Mongolia
1989 USSR withdraws.
1990 Open elections.
1992 New constitution.
1996 US defence pact.

0 400 800 Km
0 200 400 Miles

INDIA

OFFICIAL NAME
The Republic of India

CAPITAL
New Delhi

Area 3 287 263 km²
(1 269 219 sq miles)
Population 1 030 000 000
Population density 295 per
km² (765 per sq mile)
Population growth rate 1.4%
Life expectancy 57 (m); 58 (f)
Languages Hindi, English
and many local languages
Adult literacy rate 52%
Currency rupee
(US $1 = 46.8 rupees)
GDP (US million $) 468 300
GDP per head (US $) 482

Key dates

*c.*3500 BC Indus
Valley civilisation.
*c.*1500 BC Aryans
settle.
530 BC Persian
invasion.
326 BC Alexander the
Great invades.
1526 Muslim Mughal
Empire established.
1757 British East
India Company wins
Bengal.
1858 British
government control
after mutiny; Queen
Victoria named
Empress of India.
1885 Indian National
Congress founded.
1906 Muslim League
founded.

1920 Mahatma
Gandhi starts
peaceful campaign
to end British rule.
1939-45 Fights
Second World War
as one of Allies.
1947 Independence
as India and Pakistan.
1947-9 War with
Pakistan over
Kashmir.
1948 Mahatma
Gandhi murdered.
1950 Becomes
republic.
1962 Border fighting
with China.
1965 War with
Pakistan over
Kashmir.
1975-7 Political crisis;

state of emergency.
1984 More than 450
killed in attack on
Sikh Golden Temple
at Amritsar. Prime
minister Indira Gandhi
murdered; replaced
by her son Rajiv.
1990 Direct rule in
Kashmir after riots.
Ethnic riots in Punjab;
over 3500 killed.
1991 Rajiv Gandhi
killed.
1992 Hindu extremists
destroy Ayodhya
mosque; more than
1200 die in riots.
1998 Conducts
nuclear weapons
tests; accepts Test
Ban Treaty.

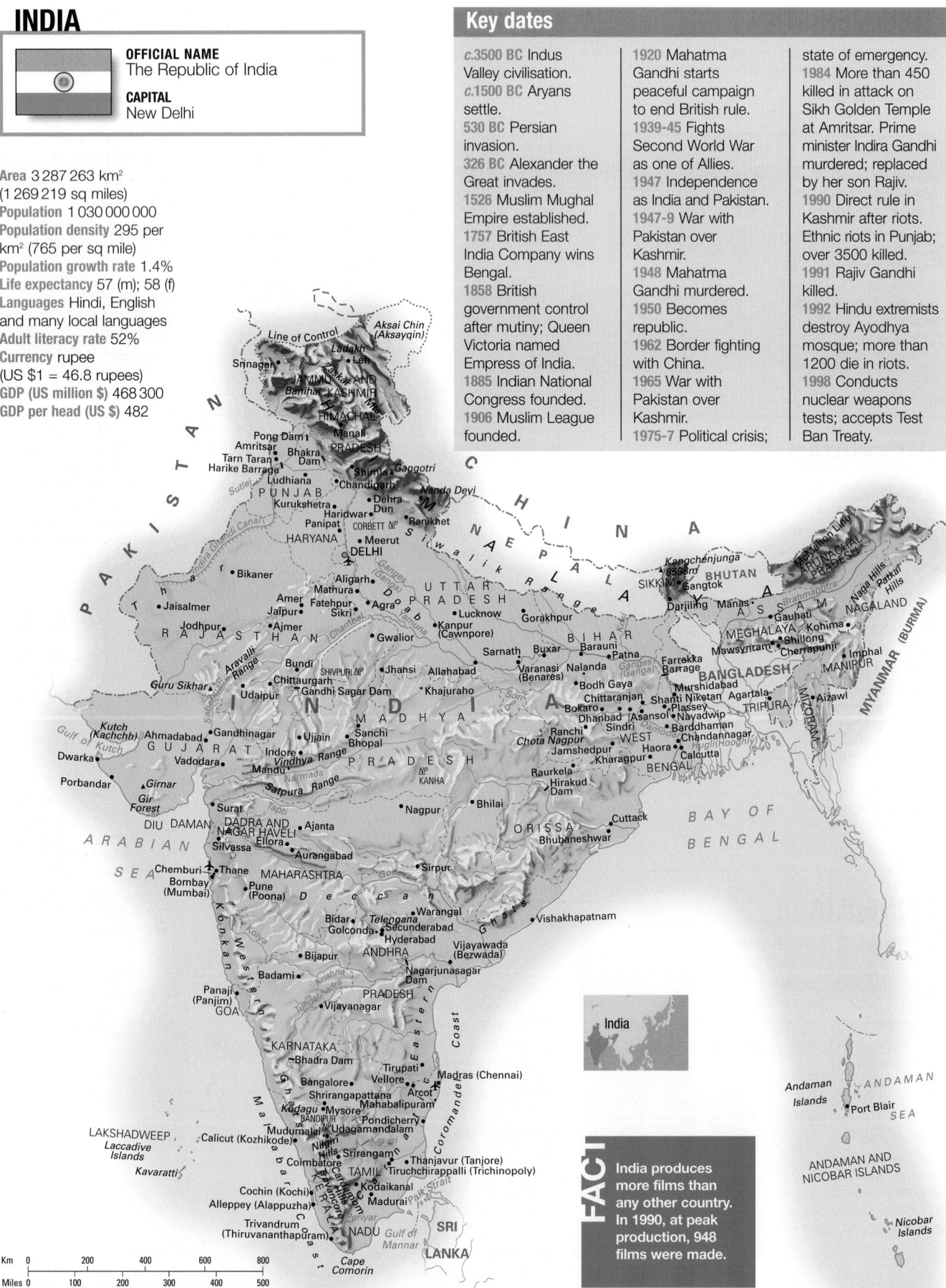

FACT
India produces
more films than
any other country.
In 1990, at peak
production, 948
films were made.

Km 0   200   400   600   800
Miles 0 100   200   300   400   500

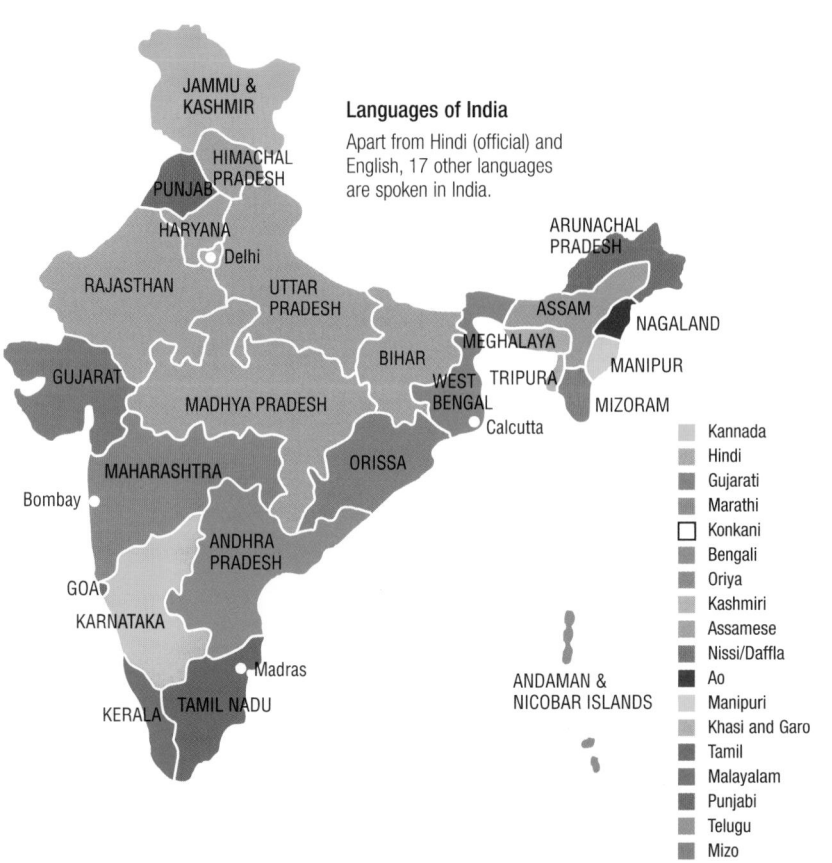

Languages of India

Apart from Hindi (official) and English, 17 other languages are spoken in India.

JAMMU & KASHMIR
HIMACHAL PRADESH
PUNJAB
HARYANA
Delhi
RAJASTHAN
UTTAR PRADESH
ARUNACHAL PRADESH
ASSAM
NAGALAND
MEGHALAYA
MANIPUR
BIHAR
TRIPURA
WEST BENGAL
MIZORAM
GUJARAT
MADHYA PRADESH
Calcutta
MAHARASHTRA
ORISSA
Bombay
ANDHRA PRADESH
GOA
KARNATAKA
Madras
KERALA
TAMIL NADU
ANDAMAN & NICOBAR ISLANDS

- Kannada
- Hindi
- Gujarati
- Marathi
- Konkani
- Bengali
- Oriya
- Kashmiri
- Assamese
- Nissi/Daffla
- Ao
- Manipuri
- Khasi and Garo
- Tamil
- Malayalam
- Punjabi
- Telugu
- Mizo

FLASHPOINT IN THE HIMALAYAS

When India and Pakistan tested nuclear weapons in 1998, it marked just the latest – if most dangerous – stage in a troubled 50-year relationship. Strife began as soon as British India was partitioned in 1947 into Muslim Pakistan and Hindu-dominated India. Then, as now, the flashpoint was Kashmir.

The 222 236 km² (85 838 sq miles) of Kashmir's mountains and valleys are peopled largely by Muslims. But Kashmir's ruler in 1947 was a Hindu prince who at independence opted to join India. A two-year war was halted in 1949 by a UN ceasefire that divided Kashmir along today's border. Pakistan was left controlling a third of the region, home to 2 million of the 6 million Kashmiris. The rest forms the Indian state of Jammu and Kashmir.

Fighting between the two countries flared again in 1965-6 and in 1971. It focused on the latter occasion mainly on East Pakistan, where India saw the chance to weaken its neighbour by helping East Pakistan to win independence.

India still keeps a large army in its part of Kashmir to suppress Islamic separatist violence that began in 1990. Ceasefires have regularly been violated; 100 were killed by shelling in 1998. However, negotiations begun in 1999 give some hope of eventual resolution to the dispute.

SRI LANKA

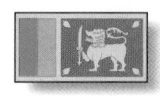

OFFICIAL NAME
Democratic Socialist Republic of Sri Lanka

CAPITAL
Colombo

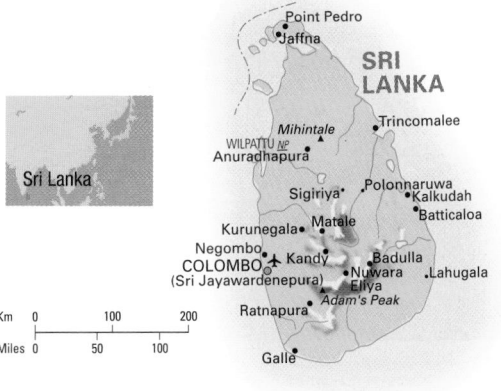

Point Pedro
Jaffna
SRI LANKA
Trincomalee
Mihintale
WILPATTU NP
Anuradhapura
Sri Lanka
Sigiriya
Polonnaruwa
Kalkudah
Batticaloa
Kurunegala
Matale
Negombo
Kandy
Badulla
COLOMBO
Nuwara
Lahugala
(Sri Jayawardenepura)
Eliya
Adam's Peak
Ratnapura
Galle

Km 0 100 200
Miles 0 50 100

Area 65 610 km² (25 332 sq miles)
Population 19 043 000
Population density 286 per km² (741 per sq mile)
Population growth rate 1.3%
Life expectancy 67 (m); 71 (f)
Languages Sinhala, Tamil, English

Adult literacy rate 90.2%
Currency Sri Lanka rupee (US $1 = 88 rupees)
GDP (US million $) 16 000
GDP per head (US $) 852

Key dates

1600-58 Portuguese rule.
1658-1795 Dutch rule.
1802-1948 British colony.
1948 Independence.
1959 Sinhalese extremist kills Prime Minister Solomon Bandaranaike.
1972 Changes name to Sri Lanka (from Ceylon).
1983 Guerrilla war starts with Tamil separatists; state of emergency.
1993 Tamil rebel kills President Ranasinghe Premadasa.

MALDIVES

OFFICIAL NAME
The Republic of Maldives

CAPITAL
Malé

Key dates

1558-73 Portuguese rule.
1573-1887 Rule by Islamic sultans.
1887 UK protectorate.
1965 Independence; leaves Commonwealth.
1968 Sultan deposed; republic established.
1982 Rejoins Commonwealth.
1988 Coup attempt by Sri Lankan mercenaries defeated by Indian army.

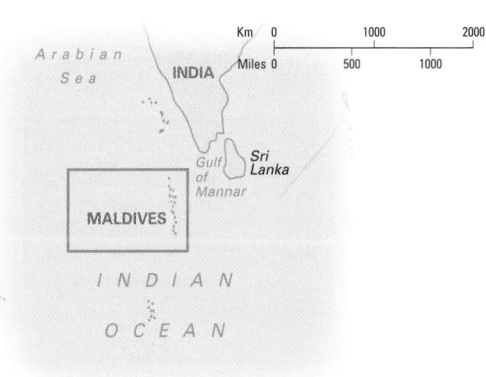

Arabian Sea
INDIA
Km 0 1000 2000
Miles 0 500 1000
Gulf of Mannar
Sri Lanka
MALDIVES
INDIAN OCEAN

Area 298 km² (115 sq miles)
Population 278 000
Population density 916 per km² (2374 per sq mile)
Population growth rate 3.2%
Life expectancy 67 (m); 67 (f)
Language Divehi (Maldivian, related to Sinhala)
Adult literacy rate 93.2%
Currency rufiyaa (US $1 = 11.77 rufiyaa)
GDP (US million $) 274
GDP per head (US $) 1079

NEPAL

OFFICIAL NAME
The Kingdom of Nepal

CAPITAL
Kathmandu

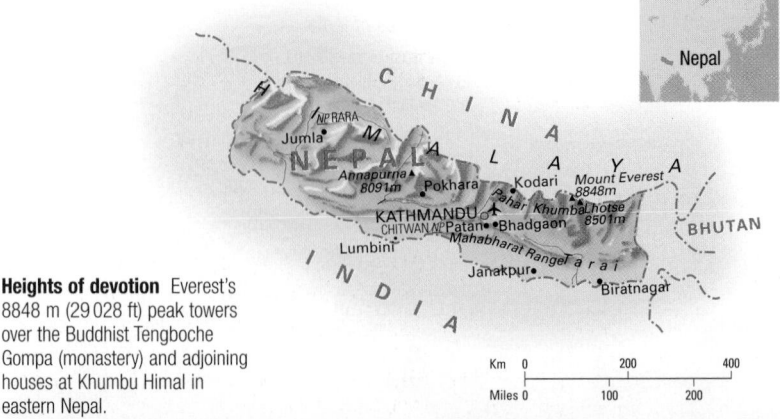

Nepal

Area 147 181 km²
(56 827 sq miles)
Population 22 367 000
Population density 148 per
km² (384 per sq mile)
Population growth rate 1.9%
Life expectancy 50 (m); 48 (f)

Languages Napali, Maithir,
Bhojpuri
Adult literacy rate 27.5%
Currency Nepalese rupee
(US $1 = 74 rupees)
GDP (US million $) 4400
GDP per head (US $) 201

Heights of devotion Everest's
8848 m (29 028 ft) peak towers
over the Buddhist Tengboche
Gompa (monastery) and adjoining
houses at Khumbu Himal in
eastern Nepal.

Key dates

1769 King of Gurkha
conquers Kathmandu.
1775 Nepal becomes
unified kingdom.
1814-16 War with British
after king tries to expand
into India; becomes
British protectorate.
1846 First Rana family
member seizes power
as prime minister.
1923 Independence.
1951 Revolution returns
power to king.
1960 Political parties
banned.
1962 New constitution;
king still holds power.
1963 Abolishes caste
system and polygamy.
1980 Pro-democracy
riots; referendum; vote
to retain status quo.
1990 Pro-democracy
riots; new constitution;
democratic monarchy.
1995 King dissolves
parliament; overruled
by Supreme Court.

BHUTAN

OFFICIAL NAME
The Kingdom of Bhutan

CAPITAL
Thimphu

Bhutan

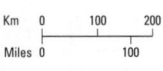

Area 46 500 km²
(17 954 sq miles)
Population 2 064 000
Population density 43 per
km² (111 per sq mile)
Population growth rate 2.2%
Life expectancy 49 (m); 52 (f)
Languages Dzongkha
(Tibetan dialect), Nepali and
others

Adult literacy rate 42.2%
Currency ngultrum
(US $1 = 46.8 ngultrums)
GDP (US million $) 294
GDP per head (US $) 147

Key dates

*c.*1630 Becomes
separate state led by
Tibetan lama.
1907 Monarchy formed.
1910 UK protectorate.
1949 Independence;
receives aid from India.
1953 Establishes
national assembly.
1959 Asylum for 4000
Tibetan refugees after
China annexes Tibet.
1990 Demonstrations by
Nepali-speakers after
enforcement of
Bhutanese customs.

BANGLADESH

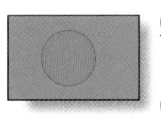

OFFICIAL NAME
The People's Republic of
Bangladesh

CAPITAL
Dhaka

Area 147 570 km²
(56 977 sq miles)
Population 126 947 000
Population density 845 per
km² (2190 per sq mile)
Population growth rate 1.2%
Life expectancy 57 (m); 56 (f)
Language Bengali
Adult literacy rate 38%
Currency taka
(US $1 = 54 taka)
GDP (US million $) 36 400
GDP per head (US $) 291

Key dates

1858 British rule begins.
1947 British India partitioned;
eastern Bengal independent
as part of Pakistan.
1971 Wins war against
West Pakistan (with Indian
assistance); becomes
independent as Bangladesh.
1975 Military coup;
President Mujib killed.
1975-9 Martial law.

1979 Elections.
1981 President Zia killed by
army rebels.
1982 Bloodless military coup.
1982-6 Martial law.
1986 Former military ruler,
Ershad, elected president.
1990 Ershad is charged
with corruption and resigns.
1996 Elections marred by
violence and alleged fraud.

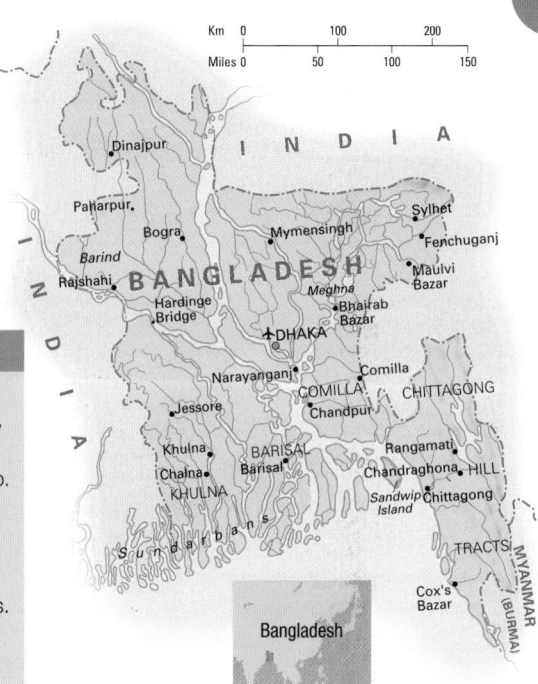

Bangladesh

MYANMAR

OFFICIAL NAME
The Union of Myanmar

CAPITAL
Yangon (Rangoon)

Area 676 553 km²
(261 218 sq miles)
Population 45 059 000
Population density 71 per
km² (184 per sq mile)
Population growth rate 2.1%
Life expectancy 57 (m); 63 (f)
Languages Myanmar
(Burmese) and other local
languages
Adult literacy rate 83.1%
Currency kyat
(US $1 = 6.6 kyats)
GDP (US million $) 5916
GDP per head (US $) 122

Key dates

1886 British take control
of Burma after three
wars; becomes
province of British India.
1937 Separated; partial
self-government.
1942-5 Occupied by
Japanese.
1948 Independence.
1962 Bloodless coup.
1974 New constitution.
1988 Military coup;
many pro-democracy
demonstrators killed.
1989 Changes name
from Burma to Myanmar.
1990 Opposition leader
Aung San Suu Kyi
arrested; wins election
landslide, but ruling
junta refuses to
recognise victory.
1991 Suu Kyi wins
Nobel peace prize.
1997 Joins ASEAN.

FACT

Myanmar is the
world's second-
largest producer
of opium for the
heroin trade,
after Afghanistan.

Myanmar

CHINA

OFFICIAL NAME
The People's Republic of China

CAPITAL
Beijing

Area 9 571 300 km²
(3 695 500 sq miles)
Population 1 274 115 000
Population density 132 per
km² (342 per sq mile)
Population growth rate 1.4%
Life expectancy 66 (m); 70 (f)
Languages Northern
Chinese (Mandarin or
putonghua), Min, Wu, Yue
(Cantonese) and others
Adult literacy rate 82.2%
Currency yuan, Hong Kong
dollar and Macau pataca
(US $1 = 8.27 yuan, HK $
7.79 or 7.95 patacas)
GDP (US million $) 993 500
GDP per head (US $) 786

Key dates

*c.*1766 BC Shang rule:
first written records.
202 BC-AD 220 Strong
empire under Hans.
1279-1368 Mongol rule.
1644-1912 Manchu rule.
1839-42 Opium War; UK
wins Hong Kong.
1900-1 Western powers
crush Boxer Rebellion.
1911 Republic declared.
1931 Japanese occupy
Manchuria.
1937 Japanese invade.
1941-5 Joins Allies in
Second World War.
1946-9 Civil war.
1949 Mao Ze-dong's
Communists defeat
Nationalists led by
Chiang Kai-shek, who
flee to Taiwan. People's
Republic proclaimed.
1950-1 Takes over Tibet.
1959 Crushes revolt in
Tibet; Dalai Lama flees.
1966 Mao instigates
Cultural Revolution.
1969 Border clashes
with USSR.
1971 Replaces Taiwan
as member of UN.
1979 Economic reforms.
1989 Pro-democracy
students massacred in
Tiananmen Square,
Beijing.
1997 UK returns Hong
Kong to China.

China's ethnic diversity

The Chinese government has officially recognised 56 ethnic groups among the hundreds that live in its country. The Han people make up 91 per cent of the total; the 'national minorities' include Mongols, Manchus, Tatars, Tibetans, Koreans, Salars, Russians, Kazakhs and Qiangs. They live in every province, and total 108 million out of China's 1.3 billion people.

Ethnic diversity has existed in China since the Qin dynasty in 221 BC, but rivalries and tensions have never disappeared. The government proclaims equality, but minorities have suffered discrimination. In particular in western provinces, where ethnic minorities often correspond to religious groupings, the discrimination has led to civil disturbance. In 1993, police battled with rioting Muslims in Qinghai province. Beijing's stated policy is to crush any unrest, and officials were told to 'wage an uncompromising struggle against separatists'.

Religious diversity of China

Some 31 per cent of China's population follow either one of the country's indigenous religions, Confucianism or Taoism, or one of the major world religions.

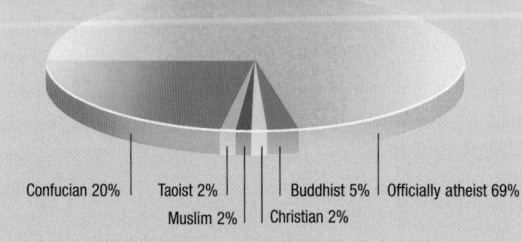

Confucian 20%   Taoist 2%   Buddhist 5%   Officially atheist 69%
                 Muslim 2%   Christian 2%

High living China is the world's most populous country and Hong Kong (below) its most crowded city. More people live in China today than inhabited the whole world 150 years ago. In parts of Hong Kong, population density exceeds 55 000 /km² (142 000 /sq mile).

RUSSIA

MONGOLIA

Qiqihar
Daqing
HEILONGJIANG
Songhai Jiang
Harbin
DONGBEI
(MANCHURIA)
JILIN
Changchun
Siping
Liaoyuan
Fengman Dam
SEA OF JAPAN

Dunhuang
Yumen
Qilian Shan

Bayan Obo
Yin Shan
Baotou
Zhangjiakou
Hohhot
Rehe Uplands
Xuanhua
Chengde
Shenyang
Fushun
Benxi
Liaoyang
LIAONING
Anshan
Fuxin
Liaodong Wan
Liaodong Peninsula
Supung Dam
NORTH KOREA

Huang He
Mu Us Shamo
Pingluo
Yinchuan
Great Wall
Datong
Shijingshan
Lugou Bridge
BEIJING (Peking)
Qinhangdao
Beidaihehaibin
Tangshan
Korea Bay
Lüshun Lüda
SOUTH KOREA

Qaidam Pendi
Qinghai Hu
Xining
Baiyin
Lanzhou
NINGXIA-HUI
Yan'an
Xi Xian
Loesslands of China
SHAANXI
Baoji
Xi'an

Shijiazhuang
Taiyuan
Yangquan
Dazhai
SHANXI
Fen He
Qiu Xian
Taihang Shan
Fengfeng
Anyang
Handan
HEBEI
North China Plain
Tianjin
Xingang
Bo Hai
Jinan
Zibo
Shengli
Weifang
Yidu
Tai Shan
SHANDONG
Jining
Yantai
Shandong Peninsula
Weihai
Qingdao
YELLOW SEA

Kaifeng
Zhengzhou
Sanmen Gorge
Luoyang
Pingdingshan
HENAN
Shangtang
Hua He
Da Yunhe (Grand Canal)
Huang He

CHINA
Qin Ling
Wei He
Han Shui
Daba Shan

JIANGSU
Nanjing
Ma'anshan
Hefei
Zhenjiang
Changzhou
Wuxi
Suzhou
Yixing
Tai Hu
Baoshan
Shanghai
Zhoushan Archipelago
ANHUI
Huangpu Jiang

Chengdu
Three Gorges Dam
Yichang
Shashi
HUBEI
Wuhan
Huangshi
Daye
Chang Jiang (Yangtze)
Huang Shan
Hangzhou
Ningbo
ZHEJIANG
EAST CHINA SEA

SICHUAN
Emei Shan 3099m
Chongqing
Dongting Hu
Yueyang
Lu Shan
Jiujiang
Poyang Hu
Jingdezhen
Nanchang
Wenzhou

Qam'do
Mekong (Lancang Jiang)

Zunyi
Wu Jiang
GUIZHOU
Xiangtan
Shaoshan
Pingxiang
Zhuzhou
Changsha
HUNAN
Hengyang
JIANGXI
Luoxiao Shan
Nanping
Fuzhou
FUJIAN

Yungui Plateau
Dongchuan
Guiyang
Huangguoshu
Dali
Er Hai
Guilin
Yangshuo
Nan Ling
Luizhou
Gui Jiang
Xiamen
Taiwan Strait
TAIWAN

MYANMAR (BURMA)
Kunming
YUNNAN
Red (Yuan) Jiang
Black (Li Jiang)
Xishuangbanna
Gejiu

GUANGXI-ZHUANG
Nanning
Xi Jiang
GUANGDONG
Conghua
Guangzhou (Canton)
Zhu Jiang (Pearl River)
Foshan
Jiangmen
Shenzhen
Zhuhai
Macau (Aomen)
Hong Kong (Xianggang)
Shantou

VIETNAM
LAOS
Maoming
Zhanjiang
Leizhou Peninsula
Hainan Strait
Gulf of Tongking
Haikou
Hainan
SOUTH CHINA SEA

China

| Km | 0 | 200 | 400 | 600 | 800 |
| Miles | 0 | | 200 | | 400 |

JAPAN

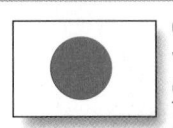

OFFICIAL NAME
Japan

CAPITAL
Tokyo

Area 377 750 km²
(145 850 sq miles)
Population 126 505 000
Population density 335 per
km² (867 per sq mile)
Population growth rate 0.4%
Life expectancy 76 (m); 83 (f)
Language Japanese
Adult literacy rate 99%
Currency yen
(US $1 = 122 yen)
GDP (US million $) 4 368 300
GDP per head (US $) 34 556

Key dates

645 First emperor.
710 First capital, at Nara.
794 Capital moved
to Kyoto.
1192-1867 Shoguns
(military leaders) rule.
1639-1853 Japan closed
to outside world.
1867-8 Revolution
restores emperor's rule;
Edo renamed Tokyo and
made capital.
1889 New constitution.
1904-5 War with Russia.
1910 Annexes Korea.
1914-18 Joins Allies in
First World War; wins
Pacific territories.

1931 Invades and
occupies Manchuria.
1937 Attacks China.
1941 Enters Second
World War, attacking US
fleet at Pearl Harbor.
1945 Atomic bombs
destroy Hiroshima and
Nagasaki; surrenders.
1946 New constitution:
emperor becomes
constitutional monarch.
1952 Occupation ends.
1956 Joins UN.
1972 Okinawa and other
islands lost in Second
World War returned.
1990s Financial crisis.

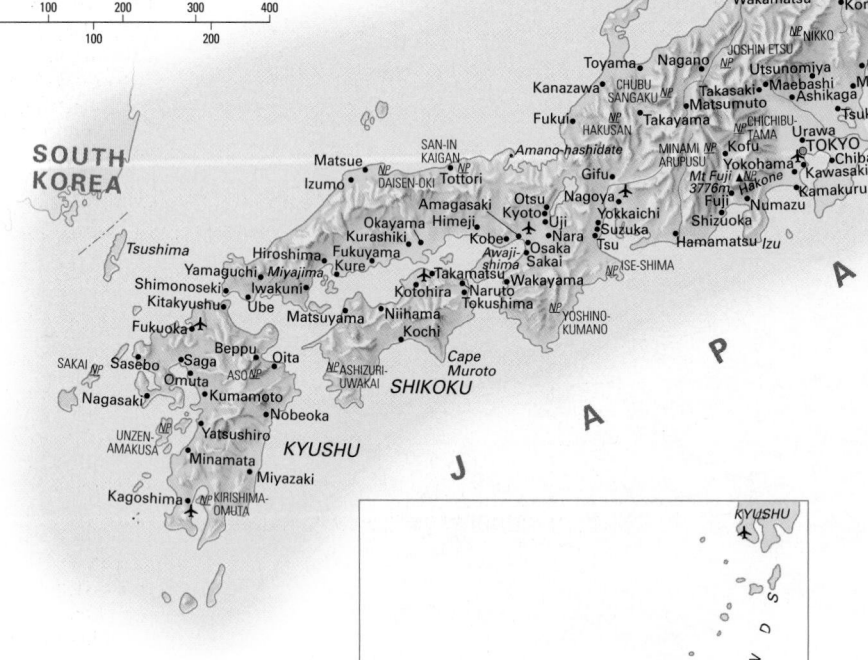

Hiroshima reborn

On August 6, 1945, the Japanese
city of Hiroshima was flattened by
an atomic bomb; 78 150 people
were killed instantly, and more than
100 000 others died later from
diseases caused by radiation.

At the time no one expected
Hiroshima to recover. Yet today it is
as vibrant and bustling as almost
any other city in Japan.
Widespread rebuilding began in
1949 and Hiroshima is now home
to more than 1 120 000 people. It
processes food, builds ships and
produces machinery, steel, motor
vehicles and furniture.

Not that Hiroshima wants to
forget its past. At the city's heart is
a memorial: 'Peace Park', with a
gutted building left just as it was
after the world's first nuclear
attack. No amount of regeneration
can erase the city's sad place in
history.

KOREA'S LONG WAIT FOR RECONCILIATION

The first major conflict after the Second World War left Korea divided. But in August 2000 some South Koreans were finally able to embrace relatives cut off by the ceasefire line. Two hundred were allowed to cross the heavily armed border by a North Korean regime shaken by the break-up of the USSR, the death of its long-time dictator and the collapse of its economy. North and South Korean leaders had already met, and the construction of a rail link between the former enemies had begun. Asia's most dangerous border was beginning to open.

Half a century before, the communist north had invaded the southern part of Korea. A US-led UN force drove the invaders back, then advanced almost to the Chinese border. China was drawn in, and its troops pushed the UN back. The three-year conflict saw the threat of nuclear war. A 1953 truce split the peninsula; despite the deaths of 37 000 GIs, this was America's first war without victory. But communist expansion was blocked – the USA had achieved its main objective, giving it the confidence to get involved in a similar war a decade later in Vietnam.

Tearful reunion Two family members, separated by the division of Korea for 50 years, greet each other during a brief border opening in August 2000.

NORTH KOREA

OFFICIAL NAME
Democratic People's Republic of Korea

CAPITAL
Pyongyang

Area 120 538 km²
(46 540 sq miles)
Population 23 702 000
Population density 194 per km² (502 per sq mile)
Population growth rate 1.8%
Life expectancy 68 (m); 74 (f)
Language Korean
Adult literacy rate 99%
Currency North Korean won (US $1 = 2.20 won)
GDP (US million $) 4381
GDP per head (US $) 187

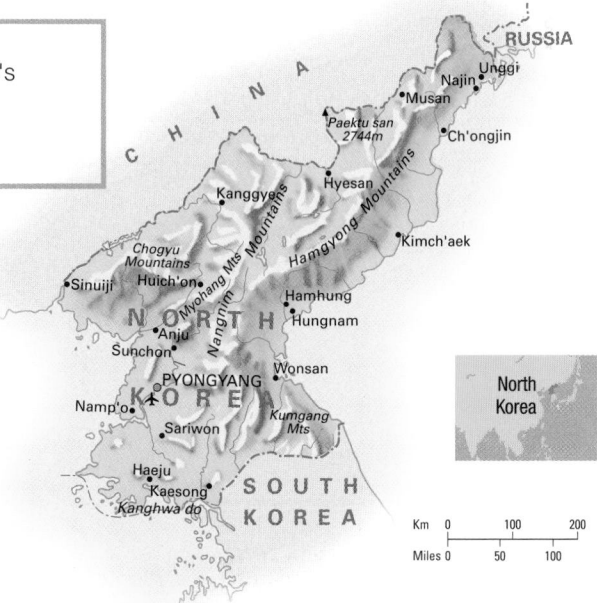

SOUTH KOREA

OFFICIAL NAME
The Republic of Korea

CAPITAL
Seoul

Area 99 392 km²
(38, 375 sq miles)
Population 46 858 000
Population density 467 per km² (1210 per sq mile)
Population growth rate 1%
Life expectancy 67 (m); 75 (f)
Language Korean
Adult literacy rate 98%
Currency South Korean won (US $1 = 1313 won)
GDP (US million $) 395 300
GDP per head (US $) 8513

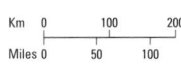

Key dates

1259-1368 Mongol rule.
1392-1910 Ruled by Yi dynasty of kings.
1910 Japan annexes.
1945 End of Second World War: Soviet forces occupy northern Korea, US forces southern Korea.
1948 Separate republics in north and south.
1950 North Korea invades South, starting Korean War; Chinese aid North Korea against US-led UN force.
1953 Ceasefire, dividing North and South Korea.
1961 Military coup in South Korea.
1979 South Korean President Park killed.
1987 New constitution in South Korea after violent protests.
1991 Both join UN. Sign non-aggression pact.
1994 Kim Il Sung, North Korean leader, dies; succeeded by his son, Kim Jong Il.
2000 North-South summit; border opened for family reunions.

Thailand, Malaysia and Singapore

THAILAND

OFFICIAL NAME
The Kingdom of Thailand

CAPITAL
Bangkok

Area 513 115 km²
(198 115 sq miles)
Population 60 606 947
Population density 119 per
km² (309 per sq mile)
Population growth rate 0.8%
Life expectancy 64 (m); 69 (f)
Languages Thai, Chinese,
Malay
Adult literacy rate 93.8%
Currency baht
(US $1 = 45 baht)
GDP (US million $) 126 200
GDP per head (US $) 2062

Key dates

1238 Sukhotai kingdom.
1350 Ayutthaya
kingdom established.
19thC Treaties recognise
Siam's independence.
1914-18 Supports Allies
in First World War.
1932 Constitutional
monarchy proclaimed.
1939 Changes name
from Siam to Thailand.
1941-5 Second World
War: occupied by Japan;
becomes unwilling ally.
1947 Military coup.
1965-72 Joins US-led
forces in Vietnam War.
1973 Civilian rule.
1976-80 Military rule.
1991 Nonviolent military
coup.

FACT Thailand is the only country in South-east Asia never to have been colonised.

EAST ASIA'S 'TIGER ECONOMIES'

Much of South-east and eastern Asia experienced 'miracle' economic growth in the 1980s, only to see it halt in the mid 90s after several high-profile financial failures, and stock market and exchange rate slumps. Leading the expansion were Thailand, Malaysia, Indonesia, Taiwan and South Korea – all at an early stage of development in the 1970s – as well as the well-established economies of Hong Kong and Singapore. They became known as the 'tiger economies'.

Thailand, for example, had a GNP growth rate of up to 10 per cent a year – several times that of the USA. Singapore became a clean, modern city and one of the world's great commercial and financial centres, with Asia's second-highest standard of living after Japan. And behind these powerhouses came China, a nation with the potential to outstrip them all.

The tiger economies' success was widely put down to 'Asian values': a combination of hard work, thrift and strong – even authoritarian – leadership. Many governments created sturdy

financial markets by encouraging savings and promoting investment. They also intervened to support certain types of business through tax credits and subsidies.

Most of the 'tigers' have improved the material lot of individual citizens, reducing gaps between rich and poor. Between 1960 and 1990 the number of people living in poverty in Malaysia, for example, dropped from 37 per cent of the population to less than 5 per cent. Life expectancy increased from 56 to 71 between 1960 and 1990. But then bust followed boom. The crisis began in

1997 and was triggered by a devaluation of the area's currencies. This caused loan defaults, since many debts were owed in foreign currencies. Land values dropped as fast as speculators had earlier sent them up. The authorities helped some troubled industries, but then the bubble burst and banks failed. As the 21st century dawned, international assistance was helping the region to regain its confidence. But some economists warned of further trouble ahead.

Annual percentage growth rate in GNP

The GNP of the 'tiger economies' grew much faster than the world average in 1980-90 (left) and 1990-98 (right).

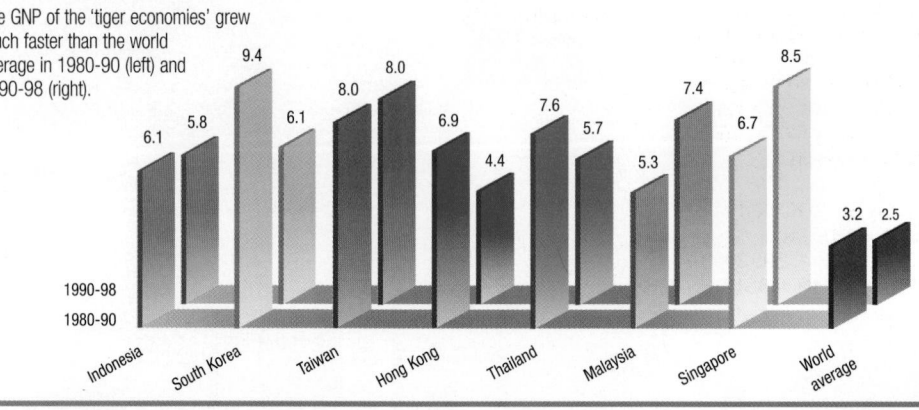

1990-98
1980-90

Indonesia 6.1 / 5.8
South Korea 9.4 / 6.1
Taiwan 8.0 / 8.0
Hong Kong 6.9 / 4.4
Thailand 7.6 / 5.7
Malaysia 5.3 / 7.4
Singapore 6.7 / 8.5
World average 3.2 / 2.5

MALAYSIA

OFFICIAL NAME
Malaysia

CAPITAL
Kuala Lumpur

Area 329 758 km²
(127 320 sq miles)
Population 22 712 000
Population density 67 per
km² (174 per sq mile)
Population growth rate 2.5%
Life expectancy 68 (m); 73 (f)
Languages Malay (Bahasa
Malaysia), English
Chinese, Tamil, Iban
Adult literacy rate 83.5%
Currency ringgit
(US $1 = 3.80 ringgits)
GDP (US million $) 81 700
GDP per head (US $) 3683

Key dates

16th-17thC Portuguese, Dutch and British settle.
1867-on British colonial rule extended.
1941-5 Japanese occupation.
1948-54 Fighting against communist guerrillas.
1957 Malaya gains independence.
1963 Malaysia (Malaya, Sabah, Sarawak and Singapore) founded.
1963-5 'Confrontation' with Indonesia.
1965 Singapore secedes from Malaysia.
1967 Founder-member of ASEAN.
1969 Anti-Chinese riots.
1987 Opposition activists arrested.

Standing tall Petronas Towers in Kuala Lumpur – the world's tallest office building in the year 2000 – symbolised Malaysia's rapid economic growth.

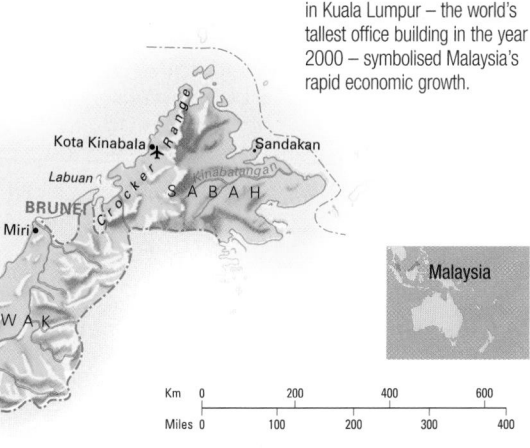

SINGAPORE

OFFICIAL NAME
The Republic of Singapore

CAPITAL
Singapore

Area 646 km²
(249 sq miles)
Population 3 894 000
Population density 5991 per
km² (15 511 per sq mile)
Population growth rate 3%
Life expectancy 74 (m); 78 (f)
Languages Malay, Chinese
(Mandarin), Tamil, English
Adult literacy rate 91.1%
Currency Singapore dollar
(US $1 = 1.81 Singapore
dollars)
GDP (US million $) 91 800
GDP per head (US $) 23 720

Key dates

1819 Raffles founds modern Singapore.
1867 Straits Settlements become British colony.
1942-5 Japanese occupation.
1946 Separate colony.
1959 Self-government.
1963 Joins Malaya, Sarawak and Sabah to form Malaysia.
1965 Secedes from Malaysia; becomes independent republic.
1991 Powers of the presidency increased.
1993 First direct election for president.

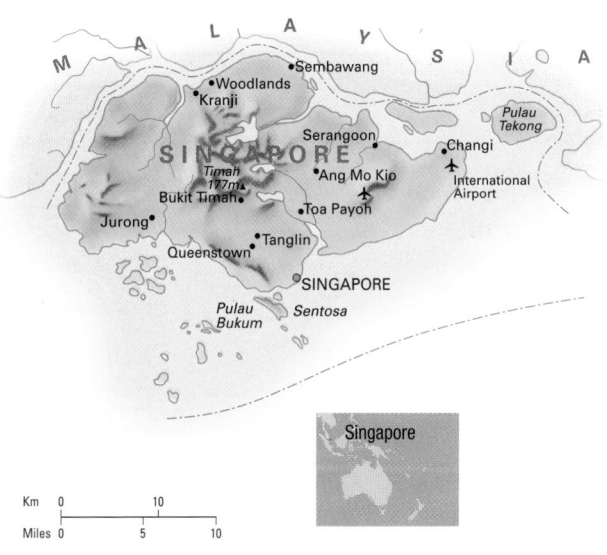

VIETNAM

OFFICIAL NAME
The Socialist Republic of Vietnam

CAPITAL
Hanoi

Area 331 114 km²
(127 844 sq miles)
Population 76 324 753
Population density 234 per km² (607 per sq mile)
Population growth rate 1.3%
Life expectancy 63 (m); 67 (f)
Language Vietnamese and many local languages
Adult literacy rate 93.7%
Currency dông
(US $1 = 14 561 dông)
GDP (US million $) 27 800
GDP per head (US $) 358

FACT The Ho Chi Minh Trail, used to supply Vietcong forces, included over 300 km (200 miles) of tunnels.

Key dates

111 BC Chinese rule.
AD 939 Independence.
1858-83 French take control.
1941-5 Second World War: Japanese control.
1945 Ho Chi Minh proclaims Democratic Republic of Vietnam.
1946 French begin to fight Vietminh forces.
1954 French defeated at Dien Bien Phu; Vietnam divided – communists control North Vietnam.
1957 Vietcong guerrillas attack South Vietnam.
1964 USA starts air strikes against North.
1973 Ceasefire; US troops withdraw.
1975 Communists take Saigon; war ends.
1976 Socialist Republic of Vietnam proclaimed.
1978-9 Attacks Khmer Rouge in Cambodia.
1979 Border war with China.
1989 Withdraws from Cambodia.
1995 Diplomatic relations with USA established.

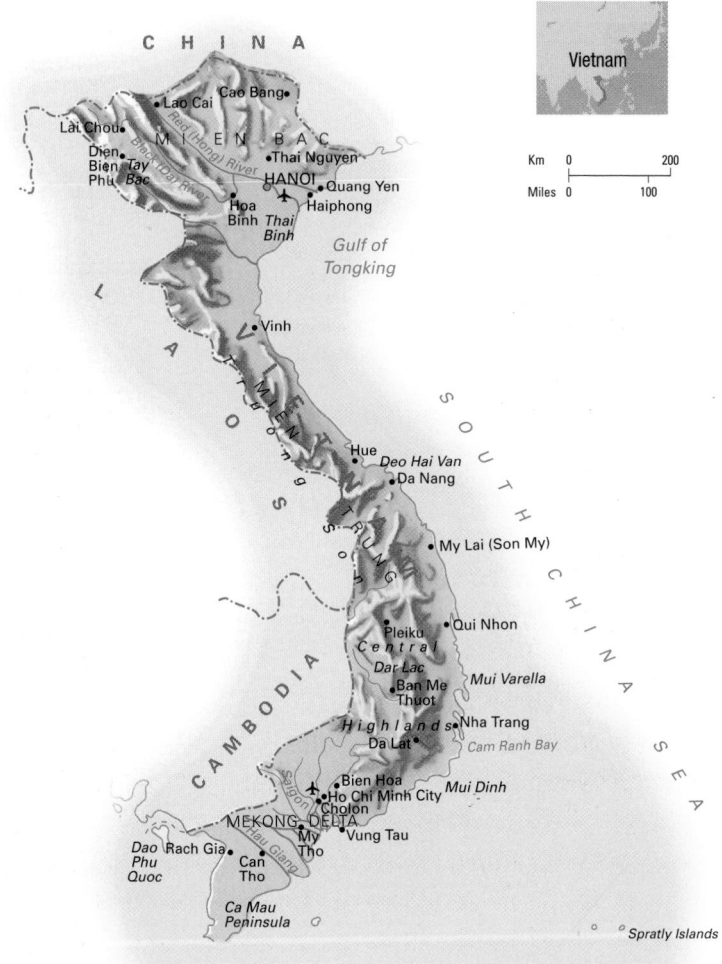

CAMBODIA

OFFICIAL NAME
The Kingdom of Cambodia

CAPITAL
Phnom Penh

Area 181 035 km²
(69 898 sq miles)
Population 10 945 000
Population density 63 per km² (164 per sq mile)
Population growth rate 4.1%
Life expectancy 50 (m); 52 (f)
Language Khmer
Adult literacy rate 35%
Currency riel
(US $1 = 3835 riels)
GDP (US million $) 3100
GDP per head (US $) 270

Key dates

7thC Khmer Empire.
1863 French establish protectorate.
1941-5 Second World War: Japanese control.
1953 Independence.
1970 Coup; monarchy abolished. Civil war.
1975 Khmer Rouge led by Pol Pot take power.
1976-8 Khmer Rouge kill more than 2.5 million.
1978-9 Vietnam helps to depose Khmer Rouge.
1992 Guerrilla war with Khmer Rouge begins.
1993 King restored.
1999 Joins ASEAN.

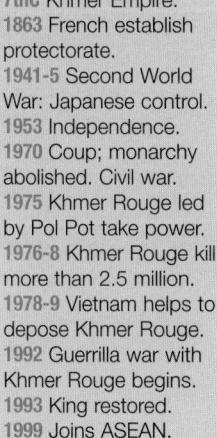

LAOS

OFFICIAL NAME
The Lao People's Democratic Republic

CAPITAL
Vientiane

Area 236 800 km²
(91 400 sq miles)
Population 5 297 000
Population density 22 per km² (56 per sq mile)
Population growth rate 2.1%
Life expectancy 49 (m); 52 (f)
Languages Lao (Laotian), French and many local languages

Adult literacy rate 56.6%
Currency new kip
(US $1 = 7600 new kips)
GDP (US million $) 1500
GDP per head (US $) 290

Key dates

1893 Becomes French protectorate.
1941-5 Second World War: Japanese control.
1949 Self-government within French Union.
1954 Full independence.
1960-73 Intermittent civil war between communist and right-wing forces.
1975 Communists seize power; Vietnam sends troops in support.
1989 Open elections.
1991 New constitution.
1997 Joins ASEAN.

TAIWAN

OFFICIAL NAME
The Republic of China

CAPITAL
Taipei

Area 36 000 km²
(13 900 sq miles)
Population 21 740 000
Population density 604 per km² (1564 per sq mile)
Population growth rate 1.2%
Life expectancy 72 (m); 78 (f)
Languages Northern Chinese (Mandarin), Taiwanese
Adult literacy rate 93.7%

Currency Taiwan dollar
(US $1 = 32.8 Taiwan dollars)
GDP (US million $) 287 000
GDP per head (US $) 13 201

Key dates

1895-1945 Japanese control after Sino-Japanese War.
1949 Chiang Kai-shek's Nationalists arrive after mainland China falls to communists.
1954 US defence treaty.
1971 Expelled from UN.
1972 US forces leave.
1979 USA ends treaty and official relations.
1987 Opposition political parties allowed.
1991 Ends state of civil war with China.
1991-2 Open elections.

SOUTH-EAST ASIA'S ROAD TO PEACE

The former French Indochina was heavily scarred by war in the 20th century. Yet, as the new century began, the old colonies of Laos, Cambodia and Vietnam were enjoying peace and economic progress.

Cambodia and Laos moved towards democracy with multiparty elections. Vietnam turned its efforts to invigorating its economy, developing tourism and an oil industry. The United States helped by dropping its 30-year trade embargo in 1994, and the following year the two former enemies re-established diplomatic relations.

The journey from colonial rule to prosperous independence was often violent for all three countries. After the Second World War, France's offer of autonomy for its Asian empire was accepted by Laos and Cambodia. But the Vietnamese wanted full independence, and fought a successful war

against the French, only to see their country divided by an anti-communist movement in the south.

Civil wars led to communist victories in 1975 in all three former colonies. The North Vietnamese and Vietcong (South Vietnamese communist guerrillas) prevailed in the 18-year Vietnam War despite American intervention. In Laos, the communist Pathet Lao took power, but ten years later introduced political liberalisation, a market economy and, in 1989, multiparty elections. In Cambodia, the extremist Khmer Rouge regime killed more than 2.5 million of its own people before it was removed by Vietnamese military intervention. Free elections were held in 1993, and the same year a new constitution restored the monarchy.

The past behind him A statue of Ho Chi Minh overshadows Bill Clinton. His visit to Vietnam in 2000 was the first by a US president since the Vietnam War.

PHILIPPINES

OFFICIAL NAME
The Republic of the Philippines

CAPITAL
Manila

Area 300 000 km²
(115 831 sq miles)
Population 74 746 000
Population density 251 per
km² (649 per sq mile)
Population growth rate 2.1%
Life expectancy 63 (m); 67 (f)
Languages Filipino (based
on Tagalog), English and
many other local languages
Adult literacy rate 94.6%

Currency Philippine peso
(US $1 = 50 pesos)
GDP (US million $) 77 500
GDP per head (US $) 1031

FACT The Jeepney – a taxi converted from an army jeep – is a mainstay of Manila's public transport system.

Key dates

1521 Magellan lands.
1565 Becomes Spanish colony.
1898 Spanish-American war: ceded to USA.
1942-5 Japanese occupation.
1946 Independence from USA.
1967 Founder-member of ASEAN.
1972-81 Martial law during fighting against Muslim separatist and communist guerrillas.
1983 Opposition leader Benigno Aquino killed.
1986 President Marcos deposed; Aquino's widow wins presidency.
1992 US forces leave.
1996 Peace treaty with Islamic separatists.
2000 Islamic separatists declare jihad (holy war); extremists take Filipino and Western hostages.
2001 President Estrada ousted; President Arroyo assumes power.

PIRATES OF THE SOUTH CHINA SEA

Piracy patrol Singaporean coast guards search the crew of a trawler suspected of piracy or smuggling. The South China Sea and other waters nearby offer pirates easy hiding among myriad uninhabited islands.

Piracy has a long history in the waters of east and South-east Asia – one that is still being written. In 1998, a Chinese ship, the *Cheung Son*, was boarded off the Chinese coast near Shanghai by 32 pirates. They bludgeoned the crew of 23 to death and threw their bodies overboard. Chinese officials later seized the ship and executed 13 of the pirates. But most of the 98 attacks in the South China Sea that year went unpunished. Ships vanished, were repainted and renamed, and sailed again under a new national flag. The *Global Mars*, a 3356-tonne tanker

hijacked in February 2000, was recovered off Hong Kong four months later; it had been newly flagged and renamed the *Bulawan*.

The sea between Hong Kong, the Philippine island of Luzon and China's Hainan island – nicknamed the 'HLH Triangle' – has been the most dangerous place in the world for pirate attacks since 1992, when naval patrols were introduced in the Malacca Straits, forcing the pirates to move on. As a result, the South China Sea has seen a rise in attacks of 61 per cent over the past decade.

To combat the problem, in 1992 the International Maritime Bureau set up a Piracy Reporting Centre, and Asian countries are currently co-ordinating their anti-piracy measures.

INDONESIA

OFFICIAL NAME
The Republic of Indonesia

CAPITAL
Jakarta

Area 1 919 317 km²
(741 053 sq miles)
Population 207 437 000
Population density 107 per
km² (276 per sq mile)
Population growth rate 0.9%
Life expectancy 61 (m); 64 (f)
Languages Indonesian
(Bahasa Indonesia, a form
of Malay) and many local
languages
Adult literacy rate 83.8%

Currency rupiah
(US $1 = 11 775 rupiah)
GDP (US million $) 153 400
GDP per head (US $) 750

FACT About 87 per cent of Indonesia's people are Muslims, making it the world's largest Islamic state.

Key dates

16th-17thC Portuguese, Dutch trading posts.
1799 Dutch rule.
1942-5 Japanese occupation.
1949 Independence.
1950 Joins UN.
1963 Dutch cede West New Guinea. Sukarno 'president for life'.
1963-5 'Confrontation' with Malaysia.
1965 Communist coup attempt; many killed. Suharto gains power.
1967 Suharto displaces Sukarno. Founder-member of ASEAN.
1976 Takes East Timor.
1991 Sumatra rebellion; East Timor massacre.
1998 Riots in Jakarta; Suharto resigns.
1999 Quits East Timor.

After the fires A Borneo villager replants after forest fires caused widespread damage in the late 1990s. Smoke spread over much of South-east Asia.

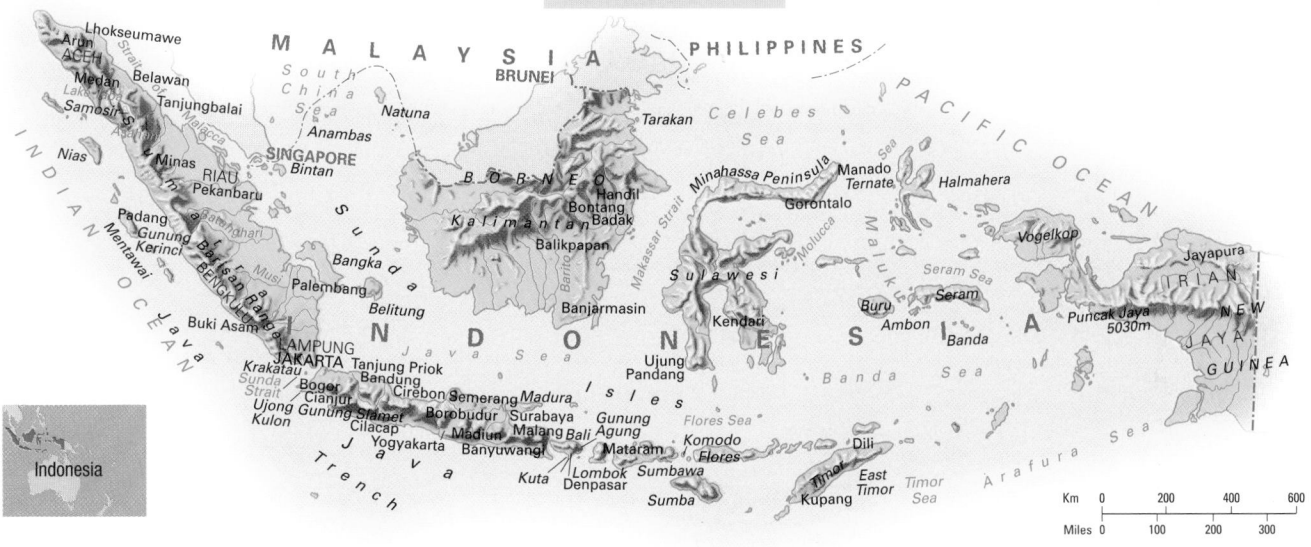

Indonesia

BRUNEI

OFFICIAL NAME
The Sultanate of Brunei

CAPITAL
Bandar Seri Begawan

Area 5765 km²
(2226 sq miles)
Population 331 000
Population density 54 per
km² (139 per sq mile)
Population growth rate 3%
Life expectancy 70 (m); 73 (f)
Languages Malay, Chinese,
English
Adult literacy rate 89%

Currency Brunei dollar
(US $1 = 1.81 Brunei
dollars)
GDP (US million $) 4850
GDP per head (US $) 15 645

Key dates

15thC First sultanate of Brunei established.
15th-16thC Controls most of north Borneo and part of Philippines.
19thC Loses much territory to Britain.
1888 Becomes British protectorate.
1929 Oil discovered.
1942-5 Japanese occupation.
1962 Abandons plans to join Malaysia.
1984 Full independence; joins ASEAN and UN.

Brunei

Australia and New Zealand

AUSTRALIA

OFFICIAL NAME
The Commonwealth of Australia

CAPITAL
Canberra

Area 7 682 300 km²
(2 966 153 sq miles)
Population 18 967 000
Population density 2 per km²
(6 per sq mile)
Population growth rate 0.8%
Life expectancy 75 (m); 80 (f)
Languages English, plus
about 200 Aboriginal and
many European and Asian
languages
Adult literacy rate 95%
Currency Australian dollar
(US $1 = 1.92 Australian
dollars)
GDP (US million $) 389 800
GDP per head (US $) 20 811

Key dates

1770 Claimed by Britain.
1788 First penal colony.
1850-90 Six colonies
gain self-government.
1870 Last convicts sent.
1901 Colonies unite as
Commonwealth
(federation) of Australia.
1902 Women win vote.
1914-18 One of Allies in
First World War.
1927 Canberra becomes
federal capital.
1939-45 One of Allies in
Second World War.
1942 Ratifies 1931

Statute of Westminster,
giving independence
within Commonwealth.
1951 Founds ANZUS
security pact with New
Zealand and USA.
1965-72 Troops fight in
Vietnam alongside US.
1967 Referendum gives
Aborigines citizenship.
1986 Australia Act ends
last British legal power.
1992 Land rights
awarded to Aborigines.
1999 Referendum vote
against republic.

The peopling of Australia

Proportion of Australians born overseas

One in five people
living in Australia have
moved there from
another country. The
figures are from 1996.

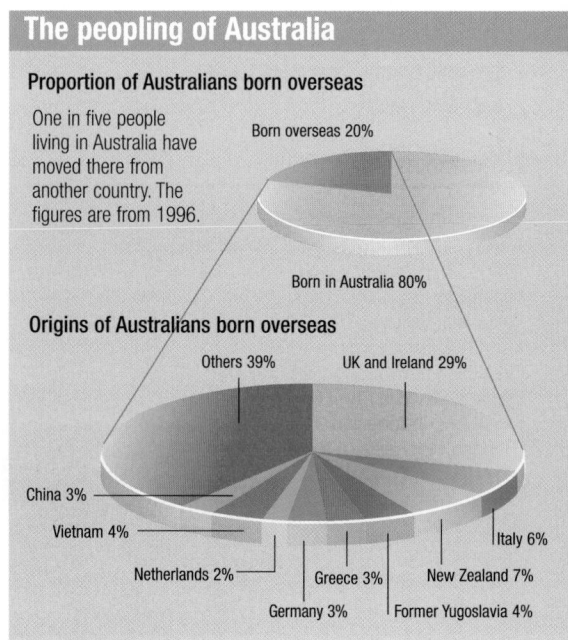

Born overseas 20%
Born in Australia 80%

Origins of Australians born overseas

Others 39% · UK and Ireland 29%
China 3% · Vietnam 4% · Netherlands 2% · Germany 3% · Greece 3% · Former Yugoslavia 4% · New Zealand 7% · Italy 6%

When the first British convict fleet landed at Sydney on January 26, 1788, Australia was considered *terra nullius* – unoccupied land. That definition of Australia remained fixed in law for more than 200 years.

The anniversary of the first convict landing has been celebrated each year since 1833; in 1931 it was named Australia Day. But as the bicentennial Australia Day approached in 1988, indigenous groups were proclaiming a quite different view of 1788. Far from being 'unoccupied', they pointed out, Australia had a native population of at least 750 000 at the time of British settlement.

Australia's Aborigines declared 1988 'a year of mourning', and conducted their own protest march for 'Freedom, Justice and Hope'. Since then, Australia Day has been turned into a community day that celebrates the cultural diversity of the nation. In 1992 the Australian High Court overturned the concept of *terra nullius* and ruled that Aborigines could claim ownership of land.

Since the Second World War, waves of new settlers – at first only from Europe, but later from a wider pool – have led to a more diverse society. About 20 per cent of today's Australians were born overseas. Besides English, more than 100 languages are now spoken. Added to those are about 200 indigenous languages spoken by the 386 000 Aboriginal and Torres Strait Islander people.

Australia used the 2000 Sydney Olympic Games to highlight its cultural diversity, and Canberra holds its own National Multicultural Festival each year. The country has also made moves to redress the historical injustices borne by indigenous people – ranging from massacres in the early years of the colony to the 'theft' of Aboriginal children to be raised by foster parents in the mid 20th century. In 1996 a parliamentary statement made a commitment to reconciliation with Aboriginal and Torres Strait Islander people, 'redressing their profound social and economic disadvantage'.

The processes of ethnic integration and reconciliation have not always been smooth, and there has often been political opposition raised against them. But Stephen Fitzgerald, a former Australian ambassador to China, says: 'We cannot clutch at . . . a white man's world now gone . . . We have to be Australian and not European.'

NEW ZEALAND

OFFICIAL NAME
New Zealand

CAPITAL
Wellington

Area 270 534 km²
(104 454 sq miles)
Population 3 811 000
Population density 14 per km² (36 per sq mile)
Population growth rate 0.9%
Life expectancy 73 (m); 79 (f)
Languages English, Maori
Adult literacy rate 99%
Currency New Zealand dollar (US $1 = 2.41 New Zealand dollars)
GDP (US million $) 52 400
GDP per head (US $) 13 825

Key dates

10thC First Maoris arrive from Pacific Islands.
1769 Capt Cook lands.
1840 Treaty of Waitangi: becomes British colony.
1852 Self-government.
1860-72 Wars over right to buy Maori land.
1893 Women gain vote.
1914-18 One of Allies in First World War.
1939-45 One of Allies in Second World War.
1947 Ratifies 1931 Statute of Westminster, giving independence within Commonwealth.
1951 Founds ANZUS security pact with Australia and USA.
1985 'Nuclear-free' policy introduced. French agents sink Greenpeace nuclear protest ship *Rainbow Warrior* at Auckland.
1988 Agrees free trade pact with Australia.
1993 Referendum in favour of proportional representation.

FACT About 75 per cent of New Zealanders live on North Island with almost a third clustered around Auckland.

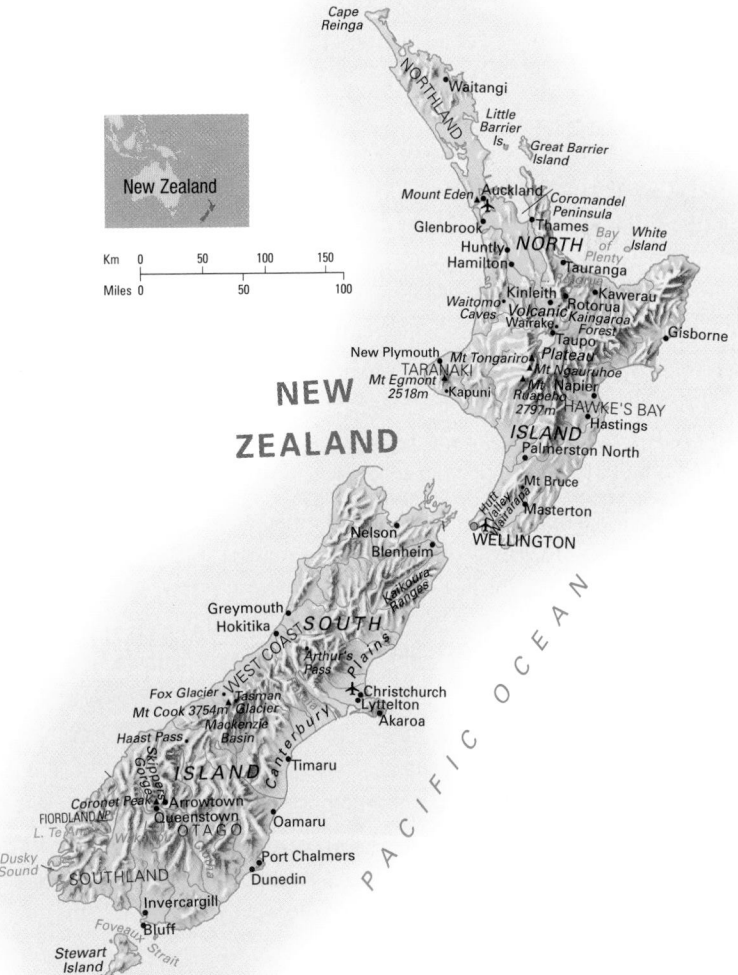

KIRIBATI

OFFICIAL NAME
The Republic of Kiribati

CAPITAL
Bairiki, on Tarawa

Independence 1979
Area 810 km²
(313 sq miles)
Population 82 000
Population density 100 per
km² (259 per sq mile)
Population growth rate 1.5%
Life expectancy 58 (m); 58 (f)

Languages I-Kiribati
(Gilbertese), English
Adult literacy rate 90%
Currency Australian dollar
GDP (US million $) 51
GDP per head (US $) 654

MARSHALL ISLANDS

OFFICIAL NAME
The Republic of the Marshall
Islands

CAPITAL
Dalap-Uliga-Darrit, on Majuro

Independence 1986
Area 180 km² (70 sq miles)
Population 61 000
Population density 339 per
km² (871 per sq mile)
Population growth rate 3%
Life expectancy 64 (m); 68 (f)

Languages English,
Marshallese, Japanese
Adult literacy rate 91%
Currency US dollar
GDP (US million $) 91
GDP per head (US $) 1649

FIJI

OFFICIAL NAME
The Republic of Fiji Islands

CAPITAL
Suva, on Viti Levu

Independence 1970
Area 18 376 km²
(7095 sq miles)
Population 806 000
Population density 44 per
km² (113 per sq mile)
Population growth rate 1.4%
Life expectancy 70 (m); 74 (f)

Languages Fijian, Hindi,
English
Adult literacy rate 91.6%
Currency Fiji dollar
(US $1 = 2.28 Fiji dollars)
GDP (US million $) 1808
GDP per head (US $) 2260

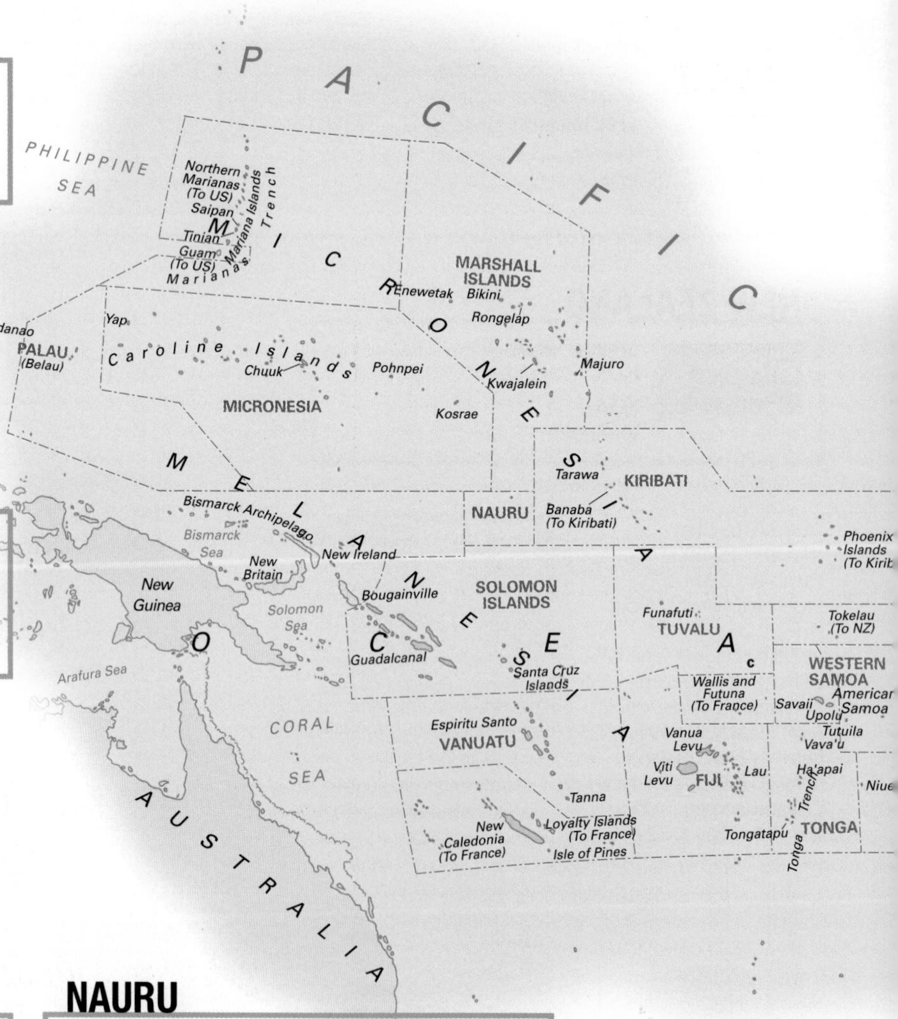

MICRONESIA

OFFICIAL NAME
The Federated States of
Micronesia

CAPITAL
Palikir, on Pohnpei

Independence 1986
Area 700 km²
(270 sq miles)
Population 116 000
Population density 157 per
km² (407 per sq mile)
Population growth rate 1.8%
Life expectancy 71 (m); 71 (f)

Languages English,
Trukese, Pohnpeian,
Yapese
Adult literacy rate 90%
Currency US dollar
GDP (US million $) 259
GDP per head (US $) 2104

PALAU

OFFICIAL NAME
The Republic of Palau

CAPITAL
Koror, on Koror island

Independence 1994
Area 508 km²
(196 sq miles)
Population 18 000
Population density 39 per
km² (102 per sq mile)
Population growth rate 2.1%

Life expectancy 60 (m); 63 (f)
Languages Palauan, English
Adult literacy rate 92%
Currency US dollar
GDP (US million $) 109
GDP per head (US $) 5450

NAURU

OFFICIAL NAME
The Republic of Nauru

CAPITAL
No official capital

Independence 1968
Area 21 km² (8 sq miles)
Population 11 000
Population density 516 per
km² (1341 per sq mile)
Population growth rate 2.3%
Life expectancy 57 (m); 65 (f)

Languages Nauruan,
English
Adult literacy rate 99%
Currency Australian dollar
GDP (US million $) 368
GDP per head (US $) 33 476

SAMOA

OFFICIAL NAME
The Independent State of
Samoa

CAPITAL
Apia, on Upolu

Independence 1962
Area 2831 km²
(1093 sq miles)
Population 169 000
Population density 59 per
km² (154 per sq mile)
Population growth rate 0.5%
Life expectancy 64 (m); 70 (f)

Languages Samoan,
English
Adult literacy rate 97%
Currency tala (Samoan
dollar) (US $1 = 3.05 tala)
GDP (US million $) 179
GDP per head (US $) 1065

PAPUA NEW GUINEA

OFFICIAL NAME
The Independent State of
Papua New Guinea

CAPITAL
Port Moresby

Independence 1975
Area 462 840 km²
(178 704 sq miles)
Population 4 702 000
Population density 10 per
km² (26 per sq mile)
Population growth rate 2.2%
Life expectancy 55 (m); 57 (f)

Languages Pidgin, English,
Motu and many local
languages
Adult literacy rate 72.2%
Currency kina
(US $1 = 3.07 kina)
GDP (US million $) 3600
GDP per head (US $) 782

TUVALU

OFFICIAL NAME
Tuvalu

CAPITAL
Vaiaku, on Funafuti

Independence 1978
Area 26 km² (10 sq miles)
Population 11 000
Population density 385 per
km² (1000 per sq mile)
Population growth rate 0%

Life expectancy 64 (m); 69 (f)
Languages Tuvaluan, English
Adult literacy rate 95%
Currency Australian dollar
GDP (US million $) 9
GDP per head (US $) 900

TONGA

OFFICIAL NAME
The Kingdom of Tonga

CAPITAL
Nuku'alofa, on Tongatapu

Independence 1970
Area 748 km²
(289 sq miles)
Population 98 000
Population density 134 per
km² (346 per sq mile)
Population growth rate 0.8%
Life expectancy 66 (m); 70 (f)

Languages Tongan,
English
Adult literacy rate 93%
Currency pa'anga
(Tongan dollar)
(US $1 = 1.92 pa'anga)
GDP (US million $) 279
GDP per head (US $) 2790

VANUATU

OFFICIAL NAME
The Republic of Vanuatu

CAPITAL
Port Vila, on Efate

Independence 1980
Area 12 190 km²
(4707 sq miles)
Population 186 000
Population density 15 per
km² (38 per sq mile)
Population growth rate 2.5%
Life expectancy 63 (m); 67 (f)

Languages Bislama,
English, French and many
local languages
Adult literacy rate 53%
Currency vatu
(US $1 = 146 vatu)
GDP (US million $) 245
GDP per head (US $) 1376

SOLOMON ISLANDS

OFFICIAL NAME
Solomon Islands

CAPITAL
Honiara, on Guadalcanal

Independence 1978
Area 27 556 km²
(10 639 sq miles)
Population 430 000
Population density 15 per
km² (39 per sq mile)
Population growth rate 3.4%
Life expectancy 68 (m); 73 (f)

Languages English,
Melanesian, Pidgin and
other local languages
Adult literacy rate 60%
Currency Solomon Islands
dollar (US $1 = SI $5.27)
GDP (US million $) 319
GDP per head (US $) 759

CANADA

OFFICIAL NAME
Canada

CAPITAL
Ottawa

Key dates

1497 John Cabot claims Canada for England.
1534-5 Jacques Cartier sails St Lawrence River.
1604 French settlement; becomes 'New France'.
1663 New France made French 'royal province'.
1670 Hudson's Bay Co sets up trading posts.
1713 Treaty of Utrecht: Britain acquires Nova Scotia, Newfoundland and Hudson Bay area.
1759 Battle of Quebec: British defeat French.
1760 British seize Montreal.
1763 All of New France becomes British.
1774 Quebec Act preserves French rights.
1791 Constitutional Act divides Quebec.
1867 Dominion (union) of Canada established.
1914-18 First World War: fights as one of Allies.
1931 Statute of Westminster gives full independence within British Commonwealth.
1939-45 Second World War as one of Allies.
1949 Newfoundland becomes tenth Canadian province.
1950-3 Korean War: troops join UN force.
1959 Saint Lawrence Seaway links Great Lakes to the Atlantic.
1980 Quebec votes against secession.
1982 Canada Act ends last British legal control.
1990 Collapse of 1998 Meech Lake Agreement to protect Quebec's culture and language.
1994 North American Free Trade Agreement with USA and Mexico.
1995 Quebec again rejects independence.
1999 Nunavut, self-governing Inuit homeland, established in North-west Territories.

Area 9 958 319 km²
(3 844 928 sq miles)
Population 30 491 000
Population density 3 per km²
(8 per sq mile)
Population growth rate 1.3%
Life expectancy 74 (m); 81(f)
Languages English, French
Adult literacy rate 99%
Currency Canadian dollar
(US $1 = 1.54 Canadian dollars)
GDP (US million $) 638 900
GDP per head (US $) 21 085

The separatist movement in Quebec

Twice in 15 years, the French-speaking province of Quebec has voted to remain part of Canada, rejecting the option of independence. But the second time, in 1995, the margin was less than 1 per cent. The urge for independence was rooted in a fierce pride in the past. Mainland Canada had been claimed for France by the explorer Jacques Cartier in 1534. 'New France'

became a French royal province, but a British victory near Quebec city in 1759 ended French rule.

Charles de Gaulle reignited old emotions in 1967 when he proclaimed 'Vive le Québec libre!' ('Long live free Quebec!'). The 1960s also saw some terrorist activity. Between the two referendums, Canada's government gave Quebec more power and money than any other

province, and made French its official language. All advertising and public signs outdoors had to be in French only. 'Language police' enforced these rules.

In today's prosperous and peaceful times, Quebec still insists on being recognised as a 'distinct society' with special rights. A new referendum is being discussed, but impatient Quebecois have nicknamed it the 'neverendum'.

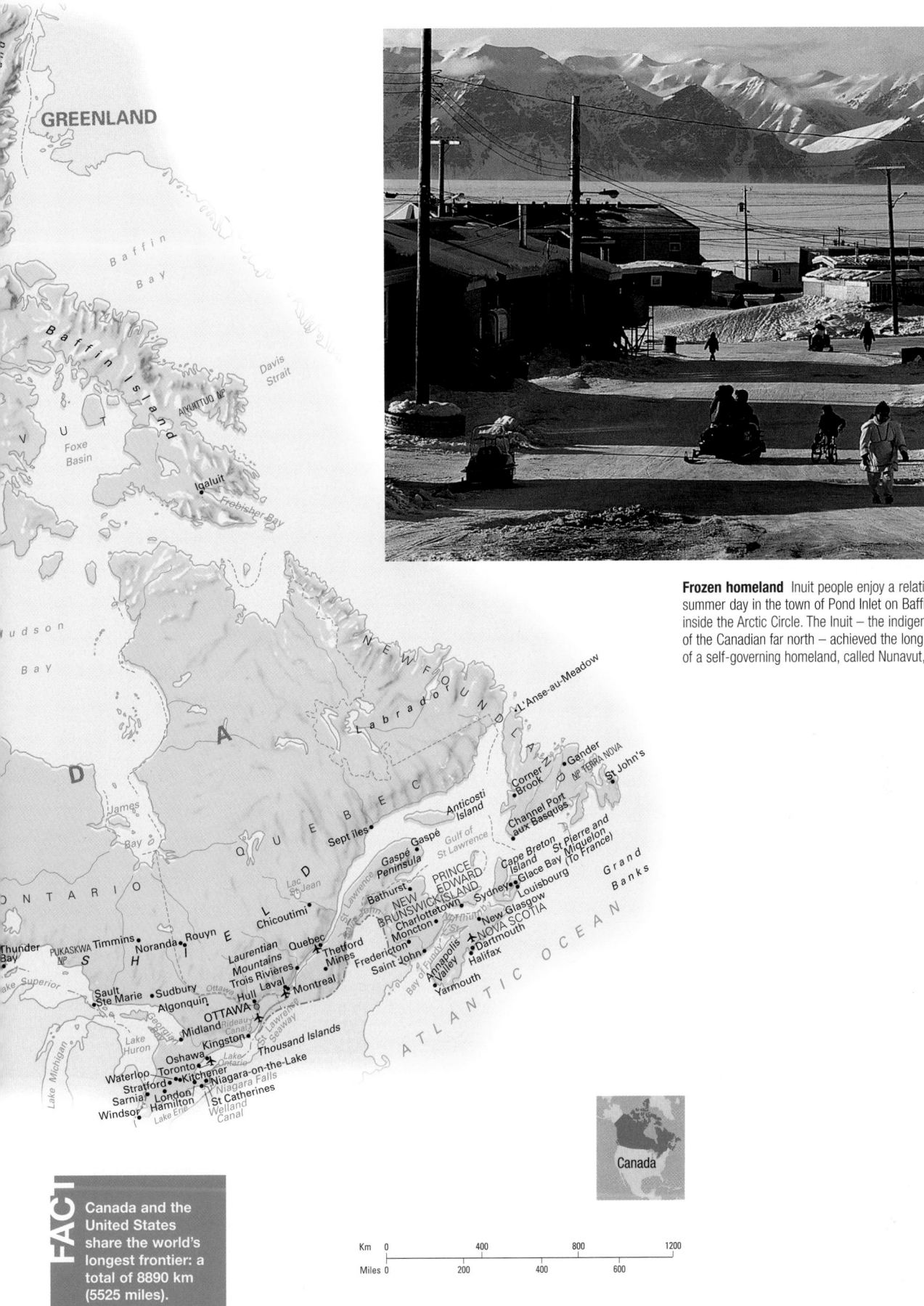

GREENLAND

Baffin
Bay

Baffin Island

Davis
Strait

AYUITTUQ NP

Foxe
Basin

Iqaluit

Frobisher Bay

Hudson
Bay

James
Bay

L'Anse-au-Meadow

Labrador

NEWFOUNDLAND

QUEBEC

Corner
Brook

Gander

NP TERRA NOVA

St John's

Anticosti
Island

Sept Îles

Channel Port
aux Basques

Gaspé
Peninsula

Gaspé

Gulf of
St Lawrence

St Lawrence

Bathurst

NEW
BRUNSWICK

Cape Breton
Island

PRINCE
EDWARD
ISLAND

St Pierre and
Miquelon
(To France)

Glace Bay
Sydney
Louisbourg

Grand
Banks

Lac
St Jean

Chicoutimi

Charlottetown

Northumberland Str.

Moncton

New Glasgow

NOVA SCOTIA

ONTARIO

Thunder
Bay

PUKASKWA
NP

Timmins

Noranda

Rouyn

Laurentian
Mountains

Quebec

Thetford
Mines

Fredericton

Dartmouth

Halifax

ATLANTIC OCEAN

Lake Superior

Sault
Ste Marie

Sudbury

Trois Rivières

Saint John

Bay of Fundy

Annapolis
Valley

Algonquin

Laval

Montreal

Yarmouth

Georgian Bay

Hull

Ottawa

OTTAWA

Rideau
Canal

St Lawrence
Seaway

Lake
Huron

Midland

Kingston

Thousand Islands

Lake Michigan

Oshawa

Toronto

Lake
Ontario

Waterloo

Kitchener

Niagara-on-the-Lake

Stratford

Niagara Falls

Sarnia

London

St Catherines

Windsor

Hamilton

Lake Erie

Welland
Canal

Frozen homeland Inuit people enjoy a relatively warm
summer day in the town of Pond Inlet on Baffin Island, well
inside the Arctic Circle. The Inuit – the indigenous inhabitants
of the Canadian far north – achieved the long-held ambition
of a self-governing homeland, called Nunavut, in 1999.

Canada

FACT

Canada and the
United States
share the world's
longest frontier: a
total of 8890 km
(5525 miles).

Km   0   400   800   1200
Miles 0   200   400   600

United States

UNITED STATES

OFFICIAL NAME
The United States of America

CAPITAL
Washington DC

Area 9 809 155 km²
(3 787 319 sq miles)
Population 281 421 906
Population density 28 per
km² (71 per sq mile)
Population growth rate 1%
Life expectancy 72 (m); 79 (f)
Languages English, Spanish
and many native languages
Adult literacy rate 95%
Currency US dollar
GDP (US million $) 9 178 000
GDP per head (US $) 33 922

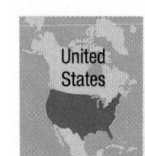

United States

Native culture A Cherokee artist from New Mexico stands beside a portrait of a warrior. The buffalo motifs emphasise the importance of the animal – as a source of food and hides for clothes and armour.

Km 0   200   400   600
Miles 0   200   400

Linguistic legacy of the Native Americans

More than 200 native groups were encountered by the first Europeans settling in what is now the United States. Columbus (who thought he had reached the Indies, or South-east Asia) called them Indians. Their ancestors had crossed the Bering Strait from Siberia tens of thousands of years before. They looked vaguely similar to Asian peoples, but during the millennia of isolation they had developed distinct languages and cultures. As many as 15 million Native Americans lived in North America in 1492; today that figure has shrunk to around 2 million.

The Native Americans' strongest legacy has proved to be their many languages. Many words were adopted by early colonists from the more than 20 languages spoken by the Algonquian group of peoples: the names of native foods such as squash, succotash, pone (corn bread), pecan and persimmon, and of animals such as moose, raccoon, opossum, chipmunk, terrapin and woodchuck. Other familiar Native American words include caucus (a political meeting), podunk (a dull, small town), hickory, moccasin and toboggan, as well as the better-

known powwow, tomahawk, teepee and totem.

The most obvious Native American names are those given to places – including 26 of the 50 states. For example, the name of Texas came from the Caddo language, meaning 'friends' or 'allies'. Tennessee was named after a Cherokee village, while Ohio is an Iroquois word for 'good river'. The Massachusett was the name of a group living around Massachusetts Bay, while the name of Wyoming comes from Algonquian words meaning 'on the great plain'. Many cities, towns and rivers also trace their

names to descriptive Native American words – for example, Chicago (Algonquian for 'place of the onion') and Mississippi (simply Algonquian for 'great river'). Among individuals immortalised are Black Warrior, a Choctaw chief, whose name in his own language was given to Tuscaloosa.

And very few Americans, setting off for a vacation trip by motor-home, know that Winnebago was the name of a plains group meaning 'people of the muddy waters' – or that Winnipeg, in Canada, similarly means 'dirty waters'.

CANADA

Duluth

MINNESOTA

St Paul
Minneapolis
Pipestone
Sioux Falls

WISCONSIN

Lake Superior

GREAT PLAINS

Muskegon
Grand Rapids
Flint
Lansing
Milwaukee
Madison
Detroit
Kalamazoo

Lake Michigan
Lake Huron

Sioux City
IOWA
Des Moines

Omaha
Lincoln
KA

M I D

Chicago
Gary
Joliet
Fort Wayne
Toledo
Cleveland
Erie
Youngstown
Akron

Lake Erie

Lake Ontario
Buffalo
Rochester
Syracuse
Utica

ILLINOIS
Springfield

Kansas City
Topeka
Jefferson City
St Louis

INDIANA
Indianapolis
Columbus
Wheeling
Pittsburgh
Gettysburg

OHIO

S T A T E S

Abilene
ANSAS
Wichita

MISSOURI
Missouri
Louisville
Frankfort
Lexington

Ohio

WEST
VIRGINIA
Charleston

Cincinnati

OKLAHOMA
Oklahoma City
Tulsa

ARKANSAS
Little Rock

KENTUCKY
MAMMOTH NP CAVE

Nashville
Knoxville

A M E R I C A

Arkansas

Memphis

TENNESSEE
Chattanooga
Huntsville

Cumberland Gap
Great Smoky Mts
Winston
Salem
Mt Mitchell
2037m
Charlotte

PENNSYLVANIA
Harrisburg

VERMONT
Montpelier
Concord
Nashua
Salem
Boston
MAINE

ACADIA NP
Portland

Saratoga Springs
Albany
Catskill Mts
West Point
Scranton
Wilkes-Barre
Palisades
Newark
New York
Long Island
East River

Springfield
Worcester
Hartford
New Haven
Bridgeport

Providence
Newport
Cape Cod

NEW YORK

Massachusetts Bay

NEW JERSEY
Trenton
Philadelphia
Wilmington
Dover
DELAWARE
Delaware Bay

Annapolis
Baltimore
Georgetown
WASHINGTON D.C.
MARYLAND

Chesapeake Bay

Shenandoah
Richmond
Williamsburg
Yorktown
Norfolk

VIRGINIA
Jamestown

Roanoke
Newport News

Raleigh

NORTH CAROLINA

Cape Hatteras

ATLANTIC OCEAN

KS
SOUTH CAROLINA
Columbia

Athens
Augusta
Atlanta

Charleston

MISSISSIPPI
Jackson
Vicksburg
Natchez

ALABAMA
Tuscaloosa
Birmingham
Montgomery

GEORGIA

Savannah

FORT
Worth
Dallas

LOUISIANA
Baton Rouge
Shreveport

New Orleans

Mobile

Okefenokee Swamp
Tallahassee

Jacksonville

Austin
Houston
San Antonio
Galveston

Gulf of Mexico

Orlando
Disney World
Tampa
St Petersburg

Cape Canaveral

Lake Okeechobee

West Palm Beach
Palm Beach
Fort Lauderdale
Miami Beach
Miami
Everglades

Corpus Christi

Key West

BAHAMAS

Alaska

Km   0   400   800
Miles 0   200   400

ARCTIC OCEAN
RUSSIA
Bering Strait
North Slope
Beaufort Sea

U.S.A.
ALASKA
Fairbanks
DENALI NP
Mt McKinley
Anchorage

CANADA

Bering Sea

Malaspina Glacier
Juneau
Gulf of Alaska

Aleutian Trench
PACIFIC OCEAN

Hawaii

Km   0   100   200
Miles 0   100

Oahu
Pearl Harbor
Honolulu
U.S.A.

Maui
NP HALEAKALA

HAWAII

Mauna Kea
4206m
Mauna Loa
4169m

Hawaii
Akaka Falls
Hilo
NP HAWAII VOLCANOES
Halemaumau
Kilauea Crater

PACIFIC OCEAN

Key dates

16thC Spanish, English and French explore North America.
1607 Chesapeake Bay colony established.
1620 'Pilgrims' found Plymouth Colony.
1624 Dutch settle in New York.
1682 French claim Mississippi valley.
1775-83 Revolution (War of Independence).
1776 Formal Declaration of Independence.
1783 Treaty recognises US independence.
1803 Louisiana Purchase of western lands from France.
1846-8 Mexican War: US wins vast territories west of Rockies.
1861-5 Civil War: Union fights secessionist Confederate States.
1865 Slavery outlawed.
1917-18 Joins Allied side in First World War.
1929 Stock market crash leads to Depression.
1941 Japanese attack Pearl Harbor, Hawaii.
1941-5 Joins Allied side in Second World War.
1950-3 Leads UN forces in Korean War.
1963 President Kennedy assassinated.
1964 Enters Vietnam War to assist South Vietnam against North.
1969 Neil Armstrong lands on Moon.
1973 Vietnam ceasefire; troops leave.
1974 President Nixon resigns over Watergate scandal.
1991 Leads international coalition in Gulf War.
1994 North American Free Trade Agreement with Canada and Mexico.
2001 President Bush resurrects the National Missile Defense System.

UNITED STATES

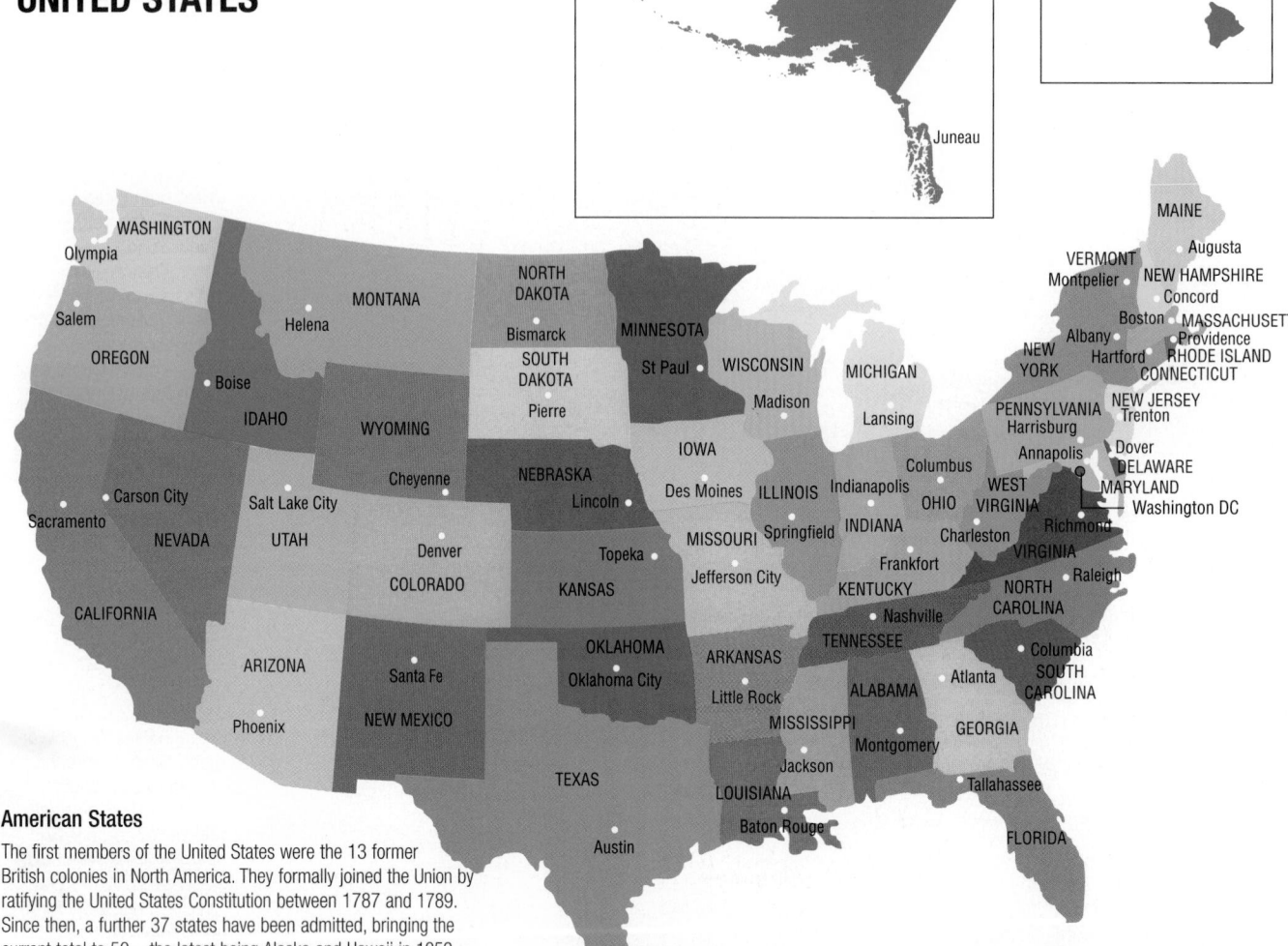

American States

The first members of the United States were the 13 former British colonies in North America. They formally joined the Union by ratifying the United States Constitution between 1787 and 1789. Since then, a further 37 states have been admitted, bringing the current total to 50 – the latest being Alaska and Hawaii in 1959.

States of the Union

Name	Nicknames	Capital	Admitted	Name	Nicknames	Capital	Admitted
Alabama	Heart of Dixie/Camellia State	Montgomery	1819	Nebraska	Cornhusker State/Beef State	Lincoln	1867
Alaska	Mainland State/The Last Frontier	Juneau	1959	Nevada	Sagebrush State/Silver State/Battleborn State	Carson City	1864
Arizona	Grand Canyon State/Apache State	Phoenix	1912	New Hampshire	Granite State	Concord	1788
Arkansas	Wonder State/Bear State/Land of Opportunity	Little Rock	1836	New Jersey	Garden State	Trenton	1787
California	Golden State	Sacramento	1850	New Mexico	Land of Enchantment/Sunshine State	Santa Fe	1912
Colorado	Centennial State	Denver	1876	New York	Empire State	Albany	1788
Connecticut	Constitution State/Nutmeg State	Hartford	1788	North Carolina	Tar Heel State/Old North State	Raleigh	1789
Delaware	First State/Diamond State	Dover	1787	North Dakota	Sioux State/Flickertail State	Bismarck	1889
Florida	Sunshine State/Everglade State	Tallahassee	1845	Ohio	Buckeye State	Columbus	1803
Georgia	Empire State of the South/Peach State	Atlanta	1788	Oklahoma	Sooner State	Oklahoma City	1907
Hawaii	Aloha State	Honolulu	1959	Oregon	Beaver State/Sunset State	Salem	1859
Idaho	Gem State	Boise	1890	Pennsylvania	Keystone State	Harrisburg	1787
Illinois	Inland Empire/Prairie State/Land of Lincoln	Springfield	1818	Rhode Island	Little Rhody/Ocean State/Plantation State	Providence	1790
Indiana	Hoosier State	Indianapolis	1816	South Carolina	Palmetto State	Columbia	1788
Iowa	Hawkeye State/Corn State	Des Moines	1846	South Dakota	Coyote State/Sunshine State	Pierre	1889
Kansas	Sunflower State/Jayhawker State	Topeka	1861	Tennessee	Volunteer State	Nashville	1796
Kentucky	Bluegrass State	Frankfort	1792	Texas	Lone Star State	Austin	1845
Louisiana	Pelican State/Sugar State/Creole State	Baton Rouge	1812	Utah	Beehive State/Mormon State	Salt Lake City	1896
Maine	Pine Tree State	Augusta	1820	Vermont	Green Mountain State	Montpelier	1791
Maryland	Old Line State/Free State	Annapolis	1788	Virginia	Old Dominion State/Mother of Presidents	Richmond	1788
Massachusetts	Bay State/Old Colony	Boston	1788	Washington	Evergreen State/Chinook State	Olympia	1889
Michigan	Great Lake State/Wolverine State	Lansing	1837	West Virginia	Mountain State/Panhandle State	Charleston	1863
Minnesota	North Star State/Gopher State	St Paul	1858	Wisconsin	Badger State/America's Dairyland	Madison	1848
Mississippi	Magnolia State	Jackson	1817	Wyoming	Equality State	Cheyenne	1890
Missouri	Show Me State/Bullion State	Jefferson City	1821				
Montana	Treasure State/Big Sky Country	Helena	1889	District of Columbia, site of Washington DC, was established by Congress in 1790-91			

MEXICO

OFFICIAL NAME
The United Mexican States

CAPITAL
Mexico City

Area 1 958 201 km²
(756, 066 sq miles)
Population 97 361 711
Population density 49 per
km² (128 per sq mile)
Population growth rate 1.5%
Life expectancy 68 (m); 74 (f)

Languages Spanish and
many local languages
Adult literacy rate 89.6%
Currency Mexican peso
(US $ 1= 9.36 pesos)
GDP (US million $) 474 900
GDP per head (US $) 4926

Key dates

250-900 Maya and other civilisations flourish.
10th-13thC Toltec empire flourishes.
14thC Aztecs found Tenochtitlan (Mexico City) and great empire.
1519-21 Cortés leads Spanish conquest.
1821 Independence from Spain.
1823 Becomes republic.
1836 Loses Texas to the USA.
1846-8 War with USA: much more territory lost.

1863-7 French troops occupy Mexico City.
1911 Revolution overthrows dictator Porfirio Diaz.
1917 New constitution introduces reforms.
1938 Nationalises foreign oil companies.
1953 Women win vote.
1970s Huge oil finds.
1985 Earthquakes kill up to 10 000 people.
1994 North American Free Trade Agreement with USA and Canada.

Fiesta! Children parade in the southern town of San Cristobal to celebrate Independence Day. It commemorates the September day in 1810 when Miguel Hildalgo, a priest, issued the first cry of defiance against Spanish rule, triggering the uprising that led to full independence 11 years later. Each year in the capital, Mexico's president re-enacts Hidalgo's call to rebellion.

CUBA

OFFICIAL NAME
The Republic of Cuba

CAPITAL
Havana

Cuba

Area 110 860 km²
(42 803 sq miles)
Population 11 160 000
Population density 100 per
km² (260 per sq mile)
Population growth rate 0.9%
Life expectancy 74 (m); 77 (f)
Language Spanish
Adult literacy rate 95.7%
Currency Cuban peso
(US $1 = 21 pesos)
GDP (US million $) 21 800
GDP per head (US $) 1960

Key dates

1492 Columbus lands
and claims for Spain.
1886 Slavery abolished.
1898 US military rule
after Spain loses
Spanish-American War.
1902 Full independence.
1906-9 US occupation.
1933 Batista in power.
1959 Revolution: Fidel
Castro deposes Batista.
1960 Pact with USSR.
US companies seized;
US trade embargo.
1961 CIA-backed Bay
of Pigs invasion fails.
1962 US–USSR crisis
over Soviet missiles in
Cuba (later withdrawn).
1976 New constitution:
socialist republic.
1987 Agreement with
USA on emigration.

Tourism helps to beat the trade ban

The collapse of the Soviet empire in 1989 was a body blow to the Cuban economy. Soviet subsidies, including the payment of inflated prices for Cuban sugar, had amounted to US $5 billion a year.

Cuba had turned to the USSR for aid and trade in the early 1960s, following a US trade embargo. This in turn was a response to a programme of nationalisation and land redistribution set up by Fidel Castro after he overthrew the dictator Fulgencio Batista in 1959. Castro's revolution hurt US businesses in Cuba, and made it seem to the USA that Communism was creeping into its 'backyard'.

Relations worsened still further after the failure of a US-backed invasion attempt at the Bay of Pigs in 1961, and during the missile crisis of 1962, when President Kennedy forced the USSR to withdraw its missiles from Cuban soil. The effectiveness of US trade sanctions can be seen today on the streets of Havana, where hundreds of ancient American cars are kept going by ingenuity and improvisation.

But what the goods blockade has stopped, the tourist trade has, at least partially, replaced. By 1997, tourism was earning Cuba more than US $1 billion a year. It may not have fitted the image of an embattled Communist society, but it brought in much-needed dollars when, in 1998, a US $5 million seaside golf course was opened at Varadero.

In 1997, a record 1.2 million foreigners visited Cuba. Significantly, 20 000 of them were American citizens. Relations between the two countries began to warm in 2000, and Castro looked forward to a further influx. 'Let them come,' he said. 'We will treat them excellently.'

JAMAICA

OFFICIAL NAME
Jamaica

CAPITAL
Kingston

Area 10 991 km²
(4244 sq miles)
Population 2 590 000
Population density 231 per
km² (598 per sq mile)
Population growth rate 0.9%
Life expectancy 71 (m); 76 (f)
Languages English and
local patois

Adult literacy rate 85%
Currency Jamaican dollar
(US $1 = 45 Jamaican
dollars)
GDP (US million $) 6700
GDP per head (US $) 2637

Key dates

1494 Columbus lands
and claims for Spain.
1655 British rule begins.
1833 Slavery abolished.
1944 Representative
parliament established.
1958-62 Part of West
Indies Federation.
1959 Full internal self-
government.
1962 Full independence
within Commonwealth;
joins UN.
1976 Takes half-
ownership of Canadian
and US bauxite mines.
1988 Hurricane Gilbert
causes severe damage.

Jamaica

HAITI

OFFICIAL NAME
The Republic of Haiti

CAPITAL
Port-au-Prince

Area 27 750 km²
(10 714 sq miles)
Population 7 803 000
Population density 276 per
km² (714 per sq mile)
Population growth rate 2%
Life expectancy 52 (m); 56 (f)
Languages French, Creole

Adult literacy rate 45%
Currency gourde
(US $1 = 24 gourdes)
GDP (US million $) 4300
GDP per head (US $) 562

Key dates

1492 Columbus lands.
1697 French control.
1804 Independence.
1915-34 US control.
1957 Dictator 'Papa Doc'
Duvalier takes power.
1971 'Baby Doc' Duvalier
succeeds his father.
1986 Military coup ousts
'Baby Doc' Duvalier.
1988-91 Series of
elections and coups.
1994 US troops enforce
civilian government.
1995 UN peace-keepers
replace US troops.

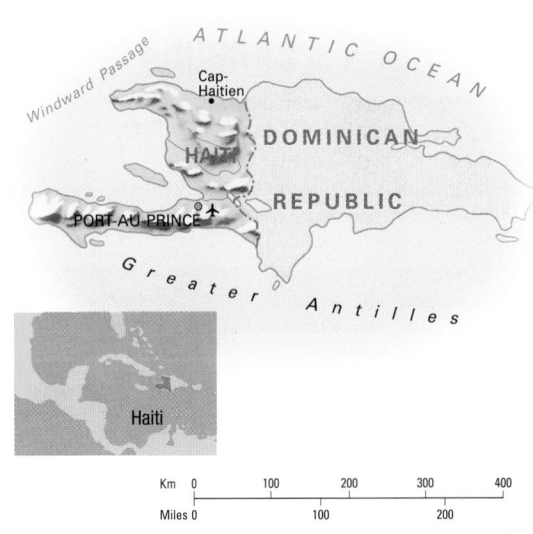

DOMINICAN REPUBLIC

OFFICIAL NAME
The Dominican Republic

CAPITAL
Santo Domingo

Area 48 422 km²
(18 696 sq miles)
Population 8 348 000
Population density 167 per
km² (434 per sq mile)
Population growth rate 2.1%
Life expectancy 68 (m); 72 (f)
Language Spanish

Adult literacy rate 82.1%
Currency Dominican
Republic peso
(US $1 = 16 pesos)
GDP (US million $) 16 900
GDP per head (US $) 2083

Key dates

1492 Columbus lands.
1496 Spanish colony.
1821 Independence, but
Haiti invades.
1844 Full independence.
1916-24 US Marines
occupy to keep peace.
1930-61 Trujillo rules as
dictator.
1962 Free elections.
1963 Military coup.
1965 US Marines put
down revolt.
1966 Constitutional
government restored.
1979 Hurricane David
causes severe damage.

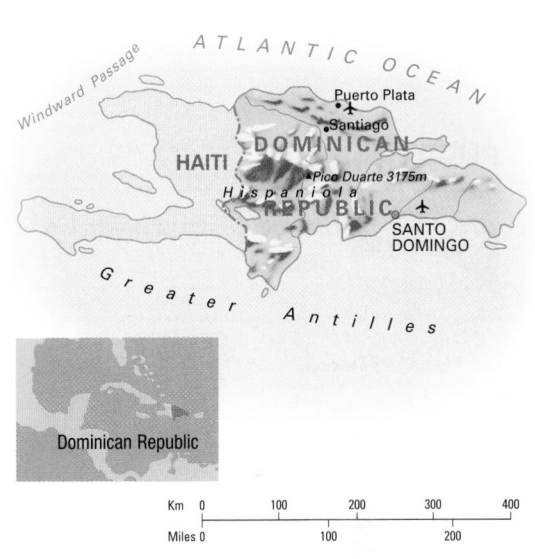

THE BAHAMAS

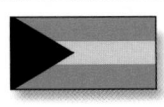

OFFICIAL NAME
The Commonwealth of The
Bahamas

CAPITAL
Nassau, on New Providence

Area 13 939 km²
(5382 sq miles)
Population 301 000
Population density 22 per
km² (56 per sq mile)
Population growth rate 1.7%
Life expectancy 68 (m); 75 (f)
Language English
Adult literacy rate 98.2%
Currency Bahamian dollar
(US $1 = 1 Bahamian
dollar)
GDP (US million $) 3946
GDP per head (US $) 13 153

Key dates

1492 Columbus lands
and claims for Spain.
17thC British settle but
Spanish forces attack.
1717 British colony.
1783 Spain gives up its
claim.
1834 Slavery abolished.
1964 Internal self-
government.
1973 Full independence
within Commonwealth;
joins UN.
1995 Refugees arrive
from Cuba and Haiti.

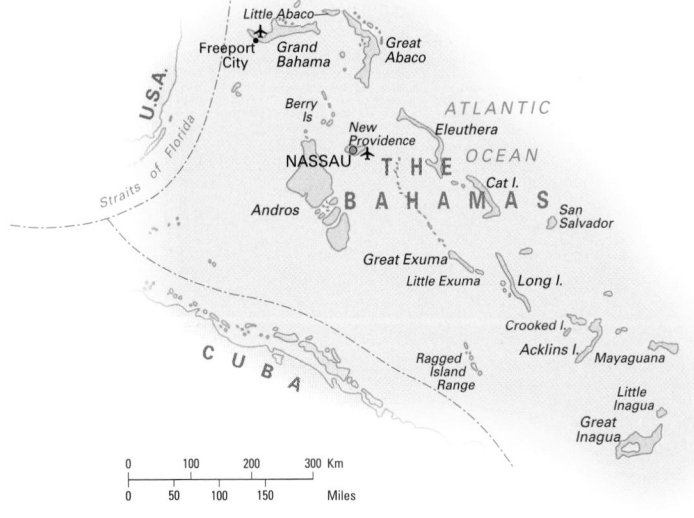

ANTIGUA & BARBUDA

OFFICIAL NAME
Antigua and Barbuda

CAPITAL
St John's, on Antigua

Area 442 km² (170 sq miles)
Population 67 000
Population density 152 per km² (394 per sq mile)
Population growth rate 0.5%
Life expectancy 74 (m); 74 (f)
Languages English, English patois
Adult literacy rate 90%
Currency East Caribbean dollar (US $1 = 2.70 East Caribbean dollars)
GDP (US million $) 603
GDP per head (US $) 9000

Key dates

1632 British colony.
1834 Slavery abolished.
1967 Self-government.
1981 Full independence within Commonwealth.
1983 Joins US-led invasion of Grenada.
1995 Takes in refugees from Montserrat following volcano eruption.

ST KITTS & NEVIS

OFFICIAL NAME
The Federation of Saint Kitts and Nevis

CAPITAL
Basseterre, on St Kitts

Area 261 km² (101 sq miles)
Population 41 000
Population density 157 per km² (406 per sq mile)
Population growth rate 0.5%
Life expectancy 67 (m); 70 (f)
Languages English
Adult literacy rate 97.3%
Currency East Caribbean dollar (US $1 = 2.70 East Caribbean dollars)
GDP (US million $) 264
GDP per head (US $) 6439

Key dates

1623 British settlement.
1834 Slavery abolished.
1967 Self-government.
1969 Anguilla becomes de facto British colony.
1980 Anguilla formally split from St Kitts & Nevis.
1983 Full independence within Commonwealth.
1998 Nevis referendum rejects secession.

PUERTO RICO

OFFICIAL NAME
Commonwealth of Puerto Rico

CAPITAL
San Juan

Status US commonwealth (dependency)
Area 9103 km² (3515 sq miles)
Population 3 522 000
Population density 387 per km² (1002 per sq mile)
Population growth rate 0.56%
Life expectancy 71 (m); 80 (f)
Languages Spanish, English
Adult literacy rate 89%
Currency US dollar
GDP (US million $) 34 700
GDP per head (US $) 9108

Key dates

1493 Columbus lands and claims for Spain.
1870 Slavery abolished.
1898 Under US rule after Spain loses Spanish-American War.
1917 Puerto Ricans given US citizenship.
1947 Gains right to elect own governor.
1952 Self-government as US dependency.
1989 Hurricane Hugo causes severe damage.
1998 Votes against independence and full statehood.

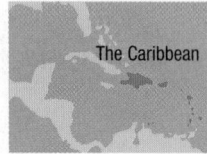
The Caribbean

ST LUCIA

OFFICIAL NAME
Saint Lucia

CAPITAL
Castries

Area 616 km² (238 sq miles)
Population 146 000
Population density 237 per km² (613 per sq mile)
Population growth rate 1.7%
Life expectancy 69 (m); 75 (f)
Languages English, French patois
Adult literacy rate 81.5%
Currency East Caribbean dollar (US $1 = 2.7 East Caribbean dollars)
GDP (US million $) 609
GDP per head (US $) 4171

Key dates

1650 French settlement after long resistance by native Carib peoples.
17th-18thC France and Britain struggle for rule.
1814 Ceded to Britain.
1834 Slavery abolished.
1958-62 Part of West Indies Federation.
1967 Self-government.
1979 Full independence within Commonwealth.

GRENADA

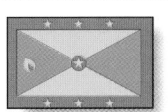

OFFICIAL NAME
Grenada

CAPITAL
St George's

Area 344 km² (133 sq miles)
Population 93 000
Population density 270 per km² (699 per sq mile)
Population growth rate 0.2%
Life expectancy 71 (m); 71 (f)
Languages English, French patois
Adult literacy rate 90%
Currency East Caribbean dollar (US $1 = 2.7 East Caribbean dollars)
GDP (US million $) 333
GDP per head (US $) 3580

Key dates

1650 French settlement.
1793 British rule.
1834 Slavery abolished.
1967 Self-government.
1974 Full independence within Commonwealth.
1979 Bloodless coup.
1983 Marxist coup put down by US-led force.
1984 Elections restore democratic rule.

BARBADOS

OFFICIAL NAME
Barbados

CAPITAL
Bridgetown

Area 431 km² (166 sq miles)
Population 267 000
Population density 617 per km² (1598 per sq mile)
Population growth rate 0.55%
Life expectancy 70 (m); 76 (f)
Language English
Adult literacy rate 97%
Currency Barbados dollar (US $1 = 1.99 Barbados dollars)
GDP (US million $) 2393
GDP per head (US $) 8962

Key dates

1627 British colony.
1838 Slavery abolished.
1951 Introduction of universal suffrage.
1958-62 Part of West Indies Federation.
1966 Full independence within Commonwealth.
1983 Joins US-led invasion of Grenada.

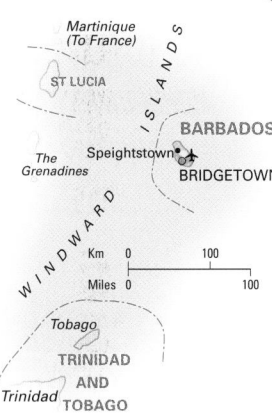

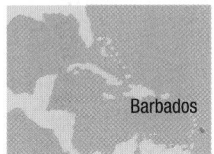

Barbados

TRINIDAD & TOBAGO

OFFICIAL NAME
The Republic of Trinidad and Tobago

CAPITAL
Port of Spain, on Trinidad

Area 5128 km² (1980 sq miles)
Population 1 289 000
Population density 250 per km² (646 per sq mile)
Population growth rate 1.2%
Life expectancy 72 (m); 72 (f)
Languages English, French, Spanish, Hindi, Chinese
Adult literacy rate 97.9%
Currency Trinidad and Tobago dollar (US $1 = 6.2 Trinidad and Tobago dollars)
GDP (US million $) 6700
GDP per head (US $) 5234

Key dates

1498 Columbus claims Trinidad for Spain.
1797 Britain captures Trinidad.
1814 Tobago ceded to Britain.
1958-62 Part of West Indies Federation.
1959 Self-government.
1962 Full independence within Commonwealth.
1976 Becomes republic.
1990 Coup attempt by Muslim extremists fails.

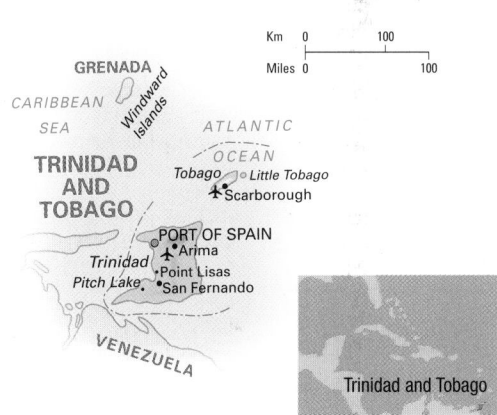

Trinidad and Tobago

DOMINICA

OFFICIAL NAME
The Commonwealth of Dominica

CAPITAL
Roseau

Area 750 km² (290 sq miles)
Population 71 000
Population density 107 per km² (276 per sq mile)
Population growth rate 0.2%
Life expectancy 72 (m); 72 (f)
Languages English, French patois
Adult literacy rate 94.4%
Currency East Caribbean dollar (US $1 = 2.7 East Caribbean dollars)
GDP (US million $) 244
GDP per head (US $) 3050

Key dates

17thC French and British settlements.
1805 British possession.
1834 Slavery abolished.
1967 Self-government.
1978 Full independence within Commonwealth.
1979 Severe hurricane.
1983 Joins US-led invasion of Grenada.

ST VINCENT & THE GRENADINES

OFFICIAL NAME
Saint Vincent and the Grenadines

CAPITAL
Kingstown, on St Vincent

Area 389 km² (150 sq miles)
Population 112 000
Population density 288 per km² (747 per sq mile)
Population growth rate 0.9%
Life expectancy 72 (m); 72 (f)
Languages English, French
Adult literacy rate 82%
Currency East Caribbean dollar (US $1 = 2.7 East Caribbean dollars)
GDP (US million $) 300
GDP per head (US $) 2678

Key dates

1783 Becomes British colony.
1834 Slavery abolished.
1958-62 Part of West Indies Federation.
1969 Self-government.
1979 Full independence within Commonwealth.
1983 Joins US-led invasion of Grenada.

HONDURAS

OFFICIAL NAME
The Republic of Honduras

CAPITAL
Tegucigalpa

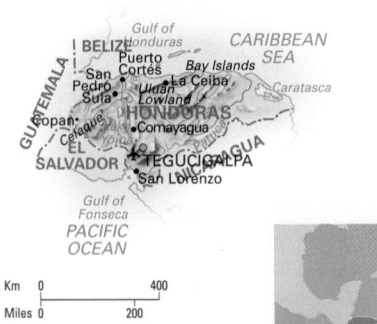

Area 112 088 km²
(43 277 sq miles)
Population 6 385 000
Population density 55 per
km² (143 per sq mile)
Population growth rate 3%
Life expectancy 65 (m); 70 (f)

Languages Spanish, English
and local languages
Adult literacy rate 72.7%
Currency lempira
(US $1 = 15.29 lempiras)
GDP (US million $) 5500
GDP per head (US $) 889

Key dates

1502 Columbus lands
and claims for Spain.
1821 Independence as
part of Central
American Federation.
1838 Full independence.
1969 Expels Salvadoran
immigrants; brief war.
1980s 'Contra' guerrillas
attack Nicaragua from
bases in Honduras.
1992 Settles El Salvador
border dispute.

BELIZE

OFFICIAL NAME
Belize

CAPITAL
Belmopan

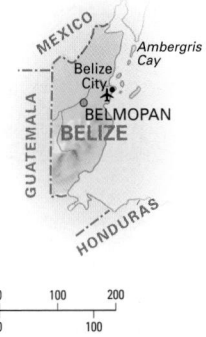

Area 22 965 km²
(8867 sq miles)
Population 235 000
Population density 10 per
km² (27 per sq mile)
Population growth rate 2.6%
Life expectancy 70 (m); 74 (f)
Languages English, Spanish,

Creole, Garifuna, Maya,
Ketchi, German
Adult literacy rate 90%
Currency Belizean dollar
(US $1 = 1.97 Belizean
dollars)
GDP (US million $) 646
GDP per head (US $) 2691

Key dates

1520s Spanish claim.
1862 Colony of British
Honduras established.
1964 Self-government.
1973 Renamed Belize.
1975 British troops help
to defend border
disputed by Guatemala.
1981 Full independence.
1991 Guatemala gives
up claims to Belize.
1993 Border dispute
with Guatemala ends.
1994 British troops go.

COSTA RICA

OFFICIAL NAME
The Republic of Costa Rica

CAPITAL
San José

Key dates

1502 Columbus lands
and claims for Spain.
1821 Independence as
part of Central
American Federation.
1838 Full independence.
1948-9 Civil war follows
disputed election.
1949 New constitution;
army abolished.
1987 President Arias
Sanchez wins Nobel
peace prize.

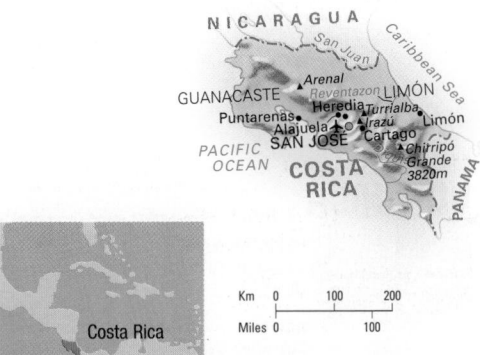

Area 51 100 km²
(19 730 sq miles)
Population 3 589 000
Population density 69 per
km² (179 per sq mile)
Population growth rate 1.5%
Life expectancy 73 (m); 78 (f)

Languages Spanish,
English patois
Adult literacy rate 94.8%
Currency Costa Rican colón
(US $1 = 323 colones)
GDP (US million $) 10 600
GDP per head (US $) 3002

A respite in Central America's years of bloodshed

The 1980s and 90s brought an
unexpected pause to the conflicts
in troubled Central America and a
Nobel peace prize for Costa Rica's
President Arias Sanchez. He drew
up a peace plan, signed in 1987
by El Salvador, Costa Rica,
Guatemala and Nicaragua.

The Central American nations,
after winning independence from

Spain in 1821, had suffered more
than 150 years of military coups,
civil wars, border conflicts and
guerrilla insurgencies.

In Nicaragua the Sandinista
guerrillas had overthrown the
dictatorship of the Somoza family
in 1979, but their policy of land
reform and nationalisation
alarmed the USA and they were

attacked by right-wing Contras,
trained and funded by the CIA.
With the country in severe
recession, the Sandinistas lost
the 1990 election. Clashes
continued, but a cease-fire
agreement was signed in 1994.

Guatemala, which had known
little but disorder and death
squads since a CIA-backed coup

in 1954, made peace with
left-wing rebels in 1996. In 1992,
El Salvador and Honduras
compromised on a long-standing
border dispute. Arias's plan had
set the mood for peace.

GUATEMALA

OFFICIAL NAME
The Republic of Guatemala

CAPITAL
Guatemala City

Area 108 889 km²
(42 042 sq miles)
Population 11 088 000
Population density 99 per
km² (257 per sq mile)
Population growth rate 2.9%
Life expectancy 62 (m); 67 (f)
Languages Spanish and
many local languages
Adult literacy rate 55.6%
Currency quetzal
(US $1 = 7.77 quetzales)
GDP (US million $) 18 100
GDP per head (US $) 1675

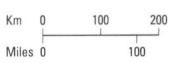

Guatemala

Key dates

1523 Spanish invasion.
1821 Independence as
part of Central
American Federation.
1839 Full independence.
1945 New constitution
brings political reforms.
1952 Land reform starts.
1954 USA backs military
coup, bringing Carlos
Castillo to power.
1985 New constitution
restores civilian rule.
1991 Belize border
dispute ends.
1993 Army removes
dictatorial president.
1996 Peace agreement
with left-wing rebels.

EL SALVADOR

OFFICIAL NAME
The Republic of El Salvador

CAPITAL
San Salvador

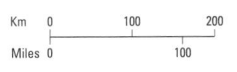

El Salvador

Area 21 041 km²
(8124 sq miles)
Population 6 154 000
Population density 287 per
km² (742 per sq mile)
Population growth rate 1.9%
Life expectancy 51 (m); 64 (f)
Languages Spanish and
local languages
Adult literacy rate 71.5%
Currencies US dollar and
Salvadorean colón
(US $1 = 8.74 colones)
GDP (US million $) 12 000
GDP per head (US $) 1990

Key dates

1524 Spanish invasion.
1821 Independence as
part of Central
American Federation.
1840 Full independence.
1931 Military coup.
1969 Brief border war
with Honduras.
1979 Fighting starts with
left-wing guerrillas.
1980 Archbishop
Romero assassinated.
1983 New constitution.
1992 Peace agreement
with guerrillas.

NICARAGUA

OFFICIAL NAME
The Republic of Nicaragua

CAPITAL
Managua

Area 120 254 km²
(46 430 sq miles)
Population 4 936 000
Population density 40 per
km² (104 per sq mile)
Population growth rate 1.8%
Life expectancy 63 (m); 69 (f)
Languages Spanish, English
and local languages
Adult literacy rate 65.6%
Currency gold cordoba
(US $1 = 13.2 gold
cordobas)
GDP (US million $) 2200
GDP per head (US $) 457

Key dates

1502 Columbus lands
and claims for Spain.
1821 Independence as
part of Central American
Federation.
1838 Full independence.
1912-33 US occupation.
1937 Anastasio Somoza
becomes dictator.
1956 Somoza killed;
succeeded by son Luis.
1967 Luis Somoza dies;
his brother Anastasio

succeeds him.
1979 Sandinistas win
17-year guerrilla war;
Somoza flees. Support
for rebels in El Salvador.
1982 'Contra' rebels
begin guerrilla offensive.
1989 Peace talks fail.
1990 Sandinista defeat
in elections. Peace
agreed with Contras.
1998 Hurricane Mitch
causes severe damage.

Nicaragua

PANAMA

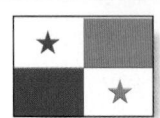

OFFICIAL NAME
The Republic of Panama

CAPITAL
Panama City

Area 75 517 km²
(29 157 sq miles)
Population 2 809 000
Population density 37 per
km² (95 per sq mile)
Population growth rate 1.3%
Life expectancy 71 (m); 76 (f)
Languages Spanish and
local languages
Adult literacy rate 90.8%
Currencies US dollar and
balboa (US $1 = 1 balboa)
GDP (US million $) 9500
GDP per head (US $) 3442

Km 0 100 200 300 400
Miles 0 100 200

Panama

Key dates

1502 Balboa visits and claims for Spain.
1821 Independence as part of Colombia.
1855 Railway built across isthmus.
1903 Independence won from Colombia through US-supported revolt; US given control of Canal Zone.
1908-28 US supervises all elections.
1914 Canal completed.
1960s Dispute with USA over Canal Zone treaty.
1968 Military coup.
1977 New Canal Zone treaty with USA.
1979 Regains control of Canal Zone from USA.

1983 General Noriega gains effective power.
1988 US courts indict Noriega for drug trafficking; USA starts economic sanctions.
1989 National Assembly names Noriega head of government and declares state of war with USA. US troops invade in order to arrest Noriega.
1990 Noriega surrenders.
1992 Noriega tried in USA and sentenced to 40 years in prison.
1999 Panama gains operational control of canal; USA retains defence rights.

Two oceans united

One British politician called it 'the greatest liberty man has ever taken with nature'. The Panama Canal linking the Atlantic and Pacific oceans took 40 000 men 10 years to complete. From 1904 to 1914, the US construction crew worked to move 315 million m³ (240 million cu yd) of earth: 6000 men died in the process. But the US government thought the prize was worth it: the canal shortened sea journeys between New York and San Francisco by some 13 000 km (8000 miles). By the end of the 20th century, it had revolutionised global economic development

by boosting world trade and creating new markets. When the USA turned control of the canal over to Panama in 1999, more than 700 000 vessels had completed the 24-hour passage, including 13 025 in 1998.

The first attempt to build a waterway through the Isthmus of Panama, by a French company in the 1880s, cost 22 000 lives before the project ended in bankruptcy. Success came after US President Theodore Roosevelt took up the challenge. Panama was then part of Colombia, which refused the USA permission to build the canal. The USA

then backed a successful Panamanian revolt. With independent Panama's enthusiastic approval, Roosevelt spent $387 million and provided America's best engineers. He also sent his country's best medical officers – chief sanitary officer Dr William C. Gorgas eliminated the twin threats of yellow fever and malaria by eradicating mosquitoes in the area.

Tight fit An ocean-going ship navigates Pedro Miguel Lock on the Panama Canal. There are three sets of locks on the canal – at its highest point, ships are 26 m (85 ft) above sea level.

VENEZUELA

OFFICIAL NAME
The Republic of Venezuela

CAPITAL
Caracas

Area 912 050 km²
(352 144 sq miles)
Population 23 706 000
Population density 25 per
km² (66 per sq mile)
Population growth rate 1.7%
Life expectancy 69 (m); 75 (f)
Languages Spanish and
local languages
Adult literacy rate 91.1%
Currency bolívar
(US $1 = 710 bolívars)
GDP (US million $) 102 800
GDP per head (US $) 4423

Key dates

1498 Columbus claims
for Spain.
1811-21 Liberated by
Simón Bolívar; part of
Greater Colombia.
1829 Full independence.
1917 Oil production
begins.
1958 Violent protests
force dictator Marcos
Perez Jiménez to flee;
democratic rule
established.
1976 Nationalises 21 oil
companies.
1989 300 die in riots
over price rises; martial
law imposed.
1992 Two attempted
military coups fail.
1994-5 Economic crisis;
civil rights suspended.

Venezuela

Km 0   400
Miles 0   200   400

COLOMBIA

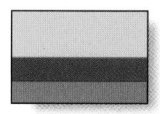

OFFICIAL NAME
The Republic of Colombia

CAPITAL
Bogotá

Area 1 141 748 km²
(440 831 sq miles)
Population 41 589 000
Population density 36 per
km² (93 per sq mile)
Population growth rate 1.5%
Life expectancy 66 (m); 72 (f)
Language Spanish
Adult literacy rate 91.3%
Currency Colombian peso
(US $1 = 2328 pesos)
GDP (US million $) 77 100
GDP per head (US $) 1888

Key dates

1525 Spanish settle.
1538 Named New
Kingdom of Granada.
1819 Liberated by
Simón Bolívar; forms
Greater Colombia.
1829-30 Venezuela and
Ecuador break away.
1903 Loses Panama.
1948-62 'La Violencia':
200 000 die in political
riots, rebellions, etc.
1957-74 Coalition rule.
1978 Begins offensive
against drug trade.
1989-90 Three
presidential candidates
assassinated.
1993 Police kill drug
baron Pablo Escobar.
1996 Emergency to fight
leftist guerrillas.

Colombia

0   400 Km
0   200   Miles

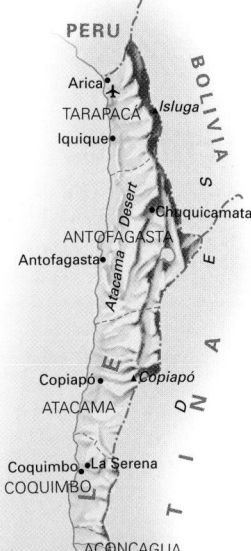

CHILE

OFFICIAL NAME
The Republic of Chile

CAPITAL
Santiago

Area 756 626 km²
(292 135 sq miles)
Population 15 018 000
Population density 20 per
km² (51 per sq mile)
Population growth rate 1.7%
Life expectancy 72 (m); 77 (f)

Languages Spanish,
Araucanian
Adult literacy rate 95.2%
Currency Chilean peso
(US $1 = 602 pesos)
GDP (US million $) 66 900
GDP per head (US $) 4514

Key dates

1541 Spaniards settle
and found Santiago.
1818 Independence
from Spain after eight-
year struggle.
1879-83 Chile wins
territory from Peru in
War of the Pacific.
1891 Civil war – more
than 10 000 killed.
1970 Marxist President
Allende elected.
1973 Allende dies in

US-backed military
coup. Pinochet heads
military junta.
1980 New constitution.
1989 Elections restore
civilian government.
1998 Pinochet arrested
in UK.
2000 UK government
allows Pinochet to
return home; charged
in Chile with murder
and kidnapping.

A CONTINENT'S SPINE

South America's Andes mountain range has always offered protection but also created problems. People sought security from persecution in the inaccessible mountains even before the Incas built their great civilisation on the high plateau of the Altiplano 800 years ago. Yet the physical barrier of the Andes range, running the length of the continent near the west coast, has blocked communications and held back modern civilisation from villages away from the sea.

Transport is difficult, with pack animals still used in some areas, and the obstacles to road and railway construction hinder economic growth in countries such as Bolivia, Peru and Ecuador. (One railway line, the Central, climbs to 4816 m [15 800 ft] – the highest standard-gauge track in the world.)

The Andes range – the world's longest at 7200 km (4475 miles) and second highest at over 6100 m (20 000 ft) – is the source of the vast Amazon and many other rivers. Its fertile soil is excellent for crops such as grain, maize, potatoes, coffee, tobacco and sugar cane, and the land yields mineral riches: oil in the foothills, gold and emeralds in Colombia, silver in Peru and Chile, and tin in Bolivia.

But the geologically young range is alive with tectonic activity. Its natural disasters have included an earthquake in Peru in 1970 that killed 50 000 people and the 1985 volcanic eruption in Colombia that cost 23 000 lives.

Young and restless The Andes are still growing, as the Pacific floor pushes under South America. The result is frequent eathquakes and volcanic disasters along the length of the range.

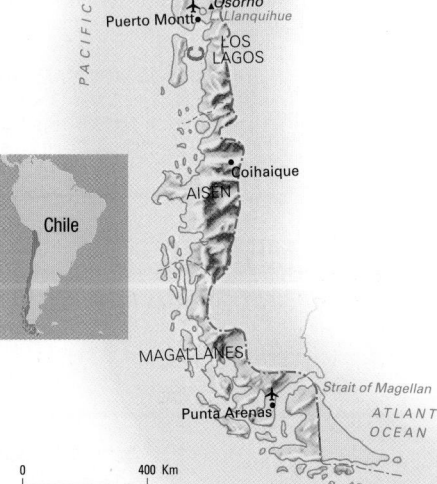

BOLIVIA

OFFICIAL NAME
The Republic of Bolivia

CAPITALS
La Paz and Sucre

Area 1 098 581 km²
(424 164 sq miles)
Population 8 137 000
Population density 7 per
km² (19 per sq mile)
Population growth rate 2.2%
Life expectancy 59 (m); 63 (f)
Languages Spanish,
Quechua, Aymara

Adult literacy rate 83.1%
Currency boliviano
(US $1 = 6.50 bolivianos)
GDP (US million $) 8400
GDP per head (US $) 1056

Key dates

15thC Inca rule.
1534 Spanish conquest.
1825 Independence.
1879-83 War of Pacific:
loses territory to Chile.
1932-5 Chaco War: loss
of territory to Paraguay.
1964-82 Military rulers.
1967 Defeat of revolt led
by Che Guevara, who
is captured and killed.
1980-3 US/EC aid halted
because of corruption.
1982 Democratic civilian
rule begins.

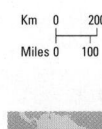

ECUADOR

OFFICIAL NAME
The Republic of Ecuador

CAPITAL
Quito

Area 272 045 km²
(105 037 sq miles)
Population 12 411 000
Population density 45 per
km² (116 per sq mile)
Population growth rate 2.3%
Life expectancy 67 (m); 72 (f)
Languages Spanish,
Quechua and other local
languages

Adult literacy rate 90.1%
Currency US dollar
GDP (US million $) 12 700
GDP per head (US $) 1043

1 Chimborazo
2 Bolivar
3 Tungurahua

Key dates

15thC Inca rule.
1534 Spanish conquest.
1822 Independence as
part of Colombia.
1830 Full independence.
1925-48 Many unstable
governments.
1941 Border war with
Peru: loses territory in
Amazon Basin.
1963 Military coup.
1966 Civilian rule re-
established; new
constitution adopted.
1972 Military coup.
1979 New democratic
constitution.
1995 Fighting with Peru
over disputed border.
1998 Emergency
economic measures.
2000 Coup deposes
president; protests over
austerity measures.

A city for all seasons
Owing to its location on
the Equator and an
altitude of 2775 m
(9250 ft), Quito's climate
can run the gamut of all
four seasons in 24 hours.

PERU

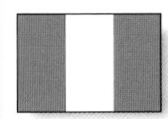

OFFICIAL NAME
The Republic of Peru

CAPITAL
Lima

Area 1 285 216 km²
(496 225 sq miles)
Population 25 232 000
Population density 19 per
km² (50 per sq mile)
Population growth rate 2%
Life expectancy 66 (m); 70 (f)
Languages Spanish,
Quechua, Aymara
Adult literacy rate 88.7%
Currency new sol
(US $1 = 3.58 new sols)
GDP (US million $) 56 200
GDP per head (US $) 2266

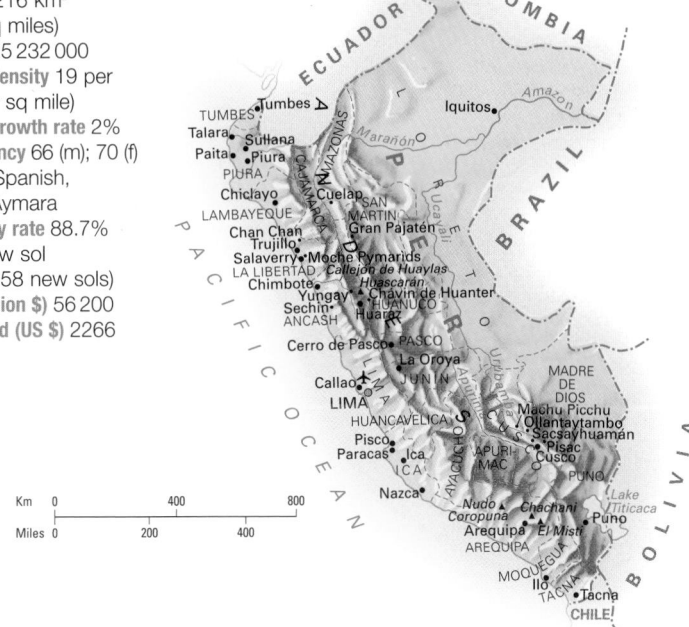

Key dates

c.1200 Inca kingdom
established.
1532-3 Conquest by
Spanish under Pizarro.
1824 Independence after
four-year war.
1879-83 War of Pacific:
loses territory to Chile.
1930 Military coup leads
to political repression.
1941 War with Ecuador:
wins Amazon territory.
1945 Open elections.
1948 Military coup.
1963 Civilian rule; social
reforms started.

1968 Military coup;
industries nationalised.
1980 Elections. 'Shining
Path' communist
guerrilla group active.
1992 'Shining Path'
leader captured.
1995 Border fighting with
Ecuador.
1996-7 Leftist Tupac
Amaru guerrillas seize
hostages; rescued by
army; guerrillas killed.
2000 President Fujimori
accused of corruption
and forced to resign.

GUYANA

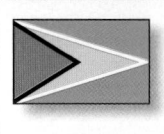

OFFICIAL NAME
The Cooperative Republic of Guyana

CAPITAL
Georgetown

Area 214 969 km² (83 000 sq miles)
Population 855 000
Population density 4 per km² (10 per sq mile)
Population growth rate 0.5%
Life expectancy 62 (m); 68 (f)
Languages English, Hindi, Urdu and local dialects

Adult literacy rate 98.1%
Currency Guyanese dollar (US $1 = 180 Guyanese dollars)
GDP (US million $) 690
GDP per head (US $) 811

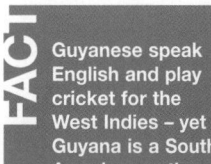

FACT Guyanese speak English and play cricket for the West Indies – yet Guyana is a South American nation.

Key dates

1581 Dutch settlement.
1814 British control.
1831 Colony of British Guyana established.
1838 Last slaves freed; indentured labourers from India (East Indians) later brought in to replace slaves.
1961 Self-government.
1962-4 Political/racial violence between black and East Indian groups delays independence.
1964 People's National Congress (mainly black) wins election over Marxist-led People's Progressive Party (mainly East Indian).
1966 Full independence within Commonwealth; renamed Guyana.
1970 Becomes republic.
1978 'Jonestown massacre' – mass suicide and murder of 911 members of the People's Temple, a US religious cult.
1988 Economic reforms and privatisation begin.

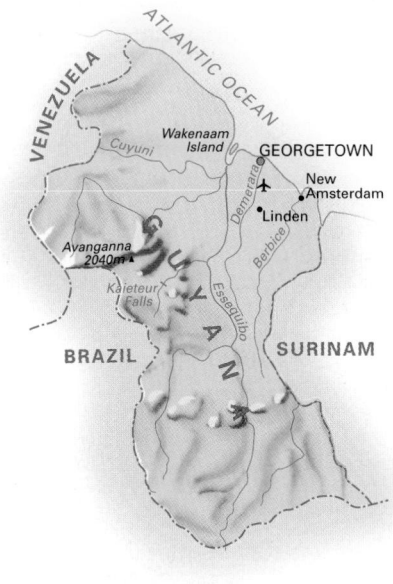

SURINAM

OFFICIAL NAME
The Republic of Surinam

CAPITAL
Paramaribo

Area 163 265 km² (63 037 sq miles)
Population 415 000
Population density 3 per km² (7 per sq mile)
Population growth rate 1.1%
Life expectancy 64 (m); 71 (f)
Languages Dutch, Hindi, Javanese, Sranang Tongo, Chinese, English

Adult literacy rate 93%
Currency Surinam guilder (US $1 = 981 guilders)
GDP (US million $) 842
GDP per head (US $) 2053

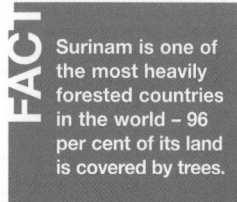

FACT Surinam is one of the most heavily forested countries in the world – 96 per cent of its land is covered by trees.

Key dates

1651 British settlement.
1667 Dutch control in exchange for New York.
1863 Slavery abolished; indentured labourers later brought in from India and Indonesia to replace slaves.
1954 Dutch Guiana gains self-government.
1975 Full independence; about two-fifths of population to emigrate to Netherlands. Name changed to Surinam.
1980 Bloodless coup.
1982-7 National Military Council governs.
1987 Antigovernment rebels cause economic chaos.
1987 Three main parties unite and win elections; new constitution.
1990 Military coup forces resignation of civilian government.
1991 New elections.
1992 Peace treaty with guerrilla groups.

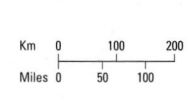

BRAZIL

OFFICIAL NAME
Federative Republic of Brazil

CAPITAL
Brasília

Area 8 511 996 km²
(3 286 500 sq miles)
Population 165 371 000
Population density 19 per
km² (49 per sq mile)
Population growth rate 1%
Life expectancy 64 (m); 70 (f)
Languages Portuguese and
local languages

Adult literacy rate 85.2%
Currency real
(US $1 = 2.22 reals)
GDP (US million $) 518 900
GDP per head (US $) 3207

Key dates

1500 Portuguese claim.
*c.*1700 Gold and
diamonds discovered.
1750 Treaty with Spain
confirms Portuguese rule.
1808-21 Rio de Janeiro is
capital of Portuguese
empire after France
invades Portugal.
1815 Declared kingdom.
1822 Independence
declared; Pedro I
crowned emperor.
1828 Loses Uruguay in
war against Argentina.
1865-70 War (with
Argentina and Uruguay)
against Paraguay;

present borders
established.
1888 Slavery abolished.
1889 Military coup
deposes emperor;
republic established.
1917-18 One of Allies in
First World War.
1930 Coup; Vargas
becomes president.
1934 New constitution;
universal right to vote.
1937 Economic crisis;
new constitution makes
Vargas dictator.
1942-5 One of Allies in
Second World War.
1945 Vargas forced to

resign by military.
1946 New constitution
restores democracy.
1951 Vargas elected
president.
1954 Military coup;
Vargas kills himself.
1960 Capital moves from
Rio de Janeiro to new
city of Brasília.
1964-85 Military rule.
1989 First direct election
of president under new
constitution.
1992 President Collor
accused of corruption;
resigns.
1994 Collor acquitted.

Urban plan A view along the
main axis of Brasília, towards
the National Congress complex,
highlights the symmetry of
Brazil's modernist capital.
Designed by architect Oscar
Niemeyer and urban planner
Lúcio Costa, the city was built in
just three years.

PARAGUAY

OFFICIAL NAME
The Republic of Paraguay

CAPITAL
Asunción

Area 406 752 km²
(157 048 sq miles)
Population 5 356 000
Population density 13 per
km² (33 per sq mile)
Population growth rate 2.2%
Life expectancy 66 (m); 70 (f)
Languages Spanish,
Guarani

Adult literacy rate 92.1%
Currency guarani
(US $1 = 3805 guaranis)
GDP (US million $) 7600
GDP per head (US $) 1455

Key dates

1537 First Spanish
settlement.
1588 Jesuits arrive;
expelled 179 years later.
1811 Independence.
1865-70 War of the
Triple Alliance: loses
territory to Brazil,
Argentina and Uruguay.
1932-5 Chaco War:
gains territory in Gran
Chaco from Bolivia.
1954 General Alfredo
Stroessner seizes
power.
1989 Coup overthrows
Stroessner.
1992 New constitution.
1993 First democratic
presidential election.

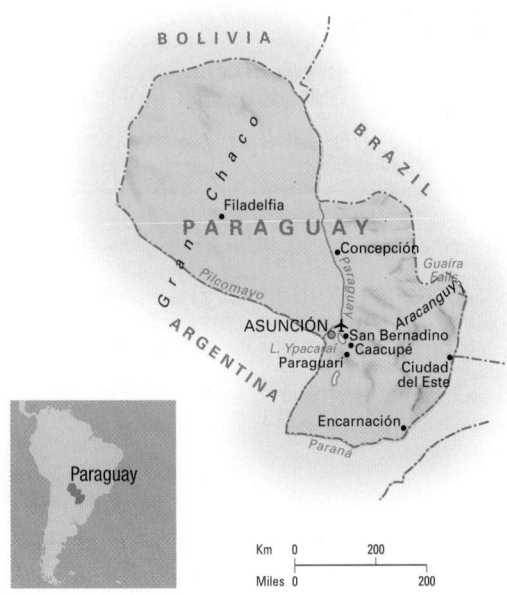

URUGUAY

OFFICIAL NAME
The Oriental Republic of
Uruguay

CAPITAL
Montevideo

Area 176 215 km²
(68 037 sq miles)
Population 3 313 000
Population density 19 per
km² (48 per sq mile)
Population growth rate 0.6%
Life expectancy 68 (m); 74 (f)
Languages Spanish,
Portuguese
Adult literacy rate 96.8%
Currency Uruguayan peso
(US $1 = 12.9 pesos)
GDP (US million $) 19 400
GDP per head (US $) 5896

Key dates

1680 Portuguese
settlement.
1726 Spanish found
Montevideo.
1777 Spanish control.
1811-20 Struggle for
independence with
Spanish, Argentine and
Portuguese forces ends
in annexation to Brazil.
1825-8 Revolt (with UK
and Argentine support)
against Brazil wins full
independence.
1836-52 Civil war
between mainly rural
Oribe and urban
Colorado groups; won
by Colorados.
1865-70 War of the Triple
Alliance: supports

Argentina and Brazil to
defeat Paraguay.
1903 President Batlle
begins reforms leading
to stable democracy.
1942-5 Supports Allies in
World War II.
1967 Tupamaro guerrilla
group becomes active.
1972 State of internal
war declared against
Tupamaros; army
stamps out their urban
terrorism.
1973 Armed forces take
control of government.
1976 Coup deposes
repressive government.
1984 Democratic
elections restore civilian
government.

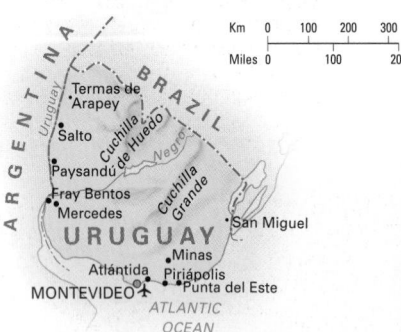

WEALTH OF THE PAMPAS

Despite the fact that its name translates as 'Land of Silver', the true wealth of Argentina lies in its soil. The pampas, a huge expanse of grassland, stretches over some 777 000 km² (300 000 sq miles) of central Argentina and into Uruguay. The Spanish introduced cattle and horses to these vast plains in the mid 16th century, and for centuries they roamed there semiwild. As well as livestock, the pampas are home to a vast array of wildlife: ostrich-like rheas, deer, guanacos (which resemble llamas), giant anteaters and maned wolves.

Only in the 19th century were the Pampas extensively settled by farmers, mainly from Europe, who established large *estancias* (cattle ranches) and farms. During those years, the hard-riding gauchos began to tame the wild horses and to round up the wild cattle. Like the cowboys of North America's Wild West, they revelled in the freedom of wide open spaces. To city dwellers, and later generations, they became cultural symbols.

The Argentinians are great meat-eaters, consuming some 70 kg (154 lb) per head a year. They are also prodigious meat-exporters, though it was not until the late 1800s, with the development of railways and refrigerated steamships, that beef exports soared, and Argentina began to amass wealth, based on the products of the pampas. Its cattle business remains immense, but modern vehicles and machinery have consigned the gaucho into a hazy and legendary past.

ARGENTINA

OFFICIAL NAME
The Argentine Republic

CAPITAL
Buenos Aires

Key dates

1516-26 Solis, Magellan and Cabot explore Rio de la Plata.
1536 Spanish settle briefly at Buenos Aires (refounded 1580).
1776 Separate Viceroyalty of La Plata.
1812-16 Jose de San Martin leads fight for independence; new state named United Provinces of La Plata.
1853 New constitution; Buenos Aires secedes.
1862 Buenos Aires rejoins as capital.
1916 First democratic elections.
1939-45 Second World War: open sympathy with Germany, but declares war on Axis in 1945.
1943 Military coup.
1946 Colonel Juan Perón made president; assisted by wife Eva, reforms economy but represses freedoms.
1952 Eva Perón dies.
1955 Perón deposed; goes into exile in Spain.
1973 Perón returns from exile; wins election.
1974 Perón dies; third wife, María, becomes president.
1976 Military coup deposes María Perón.
1982 Invades Falkland Islands; Falklands War lost to Britain. President Galtieri resigns.
1983 Democratic elections; Perónist party suffers first defeat.
1985 Five former junta members judged guilty of murder and human rights abuses.
1989 Carlos Menem elected president.
1990 Relations with Britain restored. Military coup fails.
1994 New constitution.

Area 2 766 889 km²
(1 068 302 sq miles)
Population 36 578 000
Population density 13 per km² (34 per sq mile)
Population growth rate 1.4%
Life expectancy 68 (m); 73 (f)
Languages Spanish, many other European languages and local languages
Adult literacy rate 96.2%
Currency Argentine peso (US $1 = 1 peso)
GDP (US million $) 281 900
GDP per head (US $) 7804

A piece of Europe in South America

Argentina is the only country in South America whose population is predominantly European in origin. About 85 per cent of its people trace their ancestry to Europe – mostly to Italy (35 per cent) and Spain (25 per cent). Others look back to Poland, France, Russia, Germany and the British Isles. Spanish is the official language, but German, English, French and Italian are often heard. A group of Welsh immigrants whose forebears settled in Patagonia in the 1860s have never forgotten their roots. They still bring teachers across the Atlantic, to keep Welsh a living language.

The same European origins are reflected in Argentina's culture. The capital's opera the *teatro Colón*, was shipped stone by stone, from Europe. Its opening performance, in 1908, was Verdi's *Aïda*. It was through contacts with the sports-loving British that Argentinians took up soccer, rugby, tennis and polo. But Europe is not the only influence. The tango, the best-known product of Argentina's popular culture, combines Cuban, Spanish, African and gaucho elements, and is accompanied on the bandonéon, invented by a German.

The non-European 15 per cent includes native Amerindians, people of black African origin, immigrants from the Middle East and Mestizos (people of mixed race).

Argentina

Bright barrio Not all the barrios of South America are shantytowns. The word simply means 'neighbourhood', and some, like La Boca in Buenos Aires, can be extremely smart. Many of Argentina's Italian immigrants first settled in La Boca, and they provided the barrio with its brightly painted houses and restaurants.

MOROCCO

OFFICIAL NAME
The Kingdom of Morocco

CAPITAL
Rabat

Area 710 850 km²
(274 461 sq miles)
Population 28 238 000
Population density 39 per
km² (101 per sq mile)
Population growth rate 1.4%
Life expectancy 62 (m); 66 (f)
Languages Arabic, Berber,
Spanish, French
Adult literacy rate 43.7%
Currency Moroccan dirham
(US $1 = 10.86 dirhams)
GDP (US million $) 36 500
GDP per head (US $) 1313

Key dates

680s Arab invasion.
19thC France and Spain
establish control.
1912 Divided between
French and Spanish.
1953-5 Guerrilla
liberation war.
1956 Independence from
France (small Spanish
enclaves remain).
1957 Sultan takes title
of king.
1962 New constitution.
1965-70 State of
emergency declared.
1975 Western Sahara
ceded to Morocco and
Mauritania but Polisario
Front guerrillas claim full
independence.
1979 Morocco occupies
all of Western Sahara;
Mauritania ends claim.
1991 Ceasefire in
Western Sahara.
2001 Polisario Front
threatens new war.

ALGERIA

OFFICIAL NAME
The Democratic and Popular
Republic of Algeria

CAPITAL
Algiers

Area 2 381 741 km²
(919 595 sq miles)
Population 30 774 000
Population density 13 per
km² (32 per sq mile)
Population growth rate 1.6%
Life expectancy 65 (m); 66 (f)
Languages Arabic, French,
Berber
Adult literacy rate 61.6%
Currency Algerian dinar
(US $1 = 75 dinars)
GDP (US million $) 47 200
GDP per head (US $) 1583

Key dates

7thC Arab invasion.
1518 Ottoman rule.
1830-1914 French
extend colonial control.
1954 National Liberation
Front (FLN) starts
guerrilla liberation war.
1962 Independence
from France.
1965 Military coup.
1967 Declares war on
Israel; severs diplomatic
relations with USA.
1989 New multiparty
constitution. Islamic
Salvation Front (FIS)
founded.
1991 FIS wins election.
1992 Military control;
election nullified. FIS
threatens holy war.
1996 New constitution.
1999 Terrorist amnesty,
but violence continues.

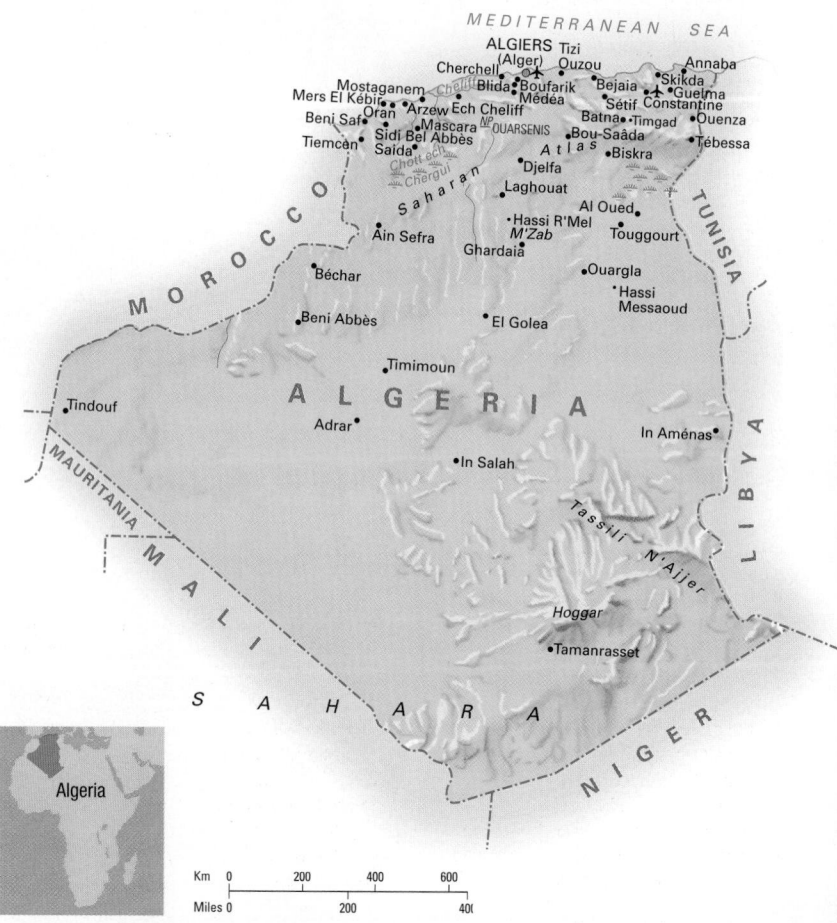

LIBYA

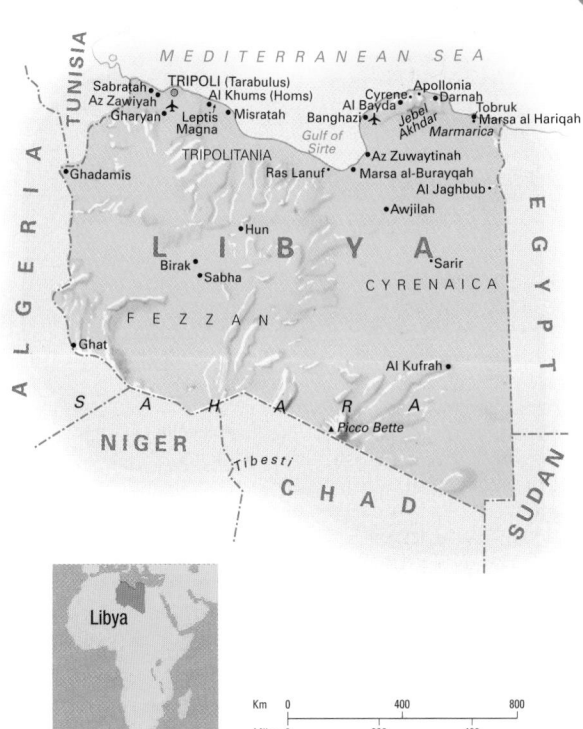

OFFICIAL NAME
The Great Socialist People's
Libyan Arab Jamahiriya

CAPITAL
Tripoli

Area 1 775 500 km²
(685 524 sq miles)
Population 5 471 000
Population density 3 per
km² (8 per sq mile)
Population growth rate 3.6%
Life expectancy 62 (m); 65 (f)
Languages Arabic, English,
Italian
Adult literacy rate 76.2%
Currency Libyan dinar
(US $1 = 0.55 dinar)
GDP (US million $) 34 970
GDP per head (US $) 6393

Key dates

640s Arab invasion.
1551 Becomes part of
Ottoman Empire.
1911 Italian invasion.
1951 Independence
gained as kingdom.
1969 Military coup led
by Colonel Gaddafi
leads to formation of
Arab Republic.
1977 Border war with
Egypt.
1983 Invades Chad.
1986 Diplomatic ties cut
by USA because of

support for terrorists.
USA attacks Libyan
boats and bases.
1987 Chad troops force
Libyan withdrawal.
1989 Further US attack.
1992 UN sanctions
imposed when
suspects, alleged to
have bombed US
airliner over Scotland,
are not handed over.
1996 UN extends
sanctions to countries
investing in Libya.

Libya

Km 0   400   800
Miles 0   200   400

TUNISIA

OFFICIAL NAME
The Republic of Tunisia

CAPITAL
Tunis

Area 163 610 km²
(63 170 sq miles)
Population 9 457 000
Population density 57 per
km² (148 per sq mile)
Population growth rate 1.1%
Life expectancy 69 (m); 73 (f)
Languages Arabic, Berber,
French
Adult literacy rate 66.7%

Currency Tunisian dinar
(US $1 = 1.41 dinars)
GDP (US million $) 20 700
GDP per head (US $) 2218

Km 0   200
Miles 0   100

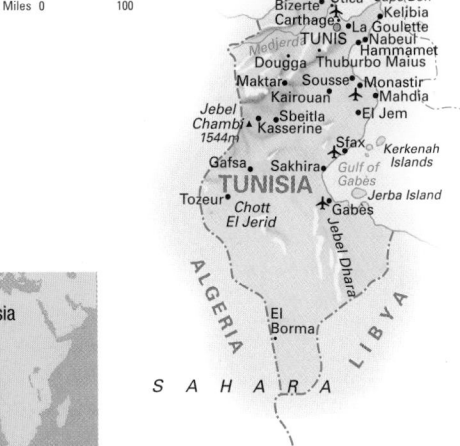

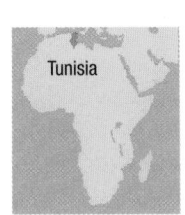

Tunisia

Key dates

7thC Arab invasion.
1574 Becomes part of
Ottoman Empire.
1881 French impose
protectorate.
1955 Internal self-
government.
1956 Full independence
from France.
1957 Republic; Habib
Bourguiba president.
1967 Joins Arab forces
in Six-Day War against
Israel.
1975 Bourguiba named
president for life.
1985-8 Cuts diplomatic
relations with Libya.
1987 Prime minister
Ben Ali deposes
Bourguiba.
1991 Measures against
Islamic fundamentalism.
1995 Signs Association
Agreement with
European Union.

THE DESERT'S ADAPTABLE HERDERS

The Bedouin, nomadic herders of
the Arabian, Sahara and Syrian
deserts, have slowly adapted to
modern life. Some still live in tents
and roam traditional areas, breeding
camels, horses, goats, sheep and
cattle. Their tribes are still led by a
sheikh and his council of elders. But
modern governments want settled
citizens, so most Bedouin have taken
to a more sedentary lifestyle.

Although many urban Bedouin earn
a living from handicrafts or manual
labour, Bedouin families produce
many doctors, lawyers, scientists
and businessmen.

The Bedouin call themselves
Ahl-el-beit (People of the Tent). They
originated in Arabia, but by the 7th
century had spread to Syria and
Egypt, then around 1050 into
Tunisia. They lived by trading in

camels, offering protection along the
caravan trade routes – and raiding
their neighbours. From the 1920s
motor transport began to move
commercial goods, and
governments put an end to
profitable theft.

The Bedouin have adjusted to
change without surrendering their
traditional values of honour, dignity,
bravery and hospitality.

EGYPT

OFFICIAL NAME
The Arab Republic of Egypt

CAPITAL
Cairo

Area 997 738 km²
(385 229 sq miles)
Population 67 226 000
Population density 66 per
km² (171 per sq mile)
Population growth rate 3.4%
Life expectancy 63 (m); 66 (f)
Languages Arabic, English,

French
Adult literacy rate 51.4%
Currency Egyptian pound
(US $1 = 3.88 Egyptian
pounds)
GDP (US million $) 89 400
GDP per head (US $) 1354

Key dates

c.3100 BC First ancient
Egyptian civilisation.
AD 639 Arab invasion.
1517 Ottoman rule.
19thC British control.
1869 Suez Canal built.
1914 UK protectorate.
1922 Independence
from Britain.
1923 Monarchy formed
under King Fu'ad I.
1948 War against Israel.
1952 Military coup; King
Farouk forced out.
1956 Seizes Suez
Canal; Britain, France
and Israel invade.

1967 Defeat in Six-Day
War with Israel.
1973 Defeat in Yom
Kippur War with Israel.
1978 Signs Camp David
Accord with Israel.
1979 Makes peace with
Israel; expelled from
Arab League (AL).
1981 Extremists kill
President Sadat.
1982 Regains Sinai.
1989 Rejoins AL.
1991 Joins US-led
coalition in Gulf War.
1997 Muslim extremists
kill 58 foreign tourists.

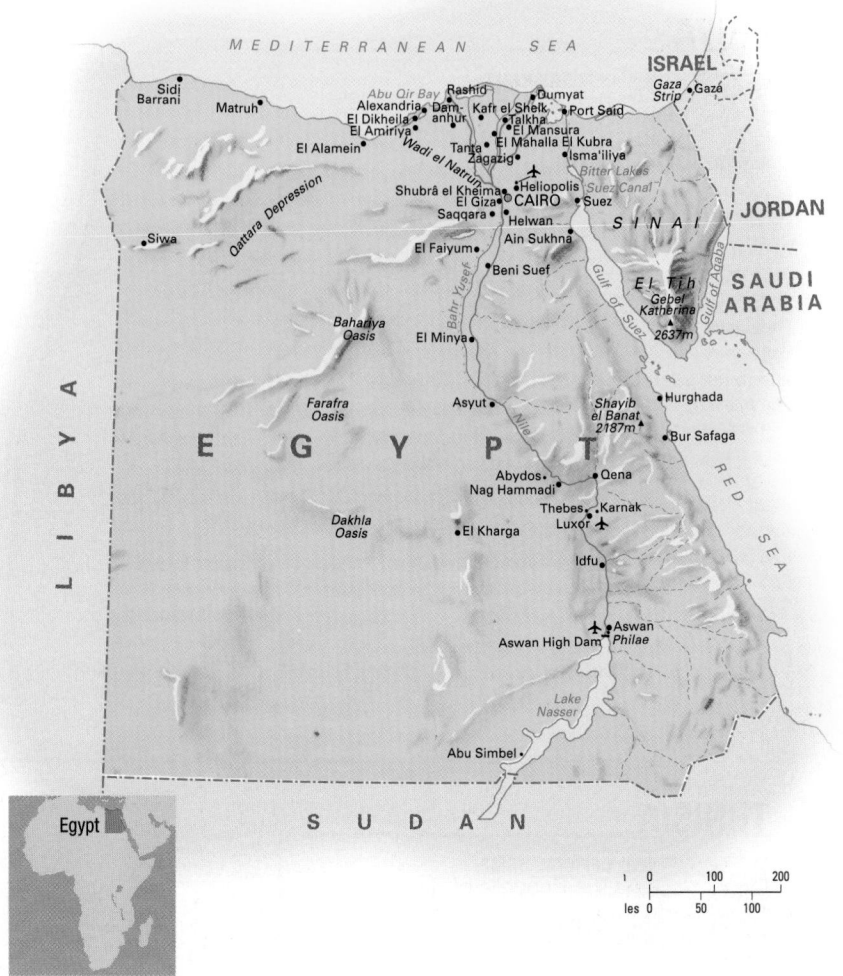

SUDAN

OFFICIAL NAME
The Republic of Sudan

CAPITAL
Khartoum

Area 2 505 813 km²
(967 500 sq miles)
Population 28 883 000
Population density 12 per
km² (30 per sq mile)
Population growth rate 0.1%
Life expectancy 49 (m); 52 (f)
Languages Arabic, English
and local languages
Adult literacy rate 46.1%
Currency Sudanese dinar
(US $1 = 258 Sudanese
dinars)
GDP (US million $) 12 300
GDP per head (US $) 424

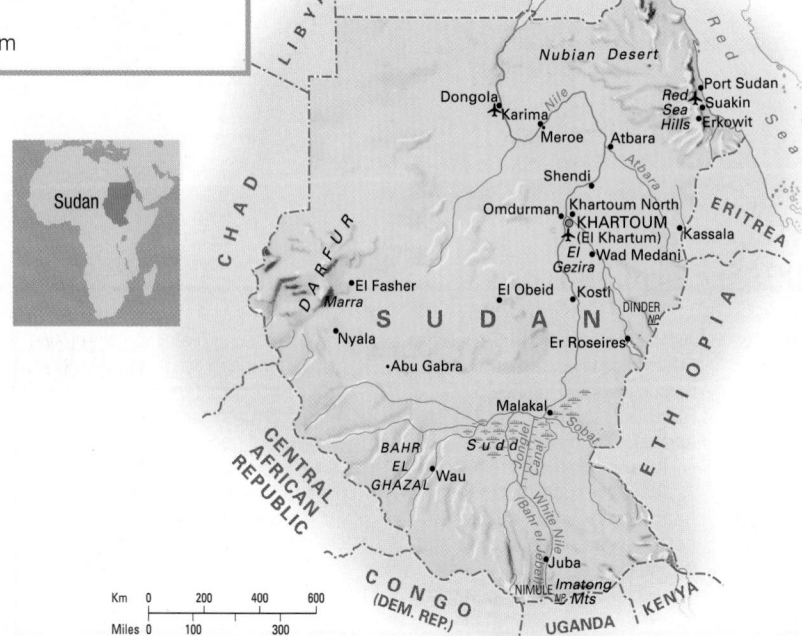

Key dates

14thC Islamic control.
1821 Egypt invades.
1881 Mahdi's revolt.
1898 British-Egyptian
victory at Omdurman.
1956 Independence
from Britain.
1958 Military coup.
1973 One-party state.
1980s-90s Droughts
cause severe famines.
1983 Imposes Islamic
law; non-Muslim Sudan
People's Liberation
Army (SPLA) starts civil
war in south.
1985 Military coup leads
to multiparty system.
1986 Elections.
1989 Military coup;
legislature replaced by
military council.
1993 SPLA ceasefire.
1994 Renewed fighting.
1998 New Islamic
constitution.

ERITREA

OFFICIAL NAME
The State of Eritrea

CAPITAL
Asmara

Area 121 144 km²
(46 774 sq miles)
Population 3 719 000
Population density 31 per
km² (81 per sq mile)
Population growth rate 2.7%
Life expectancy 48 (m); 51 (f)
Languages Arabic, Tigre,
English

Adult literacy rate 20%
Currency nakfa
(US $1 = 9.7 nakfa)
GDP (US million $) 800
GDP per head (US $) 215

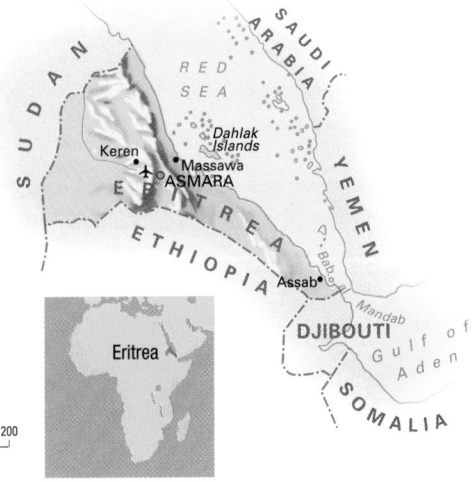

Km 0 100 200
Miles 0 100

Key dates

7thC Muslim control.
16thC Ottoman rule.
1882-9 Italian conquest.
1941 Britain invades.
1952 Becomes a
self-governing part of
Ethiopia.
1961 Civil war started
by rebel separatists.
1962 Annexed by
Ethiopia.
1991 Eritrean rebels
help to overthrow
Ethiopian government.
1993 Referendum;
independent republic.
1998-2000 Border war
with Ethiopia.

ETHIOPIA

OFFICIAL NAME
The Federal Democratic
Republic of Ethiopia

CAPITAL
Addis Ababa

Area 1 133 380 km²
(437 600 sq miles)
Population 61 672 000
Population density 53 per
km² (137 per sq mile)
Population growth rate 2.9%
Life expectancy 46 (m); 49 (f)
Languages Amharic,
English and many local
languages
Adult literacy rate 35.5%
Currency birr
(US $1 = 8.26 birrs)
GDP (US million $) 5675
GDP per head (US $) 94

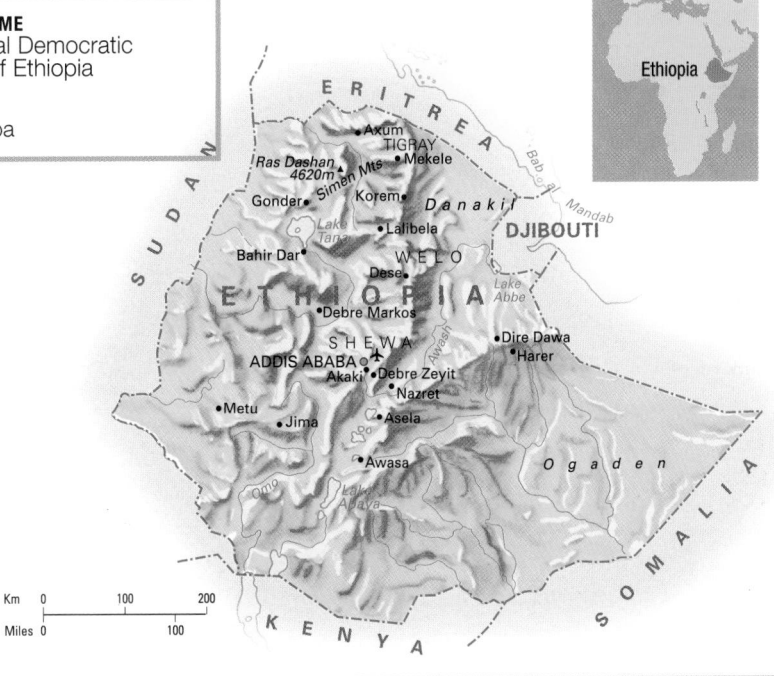

Km 0 100 200
Miles 0 100

Key dates

1889 Ethiopian Empire
united.
1930 Ras Tafari made
emperor and takes title
Haile Selassie I.
1935 Italian invasion.
1941 Liberated by British
in Second World War.
1962 Annexes Eritrea.
1974 Military coup ousts
Emperor Haile Selassie.
Start of land reform.
1977-8 War with
Somalia in Ogaden.
1980s, 90s Severe
droughts and famine.
1991 Government falls
to Tigrean, Eritrean and
other rebels.
1993 Eritrea secedes.
1995 Free elections in
Ethiopia.
1998-2000 Border war
with Eritrea.

DJIBOUTI

OFFICIAL NAME
The Republic of Djibouti

CAPITAL
Djibouti

Area 23 200 km²
(8958 sq miles)
Population 629 000
Population density 27 per
km² (69 per sq mile)
Population growth rate 4.1%
Life expectancy 47 (m); 50 (f)
Languages Arabic, French

Adult literacy rate 46.2%
Currency Djibouti franc
(US $1 = 175 Djibouti
francs)
GDP (US million $) 524
GDP per head (US $) 845

Key dates

9thC Islamic conversion.
19thC French control.
1967 Votes to keep
French links; renamed
Territory of the Afars
and Issas.
1977 Independence;
renamed Djibouti.
1979 Political parties
unite to form People's
Progress Assembly.
1992 Multiparty system.
1994 Peace accord with
Afar rebels.

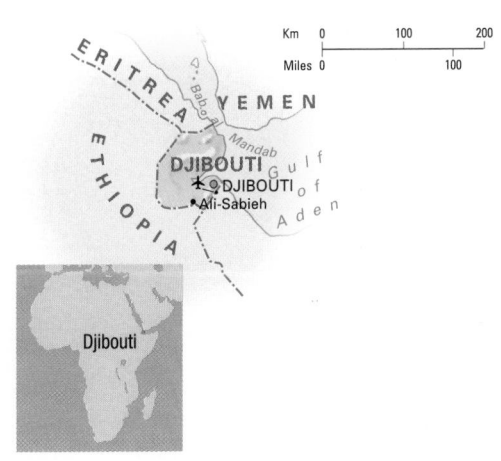

Km 0 100 200
Miles 0 100

KENYA

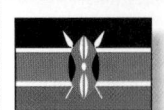

OFFICIAL NAME
The Republic of Kenya

CAPITAL
Nairobi

Area 580 367 km²
(224 081 sq miles)
Population 29 549 000
Population density 50 per
km² (129 per sq mile)
Population growth rate 2.9%
Life expectancy 57 (m); 61 (f)
Languages Kiswahili,
English, Kikuyu, Luo
Adult literacy rate 78.1%
Currency Kenyan shilling
(US $1 = 77.45 Kenyan
shillings)
GDP (US million $) 9042
GDP per head (US $) 311

Key dates

1895 British control.
1952-60 Kikuyu terrorist
group fights British rule.
1963 Independence
from Britain.
1964 One-party state.
1990 Violent democracy
demonstrations.
1991 Multiparty system
established.
1992 First open
elections take place.

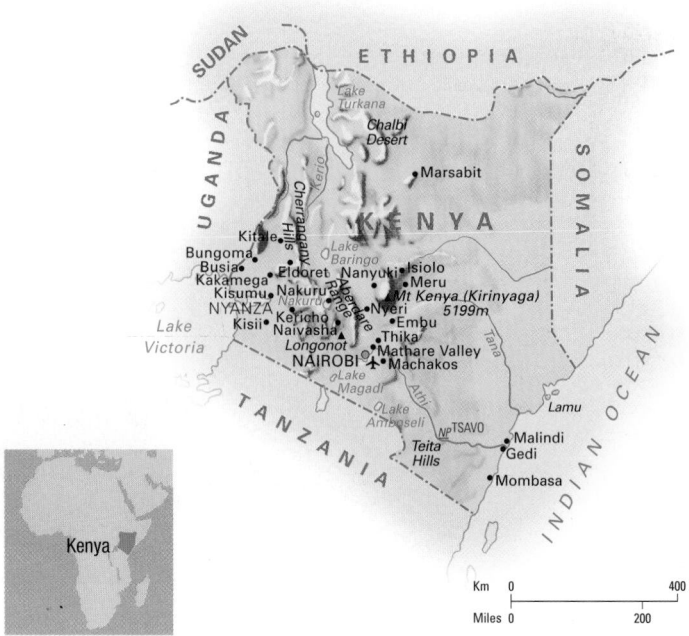

Kenya

Km 0   400
Miles 0   200

TANZANIA

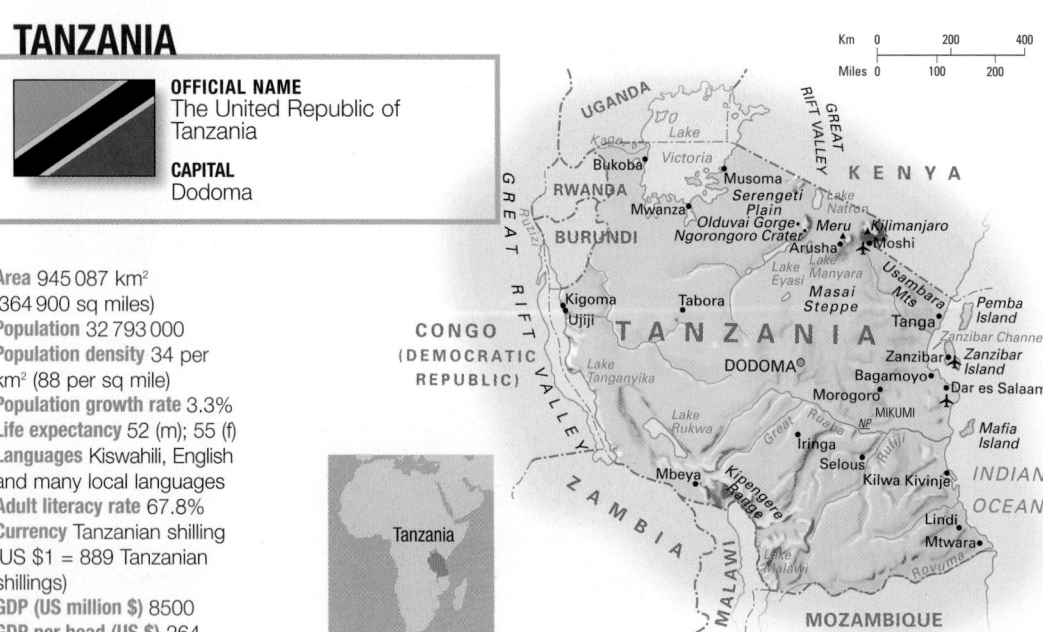

OFFICIAL NAME
The United Republic of
Tanzania

CAPITAL
Dodoma

Area 945 087 km²
(364 900 sq miles)
Population 32 793 000
Population density 34 per
km² (88 per sq mile)
Population growth rate 3.3%
Life expectancy 52 (m); 55 (f)
Languages Kiswahili, English
and many local languages
Adult literacy rate 67.8%
Currency Tanzanian shilling
(US $1 = 889 Tanzanian
shillings)
GDP (US million $) 8500
GDP per head (US $) 264

Tanzania

Km 0   200   400
Miles 0   100   200

Key dates

1880s German control
of mainland territory.
1890 Zanzibar becomes
British protectorate.
1918 British control
mainland (Tanganyika)
after First World War.
1961 Tanganyika gains
independence.
1962 Republic declared
within Commonwealth.
1963 Zanzibar gains
independence.
1964 Union of Zanzibar
and Tanganyika creates
Tanzania.
1979 Invades Uganda
to depose Idi Amin.
1992 Multiparty system
proposed.
1995 Democratic
elections held.

Happy grazing ground
Elephants wander in safety in
Kenya's Amboseli National Park,
with Kilimanjaro – Africa's
highest peak – towering in the
background. African elephants
are still widely (and illegally)
hunted for their ivory, but
their power to attract tourists
has led governments to give
them greater protection in
recent decades.

UGANDA

OFFICIAL NAME
The Republic of Uganda

CAPITAL
Kampala

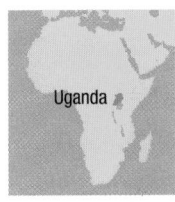

Uganda

Area 241 139 km²
(93 104 sq miles)
Population 21 620 000
Population density 87 per
km² (226 per sq mile)
Population growth rate 2.8%
Life expectancy 40 (m); 42 (f)
Languages English,
Luganda and other local
languages
Adult literacy rate 61.8%
Currency Ugandan shilling
(US $1 = 1785 Ugandan
shillings)
GDP (US million $) 6000
GDP per head (US $) 285

Key dates

19thC Powerful
kingdom of Buganda.
1894 UK protectorate.
1962 Independence
from Britain.
1963 Republic
proclaimed; kabaka
(king) elected president.
1967 Kabaka deposed.
1971 Idi Amin becomes
dictator; kills more than
300 000 Ugandans and
expels all Asians.
1979 Tanzanian troops
and Ugandan exiles
depose Amin.
1985 Military coup.
1986 Museveni made
president; peace
restored.
1995 New constitution.
1996 Free elections.

SOMALIA

OFFICIAL NAME
The Somali Democratic
Republic

CAPITAL
Mogadishu

Area 637 657 km²
(246 201 sq miles)
Population 9 240 000
Population density 14 per
km² (38 per sq mile)
Population growth rate 2.9%
Life expectancy 45 (m); 49 (f)
Languages Somali, Arabic,
English, Italian

Adult literacy rate 24.1%
Currency Somali shilling
(US $1 = 2620 Somali
shillings)
GDP (US million $) n/a
GDP per head (US $) n/a

Key dates

1880s Britain and Italy
establish colonies.
1960 Independence
from Britain and Italy.
1969 Military coup leads
to socialist republic.
1970s Severe drought.
1977-8 Invades Ogaden
region of Ethiopia but
troops driven back.
1991 Fighting between
guerrilla groups. North
claims independence
as Somaliland (not
recognised). Drought
causes serious famine.
1992 Peacekeeping
troops arrive to protect
famine-relief effort.
1994-5 UN troops leave;
rebels continue fighting.

Somalia

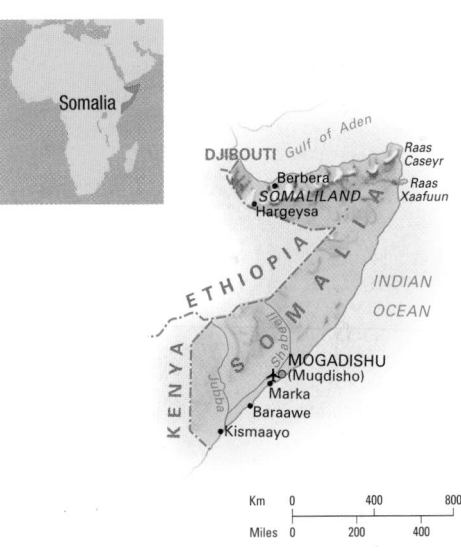

SEYCHELLES

OFFICIAL NAME
The Republic of Seychelles

CAPITAL
Victoria, on Mahé

Area 454 km²
(175 sq miles)
Population 80 000
Population density 176 per
km² (456 per sq mile)
Population growth rate 1.3%
Life expectancy 65 (m); 74 (f)

Languages Creole, English,
French
Adult literacy rate 85%
Currency Seychelles rupee
(US $1 = 6.05 rupees)
GDP (US million $) 579
GDP per head (US $) 7237

Key dates

16thC Uninhabited
islands discovered by
Portuguese.
1770 French settlement.
1814 Ceded to Britain.
1976 Independence;
becomes republic
within Commonwealth.
1977 Socialist coup
deposes first president.
1979 One-party state.
1993 New constitution:
multiparty system.

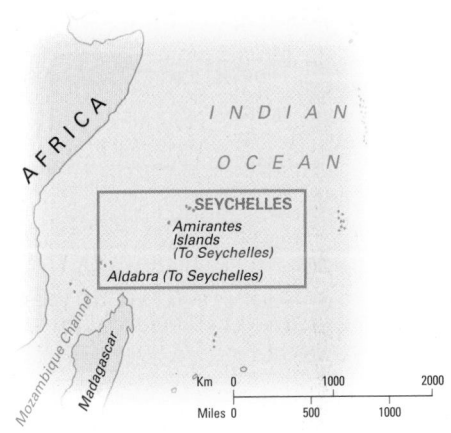

MALI

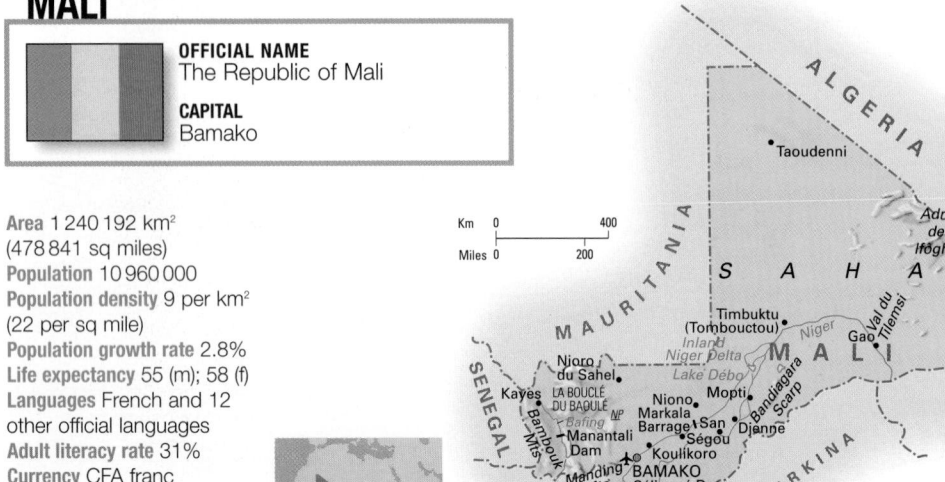

OFFICIAL NAME
The Republic of Mali

CAPITAL
Bamako

Area 1 240 192 km²
(478 841 sq miles)
Population 10 960 000
Population density 9 per km²
(22 per sq mile)
Population growth rate 2.8%
Life expectancy 55 (m); 58 (f)
Languages French and 12
other official languages
Adult literacy rate 31%
Currency CFA franc
(US $1 = 727 CFA francs)
GDP (US million $) 2859
GDP per head (US $) 267

Mali

Key dates

4th-16thC Part of
Ghana, Mali and then
Songhai empires.
1895 French control.
1904 Becomes colony
of French Sudan.
1958 Self-government
under French rule.
1959 Joins Senegal in
Mali Federation.
1960 Mali Federation
breaks up; full
independence gained
as Republic of Mali.
1968 Coup overthrows
socialist government.
1974 One-party state.
1991 Military coup.
1992 New constitution;
multiparty elections.
1992 Peace accord with
Tuareg guerrilla group.

SENEGAL

OFFICIAL NAME
The Republic of Senegal

CAPITAL
Dakar

Area 196 722 km²
(75 955 sq miles)
Population 9 279 000
Population density 47 per
km² (122 per sq mile)
Population growth rate 2.7%
Life expectancy 48 (m); 50 (f)
Languages French and
many local languages
Adult literacy rate 33.1%

Currency CFA franc
(US $1 = 727 CFA francs)
GDP (US million $) 5000
GDP per head (US $) 538

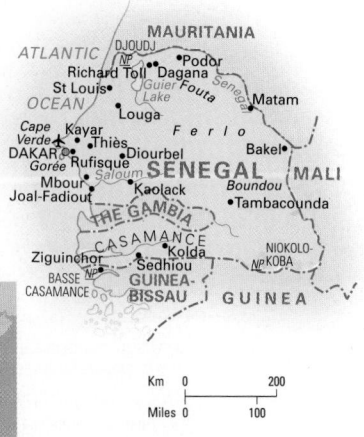

Senegal

Key dates

4th-16thC East forms
part of Ghana, Mali and
then Songhai empires.
17thC European trading
posts set up on coast.
1882 French colony.
1895 Dakar made capital
of French West Africa.
1959 Senegal and
Sudanese Republic
form Mali Federation.
1960 Full independence.
1982-9 With Gambia,
forms Confederation of
Senegambia.
1998 Sends troops to
help Guinea-Bissau to
defeat army revolt.

THE GAMBIA

OFFICIAL NAME
The Republic of The Gambia

CAPITAL
Banjul

Area 11 295 km²
(4361 sq miles)
Population 1 385 000
Population density 109 per
km² (282 per sq mile)
Population growth rate 4.1%
Life expectancy 43 (m); 47 (f)
Languages English,
Mandinka, Fula Wolof and

other local languages
Adult literacy rate 38.6%
Currency dalasi
(US $1 = 15.6 dalasi)
GDP (US million $) 375
GDP per head (US $) 304

Key dates

13th-15thC Part of Mali
Empire.
15th-18thC European
slaving posts set up.
19thC British possession
administered as part of
Sierra Leone. Made
separate colony in 1888.
1965 Independence.
1970 Republic within
Commonwealth.
1982-9 Joins Senegal
as part of Senegambia.
1994 Bloodless coup.
1996 New constitution.

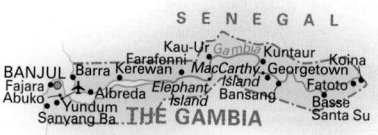

The Gambia

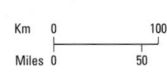

GUINEA-BISSAU

OFFICIAL NAME
The Republic of Guinea-Bissau

CAPITAL
Bissau

Area 36 125 km²
(13 948 sq miles)
Population 1 187 000
Population density 32 per
km² (83 per sq mile)
Population growth rate 1.1%
Life expectancy 41 (m); 44 (f)

Languages Portuguese,
Creole
Adult literacy rate 54.9%
Currency CFA franc
(US $1 = 727 CFA francs)
GDP (US million $) 205
GDP per head (US $) 176

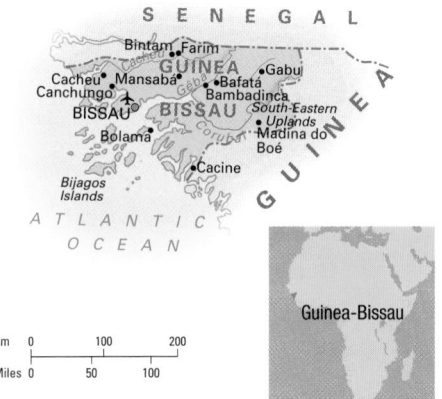

Key dates

17th-19thC Portuguese
slave-trading base.
1879 Becomes separate
Portuguese colony.
1951 Made overseas
province of Portugal.
1974 Independence
after guerrilla war.
1980 Military coup.
1984 New constitution.
1994 Open elections.
1998 Army revolt
defeated with help from
Senegal and Guinea.

MAURITANIA

OFFICIAL NAME
The Islamic Republic of
Mauritania

CAPITAL
Nouakchott

Area 1 030 700 km²
(397 950 sq miles)
Population 2 598 000
Population density 2 per km²
(6 per sq mile)
Population growth rate 2.5%
Life expectancy 50 (m); 53 (f)
Languages Arabic, French
and many local languages
Adult literacy rate 37.7%
Currency ouguiya
(US $1 = 252 ouguiyas)
GDP (US million $) 1825
GDP per head (US $) 721

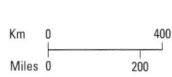

Key dates

4th-16thC Areas form
part of Ghana, Mali and
then Songhai empires.
17th-18thC European
trading posts set up.
1903 French establish
protectorate.
1958 Self-government.
1960 Independence; not
recognised by Morocco.
1965 One-party state.
1970 Morocco
recognises Mauritania's
independence.
1975 Western Sahara
ceded to Mauritania
(south) and Morocco
(north), but Polisario
Front guerrillas resist.
1978 Military coup.
1979 Mauritania ends
Western Sahara claims.
1996 Open elections.

CAPE VERDE

OFFICIAL NAME
The Republic of Cape Verde

CAPITAL
Praia

Area 4033 km²
(1557 sq miles)
Population 418 000
Population density 104 per
km² (270 per sq mile)
Population growth rate 2.3%
Life expectancy 64 (m); 71 (f)
Languages Portuguese,
Creole
Adult literacy rate 71.6%

Currency Cape Verde
escudo (US $ 1=
122 Cape Verde escudos)
GDP (US million $) 468
GDP per head (US $) 1114

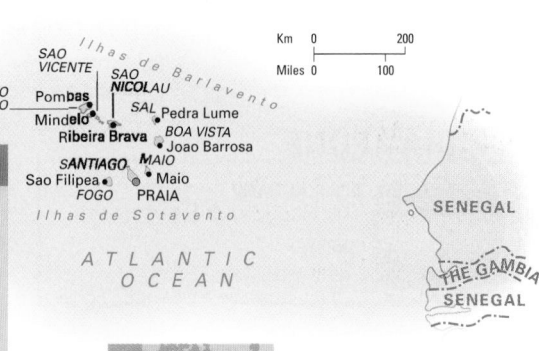

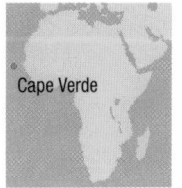

Key dates

1460s Discovered and
settled by Portuguese.
16th-17thC Prospers as
slave-trading post.
1879 Becomes separate
Portuguese colony.
1975 Independence.
1981 Plans to unite with
Guinea-Bissau ended.
1990 New constitution.
1991 Holds first
multiparty elections.

GUINEA

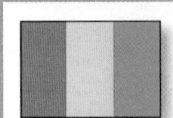

OFFICIAL NAME
The Republic of Guinea

CAPITAL
Conakry

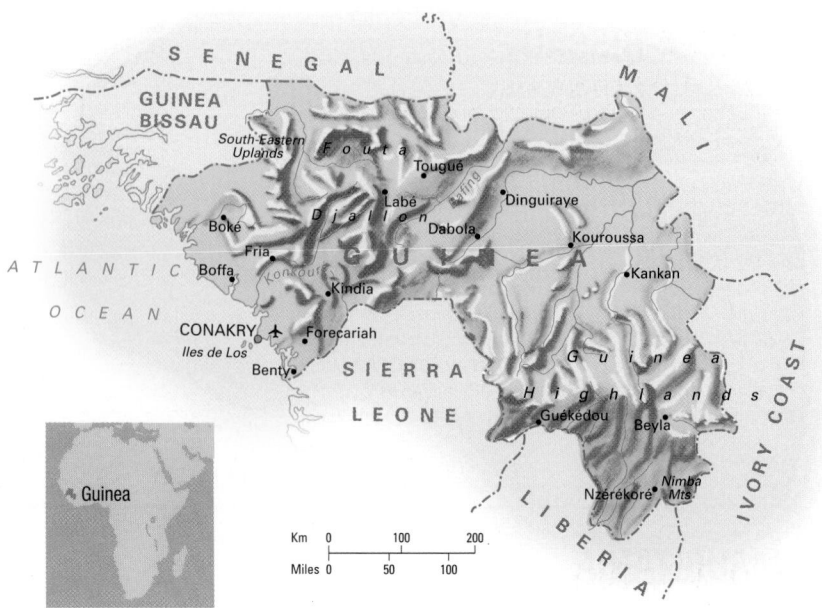

Area 245 857 km²
(94 926 sq miles)
Population 7 360 000
Population density 30 per
km² (77 per sq mile)
Population growth rate 2.9%
Life expectancy 44 (m); 45 (f)
Languages French,
Soussou, Manika and
other local languages
Adult literacy rate 35.9%
Currency Guinean franc (US
$1 = 1895 Guinean francs)
GDP (US million $) 3290
GDP per head (US $) 448

Key dates

13th-16thC Part of Mali
Empire.
1890 French colony.
1958 Independence;
Sekou Touré leads one-
party state.
1984 Bloodless coup
after Touré's death.
1990 New constitution.
1993 Open elections.
1996 Government
defeats revolt by rebels.

GHANA

OFFICIAL NAME
The Republic of Ghana

CAPITAL
Accra

Area 238 537 km²
(92 100 sq miles)
Population 19 678 000
Population density 80 per
km² (208 per sq mile)
Population growth rate 2.3%
Life expectancy 54 (m); 58 (f)
Languages English and
many local languages
Adult literacy rate 64.5%
Currency cedi
(US $1 = 7485 cedis)
GDP (US million $) 7885
GDP per head (US $) 411

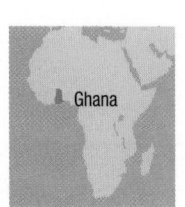

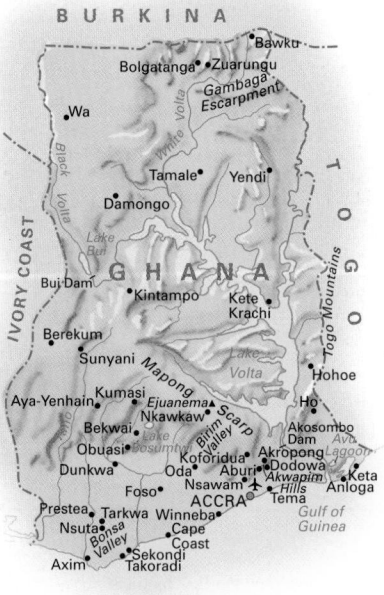

Key dates

15thC Portuguese trade;
named Gold Coast.
1642 Dutch control.
1874 British colony.
1954 Self-government.
1957 Independence
(with British Togoland).
1960 Republic; Kwame
Nkrumah president.
1964 One-party socialist
state led by Nkrumah.
1966 Military coup.
1969 New constitution;
civilian government.
1972-81 Four military
coups.
1992 New constitution:
multiparty system.
1993 Ethnic violence;
more than 1000 killed.

SIERRA LEONE

OFFICIAL NAME
The Republic of Sierra Leone

CAPITAL
Freetown

Area 71 740 km²
(27 699 sq miles)
Population 4 717 000
Population density 64 per
km² (165 per sq mile)
Population growth rate 2.5%
Life expectancy 32 (m); 36 (f)
Languages English, Mende,

Temne, Krio (Creole)
Adult literacy rate 31.4%
Currency leone
(US $1 = 1894 leones)
GDP (US million $) 702
GDP per head (US $) 153

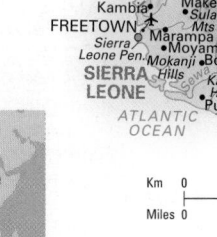

Key dates

1808 British colony.
1961 Independence.
1971 Becomes republic.
1978 One-party state.
1990s Series of military
coups and civil war
between rival groups.
1996 Ahmad Kabbah
elected president.
1997 Military coup.
1998 Nigerian troops
restore Kabbah.
1999-2000 UN force
tries to restore peace.

LIBERIA

OFFICIAL NAME
The Republic of Liberia

CAPITAL
Monrovia

Area 97 754 km²
(37 743 sq miles)
Population 2 930 000
Population density 27 per
km² (71 per sq mile)
Population growth rate 1.1%
Life expectancy 54 (m); 57 (f)
Languages English and

many local languages
Adult literacy rate 38.3%
Currency Liberian dollar
(US $1 = 41.5 Liberian
dollars)
GDP (US million $) 517
GDP per head (US $) 176

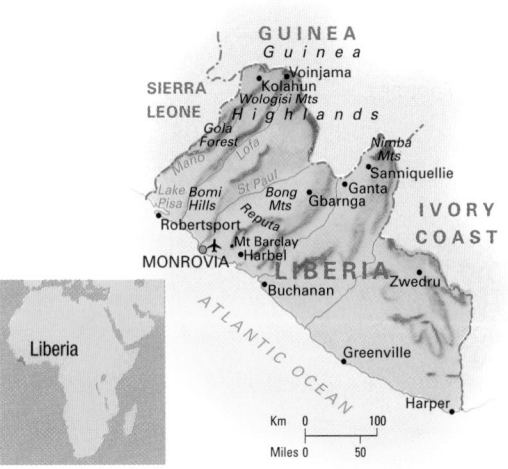

Key dates

1822 Founded by freed US slaves relocated by colonisation societies.
1847 Independent republic; constitution modelled on USA's.
1980 Military coup.
1989 Civil war begins between government and two rebel groups.
1990 President killed by rebels. Ceasefire.
1992 Renewed fighting.
1996 Peace agreement.
1997 Open elections.

IVORY COAST

OFFICIAL NAME
The Republic of Côte d'Ivoire

CAPITAL
Yamoussoukro

Area 322 462 km²
(124 503 sq miles)
Population 14 526 000
Population density 44 per
km² (115 per sq mile)
Population growth rate 0.8%
Life expectancy 50 (m); 54 (f)
Languages French and
many local languages
Adult literacy rate 40.1%
Currency CFA franc
(US $1 = 727 CFA francs)
GDP (US million $) 11 411
GDP per head (US $) 798

Key dates

1842 French protectorate.
1893 French colony.
1958 Self-government.
1960 Independence; Felix Houphouet-Boigny leads one-party state.
1990 Protests lead to multiparty elections.
1993 Houphouet-Boigny dies in office.
1999 Military coup.

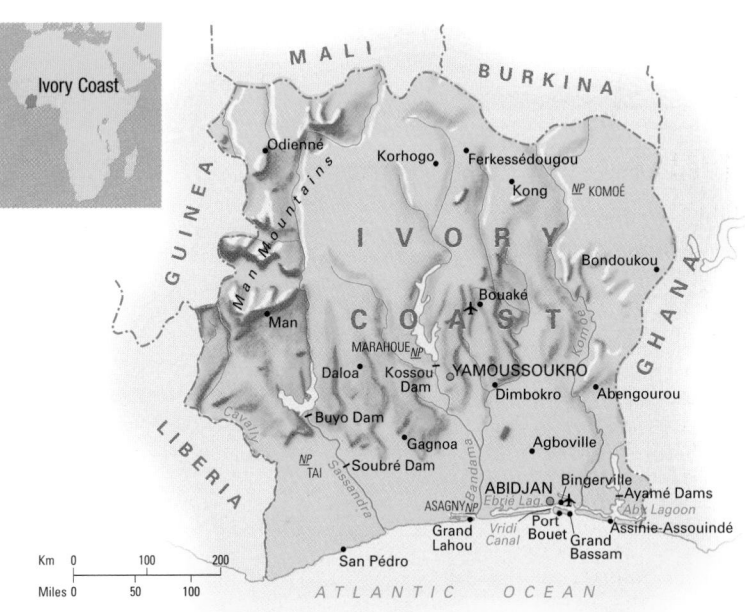

BURKINA

OFFICIAL NAME
Burkina Faso

CAPITAL
Ouagadougou

Area 274 200 km²
(105 870 sq miles)
Population 11 616 000
Population density 39 per
km² (101 per sq mile)
Population growth rate 1.5%
Life expectancy 45 (m); 47 (f)
Languages French, Mossi
and many local languages
Adult literacy rate 19.2%
Currency CFA franc
(US $1 = 727 CFA francs)
GDP (US million $) 2499
GDP per head (US $) 233

Key dates

14thC Mossi kingdom established.
mid 15thC Mossi capital at Ouagadougou.
1896 French capture Ouagadougou; set up protectorate.
1919 French colony of Upper Volta founded.
1932-47 Split between other French colonies.
1960 Independence.
1980 First of series of military coups.
1984 Changes name to Burkina Faso.
1991 New constitution; multiparty elections.

TOGO

OFFICIAL NAME
The Togolese Republic

CAPITAL
Lomé

Area 56 785 km²
(21 925 sq miles)
Population 4 512 000
Population density 77 per
km² (201 per sq mile)
Population growth rate 2.3%
Life expectancy 49 (m); 52 (f)
Languages French, Kabiye,
Ewe and other local
languages
Adult literacy rate 51.7%
Currency CFA franc
(US $1 = 727 CFA francs)
GDP (US million $) 1464
GDP per head (US $) 332

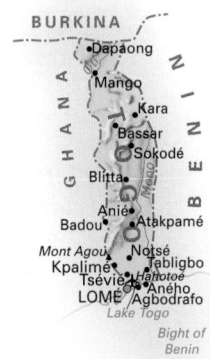

Togo

Key dates

1884 German Togo
protectorate set up.
1919 Divided between
France and Britain.
1957 British Togoland
merges with Ghana.
1960 French Togoland
independent as Togo.
1967 Military coup.
1992 Multiparty
elections approved.
1993 25 000 flee after
violent demonstrations.
1994-8 Open elections.

BENIN

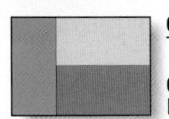

OFFICIAL NAME
The Republic of Benin

CAPITAL
Porto-Novo

Area 112 622 km²
(43 484 sq miles)
Population 6 059 000
Population density 54 per
km² (139 per sq mile)
Population growth rate 3%
Life expectancy 51 (m); 56 (f)
Languages French, Bariba,
Fulani, Fon, Yoruba
Adult literacy rate 37%
Currency CFA franc
(US $1 = 727 CFA francs)
GDP (US million $) 2261
GDP per head (US $) 374

Key dates

17thC Kingdom of
Dahomey flourishes,
based on selling slaves.
1904 French colony of
Dahomey established.
1958 Self-government.
1960 Full independence.
1972 Military coup.
1974 One-party Marxist
state proclaimed.
1975 Changes name to
Benin.
1978 New constitution
reinstates civilian rule.
1991 First free elections.

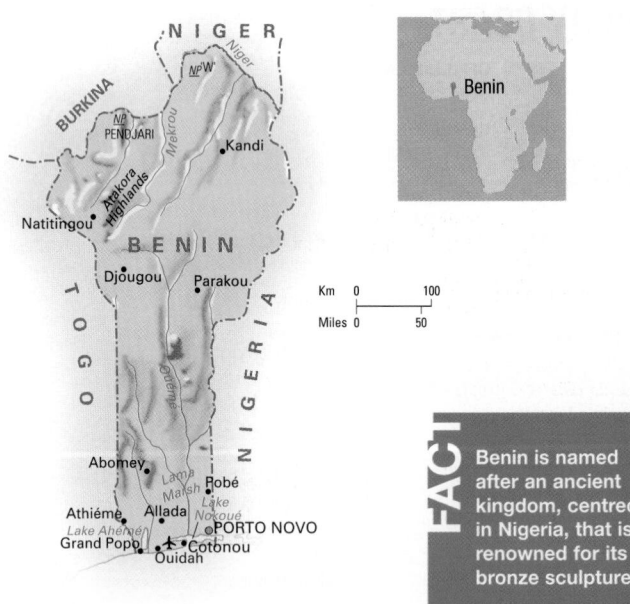

Benin

FACT Benin is named
after an ancient
kingdom, centred
in Nigeria, that is
renowned for its
bronze sculptures.

NIGER

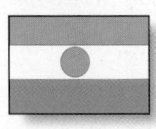

OFFICIAL NAME
The Republic of Niger

CAPITAL
Niamey

Area 1 267 000 km²
(489 191 sq miles)
Population 10 400 000
Population density 8 per km²
(21 per sq mile)
Population growth rate 3.2%
Life expectancy 45 (m); 48 (f)
Languages French and
many local languages
Adult literacy rate 13.6%
Currency CFA franc
(US $1 = 727 CFA francs)
GDP (US million $) 2000
GDP per head (US $) 198

FACT 'W' National Park,
in Niger, Burkina
and Benin, is
named after the
shape of bends in
the Niger River.

Key dates

11th-15thC Tuareg
people establish empire
around Agadez.
16thC Songhai Empire
from Mali conquers
Tuaregs.
1890s French gain
control.
1922 French colony.
1960 Independence.
1960s-70s Severe
drought causes food
shortages.
1974 Military coup;
suspends constitution.
1992 New constitution.
1993 Holds first
democratic elections.
1996 Military coup.

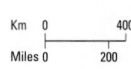

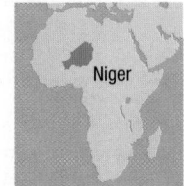

Niger

CHAD

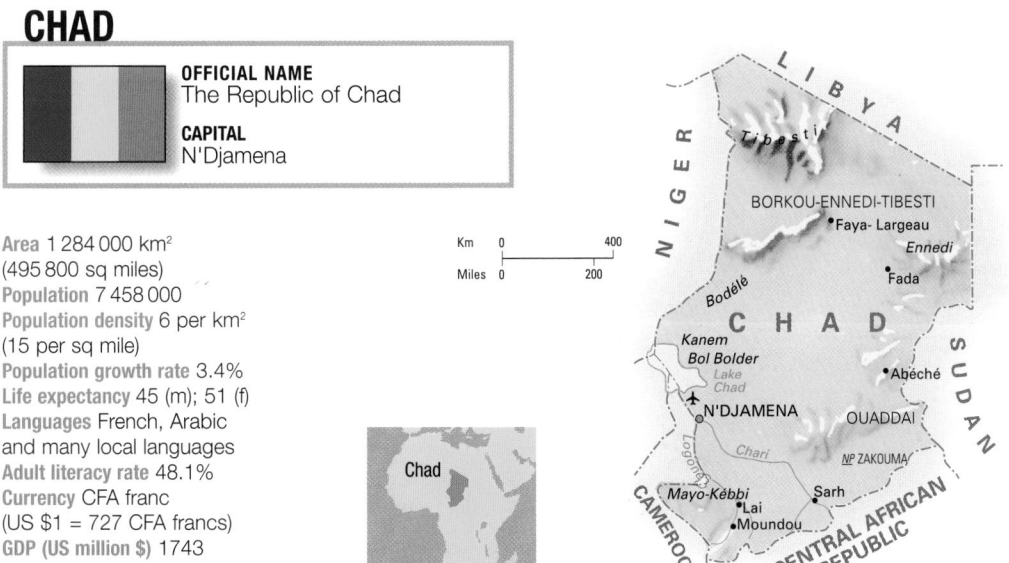

OFFICIAL NAME
The Republic of Chad

CAPITAL
N'Djamena

Area 1 284 000 km²
(495 800 sq miles)
Population 7 458 000
Population density 6 per km²
(15 per sq mile)
Population growth rate 3.4%
Life expectancy 45 (m); 51 (f)
Languages French, Arabic
and many local languages
Adult literacy rate 48.1%
Currency CFA franc
(US $1 = 727 CFA francs)
GDP (US million $) 1743
GDP per head (US $) 239

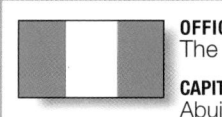
Chad

Key dates

8th-17thC Powerful
kingdoms develop on
Sahara trade routes.
1880s French claim.
1920 French colony.
1960 Independence.
1966-86 Civil wars.
1975 Military coup.
1983 Libya occupies
north; French troops
support government.
1987 Rival Chad groups
unite to drive out
Libyan forces.
1989 Chad, Libya and
France agree ceasefire.
1990 Rebels overthrow
government.
1996 New constitution.
1996-7 Presidential and
legislative elections.

NIGERIA

OFFICIAL NAME
The Federal Republic of Nigeria

CAPITAL
Abuja

Area 923 768 km²
(356 669 sq miles)
Population 108 945 000
Population density 115 per
km² (298 per sq mile)
Population growth rate 2%
Life expectancy 49 (m); 52 (f)

Languages English, Hausa,
Yoruba, Ibo
Adult literacy rate 57.1%
Currency naira
(US $1 = 124 naira)
GDP (US million $) 43 700
GDP per head (US $) 410

Nigeria

Key dates

14th-17thC Kingdoms,
including Muslim Bornu
in north-east and Benin
in south, develop.
15th-18thC European
slaving posts set up.
early 19thC Muslim
Fulani defeat Hausa to
control most of north.
1807 Britain outlaws
slave trade.
1861 UK seizes Lagos.
1900-6 All Nigeria made
British colony and
protectorate.
1954 Self-government in
three-part federation.
1960 Independence
within Commonwealth.
1960s Ethnic rivalries
lead to civil war.
1966 Military coup;
abolition of federal
system leads to riots
and countercoup.
1967 Four regions

replaced by 12 states.
Civil war after Ibo
eastern region secedes
as Biafra.
1970 Biafra defeated.
1976 Number of states
increased to 19.
1979 Civilian rule.
1983 Military coup.
1991 Capital moved
from Lagos to Abuja.
1993 Election followed
by military coup.
1995 Execution of writer
Ken Saro-Wiwa and
other Ogoni protesters
at environmental
damage. Suspended
from Commonwealth.
1998 Military ruler dies.
1999 Open presidential
election; readmitted to
Commonwealth.
2000 Introduction of
Islamic law in north
leads to ethnic tension.

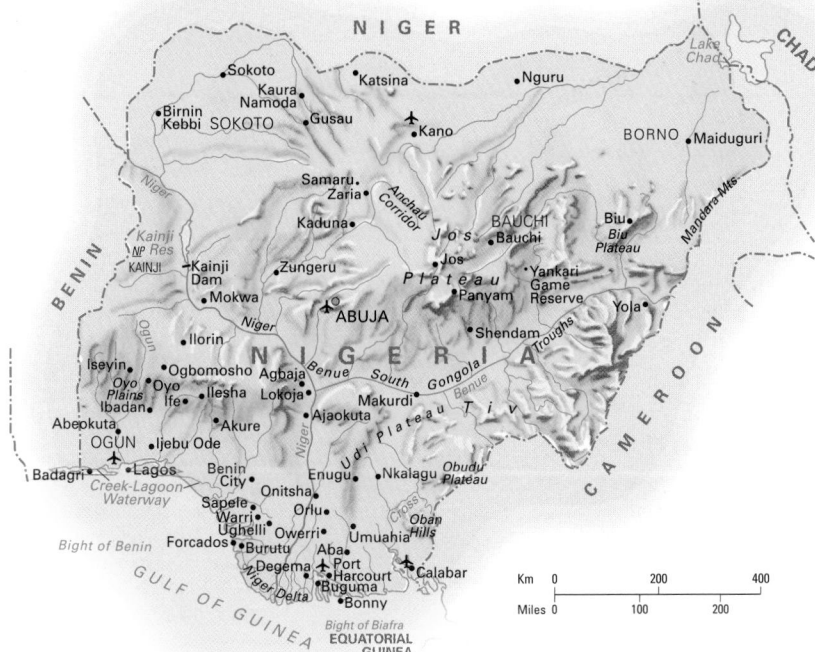

CAMEROON

OFFICIAL NAME
The Republic of Cameroon

CAPITAL
Yaoundé

Area 475 442 km²
(183 569 sq miles)
Population 14 693 000
Population density 30 per
km² (78 per sq mile)
Population growth rate 2.8%
Life expectancy 53 (m); 56 (f)
Languages English, French
and many local languages

Adult literacy rate 63.4%
Currency CFA franc
(US $1 = 727 CFA francs)
GDP (US million $) 9221
GDP per head (US $) 644

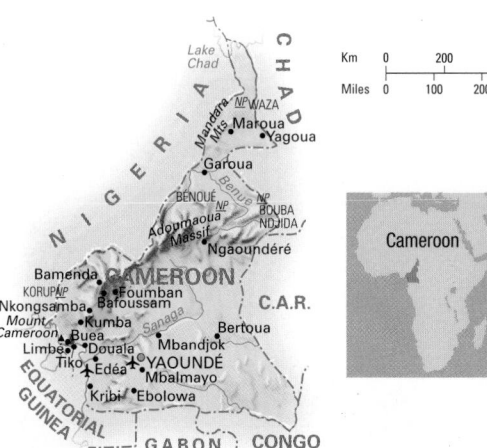

GABON

OFFICIAL NAME
The Gabonese Republic

CAPITAL
Libreville

Area 267 667 km²
(103 347 sq miles)
Population 1 385 000
Population density 4 per km²
(12 per sq mile)
Population growth rate 2.6%
Life expectancy 52 (m); 55 (f)
Languages French, Fang,
Bantu dialects
Adult literacy rate 63.2%
Currency CFA franc
(US $1 = 727 CFA francs)
GDP (US million $) 5086
GDP per head (US $) 4273

Key dates

15thC First European
slave-traders arrive.
1883 French colony.
1957 Self-government.
1960 Independence.
1964 Attempted coup.
1968 One-party state.
1990 New constitution:
multiparty system.
1993 Election; riots after
charges of vote fraud.
1995 New constitution.

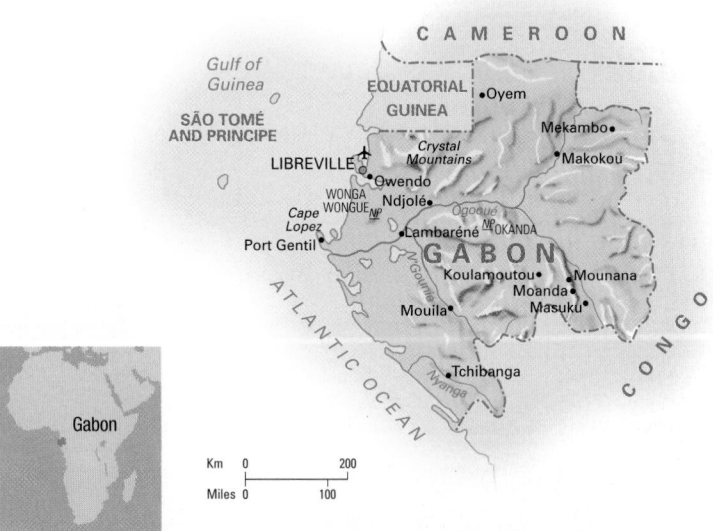

CENTRAL AFRICAN REPUBLIC

OFFICIAL NAME
The Central African Republic

CAPITAL
Bangui

Area 622 984 km²
(240 535 sq miles)
Population 3 550 000
Population density 6 per km²
(15 per sq mile)
Population growth rate 1.6%
Life expectancy 47 (m); 52 (f)
Languages French, Sango
Adult literacy rate 60%

Currency CFA franc
(US $1 = 727 CFA francs)
GDP (US million $) 1128
GDP per head (US $) 323

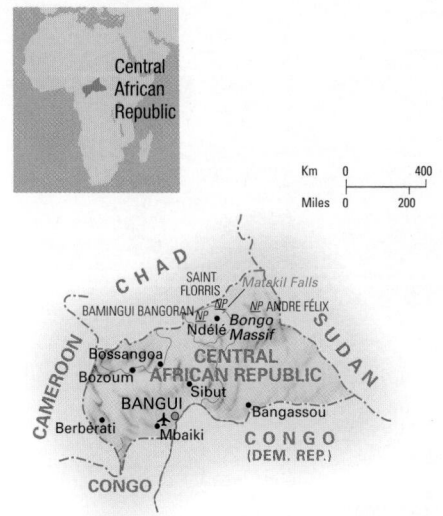

Key dates

1894 French establish
colony of Ubangi-Shari.
1958 Self-government
as Central African
Republic.
1960 Independence.
1962 One-party state.
1966 Military coup;
Jean-Bedel Bokassa
becomes president.
1976 Bokassa declares
himself emperor.
1979 Bloodless coup.
1993 Open elections;
civilian government.
1996-7 French help to
crush military revolts.

EQUATORIAL GUINEA

OFFICIAL NAME
The Republic of Equatorial Guinea

CAPITAL
Malabo

Area 28 051 km²
(10 830 sq miles)
Population 442 000
Population density 15 per
km² (40 per sq mile)
Population growth rate 2.5%
Life expectancy 46 (m); 50 (f)
Languages Spanish, French,

Fang and many local
languages
Adult literacy rate 78.5%
Currency CFA franc
(US $1 = 727 CFA francs)
GDP (US million $) 751
GDP per head (US $) 1746

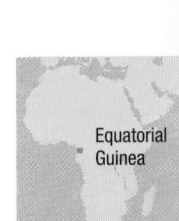

Key dates

1471 Portuguese explorers land; later claim territory.
19thC Spanish control.
1959 Spanish colony.
1968 Independence from Spain. Macias Nguema seizes power.
1979 Military coup; Obiang Nguema Mbasogo president.
1991 New constitution.
1996-9 Elections marred by allegations of fraud.

SÃO TOMÉ & PRÍNCIPE

OFFICIAL NAME
The Democratic Republic of São Tomé & Príncipe

CAPITAL
São Tomé

Area 1001 km²
(387 sq miles)
Population 144 000
Population density 140 per
km² (362 per sq mile)
Population growth rate 2.1%
Life expectancy 67 (m); 67 (f)

Languages Portuguese
and many local languages
Adult literacy rate 25%
Currency dobra
(US $1 = 8203.5 dobras)
GDP (US million $) 35
GDP per head (US $) 250

Key dates

15thC Portuguese explorers land.
1522 Becomes Portuguese province.
16thC Becomes major centre of slave trade.
1953 Portuguese troops kill protesting workers in 'Batepa massacre'.
1975 Independence.
1988 Coup attempt fails.
1991 Multiparty elections.
1995 Angolan mediation ends bloodless military coup after one week.

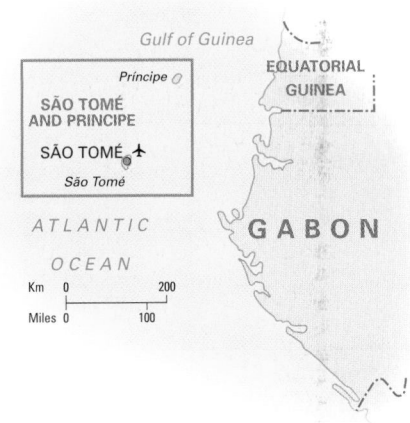

CONGO

OFFICIAL NAME
The Republic of the Congo

CAPITAL
Brazzaville

Area 342 000 km²
(132 047 sq miles)
Population 2 864 000
Population density 8 per km²
(21 per sq mile)
Population growth rate 3%
Life expectancy 48 (m); 54 (f)
Languages French, Kikongo, Lingala and other local languages
Adult literacy rate 74.9%
Currency CFA franc
(US $1 = 727 CFA francs)
GDP (US million $) 3075
GDP per head (US $) 1102

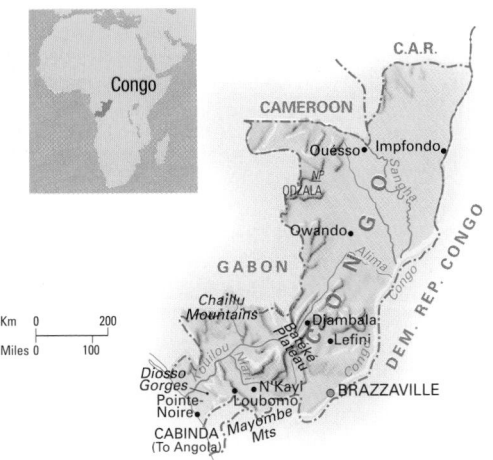

Key dates

15th-19thC European traders buy slaves.
1880 Becomes French protectorate.
1903 French colony of Middle Congo.
1958 Self-government.
1960 Independence.
1969 Military coup.
1970 Marxist government renames country People's Republic of the Congo.
1990 Government abandons Marxism.
1992 New constitution; name reverts to Republic of the Congo. First multiparty presidential election.
1993 Legislative elections.
1997 Civil war restores former Marxist Sassou-Nguesso to president.

CONGO (DEMOCRATIC REPUBLIC)

OFFICIAL NAME
Democratic Republic of the Congo

CAPITAL
Kinshasa

Area 2 344 885 km²
(905 365 sq miles)
Population 50 335 000
Population density 21 per km² (54 per sq mile)
Population growth rate 3%
Life expectancy 50 (m); 54 (f)
Languages French, Lingala, Kingwana, Tshiluba and other local languages
Adult literacy rate 77.3%
Currency Congolese franc (US $1 = 4.50 Congolese francs)
GDP (US million $) 926
GDP per head (US $) 18

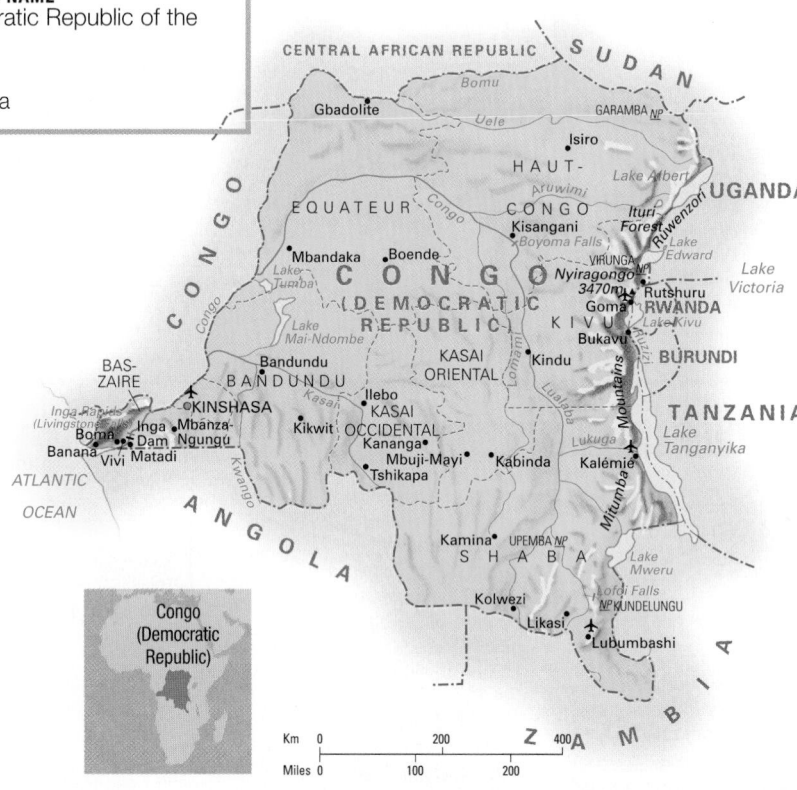

Key dates

15thC Kongo and other kingdoms established.
16th-19thC Extensive slave-trading.
1885 Congo Free State established, directly ruled by Belgian king.
1908 Control taken over by Belgian government.
1960 Independence. Copper-rich Katanga province secedes; civil war begins between rival groups.
1963 UN troops end Katanga secession.
1965 Military coup; Mobutu president.
1971 Renamed Zaire.
1977-8 Renewed war with Katanga exiles.
1996 Renewed civil war in east with rebels and Rwandan refugees.
1997 Rebels depose Mobutu; Laurent Kabila president. Name reverts to Democratic Republic of the Congo.
2001 Kabila killed; succeeded by his son.

RWANDA

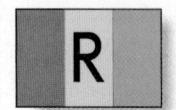

OFFICIAL NAME
The Rwandan Republic

CAPITAL
Kigali

Area 26 338 km²
(10 169 sq miles)
Population 7 235 000
Population density 251 per km² (649 per sq mile)
Population growth rate 2.7%
Life expectancy 45 (m); 48 (f)
Languages French, English, Kinyarwanda, Kiswahili

Adult literacy rate 60.5%
Currency Rwandan franc (US $1 = 431 Rwandan francs)
GDP (US million $) 2255
GDP per head (US $) 341

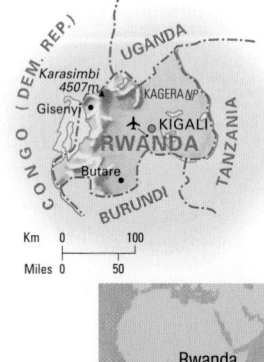

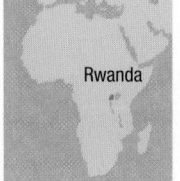

Key dates

1897 Becomes part of German East Africa.
1923 Administration by Belgium as part of Ruanda-Urundi.
1959 Hutus rebel against Tutsis; many killed or flee into exile.
1962 Independence under Hutu president.
1963 Tutsis massacred after failed coup.
1973 Military coup.
1990 Tutsi exiles begin attacks from Uganda.

1993 Peace treaty.
1994 President killed in plane crash. Hutu extremists start civil war; 500 000 (mainly Tutsi) massacred and 2 million Tutsis and Hutus flee to Zaire. Tutsi-led rebels defeat Hutus; establish government with Hutu president.
1995 Tutsi soldiers kill Hutu refugees.
1996 Many refugees flee back to Rwanda.

Ethnic violence in Central Africa

The world was shocked in 1994 by horrific images from Rwanda, as more than 450 000 Tutsis and moderate Hutus were massacred by gangs of Hutu extremists. The massacres were unleashed after the Hutu presidents of Rwanda and Burundi died when the aircraft in which they were travelling crashed under mysterious circumstances. But the conflict between Hutus and Tutsis, the major ethnic groups in both countries, dates back more than 500 years. The cattle-raising Tutsis moved into the region from Ethiopia in the 15th century and established their authority over the majority Hutu farmers.

Several Hutu uprisings in the 20th century led to mass killings on both sides. In 1994 more than a million Tutsis fled to Zaire, along with Hutus escaping reprisals, but the insanitary refugee camps brought more deaths from disease and starvation. When more than a million refugees returned to Rwanda in 1996, Hutus found their farms occupied by Tutsis. Today Tutsis control both governments, and Hutu extremists wander their ravaged lands, attacking Tutsis and Western tourists alike.

BURUNDI

OFFICIAL NAME
The Republic of Burundi

CAPITAL
Bujumbura

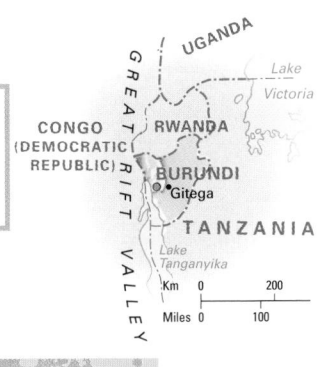

Burundi

Area 27 834 km²
(10 747 sq miles)
Population 6 483 000
Population density 226 per
km² (586 per sq mile)
Population growth rate 1.4%
Life expectancy 43 (m); 46 (f)
Languages French, Kirundi,
Swahili
Adult literacy rate 35.3%

Currency Burundi franc
(US $1 = 806 Burundi
francs)
GDP (US million $) 959
GDP per head (US $) 152

Key dates

1897 Becomes part of German East Africa.
1923 Administration by Belgium as part of Rwanda-Urundi.
1962 Independence under Tutsi control.
1972-3 Hutu revolt fails; 150 000 Hutus and 10 000 Tutsis killed.
1976 Military coup.
1981 New constitution.
1988 Army massacres thousands of Hutus.

1993 First multiparty presidential election: Hutu candidate wins but dies later in coup.
1993-6 About 150 000 die in ethnic clashes following 1993 coup.
1994 President (a Hutu) killed in plane crash; violent demonstrations.
1996 Tutsi-led military coup fails to halt ethnic violence.

ANGOLA

OFFICIAL NAME
The Republic of Angola

CAPITAL
Luanda

Angola

Area 1 246 700 km²
(481 354 sq miles)
Population 12 479 000
Population density 10 per
km² (25 per sq mile)
Population growth rate 3.2%
Life expectancy 45 (m); 48 (f)
Languages Portuguese,
Umbundo, Kimbundo,
Chokwe, Ganguela

Adult literacy rate 41.7%
Currency new kwanza (US
$1 = 18.24 new kwanzas)
GDP (US million $) 4776
GDP per head (US $) 395

1 Cuanza Norte
2 Cuanza Sul
3 Benguela
4 Huambo

Key dates

1648 Portuguese win control; trade in slaves.
1961 War of liberation. Rival groups, including MPLA and UNITA, later start fighting each other.
1975 Independence from Portugal.
1976 Soviet-backed MPLA wins civil war.
1991 Peace treaty with West-backed UNITA.
1992 Elections. Fighting resumes after UNITA rejects results.
1994 UN-negotiated peace agreement.
1998 Civil war resumes.

ZAMBIA

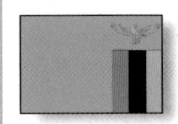

OFFICIAL NAME
The Republic of Zambia

CAPITAL
Lusaka

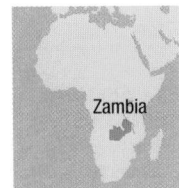
Zambia

Area 752 614 km²
(290 584 sq miles)
Population 10 407 000
Population density 14 per
km² (36 per sq mile)
Population growth rate 1.95%
Life expectancy 37 (m); 37 (f)
Languages English, Bemba,
Kaonda, Lozi, Tonga and
other local languages
Adult literacy rate 78.2%
Currency Zambian kwacha
(US $1 = 3150 kwacha)
GDP (US million $) n/a
GDP per head (US $) n/a

Key dates

1924 Becomes British protectorate of Northern Rhodesia.
1953 Federation formed with Southern Rhodesia and Nyasaland.
1964 Independence within Commonwealth as Zambia; Kenneth Kaunda president.
1970 Takes control of foreign-owned copper mines.
1972 One-party state.
1991 Multiparty elections reinstated; Kaunda defeated.
1997 Coup attempt fails.

MALAWI

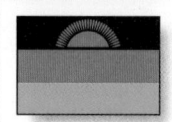

OFFICIAL NAME
The Republic of Malawi

CAPITAL
Lilongwe

Area 118 484 km²
(45 747 sq miles)
Population 10 640 000
Population density 87 per
km² (226 per sq mile)
Population growth rate 1.8%
Life expectancy 43 (m); 46 (f)
Languages English,

Chichewa and other local
languages
Adult literacy rate 56.4%
Currency Malawian kwacha
(US $1 = 79 kwacha)
GDP (US million $) 1792
GDP per head (US $) 173

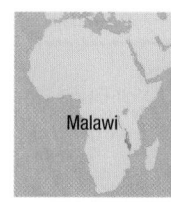

Malawi

Key dates

1891 Nyasaland made
British protectorate.
1953 Federation formed
with Northern and
Southern Rhodesia.
1964 Independence as
Malawi.
1966 One-party republic
within Commonwealth.
1971 Hastings Banda
made president for life.
1993 Multiparty system.
1994 Banda loses the
first multiparty
presidential election.

ZIMBABWE

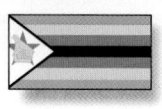

OFFICIAL NAME
The Republic of Zimbabwe

CAPITAL
Harare

Zimbabwe

Area 390 759 km²
(150 873 sq miles)
Population 13 079 000
Population density 32 per
km² (84 per sq mile)
Population growth rate 3%
Life expectancy 58 (m); 62 (f)
Languages English,
Chishona, Sindebele and
other local languages
Adult literacy rate 85.1%
Currency Zimbabwe dollar
(US $1 = 55 Zimbabwe
dollars)
GDP (US million $) 5300
GDP per head (US $) 417

Key dates

1888 Cecil Rhodes gains
mining rights.
1923 British colony of
Southern Rhodesia.
1953 Federation formed
with Northern Rhodesia
and Nyasaland.
1961 New constitution
restricts black vote.
1963 Federation ends.
1964 Named Rhodesia.
1964-74 Black activists
imprisoned.
1965 Independence
declared; unrecognised.

1966 UN sanctions.
1969 Constitution
entrenches white rule.
1970s Black groups fight
guerrilla war.
1979 Voting-rule change
gives black-majority
government. Ceasefire.
1980 Free elections;
Robert Mugabe prime
minister. Independence
as Zimbabwe.
2000-1 Mugabe enforces
land redistribution to
black population.

MOZAMBIQUE

OFFICIAL NAME
The Republic of Mozambique

CAPITAL
Maputo

Area 799 380 km²
(308 641 sq miles)
Population 17 299 000
Population density 21 per
km² (55 per sq mile)
Population growth rate 2%
Life expectancy 44 (m); 47 (f)
Languages Portuguese and
many local languages
Adult literacy rate 40.1%
Currency metical
(US $1 = 19 075 meticals)
GDP (US million $) 4037
GDP per head (US $) 238

Key dates

1505 Portuguese slave-
trading post set up.
1885 Portuguese colony
recognised.
1960s Frelimo guerrillas
start liberation war.
1974 Ceasefire; internal
self-government.
1975 Independence as

socialist republic.
1986 Plane crash kills
President Machel.
1990 One-party rule ends.
1994 First multi-party
elections.
1995 Joins the
Commonwealth.
2000-1 Severe flooding.

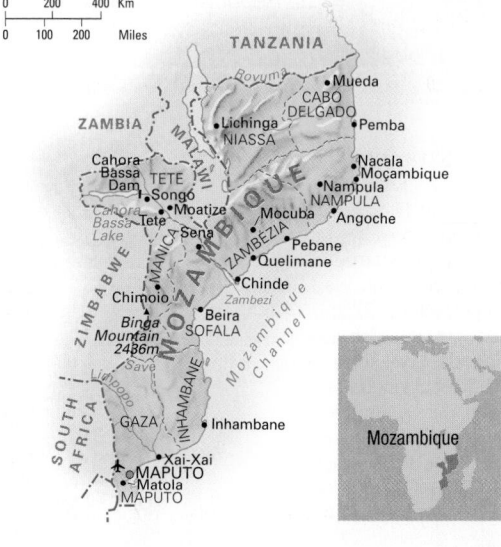

Mozambique

MADAGASCAR

OFFICIAL NAME
The Republic of Madagascar

CAPITAL
Antananarivo

Area 587 041 km²
(226 658 sq miles)
Population 15 497 000
Population density 26 per
km² (66 per sq mile)
Population growth rate 2.6%
Life expectancy 55 (m); 58 (f)
Languages Malagasy,
French, Hova and other
local languages
Adult literacy rate 45.7%

Currency Malagasy franc
(US $1 = 6320 Malagasy
francs)
GDP (US million $) 3752
GDP per head (US $) 249

COMOROS

OFFICIAL NAME
The Federal Islamic Republic
of the Comoros

CAPITAL
Moroni, on Grande Comore
(Njazidja)

Area 1862 km²
(719 sq miles)
Population 676 000
Population density 354 per
km² (918 per sq mile)
Population growth rate 2.7%
Life expectancy 55 (m); 56 (f)
Languages Comorian
(Swahili and Arabic),
French, Arabic

Adult literacy rate 57.3%
Currency Comoros franc
(US $1 = 546 Comoros
francs)
GDP (US million $) 207
GDP per head (US $) 313

Key dates

15thC Arab rule.
1843-86 French seize
control.
1961 Self-government.
1974 Christian majority
of Mayotte island votes
to stay French; others
to become independent.
1989 President Ahmed
Abdallah assassinated.
1995 French troops
invade to overthrow
military coup.
1997 Anjouan (Nzwani)
and Moheli (Mwali)
declare secession.
1999 Military coup (19th
coup or coup attempt
since independence).

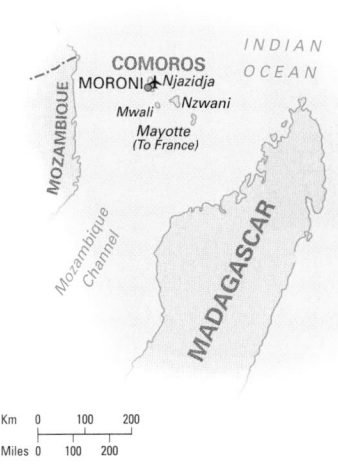

MAURITIUS

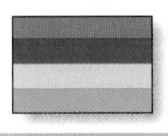

OFFICIAL NAME
The Republic of Mauritius

CAPITAL
Port Louis

Area 2040 km²
(788 sq miles)
Population 1 174 000
Population density 569 per
km² (1472 per sq mile)
Population growth rate 0.9%
Life expectancy 66 (m); 74 (f)
Languages English, Creole,
French and several Indian
and Chinese dialects
Adult literacy rate 82.9%
Currency Mauritian rupee

(US $1 = 28 rupees)
GDP (US million $) 4574
GDP per head (US $) 3943

FACT About 68 per cent
of Mauritians are
descended from
Indians who
arrived there to
work in the 1800s.

Key dates

1598 Dutch claim.
1715 French take
possession.
1810 Captured by Britain.
1814 Becomes a British
colony.
1833 Slavery abolished.
1965 Diego Garcia
island separated to
become part of British
Indian Ocean Territory.
1967 Internal self-
government.
1968 Becomes
independent within the
Commonwealth.
1992 Becomes republic.

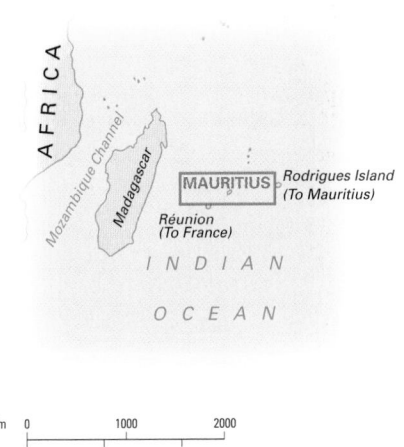

SOUTH AFRICA

OFFICIAL NAME
The Republic of South Africa

CAPITAL CITIES
Pretoria (administrative),
Cape Town (legislative),
Bloemfontein (judicial)

Area 1 219 080 km²
(470 689 sq miles)
Population 43 054 000
Population density 35 per
km² (90 per sq mile)
Population growth rate 2.4%
Life expectancy 60 (m); 66 (f)
Languages Afrikaans,
English and nine African
languages

Adult literacy rate 81.8%
Currency rand
(US $1 = 8.15 rand)
GDP (US million $) 130 100
GDP per head (US $) 3085

Key dates

1652 Dutch settle Cape.
1814 Dutch transfer
Cape Colony to Britain.
1836-8 Start of Boers'
'Great Trek' to north;
establish Natal.
1852-4 Boer colonies of
Transvaal and Orange
Free State recognised.
1868 Diamonds found.
1873-86 Gold found.
1877 Britain annexes
Transvaal.
1879 Zulus defeated in
Anglo-Zulu War.
1880-1902 Anglo-Boer
wars lead to British rule.
1910 Union of South
Africa formed from Boer
and British colonies.
1912 African [Native]
National Congress
(ANC) founded.

1914-18 First World War
fought as one of Allies.
1931 Statute of
Westminster gives
independence within
Commonwealth.
1939-45 One of Allies in
Second World War.
1948 Apartheid policy of
racial division begins.
1960 Sharpeville
massacre: 69 anti-
apartheid protesters
killed. ANC banned.
1961 Republic declared;
leaves Commonwealth.
1962 ANC leader Nelson
Mandela imprisoned.
1976 Soweto uprising
against compulsory
teaching of Afrikaans;
police kill 600 black
student demonstrators.

1986 International trade
sanctions begin. South
African forces attack
ANC bases in Botswana,
Zambia and Zimbabwe.
1990 ANC ban lifted;
Mandela freed; reform
negotiations start.
1991 Apartheid ends.
1993 Mandela and
President F. W. de Klerk
win Nobel peace prize.
'Homelands' – semi-
self-governing black
territories – abolished.
1994 Mandela elected
president in first multi-
race elections. Rejoins
Commonwealth.
1995 Truth Commission
set up to document
human rights abuses.

FACT
The world's largest
man-made hole is
an old diamond
mine at Kimberley,
500 m (1640 ft)
across and 400 m
(1310 ft) deep.

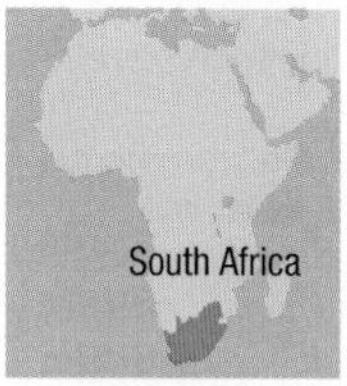

South Africa

ZIMBABWE

KALAHARI DESERT

BOTSWANA

NAMIBIA

MOZAMBIQUE

Limpopo

NORTHERN PROVINCE

Venda

Letaba Valley

Gazankulu

KRUGER NP

Pietersburg

Phalaborwa

Potgietersrus

Lebowa

Lydenburg

Komatipoort

Nelspruit

Sun City

KwaNdebele

GAUTENG

MPUMALANGA

Mmabatho

Mafikeng

Rosslyn

Brits

Rustenburg

Mamelodi

PRETORIA

Witwatersrand

Johannesburg

Kempton Park

Krugersdorp

Benoni

Springs

Carletonville

Soweto

Germiston

Secunda

Randfontein

Vanderbijlpark

Heidelberg

Potchefstroom

Sasolburg

Vereeniging

Bophuthatswana

NORTH WEST PROVINCE

SWAZILAND

SOUTH AFRICA

Welkom

Newcastle

Vryheid

Hluhluwe

FREE STATE

Rorke's Drift

Ulundi

KwaZulu

Isandhlwana

Dingaan's Kraal

St Lucia

Ladysmith

Upington

Augrabies Falls

Winburg

Qwaqwa

Richard's Bay

Griqualand West

Kimberley

Tugela

Namaland

Orange

Bushmanland

Bloemfontein

Mangaung

LESOTHO

KWAZULU-NATAL

Port Nolloth

Okiep

Hopetown

Pietermaritzburg

Valley of a Thousand Hills

Durban

Springbok

NORTHERN CAPE

Qacha's Nek

EASTERN CAPE

Griqualand East

Caledon

Gariep Dam

Carnarvon

GREAT

DRAKENSBERG

Transkei

Umtata

INDIAN OCEAN

ATLANTIC OCEAN

EASTERN CAPE

Graaff Reinet

Butterworth

Bisho

Ciskei

King William's Town

Zwelitsha

Mdantsane

East London

Saldanha

Great Karoo

Cango Caves

Grahamstown

Great Fish

Darling

Atlantis

WESTERN CAPE

Oudtshoorn

Swartkops

Hexrivier Valley

Little Karoo

TSITSIKAMA

Port Elizabeth

Table Bay

Robben Island

Cape Town

Paarl

Stellenbosch

George

Knysna

Table Mountain

Crossroads

Cape Peninsula

Simon's Town

Cape of Good Hope

Mossel Bay

False Bay

Cape Agulhas

Km 0   100   200   300

Miles 0   100   200

SWAZILAND

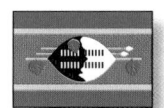

OFFICIAL NAME
The Kingdom of Swaziland

CAPITAL
Mbabane

Area 17 363 km²
(6704 sq miles)
Population 980 000
Population density 55 per
km² (142 per sq mile)
Population growth rate 1.5%
Life expectancy 55 (m); 60 (f)
Languages English, Siswati
Adult literacy rate 76.7%
Currency lilangeni (plural
emalangeni; US $1 = 8.15
emalangeni)
GDP (US million $) 1206
GDP per head (US $) 1269

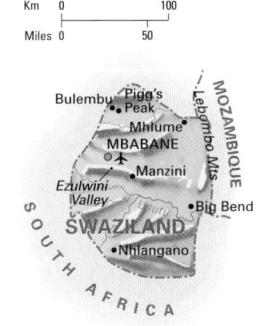

◀ Key dates

1902 British control.
1968 Independence
within Commonwealth.
1973 King assumes
absolute powers.
1978 Political parties
banned.
1993 First free elections.

Key dates ▶

1868 Basutoland made
British protectorate.
1966 Independence as
Kingdom of Lesotho.
1986 South Africa
blockades border
against African National
Congress guerrillas.
1991 Military coup.
1993 Free elections.

LESOTHO

OFFICIAL NAME
The Kingdom of Lesotho

CAPITAL
Maseru

Area 30 355 km²
(11 720 sq miles)
Population 2 108 000
Population density 68 per
km² (176 per sq mile)
Population growth rate 1.9%
Life expectancy 56 (m); 59 (f)
Languages English, Sesotho

Adult literacy rate 71.3%
Currency loti (plural maloti;
US $1 = 8.15 maloti)
GDP (US million $) 983
GDP per head (US $) 477

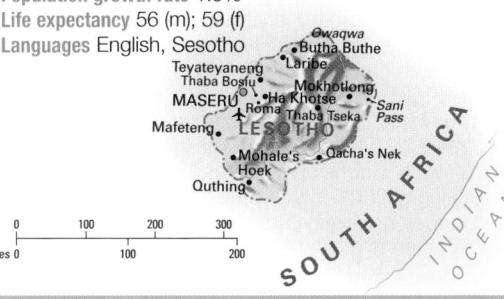

BOTSWANA

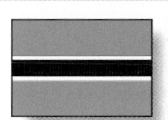

OFFICIAL NAME
The Republic of Botswana

CAPITAL
Gaborone

Area 581 730 km²
(224 607 sq miles)
Population 1 611 000
Population density 3 per km²
(7 per sq mile)
Population growth rate 2.1%
Life expectancy 56 (m); 62 (f)
Languages English,

Setswana
Adult literacy rate 69.8%
Currency pula
(US $1 = 5.68 pula)
GDP (US million $) 4700
GDP per head (US $) 2993

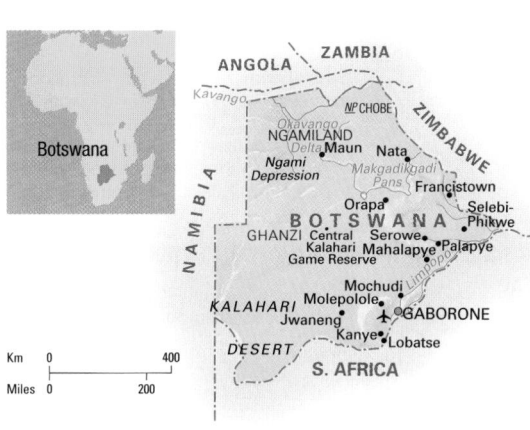

Key dates

1885 British protectorate
of Bechuanaland.
1965 Self-government.
1966 Full independence
as Botswana, within
Commonwealth.
1985-6 South African
troops raid African
National Congress
bases in Gaborone.
1994 South African
relations normalised.

NAMIBIA

OFFICIAL NAME
The Republic of Namibia

CAPITAL
Windhoek

Area 824 292 km²
(318 261 sq miles)
Population 1 695 000
Population density 2 per km²
(5 per sq mile)
Population growth rate 2.7%
Life expectancy 54 (m); 57 (f)
Languages English,
Afrikaans, German and
local languages
Adult literacy rate 62%
Currency Namibian dollar
(US $1 = 8.15 Namibian
dollars)
GDP (US million $) 3000
GDP per head (US $) 1807

1 Khomas
2 Ohanguena
3 Omusati
4 Oshana
5 Oshikoto

Key dates

1884 Germany annexes,
as South-West Africa.
1915 First World War:
South Africa invades.
1920 South Africa given
mandate under League
of Nations, but takes
total control.
1966 South-West Africa
People's Organisation
(SWAPO) starts guerrilla
independence war.
1968 UN declares name
change to Namibia.
1989 Agreement for
ceasefire and end of
South African rule.
1990 Full independence;
joins Commonwealth.
1994 South Africa
returns control of Walvis
Bay port to Namibia.

Since the 19th century, countries have increasingly recognised the benefits of international cooperation on economic, cultural, social, environmental and security matters. After the League of Nations failed to prevent the Second World War, much more effective international organisations have been set up.

The United Nations The UN is the most important example of global collaboration. Since the end of the Second World War, it has been the main international forum for airing states' concerns and grievances, for maintaining peace and security (whether by diplomacy, arbitration, peacekeeping operations or direct military intervention) and for dealing with problems that challenge all of humanity (such as global warming).

The United Nations was established on October 24, 1945, by 51 states. Today nearly every country in the world is a member – a total of 189 at the beginning of 2001. It is not a world government and it does not make laws. But member states agree to accept the obligations of the UN Charter, which sets out the basic 'rules' governing international relations.

The UN system The United Nations has six main bodies (right). Five are based at its main headquarters in New York, USA, and one – the International Court of Justice – is at The Hague, in the Netherlands. Specialised agencies (below) carry out numerous particular functions.

Security Council The UN body responsible for peace. Five of the 15 members (the USA, UK, France, Russia and China) are 'permanent', with a power of veto.

General Assembly A forum for discussing world issues. All UN members are represented, each with one vote. Unlike the Security Council, it cannot enforce decisions.

Economic and Social Council Coordinates the UN's economic and social work, monitoring issues such as human rights, the status of women, drugs and the environment.

Trusteeship Council Supervised the running of UN Trust Territories (dependencies of states defeated in the Second World War), leading them to independence. This task was completed in 1994: the Council suspended operations, agreeing to meet again only if occasion required.

International Court of Justice The UN's main judicial organ, deciding legal disputes between states. It can only hear a case if the parties agree.

Secretariat The UN's administration centre, carrying out day-to-day work and managing UN programmes. Its head is the secretary-general, appointed by the General Assembly on the Security Council's recommendation.

UN secretaries-general

1946-52	**Trygve Lie** (Norway)	
1953-61	**Dag Hammarskjöld** (Sweden)	
1961-71	**U Thant** (Myanmar [Burma])	
1972-81	**Kurt Waldheim** (Austria)	
1982-91	**Javier Pérez de Cuéllar** (Peru)	
1992-6	**Boutros Boutros-Ghali** (Egypt)	
1997-	**Kofi Annan** (Ghana)	

Autonomous organisations linked to the UN through special agreements

Name	Founded; headquarters	Principal activities/purposes
Food and Agriculture Organisation (FAO)	1945 Rome	To improve agricultural productivity, food, security and the living standards of rural populations.
International Atomic Energy Agency (IEAE)	1957 Vienna	To promote the safe and peaceful use of atomic energy.
International Civil Aviation Organisation (ICAO)	1947 Montreal	Setting international standards for the safety, security and efficiency of air transport.
International Fund for Agricultural Development (IFAD)	1977 Rome	Organising funding to raise food production and nutrition levels in developing countries.
International Labour Organisation (ILO)	1919 Geneva	To set labour standards and draw up programmes to improve working conditions around the world.
International Maritime Organisation (IMO)	1958 London	Improvement of international shipping procedures, raising of standards in maritime safety and reducing marine pollution.
International Monetary Fund (IMF)	1947 Washington DC	To promote monetary cooperation between nations, exchange-rate stability and expansion of trade.
International Telecommunication Union (ITU)	1865 Geneva	Cooperation to improve telecommunications and develop related technical facilities.
United Nations Educational, Scientific and Cultural Organisation (UNESCO)	1946 Paris	International collaboration in science, communications, education and culture; protection of the world's natural and cultural heritage.
UNIDO United Nations Industrial Development Organisation (UNIDO)	1966 Vienna	Advancement of industry in developing countries through technical assistance and advice.

Other key international organisations and alliances (see also European institutions, pp.328-9)

	Name	Founded; headquarters	Principal activities/purposes
	Asia-Pacific Economic Cooperation (APEC)	1989 Singapore	Main regional body for promoting open trade and practical economic cooperation (21 members).
	Association of South-east Asian Nations (ASEAN)	1967 Jakarta	Promotion of regional economic development and trade between member countries (10 members).
CARICOM	**Caribbean Community and Common Market (CARICOM)**	1973 Georgetown, Guyana	Coordination of economic and foreign policy (15 members; 3 associates).
	Commonwealth	1931 London, UK	Association of sovereign independent states (including the UK), nearly all once British territories (54 members).
	League of Arab States (Arab League)	1945 Cairo, Egypt	To promote closer ties among members and coordinate economic, cultural and security policies (22 members).
	North Atlantic Treaty Organisation (NATO)	1949 Brussels, Belgium	Set up to defend Western Europe and North America; now has some central European members (19 members).
OECD	**Organisation for Economic Cooperation and Development (OECD)**	1961 Paris, France	Organisation of industrialised countries for cooperation on social and economic policies (29 members).
OAU	**Organisation of African Unity (OAU)**	1963 Addis Ababa, Ethiopia	To coordinate political, economic and defence policies, and eradicate colonialism in Africa (53 members).
	Organisation of American States (OAS)	1948 Washington DC, USA	To strengthen peace and security of the Americas, and promote economic development (35 members).
	Organisation of Petroleum Exporting Countries (OPEC)	1960 Vienna, Austria	To coordinate price and supply policies of major oil-producers (11 members).
	Pacific Community	1947 New Caledonia	Regional cooperation and assistance (formerly South Pacific Commission; 27 member states and territories).

	Name	Founded; headquarters	Principal activities/purposes
	Universal Postal Union (UPU)	1875 Bern, Switzerland	Coordinating international collaboration by postal services.
	WORLD BANK GROUP	Washington DC	
	International Bank for Reconstruction and Development (IBRD; World Bank)	1945	Providing loans and technical assistance to member governments.
	International Development Association (IDA)	1960	Offering finance for development projects on interest-free terms to less-developed countries.
	International Finance Corporation (IFC)	1956	Encouraging private enterprise in developing countries.
	Multilateral Investment Guarantee Agency (MIGA)	1988	Promoting the flow of foreign direct investment to, and among, developing member countries.
	World Health Organization (WHO)	1948 Geneva	To raise the standard of health of all peoples by promoting primary health care.
	World Intellectual Property Organisation (WIPO)	1970 Geneva	Protection of intellectual property, including copyrights, trademarks, industrial designs and patents.
	World Meteorological Organisation (WMO)	1950 Geneva	Global cooperation on weather observations and the rapid exchange of weather information.
	World Trade Organisation (WTO)	1995 Geneva	To ensure fair trade between countries (successor to the General Agreement on Tariffs and Trade [GATT]).

In addition, a number of UN offices, programmes and funds (for example, the UN Development Programme, UN Children's Fund, and World Food Programme) work to improve the economic and social condition of people around the world. They are responsible to the UN General Assembly or to the UN Economic and Social Council.

European integration grew out of the desolation of two world wars and a serious economic depression in the first half of the 20th century. In 1952, a series of international agreements began which eventually led to deeper cooperation between most nations – a process from which today's European Union (EU) has evolved. At the same time, a number of other supranational bodies have been created.

The European Union

Origins The European Coal and Steel Community (ECSC) – a jointly managed market in coal and steel – was set up in 1952 by Belgium, France, Germany, Italy, Luxembourg and the Netherlands (the 'Six'). In 1958 the same nations established the the European Economic Community (EEC, or 'Common Market') and European Atomic Energy Community (Euratom), extending cooperation, making common policies and removing trade barriers. These three bodies formed what was later called collectively the European Community (EC) and, from 1993, the European Union.

The benefits of integration attracted other countries. After four waves of accessions (in 1973, 1981, 1986 and 1995), the EU now has 15 members states (see below), with 13 eastern and southern European applicant countries waiting to join.

Treaties The treaties of Paris (1951; setting up the ECSC) and Rome (1957; EEC and Euratom) have been supplemented by further constitutional measures defining the relationship and powers of the EU in relation to the member states:
- Single European Act (1986) – defined EU internal market as an area without frontiers; increased powers of European Parliament;
- Maastricht Treaty (1992) – set a timetable for European Monetary Union (EMU);
- Treaty of Amsterdam (1997) – included a new responsibility for raising levels of employment in member states.

Organisation Like any government, the EU is a system for making decisions and spending money on a joint, rather than individual, basis. It is run by five institutions:
- **Council of the EU (Council of Ministers)** The main decision-making body, made up of government ministers from all member states (participating ministers vary according to the topic under discussion). Some council decisions must be unanimous; others are by 'qualified' majority voting weighted by population.

European Commission presidents

1958-67	**Walter Hallstein** (West Germany)
1967-70	**Jean Rey** (Belgium)
1970-2	**Franco Malfatti** (Italy)
1972-3	**Sicco Mansholt** (Netherlands)
1973-7	**François-Xavier Ortoli** (France)
1977-81	**Roy Jenkins** (UK)
1981-5	**Gaston Thorn** (Luxembourg)
1985-95	**Jacques Delors** (France)
1995-9	**Jacques Santer** (Luxembourg)
1999-	**Romano Prodi** (Italy)

- **European Commission** The Brussels-based independent executive. It consists of 20 commissioners appointed by member governments, each responsible for a certain area of policy. It proposes laws (to be considered by the Council of Ministers and European Parliament), manages EU policies and international trade relations, and acts as guardian of the treaties setting up the EU.
- **European Parliament (EP)** Has 626 members (MEPs), directly elected every five years by the peoples of the member states. It normally meets for a week every month in Strasbourg, France. It gives opinions and suggests amendments to commission proposals, and in some cases jointly decides laws with the Council of Ministers.
- **Court of Justice** The supreme court of the EU. Sitting in Luxembourg, it has 15 judges (one from each member state).
- **Court of Auditors** A watchdog that monitors the EU's financial management.

The EU also has a number of supporting bodies. The **Economic and Social Committee,** an advisory body, has representatives of various economic and social groupings (workers, employers, consumers and other interests).

The **Committee of the Regions,** made up of representatives from local and regional authorities, giving them a voice in the EU system.

The **European Investment Bank,** the EU's financing institution, provides loans to promote the EU's balanced development.

The **European Central Bank,** based in Frankfurt, Germany, is responsibile for the stability of the common currency (the Euro).

The **Ombudsman** is an official who investigates alleged maladministration by the EU institutions or other bodies.

Financing EU revenues come from customs duties, levies on agricultural imports from non-members, a percentage of the proceeds of value added tax and contributions from members based on gross national product.

European Union member states, with dates of accession

	Seats in EP	Votes in Council
1958		
Belgium	25	5
France	87	10
Germany*	99	10
Italy	87	10
Luxembourg	6	2
Netherlands	31	5
1973		
Denmark	16	3
Ireland	15	3
United Kingdom	87	10
1981		
Greece	25	5
1986		
Portugal	25	5
Spain	64	8
1995		
Austria	21	4
Finland	16	3
Sweden	22	4

*West Germany until 1990.

Each member state appoints one member of the European Commission except France, Germany, Italy, Spain and the UK, which each appoint two.

Applicant countries
Bulgaria; Cyprus; Czech Republic; Estonia; Hungary; Latvia; Lithuania; Malta; Poland; Romania; Slovakia; Slovenia; Turkey

The Schengen Agreement

This agreement provides for the abolition of immigration controls at internal frontiers between member states. It began as an intergovernmental (rather than EU) arrangement in 1995, and was incorporated into the EU in the Amsterdam Treaty of 1997. But not all EU countries are yet party to it.

Major EU policies

Name	Principal activities/purposes
Common Agricultural Policy (CAP)	Regulation of agricultural market through support prices, import duties and market intervention.
Common Foreign and Security Policy (CFSP)*	Providing for member states to agree unanimously common policies and/or joint actions on international issues.
Competition Policy	Guaranteeing undistorted economic competition between equal market participants.
Economic and Monetary Union (EMU)	Promoting economic convergence; creation of a common monetary policy and single currency. That currency – the Euro – will be introduced to EMU member countries on January 1, 2002.
Employment and Social Policy	Improving living and working conditions; stimulating employment; extending social protection.
Enlargement	Helping other democratic, free-market European nations to prepare for EU membership.
Environmental Policy	Preserving the quality of the environment; protecting health; conserving natural resources.
External relations	Developing closer economic and trading ties with non-member countries and other international organisations.
Common Fisheries Policy (CFP)	Regulating access to fishing waters; conservation and management of resources; common organisation of markets.
Internal (or single) market	Creating an EU area without internal frontiers and without obstacles to free movement of goods, people, services and capital.
Justice and home affairs*	Cooperation on asylum, immigration and other issues to do with free movement of people, and on combating international crime.
Regional Policy	Promoting balanced development across the EU, mainly through Structural Funds (European Regional Development Fund; European Social Fund; guidance section of Agricultural Fund).
Research and technology	Coordinating research to strengthen the science and technology base of EU industry, mainly through joint framework programmes.
Trans-European networks	Improving the interconnection and interoperability of national transport, energy and telecommunications networks.
Common Transport Policy	Eliminating national restrictions and barriers in the operation of various means of transport.

*Policies coordinated by intergovernmental cooperation rather than centrally through the EU institutions (under the terms of the Maastricht Treaty)

Non-EU European institutions

Name	Founded; headquarters	Principal activities/purposes
Council of Baltic Sea States	1992 Stockholm, Sweden	Cooperation between the 12 states with Baltic Sea coasts in the fields of environmental protection, trade, tourism and transport infrastructure.
Council of Europe	1949 Strasbourg, France	Protection of pluralist democracy, human rights and the rule of law (41 members).
European Bank for Reconstruction and Development (EBRD)	1991 London, UK	Helps economic restructuring of former communist states in central and eastern Europe and the Soviet Union (60 members).
European Free Trade Association (EFTA)	1960 Geneva, Switzerland	Originally a 'rival' organisation to the EEC – all members apart from Norway, Denmark, Switzerland and Lichtenstein left to join the EU.
Nordic Council	1952 Stockholm, Sweden	Promoting cooperation between the parliaments and governments of Scandinavia and Iceland (five members).
Organisation for Security and Cooperation in Europe (OSCE)	1975 Vienna, Austria	The main regional instrument for early warning, conflict prevention, crisis management and post conflict rehabilitation (55 members).
Western European Union (WEU)	1954 Brussels, Belgium	Forum for cooperation on defence and security issues (ten full members).

Culture and entertainment

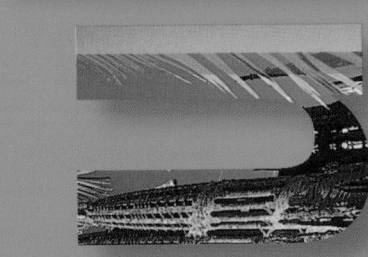

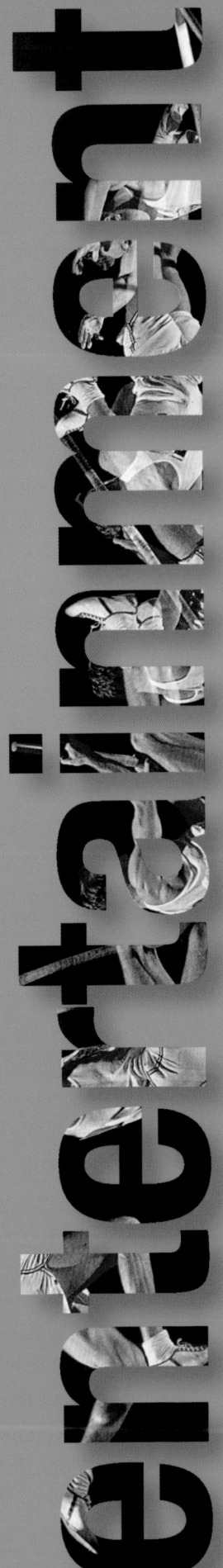

culture and entertainment

culture and entertainment

Although animals communicate, only human beings possess the mental and physical faculties to use language that is capable of conveying complex ideas and knowledge – all that makes civilisation possible. It is likely that language and thought evolved together, stimulating each other. Scientists speculate that language arose about 100 000 years ago, when the earliest human species, Homo sapiens, first left Africa, with written forms appearing about 5000 years ago.

LANGUAGE FAMILIES

Languages that appear to be historically related are grouped into families. All those in the same family are thought to have developed from a parent (proto) version of the language. They tend to have features in common, such as words with similar phonological characteristics describing similar concepts. For example, the Latin for father, *pater*, sounds similar to the equivalent word in many other languages – such as *padre* in Italian and Spanish, *père* in French and *fadar* in old German – suggesting that the languages all have a common ancestor.

At the end of the last Ice Age, 12 000 years ago, the rise in sea levels cut off many groups of people from each other, promoting the evolution of different languages and language families. Migration has led to further adaptations and amalgamations. Linguists now reckon that tens of thousands of languages have existed, but little more than 5000 have been clearly identified.

DISTRIBUTION OF LANGUAGE FAMILIES

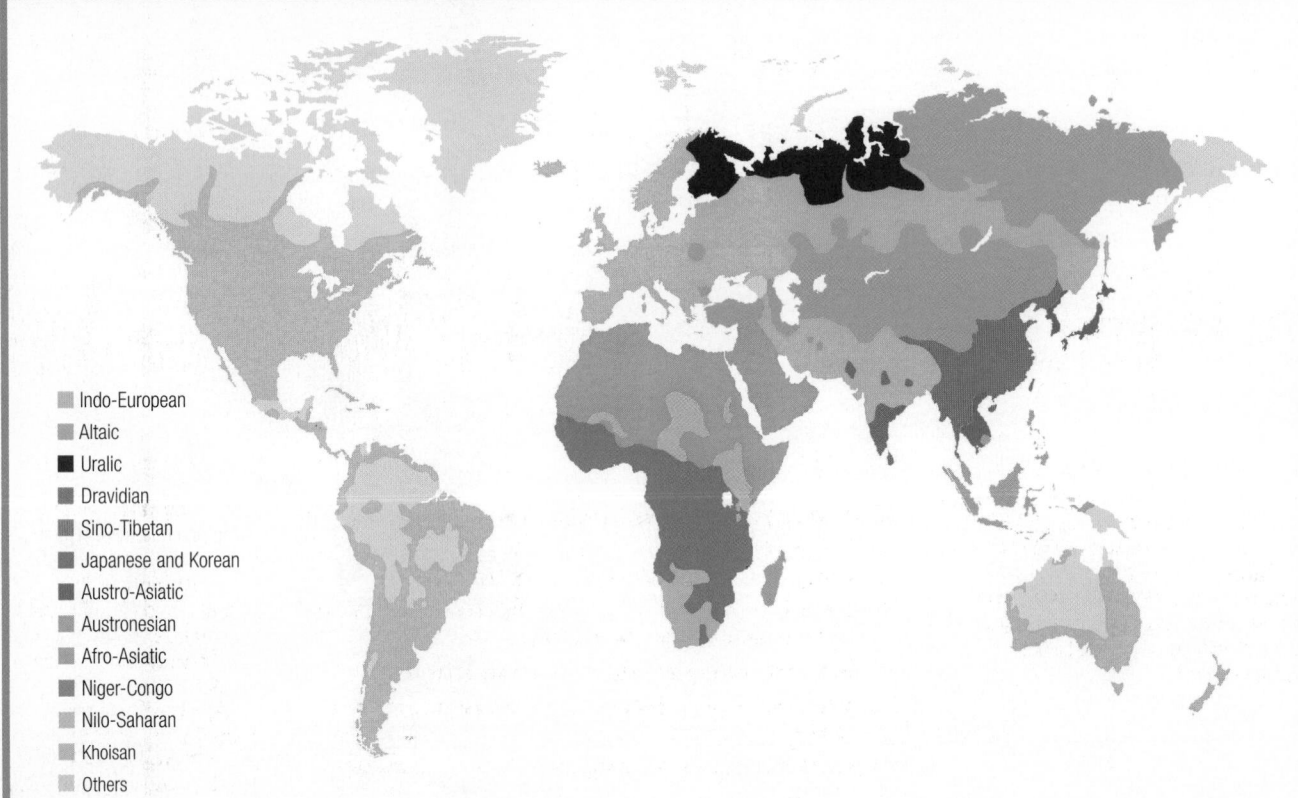

- Indo-European
- Altaic
- Uralic
- Dravidian
- Sino-Tibetan
- Japanese and Korean
- Austro-Asiatic
- Austronesian
- Afro-Asiatic
- Niger-Congo
- Nilo-Saharan
- Khoisan
- Others

The families outlined below are groups of languages related by similarities in words, phrases and inflection.

Indo-European Spoken by about half the world's population (see opposite).
Altaic More than 50 languages, including Mongolian, Tungusian (Siberia/north China) and Turkish; spoken by about 135 million.
Uralic More than 20 languages, including Estonian, Finnish and Hungarian; spoken by about 24 million people.
Dravidian 24 languages, including Tamil and Teluga; spoken by 220 million in southern India and Sri Lanka.

Sino-Tibetan More than 130 distinct languages spoken by about 1200 million people in China, Tibet and neighbouring Far Eastern countries.
Japanese and Korean Languages with no obvious links to other families, with a total of about 200 million speakers.
Austro-Asiatic (Mon-Khmer) Vietnamese, Khmer (Cambodian) and the numerous Munda languages of India, with about 110 million users.
Austronesian (Malayo-Polynesian) More than 1000 languages, including Malay, Javanese, Hawaiian and Maori, with about 270 million speakers.

Afro-Asiatic A family of 371 so far identified languages, including Arabic, Hebrew, Berber, Hausa, and Amalhric in Ethiopia; spoken by about 200 million.
Niger-Congo About 1400 languages, of which Swahili, spoken by 35 million in East Africa, is the most widely used.
Nilo-Saharan More than 30 languages spoken by about 23 million in East Africa.
Khoisan South-western African bushman languages, including Nama (Hottentot).
Others Little-studied families include the American Indian and south-east European Caucasian group, Thai and Laotian, and the 741 languages of Papua-New Guinea.

Indo-European family

By far the most widely spoken language family is the Indo-European, to which a large range of European and Asian languages belong. By the dawn of the Christian era, speakers of its varied tongues stretched from Ireland to Bengal. Basque is the only extant European language that is not part of the Indo-European group.

Since the overseas expansion of European power began five centuries ago, four Indo-European languages – French, Portuguese, Spanish, and especially English – have become the main means of communication in many parts of the globe, often killing off native tongues. In fact, more people speak an Indo-European language outside Europe and Asia: North America has the largest English-speaking population, and South America has the most Spanish speakers.

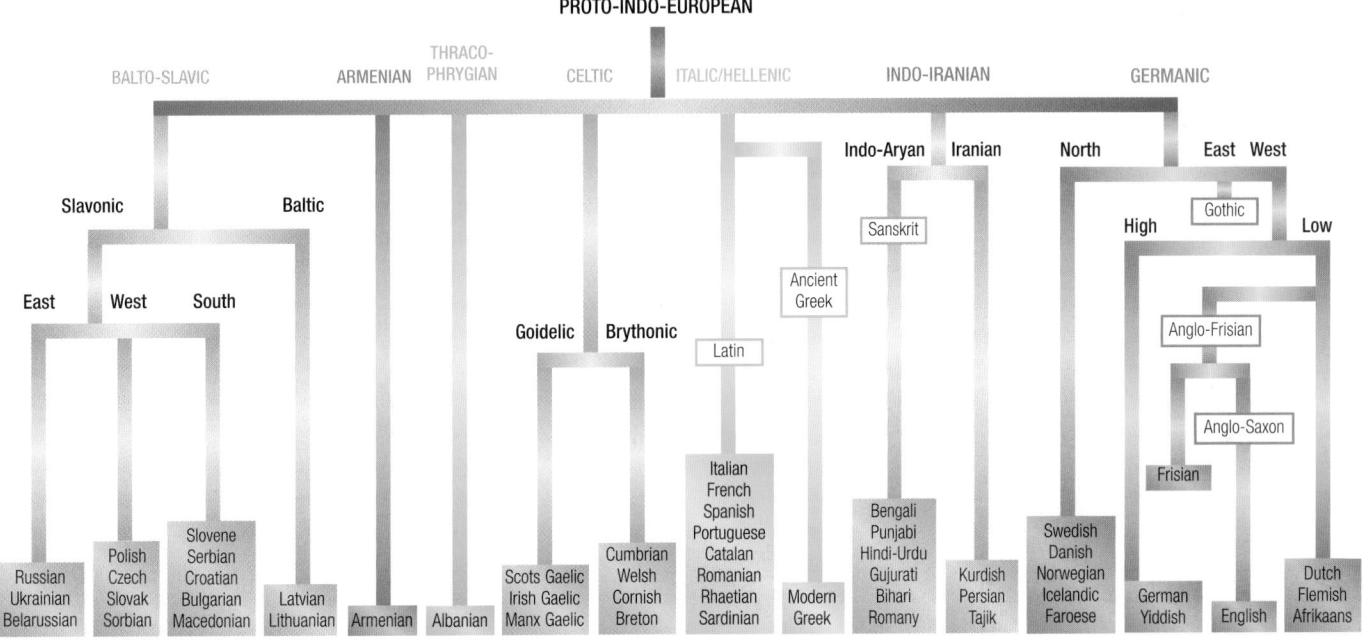

Major language speakers

Of the estimated 6000 languages spoken in the world today, only around 200 have more than 1 million speakers, and only 23 have more than 50 million. Mandarin is spoken by more people than any other language, but English is the main vehicle of international communication.

- **Mandarin Chinese** Used in northern China and by Chinese minorities across South-east Asia.
- **Spanish** Majority of speakers are in South and Central America.
- **English** The USA has the greatest number of native speakers. English is the main language of science and diplomacy.
- **Hindi** Used in India, and in Indian communities across the world.
- **Arabic** Used throughout the Arab world, and as the sacred language of the Koran.
- **Bengali** Used in Bengal and Bangladesh, and by Bengali communites worldwide.
- **Portuguese** Most speakers live in Brazil.
- **Russian** Widely used in the former republics of the USSR as well as in Russia.
- **Japanese** Majority of speakers are in Japan.
- **German** The official language in Germany, Austria, Liechtenstein and Switzerland, and widely used in Europe.
- **French** As well as its use in Europe, it is a major language in Canada, the Caribbean and many former French colonies in Africa and Asia.

KEY TERMS
- **Cognates** Words in different languages that have the same root.
- **Etymology** The origin and development of words.
- **Phonetics** Study of how sounds are articulated, perceived and combined.
- **Phonology** Study of the sound system of a language.
- **Semantics** Study of the meaning of words.
- **Semiotics** Study of human communication, particularly the use of signs and symbols.
- **Syntax** Study of the structure of phrases and sentences.

Chart data (No. of speakers, millions, as mother tongue): Mandarin Chinese 850, Spanish 332, English 330, Hindi 300, Arabic 200, Bengali 190, Portuguese 190, Russian 170, Japanese 125, German 100, French 72

see also
166-7 The prehistoric world
334-5 Writing

The oldest known writings are on clay discs from Mesopotamia, dating back to c.8000 BC. They are picture symbols, called pictograms, listing tallies of wine and oil, and reflect the commercial complexity of society in this area. Indeed, the invention of writing, allowing detailed records to be kept, was crucial to the growth of civilisation.

ASIA

Chinese pictograms

1500 BC The Chinese develop their own pictogram script, written in columns running from right to left. Originally simple pictograms, these develop into a vocabulary of about 4000 commonly used signs, known as characters.

Indus Valley pictograms

*c.*2500 BC Cities in the Indus Valley adapt Sumerian pictograms to create their own distinct writing system.

MIDDLE EAST

Aramaic

*c.*1000 BC A new alphabet develops in Aram (part of modern Syria). Aramaic script has no vowels, and reads from right to left. Part of the Old Testment is written in it.

Sabean

*c.*1000 BC The Sabean Arabs devise an alphabet, which spreads south into Africa.

Proto alphabet

Nabatean

*c.*1000 BC The Nabateans of northern Arabia create their own distinct alphabet.

3500 BC The Sumerians develop a pictogram system, which spreads via trade to Egypt and the Indus Valley civilisation in Pakistan.

2500 BC The Sumerians develop a system of signs with no apparent visual relation to objects. Written in wedge-shaped strokes, it is known as cuneiform, from the Latin *cuneus,* 'wedge'.

Sumerian pictograms | **Cuneiform**

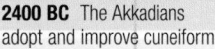

2400 BC The Akkadians adopt and improve cuneiform.

AFRICA

Egyptian hieroglyphs | **Hieratic script** | **Demotic script**

3400 BC Egyptian scribes improve pictograms to produce a script with around 2500 signs, or hieroglyphs, able to record whole sentences. This pictographic script remains in use for 36 centuries, longer than any other script has survived.

*c.*2000 BC Egyptian scribes develop the more abstract, free-flowing hieratic script.

*c.*600 BC Demotic, a faster, more abbreviated form of hieratic, is the most commonly used Egyptian script.

Phoenician script

*c.*1300 BC The Phoenicians create a 22-letter alphabet.

1500 BC The Mycenaean Greeks adapt cuneiform to their language.

Classical Greek

Etruscan

EUROPE

1750 BC Linear A ideograms are used on Crete.

1400 BC Linear B script is widely used in Minoan Greece.

1000 BC The Phoenician alphabet spreads to 'Dark Age' Greece, where writing had been forgotten after the collapse of Mycenae.

800 BC The Greeks add signs for the vowels to the Phoenician alphabet. They also change the direction of writing to read from left to right. Colonisation spreads Classical Greek script around the Mediterranean.

600 BC The Etruscans of central Italy adopt the Greek alphabet, which now has 24 letters: 17 consonants and seven vowels.

THE DEVELOPMENT OF WRITING

The earliest written messages were conveyed using pictures, from which sprang systems of pictograms, or abstract representations of objects. Gradually, these were combined into ideograms, symbols for ideas, with exact meaning often linked to context. By the start of the third millennium BC, the Sumerians were using a highly stylised system of ideograms, cuneiform script. Over the next thousand years this evolved to represent sounds in the spoken language. But its hundreds of signs made mastery a lengthy business, and its use faded. A more concise set of phonetic symbols, from which all modern alphabets stem, was not invented until the second millennium BC, by the Phoenicians.

| 3500 BC | 3000 BC | 2000 BC | 1500 BC | 1000 BC | 750 BC | 600 BC |

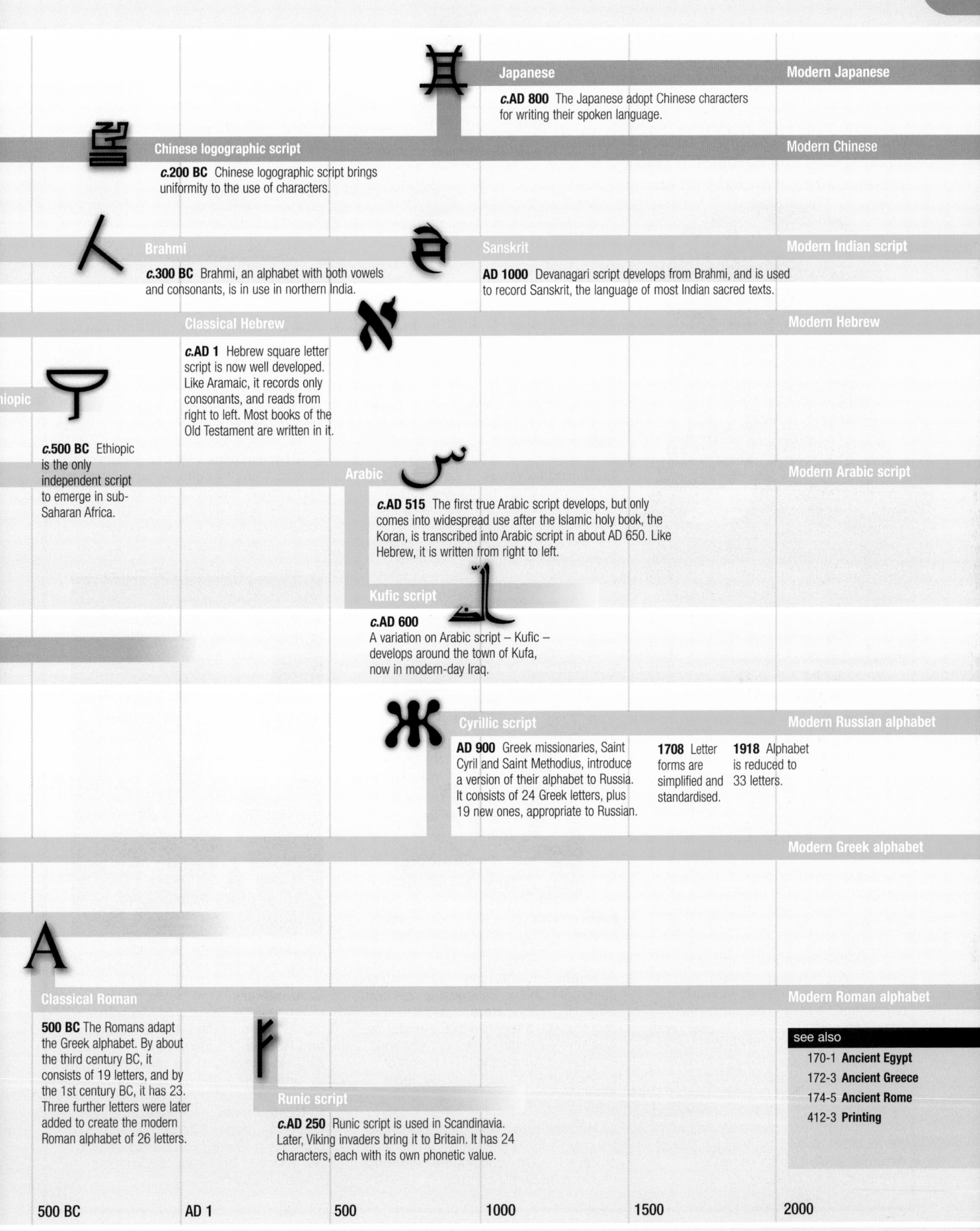

Japanese

Modern Japanese

*c.*AD 800 The Japanese adopt Chinese characters for writing their spoken language.

Chinese logographic script

Modern Chinese

*c.*200 BC Chinese logographic script brings uniformity to the use of characters.

Brahmi

Sanskrit

Modern Indian script

*c.*300 BC Brahmi, an alphabet with both vowels and consonants, is in use in northern India.

AD 1000 Devanagari script develops from Brahmi, and is used to record Sanskrit, the language of most Indian sacred texts.

Classical Hebrew

Modern Hebrew

*c.*AD 1 Hebrew square letter script is now well developed. Like Aramaic, it records only consonants, and reads from right to left. Most books of the Old Testament are written in it.

hiopic

*c.*500 BC Ethiopic is the only independent script to emerge in sub-Saharan Africa.

Arabic

Modern Arabic script

*c.*AD 515 The first true Arabic script develops, but only comes into widespread use after the Islamic holy book, the Koran, is transcribed into Arabic script in about AD 650. Like Hebrew, it is written from right to left.

Kufic script

*c.*AD 600
A variation on Arabic script – Kufic – develops around the town of Kufa, now in modern-day Iraq.

Cyrillic script

Modern Russian alphabet

AD 900 Greek missionaries, Saint Cyril and Saint Methodius, introduce a version of their alphabet to Russia. It consists of 24 Greek letters, plus 19 new ones, appropriate to Russian.

1708 Letter forms are simplified and standardised.

1918 Alphabet is reduced to 33 letters.

Modern Greek alphabet

Classical Roman

Modern Roman alphabet

500 BC The Romans adapt the Greek alphabet. By about the third century BC, it consists of 19 letters, and by the 1st century BC, it has 23. Three further letters were later added to create the modern Roman alphabet of 26 letters.

Runic script

*c.*AD 250 Runic script is used in Scandinavia. Later, Viking invaders bring it to Britain. It has 24 characters, each with its own phonetic value.

see also
170-1 **Ancient Egypt**
172-3 **Ancient Greece**
174-5 **Ancient Rome**
412-3 **Printing**

| 500 BC | AD 1 | 500 | 1000 | 1500 | 2000 |

Greek mythology focuses primarily on the activities of 12 'sky gods', believed to live on top of Mount Olympus, the country's highest mountain. Outside this official pantheon, many Greeks continued worshipping older deities. When the Romans conquered Greece, in the 2nd century BC, they adopted its gods wholesale, giving them Latin names.

The Greek pantheon
The top line of gods in the diagram are brothers and sisters. Zeus, the supreme god, fathered lesser deities with his sister and consort, Hera, and with other goddesses and mortals.

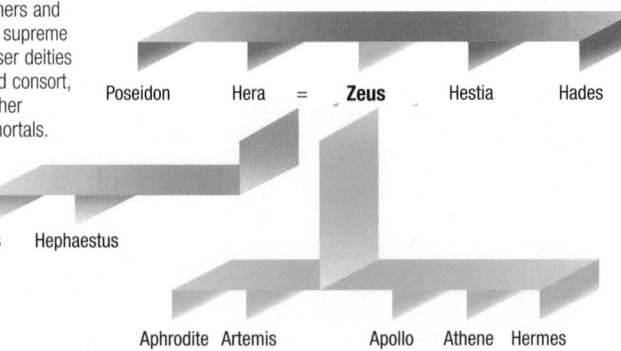

Poseidon   Hera = **Zeus**   Hestia   Hades

Ares   Hephaestus

Aphrodite Artemis   Apollo   Athene Hermes

THE TWELVE OLYMPIANS

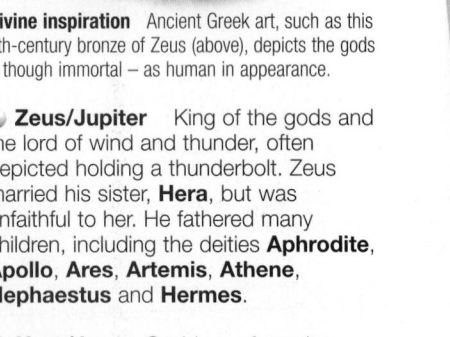

Divine inspiration Ancient Greek art, such as this 5th-century bronze of Zeus (above), depicts the gods – though immortal – as human in appearance.

⚪ **Zeus/Jupiter** King of the gods and the lord of wind and thunder, often depicted holding a thunderbolt. Zeus married his sister, **Hera**, but was unfaithful to her. He fathered many children, including the deities **Aphrodite, Apollo, Ares, Artemis, Athene, Hephaestus** and **Hermes**.

⚪ **Hera/Juno** Goddess of marriage and motherhood. Hera was jealous of her husband **Zeus**' many lovers, and devised ways to harm them and their offspring.

⚪ **Poseidon/Neptune** Ruler of the seas, usually depicted holding a trident, often with the gold chariot and white horses that he kept in his underwater palace. Poseidon was hot-tempered and constantly in conflict with his brother **Zeus**. His rages were thought to make the earth shake, causing earthquakes.

⚪ **Apollo** God of medicine, poetry and science, who could charm animals with the music of his lyre. He was the twin of **Artemis**, and was also known as **Phoebus**, 'the shining one'.

⚪ **Athene/Minerva** Goddess of wisdom and patron of architects and sculptors. Athene was born fully formed from **Zeus**' forehead. She was a warrior goddess, and is often depicted with a spear and shield.

⚪ **Aphrodite/Venus** Goddess of love, born from the foam in the sea off the island of Cyprus. Aphrodite married **Hephaestus** but deceived him with Ares, Hermes and others. Her retinue included **Eros/Cupid** and the three **Graces**.

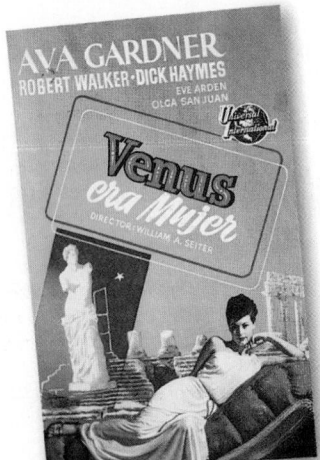

Screen goddess In the 20th century, the Roman deity Venus is still a symbol of love and beauty.

⚪ **Hephaestus/Vulcan** Blacksmith and patron of industry. Hephaestus was born lame. His mother, **Hera**, found him so ugly that she threw him to Earth, but he was later reinstated on Mount Olympus. He married **Aphrodite**. The Romans believed that his chief forge lay under Mount Etna in Sicily.

⚪ **Hades/Pluto** Ruler of the realm of the dead – the underworld – and brother of **Zeus**. Hades abducted **Persephone**, his niece, to be his consort.

⚪ **Hermes/Mercury** Quick-witted 'messenger god', son of **Zeus** by the nymph **Maia**. Hermes is often depicted with winged sandals, taking messages from Heaven to Earth.

⚪ **Artemis/Diana** Virginal goddess of hunting, twin of **Apollo**. Artemis punished the mortal **Actaeon** for spying on her while she was bathing by changing him into a stag, so that his own hounds turned upon him.

The huntress Artemis fiercely protected her chastity, and punished suitors for approaching her.

⚪ **Ares/Mars** God of war, highly revered by the Romans as Mars. They regarded him as the father of **Romulus and Remus**, the founders of Rome. In early Roman religion, he was worshipped by farmers as a god of vegetation.

⚪ **Hestia/Vesta** Goddess of hearth and home, sister of **Zeus**. Hestia was chaste and retiring. The sacred flame in her temple in Rome was regarded as Rome's 'hearth'.

OTHER IMMORTALS

Besides the Olympians, there were countless minor deities, many of whom were believed to share the Earth with man.

Dionysus/Bacchus God of theatre, wine and ecstasy; son of **Zeus** by **Semele**, princess of Thebes. Dionysus grew up wild on Mount Nysa, where he learnt to make wine. He was the focus of a major cult. Drunken female devotees were known as the **bacchantes**.

Pan/Faunus or Silvanus Patron of shepherds and god of the woods. Pan is depicted with horns and goat's legs, playing reed pipes. He was fond of chasing nymphs such as **Syrinx**, who changed into a reed to escape him.

Prometheus and the Titans The 14 Titan deities were deposed by **the Olympians**. When they challenged the new order, **Zeus** imprisoned them deep in the Earth. Prometheus alone remained loyal, so was admitted to Olympus. But he stole fire from the gods and gave it to humans. As punishment, he was chained to a rock, where an eagle gnawed his perpetually renewed liver.

Demeter/ Ceres Goddess of agriculture and fertility. When her daughter, **Persephone**, was abducted by **Hades**, Demeter stopped all crops from growing until Hades promised to return her. He agreed, provided Persephone spent four months of the year with him in the underworld. These became the winter, when the Earth remains barren.

Satyrs Half-men, half-goats. Satyrs were fertility spirits who spent their time chasing nymphs through the forest and getting drunk.

Nymphs Beautiful spirits of the air, Earth, trees and water, often loved by the gods. One nymph, **Echo**, fell in love with a mortal, **Narcissus**, who was besotted only by his own reflection.

Muses Nine goddesses of creative inspiration who accompanied **Apollo**.

Centaurs Half-men, half-horses. Centaurs were thought to possess both animal brutishness and human wisdom.

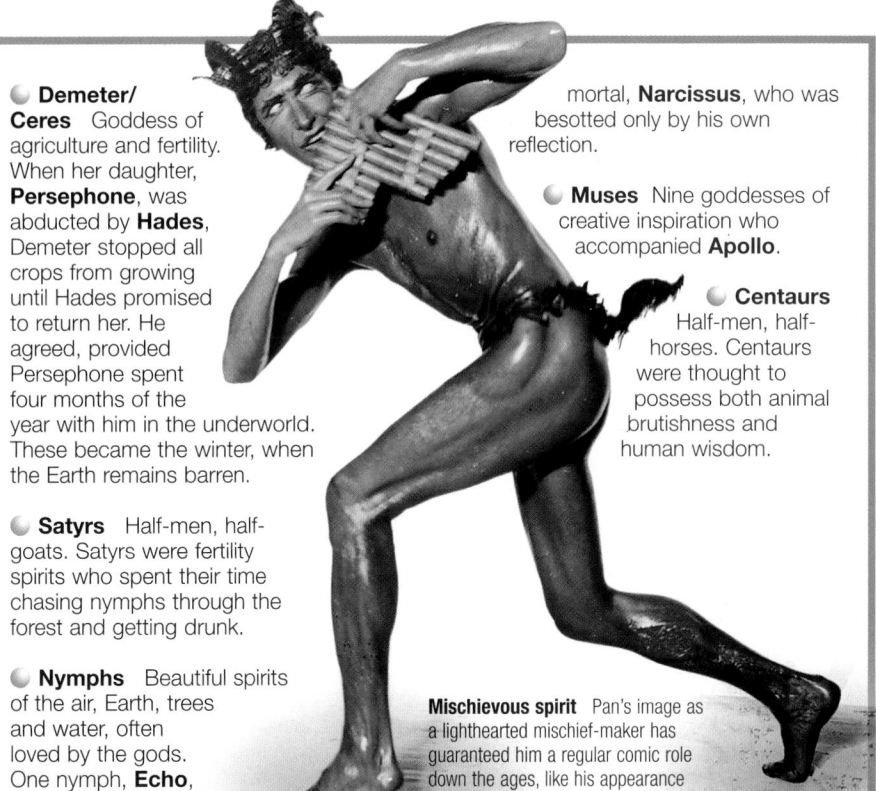

Mischievous spirit Pan's image as a lighthearted mischief-maker has guaranteed him a regular comic role down the ages, like his appearance (above) in the 1926 film, *The Magician*.

HEROES AND HEROINES

Heroes, though often half-divine in ancestry and superhuman in powers, were mortal.

Herakles/Hercules Son of **Zeus** by **Alcmene**, the Queen of Thebes. He was noted for his great strength. Driven mad by the jealous **Hera**, he killed his family, and to atone for this, undertook **12 labours**. These included capturing the man-eating horses of **Diomedes**, King of Argos, cleansing the **Augean stables**, home to 3000 oxen, and seizing **Cerberus**, the three-headed dog that guarded the underworld. He died from wearing a poisonous tunic made by the centaur **Nessus**. After his death, Zeus made him into a god.

Theseus and Ariadne Theseus, son of the Athenian king **Aegeus**, volunteered to be one of seven youths and maidens sent to Crete as an annual tribute to the **Minotaur**, a half-bull, half-human monster. Helped by the Cretan princess, Ariadne, Theseus entered the Minotaur's labyrinth and slew the beast. He then fled with Ariadne, but later abandoned her on Naxos, where **Dionysus** comforted her.

Favoured by the gods
Slaying the Minotaur (right) gave Theseus heroic status.

Jason and the Argonauts Given the task of obtaining the famed **Golden Fleece**, Jason set sail on his quest with a crew of heroes, including **Theseus**. At Colchis, Jason's destination, the king promised to surrender the Fleece if Jason could plough with wild bulls and sow with dragon's teeth. As he did so, armed men sprang from the furrows to attack him, but he tricked them into fighting each other, winning his prize.

Aeneas Son of **Aphrodite** and the Trojan **Anchises**. Aeneas escaped from the sacking of Troy (see right), and after many adventures, landed in Italy. There he married a princess, **Lavinia**, and built the city of **Lavinium**. Many noble Romans claimed him as their ancestor.

Romulus and Remus Twin sons of **Mars**. Romulus and Remus were suckled by a **she-wolf**. Legend states that they founded **Rome** in 753 BC. But the brothers quarrelled. In a rage, Romulus killed his brother, and became the city's first king.

The Trojan Horse

When the Greek queen, **Helen**, was abducted by the Trojan prince, **Paris**, Greece's armies assembled to avenge the insult. War raged for ten years, but the Greeks failed to capture the city of **Troy**. Eventually, the Trojans saw the Greeks sail away, leaving behind a huge **wooden horse**, apparently to placate the gods. Rejoicing, they dragged it inside their walls. That night, Greek soldiers hiding in the horse's wooden belly, emerged to open the gates for their returning army, who sacked the city.

see also
172-3 **Ancient Greece**
174-5 **Ancient Rome**
354-5 **Western art**
384-5 **Western literature**

All cultures have a store of myths and legends relating to religious beliefs, but the uneven spread of methods of recording them, and the development of later religions, has meant that some mythologies are much better known today than others. In Europe, the German-Scandinavian and Celtic mythologies have survived alongside the well-documented stories of the Greeks and Romans. In the Americas, the related stories of the Aztecs and the Maya gods remain among the best known.

NORSE/TEUTONIC MYTHOLOGY

The Germanic and Norse peoples of the 5th-9th centuries had a common mythology. It has survived mainly in Norse sagas, because the Vikings who created them retained their pagan beliefs for longer than did their German neighbours. Where German and Norse names differ, the Norse name is given first.

● **Odin/Wotan**   Chief of the **Vanir**, the Norse land and water gods, and creator of the world, Odin was the god of wisdom, war, art and culture. He was also a law-giver. Those who died heroically in battle would be welcomed by him to **Valhalla**, the great hall of immortality, or the feasting hall of **Asgard**, the home of the gods. Odin could change shape at will, but was often depicted as a one-eyed wanderer in wide-brimmed hat and cloak.

● **Thor/Donar**   God of thunder, fertility and, to some extent, war, the hot-tempered but dull-witted Thor is usually depicted smashing his opponents with his magic hammer, known as **Mjollnir**. Vikings often wore small hammers as amulets, invoking Thor's protection and help in defeating enemies in battle.

● **Loki**   A malevolent joker-god who is found only in Norse myth, Loki was a trickster, fraud and thief. He was regarded as the creator of chaos.

● **Baldur**   The son of **Odin** and **Frigga**, Baldur was god of peace and light. Frigga made all things on Earth promise never to harm him, but overlooked the mistletoe

plant. The evil **Loki** gave a spear made of this to the blind god, **Holdur**, who was duped into hurling it at Baldur, killing him. His death signalled the coming of **Ragnarok**.

● **Freia**   The chief goddess among the Vanir, Freia (Lady) is associated with fertility and love. She is the twin sister, or female aspect, of the god **Frey**, bringer of peace and abundance.

● **Frigga**   The Queen of Heaven and wife of Odin, Frigga was, like **Freia**, associated with childbearing and marriage. She is the chief goddess of the Norse sky gods, known as the **Aesir**.

Hanna Ralph

Mythic opera   German composer Wagner set Norse myths to music. Odin's daughter, Brunhild, appears in his *Der Ring Des Nibelungen* (above).

● **The Valkyries**   Gold-haired warrior maidens with shining armour, the Valkyries served **Odin**. Some myths describe the Valkyries as supernatural, others suggest their mortality. They rode over land and sea to give victory to heroes chosen by Odin, and took the fallen to **Valhalla**.

● **Asgard**   The heavenly home of the gods, built by giants and joined to Earth by a bridge called **Byfrost**, which is identified with rainbows or the Milky Way.

● **Ragnarok**   The name given to the final apocalypse, or 'Twilight of the gods', in which all creation, including the gods, would perish. A new world order would then arise, which in later descriptions of Ragnarok includes a single deity. This probably represents a blending into Norse myth of Christianity, which finally replaced the pagan religion in the 11th century.

● **Sigurd/Siegfried**   A descendant of **Odin**, Sigurd was persuaded by the smith **Regin** to kill the dragon **Fafnir** and win his hoard of gold. By bathing in the dragon's blood, Sigurd became invulnerable in all but one spot.

● **Beowulf**   The morality and monster-slaying of the 8th-century saga of Beowulf draws on Norse myth. The hero kills the monster **Grendel**, which has been attacking Denmark's royal court. He becomes king of the **Geats**, and dies defending his people against a dragon.

In pursuit of valour   Some Valkyries were said to have the power to kill unworthy warriors and protect those they favoured. This 1865 painting depicts a Valkyrie riding to a battlefield.

CELTIC GODS AND LEGENDS

The Celts inhabited much of western Europe before the great Germanic migrations of 200 BC to AD 400. Elements of their culture have survived in Scotland, Wales, Cornwall and Brittany, but Ireland is the best source of Celtic myths as the Irish were never conquered by Rome, and became Christians later than other Celts.

🔵 **Tuatha dé Danaan** The 'Children of the goddess **Danu**' arrived in Ireland on a magic cloud and drove out the previous inhabitants, the **Fir Bolg**. They had four magic weapons: the **Stone of Destiny** (Lia Fail), which shrieked if a true king touched it; the **spear of Lug**; the **sword of Nuadu**; and a magic inexhaustible cauldron called **Dagda**. After being driven out by invaders called **'Milesians'**, they retired underground and became the **'Little People'**, the fairies.

🔵 **Cuchulainn** The leading figure in the epic *Tain bo Cuilagne* (the Cattle Raid of Cooley), Cuchulainn, son of the god **Lug**, was a superhuman warrior. At five, he was able to fight off 150 other boys who were attacking him with spears. His fury in battle was said to be so great that it could make water boil. But he was a tragic figure. He killed his son **Conloach** in error, and lost his powers by being tricked into eating dog, a taboo meat.

🔵 **Tir nan Og** An island of the dead in the far west or underworld, Tir nan Og was a blessed place of supreme happiness to which the gods invited select heroes. It has been identified with **Avalon**, 'the island of apples', which was the final resting place of King **Arthur**.

🔵 **Arthur** The legend of Arthur was probably based on the life of an actual Romano-British leader. The son of King **Uther**

Arthurian romance The legend of Arthur inspired this stained-glass figure of Sir Lancelot by artist William Morris.

Pendragon, he was educated by **Merlin**, and declared king after pulling the magic sword **Excalibur** from its stone. He held court in splendour at Camelot, from where his knights set out on the quest for the **Holy Grail**. His best friend, **Lancelot**, fell in love with his wife, **Guinevere**, and in his old age, his son **Mordred** led a rebellion against him. Arthur crushed it, but was fatally wounded and ferried off to **Avalon**, where the 'once and future king' was said to have been healed, and from where he will one day return.

🔵 **Merlin (Myrddin)** A wise magician, Merlin was credited with helping to build Stonehenge. In spite of his wisdom, he fell for the enchantress **Nimue**, who imprisoned him inside a crystal spiral.

AZTEC/MAYA GODS AND LEGENDS

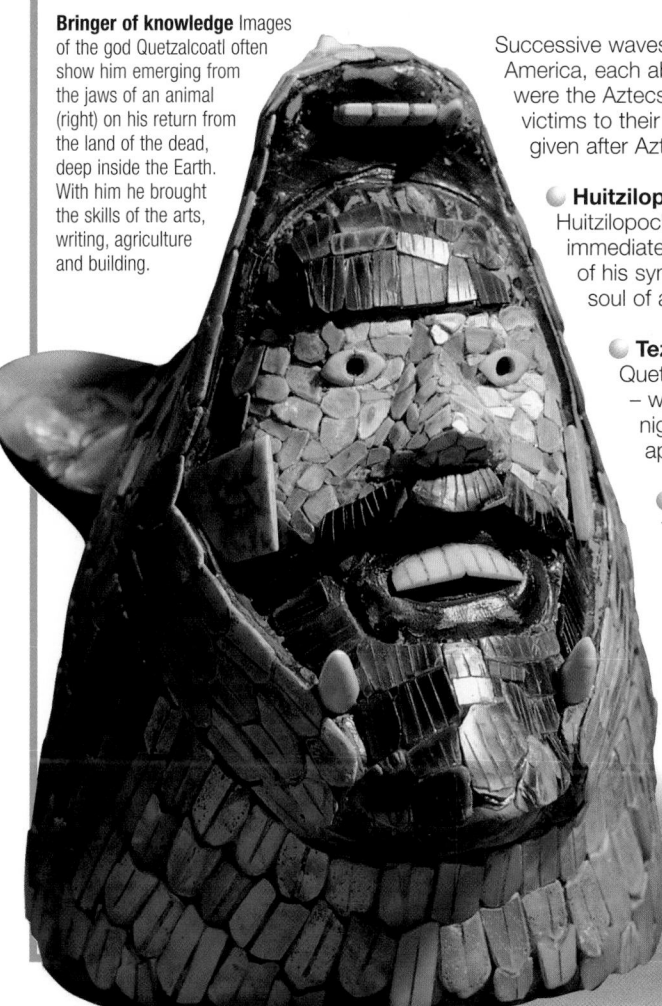

Bringer of knowledge Images of the god Quetzalcoatl often show him emerging from the jaws of an animal (right) on his return from the land of the dead, deep inside the Earth. With him he brought the skills of the arts, writing, agriculture and building.

Successive waves of invaders occupied Mexico and Central America, each absorbing earlier myths. Last and bloodiest were the Aztecs, who sacrificed tens of thousands of victims to their gods. Maya names, where different, are given after Aztec versions.

🔵 **Huitzilopochtli** A ferocious Aztec war god, Huitzilopochtli was born dressed in full armour, and immediately killed his 400 brothers and sisters. One of his symbols was the butterfly, regarded as the soul of a dead warrior.

🔵 **Tezcatlipoca** Until he was deposed by Quetzalcoatl, Tezcatlipoca – the 'Smoking Mirror' – was the sun-god. He then became god of the night and patron of witches and thieves, appearing as a jaguar or flying shadow.

🔵 **Quetzalcoatl/Kukulcàn** Quetzalcoatl – the 'Plumed Serpent' – was the god of life, sun-god and saviour. Driven out by Tezcatlipoca's intrigues, he sailed east, promising to return. Many Aztecs thought this was happening when the Spaniards under Cortés arrived in Mexico in 1519.

🔵 **Tlaloc/Chac** God of mountains, rain and springs, Tlaloc lived with his wife **Chalchiuihtlicue**, goddess of childbirth. In return for sending rain, he demanded the sacrifice of babies, which were cooked and eaten by his priests.

Days of the week

The names of weekdays have their roots in Norse and Roman myth.

Monday Norse 'moon day', Latin *lunae dies* – giving *lundi* in French.

Tuesday The day of Tiu or Tyr, a Norse war god. Tyr's Roman form, Mars, is the root of the the French *mardi*.

Wednesday Wotan's day. The Roman's 'day of Mercury' gives the French *mercredi*.

Thursday The day of Thor, or Donar, the root of Germany's *Donnerstag*. Rome's 'day of Jupiter', which became France's *jeudi*.

Friday Frigga's day. Her Roman equivalent, Venus, is the root of *vendredi* in French.

Saturday Roman Saturn's day.

Sunday The pagan day of the Sun.

see also
176-7 **Making of Europe**
190-1 **Ancient America**
336-7 **Greek/Roman myths**
384-5 **Western literature**

Religion is one of mankind's oldest and most distinctive characteristics. Archaeologists have discovered grave goods, dating back 60 000 years, which must have been intended for use in an afterlife, indicating a religious belief of which no other trace survives. Many cultures have lacked cities or literacy or even the wheel, but none has existed for long without some form of religion.

A family tree of religions

Most of the world's major religions can be placed in family groups, because they share common roots. For example, Judaism, Christianity and Islam, although now three very distinctive faiths, stem from the beliefs and rituals of people that lived in the ancient civilisations of the Middle East. Similarly, Buddhism and Jainism both spring from the teachings of men steeped in the tradition of Hinduism.

Some faiths, such as Confucianism, Taoism and Shintoism, have developed independently but show a great range of similarities, probably because they are all closely linked to the folklore of South-east Asia. All three are usually practised alongside Buddhism in their respective countries of origin.

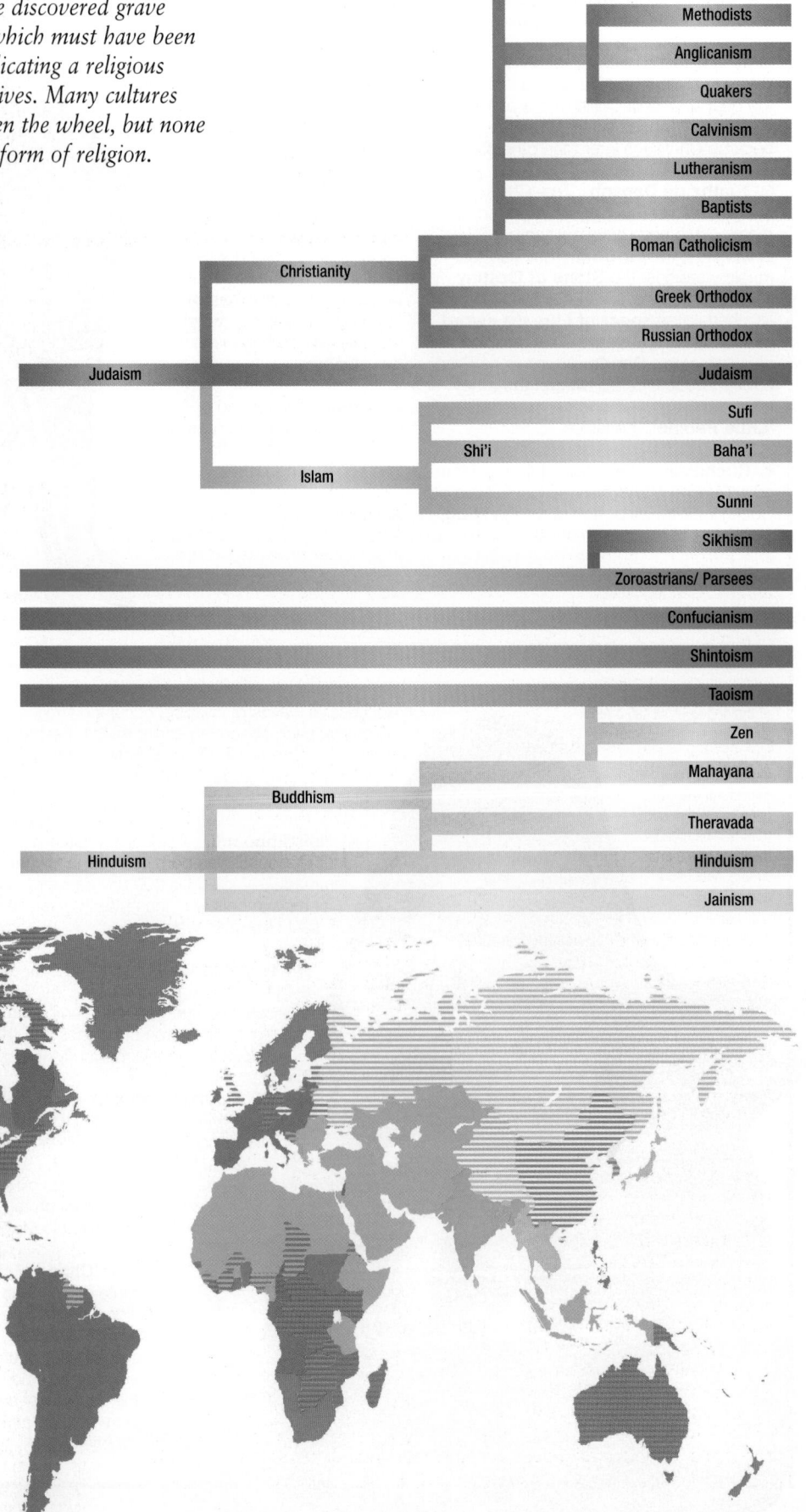

Distribution of the world's major religions

- Roman Catholicism
- Protestantism
- Orthodox Christianity
- Islam
- Hinduism
- Traditional beliefs
- Buddhism
- Judaism
- ☐ Others

JUDAISM

First of the great monotheistic religions (worshipping one God), Judaism emerged as a distinctive faith under Moses, who is believed to have received the **Ten Commandments** from God on Mount Sinai around 1200 BC. He united the Jewish people, helping his successor, Joshua, to conquer the promised land of Canaan, which the Jews renamed **Israel**. Revolt against Roman rule ended with the destruction of the Temple in Jerusalem in AD 70, and Judaism was spread around the globe by exiles.

Key beliefs Jews view the created world as essentially good, and see in human history God's divine plan.

Worship Devout Jews attend the synagogue three times a day.
🌑 In the morning and evening, they recite the basic affirmation of Judaism, the **Shema**, from in the Torah (see below).
🌑 The **Sabbath**, or day of rest, is the focal point of the week. It begins at sunset on Friday, when candles are lit, followed by prayers and a family meal.

Holy books The main holy book, the **Torah**, consists of the first five books of the Hebrew Bible, also given to Moses on Mount Sinai. The basic laws of Jewish life are found in the Torah. A collection of scholarly commentaries on these, called the **Talmud**, is also considered sacred.

God's law The Torah, hand copied onto parchment scrolls, is read out at the synagogue. No human imagery appears on the richly decorated casing, in obedience to the law not to make graven imagery.

see also
178-9 **Christianity**
196-7 **Clash of faiths**
344-7 **Western thought**
418-9 **Food**

CHRISTIANITY

Jesus Christ (c.6 BC– AD 30), the founder of the religion that bears his name, was a Jew. His controversial teachings, along with his claim to speak with God's authority, brought him into conflict with the Jewish establishment. Eventually he was arrested and crucified in Jerusalem. After the Emperor Constantine converted to Christianity in 311, it became the official faith of the Roman Empire. Followers have taken its message to all corners of the globe, so that today, Christianity is the most widespread monotheistic religion (see map, left).

Roman Catholicism Roman Catholics acknowledge the authority of the pope, who is seen as being in direct succession to St Peter, the first Bishop of Rome.

Eastern or Orthodox Church Challenges to the authority of the pope in Rome by the Orthodox Church, based in Constantinople, culminated in it breaking away in the Great Schism of 1054. Orthodoxy puts great emphasis on tradition, with icons playing a major role in worship. An icon is seen as a window to God, bringing the worshipper into the 'real' presence of the subject depicted.

Protestantism In the 16th century, the authority of the Roman Catholic Church was challenged, in a movement that became known as the **Reformation**.
Lutheranism dates from 1517, when Martin Luther attacked corruption in the Roman Catholic Church in Germany. Lutheranism stresses a personal relationship with God, and study of the Bible as the route to salvation.
Protestantism took a more puritanical, authoritarian form in **Calvinism**, founded by John Calvin the 1540s. Followers believe their salvation is entirely in the hands of an all-knowing, all-powerful God.

Anglicanism, a flexible form of Protestantism, was finalised by the Elizabethan Settlement in England in 1559. It spread around the world with English-speaking peoples.
Anabaptist sects appeared in Germany in the early 16th century. They baptised only adults, as do their successors, the **Baptists**. In the 17th century, the **Quakers** sought a more direct path to God by dispensing with churches, liturgy and clergy. **Methodists** did not take such extreme measures when they split from the Church of England in 1729, but services were simplified to give the laity a bigger role.

Key beliefs All Christians believe in the divinity of Jesus Christ, as the son of the three-in-one (triune) God. The third element in **the holy Trinity** is the Holy Spirit.
🌑 By his **crucifixion and resurrection**, Christ has shown humanity the path to eternal life.
🌑 Most Christians believe that Christ will one day return to Earth for **the Last Judgment**, to judge the living and the dead.

Worship The chief ritual, the **Eucharist** – also called the **Mass** (Roman Catholic) or **Holy Communion** (Anglican) – commemorates Jesus's Last Supper. While Orthodox and Roman Catholic Christians believe that the bread in the Mass transforms into the 'real presence' of Christ's body, Protestants regard this as a symbolic act.

Atonement To Christians, Christ's death – depicted right on an altarpiece by Rogier van der Weyden (1399-1464) – is his payment for the sins of man. By suffering, he opened up the path to salvation for all.

Holy books All Christians accept the Bible's **Old and New Testaments**, the latter recording Christ's life.
Catholics and Orthodox Christians also accept the **teachings of the early Church Fathers**, such as saints Jerome and Augustine, but Protestants usually regard the Bible as the only holy script.

ISLAM

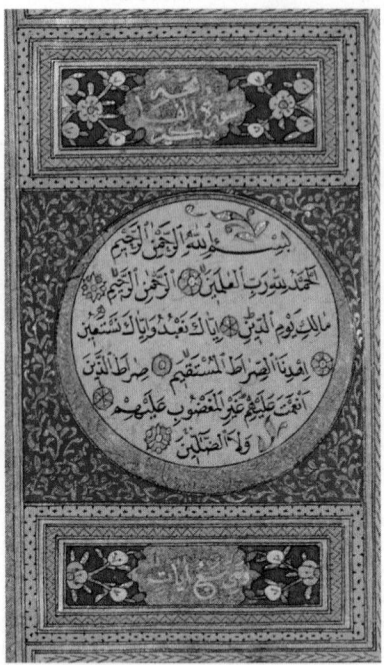

Act of devotion Muslim calligraphers produce copies of the Koran as a personal expression of faith.

Islam, meaning 'submission to God', dates from AD 622, when the Prophet Muhammad fled from persecution in Mecca, (now in Saudi Arabia) to Medina, an event known as the **Hegira**. By the time of his death in 632, all Arabia had embraced the new religion. A century later, it had spread into Spain and Central Asia. Today, about 20 per cent of the world is Muslim, and the faith is spreading faster than any other.

Islam divides into two branches: 80 per cent of Muslims are **Sunni**; the minority are **Shia**. They differ in opinion over the correct line of descent from the Prophet.

Key beliefs Muslims regard this world as good, and see or feel God's presence everywhere. However, they also view it only as a preparation for the next.
🌙 All Muslims believe in the oneness and omnipotence of God (**Allah**).
🌙 Abraham, Moses and Jesus are Muhammad's divinely inspired precursors. Muslims reject Christ's divinity – like the other prophets, he is human. Muhammad is the final and greatest prophet.

Worship Islamic observance is based on performance of the **Five Pillars**, or duties:
🌙 At least once in life, a Muslim must recite with complete conviction and understanding the profession of the faith: 'There is no God but Allah, and Muhammad is His Prophet.'
🌙 Muslims must pray five times a day: at dawn, noon, mid afternoon, sunset and bedtime. They prostrate themselves facing Mecca, the site of the Prophet's tomb.
🌙 Muslims should give alms – 2.5 per cent of all their possessions – each year to the poor and needy.
🌙 Muslims should observe the fast of **Ramadan**, the holy month, commemorating the Hegira. No food, drink or smoke may pass their lips between dawn and sunset.
🌙 Every Muslim who can should make a pilgrimage to Mecca at least once.

Holy book The **Koran** is believed to be the word of God revealed to the Prophet Muhammad. It contains 114 chapters (**suras**) giving detailed rules on every aspect of human life.

HINDUISM

Hinduism originated in northern India some 4000 years ago, and by the 11th century AD had replaced Buddhism as the dominant religion in India.

Key beliefs Behind the countless Hindu gods and goddesses lies **Brahman**, the supreme reality – infinite, impersonal, uncreated, unnameable. Buried beneath layers of egotism at the core of every human lies the divine spark, **Atman**.
🌙 The main Hindu gods – worshipped as manifestations of Brahman – are Brahma the Creator, Vishnu the Preserver and Shiva the Destroyer, who form the **Hindu trinity**, and Kali, goddess of death.
🌙 The Hindu's goal is to unite Atman with Brahman by escaping the endless cycle of life, death and rebirth (**samsara**) through spiritual liberation (**moksha**). This is obtained by different paths, or **yogas**: spiritual knowledge through meditation (jnana yoga); the yoga of devotion to a particular god (bhakti yoga); and the yoga of good work (karma yoga).
🌙 The Universe, both human and non-human, is governed by the laws of action (**karma**). Every action has its effect, good or bad, in this life or the next.
🌙 Each person has an eternal soul that can be reborn millions of times, and in millions of forms (**reincarnation**).

Worship This takes three forms:
🌙 Daily worship, or **puja**, is carried out at home, at a shrine decorated with pictures of the gods.
🌙 Worship also takes place in temples, led by a priest, or **brahmin**.
🌙 Hindus make pilgrimages to sacred sites, such as the holy city of Varanasi (Benares) on the Ganges, where many go to bathe in the sacred waters – or to die.

Holy books Hinduism has a variety of books considered holy: a collection of hymns, the **Vedas**; epic poems, the **Ramayana** and the **Mahabharata**, which includes the Bhagavad-Gita, a long account of Krishna, god of love; and philosophical writings, such as the **Upanishads**.

Elephant god Ganesh, one of the most popular Hindu gods, is revered as the Lord of Learning and Remover of Obstacles. His father, Shiva, cut off his head in error, then offered to replace it with the head of the first living thing he saw, which was an elephant.

BUDDHISM

Gautama, the Buddha or Enlightened One, was born about 560 BC in lowland Nepal. Breaking with his native Hindu tradition, he rejected the extremes of both asceticism and sensuality for the **Middle Way**, based on the Four Noble Truths (see below). Buddhism spread across India, and as far as Japan and Indonesia.

Early in its history, Buddhism split into Theravada and Mahayana Buddhism:

Theravada Buddhism Theravada, the 'Teaching of the Elders' (also known as Hinayana, the 'Lesser Vehicle'), is dominant in Sri Lanka and South-east Asia. It claims to be closest to the Buddha's original teachings and stresses the importance of meditation.

Mahayana Buddhism Mahayana, the 'Greater Vehicle', found in China, Tibet, Korea and Japan, stresses devotion and compassion. It divides into distinct schools:

Tibetan Buddhism, or Lamaism, has elaborate rituals, scriptures and monastic orders. It is led by the Dalai Lama.

Zen or **Ch'an Buddhism** originated in China and Japan. Followers work towards enlightenment through meditation.

Pure Land Buddhism also originated in China and Japan. Devotees with true faith are believed to be reborn in paradise – the Pure Land or Realm.

Key beliefs Buddhism has no personal god. The Boddhisattvas of Mahayana Buddhism resemble Catholic saints or Hindu gods, effectively being worshipped.
🙂 **Boddhisattvas** are Buddhas – of which there are many – who have turned back to the world on the cusp of enlightenment, in order to help others.
🙂 Gautama preached '**Four Noble Truths**', which are the basis of Buddhism:
1 All existence is suffering, or **dukkha** – meaning everything wrong with life, not just pain but every frustration and grief.
2 The cause of suffering is craving, or wrong desire (**tanha**).
3 Ending craving leads to enlightenment.
4 The best way to enlightenment is the **Noble Eightfold Path**.

The Noble Eightfold Path consists of Right Views; Right Intentions; Right Speech; Right Conduct, including kindness; Right Livelihood (arms or drug-dealing are unacceptable); Right Effort, meaning willing one's way; Right Mindfulness, meaning understanding of life and oneself; and Right Contemplation, including meditation.

Other aspects of Buddhist belief are:
🙂 Buddhists do not believe in an immortal soul, but in no soul (**anatta**); the idea of a separate 'self' is illusory.
🙂 Buddhists seek **nirvana** – the escape from the cycle of death and rebirth (**samsara**) by the snuffing out of individual existence and its desires and weaknesses.
🙂 Gautama attained nirvana; others can and should follow his example.
🙂 All Buddhists accept **five basic principles of life**: do not kill (Buddhists are vegetarian); do not steal; do not lie; be chaste; do not take intoxicants.

Holy books Zen Buddhists reject all writing in favour of direct experience, but other forms of Buddhism have important scriptures.

The main text of Theravada Buddhism is the three-part **Pali Canon**, written 2000 years ago in the ancient Pali language of northern India. Mahayana Buddhism has many sacred documents in different languages, the two main ones being the **Chinese Canon** and the **Tibetan Canon**. Tibetan Buddhists study texts such as the **Lotus Sutra**.

Setting an example Images of the Buddha take on many forms. The elegant, reclining Buddha is from Bangkok in Thailand. Such representations serve as inspiration, for the aim of all Buddhists is to strive to become an enlightened one, or a buddha, oneself.

SIKHISM

Sikhism originated in the 15th century AD amid conflicts between Muslims and Hindus in northern India. Offering a simple monotheism, it was intended as a peaceful middle way by its founder, Guru Nanak (1469-1539). But persecution by Muslims in the 17th century led to increasing militancy among the Sikhs.

Key beliefs Sikhs strive for union with God (**Satguru**) by adoring the Holy Name, through hard work and by being of service to others (**seva**), especially their own family.
🙂 Sikhs believe in equality, and give 10 per cent of their income to the poor.
🙂 There are no castes among the Sikhs, and men and women eat and work together.
🙂 Sikhs should rise early, bathe and then meditate on God, before going about their work.
🙂 Sikhs avoid all intoxicants, including tobacco.
🙂 Sikh men do not cut their hair, but wear it concealed under a turban, and are bearded. A dagger is carried on ceremonial occasions.
🙂 All meat has to be killed in accordance with the **Jhatka law** of the 'clean strike'.

TAOISM

Taoism, the closest thing to a native religion in China, originally had no gods, temples or priests; it was essentially a philosophical system rather than a religion. It emphasised acceptance, in the form of a yielding and joyful attitude to life. Founded in the 6th century BC by the reclusive scholar and poet, Lao Zi (Lao-Tzu) – supposedly author of its central text, the **Tao-te-Ching** – it developed further under Zhuang Zi (Chuang-Tzu) 200 years later, and rivalled Buddhism. Taoism is officially discouraged in China, but survives in Taiwan and among overseas Chinese.

Leading the faith Taoist priests (above) play a leading role in communal events, such as festivals. They are called upon to perform harmonising rites that will ensure the health, long life and prosperity of all.

Philosophy means 'love of wisdom'. Philosophers ask fundamental questions about the world and human life: Why do things happen the way they do? What can we know and how can we know it? How should we live our lives? They try to answer these questions using only the power of reason, rather than religious doctrines or scientific findings.

Plato (c.427-347 BC) Greek ▶
Plato's central belief was that all objects in this world are copies of 'Ideal Forms' that exist in an unchanging world, beyond time and space. Knowledge of these is implanted in our minds at birth, and learning is a process of uncovering this knowledge. His ideas formed the basis of much subsequent philosophical debate.

Socrates (c.469-399 BC) Greek
The ideas of Socrates are known to us entirely through the writings of his pupil Plato. He believed that true knowledge emerges through questioning and argument. He devised a method of teaching by systematic questioning – the 'Socratic method' – a technique he used with his pupils.

Aristotle (384-322 BC) Greek ▼
A pupil of Plato, Aristotle believed that the only world man could be certain of was the one he lived in, and that he found out about it through observation and experience. He decided that all things have two qualities – matter and form. Form organises matter into recognisable objects. God alone exists as 'perfect form without matter'.

St Thomas Aquinas ▶
(c.1225-74) Italian
Aquinas was inspired by the newly available translations of Aristotle's works. He believed that our senses provide our knowledge of reality. His fusion of Christianity and Aristotle's ideas is the basis for the Catholic doctrine that faith and reason are not incompatible.

St Augustine of Hippo ▼
(AD 354-430) North African
St Augustine fused ideas dominant in his time – including the idea that moral and intellectual discipline brought you closer to God – with early Christian beliefs. His ideas laid the basis for the Christian philosophy of the Middle Ages, and the Protestant beliefs of the Reformation.

René Descartes (1596-1650) French ▶
Descartes marks the beginning of modern philosophy. He set out to build a system of knowledge based solely on his own powers of reasoning. Central to his thinking were his belief that mind and body are distinct substances – a theory known as dualism – and that God implants ideas in our minds, which we can rediscover through reason.

KEY MOVEMENTS

School	Dates	Area	Key argument
Analytic philosophers	20th century	Europe	Problems can be clarified and solved by analysing the language used to express them.
Cynics	4th century BC	Greece	The distinction between true and false values is all that matters.
Empiricists	18th century	Europe	Ideas are not innate, but are acquired through the senses and experience.
Epicureans	4th-3rd centuries BC	Greece	The avoidance of suffering is the prime good in life.
Existentialists	19th-20th centuries	Europe	In a world without fixed truths, we must invent and reinvent ourselves.
Post-modernists	20th century	Europe	The meanings of words and ideas can be found only by analysing the beliefs and assumptions (structures of thought) that underlie what is being said.
Pragmatists	19th century	USA	The truth of a belief depends on the usefulness of its practical application.
Rationalists	18th century	Europe	The only reliable truths are those that can be proven logically.
Sceptics	4th-2nd centuries BC	Greece	Our senses and reason are so misleading, we cannot be certain of anything.
Scholastics	Middle Ages	Europe	Aristotle's reasoning is not incompatible with Christian faith: in fact, reason demands faith in God.
Stoics	3rdC BC-2ndC AD	Greece and Rome	The world is governed by the laws of nature, and we must accept destiny.
Utilitarians	19th century	Britain	An action is morally right if it leads to greater happiness for the greater

BC

0

000

500

500

700

John Locke (1632-1704) English
Locke believed the mind began as a blank slate, with all ideas coming from sense impressions. He divided ideas into simple and complex. Simple ideas are not imagined but received passively, such as the idea of a stone, house and so on. Complex ideas are made up of simple ideas that we imagine actively, such as honour or justice. Believing that without God morals dwindle to matters of taste, he maintained that his philosophy led to God.
▼

Benedict de Spinoza (1632-77) Dutch Spinoza believed that the Creator (God) and creation are of the same substance. This makes it impossible for mind and body to be distinct substances. Mind and body, God and nature, are two modes of the single infinite substance.
▶

Gottfried Wilhelm Leibniz (1646-1716) German Leibniz, the last great Rationalist, believed there are two kinds of truth: truths of reasoning and truths of fact. By this he meant that a statement may be true if it is internally logical (an 'analytic' statement), or if it relates to external facts that are true and verifiable (a 'synthetic' statement).
▼

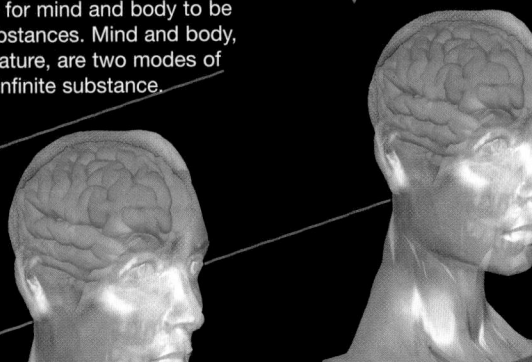

David Hume (1711-76) Scottish
Hume adapted Berkeley's reasoning to sceptical ends. As we cannot know that the material world really exists, we cannot be certain about anything. Hume applied his scepticism to questioning both God's existence and commonsense ideas of cause and effect: 'All our reasonings concerning cause and effect are derived from nothing but custom,' he observed. In practice, however, Hume relaxed his scepticism sufficiently to accept that human life does exist.
◀

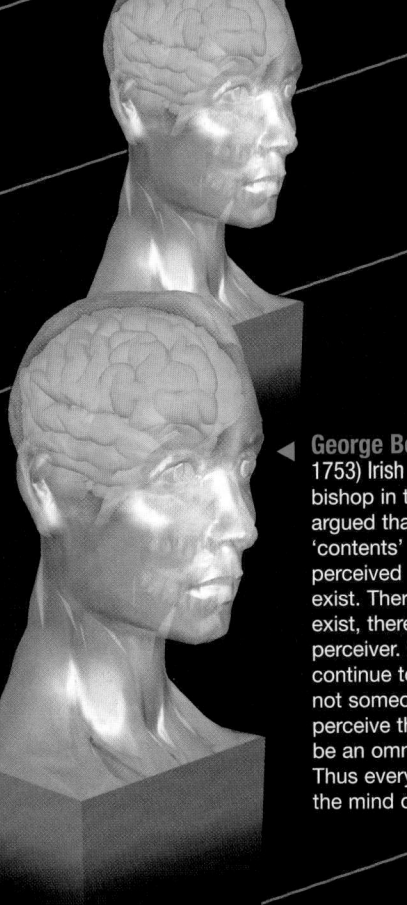

George Berkeley (1685-1753) Irish Berkeley, a bishop in the Irish Church, argued that only the 'contents' of experience perceived in our minds really exist. Therefore for things to exist, there must be a perceiver. But, since things continue to exist whether or not someone is there to perceive them, there must be an omnipresent Perceiver. Thus everything is an idea in the mind of God.

Immanuel Kant (1724-1804) German
Considered the greatest 18th-century philosopher, Kant opposed the Rationalists and the Empiricists. He believed that sensations are processed by the mind to produce experience, and that we can know only things that our senses can deal with. Other things, such as God, may exist, but we have no way of knowing about them.

KEY TO MOVEMENTS

● Belonged to no movement

● Empiricists

● Rationalists

see also
172-3 **Ancient Greece**
182-3 **The Middle Ages**
198-9 **Age of kings**
340-1 **Religions**

By the mid 18th century, as scientific knowledge grew, philosophy became less focused on solving all the mysteries of the world. It was increasingly centred on analysing the processes of human thought and reasoning, examining how our approach to the world colours our understanding of it, thus limiting our powers of objectivity.

▼ **Georg Wilhelm Friedrich Hegel** (1770-1831) German Reacting against Kant, Hegel believed that whatever is, is knowable: if something is unknowable, how can we say it exists? He thought history had a rational, understandable structure that carried all along with it in a process of destruction and creation leading to a higher state – the Absolute Idea; a process of contradiction and development (dialectical process) that leads to self-realisation.

John Stuart Mill (1806-73) ▼ British Mill, the great Utilitarian economist and political philosopher, defended the liberty of the individual against both the state and other people – as long as he 'does not make a nuisance of himself'. He was also one of the first to champion equal rights for women.

◀ **Søren Kierkegaard** (1813-55) Danish Kierkegaard rejected Hegel's concept of historical inevitability, emphasising instead the primacy of individual experience.

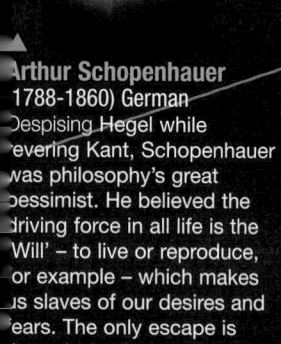

Arthur Schopenhauer (1788-1860) German Despising Hegel while revering Kant, Schopenhauer was philosophy's great pessimist. He believed the driving force in all life is the 'Will' – to live or reproduce, for example – which makes us slaves of our desires and fears. The only escape is through death – or through art, which lifts us out of ourselves.

◀ **Karl Marx** (1818-83) German Marx took Hegel's idea of the dialectical process and adapted it to explain all historical change as the result of material (economic) forces. He called this process dialectical materialism, following 'scientific' laws of development.

John Dewey (1859-1952) American ▶ Dewey was initially a follower of Hegel's ideas, but then rejected them in favour of the theory that nature as ordinarily experienced is the ultimate reality. Ideas and beliefs are true only insofar as they have observable effects in the world here and now.

KEY TERMS

Aesthetics The philosophical study of art and beauty.
A posteriori statement A statement that is validated by verification of the facts.
A priori statement A statement that is valid because of its internal logic, without reference to external facts or experience.
Dialectic Reasoning via question and answer, as used by Socrates; also the process identified by Hegel by which apparently contradictory aspects of knowledge and experience ('thesis' and 'antithesis') can produce an inclusive whole ('synthesis').
Dialectical materialism The application by Marx of Hegel's dialectic to the analysis of human history and politics.
Epistemology A branch of philosophy dealing with what we know and how we know it.
Ethics A branch of philosophy dealing with issues of right and wrong.

Logic A branch of philosophy that studies reasoned argument itself – its concepts, methods and rules.
Metaphysics An abstract branch of philosophy concerned with the ultimate nature of existence as seen from outside.
Ontology A branch of philosophy that asks what ultimately exists.
Synthetic statement A statement whose truth is determined by being tested against facts outside itself.

Friedrich Nietzsche (1844-1900) ▼
German   Nietzsche rejected
received values, especially Christian
values, with his idea of the strong-
willed Superman who could
acknowledge that the Universe is
meaningless – until
given value by
himself.
Nietzsche, too,
praised art as
humanity's
supreme
activity.
Unfortunately for
his reputation,
the Nazis later
perverted his
doctrines to
their
own
ends.

Bertrand Russell (1872-1970) English ▼
Russell, at one stage Wittgenstein's
teacher, was first and foremost a
mathematician. Using rigorous logic,
partly derived from
mathematics, he
attempted a systematic
reduction of human
knowledge, language
and experience to its
simplest elements.

Ludwig Wittgenstein (1889-1951)
German   Wittgenstein's early work
aimed to complete the work of Kant
and Schopenhauer by putting their
ideas about the unknowable worlds
on a logical basis through analysis of
language. He argued that as a
painted landscape's colours resemble
reality, so language describes the
world through the
logical forms
of words.
▶

1800

1850

Jean Paul Sartre (1905-80) French   Following
Kierkegaard, Sartre argued that in a world of
unwanted freedom, without any apparent
purpose, we must create ourselves by creating
our own values. We do this through the
choices we make – or avoid making – about
what we do in our lives.
▼

Jacques Lacan (1900-80)
French   The French
philosopher and psychoanalyst
Lacan believed that the self,
including the unconscious, is
unstable, formed by a net of
language and social custom.
The 'deconstruction' of
language and other signs is
therefore the key to all
understanding.

1900

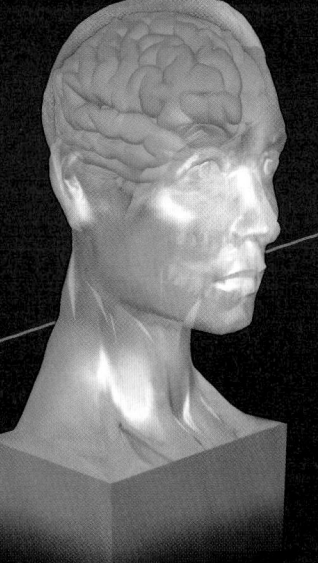

Jacques Derrida (1930-) ▶
French   A resolute opponent of
the search for ultimate
philosophical truth or meaning,
Derrida developed
'deconstruction', a technique
for analysing philosophical texts
and identifying the unstated
metaphysical beliefs behind
them. His abrasiveness and
obscurity have made him a
controversial figure.

see also
198-9 **Age of kings**
204-5 **Industrial Revolution**
348-9 **Psychology**

KEY TO MOVEMENTS

● Belonged to no movement   ● Post-modernists

● Pragmatists   ● Utilitarians

● Analytical philosophers   ● Existentialists

Psychology is the study of the mind. It covers a very wide field of investigation, from learning and perception to behavioural aspects of business and education. The application of psychological ideas to illness is called psychiatry. Both psychology and psychiatry are relatively new disciplines. Before the 1880s there was no concept that the processes of the mind could be observed and documented.

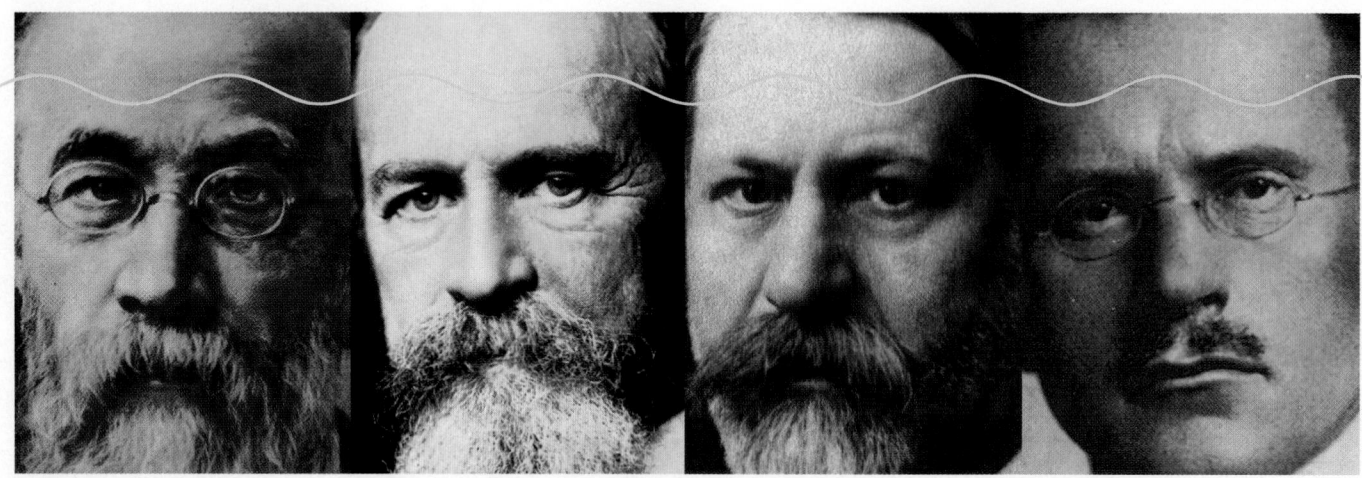

Wilhelm Wundt (1832-1920) **German**   Wundt, a professor of physiology, established the first 'laboratory for the mind' in Leipzig in 1879. He urged the practice of **'introspection'**, or self-analysis, along strict guidelines, recording and collating any findings. His book *Essentials of Physiological Psychology* (1874) helped to establish psychology as a science, and to link it closely with the study of workings of the human body.

William James (1842-1910) **American**   James' *Principles of Psychology*, published in 1890, is the first and one of the greatest studies of the subject. He was the originator of the concept of the **'stream of consciousness'**, and was concerned with exploring the nature of individuality, choice and purpose. He also developed the theory that emotions are actually the sensation of physical changes in the body, caused by exciting external events or perceptions.

Sigmund Freud (1856-1939) **Austrian**   Freud, the inventor of **psychoanalysis** (see below), coined much of the terminology still used in psychology. His theory of the development of the psyche is based on the idea that alarming early memories are repressed, potentially causing neuroses in later life. He saw the psyche as being composed of three impulses that frequently conflict: the primitive, instinctual **'id'**; the more rational **'ego'** (developing from about age two); and the **'superego'**, concerned with morality and other people.

Carl Jung (1875-1961) **Swiss** Breaking away from Freud, Jung stressed the importance of philosophical and religious as well as sexual experience. His concept of the human mind is based on the interaction between individual perception – the **'individual unconscious'** – and the shared pool of inherited memories, ideas, images and modes of thought – the **'collective unconscious'**. Jung was also the first to analyse personalities on a scale from extravert (social, impulsive and outwardly carefree) to introvert (solitary, reserved and preoccupied with the self).

Psychoanalysis

Psychoanalysis is the technique developed by Freud and his followers for the understanding and treatment of neuroses. The main technique used is analysis of what the patient says (or avoids saying) during the free association of ideas – that is, with the patient lying on a couch and talking freely of whatever comes into his or her head. Interpreting dreams and other manifestations of the unconscious also plays a part.

It is a lengthy process, and is now quite rarely practised. The aim is to uncover the memory of experiences – often from early childhood – that have been repressed, to resolve the feelings these generate, and in this way remove the cause of the neurotic behaviour. Resolution of any feelings thus exposed generally occurs through the process of transference, with emotional outbursts from the patient directed at the analyst.

Other forms of therapy

Therapists and counsellors use a wide range of techniques to resolve behavioural and psychological problems, but there are two dominant forms:

Cognitive-behavioural therapy emerged from the work of the Behaviourists (see Pavlov, above right). It is based on the principle that problems stem from faulty learning, and can be treated by conditioning the client into new ways of behaving.

Client-centred therapy originated from the work of Carl Rogers. Clients are encouraged to solve their own problems by the therapist's use of three core skills:
● *congruence* – being genuine, open and honest in their responses to the client;
● *empathy* – seeing the world from the client's point of view;
● *unconditional positive regard* – treating the client with respect and maintaining a nonjudgmental attitude.

SPECIAL BRANCHES OF PSYCHOLOGY

Abnormal The study of unusual or deviant behaviour or experiences.
Animal The use of psychological ideas to understand animal behaviour.
Business The application of psychological ideas to management and advertising.
Clinical The study of health problems such as mental disorders.

Cognitive The study of processes such as learning, memory and the acquisition of language.
Developmental The study of psychological changes over a life span.
Educational The use of psychological ideas and techniques in educational assessment and advice.

Experimental The application of scientific experimental methods and analyses to the study of the mind.
Social The study of group behaviour and human interaction.
Vocational The use of psychological techniques in assessing and developing career choices.

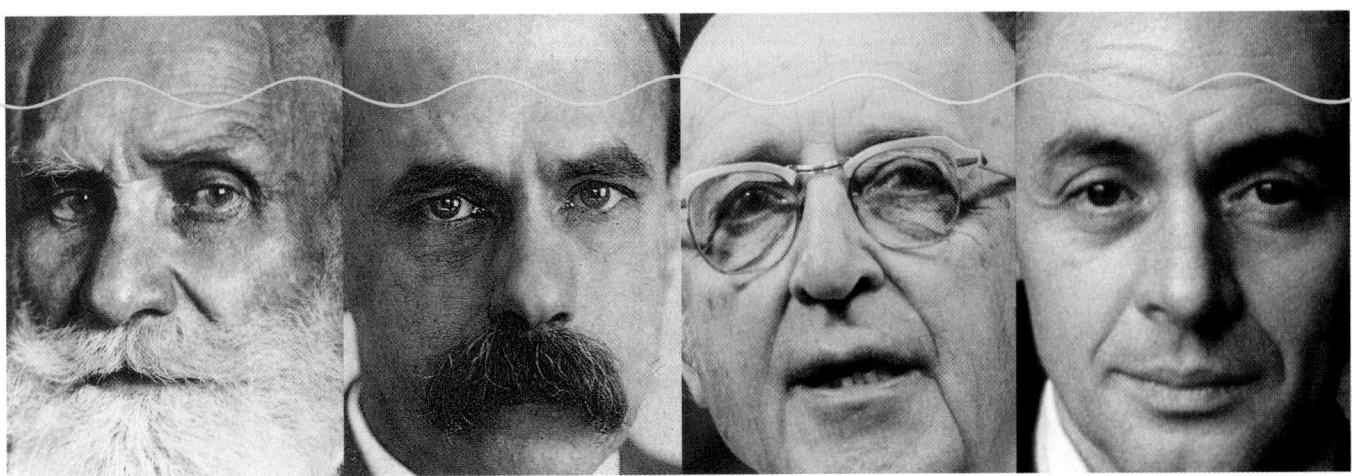

Ivan Pavlov (1849-1936) Russian
Pavlov demonstrated that if a bell was rung before dogs were fed, the dogs would soon begin to salivate (the **'response'**) at the sound of the bell alone (the **'stimulus'**). The discovery that a physical response can be evoked by a completely unconnected stimulus was called 'conditioning'. Later psychologists thought that conditioned responses, on a far more complex level, might hold the key to all human behaviour. Pavlov rejected most of the claims of the so-called **Behaviourists**.

Max Wertheimer (1880-1943) Czech/German Wertheimer and his colleagues, Kurt Koffka and Wolfgang Köhler, argued against the Behaviourists, claiming that human perception involves the isolation of meaningful patterns of information from a chaotic mass of competing stimuli. In the 1950s, their ideas led to the emergence of **Gestalt** ('form' or 'pattern') therapy. Gestalt therapists believe that in a healthy mind, input is organised into structures, and that these provoke appropriate responses.

Carl Rogers (1902-87) American
Rogers was the originator during the 1940s and 1950s of a **client-centred** approach to the practice of **psychotherapy**, which is now probably the style adopted by the majority of practitioners. He emphasised the importance of getting clients actively involved in the process and direction of their own therapy, so that they would gain a sense of positively developing their potential rather than simply being offered a 'cure'.

R.D. Laing (1927-89) British
Laing was a major figure in the 1960s and 1970s – with Thomas Szasz – in the **'anti-psychiatry' movement**, which emphasised the role played by society in creating a great deal of so-called mental illness. Laing became one of the best-known therapists of his day, developing a number of highly accessible theories based upon the use of **personal 'scripts'** and **interpersonal 'games'**, as a means of understanding and resolving problems in human behaviour.

KEY TERMS

Archetype In Jungian psychology, the primal images or ideas that underlie our notions of gods, heroes or saints.
Complex A cluster of emotionally charged ideas or perceptions which can affect behaviour or health.
Ego In Freudian terminology, the part of the psyche that consciously interacts with the outside world, conflicting with the id and the superego.
Id In Freudian terminology, the instinctual libidinous feelings at the base of every human psyche, that seek immediate satisfaction unfiltered by reason or morality.
Libido In Freudian terminology, the innate sex drive; in other schools of psychology, a more general will to survive.
Masochism Sexual pleasure or psychological relief derived from the experience of humiliation or physical pain.
Neurosis A mental disturbance due to nonphysical causes, manifested in the form of anxiety, hysterical behaviour or similar.

Oedipus complex A Freudian theory – named from a Greek myth – of the unconscious enmity a son feels towards his father as a rival for his mother's affection; the female counterpart is known as an 'Electra complex'.
Oral/anal/phallic stages Stages of sexual focus through which, according to Freud, children develop from birth to the age of six.
Paranoia Delusions of persecution or, less often, of grandeur.
Repression In Freudian and many later schools, the mechanism by which painful or embarrassing memories and ideas are suppressed in conscious memory, while continuing to influence behaviour through the unconscious.
Sadism Sexual pleasure or psychological relief derived from inflicting pain or humiliation.
Superego In Freudian terminology, the part of the psyche linked with higher feelings – altruism, ethics, conscience and guilt.

see also
346-7 **Western thought**
360-1 **Western art**
388-9 **Western literature**

The search for a framework of knowledge about the world around us began with the theorising of ancient philosophers. By the 17th century, experimentation and observation were the preferred tools of deduction. In both approaches, progress has relied on a few exceptionally creative thinkers.

Pythagoras Believed in the harmony of numbers.

MATHEMATICS

Five thousand years ago, Egyptians and Babylonians solved many problems in arithmetic and geometry, but the Greeks were the first to study pure mathematics systematically. **Thales** (c.625–c.546 BC) probably set out the first mathematical proofs based on deduction. **Pythagoras** (c.580–c.500 BC) believed numbers to be the essence of everything in nature. He or his followers devised the theorem of the right-angled triangle named after him, drawing on knowledge from Egypt and Babylon. **Euclid** (c.300 BC) wrote one of the first comprehensive geometry texts, *The Elements*. Much of it summarised earlier work, but Euclid gave proofs of many geometric theorems. His work forms the basis of today's geometry.

The Indian **Brahmagupta** (598–670) was the first to treat zero as a number with arithmetical properties. Before him, no distinction could be made between, for example, 45 and 450. The Arab scholar **Khwarizmi** (c.800–c.850) passed on Babylonian, Greek and Indian ideas in his treatises on arithmetic and algebra. The use of Arabic numerals transferred to Europe through 11th-century translations of Khwarizmi's work.

The greatest mathematical advances in Europe began later, in the 17th century. **René Descartes** (1596–1650) invented analytical geometry; **Pierre de Fermat** (1601–65) founded modern number theory; and **Gottfried Leibnitz** (1646–1716) and **Isaac Newton**

(1642–1727) independently invented the theory of calculus.

In the 19th century, **August Möbius** (1790–1868) helped to establish a branch of geometry, topology, that deals with the distortion of shapes; **George Boole** (1815–64) founded symbolic logic; and **Henri Poincaré** (1854–1912) in France explained how tiny variations in the initial conditions of an object, such as a planet or air mass, may hugely affect its later behaviour – the basis of chaos theory.

MATTER AND ENERGY

The Greek philosophers **Leucippus** (5thC BC) and **Democritus** (c.460–c.370 BC) held that everything is made of minute, invisible, indivisible particles, or atoms. But this philosophy – the basis of modern chemistry – was overshadowed for nearly 2000 years by the belief of **Aristotle** (384–322 BC) that matter is composed of four 'elements': earth, air, fire and water.

There was little advance in the study of chemistry until 1803, when **John Dalton** (1766–1844) put forward an atomic theory to explain how chemical elements combine to form compounds in fixed proportions. In the 1860s, **Dmitri Mendeleyev** (1834–1907) related the chemical properties of elements to their relative atomic mass. He created the periodic table, which lists elements in ascending order of atomic weight.

British physicist **J.J. Thomson** (1856–1940) found in 1897 that atoms can be split by physical means and are built from even smaller particles. **Ernest Rutherford** (1871–1937) and **Niels Bohr** (1885–1962) explained in 1911-13 how

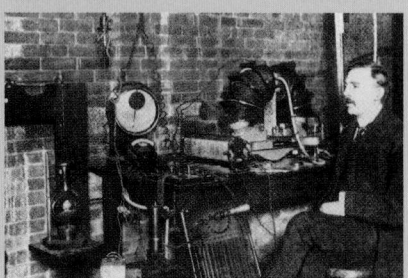

Inside the atom Ernest Rutherford discovered the structure of the atom.

atoms are built from subatomic particles. The work of all these scientists depended partly on the discovery of radioactivity by **Henri Becquerel** (1852–1908) in 1896.

Meanwhile, German physicist **Max Planck** (1858–1947) founded quantum theory: the idea that atoms emit and absorb energy in discrete particle-like bundles called quanta.

In 1905, **Albert Einstein** (1879–1955) formulated his Special Theory of Relativity, which expressed the equivalence of matter and energy by the equation $E = mc^2$. The equation's significance was realised only in the late 1930s when experiments by **Otto Hahn** (1879–1968) and **Fritz Strassmann** (1902–80), interpreted by **Otto Frisch** (1904–79) and **Lise Meitner** (1878–1968), demonstrated nuclear fission (splitting the atom) and how it released energy.

EARTH SCIENCES

For many centuries, the Biblical account of the Earth's creation was taken as the literal truth. The world was thought to be only about 6000 years old.

In 1830, Scottish geologist **Charles Lyell** (1797–1875), after studying fossils and gauging the speed that rocks change, concluded that the Earth is many millions of years old. He also argued that past geological events resulted from the same

slow processes that occur today. On the larger scale, German geologist **Alfred Wegener** (1880–1930) saw how the coasts of Africa and South America fit together like jigsaw pieces. In 1912, he suggested that the continents were the fractured remains of one vast landmass – he called it Pangaea – that began to drift apart about 200 million years ago. His theory was ridiculed until the 1960s, when

new evidence established an entirely new view of a dynamic Earth.

Environmental studies owe most to **Rachel Carson** (1907–64), who coined the term 'ecosystem' and inspired the environmental movement with her book *Silent Spring*; and **James Lovelock** (1919–), whose 1972 'Gaia hypothesis' proposed that the Earth and its creatures and plants operate as a single organism.

COSMOLOGY

Ancient philosophers watched the stars move across the sky and assumed that the Earth was the centre of the Universe, with other heavenly bodies moving around it. This belief, set out by Greek astronomer **Claudius Ptolemy** (c.AD 90–c.168), influenced European astronomers for almost 1500 years. But some Greeks – notably **Heraclides of Pontus** (4thC BC)

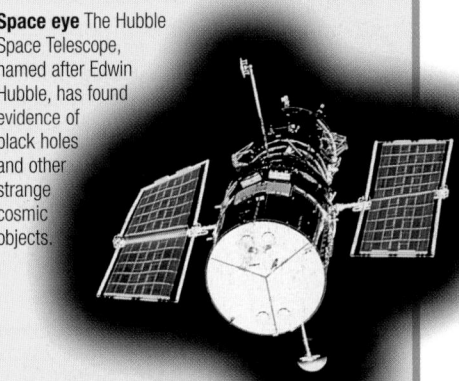

Revolutionary text Pages from Copernicus's book show the orbits of the planets around the Sun.

and **Aristarchus of Samos** (3rdC BC) – insisted correctly that the planets revolve around the Sun, not the Earth.

Nicholas Copernicus (1473–1543) was the first European astronomer to hold this view, believing that the Earth's orbit and spin are responsible for the way the planets and stars appear to move. His book *Concerning the Revolutions of the Heavenly Spheres* was published in the year he died. His ideas were suppressed by the Roman Catholic Church for more than a century.

Galileo Galilei (1564–1642) used an early telescope to observe sunspots, the

moons of Jupiter and other astronomical phenomena. He saw that Venus shows phases just like the Moon, proving that it orbits the Sun, as Copernicus said. But Galileo's *Dialogues* (1632) was also banned by the Church and the Inquisition made him recant his ideas.

Even before Galileo, German astronomer **Johannes Kepler** (1571–1630) had worked out the physical laws governing the paths of planets about the Sun. An early believer in Copernicus, he at first thought that the planets move in circular orbits, but he later refined his theories to show that the orbits are elliptical. He said there must be a force between the Sun and planets to hold them in orbit – an early description of gravity.

By far the greatest advances in cosmology were made by **Isaac Newton** (1642–1727). Apart from his discoveries about optics and his invention of calculus (see opposite), Newton devised laws of motion and gravitation that remained unchallenged for 230 years. His book the *Principia* (1687) set out three laws of motion explaining the properties of forces and the relationship between force, mass and acceleration, and also the properties of gravity. His insights at last explained the movement of the planets and other heavenly bodies, and formed the cornerstone of 'classical' physics. They have enabled us to predict the motion of all kinds of bodies, from galaxies to bicycles.

Newton's laws were only superceded when **Albert Einstein** (1879–1955) published his General Theory of Relativity in 1916. This extended Special Relativity (see opposite) to cover acceleration,

including the effect of gravity. Einstein concluded that time and space must be distorted around massive objects; that they are not constant in all situations. This knocked the bottom out of Newtonian physics, even though the difference predicted by Newton's and Einstein's equations is minute, except at the very smallest (atomic) or largest (cosmic) scale, or at speeds nearing that of light.

Scientists did not realise the true size of the Universe until 1925, when American astronomer **Edwin Hubble** (1889–1953) discovered galaxies beyond our own. By measuring the colour shift of the light in their spectrum, he realised that all stars are moving away from us and from each other – the farther away, the faster. He inferred that the Universe is expanding, and must have begun at a specific point in the past – the 'big bang'. This formed the foundation of modern cosmology.

The greatest contribution to the field since the work of Einstein has been made by British physicist **Stephen Hawking** (1942–). Hawking examined the concept of the big bang, and tried to combine quantum mechanics and relativity theory into a single theory explaining the nature and origins of the Universe.

Space eye The Hubble Space Telescope, named after Edwin Hubble, has found evidence of black holes and other strange cosmic objects.

LIFE SCIENCES

The Biblical account of the Creation – living things had existed unchanged for all time – dominated biology as much as geology. A first step towards radical change was made by Swedish botanist **Carolus Linnaeus** (1707–78), the first person to classify all living things systematically, founding the science of taxonomy.

In the late 18th century, French naturalist **Jean Lamarck** (1744–1829) developed ideas of how organisms might evolve. But British naturalist **Charles Darwin** (1809–82) revolutionised biology – and ideas about mankind's place in creation – when in 1858 he proposed a mechanism for evolution through natural selection. His plant and animal studies showed that the characteristics that help

individuals to survive in a particular habitat get passed on, and eventually become the basis for a new species or variety.

Further biological principles were discovered through working with individual organisms. **Gregor Mendel** (1823–84) began the study of heredity by experimenting with pea plants. He traced how size, colour and other traits are passed down intact from generation to generation, regardless of the environment in which the plants were reared. Sixty years later, American biologist **Thomas Hunt Morgan** (1866–1945) proved that genes – the units of heredity – are carried on minute structures, called chromosomes, inside living cells. This marked the start of the modern science of genetics.

In 1953, **James Watson** (1928–) and **Francis Crick** (1916–) looked inside chromosomes. They studied X-ray diffraction images created by **Rosalind Franklin** (1920–58) showing genetic material – molecules of DNA – and discovered the molecules' precise double-helix structure. They worked out how DNA molecules could copy themselves and pass on genetic information using chemical sequences. This theory was later confirmed by experiment, and opened the way to genetic engineering, DNA profiling, and other advances.

see also

14-15 **Planet Earth**
180-1 **The Rise of Islam**
522-3 **Mechanics**
534-5 **Relativity**

Since prehistoric times, the human form has been a central inspiration for many artists. It was the ancient Greeks who first raised sculpture to a transcendent level. The first marble figures from Greece, known as Cycladic, date from c.2500–1400 BC. Their simple, abstract forms are still appealing today. But by the 5th century BC, Greek art had taken on a new sophistication, which was to influence artists into the 15th century and beyond.

Hellenistic and Roman In the 3rd century BC, sculptors of the Hellenistic world mostly copied earlier masters. The Romans collected Greek art, but also developed genres of their own: the accurate portrait bust, the narrative relief sculpture (as in the military campaign recorded on Trajan's Column) and the mosaic. Roman painting is known only from 1st-century BC murals found at Pompeii and Herculaneum, which include vivid decorative frescoes depicting landscapes and fake architectural features.

Roman art Wall paintings in Pompeii included portraits.

| 500 BC | 0 | 250 | 500 | 750 | 1000 |

Classical Around 480 BC, Greek sculptors developed a new, realistic way of portraying the human body, keeping true to its form (naturalism). Classical sculptors adhered to strict aesthetic standards – their balanced, well-defined statues epitomise the Greek ideal of beauty and strength. The style first emerges in the *Apollo* of Piombino (of about 490 BC) and a majestic bronze god (probably Zeus) by an unknown sculptor. The male nude was perfected by two sculptors, **Polyclitus** and **Phidias**, but only clumsy Roman copies of their works survive. In the 4th century BC the softer forms of the female nude were used as a subject. **Praxiteles** created the first full-size female nude, the *Aphrodite* of Cnidus. Rivalling him was **Lysippus**, who 'modelled bronze as if it were wax'. The Classical style waned after the death of Alexander the Great in 323 BC, as art moved into the Hellenistic period.

Classical symmetry The bronze *Apollo* of Piombino displays the balance and beauty of the Greek ideal.

SCULPTURE KEY TERMS

● **Cameo** Carving on gemstone, glass or ceramic in which the background is cut away so that the design emerges in relief. The term is also often used for a portrait cut on a gemstone.
● **Chryselephantine** Statues where the flesh is covered in gold and the draperies in ivory.
● **Frieze** Horizontal band on the upper part of a wall, often decorated with carvings.

● **Intaglio** Figure or design cut into and below the surface of a metal or stone block.
● **Mobile** Sculpture consisting of individual parts suspended on wires and moved by air currents or, more recently, by motors.
● **Relief** Sculpture in which the forms project from a background. In **low relief** (bas-relief) forms project by less than half their depth; in **high relief**, by more than half.

Gothic height Tall statues with fine drapery depict *The Visitation* (c.1220) at Chartres Cathedral.

Byzantine and medieval Roman mosaic work was further developed in the Byzantine Empire in the 5th century AD. The technique added colour and splendour to the great religious buildings. Naturalism gave way to simplified, or 'stylised', images of religious icons and complex decorative patterns. In Western Europe, the main art forms to have survived are book illumination and relief sculpture in churches. From the 12th century, northern European cathedrals were decorated with stained glass, along with carvings of unnaturally tall figures in a new style known as Gothic, which stressed spirituality in its reach towards heaven.

Gothic iconography The elegant figures of the *Wilton Diptych* represent the presentation of England's Richard II to the Virgin.

International Gothic

The elaborate, graceful work of Sienese artists such as **Simone Martini** created a new style that combined the detail of Italian naturalism with the elegance of northern European Gothic forms. The style proved popular with northern courts such as that of the Duc de Berri, where the **Limbourg** brothers produced richly coloured miniature paintings. One of the greatest paintings in the style is the *Wilton Diptych* now in the National Gallery in London – the typically medieval anonymity of its creator further distinguishes the work from true Renaissance art.

1200   1300   1350

Early Renaissance The Renaissance is usually held to begin in Italy with the painter **Giotto** in the late 13th century. Renaissance artists returned to the naturalistic style of Classical art in the hope of reproducing its grandeur and beauty. Painters experimented with light and shadow to bring realistic depth to their work, and a mathematical system was invented for creating the illusion of three-dimensional space (linear perspective); the first to use perspective successfully was **Masaccio**. Italian artists of the time used tempera paint, but the Flemish painter **van Eyck** pioneered the use of oil paint, which better captured effects of light and texture.

The Classical influence was also felt by Italian sculptors. In the late 13th century, Nicola **Pisano** and his son Giovanni studied Greek and Roman sculptural forms while working on Gothic religious buildings, and modelled images of Christian saints with the naturalism of Classical times. **Donatello**'s *David* (1430–2), the first free-standing male nude since Roman times, captured a realism and vitality that was entirely new.

New depth *St Francis Honoured by a Simple Man* (1296-7) shows Giotto's ability to suggest three-dimensional form.

Sculpture facts and figures

🔵 Michelangelo's acclaimed sculpture of Moses on the gigantic tomb of Pope Julius II was originally intended to be one of 40 monumental figures carved by the artist. Lack of finance ruined plans for the other 39.

🔵 The world's most controversial sculpture is the surviving 75 m (247 ft) of a 160 m (524 ft) frieze from the 5th century BC Parthenon in Athens. In 1805, Lord Elgin, British ambassador to Constantinople, shipped it to England. The Greek government is campaigning for its return.

🔵 An ongoing sculpture of Sioux hero Chief Crazy Horse, being carved into Thunderhead Mountain, South Dakota, USA, will eventually be the tallest statue on Earth. The finished figure will measure 172 m (563 ft) high by 195 m (641 ft) across.

Artists A–C

The major figures in Western art are acclaimed for their vision, skill and innovation, and the influence they exercised on other artists.

☐ Refers to a key work.

Gianlorenzo Bernini (1598–1680) Italian
A series of life-sized statues (1618–25) assured Bernini a reputation as the leading Italian Baroque artist. In 1623, he became architect to St Peter's Basilica in Rome.
☐ Sculpture *The Ecstasy of St Teresa*

Josef Beuys (1921–86) **German**
Beuys became a major influence in 1960s conceptual art through his opposition to formalism and professionalism. His work ranged from assemblages of rubbish to perfomance pieces.
☐ Performance *How to Explain Pictures to a Dead Hare*

Sandro Botticelli (1445–1510) Italian
Botticelli painted the first female nudes for 1000 years. In 1481–2 he worked on the ceiling of the Sistine Chapel. His paintings depicting religious and mythological scenes influenced later Pre-Raphaelite and Art Nouveau styles.
☐ *Spring; Birth of Venus*

Louise Bourgeois (1911–) French-American
The disturbing, mostly abstract works of Bourgeois explore the anguish of human relationships. Bourgeois' one-woman show in New York in 1982 established her as a leading contemporary sculptor.
☐ *Here I Am, Here I Stay*

Constantin Brancusi (1876–1957) Romanian
The elegant, geometric sculptures of Brancusi were created from pure, simple shapes, mostly in marble or bronze. His work contributed to the evolution of abstract sculpture.
☐ *The Kiss*

Georges Braque (1882–1963) French
Braque's landscapes of 1908, influenced by Picasso, gave rise to the term 'Cubism'. His later, less angular still life paintings received worldwide acclaim.
☐ *The Portuguese*

Pieter Bruegel the Elder (1525–69) Flemish
Bruegel was one of the first painters to focus on landscapes and village scenes, combining close observation with fantasy.
☐ *Country Wedding; Hunters in the Snow*

Caravaggio (1571–1610) Italian
Caravaggio shocked his Baroque contemporaries with the revolutionary realism he brought to paintings of sacred themes. His use of deep contrasts of light and shade to create drama influenced painters across Europe: many travelled to Rome to see his work.
☐ *Conversion of St Paul*

Benvenuto Cellini (1500–71) Italian
Cellini was a leading sculptor of the Mannerist tradition – a Renaissance style defined by grace and sophistication. His elegant bronzes and delicate, highly wrought metalwork epitomised the luxury of Italian courtly life.
☐ *Perseus*

Paul Cézanne (1839-1906) French
Cézanne wanted to capture structure and intensity in his paintings, rather than subjective sensations. His Post-impressionist approach made him a leading contributor to the development of Cubism and abstract art.
☐ *Card Players; Mont Sainte-Victoire*

see also
172-3 **Ancient Greece**
174-5 **Ancient Rome**
182-3 **The Middle Ages**
194-5 **The Renaissance**

In the 16th century, a rejection of the Greek ideals of balance and naturalism resulted in Mannerism, characterised by crowded scenes, overdramatic gestures and poor perspective. Balance and elegance survived into the 17th century in Baroque and Classicism, and soon Dutch artists turned away from the human form to a new subject – landscape.

Baroque In the early 17th century, artists turned away from the exaggerations of Mannerism to more realistic representations of the world. The style can be seen in the 'living' feel and dramatic movement in sculptural figures by **Bernini**. In painting, Baroque is represented by grand unity – overall balance rather than focusing on a particular aspect of a scene – and the strong diagonals, curves and tonal contrasts exemplified by the work of **Caravaggio**. The uncluttered, elegant portraits of the period by **Rubens**, **Van Dyck** and **Velázquez** influenced later portrait artists such as Gainsborough.

Velázquez Portrait of the Infanta Dona Margarita of Austria.

1500

1600

High Renaissance Two centuries of experiments – with ways of depicting the human figure, perspective and oil paints – culminated in the High Renaissance, conventionally dated 1500–20. The major figures were **Leonardo da Vinci**, **Michelangelo** and **Raphael**. All produced large-scale, ambitious, complex works. Most painting was done on wooden panels or directly onto walls and ceilings, but **Giorgione** and **Titian** introduced the practice of painting on canvas. Italian Renaissance ideas began to influence German and Dutch artists, including **Dürer**.

In Italy, some artists began to depart from the established Renaissance ideas of balance and naturalism, striving instead for dramatic effects. This 'Mannerist' style also extended to the work of sculptors such as **Bellini**.

Michelangelo The figure of *David* (1501-4) became a symbol of the city of Florence.

Caravaggio Tonal contrast adds drama to *The Supper at Emmaus* (1601). Caravaggio used real people from the streets of Rome as his models.

PAINTING SUBJECTS

Religion In the Middle Ages, religious stories were artists' chief subjects. After 1800, religious commissions and works became rare. One exception to this rule is the work of Matisse, who in the 1950s designed murals and stained glass for the Chapel at Vence, southern France.

History and myth Scenes of uplifting courage, self-sacrifice or generosity, based on ancient history and myths, were once regarded as the highest art. Some offered a cloak for erotic art, with nude women painted as goddesses. Twentieth-century artists such as Picasso have at times depicted minotaurs and other creatures from their own, private mythologies.

Portraits Individual portraiture emerged in the Renaissance. Leonardo da Vinci was the first portraitist of genius, but

Raphael's portrait of Pope Leo X set new standards of realism, showing the pensive face of his patron in fine detail. The self-portraits of Rembrandt are honest paintings, 'warts and all', a style echoed by modern portraitist Lucian Freud.

Still life The first realistic paintings of inanimate objects appeared in 17th-century Spain, often in kitchen scenes (*bodegones*). The 18th-century still lifes of Chardin inspired the Impressionists, Cézanne and the Cubists.

Genre These often small-scale works depict everyday life and surroundings. The Venetian Jacopo Bassano painted animals in this style in the 16th century, but in 17th-century Holland a genre movement arose. Painters often specialised in particular themes – for example, tavern or

kitchen scenes, or musical parties. In the 18th century, Chardin and Hogarth painted famous genre scenes.

Landscape Painting landscapes was long regarded as inferior to historical or religious paintings. It started to win favour in 17th-century Holland, thanks to works by Hobbema, Vermeer and Ruisdael. They influenced English landscapists such as Gainsborough and Constable, who in turn influenced the French Impressionists.

Abstract art Shape and colour are used rather than recognisable forms. The style arose in the 1920s, led by painters such as Wassily Kandinsky, and diversified over the next 30 years, as Ben Nicholson created reliefs from geometric shapes and Jackson Pollock created 'action' paintings with drips of colour.

Classicism In the 16th and early 17th centuries, a family of three Bolognese painters called the **Carracci** looked to Michelangelo and Raphael in an attempt to revive the harmony and balance of the High Renaissance style. They influenced two French painters in 17th-century Rome, **Nicolas Poussin** and Claude Lorraine (usually known as **Claude**). Poussin founded French Classicism with austere, geometrically planned versions of classical myths. Claude painted subjects from ancient mythology set in idealised landscapes.

Poussin Nicolas Poussin painted *The Death of Germanicus* (1627) in Rome, where he spent 17 years developing his classical style.

1700

17th-century Dutch painting Painting in the Protestant Dutch Republic of the 17th century derived chiefly from the earlier Flemish realism, but was also influenced by Caravaggio's Baroque style. The Republic had no royal courts or churches to provide patronage for grand works of art – its artists painted ordinary people and everyday life. **Rembrandt**, who became Amsterdam's leading portrait painter, also recorded the progress of his own life with great perception in a series of self-portraits. **Frans Hals** portrayed Dutch dignitaries. **Vermeer** created calm interiors, while **Ruisdael**, **Cuyp** and **Hobbema** pioneered a new art form: unadorned landscape.

Hobbema *The Avenue at Middelharnis* (1689), Meindert Hobbema's best-known work, helped to popularise the landscape genre among English travellers.

Painting facts and figures

🔵 The largest painting in the world is the 600 m² (6450 sq ft) ceiling fresco in the Bishop's Palace in Würzburg, Germany. It depicts the Four Continents and was painted in 1750-1 by the Venetian, Gianbattista Tiepolo.

🔵 Pablo Picasso (1881-1973) was the most versatile and prolific artist of the 20th century. He produced 13 500 paintings, 100 000 prints, 34 000 illustrations and 300 sculptures.

🔵 The most expensive painting ever sold at auction is van Gogh's *Portrait of Dr Gachet* (1890), his patron, which reached a price of $82.5 million in May 1990 at Christie's in New York.

🔵 The world's most valuable painting is assumed to be Leonardo da Vinci's *Mona Lisa* (c.1504), kept in the Louvre, Paris. In 1960, when the painting was exhibited in the USA, it was valued for insurance purposes at $100 million.

Artists C-E

Jean-Baptiste-Siméon Chardin (1699-1779) French
Expertise with colour and skilled composition made Chardin the most successful genre and still life painter in France.
☐ *Saying Grace; Breakfast Table*

Claude Lorraine (c.1600-82) French
From his home in Rome, Claude specialised in works illustrating ancient myths. But it was the settings for these scenes – huge, formalised Roman landscapes, rich in light, shade and mood – that influenced later landscape artists such as Turner.
☐ *Cephalus and Procris*

John Constable (1776-1837) British
Constable's observations of changing light and atmosphere in the English countryside influenced other Romantic painters and the 19th-century Impressionists.
☐ *The Hay Wain*

Salvador Dali (1904-89) Spanish
Dali was a leading exponent of Surrealism, which drew images from the unconscious mind. He described his hallucinatory pictures as 'hand-painted dream photographs'.
☐ *Birth of Liquid Desires*

Jacques Louis David (1748-1825) French
The heroic subjects chosen by David, a central figure in the Neoclassical movement, expressed a self-sacrifice and devotion to duty that captured the atmosphere of revolutionary France.
☐ *Oath of the Horatii; Coronation of Napoleon*

Edgar Degas (1834-1917) French
Degas stood out among the Impressionists for his portrayal of indoor subjects, such as ballet and theatre, rather than landscape. His paintings of human figures capture a feeling of movement.
☐ *Absinthe; Rehearsal in the Opera Foyer*

Eugene Delacroix (1798-1863) French
The works of Delacroix were notorious for their violence and exoticism, influenced by a visit to Morocco. His subject matter and dramatic use of colour made him one of the most influential Romantic painters.
☐ *Death of Sardanapulus; Algerian Women*

Donatello (1386-1466) Italian
Donatello played a key role in creating the Early Renaissance style in Florence. His sculptures worked independently of their surroundings – a quality not seen since classical times.
☐ *St George*

Marcel Duchamp (1887-1968) French
Though he produced little work, Duchamp's influence as the first 'anti-artist' helped to change perceptions of what art is through acts such as exhibiting a urinal.
☐ *Nude Descending Staircase*

Albrecht Dürer (1471-1528) German
Dürer visited Italy to learn about Renaissance perspective and how to draw nudes. His sense of colour and proportion, and his engraving technique in particular, made him the greatest northern European artist of his day.
☐ *Self-portrait; Knight*

Sir Jacob Epstein (1880-1959) American-British
Epstein's sculptures – primitive-looking, distorted nudes – were criticised for offensiveness. His later naturalistic portrait busts are considered the best in the modern genre.
☐ *The Rock Drill*

see also
194-5 **The Renaissance**
196-7 **Clash of faiths**
336-7 **Greek/Roman myths**

Rococo and Romanticism moved art away from the mythological, historical and religious themes of earlier centuries. Though a strand of Greek influence still remained among the Neoclassicists, other artists began looking to contemporary literature and poetry – and to 'real life' – for their inspiration, rejecting the idealism of earlier artistic movements.

Neoclassicism From the 1760s, Europe began discovering what ancient Greek and Roman art had really looked like. Information came from the excavations at Pompeii, and from travellers' tales of Greece. This led to the rejection of Rococo in favour of a simple but grand style, again modelled on Classical sculpture. French painters such as **David** and his followers **Gérard**, **Gros** and **Ingres** produced works glorifying the French Revolution. The Italian artist **Canova**, whose works include the tomb of Pope Clement XIV, was the leading Neoclassical sculptor.

Canova The balanced beauty of the *Three Graces* (1813-16) echoes ancient Classical ideals.

1700   **1750**

Rococo Early 18th-century high society grew bored with the historical and noble themes of Baroque. Wealthy patrons began to welcome the intimate, pleasure-loving art of **Watteau**, who painted scenes of people in contemporary dress enjoying themselves. The new Rococo style – elegant, sensual and ornamental – soon spread throughout Europe. Only the serious and dignified genre scenes of **Chardin** stood apart from the new style.

Fragonard *The Swing* (c.1766), a frothy, light-hearted painting, epitomises the Rococo style.

Romanticism The Romantics rejected Neoclassicism's intellectual approach in favour of the direct expression of feelings and individual experience. The German artist **Friedrich** believed that landscape should express the artist's spiritual state, and Romantic landscapes often contained symbolic features such as ruins and twisted trees. **Delacroix** produced huge canvases often inspired by literature. Romantic painters also experimented with looser brushwork and more varied ways of applying paint. For **Turner** as for **Constable**, Dutch landscapes offered early models, but Turner soon outstripped earlier artists to pioneer an almost abstract treatment of light, colour and space.

Turner In *Rain, Steam and Speed* (1844), hazy, smudged tones give a feeling of momentum.

PAINTING KEY TERMS

Alla prima Oil-painting method in which oils are applied without underpainting.

Cartoon Full-size design for a painting.

Chiaroscuro Strongly contrasting light and shade.

Diptych Oil painting in two panels hinged together; a **triptych** has three parts, a **polyptych** four or more.

Foreshortening Perspective applied to a single object, such as an arm pointing directly at the observer.

Fresco Painting executed on plaster.

Gesso Mix of chalky pigment and glue, used to prepare canvas or panel.

Golden section Proportion of a line or rectangle divided so that smaller part is to larger as larger is to whole. Once thought to possess aesthetic power.

Grisaille Painting done entirely in shades of grey.

Ground 'Support' on which a painting is made, such as primer on canvas.

Hatching Use of fine parallel lines to suggest shading.

Icon Image of a saint or holy person, created as an object of veneration or religious comtemplation.

Impasto Thickly applied paint retaining marks of brush or other implement.

Pentimento Where the top layer of an oil painting becomes transparent with age, showing the artist's underpainting.

Picture plane Imaginary plane occupied by the physical surface of the painting. Perspective lines appear to recede from it.

Pietà Painting or sculpture of the Virgin Mary holding the dead Christ on her lap.

Primitive Originally applied to medieval Italian painters, now applied to artists who paint with childish simplicity.

Sanguine Reddish brown chalk, used for colouring.

Scumbling Brushing an opaque colour lightly over a previous layer.

Trompe l'oeil Painting that tricks the viewer into thinking that the objects exist in three dimensions.

Realism The rejection of both Neoclassicism and Romanticism in favour of the direct observation of real life was the key aim of Realism. **Courbet** believed that 'painting is essentially a concrete art and must be applied to real things'. His canvases portrayed everyday scenes, often on an epic scale. *Burial at Ornans*, showing ordinary villagers at a graveside, shocked the established art world with its 'vulgarity'. There was no recognised Realist school, but Courbet's determined rejection of established authority had a powerful influence on later art movements, from Impressionism to Cubism and beyond.

Courbet Critics disliked *Burial at Ornans* (1849-50) because it moved away from the artistic tradition of idealising life.

1800   1850

Pre-Raphaelites and Symbolism The Pre-Raphaelite Brotherhood were young painters obsessed with Romantic poetry, who wanted to return to what they saw as art's simplicity before Raphael. They included **Rossetti**, **Millais** and **Holman Hunt**. The romantic medieval style of **Burne-Jones** became associated with the movement through its similarity to Rossetti's later work. In the 1880s, the Symbolists also drew on literary sources. Inspired by the poets Baudelaire and Mallarmé, **Moreau**, **Puvis de Chavannes** and **Redon** chose their subjects from mythology and fantasy. Symbolists used light and distortion to produce a psychological impact.

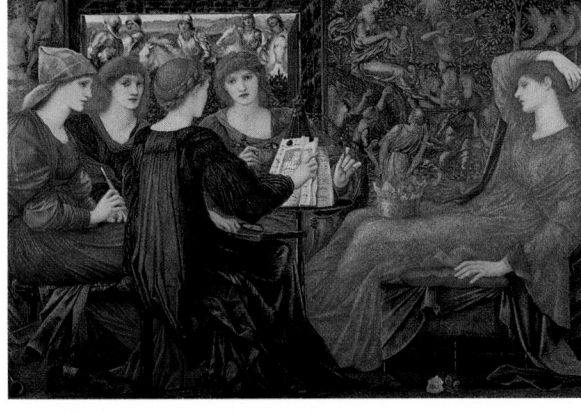

Burne-Jones *Laus Veneris* (1873-5) depicts German knight Tannhäuser discovering the home of Venus, goddess of love.

Types of paint

Acrylic A synthetic paint invented in the 1960s. Soluble in water and quick-drying, acrylics can be used as thin washes or as thick opaque impasto.

Gouache (also known as body colour or poster paint) is an opaque watercolour.

Oil The paint pigment is mixed with a drying oil, normally linseed. Oil paints, developed in Flanders around 1420, permit greater depth, subtlety and richness of colour than other media, and allow many different textures, from rough impasto to silky smoothness. Titian was the first master to exploit oil's potential fully in the 1500s, radically reworking and changing pictures as he went along.

Pastel The powdered pigment is mixed with gum or resin to bind it, and formed into sticks. Pastel was a favoured medium of the Impressionists.

Tempera The paint pigment is dissolved in water and mixed, or tempered, in egg yolk. Tempera dries very fast, so it does not allow changes to be made from the original design.

Watercolour Pigments bound with a water-soluble medium (usually gum). Lighter tones are created by thinning the paint with water so that the white of the paper shows through. Watercolours are popular with landscapists because they are convenient for outdoor use.

Artists G-K

Paul Gauguin (1848-1903) French
The Post-impressionist paintings of Gauguin show the primitive influences of Tahiti, where he spent much of his later life. His use of patterns of colour to provoke the imagination made him an influential Symbolist artist.
☐ *Tahitian Women; la Orana Maria*

Giotto di Bondone (1267-1337) Italian
Giotto introduced depth and drama to painting with his sense of perspective and realistic, expressive human figures. He was the first artist to break free from two-dimensional medieval art.
☐ *Frescoes*, Arena Chapel, Padua, Italy

Francisco de Goya (1746-1828) Spanish
Goya was a penetrating portraitist who painted his sitters in sometimes unflattering detail. He was also an early Romantic visionary whose depictions of the evils of war are unsurpassed.
☐ *Family of Charles IV; 3 May 1808*

Barbara Hepworth (1903-75) British
The leading British abstract sculptor of the 20th century explored the relationship between space and form. Hepworth based her work on the shapes of naturally weathered objects.
☐ *Single Form*

David Hockney (1937-) British
In the 1960s, Hockney emerged as a Pop Artist – a term he always rejected. Since his mid twenties, the quality of his work – from painting and fine line drawing to collage and graphic art – has earned him critical acclaim.
☐ *A Bigger Splash*

William Hogarth (1697-1764) British
Hogarth's brilliant satirical engravings and his accomplished, informal portraits made him the first great British artist.
☐ *The Rake's Progress*

Hans Holbein the Younger (c.1497-1543) German
The startling realism of Holbein's style helped him to become the leading northern Renaissance portraitist. He settled in England, and became court painter to Henry VIII.
☐ *The Ambassadors*

Edward Hopper (1882-1967) American
Hopper's paintings and etchings present an atmospheric vision of city life, depicting urban US interiors with lonely human figures. He is considered a master etcher and an outstanding figurative painter.
☐ *Nighthawks*

Jean-Auguste-Dominique Ingres (1780-1867) French
Superb draughtsmanship made Ingres the supreme exponent of French Neoclassicism. He was devoted to depicting grand mythological themes, but is better known for his nudes and portraits.
☐ *Bather; Madame Rivière*

Wassily Kandinsky (1866-1944) Russian-German
Kandinsky was the most influential early abstract theorist and painter. He believed that art should reflect inner feelings, and that colour and shape alone could create an emotional response.
☐ *Sketch for Composition IV*

Paul Klee (1879-1940) Swiss
Klee's original, inventive style made him a unique 20th-century artist. His poetic form of abstract art is sometimes described as resembling doodles.
☐ *Before the Gates of Kairouan*

The switch from the subjective, atmospheric visions of the Impressionists to the objective, structured compositions of the Post-impressionists signalled the beginnings of modern art. The intense, unrealistic colours of the Expressionists and the distorted forms of Cubism and Surrealism went on to free art from its traditional restraints.

Post-impressionism By the 1880s, some artists felt that the Impressionists' faithful rendering of nature restricted their freedom of expression, and that form and colour could be used in different ways. **Seurat** placed colours as dots so they would 'mix' in the eye of the viewer – a technique known as pointillism; **Gauguin** used flattened forms and unrealistic colours; **van Gogh** used bold, vibrant colours and thick paint; and **Cézanne** created vivid, carefully structured landscapes, still lifes and figure paintings. **Rodin** restored heroic seriousness to sculpture, but with exceptional passion and realism. His life's work, the bronze *The Gates of Hell* (started 1880), is crowded with nearly 200 dramatic figures.

Rodin *The Kiss* (1888) originated from a concept designed for *The Gates of Hell*.

1850   1875   1900

Impressionism The Impressionists rejected Romanticism's exotic subject matter and emotionalism, wanting instead to capture immediate visual 'impressions' of their subjects, and suggesting forms through fleeting effects of light. **Monet**, **Pissarro** and **Sisley** painted the same landscapes repeatedly in changing light. **Manet** and **Degas** normally painted urban or indoor scenes, as did **Berthe Morisot** and **Mary Cassatt**. The official 'Salon' rejected the Impressionists' work – the group organised eight exhibitions of their own from 1874 to 1886, after which they broke up.

Monet After creating a water garden at his house in Giverny in 1890, Monet spent 20 years painting its shimmering colours.

Fauvism At an exhibition in Paris in 1905 the wild energy, simplified forms and jarring combinations of intense colours in pictures by **Matisse**, **Vlaminck**, **Derain**, **Rouault** and **Dufy** led an art critic to dismiss the artists as *fauves* – 'wild beasts'. The movement lasted only three years, but deeply influenced the Expressionists and Abstract Expressionists.

PICASSO: ARTIST OF THE 20TH CENTURY

No other 20th-century artist rivals Spanish-born Picasso for fame, versatility, influence or number of works. His early work is often categorised into the 'Blue Period' – paintings of social outcasts in elegiac blue tones – and the 'Rose Period', depicting dancers and acrobats in warmer pinks. His studies of Cézanne and African sculpture led to the first Cubist painting, *Les Demoiselles d'Avignon* (1907), which overturned Western ideas about form and beauty with its distorted bodies and mask-like faces. Picasso later turned to sculpture, and was one of the first artists to create three dimensional works by combining miscellaneous items in ingenious ways, rather than by carving or modelling. He constructed *Head of a Bull, Metamorphosis* (1943) from bicycle parts. Though many of Picasso's works gain emotional force through images of despair, his contrasting playful style and eclecticism opened up the possibilities of modern art.

Guernica (1937) Picasso's emotional response to the German bombing of the Basque capital, Guernica, during the Spanish Civil War, expresses the horror of armed conflict.

Franz Marc *The Fate of the Animals* (1913) expresses Marc's feeling for what he called the 'inner spiritual side of nature'.

Expressionism Any work that uses distortion to reflect the state of mind of the artist can be labelled 'expressionist'. The central aim is the communication of subjective emotions through strong colours and dynamic or fantastical forms. The style underwent intense development in Germany between 1905 and 1930 among artists such as **Kirchner**, **Klee**, **Macke** and **Marc**.

Cubism Cubist painters of the early 1900s sought to depict three-dimensional objects without illusory perspective or even distinct colours. In this, Cubism marked a radical break from the idea, dating from the Renaissance, that art should reflect nature. Cubism had two phases. In Analytic Cubism an object's different aspects – sides, top and base – could all be shown at once, and the process was pushed almost to the point of total abstraction. In Synthetic Cubism, elements such as textured materials and lettering were combined (synthesised) with painting – a new technique which became known as collage.

1920   **1930**

Futurism An Italian movement originating around 1909, Futurism jettisoned as much of Italy's overwhelming artistic past as it could, inspired by contemporary life's speed and machinery. The style copied the repeating geometric planes used by Cubists to portray motion and speed. Painter and sculptor **Boccioni** was Futurism's outstanding artist, creating paintings blurred with movement and sculptures of dynamic, striding figures. Futurism died with the First World War, but had an important influence on subsequent art in Britain and Russia, and on the Dadaists.

Salvador Dali *The Metamorphosis of Narcissus* (1937) juxtaposes mundane and incongruous objects. Dali claimed that deliberately cultivated paranoia was a source of creativity.

Giacomo Balla *Velocity of Cars and Light* (1913) portrays motion with pure line and tone. Balla was a contemporary of Boccioni.

Dada and Surrealism In 1915, an art movement was founded that rejected everything – in life and in art. Its nihilism, humour and urgent desire to shock appealed to postwar disillusionment. Dada's key tenet, espoused by its most influential figure, Marcel **Duchamp**, was that art was whatever the artist said it was. After Duchamp, any object in any material was potentially a work of art. Surrealism, the fundamental aim of which was to create art direct from the unconscious, emerged in Paris in the 1920s. Surrealist artists, such as **Magritte** and **Dali**, typically used obsessively detailed images or objects in dream-like and disturbing ways.

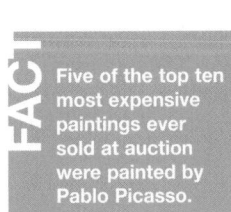

Artists K-P

Jeff Koons
(1955-) American
Koons turns banal subject matter into large, iconographic objects, often by commissioning traditional manufacturers working in materials such as metal or porcelain. His art helped to establish the term Neo-Geometricism (or 'Neo-Geo'), which refers to its unemotional, impersonal content.
☐ *Puppy*

Leonardo da Vinci
(1452-1519) Italian
Leonardo is often described as the artistic and scientific genius of the Renaissance. In his paintings, oil paint subtly models light and shade, creating pictures with mysterious landscapes and beautiful, expressive human figures.
☐ *Mona Lisa*

Roy Lichtenstein
(1923-) American
A founder and leading exponent of Pop Art, Lichtenstein uses images inspired by comic strips to create original, well-composed paintings.
☐ *Wham!*

Edouard Manet
(1832-83) French
The first Impressionist (though he never exhibited with other Impressionists) is also known as the 'first modern painter' for his choice of subjects. He painted contemporary life, rather than basing his work on traditional or moral themes.
☐ *Déjeuner sur L'Herbe*; *Olympia*

Henri Matisse
(1869-1954) French
The French Riviera provided a rich source of colour for Matisse, who built an international reputation as a modern painter equalled only by Picasso. His use of pure, vivid tones rather than natural shades inspired the Fauvism movement.
☐ *L'Escargot*

Michelangelo
(1475-1564) Italian
By his early twenties, Michelangelo had already displayed technical mastery in his sculptures of the human figure. The composition and emotional expressiveness of his statues, frescoes and architecture raised the profile of art as a profession.
☐ Sistine Chapel ceiling

Piet Mondrian
(1872-1944) Dutch
Mondrian's rigorously abstract art, with compositions of primary colours enclosed by lines, influenced graphic art and industrial design as well as later abstract art.
☐ *Composition with Red, Black, Blue and Grey*

Claude Monet
(1840-1926) French
It was Monet's painting, *Impression: Sunrise*, which gave the Impressionists their name. He specialised in depicting variations of light and atmosphere.
☐ *The Gare St Lazare*; *Rouen Cathedral*

Henry Moore
(1898-1986) British
The main works of the best-known sculptor of the 20th century represent the human form in a bold, semiabstract style, often on a huge scale. The figures reflect the curving shapes of the landscape.
☐ *King and Queen*

Piero della Francesca
(c.1415-92) Italian
Renaissance painter Piero della Francesca combined solemn grandeur with pure colour, and used classical architecture to emphasise mathematical perspective. Though influential in his own era, the level of his skill was recognised retrospectively, in the 20th century.
☐ *Legend of the True Cross* fresco cycle; *The Baptism of Christ*

see also
194-5 **The Renaissance**
348-9 **Psychology**
362-3 **Photography**

As the 20th century progressed, simplicity and minimalism became key elements in painting and sculpture. Definitions of art expanded to include video recordings, staged events and assemblages of natural objects. The act of creation is now as important as the artwork it creates.

Abstract Expressionism

Dating from the 1940s, Abstract Expressionism is the first American movement not to be influenced by European painting, although it drew on Surrealist ideas of artistic creation. Abstract Expressionists aimed for spontaneous expression at the expense of representational design. **Jackson Pollock** developed a technique of throwing or dripping paint onto a canvas – known as gestural or action painting. **Mark Rothko**'s shimmering expanses of colour are known as colour field painting. Other leading exponents include **Willem de Kooning** and **Barnett Newman**.

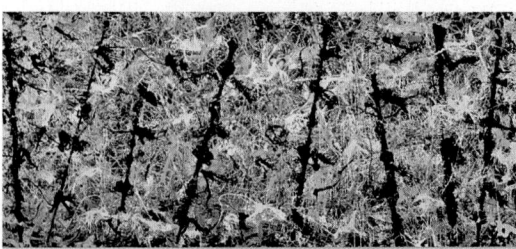

Pollock The forms within *Blue Poles: Number II* (1952) raise images from the observer's unconscious mind.

1930   **1940**   **1950**   **1960**

Brancusi The head of *Mademoiselle Pogany III* (1933) is formed by a few simple curves.

Modernism In painting, the term sums up a variety of styles from the 1920s to the 1960s, characterised by abstraction, flat colours and an emphasis on the canvas as an artificial surface. The most purely Modernist painter is **Piet Mondrian**. In sculpture, Modernism was a distinct movement, experimenting with form and structure. **Constantin Brancusi**, considered one of the 20th century's greatest sculptors, reduced his forms to near-abstract simplicity. **Henry Moore** rejected classical ideals of beauty for more vital, rougher forms based on natural shapes – human figures, shells, bones. **Barbara Hepworth** also looked to nature, but in a wholly abstract way. **Anthony Caro**'s Modernism owes more to the ideas of Pop Art, using standard industrial parts such as steel plates or aluminium tubing welded together and brightly painted.

Conceptualism Conceptualists assert that the creative act is more important than the object created; at its most extreme, it might consist of no more than an idea for a work of art. The movement includes Performance Art (events staged by the artist), Body Art (the expression of ideas – often confrontational – by the artist using his or her body), and Land Art (the creation of artworks through the interaction of the artist and the environment).

Koons *Puppy* (first made in 1992) is a 13 m (44 ft) high conceptual sculpture made of living plants.

Pop Art 'Transient, low-cost, mass-produced, young... sexy, gimmicky,' said **Richard Hamilton** of the movement he helped to create. Influenced by Dada, Pop Art took emblems of the modern world – such as comics and advertisements – and used their ideas and images to create original art. Chief proponents were **Warhol** and **Lichtenstein** in the USA; Hamilton, **Peter Blake** and **Allen Jones** in Britain.

Lichtenstein *In the Car* (1963) expresses tension between two characters in a simple, graphic image.

WHAT IS AN INSTALLATION?

Installations are works of art created in harmony with, or as part of, their setting or environment – usually a gallery. They arose in the 1960s from the belief that the context in which a work of art is viewed is as important as its content. Installation artists either totally reconstruct a room (as in the work of Russian **Ilya Kabakov**) or compose a work of art with various objects, using the room as a 'canvas' (a method exemplified by British artist **Cornelia Parker**).

Parker *Cold, Dark Matter – An Exploded View* (1991) was created by suspending pieces of wood between floor and ceiling.

VIDEO

Since the 1960s artists have exploited the expressive potential of video technology, including instant replay, continuous repetition, slow motion, large-scale and multiscreen projection, and soundtracks. Artists such as **Bill Viola** and **Sam Taylor Wood** produce work about human behaviour, relationships and identity that has an intimate, intense and sometimes disturbing effect.

Figurative painting Despite radical developments in the accepted notions of art and artworks, art representing animal or human figures (figurative art) continues to thrive – though usually in modified forms. Alongside **Francis Bacon**, **Lucian Freud** and **David Hockney**, figurative painting since the 1970s has included the Post-modernist so-called 'Neo-expressionists', such as **Anselm Kiefer** and **Julian Schnabel**.

Hockney *American Collector* (1968) displays Hockney's draughtsmanship, and his ability to convey human personality in an uncluttered, graphic style.

1970　　　　　1980　　　　　1990　　　　　2000

Minimalism Some artists reacted against Abstract Expressionism's emotiveness, believing in letting raw materials set in geometric configurations 'speak' directly to observers. This did not always work: in 1976, **Carl Andre**'s *Equivalent VIII* – 120 bricks arranged in a rectangle – attracted derision and was vandalised while on display at London's Tate Gallery.

Contemporary Art By the late 1980s, art had reached the logical conclusion of Duchamp's Dada philosophy, becoming whatever the artist wanted it to be. **Rachel Whiteread** achieved instant fame in 1992 with *Untitled (House)*, a cast of the inside of a Victorian terraced house. Much of her work concentrates on the spaces between objects, which she captures by filling them with plaster or wax to reveal something like a photographic negative of the original space. **Damien Hirst** has displayed dead animals preserved in tanks of formaldehyde to explore the themes of life and death. New technology has also stimulated developments: video recordings, films and computer-generated images have now become acceptable as artistic mediums.

Hirst Much of Hirst's work, including *The Physical Impossibility of Death in the Mind of Someone Living* (1991) (right), is intended to tap in to 'people's worst fears'.

Land Art

Some Land Art projects involve digging out and rearranging quantities of earth and rock. American **Robert Smithson**'s *Spiral Jetty* was a 457.2 m (1500 ft) long spiral of rock and salt crystals on the edge of the Great Salt Lake, Utah. British artist **Andy Goldsworthy** creates patterns and forms from materials such as leaves, pebbles and ice to express the power and transience of nature.

Goldsworthy Stone cairn constructed on Kangaroo Island, Australia.

Artists P–Z

Jackson Pollock (1912-56) American
The leading abstract Expressionist aimed for the direct expression of his unconscious. His paintings hint at gestures or forms among their coloured drips or trails.
☐ *Number 14*

Raphael (1483-1520) Italian
The limpid colours, graceful figures and symmetrical architectural backgrounds of Raphael's paintings made him a leading artist of the High Renaissance. His work inspired all of the later classical painters.
☐ *The School of Athens; Madonna della Sedia*

Rembrandt (1606-69) Dutch
The most highly regarded of the Dutch painters – a master of technique in painting and etching. Rembrandt was the first to establish a profoundly perceptive, expressive style of portraiture.
☐ *The Anatomy Lesson of Dr Tulp; Self-portrait (1658)*

Auguste Rodin (1840-1917) French
Rodin's expressive natural forms revived the popularity of sculpture among the public, and secured his reputation as the leading French Post-impressionist sculptor.
☐ *The Thinker*

Peter Paul Rubens (1577-1640) Flemish
The 'father of High Baroque style' was known for his huge, dramatic canvases, painted for courts across Europe.
☐ *Self-portrait with Isabella Brant; Arrival of the Queen at Marseilles*

Titian (c.1483-1576) Italian
One of the greatest Renaissance artists. Titian's bold brushwork revolutionised oil painting techniques. His style influenced many later painters, including Rubens and Velázquez.
☐ *Pietà*

J.M.W. Turner (1775-1851) English
Romantic painter Turner developed an almost abstract style. His use of pure light and colour prefigured the work of the Impressionists.
☐ *Steamer in a Snowstorm*

Jan van Eyck (1390-1441) Flemish
Early Renaissance painter van Eyck was the first to demonstrate technical prowess with oil paint. His works show fine detail and rich colours.
☐ *The Arnolfini Marriage*

Vincent van Gogh (1853-90) Dutch
Post-impressionist van Gogh strove to convey his inner vision through swirling colours and brushwork. His style laid the foundations of Expressionism.
☐ *Cornfield and Cypress Trees; Sunflowers*

Diego Velázquez (1599-1660) Spanish
Baroque court portraitist Velázquez eliminated props and allegory to concentrate on his sitters. His techniques influenced later painters such as Goya and Manet.
☐ *Maids of Honour*

Jan Vermeer (1632-75) Dutch
Vermeer became the leading Dutch genre painter through his expert compositional skills and use of light and shade in domestic scenes.
☐ *Girl Reading; The Kitchen Maid*

Andy Warhol (1928-87) American
From his 'Factory' studio, Warhol produced emotionless, graphic likenesses which became part of US iconography.
☐ Painting/print *Gold Marilyn Monroe*

see also

194-5 **The Renaissance**
348-9 **Psychology**
362-3 **Photography**
414-5 **Design/advertising**

The earliest photographers worked slowly – a photographic plate needed several minutes of exposure to form a clear picture. The best photographers could capture character and mood during this time. Though these skills still hold today, fraction-of-a-second exposures need the added skill of quick thinking in order to preserve the essence of a fleeting moment.

PIONEERS

In 1826, French chemist **Joseph Nicéphore Niepce** (1765-1833) produced the first fixed image on a light-sensitive pewter plate. The plate had to be exposed to a scene for about 8 hours. In 1838, **Louis-Jacques-Mandé Daguerre** (1787-1851) reduced the exposure time to 20–30 minutes by using different chemicals on a light-sensitised copper plate. The images became known as **daguerreotypes**. Two years later, **William Henry Fox Talbot** (1800-77) invented the **calotype** – a system for producing multiple copies of an image from a single negative. In the 1870s and 1880s, **Eadweard Muybridge** used fast shutter speeds and multiple cameras to capture sequences of movement clearly.

August Sander Sander's series of portraits of the residents of Cologne in the 1920s included *The Pastrycook* (1928).

Ansel Adams *The Grand Canyon from Point Imperial*, taken in 1942, shows Adams' use of tone and contrast to outline the shapes of the landscape and emphasise detail in the foreground.

Portraiture

Portrait photography developed a distinctive style as early as the 1840s. Long exposure times made most early work formal and stiff. But the best practitioners, such as **David Octavius Hill** (1802-70) and his partner, **Robert Adamson** (1821-48), could still produce results that convey a firm sense of the subject's personality and social background. The hundreds of portraits taken at their studio in Edinburgh reveal much about life in mid-Victorian Britain.

By the 1850s, a large number of portrait studios had been established. In mid-19th century Paris, many celebrities had their portraits taken by **Gaspard-Félix Turnachon** (1820-1910). His stark, simple poses are set against a plain background, lit by natural light.

Leading figures of the day also sat for **Julia Margaret Cameron** (1815-79), who took up photography as a hobby in 1864. Although her work is technically flawed, her use of large close-ups strongly evokes the character and mood of her subjects.

Another important recorder of society was **August Sander** (1876-1964). His portraits form a documentary of German life in the 1920s and 30s, during the rise of the Nazis.

Lighter cameras and more sensitive film gradually led to less static portraiture. This is evident in the dramatic portraits of **Richard Avedon** (1923-), who often photographed sitters in confrontational poses, and the homoerotic work of **Robert Mapplethorpe** (1946-89).

Landscape and architecture

Slow, often cumbersome equipment meant that static subjects, such as buildings and landscapes, were favoured in the early days of photography. The results helped to broaden people's idea of the world at a time when opportunities for travel were generally limited.

In the 1850s, the technically sophisticated work of **Francis Frith** (1822-94) offered views of the Middle East, a region then little known in the West.

This was also a time when the great open spaces of the USA were being opened up. Government expeditions sent to explore the new territories included photographers. In 1867, **Timothy O'Sullivan** (1840-82) recorded the vast spaces west of the Mississippi, and in the 1870s, **William Henry Jackson** (1843-1942) covered the American West. His pictures inspired Congress to set aside Yellowstone as the first National Park.

With his emphasis on sharpness of detail, **Edward Weston** (1886-1958) brought an element of abstraction to his landscapes, such as his 1937 series of photographs of the Mohave Desert. The work of Weston's contemporary, **Ansel Adams** (1902-84), also paid attention to sharp definition. His shots of the Yosemite Valley, California, focus on nuances of light and texture.

A common postwar theme is the city, and its encroachment upon nature. **Gabriele Basilico** (1944-) focuses on this, as do the cityscapes of **Stephen Shore** (1947-).

MODERNISTS

By the first half of the 20th century, a number of artists, particularly those involved with new movements such as **Dada** and **Surrealism** (see page 359), were experimenting with photography. Realism – the primary goal of most photography – was deliberately avoided. The main aim of most modernists was to produce abstract or surreal imagery using photographic materials and techniques.

In the early 1920s **Man Ray** (1890-1976), an American painter, developed a new technique that manipulated light to project the outline of objects directly onto photographic paper. The outline was then developed, creating abstract, otherworldly images, which he called **rayographs**. At about the same time, **Laszlo Moholy-Nagy** (1895-1946), a Hungarian, was producing similar works to Ray, which he called **photograms**.

Photomontage was another new technique, invented and developed in the 1920s by **John Heartfield** (1891-1968).

His pictures, created by assembling images from different photographs, often contained savage imagery. Heartfield and other artists such as **Max Ernst** (1891-1976) used this style to create social and political statements. Much of Heartfield's work was anti-Fascist.

Others produced pictures emphasising the decorative and abstract qualities of everyday sights and objects. The landscapes of **Franco Fontana** (1933-), an Italian, are celebrated for this.

Henri Cartier-Bresson *Sunday on the Marne River*, taken in 1938. Cartier-Bresson waited for significant moments that captured the essence of a scene.

Robert Capa A US soldier dies at the hands of a German sniper in April 1945. Capa's front line work recorded the brutal reality of war.

The social landscape

Photography was used as a means of social commentary from the start. In 1878, **John Thomson** (1837-1921) published a series of London street scenes showing aspects of city life. In the 1880s, **Peter Emerson** (1856-1936) photographed the rural life of Norfolk peasants and fishermen.

Paris was the main subject of **Eugène Atget** (1857-1927) between 1898 and 1921. The quality of his pictures of shop windows, tradespeople, historic buildings and brothels received critical acclaim after his death.

The views of the New York slums taken by **Jacob Riis** (1849-1914) in the 1880s led to housing reforms. New York life also appeared in the work of **Alfred Stieglitz** (1864-1946). Between the 1890s and the 1930s, Stieglitz's photography and writing influenced others in the field, such as **Paul Strand** (1890-1976). Strand's career as a documentary cameraman inspired him to spend his spare time taking still pictures of daily life in the USA and Europe.

In the 1920s, small, fast cameras appeared, allowing more candid shots, such as those by **Bill Brandt** (1906-83) showing the English at work. Reportage photographer **Henri Cartier-Bresson** (1908-) used a small camera to remain unobtrusive. He referred to his camera as his 'notebook', and became renowned for his ability to preserve telling moments. **Diane Arbus** (1923-71) showed the same ability in the 1960s in her contrasting portraits of the wealthy and the underprivileged.

Photojournalism

Photographs have long been used as a means of reporting news. In 1861, **Mathew Brady** (1823-96) was sent to record the conflict of the American Civil War. His unflinching portrayal of death is shocking, but there are no actual battle scenes. Equipment was too heavy and cumbersome to take into the heart of the action.

The miniature cameras of the post-First World War years revolutionised photojournalism, making it possible for pioneers such as **Alfred Eisenstaedt** (1898-1995) and **Margaret Bourke-White** (1904-71) to get closer, more involved shots of their subjects. Bourke-White produced particularly stirring pictures of the destitute in 1930s USA, and of the Second World War.

Walker Evans (1903-75) also exploited the new cameras' portability to create an intimate record of the daily struggle for survival in the depression years.

War too could now be captured in close-up. **Robert Capa** (1913-54), probably the most celebrated photographer of the genre, got as near to the frontline as any soldier. His pictures inspired the work of **Don McCullin** (1935-), best known for his graphic images of the Vietnam War.

Cameras are now highly automated, but those using light-sensitive film operate on the same principles as the cumbersome 19th-century boxes. The greatest recent advance in photography came with the advent of microchip technology, allowing images to be digitally recorded, then transferred to a computer to be displayed and manipulated.

1839-41 W.H. Fox Talbot develops the **calotype**, the first negative-positive photographic process, enabling multiple prints to be made from one negative. Exposure is reduced to 1-2 minutes.

1851 Frederick Archer invents the wet **collodion process**, giving finely detailed negatives on glass plates and much shorter exposures.

1861 The first **single lens reflex (SLR)** camera is manufactured.

1800

1850

***c.*1725** Johann Schultze discovers that exposure to light darkens silver salts.

1800 Silver salts are used by Humphrey Davy and Thomas Wedgwood to create a photographic image, but they fail to make it permanent, or 'fix' it.

1826 Joseph Nicéphore Niépce takes what will become the **oldest surviving** photograph, of his barnyard. Exposure time is several hours.

1839 Louis Daguerre patents the first practical development process, the **daguerrotype** (above). Exposure time is less than 30 minutes.

1841 Special lens for portrait photography is designed by Josef Petzval in Hungary. It greatly reduces exposure time.

1854 A camera using rolls of **light-sensitive** paper, instead of individual plates, appears.

What is film speed?

The speed of a film is a measure of its sensitivity to light, and is indicated by an ISO number – on a grading system set by the International Standards Organisation.
Slow-speed films (ISO 25-64) are less sensitive to light and need a longer exposure than 'faster' films. But they give a fine quality image, that can be enlarged without appearing grainy. They are best used in bright light, or for a stationary object, where it is possible to use a slow shutter speed.
Medium-speed films (ISO 100-200) are the most flexible, as they can be used in a wide range of lighting conditions.
High-speed films (ISO 400-1600) are the most sensitive to light and need the shortest exposure time. They are good in dim conditions and for moving subjects, where exposure time has to be short. However, prints from such films can be grainy.

Camera lenses

A lens is shaped to make the parallel rays of light entering it converge at a point behind it, known as the focus. The scale of the image formed and its perspective is affected by the distance between this focus and the lens, known as the focal length.
Normal lens (focal length 40-55 mm) has an angle of view of about 60 degrees, and forms an image similar to that seen by the human eye.
Telephoto lens (focal length 85-400 mm) has a narrow angle of view, producing close-up images of distant objects. Perspective is shortened, depth effects are reduced, and only objects close to the point of focus appear sharp.
Wide-angle lens (focal length 15-35 mm) takes in a wider view than a normal lens, but everything viewed appears smaller. Perspective is exaggerated and nearby objects are distorted.
Zoom lens incorporates a range of focal lengths. The angle of view is changed from wide-angle to telephoto by adjusting the relative position of the lens' internal components.

28 mm

135 mm

Aperture and depth of field

A camera lens can only focus precisely on one distance, and objects closer or farther away will become increasingly blurred. The distance between the nearest and farthest objects that are still reasonably in focus in an image is known as the depth of field. Depth of field varies with the size of the lens' aperture – the opening that admits light. Aperture size is adjusted not only to vary exposure, but also according to the depth of field required in the picture. It is indicated by f-numbers – also called f-stops.

f22, a small aperture setting, gives great depth of field. Objects in the background will still appear sharp.

f1.4, a wide aperture setting, gives a shallow depth of field. Only the objects that are focused upon remain sharp.

Shutter speed

When a picture is taken, the camera shutter opens, exposing the film to light. Many cameras allow the time it remains open – the shutter speed – to be varied, changing the exposure to suit the lighting conditions. Shutter speed is also determined by how much a subject is moving. Generally, the faster a subject moves, the higher the shutter speed needed.

Above 1/100th second A fast-moving subject will appear to be almost still, or 'frozen'.

Below 1/100th second The girl now appears blurred. Sometimes this is desirable, as blur implies movement.

1871 Richard Maddox replaces wet collodion with a dry **gelatin emulsion** of silver salts, the coating still used for photographic film.

1888 Kodak creates the **box 'Brownie'** camera (above). It contains a roll of negative paper, which is sent away for processing and printing.

1893 Harold Taylor designs the three-part **'Cooke Triplet' lens**, the basis of most later lens designs.

1912 Oskar Barnack produces a prototype of the first **miniature** photographic camera, still the basis of most modern camera design.

1947 Edwin Land invents the **Polaroid** 'instant' black-and-white camera. Colour Polaroid film appears in 1963.

1969 The light-sensitive **charge-coupled device (CCD)** is invented. This marks the first step in the development of **digital** cameras (see below).

1900   **1950**   **2000**

1873 Silver bromide paper is introduced for photographic prints.

1880s Improvements to gelatin emulsion reduce exposure time to a fraction of a second.

1903 The first **true colour** photographs are taken in France by Auguste and Louis Lumière, using the **Autochrome** process.

1935 The **electronic flashgun** is invented.

1936 In Germany, the Ihagee Company launches the first **35 mm SLR** camera – the Kiné Exacta. The arrival of **35 mm colour** film boosts interest in photography.

1960s High-quality **zoom lenses** for still cameras become widely available.

1996 The first mass-market **digital** still cameras start to appear in high-street shops.

Different kinds of camera

Plate camera
💧 Plate cameras are similar to the large cameras used in the 19th century. A lens and shutter is mounted at the front, with a thin lightbox at the back. In the early cameras this held a light-sensitive glass plate. In a modern version, it holds a sheet of film, one being used for each picture.

💧 Professionals use plate cameras for architectural, still life, landscape, technical and advertising work. The large film size – 13 x 10 cm (5 x 4 in) – gives high-quality prints.
💧 The position of the lens can be adjusted, so that any subject, from extreme close-ups to tall buildings, can be photographed without distortion.

Single lens reflex (SLR) camera
💧 SLR cameras have a mirror in the camera lens that directs the image to the viewfinder. This allows the user to see exactly what the lens does, making it easier to compose a picture accurately. The mirror flips up when the shutter opens, allowing light to reach the film.
💧 Lens can be changed to suit a specific purpose.
💧 Most SLRs take 35 mm film, but professionals often use 5.5 x 5.5 cm (2¼ x 2¼ in) film, for better-quality prints.

💧 Many modern SLRs contain a microprocessor that can adjust exposure time and focus automatically.

Compact camera
💧 Miniaturised compact cameras have simple 'optical' viewfinders, through which the user composes a picture before shooting it. This gives a view that is marginally different to that 'seen' by the lens.
💧 The lens usually cannot be changed. It either has a fixed focal length or is a motorised zoom.
💧 Most use the same 35 mm film as SLR models, but are simpler mechanically and are sized so that they can be carried in a pocket.

💧 The majority of functions are usually controlled by a microchip, giving automatic exposure times and focusing.
💧 Film winding and rewinding is often motorised.

APS (advanced photo system) camera
💧 APS cameras are essentially compact cameras that use 24 mm wide film in a small self-loading cassette, instead of the standard 35 mm film. The smaller cassette makes the camera easier to miniaturise.

💧 A unique feature is the ability to take 'wide-screen' and even 'panoramic' images as well as the normal format.
💧 Some APS cameras allow the film to be rewound when only part-used, then later reinserted – when it will automatically wind on to the correct position. This is possible because the cassette records all details of exposure as the film moves through the camera.

Digital camera
💧 Instead of using film, digital cameras record and store images using a charge-coupled device (CCD). This has millions of light-sensitive electronic cells which produce signals that vary according to the amount of light they are exposed to.
💧 A converter turns the image made by the electrical signals into digital form, and can convert it into an image for display.
💧 Images are viewed on a screen at the back of the camera, rather than through a viewfinder.
💧 A memory chip stores images while the camera is in use.

To store long-term, they are transferred to a removable, electronic card. When downloaded onto a computer, they can be printed using any paper.

Polaroid camera
💧 Polaroid cameras use sheets of 'instant' film that can produce a finished, printed image within minutes of exposure.
💧 Attached to each film sheet is a small pod of processing chemicals. After exposure, the film is pulled through a set of pressure rollers, that squeeze the chemicals over it.
💧 Once initial development is complete, the paper covering the print is peeled away to allow the picture to finish developing.

see also
362-3 **Photography**

Buildings are the most visible and often the most durable of human creations – the largest scale of all artistic works – and they reveal much about the culture in which they were created. Architecture, like any other art form, is subject to fashion. The style of a building may derive from a specific architect or group, or from the characteristic building techniques of a particular era and culture.

Romanesque (1000–1100) Also known as Norman, this was the second medieval style chronologically, following the Byzantine style (450–600) of the Eastern Roman Empire. It used Classical elements such as round arches in heavy-walled buildings. The massive solidity of Romanesque walls and columns was necessary to support the roofs – which were at first supported by tunnel vaults, and later by rib vaulting. Romanesque churches were lavishly decorated with religious carvings.

The Colosseum, Rome The first free-standing amphitheatre, AD 70–72; architects unknown.

Temple Concordia, Parthenon, Greece
Built by Ictinus and Callicrates, 447–432 BC.

Chartres cathedral, France c.1194–1260.

San Vitale, Ravenna, Italy 6th-century Byzantine church.

Classical Greek (c.600–300 BC) The Greeks aimed to create an ideal beauty in the design of their large public buildings. They originally built in wood, but began using stone in about 600 BC. Even early temples have a perfect symmetry, derived from strict mathematical proportion. By 490 BC the Greeks were building in marble, and were gilding temples or painting them vivid red and blue. Greek architecture reached its zenith with buildings such as the Parthenon in Athens, in which many apparently straight lines are in fact precise curves designed to counter optical distortion. The Greeks also pioneered the building of huge semicircular open-air theatres.

Roman (c.200 BC–AD 400) Roman architects borrowed many techniques – domes from the Persians, arches from the Etruscans and various architectural motifs from the Greeks. They developed new types of buildings: amphitheatres, basilicas and aqueducts. They invented concrete, with which they erected vast domes and vaults, turning architecture into a form of engineering rather than art. The Colosseum (built AD 72–82), the biggest Roman amphitheatre, seated 55 000 people on tiers. Large flat-roofed buildings called basilicas were used for public meetings. Aqueducts, such as the 47 m (155 ft) Pont du Gard (built AD 14) near Nîmes in France, carried water on raised tiers of arches.

Gothic (1150–1500) Gothic, the third medieval style, arose in northern France, possibly influenced by arches built by the Moors in Spain. Its distinguishing feature was the pointed arch, which allowed higher roofs and windows. Solid or arched 'flying' buttresses transmitted the roof's weight – and particularly the sideways forces caused by the pointed arch – to the ground. It quickly became a recognisable international style, with particularly fine examples in Germany (eg, Cologne cathedral) and Britain.

THE FIVE ORDERS

Classical Greek and Roman architects worked to set standard relationships between various elements – particularly the base, structural supports (columns) and entablature (beams) they carried. These styles are known as orders, and include precise rules for decoration and other elements. The three Greek orders are the Doric, Ionic and Corinthian. The Romans adapted these styles and added two of their own: the Tuscan and Composite.

Tuscan   **Doric**   **Ionic**   **Corinthian**   **Composite**

Gothic arches and windows

The pointed arch and window were key characteristics in Gothic architecture, and were made possible by the flying buttress, another Gothic innovation. Essentially a form of permanent external scaffolding, flying buttresses carried the weight of the roof directly to the ground. This allowed architects to reduce wall thickness and to increase the height and size of arches and windows correspondingly.

The most extreme example of the Gothic window can be seen in the Sainte Chapelle, the chapel built by Louis IX in Paris, completed in 1248. The walls are no more than frames around huge stained-glass windows, creating an airy, diaphanous building flooded with light.

In general, the lighter and higher the roof of a Gothic cathedral and the bigger its windows, the later it was built.

Florence cathedral, Italy The dome was designed by Brunelleschi, c.1420.

Villa Rotunda, Vicenza House designed by Palladio, 1550–1.

Renaissance (1400–1600) During the Renaissance, the plentiful Roman ruins in Italy inspired architects to create a style based largely on a revival of Greek and Roman principles. There was a renewed emphasis on geometric proportion, light, and authentic Classical decoration. Round arches and domes returned, as did the five orders (see left). For the first time since the Roman period, architects undertook large-scale urban planning.

Palladian (1550–1750) Architect Andrea **Palladio** created a simplified Renaissance style emphasising harmonious proportions and symmetry and restrained decoration. He was the first to use a columned temple design as a frontage – the most imitated aspect of his style. His influence in England, Ireland and North America, continued into the 19th century.

Key terms

Architrave In Classical architecture, the ledge or lintel resting on the columns.
Barrel vault Arched semicircular vaulting resting on supporting walls.
Buttress A structure built against a wall to give extra support or to transmit the outward thrust of a vault or arch.
Clerestory A windowed wall stretching above the main roof level to allow extra light into a building.
Cornice The projecting upper part of an entablature (see opposite); or a moulded horizontal projection at the top of a wall.
Cupola A small dome on a roof or turret.
Entasis The slight bulge in a column to counter the optical illusion that it is thinner in the middle.
Flying buttress A buttress in the form of a half-arch.

Gable The triangular end of a roof.
Keystone The central wedge-shaped stone at the top of an arch.
Lintel A beam or slab above an opening.
Mullion A vertical window divider.
Pediment The triangular structure above a doorway or peristyle of a Classical or Renaissance building.
Peristyle A row of columns.
Pilaster A rectangular column, with base and capital, attached to a wall.
Spandrel The triangular space between two arches, or an arch, ceiling and wall.
Stucco A mortar coating imitating stone.
Tracery The decorative stone framework of a large, usually Gothic, window.
Transom A horizontal window divider.
Tympanum The space between a lintel and the arch above it.

Architects A-H

This list covers the most successful, innovative and influential architects from the past 600 years of mainstream Western architecture.
☐ Refers to a key work.

Leon Battista Alberti (1404-72) Italian
Important in spreading knowledge of Classical architecture and as an early proponent of the idea that beauty in architecture derives from harmony and proportion.
☐ Malatesta Chapel, Rimini, Italy.

Gian Lorenzo Bernini (1598-1680) Italian
Transformed much of Rome, building palaces, churches and squares in the Baroque style on a huge and dynamic scale. He also influenced large-scale city planning across Europe.
☐ Baldacchino, St Peter's, Rome.

Donato Bramante (1444-1514) Italian
The leading architect of the High Renaissance in Rome, he favoured simple, elegant forms in a sober, Classical style. He began the rebuilding of St Peter's.
☐ Church of San Pietro in Montorio, Rome.

Filippo Brunelleschi (1377-1446) Italian
Regarded as the founder of the Italian Renaissance style. His dome for Florence cathedral (the Duomo) was a triumph of engineering. His later buildings were more purely Classical.
☐ Florence cathedral dome.

Norman Foster (1935-) British
His High Tech Post-modernist buildings make use of precision engineering and the latest technology. Many are built from modular components.
☐ Hong Kong Airport.

Ange-Jacques Gabriel (1698-1782) French
Influenced by Palladio, his work was typical of the measured and sober grandeur of French Classicism – for example, the Place de la Concorde, Paris (begun 1757).
☐ Petit Trianon, Versailles, France.

Antoní Gaudí (1852-1926) Spanish (Catalan)
Highly individual and original, he pioneered the use of fluid, organic forms in buildings in the Art Nouveau style. His influence still grows.
☐ Church of the Sagrada Familia (begun 1874), Barcelona, Spain.

Frank Gehry (1929-) American
His bold, original, often huge, Post-modernist buildings defy almost every architectural convention. He has made use of a wide variety of building materials.
☐ Guggenheim Museum, Bilbao, Spain.

Walter Gropius (1883-1969) German
Head of the Bauhaus school of architecture and design 1919-28, and emigrated to the USA in 1937. He argued for the arts to be unified, and for the use of modern materials and forms. He had a huge influence on the growth of Modernism through his teaching.
☐ Fagus Works, Alfeld-an-der-Leine, Germany.

Jules Hardouin-Mansart (1646-1708) French
His strong sense of visual drama and splendour made him the most successful architect of Lous XIV's reign. In his early career he worked in the Baroque style. Towards the end of his life, he adopted a lighter style that represented the first step towards Rococo
☐ Hall of Mirrors, Versailles, France.

During the 17th century, the purity of the Renaissance began to give way to the more ornate Baroque and Rococo styles. After revivals of the Classical and Gothic styles during the 19th century, architects in the late 19th and 20th centuries began using a range of new technologies and materials to create entirely new styles of buildings.

Romanticism/Historicism (1800–1900)

New influences from Egypt (brought back by French scholars with Napoleon's army) and Asia, and popular interest in the medieval 'Gothic' past, led to a movement of imitative architecture directly opposed to the pure style of Neoclassicism. Partly covered by the term 'Gothic Revival', it had strong Romantic and religious undertones. Characteristic features include pointed arches, battlements and finials, and elaborate surface decoration.

Art Deco (1918–1940)

Art Deco (or Style Moderne) architecture is characterised by the streamlined, mechanical shapes and repetitive, geometric decoration seen in New York's Rockefeller Center (especially the interiors), Chrysler Building and Empire State Building. Many features were constructed from chrome, enamel or glass.

St Peter's Colonnade, Rome
Bernini's novel freestanding colonnades provide a backdrop to the piazza before St Peter's.

Nash terrace, Regent's Park, London John Nash was a leading exponent of Neoclassicism.

Houses of Parliament, London Designed by Charles Barry in the Gothic Revival style.

Church of the Sagrada Familia, Barcelona Gaudí used concrete to mould organic shapes.

Baroque and Rococo (1600–1760)

Italian architect and sculptor **Bernini** established the theatrical style, elaborate surface detail and vivid wall paintings of Baroque, which became popular across Europe. In the 18th century, when an influx of wealth from colonial expansion and a growing demand for civic rather than religious buildings gave architects more freedom, a light-hearted variant of Baroque evolved in the form of Rococo. Flowing lines and elaborate, elegant decorative schemes were combined with light interiors created by including more windows.

Neoclassicism (1750–1850)

Partly as a reaction to Baroque excess, European architects such as Claude **Ledoux** looked back to Roman and Greek architecture for a 'pure' Classical style. Inspiration came from archaeological excavations, such as those at Pompeii (1748). The new movement sought to re-create Classical grandeur using simple, geometric layouts and tall Classical columns, and copied Greek or Roman decoration.

Art Nouveau (1890-1914)

Art Nouveau extended well beyond architecture, most notably into furnishings and interior design. Its roots lay in a revival of interest in the sinuous, flowing shapes of Celtic design. Technological developments in metalwork and poured concrete made possible the use of such motifs in architecture in the early 20th century. Outstanding examples are Hector **Guimard**'s Paris Métro station entrances and the organic-looking buildings of Antonî **Gaudí** in Barcelona, Spain.

Details and decoration

Arabesque A decoration using flowing curved lines, spirals and plant tendrils, often in a repeating pattern.

Cartouche A panel in the form of a curling piece of paper or a scroll, usually bearing an inscription.

Chequerwork A pattern of squares in alternating colours or materials, such as stone and brick, to produce a chessboard effect. It is used on walls and floors.

Chevron A repeating pattern of V shapes, or zigzags, common in Romanesque architecture, and revived in Art Deco.

Festoon A carved garland of fruit or flowers, often including a ribbon or bow.

Finial A carved or moulded object at the apex of a gable or pinnacle.

Fretwork Straight horizontal and vertical lines used to create a repeating geometric pattern.

Frieze A band of decorative carving near the top of a wall.

Gargoyle A water spout at roof level, often consisting of a grotesque figure.

Grotesque A decoration in which human, animal and plant forms are combined.

Mosaic Small pieces of glass or stone, called tesserae, are set in mastic to form geometric patterns or representational pictures. They can be used on floors or

walls and were a particular feature of Roman and Byzantine buildings.

Pendant A sculptural ornament suspended from the central point of a vault or ceiling. Common in Late Gothic vaulting.

Rosette A disc decorated with roses, common in Neoclassical architecture.

Running dog A repeating wave pattern, often used in a frieze and common in Classical architecture.

Scallop A carved or moulded shell.

Scroll A partly rolled scroll in relief moulding, often used in a repeating pattern. Seen on Classical columns and in Gothic vaults.

International modernism (1920–1975)

Modernism rejected ornament and links with past styles, stripping away everything except what was functionally necessary. Its main influence can be seen in commercial and industrial buildings. The Bauhaus design school, founded by **Walter Gropius** in Germany, became a centre of Modernist design. **Le Corbusier**'s principles included the 'free plan' (walls independent of the structural frame) and 'free façade' (windows positioned independently of the stucture).

Chrysler Building, New York (William Van Alen). The fan-shaped tiers are typical of Art Deco decoration.

Pluralism (1975–)

A mixture of styles, often described by the umbrella term 'Post-modernism', arose from a dissatisfaction with mainstream Modernist design. Two major schools currently exist. In the **High Tech** school, elements from previous styles are reused in new combinations made possible by technological advances. In the **Deconstruction** school, the emphasis is on movement and disorientation – fragmenting or expanding spaces through the unconventional treatment of basic elements such as floors and walls.

Robie House, Chicago Frank Lloyd Wright's first 'prairie house' has a sculptural simplicity.

La Pyramide, the Louvre, Paris (I.M. Pei). Steel struts and more than 900 pieces of glass were used to build a modern pyramid.

TODAY'S ARCHITECTURE

Early 21st-century architecture shares the 20th-century belief that the function of a building should dictate the technology and materials used to build it.

Two themes dominate. One is that in an era of permanent and ever more rapid change, architecture must be flexible and responsive, never constrained by theory. Dutch architect **Rem Koolhaas** epitomises this approach. His buildings consist of abstract forms, sometimes two or more that appear to be unrelated, but in which the internal layout is entirely logical and functional.

The second theme in contemporary architecture is to fuse conservation and innovation – to use architecture in urban regeneration and to safeguard the environment. American **Frank Gehry**'s startlingly original Guggenheim Museum in Bilbao succeeded in breathing life into a decaying industrial city as well as housing works of art. His

Experience Music Project, Seattle (Gehry)

plans for the new Guggenheim Museum in New York continue this theme on an even more dramatic scale. Similarly, Swiss architect **Jacques Herzog**'s Tate Modern gallery, built out of London's derelict Bankside power station, dovetails culture and urban renewal. And **Norman Foster**'s Reichstag (Parliament) in Berlin uses 94 per cent less energy than its 19th-century predecessor. His planned Greater London Authority Headquarters promises a virtually nonpolluting building.

Architects L–Z

Le Corbusier
(1887-1975)
Swiss/French Born Charles-Edouard Jeanneret, le Corbusier was a champion of Modernism. Early in his career, he designed influential cube-shaped white houses. Later he pioneered a more sculptural and expressive style based on abstract shapes, realised in concrete.
☐ Villa Savoie, Poissy, France.

Louis Le Vau
(1612-70) French
The first of the great French Baroque architects, and the original architect of Versailles, his most impressive work was that done on the grand scale.
☐ Château de Vaux-le-Vicomte, near Melun, France.

Adolf Loos
(1870-1933) Austrian
One of the first Modernists, he built bold, square buildings – many of them simple cubes – with no ornament, often using reinforced concrete.
☐ Steiner House, Vienna.

Michelangelo [Buonarroti]
(1475-1564) Italian
He rejected Classical notions of proportion and harmony in favour of complex and unsettling spatial effects. He used features such as columns and architraves for their visual effect as much as for structural support. His dynamic spaces influenced 17th-century architects, especially Bernini.
☐ Major contribution to St Peter's Basilica, Rome.

Ludwig Mies van der Rohe
(1886-1969)
German/American
A proponent of the International Modernist style, he created elegant buildings using materials such as glass and steel. He emphasised simplicity of design, good craftsmanship and immaculate finishes, and

his style has been imitated around the world.
☐ Lever House, New York.

Andrea Palladio
(1508-80) Italian In a series of villas, palaces and churches, he combined Classical ideas of symmetry and harmonious proportions with simplicity of layout and minimal decoration. His contemporaries considered his buildings to be unsurpassable, and his influence spread throughout Europe with the publication of his *Four Books on Architecture* (1570).
☐ Church of San Giorgio Maggiore, Venice.

Richard Rogers
(1933-) British/Italian
Exploits modern technology, selecting techniques and materials that best suit a building's function. His particular concern has been for urban renewal and the use of energy-efficient techniques.
☐ Lloyd's Building, London.

Christopher Wren
(1632-1723) English
Working in a Baroque-influenced Classical style, he built more than 50 churches in London after the Great Fire of 1666. He also designed of series of palaces. He was equally skilled on a small or giant scale.
☐ St Paul's Cathedral, London.

Frank Lloyd Wright
(1867-1959) American
The leading American Modernist of the early 20th century, he created elegant, flowing spaces rather than the harsh geometry of his European contemporaries.
■ Robie House, Chicago.

The most important developments in furniture making have taken place in the West. Popular designs – of chairs in particular – have always reflected the style of the times. Their close correspondence to architectural themes can be seen in the classical proportions and motifs of Baroque, the curves and oriental shapes of Art Nouveau and the minimalism and practicality of Modernism.

Major developments in Western furniture

China and Japan

Chinese civilisation was technically far ahead of the West almost until the end of the 18th century, yet its furniture (though often beautifully made) was not as complex as the best of the European designs. This was partly due to China's different customs – chairs were rare before the 19th century, and most tables were very low – and partly because simplicity and craftsmanship were generally prized over decoration. Ornate lacquer screens were the only exception to this rule. Japanese furniture was even more austere; the ideal house would contain only a few simple, exquisitely made items.

Renaissance (1450-1600)
Growing wealth created a demand for sophisticated furniture. Italian designs, which often tried to apply disproportionate architectural-style ornamentation to furniture, spread to Spain and France in particular. Walnut came into common use.

Baroque (17th century)
Cabinetwork became common. Wood was carved into classical columns and pediments. Polished timber was inlaid with contrasting woods or gilded. Rich decoration characterised Louis XIV furniture.

Georgian (18th century) The term 'Georgian' covers a wide range of styles in use in England such as Classical, Rococo and Gothic. Design was based on architectural rules governing proportion and ornamentation. Imported mahogany replaced walnut as the main wood for fine furniture.

French Rococo (18th century)
The heavy, elaborate Baroque style gave way to the lighter, more curved Régence. After 1735, this in turn gave way to Rococo. Under Louis XV and XVI, furniture became more elegant, with scroll, shell and floral ornaments. Gilded bronze (ormolu), lacquer and marquetry (inlay), were also used.

Arts and Crafts (1880-1900) In a reaction against industrialisation, the Arts and Crafts Movement led by William Morris advocated a return to traditional craftsmanship. A new style of plainly decorated, expensive handmade furniture emerged, which was copied cheaply by other manufacturers.

Art Nouveau (1890-1910) Wood could easily take on the shapes of Art Nouveau – organic curves based on natural forms such as tree trunks, often combined with simpler Japanese lines. Upholstery was rich in velvet and leather. The style was widely adopted in France and Belgium.

Art Deco (1930s) In the Art Deco period, furniture design was based around geometric shapes such as circles, zigzags and triangles. The style hinted at luxury with lacquered wood, opulent silver and obsidian, and stylised decorative motifs such as sunrays, leaves and animals.

Modernism (1920-50) Modernist furniture originated in Germany's Bauhaus school in about 1920, where frameworks of tubular steel were first used as a basis for light, functional designs. Ornamentation was rejected in favour of pure practicality. Upholstery was often made separately to the frame.

Shaker furniture

Shaker furniture developed separately from the evolution of European designs. The Shakers were a religious group, established in the late 18th century, who rejected worldliness in favour of a life of austerity. Their furniture reflects their spiritual beliefs. It is spare and functional but always exquisitely made. Any form of work was seen as an act of devotion to God, so a practical object was, by definition, a beautiful one. This idea was close to the philosophy of William Morris, but also became a central tenet of Modernism nearly two centuries later.

Shaker style Functional simplicity.

Furniture designers A–Z

Alvar Aalto
(1898-1976) Finnish
As an architect, Aalto worked with asymmetric forms and natural materials such as wood. He pioneered the design of mass-produced lightweight plywood furniture in the 1930s.

Robert Adam
(1728-92) Scottish
Adams saw architecture, interiors and furniture as part of a harmonious whole. His furniture designs complement his Neoclassical buildings with motifs such as palm leaves, urns and cameos.

André-Charles Boulle
(1642-1732) French
The elaborate brass and tortoiseshell inlays created by Boulle became known as Boullework. Furniture makers continued using the technique into the 19th century.

Thomas Chippendale
(1718-79) English
Chippendale's *Gentleman and Cabinet Maker's Director* (1754), contains 160 Gothic, Rococo and Chinese designs which influenced later craftsmen such as Hepplewhite and Sheraton.

George Hepplewhite
(d.1786) English
Hepplewhite made slender-legged, elegant chairs with backs in the form of a shield. His *Cabinet-Maker and Upholsterer's Guide* contains 300 designs, which were widely copied.

Arne Jacobsen
(1902-71) Danish
Jacobsen became known for his 1950s furniture, in particular for his 'Swan' and 'Egg' chairs (named for their shape), created for the SAS Royal Hotel in Copenhagen.

Charles Rennie Mackintosh
(1868-1928) Scottish
A leader of the influential 'Glasgow School' of designers. The Japanese lines and organic motifs of his slender, high-backed chairs became symbols of Art Nouveau style.

Ludwig Mies van der Rohe (1886-1969) German/American
Architect van der Rohe's cantilevered, chromed-steel and black leather 'Barcelona' chair became a design classic after its first appearance at the 1929 International Exposition in Barcelona.

Jean-Henri Riesener
(1734-1806) German/French
Reisener became cabinet-maker to King Louis XVI. His work was unsurpassed for its craftsmanship and technical sophistication.

Gerrit Rietveld
(1888-1964) Dutch
Rietveld's starkly geometric furniture, painted in bright colours, echoed the abstract painting of the 'de Stijl' artists group to which he belonged.

Eero Saarinen
(1910-61) Finnish/American
Working with American **Charles Eames** (1907-78), Saarinen was the first to use new materials such as metal tubing, foam upholstery and moulded plywood for furniture.

Thomas Sheraton
(1751-1806) English
Nothing made by Sheraton is known, but his *Cabinet-Maker and Upholsterer's Drawing Book*, a collection of much-imitated designs, contains delicate furniture lacking in superfluous ornamentation.

Philippe Starck
(1949-) French
Starck's furniture mixes minimalism with an enthusiasm for organic forms. His distinctive style and interest in designing for mass production have made him the most well-known contemporary designer.

Neoclassicism (1800-30) The term neoclassicism covers three corresponding styles – Empire in France, Regency in England and Biedermeier in Germany. All produced grand furniture with strict symmetry and decorations such as urns and medallions. Empire (named for Napoleon's reign) combined Egyptian elements with traditional Classical design.

Victorian (1830-1900) Gothic, Elizabethan, Georgian and other earlier styles were copied and combined. Furniture everywhere became more ornamental. Machinery began to replace craftsmanship, and new materials such as iron were introduced. Chairs of this era often featured elaborate upholstery.

Postwar (1945 onwards) After the Second World War, designers in the USA, Italy and Scandinavia used new production methods and materials to make practical, simple furniture, suitable for mass manufacture. Flexible laminated wood, steel frames, moulded plastic and upholstered foam cushions allowed more fluid, rounded shapes.

Post-modernism (1945 onwards) Bridging the divide between artistic innovation and market demands became a leading theme in post-modern furniture. Many designers turned to traditional styles, using elements of earlier periods such as Baroque, Arts and Crafts or Art Deco and interpreting them in modern materials such as plywood. Others produced practical designs with little ornamentation.

Ceramics, glassware and jewellery all represent a mix of art and technology that dates back to the earliest civilisations. Ceramics techniques were first perfected in China, and glass-making in the Middle East, but the focus of innovation in both has moved to Europe in the past few hundred years.

MAIN TYPES OF CERAMICS

All ceramics are made by shaping the object in wet clay; it is then heated, or fired, in a kiln to harden it. A later refinement was to apply a coating, called a glaze, after firing, to give a glass-like, waterproof surface.

Earthenware Pieces of 9000-year-old earthenware have been found in Turkey, making it the oldest type of pottery. It is fired at a relatively low 800°C (1472°F), and stays porous. Most earthenware is brown or greyish. There are several special forms:

● **Tin-glazed earthenware** has an opaque white glaze, made with tin oxide. Majolica, faience and delft are forms of tin-glazed earthenware, which is sometimes designed to mimic Chinese porcelain.

● **Creamware** is a refined cream-coloured earthenware, which is given a transparent lead glaze. It was first made in England around 1740 and is still widely produced today.

Stoneware Clay fired at 1300°C (2372°F) produces stoneware, which is very hard, fine-grained, and either whitish, grey or brown. It originated in China in about 1400 BC, and is naturally waterproof, although a decorative glaze may be applied.

Porcelain Potters in Tang-dynasty China invented porcelain, by firing a mixture of ground-up china stone (petuntse) and china clay (kaolin) at more than 1400°C (2552°F). It is hard, usually translucent, and often glazed for decoration. Chinese porcelain is called **hard paste**. From 1710, Meissen in Germany made it.

● In late-16th-century Europe, attempts to duplicate hard paste produced an artificial, or **soft paste**, porcelain.

● About 1794, Spode in England created a less brittle form of porcelain, called **bone china**, by adding ground bones to the clay.

CHINESE CERAMIC PERIODS

Chinese pottery and porcelain evolved through a series of technical and artistic phases over several thousand years. They are defined by the Imperial dynasty in which they were made.

● **618-907 Tang** The Tang period saw the first known use of porcelain. Coloured glazes were also developed in this period; they were dappled or splashed on to pottery.

● **960-1279 Song** The Song, or Sung, is considered the classic period, with simple forms and decoration. Among many highly prized glazes of this period was a transparent green called celadon. The finest Song pottery was made near the Imperial capital, Hangchow.

● **1280-1368 Yuan** More elaborate decoration was introduced in Yuan dynasty ceramics, including the first blue-and-white patterns. Translucent white porcelain was also made in much greater quantities than before.

● **1368-1644 Ming** Famed partly because it was the first Chinese porcelain to be exported widely to the West, Ming-dynasty items tend to be large, with elaborate and colourful decoration. Blemishes were prized as evidence of the potter's spontaneity.

● **1644-1912 Qing (Ch'ing)** The vigour of Ming designs gave way to more carefully made Qing goods. Output was boosted to meet the growing European demand, especially for blue-and-white porcelain.

Staffordshire dogs From the 17th century onwards, the Staffordshire potteries in north-west England produced vast numbers of ornamental figures – human and animal – in stoneware and earthenware. Many, such as these mid-19th-century earthenware greyhounds, commemorated real events or people.

Major European pottery and porcelain factories

Factory	Location	Date founded	Notable products and special features
Delft	Netherlands	17th century	Imitations of Chinese porcelain; tiles. Most decoration blue on white tin glaze.
Staffordshire	England	17th century	Red and brown-glazed stoneware replaced by near-porcelain quality in 1690s.
Meissen	Dresden, Germany	1710	Elaborate and brilliantly coloured figures. European pioneer of hard-paste porcelain.
Chelsea	London, England	1743 (-84)	Figure groups in a light, informal style. First English porcelain manufacturer.
Sèvres	Paris, France	1756	Ornate figure groups; formal services; vases. Europe's leading factory until Revolution.
Wedgwood	Staffordshire, England	1759	Creamware; white unglazed stoneware; black basalts; coloured jasper ware.
Minton	Staffordshire, England	1796	Dinnerware in earthenware, bone china and porcelain. Populariser of willow pattern.
Doulton	Lambeth, London	1818	'Studio' art pottery (from 1860s); fine porcelain (from 1882); tile panels (from 1900).

GLASS MAKING

Glass is made by heating a mixture of silica-containing material (usually sand) and an alkaline 'flux' such as soda or potash. The mixture melts and 'vitrifes' (becomes glassy) at about 1100°C (2012°F) – below silica's normal melting point. Extra ingredients may be added to give special properties. The glass is shaped while hot, allowed to harden, and then may be decorated.

◗ **Blown glass** An object is formed from molten glass by blowing air through a pipe. Glass-blowing was invented in Syria around 50 BC, and allows a wide range of shapes and styles to be made.

◗ **Cased and cameo glass** Layers of coloured glass are blown inside each other. By cutting away parts of the outer layers, the inner colours can be seen. In cameo glass, the layers are generally opaque and the decoration elaborate. It was known to the ancient Egyptians and Romans, and became popular in France during the 19th century.

◗ **Craquelure** The surface of a piece is fissured with tiny cracks, like shattered ice. Craquelure was a popular form of decoration in 16th-century Venice, and was revived in 19th-century England.

◗ **Cut glass** A grinding wheel is used to give glass faceted shapes that make it sparkle. This was done as early as the 8th century BC, but was not perfected until the 18th century in England.

◗ **Engraved glass** The surface of a piece is decorated with a finely detailed design cut by a sharp point, often a diamond, or by a rotating copper wheel. The technique reached heights of great sophistication in Germany during the 17th and 18th centuries.

◗ **Enamelled glass** Glass is decorated with enamel paints. Widely used by the the ancient Romans and in 15th-century Venice, the technique has remained popular.

◗ **Lead crystal** Lead oxide is added to the glass mixture, to make a particularly heavy, brilliant and transparent glass. A 17th-century English invention, it mimics 15th-century Venetian 'cristallo'.

◗ **Pressed glass** Molten glass is moulded to form its outer shape; a shaped metal arm, or plunger, then forms the interior. It is a fast and simple technique developed in the USA in the early 19th century. Pressed glass may mimic cut glass, but the moulded edges of the facets are less sharp.

Encased Flavio Poli used the ancient technique of cased glass – where one layer of colour sits inside another – to create these distinctly modern-looking vases in the 1950s.

JEWELLERY

Jewellery has been worn for personal adornment, as a sign of power or status, or for religious or magical purposes in almost every society for thousands of years. Up to the 19th century, many items embodied a theme or message – often engraved, or spelt out by the arrangement of gemstones.

The 19th and 20th centuries saw a huge growth in the use of jewellery by the newly prosperous middle classes. Industrial techniques and new materials also allowed a wider range to be made cheaply. In the 20th century, low-cost 'costume' jewellery became popular.

Jewelled leopard The Duchess of Windsor's 'big cats' were made by Cartier between 1949 and 1966.

Influential jewellers and firms included:
◗ **Cartier** (founded 1847) French In the early 20th century, the firm became internationally famous for its Art Deco jewellery and watch designs.
◗ **Peter Carl Fabergé** (1846-1920) Russian His most famous works were the 56 jewelled Easter eggs that he fashioned for the Russian royal family.

◗ **Alphonse Fouquet** (1828-1911) French He produced Renaissance-style designs with carved gemstones. His son **Georges** (1862-1957) designed Art Nouveau pieces.
◗ **René Lalique** (1860-1945) French A leading Art Nouveau jeweller, Lalique had switched to designing glassware by 1910.
◗ **Alphonse Mucha** (1860-1939) Czech-born Best known for his Art Nouveau illustrations, Mucha designed jewellery for Fouquet in Paris and later for Tiffany.

◗ **Tiffany & Co** (founded 1837) US **Louis Comfort Tiffany** (1848-1933) brought the firm founded by his father to prominence. Famous for its glassware and lamps, from 1902, it concentrated on jewellery.
◗ **Van Cleef & Arpels** (founded 1906) French The firm introduced 'invisible' gem settings, in which the metal clasps holding the stones are hidden.

Jewellery records

The **greatest jewellery sale**, of the late Duchess of Windsor's jewels in Geneva, Switzerland, in 1987, totalled $53 million. The **biggest rough diamond** was the Cullinan, found in South Africa in 1905; it weighed 3106 carats (621 g). The **largest cut diamond** – the 530-carat (106 g) Star of Africa, part of the British crown jewels – was cut from it. The **highest priced pearl** was the 75-carat (15 g) La Régente, which sold for almost US $865 000 in 1988.

Modern artistry Late-20th-century jewellers may use similar skills to an engineer. Jacqueline Mina has constructed this necklace to hang smoothly down one side, then splay out as it turns upwards.

see also
38-9 **Earth's treasures**
186-7 **China and Japan**
414-5 **Design/advertising**

The early Christian Church absorbed and adapted the pagan music of antiquity and the East. Yet the development of Western church music led, in turn, to new realms of expression and technique in secular music over the next centuries. These reached a pinnacle during the 18th-century 'Classical' period, with the works of Mozart.

Middle Ages The earliest medieval church music was a chant called plainsong, sung alternately by priest and choir. Most music had a single melodic line (monophony), but from about the 9th century music with two or more melodies sung simultaneously (polyphony) developed. By 1100, a system for writing down music had been devised (it was previously passed on orally).

Medieval troubadors
From a 14th-century German manuscript.

Renaissance In the Renaissance, instrumental music emerged as a separate style from vocal music, and music was written specifically for particular instruments. The northern European tradition of elaborate polyphony merged with the southern (mainly Italian) taste for chords and harmonies. The madrigal, a form of secular song in five or six parts, was invented in about 1530 in the Netherlands and Italy. It became popular in Elizabethan England, and increased the trend towards secular music.

Early Baroque The Baroque style emerged in Italy during the early 1600s. It rejected Renaissance serenity for dramatic contrasts in tone, volume and pace. A new style of religious music developed – oratorio – written for solo voices, chorus and orchestra. New instrumental forms also emerged: the sonata (for solo instruments) and the concerto (for a solo instrument with orchestra). Instrumental music gained in popularity through the widespread use of the harpsichord and organ. The most celebrated violins and cellos ever made were produced during this period by Nicolo Amati of Cremona in Italy, whose pupils included Antonio Stradivari.

Italian viola Made by Gaspar da Salo *c*.1600.

800

1200

1500

1600

840-50 Earliest treatise on Gregorian chant.
*c.*1100 Troubadours (wandering poet composers) first appear in southern France.

12th century Hildegard of Bingen publishes 77 musical poems.
Early 14th century Composer Philippe de Vitry publishes *Ars Nova* ('New Art') outlining new forms of musical harmony.

1570 Palestrina's *Missa Brevis* first performed.
1573 Thomas Tallis composes *Spem in alium*, a motet for 40 voices.
1592-5 William Byrd composes his three Masses.

1607 Monteverdi's opera *L'Orfeo* produced in Mantua.

KEY TERMS

Alto An abbreviation of contralto.
Aria An extended vocal solo, often with orchestral accompaniment, in opera, oratorios and cantatas.
Bagatelle Short, light instrumental piece, often for piano.
Baritone Man's middle-range singing voice, between tenor and bass.
Bass Man's lowest-range singing voice.
Cantata Vocal music with an orchestral accompaniment.
Chamber music Music written for a small group of performers, usually three to eight players. The term originally meant music for performance in a private salon or room.
Continuo An abbreviation for 'basso continuo', denoting a continuous bass part running through a piece, usually on keyboard. It is common in Baroque work.
Contralto Lowest female singing voice.
Countertenor High male singing voice at alto pitch.

Duet A piece of music written for two performers or two instruments.
Fantasia Piece in an improvisatory style.
Fugue A piece of music with several lines of melody built up in sequence then repeated, overlapping one another.
Gregorian chant Plainsong named after Pope Gregory the Great, who organised a review of church music in the 6th century.
Impromptu Short improvised piece.
Libretto The text of an opera or oratorio.
Lieder German 'songs', especially 19th-century solo and piano songs.
Madrigal Unaccompanied song for four or five voices with secular text.
Mezzo-soprano A female singing voice between soprano and contralto.
Movement Symphonies and concertos are divided into sections, or movements, each with its own pace, theme and mood.
Nocturne A dreamy musical piece, often for piano, that evokes the night.

Pitch The highness or lowness of a note.
Prelude Short instrumental piece.
Quartet A group of four musicians; a piece written for four instruments.
Quintet A group of five musicians; a piece written for five instruments.
Requiem A Mass for the Dead.
Septet A group of seven musicians; a piece written for seven instruments.
Sextet A group of six musicians; a piece written for six instruments.
Soprano Highest female singing voice.
Symphony A major orchestral piece, normally in three or four movements.
Syncopation Stressing of normally unstressed beats of metre.
Tenor Highest normal male singing voice.
Toccata A keyboard piece that shows the player's touch and dexterity.
Treble Soprano-like child's singing voice.
Trio A group of three musicians; a piece written for three instruments.

Late Baroque Baroque music reached its finest expression during the late 1600s and early 1700s, in the work of **Bach** and **Handel**. Bach wrote mainly church music (particularly Passions, religious cantatas and organ pieces) while Handel's work was mostly dramatic (opera, oratorios and secular cantatas). Both composers brought the twin traditions of polyphonic melody and harmonic chords together in a highly sophisticated way. Both also helped to develop a clear and formal system of key changes and scales that gave music a new technical precision.

Baroque style 17th-century music wove around base lines played on a keyboard such as this organ of c.1627.

Classical During the 1700s and early 1800s, music retained much of the formality of Baroque music. It was emotionally restrained, with a new emphasis on a single tuneful melody in place of Baroque polyphony. The symphony became the most important orchestral form; the sonata emerged as the most important form in instrumental music as a whole. The sonata reached perfection in late-18th-century Vienna – by then the world's music capital – in the work of **Haydn**, **Mozart**, **Gluck** and the young **Beethoven**.

Mozart From the age of four, Mozart performed as a pianist. He began composing at five.

1650
1674 Jean-Baptiste Lully's opera *Alceste* first performed.
1689 Henry Purcell's opera *Dido and Aeneas* written.

1700
1721 J.S. Bach's *Brandenburg Concertos* first performed.
1721 Vivaldi's *Four Seasons* published.
1742 Handel's *Messiah* premiered.
1791 Mozart's *The Magic Flute* first performed in the year of the composer's death.

NOTATION GLOSSARY

Musical notes symbolise the duration of a sound, and the five-line stave denotes the sound's pitch (its level on the musical scale). Key signatures are symbols on the stave at the beginning of a piece of music that alter its tone, while keeping the sounds of the notes complementary to one another.

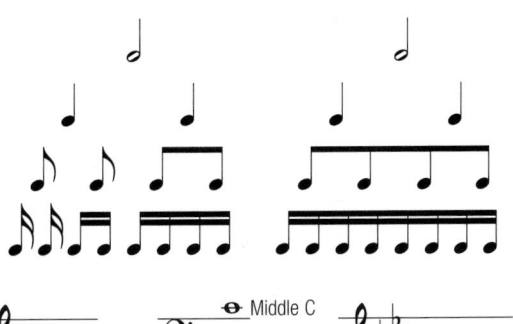

Semibreve whole note (4 counts)
= **Two minims** ½ note
= **Four crotchets** ¼ note
= **Eight quavers** ⅛ note
= **Sixteen semiquavers** 1/16 note
♭ flat (½ tone lower)
♯ sharp (½ tone higher)

Treble clef Middle C

Bass clef Middle C

Key signature E flat major

The following A-Z is a guide to the principal classical composers.
☐ Refers to a key work.

J.S. Bach
(1685-1750) German
An outstanding organist, Bach had a great command of counterpoint (combining melodies), a characteristic of the Late Baroque era. Among his works are fugues and preludes for the organ, and church cantatas.
☐ *Brandenburg Concertos; B Minor Mass*

Ludwig van Beethoven
(1770-1827) German
Beethoven's compositions progressed from classical works to passionate music that shocked his contemporaries and bridged the Classical-Romantic divide. He is known for symphonies, concertos and sonatas. Many of his masterpieces were written after he became deaf.
☐ *Symphony No 3* (Eroica), *Piano Sonata No 14* (Moonlight)

Johannes Brahms
(1833-97) German
Brahms is known for his original rhythms and counterpoint. He composed symphonies, concertos, piano and chamber music, and many songs. He also wrote the world's most famous lullaby, *Wiegenlied*.
☐ *Clarinet Quintet*

Benjamin Britten
(1913-76) English
Britten's Modernist music often uses discordant sounds to create moods, as in his operas, but he also wrote church music. He co-created the annual Aldeburgh Festival.
☐ Opera *Peter Grimes*

Frédéric Chopin
(1810-49) Polish
A Romantic who combined exceptional piano technique with creative harmonies and beautiful melodies. Chopin wrote many short pieces, including the 'Minute Waltz' and nocturnes, preludes and mazurkas.
☐ *Nocturnes*

Aaron Copeland
(1900-90) American
Copeland's compositions were inspired by jazz, cowboy songs and US folk music. Besides symphonies and piano works, he wrote music for ballets and Hollywood films.
☐ Ballet *Appalachian Spring*

Antonin Dvorak
(1841-1904) Czech
A Romantic known for joyous melodies, Dvorak used folk tunes in many works, including the *New World Symphony*. He also wrote operas, concertos and piano music.
☐ *Slavonic Dances*

Edward Elgar
(1857-1934) English
A Late Romantic, Elgar developed a heroic 'national' style in his five *Pomp and Circumstance* marches. His melodic music created different moods in symphonies, oratorios, concertos and sonatas.
☐ *Enigma Variations*

George Frideric Handel
(1685-1759) German/English
Handel is best known for the *Messiah* and other religious oratorios in the British choral tradition. He also wrote opera, coronation anthems and inspirational music in many forms.
☐ *Water Music*

Joseph Haydn
(1732-1809) Austrian
Haydn greatly advanced the forms of the symphony and string quartet during the Classical era. His music often humorously imitated everyday sounds (such as a clock, hen and donkey).
☐ 'Paris Symphonies' Nos 82-87

The formal beauty of 18th-century compositions gave way to the 'Romantic' period, in which emotional expression was paramount. The symphony came into its own, and some of the finest operas were written. The 20th century saw music develop in a wealth of ways – the 12-tone scale, folk influences, electronic sound, and even Orthodox church music each played a significant role.

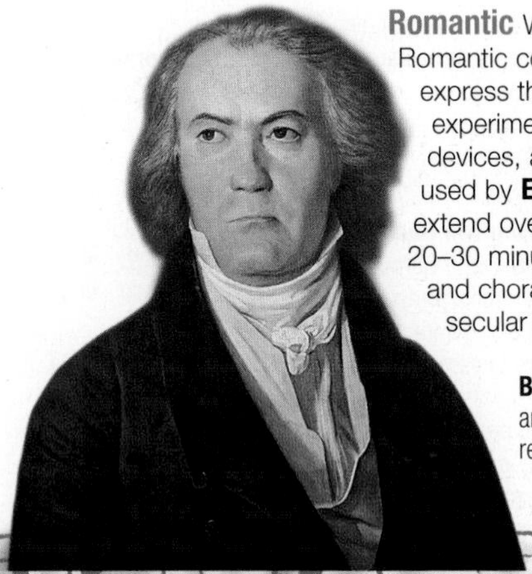

Romantic Working during the early to mid 1800s, Romantic composers sought dramatic ways to express their feelings. Rhythmic energy and experimentation became important expressive devices, as did the unusual, dissonant chords used by **Beethoven**. Symphonies began to extend over an hour in length, in contrast to the 20–30 minutes of the Classical period. Chamber and choral music declined in importance, while secular song remained popular.

Beethoven The forward-looking compositions and wide influence of Beethoven secured him a reputation as the greatest composer of all time.

Late Romantic As the 19th century drew to a close, Romantic composers wrote for increasingly large orchestras, and experimented with new kinds of expressive effects. Whereas previous composers had used dramatic key changes and dissonant chords for expressive effect, **Wagner** used them continuously to create emotional weight and tension. **Debussy** and **Ravel** introduced novel rhythm patterns and new types of harmony, some based on unconventional scales. Nationalism had a major impact. Folk melodies and popular song inspired the music of **Sibelius**, **Dvorak**, **Elgar**, and **Richard Strauss**.

Strauss Distinctive compositions such as *The Blue Danube* (1867) earned Johann Strauss the sobriquet 'the waltz king'.

1800

1800 The Romantic style is introduced with Beethoven's *Symphony No. 1*.
1816 Rossini's *The Barber of Seville* premiered.
1830 Berlioz composes the *Symphonie Fantastique*; Chopin writes his first mazurka.

1850

1853 First performance of Verdi's opera *Rigoletto*.
1859 Wagner premieres *Tristan und Isolde*.
1871 Verdi's *Aida* first performed.
1892 Tchaikovsky's *The Nutcracker* is premiered.

A GUIDE TO THE ORCHESTRA

The musicians in a full orchestra are always seated in a standard arrangement by instrument. The treble instruments are generally to the left, and the bass instruments to the right. The exact seating arrangements depend on the piece being performed: sometimes, for example, percussion might occupy more space.

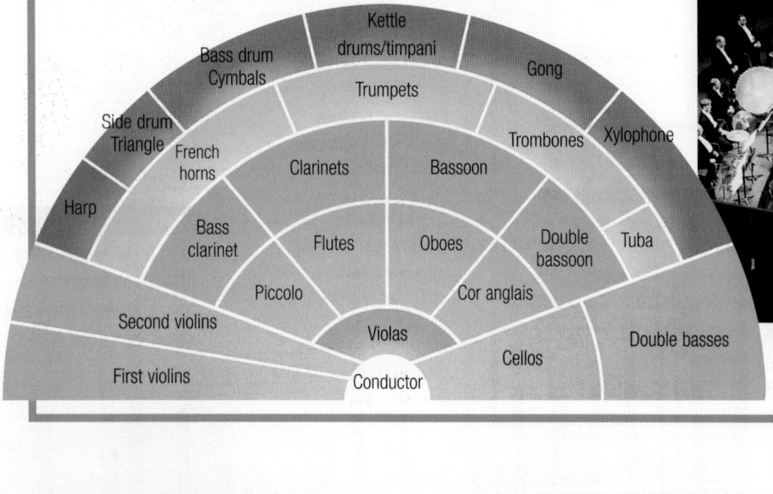

Kettle drums/timpani
Bass drum
Cymbals
Trumpets
Gong
Side drum
Triangle
French horns
Clarinets
Bassoon
Trombones
Xylophone
Harp
Bass clarinet
Flutes
Oboes
Double bassoon
Tuba
Piccolo
Cor anglais
Second violins
Violas
Cellos
Double basses
First violins
Conductor

Making music Modern symphony orchestras are seated in a schematic arrangement to ensure a full, balanced sound.

Modernism In 1913 *The Rite of Spring by* **Stravinsky** caused a riot at its Paris premiere because it rejected all traditional rhythm, instead juxtaposing discordant 'blocks' of music. Other composers, such as **Schoenberg**, adopted the 12-tone scale for whole pieces rather than short sections. Or, like **Bartók** or **Gershwin**, added influences from folk music or jazz. After 1945, **Stockhausen** and others carried this Modernist experimentation to new levels, with music composed from a wide variety of electronic and mechanical sounds completely unrelated to conventional musical instruments.

Post-modernism In the late 20th century, some composers returned to writing more accessible, harmonic music. Current music includes a range of approaches, from the trance-like minimalism of **Glass** or **Reich** to the Post-modernist revival of older musical forms, such as Orthodox church music (**Tavener**).

Tavener Stravinsky's music and Russian Orthodoxy inspired John Tavener's later compositions, such as *The Protecting Veil* (1989) and *Mary of Egypt* (1992).

Stravinsky Russian ballets such as *The Firebird* (1910) made Stravinsky's modern style popular.

1900

1960

1913 First performance of Stravinsky's *The Rite of Spring*.
1921 Arnold Schoenberg formulates the 12-tone scale, later adopted by Berg and Webern.
1924 Premier of George Gershwin's *Rhapsody in Blue*.

1961 Britten's *War Requiem* is premiered.
1984 Premier of Philip Glass's opera *Akhnaten*.
1988 Steve Reich composes *Different Trains*.
1989 Premier of John Tavener's *The Protecting Veil*.
1992 Henryk Górecki's *Symphony No 3* first performed.

Opera

Opera is generally said to have originated with Monteverdi, some 400 years ago. In the 18th century, Handel developed the genre with superb solo arias and Gluck's *Orfeo* showed how a libretto's musical and dramatic possibilities could be fully exploited. Haydn's operas were eclipsed by Mozart's later works of genius.

The two greatest opera composers of the 19th century were Verdi and Wagner. Verdi's genius emerged in *Rigoletto*, *La Traviata*, *Il Trovatore* and *Aïda*. After a 16-year gap he produced *Otello* (1887), with its varied, dynamic and tragic score.

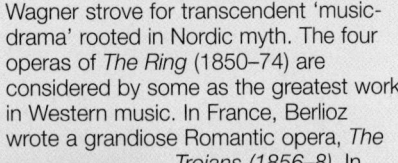

Wagner strove for transcendent 'music-drama' rooted in Nordic myth. The four operas of *The Ring* (1850–74) are considered by some as the greatest work in Western music. In France, Berlioz wrote a grandiose Romantic opera, *The Trojans (1856–8)*. In 1875 came Bizet's popular, passionate opera *Carmen*, Johann Strauss's archetypal Viennese operetta *Die Fledermaus* (The Bat), and the social satire of English operetta *HMS Pinafore* by Gilbert and Sullivan. At the turn of the century, Puccini dominated Italian opera with the popular works *La Bohème* (1896) and *Tosca* (1900).

Singing opera The voice of tenor Luciano Pavarotti is acclaimed for its purity of tone.

Composers L-Z

Franz Liszt
(1811-86) Hungarian
Liszt invented the symphonic poem, or tone poem – an orchestral composition inspired by subject matter such as literature or poetry, intended to evoke mental pictures. A great pianist, his works include 20 Hungarian Rhapsodies inspired by gypsy music.
☐ *Transcendental Studies*

Felix Mendelssohn
(1809-47) German
Mendelssohn's music combines Romantic passion with Classical form. He created melodies for overtures, including the Scottish-inspired *Fingal's Cave*, symphonies, concertos, sonatas and other forms.
☐ *Italian Symphony*

Wolfgang Amadeus Mozart
(1756-91) Austrian
A musical prodigy, Mozart developed the concerto form and wrote jubilant operas, such as *The Magic Flute*. His emotional music enriched many other musical forms – he was the only composer to write in every musical genre of his day.
☐ *Piano Concerto No 21 in C* (Elvira Madigan), opera *The Marriage of Figaro*

Giacomo Puccini
(1858-1924) Italian
An opera composer renowned for his flowing and dramatic melodies. Puccini based his emotionally charged music on stories of love, tragedy and violence in such operas as *Madame Butterfly*.
☐ Opera *La Bohème*

Franz Schubert
(1797-1828) German
Schubert composed more than 600 songs, which are noted for their memorable melodies. His other works included many symphonies, such as the 'Unfinished Symphony', piano sonatas, chamber music and overtures.
☐ *Quintet in C*

Richard Strauss
(1864-1949) German
A conductor and Late Romantic composer influenced by Wagner, Strauss was noted for his dramatic operas. He advanced the symphonic poem form and composed songs.
☐ Opera *Der Rosenkavalier*

Igor Stravinsky
(1882-1971) Russian
Stravinsky was a Modernist who used innovations of harmony and rhythm for ballet music. His dramatic, dissonant compositions created a completely new musical style.
☐ Ballet *The Firebird*

Peter Tchaikovsky
(1840-93) Russian
Melodic, emotional music made Tchaikovsky renowned for ballets such as *Swan Lake*. His *Piano Concerto No. 1* is the world's most popular and most recorded concerto.
☐ Ballet *Romeo and Juliet*

Giuseppe Verdi
(1813-1901) Italian
Verdi's powerful Romantic operas mix memorable arias with dramatic Italian moods. His 'Chorus of the Hebrew Slaves' in *Nabucco* became an anthem for Italian independence.
☐ Opera *La Traviata*

Richard Wagner
(1813-83) German
The theories of composer and conductor Wagner influenced the harmony, orchestration and structure of future opera. He united music, drama and other arts to create what he described as 'music-drama' – a term he preferred to opera.
☐ Opera cycle *Der Ring des Niebelungen*.

see also

338-9 **World mythology**
382-3 **Dance**
406-7 **Radio**
564-5 **Recorded sound**

At the turn of the 20th century, popular music existed in the form of light opera or 'operetta', and the theatrical entertainment prevailing in British music halls and in vaudeville in the USA, which attracted large and enthusiastic audiences. Fifty years later, the Western world's teenagers bopped to rock'n'roll. The catalyst for this transformation came when the descendants of west African slaves introduced the USA to the rhythm of jazz.

1900-1919

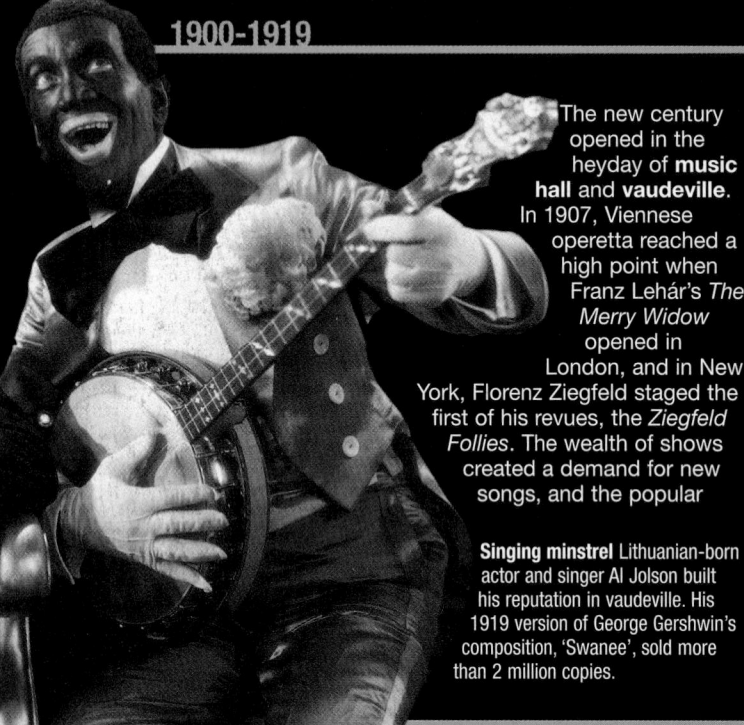

The new century opened in the heyday of **music hall** and **vaudeville**. In 1907, Viennese operetta reached a high point when Franz Lehár's *The Merry Widow* opened in London, and in New York, Florenz Ziegfeld staged the first of his revues, the *Ziegfeld Follies*. The wealth of shows created a demand for new songs, and the popular

Singing minstrel Lithuanian-born actor and singer Al Jolson built his reputation in vaudeville. His 1919 version of George Gershwin's composition, 'Swanee', sold more than 2 million copies.

music business began in New York's Tin Pan Alley, a street named for the constant pounding of pianos by songwriters demonstrating their work to publishers.

At the same time, a craze for **ragtime** gripped the USA. The 'ragged time' (syncopated) tunes were influenced by folk tradition, minstrel shows and marching bands. Scott Joplin's 'Maple Leaf Rag' (written in 1899) sold more than a million copies as sheet music. In 1911, songwriter Irving Berlin's long career began with the hit 'Alexander's Ragtime Band'.

Behind the scenes, rhythms brought to the USA by African slaves could be heard in New Orleans' brothels, where black musicians entertained the clients, and elsewhere. Their improvised music, influenced by blues and ragtime, became known as **jazz**. Jazz didn't remain behind closed doors – a group of white southerners formed The Original Dixieland Jazz Band in 1912 and entertained the rest of the city. The jazz sound drifted north, played by bands on Mississippi riverboats, and when the New Orleans' red light district closed in 1917, the Dixieland band travelled to New York.

Soon, Dixieland jazz became known across the USA. In 1922 the Cotton Club jazz venue opened in New York, making the new sound fashionable. US troops took jazz across the Atlantic to Europe during the First World War.

1920-1929

Musical comedy continued to develop alongside jazz. Broadway, the Manhattan theatre district, enjoyed its heyday in the 1920s. Memorable songs caught the public imagination in light entertainment shows such as *Lady Be Good* (1924) – **George Gershwin**'s first major musical. Gershwin's music fused classical music, popular music and jazz to create a new, distinctively American sound. In the same year, US bandleader Paul Whiteman commissioned Gershwin to write his most famous piece of music, 'Rhapsody in Blue'. By 1925, Broadway had 80 theatres, and between 1927 and 1928, 280 new productions opened, including **Jerome Kern**'s *Show Boat*, with plotting and characterisation that set new standards for the stage musical.

By the twenties, the centre of the jazz world had shifted from New Orleans to the speakeasies of Prohibition-era Chicago, where **Louis Armstrong**, **Bix Beiderbecke** and **Jelly Roll Morton** became the new giants of jazz. A new style of solo improvisation earned trumpeter, cornet player and gravelly voiced singer Armstrong worldwide acclaim. Vocalist **Bessie Smith** made a series of recordings with the top musicians of the decade, including Armstrong, which earned her the nickname 'Empress of the Blues'. In 1927, **Al Jolson** starred in the first 'talkie', *The Jazz Singer*, and Bix Beiderbecke recorded the jazz classic 'Singin' the Blues'. Standards of musicianship reached a pinnacle, and the decade as a whole

became known as the 'jazz age'. As the jazz craze spread across the USA, a new type of music crept onto the radio in the south and midwest USA – **country music**. The nostalgic rural songs, rooted in the folk tradition of English, Scottish and Irish settlers, told moral tales, accompanied by guitars and fiddles.

In 1925 the country music showcase *Grand Ole Opry* was first broadcast from Nashville, Tennessee. The show proved a hit with the burgeoning radio audience, and was to establish country music as a new American genre.

Talking jazz Singer, trumpeter and cornet player Louis 'Satchmo' Armstrong created 'scat' – a vocal style which imitated musical instruments.

Musicals now moved onto the big screen in lavish Hollywood productions. Radio star **Bing Crosby** introduced his smooth looks and crooning voice in *King of Jazz* (1930). *The Gay Divorcee* (1934), based on a **Cole Porter** story, and *Top Hat* (1935) by **Irving Berlin** entertained with pure escapism. In 1935, Gershwin's 'folk opera', *Porgy and Bess*, opened on Broadway – a mixture of operatic style, popular music and jazz.

The end of Prohibition in 1933 forced many musicians out of the illegal drinking clubs and into the open. Jazz adapted its style for wider appeal, tailoring itself to the dance hall in the form of big bands and swing. Bandleaders **Count Basie**, **Duke Ellington** and **Paul Whiteman** led the change. Vocalist **Billie Holiday** dominated the decade with her jazz interpretations

of popular songs, recording with saxophonist **Lester Young**, whose light tone influenced soloists such as Charlie Parker. In 1934, **Fats Waller** introduced his humorous vocal jazz style, and three years later, **Glenn Miller** began leading orchestras in his distinctive style of swing.

Big-band leader Trombonist Glenn Miller put the swing into dance orchestras with his innovative arrangements.

1940-49

Hollywood continued to create star vocalists such as **Ella Fitzgerald** and **Frank Sinatra**. In 1942, Irving Berlin's genius for melody produced the song 'White Christmas'; Bing Crosby's version has sold more than 30 million copies.

The smoothness of swing provoked a jazz rebellion in the form of **bebop**, or 'hot jazz' – an experimental form with complex rhythms and harmonies, led by

Ol' Blue Eyes Frank Sinatra recorded his first hit, 'All or Nothing at All', in 1943. He remained a top concert performer into the 1990s.

saxophonist **Charlie Parker**, trumpeter **Dizzy Gillespie** and guitarist **Charlie Christian** – the first to use electrical amplification. At the same time, **Woody Guthrie**'s songs, such as 'This Land is Your Land', caused a quiet revolution in folk music, expressing popular sentiments about the Great Depression and the suffering of the poor. His writing was to influence Bob Dylan and a host of folk singers 20 years later.

The mixing of musical styles opened up new avenues. Under the influence of swing, country music was transformed: **western swing** emerged, with amplified guitars and strong dance rhythms, and **honky tonk** developed in the hands of US singers such as **Hank Williams**.

In 1949, US magazine *Billboard* christened a new fusion of blues, boogie-woogie, jazz and mainstream pop music: **rhythm and blues**.

1950-59

Rhythm and blues, characterised by the rolling guitar rhythms of **Jackie Wilson** and the laid-back style of **B.B. King**, became big business in the USA in the early 1950s. Country music also became increasingly commercial. **Johnny Cash** began recording in 1955, and in 1957 **Patsy Cline** won the talent competition that launched her career.

A mixture of black rhythm and blues and white country music produced the dominant style of the new decade – **rock'n'roll**. The regular beat and young lyrics appealed to teenagers, and the first music charts, which appeared in the USA in the late 1940s and in Britain in 1952, confirmed its popularity. In 1955, **Bill Haley**'s 'Rock Around the Clock' reached number 1 – sales eventually topped 22 million. In the same year, the manic piano style and outrageous clothes of **Little Richard** made 'Tutti Frutti' a hit, and **Chuck Berry** made his debut with 'Maybellene'. The rock'n'roll of Berry and rhythm and blues of B.B. King became two of the most important influences on the popular music of the 1960s.

In 1956, **Elvis Presley** released 'Heartbreak Hotel'. Because he was white and sounded black, he captured the spirit of rock'n'roll, and became the biggest-selling artist in the history of popular music. In 1957, **Jerry Lee Lewis**

released the classic rock'n'roll tracks 'Whole Lotta Shakin' and 'Great Balls of Fire'. In the same year, **Buddy Holly** and The Crickets set trends that still persist in popular music with the release of 'Peggy Sue', using a line-up of two guitarists, a bassist and a drummer, and studio techniques such as double-tracking.

Just one year after Buddy Holly's death in a plane crash in 1959, popular music began to take a new direction.

American dream Elvis Presley produced 14 consecutive million-selling records before he was conscripted into the US army in 1958.

n the 1960s, the folk tradition gave pop music a new focus by introducing a social conscience into modern lyrics. In combination with teenage angst, this led to the rebelliousness of punk and heavy rock in the 1970s. Reacting against such intensity, disco, and later electronic pop, attracted wide appeal. By the end of the 20th century, a huge variety of musical styles catered for every taste and cultural niche.

1960-1969

In the USA, rock'n'roll gave way to a revival of **folk** and pure **rhythm and blues**, styles more suited to a decade of political protest. Singers **Bob Dylan**

Voice of a generation Bob Dylan's songwriting was heavily influenced by the socially-conscious style of 1940s singer Woody Guthrie.

and **Joan Baez** led the movement. Dylan's 'Blowin' in the Wind' (1962) became a civil rights anthem.

By the middle of the decade, the rise of the small Motown record label in Detroit led to its name becoming a byword for **soul** music – a new singing style with its roots in the gospel tradition. **Stevie Wonder**, the **Supremes**, **Marvin Gaye** and **Gladys Knight** popularised the Motown sound.

In Britain, The **Beatles** created their own musical style with a blend of clear melodies and complex rhythms. Their 1963 single 'From Me to You' began an unbroken run of UK number one hits that dominated the decade, lasting until 1967. Paul McCartney and John Lennon were the group's chief lyricists. Their compositions included 'Please Please Me' and 'Hey Jude'. The Beatles stopped performing as a band in 1969.

Rock music continued to develop in Britain, where **Jimi Hendrix** worked on his experimental guitar technique, and the **Rolling Stones** created a mix

of rhythm and blues and rock'n'roll. In 1968, a heavier rock style began to emerge in the music of **Led Zeppelin**.

The fab four The Beatles created the first 'concept' album, *Sgt. Pepper's Lonely Hearts Club Band* (1967) – a collection of songs connected by a narrative thread.

1970-1979

The Led Zeppelin rock style became known as **heavy metal**, and throughout the 1970s, new groups such as **Van Halen** (formed in 1974) and **Def Leppard** (1977) adopted the sound. A mixture of rock and melodic pop produced the **glam rock** of **Elton John** and **David Bowie**, with flamboyant stage costumes and make-up.

In contrast, disco music became an international force, with a pop beat designed for dancing and an emphasis on slick studio production. The well-produced vocal harmonies of Swedish group **Abba** made them a Europe-wide success with sing-along hits such as 'Dancing Queen' (1976).

West Indian rhythms fused black disco with soul to create **reggae**, with a strong off-beat and heavy bass line. Jamaican musician **Bob Marley** popularised the sound worldwide with hits including 'Get Up, Stand Up' (1973) and 'No Woman No Cry' (1975).

Meanwhile, musicals are brought up to date with *Jesus Christ Superstar*, which opened in London in 1973.

In the second half of the decade, the spirit of youth rebellion arose again, this time in the form of aggressive, thrashing **punk** rock. Leading the new genre, the **Sex Pistols** attacked contemporary Britain in the lyrics of

'Anarchy in the UK' (1976) and 'God Save the Queen' (1977).

Reggae star Bob Marley made his first record at the age of 19. In 1965, he formed his group, The Wailers, with 'Bunny' Livingstone and Peter Tosh.

1980-1989

Punk survived into the 1980s in Britain, metamorphosing into fast, distorted, uncommercial hardcore, but a backlash soon began in the London clubs. **Spandau Ballet** and **Duran Duran** drew on glam rock to perform the melodic pop of the **New Romantics** dressed in elaborate clothes and make-up. Thrashing guitars were abandoned for synthesisers by **Depeche Mode**, and computer-based German band **Kraftwerk** enjoyed a new popularity.

In the USA, vocal soloists took the lead. **Madonna** Ciccone's debut album (*Madonna*, 1983) produced five US hit singles, including 'Holiday' and 'Lucky Star' (1984). Only two other vocalists could compete: **Prince**, who had US number ones with 'Let's Go Crazy' (1984) and 'When Doves Cry' (1985), and **Michael Jackson**, whose *Thriller* (1982) became the most successful

Into the groove Madonna became known for her extravagant costumes and provocative personae during the 1990 Blonde Ambition tour. The 1991 film *In Bed With Madonna* recorded behind-the-scenes footage of the tour.

album of all time, selling 42 million copies by the early 1990s.

In New York, **rap** emerged: rhythmic chanting of streetwise lyrics over a heavy, rhythmic backing track. Its distinctive style spawned a host of pop subcultures, including **hip-hop**, which took its percussive effect from 'scratching' (manually rotating) vinyl records – extracting ('sampling') musical phrases to create new tracks, set to an electronic drum beat.

Digital sampling using computer technology opened up new forms of dance music. In Chicago, a mix of black disco and pop, using studio sampling and dubbing, became known as **house** music, named after the dance club Warehouse.

From Chicago house music, **acid house** evolved, stripping away vocals and melodies and replacing them with the distinctive acid sound of the Roland 303 synthesiser.

In the late 1980s, New York club Paradise Garage brought a new sound to dance music – the rhythmic but soulful **garage**.

1990-1999

In the early 1990s in Seattle, heavy rock and punk combined to create **grunge** – fast, thrashing rock with melodic overtones. The sound brought commercial success for **Nirvana**, and their *Nevermind* album (1991) popularised grunge worldwide.

British pop musicians reacted against grunge with the distinctive sound of **Britpop**. Beatles-influenced group **Oasis** and **Blur** – influenced by earlier British bands Madness and The Kinks – competed for the top chart position. By 1997, US influences had diluted the style.

Dance music and rap continued to develop derivative styles. As the 1980s ended, the minimalist electronic sound of **techno** jumped from its birthplace in Detroit to Europe. There, beefed up with stronger beats and bass lines, it evolved into **hardcore** and, by the mid-1990s, **jungle** music. Rap evolved into **ragga** – rapping in Jamaican patois.

In the pop charts, mainstream solo vocalists and 'teen' bands dominated. **Madonna**'s sound matured with her *Ray of Light* album (1998), an introspective though 'danceable' selection of tracks.

The Canadian singer, **Celine Dion**, recorded 'Because You Loved Me'

(1996), the highest-selling adult contemporary single ever, and a year later she could be heard on radio stations the world over singing 'My Heart Will Go On', the theme tune to the film *Titanic*.

In Britain, a female quintet, the **Spice Girls** eclipsed the success of popular boybands such as **Take That**

when sales of their albums *Spice* (1996) and *Spiceworld* (1997) made them the most commercially successful UK pop artists of the decade.

Reach for the stars S-Club 7 is an example of the carefully constructed, expertly marketed, clean-cut boy/girl band of the late 1990s.

The roots of dance lie in the celebration of ritual and religion. The ancient Greeks considered it a vital part of education, and formalised traditions appeared in India, Korea and Manchuria 2000 years ago. Social dancing appeared much later: in Europe, folk dancing spread through all strata of society in the 14th century. The more restrained dances of the royal courts developed into ballet.

BALLROOM

Couple-dancing became popular in Europe in the 14th century, and by the 17th century, new styles had begun to evolve. The courtly **minuet** began in France in 1663, followed by the lively **gavotte** in 1696. The **waltz** evolved in Austria in 1781 from German peasant dances. During the 19th century it became a ballroom dance.

Bohemian folk dancing created the three quick steps and a hop of the **polka**.

In the years before the First World War, several new styles became popular. Harry Fox introduced the **foxtrot** in the 1913 Ziegfeld *Follies* revue. The tilting body movements of the **maxixe**, a mixture of polka and African-influenced Brazilian dance, laid foundations for the **samba**.

The **tango** reached the ballrooms in 1913, having developed in Buenos Aires. Later styles evolved from Latin America, including the swaying Afro-Cuban **rumba** (1922) and the modern **salsa** (1962), which was influenced by jazz and rock.

The foxtrot A combination of walking and faster steps and turns are performed to a syncopated rhythm.

BALLET

The Paris Opéra's 1832 production of *La Sylphide* began the first era of ballet – the romantic style – based on stories of passionate but chaste love, with a female lead. The genre reached its peak with *Giselle* (1841). Dancing on 'points' (shoes with the toes blocked in) was introduced by Marie Taglioni, who starred as the first La Sylphide.

In Russia, the Imperial Ballet Company (founded in 1738, now known as the Mariinskiy Ballet) and the Bolshoi Ballet (1776) established the formal, enduring genre of classical ballet. Russian composer Tchaikovsky and French choreographer Marius Petipa characterised the style with *Sleeping Beauty* (1890), *The Nutcracker* (1892) and *Swan Lake* (1895). Russia continued to lead the way in the first

Classical steps
Charle-Louis Beauchamp invented the five positions of classical ballet in 1661.

years of the 20th century with the innovative music and scenery of the Ballet Russes founded by Sergei Diaghilev in 1909. The company introduced new ideas, using folk influences in *The Firebird* (1910) and separating music and narrative in *L'Après-midi d'un faune* (1912).

Russian-born George Balanchine re-created classical ballet in a modern style with the New York City Ballet (1948). His *Serenade* (1934) relied on the audience to interpret the loose narrative.

In the latter years of the 20th century, American choreographers Twyla Tharp and Mark Morris have taken ballet to a wider audience by combining it with popular contemporary dance.

CULTURAL

Many dance styles are particular to specific communities, and originate from national folk dances. The 2000-year-old Indian classical dance tradition of **Bharata natyam** is based on narratives recounting the exploits of the gods. Facial gestures are as important as the movements and stamping rhythms.

Eastern courtly dances are still performed in Japan, where they are known as **bugaku**. Dancers wear elaborate character masks, and follow traditional, geometric movements cued by drum beats. The style has two forms, corresponding to the musical traditions of China and Korea.

A mixture of Arabic and Spanish folk traditions produced **flamenco**, the dance of the Andalusian gypsies, first performed

professionally in the 19th century. Toe and heel clicking and graceful arm movements accompany a song (*cante*), and are *grande* (anguished) or *chicho* (light and lively) in expression.

Bharata natyam Expressive movement and improvised rhythms are used to tell a story.

DANCE CRAZES

Dance crazes developed in tandem with the evolution of popular music. In 1900, just as jazz was beginning to emerge, Afro-Americans created a satirical mimicking of white ballroom dancing, the **cakewalk**. Couples formed a square with the men on the inside, and strutted around the square to music. Couples with the best style won a cake. The 1920s **Charleston** also owed its popularity to the stage – its appearance in the musical *Running Wild* (1923) brought this black folk dance into the dance halls.

The influence of African dance continued into the swing era of the 1930s and 1940s in the high lifts and fast footwork of **jitterbug** and **jive**. US troops took the new styles to Europe during the Second World War. By the 1950s, **rock'n'roll** swept across the USA and Europe, retaining the traditional ballroom hold but adding pivoting, sliding and high throws.

Films and television popularised the bent knees and swaying hips of the **twist**, originated by US singer Hank Ballard in 1958, and made **disco** an international craze in 1977 with the film *Saturday Night Fever*. From disco, **breakdancing** evolved in New York in the late 1970s, with robotic walking and fast body spins resting on the neck and shoulders. By the 1990s, techno music dance parties in Europe and the USA had created **rave**, a euphoric style driven by interpretation of the music's regular, heavy bass beat.

see also
376-7 **Classical music**
378-81 **Popular music**
394-9 **Cinema**

Synchronised steps Line dancing evolved during the 1970s from fad dances such as Bus Stop and The Mashed Potato.

FILM

In the 1930s and 40s, Busby Berkeley set a new trend in Hollywood musicals with lavish sets and vast numbers of dancers. Berkeley's dance routines often created a kaleidoscopic effect when filmed from above, as in **Footlight Parade** in 1933. In the same year, the partnership of Ginger Rogers and Fred Astaire began in **Flying Down to Rio**. It continued for another nine films, eight of which were collaborations between choreographer Hermes Pan and Astaire. The dancing of Astaire in the 1930s, and of Gene Kelly in the 1940s and 1950s, revolutionised the film musical with innovative routines. Kelly co-directed and starred in **Singin' in the Rain** (1952), one of the most popular musicals ever produced. In 1957, Jerome Robbins choreographed the Broadway show **West Side Story**, introducing a mixture of jazz dance and modern ballet to a mass audience. Choreographer Bob Fosse won acclaim for his stylised routines in **Cabaret** (1972).

Legendary duo The effortless style of Fred Astaire and Ginger Rogers heralded a new dance era.

CHOREOGRAPHY

The most influential figures in 20th-century ballet, **Michel Fokine** (1880-1942) and **George Balanchine** (1904-83), worked with the Ballet Russes early in their careers. Fokine moved away from the classical style. Balanchine concentrated on pure dance with no narrative, and minimal costumes and scenery.

The freer, naturalistic style of **Isadora Duncan** (1877-1927) established the foundations of modern dance. Leading choreographer of the modern style, **Martha Graham** (1894-1991), expressed emotion through movement centred in the solar plexus. She themed many of her dances around the women of Greek mythology. **Merce Cunningham** (1919-) founded a post-modern alternative to Graham's style, creating steps separately from the musical score, free of dramatic narrative.

In the 1970s, **Twyla Tharp** (1941-) worked in jazz and ballet, and on Broadway, bringing classical techniques

Frederick Ashton British choreographer Ashton's witty, romantic reworkings of classical favourites helped to popularise ballet in the mid 20th century.

to modern dance. The mixing of styles continues in the work of **Mark Morris** (1956-), who creates unconventional, often comical performances.

The earliest literature of many cultures includes founding myths that were collected together into epic narratives – the Iliad *(ancient Greece), the* Aeneid *(ancient Rome),* Beowulf *(England), the* Poema del Cid *(Spain), the* Chanson de Roland *(France) and the* Nibelungenlied *(Germany). Other forms of poetry also evolved as did prose narrative and non-fiction. In the 14th century, European writers began to rediscover the literature of the classical Greeks and Romans, and used it as their model.*

How the novel evolved Prose writing emerged in ancient Greece, but the novel took much longer to evolve as an art form. Many strands contributed to the emergence of the novel in 16th-century Europe. Writers drew on the traditions of sagas and romances, biographical sketches, and diaries and journals. The term novel comes from the Italian *novella*, meaning 'story' or 'piece of news'. It came to be used to describe stories about everyday life, sometimes based on contemporary incidents or events, so distinguishing them from romances, which were set in the past.

Dante Alighieri

Geoffrey Chaucer

Homer

800 BC			19 BC		AD 900		1300	

c.800 BC Homer compiles the *Iliad* and the *Odyssey*, the greatest Greek epic poems, cornerstones of later Western literature.

c.450 BC Herodotus writes the first major Greek prose, a history of the Persian Wars.

c.300 BC The poet Theocritus invents the pastoral, a country idyll based on a fantasy world, peopled by shepherds and shepherdesses.

19 BC Virgil dies just before completing his epic masterpiece the *Aeneid*.

8 BC Horace, noted for his *Odes* and *Satires,* dies. Ovid is exiled, possibly for his scandalous love poetry, *Ars Amatoria.* He dies in AD 18.

c.AD 900 The Old English epic *Beowulf* is written down, but probably dates back to c.750.

c.1120 *Chanson de Roland*, one of the earliest French romances appears. Like much work of this period, the author is unknown.

1307 Dante begins the *Divine Comedy*, the first great epic poem in Italian.

1387 Chaucer starts the *Canterbury Tales*, among the first poems written in English.

Classical literature Ancient Greece produced some of the earliest poetry of any note, largely in the form of the *Iliad* and the *Odyssey*, two epic works by **Homer** that explored themes of love, honour, vengeance and death. Later poets focused on shorter lyric verse, such as the pastoral fantasies of **Theocritus**.

The *Odyssey* Homer's epic recounted Odysseus's escape from the Cyclops.

The Greeks were also responsible for the first history and scientific texts. **Herodotus**, considered the 'father of history', was a masterly writer of prose.

Rome aimed to rival the Greek output. This was largely achieved by the poets **Virgil**, **Horace** and **Ovid** under the patronage of the Emperor Augustus (27 BC-AD 14). Virgil is recognised as Rome's greatest poet, but Horace is the finest stylist, and, with Ovid, influenced 18th-century English poetry.

The Romans, too, wrote prose histories. **Caesar** described his own exploits in *The Gallic Wars*, while **Tacitus** and **Suetonius** chronicled the emperors, and **Cicero**, the master of oratory, provided sharply observed social commentary in his letters.

Medieval romances and epics Sagas, prose narratives about the exploits of well-known kings and warriors, were popular in medieval Iceland and Scandinavia. Until the 12th century they existed only in oral form.

Romances – long poetic tales of knightly valour – first appeared in France and Germany in the 12th century. Although written to entertain, they also have a moral point. Some of the best known are *Chanson de Roland*, and the allegorical *The Romance of the Rose*, with its theme of idealised 'courtly love', a central topic of much 12th-century poetry. English romances appeared in the 13th century, and included the chivalric *Sir Gawain and the Green Knight*. By the 15th century, romances were being written in prose.

Narrative poetry was widely written, and culminated in the work of **Dante** and **Chaucer**, who were also among the first poets to write lyric poetry to be read rather than sung. In 14th-century Italy, there was a fashion for the prose short story, or **novella**. These were often published in collections, such as **Boccaccio**'s the *Decameron*.

Pseudonyms

● **Anthony Burgess** John Wilson, forbidden to write while in the British colonial service, became famous as Anthony Burgess for *A Clockwork Orange*, *Enderby* and *Earthly Powers*.
● **Izak Dinesen** Karen Blixen wrote *Gothic Tales* as Izak Dinesen in order to escape the name of a husband she loathed.
● **George Elliot** Mary Ann Evans masked her gender with a male pseudonym to help to secure publication of her novels. Sales fell briefly when her identity was revealed.

● **George Orwell** Eric Blair chose the surname Orwell because 'O' seemed to him to be the best initial for catching a buyer's attention.
● **George Sand** Armandine Dudevant took a man's name so that she would be taken seriously when she began writing romantic novels in the 1830s.
● **Stendhal** Henri Beyle, author of *The Scarlet and Black*, adopted his *nom de plume* when he was serving as a French consul in Italy.

William Shakespeare

1400	1500		1600		

c.1477 William Caxton sets up a printing press in London. He publishes many of his own translations of French works, which strongly influence 15th-century English prose.

1579 *Euphues, the Anatomy of Wit* by John Lyly, the first English picaresque novel, is published.

1590 Sir Philip Sidney's *Arcadia* and the first three books of Edmund Spenser's the *Faerie Queene* are published.

1605 The first part of *Don Quixote* by Cervantes appears.

1609 The complete *Sonnets* of William Shakespeare are published. They form the longest sonnet cycle in English.

1667 Milton finishes *Paradise Lost*, his great religious epic.

Dante's *Inferno* One of the punishments described by Dante, illustrated by William Blake.

The Renaissance The rediscovery of classical literature began in 14th-century Italy and resulted in a different world view from that of medieval feudalism. Classical culture emphasised the importance of the individual, which contributed to an introspective approach to writing. Lyric poetry, including songs, and religious and mystical poems, flourished, as did the love poem in sonnet form. The sonnet was developed in the 14th century by **Petrarch** in Italy and **Ronsard** in France, and perfected by **Shakespeare**. **Spenser**'s *The Faerie Queene* brought the chivalric epic tradition to an end.

An early form of the novel, known as picaresque, appeared in 16th-century Spain, in which a roguish hero romps through a series of self-contained adventures. **Cervantes**' romance *Don Quixote* is the best example.

In the 17th century, English poets **Donne**, **Marvell** and **Herbert**, wrote verse focused on analysis of the heightened emotions aroused by love and religion. The group later became known as the Metaphysical Poets. **Milton** revived the epic with *Paradise Lost*.

Writers A–G

The following poets and novelists helped to shape the course of Western literature.
☐ Refers to a major work.

Jane Austen
(1775-1817) British
In her concentration on ordinary characters in everyday situations, Austen created a microcosm of the larger world.
☐ *Pride and Prejudice*

Emily Brontë
(1818-48) British
Wrote poetry and one novel, in which she showed a deep love of nature and understanding of human passion. She was one of the first novelists to refrain from judging the behaviour of her characters.
☐ *Wuthering Heights*

Lord Byron
(1788-1824) British
Romantic poet whose verse melodramas caught the imagination of Europe. His work influenced Romanticism in poetry, music and painting.
☐ *Don Juan*

Miguel de Cervantes
(1547-1616) Spanish
In *Don Quixote*, Cervantes ridiculed the chivalric code and the whole romance tradition. It is the most translated book after the Bible. He also wrote plays and poems.
☐ *Don Quixote*

Geoffrey Chaucer
(1343-1400) English
Considered one of the finest poets in English literature. He was the first English poet to develop the use of the ten-syllable line, which evolved into the heroic couplet.
☐ *Canterbury Tales*

Dante Alighieri
(1265-1321) Italian
The first major author to write in Italian rather than Latin. He wrote one of the greatest of all narrative poems, and influenced Chaucer among others.
☐ *Divine Comedy*

Charles Dickens
(1812-70) British
In novels that move between high farce and grim reality, Dickens

created a model of society in his time.
☐ *Oliver Twist*

Fyodor Dostoyevsky
(1821-81) Russian
One of the first novelists to explore the ambiguities of the human psyche. His novels deal with universal themes of sin, suffering, guilt, conscience and the search for faith.
☐ *Crime and Punishment*

George Eliot (Mary Ann Evans) (1819-80) British
Eliot introduced several plot strands and a variety of characters, and developed the psychological analysis of characters. She also used her work to discuss moral and social problems in Victorian England.
☐ *Middlemarch*

Thomas Stearns Eliot
(1888-1965)
American/British
A founding Modernist poet and dramatist. Eliot revolutionised poetry through his insistence on the use of new forms and rhythms, and modern subject matter, such as the industrial city.
☐ *The Waste Land*

Gustave Flaubert
(1821-80) French
A perfectionist who spent hours on every sentence, Flaubert's psychological insight and piling up of precise detail – based on extensive research and observation – made him an influential early realist.
☐ *Madame Bovary*

Gabriel García Márquez
(1928-) Colombian
Through short stories and novels set in his native Colombia, García Márquez became a leading practitioner of magic realism.
☐ *One Hundred Years of Solitude*

see also
174-5 **Ancient Rome**
194-5 **The Renaissance**
338-9 **World mythology**
390-3 **Drama**

Eighteenth-century writers were influenced by Classicism, drawn by the order, harmony and moral sense that they found in early Roman models. The novel took shape in its modern form. Towards the end of the century there was a reaction against the discipline of Classicism as writers produced work which emphasised the importance of imagination.

Forms of poetry

Allegory Story in verse or prose in which characters and incidents have one or more symbolic meanings in addition to the literal meaning.
Dramatic monologue Poem in which a speaker reveals his or her inner thoughts and ideas to an audience.
Elegy Reflective poem usually dealing with death and mortality.
Epic Long narrative poem, often celebrating the feats of heroes, and often about the founding of a race or nation. Homer's *Iliad* and Virgil's *Aeneid* are

ancient epics; Tolstoy's *War and Peace* is an epic in modern form.
Epigram Short poem ending with a witty saying.
Free verse Verse without metre or rhyme.
Lyric Originally a poem sung to a lyre; now a non-narrative poem expressing an individual's ideas and feelings.
Soliloquy An interior monologue in which a character examines his or her thoughts and feelings.
Sonnet Poem of 14 lines usually ending in a rhyming couplet.

Voltaire   Jane Austen

1700

1719 Daniel Defoe's *Robinson Crusoe* appears.

1726 *Gulliver's Travels*, Jonathan Swift's satirical masterpiece, is published.

1731 Abbé Prévost's *Manon Lescaut* establishes the novel in France.

1740 Henry Fielding's novel, *Joseph Andrews* is published, followed by *Tom Jones* in 1749.

1747 Samuel Richardson produces *Clarissa*, considered his finest work.

1755 Samuel Johnson finishes his *Dictionary of the English Language*.

1759 First instalments of Laurence Sterne's *Tristram Shandy* appear.

1774 Goethe's *Sorrows of Young Werther* introduces the first romantically morbid young hero.

1789 *The Power of Sympathy*, by William Hill Brown, is the first American novel.

Classicism Literature, particularly in England and France in the late 17th and 18th century, was characterised by a passion for clarity of form, and a strong sense of reason and order. Styles followed those of the ancient Greeks and Romans, who were much admired. In England, poets such as **Dryden** and **Pope** produced satirical verse in heroic couplets, modelled on the poetry of Virgil and Ovid. The French classical scholar and poet **de la Fontaine** drew on classical forms and sources for many of his *Fables*.

Satire was a common element in literature of this time. In addition to verse, there was a large body of satirical prose, such as **de la Bruyère**'s *The Characters, or the Manner of the Age* and **Swift**'s *Gulliver's Travels*. Prose in general flourished. Many modern forms, including the novel, biography, travel writing and journalism, developed.

The essay was popular, and owed much to the growth of journalism, with the increasing number of periodicals offering opportunity for publication. **Johnson**, a leading satirist and prose stylist, was noted for his *Rambler* and *Idler* essays.

The rise of the novel The novel became established in its modern form in the 18th century, largely in England and France. **Defoe** and **Richardson**'s set the format in England, and **Fielding** took it further, with more complex plots and greater realism. **Sterne**'s *Tristram Shandy* dispensed with a chronological framework to present life as a jumble of unrelated events. The early 19th century brought **Austen**'s detached, ironic dissections of human motivation and folly.

Psychological insight was already a noted quality of some of the earliest French novels, such as those of **Madame de la Fayette**, written in the late 17th and early 18th centuries. **Abbé Prévost**'s *Manon Lescaut*, published in 1731, foreshadowed Romanticism. By the mid 18th century, political and philosophical writers like **Voltaire** and **Rousseau** were using fictional situations as a vehicle for their ideas on the importance of emotions and individualism.

Tristram Shandy An illustration from 1786.

Children's classics

Books written specifically for children first appeared in the 18th century. During the 19th century the major genres became established. F.R. Marryat pioneered the boys' adventure story with *Masterman Ready* (1841), followed by R.M. Ballantyne's *The Coral Island* (1857). In 1857, Thomas Hughes's *Tom Brown's Schooldays* established the vogue for school stories. C.M. Yonge's *The Daisy Chain* (1856) and Louisa May Alcott's *Little Women* (1868) brought in the family saga. Anna Sewell's *Black Beauty* (1877) provided a model for animal stories.

In the early 20th century, Kenneth Grahame's *Wind in the Willows* (1908), A.A. Milne's *Winnie the Pooh* (1926) and Arthur Ransome's *Swallows and Amazons* (1930) became classics. Fantasy was established as a leading genre by J.R. Tolkien with *The Hobbit* (1937) and *Lord of the Rings* (1954-5). C.S. Lewis combined fantasy with adventure and allegory in *The Lion, the Witch and the Wardrobe* (1950).

At the beginning of the 20th century, Helen Bannerman and Beatrix Potter successfully championed the idea of books in which text and illustrations are of equal importance.

William Wordsworth

Wolfgang von Goethe

1800

1820

1798 Publication of *Lyrical Ballads*, by William Wordsworth and Samuel Taylor Coleridge, launches English Romanticism.

1811 *Sense and Sensibility*, Jane Austen's first major work, is published.

1812 Lord Byron's *Childe Harold* triggers a new phase of English Romanticism.

1818 Mary Shelley publishes her Gothic novel, *Frankenstein*.

1821 The first great American novel, James Fenimore Cooper's *The Spy*, appears.

1823 Alexander Pushkin begins the verse novel *Eugene Onegin*.

Romanticism Romanticism represented a backlash against the formality of the Classicists. It idealised 'nature', and stressed the importance of individual experience. Lyric poetry was revived throughout Europe: short verses were the perfect vehicle for poets who wanted to present delicate sketches of fleeting emotion. German poets, such as **Hölderlin** and **Goethe** led the way. The first major English Romantics – **Blake**, **Coleridge** and **Wordsworth** – followed, inspiring a second generation, including **Byron**, **Shelley** and **Keats**. **Hugo** was the main influence in France.

Idealisation of the past led to a vogue for historical fiction: **Scott**'s novels and poems were an influence on the great Russian poet, **Pushkin**. An obsession with darker emotions fuelled the Gothic novel, such as those of **Shelley** in England, and **Poe** in the USA.

By 1830, Romanticism was shaping the work of some of the first American literary giants. **Thoreau**, **Hawthorne** and **Melville** treated the natural world as symbolic of the spiritual world, and came to be known as romantic symbolists.

Childe Harold's Pilgrimage Byron's poem provided a model for the romantic hero.

Writers G–N

Wolfgang von Goethe
(1749-1832) German
A poet, dramatist and novelist, Goethe was a leading figure in the German Romantic movement, although his dramatic and lyrical verse transcended any romantic/classical divide. He transformed German poetry, raising it to among the world's greatest.
☐ *The Sorrows of Young Werther*

Nathaniel Hawthorne
(1804-64) American
One of the finest early American novelists, Hawthorne was preoccupied with themes of sin, conscience and ancestral guilt. His classical style and use of allegory influenced other American writers such as Melville and Henry James.
☐ *The Scarlet Letter*

Seamus Heaney
(1939-) Irish
Heaney's earlier poetry drew on rural Ireland and expresses a strong sense of physical environment. His later works deal increasingly with Ireland's political problems.
☐ *Selected Poems 1966-87*

Ernest Hemingway
(1899-1961) American
A writer of novels and short stories, Hemingway's economic style, terse dialogue and characterisations have made him one of the most influential and imitated writers of his time.
☐ *A Farewell to Arms*

Homer
(*c*.800 BC) Greek
The stories in Homer's epics had been told many times, but he transformed his source material through poetic power and the development of character. The Greeks admired him above all other poets.
☐ *Odyssey*

Victor Hugo
(1802-85) French
A central figure in the Romantic movement and often considered France's greatest lyric poet. He experimented with language and rhythm in his poetry, while his novels have an epic sweep.
☐ *Les Misérables*

Henry James
(1843-1916) American
In his novels, short stories and plays, James explored the clash between the American and European character and the impact of old and new cultures on each other. He explored characters' inner selves confronted with difficult moral choices.
☐ *The Portrait of a Lady*

James Joyce
(1882-1941) Irish
Modernist who revolutionised the structure of the novel and pushed language to the limits of communication. His use of the 'stream of consciousness' technique influenced many writers, including Virginia Woolf and William Faulkner.
☐ *Ulysses*

Thomas Mann
(1875-1955) German
Modernist novelist who chronicled the decline of the German bourgeoisie, the creative anguish of artists and the perils of Nazism.
☐ *The Magic Mountain*

Herman Melville
(1819-91) American
Created the mixed-genre romantic/symbolic novel, and increased the scope and stylistic range of American fiction.
☐ *Moby Dick*

John Milton
(1608-74) English
Wrote poetry in a variety of forms, including sonnets and a masque. His greatest achievement was to produce the finest post-classical epic poem. His work mixes passion with self-discipline, and was an influence on the Romantics.
☐ *Paradise Lost*

see also

198-9 **Age of kings**

390-3 **Drama**

In an era of rapid industrialisation, Romanticism seemed too escapist. Nineteenth-century novelists wanted to describe the real world and the social forces at work in it. This trend was overturned in the early 20th century by writers who wanted to make a complete break with the past. At the end of the century, poets and novelists experimented with a range of approaches, including parody, pastiche and a mixture of traditions.

Key terms

Alliteration A repetition of consonants in nearby words, especially at the start of words: '...rifles rapid rattle...'
Assonance Two or more nearby words that contain a similar vowel sound: '...swimmers into cleanness leaping...'
Blank verse Verse that does not rhyme but has metre.
Foot A group of two to four syllables making up a unit of rhythm in verse.
Hexameter Verse with a six-foot line.
Iambic A foot consisting of two syllables, in a short-long combination.

Irony Language expressing a meaning other than the literal: 'big deal'.
Metaphor Figure of speech in which one object is described in the terms of another: 'A river of men poured across the bridge.'
Metre Sound patterns formed by stressed and unstressed syllables. Metre underpins rhythm and so most poetry.
Pentameter Verse with a five-foot line.
Simile Figure of speech in which a comparison is used to intensify an image: 'The moon hung like a cheap earring'.

Leo Tolstoy

James Joyce

Virginia Woolf

1830   1850   1900

1837 The first instalments of *Oliver Twist* appear, confirming Charles Dickens as the century's most popular writer.

1855 The first edition of Walt Whitman's *Leaves of Grass* pioneers free verse.

1857 Gustave Flaubert's *Madame Bovary* outrages public morals by its nonjudgmental analysis of its heroine's adultery.

1859 Charles Darwin publishes his radical theory of evolution in *The Origin of Species*, precipitating the loss of old religious certainties.

1863 The first episodes of Leo Tolstoy's epic novel *War and Peace* appear.

1872 George Eliot completes *Middlemarch*, considered by some the greatest English novel of its time.

1915 D.H. Lawrence's novel *The Rainbow* is seized by police for obscenity.

1922 T.S. Eliot's *The Waste Land* and James Joyce's *Ulysses* are published. Marcel Proust finishes *Remembrance of Things Past*.

1926 Ernest Hemingway's *The Sun also Rises* captures the disillusion of the postwar generation.

Realism Around 1830, many writers, particularly novelists in England, France and the USA, began to look to ordinary people and daily life – usually middle and lower-class – for their subject matter. Some aimed at reform by exposing social ills.

Dickens' work focuses sharply on contemporary society. But it was **Eliot**, and later **Hardy**, who gave a more objective portrait of mid-19th-century England, as did **Balzac** and **Flaubert** in France. Many, like the American **Twain**, highlighted the comic and absurd.

By the late 19th century, **James** and **Dostoyevsky** were enriching the strong characterisation central to Realist work with deep psychological analysis. In France, the more documentary style of **Zola** and **Maupassant** heralded a new movement known as Naturalism.

Great Expectations Pip speaks to Miss Haversham.

Modernism The First World War brought sweeping social and cultural change and a sense of anger. Modernists rejected tradition in favour of experimental techniques and contemporary subjects.

Proust and **Conrad** broke free of chronological sequence in the plots of their novels. **Joyce** and **Woolf** portrayed their characters through the 'stream of consciousness' technique – the unedited flow of thoughts and feelings running through a character's mind.

Poets such as **Pound** and **Eliot** cast aside traditional metre. **Williams**, writing in prose and verse, emerged as a leading Modernist in the USA.

The Museyroom A scene from Joyce's *Finnegan's Wake* illustrated by John Glashan.

Travel writing

Since an unknown Egyptian wrote *The Journeying of the Master of the Captains of Egypt* in the 14th century BC, authors, explorers and scientists have recorded their travels. Early examples include the *History* of Herodotus (*c.*485-425 BC) describing Egypt and Africa, and *Description of Hellas* (2nd century AD) by the Greek writer Pausanias.

The merchant Marco Polo published an account of his 24 years travelling in China and India in the 13th century. European explorers in the 16th century recorded their voyages. Hakluyt's *Principall Navigations, Voiages and Discoveries of the English Nation* (1598) is a large collection of these accounts.

The 19th-century German explorer and scientist Alexander von Humboldt published 35 volumes of his travels and scientific reports, *Voyage aux régions equinoxiales du Nouveau Continent*. It is the largest body of travel writing produced by one person. In 1872 Francis Galton published the first survival guide, *Art of Travel; or Shifts and Contrivances Available in Wild Countries*.

Notable travel writers of the 20th century include Freya Stark, Wilfred Thesiger, Thor Heyerdahl and Eric Newby.

Saul Bellow

1930

1937 *Spain*, W.H. Auden's poem about the Spanish Civil War, speaks for a generation about the rise of fascism.

1949 Orwell publishes *1984*, a political satire awakening the West to the evils of Stalinism.

1950

1955 The paedophile hero of Vladimir Nabokov's *Lolita* creates scandal.

1957 Patrick White emerges as a major novelist with *Voss*, his heroic tale of life in Australia's outback.

1968 *One Hundred Years of Solitude* by Gabriel García Márquez signals the emergence of magic realism.

1980

1981 Salman Rushdie's *Midnight's Children* marks the arrival of Postmodernism in Anglo-Indian fiction.

20th century Although the effects of Modernism were far-reaching, many novelists continued with more traditional forms. In the USA **Dreiser** wrote naturalistic novels based on documentary evidence such as newspaper reports and official archives. **Lawrence** analysed the mood of self-destruction of his times. **Scott Fitzgerald** expressed the disillusion felt by the generation that had been through the First World War.

In the 1930s, the poet **W.H. Auden** reacted against Modernism, seeing it as academic, elitist and difficult to understand. His work addressed political and social issues, and he used traditional poetic forms, metre and rhythms in order to make his work intelligible to as wide an audience as possible.

The trend towards intelligibility in poetry continued in the following decades, in the Neo-romanticism of **Dylan Thomas** in the 1940s, and the protests of the Beat Poets in the 1960s. **Frost** became the USA's unofficial poet laureate.

In the 1950s, the antihero and the nonhero first appeared in the novels of American authors **Bellow**, **Roth** and **Updike**.

In France, the *roman nouveau* (the new novel, or antinovel) appeared. Influenced by Modernism, authors such as **Duras** and **Mauriac** strove for a kaleidoscope of impressions in an attempt to imitate the way we experience life.

In the 1980s the name **magic realism** was given to a type of fiction in which the real is mixed with the fantastic, dreamlike and inexplicable. **García Márquez** is a leading exponent, and **Carter**, **Grass** and **Rushdie** have all used its techniques.

Writers O–Z

George Orwell
(1903-50) British
Early work included semi-autobiographical and comic novels, but he is best known for his later political novels and for his journalism.
☐ *1984*

Ezra Pound
(1885-1972) American
Through his poetry, criticism, and championing of contemporaries such as Eliot and Joyce, he helped to create the Modernist revolution. His translations of the poetry of ancient civilisations such as Greece and China revived interest in these cultures.
☐ *Cantos*

Marcel Proust
(1871-1922) French
Prolific writer of short stories and novels. The nonlinear treatment of time, detailed analysis of character's observations and thought processes, and original style were major influences on 20th-century writers.
☐ *Remembrance of Things Past*

Alexander Pushkin
(1799-1837) Russian
Although he was influenced by Western models, Pushkin forged a distinctly Russian style. His poetry established Russian as a literary language, and as such he is often seen as the founder of Russian literature.
☐ *Eugene Onegin*

Salman Rushdie
(1947-) Indian/British
Among the most celebrated and controversial of contemporary writers, Rushdie draws on Indian memories, legends and Muslim theology.
☐ *Midnight's Children*

William Shakespeare
(1564-1616) English
Considered the world's greatest dramatist, Shakespeare was also a true Renaissance poet. His output included long narrative poems based on classical myths, and a 156-sonnet cycle.
☐ *Sonnet XVIII*

Alexander Solzhenitsyn
(1918-) Russian
In novels and histories that chronicle life in Stalinist Russia, Solzhenitsyn sought to make literature a weapon against oppression.
☐ *The Gulag Archipelago*

Leo Tolstoy
(1828-1910) Russian
Wrote novels, short stories, plays and essays. Tolstoy's major novels – great, gaudy portraits of Russian society – are considered among the greatest ever written.
☐ *War and Peace*

Virgil
(70 BC-19 BC) Roman
The greatest Latin poet, Virgil created for the new Roman Empire a national epic to rival Homer's. His pastoral poetry has often appealed more to later generations.
☐ *The Art of Husbandry*

Walt Whitman
(1819-92) American
Whitman's vigorous poetry is marked by its pioneering free verse and unabashed celebration of sexuality. His style was a strong influence on Modernist poets.
☐ *Leaves of Grass*

William Wordsworth
(1770-1850) British
Cofounder of English Romanticism with Coleridge, Wordsworth created a simple poetry, based on language as it is used in everyday speech.
☐ *The Prelude*

William Butler Yeats
(1865-1939) Irish
Yeats moved from romantic themes in his early work to subjects as diverse as Irish folklore, political themes and the occult, which he treated in diction and rhythms close to common speech.
☐ *The Winding Stair*

see also
204-5 **The Industrial Revolution**
348-9 **Psychology**
390-3 **Drama**

Drama as plays performed by individual actors began with the ancient Greeks. Early Greek drama evolved from religious festivals at which choruses of masked male actors recited or sang stories about the misfortunes of the heroes of myth and history. About 550 BC, a Greek poet *called Thespis stepped forward from the chorus to recite speeches, becoming the first actor. He also exchanged lines with the leader of the chorus, creating the first instances of stage dialogue.*

Roman The Romans built fine theatres, but their drama was derived from the Greeks. **Plautus** is known for topical comedies. The philosopher and politician **Seneca** wrote nine tragedies. They were never staged at the time, but were used as models by Renaissance dramatists. What pleased the Roman public most – apart from gladiatorial combat – was 'pantomime', a mixture of farce, song and mime.

▼

Classical Greek Ancient Greek theatre took three forms: tragedy, satire and comedy. Tragedy involved a hero pitted against the forces of fate, such as in **Sophocles**'s Oedipus plays. It explored themes of divine law, free will, fate, justice and retribution. **Aeschylus** and **Euripides** explored the use of character and experimented with the chorus. Satire, then as now, ridiculed and criticised public figures, in the work of dramatists such as **Aristophanes**. **Menander** was the first prominent writer of comedy, in which stock character types representing human follies were set against each other in order to make fun of them.

Medieval (11th–14th century) From 1100, new forms of drama developed in Europe. Plays based on Bible stories – called mystery or miracle plays – were performed, first as tableaux in churches, then outdoors. In some places these were collected into cycles of plays, such as the York Cycle in England. Plays portraying Christ's crucifixion were known as passion plays; the Oberammergau Passion Play (1634) is still performed. Alongside these emerged plays in which virtues and vices were personified in order to teach a moral lesson, known as morality plays.

Theatre design – stage and audience

The ancient Greek amphitheatre Large open-air amphitheatre that provided a model for later theatre design.

Elizabethan theatre Separated players from the ground-level, standing audience using a raised stage, and created a backdrop.

The Parisian Palais-Royal (1641) Originated the traditional design of a proscenium to frame the action, and movable scenery.

Theatre-in-the-round In use since the 1930s, this allows a close rapport between audience and performers.

Elizabethan (16th-17th century) In England, a strong theatre tradition grew out of a revived interest in classical, especially Roman, drama combined with the medieval tradition of miracle and morality plays. Several major playwrights emerged from a large and diverse group of dramatists. **Christopher Marlowe** revolutionised theatre by probing his tragic heroes' inner conflicts and showing the expressive versatility of blank verse. **William Shakespeare**'s poeticism gave his plays atmosphere and emotional force. He broke the rules of classical drama by interweaving plots with subplots, moving the action from place to place, and introducing comic elements into tragedies. His rival **Ben Jonson** followed the classical tradition more closely, using satirical comedies to attack vices such as greed and hypocrisy. In the early 17th century, 'revenge' tragedy became popular, seen in Shakespeare's later tragedies and the plays of **John Webster**.

Restoration (17th-18th century) After the English monarchy returned, playwrights such as **William Wycherley** and **William Congreve** wrote comedies that caricatured the morals and behaviour of upper-class society. This type of comedy became known as comedy of manners. In the 18th century **Richard Sheridan** and **Oliver Goldsmith** continued this tradition. Tragedy took the form of 'heroic drama' – plays written in rhyming couplets, with the emphasis on spectacle, extreme passions and violent exchanges between characters. **John Dryden** was the leading exponent.

▲ **French golden age** (17th century) Theatre in 17th-century France modelled itself closely on classical drama. Tragedy pointed out the consequences of people's follies, while comedy ridiculed them. Plays also followed Aristotle's rules of unity of action, time and place – the action must be based on one incident (no subplots) and take place in one setting and in the space of one day. **Pierre Corneille** established the French classical tradition, but was eclipsed by **Jean Racine**, whose tragedies were written in formal verse. **Jean-Baptiste Molière** wrote satirical comedy, such as *Le Misanthrope* in which he attacked the hypocrisy of groups such as the clergy.

SHAKESPEARE

William Shakespeare (1564-1616) produced 37 plays between 1590 and 1616, some in collaboration with others. He drew on a range of sources – the plays of Seneca and Plautus, medieval morality plays, Italian *commedia dell'arte*, historical chronicles and folk traditions. From these styles, which influenced his plots, characterisation and use of rhetorical and theatrical devices, he produced highly original drama.

● Early comedies
The Two Gentlemen of Verona (1590-1)
The Taming of the Shrew (1593)
The Comedy of Errors (1594)
Love's Labour's Lost (1594-5)

● Histories
Henry VI, Parts I, II and III (1592)
Richard III (1592-3)
King John (1595)
Richard II (1595)
Henry IV, Parts I and II (1596-7)
Henry V (1598)
● Later comedies
A Midsummer Night's Dream (1595-6)
The Merchant of Venice (1596-7)
The Merry Wives of Windsor (1597-8)
Much Ado About Nothing (1598)
As You Like It (1599)
Twelfth Night (1601)
Troilus and Cressida (1602)
Measure for Measure (1603)
All's Well That Ends Well (1604-5)

● Tragedies
Titus Andronicus (1592)
Romeo and Juliet (1595)
Julius Caesar (1599)
Antony and Cleopatra (1606)
Coriolanus (1608)
Hamlet (1600-1)
Othello (1603-4)
Timon of Athens (1605)
King Lear (1605-6)
Macbeth (1606)
● Late plays
Pericles (1607)
The Winter's Tale (1609)
Cymbeline (1610)
The Tempest (1611)
Henry VIII (1613)

The conventions of the classical age survived into the 19th century, but 20th-century theatre broke away from traditional forms to explore ways of making drama more closely represent real life. The emphasis moved away from clever plotting towards the expression of inner feelings or satirical social and political comment. By the end of the century, a broad range of alternative theatre groups existed alongside the mainstream.

Japanese Noh plays (17th-19th century) Noh plays originated in Japanese courtly circles in the 14th century, and flourished in the 17th-19th centuries. The subjects were taken from classical Japanese literature, with stately dances performed to an accompaniment of drums and flute. Language was sonorous and honourable for all characters.

▼

▲

Romanticism (mid 18th-19th century) Dramatists reacted against the virtues of reason and respect for convention of the classical age. In Germany **Johann Wolfgang von Goethe** and **Friedrich Schiller** produced work that promoted feelings and imagination. In Britain and the USA this trend produced a shift from tragedy to melodrama, plays with simple plots and strong emotional appeal, with a musical accompaniment to heighten the mood. Towards the end of the century the satirical comedies of **Oscar Wilde** and **Arthur Pinero** became popular.

Social realism (late 19th-early 20th century) Dramatists turned their attention to the ills of society, in plays that were true to life but selective in presenting only what was essential – a style known as realism. **Henrik Ibsen, George Bernard Shaw, John Synge** and **Eugene O'Neill** wrote realist drama. **Chekhov** took realism further in plays that presented life as it is in every detail and in which atmosphere and the inner lives of characters are more important than plot –– known as naturalism. Another related style, seen in some of **Strindberg's** plays, was symbolism, in which truth is presented through allegorical means.

▼

KEY DRAMATISTS

Since the expansion of theatrical forms during the 17th century, several playwrights have stood out for their skills of dramatic interpretation and their ability to reflect contemporary concerns.

Samuel Becket (1906-89) Irish The plays of Beckett are characterised by their themes – the failure of human communication and the pointlessness of human endeavour – and well-honed prose. ■ *Waiting for Godot*
Anton Chekhov (1860-1904) Russian Collaboration with Stanislavsky in 1898 brought Chekhov his first successes. His emphasis on atmosphere rather than

action influenced later playwrights such as Pinter. ■ *The Cherry Orchard*
Wolfgang von Goethe (1749-1832) German Goethe was a supreme dramatist, whether reworking ancient tragedies or compiling his Romantic masterpiece ■ *Faust*
Maxim Gorky (1868-1936) Russian Political activist Gorky

The actor's role John Gielgud and Ralph Richardson bring David Storey's characters to life in *Home.*

wrote about social outcasts. He was exiled for his revolutionary fervour. ■ *The Lower Depths*
Henrik Ibsen (1828-1906) Norwegian The controversial subject matter and uncomfortable endings of Ibsen's plays

Theatre of the Absurd In Paris in the 1950s, a type of drama developed in which motiveless characters and non-existent plots were used to express life's final futility. The leading exponents were Irish writer **Samuel Becket**, and Romanian-born **Eugene Ionesco**. Other playwrights linked to the Theatre of the Absurd are **Harold Pinter**, **Edward Albee** and **Tom Stoppard**. Eastern European dramatists such as **Vaclav Havel** used the style of Theatre of the Absurd to satirise society under communist rule and the struggle of the individual against bureaucracy.

▼

Political satire (early 20th century) After the First World War, European chaos was mirrored in theatre. **Bertolt Brecht** emerged as the leading German playwright. He introduced epic theatre, in which the audience is encouraged to watch a play without becoming emotionally involved, so that they can think about its themes objectively. Devices such as songs, banners and masks create a distancing or 'alienation' effect which reminds the audience that the action in front of them is a performance, rather than reality. In prerevolutionary Russia **Maxim Gorky** depicted social misery in *The Lower Depths*. In Soviet Russia, **Mikhail Bulgakov** produced satirical plays such as *The Day of the Turbins*. In Paris, **Alfred Jarry** attacked bourgeois conventions in his satirical farce *King Ubu*.

Since 1950 **Arthur Miller** and **Tennessee Williams** emerged as the leading playwrights in 1950s America. Both portrayed a society that was decadent and obsessed with power. In Britain, **John Osborne**'s plays challenged the established social order. During the 1970s and 1980s the theme of disillusionment continued in the work of **David Mamet** in the United States, and **David Hare** in Britain. **Neil Simon** (American) and **Alan Ayckbourn** (British) produced domestic comedies about deteriorating relationships. During the 1960s, small alternative or fringe theatre companies emerged in response to rising production costs and the competition from television. They used alternative venues such as cafes and pubs, and many tackled social and political issues, while minorities such as ethnic groups and AIDS campaigners used theatre to fight discrimination.

were unique in European drama. Ibsen is the father of modern realist theatre, although his late work grew increasingly symbolist. ■ *Hedder Gabler*
Arthur Miller (1915-) American Miller explores human relationships through the themes of guilt and of responsibility to self and society. ■ *Death of a Salesman*
Jean-Baptiste Molière (1622-73) French Molière's depictions of human follies raised comedy to the same level as tragedy. ■ *The Misanthrope*
Eugene O'Neill (1888-1953) American The down-to-earth dramas of O'Neill were the antithesis of contemporary

Broadway's melodrama and romanticism. ■ *Long Day's Journey into Night*
Harold Pinter (1930-) British Pinter uses everyday language and silences to convey his characters' thoughts. His plays explore the problems of identity and communication. ■ *The Caretaker*
Jean Racine (1639-99) French The tragedies of Racine were based on historical and classical subjects. ■ *Phedre*
August Strindberg (1849-1912) Swedish Strindberg experimented with a variety of theatrical styles, including naturalism. His later works were themed around religion and symbolism. ■ *Miss Julie*

see also
204-5 **Industrial Revolution**
212-13 **Between the wars**
384-9 **Western literature**

The story of film-making is one of rapid technical change and of the supremacy of Hollywood: within 20 years of the invention of the motion picture, the industry had become a huge business with Hollywood at its heart. By the 1920s, film had become the most important new medium of the 20th century.

Swashbuckling hero Douglas Fairbanks Sr, whose graceful athleticism in films such as *The Mark of Zorro* (1920, left) made him a heartthrob, was one of the earliest stars to experience public interest in his personal life.

1893 In the USA, Thomas Edison patents the peephole Kinetoscope and makes the world's first moving picture (of a man sneezing).
1895 Louis and Auguste Lumière open a cinema in Paris.
1897 Georges Méliès opens a film studio in Paris, and goes on to make 500 short films.

1903 *The Great Train Robbery*, in 12 minutes and 14 scenes, establishes scripted narrative film.
1905 A permanent cinema opens in Pittsburgh, USA.
1908 D.W. Griffith, the 'father of film', joins Biograph studio as a director.
1909 Studios create the 'star system' by exploiting the popularity of actors and actresses to attract film audiences.

1911 Film studios are set up in Hollywood; among the earliest is Keystone Pictures, founded by directors Cecil B. DeMille, D.W. Griffith and Mack Sennett.
1914 *The Squaw*, the first Hollywood feature-length Western, opens.
1915 Griffith's epic *Birth of a Nation* and Charlie Chaplin's *The Tramp* are released.
1917 Chaplin signs the first $1 million film contract.

1919 Chaplin, Mary Pickford and Douglas Fairbanks Sr. found United Artists studio: film stars become superstars.

1890

1900

1920

Birth of the cinema The Lumière brothers' Cinematograph (left) could both record and project moving images. Their first film (1895) showed workers leaving the Lumière factory.

FACT Charlie Chaplin's trademark bowler hat and walking cane were sold for £44 750 at auction in 1995.

1920 *The Mark of Zorro* starts a trend for swashbuckling epics.
1921 *The Four Horsemen of the Apocalypse* makes a worldwide romantic idol of Rudolf Valentino. His early death in 1926 brings mass hysteria to the USA.
1923 *The Covered Wagon* establishes the Western as a staple genre: until the mid 1950s, a quarter of Hollywood films are Westerns. The Hollywood studio system is founded with the opening of Warner Bros.
1924 New studios Columbia and MGM are established.

1925 Chaplin directs and stars in *The Gold Rush*. King Vidor's antiwar film *The Big Parade* opens. Sergei Eisenstein pioneers new framing and editing techniques in *Battleship Potemkin*.
1927 Birth of the 'talkies' with *The Jazz Singer*.
1928 Mickey Mouse makes his debut in *Steamboat Willie*, the first cartoon with sound.
1929 *Wings* wins the first Academy Award ('Oscar') for best film.

Global celebrity Charlie Chaplin directed many of the films he starred in, including *The Gold Rush* (left) in 1925. Chaplin went to Hollywood in 1914; by 1916 he had made more than 50 silent films. The silent genre, understood across the world, made Chaplin the first international movie star.

DIRECTION

Most 1920s and 1930s film directors were no more than glorified technicians employed by studios to create showcases for star performers. But a few exceptional talents began to establish the artistic importance of film direction.

D.W. Griffith, in his epics *The Birth of a Nation* (1915) and *Intolerance* (1916), established the basic 'language' of film: long scenic shots, close-ups, fading in and out at the beginning and end of scenes, and crosscutting (editing together) scenes from different locations. **Cecil B. DeMille**, best known for directing biblical epics such as *The Ten Commandments* (1923), produced and wrote his films, as did French director **Jean Renoir** (*La Grande Illusion*, 1937).

Russian director **Sergi Eisenstein** borrowed ideas from modernist art and music to create 'montage' – editing a series of different shots together into 'conceptual' scenes, the themes of which are perceived in the mind of the viewer. The technique was used to its greatest effect to dramatise a massacre at Odessa in the Russian Revolution propaganda film *Battleship Potemkin* (1925).

In 1929, **Alfred Hitchcock** explored the use of sound for dramatic effect in *Blackmail*, Britain's first 'talkie', in which a woman's thoughts are heard by the audience.

By the late 1950s, directors were acknowledged as a creative force, each with a recognisable personal style as well as technical mastery.

Hitchcock became known for moments of suspense, **John Cassavetes** for low-budget techniques such as hand-held cameras and grainy prints. **François Truffaut** filmed on location, abandoning smooth narratives for disconnected scenes (*Jules et Jim*, 1962). In Italy, **Federico Fellini** excelled in subversive fantasy (*La Dolce Vita*, 1960).

In contemporary cinema, the name of the director indicates the style of a film, and helps to ensure a level of success at the box office. **Stephen Spielberg**, the most commercially successful contemporary director, is best known for his blend of sentiment and adventure (*E.T. The Extra-Terrestrial*, 1982; *Jurassic Park*, 1993).

1930

1930 The golden age of Hollywood and the studio system begins: movies become the world's favourite entertainment. Greta Garbo utters her first screen words (*Anna Christie*). Marlene Dietrich debuts (*The Blue Angel*). Gangster films are pioneered with *Little Caesar*, starring Edward G. Robinson. John Wayne stars for the first time in *The Big Trail*.

1931 The horror film is established with *Dracula*, starring Bela Lugosi, and *Frankenstein*, starring Boris Karloff.
1932 Tarzan series begins with Johnny Weissmuller in *Tarzan the Ape Man*.
1933 *Flying Down to Rio* introduces the first of ten Ginger Rogers/Fred Astaire films. New standards in special effects are set with *King Kong*. The Marx Brothers' *Duck Soup* opens.

1934 French director Jean Vigo establishes an international reputation with *L'Atalante*. Six-year-old Shirley Temple stars in *Stand Up and Cheer*.
1935 Colour feature films are introduced with *Becky Sharp*. Alfred Hitchcock's spy thriller *The 39 Steps* opens.

1937 Jean Renoir directs one of the definitive French masterpieces, *La Grande Illusion*.
1939 *Gone with the Wind*, *Stagecoach* and *The Wizard of Oz* are released.

Romantic lead Errol Flynn was chosen over contender James Cagney for the role of Robin in the popular 1938 version of *The Adventures of Robin Hood*.

Who's who – stars' stage names

Stage name	Real name	Stage name	Real name
Joan Crawford	Lucille Le Sueur	**Groucho Marx**	Adolph Marx
Tony Curtis	Bernard Schwarz	**Marilyn Monroe**	Norma Jean Baker
Marlene Dietrich	Marie Losch	**Mary Pickford**	Gladys Smith
Diana Dors	Diana Fluck	**Ginger Rogers**	Virginia McMath
Kirk Douglas	Yussur Demsky	**Mickey Rooney**	Joe Yule
Douglas Fairbanks	Julius Ullman	**Barbara Stanwyck**	Ruby Stevens
Greta Garbo	Greta Gustafsson	**Robert Taylor**	Spangler Brough
Cary Grant	Alexander Leach	**John Wayne**	Marion Morrison
Rita Hayworth	Margarita Cansino	**Loretta Young**	Gretchen Belzer
Carole Lombard	Jane Peters		

see also
378-81 **Popular music**
382-3 **Dance**
400-1 **Behind the scenes**
496-7 **Information economy**

Throughout the 1950s, Technicolor epics and technical advances such as 3-D, Cinerama and Cinemascope expanded the possibilities of film. The following decade marked the end of the studio system and the rise of independent film-makers, and brought the first explorations of sex and violence to the big screen.

1940 *The Grapes of Wrath* reflects on the Depression. Bing Crosby and Bob Hope make *The Road to Singapore*, the first of seven 'Road' films.
1941 In *Citizen Kane*, director Orson Welles uses innovative overlapping dialogue, multiple character viewpoints and flashbacks to create a dark mood.

1942 *Casablanca* opens.
1945 The French historical epic *Les Enfants du Paradis* is released.
1946 Post-war American realism begins with the hope-in-despair themes of *The Best Years of Our Lives* and *It's a Wonderful Life*. *Great Expectations* and *Brief Encounter* inaugurate a golden age of British film-making.

1947 In the USA, the hunt for Communist influences in Hollywood ends many careers.
1949 The first of the classic Ealing comedies are made in London: *Passport to Pimlico*, *Kind Hearts and Coronets*, *Whisky Galore!*

1950 Melodrama and black humour come together in *Sunset Boulevard*. Marilyn Monroe makes her debut in *All About Eve*.
1951 Marlon Brando makes his screen debut in *Streetcar Named Desire*.
1952 A high point of the Hollywood musical is reached with *Singin' in the Rain*, starring Gene Kelly. The Western matures with *High Noon*.
1953 In the Japanese film *Tokyo Story*, director Yasujiro Ozu abandons camera movements such as panning and keeps every frame still, to record family relationships in close detail.

1955 James Dean appears in *East of Eden* and *Rebel Without a Cause*.
1956 The sci-fi boom begins with *Invasion of the Body Snatchers*. DeMille directs his second version of *The Ten Commandments*.
1958 *Carry On Sergeant* is released, the first of 30 Carry Ons made over the next 34 years.
1959 French 'nouvelle vague' (new wave) is launched by François Truffaut's *Les Quatre Cent Coups*.

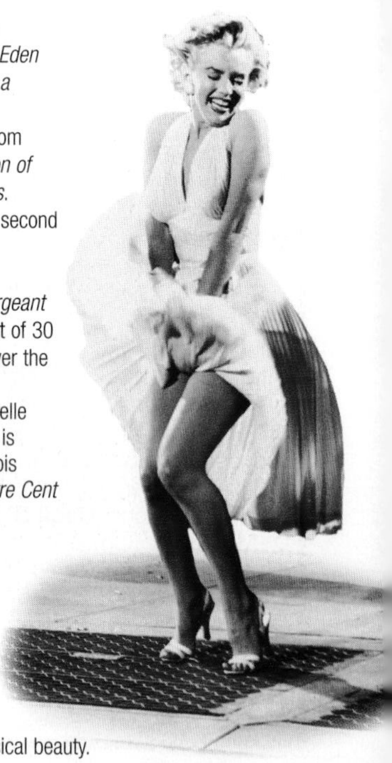

Hollywood icon
Death at a young age made Marilyn Monroe a symbol of Hollywood's exploitation of physical beauty.

1940

1950

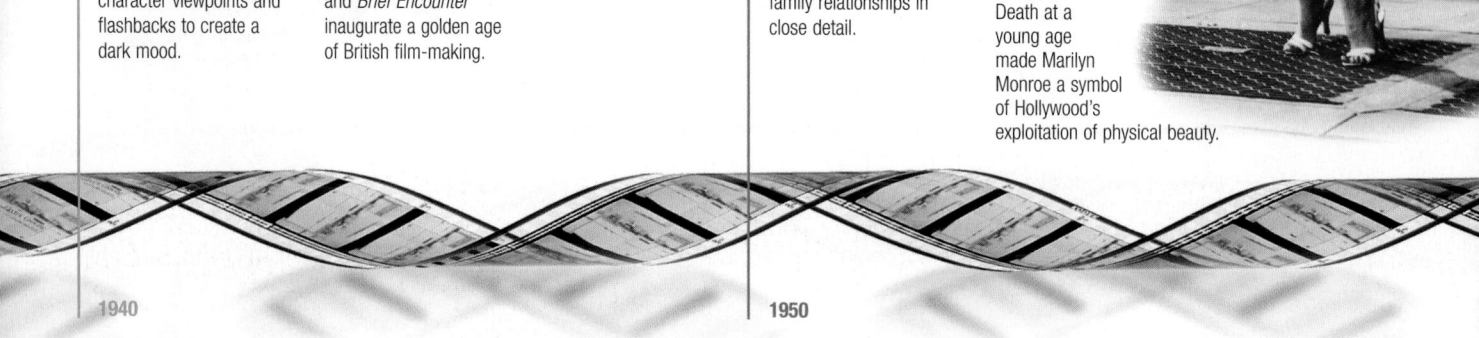

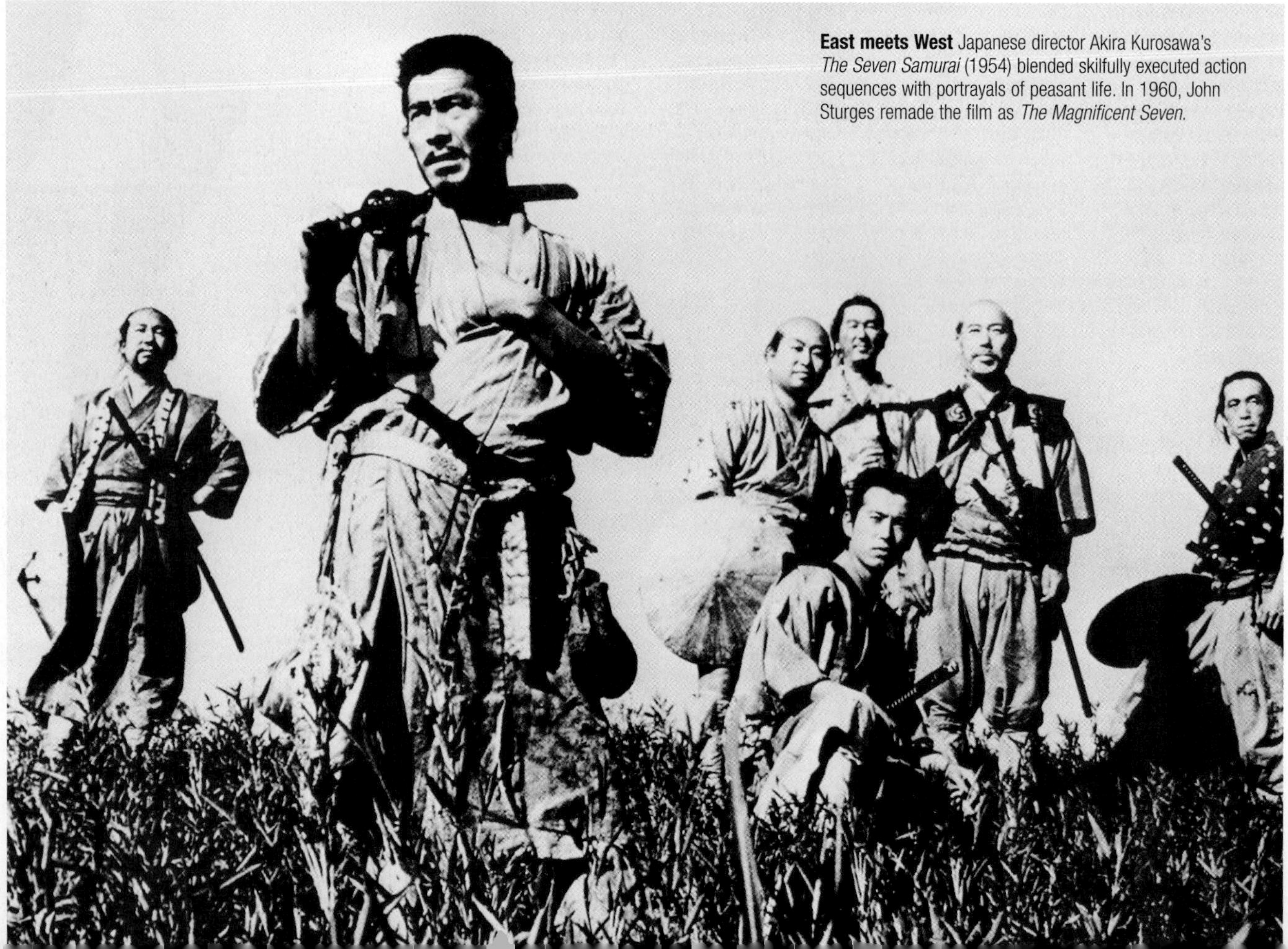

East meets West Japanese director Akira Kurosawa's *The Seven Samurai* (1954) blended skilfully executed action sequences with portrayals of peasant life. In 1960, John Sturges remade the film as *The Magnificent Seven*.

FILM ACTING

In the earliest days of the cinema, stage acting techniques were transferred wholesale to the screen. But the grand theatrical gesture is rarely convincing on film, and as a result the trend in screen acting has consistently been towards greater naturalism – performers 'react' rather than 'act'.

This ability to appear natural in front of the camera – to project a personality that the audience identifies with and warms to – has been the hallmark of almost all the great film stars. From **Buster Keaton**'s silent comedies to **John Wayne**'s action heroes, the best film actors have been able to conjure up an unmistakable screen presence. **Greta Garbo** was undistinguished as a stage performer in her native Sweden, but on the screen, she had a magnetic persona.

In the 1920s, German cinema led a reaction against naturalistic acting, using exaggerated bodily and facial gestures, deliberately emphasised by camera angles. The technique was later used by Russian director Sergei Eisenstein in *Ivan The Terrible* (1944).

In the early 1950s, many film actors were influenced by 'Method', a technique based on the theories of the Russian theatre director Konstantin Stanislavsky. The Method required actors to recall emotions and reactions from their past experiences and to use them in their performances; in short, to bring even greater realism to the screen.

Method acting's leading exponent was **Marlon Brando**, whose seemingly halting performances in films such as *On the Waterfront* (1954) and *The Godfather* (1972) were in fact the product of rigorous training by the Polish-born Lee Strasberg, founder of the Actors Studio in New York. The idea was to 'fake' as little as possible. This pursuit of realism was taken further in later years by **Robert De Niro** (also trained by Strasberg) who, in preparation for his Oscar-winning role as a dissolute boxer in *Raging Bull* (1980), put on nearly 27 kg (60 lb) in weight.

The close-up intimacy of film and the public interest in celebrities' private lives has often meant that established stars bring their personal stamp, or image, to a part. For some, this results in typecasting – for example, John Wayne was repeatedly cast as a solitary cowboy, **Arnold Schwarzenegger** is mainly associated with action-adventure movies and **Jim Carrey** with zany, slapstick comedies.

The film actor's task has always been hampered by the peculiar demands of the medium. On stage, a performance is concentrated into a few hours. On film, it is assembled piece by piece, often over several months and in a different sequence to the progression of the story. Creating a convincing character in these disjointed circumstances is the unique challenge facing any film actor.

1960 Hitchcock releases *Psycho*.
1961 *West Side Story* is the first modern musical.
1962 Sean Connery stars in the first Bond film, *Dr No*. The epic returns with *Lawrence of Arabia*.
1963 The $44 million *Cleopatra* almost bankrupts Fox studios.

1965 *The Sound of Music*, the biggest grossing musical of all time, opens.
1966 The licentiousness of the 1960s is epitomised in *Blow-Up*, and the following year in *The Graduate*.

1967 The trend for violence as glamour begins with *Bonnie and Clyde*.
1968 A new film classification system introduces the X film.
1969 Cinema meets the counterculture in *Easy Rider*.

Spaghetti Western In *The Good, the Bad and the Ugly* (1966), Clint Eastwood's edgy, justice-dispensing character became a model for later fictional cowboys and private detectives.

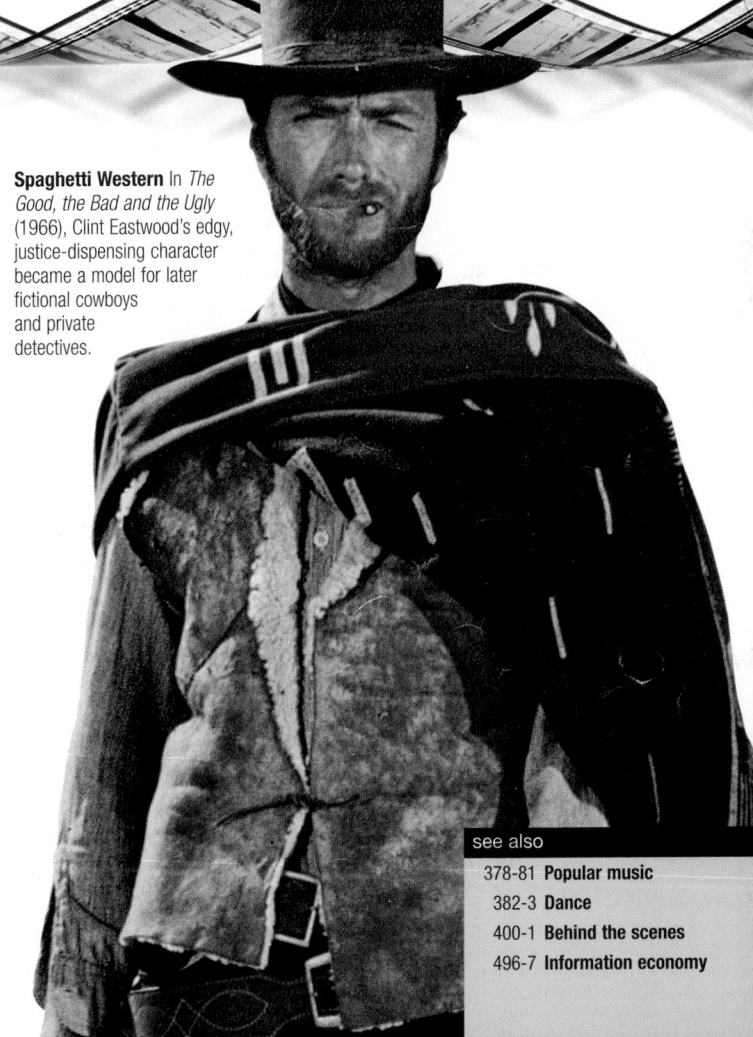

Artistic control François Truffaut argued that the director should be the main creative force behind a film – a concept labelled *nouvelle vague* (new wave). He used flowing camera movements and voice-over narrative to capture feelings in *Jules et Jim* (1962).

see also
378-81 **Popular music**
382-3 **Dance**
400-1 **Behind the scenes**
496-7 **Information economy**

From the 1970s, levels of explicit, gritty screen violence, sex and horror rose continually, and they have become leading themes in contemporary cinema. Today, digital technology has turned the adventure story into a high-tech blockbuster spectacular.

1970 *Airport* launches the disaster movie.
1971 Woody Allen's *Bananas* is released. The violence in *Dirty Harry*, *The French Connection*, *Straw Dogs* and *Clockwork Orange* shock audiences.
1977 *Star Wars* introduces the high-tech sci-fi spectacular.
1979 *Apocalypse Now* explores the US trauma of the Vietnam War.

1981 Steven Spielberg collaborates with George Lucas (as producer) to make the adventure film *Raiders of the Lost Ark*.
1984 Big-budget violence and special effects reach new heights in *The Terminator* (James Cameron).
1985 Independent film company Merchant Ivory begins a series of classic literary adaptations with E.M. Forster's *A Room With a View*. Digital technology is first used in *The Young Sherlock*

Holmes to create a sword-wielding knight made of stained glass.
1989 In *The Abyss* (James Cameron), new digital techniques are used to conjure up a creature out of sea water.

Big-budget thrills
Terminator 2: Judgement Day (1991), starring Arnold Schwarzenegger (right), was the first $100 million budget film. But sci-fi special effects are less expensive than the water-based effects used in films such as *Titanic*.

1992 Quentin Tarantino uses violence as a central theme in *Reservoir Dogs*.
1993 Digital technology creates realistic dinosaurs and mixes them with live action in Steven Spielberg's *Jurassic Park*.
1995 *Toy Story* is the first digitally animated full-length feature film.
1996 Comedian Jim Carrey commands the first $20 million salary, for *The Cable Guy*.
1997 *Titanic* (James Cameron) becomes the most expensive film ever made ($200 million).
1999 *Star Wars Episode 1 – The Phantom Menace* breaks the film sequel tradition to provide a prequel to the classic 1970s sci-fi epic.

2000 The epic picture in the style of *Ben-Hur* is revived by Ridley Scott in *Gladiator*. Ang Lee's *Crouching Tiger, Hidden Dragon* creates a new form of martial arts film: the central characters are strong women, and the film has an emotional depth lacking in other 'action' pictures.

1970   1980   1990

Digital effects In *Gladiator*, released in 2000, computer technology was used to build up images, as in this scene where the actors fight a 'virtual' tiger.

FILM GENRES

There can be no definitive list of film genres, and the boundaries between them are often blurred. Listed here are films that broke new ground and spawned imitators.

Action-thrillers
Fast-paced, violent and often sexually explicit, the action-thriller is a relatively recent phenomenon, largely launched by the James Bond series in the early 1960s.
Goldfinger (1964)
Deliverance (1972)
Die Hard (1988)
Terminator 2 (1991)
Speed (1994)

Adventure
The improbable adventures of dashing characters were a mainstay of 1930s Hollywood. The genre was reinvigorated by the Indiana Jones trilogy in the 1980s.
The Black Pirate (1926)
Mutiny on the Bounty (1935)
The Prisoner of Zenda (1937)
The Adventures of Robin Hood (1939)
Raiders of the Lost Ark (1981)

Adventure Harrison Ford in *Raiders of the Lost Ark.*

Cartoons and animation
Walt Disney's *Snow White and the Seven Dwarfs*, made in the face of great scepticism, showed the potential of animation.
Snow White and the Seven Dwarfs (1937)
Who Framed Roger Rabbit? (1988)
Toy Story (1995)
Chicken Run (2000)

Comedy
Silent movies lent themselves naturally to visual comedy, but the coming of sound in the late 1920s changed the emphasis to dialogue.
The General (1927)
Bringing Up Baby (1938)
Some Like It Hot (1959)
Annie Hall (1977)
Four Weddings and a Funeral (1994)

Cult
This category covers films with limited commercial appeal, which often deal with bizarre or freakish subjects.
Freaks (1932)
The Valley of the Dolls (1967)
Pink Flamingos (1984)

Drama
As a genre, drama films are those that deal seriously and more or less realistically with serious, normally adult issues. Drama is, for the most part, the single largest category of film, and contains some of the most memorable movies ever made.
Grand Hotel (1932)
La Règle du Jeu (1939)
Citizen Kane (1941)
The Misfits (1961)
Schindler's List (1993)

Fantasy
Fantasy films are those in which the laws of reality have been suspended and anything can happen (with special effects well to the fore). They have mostly tended to be children's films.
King Kong (1933)
The Wizard of Oz (1939)
E.T. The Extra-Terrestrial (1982)
Batman (1989)
Jurassic Park (1993)

Gangster
Gangster films and their offshoots – detective and crime films – began to emerge in the 1930s, largely in response to the lawlessness of American Prohibition. They rival the Western as the definitive film form. In the 1940s, many gangster movies also epitomised the stark, pared-down style of *film noir*.
Scarface (1932)
Double Indemnity (1944)
The Big Sleep (1946)
The Godfather (1972)
LA Confidential (1997)

Horror
Being a visual medium film is particularly suited to horror. Some of the most arresting horror films could be termed psychological thrillers, but recent trends have been towards ever-more explicit levels of horror and violence.
Nosferatu (1922)
Psycho (1960)
The Exorcist (1973)
Halloween (1978)
The Silence of the Lambs (1991)

Musicals
Sound was introduced in 1927 with *The Jazz Singer*, a silent film with several musical numbers sung by Al Jolson. It was an immediate sensation. The film musical built on a rich stage tradition to include lavish dance sequences.
42nd Street (1933)
Top Hat (1935)
Yankee Doodle Dandy (1942)
Singin' in the Rain (1952)
The Sound of Music (1965)

Period and history films
These overlap with drama and, frequently, with fantasy films, but a recurring element is the epic: lavish, spectacular and not always historically accurate.
The Birth of a Nation (1915)
Anna Karenina (1935)
Ben-Hur (1959)
Lawrence of Arabia (1962)
Shakespeare in Love (1998)

Romance
Romance is a central element of many films, but surprisingly few are exclusively (or almost so) love films.
Wuthering Heights (1939)
Waterloo Bridge (1940)
Brief Encounter (1946)
When Harry Met Sally (1989)
The Bridges of Madison County (1995)

Science fiction
From the late 1960s sci-fi moved up from B-movie status thanks to the increasing sophistication of special effects.
Planet of the Apes (1967)
2001: A Space Odyssey (1968)
Star Wars (1977)
Blade Runner (1982)
Independence Day (1996)

War
After the First World War, war became a frequent subject for the movies.
All Quiet on the Western Front (1930)
La Grande Illusion (1937)
Apocalypse Now (1979)
Das Boot (1981)
Saving Private Ryan (1998)

Western
The Western rapidly became the definitive form of American film. Its golden age ended in the 1960s.
Stagecoach (1939)
High Noon (1952)
The Searchers (1959)
A Fistful of Dollars (1964)
Unforgiven (1992)

Horror Linda Blair in *The Exorcist*, still considered the most frightening film ever.

In the 1970s, the film industry struggled to compete against television and video entertainment. New technology revived its fortunes: money lavished on postproduction effects has created a new realm of cinematic experience. The USA is still the industry's leading investor.

FILM PRODUCTION

A film can take several years to progress through its three stages:

Preproduction
- Producer (or director, actor or other interested party) sells an idea or script to a studio. The producer is then responsible for all practical business in making the film.
- Producer supervises hiring of a director and actors.
- Technical crews are employed.
- Writers refine or rewrite original script.
- Producer and studio agree a budget and arrange finances.

Production
- Set designers create sets.
- Director and technical crew determine lighting, sound and camera positions.
- Director supervises creative aspects of the filming and instructs the actors as scenes are shot.
- Additional dialogue and sounds added.
- Special effects added.

Postproduction
- Film editor trims and assembles film shots, shaping the completed work.
- Music added.
- Duplicate prints made for distribution.
- Promotion done, mainly via advertising.
- Preview audiences attend test screenings, which can lead to changes.
- General release in cinemas.
- Videos and DVDs produced and sold.
- Deals negotiated for spin-off products.

Global cinema admissions

	Country	Number of admissions sold in 1999 (in millions)
1	India	7700
2	USA	1377
3	Indonesia	247
4	France	169
5	China	159
6	Japan	153
7	Germany	150
8	UK	135
9	Italy	120
10	Spain	112

The film industry worldwide

Investment in film is not necessarily linked to the number of films produced by a country. India produces more films than any other country, but low production budgets keep their annual investment down to the equivalent of around $52.2 million (1998).

Number of films produced by country (1998):

1	India	693
2	USA	661
3	Japan	249
4	France	182
5	Germany	119
6	Italy	92
7	Hong Kong	91
8	UK	87
9	China	80
10	Spain	65

Feature film investments by country (1998):

		$ million
1	USA	9254.0
2	France	963.4
3	Japan	889.6
4	UK	717.3
5	Italy	361.6
6	Germany	342.5
7	Spain	206.4
8	Canada	193.0
9	Australia	104.6
10	Brazil	77.2

HOW MUCH IT COSTS

A typical Hollywood production, *Spy Kids* (2001), cost $30 million and employed a film crew of about 200. The term 'blockbuster' is applied to any film costing more than $100 million. Disney's animated *Dinosaur* (2000) cost about $285 million. At the other end of the scale, the 1999 independent success, *The Blair Witch Project*, was produced for only $60 000. British hit *The Full Monty* (1999) cost $3.5 million, and was shot in 40 days – Hollywood films normally take several months to shoot.

There are great disparities in leading actors' pay, with established stars commanding huge sums. Mel Gibson earned $40 million for *Lethal Weapon 4* (1998); Julia Roberts earned $17 million for *Runaway Bride* (1999). Newcomer Leonardo DiCaprio received only $2.5 million for *Titanic* (1997), but $20 million for *The Beach* (1999).

INDIAN CINEMA

India's film industry originated in 1913 with Dadasaheb Phalke's silent film *Raja Harishchandra*. By the late 1920s the nation was turning out more films than the UK. In 1934, the Bombay Talkies company established a commercial film style nicknamed 'Bollywood', and created the first Indian film stars, Ashok Kumar and Devika Rani. In Bollywood, historical or romantic plots are subordinate to song and dance and lavish costumes. In the 1970s, it began to explore the Western themes of violence and sexuality, even making an Indian 'Western', *Sholay* (1975). Bollywood movies are made for a domestic audience. In contrast, Indian 'art' movies with social themes, such as Satyajit Ray's *Pather Panchali* (1955), have received international acclaim.

Changing tastes Family dramas such as *Papa Kahte Hain* (below), based on the American film *My Father the Hero*, are gradually becoming more popular in Bollywood than song-and-dance films.

Top grossing films

At US box office (all figures based on year 2000 average ticket price of $5.35):	Takings ($ million)
1 Gone With the Wind (1939)	1083.3
2 Star Wars (1977)	968.9
3 The Sound of Music (1965)	803.5
4 E.T. The Extra-Terrestrial (1982)	745.8
5 The Ten Commandments (1956)	718.5
6 Jaws (1975)	702.5
7 Titanic (1997)	685.3
8 Doctor Zhivago (1965)	664.1
9 The Jungle Book (1967)	594.1
10 Snow White and the Seven Dwarfs (1937)	583.2

Globally:	Takings ($ million)
1 Titanic (1997)	1835.4
2 The Phantom Menace (1999)	923.1
3 Jurassic Park (1993)	920.1
4 Independence Day (1996)	813.2
5 Star Wars (1977)	798.0
6 The Lion King (1994)	766.9
7 E.T. The Extra-Terrestrial (1982)	704.8
8 Forrest Gump (1994)	679.7
9 The Sixth Sense (1999)	672.8
10 The Lost World: Jurassic Park (1997)	614.4

FILM CREDITS – WHO DOES WHAT?

Best boy Assistant chief lighting technician – usually to the gaffer, although the term is often used for the second-in-command of a group. There are no best girls: female chief assistants are also called best boys.

Boom operator Sound-crew member who operates a long pole with a microphone on the end.

Clapper loader Person who loads film into camera magazines and operates the clapper – a board filmed at the start of a shot which identifies it by a take number, and the date and time. A hinged stick on top of the board is 'clapped' to provide audio-visual synchronisation. Also known as loaders, as they often concentrate on loading film and delegate clapperboard responsibilities.

Dolly operator A grip who moves cameras around on wheeled trolleys (dollies).

Focus puller Camera-crew member who adjusts the focus of the camera during filming.

Gaffer The chief lighting technician.

Grip In the USA, a person responsible for producing and maintaining production equipment on the set. Duties include erecting scaffolding or laying dolly tracks (rails on which a camera can be moved). In the UK, a grip only works with equipment on which the camera is mounted.

Key grip The chief grip, who works closely with the gaffer. May double as a construction coordinator or as back-up for camera crew.

Props Person who buys or acquires all the props needed for a production.

Set dresser Person who arranges pictures, curtains and other items of scenery on the sets.

TECHNOLOGICAL INNOVATION

The major cinematic innovations of the early 20th century were sound (1926) and Technicolor (1932). The threat of colour television in the 1950s spurred further advances, including three-dimensional cinematography (3-D) and the curved screen of three-camera Cinerama, both in 1952, and the first CinemaScope widescreen film in 1953. The 1960s brought the beginnings of animatronics – moving mechanical models – developed by Walt Disney.

A new format, IMAX ('image maximum'), began operating in 1970. IMAX uses 70 mm film (ten times larger than conventional 35 mm film) and projects onto a giant screen, accompanied by six-channel digital sound.

Computer technology has brought a new sophistication to film production. The most spectacular developments have arisen from digital technology:

animation 3-D figures can now be mapped out and manipulated using computer software. For complex figures, clay models can be scanned directly into a computer. Jurassic Park (1993) included just 6 minutes of digital animation. The first film to use the technique throughout, Disney's 77-minute Toy Story (1995), took four years to produce. Disney's Dinosaur (2000), a combination of live-action film and computer-generated figures, required 3.2 million hours of computer processing.

enhancement Damaged film can be restored using computer software. Black-and-white films can be coloured.

postproduction Images from digital cameras allow editing on computer. Future cinemas will use digital projectors, eliminating film reproduction, shipping and storing.

special effects Digital graphics can create a range of effects, including morphing – the gradual transformation of one image into another, such as the cyborg shape-shifting sequences in the action film Terminator 2: Judgment Day (1991); and cloning – duplicating images to create crowd or battle scenes, as used in the historical film Elizabeth (1998).

Powerful projection The huge screens used to show IMAX films measure 5.6 m high by 21.5 m wide (51 x 70 ft).

FACT The notorious financial flop, Heaven's Gate (1980), forced the sale of the United Artists studio.

see also
394-9 **Cinema**
496-7 **Information economy**
562-3 **Digital communications**
564-5 **Recorded sound**

Televisions are found in 98.1 per cent of US homes, with 35 per cent owning two sets and 41 per cent three or more. Worldwide in 2000, some 33 000 television stations produced 48 million hours of programmes. TV sets are already offering the Internet and email, and the near future will usher in interactive television.

Coronation of George VI In
1937, the BBC makes one of
the earliest outside broadcasts.

1925 Scottish engineer and
inventor John Logie Baird
transmits a television picture
of office boy William Taynton).
1928 General Electric in the
USA begins regularly
scheduled TV programmes (a
half-hour three times a week)
at its radio station WGY in
Schenectady, New York.
The BBC begins daily TV
transmissions in the UK.
1936 The BBC begins regular
public television service.
1938 The USA has about
100 television sets in use;
US company NBC broadcasts
a feature film (*The Scarlet
Pimpernel*).
1939 Television is
demonstrated to millions for
the first time, at the New York
World's Fair.

Truth or Consequences NBC's
show becomes the world's first
sponsored TV progamme, in
1941. Advertisers include Adam
Hats, Bulova Watches, Botany
Worsted and Ivory Soap.

1940 Experimental colour
broadcasts are made from New
York's Chrysler Building by CBS.
1941 NBC and CBS begin
regular television transmission
in USA.
1944 A television soap opera,
Painted Dreams, begins in the
USA; it was also radio's first
soap in 1930.
1949 In the USA, network
television linking stations
around the country is
launched and cable television
is introduced.

I Love Lucy Within six months of
its debut, the comedy series was
watched in more than 10 million
US homes.

1953 Around 1 million TV sets are
bought by the British to watch the
coronation of Elizabeth II.
US politician Richard Nixon's popularity
is boosted after some 60 million
Americans watch him saying that his
only personal political gift was his
dog, Checkers.
1954 US politician Joseph McCarthy's
televised claims of Communist
infiltration of the US Army are shown
to be based on falsified evidence.
1955 Commercial television begins in
the UK with ITV; Gibbs SR Toothpaste
is the first commercial.

Man on the Moon A world audience estimated a
500 million watch as the US Apollo 11 spacecraf
lands on the Moon in 1969, and astronaut Neil
Armstrong takes the first lunar walk.

1962 First transatlantic satellite transmission
of television programmes, by Telstar
communication satellite built by American
telecom company AT&T.
1963 Millions around the world follow the
aftermath of the assassination and the funeral o
US President John F. Kennedy, and millions of
Americans see a murder on live TV as Lee
Harvey Oswald, Kennedy's suspected assassin,
is shot by Jack Ruby.
1964 Some 73 million Americans watch The
Beatles' first US television appearance, on the
Ed Sullivan Show.
1967 BBC2 begins a scheduled colour TV
service, Europe's first.
Some 400 million people worldwide watch the
first global satellite TV programme, *Our World*,
featuring The Beatles playing 'All You Need Is
Love' in England.
1969 Television records US astronaut Neil
Armstrong taking the first steps on the Moon.

Drama

Early dramas consisted of filmed versions
of theatrical productions, such as the 1937
BBC version of George Bernard Shaw's *How
She Lied to Her Husband*. The 1960s saw
the introduction of drama series and more
action, and today drama encompasses any
fiction series generally.

1961 *The Avengers* adventure-drama
series begins.
1963 *Doctor Who* popularises science
fiction; *Star Trek* begins in the USA in 1966.
1965 *I Spy* debuts in the USA, introducing
the first black hero.

1970 *The Six Wives of Henry VIII* is the first
historical drama.
1971 *Upstairs, Downstairs* reflects on changes
in British society. The series, which finished in
1975, was watched by 300 million viewers in
50 countries. Unlike earlier costume drama
series, it was written specifically for TV.
1972 The 26-part *War and Peace* establishes
a new way of showing literary works.
1978 *Dallas* is first shown in the USA. It runs
for another 13 years and is broadcast in
more than 130 countries.
1998 The first ever 60-second sitcom, or
blipcom, airs on the US network TV Land.

Documentaries

Documentaries were popularised by the cinema in the 1930s. Two decades later TV began to use the form to highlight political and social problems.

1954 *Zoo Quest* introduces the naturalist David Attenborough on television.
1958 *Whicker's World* – a mix of travel and celebrity interviews – begins, presented by Alan Whicker.
1964 The camera takes an intimate look at a working-class family in *The Family*; *Seven Up* follows the lives of children from different social backgrounds.
1969 *Civilisation* brings high-brow art and culture to the British people.
1973 The Second World War is seen from the viewpoint of all countries involved in *The World at War*.
1974 *Ascent of Man* retraces human history.
1992 *The Secret History: Bloody Sunday* exposes events in Northern Ireland.
1999 Outer space is explored in *The Planets*.
2000 The BBC makes use of computer animatronics in its *Walking With Dinosaurs* 'docudrama' series.

Sport

Sport has been a staple of television since its early days. Today, the impact of every major sporting event can be measured by the size of its television audience (138.5 million people watched the 1996 US Super Bowl and 38 billion the 1998 football World Cup final).

1931 The world's first broadcast sporting event is the Derby from Epsom on the BBC.
1933 The first boxing match is televised, from the BBC's studios.
1936 The Berlin Olympics are televised throughout Germany.
1937 The BBC televises the Wimbledon tennis championships.
1938 The BBC televises the University Boat Race, FA Cup Final and Test cricket.

1958 BBC starts *Grandstand*, now the world's longest-running sports programme.
1963 The first ever instant replay is shown; US viewers watching the Army-Navy American football match see the same touchdown twice broadcast back-to-back.
1964 the BBC's *Match of the Day* is first shown.
1968 The BBC shows live colour pictures of the Olympic games in Mexico. At the previous Games, in Tokyo, black-and-white film had to be flown back to London.
1991 Sky Sports is launched as the first channel dedicated exclusively to sports.
1999 Sky broadcasts the first pay-per-view football match: Oxford United v Sunderland for £7.95.

see also
404-5 **TV broadcasting**
496-7 **Information technology**
562-3 **Digital communications**

Vietnam War In the early 1970s, daily US news coverage of American casualties and pictures of the fighting in South Vietnam led to widespread public pressure to end the military effort. In January 1973 a cease-fire ended 12 years of war.

1970 The events of a Palestinian terrorist attack on Israeli athletes at the Munich Olympics are broadcast around the world.
A videodisc is demonstrated in Germany.
1972 Home Box Office (HBO) in USA is the world's first subscription cable television service.
Ceefax teletext information is introduced by the BBC.
1973 Americans watch the Senate hearings on the Watergate political scandal that would force president Richard Nixon to resign on live television the following year.
Also in the USA, the 12-hour slavery saga *Roots* (shown in regular episodes) achieves audiences of 130 million.

Royal wedding The 1981 wedding in London of Prince Charles and Lady Diana Spencer is viewed around the world by 700 million people.

1980 Cable News Network (CNN) begins 24 hour newscasts in USA.
1983 More than 107 million people in the US watch the final episode of the comedy series *M*A*S*H*, still a US record for a single programme.
1984 The Live Aid charity rock concerts, linking London and Boston by TV satellite, are seen live by about 1.8 billion people worldwide, raising approximately $50 million for famine relief in Africa.
1985 Cable television shopping channels begin in USA.
1989 Sky TV, the first UK satellite television channel, is launched.

Interactive television In 1999, Sky TV launched services that the viewer could control through their handset. Email through the television is now also available.

1991 The Gulf War, covered mainly by CNN, is the first war followed live worldwide.
1997 The funeral of Diana, Princess of Wales, is seen by an estimated 2.5 billion people around the world.
1998 Digital television is introduced, with potential for hundreds of new channels.

New millennium
Fireworks ring in the New Year 2000 in Sydney, Australia, as part of celebrations that are broadcast worldwide.

In 1884, a German student called Paul Nipkow invented the Nipkow disc, a device which scanned images mechanically and translated them into electronic impulses. Karl Ferdinand Braun, another German, invented the cathode-ray tube 13 years later. But it would be more than a quarter of a century before the first television broadcasts were made.

1922 In Idaho, USA, high-school student Philo Farnsworth makes an **electronic image scanner**, using a cathode-ray tube.
1925 John Logie Baird demonstrates his **mechanical television**, using a Nipkow disc with lenses to scan the image.
1927 Farnsworth builds the first **electronic television**, using his 'Image Dissector' camera tube and a cathode-ray tube.
1929 Baird begins experimental transmissions for the British Broadcasting Corporation (BBC).

First pictures Scottish inventor John Logie Baird (centre) is the first person to produce a TV image of a human face.

1930 Farnsworth patents his electronic system. Various cameras developed by other companies over the next few years are found to infringe his patents.
1936 The BBC starts the first regular **high-definition television** service (with 405-line images).
1939 In New York, the World's Fair introduces television to the American public.

Outdoor coverage BBC outside broadcasts begin in 1931.

1948 Cable is first used to distribute TV in areas of the USA with poor reception.

1920   1930   1940

FROM TV CAMERA...

When an image is filmed by a TV camera, it is split into easily decodable pieces of information before being transmitted across the air on radio waves.

Encoding colour Light from an image passes through the camera lens, and is split by special mirrors into its red, green and blue components. These are focused as red, green and blue images on light-sensitive targets in three separate tubes.

Scanning the images The primary coloured image on each target is scanned into 625 horizontal lines: the brightness of each line is recorded as an electrical signal. A synchronisation circuit ensures that each tube scans the same line of the image at the same time, so that when the signals from the three tubes are combined they give information about the same part of the image.

Transmitting the image The red, green and blue signals from the camera tubes are brought together and encoded as colour and brightness. This information is then combined with an audio signal, the synchronisation signal and a radio wave for transmission. The radio wave has a frequency specific to the television channel.

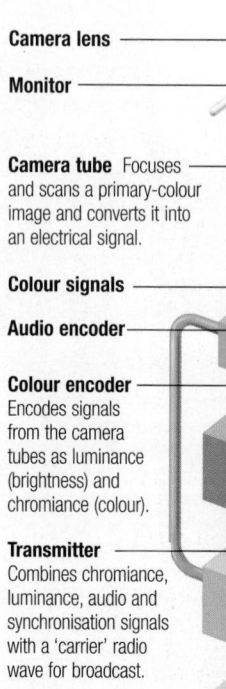

Camera lens

Monitor

Camera tube Focuses and scans a primary-colour image and converts it into an electrical signal.

Colour signals

Audio encoder

Colour encoder Encodes signals from the camera tubes as luminance (brightness) and chromiance (colour).

Transmitter Combines chromiance, luminance, audio and synchronisation signals with a 'carrier' radio wave for broadcast.

Flat-screen technology

Traditional televisions are bulky because they have to house a cathode-ray tube (see below), but in the 1980s manufacturers began producing television sets with screens only a few centimetres deep. The majority of these 'flat-screen' televisions use plasma display panels (PDPs). A PDP is made up of thousands of tiny units called pixels, stacked alongside each other in horizontal lines (a PDP has about 1100 lines, compared with the 625 of the screen of a cathode-ray tube). Each pixel consists of three bricklike subpixels; one red, one green and one blue, sandwiched between horizontal and vertical electrodes. A current passed between these electrodes causes the red, green or blue coating of the subpixel to glow: the higher the current, the brighter the glow. The brightness of each subpixel decides the overall brightness and colour of a pixel. And the arrangement of pixel illumination across the screen creates the image.

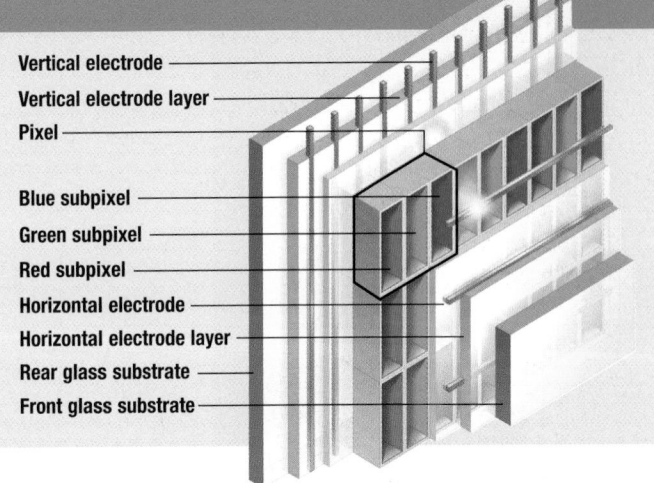

Vertical electrode
Vertical electrode layer
Pixel
Blue subpixel
Green subpixel
Red subpixel
Horizontal electrode
Horizontal electrode layer
Rear glass substrate
Front glass substrate

1951 Regular **colour television** broadcasts start in the United States.
1956 The Ampex Corporation of California demonstrates a **videotape recorder**. Soon, videotape replaces film in television production.

1962 The Telstar satellite transmits the first **live television** between the United States and Britain.
1967 The BBC begins Europe's first regular colour broadcasts.
1969 Americans George Smith and Willard Boyle invent the **charge-coupled device** (CCD).

1972 Domestic videotape recorders are launched.
1974 The BBC begins Ceefax, the world's first **teletext** service.
1975 In the United States, the first **satellite television** service is relayed locally by cable. Satellite services are broadcast to domestic televisions in 1980.

1986 The BBC's Nicam **stereo sound** system is adopted throughout Europe.
1989 Japan first broadcasts 1000-line **high-definition** television (HDTV).

1994 Satellite **digital television** broadcasts begin in the United States.
1998 Digital television is first broadcast from terrestrial transmitters.

1950 | 1960 | 1970 | 1980 | 1990

Miniature TV British inventor Clive Sinclair introduces the pocket television in 1966.

Global broadcasting Live news coverage now connects the world's major countries.

...TO TV SET

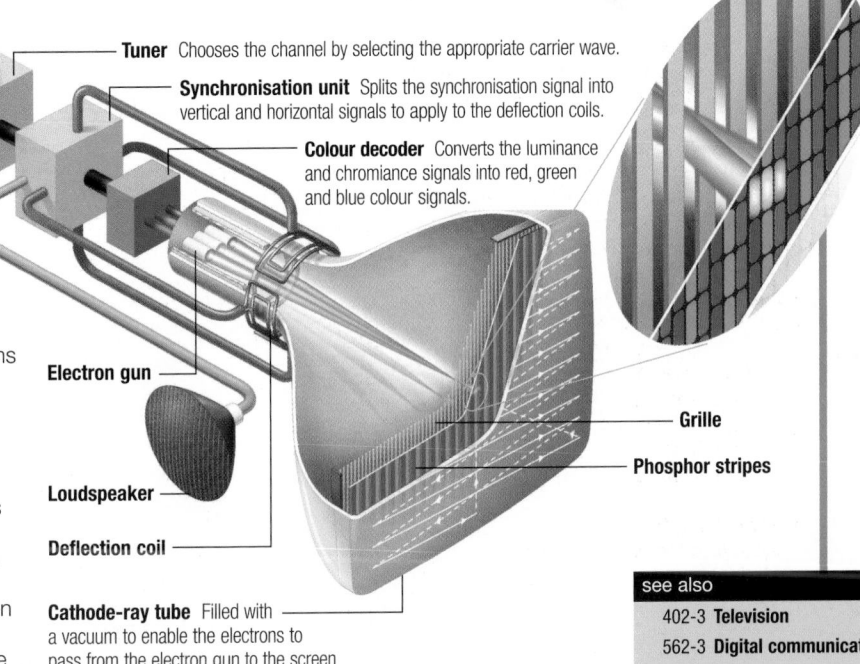

When you switch on a TV set, the composite signal sent by the broadcaster is picked up through an aerial or satellite dish and separated from the carrier radio wave. The different components of the signal have to be decoded to re-create the image.

Decoding colour A colour decoder unscrambles the colour and brightness signals for red, green and blue and feeds them into the picture tube. Three electron guns inside the tube (one for each primary colour) emit narrow beams of electrons, which are accelerated towards the screen by high voltage. Electromagnetic deflection coils bend these electronic beams so that they can be relayed across the screen.

Re-creating the image The inside of the screen is coated with very thin, vertical stripes of red, green and blue phosphors, which glow when struck by an electron beam. Grilles with vertical apertures are positioned between the electron guns and the screen to ensure that the rays from each gun reach only phosphor stripes of the corresponding colour. As the colours in the phosphor glow, the image is re-created.

Tuner Chooses the channel by selecting the appropriate carrier wave.
Synchronisation unit Splits the synchronisation signal into vertical and horizontal signals to apply to the deflection coils.
Colour decoder Converts the luminance and chromiance signals into red, green and blue colour signals.
Electron gun
Loudspeaker
Deflection coil
Cathode-ray tube Filled with a vacuum to enable the electrons to pass from the electron gun to the screen without interference from other particles.
Grille
Phosphor stripes

Just 25 years after Guglielmo Marconi's first radio transmission in 1901, broadcasting stations had been established throughout Europe, and in Australia, Canada, India, Japan, Mexico and New Zealand. By the year 2000, radio had become a worldwide service, with 43 973 radio stations producing an annual 65.3 million hours of programming.

BBC news and current events

John Reith, first director of the BBC (1922–38), set high standards for the new company with a remit to educate, inform and entertain.

Key dates

1924 George V's first broadcast, from the British Empire Exhibition.
1926 The General Strike prompts the BBC to produce five news bulletins a day.
1932 George V inaugurates the royal Christmas message, with a speech written by Rudyard Kipling.

1934 The royal wedding of the Duke of Kent and Princess Marina is broadcast.
1940 On June 18, British prime minister Winston Churchill gives his 'This was their finest hour' speech, raising military and public morale on the eve of the Battle of Britain.
1957 The *Today* news and current affairs programme is first broadcast.
1978 Regular broadcasts begin from the House of Commons.
1994 The 24-hour news and sport service Radio 5 Live is launched.

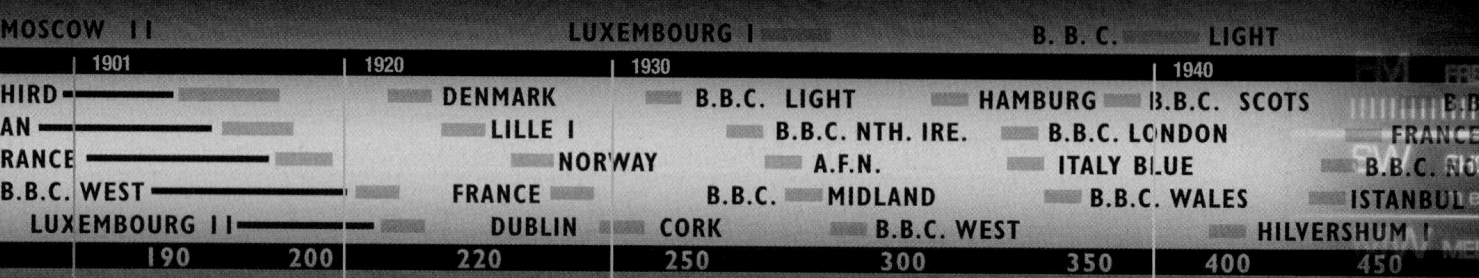

MOSCOW II   LUXEMBOURG I   B. B. C.   LIGHT

1901   1920   1930   1940

HIRD — DENMARK — B.B.C. LIGHT — HAMBURG — B.B.C. SCOTS — E.B
AN — LILLE I — B.B.C. NTH. IRE. — B.B.C. LONDON — FRANCE
RANCE — NORWAY — A.F.N. — ITALY BLUE — B.B.C. NO
B.B.C. WEST — FRANCE — B.B.C. MIDLAND — B.B.C. WALES — ISTANBUL
LUXEMBOURG II — DUBLIN — CORK — B.B.C. WEST — HILVERSHUM

190   200   220   250   300   350   400   450

1901 Guglielmo Marconi sends the first transatlantic radio signal from Cornwall, England, to Newfoundland in North America.
1906 The world's first radio transmission of speech and music is made from Brant Rock in Massachusetts, USA.
1915 The First World War introduces propaganda to the radio waves. Germany sends Morse code 'news' transmissions to neutral countries.

1920 US radio station KDKA broadcasts the world's first regularly scheduled programmes from Pittsburgh, Pennsylvania.
In the UK, the Marconi Company makes the first scheduled broadcasts.
1922 The British Broadcasting Company (BBC) is founded. In the USA, there are now 564 licensed radio stations. France begins broadcasting from the Eiffel Tower.
1923 Outside broadcasts are introduced in the UK with a performance of *The Magic Flute* from Covent Garden. Transmissions begin to cross the waters, from continental Europe to the UK, and from the UK to the USA. Three million Americans own radios.
1924 Commercial sponsorship of programmes begins in the USA. In the UK, the Greenwich time signal 'pips' are first broadcast, and a ground-breaking live commentary covers the Lord Mayor's Show.
1926 Organised broadcasting begins in India.
1927 The NBC and CBS networks begin broadcasting in the USA.
1929 About 14 million Americans own radios.

1931 Radio Normandy begins in France, and is the first commercial station to broadcast to the UK.
1932 BBC Empire Service is launched, forerunner of the World Service.
1933 Franklin D. Roosevelt begins 'fireside chats' on US radio.
1936 BBC broadcasts Edward VII's abdication speech.
1938 Foreign-language services begin at the BBC. On CBS in the USA, Orson Welles' dramatisation of H.G. Wells' novel, *The War of the Worlds*, causes panic among listeners, who believe that the simulated

news broadcast is real.
1939 BBC broadcasts Neville Chamberlain's declaration of war on Germany. British households can tune in to the traitorous Lord Haw-Haw (William Joyce) broadcasting German propaganda to Britain from Radio Hamburg. The USA has 40 million radio sets in use; Germany 10 million.

Creating panic Orson Welles announced an imminent Martian attack on planet Earth in his dramatisation of *War of the Worlds* on US radio (1938).

1940 Commercial FM radio, with a higher quality audio signal, begins in the USA.
1942 The US government's *Voice of America* is launched during the Second World War to broadcast to the population of Germany.
1944 'Disc jockeys' are introduced on US stations.
1946 An annual BBC licence fee covering radio and television is introduced in the UK, costing £2.

Underground tactics
During the Second World War, political leader Charles de Gaulle broadcast to the French resistance movement from Britain.

Longest-running programmes

◐ **Music:** *Grand Ole Oprey* (USA), first broadcast in 1925, and *Desert Island Discs* (UK), which began in 1942. Both programmes are still running.
◐ **Talk:** Alistair Cooke's US affairs programme *Letter from America* (UK), which was first broadcast in 1946, and now attracts an audience of 34 million listeners worldwide.
◐ **Comedy:** *Amos and Andy* (USA) ran from 1928 until 1960.
◐ **Drama:** *The Archers* (UK), set in the fictitious rural village of Ambridge. The series had produced 13169 episodes by its 50th anniversary on January 1, 2001.
◐ **Political reportage:** *The Week in Parliament* began in 1929 and continues today under the title *The Week in Westminster*.

The British comedy tradition

Britain has a long tradition of radio comedy, which has given rise to some unforgettable catch phrases. The catch phrase was born at the beginning of the Second World War with Arthur Askey's 'I thang-you' on *Band Waggon*, and the typically British chit-chat in *ITMA* (It's That Man Again). *ITMA* was the BBC's most popular comedy programme, attracting 20 million listeners. It ran until 1949. Even when television became widespread, the impact of radio on listeners' imaginations kept the comedy tradition alive.

Most popular comedy shows
1938 *Band Waggon*
1939 *ITMA*
1947 *Take It From Here*
1950 *Life with the Lyons*
1951 *Crazy People* (later known as *The Goon Show*)
1954 *Hancock's Half-Hour*
1962 *The Men from the Ministry*
1964 *I'm Sorry I'll Read That Again*
1975 *The News Huddlines*
1976 *I'm Sorry I Haven't A Clue*
1999 *The Weekend Starts Here*

1950 Radio Free Europe, a private US station supported by the US government, begins broadcasting to European countries. Foreign-language programming has become well established: the USA and the Soviet Union are each transmitting more than 500 hours of foreign-language programmes a week; Britain is producing 600 hours a week.
1957 The world's first transistor radio, the Sony TR63, is introduced in Japan.

1960 Stereo broadcasting on FM stations begins in USA.
1964 Radio Caroline uses unauthorised wavelengths to broadcast pop music to the UK from a ship anchored at sea, outside territorial waters, setting a precedent for similar 'pirate' stations.
1966 The BBC is authorised to establish nine local BBC radio stations; the first, Radio Leicester, begins broadcasting in 1967.
1967 The BBC creates a pop music station, Radio 1, and other services are renamed: the Light Programme becomes Radio 2, the Third Programme becomes Radio 3 and the Home Service becomes Radio 4.

1973 LBC (London Broadcasting Company) becomes the first independent local radio station. Capital Radio introduces radio commercials to the UK.

Rousing talk Adrian Cronauer's upbeat radio broadcasts helped to keep up the spirits of US troops during the Vietnam War (1954–75). The film *Good Morning Vietnam!* (1988) was loosely based on Cronauer's experiences.

1981 The Soviet Union is now producing more than 2000 hours of foreign-language programmes a week, ahead of Britain (nearly 750 hours) and the USA (nearly 2000 hours).

Man of letters
Alistair Cooke was born in Manchester, but studied at Yale and Harvard. Since emigrating to the USA in 1937, he has commented on American affairs for the BBC.

1990 The average US household owns five radios.
1991 The Independent Radio Authority (IRA) is formed in the UK to regulate independent radio stations.
1994 The USA has 10057 commercial radio stations.
1995 The BBC launches digital radio to improve sound quality.
1997 The USA's Federal Communications Commission approves the introduction of satellite radio stations.

FACT The first radio commercials were broadcast in the USA in 1922.

see also
408-9 **Radio broadcasting**
562-3 **Digital communications**
564-5 **Recorded sound**

Radio waves, like light and sound waves, are part of the electromagnetic spectrum. They lie at one end of it, where the waves have the lowest frequency and longest wavelength. Starting in the late 19th century, it was discovered how to harness these waves to transmit sound signals – first the dots and dashes of Morse code, then later the human voice itself.

Broadcasting and receiving

How radio signals are broadcast
First, a radio, or carrier, wave is created, then modulated to carry sound. This creates a radio signal, which is fed to an aerial and transmitted.

● **Oscillator** Generates the carrier wave, an electric current oscillating rapidly at a precise radio frequency.
● **Sound signal** A microphone converts sound waves into electric signals of varying voltage.
● **Amplifier** Increases the strength of the sound signal.
● **Transmitter** Superimposes the sound signal onto the carrier wave. It then feeds the signal to the aerial on the transmitter mast.

How radio signals are received
Signals picked up by the aerial are tuned to filter out those of unwanted frequency. The sound signal is fed to the speaker.

● **Radio aerial** Radio waves induce minute currents oscillating at the same frequency as incoming carrier-wave signals.
● **Tuner** Selects the desired frequency.
● **Radio-frequency amplifier** Boosts the strength of the signal.
● **Demodulator** Separates the sound signal from the carrier wave.
● **Audio amplifier** Boosts the sound signal and feeds it to the loudspeaker.

1850   1900

Coherer Marconi's own coherer (the glass tube) and tapper.

Diode valve Fleming's invention improved reception.

1864 Scottish physicist James Clerk Maxwell publishes his theory of **electromagnetic waves.**
*c.*1888 German physicist Heinrich Rudolph Hertz builds a simple **transmitter** – a spark transmitter – able to form radio waves, thereby proving Maxwell's theory. He measures the waves' length, speed and other physical properties, but can see no practical use for them.

1890 French engineer Edouard Branly invents the **'coherer'**, a device that detects radio waves.
1895 Working separately, the Italian Guglielmo Marconi and the Russian Alexander Popov are the first people to use a spark transmitter to send **radio waves** over a distance, then detect them with a coherer.

1901 Marconi sends a radio signal **across the Atlantic**, from Cornwall to Newfoundland.
1902 Danish engineer Valdemar Poulsen invents a high-frequency **electronic oscillator** for generating radio waves.
1904 British electrical engineer John Ambrose Fleming invents the **diode electronic valve**, which is more sensitive to radio waves than the coherer.

1905 Canadian-born, former university professor, Reginald Fessenden, builds a transmitter that can be used to broadcast the **human voice**.
1906 American H.H.C. Dunwoody invents the crystal and wire **'cat's whisker'** radio.
1907 American inventor Lee de Forest unveils the **audion (triode) electronic valve**, an improvement on Fleming's diode for detecting radio waves.

*c.*1909 In San Francisco, California, the station KCBS makes the first regular **radio broadcasts**.

29 000km

UHF (ultra high frequency) signals These are used for television and digital radio broadcasts. Frequency: above 300MHz.

500km

Finding a frequency
Radio waves are a form of electromagnetic radiation occurring at the longest-wavelength end of the spectrum. They are generated by radio transmitters, which broadcast a carrier wave continuously. Radio waves may be reflected or bent by the ground or atmosphere, depending on the wave's frequency or wavelength. The frequency spectrum is regulated by international agreement, with frequencies reserved for military use, police, radar and other services. Radio stations are allocated frequencies depending on availability and the power of their transmitter.

Short-wave signals These bounce off the ground and the layer in the Earth's atmosphere known as the ionosphere, and can travel to any part of the Earth. They are used for international broadcasting but are subject to interference. Frequency: 3-30MHz.

Medium-wave signals At night these bounce off the lower part of the ionosphere to travel several hundred kilometres. In the day they travel along the ground. They are suitable for radio stations requiring medium-quality sound but they are not suitable for stereo broadcasting. Frequency: 300kHz-3MHz.

200km

120km

70km

AM, FM AND DIGITAL

There are three ways in which a radio wave can be modulated to carry an electric sound signal. The most used are amplitude modulation (AM) and frequency modulation (FM), which work by modifying characteristics of the carrier wave to mirror those of the sound signal:

● **Amplitude modulation (AM)**   Alters the amplitude, or power, of the carrier wave so that it varies with the voltage of the sound signal: the higher the voltage, the greater the amplitude of the carrier wave. AM needs relatively simple receivers, but is subject to static interference from lightning storms.

● **Frequency modulation (FM)**   Alters the frequency of the carrier wave so that it varies with the voltage of the sound signal: the higher the voltage, the higher the frequency of the wave. The receivers are more complex, but produce a better-quality sound than AM. However, interference, caused by signals bouncing off hills and buildings, is still a problem.
● **Digital audio broadcasting (DAB)** Uses digital technology to convert details of a sound wave into a series of digital bits, then transmits this sequence. Receivers are complex and use microchips, but interference and distortion are virtually eliminated.

Amplitude and frequency   Electromagnetic waves have both amplitude (reflecting the size or strength of the wave) and frequency. AM transmissions modify the carrier wave's amplitude to match the voltage of the sound signal; FM transmissions modify its frequency.

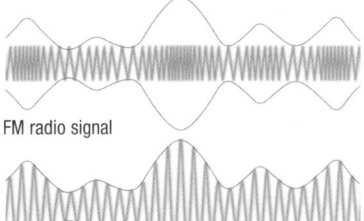

FM radio signal

AM radio signal

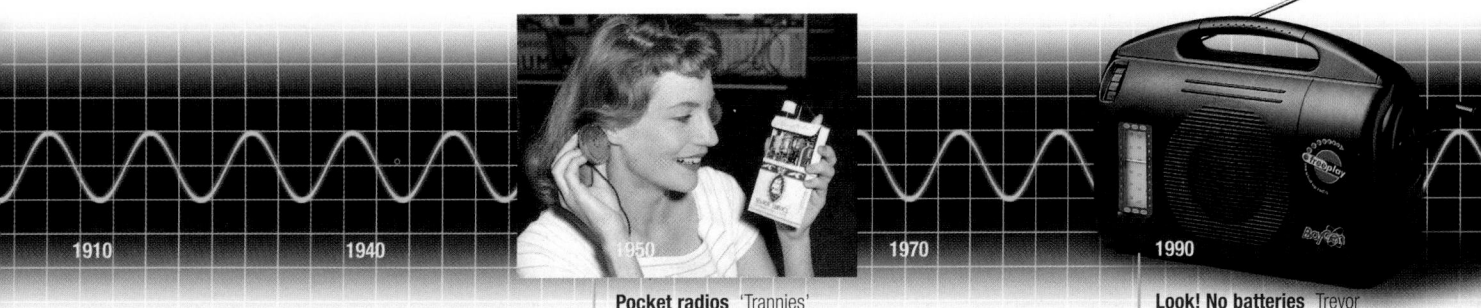

1910   1940   1950   1970   1990

Pocket radios 'Trannies' revolutionised radio listening.

Look! No batteries Trevor Baylis's clockwork radio.

1912-23 American engineer Edwin Howard Armstrong builds a succession of electronic circuits, which lead to him producing the first **portable radio** in 1923.
1929 American Paul Gavin makes the first **car radio**, the Motorola.
1930s Edwin Armstrong patents a **frequency modulation (FM)** system. He transmits FM broadcasts from station W2XMN, near New York.

1940s The first regular **FM broadcasts** occur on US commercial radio.
1947 American scientists John Bardeen, Walter Brittain and William Shockley invent the **transistor** to amplify signals. This eliminates the bulky vacuum tube.

1950s Experimental **stereophonic broadcasts** take place in the USA.
1955 Pocket transistor radios on sale in the USA.
1955 The BBC's first FM broadcast takes place; **stereo FM** follows in 1962.

1975 Experimental **digital radio** broadcasts take place in the UK.
1988 BBC stations launch the **Radio Data System** (RDS) – traffic news, channel data and automatic tuning for car radios.

1991 British inventor Trevor Baylis unveils his wind-up **clockwork radio**.
1995 Regular digital radio broadcasts start in Britain and Canada.
1996 Web radio stations broadcast over the Internet.

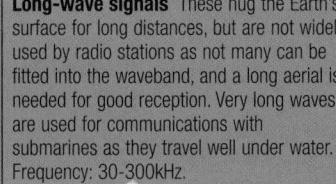

Long-wave signals   These hug the Earth's surface for long distances, but are not widely used by radio stations as not many can be fitted into the waveband, and a long aerial is needed for good reception. Very long waves are used for communications with submarines as they travel well under water. Frequency: 30-300kHz.

VHF (very high frequency) signals   FM radio works on VHF signals. These generally travel only as far as the horizon and may reflect from buildings or the ground, but carry a lot of information so can be used for high-quality stereo broadcasts. Frequency: 30-300MHz.

The oldest known written news reports – ancient Rome's Acta Diurna ('Daily Events') – were hung in prominent places for all citizens to read. But after the Roman Empire disintegrated it was more than 1200 years before written news reached the general public again.

NEWSPAPERS AND MAGAZINES

News became widely available in pamphlets covering current events in the 16th century. During the following century, newspapers, magazines and illustrated narrative strips became well established. From 1618, the Dutch pioneered weekly newspapers with *corantos* ('current news'), translated into English and French and circulated widely through trading links. Broadsheets appeared independently at around the same time in Japan. The first British newspaper was the *Weekley Newes* (1622), and the first in North America *Publick Occurrences* (1690).

Top newspaper and magazine circulation by country

Country	Largest magazine	Circulation	Largest newspaper	Circulation
Brazil	*Veja*	1.12 million (pw)	*Folha de Sao Paolo*	449 000
Canada	*Reader's Digest*	1.01 million (pm)	*Toronto Star*	460 000
France	*Télé 7 Jours*	2.56 million (pw)	*Ouest France*	758 000
Germany	*TV Movie*	2.59 million (fortnightly)	*Bild*	4.23 million
Italy	*L'Espresso*	388 000 (pw)	*Corriere della Sera*	1.08 million
Japan	*Young Jump*	1.96 million (pw)	*Yomiuri Shimbun*	10.22 million
Spain	*Hola*	760 000 (pw)	*El Pais*	410 000
UK	*What's on TV*	1.74 million (pw)	*News of the World*	4.07 million
USA	*Modern Maturity*	20.6 million (pm)	*Wall Street Journal*	1.95 million

such as the *Gentleman's Journal* (1692) and the *Ladies' Mercury* (1693). *The Gentleman's Magazine* followed in 1731. North America's first, the *American Magazine* (1741), lasted just three months, but by the turn of the century there were more than 100 titles in the US.

The age of the press barons By 1855 all of today's leading British quality dailies – *The Times*, *The Observer*, *The Guardian* and *The Daily Telegraph* – had been established. In the US, the reputations of the *New York Times* and *The Washington Post* were growing. By the end of the century, modern journalism began to evolve, shaped by a handful of powerful businessmen. The faltering *New York World* owed its revitalisation to Joseph Pulitzer. Under his management, the newspaper produced the world's first colour supplement (1893) and regular comic strip (1895). Pulitzer's competition came in the form of William Randolph Hearst and his *Morning Journal*. Hearst introduced sensationalist stories with banner headlines and lavish pictures, a style of news reporting that came to be known as 'yellow journalism'.

In Britain, Lord Northcliffe (Alfred Harmsworth) introduced the small-format US-style tabloid, the *Daily Mail* (1896) – the first paper in the world to reach a circulation of more than 1 million copies a day, and the *Daily Mirror* (1903), also selling a million copies a day by 1914. Lord Beaverbrook (Max Aitken) took over the competing *Daily Express* in 1919 and raised its circulation to a record-breaking 2.25 million copies a day. Today's largest circulation figures belong to the tabloid *News of the World* (founded in 1843), which sells just over 4 million copies a week.

The rise of photojournalism
Photojournalism took off in the 1920s with the appearance of *Time* (1923), the *New Yorker* (1925) and *Life* (1936) in the USA, and *Picture Post* (1938) in Britain. Postwar depression was lifted in Germany with *Stern* magazine (1948), and France began *Paris Match* (1949).

Gallic style *Paris Match* introduced photojournalism to France more than 50 years ago and is still a best-selling magazine.

Reading for leisure Intellectual journals published in England, France, Germany and Italy in the 1660s marked the beginning of the magazine industry. The first entertainment magazine, *Le Mercure Galant*, with court news, anecdotes and poetry, appeared in France in 1672. By the end of the century, England had produced periodicals

Man of influence
William Randolph Hearst's sensationalist treatment of Cuba's struggle for independence helped to provoke the Spanish-American War.

Breaking news In 1972, *The Washington Post*'s investigation into a break-in at the Democratic Party's Watergate headquarters implicated the Republicans, forcing President Nixon to resign.

Newspaper launch dates

Date	Newspaper	Country
1785	*The Times*	UK
1791	*The Observer*	UK
1821	*The Guardian*	UK
1838	*Bombay Times*	India
1851	*New York Times*	USA
1855	*The Daily Telegraph*	UK
1874	*Yomiuri Shimbun*	Japan
1876	*Corriere della Sera*	Italy
1877	*The Washington Post*	USA
1888	*Financial Times*	UK
1889	*Wall Street Journal*	USA
1918	*Pravda*	Russia
1923	*Hindustan Times*	India

COMIC CHARACTERS

Character	Cartoonist	Date	Country
Little Orphan Annie	Harold Gray	1924	USA
Blondie	Chic Young	1929	USA
Popeye	Elzie C Segar	1929	USA
Tintin	Hergé	1929	Belgium
Dick Tracy	Chester Gould	1931	USA
Li'l Abner	Al Capp	1934	USA
Peanuts	Charles Schulz	1950	USA
Andy Capp	Reg Smythe	1957	UK
Astérix	Albert Uderzo	1959	France
Doonesbury	Garry Trudeau	1970	USA
Garfield	Jim Davis	1978	USA
Dilbert	Scott Adams	1988	USA

Press records

◉ **The country with the largest number of newspapers** is India, which has 4235 titles – mostly regional.
◉ **The world's best-selling magazine** is the *Reader's Digest*, which sells 27 million copies per month in 18 languages. The US edition alone sells 15 million copies per month.
◉ **The oldest surviving daily newspaper** is Austria's *Wiener Zeitung*, established in 1703.
◉ **The oldest surviving weekly newspaper** is Sweden's *Post-och Inrikes Tidningar*.

ILLUSTRATORS AND CARTOONISTS

Illustrating publications for widespread circulation required a broad range of artists with many different skills. The 19th-century newspaper industry needed factual illustrations, and sent reporters such as Thomas Nast out into the field to capture real events in pen and ink. Illustration for entertainment began even earlier, with the caricatures drawn by Arthur Pond for Britain's *London Magazine* in the 1740s. Their broad appeal created a market for satirical magazines such as *Punch* (1841). By 1865 the comic strip arrived, with the German pictorial narrative *Max und Moritz*, drawn by Wilhelm Busch.

Comic-strip hero Tintin and his dog Milou (known as Snowy in the UK and USA) first set out on their adventures in 1929. Since then, 25 million copies of the comic-strip stories have been sold.

Leading illustrators

◉ **George Cruikshank** (1792-1878) British
Great technical facility and robust satire made Cruikshank the leading political cartoonist of his day. He also illustrated more than 850 books, and is well known as the illustrator of Charles Dickens' *Sketches by 'Boz'*.
◉ **Hergé (Georges Remi)** (1907-83) Belgian
The writer and illustrator who created Tintin and his moral adventure stories, Hergé is widely credited as the finest exponent of the *bande dessinée* (strip cartoon).
◉ **Thomas Nast** (1840-1902) German (naturalised American)
The political cartoonist who created the donkey symbol for the Democratic political party and the elephant for the Republicans. His caricatures helped to expose political corruption in the New York administration.
◉ **Frederic Remington** (1861-1909) American
The best known illustrator of the American West, whose drawings of soldiers, cowboys and Native Americans shaped popular views of the West for decades.
◉ **Norman Rockwell** (1894-1978) American
Chronicler of middle America, whose covers for *The Saturday Evening Post* magazine, drawn over a period of 47 years, became an American institution.
◉ **Charles Schulz** (1922-2000) American
Creator and cartoonist of *Peanuts*, the world's most popular comic strip.
◉ **James Thurber** (1894-1961) American
Writer and illustrator famous for his cartoons of the frustrated, daydreaming urban man.

Small-town style Norman Rockwell sold his first cover to *The Saturday Evening Post* in 1916. He went on to draw another 316 covers.

The invention of printing in the mid 15th century was crucial to the development of Western civilisation. It allowed mutiple copies of books to be made, speeding up the flow of new ideas to a Renaissance world eager for knowledge. Technolology since has been driven by ever increasing demand – today there are presses producing around 90 000 newspapers per hour.

Typesetting

Traditionally, the arrangement of letters into words, lines and pages was a mechanical process, with lines of type set by printworkers called compositors and cast in molten or 'hot' metal to make a printing plate. Computer technology has transformed this process:

⬤ Working from personal computers (PCs), operators use desktop publishing (DTP) software programmes to set type, lay out pages and incorporate digital images from a scanner. The completed pages are then stored as a computer document, or file.

⬤ The computer files are transferred, or downloaded, into an image processor to be prepared for printing. Each page, which will have been made up of separate elements, such as type, photographs and drawn illustrations, is converted into a single image.

⬤ A phototypesetter, also known as an imagesetter, is used to print the page either onto paper, so it can be looked through for errors ('proofing'), or onto photographic film, from which a final, high-qualitly print can be made.

Typefaces

The alphabet has been styled in many thousands of ways to suit changes in fashion and technology. This bewildering range can be grouped into just eight basic types:

Gothic type reflects the handwriting of late medieval Germany, where it originated.

Old Style is also based on writing, that of 18th-century, Italian formal documents.

Transitional type, with its distinct, crisp horizontals and verticals, relates to the growing use of the printing machine.

Modern, with its contrasting thick and thin strokes, owes much to the late 18th-century vogue for classical styling.

Egyptian type is a machine-crafted style. It is bold, with serifs having a similar weight to the rest of the letter.

Sans serif styles are bolder still, with extras, such as serifs disappearing altogether.

Script type is machine-made, but mimics handwriting.

Optical character recognition (OCR) type is styled so that it is easy to scan and record digitally.

𝕬𝕒 Gothic or black letter **𝕺𝕷𝕯 𝕰𝖓𝖌𝖑𝖎𝖘𝖍** (15th-16th century)

Aa Old Style **Caslon** (1722)

Aa Transitional Baskerville (1760)

Aa Modern **Bodoni** (1790)

Aa Egyptian or slab serif **Rockwell** (1855)

Aa Sans serif **Gill Sans** (1928)

Aa Script *Kuenstler Script*

Aa OCR face Geneva

Display face Fat, rounded type, popular for posters and billboards in the 19th century, was well suited for cutting onto wooden printing blocks (above).

c.8th century AD The Chinese print on paper and cloth (right), using ink-brushed **woodblocks**, with a mirror image of the text in relief.

c.12th century Arab traders introduce **paper** to Europe.

c.1453-55 Johann Gutenberg pioneers **'movable' metal type**. Assembled in a frame for printing, the type could then be separated and reused.

1477 First use of engraved metal plates – known as **gravure printing** – enabling fine line illustrations, for printing maps.

c.1725 Scotsman William Ged develops a process for making **duplicate** (stereotype) **printing plates** from plaster of Paris, with the print area in relief.

1775 Standard type sizes, now used worldwide, are introduced in France by François-Ambroise Didot.

c.8th centuryAD   c.1040   c.12th century   **1400**   1403   1453-55   1476   1477   *1600*1642**1700**c.1725   1768   1775

c.1040 Movable type develops in China. Each Chinese character, moulded from clay and glue, is baked to form a hard 'type', then mounted on a metal plate.

1403 Cast **metal type** is first used in Korea.

1476 William Caxton sets up the first **printing press** in London. Chaucer's *Canterbury Tales* is among the 100 books he published.

1642 Development of the **mezzotint process** for printing graduated tones ('halftones'), enabling light and shadow in engravings.

1768 Aquatint engraving on copper is invented, giving prints that look like watercolours.

Printing processes

Lithography (litho), the most versatile printing process, works on the principle that oil and water will not mix. The image areas – type and illustrations – are produced as film, and transfered to a flat metal plate. The plate is then treated so that only the image areas will attract the greasy ink. In the 'offset litho' process the ink is transferred, or offset, onto a rubber roller, or 'blanket', and then to the paper. It gives a clearer, sharper result than printing direct from the plate.

Letterpress, the earliest form of printing, is a 'relief' print process, in which the type is raised from the surface; a roller deposits ink only on the raised surface, onto which paper is pressed. More costly than offset litho, it is now used for specialist printing.

Photogravure (gravure) is the reverse of letterpress printing: the printable image is photographically etched onto a cylinder, leaving tiny hollows ('cells') wherever ink is to be transferred to paper. On the press, the cylinder is coated with ink; this is then scraped off the surface, but remains in the hollows. The paper absorbs the ink from the hollows. Gravure is used to print material that requires a high print quality, such as art and photographic books.

cyan

magenta

yellow

black

combined

Printing colour

To enable different tones of colour to be adjusted, a single multicoloured image is converted at printing stage into separate colour images – usually the 'four process' colours: cyan (greenish blue), magenta (purplish red), yellow and black. When these are printed together in varying strengths, they give the full range of coloured tones.

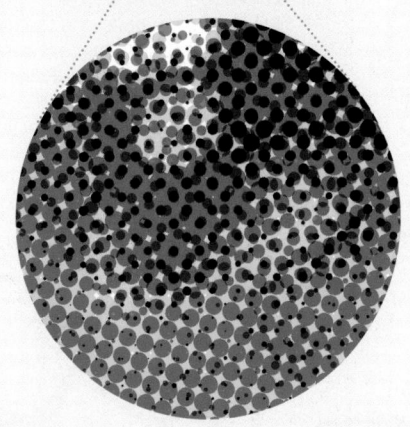

Illustrations

Engraving (left) The metal plate for printing was traditionally etched by hand. Today the design is etched photographically and printed by letterpress.

Halftone (above) A representation of an image is made, in which colour density is converted into different sized dots. This is done by copying it through a grid-like halftone screen, or electronically using a digital scanner.

see also

334-5 **Writing**

496-7 **Information economy**

The bound book

High-quality hardback books, like this one, are usually constructed using the 'case binding' method. The pages are machine sewn together with thread, and a cover is glued to the spine of the book. 'Perfect binding' is used in less expensive editions and most paperbacks: the pages are held along the spine by glue. In some books, words or decoration are stamped on the cover in silver or gold foil, a process known as 'blocking'.

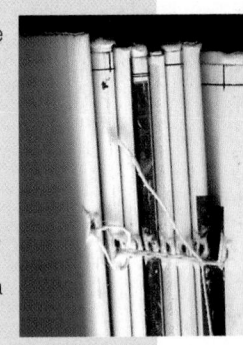

c.1810 In Germany Friedrich Koenig's steam-powered **cylinder printing press** greatly increases efficiency and clarity.

1852 William Fox Talbot develops a **photo-engraving process** for reproducing images.

1865 A high-speed **rotary press**, printing paper fed from a reel. or 'web' is developed.

1880s Typesetting machines such as **Linotype** (1884) and **Monotype** (1887) increase efficiency.

1939 First **mechanical photo-typsetting machine** transfers type onto photographic film, used to make printing plates.

1984 Desktop publishing (DTP) software enables digital typesetting and page make-up to be processed on personal computers.

1800 1810   1822   1852   c.1855 1865   1880s **1900** 1905 1939   c.1980 1984   **2000**

1822 American William Church invents the first **typesetting machine**.

c.1855 Photolithography is developed in France by Alphonse Poitevin, using plates prepared photographically.

1905 Offset litho, in which the inked image on a plate is transferred onto a roller, improves quality of litho printing.

c.1980 Digital colour scanners, storing images in computers, are used commercially.

Design consists of the drafting and planning of a product for industrial production. There are three aspects of a product that the designer is particularly concerned with: the object's appearance; the way it functions; and the marketing angle.

INDUSTRIAL DESIGN

In 1907, German electrical business AEG employed architect and designer Peter Behrens (1868-1940) as artistic adviser. Over the next seven years he designed factories, products, advertising material, catalogues and price lists. He gave AEG a uniform image, or corporate identity, as a way of promoting sales, and defined the role of the designer within the whole industrial and marketing process.

During the 1920s and 1930s, European designers were concerned with the functional aspects of products. In the USA, emphasis was put on a product's style and looks as a way of maximising sales. By the 1950s, people had acquired the basic necessities, and the emphasis shifted to producing new, improved models and versions in order to keep consumers interested. Japan began to compete with the USA in the areas of transistor and television technology and miniaturisation. Italy and the Scandinavian countries emerged as major design nations. By the late 20th century, new materials and technologies, and a keen awareness of the impact of style on sales, had transformed traditional products in every field.

All classic designs have one feature in common – long-term survival. The Anglepoise lamp, designed in 1934 by George Carwardine, is based on the articulations of the human arm. Its simple, functional design has been copied ever since. The BMC Mini was designed in 1959 by Alec Issigonis for the British Motor Corporation. Fitting the engine transversely enabled the tiny 3 m (10 ft) long mini to take four people. Newly invented rubber-cone suspension drastically reduced vibration from its small wheels.

▲ **Computer revolution**
The iMac's internal modem revolutionised computer design. There are few wires to break up its compact, elegant shape.

◀ **Cool juicer** In his spidery redesign of a lemon squeezer, designer Phillipe Starck transformed a mundane kitchen implement into a style icon.

◀ **Easy riding** The use of lightweight materials, advanced suspension, and gear sprockets that give up to 30 gears has transformed the bicycle into a vehicle that can be ridden over the roughest and steepest terrain.

Tizio lamp Richard Sapper's modern version of the anglepoise lamp has counterbalanced arms to improve stability. It has no internal wiring: the metal arms conduct electrical energy from a transformer in the base.

▲ **Filmless photography**
The digital camera records an image onto a disc, doing away with the need for buying and developing film.

London Eye Architects Julia Barfield and David Marks combined high-tech design and precision engineering to create the largest rotating wheel ever built, standing 135 m (443 ft) and weighing 1600 tonnes.

A VISUAL MESSAGE

Graphic design covers all areas of visual communication, including typography, advertisements, corporate identities and computer graphics.

The modernisation of type and page design began with William Morris (1834-96), leader of England's Arts and Crafts Movement. His approach to typography, in

Effective subtlety In 1960, designer Paul Rand associated the IBM logo with new technology by introducing stripes to suggest scan lines.

the books produced by his Kelmscott Press, was that it should be clear, beautiful and unadorned.

By Morris's time, the association of particular type, colours and logos with specific products had already begun. The early packaging of brands such as Colman's Mustard (created in 1823) is still familiar. In the 20th century, type styles derived from the 1920s German Bauhaus school – clear and simple, conveying a short, forceful message – have been an overwhelming influence on all areas of graphic design.

Company logos represent the epitomy of the simple visual message, and classic logos retain their meaning over time. The Coca-Cola typography was designed in 1887 by Frank M. Robinson, and now associates coke with heritage and authenticity. The Olympic rings were designed in 1913 by Pierre de Coubertin. The interlocking rings represent the union of

FedEx success A change of colours in the Federal Express logo saved the company $10 million in reproduction costs. Look between the E and the X for a hidden symbol.

the five continents; at least one of each of their colours can be found in every national flag. The Mercedes-Benz three-pointed star was designed in around 1890 by Gottlieb Daimler. He originally doodled the star on a postcard as a symbol of luck for his new company, using it as the official logo from 1909. The symbol created such a strong corporate image that Benz kept it when the two companies merged in 1924.

ADVERTISING

Modern advertising techniques originated in the 1920s, when psychological research led to two specific methods of selling products. 'Reason-why' advertising appealed to the rational mind by listing a product's practical advantages. Atmospheric advertising played on the consumer's emotions. These concepts, combined with the arrival of television advertising on US station NBC in 1939, laid the foundations for today's industry.

In 1954, US agency chief Rosser Reeves developed reason-why advertising further with the concept of USP – the Unique Selling Proposition: focusing on the specific benefit that sets a product apart from the competition. He advertised chocolate M&Ms on the basis of their unique sugar coating – they 'melt in your mouth, not in your hand'. In 1959, William Bernbach used the same technique to produce the most successful US car advertising campaign ever for the Volkswagen Beetle. He reversed the trend of promoting a car's superiority and sexiness, concentrating instead on the Beetle's quality and compactness with the headline 'Think small'.

Britain followed the USA's lead. The first television commercial, for Gibbs SR toothpaste, appeared in 1955. By the 1960s, the immediacy of television

Put a tiger in your tank The ESSO tiger, a metaphor for power, first appeared in 1951.

combined with the proliferation of goods on the market forced advertisers to look for new ways of differentiating between products. British agency boss David Ogilvy moved away from the USP concept by concentrating on a product's personality, or 'brand image'. He created company icons: US Schweppes president, Commander Whitehead, became 'The Man from Schweppes', and a liveried chauffeur became a symbol for Imperial Whiskey.

In the 1980s, social aspirations became the driving force in 'lifestyle' advertising. In 1987, after 20 years promoting Gold Blend as a coffee, Nescafé repackaged it as a vital item for a sophisticated couple, and sales rose by 70 per cent. Designers took sophistication a step further with art-driven adverts such as Guinness's film of Polynesian surfers (1999).

Spending on advertising, UK

Product or sector	Amount spent in 1999
1 Retail & mail order	£1195 m
2 Cars	£687 m
3 Food	£616 m
4 Finance	£545 m
5 Toiletries	£350 m
6 Leisure equipment	£349 m
7 Holidays/travel	£282 m
8 Drink	£281 m
9 Household stores	£259 m
10 Publishing	£253 m

The surfer The 1999 Guinness advert, voted the greatest TV advert of all time by British viewers, associated the anticipation of a great surfing wave with the wait for a slow-drawing pint of Guinness.

Global spending on advertising

The top spenders on advertising worldwide in 1999 were:

Name	Country	Amount spent
1 Proctor & Gamble	USA	US $4.69 bn
2 General Motors	USA	US $4.1 bn
3 Unilever	UK/Holland	US $3.69 bn
4 Ford	USA	US $2.42 bn
5 Philip Morris	USA	US $2.12 bn

see also
370-1 **Furniture**
402-3 **Television**
412-3 **Printing**

For centuries, fashion was created by the rich for the rich. Then, in the mid-19th century, Charles Worth opened the first Paris couturier house, and the professional designer was born. It took nearly 100 years for fashion to become part of most people's lives. Since the 1950s, new levels of prosperity, mass production and instant communication have allowed fashion to grow into a global industry.

CROWNING GLORY

Hairstyles have always mirrored fashion in clothes. In the mid-19th century, men's hair was short, bushy sideburns often being the only decorative touch. Women's hair was long, but usually worn pinned up.

After the First World War, short hair became a symbol of a new sense of independence for women. The 1920s flapper favoured the short 'Eton crop'. This could be softened by a 'permanent wave'. First tried in 1872, the perm was ideal for short styles.

In the 1960s, while their mothers used curlers to give their hair a wavy softness, young women had short,

Punk style The spiked, brightly coloured Mohican look had a unisex appeal.

asymmetric cuts to complement the clean, straight lines of the miniskirt. Men wore their hair long.

The desire of youth to shock reached its exteme in the 1970s with the punk look.

1850s men's fashion — **A bustle skirt** — **A hobble skirt with flounces by Poiret** — **A flapper dress**

*c.*1850 Men wear fitted coats over straight trousers, usually in dark, sober colours. Gradually the three-piece lounge suit, ties, bowler hats (derby in the USA), felt hats (the homburg) and straw boaters start to become fashionable.

Women wear large, shaped skirts supported by layers of underskirts and horsehair padding. These are soon replaced by a lighter framework of steel

hoops – the crinoline. Skirts are lavishly decorated with lace and ruffles.

A very narrow waist is essential to the succes of the look, and as skirts become wider – sometimes reaching 9 m (30 ft) in circumference – corsets grow tighter. Small hats and laced, heeled ankle boots complete the look.

Mass production helps to make the latest fashions more widely available.

*c.*1870 Tight corsets, ballooning sleeves, high necklines and sweeping full-length skirts with a rear bustle create a high point in impractical women's fashion. Any attempts to introduce more 'rational' attire for women, such as knickerbockers and bloomers, are largely greeted with derision.

*c.*1890 Dresses and skirts with a slimmer outline appear, though 'the tyranny of the corset' continues.

*c.*1905 Higher waistlines and straighter, simpler skirts and dresses proliferate, though dresses remain full length, and hats become more lavish.

1910s The high-waisted 'hobble skirt', pinched at the ankles, is introduced by **Paul Poiret**. Skirts inch up. By the end of the decade, women's clothes are more functional, with calves, arms and necks now generally on view.

1920s Hemlines rise, and less formal, yet still elegant clothes become popular. Women favour the corsetless, flat-chested look, with its short, drop-waisted, straight skirts, seen in the strikingly simple designs of **Coco Chanel**.

The casual look for men includes wide-legged trousers, known as Oxford bags, knee-length golfing trousers, or plus fours, turn-ups and tweed jackets.

1930s As skirts begin to grow longer and straighter, a more womanly shape returns. Shoulders widen, waists get narrower, and the bosom reappears. The striking gowns of **Elsa Schiaparelli** capture the elegance and glamour of the period.

Mass production and use of cheaper, synthetic fabrics, such as rayon, bring the styles of the rich within easy reach of young working-class people.

Levi Strauss and the jeans revolution

In the mid 19th century, a German-born immigrant to the United States called Levi Strauss began producing hard-wearing trousers for Californian goldminers. He used a heavy canvas called *jene fustian*, or jean cloth, produced in Genoa, Italy, and originally intended for wagon covers

In 1873 Levi Strauss patented his design. They became known as Levi's and were standard workwear for labourers. Later, jean cloth was replaced by a French fabric, *serge de Nîmes*, which became corrupted to 'denim'.

By the 1930s jeans had been adopted as casualwear in the USA. In the 1960s young people everywhere wore them as a symbol of defiance. By the1970s they had gained acceptance among all groups and for all types of occasions, and in the1980s the first 'designer' jeans appeared.

see also

204-5 **Industrial Revolution**
212-3 **Between the wars**

Christian Dior's New Look **The miniskirt** **Smock and flares** **Yves St Laurent suit** **1990s street fashion**

1940s Wartime brings clothes rationing, followed by 'Utility' fashion in 1942, with **Norman Hartnell** and others aiming to provide attractive, practical garments on a very tight budget.

Austerity is swept aside in 1947 by the stylish extravagance of the 'New Look' from **Christian Dior**. Gathered into a narrow waist, his long, full skirts take up to 25 m (27 yd) of fabric to create.

1950s Mass-market fashion booms, with 'youth' styles, such as jeans and T-shirts, having a major impact on the mainstream. All ages gradually begin to dress more casually. Even leading Paris couturier **Hubert Givenchy** is noted for his relaxed mix-and-match skirts, slacks and blouses.

New materials such as nylon and synthetic silks provide colourful, creaseproof, popular clothes.

1960s Paris also aims at the young. **Pierre Cardin** styles a collarless jacket that is popularised by The Beatles, and, in 1965, **André Courrèges** launches the miniskirt. **Mary Quant** designs simple, colourful clothes that give women a more youthful look.

Hippie culture in the late 1960s leads to men adorned in as much silk and finery as women. Loose-fitting clothes and long flowery skirts appear.

1970s The decade starts with brief, close-fitting shorts, known as hot pants, and platform boots. Smocks and flared trousers and ruffles and flounces proliferate, influenced by the 'glam rock' vogue in music.

Vivienne Westwood and her partner, **Malcolm McLaren**, create the punk look: ripped clothes held together by safety pins and chains, and ghoulish make-up.

1980s The miniskirt is back in fashion. Shoulders expand, waists shrink, and ruffles disappear. 'Power-dressing', for both sexes, is in vogue, epitomised by the suits of **Giorgio Armani** and **Yves St Laurent**.

Japanese styling is evident, notably in the clothes of **Issey Miyake**, with their crisp layering and folding of fabrics.

'Supermodels' emerge, influencing notions of beauty.

1990s A bewildering array of styles emerges, with the emphasis on loose, unstructured, casual-looking clothes. New elasticated materials provide added comfort. A mixing of styles is seen, such as long, straight skirts worn with trainers, and blazers worn with lace skirts and thick-soled boots.

Teenagers go for the unisex styles of 1970s retro (hippy styles) and the baggy, ill-fitting grunge look.

Food long ago evolved beyond the basic function of sustaining life. It defines social groups, reflects religious attitudes and moral beliefs governing what can be eaten, and in the rituals of meal times promotes social cohesion. History, culture and technology have profoundly affected how we obtain, prepare and consume food.

Food and major religions

Buddhism The killing of animals is not permitted. Buddhists are vegetarian.
Christianity No overall rules, but some avoid meat on Fridays, especially Good Friday when Christ was crucified.
Hinduism Beef is forbidden because cattle are held to be sacred. Many sects are fully vegetarian.
Islam Pork, alcohol and the flesh of any animal found dead are forbidden; other meat must be *halal* – from animals killed in a prescribed manner.
Judaism Strict laws govern *kosher* (permitted 'pure') food. Meat must be from cloven-hoofed animals that chew the cud and have been killed by a *shohet* (trained ritual slaughterer). Shellfish and fish without skins and scales are forbidden. Meat and dairy foods must not be mixed.

Cuisines of the world Each of the world's societies has its own distinctive cuisine, based on climate, available food resources and culture.

Western Europe is divided in its cuisine by the northern limit of the growth of olive trees. To the south, the main cooking fat is olive oil, to the north butter and other animal fats. Other defining features are available vegetables: root vegetables are much used in the north, often in hearty stews, garlic and tomatoes in the south.

Central Europe still shows the influence of the former Austro-Hungarian Empire in its cuisine, including variations of paprika-laden goulash. Austria's link to Germany is seen in such dishes as *Apfelstrudel*, sausages and *Wienerschnitzel*. Coffee reached Continental Europe from Turkey through this region.

Middle East and North Africa derive their cuisine from the Ottoman Empire. Lamb dishes predominate, and olives, yoghurt, nuts, vine leaves, couscous and rice are some of the common local ingredients. Sweets are extremely sweet – as in *halva*, which combines sugar, sesame seeds and almonds.

India is well known for its use of spices to produce a wide range of subtly flavoured dishes; the taste tends to be hottest in the south. Chicken and lamb are favourite ingredients, but poverty and religion restrict meat-eating: strict Buddhists and many Hindus eat no meat, Muslims no pork. Milk and curds are widely used.

FAST FOOD

The first 'fast food' was the sandwich, reputedly invented 250 years ago by the 4th Earl of Sandwich, who put a slice of beef between two pieces of bread in order to avoid losing time at the gaming table. But today's fast food is a 20th-century American invention.

The first hamburger chain, White Castle, began selling 5 cent square hamburgers in 1921; it still sells 500 million a year. Many fast-food chains had small beginnings. Colonel Harland Sanders opened his first fried chicken shop in Corbin, Kentucky, in 1952, when he was 65, using his $105 social security cheque. Twelve years later he sold the company for $2 million. In 2000, KFC was serving more than 2 billion chicken meals annually in 82 countries.

In a similar way, two college students, Frank and Dan Carney, borrowed $600 from their mother to begin Pizza Hut in 1958 in Witchita, Kansas. By 2000, Pizza Hut had 12 000 outlets worldwide and was selling 1.7 million pizzas a day.

The two biggest hamburger chains also began in the 1950s: Burger King in Miami in 1954, and McDonald's in 1955 in San Bernadino, California. In 2000, Burger King's 11 340 restaurants around the world were visited by 15 million customers a day and sold a total of 2.6 billion hamburgers. In 1999, McDonald's served 15 billion customers –

43 million people a day – in more than 28 000 restaurants worldwide. In the UK 2.5 million people visit McDonald's every day.

Key dates

600s Forks used in the Middle East.
1589 Forks first used at the French court.
1609 Tea from China shipped to Europe.
1650 Tea introduced into England. First English coffee house opens.
1809 Nicolas Appert (France) preserves food in heat-sterilised bottles; canning is patented in England.
1840 Afternoon tea established in England.
1851 First refrigerated railway car (USA).
1868 First 'Pullman' railway dining car.
1880 Tinned fruits and meats on sale.

1890 First cafeterias and diners in USA.
1908 First tea bags introduced in USA.
1930 Birdseye introduces frozen foods.
1936 First in-flight meals (American Airlines). Food blender introduced
1937 Instant coffee invented in Switzerland.
1953 USA has about 17 000 supermarkets.
1954 Frozen 'TV dinners' launched in USA.
1990 UK approves first genetically modified food item, a variety of yeast.
1994 First genetically modified tomato produced in USA.

Sealed in a can
The advent of tinned food added variety to the daily diet.

China and Japan share rice and noodles as staples, but China is so vast that it has many regional cuisines. The emphasis is on balance – the principles of yin and yang – with the right mix of staples and vegetables/meat for health. Japan's formal culture means that the presentation of food is as important as its taste.

South-east Asia is noted for its fish and seafood, rice and noodle dishes and for such local and introduced spices as ginger, galangal, lemongrass and chilli. Chinese cooking has influenced dishes in much of South-east Asia, and French that of Indo-China. Fermented fish sauce is widely used as a flavouring.

North America uses local ingredients such as corn, but there are few truly native recipes. Immigrants have created the world's most varied cuisine, including Cajun, Tex-Mex and 'fusion' cooking. Many 'ethnic' dishes such as chop suey and deep-pan pizza are unknown in their supposed country of origin.

Central and South America have combined the inherited cuisines of Spain, Portugal and other European nations with such local ingredients as beans, maize, chilli peppers and plantains, and indigenous cooking methods. Seafood is plentiful in the Caribbean, beef and lamb in South America.

FOOD AND EXPLORATION

Throughout history, people have transplanted foods from one place to another. As a result, many foods are now grown thousands of miles from their place of origin.

For example, Alexander the Great introduced apricots to Greece from Asia about 300 BC, and Europeans took radishes to China around AD 700. The Romans systematically took foods to lands they conquered, such as orange trees from India to plant in North Africa in the 1st century. The Moors of North Africa then took orange trees to Spain by about the 8th century (along with

olives and spinach), and by 1493 Columbus had shipped Spanish oranges to the West Indies.

Columbus was a keen collector of exotic foods, shipping home maize, pineapples and beans. The Spanish found the Aztecs using chocolate around 1500 and took that home. The French introduced large-fruited North American strawberries to Europe in 1624.

English explorer Francis Drake took sassafras (and tobacco) from Virginia to England. Captain William Bligh's purpose, during the voyage that ended in the *Bounty* mutiny, was to introduce breadfruit

trees from Tahiti to the West Indies to feed plantation slaves.

Some foods made a two-way trip. The turkey was taken home from Mexico by Spanish conquistadors about 1519, and English colonists later shipped it to their North American colonies. The Spanish introduced the potato to Europe from South America in the 16th century, and it returned west with the English to North America as a 'new' crop. Italian explorers shipped tomatoes grown by the Incas and Aztecs to Italy about 1550; Europeans took them to the USA in the late 18th century.

Almost every country on Earth has its own kinds of alcoholic drink. European nations in particular have a long tradition of producing various beers, wines and spirits. Climate plays an important role in what is made – and drunk – whereby its effect on the ability to grow certain ingredients.

MAJOR WINE-PRODUCING REGIONS OF THE WORLD

Most wine is produced between 30° and 50° N and 30° and 50° S of the Equator. Areas within these bands of latitude have the combination of warm summers and relatively mild winters needed to grow high-quality wine grapes. Location and soil type are also important. Valleys give protection from wind and frost, and thin soil with good drainage force vines to root deeply, protecting them from excessive damp, and letting them draw water from deep subsoil during droughts.

France produces slightly less wine than Italy, but is still the world's leading wine producer in terms of quality and variety. Bordeaux and Burgundy are the two most important regions.

Germany has a climate that mainly suits the cultivation of white grapes. The best vineyards are found in the west of the country. **Austria** makes similar wines to Germany's, although because of the marginally warmer climate they tend to be slightly richer and fuller.

South-east Europe
Wine has been made in Eastern Europe for centuries, but its quality is very varied. **Hungary** is best known for the red Bull's Blood, made around the ancient fortress town of Egar, and the dessert wine Tokaji Aszú. **Bulgaria** has, since the 1970s, built up a big export trade in wine made from Western grape varieties such as Cabernet Sauvignon. **Romania** produces wines using Pinot Noir and other Western varieties, and has great potential according to many experts.

Saale-Unstrut · Saxony · Ahr · Mittelrhein · Rheingau · Rheinhessen · Mosel-Saar-Ruwer · Pfalz · Franken · Württemberg · Baden · Hessische Bergstrasse · Champagne · Alsace · Loire Valley · Burgundy · Jura · Bordeaux · Bergerac · Cahors · Savoie · Rhône Valley · Valle d'Aosta · Trentino-Alto Adige · Lombardy · Piedmont · Friuli-Venezia Giulia · Veneto · Emilia-Romagna · Gascony and the South-West · Languedoc-Roussillon · Provence · Tuscany · Marches · Umbria · Abruzzi · Douro · Rioja and Navarra · Dão · Bairrada · Penedés and Cava · Tarragona · Corsica · La Mancha · Valencia · Valdepeñas · Montilla-Moriles · Jerez · Sardinia · Campania · Apulia · Calabria · Sicily

Portugal has long been a wine producer, but until recently most of its table wine was for local consumption. Vinho Verde and Dao are the best-known styles outside Portugal, along with the fortified wines Madeira (from the island of the same name) and Port (from the Douro valley).

Spain is more heavily planted with vines than any other country, yet yields are low because of the blistering summer heat. The best wine is generally produced in the cooler north and in the Jerez area where sherry is made.

Italy was called 'the land of the vine' by the ancient Greeks because of the ease with which wine grapes grow there. It produces more wine each year than any other single country. The most prestigious regions are in the north, especially in Piedmont.

Principal grape varieties

Only about 50 of the 5000 or so known grape varieties are used in wine-making. Red and rosé wines are produced almost exclusively using red ('black') grapes, while white wine, including Champagne, can be made from both white and red grapes.

Red grapes
Cabernet Sauvignon is the principal grape of the Bordeaux region of France, now widely grown around the world.
Merlot is another major Bordeaux grape that is cultivated worldwide.
Pinot Noir is the great red Burgundy grape, also used for Champagne. Difficult to grow, it is less successful elsewhere.
Sangiovese is Italian and used for Chianti.

Syrah is the red grape of the northern Rhone Valley, now better known as Shiraz, one of Australia's most successful grapes.
Tempranillo is the delicate, aromatic grape used in Spain to make red Rioja.

White grapes
Chardonnay makes white Burgundy, Champagne and many New World wines.
Chenin Blanc is the main white grape of the Loire region, where it is used to make both dry and sweet wines.
Riesling is the great grape of Germany, producing high-quality dry and sweet white wines.

Sauvignon Blanc is a major French grape, planted in Bordeaux and the Loire. It is now also commonly grown in the New World, particularly in New Zealand.
Sémillon is at its best in the sweet Sauternes of Bordeaux, although it is also used to make soft dry whites in France and the New World, particularly Australia.

Riesling country
The Rhine valley boasts Germany's finest vineyards.

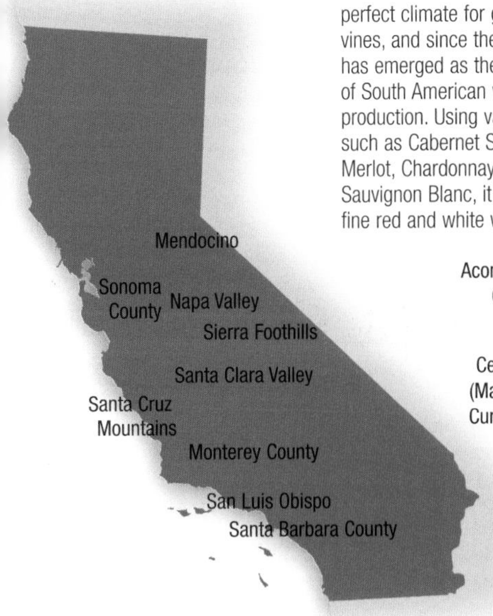

Chile has wide areas with a perfect climate for growing vines, and since the 1980s has emerged as the superstar of South American wine production. Using varieties such as Cabernet Sauvignon, Merlot, Chardonnay and Sauvignon Blanc, it produces fine red and white wines.

Argentina is the world's fifth-biggest producer of wine, but much of it is of mediocre quality. Vines are widely grown in many parts of western Argentina, but mainly around Mendoza in the Andes foothills.

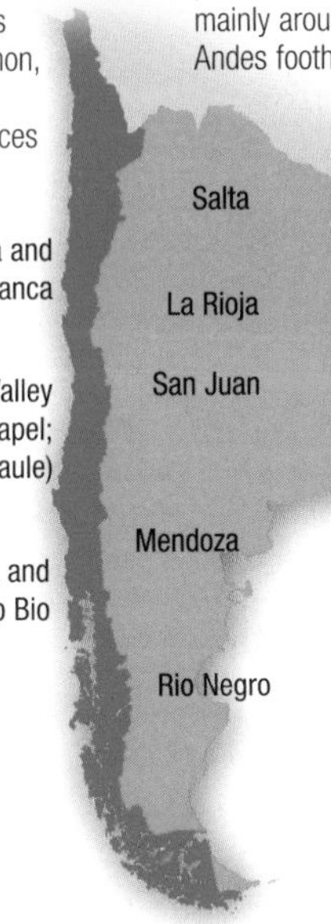

South Africa was once known only for its dessert wines. Today it makes wine from many varieties of grape, including some very good reds from Pinotage and Cinsaut and dry whites from Colombard and Steen (Chenin Blanc).

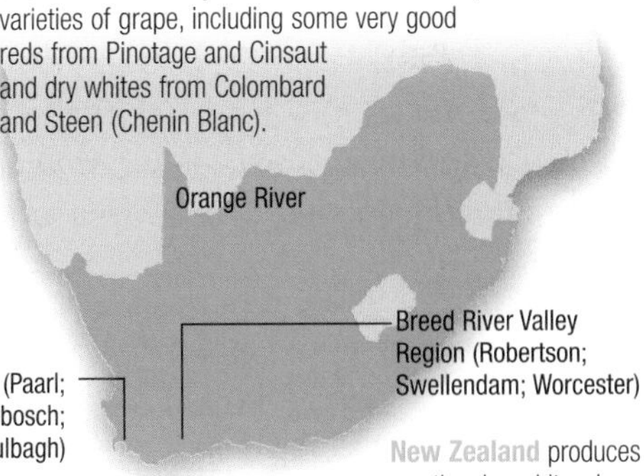

Mendocino
Sonoma County
Napa Valley
Sierra Foothills
Santa Clara Valley
Santa Cruz Mountains
Monterey County
San Luis Obispo
Santa Barbara County

Salta
La Rioja
San Juan
Mendoza
Rio Negro

Aconcagua and Casablanca
Central Valley (Maipo; Rapel; Curicó; Maule)
Itata and Bio Bio

Orange River

Coastal Region (Paarl; Stellenbosch; Swartland; Tulbagh)
Breed River Valley Region (Robertson; Swellendam; Worcester)

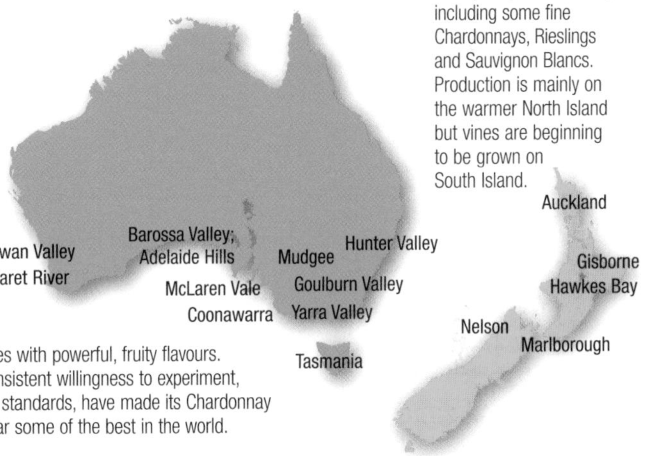

The USA produces a wide variety of wines, mostly in California (above), where the climate is ideal for vine-growing. Newer areas are being developed in the Pacific North-west – especially in Washington state, Oregon and Idaho – and in the North-east, including New York state, where wine was first made in the 17th century.

New Zealand produces mostly crisp white wines, including some fine Chardonnays, Rieslings and Sauvignon Blancs. Production is mainly on the warmer North Island but vines are beginning to be grown on South Island.

Auckland
Gisborne
Hawkes Bay
Nelson
Marlborough

Swan Valley
Margaret River
Barossa Valley; Adelaide Hills
McLaren Vale
Coonawarra
Mudgee
Goulburn Valley
Yarra Valley
Hunter Valley
Tasmania

Australia is known for wines with powerful, fruity flavours. The Australian industry's consistent willingness to experiment, together with high technical standards, have made its Chardonnay and Shiraz wines in particular some of the best in the world.

BEER

Beer is brewed and drunk much more widely than wine, because the grains used to make it do not need such warm conditions as grapes. China and the USA brew the most beer, but the greatest drinkers per head are the Czechs and the Irish. The average Czech drinks 162 litres (285 pints) of beer a year. in Ireland the figure is 151 litres (266 pints), while in Britain it is 99 litres (174 pints).

Most beer is made from barley, sprouted and roasted to make malt, but wheat, maize or rice may also be used. Hops (the dried flowers of the hop plant) are added to give flavour before fermentation with yeast.

Types of beer The main distinction is between top-fermented beers, in which the yeast forms a thick, frothy mass at the top of the fermentation tank, and bottom-fermented beers, or lagers, in which the yeast sinks to the bottom and ferments there. 'Ale' once meant beer brewed without hops, but today can refer to almost any top-fermented beer.
Bitter is the classic British draught beer. It is top-fermented and flavoured using bitter English hops. It is amber in colour and has 3-5 per cent alcohol.
Pale ale, or light ale, is the name given to light-coloured bottled bitter.

Bavarian celebration The Oktoberfest in Munich is the world's premier beer festival. Germans come third in the world league table of beer drinkers, consuming 127 litres (223 pints) per person per year.

Strong ale is a style of bitter with more than 5 per cent alcohol and a fuller flavour given by extra hops.
Brown ale is made medium-sweet by adding crystal malt and extra sugar.
Mild ale is similar but weaker and darker.
Stout has a rich flavour and an almost black colour from adding black or chocolate malt. It is top-fermented.
Lager, or pilsner, is the main beer made in Continental Europe, the USA and most other parts of the world. It is flavoured with hops that are less bitter and more aromatic than English hops. The alcohol content ranges from about 3 per cent up to 5-7 per cent or more.

Spirits

Spirits are made by distilling a weak alcoholic liquid, or a fermented mash of plant ingredients and water, to produce a drink with a high alcohol content. The fermented material can be any grain, fruit or vegetable. Raw distilled spirit contains about 60-80% alcohol; it is generally watered down before bottling.

Spirit	Main ingredients; flavourings (if any)
Aquavit	Grain or potatoes; caraway seed
Arrack	Rice, molasses or palm-juice
Bourbon	Maize with malted barley and/or rye
Brandy	Grapes or wine
Calvados	Apples
Gin	Rye, maize, etc; juniper berries
Grappa	Grape skins
Kirsch	Cherries
Ouzo	Grapes; aniseed
Rum	Sugar cane or molasses
Schnapps	Grain or potatoes
Slivowitz	Plums
Tequila	Maguey (agave) plant
Vodka	Grain or potatoes
Whisk[e]y	Barley (malted or unmalted) or rye

see also
245 **Czech Republic**
418-19 **Food**
540-1 **Chemistry of compounds**

Football is the most popular team sport in the world. In 1904 the game's governing body FIFA (Fédération Internationale de Football Association) was founded by just seven countries – today it boasts more than 200 member nations around the globe.

The aim of the game

Two teams compete to score goals; a goal is scored by a player kicking, heading or otherwise deflecting the ball with any part of his body other than his hands or arms over the goal line between the posts and under the crossbar. There are 11 players on each team: one goalkeeper and ten outfield players (with attacking, midfield or defensive roles). During the game, players can be replaced by substitute players; each team can use up to three substitutes. A player who has been replaced takes no further part in the game. Teams change ends at half-time.

Duration and extra time

Most football games last for 90 minutes (two 45 minute halves, with an interval). If at the end of that time the scores are level, the game is declared a draw. In knock-out competition, however, if the score is even at the end of play, extra time may be played, generally for 30 minutes. Further stalemate can lead to a replay or a 'penalty shoot-out': each team gets five penalty shots at goal. If the score is still level at the end of the latter then the first team to miss a penalty loses. Sometimes the first goal scored in extra time (the so-called 'golden goal') is used to settle a match.

Officials and sanctions

A football match is controlled by a referee, two assistant referees who patrol the touchlines and a fourth official. The main sanctions issued by the referee are:

● **Yellow card** A 'caution' given to a player for flouting the rules or for dissent. Too many yellow cards over time can lead to suspension by the football authorities.

● **Red card** This is issued to a player for two yellow card offences in the same game, or a particularly serious or violent infringement; the player is sent off the pitch and suspended.

Foul play, whether deserving of a card or not, is penalised by a free kick being given to the opposition from the point where the infringement was made. The opposition must retreat 9 m (10 yd) from the ball. If a foul is committed inside the penalty box then the opposition is awarded a penalty kick, which is taken from the penalty spot directly in front of the goal.

The playing area

Almost all football pitches are made of turf. Sizes vary but those used for international matches must be 100-110 m x 64-75 m (110-120 yd x 70-80 yd).

Corner If the ball is knocked over the goal line outside the goal by a player of the defending team, then the referee calls for a corner kick to be taken (if it is knocked over by an attacking player then it is a goal kick instead). A corner kick, or corner, is taken by a member of the attacking side with the ball placed inside the marked quarter circle (radius 90 cm [3 ft]).

Centre circle Radius of 9.15 m (10 yd); a centre spot marks the kick-off point for the start of the game, the restart after half-time and after a goal is scored.

Goal line

Touchline

Halfway line

Equipment

Ball An air-filled rubber bladder with an outer casing of leather or artificial material, measuring 21.5-22.5 cm (8$\frac{1}{2}$-8$\frac{3}{4}$ in) across, and weighing 400-450 g (14-16 oz).
Boots Lightweight and made of leather with six screw-in studs on the sole. Some football boots have metal toecaps.
Shin pads Worn beneath the socks to protect the fronts of the lower legs from injury.

World Cup holders

The World Cup is held every four years. Japan and South Korea will host it in 2002, and Germany in 2006.

Year	Result of the final
1930	Uruguay 4-2 Argentina
1934	Italy 2-1 Czechoslovakia
1938	Italy 4-2 Hungary
1950	Uruguay 2-1 Brazil
1954	W Germany 3-2 Hungary
1958	Brazil 5-2 Sweden
1962	Brazil 3-1 Czechoslovakia
1966	England 4-2 W Germany
1970	Brazil 4-1 Italy
1974	W Germany 2-1 Holland
1978	Argentina 3-1 Holland
1982	Italy 3-1 W. Germany
1986	Argentina 3-2 W Germany
1990	W Germany 1-0 Argentina
1994	Brazil 0-0 Italy (3-2 pen)
1998	France 3-0 Brazil

Team formations

Today's favoured options for the deployment of players include a formation using four defenders, four midfield players and two attackers, known as 4-4-2, and other structures such as 4-2-4, 4-3-3, or 3-5-2 (using defenders as back-up attackers, called 'wing backs'). The choice depends on the attributes of the players available and the assessment of the opposition.

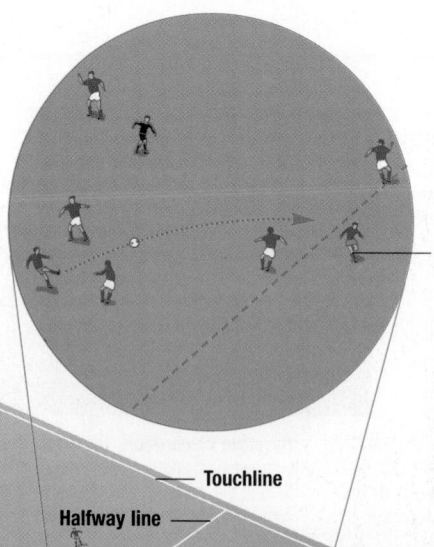

Fouls

Handball Apart from goalkeepers, players are not allowed to touch the ball with their hands or arms, except for 'throw-ins' after the ball has gone over the touchline. A goalkeeper may not handle the ball outside the penalty area or if it has been kicked (rather than headed) back by a teammate.

Offside A player is offside if, while he is in the opponents' half, a pass is made to him from a colleague when there is only one defending player (which may be the goalkeeper) between himself and the goal line. He is not offside if there is a second defender in line with or in front of him at the moment the passing player hits the ball.

Reckless tackling This is judged by the referee, whose decision is final.

Goal The two goalposts are 7.3 m (24 ft) apart and topped by a crossbar 2.4 m (8 ft) high.

Penalty spot

Goal area 5.5 m (18 ft) long and 18.3 m (60 ft) wide.

Penalty area 16.5 x 40.2 m (54 ft x 132 ft). The penalty spot is 11 m (36 ft) from the goal.

Division One/Premier and FA Cup winners

League champions

Year	Winner
1970	Everton
1971	Arsenal
1972	Derby County
1973	Liverpool
1974	Leeds United
1975	Derby County
1976-7	Liverpool
1978	Nottingham Forest
1979-80	Liverpool
1981	Aston Villa
1982-4	Liverpool
1985	Everton
1986	Liverpool
1987	Everton
1988	Liverpool
1989	Arsenal
1990	Liverpool
1991	Arsenal
1992	Leeds United
1993-4	Manchester United
1995	Blackburn Rovers
1996-7	Manchester United
1998	Arsenal
1999-2001	Manchester United

Most championships won since the First Division began (in 1889)

18	Liverpool
14	Manchester United
11	Arsenal
9	Everton
7	Aston Villa

FA Cup winners

Year	Winner
1970	Chelsea
1971	Arsenal
1972	Leeds United
1973	Sunderland
1974	Liverpool
1975	West Ham United
1976	Southampton
1977	Manchester United
1978	Ipswich Town
1979	Arsenal
1980	West Ham United
1981-2	Tottenham Hotspur
1983	Manchester United
1984	Everton
1985	Manchester United
1986	Liverpool
1987	Coventry City
1988	Wimbledon
1989	Liverpool
1990	Manchester United
1991	Tottenham Hotspur
1992	Liverpool
1993	Arsenal
1994	Manchester United
1995	Everton
1996	Manchester United
1997	Chelsea
1998	Arsenal
1999	Manchester United
2000	Chelsea
2001	Liverpool

Division One/Premier records

Clubs winning the most First Division/Premier League matches (1889-2000)

Club	Played	Won	Drew	Lost
Everton	3796	1557	931	1308
Liverpool	3412	1552	852	1008
Arsenal	3412	1470	888	1054
Aston Villa	3462	1456	779	1227
Manchester United	3056	1358	784	914

European Championships

Year	Winner	Year	Winner
1960	USSR	1980	W. Germany
1964	Spain	1984	France
1968	Italy	1988	Holland
1972	W Germany	1992	Denmark
1976	Czechoslovakia	1996	Germany
		2000	France

Diego Maradona
(1960–) Argentinian
Acknowledged by the mid 1980s as the world's best player, Maradona created controversy during the 1986 World Cup in which Argentina defeated England when he apparently used his hand to score a goal – an action he later ascribed to 'the Hand of God'.

Euro stars Frenchman Lilian Thuram (right) tackles Italian Roberto Baggio. Tackles are fair if the referee judges that the player is not careless, reckless or uses excessive force.

Alfredo Di Stéfano
(1926–) Argentinian
Alfredo Di Stéfano is best remembered for his goal-scoring achievements for Real Madrid in the 1950s. 'The Blond Arrow', as he was nicknamed, took the team to five consecutive European Cup successes. A combination of injury, nationality issues and sheer bad luck meant that he never got to play in the World Cup.

LEGENDS
Pelé (Edson Arantes do Nascimento)
(1940–) Brazilian
Widely considered the greatest attacking player ever, in 1969 Pelé became the first player to score 1000 goals in first-class games, and scored 1283 in total.

American football evolved from rugby in the 1800s. Today, it is run by the National Football League (NFL). As well as being the USA's most popular professional sport, it is played in over 650 American colleges, which compete yearly for the Rose Bowl.

The aim of the game
American football is played between two teams of up to 45 players (including substitutes). Only 11 players from each team are on the field ('gridiron') at any one time. The object is for players to gain ground up the field and score points, either by carrying or catching the oval ball over the opponents' goal line for a touchdown or by kicking the ball over the crossbar between the goalposts.

The sequence of play
The game is divided into four 15 minute quarters, with a half-time interval. Each quarter starts with one team kicking the ball to the other team, which is then allowed four attempts (downs) to advance 10 yd (9 m) or more up the field with the ball. If they succeed, they get four more downs; if they fail, their opponents win possession. A down ends when a player with the ball is stopped by opposing players or goes out of bounds, or if a pass is thrown and missed.

The roles of different players
Each team has three separate groups of players:
◉ **Offense** When a team wins possession, they put their offense on the field. The offense's job is to move the ball forward, either by running with it or by one player throwing it and another catching it. The 11 men in the offense are led by the quarterback, who is the playmaker and throwing specialist. He is supported by three receivers, whose job it is to run into space upfield and

catch the ball. The quarterback is protected from the front by a line of five players (the centre, the right and left tackles, and the right and left guards) and from behind by two players; the fullback and tailback (also known as running backs). Sometimes the quarterback will opt to give the ball to the running backs to run with rather than attempting to throw it.
◉ **Defense** The job of the defense is to prevent the opposition's offense from moving the ball forward. This is done most effectively by tackling ('sacking') the quarterback before he can make a throw or pass.
◉ **Special team** This group comes onto the field for kicking situations: to start or restart play; to kick at goal; or to gain ground by punting the ball upfield.

The playing area
The American football field, or gridiron, is covered by grass or an artificial alternative called AstroTurf. It is measured in yards and is 100 yd (91 m) long by 53½ yd (49 m) wide.

Super Bowl winners
Begun in 1967, this game between the champions of the professional American and National Football Conferences (the AFC and NFC, which together comprise the NFL) is now the USA's biggest sporting event.

Year	Champion		Year	Champion
1967-8	Green Bay Packers		1989-90	San Francisco 49ers
1969	New York Jets		1991	New York Giants
1970	Kansas City Chiefs		1992	Washington Redskins
1971	Baltimore Colts		1993-4	Dallas Cowboys
1972	Dallas Cowboys		1995	San Francisco 49ers
1973-4	Miami Dolphins		1996	Dallas Cowboys
1975-6	Pittsburgh Steelers		1997	Green Bay Packers
1977	Oakland Raiders		1998-9	Denver Broncos
1978	Dallas Cowboys		2000	St Louis Rams
1979-80	Pittsburgh Steelers		2001	Baltimore Ravens
1981	Oakland Raiders			
1982	San Francisco 49ers			
1983	Washington Redskins		**Most Super Bowl wins**	
1984	Los Angeles Raiders		Dallas Cowboys	5
1985	San Francisco 49ers		San Francisco 49ers	5
1986	Chicago Bears		Pittsburgh Steelers	4
1987	New York Giants		Green Bay Packers	3
1988	Washington Redskins		Washington Redskins	3

Joe Namath
(1943–) American

Namath is acknowledged as one of the best passers in the game. As quarterback, he led the New York Jets to the 1969 Superbowl championship, after which he was named the game's most valuable player, and made 173 touchdowns in a career lasting 23 years.

Body armour
All American footballers wear a helmet, and protective pads on their thighs, hips, knees, groin, ribs, arms and shoulders. Some also wear padded fingerless gloves.

50 yd (45.7 m) line This is the halfway line. Lines are numbered downwards from this towards the goal line at 10 yd (9 m) intervals.

End zone The ball must be carried into or caught in this 10 yd (9 m) area behind the goal line for a touchdown to be scored.

Hashmarks These divide the pitch up into yards.

Defence

Offense

Quarterback

Joe Montana
(1956–) American

This quarterback played for San Francisco 49ers and Kansas City Chiefs between 1979 and 1994. He led the 49ers to four Superbowl championships, in one of which he orchestrated a 92 yd (84 m) winning drive in the closing seconds.

Scoring
Touchdown This is worth six points. Following a touchdown, a conversion kick, worth one point, is taken from in front of the goalposts. Alternatively, players may attempt to carry or pass the ball into the end zone for two points.
Field goal This is a placement or drop kick that passes between the goalposts, and is worth three points. It may be attempted at a third or fourth down if the offense does not expect to make the distance required for another first down.
Safety This is worth two points. It is scored by the team playing defense if one of the offense is stopped inside his own end zone while in possession of the ball.

Goalposts
Two uprights, 30 ft (9 m) tall and 18 ft (5.6 m) apart, extend from a crossbar resting on a 10 ft (3 m) high support pole.

Rugby

The sport of rugby was invented at Rugby school in England, where it was first played in 1823. The Rugby Football Union was established in 1871. In 1895, a split between clubs over whether or not players should be paid led to the creation of the Rugby Football League and the development of Rugby League as a separate game.

Union World Cup

Year	Winner
1987	New Zealand
1991	Australia
1995	South Africa
1999	Australia

The aim of the game
Rugby Union, the older of the two forms of rugby, is played between two teams of 15 players (or sometimes seven a side, known as 'sevens'). The aim is to score points by carrying the ball across the opponents' goal line and 'touching it down' to the ground, or by kicking it over the crossbar between the goalposts.

How rugby is played
A game is played over two 40-minute halves; teams change ends at half-time. Each half begins with one team taking a place-kick from the centre spot (kick-off), with the opposing team on or behind their 10 m (10 yd) line. After the kick-off, the side in possession works the ball towards their opponents' goal line by running with it, passing it sideways or backwards, or kicking it, with the aim of scoring. The other team attempts to stop them and, if possible, win back possession.

Scrums and line-outs
A scrum is made of the eight forwards from each side. The front rows of three players lock their heads together and the ball is thrown between them. The players then try to heel the ball backwards out to their own team. A scrum is called if:
- A player passes the ball forwards;
- A player is tackled and fails to release the ball promptly after hitting the ground;
- A player knocks the ball forwards onto the ground with his hand or arm (knock-on);
- The ball is passed by one player while another of his team is in front of him (offside).

A line-out is called when the ball goes over a touchline. Players from each side form two parallel lines, at right angles to the touchline. The ball is thrown between the lines by the hooker from the team that did not kick the ball out. Likewise, the ball is thrown into a scrum by the scrum half of the team infringed against.

RUGBY LEAGUE

Rugby League is a 13-a-side game, with six forwards and seven backs, including the scrum half. While rugby union was strictly amateur until 1995, rugby league has been both amateur and professional from the beginning. It is played mostly in the north of England and in Australasia. Other major differences between the sports are that in rugby league a try is worth four points and all kicked goals (including conversions) are worth two. Also, the team in possession of the ball can be tackled five times in succession, but on the sixth tackle must concede possession to the opposition.

AUSTRALIAN RULES FOOTBALL

Australian Rules football developed from rugby. It is played on an oval pitch, up to 185 m (606 ft) long by 155 m (508 ft) wide; at each end are two goalposts, each flanked by a 'behind' post. The game is played between two teams of 18 players; players may run with the ball, kick it and hit it with their hands, but cannot throw it. A ball kicked between the goalposts scores a goal worth six points; if it passes between a goalpost and a behind post (outside each goalpost), it earns one point.

The playing area – rugby union
Pitches never exceed 100 m x 69 m (110 yd x 75 yd) between goal lines.

Goalposts 5.6 m (18.5 ft) apart with a crossbar 3 m (10 ft) from the ground.

Dead ball line

Goal line

10 m (10 yd) line

Halfway line

22 m (25 yd) line This marks the limiting distance from his own goal line that a player may kick the ball into touch.

Touchline

In-goal area This varies in size between pitches but is never more than 69 m x 23 m (75 yd x 25 yd).

Colin 'Pinetree' Meads
(1936–) New Zealand

Between 1967 and 1972, Meads played for the New Zealand All Blacks a record 55 times. The team's finest ever all-rounder, he is widely credited with having driven the All Blacks' rise to dominate international rugby.

Scoring
Try To score a try, worth five points, a player must put the ball on the ground in the opposition's in-goal area. He must be touching the ball when it hits the ground. A try is followed by a conversion kick, worth two points. This is taken from a point in line with where the try was scored.

Drop goal This is a drop kick that passes over the crossbar and between the goalposts. It is worth three points.

Penalty kick This is worth three points. It is awarded against a foul and taken from the point on the ground where the foul occurred.

LEGENDS

Gareth Edwards
(1947–) Welsh

Gareth Edwards played his first rugby union game for Wales in 1967 at the age of 19 and became their youngest-ever captain a year later. He went on to make 53 consecutive appearances in international matches – a Welsh record – and never missed a game in his career for his country.

Fouls Fouls are illegal tackles and dangerous play. They include hacking at the shins, stamping and high tackles around the head or neck.

Players
Forwards Numbered 1 to 8, they play in the scrum and line-outs.

Backs These players stand behind the scrum and are involved in most of the running and passing play.

Scrum half This player tries to retrieve the ball from the scrum to pass it to the other backs.

Cricket

Cricket has existed since the 13th century. The first laws of the modern game were enshrined in 1787 with the formation of the Marylebone Cricket Club (MCC). The MCC, based at Lord's in London, still has responsibility for the Laws of Cricket – the game's official rule book.

The aim of the game Cricket is played between two sides of 11 players. Each side bats and fields in turn. To win, one side must accumulate more runs than the other, and get all of the opposing batsmen out. If, at the close of play, the side batting second fails to reach the first side's score but still has batsmen who are not out, then the game is a declared a 'draw'.

How cricket is played The bowler throws the ball overarm to the batsman, who then tries to hit it to obtain runs. Six runs are awarded for hitting the ball out of the playing area without it touching the ground; four if it bounces on the way. Runs may also be scored by running (see below) or awarded if the bowler is judged by one of the two umpires to have bowled too far wide of the batsman (wide) or infringed the rules in any other way (no-ball).

- Bowling is divided into periods of six balls (overs); bowlers bowl for one over at a time, two bowlers alternating over a period of time.
- The batting side has a batsman at each wicket. When a batsman is out, he is replaced until all players have batted. The time that one side bats is called its innings. In Test matches, each side plays two innings.
- Batsmen are out: if they miss the ball and it hits the stumps (bowled); if they hit the ball and it is caught by one of the fielders before it touches the ground; if the batsman runs but fails to reach the popping crease before a fielder breaks the wicket at that end with the ball (run out); if the wicketkeeper hits the stumps with the ball when the batsman is outside his popping crease (stumped); or if the bowled ball hits the batsman's pad or body, but would have hit the stumps if the batsman had not been in the way (LBW – leg before wicket). Other reasons for a batsman's dismissal include handling the ball, obstructing a fielder and hitting the ball twice.

Cricket Test match records

Test matches (international games) have been played since 1877.

Consecutive Test series wins 8 – England, 1884-90
Consecutive Test series lost 10 – New Zealand, 1950-9
Biggest Test win England by an innings and 579 runs v Australia on August 20, 1938
Highest match aggregate 1981 runs by South Africa and England (drawn) in Durban, March 3, 1939
Highest innings total 952 for 6 declared by Sri Lanka v India at Colombo, August 2, 1997
Most Test matches played by one player 156 – Allan Border (Australia) 1978-94
Most Test runs scored by one player 11 174—Allan Border (Australia) 1978-94
Highest individual Test score 375 – Brian Lara (West Indies) v England at St John's, 5th Test, 1993-4

LEGENDS

William Gilbert Grace
(1848–1915) English

W.G. Grace broke all records with bat and ball between 1865 and 1899, scoring more than 54 000 runs in all (including 126 centuries), and taking more than 2800 wickets. His batting record remains the fifth-highest career total in first-class cricket.

LEGENDS

Sir Donald Bradman
(1908–2001) Australian

Universally acknowledged as the greatest batsman ever. At his last Test match in 1948 he needed to score just five runs to average 100 runs each time he batted. Instead, a stunned crowd saw him bowled second ball, so he only averaged 99.94. No one before or since has come anywhere near this figure.

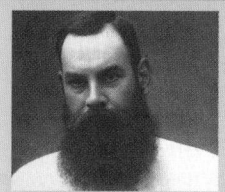

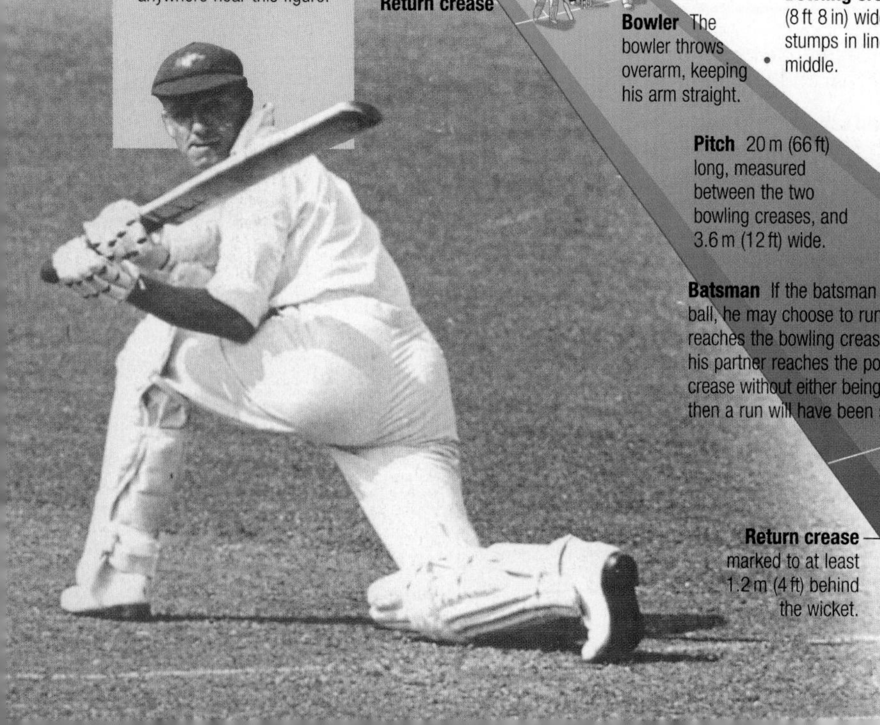

Cricket World Cup Champions

Year	Champion
1975*	West Indies
1979	West Indies
1983	India
1987	Australia
1992	Pakistan
1996	Sri Lanka
1999	Australia

*First year of competition

Equipment

Ball Wood in leather with a straight stitched seam, weighing 155 g (5 1/2 oz) and 7.3 cm (2 7/8 in) in diameter.
Bat Made from willow; no more than 96.5 cm (3 ft 2 in) long, and 10.8 cm (4 1/4 in) at its widest.
Protective gear Batsmen need pads and gloves on their legs and hands, and an abdominal guard; wicketkeepers wear especially thick gloves.

Playing area Can be any shape, but usually oval. Size varies, but ideally there should be 69 m (226 ft) of ground in any direction from the pitch or wicket.

Field positions There are many fielding positions. The captain and bowler place the fielders according to their tactics.

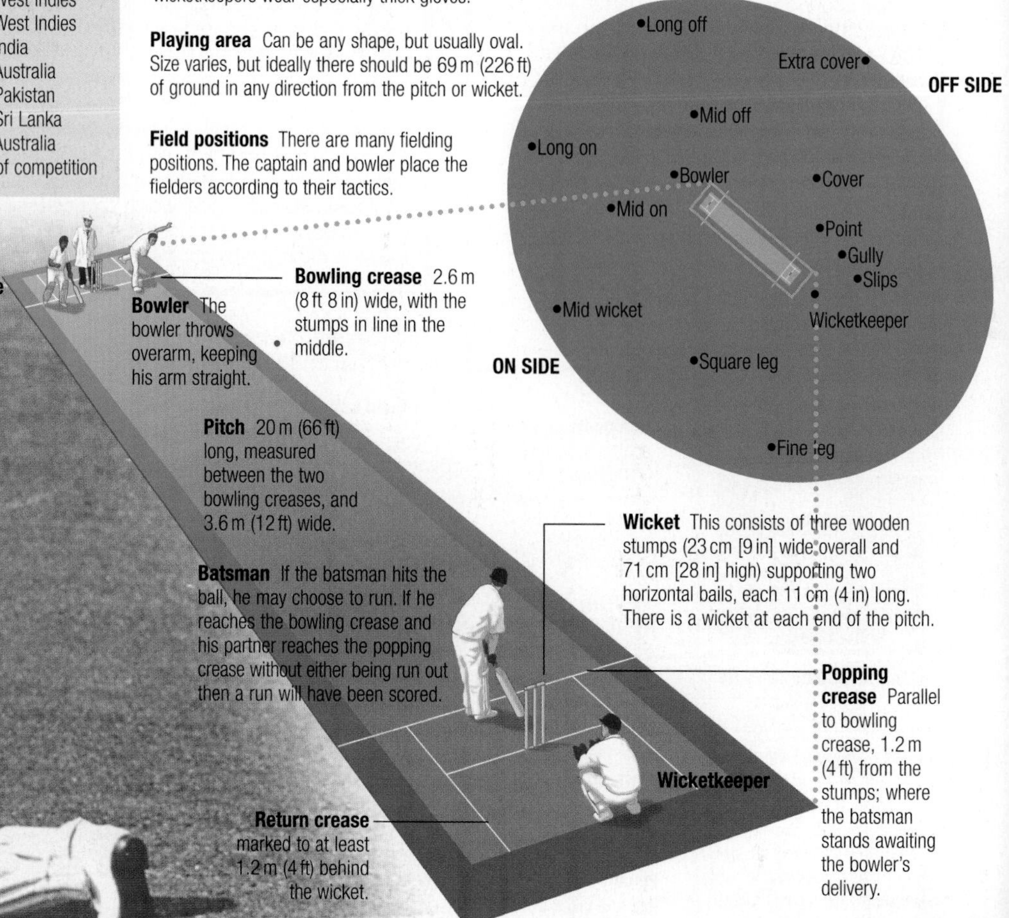
Long off
Extra cover
OFF SIDE
Mid off
Long on
Bowler
Cover
Mid on
Point
Gully
Slips
Mid wicket
Wicketkeeper
ON SIDE
Square leg
Fine leg
Return crease
Bowling crease 2.6 m (8 ft 8 in) wide, with the stumps in line in the middle.
Bowler The bowler throws overarm, keeping his arm straight.
Pitch 20 m (66 ft) long, measured between the two bowling creases, and 3.6 m (12 ft) wide.
Wicket This consists of three wooden stumps (23 cm [9 in] wide overall and 71 cm [28 in] high) supporting two horizontal bails, each 11 cm (4 in) long. There is a wicket at each end of the pitch.
Batsman If the batsman hits the ball, he may choose to run. If he reaches the bowling crease and his partner reaches the popping crease without either being run out then a run will have been scored.
Popping crease Parallel to bowling crease, 1.2 m (4 ft) from the stumps; where the batsman stands awaiting the bowler's delivery.
Wicketkeeper
Return crease marked to at least 1.2 m (4 ft) behind the wicket.

Baseball

The official US national sport, baseball developed from the old English game of rounders, which arrived in the 18th century with the first settlers. Baseball's most prestigious tournament, the World Series, began in 1903. It is played at the end of the season between eight teams; the top four from both the National and American leagues.

Baseball World Series Champions

Year	Champion				
1970	Baltimore Orioles	1982	St Louis Cardinals	1995	Atlanta Braves
1971	Pittsburgh Pirates	1983	Baltimore Orioles	1996	NY Yankees
1972	Oakland A's	1984	Detroit Tigers	1997	Florida Marlins
1973	Oakland A's	1985	K'sas City Royals	1998	NY Yankees
1974	Oakland A's	1986	NY Mets	1999	NY Yankees
1975	Cincinnati Reds	1987	Minnesota Twins	2000	NY Yankees
1976	Cincinnati Reds	1988	LA Dodgers		
1977	NY Yankees	1989	Oakland A's		**Most Series won since**
1978	NY Yankees	1990	Cincinnati Reds		**the tournament began**
1979	Pittsburgh Pirates	1991	Minnesota Twins	NY Yankees	26 wins
1980	P'delphia Phillies	1992	Toronto Blue Jays	St Louis Cardinals	9 wins
1981	LA Dodgers	1993	Toronto Blue Jays	Phil/KC/Oakland A's	9 wins
		1994	No series	Br'klyn/LA Dodgers	6 wins

The aim of the game Baseball is played by two teams of nine players, each batting and fielding in turn. Balls are thrown or 'pitched' by a pitcher to the opposing batsman. Batsmen attempt to hit the ball into the field and run round a series of 'bases', touching each on the way, to score a run. The team which scores the most runs wins.

How baseball is played The pitcher throws the ball towards the batter, who is standing on the home base plate. The pitcher aims at the area over the home plate, at a height between the batter's armpits and knees. This area is known as the strike zone.

If the ball is pitched outside the strike zone, and the batter does not swing at it, the pitch is declared a 'ball'; after four balls, the batter advances to first base. If the ball is pitched inside the strike zone, but the batter either: does not swing at it; swings at it but misses; or hits it beyond the foul lines the pitch is declared a 'strike'. After three strikes a batter is out.

Batters who hit a ball inside the field can start running to first base, or farther if they have time before the ball is fielded. Batters who have reached a base can proceed to the next base when a subsequent batter hits the ball. Only one runner can occupy a base at one time. Batters who hit the ball far enough to run round all four bases in one go score a home run. A home run is always scored if a batter hits the ball outside the field.

In addition to the 'three strikes' dismissal, a batter can also be out if the ball is caught before it touches the ground, or if a fielder in possession of the ball touches (tags) him or first base before he can reach it. Base runners making their way round the bases can also be put out by being tagged by a fielder.

The game is divided into nine periods of play, known as innings. Each innings is divided into two halves, with one team batting and the other fielding in turns. To end their half of the innings, the fielding side must put three players of the batting team out.

Equipment

Ball A cork core in rubber casing, wound with yarn and covered with leather. It weighs 142-156 g (5-5$^{1}/_{2}$oz) and is 7.3 cm (2$^{7}/_{8}$in) in diameter.

Bat A smooth, round, solid wooden (or aluminium) stick, not more than 107 cm (42 in) long and 6.9 cm (2$^{3}/_{4}$in) in diameter at the thickest part.

Protective gear Fielders wear a padded leather glove, for catching the ball; the larger glove worn by catchers and first basemen is known as a mitt. Catchers and batters wear helmets and other special protective gear.

Playing area The playing area, or pitch, covers about 2 acres. It is made up of an infield, or 'diamond', 27 m (90 ft) square, and an outfield. The outfield is split in two by an arc called the grass line, running 29 m (95 ft) from the pitcher's plate.

Field positions Three fielders stand in an arc beyond the grass line, and are known as the right outfielder, centre outfielder and left outfielder.

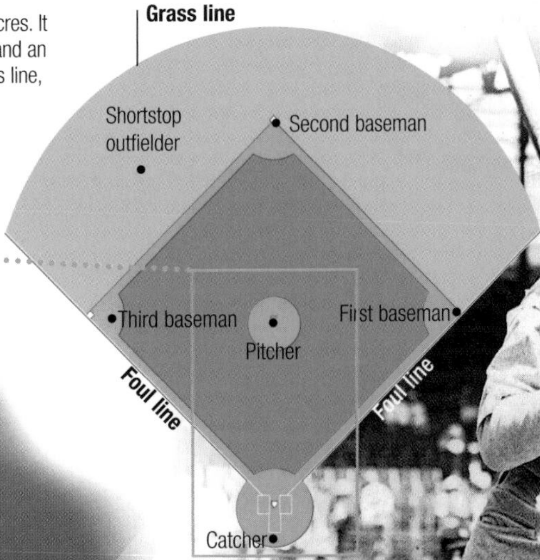

Bases The four corners of the diamond are named anticlockwise as home base, first base, second base and third base; home base is a slab of white rubber, the other bases are marked by a white canvas bag. The distance between each base is 27 m (90 ft).

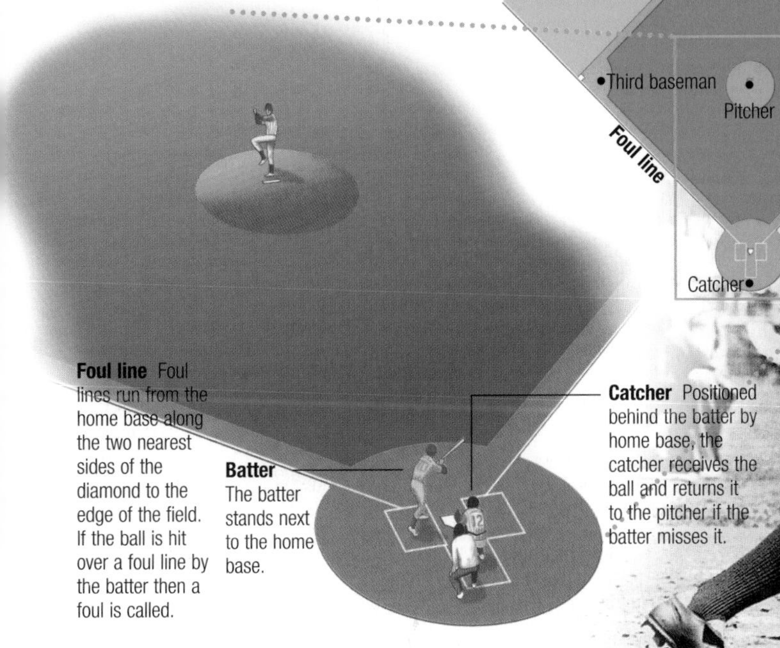

Grass line

Shortstop outfielder

Second baseman

Third baseman

Pitcher

First baseman

Foul line

Foul line

Catcher

Foul line Foul lines run from the home base along the two nearest sides of the diamond to the edge of the field. If the ball is hit over a foul line by the batter then a foul is called.

Batter The batter stands next to the home base.

Catcher Positioned behind the batter by home base, the catcher receives the ball and returns it to the pitcher if the batter misses it.

LEGENDS

Joe DiMaggio
(1914–99) American

'Joltin' Joe' played with just one team, the New York Yankees (1936-51). In 1941 he set a record by getting hits at least once in 56 consecutive games, and during his career hit 361 home runs. He was also an outstanding centre fielder.

LEGENDS

Babe (George Herman) Ruth
(1895–1948) American

Played for the Boston Red Sox and New York Yankees. Best remembered for his record-setting home run hitting ability, with 60 home runs in 1927 and 714 in all.

Games similar to basketball have been played for centuries; the oldest known version, called Pok-ta-Pok, was played by the Olmecs of Mexico 3000 years ago. The modern game was invented in 1891 by a Canadian – Dr James Naismith – at the YMCA Training School in Massachussets, USA. His aim was to revive his pupils' interest in sport.

The ball Round, with an outer surface of leather, rubber or synthetic material. It weighs 567-650 g (20-23 oz) and is 24-25 cm (9$\frac{1}{2}$-9$\frac{3}{4}$ in) wide.

High and mighty Apart from skill, height is a basketball player's most important attribute. Few of today's professionals are under 1.8 m (6 ft) tall.

The aim of the game
In basketball, two teams aim to score points by throwing the ball into their opponents' basket while stopping the other side from scoring. Players can throw, bounce ('dribble') and pass the ball, but cannot carry or kick it. Basketball is a noncontact sport, and players have a 'personal' space which others may not violate deliberately.

How basketball is played
The referee starts the game by tossing the ball into the centre circle, between the two opposing centres (jump ball). The team that gets the ball tries to advance it towards their opponents' basket. Goals, known as 'baskets', are scored for throwing a ball into a basket. They are worth two or three points depending on the player's distance from the basket. A basket from a free throw (awarded for fouls) is worth one point. After a basket is scored, play is restarted by the defending team from behind its end line.

Duration, teams and time rules
Amateur basketball games comprise two halves of 20 minutes each; professional games four periods of 12 minutes each. If a game ends in a draw, 5 minute periods may be played until there is a winner. There are two teams of ten for amateur games; 12 for professional games. Only five players from each team are allowed on the court at any time: two forwards, a centre (usually the tallest player) and two guards.

There are three time rules:
- **30 second rule** A team must shoot at the basket within 30 seconds of gaining possession of the ball.
- **10 second rule** A team gaining possession of the ball in its half of the court (back court) must get it into the other side (front court) within 10 seconds.
- **3 second rule** A player in possession of the ball may not be in the opposing side's restricted area for more than 3 seconds.

Basketball court dimensions 28 x 15 m (31 x 16 yd)

Three point line Semicircle with a radius of 6.25 m (20 ft 6 in) from the point on the floor directly beneath the centre of the basket. Baskets scored from outside this line are worth three points. Those scored from inside it are worth two.

Basket 45 cm (1 ft 6 in) in diameter; 3.05 m (10 ft) from the ground.

Centre line

Centre circle 3.6 m (4 yd) in diameter.

Restricted area

Free throw line This is 5.8 m (19 ft) from the end line, and 3.6 m (4 yd) long. Free throws are taken from within the semicircle behind this line.

Side line

End line

Fouls There are two types of foul; personal fouls (illegal body contact) and technical fouls (for example, bad sportsmanship). Fouls are penalised by free throws. Players committing five (amateur) or six (professional) personal fouls are sent off for the rest of the game.

Backboard Positioned at the centre of each back line. 1.8 m (5 ft 11 in) long and 1.2 m (3 ft 11 in) high, its lower edge is 2.9 m (9 ft 6 in) from the floor.

LEGENDS

Michael Jordan
(1963–) American

In his 13 seasons with the Chicago Bulls, Jordan led the team to six National Basketball Association (NBA) championships (1991-3 and 1996-8). His career average of 31.5 baskets a game is the best in NBA history.

Hockey

Hockey developed in Britain in the 1800s from the older games of shinty, hurling and bandy. The sport's first governing body was the English Hockey Association, formed in 1875. Today, it is run by the Fédération Internationale de Hockey (FIH), based in Belgium.

Olympic gold medal winners

Men's hockey became an Olympic sport in 1908 and, until the 1970s, was dominated by India and Pakistan. Women's hockey was admitted in 1980.

Men		Women	
Year	Nation	Year	Nation
1980	India	1980	Zimbabwe
1984	Pakistan	1984	Netherlands
1988	Great Britain	1988	Australia
1992	Germany	1992	Spain
1996	Netherlands	1996	Australia
2000	Netherlands	2000	Australia

Equipment The hard ball is about 7 cm (2³/₄ in) across and has a covering of rubber, leather or synthetic material. Most sticks are made of ash wood with a cane handle.

The aim of the game Hockey is played by two teams of 11 players on a grass or synthetic pitch measuring 91.4 x 55 m (100 x 60 yd). The object is to score points by hitting the ball with a wooden stick into the opposition's goal. Each goal is worth one point and the team with the most points at the end of 70 minutes of play (two 35 minute periods with a half-time interval) is the winner. For a goal to count, the shooting player must be inside an area in front of the goal known as the shooting circle, actually a half-lozenge shape marked by a line 14.6 m (16 yd) from the goal itself. The game is started, and restarted after each goal and at half-time, from the centre of the pitch.

Players, rules and penalties

● **Players** Players are classified as attackers, midfield players and defenders, but adapt their positions according to immediate needs. Only the goalkeeper is allowed to touch the ball with the feet.
● **Offside** When an attacker plays the ball within 25 yards of the opposition's goal, any other attacker must be behind the ball, or there must be at least two opposition defenders between the goal and the attacker not playing the ball.
● **Other fouls** These include using the stick to trip or hit another player, and hitting the ball above shoulder height.
● **Officials** Fouls are judged by two umpires, one for each half of the field.
● **Penalties** Fouls are penalised by a free hit for the opposition. This is taken from the penalty spot (for an offence within the shooting circle) or from a point on the goal line (penalty, or short corner).
● **Bully off** This restarts the game when both teams have breached the rules, or an injury or other event has stopped play. Two opposing players tap sticks together then hit the ground three times before battling for the ball dropped between them.

Ice hockey

Ice hockey was invented in the 1850s in Canada, where it is now the national game. It is the fastest team sport of all – players can reach speeds of more than 48 km/h (30 mph), and the puck may travel at up to 190 km/h (118 mph).

The aim of the game Ice hockey developed from hockey and shares the same basic objective; to score more goals than the opposition. Beyond that, ice hockey differs in a number of ways. It is a contact sport, where 'checking' an opponent to take them out of play is a legitimate tactic. The offside rule is different, and infringements are penalised differently. Ice hockey teams contain up to 18 members, but no more than six may be on the ice at any time. These are the goaltender, right and left defence, centre, right wing and left wing. A game lasts for an hour, split into three 20 minute periods.

Officials and rules The officials are: a referee, two linesmen and goal judges, a scorer, game timekeeper and penalty timekeeper. Infringements include:
● **Icing** This occurs when one team shoots the puck from its defensive zone over the other team's goal line.
● **Offside** A player is offside if he takes a pass that has crossed both blue lines (or the centre line and one blue line in Canadian and professional games). A player who enters the attacking zone ahead of the puck is also offside. Offside is penalised with a face-off – the puck is dropped between two players, who then compete for it. Face-offs also penalise icing and restart the game after a goal.
● **Fouls** These include elbowing, charging and 'high-sticking'. The offending player is sent off for 2 minutes.

Well covered Players wear helmets and around 11 kg (25 lb) of body armour for protection from the puck and each other.

Olympic men's champions

Men's ice hockey was played in the summer Games of 1920, and has been part of the winter Olympics since 1924. Women's teams joined in 1998, when the USA won.

Year	Gold medal	Year	Gold medal
1920	Canada	1964	USSR
1924	Canada	1968	USSR
1928	Canada	1972	USSR
1932	Canada	1976	USSR
1936	UK	1980	USA
1948	Canada	1984	USSR
1952	Canada	1988	USSR
1956	USSR	1992	Unified Team
1960	USA	1994	Sweden
		1998	Czech Rep.

Playing area A rectangular rink measuring 61 x 26 m (200 x 85 ft), with rounded corners. The rink is crossed by two blue lines, dividing it into three sections: the defensive zone, neutral zone and attacking zone.
Goals 1.8 m (6 ft) wide and 1.2 m (4 ft) high; positioned 3.4 m (11 ft) from each end of the rink, in the centre of the goal line.

LEGENDS

Wayne Gretzky
(1961–) Canadian

Wayne Gretzky has been the American/Canadian NHL's regular season highest-scoring player ten times in his career (1981-7, 1990-1 and 1994). He holds the all-time record for the most goals in one season (100 in 1983-4), and on March 29, 1999, became the highest-scoring player ever in professional ice hockey with his 1072nd career goal.

Equipment Ice hockey sticks are usually made from laminated wood, and measure 135 cm (4 ft 5 in) from the 'heel' to the end of the handle. The blade is 30 cm (1 ft) long. Goaltender's sticks have thicker blades and a wide lower shaft. The puck is 2.5 cm (1 in) thick and 7.5 cm (3 in) across. It is made from vulcanised rubber.

Golf probably originated in Scotland – there is documentary evidence of it being banned there in 1457 and later played by Scottish royalty, including King James IV and Queen Mary. The rules of the modern game are kept by the Royal and Ancient Golf Club of St Andrews in Scotland, which is considered by most countries to be the sport's governing body.

The aim of the game
Golf is played by individual competitors on a large outdoor course, usually made up of 18 sections, called holes. The object is to hit the ball, using specialised clubs, from the starting point (tee) of a section into the hole at the end. Players are marked on the number of hits (strokes) that they take to complete each hole; the fewer the better. There are two ways of deciding the winner of a game. The method most often used in professional tournaments takes the winner to be the person who played the fewest strokes in total over the 18 holes. The second method – called match play – awards the game to the player who wins the most holes overall (a hole is won by the player that completes it in the fewest strokes).

The golf course
The holes that comprise a golf course are divided into three sections (tee, fairway and green) and dotted with various hazards.

Tee The tee is the area marking the starting place for the hole to be played (in this picture it is obscured by trees); the first play for a hole is known as the tee shot. 'Tee' is also the word used for the small peg on which the ball is placed for the tee shot.

Fairway This area of mown grass between the tee and the green varies in length. If the green cannot be reached in one shot, this is where golfers aim to play.

Green The green is a closely mown and carefully tended area around the hole. The hole is 11 cm (4^1/$_4$ in) wide, 10 cm (4 in) deep and marked with a flag known as the pin. The green is usually roughly circular in shape but rarely level, increasing the difficulty of putting the ball into the hole.

Hazards Various obstacles are positioned to catch wayward shots and make it difficult for players to proceed. The most common are sand traps, or 'bunkers', rough surrounding ground ('rough') and water obstacles such as ponds and streams.

US Open
First played in 1895.

Year	Winner
1970	Tony Jacklin
1971	Lee Trevino
1972	Jack Nicklaus
1973	Johnny Miller
1974	Hale Irwin
1975	Lou Graham
1976	Jerry Pate
1977	Hubert Green
1978	Andy North
1979	Hale Irwin
1980	Jack Nicklaus
1981	David Graham
1982	Tom Watson
1983	Larry Nelson
1984	Fuzzy Zoeller
1985	Andy North
1986	Raymond Floyd
1987	Scott Simpson
1988	Curtis Strange
1989	Curtis Strange
1990	Hale Irwin
1991	Payne Stewart
1992	Tom Kite
1993	Lee Janzen
1994	Ernie Els
1995	Corey Pavin
1996	Steve Jones
1997	Ernie Els
1998	Lee Janzen
1999	Payne Stewart
2000	Tiger Woods
2001	Retief Goosen

LEGENDS

Gary Player
(1936–) South African

Winner of more than 100 tournaments in the 1960s and 1970s, including all four major championships: the US Masters (1961, 1974, 1978); US PGA (1962, 1972); US Open (1965); and British Open (1959, 1968, 1974). He is best remembered for the phrase: 'The more I practise, the luckier I get'.

Playing terms

Par The number of strokes that golfers of high ability ought to take to complete the hole. The hole above is a par four – a good golfer should take four shots from tee to putting the ball in the hole.

Bogie The term for a hole completed in one stroke over par – in this case, five shots. The player's first drive goes into the rough and the third into a bunker.

Birdie The term for a hole completed in one stroke under par – in this case three shots.

Eagle A hole completed in two under par – in this case two shots. The player makes a very long and well-positioned first drive and the second shot lands in the hole.

Handicap An advantage or compensation given according to a golfer's ability or experience, to even the chances of winning. A handicap is determined by the number of strokes the golfer takes to complete a round: for example, players who go round a par 70 course in 80 strokes have a handicap of 10. Players with a higher handicap than their opponents receive an allowance of shots equal to the difference.

Jack Nicklaus
(1940–) American

The 'Golden Bear', as he is known, is considered to be the most talented golfer of the 20th century. Between 1962 and 1986 he set a record by winning 18 titles at professional golf's premier events, or Major championships.

US Masters

First played in 1934.

Year	Winner
1970	Billy Casper
1971	Charles Coody
1972	Jack Nicklaus
1973	Tommy Aaron
1974	Gary Player
1975	Jack Nicklaus
1976	Raymond Floyd
1977	Tom Watson
1978	Gary Player
1979	Fuzzy Zoeller
1980	Seve Ballesteros
1981	Tom Watson
1982	Craig Stadler
1983	Seve Ballesteros
1984	Ben Crenshaw
1985	Bernhard Langer
1986	Jack Nicklaus
1987	Larry Mize
1988	Sandy Lyle
1989	Nick Faldo
1990	Nick Faldo
1991	Ian Woosnam
1992	Fred Couples
1993	Bernhard Langer
1994	José María Olázabal
1995	Ben Crenshaw
1996	Nick Faldo
1997	Tiger Woods
1998	Mark O'Meara
1999	José María Olázabal
2000	Vijay Singh
2001	Tiger Woods

British Open

The oldest of the four Major tournaments, which began in 1860.

Year	Winner
1970	Jack Nicklaus
1971	Lee Trevino
1972	Lee Trevino
1973	Tom Weiskopf
1974	Gary Player
1975	Tom Watson
1976	Johnny Miller
1977	Tom Watson
1978	Jack Nicklaus
1979	Seve Ballesteros
1980	Tom Watson
1981	Bill Rogers
1982	Tom Watson
1983	Tom Watson
1984	Seve Ballesteros
1985	Sandy Lyle
1986	Greg Norman
1987	Nick Faldo
1988	Seve Ballesteros
1989	Mark Calcavecchia
1990	Nick Faldo
1991	Ian Baker-Finch
1992	Nick Faldo
1993	Greg Norman
1994	Nick Price
1995	John Daly
1996	Tom Lehman
1997	Justin Leonard
1998	Mark O'Meara
1999	Paul Lawrie
2000	Tiger Woods

The perfect drive To hit the ball hard (drive), the golf player swings the club right back round the body, then swings forward to strike the ball and follow through in one smooth action, transferring weight to the front foot and unwinding the hips as the club swings all the way round to end up down the back.

Clubs Players carry a range of clubs, each designed for different types of stroke. There are three main types of golf club:

⚫ **Woods** Generally used for power shots, and, in spite of their name, usually made of metal. They have large heads and longer shafts than other clubs, and are numbered 1 to 5. No.1, or the 'driver', is used for the tee shot; any wood, including the driver, may be used for distance shots off the tee.

⚫ **Irons** Numbered 1 to 9 and used for shorter precision shots. A no.1 iron hits the ball lower and further than a no.2, which hits lower and farther than a no.3, and so on. There are two other clubs known as wedges. They are the sand wedge for getting balls out of bunkers, and the pitching wedge for chipping the ball up onto the green.

⚫ **Putters** Used on the green for hitting the ball along the ground (putting) towards the hole. They are not numbered but there are many different designs.

Players can take a maximum of 14 clubs on a round (usually three or four woods, nine or ten irons and a putter). Clubs are carried by an assistant called a caddie.

Tiger Woods
(1975–) American

Tiger Woods turned professional in 1996. In June 2000, he won the US Open by 15 strokes, the biggest margin ever in a Major tournament. In July of the same year, he won the US PGA Championship, making him the youngest player ever to have won all four of professional golf's Major championships.

US PGA Championship

The first championship was held in 1916.

Year	Winner
1970	Dave Stockton
1971	Jack Nicklaus
1972	Gary Player
1973	Jack Nicklaus
1974	Lee Trevino
1975	Jack Nicklaus
1976	Dave Stockton
1977	Lanny Wadkins
1978	John Mahaffey
1979	David Graham
1980	Jack Nicklaus
1981	Larry Nelson
1982	Raymond Floyd
1983	Hal Sutton
1984	Lee Trevino
1985	Hubert Green
1986	Bob Tway
1987	Larry Nelson
1988	Jeff Sluman
1989	Payne Stewart
1990	Wayne Grady
1991	John Daly
1992	Nick Price
1993	Paul Azinger
1994	Nick Price
1995	Steve Elkington
1996	Mark Brooks
1997	Davis Love III
1998	Vijay Singh
1999	Tiger Woods
2000	Tiger Woods

Tennis originated in the monasteries of 11th-century France, where the indoor game now known as real tennis was first played. The modern game of lawn tennis was not created until 1873 in England; its first championships were held at Wimbledon in 1877. The first international lawn tennis competition was the Davis Cup tournament, which started in 1900 and is played between national teams.

The aim of the game Tennis is played with a racket and a ball on an indoor or outdoor court between two opponents (singles) or two pairs (doubles). Points are scored by hitting the ball over the net into the receiving player's half of the court in such a way that it cannot be successfully returned.

Service The game begins with one player serving. He or she stands behind the baseline, tosses the ball into the air and strikes it into the receiver's side of the court. The server has two chances to make a valid serve; if they fail they lose the point – a double fault. Service alternates between players with each game.

Let If a serve touches the net before landing in the receiver's court, a let is called and the serve is replayed.

Strokes These include the forehand, backhand, lob, overhead smash (hit like a serve), drop shot and volley.

Scoring A game is played to four points, designated by the terms 15, 30, 40 and game. A player who does not score a point remains on nil or 'love'. If the score becomes 40-all, a 'deuce' is called. A game must be won by two clear points, so play continues from deuce until one player leads by that margin.

Set and match Games are grouped into sets. To win a set a player must have won six games and lead by at least two. If the score reaches six games each, a tie break game may be played to determine the winner of a set. Each match has a maximum of five sets for men, and three for women and mixed doubles.

Officials An umpire, referee, and line judges decide whether or not a ball is out of play. In professional tournaments, electronic devices may also be employed for this purpose.

Grand Slam title holders

A Grand Slam is achieved by holding all four Major titles – the Australian Open, French Open, Wimbledon and the US Open – at the same time.

Men's Singles

Donald Budge	1938
Rod Laver	1962, 1969

Women's Singles

Maureen Connolly	1953
Margaret Court	1970
Martina Navratilova	1983/4
Steffi Graf	1988, 1993/4

Wimbledon singles champions

Year	Men	Ladies
1950	Budge Patty	Louise Brough
1951	Dick Savitt	Doris Hart
1952	Frank Sedgman	Maureen Connolly
1953	Vic Seixas	Maureen Connolly
1954	Jaroslav Drobny	Maureen Connolly
1955	Tony Trabert	Louise Brough
1956	Lew Hoad	Shirley Fry
1957	Lew Hoad	Althea Gibson
1958	Ashley Cooper	Althea Gibson
1959	Alex Olmedo	Maria Bueno
1960	Neale Fraser	Maria Bueno
1961	Rod Laver	Angela Mortimer
1962	Rod Laver	Karen Hantze-Susman
1963	Chuck McKinley	Margaret Smith
1964	Roy Emerson	Maria Bueno
1965	Roy Emerson	Margaret Smith
1966	Manuel Santana	Billie Jean King
1967	John Newcombe	Billie Jean King
1968	Rod Laver	Billie Jean King
1969	Rod Laver	Ann Haydon-Jones
1970	John Newcombe	Margaret Smith Court
1971	John Newcombe	Evonne Goolagong
1972	Stan Smith	Billie Jean King
1973	Jan Kodes	Billie Jean King
1974	Jimmy Connors	Chris Evert
1975	Arthur Ashe	Billie Jean King
1976	Bjorn Borg	Chris Evert
1977	Bjorn Borg	Virginia Wade
1978	Bjorn Borg	Martina Navratilova
1979	Bjorn Borg	Martina Navratilova
1980	Bjorn Borg	Evonne Goolagong Cawley
1981	John McEnroe	Chris Evert Lloyd
1982	Jimmy Connors	Martina Navratilova
1983	John McEnroe	Martina Navratilova
1984	John McEnroe	Martina Navratilova
1985	Boris Becker	Martina Navratilova
1986	Boris Becker	Martina Navratilova
1987	Pat Cash	Martina Navratilova
1988	Stefan Edberg	Steffi Graf
1989	Boris Becker	Steffi Graf
1990	Stefan Edberg	Martina Navratilova
1991	Michael Stich	Steffi Graf
1992	André Agassi	Steffi Graf
1993	Pete Sampras	Steffi Graf
1994	Pete Sampras	Conchita Martinez
1995	Pete Sampras	Steffi Graf
1996	Richard Krajicek	Steffi Graf
1997	Pete Sampras	Martina Hingis
1998	Pete Sampras	Jana Novotna
1999	Pete Sampras	Lindsay Davenport
2000	Pete Sampras	Venus Williams
2001	Goran Ivanisevic	Venus Williams

Playing surface Clay, plastic carpet or grass. 23.8 m (78 ft) x 8.2 m (27 ft) for singles; 11 m (36 ft) wide for doubles.

Net 91 cm (3 ft) high, suspended from a cord or cable between two posts, set 91 cm (3 ft) outside each doubles sideline.

Umpire

Service line

Sideline (doubles)

Sideline (singles)

Service court
For a service to be valid, the player must be behind the baseline and the ball played into this rectangle from right of the centre mark (or the rectangle next to it from left of the centre mark).

Centre mark

Baseline

Equipment

Ball About 6.35 cm (2½ in) in diameter and weighing approximately 56.7 g (2 oz), it is hollow, with a cover of wool and manmade fibre over inflated rubber.

Racket With a maximum length of 81.5 cm (32 in), the oval head must not be more than 39.4 cm (15½ in) and 29.2 cm (11½ in) wide. It is usually strung with gut or a synthetic material, such as nylon.

Pete Sampras
(1971–) American

Pete Sampras is the most successful player of recent years. His victory in the 2000 Wimbledon men's singles was not only his seventh in that tournament, but also his 13th Major tournament title – an all-time men's record.

Davis Cup

Year	Winning team
1970	United States
1971	United States
1972	United States
1973	Australia
1974	South Africa
1975	Sweden
1976	Italy
1977	Australia
1978	United States
1979	United States
1980	Czechoslovakia
1981	United States
1982	United States
1983	Australia
1984	Sweden
1985	Sweden
1986	Australia
1987	Sweden
1988	W Germany
1989	W Germany
1990	United States
1991	France
1992	United States
1993	Germany
1994	Sweden
1995	United States
1996	France
1997	Sweden
1998	Sweden
1999	Australia
2000	Spain

Hi-tech rackets

Graphite, titanium and glass fibre frames make modern tennis rackets much stronger than the wooden and metal ones they replaced. As a result, today's rackets can be strung much tighter, greatly increasing the speed of the ball.

Squash

Squash was created at Harrow School, England, in the mid 19th century, and by the early 1900s was a favourite school game. The modern rules were not set until after the First World War. Its popularity grew rapidly in the 1920s, when formal competitions were established.

Squash is played in an enclosed court between two players. One serves against the front wall and the other tries to return before the ball can bounce twice. Shots may be glanced off the back and side walls, as long as the ball reaches the front wall without first touching the ground or going above the front, side or back wall lines. Only the server wins points, the receiver having to win a rally to gain service.

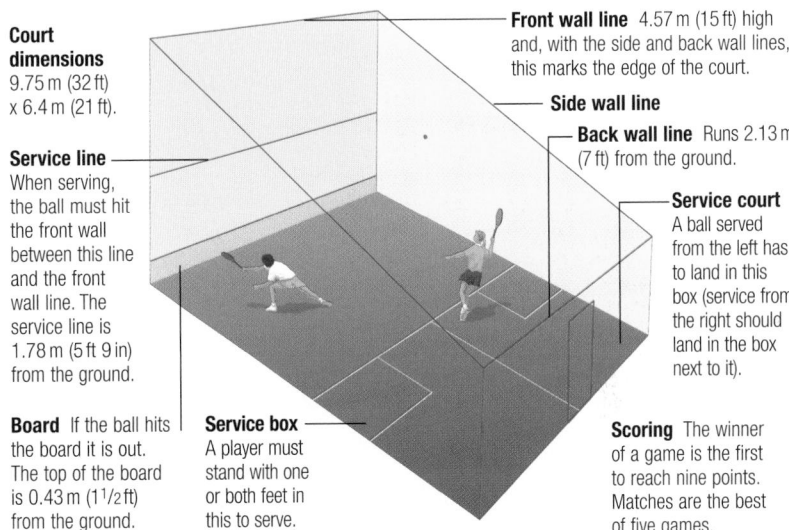

Court dimensions 9.75 m (32 ft) x 6.4 m (21 ft).

Service line When serving, the ball must hit the front wall between this line and the front wall line. The service line is 1.78 m (5 ft 9 in) from the ground.

Board If the ball hits the board it is out. The top of the board is 0.43 m (1 1/2 ft) from the ground.

Service box A player must stand with one or both feet in this to serve.

Front wall line 4.57 m (15 ft) high and, with the side and back wall lines, this marks the edge of the court.

Side wall line

Back wall line Runs 2.13 m (7 ft) from the ground.

Service court A ball served from the left has to land in this box (service from the right should land in the box next to it).

Scoring The winner of a game is the first to reach nine points. Matches are the best of five games.

Badminton

Badminton is a singles or doubles game played on an indoor court with rackets and a shuttlecock. The object is to strike the shuttlecock over the raised net and score points by grounding it in the opponents' half of the court or by forcing an error. As in squash, only the server can score points.

Equipment
Shuttlecock A half-sphere of cork or plastic, with a feather or nylon skirt.
Racket 66 cm (26 in) long, and 21 cm (8 1/2 in) at the broadest point of the head.

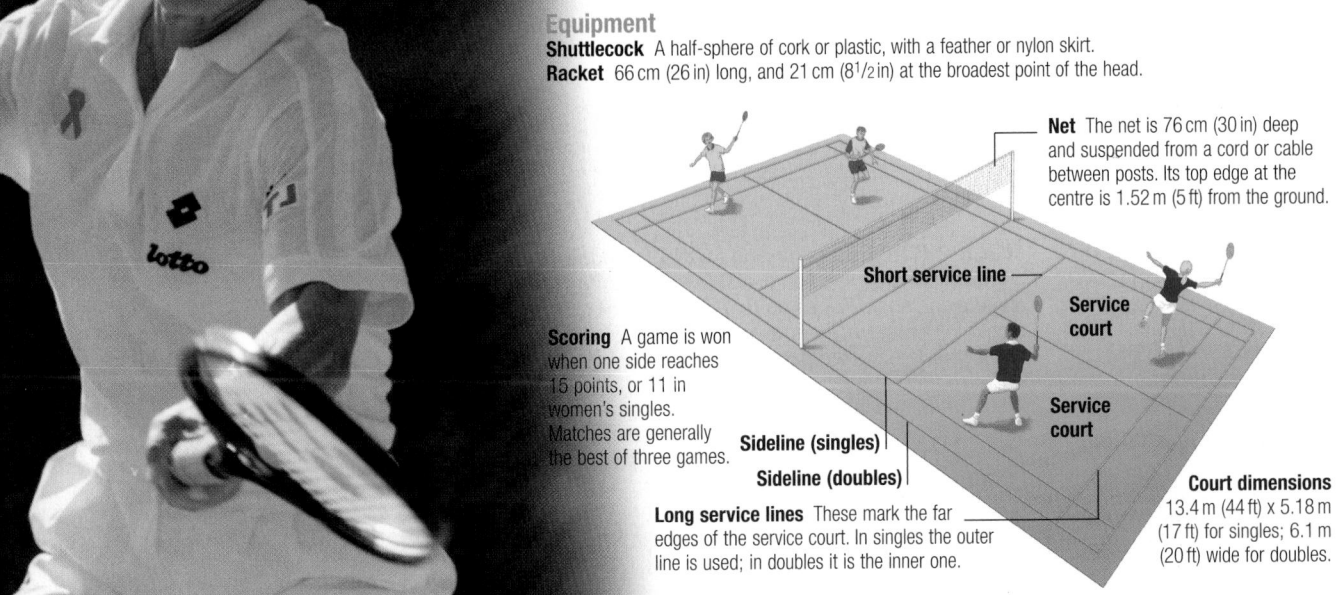

Scoring A game is won when one side reaches 15 points, or 11 in women's singles. Matches are generally the best of three games.

Short service line

Net The net is 76 cm (30 in) deep and suspended from a cord or cable between posts. Its top edge at the centre is 1.52 m (5 ft) from the ground.

Service court

Service court

Sideline (singles)

Sideline (doubles)

Long service lines These mark the far edges of the service court. In singles the outer line is used; in doubles it is the inner one.

Court dimensions 13.4 m (44 ft) x 5.18 m (17 ft) for singles; 6.1 m (20 ft) wide for doubles.

Athletics are the oldest forms of organised sport, originating in ancient Greece at least 3500 years ago. Contested between individuals and teams, they include track and field events. The most important meeting in the athletics calendar is the Olympic Games. The Greek Olympics were held in honour of the god Zeus at Olympia until AD 394; the modern Games began in Athens in 1896, and are now held every four years.

Field events These take place within the running track's perimeter. The object of all field events is either to jump or throw an object farther than other contestants.

Javelin This event involves throwing a long metal spear weighing 800 g (28 oz) for men or 600 g (24.7 oz) for women.

Discus A throwing event in which a wooden and metal or plastic disc, weighing 2 kg (4¹/₂ lb) for men or 1 kg (2¹/₄ lb) for women, is lodged between the palm of the hand and the forearm, then launched by the athlete after a series of spins around the throwing circle.

Hammer A metal ball, attached to a long wire handle, is swung around the athlete's body several times before being released.

Shot put This entails pushing a heavy, metal ball 7.26 kg (16 lb) for men or 4 kg (8 lb 13 oz) for women) from a resting position on the shoulder as far as possible through the air, from within a throwing circle of just over 2 m (6¹/₂ ft) in diameter.

Long jump After a short run-up to a take-off board, athletes leap forward, trying to clear the longest possible distance, without touching the ground.

High jump In this event competitors aim to leap over a crossbar without knocking it off its supports.

Triple jump This is similar to the long jump, but with a more complicated hop, step and jump sequence of manoeuvres.

Adopted standard Swede Kajsa Bergqvist clears the bar with a Fosbury flop. The technique was first used by the American athlete Dick Fosbury in the 1968 Olympics.

Pole vault The pole vault involves clearing a high crossbar resting on uprights by using a flexible pole for propulsion. The athlete swings upwards towards the crossbar, arching over it feet first before landing.

Shot put

Javelin

Hammer
Discus

High jump

Triple jump

Long lump

Pole vault

Steeplechase
water jump

Finish
line

Jesse Owens
(1913–80) American

In the 1935-6 season, Jesse Owens set three world records and equalled another which lasted for 25 years. He became world famous as the star of the 1936 Olympic Games in Berlin, where he won four gold medals. Because he was a black athlete, this success greatly embarrassed the Nazi government.

Sprinting The shortest running races are known as sprints. Sprints are run over 100 m, 200 m and 400 m.

Hurdles This combines sprinting with jumping over barriers set at specific heights. Hurdles are normally run over 110 m and 400 m.

Relays These are races between teams of four runners. The first runner runs to the second, who runs to the third and so on. A baton is passed from the approaching to the leaving runner. Relays are run over 100 m and 400 m.

Middle-distance running The two standard middle-distance races are held over 800 m and 1500 m.

Long-distance running Long-distance track races range from 1 mile through 2000 m, 3000 m, 5000 m, 10 000 m, 20 000 m and 25 000 m. The marathon, at 42 195 m (26 miles 385 yd), is a road race, which may or may not end on the athletics track.

Steeplechase This combines long-distance running with hurdles and water-jump obstacles. Steeplechases are run over 2000 m and 3000 m.

Track events Most running events in outdoor competition take place on a 400 m oval track with six or eight lanes. Races up to 110 m are run on a straight course. Races above that length involve running on the curved part of the course, where the distance around the outside of the track is greater than that on the inside. Therefore athletes in races over 110 m start in a staggered line, so each runs an equal distance. Races over 400 m are run in lanes only as far as the first bend, so athletes are able to manoeuvre from the outside to the inside of the track. A single finish line at the end of one straight serves all races.

Races that take place off the athletics track include the marathon and most walking races. In sporting terms, walking is defined as moving with always at least part of one foot on the ground. Standard races for walking are over 20 km, 30 km, 50 km or 2 hours.

Combined events In combined events – the triathlon, pentathlon, heptathlon and decathlon – athletes compete in several disciplines of both track and field over a period of up to two days. Points are awarded for each event and the highest collective score determines the winner.

World outdoor record holders

Men track

Event	Record holder	Nation	Time	Date
100 m	Maurice Greene	USA	9.79	1999
200 m	Michael Johnson	USA	19.32	1996
400 m	Michael Johnson	USA	43.18	1999
800 m	Wilson Kipketer	Denmark	1:41.11	1997
1000 m	Noah Ngeny	Kenya	2:11.96	1999
1500 m	Hicham El Guerrouj	Morocco	3:26.00	1998
1 mile	Hicham El Guerrouj	Morocco	3:43.13	1999
2000 m	Hicham El Guerrouj	Morocco	4:44.79	1999
3000 m	Daniel Komen	Kenya	7:20.67	1996
5000 m	Haile Gebrselassie	Ethiopia	12:39.36	1998
10 000 m	Haile Gebrselassie	Ethiopia	26:22.75	1998
20 000 m	Arturo Barrios	Mexico	56:55.6	1991
25 000 m	Toshihiko Seko	Japan	1:13:55.8	1981
Marathon	Khalid Khannouchi	Morocco	2:5:42.00	1999
110 m hurdles	Colin Jackson	UK	12.91	1993
400 m hrdles	Kevin Young	USA	46.78	1992
Steeplechase	Barnard Barmasai	Kenya	7:55.72	1997
4 x 100 m relay		USA	37.40	1992
4 x 400 m relay		USA	2:54.20	1998
4 x 800 m relay		UK	7:03.89	1982

Men field

Event	Record holder	Nation	Distance	Year
High jump	Javier Sotomayor	Cuba	2.45 m (8 ft 1/2 in)	1993
Long jump	Mike Powell	USA	8.95 m (29 ft 4 1/2 in)	1991
Triple jump	Jonathan Edwards	UK	18.29 m (60 ft 1/4 in)	1995
Discus	Juergen Schult	E Germany	74.08 m (243 ft 0 in)	1986
Hammer	Yuri Sedykh	USSR	86.74 m (284 ft 7 in)	1986
Shot put	Randy Barnes	USA	23.12 m (75 ft 10 1/4 in)	1990
Javelin	Jan Zelezny	Czech Rep.	98.48 m (323 ft 1 in)	1996
Pole vault	Sergei Bubka	Ukraine	6.14 m (20 ft 1 3/4 in)	1994
Decathlon	Thomas Dvorak	Czech Rep.	8994 points	1999

Women track

Event	Record holder	Nation	Time	Date
100 m	Florence Griffith-Joyner	USA	10.49	1988
200 m	Florence Griffith-Joyner	USA	21.34	1988
400 m	Marita Koch	E.Germany	47.60	1985
800 m	Jarmila Kratochvilova	Czechoslovakia	1:53.28	1983
1000 m	Svetlana Masterkova	Russia	2:28.98	1996
1500 m	Qu Yunxia	China	3:50.46	1993
1 mile	Svetlana Masterkova	Russia	4:12.56	1996
2000 m	Sonia O'Sullivan	Ireland	5:25.36	1994
3000 m	Junxia Wang	China	8:06.11	1993
5000 m	Bo Jiang	China	14:28.09	1997
10 000 m	Junxia Wang	China	29:31.78	1993
Marathon	Tegla Loroupe	Kenya	2:20:43.00	1999
100 m hurdles	Yordanka Donkova	Bulgaria	12.21	1988
400 m hurdles	Kim Batten	USA	52.61	1995
Steeplechase	Casandra Cristinalloc	Romania	9:40.20	2000
4 x 100 m relay		E.Germany	41.37	1985
4 x 400 m relay		USSR	3:15.17	1988
4 x 800 m relay		USSR	7:50.17	1984

Women field

Event	Record holder	Nation	Distance	Year
High jump	Stefka Kostadinova	Bulgaria	2.09 m (6 ft 10 1/4 in)	1987
Long jump	Galina Chistyakova	USSR	7.52 m (24 ft 8 1/4 in)	1988
Triple jump	Inessa Kravets	Ukraine	15.50 m (50 ft 10 1/4 in)	1995
Discus	Gabriele Reinsch	E. Germany	76.80 m (252 ft 0 in)	1988
Hammer	Mihaela Melinte	Romania	76.07 m (249 ft 7 in)	2000
Shot put	Natalya Lisovskaya	USSR	22.63 m (74 ft 3 in)	1987
Javelin	Trine Hattestad	Norway	68.91 m (226 ft 1 in)	1987
Pole vault	Stacy Dragila	USA	4.60 m (15 ft 1 in)	2000
Heptathlon	J Joyner-Kersee	USA	7291 points	1988

LEGENDS

Bob Beamon
(1946–) American

At the 1968 Olympics in Mexico City, Bob Beamon leapt a record-shattering 8.9 m (29 ft 2 1/2 in) in the long jump. This was an amazing 55.25 cm (21 3/4 in) more than anyone had ever jumped before. His record stood unbroken for 23 years.

Achieving greater heights
Technology has helped pole vaulters improve their performances. Today's glass fibre poles are far stronger and more flexible than the wooden ones of a century ago, and give much greater lift.

LEGENDS

Roger Bannister
(1929–) British

Bannister was the first person ever to run the mile in under 4 minutes, a feat previously considered humanly impossible. On May 6, 1954, he won a race over that distance with a time of 3 minutes

The modern Olympics were the idea of Pierre de Coubertin, a French aristocrat. They began in 1896 and, excepting the two World Wars, have been held every four years since.

1896
Athens

245 men from 14 nations competed. The **marathon** was born. **American students** dominated the athletics.

Most medals
German gymnast **Hermann Weingärtner** won three golds, two silvers and a bronze.

Local hero The first modern marathon was won, appropriately, by a Greek, Spiridon Louis.

1900
Paris

1319 people from 22 countries entered. The Games were eclipsed by the Great Exhibition. **Women competed** for the first time.

Most medals
Irving Baxter (USA) won two golds and three silvers in athletics.

1904
St Louis

687 competitors from 13 nations took part. 525 of the competitors were from the USA and **some events included only Americans**.

Most medals
Anton Heida (USA) won five golds and a silver in men's gymnastics.

1908
London

2035 men and women from 22 countries took part. The Games were marred by allegations of **bias by the British judges**, particularly against the American athletics team, who at one point threatened to withdraw.

Memorable event
Dorando Pietri, a sweetshop owner from Capri, Italy, collapsed four times just yards from the finish of the marathon, and was helped over the line to win. Despite protests, he was disqualified.

Most medals
Mel Sheppard (USA) won golds in three of the men's athletics events.

1912
Stockholm

2547 competitors from 28 countries took part. **Swimming and modern pentathlon** were included for the first time, and **gymnastics** became popular as a spectator sport, with 1000 competitors from 13 countries entering those events. **Electronic timing devices** were used for the first time.

Memorable event
Jim Thorpe (USA) won gold in the pentathlon and decathlon, but was ordered to return his medals six months later when it transpired that he had been paid a small sum for playing baseball years before.

Most medals
Hannes Kolehmainen (Finland) won three gold medals, for the 5000 m, 10 000 m and the 8000 m cross country.

1920
Antwerp

2669 competitors from 29 nations entered. Antwerp was chosen in honour of the Belgian people, who had lived under enemy occupation for four years of the First World War. **Germany, Austria, Bulgaria, Hungary and Turkey** were not invited.

Memorable event
Oscar Swahn (Sweden) became the **oldest Olympic medallist ever** when he won a silver in the running deer team shooting event (since discontinued) aged 72. Four years earlier, he had won gold in the same event, making him the **oldest Olympic gold medallist** as well. Both records still stand.

Most medals
Willis Lee (USA) won five golds, one silver and one bronze in the shooting events.

1924
Paris

3092 people from 44 countries competed. The **Olympic motto** *citius, altius, fortius* ('faster, higher, stronger') was coined. French fans caused outrage by booing other countries' national anthems.

Memorable event
American swimmer **Johnny Weissmuller** won gold medals in the 100 m and 400 m freestyle, and 4 x 200 m freestyle relay events. He went on to win two more golds in the 1928 Amsterdam Olympics before achieving even greater fame as Hollywood's best-known Tarzan.

Most medals
Ville Ritola (Finland) won four golds and two silvers in distance running events. His teammate, **Paavo Nurmi**, won five golds.

1928
Amsterdam

3014 competitors from 46 countries took part. This was the first year that **women competed in athletics** events, although they had previously featured in tennis, golf, swimming, archery, fencing and yachting. **Germany** was invited to the Games for the first time since the First World War.

Memorable event
Centre-forward **Dhyan Chand** brought gold to the Indian men's hockey team for the first time. Chand went on to win golds in 1932 and 1936; over the course of the three Olympics, his team scored 102 goals and conceded just three.

Most medals
Swiss gymnast **Georges Miéz** won three golds and one silver.

1932
Los Angeles

Just 1408 people from 37 nations competed as a result of the Great Depression. **Automatic timing devices** and the **photo-finish camera** were introduced, as were **podiums** for award ceremonies and the playing of **winners' national anthems**. The 50 km walk marked the entry of **walking** as an Olympic sport.

Memorable event
Mildred Didrikson (USA) was the star of the Games, winning gold in the javelin and 80 m hurdles and silver in the high jump. She later became one of the finest women golfers of all time and, in 1950, was voted the best woman athlete of the half-century.

Most medals
Male gymnast **István Pelle** (Hungary) won two golds and two silvers.

1936
Berlin

3738 competitors from 49 nations entered. The Berlin Games were the **first to be televised**.

Memorable event
Adolf Hitler tried to turn the Games into a Nazi propaganda event, but was thwarted by the success of non-Aryan athletes. Afro-Americans took gold medals in every track event from 100 m to 800 m.

Most medals
Jesse Owens (USA) won golds in the 100 m, 200 m, long jump and sprint relay.

Olympic flame Berlin's Games were the first to be preceded by the torch relay.

1948
London

4099 people from 59 countries took part. **Germany and Japan** were not invited and the **USSR** did not send a team. Communist countries were involved for the first time and the London Games saw the first **defections of participants**.

Memorable event
The moving **opening ceremony**, in which the teams of all 59 nations marched one after the other, did much to heal the wounds of war. The Games were watched by half a million people on Britain's 80 000 television sets.

Most medals
Thirty-year-old Dutch mother of two **Fanny Blankers-Koen** won golds in the 100 m and 200 m sprints, 80 m hurdles and 4 x 100 m sprint relay.

1952
Helsinki

4925 athletes from 69 nations entered. The **USSR** competed for the first time and, despite fears that there would be problems, Soviet and American athletes got on well together. The Games were **superbly organised**, leading some commentators to suggest that they should always be held in Scandinavia.

Memorable event
Czech runner **Emil Zatopek** completed an incredible treble, taking gold in the 5000 m, 10 000 m and marathon. His wife Dana won a gold medal in the javelin.

Most medals
Gymnast **Maria Gorokhovskaya** (USSR) won seven medals (two golds and five silvers); the most ever won by a woman in a single Games.

1956
Melbourne

3342 competitors from 72 nations entered. This was the **first Olympics held in the Southern Hemisphere**. The **equestrian events** took place in Stockholm because of Australian quarantine laws.

Most medals
Gymnasts **Viktor Chukarin** (USSR) and **Ågnes Keleti** (Hungary) each won four golds and two silvers.

Dawn Fraser The Australian swimmer began her Olympic career by winning two golds and a silver.

1960
Rome

5348 athletes from 83 nations participated. Some events were held in **brand-new facilities**, others in **ancient stadia**. The wrestling, for instance, took place in the Basilica of Maxentius, where Romans had held similar contests 2000 years before. This was the last Games to which **South Africa** was invited for 32 years. It was followed by the first **Paralympics**.

Memorable event
Cassius Clay won boxing gold in the light-heavyweight division for the USA. He changed his name to Muhammad Ali in 1964.

Most medals
Gymnast **Boris Shaklin** (USSR) won four golds, two silvers and a bronze.

1964
Tokyo

5140 competitors from 93 countries took part. These were the **first Games held in Asia**. Two new sports, **judo and volleyball**, were introduced, and three competitors received their **third successive Olympic golds**; swimmer Dawn Fraser (Australia), showjumper Hans Winkler (Germany) and sculler Vyacheslav Ivanov (USSR). **Don Schollander** (USA) won four swimming golds.

Memorable event
The **Japanese** used the Games to **put the war behind them**. A student born near Hiroshima on the day the atomic bomb fell lit the flame.

Most medals
Larissa Latynina (USSR) won two golds, two silvers and two bronzes in the women's gymnastic events.

1968
Mexico City

5531 people from 112 nations competed. The choice of Mexico City was controversial because of the **high altitude**. The low air density meant that **world records in sprint events** tumbled, while distance running became more difficult. Sprinters John Carlos and Tommie Smith gave **black power salutes** on the podium.

Memorable event
Bob Beamon (USA) beat the world long jump record by 55.25 cm (21³/₄ in). Upon realising what he had achieved, he suffered a seizure and collapsed but later recovered to claim his gold medal.

Most medals
Gymnast **Mikhail Voronin** (USSR) won two golds, four silvers and a bronze.

1972
Munich

7123 competitors from 121 countries entered. Full-scale **drug testing began**. The USA lost the basketball final for the first time, to the USSR.

Hostage crisis Eleven members of the Israeli team were murdered by Palestinian terrorists.

Memorable event
Olga Korbut (USSR) charmed television audiences around the world on her way towards winning three gymnastics gold medals.

Most medals
American Swimmer **Mark Spitz** won seven golds – the most won by one person in a single Olympic Games.

1976
Montreal

6028 athletes from 82 countries entered. The Games were **boycotted by African nations** in protest at the International Olympic Committee's refusal to bar New Zealand, after a rugby tour of South Africa by its All Blacks team. Poor planning and corruption meant that the Games were a **financial disaster**.

Memorable event
Caribbean men took gold in the sprint events and 800 m. The 100 m was won by Hasely Crawford (Jamaica), the 200 m by Don Quarrie (Trinidad and Tobago) and the 400 m and 800 m by Alberto Juantorena (Cuba).

Most medals
Gymnast **Nikolai Andrianov** (USSR) won four golds, two silvers and a bronze.

1980
Moscow

5217 people from 80 countries competed. The **USA, Canada, West Germany and Japan boycotted** the Games in protest at the Soviet invasion of Afghanistan. Despite this, more world records were set than in 1976. **East German women** won 11 golds on the running track, setting seven world records in the process.

Memorable event
British runners **Steve Ovett and Sebastian Coe** battled it out in the middle-distance finals. Ovett took gold and Coe silver in the 800 m before the honours were reversed in the 1500 m.

Most medals
Gymnast **Aleksandr Dityatin** (USSR) won eight medals (three golds, four silvers and a bronze); the most by any man in a single Games.

1984
Los Angeles

6797 athletes from 140 nations took part. There was a **boycott by the USSR** as revenge for the Moscow boycott four years earlier. The Games took place in the same stadium as in 1932. **Daley Thompson** (UK) won gold in the decathlon for the second Olympics in succession.

Memorable event
The American athlete **Carl Lewis** delighted home fans by taking gold medals in four events; the 100 m, 200 m, long jump and 4 x 100 m relay.

Most medals
Male gymnast **Li Ning** (China) won three golds, two silvers and a bronze.

1988
Seoul

8465 people from 159 nations competed. **Florence Griffith-Joyner (Flo Jo)** won three golds and a silver for the USA.

Fallen hero Canadian Ben Johnson won the 100 m in a world record time but was stripped of his gold three days later after testing positive for steroids.

Most medals
Swimmer **Matt Biondi** (USA) won five golds, a silver and a bronze. Another swimmer, **Kristin Otto** (Germany), won six golds – the most by any woman in a single Olympics.

1992
Barcelona

9364 competitors from 169 countries took part. Former Soviet republics competed as the **Unified Team** under the Olympic flag, and came top of the medal table. A **united German team** took part, and **South Africa** returned to Olympic competition following the ending of apartheid.

Memorable event
Cyclist Chris Boardman (UK) unveiled a controversial **bicycle design**. Made from carbon fibre, titanium and aluminium, and with a one-piece frame and disc wheels, it was more aerodynamic than the traditional bicycles used by other competitors.

Most medals
Male gymnast **Vitaly Shcherbo** won six golds for the Unified Team.

1996
Atlanta

10 744 competitors from 197 countries entered. **Michelle Smith** (Ireland) became the first Irish medal winner, with three swimming golds.

Memorable event
A **bomb** went off in the Centennial Olympic Park killing one person.

Most medals
Russian gymnast **Alexei Nemov** won two golds, a silver and three bronzes.

Michael Johnson The American completed an unprecedented double by winning the 200 m and 400 m sprints. He finished the 200 m final in a world record time.

2000
Sydney

10 651 athletes from 199 nations took part. The **triathlon** was held for the first time and **taekwondo**, which had been a demonstration sport in the 1988 and 1992 Olympics, was first fought for medals. Aboriginal Australian **Cathy Freeman** thrilled the home crowd by winning the 400 m.

Memorable event
British rower **Steve Redgrave** became the first competitor to collect five consecutive Olympic gold medals.

Most medals
Alexei Nemov topped the tables again, matching his 1996 total of two golds, a silver and three bronzes.

2004
Athens

In 2004, the Olympics will return to the city of their birth. 296 events in 28 sports will be held (at the 1896 Games there were just 43 events in nine sports), and more than 11 000 athletes from 199 nations are expected to enter. The Games will run from **August 13 to 29** in facilities that will include a newly renovated Panathenaic Stadium – the place where the first modern Olympics were held.

Gymnastics, particularly in the women's events, involves considerable artistry as well as strength, suppleness, coordination and balance. It dates back to ancient Greece, but modern techniques only started to develop in the 19th century, particularly in Germany and Sweden. The International Gymnastics Federation was founded in 1891, and the sport featured in the first modern Olympic Games in 1896.

Scoring

Competitions are judged both as individual and team events. Competitors must perform a required number of specific moves, which are graded by difficulty, for which points are awarded on a scale of 0 to10 – 10 being a perfect score. Judging is subjective. Judges deduct points for flaws or omissions, and award bonus points for exceptional performance.

LEGENDS

Nadia Comaneci
(1961–) Romanian
(American from 1989)

Comaneci made history at the 1976 Olympic Games by becoming the first gymnast ever to score a perfect 10. She won six medals in those Olympics and four more in 1980.

2000 Olympic Games

Men's Event	Gold medallist	Nation
All-around	Alexei Nemov	Russia
Floor exercises	Igors Vihrovs	Latvia
Vaulting horse	Gervasio Deferr	Spain
Parallel bars	Xiaopeng Li	China
Horizontal bar	Alexei Nemov	Russia
Pommel horse	Marius Urzica	Romania
Rings	Szilveszter Csolany	Hungary
Trampoline	Alexander Moskalenko	Russia
Men's Team		China

Women's Event	Gold medallist	Nation
All-around	Simona Amanar	Romania
Floor exercises	Elena Zamolodchikova	Russia
Vaulting horse	Elena Zamolodchikova	Russia
Asymmetric bars	Svetlana Khorkina	Russia
Balance beam	Xuan Liu	China
Trampoline	Irina Karavayeva	Russia
Women's Team		Romania

Rhythmic gymnastics Event	Gold medallist	Nation
All-around	Yulia Barsukova	Russia
Women's Team		Russia

LEGENDS

Vitaly Shcherbo
(1972–) Belarussian

Vitaly Shcherbo won six gold medals at the Barcelona Olympics in 1992, becoming the first gymnast ever to gain so many golds in a single Games.

LEGENDS

Nikolai Andrianov
(1952–) Russian

The man who put men's gymnastics on the map, Andrianov was winner of 15 Olympic medals between 1972 and 1980, as well as three world and eight European championships.

Competition

Gymnasts perform on various pieces of apparatus. Medals are awarded for individual exercises and combined scores of all of the exercises performed. Competition gymnastics differs between the sexes, with men using some pieces of apparatus and women others. Both sexes do floor exercises.

Rings Male gymnasts perform a series of forward and backward gyrations, hanging from two suspended rings 2.75 m (9 ft) from the floor.

Vaulting horse This apparatus is used by both men and women. Gymnasts take off from a springboard and vault lengthways over the 'horse', making contact with their hands. A variety of different vaults may be performed, including cartwheels and handsprings. The horse is set at a height of 1.35 m (4 1/2 ft) for men and 1.3 m (4 ft) for women.

Parallel bars Men perform a series of swinging moves and balances on these two bars 1.75 m (5 ft 9 in) from the floor.

Pommel horse The pommel horse is similar to a vaulting horse, but has two handles attached. Male competitors perform a series of swinging movements, keeping their feet and legs clear of it.

Horizontal bar The bar is set 2.55 m (8 ft 4 in) off the ground. Male gymnasts use it to perform a routine of swinging movements.

Balance beam Continuous turns and leaps are performed by women gymnasts on a wooden beam, 5 m (16 1/2 ft) long and 10 cm (4 in) wide, and 1.2 m (4 ft) off the floor.

Asymmetric bars Continuous swinging movements are performed by female gymnasts over, under and between these two parallel, flexible bars, one 2.4 m (8 ft) and the other 1.6 m (5 ft 3 in) from the floor.

Rhythmic gymnastics This is performed by women to music, using various hand-held accessories – a rope, ribbon, hoop, ball and club. It became an Olympic event in 1984.

Floor exercises These comprise acrobatic routines, including somersaults, twists and leaps, on a mat 12 m² (40 sq ft) in area.

Weightlifting

The modern sport of weightlifting dates from the late 19th century. The first World Championships were held in 1891 and, like gymnastics, weightlifting was included in the first modern Olympics of 1896.

Competitions Contestants compete in classes based on their bodyweights. They are allowed three attempts to lift individually chosen weights, which are increased progressively. The rankings are decided from each competitor's best lift. In the World Championships, separate titles and medals are awarded for both the snatch and clean-and-jerk lifts (see right), as well as for a combination of the two. In Olympic competition, the combined result of both lifts decides the medals.

Equipment

Bar A steel bar, 2.2 m (7 ft 4 in) long and weighing 22 kg (48 1/2 lb), is the main piece of equipment. A combination of discs of different weights is loaded at each end and secured by collars.
Disc weights Ranging from 0.25 kg (1/2 lb) up to 25 kg (56 lb), these are generally made of iron. Rubber or plastic-covered weights that are colour-coded are normally used in top-class competitions. The covers help to prevent damage to the floor or weights if they are dropped.
Belt A wide belt may be worn by the weightlifter to support the back and protect it from injury.

The two standard weightlifting techniques

'Clean-and-jerk' movement The competitor lifts the barbell from the floor to rest on the shoulders, before pushing it up above the head on outstretched arms. This technique is considered the easier of the two.

'Snatch' movement Starting in a squat position, the lifter hoists the barbell above the head from the floor in a single movement.

The term martial arts is used to describe various combat techniques that originated in the Far East. Some are practised as a means of self-defence and others as competitive sports. Two – judo and tae kwon do – have become Olympic sports.

Karate This originated in Japan as a system of unarmed self-defence. The modern sport involves two opponents delivering kicks and punches in order to block one another's blows. Each combatant tries to score points by attacking particular areas of their opponent's body, superior technique counting for more than actual physical contact. Degrees of proficiency are indicated by the colour of a contestant's belt – the highest being black.

Aikido Primarily defensive and non-competitive, aikido was developed in Japan in the 20th century, and is considered the gentlest martial art. Attacks by an opponent are deflected with throws and immobilising actions based on circular movements, to turn an assailant's own momentum against him.

Kendo A traditional Japanese form of fencing, kendo uses a wooden sword called a shinai, made of strips of bamboo tied together with waxed cord. Its length must not exceed 118 cm (47 in). Competitors, known as kendoka, wear elaborate protective equipment, and may only deliver a limited range of cuts and thrusts to score points.

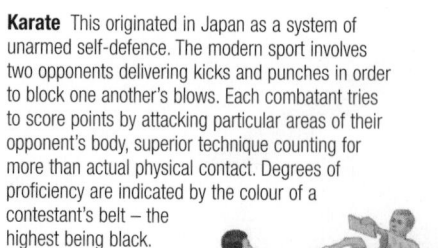

Judo Derived from the ancient Japanese martial art of ju-jitsu, judo is a form of wrestling in which an opponent's strength and weight are directed against him, in order to throw or immobilise him for a specified time. Points are awarded for superior technique. Contests, men's lasting 5 minutes and women's four, fall into one of 14 weight divisions – seven each for men and women. The judoki, or combatants, wear loose-fitting, belted jackets and trousers. As in karate, belt colour denotes grade or skill level.

Tae kwon do Like karate, the Korean martial art of tae kwon do includes punching and flying kicks. It was introduced into the Olympic Games in Sydney in 2000, with four weight classes each for men and women. Contests are scored over three rounds by awarding a point for each legitimate blow and deducting a point for each penalty. When a contestant is knocked down – a knockout being the ultimate aim – the referee begins a 10 second count.

Kung fu Kung fu employs a whole array of acrobatic movements, blows and holds. It originated in China and has many different styles, which divide broadly into two categories, 'soft' and 'hard'. Soft styles tend to concentrate on redirecting an opponent's energy and momentum to unbalance them or bring them within striking range. Hard styles emphasise direct attack, with greater force in blows and other movements.

Judo belts

Degrees of proficiency in judo are indicated by the colour of the belt a judoka wears: white (for novices), then yellow, orange, green, blue, brown and black. The levels of black belt are designated by dan grades: first to fifth dan wear black belts, sixth to ninth wear red and white, and tenth wears red.

Boxing

In the 18th and 19th centuries brutal, bare-fisted fights were a popular form of entertainment. The sport was transformed in 1867, when the Marquis of Queensberry established the strict rules that still govern the sport today. Boxers now wear padded gloves, gumshields and, in amateur bouts, headguards, and rounds may last no more than 3 minutes. Some amateur contests consist of just three rounds; professional contests can have as many as 12.

World heavyweight champions

All championships were undisputed until 1978. Separate titles have since been awarded by the International Boxing Federation, World Boxing Association and World Boxing Council.

Year	Champion
1882-92	John L Sullivan
1892-7	James J Corbett
1897-9	Robert Fitzsimmons
1899-1905	James J Jeffries
1905-6	Marvin Hart
1906-8	Tommy Burns
1908-15	Jack Johnson
1915-19	Jess Willard
1919-26	Jack Dempsey
1926-8	Gene Tunney
1928-30	No holder
1930-2	Max Schmeling
1932-3	Jack Sharkey
1933-4	Primo Carnera
1934-5	Max Baer
1935-7	James J Braddock
1937-49	Joe Louis
1949-51	Ezzard Charles
1951-2	'Jersey' Joe Walcott
1952-6	Rocky Marciano
1956-9	Floyd Patterson
1959-60	Ingemar Johansson
1960-2	Floyd Patterson
1962-4	Sonny Liston
1964-7	Cassius Clay (Muhammad Ali)
1970-3	Joe Frazier
1973-7	George Foreman
1974-8	Muhammad Ali
1978-9	Muhammad Ali (WBA)
1978	Leon Spinks (WBA, WBC)
	Ken Norton (WBC)
1978-83	Larry Holmes (WBC)
1979-80	John Tate (WBA)
1980-2	Mike Weaver (WBA)
1982-3	Michael Dokes (WBA)
1983-4	Gerrie Coetzee (WBA)
1983-5	Larry Holmes (IBF)
1984	Tim Witherspoon (WBA)
1984-5	Greg Page (WBA)
1984-6	Pinklon Thomas (WBC)
1985-6	Tony Tubbs (WBA)
1985-7	Michael Spinks (IBF)
1986	Tim Witherspoon (WBA)
	Trevor Berbick (WBC)
1986-7	Mike Tyson (WBC)
	James 'Bonecrusher' Smith (WBA)
1987	Tony Tucker (IBF)
1987-90	Mike Tyson
1990	'Buster' Douglas
1990-2	Evander Holyfield
1992-3	Riddick Bowe (IBF, WBA, WBC; latter title removed in 1992)
1992-4	Lennox Lewis (WBC)
1993-4	Evander Holyfield (IBF, WBA)
1994	Michael Moorer (IBF, WBA)
1994-5	Oliver McCall (WBC)
	George Foreman (IBF, WBA)
1995	Frans Botha (IBF)
1995-6	Bruce Seldon (WBA)
	Frank Bruno (WBC)
1996	Mike Tyson (WBA, WBC)
1996-7	Michael Moorer (IBF)
1996-9	Evander Holyfield (IBF, WBA)
1997	Lennox Lewis (WBC; title removed in 2000)
1999-2001	Lennox Lewis (IBF, WBA)
2000-1	Evander Holyfield (WBA)
2001-	John Ruiz (WBA)
2001-	Hasim Rahman (IBF, WBC)

LEGENDS

Rocky Marciano
(1923–69) USA

Rocky Marciano took the world heavyweight crown in 1952, and kept it until he retired in 1956 at the age of 32. His extraordinary professional record of 49 bouts and 49 victories included 43 knockouts.

Winning on points

Each boxer is awarded up to 10 points by the referee or judges at the end of every round for skill in landing legitimate punches during that period. To score points, a punch with the knuckle part of the glove must connect with an opponent's upper body, or the front or side of his head. If there is no knockout, retirement, or stoppage by the referee, then the boxer with the highest number of points at the end of the contest is declared the winner.

LEGENDS

Muhammad Ali
(1942–) USA

Muhammad Ali first came to prominence by becoming Olympic light-heavyweight champion in 1960. He then turned professional, taking the world heavyweight title in 1964. In a subsequent flamboyant and extrovert career, he lost, but twice regained the heavyweight crown.

Classifying boxers

Boxers are classified by weight and may not fight in a category lighter than their own. The divisions are:

Heavyweight	Over 88 kg (194 lb)
Cruiserweight (Junior heavyweight)	Up to 88 kg (194 lb)
Light heavyweight	Up to 79.4 kg (175 lb)
Super middleweight	Up to 76.2 kg (168 lb)
Middleweight	Up to 72.6 kg (160 lb)
Super welterweight (Junior middleweight)	Up to 69.9 kg (154 lb)
Welterweight	Up to 66.7 kg (147 lb)
Super lightweight (Junior welterweight)	Up to 63.5 kg (140 lb)
Lightweight	Up to 61.2 kg (135 lb)
Super featherweight (Junior lightweight)	Up to 59 kg (130 lb)
Featherweight	Up to 57.2 kg (126 lb)
Super bantamweight (Junior featherweight)	Up to 55.3 kg (122 lb)
Bantamweight	Up to 53.5 kg (118 lb)
Super flyweight (Junior bantamweight)	Up to 52.2 kg (115 lb)
Flyweight	Up to 51 kg (112 lb)
Light flyweight (Junior flyweight)	Up to 49 kg (108 lb)
Straw-weight	Under 47.6 kg (105 lb)

LEGENDS

Joe Louis
(1914–81) USA

Nicknamed 'the Brown Bomber', Joe Louis was world heavyweight champion from 1937 until 1949. During his long reign, he defended the title 25 times, scoring 21 knockouts. He subsequently came out of retirement but, in his last fight of consequence in 1951, was beaten by future champion, Rocky Marciano.

Competitive motor racing takes many forms, the most popular being Formula One Grand Prix. Stock car racing, rallying and, in the United States, Indy car racing also enjoy a large following. In every type of motor racing, cars must meet certain criteria before being allowed to compete.

Formula One Grand Prix Grand Prix racing cars are light, single-seat vehicles, with a one-piece chassis, made of ultrastrong materials, such as carbon fibre. Aerofoils help to provide stability. Sets of rules (known as formulas) governing design and construction are laid down for each category of Grand Prix motor racing. To be eligible to compete in official Formula One races, a car must conform to the following technical and safety specifications:

- It must weigh no less than 600 kg (1344 lb) and be no more than 1.8 m (5 ft 10³/₄ in) wide (there is no limit on length).
- Its engine must be 4-stroke and have 10 cylinders, each with no more than 5 valves.
- The cylinder capacity of the engine must not exceed 3 litres.
- The engine must not be supercharged (turbocharged).
- The bodywork must not cover any part of the wheels.
- The fuel tank must be a single rubber bladder.
- It must be fitted with roll-over bars and front and side deformable structures, which must survive designated load and impact tests.
- It must have at least two rear-view mirrors, and a rear light for racing in poor visibility.
- It must carry an accident data recorder.

Grand Prix circuits

A World Championship title has been awarded for Formula One drivers every year since 1950. The winner is selected on points, which are awarded for performance in a number of Grand Prix races, over distances from 240 to 320 km (149 to 199 miles), and held from March to October at circuits all around the world.

The maximum number of championship events in one season is 17 and the minimum is eight. The Grand Prix events of the 2001 season were:

Australian (Melbourne)
Malaysian (Kuala Lumpur)
Brazilian (São Paolo)
San Marino (Imola)
Spanish (Barcelona)
Austrian (Spielberg)
Monaco (Monte Carlo)
Canadian (Montreal)
European (Nurburgring, Germany)
French (Magny Cours)
British (Silverstone)
German (Hockenheim)
Hungarian (Hungaroring)
Belgian (Spa Francorchamps)
Italian (Monza)
United States (Indianapolis)
Japanese (Suzuka)

Racing teams A professional racing team consists of many people apart from the driver. Each car at a Formula One event has at least 20 mechanics on hand in special off-track areas known as pits. Their job is to keep both the car and driver performing at optimum level. They prepare the car before a race, and can quickly service and refuel it, if necessary, during the event. A skilled pit crew usually manages to change all tyres and refuel in the space of 5-10 seconds.

LEGENDS

Juan Manuel Fangio
(1911–95) Argentinian

Known as the 'Maestro', he began his motor racing career as a mechanic, before turning to driving and going on to win the world championship a record five times between 1951 and 1957, including four times in a row from 1954 to 1957.

Grand Prix car design
Three-quarters of a century have seen huge changes in racing car engines and body shapes.

Formula One champions

Year	Champion	Nation	Year	Champion	Nation
1950	Giuseppe Farina	Italy	1975	Niki Lauda	Austria
1951	Juan Fangio	Argentina	1976	James Hunt	UK
1952	Alberto Ascari	Italy	1977	Niki Lauda	Austria
1953	Alberto Ascari	Italy	1978	Mario Andretti	USA
1954	Juan Fangio	Argentina	1979	Jody Scheckter	S Africa
1955	Juan Fangio	Argentina	1980	Alan Jones	Austria
1956	Juan Fangio	Argentina	1981	Nelson Piquet	Brazil
1957	Juan Fangio	Argentina	1982	Keke Rosberg	Finland
1958	Mike Hawthorn	UK	1983	Nelson Piquet	Brazil
1959	Jack Brabham	Australia	1984	Niki Lauda	Austria
1960	Jack Brabham	Australia	1985	Alain Prost	France
1961	Phil Hill	USA	1986	Alain Prost	France
1962	Graham Hill	UK	1987	Nelson Piquet	Brazil
1963	Jim Clark	UK	1988	Ayrton Senna	Brazil
1964	John Surtees	UK	1989	Alain Prost	France
1965	Jim Clark	UK	1990	Ayrton Senna	Brazil
1966	Jack Brabham	Australia	1991	Ayrton Senna	Brazil
1967	Denis Hulme	N. Zealand	1992	Nigel Mansell	UK
1968	Graham Hill	UK	1993	Alain Prost	France
1969	Jackie Stewart	UK	1994	Michael Schumacher	Germany
1970	Jochen Rindt	Austria	1995	Michael Schumacher	Germany
1971	Jackie Stewart	UK	1996	Damon Hill	UK
1972	Emerson Fittipaldi	Brazil	1997	Jacques Villeneuve	Canada
1973	Jackie Stewart	UK	1998	Mika Hakkinen	Finland
1974	Emerson Fittipaldi	Brazil	1999	Mika Hakkinen	Finland
			2000	Michael Schumacher	Germany

TYRES

Grand Prix racing tyres are designed to cope with either wet or dry conditions. Wet-weather tyres have grooves to help water to drain clear and prevent skidding. Tyres for dry weather, called slicks, grip by heating up and becoming sticky. Slicks were totally smooth until 1998 when regulations were changed to improve safety. Now they must have grooves running around them. Formula One tyres wear down quickly and are changed at least once during a race.

Bugatti Type 35 Designed in 1924, this was one of the first-ever single-seat racers. With a 1991 cc, 135 brake horse power (bhp) engine, it dominated Grand Prix racing from 1927 to 1931.

Alpha Romeo 158 In 1950 this car, already 13 years old, stormed to victory in the first-ever Formula One championship. At 1500 cc, its engine was smaller than the earlier Bugatti but more powerful, developing over 350 bhp.

Vanwall The Vanwall was launched in 1957. Its teardrop shape was so streamlined that it proved capable of beating more powerful cars, starting a trend towards increasingly aerodynamic designs.

Rallying Competition rallying involves driving over a series of timed stages, either on roads, private tracks or race tracks, usually over a period of three days. Each car is manned by a team consisting of a driver and a navigator. The most famous long-distance race is the Monte Carlo Rally, which took place for the first time in 1911. Other major events include the Acropolis Rally, Safari Rally and Cyprus Rally.

Pit stop Jeff Gordon pulls in for a tyre change at Sonoma, California. As with Formula One, changing a stock car tyre involves replacing the entire wheel.

Indy car racing
Indy car racing is the leading single-seat racing class in the United States. The cars resemble those used in Formula One races, but with engines up to almost 5000 cc. Races, covering distances of between 125 and 500 miles (201 and 805 km), take place on road circuits or banked, oval tracks. The Championship Auto Racing Teams, Inc. (CART) organises all Indy car racing events except the Indianapolis 500, which is sanctioned by the United States Auto Club.

The Indianapolis 500 is the major race in the United States, and was part of the World Drivers' Championship until 1960. It takes place on the Indianapolis Motor Speedway, and, in terms of attendance, is the largest single-day sporting event in the world. The first driver to complete 200 laps around the track – a distance of 500 miles (805 km) wins the race.

Stock car racing
Stock cars are heavy, single-seat saloon vehicles, weighing up to 1700 kg (3809 lb), which look generally like production cars but have been modified to increase power and speed. Most major stock car races are held on oval, paved tracks. In the USA the main races comprise the Winston Cup series (first held in 1949), the Busch series and ASA series. The National Association for Stock Car Auto Racing (NASCAR) is the sport's regulatory body.

High flier Norwegian Champion Petter Solberg takes a jump in his Ford Focus during the 2000 Kenya Rally. Many modern rallies are competed between highly modified versions of everyday road cars. The sport is a test of a car's endurance as much as speed.

LEGENDS

Ayrton Senna
(1960–94) Brazilian

Ayrton Senna was three times world champion – in 1988, 1990 and 1991. Overall, he won 41 Grand Prix races in 161 starts, including a record six wins at Monaco. He was killed after crashing off the Imola circuit during the 1994 San Marino Grand Prix.

Indianapolis 500 and NASCAR Winston Cup

The Indianapolis 500 is raced yearly at the end of May as part of the US Memorial Day celebrations. It was first held in 1911.

Year	Champion	Year	Champion
1970	Al Unser	1986	Bobby Rahal
1971	Al Unser	1987	Al Unser
1972	Mark Donohue	1988	Rick Mears
1973	Gordon Johncock	1989	Emerson Fittipaldi
1974	Johnny Rutherford	1990	Arie Luyendyk
1975	Bobby Unser	1991	Rick Mears
1976	Johnny Rutherford	1992	Al Unser, Jr
1977	A J Foyt	1993	Emerson Fittipaldi
1978	Al Unser	1994	Al Unser, Jr
1979	Rick Mears	1995	Jacques Villeneuve
1980	Johnny Rutherford	1996	Buddy Lazier
1981	Bobby Unser	1997	Arie Luyendyk
1982	Gordon Johncock	1998	Eddy Cheever
1983	Tom Sneva	1999	Kenny Brack
1984	Rick Mears	2000	Juan Montoya
1985	Danny Sullivan	2001	Helio Castroneves

The NASCAR Winston Cup has been awarded since 1949. Until 1970, it was known as the Grand National series.

Year	Champion	Year	Champion
1970	Bobby Isaac	1986	Dale Earnhardt
1971	Richard Petty	1987	Dale Earnhardt
1972	Richard Petty	1988	Bill Elliott
1973	Benny Parsons	1989	Rusty Wallace
1974	Richard Petty	1990	Dale Earnhardt
1975	Richard Petty	1991	Dale Earnhardt
1976	Cale Yarborough	1992	Alan Kulwicki
1977	Cale Yarborough	1993	Dale Earnhardt
1978	Cale Yarborough	1994	Dale Earnhardt
1979	Richard Petty	1995	Jeff Gordon
1980	Dale Earnhardt	1996	Terry Labonte
1981	Darrell Waltrip	1997	Jeff Gordon
1982	Darrell Waltrip	1998	Jeff Gordon
1983	Bobby Allison	1999	Dale Jarrett
1984	Terry Labonte	2000	Bobby Labonte
1985	Darrell Waltrip		

Lotus-Ford 72 At the end of the 1950s, Formula One designers began to put the engine at the back rather than the front of the car. This made it easier for the driver to lean back into the increasingly streamlined contours of the car. By 1970, when the Lotus-Ford 72 came out, drivers were able to lie virtually flat, reducing drag to a minimum.

Tyrell-Ford P34 This car was launched in 1976, by which time front and rear 'wings', or aerofoils, had become standard on Formula One cars. Aerofoils improved stability and roadholding, enabling cars to take corners faster. The P34's four 10-inch front wheels were intended to improve cornering still further but put too much stress on the tyres. After two years, the design was abandoned.

Ferrari F1-2000 Today, Formula One cars are more streamlined, powerful and lightweight than ever. The Ferrari F1-2000 weighs just 600 kg (1348 lb), yet its 2997 cc engine can develop 770 bhp, enabling it to accelerate from 0-160 km/h (0-100 mph) in just 3.7 seconds.

Motorcycling

The earliest recorded motorcycle race was in France in 1896, from Paris to Nantes and back. The following year, the first competition on a purpose-built track took place in Surrey, England. Today, motorcycle racing exists in a number of forms, with machines designed to cope with a wide variety of racing conditions.

There are five main categories of motorcycle racing:

● **Circuit racing** This is competed over purpose-built tarmac tracks with bikes designed almost solely for speed.

● **Road racing** This takes place on open roads using the same sort of bikes as circuit racing. The most famous road race is the Isle of Man TT.

● **Motocross** Also known as scrambling, motocross takes place over natural terrain. The bikes have long front forks, improved suspension and knobbly tyres for riding over rough ground.

● **Trials** Trials are also run over natural terrain, but with additional artificial hazards. The bikes used are the same as in motocross.

● **Speedway** This is raced over flat, oval-shaped dirt tracks for short distances. Speedway bikes have long front forks and knobbly tyres but almost no suspension.

500 cc World Champions

The international governing body of motorcycle racing – Fédération Internationale Motocycliste (FIM) – began running World Championships for circuit racing in 1949. Titles are awarded in 125 cc, 250 cc and sidecar racing categories as well as 500 cc.

Year(s)	500 cc winner	Manufacturer
1970-2	Giacomo Agostini	MV
1973-4	Phil Read	MV
1975	Giacomo Agostini	Yamaha
1976-7	Barry Sheene	Suzuki
1978-80	Kenny Roberts	Yamaha
1981	Marco Lucchinelli	Suzuki
1982	Franco Uncini	Suzuki
1983	Freddie Spencer	Honda
1984	Eddie Lawson	Yamaha
1985	Freddie Spencer	Honda
1986	Eddie Lawson	Yamaha
1987	Wayne Gardner	Honda
1988-9	Eddie Lawson	Yamaha
1990-2	Wayne Rainey	Yamaha
1993	Kevin Shwantz	Suzuki
1994-8	Michael Doohan	Honda
1999	Alex Criville	Honda
2000	Kenny Roberts, Jr	Suzuki

LEGENDS

Giacomo Agostini
(1943–) Italian

Between 1965 and his retirement in 1977 Agostini won 15 world racing titles and 122 Grands Prix in the 350 cc and 500 cc categories, setting an unbeaten record.

Turn of speed Motorcycle racers wear heavy protective gear, including leather outfits with extra padding around the elbows and knees.

Cycling

Soon after the bicycle was invented people started using it to race against each other. The first organised bicycle race took place in the Parc St Cloud, Paris, in 1868. Cycling was included in the first modern Olympics in 1896 and remains part of the Games today.

Cycle racing takes place on roads or on tracks in specially designed stadia called velodromes. Road races include time trials, massed starts, criteriums (run over a relatively short closed course) and stage races. Cross-country racing, or cyclo-cross, covers rough terrain and often requires riders to dismount and carry their cycles over certain stretches of the course.

LEGENDS

Eddy Merckx
(1945–) Belgian

Merckx won the Tour de France a joint record five times between 1969 and 1974, as well as the Giro d'Italia (another classic race) on five occasions (1968, 1970 and 1972-4).

Out in front Eddy Merckx leads the Tour de France – the world's best-attended sporting event with more than 10 million spectators every year.

Tour de France

The Tour de France, which began in 1903, takes place annually in July, incorporating time trial and endurance cycling. The 4800 km (3000 mile) course, run over 21 stages, varies each year, often taking in adjoining countries but always ending in Paris. The overall leader wears the coveted 'yellow jersey'.

Year(s)	Winner	Nation	Year(s)	Winner	Nation
1950	F Kübler	Swtzrlnd	1975	Bernard Thévenet	France
1951	Hugo Koblet	Swtzrlnd	1976	Lucien van Impe	Belgium
1952	Fausto Coppi	Italy	1977	Bernard Thévenet	France
1953-5	Louison Bobet	France	1978-9	Bernard Hinault	France
1956	Roger Walkowiak	France	1980	Joop Zoetemelk	Holland
1957	Jacques Anquetil	France	1981-2	Bernard Hinault	France
1958	Charly Gaul	Lxmbrg	1983-4	Laurent Fignon	France
1959	F Bahamontès	Spain	1985	Bernard Hinault	France
1960	Gastone Nencini	Italy	1986	Greg LeMond	USA
1961-4	Jacques Anquetil	France	1987	Stephen Roche	Ireland
1965	Felice Gimondi	Italy	1988	Pedro Delgado	Spain
1966	Lucien Aimar	France	1989-90	Greg LeMond	USA
1967	Roger Pingeon	France	1991-5	Miguel Induráin	Spain
1968	Jan Janssen	Holland	1996	Bjarne Riis	Denmark
1969-72	Eddy Merckx	Belgium	1997	Jan Ullrich	Germany
1973	Hugo Koblet	Swtzrlnd	1998	Marco Pantani	Italy
1974	Eddy Merckx	Belgium	1999-	Lance Armstrong	USA

Cycling velodrome The velodrome is a banked oval track, usually made of wood, for high-speed racing. Cyclists can reach 60 km/h (37 mph) in sprint competitions. The bicycles used have just one gear and no brakes.

Pursuit racing Riders or teams start opposite one another, then race to win by catching their opponents or completing the course in a faster time than them.

Time trial Cyclists race alone against the clock.

Start lines

Points racing Riders try to win sprints every few laps to gain points. If a rider finishes the race a lap or more ahead, he or she wins regardless of points scored.

Match sprint Riders begin from the same start line, jockey for position over two or three laps then sprint for the finish.

Sailing

The sport of sailing began in the Netherlands in the 1500s, and the first yacht club opened in Cork, Ireland, in 1720. Today, there are two recognised types of competition sailing: fleet racing (the predominant form) – where all competing boats sail against each other at one time; and match racing – one-on-one racing (and a more tactical contest) between two boats.

Sailing races vary from competitions over a few miles to journeys round the world. The length and direction of races are set by race organising committees.

Other than sailboards, there are two main types of boat used in races:

● **Racing dinghy** A small craft with a crew of one or two. It is fundamentally unstable and depends on the skill of the crew to keep it upright. Apart from the centreboard, which projects under the keel to prevent too much sideways drift, it has no ballast other than the distribution of the crew's weight to prevent the wind knocking it down.

● **Keelboard boat** A powerful, ocean-going yacht, which can race many thousands of miles with a crew of up to twelve. The keel is heavily weighted, so it is more stable than a racing dinghy.

OLYMPIC RACING CLASSES

There are nine classes of boat in sailing events at the Olympic Games. All compete in fleet races, apart from the Soling class boats, which sail in match races.

Mistral One-person sailboard used for male and female windsurfing events.

Laser One-person racing dinghy used for competitions open to both men and women. It is 4.25 m (13 ft 11 in) long and weighs 59 kg (130 lb).

Europe One-person racing dinghy used for female competition only. It is 3.35 m (11 ft) long and weighs 45 kg (99 lb).

Finn One-person dinghy raced by men. It is 4.5 m (14 ft 9 in) long and weighs 126 kg (278 lb).

470 Two-person dinghy used for separate male and female competitions. It is 4.7 m (15 ft 6 in) long and weighs 120 kg (264 lb).

Tornado Two-person catamaran (boat with two hulls); 6.1 m (20 ft) long and raced by men and women in a mixed event.

49er Two-person, high performance dinghy used in mixed competition. It is 4.9 m (16 ft 1 in) long and weighs 127 kg (280 lb).

Soling Three-person keelboat and largest of the Olympic-class boats. It is 8.2 m (26 ft 11 in) long and weighs 1035 kg (2282 lb).

Star Two-person keelboat used for mixed competition. It is 6.9 m (22 ft 8 in) long and weighs 676 kg (1490 lb).

America's Cup winners

Year	Winner	Nation	Year	Winner	Nation
1851	*America*	USA	1934	*Rainbow*	USA
1870	*Magic*	USA	1937	*Ranger*	USA
1871	*Columbia & Sappho*	USA	1958	*Columbia*	USA
1876	*Madeline*	USA	1962	*Weatherly*	USA
1881	*Mischief*	USA	1964	*Constellation*	USA
1885	*Puritan*	USA	1967	*Intrepid*	USA
1886	*Mayflower*	USA	1970	*Intrepid*	USA
1887	*Volunteer*	USA	1974	*Courageous*	USA
1893	*Vigilant*	USA	1977	*Courageous*	USA
1895	*Defender*	USA	1980	*Freedom*	USA
1899	*Columbia*	USA	1983	*Australia II*	Australia
1901	*Columbia*	USA	1987	*Stars & Stripes*	USA
1903	*Reliance*	USA	1988	*Stars & Stripes*	USA
1920	*Resolute*	USA	1992	*America*	USA
1930	*Enterprise*	USA	1995	*Black Magic 1*	NZ
			2000	*New Zealand*	NZ

AMERICA'S CUP

This sailing challenge started in 1851, when a 170 ton schooner, *America*, defeated 14 Royal Yacht Squadron boats in a race round the Isle of Wight as part of the Great Exhibition celebrations. The race is run every few years between two boats from different countries: the previous winner and one challenger, chosen by virtue of winning a 'Challenger Selection Series' of races. The Cup race takes place in the holding country's home waters, and has the third largest TV audience of any sporting event after the Olympic Games and football World Cup.

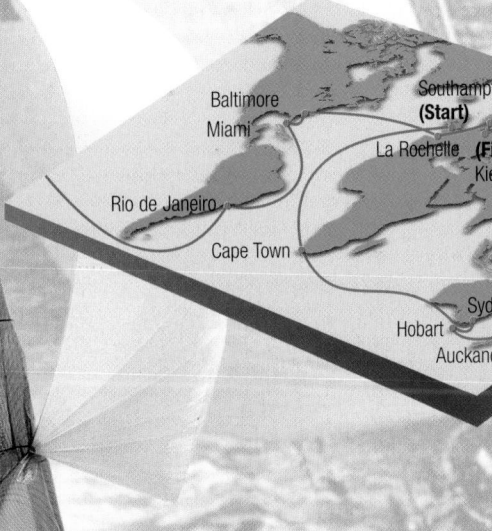

The longest race on Earth
The Whitbread Round The World Race is held every four years. In 1998, it was entered by 10 yachts with crews of six to 12 people, and lasted for more than four months.

Swimming and diving

The earliest reference to competitive swimming dates from ancient Japan in 36 BC. Races became popular in Britain in the 18th century, and swimming was first formalised as a sport in London in 1869 with the creation of the Metropolitan Swimming Clubs Association, later to become the Amateur Swimming Association (ASA). It was included as an Olympic sport from 1896, although the first world records were not recognised until 1908. Highboard platform diving joined the list of Olympic sports in 1904 and springboard diving was included four years later.

LEGENDS

Mark Spitz
(1950–) American

At the 1972 Munich Games Spitz became the first competitor to win seven gold medals in a single Olympics: two golds in freestyle events, two in butterfly events and three in team relays. To cap it all, they were all world records.

LEGENDS

Shane Gould
(1956–) Australian

At the age of 15 and having already set every world women's freestyle record from 100 m to 1500 m, Gould collected three gold medals, one silver and one bronze at the 1972 Munich Olympics. She retired from competitive swimming after her Olympic success.

Swimming events The basic strokes in swimming are front crawl (the fastest, also called freestyle), backstroke (back crawl), breaststroke and butterfly. Competitions are held in long-course pools (50 m/164 ft) and short-course pools (25 m/82 ft), with up to ten lanes.

Olympic competition takes place in long-course pools over the following distances:
freestyle 50 m, 100 m, 200 m, 400 m, 800 m (women only), 1500 m (men only).
breaststroke 100 m, 200 m.
backstroke 100 m, 200 m.
butterfly 100 m, 200 m.
individual medley 200 m, 400 m.
medley relay 4 x 100 m.
freestyle relay 4 x 100 m, 4 x 200 m.
Medleys are races where a certain distance is swum in each of the four strokes.

Water ballet Synchronised swimming demands artistry rather than speed and endurance. Competitors perform rhythmic routines to music, and points are awarded for interpretation and style. It was introduced into the Olympics in 1984.

World records

Men's Event	Record holder	Nation	Time
50 m freestyle	Alexander Popov	Russia	21.64
100 m freestyle	P van den Hoogenband	Netherlands	47.84
200 m freestyle	P van den Hoogenband	Netherlands	1:45.35
400 m freestyle	Ian Thorpe	Australia	3:40.59
800 m freestyle	Kieren Perkins	Australia	7:46.00
1500 m freestyle	Kieren Perkins	Australia	14:41.66
100 m backstroke	Lenny Krayzelburg	USA	53.60
200 m backstroke	Lenny Krayzelburg	USA	1:55.87
100 m breaststroke	Roman Sloudov	Russia	1:00.36
200 m breaststroke	Mike Barrowman	USA	2:10.16
100 m butterfly	Michael Klim	Australia	51.81
200 m butterfly	Tom Malchow	USA	1:55.18
200 m ind. medley	Jani Sievinen	Finland	1:58.16
400 m ind. medley	Tom Dolan	USA	4:11.76

Men's relay			
4 x 100 m freestyle		Australia	3:13.67
4 x 200 m freestyle		Australia	7:07.05
4 x 100 m medley		USA	3:33.73

Women's Event	Record holder	Nation	Time
50 m freestyle	Ingede Bruijn	Netherlands	24.32
100 m freestyle	Ingede Bruijn	Netherlands	53.83
200 m freestyle	Franziska van Almsick	Germany	1:56.78
400 m freestyle	Janet Evans	USA	4:03.85
800 m freestyle	Janet Evans	USA	8:16.22
1500 m freestyle	Janet Evans	USA	15:52.10
100 m backstroke	Cihong He	China	1:00.16
200 m backstroke	Kristina Egerszegi	Hungary	2:06.62
100 m breaststroke	Penelope Heyns	South Africa	1:06.52
200 m breaststroke	Penelope Heyns	South Africa	2:23.64
100 m butterfly	Ingede Bruijn	Netherlands	56.61
200 m butterfly	Susan O'Niell	Australia	2:05.81
200 m ind. medley	Yanyan Wu	China	2:09.72
400 m ind. medley	Yana Klochkova	Ukraine	4:33.59

Women's relay			
4 x 100 m freestyle		USA	3:36.61
4 x 200 m freestyle		GDR	7:55.47
4 x 100 m medley		USA	3:58.30

DIVING

Diving involves precision timing and technique. In competition, divers usually leap from a firm platform 5 m (16 ft 4 in) or 10 m (32 ft 8 in) above the water; or from a flexible springboard 1 m (3 ft 3 in) or 3 m (9 ft 8 in) above the water.

Groups of dive
There are six groups based on take-off position and dive direction.
- **Forward** The diver faces the water, then dives rotating forward.
- **Backward** The diver faces away from the water for take-off, then dives and rotates backward.
- **Reverse** The diver faces the water, but dives rotating backward.
- **Inward** The diver faces away from the water, then dives rotating forward.
- **Twist** While performing one of the above types of dive, the diver also swivels the body on its long axis.
- **Armstand** Take-off is from a handstand position.

Perfect entry Keeping the body straight and feet pointed and held together ensures almost no splash when the diver hits the water.

Diving positions
There are three diving positions in the air:
- **Straight** The body remains straight.
- **Pike** The body bends at the hip but the knees remain straight.
- **Tuck** The knees are drawn up to the chest, and the lower legs are clasped with the arms.

Scoring
In competition, divers perform a number of listed dives, rated for their degree of difficulty, as well as several of their own choice. Three or more judges score each dive, with attention paid to take-off, posture in the air, execution of the prescribed movements and entry into the water.

Scores for each dive are added and multiplied by the degree of difficulty. The diver with the highest score for all dives at the end of the contest wins.

References to competition rowing can be found in Greek and Roman literature. Competitions have been held on the River Thames for centuries; today both the University Boat Race and Henley Royal Regatta are held there. Rowing became an Olympic sport in 1900.

Competition Racing craft, called shells, range in length from 7 m (24 ft) to 18 m (60 ft), depending on the number of crew members (single, pair, four or eight). A helmsman, called the coxswain (cox), is carried for some events. In rowing, a single oar is worked with both hands. The use of two oars, one in each hand, is called sculling. In the Olympics and most other competitions, all races take place over a 2000 m (2200 yd) straight course, each crew or sculler racing in a separate, marked lane. The exceptions are the two most famous rowing events, the University Boat Race and Henley Royal Regatta, where the courses are 6779 m (4 miles 374 yd) and 2112 m (1 mile 550 yd) respectively. The annual University Boat Race has been won by Cambridge 77 times and Oxford 69 times with one dead heat.

LEGENDS

Steven Redgrave
(1962–) British

In the men's coxless fours event at the 2000 Olympic Games in Sydney, Australia, Redgrave earned a record-breaking fifth consecutive Olympic gold medal. His previous golds were for the coxed fours in 1984, and coxless pairs in 1988, 1992 and 1996. In the 1986 Commonwealth Games, he won a record three gold medals.

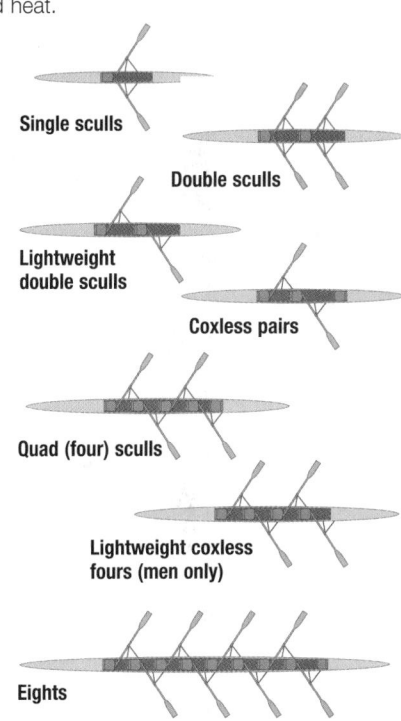

- Single sculls
- Double sculls
- Lightweight double sculls
- Coxless pairs
- Quad (four) sculls
- Lightweight coxless fours (men only)
- Eights

2000 Olympic rowing

Men's Events	Gold medallist(s)	Time
Single sculls	New Zealand (Rob Waddell)	6:48.90
Double sculls	Slovenia	6:16.63
Lightweight double sculls	Poland	6:21.75
Quadruple sculls	Italy	5:45.56
Coxless pairs	France	6:32.97
Coxless fours	UK	5:56.24
Lightweight coxless fours	France	6:01.68
Coxed eights	UK	5:33.08

Women's Events	Gold medallist(s)	Time
Single sculls	Belarus (Ekaterina Karsten)	7:28.14
Double sculls	Germany	6:55.44
Lightweight double sculls	Romania	7:02.64
Quadruple sculls	Germany	6:19.58
Coxless pairs	Romania	7:11.00
Coxed eights	Romania	6:06.44

There are three basic kinds of skiing: Alpine (downhill and slalom racing); Nordic (cross-country skiing and ski jumping); and freestyle, which focuses on acrobatics.

Nordic skiing

Skiing originated in Scandinavia as a way of getting around in snow-covered landscapes. The modern sport of cross-country skiing developed from this tradition. The other Nordic skiing sport is ski jumping.

Cross-country skiing Competitors race on lightweight, narrow skis over distances of 10-50 km (6.2-31 miles), propelling themselves with the aid of sticks. Events are contested in two disciplines: classical, in which skiers must push the toe ends of their skis almost diagonally outwards as they stride, and freestyle, where no restriction is placed on the type of stride used.

Ski jumping In this sport competitors glide down a prepared steep incline to a take-off point up to 90 m (295 ft) high. They are judged on the length of their jump, style of execution, coordination and balance. Jumps of more than 150 m (490 ft) can be achieved. Ski-jumping skis are about 244cm (8 ft) long, making them the longest variety of all. They are also wider and heavier than any other skis.

FREESTYLE SKIING

Freestyle skiing developed in the 1960s. There are three events: moguls, in which skiers race down a course with large bumps of hard-packed snow; aerials, where they perform acrobatic jumps; and ballet, which takes place on smooth slopes to music. Mogul and aerial skiing are Olympic events.

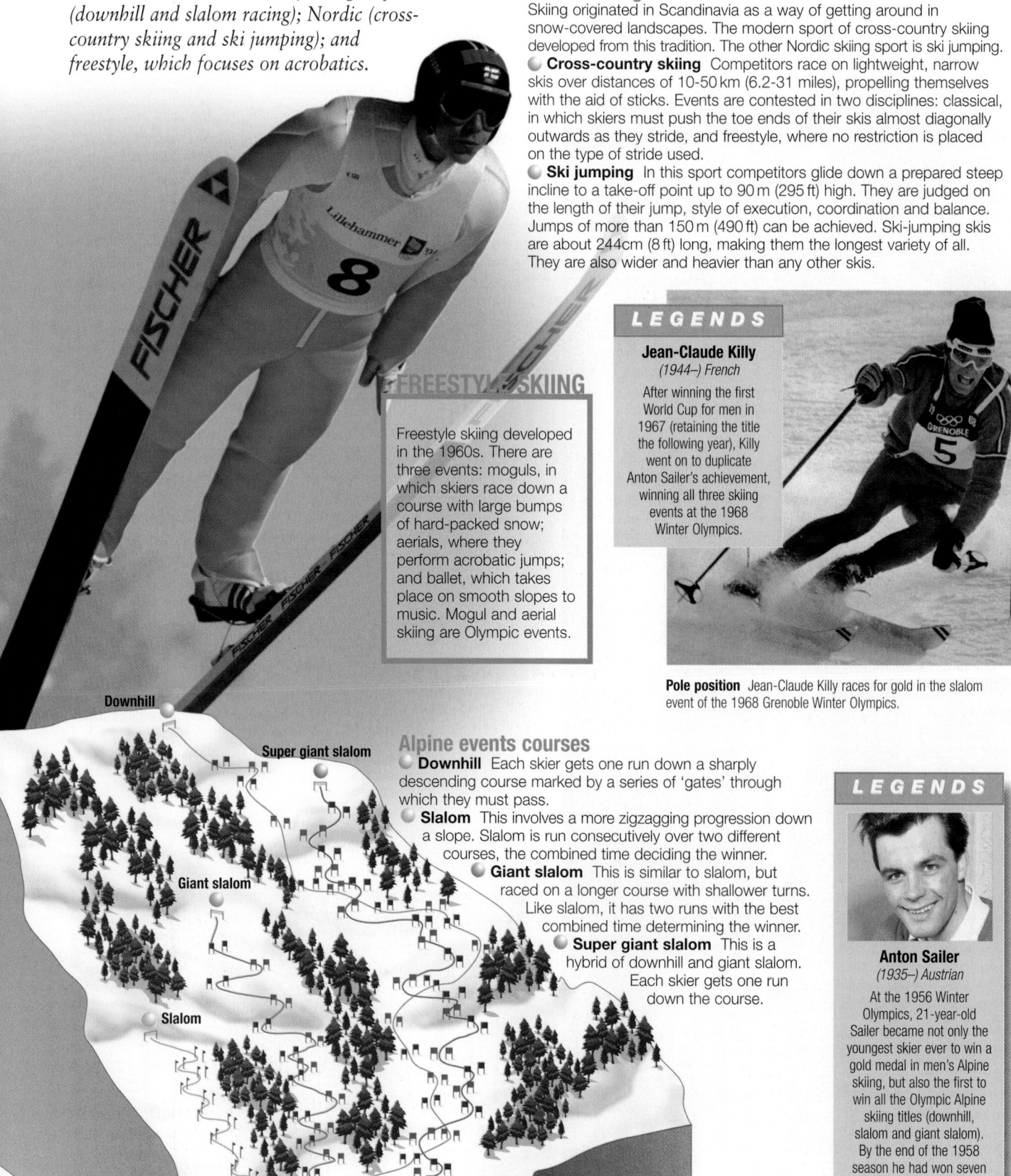

LEGENDS

Jean-Claude Killy
(1944–) French

After winning the first World Cup for men in 1967 (retaining the title the following year), Killy went on to duplicate Anton Sailer's achievement, winning all three skiing events at the 1968 Winter Olympics.

Pole position Jean-Claude Killy races for gold in the slalom event of the 1968 Grenoble Winter Olympics.

Alpine events courses

Downhill Each skier gets one run down a sharply descending course marked by a series of 'gates' through which they must pass.

Slalom This involves a more zigzagging progression down a slope. Slalom is run consecutively over two different courses, the combined time deciding the winner.

Giant slalom This is similar to slalom, but raced on a longer course with shallower turns. Like slalom, it has two runs with the best combined time determining the winner.

Super giant slalom This is a hybrid of downhill and giant slalom. Each skier gets one run down the course.

Downhill
Super giant slalom
Giant slalom
Slalom

LEGENDS

Anton Sailer
(1935–) Austrian

At the 1956 Winter Olympics, 21-year-old Sailer became not only the youngest skier ever to win a gold medal in men's Alpine skiing, but also the first to win all the Olympic Alpine skiing titles (downhill, slalom and giant slalom). By the end of the 1958 season he had won seven world titles.

Figure skating originated in Britain in the early 1700s, and speed skating in the Netherlands at about the same time. The first ice-skating club was formed in Edinburgh, Scotland, around 1742. Artificial rinks did not appear until 100 years later, however.

1998 Winter Olympics

Men's Alpine skiing

Event	Gold medallist	Nation	Time
Downhill	Jean-Luc Cretier	France	1:50.11
Super giant slalom	Hermann Maier	Austria	1:34.82
Giant slalom	Hermann Maier	Austria	2:38.51
Slalom	Hans-Petter Buraas	Norway	1:49.31
Combined	Mario Reiter	Austria	3:08.06

Women's Alpine skiing

Downhill	Katja Seizinger	Germany	1:28.89
Super giant slalom	Picabo Street	USA	1:18.02
Giant slalom	Deborah Compagnoni	Italy	2:50.59
Slalom	Hilde Gerg	Germany	1:32.40
Combined	Katja Seizinger	Germany	2:40.74

Ski jumping

Individual	Gold medallist	Nation	Points
Normal hill	Jani Soininen	Finland	234.5
Large hill	Kazuyoshi Funaka	Japan	272.3

Team			
Large hill	Japan		933.0

BOBSLEIGH

A crew of two or four take a running start with a sleigh, then sit in it and slide down an ice chute with banked walls, using steering and the distribution of their weight to help to guide the bob in bends. Braking is against the rules. It is allowed only to stop the bob at the end of a run or to correct skids. The number of runs in a competition varies; the winning team is the one with the lowest combined time at the end. Courses are typically 1.2-1.5 km (0.75-1 mile) long.

LUGE

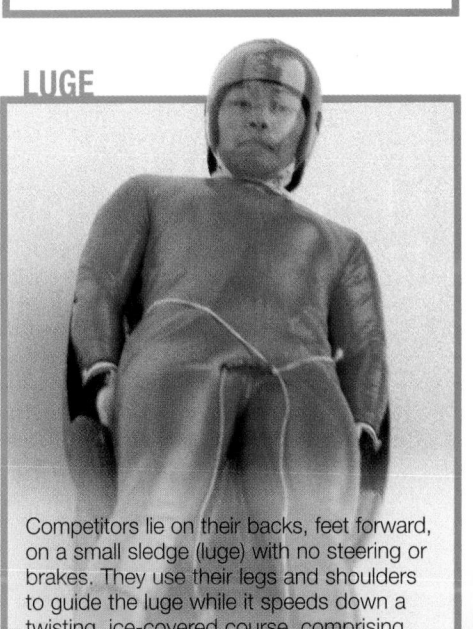

Competitors lie on their backs, feet forward, on a small sledge (luge) with no steering or brakes. They use their legs and shoulders to guide the luge while it speeds down a twisting, ice-covered course, comprising turns, curves and straight stretches, and the best time determines the winner. Courses are typically 1-1.5 km (0.6-1 mile) long and speeds can reach about 112 km/h (70 mph).

Figure skating and ice dancing

Competiton is on rinks of 60 m x 30 m (196 ft x 98 ft).

● **Figure skating** In Olympic competition the men's, women's and pairs events each consist of a short programme, during which skaters must perform eight different prescribed elements made up of jumps, spins, step sequences, spirals and linking movements, and a free-skating programme, where they select their own elements. The short programme makes up a third of their final score; the free-skating programme two-thirds.

● **Ice dancing** This pairs event has four parts, all set to music. Competitors must perform two compulsory dances (the rhythm and tempo of which are defined), one original dance (also to a prescribed rhythm) and one free dance (to music chosen by the pair). The free dance accounts for half of the final score.

Skating moves

There are several moves. The most common ones are:

● **Axel** A flying spin where the skater skates forwards into the take-off (in all other flying spins the skater skates backwards into the take-off).

● **Lutz** A flying spin with the take-off from the back of one skate and the landing on the back of the other.

● **Camel spin** A spin on one leg, with the other at right angles to the ice.

● **Death spiral** The man spins, holding his partner's hands as she glides on one skate in an almost horizontal position.

Speed skating

This racing on ice takes place over courses ranging from 500 m (546 yd) to 10 000 m (6.2 miles) in length. Speed skates have longer blades than figure or ice-dancing skates.

LEGENDS

Irina Rodnina (1949–) and **Aleksandr Zaitsev** (1952–) Russian

Rodnina and Zaitsev won Olympic gold in the figure-skating pairs twice, in 1976 and 1980, and topped the World Championships every year from 1973-8. Rodnina also won an Olympic gold for the figure-skating pairs in 1972 with Alexei Ulyanov, and held the World Championship title with him from 1969 to 1972.

Winter Olympics

Figure skating 1998

Event	Gold medals	Nation
Men's singles	Ilya Kulik	Russia
Women's singles	Tara Lipinski	USA
Pairs	Oksana Kazakova & Artur Dmitriev	Russia
Ice dancing	Pasha Grishuk & Evgeny Platov	Russia

LEGENDS

Jayne Torvill (1957–) and **Christopher Dean** (1958–) British

This ice dancing pair won the World Championship four times in a row (1981-4), and the European championship in 1981, 1982, 1984 and 1994. In 1984, they won gold at the Olympics with an unprecedented perfect score of six marks from every judge for artistic impression.

Perfect start Torvill and Dean begin their gold-medal-winning performance at the 1984 Winter Olympics in Sarajevo.

The modern organisation of horse racing dates from 1750 when the Jockey Club was established in England. Today the sport is popular in many countries but its strongholds are the UK, USA, Ireland and France. There are two main forms of horse racing; flat racing and racing over jumps.

Red Rum
This steeplechase racing horse won the English Grand National at Aintree a record three times: in 1973, 1974 and, as a 12-year-old, in 1977. In both of the intervening years he finished second. He died in 1995, aged 30, and is buried at Aintree racecourse near to the winning post.

WEIGHING IN

Horses are required to carry weights determined by distance and their age and sex (females carry less, as do younger horses up to five years old). Jockeys and their equipment (including saddle, but not hat) weigh 'out' before a race, and weigh 'in' after it. This ensures that they:
Meet the designated weight (any remainder is made up with weights added into the saddle);
Cannot shed weights during the race, which would give their horse an advantage.

Lester Piggott
(1935–) British
By the time Piggott retired as a flat racing jockey in 1995 he had been the champion jockey in England on 11 occasions. He won the Derby a record nine times, the St Leger eight times, the Oaks six times, the 2000 Guineas five times, and the 1000 Guineas twice.

Major international flat races

Race	First run	Course	Distance
Melbourne Cup	1861	Flemington Pk, Victoria, Aus	3.2 km (2 miles)
Kentucky Derby	1875	Louisville, USA	2.4 km (1.5 miles)
Prix de l'Arc de Triomphe	1920	Longchamp, Paris, France	2.4 km (1.5 miles)
Breeders' Cup	1984	Various venues in the USA and Canada; seven races	Various
Dubai Cup	1996	Dubai, UAE	2 km (1.25 miles)

Flat racing A flat race is any race between thoroughbred horses over a course without obstacles. A thoroughbred is a horse registered in official national stud books whose parentage traces back to any of three Arabian 'founding sires' (the Godolphin Barb, Byerly Turk and Darley Arabian) brought to Britain between 1690 and 1730.

Racing over jumps Horse races over jumps fall into one of two categories:
● **Steeplechasing** The jumps in steeplechasing vary in size, but may be up to 1.6 m (5 ft 2 in) wide and 1.8 m (6 ft) high. Some have ditches preceding or following them. The earliest steeplechases were across open country, with church steeples used as landmarks.
● **Hurdling** The jumps (hurdles) in hurdling are narrow and set with the top edge 107 cm (3 ft 6 in) from the ground.

HARNESS RACING

In harness racing, horses pull a light, two-wheeled vehicle (called a sulky) with a driver round a track. They trot or pace at speeds of up to 48 km/h (30 mph) or more. Trotting and pacing entail different leg movements. Races are usually staged over distances between 1.6 km (1 mile) and 2.4 km (1.5 miles).

Harness racing is for standard-bred horses, who have a more robust build than thoroughbreds. It is particularly popular in the United States, Australia and New Zealand.

Racing terminology

● **Stakes race** For stakes races, the owner usually must pay a fee to run a horse. Entry fees, together with a contribution from the track, constitute the prize money for the winning and placed horses. Some stakes races are by invitation and require no payment or fee.
● **Handicap race** In handicap races, horses with a better racing record are handicapped by being given extra weights to carry.
● **Match race** A race between two horses, usually the most successful runners of a particular season.
● **Walkover** This happens when all but one horse has been withdrawn from a race. Horses may be withdrawn up to several hours before the start of a race.

Major UK races

Classic flat races for three-year-olds

Race	First run	Course	Distance
St Leger	1776	Doncaster, S Yorks	2.8 km (1³/4 miles)
Oaks (fillies only)	1779	Epsom, Surrey	2.4 km (1¹/2 miles)
Derby	1780	Epsom, Surrey	2.4 km (1¹/2 miles)
2000 Guineas	1809	Newmarket, Suffolk	1.6 km (1 mile)
1000 Guineas (fillies only)	1814	Newmarket, Suffolk	1.6 km (1 mile)

Royal Ascot (flat races)

Race	First run	Course	Distance
Ascot Gold Cup	1807	Ascot, Berkshire	3.6 km (2¹/4 miles)
St James's Palace Stakes	1834	Ascot, Berkshire	1.6 km (1 mile)
Coronation Stakes	1840	Ascot, Berkshire	1.6 km (1 mile)

Steeplechases and hurdles

Race	First run	Course	Distance
Grand National	1837	Aintree, Liverpool	7.2 km (4¹/2 miles)
Cheltenham Gold Cup	1924	Cheltenham, Gloucs	5.2 km (3¹/2 miles)
Champion Hurdle	1927	Cheltenham, Gloucs	3.2 km (2 miles)

Equestrian sports

There are three main branches of equestrian sports: showjumping, three-day eventing and dressage, each with individual and team competitions. In all equestrian events, riders must wear formal dress.

Dressage This competition tests a horse's obedience and the rider's control. It comprises a series of set movements by the horse at walk, trot and canter gaits. Each movement is judged for balance and harmony between horse and rider, and smooth transitions from one pace or movement into the next. Olympic rules decree that none of the dressage movements can be tricks – each must be a natural movement for the horse.

Three-day event This tests the abilities of a horse and rider in dressage, cross-country and showjumping. Competitors do not win points, but incur penalty points. The winners have the fewest penalty points at the end. In dressage, each rider and horse are required to perform a prescribed set of 20 movements. The cross-country event comprises four parts: two road and track sections; one steeplechase; and one cross-country course with up to 35 obstacles. Showjumping features 10–12 obstacles designed to test a horse's stamina and agility after the previous demands of the competition.

2000 Olympic Games

Individual competition	Gold medallist	Horse	Nation
Showjumping	Jeroen Dubbeldam	Sjiem	Netherlands
Dressage	Anky van Grunsven	Bonfire	Netherlands
Three-day event	David O'Connor	Custom Made	USA

Team competition	Gold medallist
Showjumping	Germany
Dressage	Germany
Three-day event	Australia

Showjumping This involves riding a horse over a course which typically incorporates 15-20 obstacles (including triple bars, parallel rails, water jumps and walls) within a specified time. The winning competitor is the rider with the fewest number of penalties, or 'faults', given for knocking down or refusing to jump fences. In the event of a tie, another round of the course, or 'jump-off', is conducted.

Showjumping arena This 120 x 80 m (394 x 262 ft) field contains five categories of jumps, each designed to test different aspects of horse and rider's skill and athleticism.

Combination Two or three jumps (elements) set a stride or two apart.

Vertical An upright gate or fence that tests precision and agility.

Wall No higher than 1.7 m (5 ft 8 in), this is built to look like real brick or stone.

Water jump A low hedge or fence followed by shallow water that may be up to 4.5 m (15 ft) wide.

Start

Spread A wide fence that requires power from a horse to stretch across the gap, and control in order to get back into its rhythm before the next jump.

Finish

LEGENDS

Mark Todd
(1956–) New Zealander

Todd won the individual three-day event gold medal at the 1984 and 1988 Olympic Games, and helped New Zealand to win the three-day event team title at the World Championships in 1990. He won individual golds for three-day eventing at several Badminton and Burghley horse trials.

LEGENDS

Alwin Schockemöhle
(1937–) German

Alwin Schockemöhle won his first Olympic gold medal for showjumping in 1960 with the German team; his second came in 1976, this time an individual gold. He completed the 1976 Olympic final with zero faults, making him one of only three people ever to achieve this.

The global economy

The global economy

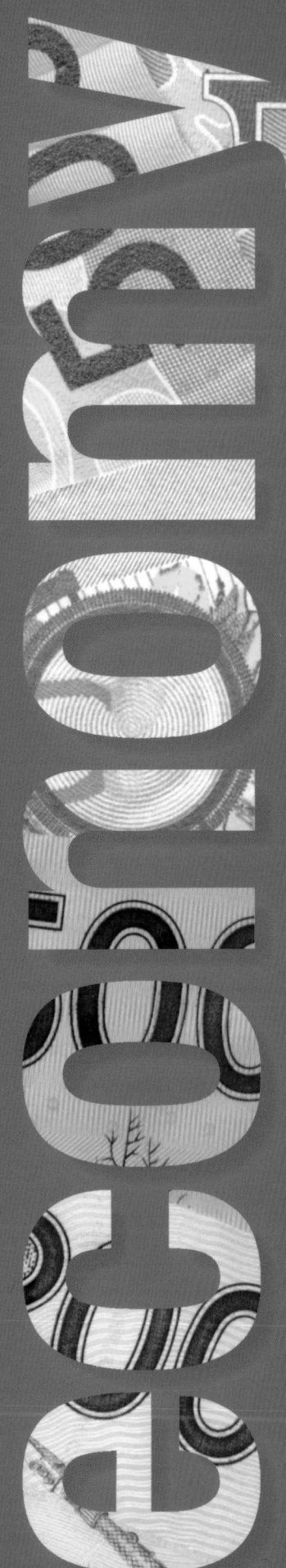

The global economy

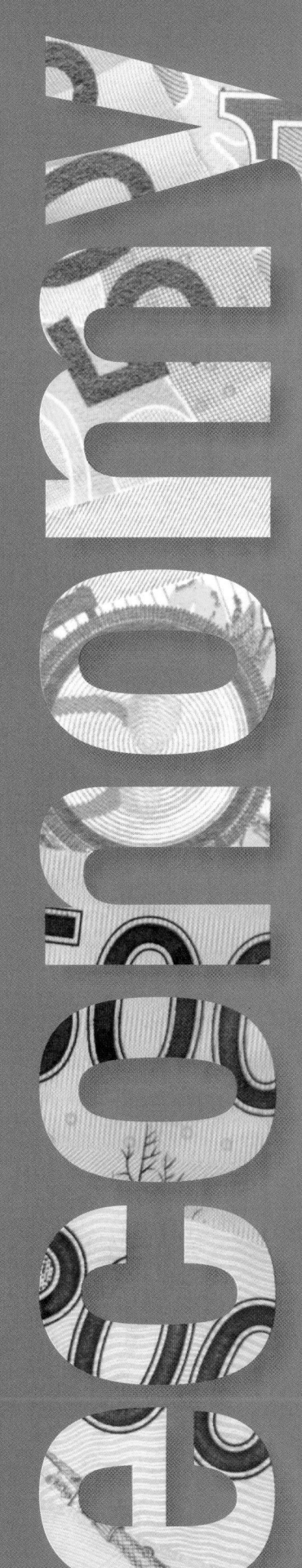
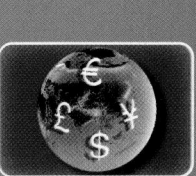

Wealth map of the world ▶

The wealth of a country can be measured by calculating its gross domestic product (GDP) – the total market value of the goods and services it produces during a year. The ten biggest economies, measured by GDP, control most of the world's trade, making them wealthier than other nations. Organisations such as the World Bank and United Nations move capital in the form of loans or aid from rich to poor countries in an effort to raise global standards of living.

THE MEASUREMENT OF WEALTH

The figures added together to create GDP include the monetary value of a country's spending (government and private), investment goods (capital in the form of machines, factories and houses) and net exports (the value of exports minus the value of imports). Exports include earnings from goods, such as cars or food, and services, such as insurance and freight transport.

Governments keep track of their country's income and outlay in a current account. Borrowing foreign funds for investment in domestic industry leads to economic growth, raising national income in the longer term.

Standards of living A country's standard of living is calculated by dividing its GDP by its population figure, to give a figure for GDP per person. If GDP grows at a higher rate than the population, the income per person is higher and living standards are said to be rising; if the population grows faster than the GDP, living standards are falling.

Economic development Around 75 per cent of the world's population live in developing countries – countries that are working towards improved living standards but have yet to achieve economically viable levels of industrial production. International agencies such as the United Nations and the World Bank encourage economic growth in developing countries, transferring capital from developed economies in two ways: through technical and medical aid, and through loans for investment in health, education and facilities such as roads and airports.

Projects have met with mixed success. Financial aid for building projects has often been tied to design and construction companies from developed countries, preventing local people from gaining employment and training. Loans have been wasted by poor planning, and unscrupulous heads of state have used the money to buy luxuries or arms from developed countries. A few developing countries, such as China, India and South Korea, have used loans more successfully, and transformed their economies during the last half of the 20th century by increasing trade.

THE DISTRIBUTION OF WEALTH

The map below gives a guide to global wealth. The higher the GDP per capita, the higher the standard of living. The 13 richest countries (those with the highest national GDPs) and Russia are ranked in terms of industrial output.

GDP per capita (in US dollars)

More than 18 000

10 000–18 000

4000–10 000

1000–4000

Less than 1000

Canada
8 GDP: $638 billion
10 Industrial output: $177 billion
Goods export: 4.06 per cent of world total
Services export: 2.01 per cent of world total
Total imports: $220 183 million
Current account balance:
−$11.2 billion

USA
1 GDP: $9178 billion
1 Industrial output: $2055 billion
Goods export: 15.32 per cent of world total
Services export: 20.26 per cent of world total
Total imports $1059 million
Current account balance:
−$220.6 billion

Brazil
10 GDP: $519 billion
8 Industrial output: $223 billion
Visible exports: 1.05 per cent of world total
Invisible exports: 0.49 per cent of world total
Total imports: $52 059 million
Current account balance:
−$33.8 billion

World debt

In the early 1980s, world recession and high interest rates lowered export earnings, leaving many developing countries unable to keep up with loan repayments. When oil prices fell in 1985, oil-producing nations began struggling to meet repayments on loans originally taken out during the 1970s oil boom. At the end of the 20th century, repayments had to be rescheduled over longer periods.

Highest foreign debts in millions of US dollars, 1999

1	Brazil	244 673	6	Argentina	147 880	11	Poland	54 268
2	Russia	173 940	7	South Korea	129 784	12	Philippines	52 022
3	Mexico	166 960	8	Turkey	101 796	13	Malaysia	45 939
4	China	154 223	9	Thailand	96 335	14	Chile	37 762
5	Indonesia	150 096	10	India	94 393	15	Venezuela	35 852

UK
4 GDP: $1463 billion
5 Industrial output: $392 billion
Goods export: 5.57 per cent of world total
Services export: 10.98 per cent of world total
Total imports $317 968 million
Current account balance:
−$0.8 billion

Spain
9 GDP: $588 billion
9 Industrial output: $178 billion
Goods export: 2.30 per cent of world total
Services export: 2.48 per cent of world total
Total imports: $144 436 million
Current account balance:
−$1.6 billion

France
5 GDP: $1445 billion*
6 Industrial output: $381 billion
Goods export: 5.56 per cent of world total
Services export: 5.76 per cent of world total
Total imports $216 621 million
Current account balance:
+$40.2 billion
(*including overseas départements)

Italy
6 GDP: $1176 billion
7 Industrial output: $359 billion
Goods export: 4.33 per cent of world total
Services export: 4.63 per cent of world total
Total imports: $216 621 million
Current account balance:
+$20.0 billion

Germany
3 GDP: $2149 billion
3 Industrial output: $695 billion
Goods export: 9.64 per cent of world total
Services export: 6.34 per cent of world total
Total imports: $472 161 million
Current account balance:
−$3.4 billion

Russia
24 GDP: $190 billion
12 Industrial output: $116 billion
Goods export: 1.28 per cent of world total
Services export: 0.67 per cent of world total
Total imports: $40 429 million
Current account balance:
+$2.1 billion

South Korea
12 GDP: $395 billion
11 Industrial output: $171 billion
Goods export: 2.15 per cent of world total
Services export: 1.09 per cent of world total
Total imports: $119 750 million
Current account balance:
+$40.6 billion

Japan
2 GDP: $4368 billion
2 Industrial output: $1513 billion
Goods export: 6.03 per cent of world total
Services export: 10.60 per cent of world total
Total imports: $311 262 million
Current account balance:
+$120.7 billion

China
7 GDP: $994 billion
4 Industrial output: $453 billion
Goods export: 3.09 per cent of world total
Services export: 1.15 per cent of world total
Total imports: $165 788 million
Current account balance:
+$29.3 billion

Australia
13 GDP: $390 billion
15 Industrial output: $101 billion
Goods export: 1.13 per cent of world total
Services export: 0.88 per cent of world total
Total imports: $69 135 million
Current account balance:
−$18.1 billion

India
11 GDP: $468 billion
13 Industrial output: $107 billion
Goods export: 0.76 per cent of world total
Services export: 0.53 per cent of world total
Total imports: $44 889 million
Current account balance:
−$6.9 billion

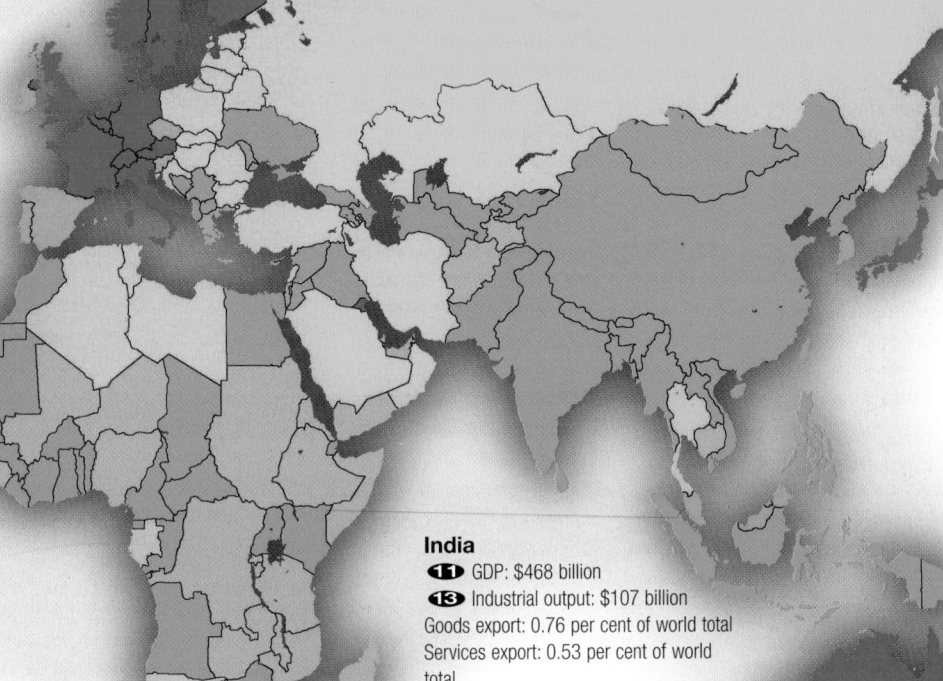

The Human Development Index

The Human Development Index is produced annually by the UN. It measures economic development in terms of the improvement of quality of life, combining statistics for GDP per capita, life expectancy, education and adult literacy. On a scale of 1 to 100, development falls into three categories: high (80 to 100), medium (50 to 80) and low (below 50).

Highest (1998)	
Canada	93.5
Norway	93.4
United States	92.9
Australia	92.9
Iceland	92.7
Sweden	92.6
Belgium	92.5
Netherlands	92.5
Japan	92.4
United Kingdom	91.8

Medium	
Ecuador	72.2
Jordan	72.1
Armenia	72.1
Albania	71.3

Lowest	
Ethiopia	30.9
Burkina Faso	30.3
Niger	29.3
Sierra Leone	25.2

see also
456-7 **International finance**
458-9 **Money and markets**
460-1 **Trade and banking**
462-3 **Principles of economics**

The international financial system is managed by monetary organisations and governments. They issue currency and regulate its exchange between countries. Since the 1960s, with the growth of computer technology, exchanging currencies has become faster and easier. This has enabled businesses and individuals hoping to raise capital or to invest large sums of money to look abroad for the best deal.

MANAGING INTERNATIONAL CURRENCIES

Purchasing goods or services in a foreign country usually requires payment in the local currency. At some point, travellers must exchange their own national currency for that of the country they are visiting. In order for this exchange to be fair, the international financial system sets globally acceptable rates of exchange between currencies.

Exchange rates The exchange rate is the ratio at which a country's units of currency can be exchanged for units of another country's currency. A favourable rate of exchange makes more foreign money available per unit of domestic money. In this situation, the domestic currency will be in demand in other countries, and is said to be 'strong'. Factors which attract foreign confidence in a currency and contribute to its strength include political stability, a low rate of inflation – which keeps prices low – and higher-than-average interest rates, which give a good rate of return on foreign investments.

Reserve currencies Currencies which attract long-term international confidence are known as reserve currencies, because governments and financial institutions worldwide build up supplies to use in international trade. The key reserve currency is the US dollar, which finances more than 50 per cent of the world's trade.

Keeping control A strong currency can have disadvantages as well as benefits. A favourable rate of exchange means that people can purchase more imported goods and services for their money than domestic products. As the market for domestic products shrinks, fewer manufacturing staff are required, and unemployment rises.

To avoid this problem, national governments try to keep their currencies stable. Methods of controlling a strong currency include limiting imports or imposing tariffs on them, and lowering interest rates. This drives investors abroad, lowers the value of the domestic currency against other currencies and stimulates exports.

Malaysian stock market There are almost 50 financial markets around the world, mostly concentrated in developed or rapidly developing countries.

THE MAJOR FINANCIAL MARKETS

In 1992 the global capital markets were estimated to be worth $35 trillion – by 1999 the figure had risen to more than $80 trillion. The domestic and international finances of the largest global centre, New York, were valued at almost $17 billion at the end of 1999. The numbered symbols on the map below show the rankings of the main cities of the international financial system in specific areas of financial management. The clocks show the time differences between them.

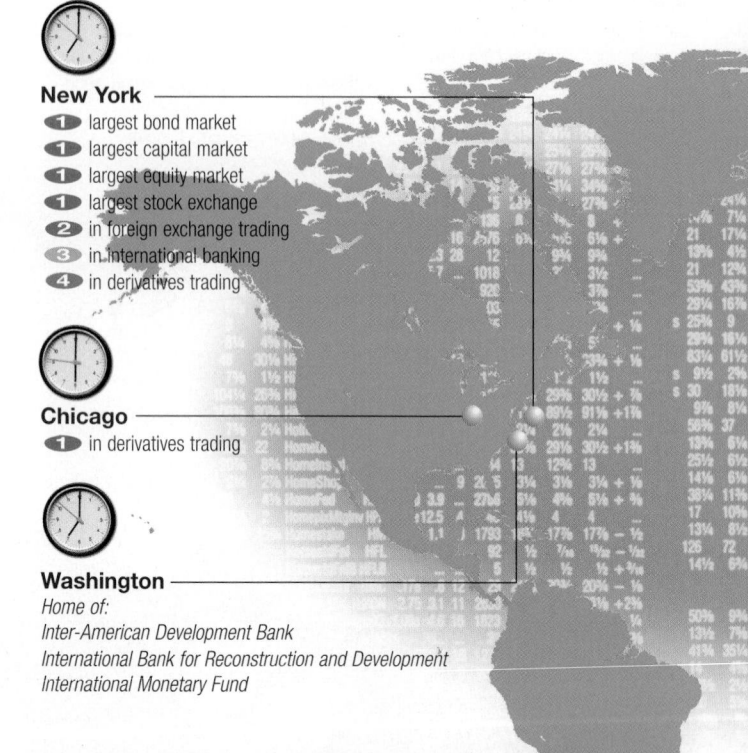

New York
- ① largest bond market
- ① largest capital market
- ① largest equity market
- ① largest stock exchange
- ② in foreign exchange trading
- ③ in international banking
- ④ in derivatives trading

Chicago
- ① in derivatives trading

Washington
Home of:
Inter-American Development Bank
International Bank for Reconstruction and Development
International Monetary Fund

The Big Mac index

In the 1980s, the *Economist* magazine in London launched the Big Mac index as a way of comparing the purchasing power of the world's currencies. A Big Mac is a good indicator because it is one of the few products which is identical the world over. In the United States in April 2001, $2.54 would buy you a McDonald's Big Mac. In Switzerland, the same burger cost the equivalent of US$3.65; in Malaysia, it cost just US$1.19. In other words, you could purchase more for your dollar in Malaysia than in the USA, and considerably more than in Switzerland. If a currency has a higher purchasing power in its own country than elsewhere (making a Big Mac cheap), it is said to be undervalued: you need to spend more of it to buy the same thing in other countries. If the currency buys less in its own country than elsewhere (making a Big Mac expensive), it is overvalued.

The price of a Big Mac, April 2001
Showing percentage under or overvalued against US$

	US$	%		US$	%
United States	*2.54*	*0*			
Australia	1.52	−40	Japan	2.38	−6
Canada	2.14	−16	Malaysia	1.19	−53
China	1.20	−53	Russia	1.21	−52
Denmark	2.93	+15	Switzerland	3.65	+44
Euro area	2.27	−11	United Kingdom	2.85	+12

London
Leading global financial centre
Home of European Bank for Reconstruction and Development
- 1 in eurobonds
- 1 largest European futures and options exchange
- 1 in foreign exchange trading
- 1 insurance centre
- 1 in international banking
- 2 in derivatives trading
- 3 largest stock exchange

Frankfurt
Leading European financial centre
Home of European Central Bank
- 3 in derivatives trading
- 4 in international banking

Geneva
Home of World Trade Organisation

Basel
Home of Bank for International Settlements
- 6 in foreign exchange trading

Paris
Home of OECD
- 5 in derivatives trading
- 7 in international banking

Hong Kong
- 2 largest Asia-Pacific financial centre
- 2 largest Asian stock market
- 2 in foreign exchange trading
- 4 in international banking

Taiwan
- 3 largest Asian stock market

Tokyo
- 1 largest Asia-Pacific financial centre
- 1 largest Asian stock market
- 2 largest stock exchange
- 2 largest capital market
- 2 in international banking
- 3 in foreign exchange trading

Manila
Home of Asian Development Bank

Singapore
- 3 largest Asia-Pacific financial centre
- 4 in foreign exchange trading
- 5 in international banking

see also

326-7 **International organisations**
328-9 **European institutions**
454-5 **Wealth map of the world**
460-1 **Trade and banking**

KEY TERMS

● **Capital market** The trade in government and company securities (documents of ownership of financial assets, such as bonds and shares) to raise finance for long-term political or business plans.

● **Derivatives** Financial products which take on the monetary risk associated with buying and selling. For example, *futures* – which allow the purchase or sale of a product or asset at a fixed price before delivery to avoid later price or exchange rate fluctuations, and *swaps* – which switch fluctuating interest rates to fixed rates, or vice versa, to minimise liabilities.

● **Equities** Ownership rights to companies, such as shares, which yield dividends (payments drawn from profits).

● **Eurobonds** Bonds or cash held outside the country which issued them. The USA began using this European concept in the 1970s, depositing dollars outside the country (Eurodollars) to avoid domestic financial regulations.

The euro

The introduction of the euro in 12 European states between 1999 and 2002 eliminated exchange rates between member countries. The single currency aimed to stabilise prices and cut the cost of financial transactions, creating a currency able to compete against the US dollar. Its predicted downside was its inability to cope with economic problems in single countries. Previously that had been dealt with by stabilising national currencies.

Global financial institutions

The international financial system is regulated by organisations which work towards raising the global standard of living. The following institutions promote global trading and financial communications, and stimulate the economies of underdeveloped countries.

Asian Development Bank (ADB) Founded 1966. Stimulates economic growth in Asia and the Far East through loans and technical assistance.

Bank for International Settlements (BIS) Founded 1930. Made up of the directors of the central banks of the main trading states, which facilitates financial settlements and undertakes economic research.

European Bank for Reconstruction and Development (EBRD) Founded 1991. Assists economic reform in Central and Eastern Europe.

European Central Bank (ECB) Founded 1998. Sets interest rates for the euro.

Inter-American Development Bank (IDB) Founded 1959. Finances economic and social development in the Americas.

International Bank for Reconstruction and Development (IBRD) (World Bank) Founded 1945. Provides long-term investment, technical aid and economic advice to developing countries.

International Monetary Fund (IMF) Founded 1947. A United Nations agency which promotes monetary cooperation, world trade and foreign exchange stability. Finances loans to member countries experiencing financial difficulties.

Organisation for Economic Cooperation and Development (OECD) Founded 1961. Promotes international agreement on economic and social policies among member countries, with the aim of achieving economic growth and high employment.

World Trade Organisation (WTO) Founded 1995. Administers international trade agreements, resolves disputes and reduces trade barriers.

Money evolved as a more convenient way of exchanging goods than barter. Early coins were valued for their precious-metal content. Today's currency is worth little in itself, but is accepted as a means of payment by government order. New methods of payment led to the growth of the money markets, which trade items of monetary value, from currency and gold to shares in companies and bonds – certificates of debt.

WHAT IS MONEY?

Money is a universally accepted medium of exchange for goods and services. It is quicker and easier to use than bartering. Barter is inefficient because it involves finding someone who is selling what you want and who wants what you have for sale. It also requires the creation of a complex system of comparative values between different types of goods.

Metal coins have endured as a medium of exchange since the 8th century BC because they have many convenient characteristics:

● Metal can be shaped into small denominations, making coins portable and suitable for small transactions.
● The precious metals originally used in coin manufacture gave them a high intrinsic value relative to their size and weight.
● Coins are durable, and recyclable – they can be melted down and restruck.
● Branded metal discs are difficult to counterfeit.

For larger transactions, the exchange of paper money proved more convenient. Paper notes represented a promise by the issuer to pay the bearer a certain value in gold or silver, and became widespread in the 18th century.

The link between hard currency and precious metal began to disappear after the First World War. Gold exports had been restricted during the war, and natural resources were dwindling. Many bank clients did not require access to gold, and it became unnecessary for banks to maintain huge reserves to back up their currency. The 'promise to pay' is no longer valid – most modern currency is not backed by precious metal. It derives its value from a fiat – a government order which declares it legal tender – and is known as fiat money.

Today, the purchase of goods and services does not rely on hard currency. Cheques, originating from 17th-century banker's orders, and credit cards, a 20th-century invention, have made payment without cash easy and efficient.

Changing faces Since the Middle Ages, money has progressed from pure gold to plastic. A 16th-century Spanish doubloon contrasts with a Diner's Club card – the world's first credit card. In 1951, the Diner's Club issued the card to 200 customers, who could use it to pay at 27 restaurants in New York.

| Before 1000 BC | c.800–500 BC | AD 1100 | 1500 |

Early money
Decorative tools and weapons and objects of religious and ceremonial significance are widely accepted as payment.

In Europe, metal rings and spirals are exchanged between traders.

In India, China and the Middle East, cowrie shells are exchanged as a form of payment. As trade develops, the use of cowrie shells circulates around Asia, Africa and the Pacific Islands.

Metal money
The first coins with values fixed by their country of issue appear. Chinese traders exchange copper discs. In Lydia (modern Turkey), merchants strike high-value coins from electrum, an alloy of gold and silver.

7th century BC Aegean city-states issue precious-metal coins bearing state emblems.

6th century BC The first pure gold and silver coins are produced in Lydia, each with a guaranteed weight and stamped with the insignia of King Croesus.

International systems
Bills of exchange – written promises to pay at a future date – are issued by merchants and banks to provide credit for trade. In France, bills of exchange are traded, a practice which contributes to the later emergence of the stock exchange.

1252 The city of Florence mints *fiorini d'oro* (gold flowers) – gold coins bearing the image of a lily. Their use in international trade makes them valuable across Europe. Outside Italy, they are known as florins.

Capital markets
Joint-stock companies appear when multiple owners subscribe capital to fund a new business. The companies are chartered by European heads of state to explore and colonise new territory.

1555 English merchants trading in Russia form the first joint-stock company, The Muscovy Company. Each merchant owns a share of the company's assets and profits.

1600 The joint-stock East India Company is formed to trade in East and South-east Asia.

Modern-day barter
A travelling merchant presents his wares to the market overseer in Sokoto, Nigeria, where gold and kola nuts are exchanged for weapons and salt, sold in the form of cones (foreground).

Medieval desk job Italian tellers wait for custom in a 14th-century bank. In the Middle Ages, trade in wheat and wool made Italy wealthy.

MONEY MARKETS

Institutions which buy and sell currency and short-term finance are known as money markets. Market dealers trade in gold bullion, foreign currency and short-term securities – documents which guarantee the later repayment of a debt or claim, such as bonds or stocks and shares.

Gold bullion market Bars or ingots of gold are mainly traded for use in the manufacture of coins, industrial components and jewellery. The major bullion markets are in Hong Kong, London and New York.

Foreign exchange market Foreign exchange dealers buy and sell currencies. The US dollar is the main medium of exchange: currencies are exchanged for dollars, which are then exchanged for another currency.

Securities market The buying and selling of securities takes place in **stock exchanges**. Deals are administered by brokers, who buy and sell on behalf of clients and charge a commission for their services. The world's largest stock exchanges are in London, New York and Tokyo.

On-screen trading In 1983 the Toronto stock exchange introduced electronic trading, giving members instant access to trade information on computer screens. By 1985 Toronto had forged trading links across North America. The system was adopted worldwide, accelerating trade and widening its scope.

Key terms

Bonds Certificates of government or corporate debt which will be repaid at a fixed interest rate after a fixed period of time.

Stocks and shares Shares are portions of capital subscribed in return for part ownership of a company. Stocks are groups of shares; in Britain, the term can refer specifically to fixed interest loans made to companies, local authorities or governments.

FACT The first stock exchanges appeared in Antwerp (1531), Hamburg (1558) and Amsterdam (1611). The London stock exchange opened in 1773, and New York's in 1817.

Valueless money In the 1920s, the German government printed money in an effort to fulfil wartime reparation payments. As the country's stock of currency rose, so did prices. In 1923, inflation reached a peak of 332 per cent per month, rendering the German currency worthless.

see also
454-5 **Wealth map of the world**
456-7 **International finance**
460-1 **Trade and banking**
462-3 **Principles of economics**

1657 | **1700** | **1920s** | **1975**

Banking and paper money
The Bank of Stockholm begins operating – the first bank to be founded with a lending department. In 1661 it issues Europe's first banknotes. In 1664, bad debts drive the bank into insolvency.

1668 The demise of the Bank of Stockholm leads to the formation of the world's first central bank – the state-owned Bank of Sweden.

1694 The Bank of England is founded, and helps to establish the City of London as a centre of global financial activity.

Bursting bubble
Lack of regulation encourages French and British joint-stock companies to engineer wild speculation in their shares by promising rich rewards to investors.

1720 Britain's South Sea Company offers shares to the public. The company encourages rumours of enormous future profit, bribing politicians to promote the business. The share price rises from £128 in January to £1000 in August. In September, investors lose confidence in the deal – the bubble bursts and share prices crash.

Market crash
Easy credit in 1920s USA drives investors to borrow to buy stocks. Share values climb steeply.

1929 The USA's central banking regulator, the Federal Reserve, brings the financial speculation to an end by tightening credit.

October 24, 1929: Black Thursday Investors lose confidence and begin selling shares; the following Tuesday, the market collapses. The USA calls in its international loans, and European banks close, unable to fulfil their obligations. Private investors withdraw their savings, leading to a worldwide economic crisis.

Deregulation
May 1: May Day The New York stock exchange abolishes fixed commission charges for brokers, allowing them to negotiate competitive rates.

October 1986: Big Bang The London stock exchange abolishes fixed charges for brokers. Its unique system of jobbers (who buy and sell shares) and brokers (who liaise between jobbers and the public) ends when the two jobs are merged. This allows brokers to deal directly in shares, and promotes market growth.

Gold standard

Until 1937, the monetary systems of many countries followed a common standard, under which the basic unit of currency was equal to a fixed weight of gold. Each coin or banknote in circulation had to be backed by an equivalent value of gold kept in the vaults of the central bank. Gold had a common value in all countries, making the exchange of payments easier.

Britain introduced the gold standard in 1821. By 1900, most of the world's leading economies had joined. It was suspended during the First World War, and gradually abandoned after the Great Depression of 1929.

Almost 80 per cent of the world's goods and services are produced by one-sixth of its people – who bank 80 per cent of the world's wealth. The trading of surplus goods and services finances future production, lowering costs, creating economic growth and raising the national income. A country's prosperity can be measured, in part, by the strength and size of its banking system.

WHY TRADE?

Few countries could retain a good standard of living without international trade. Using domestic raw materials alone, each country could only produce a limited selection of goods. World trade makes a vast diversity of raw materials available – from Middle Eastern oil to timber grown in the forests of Norway. It also allows the wide distribution of the different types of goods manufactured in different countries. Trade also benefits domestic industry:

◖ Money flows in from payments for exported goods and services.
◖ Imported raw materials stimulate domestic production and the export of manufactured goods.
◖ Increased industrial production expands service industries in areas such as banking, goods transport and insurance.
◖ Employment rises as industries hire labour to keep up with the expansion in goods and services.

Prosperity through specialisation Countries take advantage of local raw materials and specialist skills to produce particular types of goods. For example, Indonesia specialises in timber and wood products, Japan in electronic goods. When raw materials and skills are easily available, the average cost of production lowers and productivity rises, leading to a goods surplus. The surplus can be traded for products from other countries that would be expensive to produce at home. In this way, international trade lowers the cost of production worldwide, the average worker can buy more goods for his or her money, and standards of living improve.

Protectionism versus free trade

Protectionism
To protect domestic industry against foreign competition, governments create trade barriers. Barriers include *tariffs* – customs duties or taxes levied on imports to raise their selling price, and *quotas* – limits on the quantity of imports of certain goods.

Pros
◖ Domestic producers have less competition.
◖ The country's balance of trade (profits earned from the sale of goods) improves.
◖ New domestic industries can be protected until they become established.

Cons
◖ Other nations retaliate with trade barriers.
◖ Some domestic industries become monopolies.
◖ Consumers face fewer choices and higher prices.

Free trade
Trading goods between countries without trade barriers increases world production. The World Trade Organisation, established in 1995, works towards the global removal of barriers.

Pros
◖ Exports increase, stimulating industrial output.
◖ Consumers enjoy a wider selection of goods, many at lower prices.
◖ Countries become increasingly specialised in the type of goods and services they produce.

Cons
◖ Imports may exceed exports, so money flows out to pay for foreign goods.
◖ If particular goods can be produced more cheaply in other countries, domestic industries suffer through competition from lower-priced imports.

International trading cooperation

Free trade is easier to sustain across associations of countries rather than across the world. Two main types of free trade association exist:

Free trade area An association of countries which agrees to remove tariffs, quotas and export incentives in trade with members, while maintaining tariffs and quotas against non-member countries. One example is the North American Free Trade Association, formed by Canada, the USA and Mexico in 1994.

Customs union An association of countries which agrees to remove trade barriers between members and erects a common tariff against non-members. The European Union (EU), founded in 1993, is an example of a customs union. It has common commercial, agricultural, security and transport policies between members, in addition to free trade.

BANKING

BANKING

In most countries, the flow of money is controlled by a central bank, which supports a system of commercial banks, investment banks and universal banks.

Central banks hold reserve stocks of gold and foreign currencies, and support commercial banks by providing short-term advances when a bank's reserves are low. They also transfer gold and currency to and from other central banks and international financial institutions. The main aim of a central bank is to keep employment and production high and stabilise prices by regulating monetary conditions. Their methods include:
- Controlling the money supply by issuing notes, buying or selling government securities, and managing national debt.
- Advising government on money supply, rates of interest, exchange and inflation.
- Setting national interest rates.
- Intervening in the money markets to stabilise the exchange rate of the national currency.

Commercial banks deal with the public at local branches through cheque accounts – taking deposits, making loans and exchanging foreign currency. They are businesses, set up to make a profit. Commercial banks are also known as retail, deposit or credit banks. In the USA they are also called member banks (referring to membership of the central Federal Reserve Board).

Investment banks deal in shares and bonds, advising clients on how and when to issue them and underwriting their issue (promising to pay for any unpurchased shares or bonds). They do not take deposits from the public. In the UK, investment banks are known as issuing houses or merchant banks.

Universal banks combine the functions of commercial and investment banks, taking deposits from and making loans to the public, and underwriting securities. They also offer insurance, asset management and financial advice.

Influential central banks

Federal Reserve Board (USA) Founded in 1913; based in Washington, D.C. Known as 'The Fed'. Determines the policy of 12 regional central banks (federal reserve banks) across the USA, making it the largest central banking body in the world. Accountable to US Congress.

Bank of England (Britain) Founded in 1694; based in London. The most influential bank of the 18th century: became a model for other central banks. Privately owned until 1946, when it was nationalised. Assumed independent responsibility for setting interest rates in 1997.

Deutsche Bundesbank (Germany) Founded in 1875; based in Frankfurt. Germany's central bank and the most important bank in the euro zone. State controlled until 1945: now independent. Operates through nine Land Central Banks in Germany.

International commercial banks

In the 1960s, banks began to establish overseas agencies, offices, and branches. Today, the number of foreign commercial banks in a city's financial district is a measure of its stature in world trade. The presence of more than 500 foreign commercial banks in London by the mid-1990s indicated the City's wide financial influence.

International commercial banks are known as wholesale banks because they deal with financial institutions such as large corporate customers and government agencies. They finance import and export through bills of exchange, lend to overseas clients, and deal in the global currency markets.

The world's largest banks

Large bank reserves are a sign of high industrial output and a growing economy. In the 1960s, the USA's banks were the largest, worldwide. By the 1980s, high productivity allowed Japan to take over this position. After a pronounced economic recession in Japan in the 1990s, American banks resumed their status as the dominant force in international banking.

Capital (billion US$), 1999

1	Citicorp	USA	41.9
2	BankAmerica Corp	USA	36.9
3	HSBC Holdings	Britain	29.4
4	Crédit Agricole	France	25.9
5	Chase Manhattan Corp	USA	25.1
6	Industrial and Commercial Bank of China	China	22.2
7	Bank of Tokyo-Mitsubishi	Japan	22.1
8	UBS	Switzerland	20.5
9	Sakura Bank	Japan	20.0
10	Bank One Corp	USA	19.7

Balance of payments

Just as commercial firms balance their books annually, the government of each country produces an annual balance of payments account recording its transactions with foreign countries. This has two components: the current account and the capital account. The sum of these two balances is always zero.

- **Current account** Four figures make up the balance of the current account:
  - The monetary difference between imports and exports (known as the balance of trade).
  - Earnings from services (such as insurance, shipping and tourism), minus payments made for services.
  - Investment income – earnings from investments in foreign countries.
  - Transfers – payments from the government to individuals (such as welfare allowances, subsidies).

- **Capital account** A record of transactions involved in capital purchases – for example, the private or government purchase of securities or industrial equipment.

FACT The Bank of England was established by 1268 merchants to finance a £1.2 million loan to William III, to pay for his wars against France. The king paid 8 per cent interest on his loan.

Economics investigates the production, distribution and consumption of wealth. Microeconomics looks at individuals, groups of consumers, companies and industries, while macroeconomics operates on a larger scale, studies the global economy and the complex internal and external interaction of countries or communities of states with common economic policies, such as the European Union.

The basic economic problems

At the heart of economics is the idea that economic resources (land, skilled workers, fuel supplies and so on) are finite, while people's wants are infinite. Moreover, the availability of some resources is uneven, so while populations in developed countries have plentiful food supplies, the people in many developing countries starve.

Supply and demand The allocation of scarce resources takes place largely in the market, which is not so much a place as an arrangement between people wanting to sell goods or services and those who want to buy them, and who have an agreed means of exchange, such as money. The market is governed by the laws of supply and demand. Supply is the amount of a commodity that producers will supply at a certain price, and demand is the amount people are willing to buy at a given price. Producers can put an accurate price on the goods they sell by analysing supply and demand.

Where supply meets demand The example below shows the supply and demand data for a motor company producing a new vehicle. Analysis of supply shows that at a price of £5000 each, the company can viably produce 400 000 vehicles; at a price of only £2000, the number of vehicles goes down to 100 000. Analysis of demand, by contrast, shows that a price of £5000 will attract only 200 000 customers, whereas a price of £2000 will attract 400 000. There is just one 'equilibrium price': at £4000, the number of vehicles the company can economically produce at that price equals the number of vehicles customers are willing to buy at the same price.

BOOM AND SLUMP

Free market economies experience fluctuations in economic activity, known as booms and slumps. These often shadow each other in countries with similar economic systems. A boom is a long period of expansion – in which goods and services produced (the gross domestic product, GDP) increase – combined with a rise in employment, which raises the demand for goods. There are usually also increases in interest rates. The downside of a boom may be:

● **Inflation** This is a general rise in prices over a long period, which may be caused by increased demand, or by a rise in costs of the raw materials and labour. Typically, it would be followed by…

● **Deflation** If demand falls, because it is satisfied, or interrupted by some outside event, there may be a sustained fall in prices, which causes output to fall and unemployment to rise.

● **Stagflation** Employment may stagnate or fall while prices are rising. This occurred in Western economies during the 1970s.

● **Recession** A sudden, shortlived decline in economic activity. There may be a sharp fall in production and a rise in unemployment.

● **Depression** A more prolonged version of the latter, the most notable example of which was during the 1930s.

Fluctuations in GDP in the United States

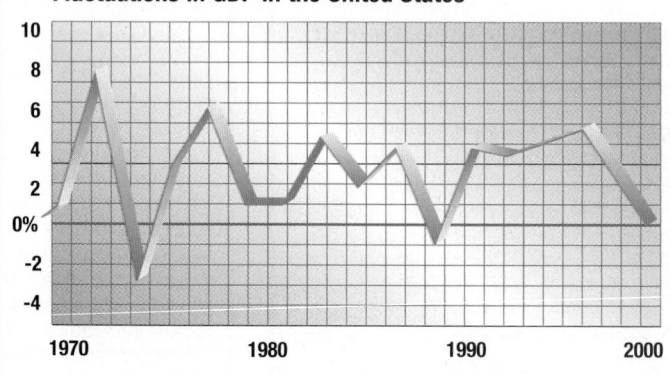

KEY TERMS

● **Capital** Any material wealth that can be used to produce further wealth (profit). Capital may exist in the form of money or property. Farms, factories, machinery, buildings and exchangeable notes and coins are all forms of capital.

● **Land** All natural resources owned by an individual, partnership, company or nation, including any part of the sea or outer space.

● **Money supply** An economy's stock of assets which can be exchanged for goods and services, including notes, coins, and bank deposits and accounts.

● **National income** The incomes of all residents of an economy added together.

● **Reserves** The total amount of foreign currency and gold kept by a country for the settlement of foreign debts in the eventuality of them being called in.

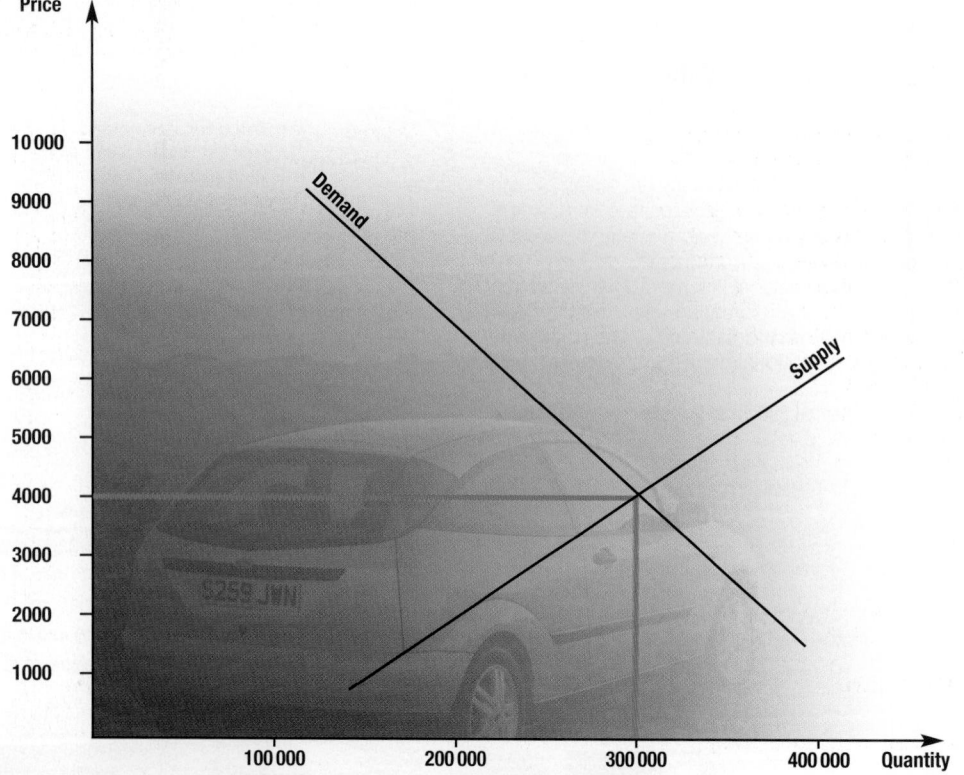

Key economic theories

Economic theorists do two things – analyse the system, like scientists, and come up with ways of changing and improving it, like politicians. The story of economic thought is a story of that process of observation and intervention. Some economists do one or the other, while some try to do both.

Mercantilism
Key idea: Government should intervene in economic activity to increase national wealth.

Laissez-faire
Key idea: The economy is self-regulating and government should leave it alone.

Malthusian economics
Key idea: Population increases faster than the increase in the output of food supplies.

Classical economics
Key idea: Knowledge of manufacturing and the role of labour are the key to understanding how society will develop.

Economic determinism
Key idea: The free market system is merely a stage in the process of economic development.

Macro-economics
Key idea: Putting a figure on the output of all factories, industries and other work units can help decision-making by government.

Technostructure
Key idea: Modern economies produce ever larger corporations which operate as monopolistic power systems.

Monetarism
Key idea: An increase in the supply of money is a major cause of inflation.

Gerard Malines
(1586–1641)
English merchant and government official. Published *The Centre of the Circle of Commerce* (1623).
His arguments:
- Import tariffs should be raised and gold bullion exports banned.
- Government should control foreign currency dealing.

Adam Smith
(1723–90)
Scottish professor of philosophy. Published *An Inquiry into the Wealth of Nations* (1776).
His arguments:
- The self-interest of ordinary people can contribute to the wealth of the economy.
- Division of labour: productivity is increased by specialisation.

Thomas Malthus
(1766–1834)
English parson and mathematician. Published *Essay on the Principle of Population* (1798).
His arguments:
- An exploding population will result in mass starvation.
- Individual restraint on the size of families is the only way to avert catastrophe.

David Ricardo
(1772–1823)
European financial market trader. Published *Principles of Political Economy and Taxation* (1817).
His arguments:
- The value of all goods derives from the effort put into producing them.
- A theoretical model of the economy needs to be built in order to study it.

Karl Marx
(1818–83)
German journalist and philosopher. Published *Das Kapital (Capital)* (1867).
His arguments:
- Industrialisation concentrates capital in the hands of fewer and larger firms.
- Workers are not paid; they choose to sell their services to an employer.

John Maynard Keynes
(1883–1946)
English mathematician. Published *A General Theory of Employment, Interest and Money* (1936).
His arguments:
- There is no inherent tendency for unemployment to fall.
- Spending on public works can generate an economic upturn.

John Kenneth Galbraith
(1908–)
American. Published *American Capitalism* (1952).
His arguments:
- Large companies become preoccupied with their own survival.
- Advanced economies create false demands.

Milton Friedman
(1912–)
American. Published *Inflation, Causes and Consequence* (1963).
His arguments:
- Control of the money supply is needed to control inflation.
- High pay is industry's reward to risk-takers.

see also
454-5 **Wealth map of the world**
456-7 **International finance**
458-9 **Money and markets**
460-1 **Trade and banking**

TYPES OF ECONOMIC SYSTEM

Economies are classified according to whether a free market economy operates or whether there is state intervention. In practice, most countries' economies have a degree of both.
- **Free market economy** Minimal government control. The laws of supply and demand determine how the country's resources are allocated and to whom. This system is also called 'capitalism' because capital may be owned and controlled by any individual.
- **Mixed economy** An active private sector coexists with a degree of central planning. Entrepreneurs produce and sell goods according to the laws of supply and demand, and may own capital and employ workers. The state also owns capital and may own and operate industries or sectors, such as transport, education or the health system.
- **Planned economy** All economic resources – land, property, and capital – are owned by the state. The government plans how these resources, including labour, will be allocated, what farmers and factories will produce, and how and to whom the goods they produce will be distributed. This type of economy is called 'communist' because all capital is communally owned.

Estimated state intervention, per cent

Singapore USA UK Germany France Sweden China North Korea
0 10 20 30 40 50 60 70 80 90 100

Free market economy   **Mixed economy**   **Planned economy**

Economic activities

People produce wealth by selling goods or services. Economists group economic activities into three sectors (below). Most developing economies rely heavily on one primary-sector activity, while advanced economies range across all three.

Primary sector	Agriculture, Fishing, Mining and quarrying
Secondary sector	Manufacturing, Construction, Energy and water
Tertiary sector	Services (insurance, distribution, transport, education, healthcare)

The world produces enough food for everyone to receive an adequate diet, but food shortages and famines still occur. The main causes include overpopulation, particularly in India and China, drought, which has repeatedly occurred in sub-Saharan Africa, and war. Famines induced by human conflict have provoked international action to alleviate hunger, made possible by new agricultural practices and improvements in global communication.

THE GREEN REVOLUTION

Hunger became a global issue in the wake of the First and Second World Wars. International armed conflict disrupted food supplies, highlighting the need for an agency to ensure that every country could meet its food requirements. In 1945, the United Nations' Food and Agriculture Organisation (FAO) was established, with the intention of raising levels of food production and nutrition worldwide.

A new initiative

An acceleration in population growth after the Second World War reached its peak in the early 1960s. In 1963 the FAO launched the Green Revolution, aiming to provide enough food to cater for future population expansion. They developed higher-yielding varieties (HYVs) of cereals such as rice, wheat and corn through selective breeding (interbreeding different varieties to encourage desirable qualities). HYVs produced three crops annually on the same land. Farmers were also encouraged to use high levels of fertilisers and pesticides to improve yields.

By the 1980s, wheat and rice yields had increased dramatically; some developing countries produced a surplus for the first time. The increased income led to the mechanisation of more farms, further increasing yields. Agrochemical companies making fertilisers and pesticides grew into large businesses.

The disadvantages

Overall, wealthier farmers benefited from the initiative more than poorer ones, who were unable to afford the new HYV seeds, fertilisers and pesticides. Mechanisation led to unemployment, and repeated cropping damaged the soil. Chemical fertilisers and pesticides were found to be toxic to workers and caused pollution. Some authorities believe the answer to world food shortages now lies in a new revolution based on genetically modified (GM) crops.

Global calorie consumption

According to the United Nations, an average adult should consume a minimum of 2400 Calories per day to lead a healthy, active life. Those who are more active, or live in colder climates, require more calories than those who are less active, or live in the tropics. In countries where the average daily consumption is 2000 Calories or less (2000 Calories is equivalent to 2.2 kg/5 lb of potatoes or 1.4 kg/3 lb of rice), the majority of the population is chronically malnourished. Some 800 million people in the developing world do not get enough to eat. In the developed world, about 34 million people have poor diets and unreliable food supplies.

Calories consumed per day per person

- Over 3000
- 2800-3000
- 2600-2800
- 2400-2600
- 2200-2400
- 2000-2200
- Less than 2000

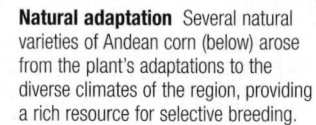

Human intervention Cross-fertilising strains of rice improves the crop's yield and disease resistance.

Genetically modified crops

Advances in biotechnology have made it possible to alter the genes of a plant so that it exhibits a particular characteristic. The desired gene is taken from one organism and inserted into another organism. For example, a gene conferring resistance to an insect pest can be transferred from a bacterium to maize.

Advantages
- Disease-resistant and pest-resistant GM crops reduce the need for chemical sprays.
- Crops are more productive, and the produce has a longer shelf-life.

Disadvantages
- The long-term effect on humans and the environment are unknown.
- The developing world, who would benefit the most from GM crops, cannot afford them.
- GM crops decrease biodiversity.

Natural adaptation Several natural varieties of Andean corn (below) arose from the plant's adaptations to the diverse climates of the region, providing a rich resource for selective breeding.

Worst famines of the 20th century

Most of the worst famines of the last century had a man-made cause. Although crop failure and distribution problems were contributory factors, lack of food has usually been connected to the disruptions to agriculture caused by unsuccessful government policies or war.

1921–3	**Russia**	The effects of a drought are exacerbated by the Bolshevik government, who order the surrender of rural grain supplies for consumption in the cities. Poverty and food shortages lead to the death of 6 million peasants.
1933–8	**Russia**	From 1929 to 1933, Stalin orders small farms to group into collectives, which are forced to supply grain to the government at low prices. Famine follows, resulting in 5 million deaths in the Caucasus and Ukraine.
1943	**Bengal**	As a result of wartime food shortages after the Japanese conquest of Burma, 1.5 million people die.
Late 1940s	**China**	Drought coupled with the disruptions caused by civil war between the Communists and Nationalists kills about 5 million.
1958–61	**China**	Around 20 million die as a result of Mao Ze-dong's 'Great Leap Forward', in which nationalisation of all farms, and experimental systems for planting crops, fail to produce results.
1967–70	**Nigeria**	A million people starve to death during civil war in the province of Biafra.
1984	**Ethiopia**	Since 1975, when the state took over all land ownership, peasants have been forced to sell grain to the government at below market prices. Harvests decline, and drought finally brings famine, killing nearly a million.

Organic farming

Organic farming aims to produce food without the use of agrochemicals, and with minimal damage to the environment. Soil is fertilised with manure or organic compost. Crop rotation techniques and natural pest-eating predators are used to minimise plant diseases and pest damage.

Advantages
- Improves soil structure
- Reduces pollution
- Benefits wildlife

Disadvantages
- Crop yields are lower than those of conventional farms
- Produce is expensive
- Natural pest control is not effective in tropical climates

see also
466-7 **Man the grower**
468-9 **Fruits of the earth**
470-1 **Breeding and rearing**
546-7 **Inherited characteristics**

About 8000 years ago, mankind ceased to be hunter-gatherers and turned to agriculture. This allowed settled communities to form. From these, towns and cities grew, along with government, trade and economy. But the availability of food has continued to restrict the size of human populations. The application of science by the wealthier nations, mainly in the form of fertilisers and mechanised machinery, has helped to boost agricultural output – worldwide food production has doubled in the last 50 years.

Norfolk 'four-course' rotation system

By 1800, most farmers in Britain were practising a new system of crop rotation, first used on farms in Norfolk. By 1900, it had been adopted across much of continental Europe. The system allowed all fields to be used every year without exhausting the soil. Crops were rotated over a four-year period:

Year 1 Wheat is sown.

Year 4 The clover and rye from year three are left for grazing. The clover adds nitrogen to the soil, and droppings from the grazing animals further enrich it, helping to improve yields of wheat the following year.

Year 2 Root vegetables are grown, then harvested to provide winter fodder for livestock. Previously, livestock did not survive the winter. They can now be fattened up and sold the following spring.

Year 3 Manure, provided by the overwintering livestock, is used to fertilise the soil, and spring wheat or barley is sown, along with an undersowing of clover and rye.

Prehistoric times
People lead a nomadic, hunter-gatherer lifestyle, trapping wild animals for meat and skins, and gathering roots, fruits and cereals from the wild.

*c.*3000 BC The Egyptians use a water-lifting device (the *shaduf*) to redirect Nile water to irrigate crops. This increases yield, leading to food surpluses.

*c.*1000 BC Rye and oats are cultivated in northern Europe.

*c.*600 Crop rotation is practised in China.

800 In Europe, the open (shared) field system is becoming established.

1700s The modern agricultural revolution begins in Britain.
1701 Jethro Tull develops the horse-drawn seed drill, sowing seed in rows and reducing waste.

1730s The Norfolk rotation system is introduced.

| 6000 BC | 3000 BC | 1000 BC | 0 | 1000 | 1500 | 1700 | 1750 |

*c.*5000 BC Wet rice farming begins in China.

*c.*3500 BC Maize is widely cultivated in the Americas.

*c.*1600 BC Vines and olives are cultivated in Crete.

AD 65 Roman farmer Lucius Columella writes *De Re Rustica* (*On Rural Things*), a treatise on agriculture.

*c.*1100 Champa, or early ripening rice, is planted widely in China.

1500s Potatoes, tomatoes and maize are introduced to Europe from the New World.

*c.*1760 Robert Bakewell (1725–95) introduces scientific stock breeding; his 'New Leicester' sheep are heavier and fatter.

EVOLUTION OF THE PLOUGH

The earliest farmers simply hoed the ground with a wooden digging stick. Ox-drawn wooden ploughs, invented in Mesopotamia about 3500 BC, broke up a deeper layer of soil and dug in the remains of previous crops, enriching the soil.

The Egyptians added a sharp flint cutting edge. The iron digging blade, or share, was introduced in China around 500 BC and later used by the Romans. It lasted longer than a wooden blade and was also heavy enough to dig deep into the wet, dense soil of northern Europe. Even in pre-Roman Britain, iron-tipped wooden ploughs were in use.

About 1000 BC, the Chinese invented the curved mouldboard to turn over the cut earth; it was not used in Europe until about AD 600, when heavy ploughs were introduced in north-eastern Europe. They had a vertical iron front cutting blade – the coulter – with a horizontal iron ploughshare and a mouldboard. They also often had wheels, making them easier to control.

Apart from the horse collar, which allowed horses to replace oxen, ploughing saw little change until the 18th century. The first all-iron plough, made by Robert Ransome in 1808, was followed in 1837 by John Deere's steel plough, which helped to transform the American prairies. Then came power: stationary steam engines pulling the plough by cable in 1860, the first petrol tractor in 1892 and Ford's mass-produced model in 1916.

Mouldboard turns over soil.

Coulter makes first cut.

Plough The plough's basic form has changed little in 1400 years, apart from steel replacing wood.

Ploughshare cuts furrow.

FACT The average American farmer of 1850 grew enough food to feed five people; today he produces enough for almost 80 people.

Modern farming

Britain began the agricultural revolution, but modern mechanised farming originated in the United States. It became established in the mid 19th century, stimulated by labour shortages, plentiful flat land with no tradition of small-scale ownership, and rail transport. Farm machines – culminating in the combine harvester – were powered at first by horses, then by steam and finally by internal-combustion engines. Mechanisation was not the only step forward: chemical fertilisers were used increasingly to boost soil fertility from the late 19th century, and especially after German chemist Fritz Haber invented a process for making ammonia from air in 1913. Then, after the discovery of the insecticide DDT in 1939 and of 2,4-D, the first selective weedkiller, in 1945, farmers became as dependent on chemicals as on machines.

Prairie leviathans Modern combine harvesters cut a 6 m (20 ft) swathe through cornfields. Operated by one man, they reap, thresh and store the grain, then offload it into trucks.

1830s American farmer Cyrus McCormick invents the harvesting machine, or reaper. Hiram Moore and John Hascall patent the first horse-drawn combined reaper-thresher, or combine harvester. John Deere invents the steel plough.

1862 American engineer L.O. Colvin invents the milking machine, with elastic tubes, pumped by bellows, attached to milking cows.

1916 Ford starts to mass-produce all-purpose tractor.

1940s Battery farming for the production of eggs begins in the USA.

1960s The 'Green Revolution' sees the development of higher-yielding hybrid crops, and the introduction of chemical fertilisers in developing countries helps to increase productivity.

1800   1850   1900   1925   1950   1975   1990

1786 Scotsman Andrew Meikle invents the horse-driven threshing machine, which separates grain by rubbing it through rollers.

1801 The first General Enclosure Act simplifies and speeds up process of land enclosure in Britain.

1884 Australian Hugh McKay invents the first modern combine harvester.

1920s Modern combine havester, with huge revolving blades, can process up to 0.8 ha (2 acres) of cereal crops an hour.

1945 Intensive farming is introduced for pig, poultry and milk production. Large numbers of animals are kept in controlled feeding and temperature environments.

1980s The popularity of organic foods grows in the developed world, reflecting concern about modern agricultural practices.

1990s Genetically modified food crops are field-tested.

Shared fields to enclosures

Strip-farming dominated much of northern Europe from the Middle Ages. Big 'open' fields were divided into narrow strips; each farmer would work a number of strips scattered across three fields. The crops were rotated: wheat one year, vegetables and barley the next, then a fallow year for the soil to recover. Livestock grazed common land, woods and harvested fields.

Land enclosures ended the medieval layout of arable land. The new landlords farmed for profit. Open fields and commonly held land passed into private ownership. This change had started as early as the 12th century, but did not gather pace until the 17th and 18th centuries. Although overall productivity increased, tenant farmers were often inadequately compensated for the loss of grazing rights on common land.

Terracing Horizontal miniature fields or terraces make land available for farming on hill slopes. They also help to retain water. Crops that need plenty of moisture are often grown on terraces in mountainous regions – as on these 2000-year-old rice terraces near Banaue, on Luzon island in the Philippines.

Plants have been cultivated as food for about 10 000 years. Until recently, however, the diet of a particular region was more or less based on what grew under local climate and soil conditions. In the 20th century, science, along with a revolution in communications and transport, has created a lucrative global market in fruit and vegetables. Almost anything is now available anywhere at any time – for a price.

Roots The swollen, starchy roots, or tubers, of the potato, sweet potato and yam plants play a major role both as cash crops in the world economy, and in providing basic nourishment for growing populations.

Potatoes First cultivated by the people of the Andes in South America, they were brought to Europe in the 16th century. By the 19th century, they had become a staple food from Ireland to Siberia.

World production, 2000:
308.2 million tonnes

Sweet potatoes A native of tropical America, they are a food staple in the southern United States, where they are also fed to livestock. In Japan they are used to make alcohol.

World production, 2000:
141.1 million tonnes

Yams The edible tubers of various tropical vines belonging to the genus *Dioscorea*, they are eaten as vegetables in the tropics. In eastern Asia, they are used for medicinal purposes, such as helping the digestion.

World production, 2000:
37.8 million tonnes

Fruit Fruit is cultivated commercially in most climate zones, from tropical to cool temperate. It is an important source of vitamins and minerals.

Apples Originally from Afghanistan, apples are now grown in most temperate regions of the world. A large part of the European crop is used for cider-making.

World production, 2000:
60 million tonnes

Bananas Now grown in tropical climates, from Africa to the West Indies to Taiwan, bananas probably originated in South-east Asia. Plants bear up to 200 fruits. They are harvested while still green and ripen later.

World production, 2000:
58.7 million tonnes

Tomatoes Native to South America, tomatoes were once thought to be poisonous, and until the 18th century were grown only for decoration. They are now cultivated worldwide, often under glass.

World production, 2000:
100.8 million tonnes

Grains Grains have been cultivated since prehistoric times as a staple food, with stalks and straw used for fodder. They are largely grown in temperate zones with moderate rainfall.

Wheat The cultivation of wheat can be traced back to ancient Egypt. The soft grains are used to make flour for bread, whilst flour from the harder, glutinous grains makes pasta, semolina and breakfast foods.

World production, 2000:
580 million tonnes

Rice For about half the world's population, rice is the main source of nourishment. This native of South-east Asia needs warm, wet conditions.

World production, 2000:
597.2 million tonnes

Maize Also known as corn, maize is native to North America. It needs a sunny growing climate. It can be eaten as a vegetable, oil can be extracted from it, and it can be ground to make cornflour.

World production, 2000:
589.3 million tonnes

Pulses Pulses are the edible seeds of leguminous plants, one of the historic staple foods in Asia. They are increasingly used worldwide as part of a vegetarian diet for their high protein content.

Lentils Native to southern Asia, lentils are one of the oldest known foods. Archaeologists have found them discarded at Bronze Age sites. They are widely used in African, Indian and Middle Eastern cooking.

World production, 2000:
3.2 million tonnes

Peas The small, round, green seeds of the pea plant are grown throughout the temperate regions of the world. There are a number of varieties, some of which have edible pods.

World production, 2000:
17.9 million tonnes

Beans An important source of protein, some, such as runner beans, have edible pods; others, such as kidney and broad beans, have edible seeds. Many are preserved by drying.

World production, 2000:
23.4 million tonnes

Other major crops In addition to the main staples mentioned above, there is an array of other important crops that are vital to the economies of the various countries that cultivate them.

Coconuts The milk contained in the coconut shell is used in cooking and as a drink, and the flesh is eaten. Coir, used in matting, comes from the husk, and chopped shell is used as a soil cover by gardeners.

World production, 2000:
58.4 million tonnes

Sugar The world's major source of sugar is sugar cane, a giant tropical grass. The tuberous sugar beet is the main native source of sugar in colder, temperate climates.

World production, 2000:
1531.7 million tonnes

Cocoa beans The seeds of the tropical cacao tree are roasted and ground to make cocoa powder, from which chocolate is made. The Aztecs introduced it to the Spanish in the 16th century.

World production, 2000:
3.1 million tonnes

Top producers

The figures given below are for the year 2000, and include crops for both home consumption and export. Many third-world countries are concentrating increasingly on export. This often means that the best land is reserved for growing high-priced 'luxury' produce to sell to the West. Hopefully, this should generate a healthy profit plus sufficient to buy in any necessary staples that can no longer be home-grown. Frequently, however, the focus on cash crops leads to a deterioration in the local diet.

Coffee (million tonnes)
Brazil	2.1
Colombia	0.6
Indonesia	0.5
Vietnam	0.4
Mexico	0.3

Maize (million tonnes)
USA	253.2
Brazil	32.0
Mexico	18.8
France	16.4
Argentina	16.0

Rice (million tonnes)
China	198.7
India	129.0
Indonesia	50.8
Vietnam	30.5
Bangladesh	29.8

Sugar (million tonnes)
Brazil	19.2
EU	17.9
India	14.3
China	8.9
USA	7.2

Tea (million tonnes)
India	0.9
China	0.7
Kenya	0.3
Sri Lanka	0.3
Turkey	0.2

Wheat (million tonnes)
China	109.7
EU	103.8
USA	69.4
India	65.9
Russia	27.0

Grapes The green and purple berries of *Vitis vinifera* have been cultivated in the warmer parts of southern Europe and the Middle East for thousands of years. The bulk of the crop is used in wine-making.

World production, 2000: 62.3 million tonnes

Oranges Originating in South-east Asia, oranges first came to Europe in the Middle Ages. They grow well in the tropical and subtropical regions of the Americas, the Mediterranean, Australia and South Africa.

World production, 2000: 66.1 million tonnes

Olives Prized for their fruit and oil, olives have been grown in the eastern Mediterranean for at least 3000 years. The countries round the Mediterranean are still the leading producers.

World production, 2000: 13.7 million tonnes

Oats Higher in fat and protein than other cereals, oats grow well in the cool regions of Russia and North America. They are used for breakfast cereals, and as an ingredient in processed foods, such as peanut butter.

World production, 2000: 26 million tonnes

Barley First grown in ancient Egypt, barley is now mostly grown in Europe. It is one of the most hardy of cereals. It is a basic ingredient of malting and brewing: over 10 per cent of the world's output is used in this way.

World production, 2000: 132.9 million tonnes

Rye A cold-resistant cereal, rye is native to northern Europe, where it is grown as animal fodder. It is also used to make 'black' breads, flakes for breakfast cereal, and is used with barley to make rye whisky.

World production, 2000: 20 million tonnes

see also
470-1 **Breeding and rearing**
472-3 **Harvesting the seas**

Soya beans These versatile beans have a high protein content. They can be eaten as a vegetable, used to produce cooking oil, flour, soy 'milk' or meat-substitute, or fermented for soy sauce.

World production, 2000: 161 million tonnes

Groundnuts Also known as peanuts, groundnuts are natives of tropical South America, and are a concentrated source of fat, protein and calories. The largest producers are the USA, India, China and West Africa.

World production, 2000: 34.5 million tonnes

Chickpeas A native of Asia, but now widely grown elsewhere. chickpeas are also known as gram or garbanzo. They are usually sold in dried form. Chickpeas can also be ground and made into flour.

World production, 2000: 8.8 million tonnes

FACT In Brazil a motor fuel called bagasse is derived from sugar.

Coffee Seeds from trees of the *Coffea* species are roasted to make coffee beans. Coffee drinking originated in Arabia and was introduced into Europe in the 17th century.

World production, 2000: 7.1 million tonnes

Tea The drink is made from the dried leaves of the *Camellia sinensis* shrub, widely cultivated in eastern Asia. The drink was introduced from China to Europe in the 17th century.

World production, 2000: 2.9 million tonnes

Pepper Pepper grows on a climbing vine native to India's Malabar coast. From classical times, it was traded with Europe, where its value was so great that it was used as a medium of exchange.

World production, 2000: 248 570 tonnes

Vanilla Used for flavouring, vanilla extract comes from the pods of tropical climbing orchids, native to Central America. The Spanish brought it to Europe from Mexico.

World production, 2000: 5312 tonnes

Livestock provides mankind with food, clothing and muscle power. Scientific breeding and advances in veterinary medicine are now helping to create more profitable animals, but there can be an unforeseen price to pay for this, in the form of poorer quality meat, and the spread of deadly disease across species.

Cattle

Beef cattle Because beef cattle are bred for meat production, they have heavy, well-developed muscle tissue, and need large bones to support it. They are particularly big around the loins and hindquarters, where the meat of greatest financial value is found.

● **Aberdeen Angus** The black, heavily built Aberdeen Angus breed originated in Scotland. It is widely reared for its high quality meat.
● **Beefmaster** A Brahman-Hereford-Shorthorn cross, the Beefmaster was first bred in Texas in 1908. Red, often with white markings, it is hardy, fertile and gives low-fat meat.
● **Brahman** Mainly farmed for cross-breeding. Brahman cattle are sacred to Hindus, who only use them for milk.
● **Brangus** A Brahman-Aberdeen Angus cross, the Brangus was bred to be fertile and hardy by the United States Department of Agriculture in 1932. It is black and lacks horns.
● **Charolais** The French Charolais breed is frequently used for cross-breeding. Most are white or pale cream, with the odd black marking.
● **Chianina** Originally bred as draught animals in Tuscany, Chianina are particularly good meat producers. They are white or light grey.
● **Hereford** Being hardy and quick to mature makes the Hereford a popular breed. It is red and white.
● **Simmenthal** Red with white markings, the Swiss Simmenthal breed is used extensively for cross-breeding.

Dairy cows These produce 10-15 litres (2.2-3.3 gallons) of milk each day for about ten months after the birth of a calf. Unlike beef cattle, they are tall and fine-boned with large udders.

● **Ayrshire** The heavy-set Scottish Ayrshire has a markedly high milk yield. Red or brown, it has white markings.
● **Brown Swiss** Only classified as a dairy breed in the USA, the Brown Swiss cow is reared elsewhere for its rich, dense meat. It ranges from milky to dark, dusky brown.
● **Friesians** Usually with black and white markings, the Friesian is a native of the Netherlands. It gives high yields of milk and butterfat.
● **Guernsey** Fawn with white markings, the Guernsey cow produces milk that is especially high in butterfat.
● **Jersey** Milk from Jersey cows contains 50 per cent more cream than that from other breeds. Colouring ranges from light grey to dark fawn.

Milk and meat Some breeds of cattle are good for both meat and milk. Or, they give high milk yields when reared in one part of the world, but are better at developing muscle for beef under different conditions.

● **Milking Shorthorn** Red, with a few white markings, Milking Shorthorns are highly fertile and long-lived.
● **Red Poll** Red or cream-coloured with no horns, the Red Poll was first bred in East Anglia in the 1860s.

The versatile cow Although cattle are reared primarily for food, there are a number of valuable by-products:

● **Beef tallow** provides glycerine for lipstick and hand creams and is an ingredient of shampoos, other cleaning agents and antifreeze.
● **Bonemeal,** made of ground up bones and hooves, is no longer used as fodder in most countries, but can be used as a fertiliser by, for example, gardeners on their own property.
● **Casein** is the main protein in milk, and the chief ingredient in cheese. It is also used in cosmetics, paint and glue, and as a protein supplement to treat malnutrition. When mixed with rennin, an enzyme, it can be used to make plastic objects such as buttons.
● **Gelatin,** made from hide and bone, is used as a setting agent in cooking, for example in preparing mousses, jellies or jam. Photographic film also contains gelatin, and pills and capsules are often coated with it.
● **Glue** is made from collagen, a mixture of bone and tissue.
● **Leather** includes soft, fine calfskin and the tougher hides, which are used to make durable goods such as the soles of shoes.

Beef facts

Biggest beef producers (1999)

		thousand tonnes
1	USA	12 050
2	EU	7 609
3	Brazil	6 182
4	China	4 674
5	Argentina	2 650

Biggest beef exporters (1999)

		thousand tonnes
1	Australia	1 289
2	USA	1 141
3	Brazil	615
4	EU	600
5	Canada	540

Dairy facts

Biggest dairy product producers (1999)

		thousand tonnes
1	EU	121 078
2	USA	77 773
3	India	37 750
4	Russia	32 415
5	Brazil	22 604

Biggest consumers of milk (1999)

		litres per capita
1	South Africa	683
2	Finland	181
3	Canada	178
4	Ireland	144
5	Sweden	134

Sheep

It is estimated that there are about 1.2 billion sheep worldwide. In Australia, they outnumber humans by about ten to one. Breeds are classified according to whether they have fine, medium or coarse wool.

Cheviot Large, with a white face and black muzzle, the Cheviot is a Scottish breed. It produces prime quality lamb, and especially strong wool, which is often blended with other yarns for durability.

Columbia Originally from the USA, Columbia sheep are a Rambouillet-Lincoln cross. They have a large frame and a white face. Their fleeces can weigh up to 7 kg (16 lb).

Hampshire The large-framed, white-faced Hampshire breed is mainly reared for its meat and for cross-breeding.

Karakul A native of Asia, Karakuls produce quality meat, and coarse, brown or grey wool used in carpets.

Lincoln With the longest hair of any sheep breed, the fleece from a Lincoln can weigh over 9 kg (20 lb). But the wool is coarse, and only suitable for making carpets.

Merino First bred in Spain in the 12th century. Merino sheep produce fine wool fibres of very high quality. The white fleece can weigh up to 5 kg (11 lb).

Rambouillet Largest of the fine wool breeds of sheep, the Rambouillet originated in France. The soft, white fleece can weigh up to 8 kg (18 lb).

Southdown Small with brown markings on the face and legs, Southdown sheep were first bred in Sussex. They mature early, producing fleeces that can weigh up to 3 kg (7 lb).

Lamb and wool facts

Biggest lamb producers (1999)		Biggest wool producers (1998)	
	thousand tonnes		thousand tonnes
1 China	1 250	1 Australia	700
2 EU	1 058	2 China	277
3 Australia	608	3 New Zealand	261
4 New Zealand	498	4 Uruguay	78
5 Pakistan	301	5 Argentina	68

Pigs

Pigs are farmed in almost all parts of the world, though not in Muslim or Jewish communities.

Berkshire An English breed, the medium-sized Berkshire is black with a white face, tail tip and feet. Its meat is sold as pork, and processed into bacon.

Duroc Originally bred in the USA in the late 19th century, the hardy Duroc gives high quality pork and lard. Colouring varies from light yellow to dark red.

Hampshire Black, with a white 'belt' across its forelegs and shoulders, the medium-weight Hampshire has a distinctive long body.

Yorkshire or Large White A large, pale animal, sometimes with dark markings, the Yorkshire is an English-Chinese cross. It is a major provider of pork and bacon, and is frequently used for cross-breeding.

The profitable pig
Pigs grow quickly and provide a wide range of meat and other products:

Bacon is fatty meat from the back and sides, that is salted, and often smoked.

Bristles are used to make paint brushes.

Lard, a soft, white fat, is widely used for cooking.

Pigskin is used for high quality, leather goods.

Pig facts

Biggest pork producers (1999)			Biggest pork exporters (1999)		
		thousand tonnes			thousand tonnes
1	China	39 858	1	Denmark	1 230
2	USA	8 785	2	Netherlands	1 164
3	Germany	3 940	3	Belg/Lux	647
4	Spain	2 900	4	France	570
5	Brazil	1 752	5	Canada	502

Chickens

The recognised types are either American, English, Mediterranean, and Asiatic; all the common breeds are variations of these four. There are more than 5 million commercially kept chickens worldwide, the majority of which are reared for meat production.

Cornish The Cornish is often used in cross-breeding to produce meaty birds.

Leghorn The Italian Leghorn breed is one of the most prolific egg-layers.

New Hampshire A meaty bird, the New Hampshire is also a good producer of eggs.

Rhode Island Red North American breed. One of the best-known chickens. Valued for its high-quality meat.

see also
468-9 **Fruits of the earth**
472-3 **Harvesting the seas**

Harvesting the seas ▶

Fishing has grown from supplying local needs into a major commercial enterprise. At the end of the 20th century, it was estimated that around 5 million people worldwide made a living from fishing, and for many countries, such as China, trade in fish and fish products is vital to their economy.

MAJOR WORLD FISHERIES

In all the major fisheries of the world, catch sizes are increasing faster than breeding is capable of replenishing stocks. An outright ban has been placed on the fishing of endangered species in some areas. Catch sizes for 1996 by specific countries in each area are given below:

Pacific north-east

Major species: Alaskan pollock, sockeye and pink salmon, cod, hake, crabs and shrimps. Pollock, salmon and shellfish catch much reduced.
Catch (thousand tonnes):
USA (2592), Canada (237).
Status: Overfished.

Atlantic north-west

Major species: Haddock, hake, herring, shrimps, lobster, clams and cockles. Cod fishing is currently banned.
Catch (thousand tonnes):
USA (1206), Canada (624).
Status: Overfished.

Atlantic north-east

Major species: Cod, haddock, herring, whiting, salmon (90 per cent reared) and capelin.
Catch (thousand tonnes):
Norway (2630), Iceland (2039), Denmark (1681), UK (861).
Status: Overfished.

Atlantic eastern central

Major species: Sardine, herring, anchovy, European pilchard, mackerel, cod, hake and tuna.
Catch (thousand tonnes):
Morocco (600), Ghana (399), Senegal (389), Spain (303), Nigeria (170).
Status: Overfished.

Pacific north-west

Major species: Japanese anchovy, largehead hairtail, squid, salmon, Alaskan pollock and mackerel.
Catch (thousand tonnes):
China (12,393), Japan (5203), Russia (3097), Korea (1933), Korea (1622).
Status: Stocks in decline.

Indian ocean west

Major species: Herring, sardine, anchovy, Indian mackerel, tuna and shellfish.
Catch (thousand tonnes):
India (2029), Pakistan (395), Iran (242), Sri Lanka (210), Oman (122).
Status: Stocks in decline.

Indian ocean east

Major species: Herring, mackerel, tuna, lobster and shrimp.
Catch (thousand tonnes):
Thailand (835), India (812), Myanmar (626), Indonesia (629), Malaysia (494).
Status: Stocks in decline.

Pacific western central

Major species: Tuna, herring, redfish, mackerel and shrimp. Tuna stocks are rapidly diminishing.
Catch (thousand tonnes):
Indonesia (2757), Thailand (2099), Philippines (1606), Vietnam (684).
Status: Stocks in decline.

Pacific south-east

Major species: Peruvian anchoveta (sardines, herrings and anchovies), South American sardine, Chilean jack mackerel, tuna and squid.
Catch (thousand tonnes):
Peru (9486), Chile (6688).
Status: Stocks in decline.

Atlantic south-west

Major species: Argentinian hake, blue whiting, squid and shellfish (the largest fishery in the Southern Hemisphere).
Catch (thousand tonnes):
Argentina (1226), Brazil (620).
Status: Stocks in decline.

Overfishing

Decades of overfishing have led to declining or static fish stocks in around 60 per cent of the world's fisheries. Several factors are responsible for this crisis:
- The demand for fish is rising rapidly.
- The world's fishing fleet has expanded six-fold since 1970.
- Large factory supertrawlers have been introduced in most of the world's fisheries.
- Technology for finding and catching fish has improved greatly.

A number of strategies to reverse the decline in fish stocks have recently been implemented. These include: setting up of fishing quotas; controlled net-mesh size to prevent capture of juvenile fish; fishing bans; and fish farming.

With effective management of depleted stocks, it is hoped that there will be an increase in world annual fish production to 144 million tonnes by 2010; without it there will be a shortfall of 20 million tonnes.

	Catch (thousand tonnes)	
	1955	1996
Atlantic north-west	2 645	2 114
Atlantic north-east	6 937	10 938
Atlantic south-west	215	2 256
Atlantic eastern central	340	2 999
Indian ocean west	706	3 901
Indian ocean east	434	3 747
Pacific north-west	6 334	24 768
Pacific western central	1 021	8 911
Pacific south-east	311	17 558
Pacific north-east	416	2 714

METHODS OF FISHING

Modern fishing fleets use sophisticated equipment for locating and hauling in fish. Aerial surveillance, along with computer-controlled, satellite and sonar tracking devices, and enormous nets ensure that catches are large.

1 Drift netting Long curtain-like nets of strong plastic webbing are suspended vertically across the ocean. They either drift along freely, or are fixed in position by weights on the seabed. Dolphins and turtles die when they become entangled in them. A UN resolution bans the use of nets over 2.5 km (1 1/2 miles) long.

2 Purse-seining Wire ropes pass through rings around the edge of the circular purse-sein net, which is towed around a shoal then pulled shut, like a draw-string purse, to trap the fish. Most of the world's annual fish yield is caught in this way.

3 Long-lining 'Long-lines', attached to hundreds of shorter lines with baited hooks, are allowed to drift to catch surface fish, such as tuna and salmon, or are spread along the ocean floor to catch groundfish, such as cod and halibut. Motorised winches haul in the heavy catch.

4 Trawling A huge cone-shaped net is dragged along the bottom of the ocean, taking everything in its path. Trawling is the main commercial method of fishing in north-west Europe.
Factory ship Giant trawlers can catch huge shoals of fish, then process, freeze and even package them onboard. This allows them to fish in deep water, far from home, for months at a time.

Potting Small cages, made of wood, wicker, wire, or plastic, catch lobsters and crabs off rocky coastlines. These traps are set up in lines with their positions marked by floats.

see also

96-9 **Fishes**
468-9 **Fruits of the earth**
470-1 **Breeding and rearing**

WORLD FISHING FLEETS

In 1996, the world fishing fleet was estimated to comprise 1.2 million decked vessels, most of which were operating in Asia. The United Nations has since estimated that a third of these ships would have to stop operating in order to halt the current decline in global fish stocks.

FISH FARMING

Twenty per cent of the fish we eat comes from aquaculture, the intensive cultivation of fish. Fish eggs are placed in warm water tanks until they hatch into fry, and then reared in freshwater or seawater tanks or cages.

Asia has a long tradition of carp farming, and now produces 90 per cent of the world's output. Salmon and trout fisheries, which originated in Norway and Scotland, also flourish today in Chile and Canada, both major producers for the European market. The tilapia, a perch-like fish, is being successfully cultivated in parts of Africa.

Fishing activity

Fishing activity is highly regionalised, with about ten countries accounting for almost 70 per cent of the world's total catch.

Top ten fishing countries (1997)

Country	Catch (million tonnes)
China	36.3
Peru	7.9
Japan	6.7
Chile	6 1
USA	5.4
India	5.3
Russia	4.7
Indonesia	4.4
Thailand	3.5
Norway	3.2

World's favourite fish

The popularity of some species has led to scarcity, and hence rising prices. Fish farming has helped to counter this trend to some degree, and may become the main way of replenishing the stocks of some species.

World's favourite fish (1996)

Species	Consumption (thousand tonnes)
Anchoveta (sardine, and anchovy)	8864
Alaskan pollock	4533
Chilean jack	4379
Atlantic herring	2331
Chub mackerel	2168
Capelin	1527
South American pilchard	1494
Skipjack tuna	1480
Atlantic cod	1329
Largehead hairtail	1275
Japanese anchovy	1254

Who are eating the fish?

The countries where fish forms a major part of the daily diet are not necessarily the same as those that have the largest catches. Many countries fish primarily for export. Japan is the biggest seafood importer, taking 30 per cent of world supplies of tuna.

Top ten fish-eaters (1997)

Country	Consumption (kg per capita)
Iceland	99.3
Japan	67.6
Portugal	59.2
South Korea	51.2
North Korea	46.3
Norway	45.3
Gabon	44.0
Guyana	42.1
Spain	41.0
Philippines	33.5

Water is a limited resource, which needs to be carefully managed. Its natural abundance in a region, and how it is collected, stored and distributed, has a major impact on a country's economy, determining what crops can be grown, and whether there is sufficient to meet domestic and industrial demands. The establishment of some of the first civilisations in the Middle East was due to the inspired use of Nile floodwater for irrigation.

THE WATER WE USE

If water is to be available on demand all year round, it needs to be collected and stored. How this is done varies around the world, according to climate and geography.

In **Asia**, water from heavy rainfall and river run-offs during the monsoon season is collected and stored in aquifers and reservoirs for use in the dry season. China, for example, has over 80 000 reservoirs.

In **some tropical areas** and islands, such as Bermuda, where surface and ground water is limited, each household has its own tank in which to collect and store rainwater.

In **European temperate zones** resources are distributed through river basins, often via man-made canals and reservoirs. Aqueduct systems have been built to reach the major cities, such as Marseilles and Vienna.

In **North America**, Canada has the largest number of inland lakes in the world. The Ogallala Aquifer, the largest source of ground water in the USA, extends for over 400 000 sq miles under the central plains, and supplies major cities via extensive aqueduct systems.

South America is largely drained by the Amazon, Orinoco and Paraguay-Parana rivers. Most of its permanent lakes are high in the Andes.

In **Africa**, vast areas suffer low or irregular rainfall. Since the 1950s dams and reservoirs have been built, but in some parts, such as in Ethiopia, people still have to walk for miles to reach the nearest tap or well.

In **Australia**, 70 per cent of water reserves are located beneath the vast plains in the Great Artesian Basin – the world's largest area of artesian water (see below, right).

WORLD WATER DISTRIBUTION

Plentiful water all year round
The equatorial rain forests of South America and South-east Asia receive heavy daily rainfall. Countries like Thailand, Malaysia and Indonesia have harnessed such climatic conditions to cultivate oil palms and extensive rubber tree plantations.

Marginal water in the growing season
Grasslands in the centre of large continents tend to have a drier climate than areas nearer the sea. Dry winters are followed by limited rainfall in spring and early summer. They are generally farmed for cereals and livestock.

Markedly seasonal water supplies
Large areas of the Indian subcontinent and southern China have a tropical monsoon climate, where 80 per cent of rainfall occurs during a three-month period each year. Such a climate is ideally suited to the cultivation of rice.

Constant water deficit
Little will grow in deserts, but some of the countries of the Arabian peninsula have harnessed nonconventional water sources. They obtain fresh water through the desalination and purification of sea water (see box, right).

● **The world's largest reservoirs**

Williston Lake
(70 300 million m³)
Canada

Manicouagan
(141 900 million m³)
Canada

Guri
(135 000 million m³)
Venezuela

Making water available to drink

The water in most rivers and lakes is clean enough to support wildlife, but before it flows out of the tap it must be made safe for human consumption. This is achieved at a water treatment plant, in a series of steps:

1 Once any floating debris has been filtered off, the water is pumped into large, open storage reservoirs. Here heavier particles sink to the bottom, and the large, exposed surface area allows oxygen in the air to act on the other impurities, and to start breaking them down.

2 Water is then pumped into the treatment plant. Ozone gas is passed through it, which helps to destroy impurities such as pesticides or nitrates.

3 The next step is to pass the water through a filter bed containing coarse sand. As the water percolates down, the grains of sand trap debris along with bacteria and other microorganisms.

4 The water that emerges is now given a further dose of ozone, before it flows on to another filter bed, containing a thin layer of granular activated carbon (GAC). Here all remaining dissolved impurities are removed. The tiny carbon granules can absorb harmful substances in the way that a sponge can soak up liquid.

5 The water is now clean enough to drink. To ensure that it remains fresh, a small dose of chlorine is added to disinfect it, plus a little sodium sulphite to eliminate the chlorine taste. The water is stored in covered service reservoirs, before being pumped to our taps.

The dying sea

The Aral Sea was once the world's fourth largest lake. But from the 1960s on, the rivers feeding it were diverted to irrigate the cotton fields of Kazakhstan and Uzbekistan. The sea began to recede, and its dwindling waters were irredeemably polluted with pesticides and other agrochemicals. The Aral is now an ecological disaster zone. It will almost certainly disappear by 2015, leaving a poisonous desert in its place.

How we use our water

More than 90 per cent of world water consumption goes to agriculture (see below). Domestic use accounts for less than 3 per cent, with only a little more being consumed by industry. The major industrial use of water is for cooling in nuclear and other thermal power plants, and for turning turbines in hydroelectric plants. Other heavy industrial users are the chemical, oil, paper and machinery manufacturing sectors.

World water consumption

93.4% Agriculture
3.8% Industry
2.7% Domestic

Water consumption patterns

The pattern of water use varies in different parts of the world. For example, in the developed world – Western Europe and North America – industry often makes just as much, if not more, demand on water resources than agriculture.

Water consumption by continent (billion m³)

	Agriculture	Domestic	Industry
Africa	120	6	6
Asia	1500	50	80
Europe	230	50	270
North America	400	90	650
Oceania	14	1.5	10
South America	60	7	12

Krasnoyarsk
(73 300 million m³)
Russia

Bratsk
(169 000 million m³)
Russia

Lake Nasser, High Aswan Dam
(162 000 million m³)
Egypt

Lake Volta, Akosombo Dam
(148 000 million m³)
Ghana

Lake Victoria, Owen Falls Dam
(204 800 million m³)
Uganda, Kenya and Tanzania

Kariba Lake
(160 400 million m³)
Zimbabwe and Zambia

Land irrigation

UNESCO estimates that nearly half the world's crop production, in terms of value, comes from irrigated land. Without irrigation, many nations would find it impossible to feed their populations or develop their economies. In China and India, the high yield of rice is totally dependent upon controlled floods, which irrigate the river plains in the dry season. Egypt would be as infertile as the Sahara Desert without the heavy monsoon rains from the East African highlands which flood the River Nile. The water is stored, via the Aswan High Dam, in the Lake Nasser reservoir. The thriving fruit farms of California are dependent on water brought from the Colorado river via a 390 km (242 mile) long aqueduct.

see also

42-3 **Rivers**
44-5 **Lakes**

Artesian wells

When ground water seeps into a porous layer of rock (an aquifer), which is sandwiched between two layers of nonpermeable rock, pressure begins to build up. A hole drilled through into the aquifer will release that pressure, and the water will shoot upwards to the surface, where it can be collected. This is known as an artesian well, a name derived from the Artois region of France, where the first one was bored in 1126.

Desalination

Desert countries of the Arabian peninsula boost their supply of fresh water by desalinating and purifying sea water. This involves distillation, where the sea water is heated to 80°C (176°F), and the vapour given off – which contains very little salt – is condensed and collected. This process is repeated to produce water of acceptable drinking quality. Sometimes an alternative method is used: sea water is force through a special membrane, which traps salt, allowing only pure water through.

The development of motorised road transport was one of the defining features of the 20th century. It brought unprecedented mobility to millions and created a huge industry out of the inventions of workshop pioneers. The first internal-combustion engines were built to power factory machines. When they were fitted to a bicycle and to a four-wheeled carriage, the results were the first motorcycle and the 'horseless carriage' – the first motor car.

THE MOTOR CAR MATURES

The motor car was not a single development but the sum total of hundreds – even thousands – of individual inventions. The key ones, however, were the compact petrol-fuelled internal-combustion engine and the pneumatic (air-filled) tyre. Although these were both invented in 19th-century Europe and first brought together in Germany and France, the United States took the lead in car manufacturing and use early in the 20th century. Public demand for fast, easy and cheap personal transport was met by mass-production techniques first introduced there, and the opening up of oil fields made cheap fuel available to power the new freedom of the road.

A century later, cars were far more sophisticated machines (see page 478), but were well on the way to becoming victims of their own success. The 20 000 cars on the world's roads in 1900 had grown to more than 230 million by 2000. Dwindling world oil reserves and fears about pollution and global warming were forcing manufacturers to seek viable alternatives to the petrol engine, while trying to cut fuel consumption and pollution from existing designs. Meanwhile, in developing countries, car ownership remains a distant dream for vast numbers of people.

Liberating cycle The bicycle brought women new freedoms in the late 19th century. They dressed accordingly, abandoning long skirts for the more practical knickerbockers.

Evolution of the bicycle

1790 The French 'Celerifère'. Looking like a wooden scooter, it has a fixed front wheel, and no seat or pedals.
1818 Baron Karl von Drais adds a seat and steerable front wheel to make the 'Draisienne', or hobbyhorse.
1839 Scotsman Kirkpatrick Macmillan builds a cycle with pedals, connecting rods and cranks to turn the rear wheel.
1861 Frenchman Pierre Michaux adds pedals linked to the front wheel of a Draisienne. He calls it the 'Vélocipède'.
1870 The Vélocipède is developed into the 'high' bicycle, or 'penny-farthing'. Its large front wheel increases speed.
1879 Englishman Henry Lawson patents the 'Bicyclette', a chain-driven bicycle with same-sized wheels.
1885 In Britain, J.K. Starley produces the first successful 'safety bicycle', with simple gears and suspension.
1888 Scottish inventor John Dunlop patents the pneumatic tyre for bicycles. It is used for motor cars from 1895.
1909 Dérailleur gears are introduced, moving the driving chain on sprockets.
1938 Epicyclic gears, contained in the rear wheel hub, are introduced.
1973 The 'mountain bike' – with a large number of gears and heavily ridged tyres suitable for rough terrain – is introduced.
1980s Professional racing bicycles make use of lightweight carbon-fibre composites, later incorporated into the design of leisure bicycles.

Horseless carriage This 1886 Daimler, the first four-wheeled petrol-driven carriage, had its engine suspended at the back. It was capable of 19 km/h (12 mph).

Putting the world on wheels More than 15 million Model T Fords were built in the 20 years the car was in production.

Beetling to success Although developed before the Second World War, the Volkswagen 'Beetle' did not go into mass production until after the war.

Daimler

Model T Ford

Volkswagen

| 1860 | 1880 | 1900 | 1910 | 1920 |

1860 Etienne Lenoir of France builds the first practical internal-combustion engine; a stationary industrial gas engine, it has limited commercial success.

1876 Nikolaus Otto of Germany develops the four-stroke internal-combustion gas engine, the basis of the modern car engine.

1883–5 In Germany, engineers Gottlieb Daimler (with Wilhelm Maybach) and Karl Benz develop the first petrol engines.

1890 René Panhard and Emile Levassor of France build the first purpose-designed petrol-engined car.

1892 The German engineer Rudolf Diesel patents the compression-ignition engine.

1901 Gottlieb Daimler's son Paul builds the first Mercedes. Its steel chassis makes it the forerunner of the modern steel-bodied car.

1901–6 American Ransome E. Olds builds 18 000 Oldsmobiles by mass-production methods, using bought-in components.

1908 Henry Ford introduces the mass-produced Model T.

1911 The Studebaker Company in the United States offers deferred payment plans for car purchases.

1913 Henry Ford revolutionises car-manufacturing with his moving production line for Model Ts. Production increases to over 240 000 cars a year; the price drops from US$850 to US$260 by 1925.

1920s Buses and lorries are made with diesel engines.

1922 Low-pressure 'balloon' tyres bring greater comfort.

1928 The last Model T Ford is produced.

1935 In Germany, Ferdinand Porsche unveils the rear-engine Volkswagen ('people's car').

Horse-drawn carriages

By the late 19th century, horse-drawn carriages had evolved from crude wagons to become highly sophisticated vehicles in a variety of designs for special purposes. Some showed signifiicant technical innovations. The brougham of 1838, for example, had no separate chassis. Instead, the rear axle and suspension, and the front undercarriage, were mounted directly on the body – a principle used in many modern cars.

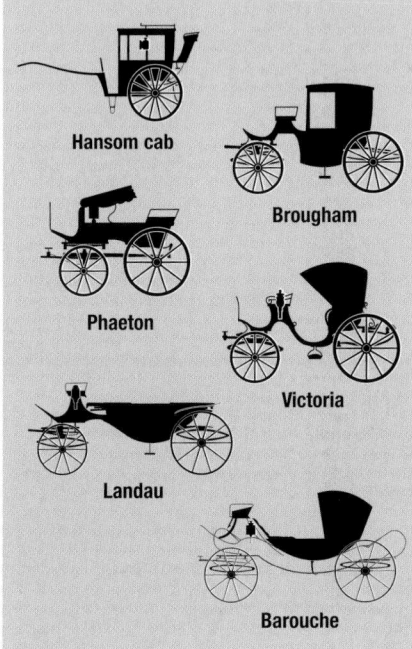

Hansom cab

Brougham

Phaeton

Victoria

Landau

Barouche

Brief history of the motorcycle

Just as the car developed from the motorised 'horseless carriage', the motorcycle was born from the combination of the bicycle with a particularly compact version of the internal-combustion petrol engine.

1885 Gottlieb Daimler produces the world's first motorcycle by mounting a petrol-powered internal-combustion engine on a wooden-framed bicycle. Independently, Karl Benz installs a petrol engine in a tricycle.

1894 The Hildebrand brothers and Alois Wolfmüller manufacture a two-cylinder, four-stroke motorcycle capable of 39 km/h (24 mph).

1895 The compact French-developed de Dion-Bouton engine sets the standard for four-stroke motorcycle engines.

1903 The Honold-Bosch high-tension magneto provides much-improved fuel ignition.

1907 Harley-Davidson builds the first two-cylinder V-twin motorcycle engine.

1911 Variable-speed gears and clutch are introduced.

1913 A motorcycle is timed for the first time at more than 160 km/h (100 mph).

1914 The first production motorcycle with an electric starter – the Indian Hendee Special – is introduced.

1914 Drum (internal expanding) brakes are introduced for motorcycles.

1947 The first motor scooters – Vespa and Lambretta – with small wheels, a low-powered enclosed engine, and an open frame and running board, are launched.

1959 Japanese manufacturers start to dominate the world motorcycle market.

1968 The first production motorcycle with disc brakes – the Honda CB750.

1980s High-performance motorcycles with turbocharged engines are introduced.

1990s Fuel injection is introduced for some motorcycle engines.

Poor man's car The motorcycle and sidecar, such as this BSA of 1922 with its own hood, provided motor transport for families who could not afford a car.

see also
478-9 **The modern car**
480-1 **Trains**
500-1 **Fossil fuels**

All fins and chrome Cadillac stylist Harley Earl introduced large tail-fins in 1948. This 1959 Eldorado was one of the last models to bear his hallmark so prominently.

Mini Minor The Mini started a trend for front-wheel-drive compact cars. Among its revolutionary features were a space-saving transverse (sideways-mounted) engine and rubber suspension.

People carrier The Renault Espace created a new kind of large family car – part estate car, part minibus.

Cadillac

Mini

Renault Espace

| 1940 | 1950 | 1960 | 1970 | 1980 | 1990 |

1948 New tyre designs improve car performance and road handling. The French company Michelin introduces safer and longer-lasting radial tyres. In the United States, the Goodyear company introduces the convenient tubeless tyre.

1951 Dunlop introduces disc brakes. Pads operated by hydraulics grip each side of a disc attached to the wheels.

1959 The British Motor Corporation unveils the revolutionary Austin-Morris Mini, designed by Greek-born engineer Alec Issigonis.

1965 American lawyer Ralph Nader publishes his book *Unsafe at Any Price*, criticising car safety standards. It leads to much stricter safety regulations governing car design, and to the use of seat belts and airbags.

1970 US federal laws require big cuts in car exhaust pollution, leading to the introduction of catalytic converters to clean up exhaust gases.

Mid 1970s World fuel crises slow down the growth of the car industry and give a new impetus to small, fuel-efficient cars.

1980 Japanese car output exceeds that of the United States for the first time.

1980 Renault of France launches the Espace, setting a new trend for 'people carriers'.

1997 Mercedes-Benz's A-class is the first small runabout from an up-market car manufacturer.

1997 Toyota and Honda of Japan introduce highly fuel-efficient 'hybrid' petrol-electric cars.

Over 500 million cars use the world's roads, and problems of pollution and threatened fuel shortages face car manufacturers and users alike. For makers there is constant pressure to devise ways to engineer safer, cleaner and more economical cars, and to build in designs and gadgets with customer appeal.

Car systems Today's cars are recognisably descendants of Panhard and Levassor's 1890 vehicle, though generally they have a one-piece 'monocoque' body with no separate chassis, and the individual systems are vastly more complex than in 1890. Most medium to large cars have an engine at the front driving the rear wheels, but small and medium-sized cars commonly have front-wheel drive. In some cars and all-terrain vehicles a transfer gearbox divides power between all four wheels. Safety systems are of major importance: side-impact bars, crumple zones, collapsing steering columns, airbags and ABS braking all help to protect car users.

FOUR-STROKE ENGINE CYCLE

Most petrol-driven cars have a four-stroke engine. The power stroke, which provides the driving force, occurs once every two complete turns of the crankshaft. For smooth, continuous power delivery, most engines have four, six, eight or even more cylinders that fire in turn.

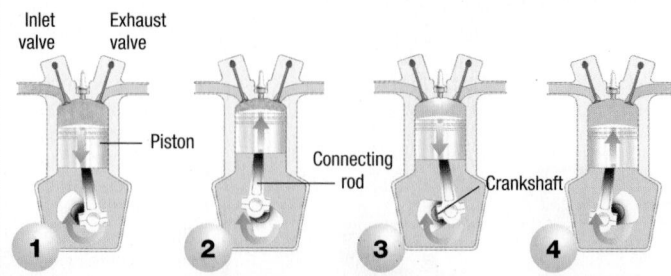

1 Intake or induction Inlet valve is open. Exhaust valve is closed. Piston moves down. Petrol-air mixture is drawn in.

2 Compression Inlet and exhaust valves are closed. Piston moves up. Petrol-air mixture is compressed.

3 Power Inlet and exhaust valves are closed. Spark plug ignites petrol-air mixture. Piston is driven down by expanding burning gases.

4 Exhaust Inlet valve is closed. Exhaust valve is open. Piston moves up. Exhaust gases are driven out.

Fuel system The fuel pump draws fuel from the tank. Fuel and air are then mixed in the correct proportions and fed into the engine. Most often nowadays, fuel injection is used; this squirts a measured amount of fuel directly into the air stream entering the engine.

Engine Chains, belts or geared shafts operate the inlet and exhaust valves and time the delivery of electric current to the spark plugs.

Electrical system The battery supplies power when the car is not running. Once the engine is started the alternator generates enough electricity to run all the electrical systems and accessories, and keeps the battery fully charged.

Exhaust system An arrangement of pipes takes burned exhaust gases from the engine. One or more silencers smooth the flow to reduce noise. In most new cars a catalytic converter chemically changes some of the gases to less-polluting carbon dioxide and water.

Starter motor This electric motor turns the engine's flywheel through its cycle until the engine starts to turn under its own power.

Cooling system Some car engines are air-cooled, but usually water circulates through channels in the engine and then through the radiator, where air blown by a fan dissipates the excess heat.

Ignition system The engine needs carefully timed sparks to ignite the fuel-air mixture. This used to be done with a coil and distributor, but most new cars have electronic ignition.

Gearbox The gears give varying output speeds for a given engine speed. An automatic transmission automatically changes the gear ratio according to road speed and engine load, usually under electronic control.

Suspension and steering Springs and shock absorbers attach each wheel to the body and keep it stable as the car travels over uneven surfaces. Many cars have power-assisted steering to reduce effort.

Wheels and tyres Car wheels are made from pressed steel or cast lightweight alloy. The tyre tread pushes surface water aside, and is braced with steel or fibre cords to stop it distorting.

Brakes Disc brakes have twin pads that press on either side of a metal disc. Drum brakes have horseshoe-shaped linings that press outwards onto the inner surface of the brake drum; these are more efficient for parking and are often fitted at the rear.

Alternative power for vehicles

Dwindling oil reserves and the need to reduce the emissions of carbon dioxide and other 'greenhouse' gases are forcing car manufacturers to seek alternatives to the traditional internal-combustion engine. One approach is to develop efficient 'lean-burn' engines; another is to use wholly new fuels or technologies – or both.

Electric vehicles (EV)
EVs are powered by an electric motor driven by electricity from batteries.

Pros:
- No greenhouse gases emitted
- Can be refuelled (recharged) at home

Cons:
- Limited range
- Lengthy daily recharging needed
- Generating power to recharge batteries may produce greenhouse gases

Hybrid electric vehicles (HEV)
A battery-powered electric motor drives the car at low speed or when necessary assists a small internal-combustion engine – which also recharges batteries.

Pros:
- Reduced fuel consumption
- Good range

Cons:
- Some emissions from the internal-combustion engine
- Complex

Liquefied petroleum gas (LPG)
This by-product of the petroleum industry is used to power an internal-combustion engine.

Pros:
- Reduced fuel costs
- Reduced greenhouse gas emissions

Cons:
- LPG is a fossil fuel with finite reserves
- Needs a special pressurised fuel tank

Fuel cell
Hydrogen from the electrolysis (electrical splitting) of water is combined with oxygen from air to generate electricity to power a motor.

Pros:
- No carbon dioxide emitted (only by-product is water)
- Good fuel economy and range
- Almost silent

Cons:
- Hydrogen is currently more expensive than petrol

Ethanol
Used on its own or mixed with petrol to power an internal-combustion engine, ethanol (ethyl alcohol) is a renewable fuel made from maize and other crops.

Pros:
- Made from a renewable resource
- Reduced greenhouse gas emissions

Cons:
- Limited public refuelling sites

see also
476-7 **Road transport**
480-1 **Trains**
500-1 **Fossil fuels**

The world's biggest vehicle manufacturers

	Group	Units sold 1998 (millions)	Turnover US$ (billions)	Major marques
1	General Motors	8.1	126	Buick, Cadillac, Chevrolet, Opel, Saab, Vauxhall
2	Ford	6.8	119	Ford, Jaguar, Land Rover, Lincoln, Mazda, Volvo
3	Toyota	5.2	109	Daihatsu, Lexus, Toyota
4	Volkswagen	4.6	62	Audi, Bentley, Seat, Skoda, Volkswagen
5	Daimler Chrysler	4.5	111	Chrysler, Dodge, Jeep, Mercedes, Smart
6	Nissan	2.5	58	Infiniti, Nissan
7	Honda	2.3	45	Acura, Honda
8	PSA Peugeot Citroën	2.3	29	Citroën, Dacia, Peugeot
9	Renault	2.1	35	Alpine, Renault
10	Mitsubishi	1.8	32	Mitsubishi

The world's busiest road networks

		thousand km travelled per year per km of road
1	Indonesia	8134
2	Hong Kong	6071
3	Bahrain	2808
4	Mongolia	2169
5	Israel	2096
6	Thailand	1546
7	Portugal	1297
8	United Kingdom	1089
9	Belgium	1074
10	Germany	889

Car ownership The United States is by far the world leader in car ownership, with more than 130 million cars on its roads. However, a number of smaller countries have more cars per thousand population, as shown below. In Britain, there are almost 23 million cars – 385 per thousand people.

The world's longest road networks

		thousand km			thousand km
1	United States	6348	6	Australia	913
2	India	3320	7	Canada	902
3	Brazil	1980	8	France	893
4	China	1210	9	Germany	656
5	Japan	1152	10	Italy	655

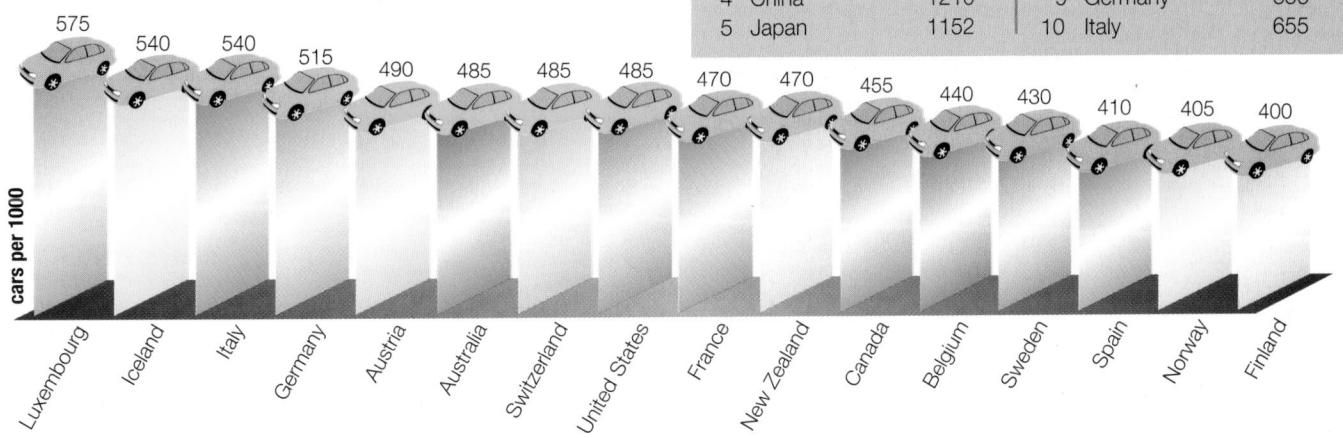

cars per 1000

Luxembourg	Iceland	Italy	Germany	Austria	Australia	Switzerland	United States	France	New Zealand	Canada	Belgium	Sweden	Spain	Norway	Finland
575	540	540	515	490	485	485	485	470	470	455	440	430	410	405	400

The train was the first truly mass means of transport. Hundreds of thousands of kilometres of track were built on almost every continent during the 19th century, opening up many remote areas and driving economic development. Despite competition from road and air transport, railways still thrive in hauling heavy cross-country freight, in transporting millions of commuters, and in linking at high speed city-centres up to 1000 km (600 miles) apart.

Steep climb San Francisco's cable cars make light work of the city's hills. The carriage clamps onto a moving cable driven from a central engine-house.

Trams, trolley buses and light trains

The first horse-drawn tram service started in New York City in 1852. The trams ran along rails set into the road. Almost 20 years later cable cars – trams pulled by a continuously moving cable housed in a trough in the road – were introduced in the hilly city of San Francisco.

City transport evolved in the late 19th century with such innovations as steam trams, battery-powered electric trams and trams powered from overhead electric cables – with power transmitted to the tram via a 'trolley', a pole topped with a metal wheel that ran along the cable. A similarly powered electric 'trolley bus' service started in British cities in 1911, running until the introduction of diesel-engined buses in the late 1940s.

In these days of traffic congestion and pollution, cities worldwide have modernised, extended or reintroduced their tram systems in an effort to improve urban environments. Elsewhere, futuristic-looking overhead railway systems, such as London's Docklands Light Railway and the SkyTrain in Vancouver, provide the answer.

1825 British engineer George Stephenson runs the first public steam train, using his engine *Locomotion*. Passengers travel at up to 24 km/h (15 mph) between Stockton and Darlington in northern England.

1830 The Liverpool and Manchester Railway opens, using Stephenson's *Rocket* – the true birth of the railways.

The Baltimore and Ohio Railroad is the first railway in the United States. It uses the locomotive *Tom Thumb*.

Iron horse The railroad opened up the American West.

1869 In the USA, the first transcontinental railway is created when the Union Pacific and Central Pacific railroads link up in Utah.

American inventor George Westinghouse patents the pneumatic (air) brake for trains.

1896–7 The first underground railway in continental Europe opens in Budapest, Hungary. The first in the USA, where it is called the subway, opens in Boston.

1800

1801 Cornishman Richard Trevithick builds the first steam locomotive, able to pull a 10-tonne load at 8 km/h (5 mph).

1829 Stephenson and his son Robert build the *Rocket*, which reaches the astonishing speed of 38 km/h (24 mph).

1850 Britain has more than 9600 km (6000 miles) of railway track; the USA has 14 500 km (9000 miles).

1850

1863 The world's first underground railway opens in London. The 6 km (4 mile) line (the Metropolitan Railway) runs from Paddington to Farringdon, via Euston and King's Cross mainline stations.

1890 The world's first deep-level electric underground railway – nicknamed the 'Tube' – starts operating in London.

1900

1900 The *Métropolitain* (or 'Métro') underground railway opens in Paris.

Power on wheels Stephenson's *Rocket* was the fastest and most powerful locomotive of its day. The Stephensons went on to supply many European railways.

Smoky journey London's underground railway – the first in the world – used coal-fuelled steam engines.

Modern train technologies

● **Magnetic levitation trains** 'Maglev' trains can travel at more than 500 km/h (310 mph). The trains 'float' 1–10 cm (½–4 in) above a guideway, kept aloft by a powerful magnetic field. Speed is regulated by means of an alternating current fed to magnets placed along the guideway, so that their magnetic field 'travels' along the track. These trains are still experimental.

● **Tilting trains** The overall speed of conventional trains is limited by their ability to negotiate curves. They can reach 235 km/h (145 mph), but are limited to 145 km/h (90 mph) on many bends. A tilting train can travel around corners 25–40 per cent faster. The train's undercarriage is fitted with a computerised device which controls pistons to adjust the angle at which the carriages tilt.

● **Monorail** Monorail train systems, such as those in Tokyo and Sydney, are electrically powered and run at relatively low speeds. Some systems use an overhead rail, from which the train is suspended, while others use a single undercarriage rail with guidewheels to stabilise the carriages.

● **Automatic light railway** This is well suited to city environments because it minimises disruption during construction: the Docklands Light Railway in London connects the City and Docklands business districts. The driverless trains are operated from a central control room by a computerised system.

● **High-speed trains** The Japanese 'Bullet', French TGV and other high-speed trains have a powerful electric engine at each end and run on special tracks with gentle curves. Signalling data is transmitted to the train via computers. TGV carriages are linked by four-wheel 'trucks' instead of having separate sets of bogies, aiding stability.

● **The world steam speed record**, 203 km/h (126 mph), was set in Britain in 1938 by the engine *Mallard* (above).

● **The fastest trains in regular service** are the French TGVs, which now consistently average speeds of 300 km/h (186 mph).

● **The world speed record for a maglev train** was set in Japan in 1999. Travelling on an 18 km (11 mile) test track, the five-coach train reached 552 km/h (343 mph).

● **The world's longest railway line**, the Trans-Siberian Railway, runs about 9300 km (5780 miles) from Moscow to Vladivostok.

● **The longest stretch of straight track**, across the Nullarbor Plain in Australia, runs 478 km (297 miles) without a bend.

● **The world's longest railway tunnel**, the Seikan, links the Japanese islands of Honshu and Hokkaido. It is 53.9 km (31.1 miles) long; its lowest point lies 240 m (787 ft) below sea level.

1916 After 25 years' work, the Trans-Siberian Railway is completed across Russia.

1928 Union Limited and Union Express launch a railway service between Cape Town and Johannesburg, using bright-blue luxury carriages. The service is officially renamed the Blue Train in 1946.

1940 In the USA, the Santa Fe Railroad opens the first regular diesel-electric freight service.

Tilting train This Swedish X-2000 train, like the innovative Italian Pendolino, senses curves in the track ahead, and a computer causes the carriages to tilt accordingly.

1900

1950

1901 The first monorail system opens in Wuppertal, Germany.

1930s The first lightweight, high-speed diesel trains enter service in Germany and the United States.

1964 Japan introduces the Shinkansen ('Bullet') train, capable of travelling at 209 km/h (130 mph).

1988 The Pendolino high-speed train enters service in Italy. It is the first commercially successful tilting train that is able to reach high speeds on standard track.

2000AD

Rail safety

Safe train operation depends on effective signalling. Most systems use red, yellow and green signals, like traffic lights, but rely on drivers remaining alert and responding to the signals. Automatic protection systems help to reduce the risk of human error.

● **Automatic Warning System (AWS)** Passing a yellow or red signal activates a hooter or buzzer in the driver's cab. If the driver fails to cancel the warning sound, the brakes are applied automatically.

● **Train Protection and Warning System (TPWS)** Unlike AWS, TPWS cannot be overridden by the driver. It initiates automatic braking of the train if it is about to pass a red signal or exceed the speed limit on a curve.

● **Automatic Train Protection (ATP)** This is the most effective and expensive system. Trackside equipment monitors the speed of the train and transmits a calculated 'safe' speed to a display in the cab. If the driver exceeds this speed, automatic braking is applied.

1983 The French TGV (*Train à Grande Vitesse*) service starts running between Paris and Lyon. The trains attain an average speed of 260 km/h (162 mph).

1994 The 50 km (31 mile) Channel Tunnel rail link connects Britain with France, carrying high-speed passenger, car and lorry-transporting trains.

2000 By the turn of the century there are more than 1.2 million km (750 000 miles) of mainline rail track around the world.

Streamlined for speed The TGV streaks through France at up to 400 km/h (250 mph).

People built primitive boats before even the first land vehicles – they had to, because rivers, lakes and seas presented otherwise uncrossable obstacles. The ability to build and skilfully sail ships led to political and economic expansion, as exploration was followed by the spread of civilisations and the growth of trade. Many of the world's greatest empires – from the Mediterranean to the Far East, from ancient Greece and Rome to Spain and Britain – were created largely by naval power and consolidated through marine trade.

The evolution of sails and rigging

The first sails, used on ancient Egyptian vessels, were rectangular and hung from a horizontal spar, or 'yard'. Such a 'square rig' gives good speed if the wind comes from more or less behind the vessel, but it cannot sail into the wind. The problem was solved about the 5th century AD by Arab shipbuilders with the lateen sail, which was triangular and hung from an angled spar. By deflecting the wind, it enabled ships to sail at an angle into the wind. From then on, the history of sail was largely a matter of refining these two systems – often in combination – up to the speedy clippers of the 19th century and today's sailing yachts. Even modern racing yachts, fore-and-aft rigged with descendants of the lateen sail, use a modern derivative of the square rig – the spinnaker – when running downwind.

Lateen-rigged ships, based on the Arab dhow, were built in the western Mediterranean from AD 1200. They could sail at an angle into the wind.

Portuguese caravel of the 15th century enlarged upon the lateen rig to produce a highly manoeuvrable light ship. Similar ships took Columbus to the New World.

Galleon combined the lateen rig for manoeuvrability and square rig for speed before the wind. It was used for trade and as a warship from the mid 16th century.

Four-masted barque was among the fastest type of 'clipper' ship. It was mainly square-rigged, designed to speed downwind with cargoes of tea, spices or wool.

Types of yacht

Most modern yachts are fore-and-aft rigged, with the sails fixed at the forward edge to a mast or to a rope or cable known as a stay. The mainsail may be a simple triangle – 'Bermuda-rigged' – or, in the gaff rig, have the top part 'cut off' and hung from a short angled spar called a gaff.

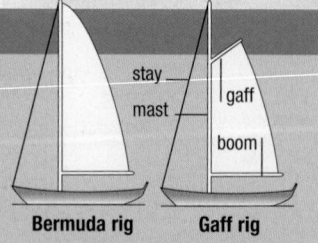

stay / mast / gaff / boom

Bermuda rig   **Gaff rig**

*c.***3200 BC** The ancient Egyptians make boats from wooden planks and use sails to harness the wind (above).

*c.***1000 BC–AD 1000** The ancestors of Pacific islanders make long ocean voyages in outrigger canoes.

*c.***AD 400–500** Arab shipbuilders develop wooden dhows with caulked (filled) joints. They are the first craft with triangular 'lateen' sails, able to sail into the wind.

*c.***1450** The first full-rigged ships are built in the Mediterranean. They combine the rudder, forecastle and poop (stern) of the cog with the light structure of lateen rigs. They have three masts, with a lateen sail on the aft or mizzen mast and rectangular sails on the others. These ships begin the great era of European exploration.

17th and 18th centuries The design of naval and merchant ships diverge for the first time since the war galleys of ancient Greece. Large cargo ships, known as East Indiamen, are developed for trade with the Far East; they are much broader than warships. Warships range from large men-of-war, carrying more than 100 guns, to light, fast, highly manoeuvrable frigates with fewer than 50 guns.

| 2000 BC | AD 1000 | 1500 | 1700 |

*c.***2500–1200 BC** The Minoans of Crete and Mycenaeans of mainland Greece build broad-beamed seagoing cargo ships with a single sail. Narrow, faster galleys, propelled by oarsmen, are developed as warships.

*c.***700–500 BC** The Greeks build biremes – fighting galleys with two banks of oars on each side – and later triremes, with three banks of oars. These ships are up to 38 m (125 ft) long, and manned by 200 men. They can reach 7 knots (13 km/h).

8th–10th centuries The Vikings cross the North Atlantic in longships (below). Up to 30 m (100 ft) long, the longships are steered using an oversized oar, or sweep, as a rudder.

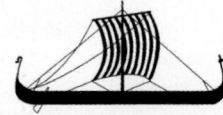

*c.***1200** Cogs, sturdy single-sailed ships with high 'castles' at bow and stern, are built in northern Europe. They have a rudder instead of a steering oar. Lightweight lateen-rigged craft appear in the Mediterranean.

Chinese junks (right) trade as far afield as India and east Africa. Their linen or matting sails, stiffened with bamboo battens, are easy to manipulate. Bulkheads divide the hull into watertight compartments.

*c.***1550** European shipbuilders develop the sturdy galleon, with a low forecastle and high, roomy poop. The largest have four masts.

1769 The biggest warship of the age of sail – the Spanish *Santissima Trinidad* – is launched. It is armed with up to 144 guns.

1776 American engineer David Bushnell builds the first practical one-man submarine. Named the *Turtle*, it has buoyancy tanks and is hand-propelled by the occupant.

A ship of the line HMS *Victory* became famous as Nelson's flagship at the Battle of Trafalgar (1805), and remains the oldest commissioned warship in the world. It was launched in 1765, and is shown here in the Mediterranean in the 1780s in a painting by Monamy Swaine. *Victory* was a 'first-rate' ship, built to carry 100 guns on three main gun decks plus the quarter deck (near the stern) and the forecastle. It took the timber of 6000 trees, mostly oaks, to build *Victory*, which is 69 m (227 ft) long and displaces 3556 tonnes. It is a so-called 'ship-rigged' vessel, meaning that it has three masts plus a bowsprit. Each mast – made of light and supple pine or fir – has three sections, supporting horizontal spars or yards, from which the sails hang. In very light winds, a fourth, 'royal' yard and sail could be hoisted to the top of each mast.

see also

192-3 **Age of exploration**
484-5 **Steamships to hydrofoils**
486-7 **Navigation**

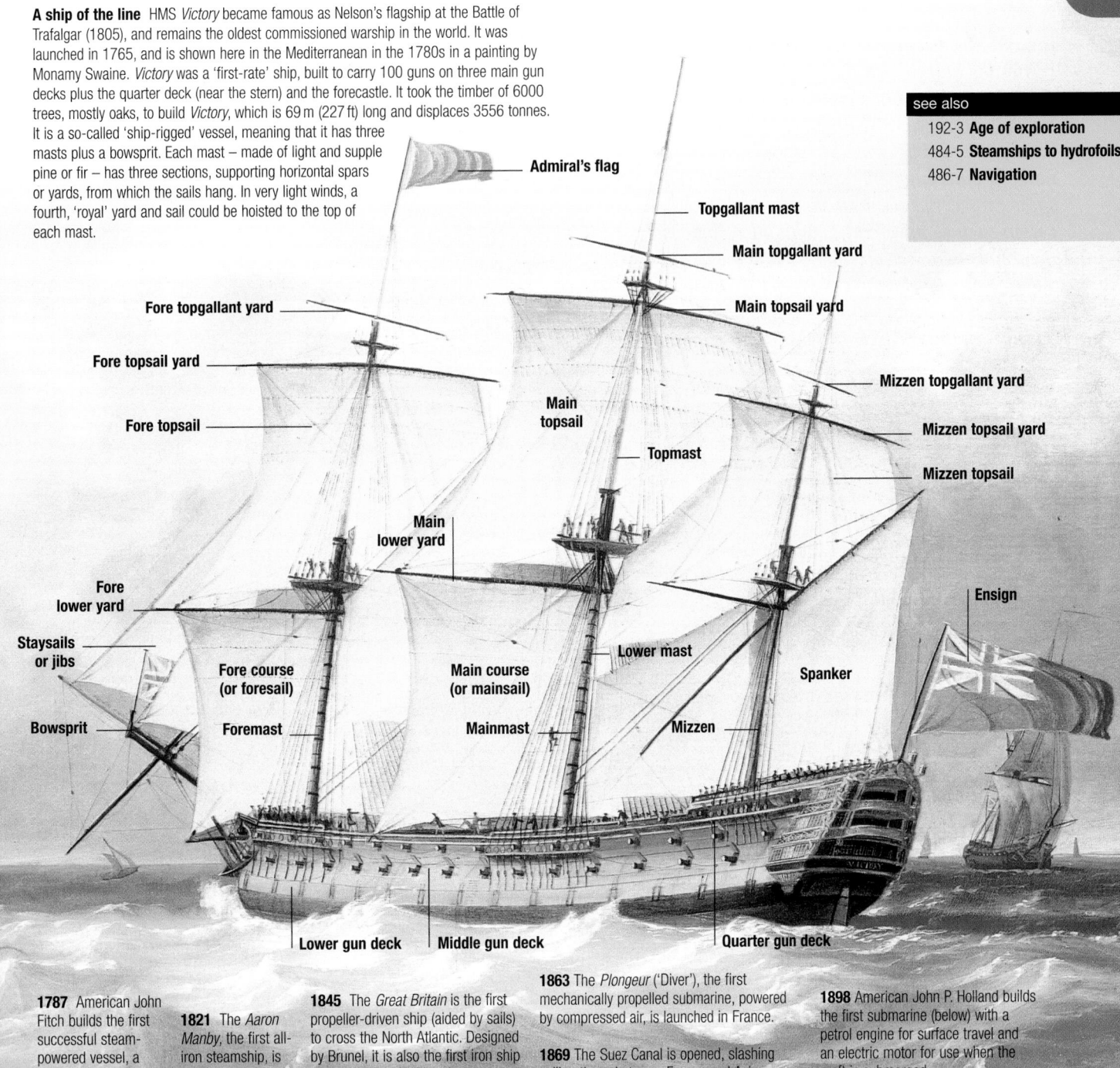

Admiral's flag

Topgallant mast

Main topgallant yard

Fore topgallant yard

Main topsail yard

Fore topsail yard

Mizzen topgallant yard

Fore topsail

Main topsail

Mizzen topsail yard

Topmast

Mizzen topsail

Main lower yard

Fore lower yard

Lower mast

Ensign

Staysails or jibs

Spanker

Fore course (or foresail)

Main course (or mainsail)

Bowsprit

Foremast

Mainmast

Mizzen

Lower gun deck

Middle gun deck

Quarter gun deck

1787 American John Fitch builds the first successful steam-powered vessel, a paddle boat.

1821 The *Aaron Manby*, the first all-iron steamship, is launched in Britain.

1845 The *Great Britain* is the first propeller-driven ship (aided by sails) to cross the North Atlantic. Designed by Brunel, it is also the first iron ship with watertight bulkheads.

1863 The *Plongeur* ('Diver'), the first mechanically propelled submarine, powered by compressed air, is launched in France.

1869 The Suez Canal is opened, slashing sailing times between Europe and Asia.

1898 American John P. Holland builds the first submarine (below) with a petrol engine for surface travel and an electric motor for use when the craft is submerged.

1800   1850   1890

1800 American engineer Robert Fulton builds the first submarine with a compressed air supply and hydroplanes to make the craft rise or fall in the water.

1807 Fulton develops the *Clermont*, the first commercially successful steamboat.

1836 The marine screw propeller, a major advance in maritime propulsion, is patented in Sweden and Britain.

1837 British engineer Isambard Kingdom Brunel launches the first ocean-going steamship, the *Great Western*. It is propelled by side-paddles.

1854 The Boston-built clipper *Lightning* sets a world record during a passage from Boston to Liverpool, when it sails 436 nautical miles (807 km) in 24 hours, reaching speeds of 21 knots (39 km/h). The slender clippers have three, four or even five masts, with up to 35 sails.

1880s–90s British engineer Charles Parsons develops the marine steam turbine engine. In 1894 he installs it in his 31.6 m (104 ft) launch the *Turbinia*, capable of 34.5 knots (64 km/h).

1890s Thames sailing barges (left) carry cargoes along the south-east coast of England. They are still being built as late as the 1920s.

Even in this age of mass air travel, shipping still carries the bulk of the world's trade. At the same time, demand for holidays at sea has led to the building of huge cruise liners, able to carry more than 3000 passengers and equipped with a vast range of entertainment facilities. The desire for speedy travel has been satisfied by high-tech vessels such as hovercraft, multihulled ships and hydrofoils. Nor has air power made the world's navies redundant, although fast patrol boats, aircraft carriers and submarines have replaced heavily armoured 'dreadnoughts' (battleships).

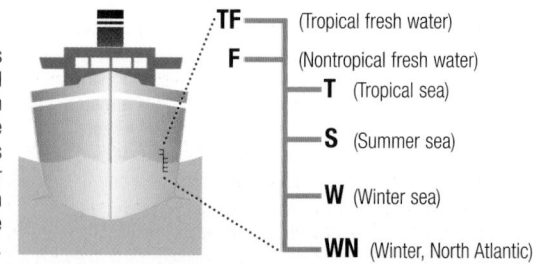

Plimsoll line These lines painted on a ship's hull show the maximum depth it can safely ride in the water when loaded. Ships sit higher in cold, salt water than in warm or fresh water, so the Plimsoll line shows a series of depths.

TF — (Tropical fresh water)
F — (Nontropical fresh water)
T — (Tropical sea)
S — (Summer sea)
W — (Winter sea)
WN — (Winter, North Atlantic)

Atlantic queen Launched in 1934, the *Queen Mary* (above in New York harbour) won the Blue Riband two years later and kept it for 16 years.

The Blue Riband

A group of transatlantic shipping companies introduced the Blue Riband award in 1833 – before the days of steamships – for liners making the fastest crossings between Europe and North America. Today, the rules state that the vessels must be proper passenger ships, not small boats, in order to rule out specially built competitors.

Blue Riband holders since 1900 (*in order of speed; route lengths varied*)

Ship	Line	Year	Duration (days:hrs:mins)	Speed (knots)
Deutschland	Hamburg America	1900	5:15:46	22.42
Kaiser Wilhelm II	North German Lloyd	1904	5:12:44	23.12
Lusitania	Cunard	1907	4:19:52	23.99
Mauritania	Cunard	1908	4:20:15	24.86
Bremen	North German Lloyd	1929	4:17:42	27.83
Europa	North German Lloyd	1930	4:17:06	27.91
Rex	Italian Line	1933	4:13:58	28.92
Normandie	French Line	1935	4:03:02	29.98
Queen Mary	Cunard White Star	1936	4:00:27	30.14
United States	United States Line	1952	3:12:12	34.51
Hoverspeed Great Britain	Hoverspeed	1990	3:07:54	36.60
Cat-Link V	Scandlines	1998	2:20:09	41.28

Key measurements

Deadweight tonnage (dwt) A ship's total carrying capacity, including crew, passengers, supplies, fuel and spare parts as well as cargo. Measured in tonnes, it is used for tankers and cargo ships.
Displacement tonnage The weight, measured in tonnes, of the water a ship displaces. It is used mostly for naval ships.
Gross tonnage (grt) A measure of the volume of the space within a commercial ship's hull. It has nothing to do with weight. One grt equals 100 cu ft, or about 3 m³.
Nautical mile Still used both at sea and in the air, it equals 1852 m (6076 ft, or about 1.15 land miles). A **knot** is a speed of one nautical mile per hour.
Net tonnage A similar measurement of volume to gross tonnage, this is based on passenger and cargo space only, excluding the engine room and fuel store. It is used when calculating harbour fees and taxes.

1900	1910	1930	1940	1950

1902 Germany launches the *Preussen*, still the biggest sailing ship ever built. It is 132 m (433 ft) long, with five masts and a steel hull.

1906 The first full-sized, self-propelled hydrofoil is successfully tested by Italian engineer Enrico Forlanini.

1908 Britain launches the first diesel-powered submarine.

1914–18 During the First World War, Germany proves the effectiveness of naval submarines by sinking many Allied ships.

1916 The British Navy commissions HMS *Argus*, the first aircraft carrier. It is converted from a passenger liner.

1937 In Germany, the first commercial hydrofoil service starts.

The world's biggest merchant fleets

Number of vessels over 100 grt (1999)
1	Japan	8462
2	Panama	6143
3	United States	5642
4	Russia	4694
5	China	3285

1939–45 The Second World War proves the importance of submarines and aircraft carriers in naval warfare.

1954 The United States launches the world's first nuclear-powered ship – the submarine *Nautilus* – which sets new underwater speed and endurance records.

1959 British inventor Christopher Cockerell builds a full-sized hovercraft – the first truly amphibious craft.

HOVERCRAFT

Hovercraft ride on a cushion of air, which allows them to travel over water, swamps, beaches or fairly level land. Powerful fans, driven by gas-turbine or lightweight diesel engines, pump air into a hollow chamber formed by the flexible skirt around the craft. The air escapes from there into the wider space between the hull and the ground or water, forming the air cushion on which the craft rides. Propellers above the stern push it forward and rudders in the airflow give steering. Top speeds may approach 70 knots (130 km/h). For extra manoeuvrability there are swivelling air nozzles, known as thrusters, on each side of the bow. Like hydrofoils, hovercraft are used as military patrol craft as well as short-distance car and passenger ferries.

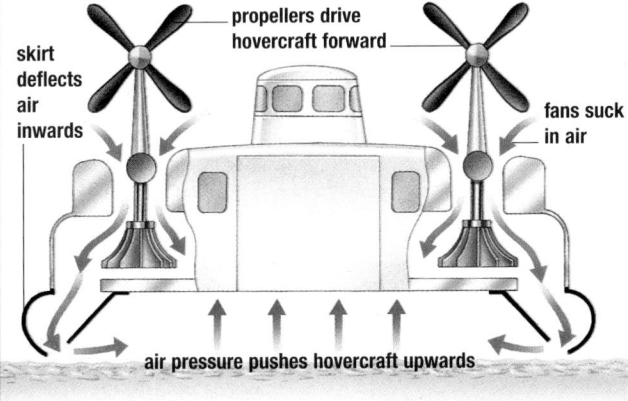

skirt deflects air inwards

propellers drive hovercraft forward

fans suck in air

air pressure pushes hovercraft upwards

Supercarrier The two nuclear reactors on board the *Nimitz*-class USS *John C. Stennis* will power it for about a million nautical miles (1.85 million km) before refuelling. The ship cruises at more than 30 knots (55.5 mph) and is operated by a crew of 6250. The flight deck covers an area of 1.8 ha (4.5 acres). The carrier was commissioned in 1995.

How a hydrofoil works

A hydrofoil uses the same principle as an aircraft. It has a foil or 'wing' mounted underneath the hull which 'flies' through the water, creating lift. When there is enough lift to raise the main hull above the water level, drag is greatly reduced, and cruising speeds of 55 knots (100 km/h) are possible in calm waters. Powered by diesel or gas-turbine engines and mostly used as short-distance passenger ferries, hydrofoils are also used as ocean-going military patrol boats and for carrying guided missiles. A hydrofoil with fully submerged foils and an automatic stabilising system to keep it level can operate in rougher water than the conventional surface-piercing type, with V-shaped foils, shown here.

flow of water over foils near bow and stern due to movement of craft

lift created by flow of water over foils

foils

turbine or diesel-powered water-jets drive craft forward

see also
482-3 **The age of sail**
486-7 **Navigation**

1970	1980	1990	2000

1970s to 90s The United States navy launches its *Nimitz*-class aircraft carriers. At 100 000 tonnes, these vessels are the world's biggest warships.

1980 Japanese coastal vessels fitted with computer-controlled rigid vertical sails, or foils, show a fuel saving of up to 50 per cent.

1976 The largest ship afloat, the supertanker *Seawise Giant*, is launched; it is enlarged and renamed *Jahre Viking* in 1980. Its deck covers more than 30 000 m² (320 000 sq ft) – equal to nearly 400 football pitches – and it has a deadweight tonnage of 564 763 tonnes. When fully laden, it draws too much water to pass through the English Channel.

1985 The ROV (remotely operated vehicle) *Argo* discovers the wreck of the liner *Titanic* (which sank in 1912) 3738 m (12 263 ft) deep on the Atlantic seabed.

1999 The *Voyager of the Seas* is launched. The world's biggest passenger ship, it has berths for 3800 passengers.

Jahre Viking At 458.5 m (1504 ft), it is as long as 43 buses nose to tail.

Electronic systems can plot the position of a seaborne vessel or aeroplane to within a few metres, using reflections of radio waves bounced against fixed beacons or satellites. Before this technology became available, ocean voyagers had to rely on wind direction, astronomical observation or dead reckoning to calculate their position and direction.

The principles of plotting a course

The 'fixed' positions of the Sun and the stars offered the most reliable reference points for medieval sailors. Latitude – the distance north or south of the Equator – could be calculated by measuring the altitude of the Pole Star or the noonday Sun and consulting almanacs which plotted the celestial positions for each day in the year. Longitude – the distance east or west of the meridian line at Greenwich – could be determined by comparing local time with the time at a known meridian (the Earth rotates by 15 degrees each hour). Today, navigators still use fixed reference points in the sky – satellites, rather than stars – which receive and reflect radio waves to pinpoint their position anywhere on Earth.

Plotting a course without reference to the stars or satellites is known as dead reckoning. Measurements of direction and speed are used to gauge the position of a ship or aircraft in relation to a fixed starting point.

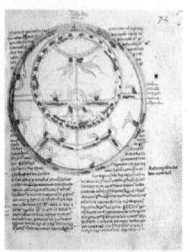

Ancient astronomy
A Christian Greek manuscript (above) explains the complex workings of an astrolabe (below right).

The astrolabe

Ancient Greek astronomers used the astrolabe to calculate the time using the position of the Sun or the stars. Movable discs mapped out the stars on the face of the astrolabe. When the device was hung freely from the thumb-ring at the top, the metal rule across the face could be aligned between the human eye and a celestial body, and the discs rotated to correspond with its angle. The time could then be read on a scale around the circumference. Medieval European sailors adapted the idea, creating the quadrant – a quarter circle with pinholes on one edge for sighting stars, and a plumb line to measure the angle of elevation using a 90° scale.

Late 10th century
Viking sailors calculate latitude by observing the position of the Pole Star.

Key terms

● **Log** A rotating paddle or propeller – or an electronic system such as sonar – which measures a ship's speed. Can also measure the distance travelled through water.

● **Loran** (long-range navigation) A system in which an on-board receiver pinpoints its position by measuring the time difference between long-wave radio signals emitted by a connected series of land stations. Loran is being superseded by satellite navigation.

● **Radar** (radio detection and ranging) The transmission of radio waves and detection of their reflection from ships and other objects, showing their distance and direction on a screen.

● **Radio navigation** The use of radio waves for navigation. The VOR (VHF omnidirectional radio) system used by aircraft, for example, broadcasts signals from radio beacons in known positions along air corridors. Aircraft follow the signals from one beacon to the next.

● **Sextant** An instrument used to calculate a ship's position. It has a curved scale with a fixed, half-silvered mirror, a movable arm with a second mirror, and an eyepiece. Looking through the eyepiece, the mirror image of the Sun or a star is aligned with the horizon by moving the arm, then a reading of its angle of altitude is taken from the scale and checked against latitude and longitude tables.

● **Sonar** An underwater device that works by echo location. It uses reflected sound waves in the same way that radar uses reflected radio waves to show the direction and distance of objects.

● **Transponder** The receiver-transmitter in an aircraft that detects, boosts and retransmits radar signals, automatically identifying the aircraft on air-traffic control screens.

Hadley's quadrant

In 1730, John Hadley invented a revolutionary device: a 45 degree quadrant with a movable mirror which reflected a celestial body onto a half-silvered mirror opposite the eyepiece. The half-silvered mirror allowed enough light through to keep the real horizon visible. Hadley's invention became a standard device, and developed into the sextant.

1569 Flemish cartographer Gerardus Mercator publishes the first atlas of the world. He devises a way of representing the spherical surface of the Earth on a flat piece of paper – the Mercator projection.

c.1666 English scientist Robert Hooke invents the reflecting quadrant, with a movable mirror to line up the Sun or a star with the horizon.

0	500	1000	1500	1600	1700

< At least 1000 BC Pacific islanders navigate great distances using the stars and memorised patterns of ocean swells.

c.200 BC The astrolabe is invented in Greece.

c.AD 850 Arab seamen develop the marine astrolabe – a simplified version of the astronomical astrolabe. It is used to measure the position of the Sun or Pole Star above the horizon.

c.1100 The compass, made with the naturally magnetic mineral lodestone (iron oxide), is used first by Chinese and then by European and Arab navigators.

1594 Englishman John Davis invents the backstaff, a rod with a crosspiece which lines up with the Pole Star or the Sun and measures their angle above the horizon.

c.1677 Isaac Newton builds a reflecting quadrant with two mirrors. The angle measured is doubled to give altitude, so the scale reduces in size to 45°. (The device is later known as an octant.)

HOW GPS WORKS

The Navstar global positioning system (GPS) was set up by the United States Department of Defense to provide all-weather navigation information for its ground, sea and air forces. It was later opened up to civilian use, and is now used by a range of organisations, from fishing fleets to the emergency services.

The system uses 24 satellites launched into orbits about 20 000 km (12 500 miles) above the surface of the Earth. They each circle the Earth every 12 hours, transmitting signals regulated by atomic clocks, and are accurately tracked. GPS receivers on Earth, which can be the size of a mobile phone, measure the precise time the signals take to arrive from at least three of the satellites – and hence the exact distance of each satellite.

The receiver uses a built-in electronic almanac, which stores the exact position of each satellite, to calculate its position to within a few metres. It can also calculate a course to a chosen destination. The receiver's built-in clock is also synchronised by satellite. Correction signals are sent out whenever the slightest deviation in a satellite's orbit is detected.

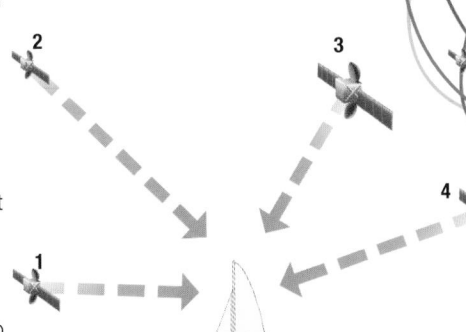

Long-distance 'fix' At least four of the Navstar satellites are within line of sight of any point on Earth at a time (above and left). The precise time their signals take to reach the receiver indicates their distance, giving a precise location instantly.

The longitude prize

Until the 18th century, inaccurate timekeeping during sea voyages made longitude calculations unreliable. In 1714 the British government offered £20 000 to anyone who could solve the problem. Yorkshire-born carpenter John Harrison spent more than 30 years tackling the challenge, crafting clocks of increasing intricacy. By 1759, he had created a chronometer accurate to within 5 seconds on a journey between Plymouth and Jamaica. The prize money was withheld until 1773 because of controversy over Harrison's lack of formal education and secrecy about his technical methods.

Perfect timing Harrison did not provide any technical plans for his 1759 chronometer (left), making it difficult to copy.

Air traffic control

Over land, commercial aircraft keep to air corridors, marked by radio beacons. They are directed along these by ground controllers using radar, and there are strict rules about how far apart vertically and horizontally the planes are allowed to fly. Over the oceans, the corridors are wider than over land, and other navigation systems, such as Loran, are used.

Near airports, aircraft circulate close together in stacks before being directed onto the glide path, which leads to the landing runway. Landing systems at the airport transmit two accurate radio beams: one indicating the centre line of the runway, the other giving the correct landing angle. Instruments on board the aircraft warn the pilot of any deviation from the correct path. The signals can be fed to an autopilot to land an aircraft safely in zero visibility more accurately than a human pilot.

1908 German Hermann Anschtz-Kaempfe and American Ambrose Sperry independently invent the gyrocompass, which works on the principle that a spinning gyroscope always points to true north.

c.1950 The first accurate inertial guidance system (IGS) is developed. The system (usually for an aircraft, rocket or submarine) uses dead-reckoning techniques.

1978–95 The United States Department of Defense sets up the Navstar global positioning system (GPS), using monitors (left) to connect with satellites to provide precise navigation. The system is first used by US military forces.

1800	1900	1950	2000

1757 British naval captain John Campbell extends Hadley's quadrant scale to 60°. Long lunar distances and local time can now be calculated. The device, known as a sextant, can be used in conjunction with celestial tables to work out latitude and longitude.

1767 *The Nautical Almanac* is published in Britain, supervised by the Astronomer Royal. It provides the first accurate tables showing the positions of celestial bodies throughout the year.

1887 German physicist Heinrich Hertz discovers radio waves. He demonstrates that radio waves can be refracted in the same way as light waves, taking the first step in the development of radar technology.

1939 Radar systems are installed in military equipment by Britain, France, Germany, Italy, Japan, the Soviet Union and the United States.

1964 The US Navy launches its Transit satellites, the first satellite navigation system.

see also
30-4 **Structure of the Earth**
406-9 **Radio**
528-9 **Electromagnetism**
592-3 **The night sky**

In 1999, 1.6 billion people flew on scheduled flights worldwide. A little over 200 years earlier, aviation history began when two Frenchmen drifted just a few kilometres in a hot-air balloon. The intervening years have produced aircraft as diverse as the tiny microlight – little more than a giant kite fitted with an engine – airliners that carry hundreds of passengers and jet fighter planes capable of speeds of more than 3200 km/h (2000 mph).

Ferdinand, Count von Zeppelin (1838–1917)

German
Zeppelin, a general in the German army, retired early in order to devote himself to designing and building the rigid-framed dirigible airships that would come to bear his name. His vast, cigar-shaped craft – first flown in 1900 – were the first commercially viable airships. German military Zeppelins bombed London during the First World War.

George Cayley (1773–1857)

British
Cayley was a Yorkshire baronet who was passionate about flight. Today, he is widely recognised as the father of the science of aerodynamics. He worked out the main principles of flying, and wrote about parachutes and helicopters. But the engines of his day were not capable of getting a craft airborne. He built a number of gliders, one of which in 1853 carried his coachman a distance of some 400 m (1300 ft), but it had no flight controls.

Louis Blériot (1872–1936)

French
Blériot's hop from Calais to Dover in 1909 was the first international aeroplane flight over water. His craft were among the first successful monoplanes, and in 1908 he introduced flap-type ailerons for flight control.

Junkers J1
Germany, 1915
The J1 was the first all-metal aeroplane with cantilever wings entirely supported by an internal framework rather than by external struts or cables.

Fokker EI/III
Germany, 1915
'Flying Dutchman' A.H.G. Fokker's pioneer fighter planes enabled the pilot to fire a machine gun ahead without hitting the propeller blades.

1750 | 1800 | 1900 | 1925

October 15, 1783
In Paris, the first-ever manned flight takes place. Jean-François Pilâtre de Rozier rises 25 m (80 ft) in a tethered hot-air balloon built by the Montgolfier brothers.

November 21, 1783
Again in Paris, the first manned free (untethered) flight takes place, as before in a Montgolfier balloon. The passengers, Pilâtre de Rozier and François-Laurent, marquis d'Arlandes, spend 25 minutes in the air.

December 1, 1783
Frenchmen Jacques Charles and Nicolas Robert make the first manned flight in a hydrogen-filled balloon, designed and built by themselves.

1799
In Britain, Sir George Cayley produces the first designs for a winged aircraft powered by propellers.

1849
An unmanned Austrian balloon makes the first aerial bombing raid in history, against Venice.

1853
Frenchman Henri Giffard makes the first powered flight, in a steam-powered dirigible (steerable airship).

Sir George Cayley's coachman makes the first manned but uncontrolled flight by a winged glider.

1891–6
German engineer Otto Lilienthal makes several controlled glider flights.

1900
In Germany, a Zeppelin airship takes its first flight.

December 17, 1903
In the USA, the Wright brothers achieve the first powered, manned flight.

1909
Frenchman Louis Blériot flies an aeroplane across the Channel from France.

The Zeppelin *Deutschland* enters commercial service.

1914
The world's first regular passenger aeroplane goes into service, flying across Tampa Bay, Florida.

1914–18
During the First World War, rapid technological advances result from the extensive use of fighters, bombers and reconnaissance planes – as well as bombing and reconnaissance balloons and airships.

1919
The British *R34* makes the first transatlantic crossing by an airship.

British aviators John Alcock and Arthur Whitten Brown make the first nonstop transatlantic flight by aeroplane.

1927
American aviator Charles Lindbergh makes the first solo nonstop transatlantic flight by aeroplane.

Wright brothers

Wilbur (1867–1912) and Orville (1871–1948); American
The Wright brothers' first successful controlled flight in a powered heavier-than-air craft, in 1903, was the culmination of years of preparation. They had experimented extensively with wings and rudder controls, and built their own lightweight petrol engine. They went on to set up their own aircraft-manufacturing company in 1909.

Wright brothers' *Flyer* (1903)

Concorde
Britain/France, 1976
The first supersonic airliner has a cruising speed of 2330 km/h (1450 mph). Its high cost, along with environmental problems, limited production to 16 aircraft. A fatal accident in 2000 grounded the entire fleet for more than a year.

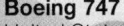

see also
486-7 **Navigation**
490-1 **The age of air travel**
492-3 **First steps in space**
494-5 **Cooperation in space**

de Havilland Comet
Britain, 1952
The Comet was the first jet airliner. A series of accidents, caused by metal fatigue, grounded the first model, but an improved version was rolled out in 1958.

Boeing 747
United States, 1970
The 747 was the first commercial jumbo-jet airliner, able to carry almost 500 passengers and powered by large-diameter turbofan engines. More than 1200 aircraft had been built by 2000.

Douglas DC3 ('Dakota')
United States, 1936
The twin-engined 21-seater DC3 airliner (also called the Dakota) became one of the most widely used transport aircraft in the world. Some DC3s are still in service today.

F-100 ('Super Sabre')
United States, 1953
The F-100 fighter made history as the first supersonic production aircraft.

Boeing 247
United States, 1933
The first modern airliner, the Boeing 247 was a twin-engined all-metal monoplane carrying ten passengers at 300 km/h (185 mph).

Hawker Siddeley Harrier
Britain, 1966
This was the first operational V/STOL (vertical/short takeoff and landing) military aircraft, widely flown from land and aircraft carriers.

Airbus A380
Britain/France/Germany/Spain, 2006 (scheduled)
The European consortium's double-deck 'superjumbo' will seat up to 1000, and may provide restaurants, shops, a gym and sleeper cabins.

1950 **1975** **2000**

1930
British engineer Frank Whittle patents his gas turbine (jet) engine design.

1935
A French-built Breguet-Dorand craft makes the first controlled flight by a helicopter.

1937
The hydrogen-filled German airship *Hindenburg* explodes in the United States, and passenger-carrying airships cease service.

1939
Russian-born American engineer Igor Sikorsky builds and flies the first single-rotor helicopter.

The Heinkel He-178, built in Germany, becomes the first successful jet aircraft.

1939–45
Advances during the Second World War include the first jet fighter, airborne radar and naval air power.

1947
American Chuck Yeager breaks the sound barrier in a Bell X-1 rocket plane.

1952
The British de Havilland Comet launches the first jet-airliner service.

1959
The Boeing 707 jet starts services in North America and across the Atlantic.

1960s
The development of highly efficient turbofan engines makes it possible to build wide-bodied 'jumbo-jet' airliners, heralding the era of low-cost mass air travel.

1976
Air France and British Airways start operating supersonic passenger services using Concorde, which makes the Atlantic crossing in just three and a half hours.

1999
Bertrand Piccard of Switzerland and Briton Brian Jones succeed in making the first nonstop round-the-world flight in a balloon, the Breitling Orbiter 3.

Air-speed records

Pilots have pushed aircraft to the limits of speed ever since the earliest days of flying, and in the process have stimulated far-ranging design and engineering improvements. Most of the records set here (over a timed, measured course) were achieved in military aircraft.

			km/h	(mph)				km/h	(mph)
1905	W. Wright	United States	61.2	(38.0)	1955	H.A. Hanes	United States	1323.3	(822.26)
1912	J. Vedrines	France	174.1	(108.18)	1956	L.P. Twiss	Britain	1821.99	(1132.13)
1922	W. Mitchell	United States	358.84	(222.97)	1957	A.E. Drew	United States	1943.44	(1207.6)
1932	J.H. Doolittle	United States	473.76	(294.38)	1958	W.W. Irwin	United States	2259.66	(1404.09)
1933	J. Wedell	United States	490.82	(304.98)	1959	G. Mosolov	Soviet Union	2388.03	(1483.85)
1939	F. Wendel	Germany	755.14	(469.22)	1959	J.W. Rogers	United States	2455.79	(1525.96)
1945	H.J. Wilson	Britain	975.66	(606.25)	1961	R.B. Robinson	United States	2585.12	(1606.32)
1948	R.L. Johnson	United States	1079.84	(670.98)	1962	G. Mosolov	Soviet Union	2680.99	(1665.89)
1952	J.S. Nash	United States	1124.13	(698.5)	1965	R.L. Stephens	United States	3331.5	(2070.1)
1953	F.K. Everest Jr	United States	1215.28	(755.14)	1976	E.W. Joersz	United States	3529.56	(2193.16)

Modern passenger aircraft travel at speeds ranging from around 320 km/h (200 mph) to Concorde's supersonic 2179 km/h (1354 mph) – more than twice the speed of sound. Advanced engine technology and streamlining take advantage of the natural forces of air pressure, gravity and friction to lift and support 350 tonne jumbo jets, and the safety and comfort of the aeroplane attracts millions of travellers every year.

HOW A PLANE FLIES

Four different forces act on an aircraft:

⬤ **lift** – an upward force created by the movement of air around the aircraft's wings.
⬤ **gravity** – the natural force due to the aircraft's weight, which pulls it downwards.
⬤ **thrust** – the forward force created by the aircraft's engines, which moves it forwards.
⬤ **drag** – the frictional force of air moving past the aircraft, which slows it down.

During steady, level flight, lift is equal to gravity and thrust is equal to drag, but to take off, a plane has to push these forces out of balance.

Taking off The cross-sectional shape of a wing is known as an aerofoil – the curved front and top taper to a thin, streamlined back. The shape acts with air pressure to create lift.

When an aircraft is at a standstill, the air pressure on the top and bottom surfaces of its wings is equal. As the plane speeds along the runway during take-off, air flowing under the flat lower surface of each wing moves a shorter distance – and more slowly – than the air passing over the longer, curved top surface. The air molecules under the lower surface bunch closer together, raising the air pressure. The difference in pressure above and below the wing pushes it upwards. Once an aircraft reaches a certain speed – 290 km/h (180 mph) for a Boeing 747 – lift exceeds the force of gravity, thrust overcomes drag, and it rises into the air.

Steering The pilot uses movable metal plates known as control surfaces to balance the aircraft and change its direction. They work by causing upward, downward or sideways pressure from air moving past the wing. The tail also has control surfaces: an upright fin (rudder), which stops the plane slewing from side to side, and horizontal tail planes (elevators), which move the nose up and down and prevent the aircraft from rocking.

Thrust As well as steering the plane and keeping it aloft, the wings hold fuel tanks and engines. Jet engines expel pressurised gas at a speed of more than 2000 km/h (1240 mph).

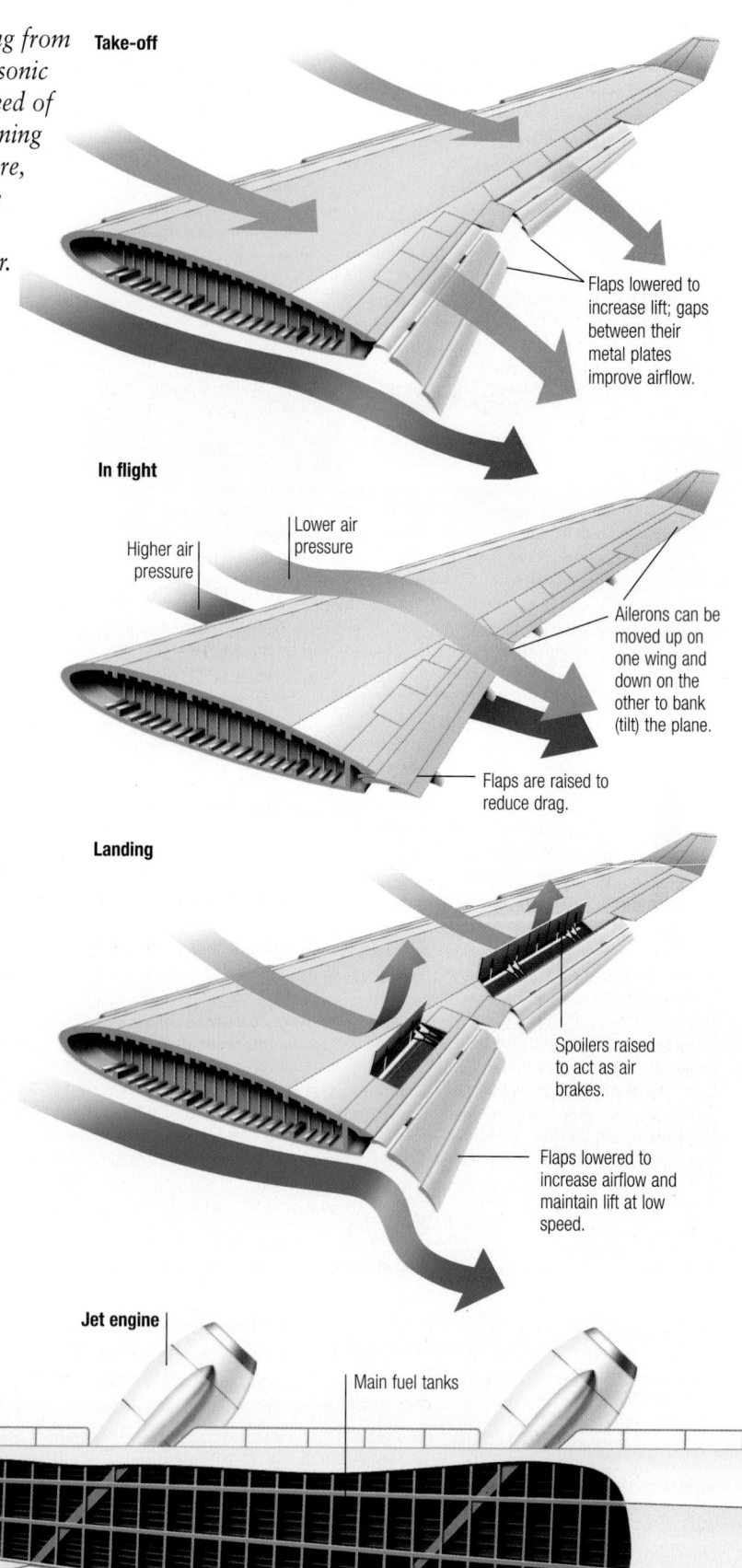

Take-off

Flaps lowered to increase lift; gaps between their metal plates improve airflow.

In flight

Higher air pressure

Lower air pressure

Ailerons can be moved up on one wing and down on the other to bank (tilt) the plane.

Flaps are raised to reduce drag.

Landing

Spoilers raised to act as air brakes.

Flaps lowered to increase airflow and maintain lift at low speed.

Jet engine

Main fuel tanks

AIRCRAFT ENGINES

Piston engine The thrust of a piston engine is created by its propeller, which pushes air back like a fan and creates an equal and opposite forward thrust. Today, only light aircraft use piston engines. Most aeroplanes use some kind of gas turbine (jet) engine.

Turboprop engine Like a piston engine, this has a propeller, but it is driven by a gas turbine, which also produces some direct thrust from its exhaust gases. It is efficient and economical only at relatively low speeds, and is used mainly for airliners operating on short routes.

Turbojet engine This is a 'pure' gas turbine, which derives its power from the burned gases shooting from its rear. It is powerful, but noisy, and uses a lot of fuel. It is used mainly in supersonic and military aircraft. Some jet engines have an 'afterburner', which burns extra fuel in the exhaust to boost thrust.

Turbofan engine This is used in most modern airliners as it combines great power with fuel economy and relatively low noise. It has a gas turbine, which serves partly to drive a large fan. Air from this fan forms a rapidly moving column round the exhaust jet – providing about 75 per cent of the thrust and also masking the noise.

Turbofan engine

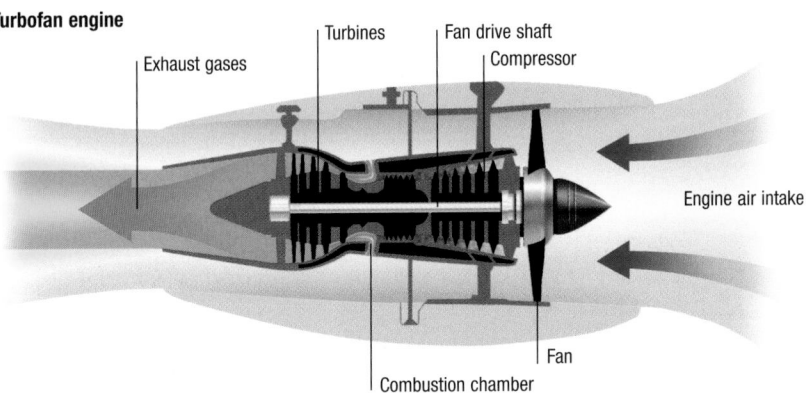

Exhaust gases | Turbines | Fan drive shaft | Compressor | Engine air intake | Fan | Combustion chamber

THE AGE OF THE GLOBETROTTER

With the development of the jet airliner in the late 1950s, the world became a smaller place. Crossing the Atlantic by jet plane took about one-sixteenth of the time it had taken by boat – just seven or eight hours (in 1976, with the introduction of commercial supersonic flights on Concorde, the time was reduced to just three hours). Travellers could reach Australia in about 24 hours by air, instead of weeks by sea.

As airports opened all over the world and intense competition among the airlines brought ticket prices down, holidays abroad became a reality for many people. In 1999 more than 9 million British tourists flew to Spain.

Ensuring that the skies remain safe is the job of air-traffic control. At London's Heathrow Airport, air-traffic controllers at the height of the tourist season deal with more than 1000 flights a day, with one flight taking off every two minutes.

How a helicopter flies

A helicopter generally has one propeller-like rotor on a vertical shaft. The rotor is, in fact, a rotating wing, shaped like an aerofoil, which when under power creates lift.

A complex gearing mechanism allows the rotor to be tilted forward, backward or to the side. This provides horizontal thrust, allowing the helicopter to move in any direction.

As the rotor turns, it tends to make the helicopter's fuselage turn in the opposite direction. Most helicopters have a small tail rotor to create side thrust, which counteracts this tendency.

Twin-rotor helicopters have two rotors turning in opposite directions: their turning forces cancel each other out, and no tail rotor is needed.

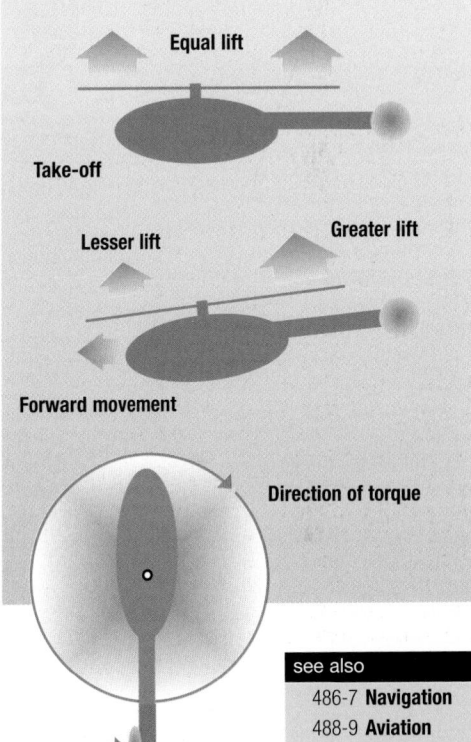

Equal lift / Take-off / Lesser lift / Greater lift / Forward movement / Direction of torque / Sideways thrust from tail rotor

see also
486-7 **Navigation**
488-9 **Aviation**
522-3 **Mechanics**

World's busiest airlines

Domestic and international passengers

		million (1999)
1	Delta Air Lines	105.5
2	United Airlines	87.0
3	American Airlines	81.5
4	Northwest Airlines	57.5
5	US Airways	55.8
6	Continental Airlines	44.0
7	Nippon Airlines	42.7
8	Lufthansa	42.1
9	Air France	37.0
10	British Airways	36.6

World's busiest airports

Domestic and international passengers

		million (1999)
1	Atlanta	77.6
2	Chicago, O'Hare	72.6
3	London, Heathrow	62.0
4	Los Angeles	61.8
5	Dallas–Fort Worth	56.3
6	Tokyo, Haneda	54.3
7	Frankfurt	45.4
8	Paris, Charles de Gaulle	43.4
9	San Francisco	40.0
10	Denver	38.0

Most frequent fliers

Air travel by country

		annual passenger km, billion
1	United States	984.7
2	Japan	154.4
3	United Kingdom	152.1
4	Germany	90.4
5	France	89.3
6	China	75.3
7	Australia	73.7
8	Netherlands	69.1
9	Canada	63.8
10	Singapore	58.1

Much of the early impetus for space travel came from Cold War political rivalry between the United States and the Soviet Union. The Russians took the lead when they put the first man in space in 1961. This prompted President Kennedy to commit the USA to a programme to land men on the Moon within the decade. American industrial resources enabled it to overtake its rival, and the Soviet focus shifted to long-term space stations.

Spin-offs from space

The space programme raised thousands of technological problems, needing new materials, new miniaturised sensors and new electronic systems. Many of these technologies have now become a part of everyday life. Despite common belief they did not include nonstick pans, but did include:
● **bar codes** These are based on NASA systems for keeping track of the millions of spacecraft parts.
● **quartz watches** They were first used on Apollo flights.
● **miniature artificial heart** This was developed from fuel-pump technology used in the space shuttle.
● **charge-coupled devices** Based on satellite sensors, these are used in video cameras and to detect cancers.
● **water-cooled suits** Originally used by astronauts, they are now available for medical and other applications.
● **fire-retardant metallic materials** Now used to protect fire-fighters, they were first used in space.
● **pressurised ball-point pens** These pens, which can write upside-down, were first used by Apollo astronauts.
● **cordless electric drills** They were first used by Apollo astronauts to gather moon rocks.

Konstantin Tsiolkovsky
(1857–1935)
Russian physicist and teacher
In 1903, Tsiolkovsky published a theoretical paper on rocketry. He later forecast space travel and suggested the use of liquid fuels and multistage rockets.

Robert Goddard
(1882–1945)
American physicist
Goddard experimented with solid and liquid-fuelled rockets, developing propellant pumps and gyroscopic controls. He launched his first 1.2 m (4 ft) liquid-fuelled rocket to a height of 56 m (184 ft) in 1926. His achievements were only appreciated after his death.

Wernher von Braun
(1912–77)
German engineer
Von Braun led the team that built the V2 rocket, used against Allied cities in the last year of the Second World War. Von Braun surrendered to the United States Army at the end of the war, and later led the NASA team that developed the Saturn rockets that took the first men to the Moon.

Yuri Gagarin
(1934–68)
Soviet cosmonaut
Soviet Air Force pilot Gagarin (above) made history when he piloted his *Vostok 1* spacecraft into Earth orbit on April 12, 1961, becoming the first person in space. He remained in orbit for just over 89 minutes, travelling at a speed of about 27400km/h (over 17000mph). From start to finish, the whole mission lasted 1 hour 48 minutes. Gagarin died in an aircraft crash while training for another space mission.

John Glenn
(1921–)
American astronaut
Glenn was the first American to orbit the Earth (which he did three times over about four hours), in the Mercury capsule *Friendship 7* on February 20, 1962. Glenn left the astronaut programme in 1964 and later became a United States senator. He returned to space, aged 77, in 1998 on board the space shuttle *Discovery*, becoming the oldest man in space.

Neil Armstrong
(1930–)
American astronaut
Armstrong was the first man to set foot on the Moon. A United States Navy pilot and civilian test pilot before he became an astronaut, in 1966 Armstrong and a co-astronaut performed the first successful space docking manoeuvre. Three years later, Armstrong commanded the Apollo 11 lunar landing mission. After this, Armstrong did not go into space again.

Saturn V rocket with Apollo spacecraft

February 3, 1966
The Soviet Luna 9 probe makes the first soft landing on the Moon.

December 21, 1968
The Apollo 8 mission is the first manned mission to orbit the Moon. After ten orbits and six days it splashes down in the Pacific, within 5km (3 miles) of its target.

October 4, 1957
The 'space age' begins with the launch of the first artificial satellite, the 85kg (185lb) Soviet *Sputnik 1*.

June 16, 1963
Russian Valentina Tereshkova becomes the first woman in space.

1965

1960

March 18, 1965
Russian Alexei Leonov makes the first 'space walk' from *Voskhod 2* orbiting 2500km (300 miles) above Earth.

January 27, 1967
Fire on board an Apollo capsule during launch-pad tests kills three astronauts. This delays the Apollo programme while parts of the capsule are redesigned.

July 20/21, 1969
Americans Neil Armstrong and 'Buzz' Aldrin are the first humans to set foot on the Moon, during the Apollo 11 mission.

1805
English artillery officer William Congreve builds the first modern military rockets. Measuring 100cm (40in) long, with a range of 1800m (5900ft), they are used with limited success at the Battle of Waterloo in 1815.

May 5, 1961
Alan Shepard is the first American in space. His sub-orbital flight reaches a height of 100km (62 miles) above the Earth's surface.

May 25, 1961
In the United States, President Kennedy in an address to Congress sets his country the challenge of landing a man on the Moon and returning him safely to Earth before the end of the 1960s.

July 14, 1965
Mariner 4, an unmanned American spacecraft, flies by Mars and sends back photographs.

Moonwalking Apollo astronauts explore the Moon at last in July 1969.

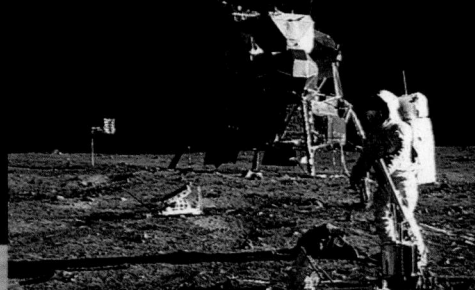

Manned Apollo flights

Between May 1964 and April 1968, there were nine unmanned suborbital and orbital flights around the Earth to test various components of the Apollo system. On January 27, 1967, a fire in the command module (probably caused by a spark in the pure-oxygen atmosphere) killed the crew, Virgil Grissom, Edward White and Roger Chaffee. They were training for the first planned manned Apollo Earth-orbit flight, mission AS-204, scheduled for February 21, 1967. Resulting modifications to electrical and air-supply systems delayed the Apollo programme by over a year.

Mission	Dates	Crew	Destination	Notes
Apollo 7	October 11–22, 1968	Walter Schirra, Donn Eisele, Walter Cunningham	Earth orbit	First manned Apollo test flight. Delayed over a year by January 1967 fire.
Apollo 8	December 21–27, 1968	Frank Borman, James Lovell, William Anders	Lunar orbit	First manned lunar flight, using command/service module only.
Apollo 9	March 3–13, 1969	James McDivitt, David Scott, Russell Schweickart	Earth orbit	First flight test of lunar module (the module that will be used for landing on the Moon), including separation and redocking.
Apollo 10	May 18–26, 1969	Thomas Stafford, John Young, Eugene Cernan	Lunar orbit	First flight test of lunar module in lunar orbit.
Apollo 11	July 16–24, 1969	Neil Armstrong, Michael Collins*, Edwin ('Buzz') Aldrin	Sea of Tranquility	First lunar landing.
Apollo 12	November 14–24, 1969	Charles Conrad, Richard Gordon*, Alan Bean	Ocean of Storms	Second lunar landing. Brought back parts of old *Surveyor 3* probe.
Apollo 13	April 11–17, 1970	James Lovell, John Swigert, Fred Haise	(Lunar swingby)	Lunar landing cancelled after explosion in fuel cell severely damaged craft.
Apollo 14	January 31–February 9, 1971	Alan Shepard, Stuart Roosa*, Edgar Mitchell	Fra Mauro	Third lunar landing. Hand-pulled 'lunar cart' used.
Apollo 15	July 26–August 7, 1971	David Scott, Alfred Worden*, James Irwin	Hadley Rille	Fourth lunar landing. Powered Lunar Rover used. Lunar subsatellite released.
Apollo 16	April 16–27, 1972	John Young, Thomas Mattingly*, Charles Duke	Descartes	Fifth lunar landing. Lunar Rover used. Lunar subsatellite released
Apollo 17	December 7–19, 1972	Eugene Cernan, Ronald Evans*, Harrison Schmitt	Taurus-Littrow	Final lunar landing. Lunar Rover used. Schmitt was the first professional geologist on the Moon.

*Command module pilot – remained in lunar orbit while other crew members landed; in all crew lists, the mission commander is named first.

see also

26–7 **The Moon**
494-5 **Cooperation i**

Contact in space
A commemorative United States stamp marks the 1975 docking of the Apollo and Soyuz spacecrafts.

US 10c
APOLLO SOYUZ 1975

970–2
hree unmanned Soviet lunar robes return soil samples to arth. Two of them use remote-controlled rover vehicles.

1971–82
A series of Soviet Salyut space stations are launched, operating for up to five years. Crews spend up to eight months on board.

February 5, 1974
The American probe *Mariner 10* flies past Venus on its way to a rendezvous with Mercury, which it reaches on March 29.

July 20, 1976
The Americans launch *Viking 1* and, six weeks later, *Viking 2* to land on Mars. They send back images and data, but report no signs of life.

April 19, 1971
The Soviet Union launches the first Earth-orbiting space station, Salyut 1.

June 7, 1971
Three Soviet cosmonauts are killed when air leaks from their Soyuz 11 during re-entry.

November 13, 1971
The American probe *Mariner 9* orbits Mars and for 11 months transmits data and images of the planet and its moons.

May 14, 1973
The first American space station, Skylab, is launched, but is damaged. Repairs are successfully carried out in orbit.

December 3, 1973
After a 21 month flight, the American probe *Pioneer 10* passes by Jupiter. It is followed in 1974 by *Pioneer 11*.

1975

July 17, 1975
An American Apollo capsule successfully docks with a Soviet Soyuz craft. This is the first step towards international space stations.

October 21, 1975
The Soviet *Venera 9* lander sends the first images of the surface of Venus.

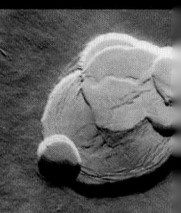

Olympus Mons Viking stunning image of the c on Mars' highest moun

Space exploration continues, but marked by increasing international cooperation rather than the old Cold War rivalries. After Apollo's success, it was time to develop a reusable craft to bring down the enormous costs of space travel. At the same time, ever-closer investigations of other planets continued, and increasingly sophisticated telescopes and other instrumentation were sent into space.

The space shuttle

The space shuttle, first launched in 1981, made history as the first reusable spacecraft. A cross between a rocket and a glider, its proper name is the Space Transportation System (STS).

On lift-off, the main craft is dwarfed by the huge external fuel tank, which supplies the three main engines; it is discarded just before reaching orbit. The craft also has two external solid-fuel booster engines that are ditched soon after lift-off. The shuttle's own tanks contain enough fuel for manoeuvring in orbit and for re-entry.

The craft has a large payload bay for carrying satellites and space probes to be launched from orbit. This is also where the crew repair satellites that have been retrieved by a robot arm. The shuttle was designed for launching and servicing military satellites as well as for civilian use.

The craft re-enters the Earth's atmosphere belly-first (protected by a ceramic tile heat shield), then glides down to land like an aircraft.

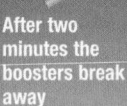

The main fuel tank is jettisoned shortly before reaching orbit

After two minutes the boosters break away

Launch

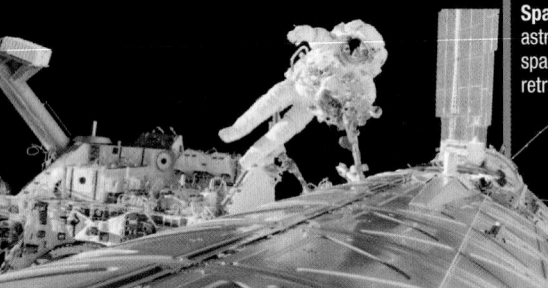

Space walk An astronaut, tethered to the space shuttle, works on a retrieved satellite in orbit.

Orbiters and landers to Mars and beyond

Galileo Launch date: October 1989
Galileo has been orbiting Jupiter since December 1995 and continues to send images and data.

Mars Observer Launch date: September 1992
Mars Observer was scheduled to start orbiting Mars in the late summer of 1993, but communication was lost just three days before it was due to enter orbit.

Mars Global Surveyor Launch date: November 1996
Global Surveyor went into orbit around Mars on September 11, 1997. It continues to provide maps of the surface of Mars, showing the distribution of minerals.

Mars Pathfinder Launch date: December 1996
Pathfinder landed on Mars on July 4, 1997. It took photographs of the site and released a six-wheeled, 63 cm (25 in) Sojourner vehicle equipped to analyse rocks.

Cassini-Huygens Launch date: October 1997
The Cassini orbiter is due to go into Saturn orbit in July 2004 and send the European-built Huygens probe into the atmosphere of Saturn's moon Titan four months later.

Mars Odyssey Launch date: April 2001
Mars Odyssey's mission is to map the surface of Mars, to assess it for hazards for any future human exploration and to establish evidence of potential water resources.

Mars Exploration Rovers Launch date: summer 2003
The two powerful Exploration Rovers are due to reach the surface of Mars in January or February 2004. The identical craft will land in different regions and carry out analysis of soil and rocks, searching for evidence of liquid water.

April 24, 1990
The United States and European Space Agency launch the Hubble Space Telescope. Results are disappointing. The mirror is found to have a tiny inaccuracy and the images are not as clear as expected.

August 10, 1990
The United States probe *Magellan* enters the orbit of Venus and begins a radar survey of the planet's surface.

October 6, 1990
The European probe *Ulysses* goes to study the Sun's poles.

December 1993
Orbiting American astronauts carry out repairs to the Hubble Space Telescope, correcting the fault in the mirror.

1990

January 28, 1986
The explosion of the space shuttle *Challenger*, 73 seconds after its tenth lift-off, kills all seven crew. It is caused by a fuel leakage.

February 20, 1986
The first part of the Soviet space station Mir is launched; it will last for 15 years.

April 12, 1981
The United States space shuttle *Columbia* makes its first 54-hour space flight. Many further flights follow, for civilian and military purposes, including the launch and repair of satellites.

1977
The United States makes test glides and landings of the space shuttle *Enterprise*, launching it from an aircraft.

1977
The United States launches two deep-space *Voyager* probes. *Voyager 1* uses a rare alignment of four outer planets and their gravity to 'sling-shot' it from one planet to the next.

1980

1979–89
The *Voyager* space probes send back detailed images of Jupiter, Saturn, Uranus and Neptune.

The International Space Station

A Russian rocket launched in November 1999 carried into space the first part of what is due to be the biggest space structure ever built – the International Space Station (ISS), also known as space station Alpha. When completed in about 2005, it will be as big as a football pitch, orbiting at an altitude of about 350 km (220 miles). It will have 6500 m² (70 000 sq ft) of power-generating solar panels, and will be a bright moving object in the night sky.

Collaborators from a number of countries are building various laboratory, control and living modules, which will be attached to a central girder-like truss. Up to seven specialists at a time will be able to conduct research into a wide range of fields. Floating 'personal satellite assistants' – spherical electronic robots 15 cm (6 in) across – will aid crew communications.

American space shuttles and Russian Soyuz spacecraft are the initial means of getting to and from the station, but a new highly efficient shuttle, the X-38, is being developed in the United States. It will dramatically reduce the cost of launching each tonne of payload into space, and will also act as a 'lifeboat' in case of emergency.

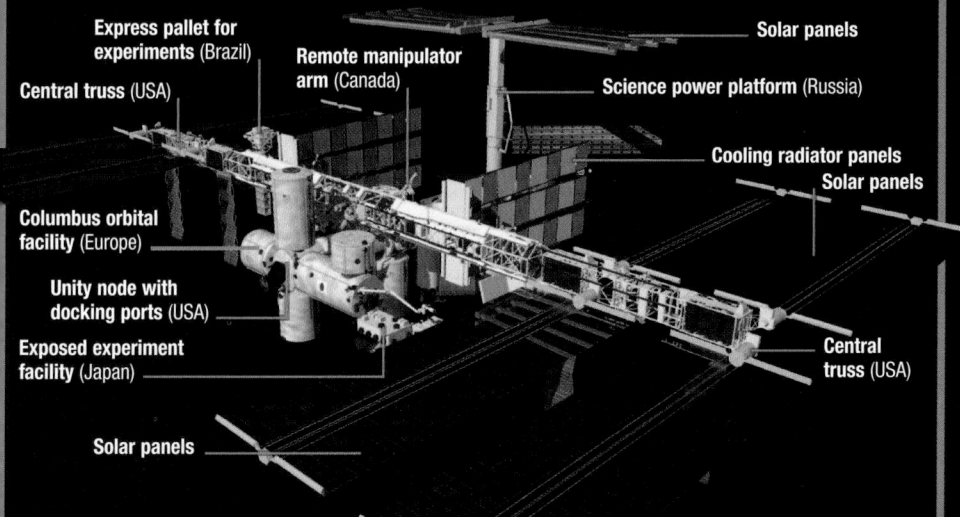

Express pallet for experiments (Brazil)
Central truss (USA)
Remote manipulator arm (Canada)
Solar panels
Science power platform (Russia)
Cooling radiator panels
Solar panels
Columbus orbital facility (Europe)
Unity node with docking ports (USA)
Exposed experiment facility (Japan)
Central truss (USA)
Solar panels

● **Mountains of the Moon** American astronaut John Young's six trips into space are a record. He also reached the highest lunar altitude when he stood with Charles Duke at 7830 m (25 688 ft) on the Descartes Highlands.

● **'Sling-shot' effect** If a space vehicle approaches a planet at the correct angle and distance, the planet's gravitational pull not only changes its direction, but also speeds it up. The planet slows down a tiny amount in compensation. This 'sling-shot' effect has been used a number of times – notably with *Voyager 1*, which passed four planets in 1979–89.

● **Space feud** Cosmonauts Valentin Lebedev and Anatoly Berezovoi got on each other's nerves on board Mir in 1982. They hardly spoke to each other for 211 days.

● **Heat of entry** Rather like a giant meteor, a spacecraft entering Earth's atmosphere compresses and heats the air in front of it. The space shuttle uses a protective shield of heat-resistant tiles made of silica fibres, but most earlier spacecraft had layers of 'ablative' coatings that simply burnt off slowly.

● **Space junk** About 300 satellites orbit the Earth, but they share space with more than 20 000 identified pieces of space junk. These include satellite and rocket parts, lost tools, paint flecks and even discarded human waste.

March 22, 1995
Russian Valeri Polyakov returns to Earth after setting a new record for manned space flight of more than 14 months aboard Mir.

December 7, 1995
The American probe *Galileo*, launched on October 18, 1989, reaches Jupiter. One section goes into orbit while the other enters the planet's atmosphere. It transmits data for more than an hour as it descends. The orbiter goes on to send detailed images of Jupiter and its moons.

95

June 25, 1997
An unmanned supply craft collides with Mir, damaging the space station's power supply, disabling its computer and endangering the crew's lives. Later repairs allow Mir to continue operating.

October 15, 1997
The American *Cassini* probe, with the European *Huygens* lander, is launched on a flight to Saturn. It is expected to go into orbit around Saturn in 2004.

July 4, 1997
The United States *Pathfinder* lands on Mars and explores the site with the tiny Sojourner rover.

February 18, 1998
Voyager 1 becomes the most distant space probe, overtaking *Pioneer 10*. By the year 2000 it is more than 12 billion km (7.5 billion miles) away.

October 29–November 7, 1998
John Glenn, the first American in orbit, joins a space shuttle flight to become the oldest person to go into space.

November 20, 1998
A Russian rocket launches the first section of the International Space Station (ISS). Three weeks later Americans launch the next.

January 3, 2000
Galileo passes close to Jupiter's moon Europa. Its radar detects evidence of salty water below Europa's frozen surface.

November 2, 2000
An American astronaut and two Russians begin the first full-scale mission on board the International Space Station.

2000

March 23, 2001
Mir re-enters the atmosphere and crashes into the Pacific Ocean.

Information, and the technologies involved in processing and transmitting it, are a major source of economic power. Virtually every business depends on communication technology, from telephones to computers and the Internet. Corporations that own and sell information and entertainment – media businesses – have become richer and more powerful than many small nations, and their spread is increasingly global.

THE RISE AND RISE OF THE MEDIA

Three factors fed the rising importance of the information and entertainment industries during the 20th century:
- a rising demand from consumers with increasing spare time;
- a growth in the amount of information (from academic research to pure entertainment) being created;
- technological advances in the delivery of the information.

The technological factor became overwhelming with the development of personal computers and particularly the Internet in the 1980s and 1990s, leading to a vast growth in the accessibility of information – the so-called 'information revolution'.

Creating a global marketplace

One important effect of new technology was to blur the distinction between different media, encouraging large-scale mergers of media and entertainment businesses (see below). Some forecasters predict a future in which television and radio programmes and cinema films are distributed over a superfast version of the Internet, newspapers and magazines are delivered in the same way, and

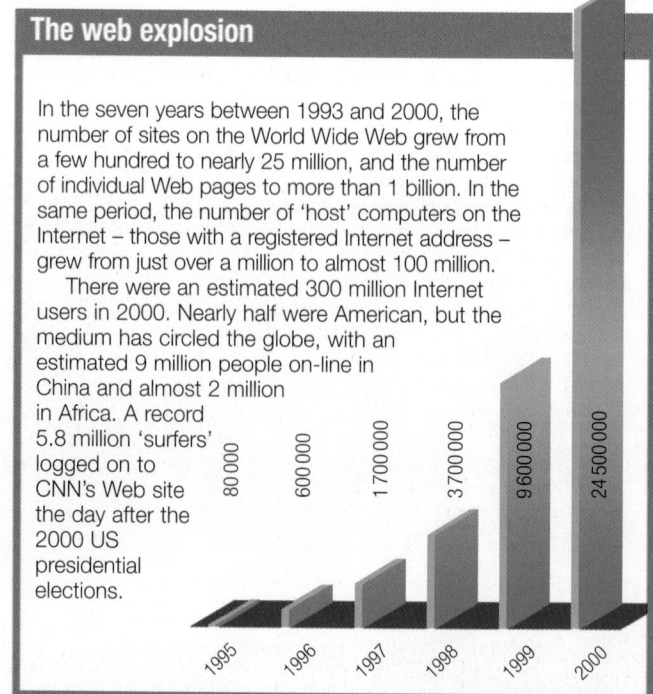

The web explosion

In the seven years between 1993 and 2000, the number of sites on the World Wide Web grew from a few hundred to nearly 25 million, and the number of individual Web pages to more than 1 billion. In the same period, the number of 'host' computers on the Internet – those with a registered Internet address – grew from just over a million to almost 100 million.

There were an estimated 300 million Internet users in 2000. Nearly half were American, but the medium has circled the globe, with an estimated 9 million people on-line in China and almost 2 million in Africa. A record 5.8 million 'surfers' logged on to CNN's Web site the day after the 2000 US presidential elections.

| 80 000 | 600 000 | 1 700 000 | 3 700 000 | 9 600 000 | 24 500 000 |
| 1995 | 1996 | 1997 | 1998 | 1999 | 2000 |

'e-books' replace the printed version. The Internet has also begun to affect traditional methods of selling – millions now shop on-line for goods as varied as cars, computers and groceries. In 1999 alone, new 'dot.com' businesses fuelled stock markets by several trillion US dollars – only to see a slump the next year as investors realised how long it might take for such firms to come into profit.

GLOBAL MEDIA GIANTS

The trend towards business mergers that began in the 1980s has created several giant media firms. The six biggest span the world in a wide range of media, with interests in areas such as book publishing, the music industry and TV networks.

Viacom

A US company, Viacom acquired the Hollywood studio Paramount and the video retailer Blockbuster in 1994. In 2000 it completed a US$50 billion merger with CBS Corporation. Businesses include:
Film: Paramount Pictures; United Cinemas International (partly owned)
Broadcasting: CBS Television, with 39 stations and more than 200 affiliates; cable networks MTV, Nickelodeon, Showtime and VH1; Infinity Broadcasting, with 180 radio stations
Book publishing: Simon & Schuster; Pocket Books; Scribner
Other: Paramount theme parks; Blockbuster video stores; the largest outdoor advertising sites in North America
Worth: In 1999, Viacom and CBS together had revenues of US$12.8 billion and profits of $2.09 billion.

Vivendi Universal

Created in 2000 by the merger of French firms Vivendi (with businesses ranging from telecommunications to water supply) and Canal Plus (television) with Seagram of Canada. Businesses include:
Films: Universal Studios; Canal Plus; United International Pictures (partly owned); Cineplex Odeon cinema chain
Broadcasting: Universal Television; Canal Plus; 24.5 per cent stake in BSkyB television; USA network
Music: Universal Music Group, including MCA, Polygram, Island Records, Motown, Decca
Book publishing: Havas (France), with 60 imprints
Internet: Part of Vizzavi (Internet portal); MP3.com (music site)
Other: Universal Studios theme parks; mobile and other telecommunications networks
Worth: The combined company has revenues of US$55 billion. In 1999 Vivendi alone had sales of US$41 billion.

Bertelsmann

A German company, Bertelsmann owns the world's largest book-publishing group and Europe's biggest broadcasting corporation. Businesses include:
Broadcasting: Television channels RTL (Germany), M6 (France) and part of Channel 5 (Britain); 17 radio stations
Music: More than 200 music labels, including RCA and Arista (USA) and Ariola (Germany); BMG Music Publishing (Britain)
Magazines and newspapers: Gruner & Jahr, with more than 80 magazines; ten newspapers in Germany and Eastern Europe, including *Berliner Zeitung*
Book publishing: Random House and Transworld groups (USA and UK), including Knopf, Crown, Bantam, Doubleday, Dell, Jonathan Cape, Century, Hutchinson, Ebury Press and Corgi; Berlin, Goldmann, and Siedler (Germany); Plaza & Janés (Spain); Sudamericana (Argentina); book clubs in many countries; Internet stores BOL.com and Barnes&Noble.com
Internet: Comundo (Internet access); Lycos (search engine)
Worth: In 1999 Bertelsmann had revenues of US$14.8 billion, assets of US$10.4 billion and profits of US$372 million.

LEADERS IN THE INFORMATION ECONOMY

The degree to which a nation participates in the information technology revolution is measured by the Information Society Index – a measure of people's 'information wealth'. The index is based on four main factors:
• Computer infrastructure, including the number of PCs in homes, schools and businesses.
• Information access, including television, radio, telephones and fax machines.
• Internet access, including the use of e-commerce
• Social factors such as levels of school enrolment, press freedom and civil liberties.

1999 rank	2000 rank	Country	2000 score
1	1	Sweden	6496
4	2	Norway	6112
3	3	Finland	5953
2	4	United States	5850
5	5	Denmark	5837
12	6	United Kingdom	5662
8	7	Switzerland	5528
9	8	Australia	5382
11	9	Singapore	5269
7	10	Netherlands	5238
10	11	Japan	5182
6	12	Canada	5126
13	13	Germany	4937
16	14	Austria	4868
14	15	Hong Kong	4745
17	16	New Zealand	4483
15	17	Belgium	4439
18	18	Taiwan	4296

Silicon Valley

The information technology (IT) industry has created several economic boom areas, most famously Silicon Valley, near San Francisco, California. It began in 1953 when Stanford University leased some of its land in Palo Alto for a high-tech industrial park. Soon companies such as Hewlett-Packard and IBM had bases there; more quickly followed, attracted by the facilities and highly skilled manpower available, the proximity of advanced research centres and the opportunity to do business with each other.

The Silicon Valley name, derived from the material used for microchips, was coined by journalist Don Hoefler in 1971. Today, 4000 IT companies are based between San Francisco and San Jose, accounting for 40 per cent of California's export trade. Similar areas soon grew in New York City (nicknamed 'Silicon Alley'), Scotland ('Silicon Glen') and Bangalore, India ('Silicon Plateau').

Media mogul Rupert Murdoch (1931–) inherited the *Melbourne News* in 1952 and started to build a media empire. He took over often weak newspapers in Britain, the USA and elsewhere, and made them successful. Buying 20th Century Fox in 1985 took him into film and television, and in 1989 he began building a global satellite TV network.

see also
394-401 **Cinema**
402-4 **Television**
410-1 **Newspapers**
566-7 **The Internet**

Media and sport Ted Turner of CNN bought the Atlanta Hawks basketball team in 1977.

News Corporation

Headed by Rupert Murdoch and based in Australia, this is the world's leading publisher of English-language newspapers, selling 40 million copies a week. It is also a major television operator, film-maker and book publisher. Businesses include:
Films: 20th Century Fox
Broadcasting: Fox Network, with 22 television stations (USA); Sky Global Networks (satellite), including British Sky Broadcasting (BSkyB), Star TV and Phoenix (Asia), and Foxtel (Australia)
Newspapers and magazines: *The Australian* and *Daily Telegraph* and *Sunday Telegraph* (Australia); *The Times*, *Sunday Times*, *The Sun* and *News of the World* (UK); *New York Post* (USA); numerous other newspapers in Pacific region; *TV Guide* (USA; partly owned)
Book publishing: HarperCollins (USA and UK)
Sport: Los Angeles Dodgers (baseball); National Rugby League (Australia); football teams in UK
Worth: In 1999, News Corporation had revenues of US$13.7 billion, assets of US$35.7 billion and profits of US$685 million.

AOL Time Warner

This media giant was created in 2001 by the merger of Internet firm America Online (AOL) with Time Warner, the world's largest media company. Businesses include:
Films: Warner Bros; Hanna-Barbera; Castle Rock; Cinemax
Broadcasting: Cable News Network (CNN); Cartoon Network; Home Box Office (HBO); Turner Broadcasting System (TBS); Turner Network Television (TNT); Time Warner Cable network
Music: Warner Bros records; Atlantic; Elektra
Magazines: *Time*; *People*; *Sports Illustrated*; *Fortune*; 30 others
Book publishing: Little, Brown; Warner Books; Time Life
Sports: Atlanta Braves (baseball); Atlanta Hawks (basketball)
Internet: America Online (AOL); CompuServe; Netscape
Other: Theme parks; Warner Bros studio stores in 30 countries
Worth: The combined company has a stock-market value of US$350 billion and revenues of US$30 billion.

Walt Disney

As well as the entertainment businesses usually associated with the Disney name, this US company also makes compact discs and audio cassettes, and produces musicals. Businesses include:
Films: Walt Disney; Miramax; Touchstone; Buena Vista
Broadcasting: Radio and television stations including ABC network; Disney Channel; ESPN (sports); SoapNet
Music: Buena Vista Music Group; Walt Disney Records
Internet: Part of Infoseek (search engine); other Internet sites
Other: Disney and Disney-MGM theme parks; Walt Disney Theatrical Productions
Worth: In 1999, Walt Disney's revenues were US$23.4 billion, with profits of US$1.3 billion and assets of US$43.7 billion.

Shakespeare in Love Miramax's blockbuster of 1998.

The world's most developed economies are its most voracious consumers of energy. Every year, the USA consumes energy in all its forms equivalent to around 8 tonnes of oil per head of population; its poorer neighbour Mexico consumes the equivalent of just 1.5 tonnes per head. Most of this energy is created by burning non-renewable resources such as oil and coal – how long these will last depends on the speed of industrialisation in currently underdeveloped countries, and on global efforts to conserve energy by using it more efficiently.

Key to the map

The colours below represent average energy consumption in each country. For countries shown in grey, no statistics are available.

Tonnes of oil equivalent (toe) consumed per person per year, 1998

0-0.99		3-3.99
1-1.99		4-4.99
2-2.99		5-5.99

Measuring world energy consumption

Global energy consumption is measured in tonnes of oil equivalent, which includes all forms of energy, from fossil fuels to alternative resources such as nuclear, hydroelectric, geothermal, wind and solar power. In 1998, the world consumed energy equivalent to more than 9.5 billion tonnes of oil – each person consumed an average of more than 1.6 tonnes of energy.

Biggest per capita consumers of energy

Measured in tonnes of oil equivalent per capita, 1998

1	Qatar	20.41	11	Trinidad & Tobago	6.96
2	United Arab Emirates	10.04	12	Brunei	6.61
3	Bahrain	9.72	13	Finland	6.49
4	Iceland	9.59	14	Sweden	5.93
5	Netherlands Antilles	8.13	15	Norway	5.75
6	United States	8.11	16	Belgium	5.72
7	Kuwait	7.82	17	Australia	5.60
8	Luxembourg	7.79	18	Saudi Arabia	4.98
9	Canada	7.73	19	Netherlands	4.74
10	Singapore	7.68	20	Gibraltar	4.60

North America
(includes Mexico)
Total energy consumption:
2563.96 million toe
Energy consumption per capita:
5.80 toe

Biggest overall consumers of energy

Measured in millions of tonnes of oil equivalent, 1998

1	United States	2181.80	11	Italy	167.93
2	China	1031.41	12	South Korea	163.38
3	Russia	581.77	13	Mexico	147.83
4	Japan	510.11	14	Ukraine	142.94
5	India	475.79	15	Indonesia	123.07
6	Germany	344.51	16	Spain	112.78
7	France	255.67	17	South Africa	110.99
8	Canada	234.33	18	Australia	105.01
9	United Kingdom	232.88	19	Saudi Arabia	103.23
10	Brazil	174.96	20	Iran	102.15

A breakdown of global energy resources

Fossil fuels – non-renewable resources which will eventually run out – are currently used to produce more than 80 per cent of the world's energy. Alternative, renewable resources such as solar and water power will eventually have to replace fossil fuels as the world's major energy resource.

South and Central America (includes the Caribbean)
Total energy consumption:
444.20 million toe
Energy consumption per capita:
1.10 toe

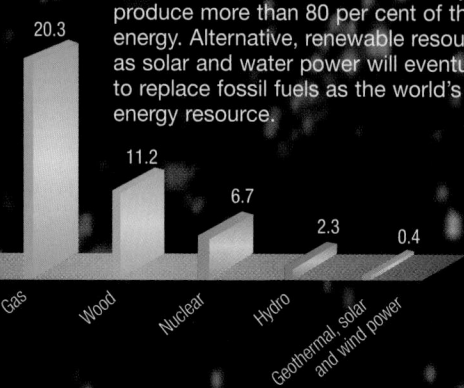

Percentage of world energy production (1998)

Oil	Coal	Gas	Wood	Nuclear	Hydro	Geothermal, solar and wind power
35.7	23.3	20.3	11.2	6.7	2.3	0.4

Which countries use energy most efficiently?

The energy efficiency of a country can be measured by calculating how much energy it uses to produce each unit of its gross domestic product, or GDP (the total market value of goods and services produced inside its borders). Dividing the country's annual energy consumption (in tonnes of oil equivalent) by its GDP (in thousands of US dollars), produces an 'energy intensity' figure: the lower the energy intensity figure, the more efficiently the country uses energy. Various factors influence efficiency, including the ratio of industrial activity (high-energy) to economic activity (low energy), and the use of conservation measures such as building insulation.

Global energy intensity figures, 1998

1	Switzerland	0.11	5	Norway	0.16	8	United Kingdom	0.21	11	Uruguay	0.26
2	Denmark	0.13	6	Germany	0.18	9	Finland	0.22	12	Argentina	0.27
3	Italy	0.14	7	France	0.19	9	Gabon	0.22	12	Australia	0.27
4	Austria	0.15	7	Spain	0.19	10	Israel	0.24	13	Greece	0.28
4	Japan	0.15	8	Luxembourg	0.21	11	Belgium	0.26			
5	Hong Kong	0.16	8	Netherlands	0.21	11	Portugal	0.26			
5	Ireland	0.16	8	Sweden	0.21	11	Slovenia	0.26			

The USA is joint 16th with Panama, at a figure of 0.31.

Europe (includes Russia)
Total energy consumption: 2572.93 million toe
Energy consumption per capita: 3.40 toe

China, North and South Korea and Japan
Total energy consumption: 1776.52 million toe
Energy consumption per capita: 2.69 toe

Middle East and Turkey
Total energy consumption: 428.20 million toe
Energy consumption per capita: 1.67 toe

Central Asia (ex Soviet republics)
Total energy consumption: 108.33 million toe
Energy consumption per capita: 1.16 toe

Southern Asia and the Pacific
Total energy consumption: 998.89 million toe
Energy consumption per capita: 0.55 toe

Africa
Total energy consumption: 481.50 million toe
Energy consumption per capita: 0.64 toe

Australia and New Zealand
Total energy consumption: 122.17 million toe
Energy consumption per capita: 5.06 toe

see also
500-1 **Fossil fuels**
502-3 **Nuclear power**
504-6 **Renewable energy**

Almost 80 per cent of the energy consumed globally is produced by burning fossil fuels – coal, oil (petroleum) and natural gas – the remains of living organisms that have been buried in the Earth for millions of years. Fossil fuels are the cheapest and most effective way of producing energy, but resources are finite, and are steadily being used up.

Carbon dioxide levels

Burning fossil fuels releases carbon dioxide, which contributes to global warming by trapping infrared radiation in the atmosphere – known as the 'greenhouse effect'. China, the Middle East and the former USSR produce the largest amounts of carbon dioxide in relation to the amount of energy they create.

Production of CO_2 in tonnes of CO_2 per tonne of oil equivalent, 1998

North Korea	3.63	South Africa	3.19	Israel	3.00	Morocco	2.86
Macedonia	3.40	Estonia	3.17	Gibraltar	2.98	Lebanon	2.84
Poland	3.32	Libya	3.11	Czech Republic	2.94	Iraq	2.83
Kazakhstan	3.23	Greece	3.06	Ireland	2.90	China	2.77

How a refinery works

Oil refineries separate out the chemical components, or fractions, of crude oil. Each fraction vaporises (boils) at a different temperature. Crude oil is heated until it begins to vaporise, then fed into the bottom of a distillation tower. Oil vapour rises up the tower as it cools, condensing into different liquids at different levels and remaining gaseous at the top. Each fraction forms a different end product.

Vapour rises up through perforated condensation trays placed at different heights in the tower.

Crude oil is heated to 400°C (750°F) on its way to the distillation tower.

The heaviest, least volatile fractions can be broken up into lighter, more useful fuels by subjecting them to further heat and pressure – a process known as cracking.

Gaseous fractions are drawn from the very top of the distillation tower.

The liquid fractions with the highest boiling point (including petrol) are drawn from the top trays.

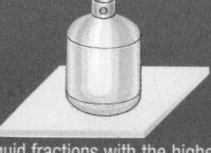

Gases such as butane, ethane, ethylene, methane and propane are used as bottled fuel, and as raw material for the production of petrochemicals.

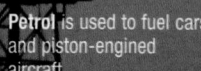

Petrol is used to fuel cars and piston-engined aircraft.

Paraffin is used as fuel for jet aircraft and heating and lighting, and as a solvent.

Diesel oil is used to power lorries and tractors.

Heating oil fuels heating systems in buildings.

Lubricating oil is used to keep machinery running smoothly.

Fuel oil is a heavy grade oil used to fuel ships.

Bitumen is used for road surfacing and waterproofing.

13th century The first commercial coal mines go into operation in England and Belgium.

Early 17th century Coal overtakes wood and charcoal as the most-used industrial fuel in England.

Late 18th century In Britain, American scientist Benjamin Thompson invents efficient coal grates, stoves and chimneys.

1821 William Hart digs the first natural gas well, 8 m (26 ft) deep, at Fredonia, New York.

1855 Robert Bunsen, a German chemist, invents an efficient gas burner for use in cookers and gas fires.

400BC   0   1200s   1500s   1600s   1700s   1800s

370 BC First known use of coal as a fuel in China.

Before 16th century Native Americans use oil from pools and

1765 In England, coal gas is used to light the offices of a mine near

1815 British scientist Humphrey Davy invents the safety lamp, making

c.1850 Processes are developed for distilling paraffin from

1859 Edwin Drake drills the first oil well, at Oil Creek,

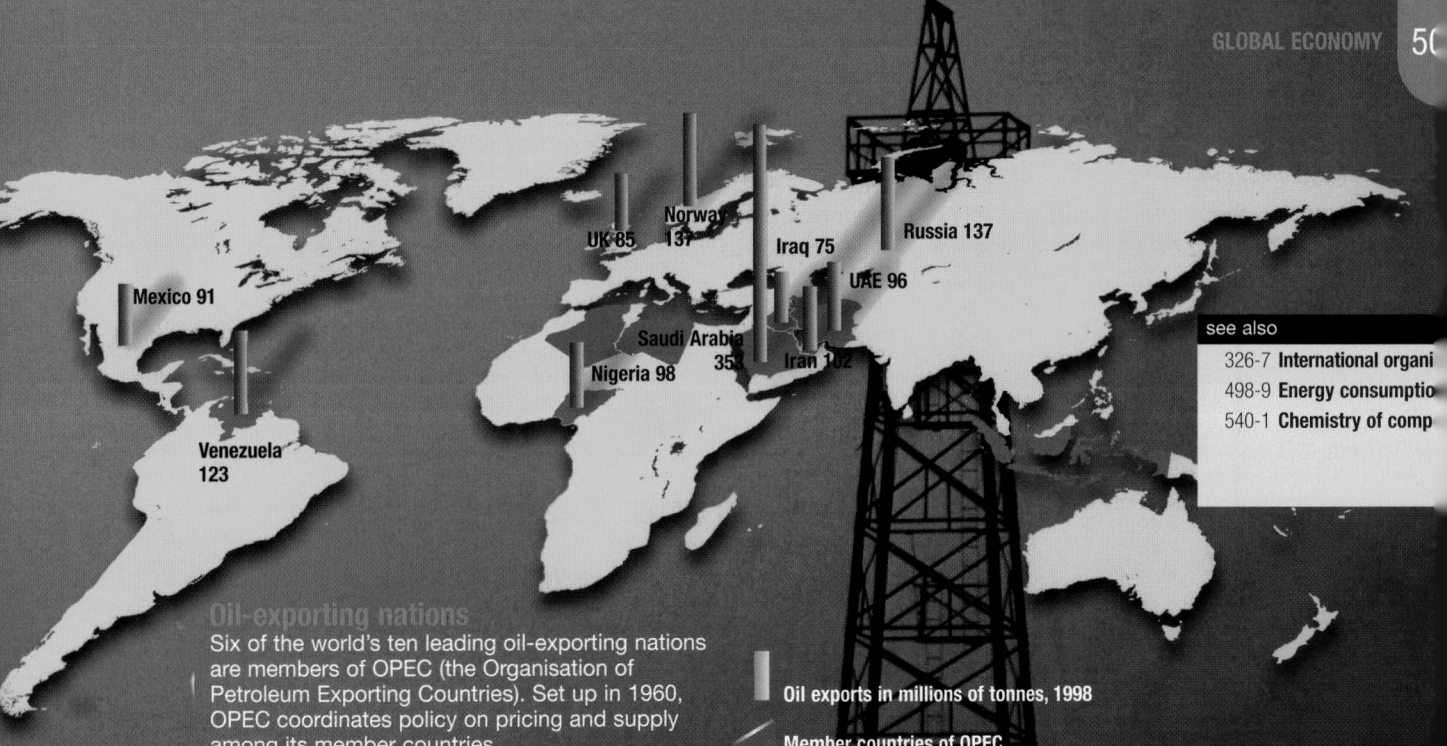

Oil-exporting nations

Six of the world's ten leading oil-exporting nations are members of OPEC (the Organisation of Petroleum Exporting Countries). Set up in 1960, OPEC coordinates policy on pricing and supply among its member countries.

Oil exports in millions of tonnes, 1998

Member countries of OPEC

see also

326-7 International organi

498-9 Energy consumptio

540-1 Chemistry of comp

Oil

About 95 per cent of the world's oil has been produced by 5 per cent of its oil fields. Two-thirds of the largest fields have been found in the Middle East. Scientists estimate that reserves will run out before 2060.

Top producers, 1996 million barrels per day		Top consumers, 1996 million barrels per day	
1	Saudi Arabia 9.23	1	USA 17.81
2	USA 8.00	2	Japan 5.55
3	Russia 6.17	3	China 4.11
4	Iran 3.80	4	Germany 2.92
5	Mexico 3.50	5	Russia 2.46
6	Venezuela 3.34	6	South Korea 2.02
7	Norway 3.22	7	France 2.01
8	China 3.21	8	Italy 1.98
9	UK 2.80	9	India 1.82
10	UAE 2.71	10	Canada 1.82

Natural gas

Russia and the Middle East originally contained the world's largest natural gas reserves. Only 14 per cent of global reserves have been used up, but it is estimated that remaining reserves are likely to run out before 2115.

Top producers, 1996 billion m³		Top consumers, 1996 billion m³	
1	Russia 551.3	1	USA 612.4
2	USA 543.8	2	Russia 364.7
3	Canada 160.4	3	UK 88.7
4	UK 90.3	4	Germany 79.5
5	Algeria 72.8	5	Canada 70.3
6	Indonesia 68.4	6	Japan 69.5
7	Netherlands 63.6	7	Ukraine 68.8
8	Uzbekistan 51.1	8	Italy 57.2
9	Iran 50.0	9	Iran 51.7
10	Saudi Arabia 46.0	10	Uzbekistan 47.0

Coal

Coal reserves exist in every continent, including Antarctica, but technology and economics will only allow the recovery of 7 per cent. Estimates of when reserves will run out range from 2250 to around 3400.

Top producers, 1996 million tonnes		Top consumers, 1996 million tonnes	
1	China 625.7	1	China 615.4
2	USA 589.6	2	USA 533.7
3	India 147.8	3	India 153.6
4	Australia 147.5	4	Russia 102.8
5	South Africa 118.3	5	Japan 88.4
6	Russia 104.6	6	South Africa 87.9
7	Poland 76.3	7	Germany 84.7
8	Germany 61.3	8	Poland 60.9
9	Canada 41.1	9	Australia 45.8
10	Ukraine 39.6	10	UK 40.7

1872 The first natural gas pipelines are constructed in Pennsylvania and New York.

1890 The process for making smokeless fuel (Coalite) from coal is patented.

1900s

1913 The invention of thermal cracking (see How an oil refinery works, opposite) boosts the output of petrol from each barrel of crude oil.

1948 The Al-Ghawar oil field is discovered in Saudi Arabia. It later proves to be the world's largest oil field, containing 82 billion barrels.

1973 The Arab-Israeli war provokes a world energy crisis when Arab nations stop exporting oil to the USA, Israel's ally.

1991 Iraq releases almost a million tonnes of crude oil into the sea during the Gulf War – the biggest-ever oil spill.

2000

1882 Thomas Edison builds the world's first large-scale electricity generating station in New York.

1908 The first big discovery of oil is made in the Middle East, in Persia (Iran)

1940s Cracking is used to boost the output of aviation fuel in the Second World War

1970s The 5470 km (3400 mile) Northern Lights gas pipeline, from the Arctic Circle to Europe, is built

1974 The Organisation of Petroleum Exporting Countries quadruples oil prices. Global economic recession follows

1990s Asia, Europe and the USA research Clean Coal Technologies (CCTs) to reduce emissions and increase efficiency

Nuclear power is generated by the fission, or splitting apart, of atoms of uranium or plutonium. The process releases huge amounts of energy using small amounts of raw material: the fission of 1 kg (2.2 lb) of uranium releases as much energy as burning 2000 tonnes of coal or 8000 barrels of oil.

Types of nuclear reactor

Pressurised water reactor (PWR) The most common design for nuclear reactors (also known as light water reactors) uses high-pressure water as a coolant. The coolant removes heat from the reactor's core and channels it into a heat exchanger which produces steam. The steam spins turbines to generate electricity.

Boiling water reactor (BWR) This is another type of light water reactor. The coolant is passed through the core and allowed to boil, producing steam.

Pressurised heavy water reactor (PHWR) The coolant is 'heavy water': processed water with a higher molecular weight than ordinary water.

Light water graphite reactor (LWGR) LWGR fuel rods are contained in individual pressure tubes surrounded by water (the coolant) and graphite (the moderator, which slows the neutrons and thus increases the process of fission).

Gas-cooled reactor (GCR) GCRs use pressurised carbon dioxide as a coolant instead of water.

Advanced gas-cooled reactor (AGR) Advanced GCRs work in the same way as ordinary GCRs, but use chemically manufactured enriched uranium as fuel. Enriched uranium is about five times more concentrated than natural uranium.

Fast breeder reactor (FBR) Breeder reactors produce more fuel (in the form of plutonium) than they consume. FBRs do not use a moderator so the neutrons are able to travel faster. The original fuel is a type of uranium which becomes unstable when bombarded by fast neutrons, and decays into plutonium.

Creating power: the chain reaction

Atoms are composed of electrons surrounding a nucleus which contains protons and neutrons. Bombarding an atom with neutrons splits the nucleus into two parts. This process, called fission, releases energy (as heat) and radioactivity, and it frees up more neutrons. The neutrons can be captured and used to bombard further atoms, continuing the process in a chain reaction. Fission is regulated by substances known as moderators (usually water or metal) which slow the neutrons down to improve their chances of hitting nuclei. If the energy is contained and controlled, it provides a source of power; if it is not contained, it causes a huge 'atomic' explosion.

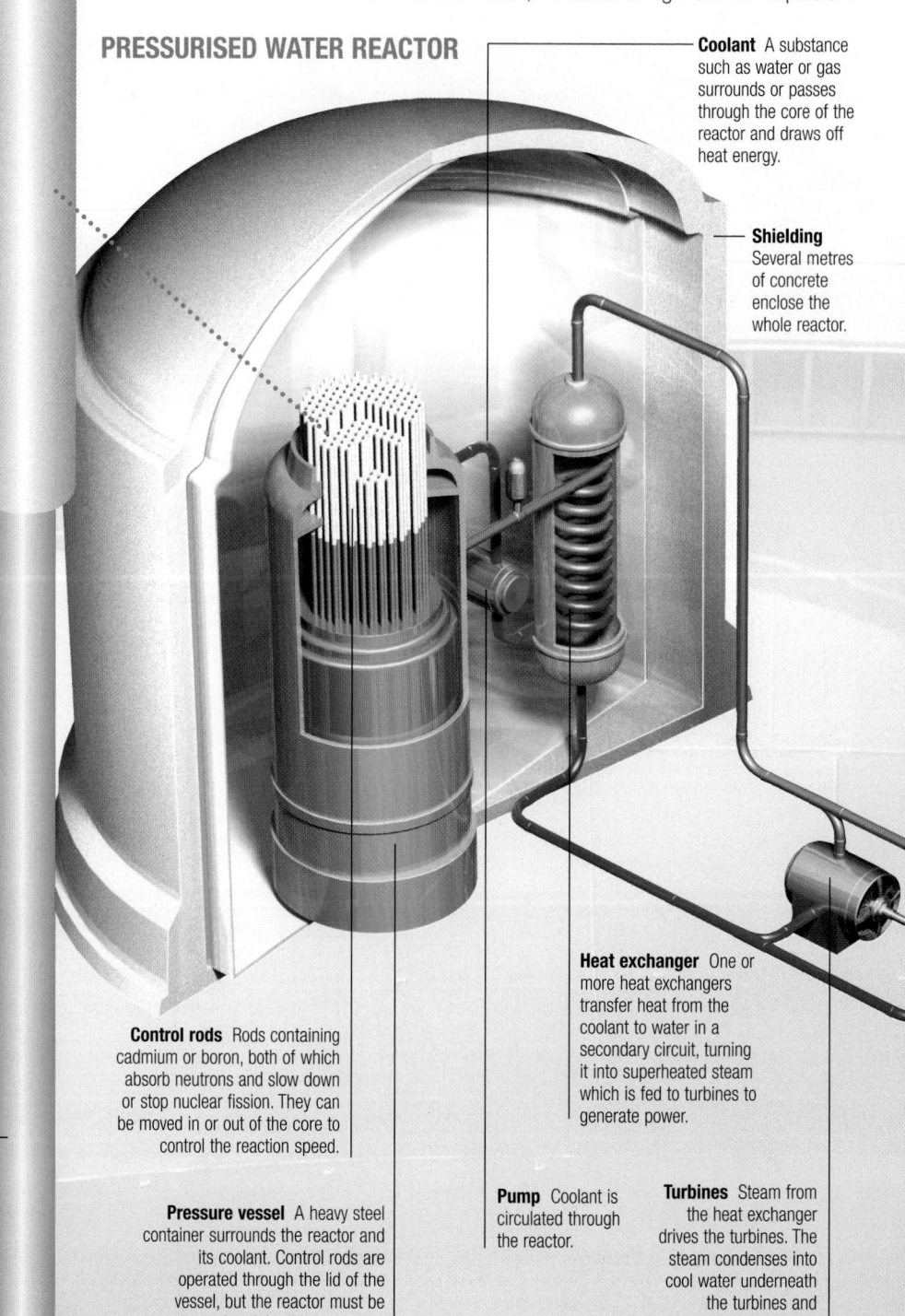

PRESSURISED WATER REACTOR

Coolant A substance such as water or gas surrounds or passes through the core of the reactor and draws off heat energy.

Shielding Several metres of concrete enclose the whole reactor.

Heat exchanger One or more heat exchangers transfer heat from the coolant to water in a secondary circuit, turning it into superheated steam which is fed to turbines to generate power.

Control rods Rods containing cadmium or boron, both of which absorb neutrons and slow down or stop nuclear fission. They can be moved in or out of the core to control the reaction speed.

Fuel rods Nuclear fuel – usually uranium oxide pellets – is contained in rods about 4 m (13 ft) long by 1 cm (½ in) in diameter. These are surrounded by a moderator substance which slows the neutrons down (fast-moving neutrons bounce off uranium atoms instead of penetrating them).

Pressure vessel A heavy steel container surrounds the reactor and its coolant. Control rods are operated through the lid of the vessel, but the reactor must be stopped and the lid removed to allow refuelling about once a year.

Pump Coolant is circulated through the reactor.

Turbines Steam from the heat exchanger drives the turbines. The steam condenses into cool water underneath the turbines and circulates back into the reactor core.

Leading producers of nuclear power

Percentage of domestic electricity supplied by nuclear power, 1998

1	France	77	7	UK	28
2	Sweden	47	8	USA	19
3	Ukraine	44	9=	Canada	13
4	South Korea	38	9=	Russia	13
5	Japan	32		Rest of the world	10
6	Germany	29		World total	17

The most common types of power reactor used by leading producers

Overall, the pressurised water reactor is the most widely used around the world. France, the second largest producer of nuclear power, and Russia have the only fast breeder reactors.

	Country	PWR	BWR	GCR	PHWR	LWGR	AGR	FBR	Production in million MW hrs
1	USA	69	34						714
2	France	58						1	388
3	Japan	23	27						332
4	Germany	14	6						162
5	Russia	13				15	14	1	104
6	UK	1		20					100
7	South Korea	12			4				90
8	Ukraine	13			1				75

FOR AND AGAINST

Pros
- Nuclear power uses less raw material than fossil fuel.
- It does not release uncontrolled harmful emissions into the atmosphere, unlike fossil fuels. In 2000, British Energy saved 40 million tonnes of CO_2 – equivalent to removing nearly two-thirds of cars in the UK – by using nuclear means rather than fossil fuels to produce power.

Cons
- Nuclear power stations are expensive to build.
- Public concern has led to protests over the storage of highly radioactive waste and the danger it poses to human health. The exposure of humans to radiation as a result of malfunctions at power stations has provoked calls for the closure of all nuclear plants.
- The gathering of raw material for nuclear power production risks the possibility of its appropriation for the unlicensed manufacture of nuclear weapons.

Key dates

1905 Albert Einstein's Special Theory of Relativity suggests that mass (matter) can be converted into energy.

1938 German scientists Otto Hahn and Fritz Strassmann split uranium atoms by bombarding them with neutrons. The process involves the loss of mass, which is converted into energy, confirming Einstein's theory.

1942 A team led by Enrico Fermi at the University of Chicago build a nuclear reactor and create the first man-made uranium chain reaction. This is the birth of the nuclear age.

1943–5 Reactors are built at Hanford, Washington State, USA, to manufacture plutonium for use in atomic bombs.

1952 An experimental dual-purpose breeder reactor is built in Idaho, USA – it produces both electricity and plutonium fuel.

1956 The first full-scale nuclear power station opens in Britain at Calder Hall, near Sellafield. The following year, a reactor overheats, setting the core on fire and releasing radioactivity into the local area.

1957 A chemical explosion in radioactive waste tanks at a plant near Chelyabinsk, USSR, contaminates a wide area in the Urals.

1979 Malfunction and operator error cause the loss of coolant in a reactor at Three Mile Island in Pennsylvania, USA, leading to the overheating and partial meltdown of its core.

1986 A reactor explodes at Chernobyl, Ukraine, killing 32 people and spreading radioactivity as far as France and Italy. Radiation sickness later kills many more people in the surrounding area.

1999 Operator error causes an uncontrolled chain reaction at the Tokaimura processing plant in Japan. Three workers are irradiated: two later die; hundreds more are exposed.

see also
498-9 **Energy consumption**
532-3 **Radioactivity**
534-5 **Relativity**

Dealing with the waste

Levels of radioactivity deplete over time. The toxic radioactive waste produced by nuclear fission is categorised as low, intermediate or high-level, depending on how long it is likely to remain dangerous. Low and intermediate-level waste includes items such as discarded protective clothing and the sludges and resins arising from the reaction process. Low-level waste is incinerated, compressed and stored underground. Intermediate-level waste is shielded in drums and placed inside a concrete or bitumen chamber.

High-level waste includes dangerous isotopes (see page 532), whose radioactivity lasts in some cases for hundreds or even thousands of years. These are currently stored in liquid form in stainless-steel tanks at specialised waste disposal sites. The liquid continues to emit heat, and has to be continually cooled.

Long-term plans have been made to store high-level waste inside solid glass blocks and keep it above ground for 50 years before disposal. This will allow its radioactivity to decay to lower levels. It could then be stored in the same way as intermediate-level waste.

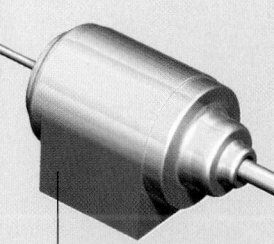

Generator The electricity generated provides a local or national supply. The output of a typical commercial nuclear power station is usually between 600 and 1000 megawatts.

Geiger counting Radiation levels are periodically checked at disposal sites such as this low-level waste site in Hanford, USA.

The unrelenting global demand for energy, and the knowledge that fossil fuel reserves will not last forever, has led to a hunt for renewable resources. The use of hydroelectricity is well established. In countries such as Norway and Brazil, it accounts for more than 90 per cent of domestic electricity generation. The oil crisis of the 1970s created renewed interest in wind power, a field now led by Germany, the USA, Denmark and India.

AD 1000   1800

915 Windmills are used to grind grain in Seistan, Persia.

12th century Windmills become common in Europe, particularly in the Netherlands where they are used for draining marshes.

1891 An experimental hydroelectric power plant is built in Germany.

1893 The world's first major hydroelectric plant is built at Niagara Falls on the US-Canadian border.

HYDROELECTRICITY

Hydroelectric power stations use the power of falling water to drive a turbine coupled to an electric generator. Stations are built at natural waterfalls, such as Niagara Falls on the US-Canadian border, or by constructing a dam across a river and controlling the water flow through artificial channels.

In areas where the demand for electricity varies throughout the day, pumped-storage hydroelectric plants are used. In periods of low demand, surplus power generated by the plant is used to reverse the water flow and fill an artificial reservoir behind the dam. The stored water is released at times of peak demand to provide extra power.

● **Pros** Running costs are low and hydroelectric plants do not produce harmful emissions. Constructing dams helps to regulate seasonal flooding and provides water for irrigation.

● **Cons** Construction costs are high. Dams may flood large areas of land, upsetting the local ecological balance.

● **Biggest plants** The Itaipú plant on the Paraná River (Brazil-Paraguay border) has a capacity of 12 600 megawatts. The Three Gorges project on the Yangtze River in China, due for completion in 2009, will have a capacity of 18 200 megawatts.

A river of energy The 7744 m (25 500 ft) stretch of dams which make up the Itaipú complex on the Brazil-Paraguay border are connected to 18 generating units with a capacity of 700 MW each. The energy captured from the Paraná River supplies 25 per cent of Brazil's power, and 78 per cent of Paraguay's power.

Leading producers of hydroelectricity for domestic use, 1998

Total production of hydroelectricity in million megawatt hours
World total: 2643

Percentage of domestic power generation provided by hydroelectricity
World total: 18.4 per cent

Generating power A hydroelectric plant (right) creates energy by trapping a river behind a dam and controlling its onward flow.

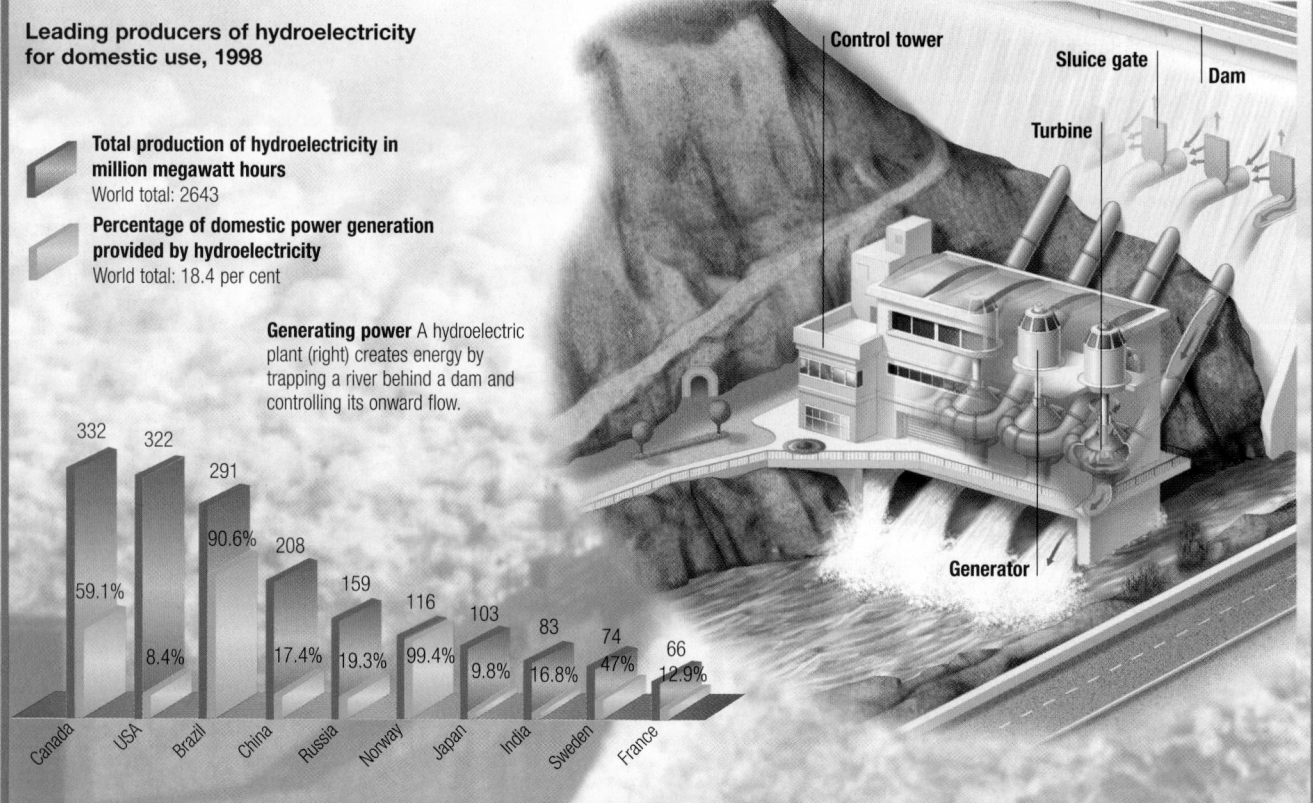

Control tower

Sluice gate

Dam

Turbine

Generator

Country	Production	Percentage
Canada	332	59.1%
USA	322	8.4%
Brazil	291	90.6%
China	208	17.4%
Russia	159	19.3%
Norway	116	99.4%
Japan	103	9.8%
India	83	16.8%
Sweden	74	47%
France	66	12.9%

1900   1940   1960   1980

1904 The world's first geothermal power plant opens at Larderello, Italy, with a generating capacity of 250 kW.

1941 The first modern wind turbine is built in Vermont, USA, generating 1250 kW.

1960 The first thermal power plant using solar energy is built in the Soviet republic of Turkmenistan.

1967 Construction of the first major tidal power plant is completed in the Rance estuary, near St Malo, France.

1982 The 10-MW Solar One power plant begins operating in the Mojave Desert, California. By the 1990s, another eight solar plants have been built in the Mojave.

see also
26-7 **The Moon**
54-5 **Weather**
498-9 **Energy consumption**

TIDAL AND WAVE POWER

Specialised hydroelectric plants harness the power of tides using dams constructed across river estuaries. During the flood tide, sluice gates are opened, allowing water to flow through the dam. At high tide, the gates are shut, trapping the water, which is released in a controlled flow as the tide ebbs.

Power plants have also been designed to harness the energy in the rise and fall of sea waves on ocean coasts. The movement of the waves compresses air inside covered chambers, pushing and pulling the air through reversible turbines. This technology is currently experimental, but its global energy potential is estimated at 2-3 million megawatts.

Pros Tidal and wave power plants do not produce harmful emissions, and offer a vast, sustainable resource.

Cons Tidal power is suitable only where the tidal range (the difference between high and low tide) is 6 m (20 ft) or more. Energy output varies because tides vary in height from day to day and season to season. Wave power energy output is also inconsistent because the size of waves varies. Power plants may cause ecological harm to the shoreline by altering tidal levels in estuaries and along coastlines. Ring-shaped offshore 'tidal lagoon' plants are currently being planned, which may solve this problem.

Biggest plants The Rance estuary, near St Malo, Brittany, is the world's largest working tidal plant, with 24 turbines and a total capacity of 240 megawatts. The Azores, Portugal, have the world's largest wave installation, with a total power capacity of 1 megawatt.

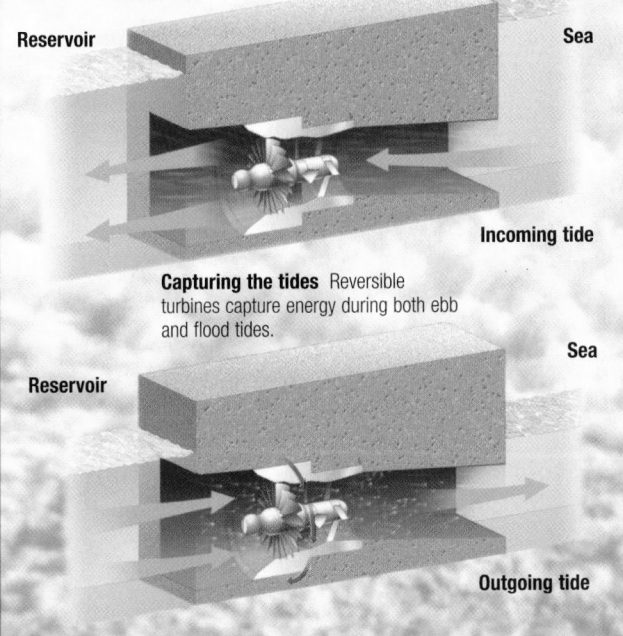

Capturing the tides Reversible turbines capture energy during both ebb and flood tides.

Reservoir — Sea — Incoming tide
Reservoir — Sea — Outgoing tide

WIND POWER

Most modern wind turbines have a three-bladed propeller, up to 100 m (330 ft) across, attached to a generator. Computer control keeps the propeller facing the wind and adjusts its direction according to the wind strength. Generators can have a capacity of up to 4 megawatts each, though 250-500 kilowatts is more usual. They are often grouped together in 'wind farms' on windy ridges, plains or coasts, or offshore.

The total worldwide energy capacity of wind turbines has increased by more than 25 per cent a year since 1997. In the year 2000, it was estimated at more than 10 000 megawatts – ten times the capacity of 1990 – and rapidly increasing.

Pros The cost of running wind farms is competitive with the best coal or gas-powered generating stations, and wind turbines do not create harmful emissions.

Cons Power output varies, depending upon the strength of the wind. The turbine blades and their mechanical gearboxes are noisy. The turbines also take up a great deal of space, and are often considered unsightly. They can pose a threat to birds.

Biggest plants The largest wind farms – about 5000 turbines each – are in Altamount Pass and Tehachapi Pass, California. In combination with smaller Californian wind farms in San Gorgonio Pass, Pacheco Pass and Solano, they generate 30 per cent of the world's wind power. In 1995, Californian wind power capacity reached 2.9 billion kilowatt hours of electricity a year – enough to supply 500 000 homes.

Coastal power Nine 300 kW turbines began operating at Blythe Harbour in Northumberland, UK, in 1993. In 2000, two 2 MW turbines were built half a mile offshore. The Blythe turbines capture enough energy to supply 5000 homes.

By the end of the 20th century, several viable alternatives to fossil fuels had emerged. Solar power heats water in more than a million homes in Greece. Iceland capitalises on its natural geothermal resources to heat 85 per cent of its houses. Biomass energy, produced by the burning or chemical processing of organic matter, provides 15 per cent of domestic power in Scandinavia, and is the main energy source for millions of villagers in China and India.

SOLAR POWER

Two solar technologies are being developed. *Solar thermal* employs mirrors to focus the Sun's rays onto a heat collector, which boils water directly, or heats an intermediate fluid such as oil, which is then used to generate steam to drive a turbine.

Solar electric exploits the principle that combinations of certain dissimilar materials, such as silicon and boron, create an electric charge when light is applied to them. This photoelectric effect, which can convert sunlight directly into electricity, is used for household energy supplies, and to power calculators, satellite phones and experimental cars.

⬤ **Advantages** Solar energy is an endlessly sustainable power source, which causes no pollution.

⬤ **Disadvantages** Large power plants cover huge expanses of land; generators produce power only during daylight hours, and are only practicable in areas with plentiful sunshine.

⬤ **Biggest plant** A series of nine solar-power plants in the Mojave Desert, California, with computer-controlled parabolic mirrors, covers 400 hectares (1000 acres). It has a total output of 354 megawatts – enough to supply power to 500 000 people.

Under the African sun A reliance on wood for fuel has led to deforestation and inadequate energy supplies in the Sudan. In the 1990s, relief agencies and the United Nations Environment Programme began installing solar panels in Sudanese villages to power essentials such as lighting, refrigeration and water pumps.

Concentrated energy A giant parabolic reflector, built in 1969 in the Pyrenees mountains at Odeillo, France, directs the sun's rays to a single focal point, where a receiver collects the energy. The parabola receives sunlight from 63 heliostats (computer-controlled mirrors which move to reflect sunlight at a constant angle) positioned on a hillside opposite. Temperatures usually reach between 800°C and 2500°C, providing a maximum power of 1000 kW.

GEOTHERMAL POWER

In regions with high levels of volcanic activity, the heat of rocks and underground water is used to produce electricity. Any naturally occurring steam is transported in pipes to the surface, where it drives turbines which generate electricity. Holes are also drilled down to hot rocks, then water is run across them to produce steam. In 1998, the worldwide capacity of geothermal power reached 8240 megawatts.

Advantages Geothermal power uses less land area per megawatt than almost any other kind of power plant, and supplies energy 24 hours a day.

Disadvantages Natural sources of steam are quite rare, and the energy they supply is not a truly renewable resource – natural hot spots can cool, and take thousands of years to regenerate; power plants can be noisy, and their pipes often become corroded by water-borne minerals.

Biggest plant The world's largest developed geothermal field, The Geysers in California, is capable of generating up to 1900 megawatts, but there are restrictions on energy production in order to prolong the life of the plant.

Leading geothermal power producers, 1998
Capacity in megawatts

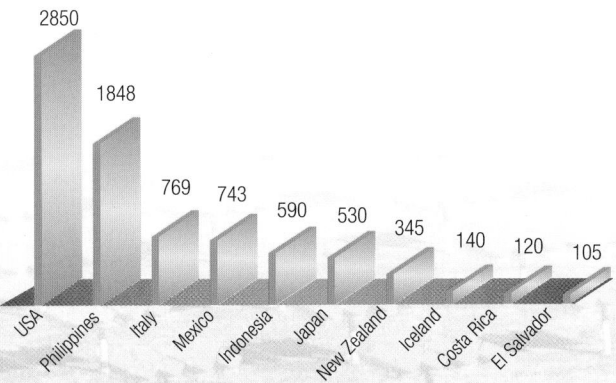

2850 USA
1848 Philippines
769 Italy
743 Mexico
590 Indonesia
530 Japan
345 New Zealand
140 Iceland
120 Costa Rica
105 El Salvador

Steam power Planning for the Wairakei geothermal energy plant on New Zealand's North Island began in 1947, after sustained dry weather led to a hydro-electricity shortage. The Wairakei plant began operating in 1958; 40 years later, its operating capacity reached just over 160 megawatts.

BIOMASS

Power is generated from decaying organic matter and waste, such as plants, wood, straw, manure and household rubbish. These are known collectively as biomass. Techniques for converting biomass into energy include:

Tapping biogas Decaying animal waste and buried rubbish give off methane gas, which is collected and burned as fuel in specially designed biogas digesters.

Combustion Burning household rubbish, rather than dumping it, can contribute to a city's energy supply. Each tonne of refuse can produce up to 400 m^3 (14 000 cu ft) of methane.

Alcohol fermentation During fermentation, enzymes break down plant starches into simpler compounds, eventually producing ethanol, a high-octane fuel. A small quantity of ethanol is frequently blended into the petrol used in cars.

Plant oil processing Removing glycerine from vegetable oil leaves a clear liquid, known as biodiesel. This is burned as diesel fuel.

Advantages Resources are endlessly renewable. Combustion reduces waste, and biofuels reduce pollution.

Disadvantages Combustion creates gases which pollute the environment; methane collected through biogas digesters also contributes to global warming, if released.

Leading producers The USA has 70 biogas sites. The largest – in the Puente Hills, California – generates 46 megawatts. Most of the world's 350 combustion plants are in Europe and Japan: Germany burns about 5.5 million tonnes of refuse a year; Japan burns about half a million. Brazil produces around 11 billion litres of liquid biofuel (ethanol and diesel) a year; the USA produces around 4 billion litres.

Recycling success More than 2.5 million household biogas plants have been installed in India since 1980. In many communities, biogas digesters attached to toilets use human waste to create energy for lighting and cooking. This helps improve hygiene, and frees up animal manure for use as fertiliser.

see also
498-9 **Energy consumption**
502-3 **Nuclear power**
504-5 **Renewable energy**

More than 2500 minerals have so far been identified. Their widespread occurrence and durability made them ideal for trading in the ancient world – bars of metal were exchanged for goods in Egypt as early as the 4th millennium BC. Today, minerals and metals – even precious substances such as diamond and silver – are more vital to the global economy for their broad industrial applications than as a medium of exchange.

MINING TERMS

● **Dredging** A grab, scoop, or continuous chain of buckets is used to dig mineral-bearing sand, gravel, or mud from the bed of a natural or man-made lake or river.

● **Open-cast mining** Explosives and heavy machinery are used to remove 'overburden' (surface rock above the target ore), and dig ore from thick seams close to the Earth's surface.

● **Placer mining** Less dense deposits of sand or gravel are separated from minerals using water: the lighter waste is washed away, leaving the heavier minerals.

● **Pumping** A mineral is separated from any soluble material around it, by pumping mineral-bearing water (including seawater) over it in a processing plant.

● **Quarrying** A similar method to open-cast mining (see above), quarrying is used to extract minerals, where there is little or no overburden.

● **Sluicing** A larger-scale version of placer mining (see above), sluicing employs a trough, called a riffle box, with grooves at the bottom in which the mineral particles collect.

● **Strip mining** Shallow minerals are dug out in successive parallel strips. As each strip is removed, overburden is used to fill in the previous hole.

● **Underground mining** A vertical or horizontal shaft is dug into the ground, with passages branching off it, that are called levels or drifts. Ore is extracted using the room-and-pillar method, in which sections of ore are left uncut, so that they act as pillars to support the rock above.

● **Caving** A body of ore is undercut, causing it to collapse into pieces for easy transport.

Precious metals and minerals

Scattered deposits of diamond, gold and silver were discovered in river beds in ancient times. The Romans began mining gold and silver in Spain in the 1st century BC. Platinum mining began after the first deposits were discovered in Colombia in the 16th century. Diamond mining began with the first discovery of rock-bound specimens in South Africa in 1870.

Diamond

The hardest naturally occurring substance. Only 23 per cent of diamonds are clear enough to be gem quality; the rest are used to make cutting and grinding tools.
Occurrence: Alluvial sediments; glacial till; occasionally found in kimberlite rocks.
Known world reserves: 1900 million carats (1 carat = 0.2 g; 5000 carats = 1 kg)
Annual production: 120 million carats
Largest producers: Australia, 34.3 per cent; Democratic Republic of the Congo, 18.8 per cent; Russia, 16.3 per cent; Botswana, 16 1 per cent.

Gold

Good conductor of electricity: used for non-corroding electrical contacts in electronic equipment.
Occurrence: Alluvial sediments; veins in rocks; often associated with quartz and pyrite or copper and lead deposits.
Known world reserves: 46 000 tonnes
Annual production: 2375 tonnes
Largest producers: South Africa, 20.5 per cent; USA, 14.8 per cent; Australia, 12.8 per cent; Canada: 7.1 per cent; China: 7 per cent.

Platinum group

Six metals – iridium, osmium, palladium, platinum, rhodium and ruthenium – have similar properties and are usually found together. They are used as catalysts in industrial processes and car exhausts.
Occurrence: Alluvial sediments; in rocks, associated with chromite and norites, or combined with arsenic as sperrylite.
Known world reserves: 71 000 tonnes
Annual production: 355 tonnes
Largest producers: Russia, 46.9 per cent; South Africa, 46.3 per cent.

Rock-bound gems Diamonds (background) are only found in volcanic pipes of kimberlite rock – a type of peridotite – and were formed at depths of 100 to 200 km (60 to 125 miles).

Silver

Used in electric circuits – silver's electrical conductivity is the highest known of all metals. Also used in photographic materials for its light sensitive properties.
Occurrence: Ore veins, often with copper, lead or zinc. Sometimes found as argentite (silver sulphide); more rarely found as native (pure) silver.
Known world reserves: 280 000 tonnes
Annual production: 16 000 tonnes
Largest producers: Mexico, 16.9 per cent; Peru, 12.7 per cent; China, 8 per cent; Canada, 7.8 per cent; Australia, 7.5 per cent; Chile: 7.5 per cent.

Non-metals

Fluorspar was the first non-metal to find an industrial application. It has been used in metallurgy since its discovery in the 12th century. The first artificial fertiliser, made from phosphates, was manufactured in England in 1843, and widespread use of sulphur in chemical processing began in 1891, when a new method of extracting it in pure form was devised.

Fluorspar

Used in the steel industry to remove impurities. Contains fluorine, used in plastics, refrigerants, and rocket and nuclear reactor fuel.
Occurrence: Found in sulphide deposits.
Known world reserves: 218 million tonnes
Annual production: 3.9 million tonnes
Largest producers: China, 51.7 per cent; Mexico, 14.4 per cent; South Africa, 5.5 per cent.

Phosphate

Used mainly as fertiliser in the form of phosphoric acid.
Occurrence: Found in marine sediments such as limestone and shale, with calcium and magnesium.
Known world reserves: 11 345 million tonnes
Annual production: 140 million tonnes
Largest producers: USA, 32.2 per cent; China, 17.9 per cent; Morocco, 15.9 per cent; Russia, 6.8 per cent.

Potash

Minerals containing potassium are known as potash, though the term refers specifically to potassium carbonate or hydroxide. Potassium carbonate is used as fertiliser, and in detergent and glass manufacture.
Occurrence: Derived from sylvite, which is found in underground salt beds.
Known world reserves: 8380 million tonnes
Annual production: 25.1 million tonnes
Largest producers: Canada, 34.8 per cent; Germany, 13.7 per cent; Russia, 12.6 per cent; Belarus, 12.5 per cent; Israel, 6.2 per cent; USA, 5.4 per cent.

Sulphur

Used to make sulphuric acid, important in the production of batteries, drugs, detergents, explosives, fertilisers, and pigments and dyes. Also used in oil refining and metallurgy.
Occurrence: Found as sulphide in crude oil and natural gas, and in many minerals, including pyrite and gypsum; also is a by-product of metal smelting.
Known world reserves: 1400 million tonnes
Annual production: 55.3 million tonnes
Largest producers: USA, 21.4 per cent; Canada, 17.2 per cent; China, 12.5 per cent; Russia, 6.9 per cent.

Metals

Metalworking is one of the oldest industries – smelting (heating rocks to extract pure metal) first occurred in Turkey and Mesopotamia in about 5000 BC. Today, all the metals listed below are economically important for their use in machinery, and in the production of electricity and nuclear power.

Aluminium

Alloys of aluminium are as strong as steel, but much lighter and non-corroding: they are used to build aircraft and ships, and in cables, drink cans and kitchen utensils.
Occurrence: Found in bauxite, an impure form of alumina (aluminium oxide).
Known world reserves: 4250 million tonnes
Annual production: 22.9 million tonnes
Largest producers: Australia, 35 per cent; Guinea, 14.5 per cent; Brazil, 10.5 per cent.

Chromium

Used to harden steel and make it corrosion-resistant.
Occurrence: Found in chromite, an oxide of chromium and iron.
Known world reserves: 350 million tonnes
Annual production: 3.6 million tonnes
Largest producers: South Africa, 45.3 per cent; Kazakhstan, 12.1 per cent; India 11.6 per cent.

Copper

Good electrical conductor: used in cables. Alloyed with zinc to make brass, and with tin to make bronze.
Occurrence: Found in sulphide ores, such as bornite, chalcocite and chalcopyrite, and in oxides, such as cuprite and malachite.
Known world reserves: 330 million tonnes
Annual production: 11.5 million tonnes
Largest producers: Chile, 29.4 per cent; USA 16.5 per cent; Canada, 6 per cent; Indonesia, 5.4 per cent; Australia, 5 per cent.

Early industry Copper-working began 9000 years ago in south-eastern Turkey. Its electrical conductivity, second only to silver, was not discovered until the 19th century.

Iron

The most important industrial metal, iron is alloyed with small amounts of carbon, silicon and other metals to make a wide range of steels.
Occurrence: Mainly found in oxides such as haematite, magnetite and limonite, and in the sulphide pyrite.
Known world reserves: 68 700 million tonnes
Annual production: 601 million tonnes
Largest producers: China, 23 per cent; Brazil, 16.8 per cent; Australia, 13.9 per cent; Ukraine, 9.9 per cent; Russia, 6.4 per cent; India, 6.4 per cent.

Lead

Used in batteries, as it resists acid corrosion.
Occurrence: Found in the sulphide galena. More than 50 per cent of industrial lead is extracted from recycled scrap.
Known world reserves: 65 million tonnes
Annual production: 3.1 million tonnes (excluding recycled scrap)
Largest producers: China, 21.1 per cent; Australia, 18.2 per cent; USA ,15.1 per cent; Peru, 8.4 per cent; Canada, 6.9 per cent.

see also
38-9 **Earth's treasures**
538-9 **The periodic table**

Magnesium

Alloyed with aluminium or zinc, or both, to make strong, light materials for use in aircraft and cars.
Occurrence: Found as chloride in seawater, as carbonate in dolomite and magnesite, as chloride in carnallite, and in many other minerals.
Known world reserves (magnesite): 2500 million tonnes
Annual production: 19 million tonnes
Largest producers: China, 43.4 per cent; Russia, 14.3 per cent; Turkey, 12.6 per cent; North Korea, 7 per cent.

Manganese

Used for strengthening steel during refining. In alloy steel, used to make safes and heavy-duty machines.
Occurrence: Found in iron ores; deep sea-bed nodules contain up to 20 per cent manganese.
Known world reserves (land only): 660 million tonnes
Annual production: 9.6 million tonnes
Largest producers: Ukraine, 26.1 per cent; China, 23.8 per cent; South Africa, 12 per cent.

Nickel

Used in the manufacture of stainless steels.
Occurrence: Found in pentlandite, a sulphide of nickel and iron; some also found in deep sea-bed nodules.
Known world reserves (land only): 40 million tonnes
Annual production: 1.1 million tonnes
Largest producers: Russia, 21.4 per cent; Canada, 18.1 per cent; New Caledonia, 11.8 per cent; Australia, 11.6 per cent.

Tin

Used as a corrosion-resistant plating metal and in alloys, including solders, bronze and pewter.
Occurrence: Found as cassiterite, an oxide of tin.
Known world reserves: 7.8 million tonnes
Annual production: 215 000 tonnes
Largest producers: China. 32.2 per cent; Indonesia, 24.9 per cent; Peru, 12.5 per cent; Brazil, 8.4 per cent.

Titanium

Light, strong, corrosion and heat-resistant: used to build aircraft and spacecraft.
Occurrence: Found as titanium oxide in ilmenite (with iron) and rutile; small amounts found in titaniferous iron ore.
Known world reserves: 183 million tonnes
Annual production: 2.5 million tonnes
Largest producers: Australia, 31.5 per cent; Canada, 21.2 per cent; South Africa, 17.7 per cent; Norway, 9.3 per cent.

Tungsten

Has the highest melting point of all metals: used in filament lamps and to make tungsten carbide, a hard substance for cutting tools.
Occurrence: Found as scheelite (calcium tungstate) and wolframite (iron manganese tungstate).
Known world reserves: 2 million tonnes
Annual production: 34 600 tonnes
Largest producers: China, 73.1 per cent; Russia, 12.7 per cent.

Uranium

Used mainly as nuclear fuel.
Occurrence: Most commonly found as pitchblende, a form of uraninite, containing uranium dioxide.
Known world reserves: 2.6 million tonnes
Annual production: 34 800 tonnes
Largest producers: Canada, 33.3 per cent; Australia, 14.7 per cent; Niger, 10.1 per cent; Namibia, 7.8 per cent; USA, 6.2 per cent.

Zinc

Used to galvanise metal (gives a rustproof coating); also used in alloys such as brass, and in solders.
Occurrence: Found as sphalerite (zinc blende), a sulphide usually with lead and silver.
Known world reserves: 190 million tonnes
Annual production: 7.5 million tonnes
Largest producers: China, 16.3 per cent; Canada, 15 per cent; Australia, 14.2 per cent.

Flash-point Magnesium (above) was once used for flash photography. When lit, it burns with an intense white flame.

Science and invention

science and technology

Mathematics is the study of numbers, shapes and quantities. It forms a part of other disciplines, from physics, chemistry and biology to computing, economics and management theory, and is an essential tool for understanding the world. It even extends into aesthetics through concepts such as the 'golden ratio', creating pleasing proportions in art and architecture.

Branches of mathematics

Mathematics is divided into two major areas: pure and applied.

● **Pure mathematics** is the study of mathematical theory without considering any particular practical applications.

● **Applied mathematics** is the use of mathematics in other activities, including scientific disciplines such as physics, chemistry or biology.

The main branches of pure and applied mathematics are:

● **Arithmetic** The study of numbers and the relationship between them, including their addition, subtraction, multiplication and division.

● **Algebra** The use of letters or symbols in calculations as substitutes for any unknown numbers.

● **Calculus** The study of continuous change, such as curving lines on graphs, using algebra.

● **Geometry** The study of points, lines, angles, surfaces and solids, and the relationships between them.

● **Probability** The study of random events, and ways of calculating the likelihood of their happening.

● **Set theory** The study of sets. A set is any group of specified elements – for example, all people aged over 50 – where there is a rule determining whether or not an element is a member of the set.

● **Statistics** The collection, organisation and interpretation of numerical data.

● **Trigonometry** The study of angles and triangles, and their application to problems in geometry and other areas.

Pi (π)

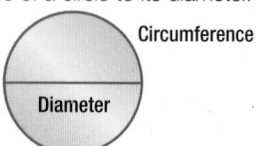

An irrational, or inexact, number (see below), π or *pi* is defined as the ratio of the circumference of a circle to its diameter.

Circumference

Diameter

● It is one of the most important numbers in mathematics, used to calculate the lengths of curves, the areas of curved surfaces and the volumes of solids. It even appears in formulas describing the vibration of strings and the motion of pendulums.

● As an irrational number it cannot be represented as a fraction, although the improper fraction $^{22}/_7$ is sometimes used to show its approximate value.

● To the first **120** decimal places, its numerical value is:

3.14159265358979323846264338327950288419716939937510582097494459230781640628620899862803482534211706798214808651328230 6647

NUMBERS OF DIFFERENT KINDS

The simplest numbers are **natural (or whole) numbers**, used for counting things in whole amounts. They are the first numbers that children learn – **1, 2, 3, 4, 5, 6, 7** and so on.

● **Integers** A refinement on natural numbers, integers are numbers used for counting whole steps backwards or forwards, upwards or downwards.

An integer consists of a natural number with a plus or minus sign in front of it: –7, –6, –5, –4, –3, –2, –1, 0, +1, +2, +3, +4, +5, +6, +7. In practice, of course, positive integers are normally written without the plus sign.

● **Real numbers** All the numbers that exist, not just integers, but also the limitless supply of other numbers that lie in between each pair of integers, are described as real numbers These are expressed as fractions or decimals: **6.989**, **5⁵/₈** and so on.

● **Prime numbers** A whole number that can only be divided exactly by itself and by 1, is known as a prime number.
Example: The first 20 prime numbers are: **2, 3, 5, 7, 11, 13, 17, 19, 23, 29, 31, 37, 41, 43, 47, 53, 59, 61, 67, 71**.

● **Factors** A factor is any number that divides exactly into another number.
Example: The factors of **12** are **1, 2, 3, 4, 6** and **12**.
A factor that is also a prime number is called a prime factor.
Example: **2** and **3** are prime factors of **12**.

● **Perfect numbers** Natural numbers that equal the sum of all their factors are called perfect numbers.
Example: **28** is a perfect number because 1, 2, 4, 7 and 14 are its factors, and 1 + 2 + 4 + 7 + 14 = 28.
The first six perfect numbers are: **6, 28, 496, 8128, 33550336, 8589869065**.

● **Infinity** The number that is too large to count, found at the theoretical end of the line of real numbers, is infinity. It is represented by the symbol ∞.

● **Irrational numbers** Most numbers (known as rational numbers) can be expressed exactly, using decimals or fractions. But a few have precise values that can never be written down in this way. These are irrational numbers.
Example: The square root of **2** is irrational. An approximate value is **1.41421356237309504880168872420 97**.

You could keep adding more and more digits to this number, and still never write it down exactly.

● **Recurring numbers** Expressed as decimals, some rational numbers have an infinite expansion – the numbers after the decimal point do not come to an end.
Example: Whereas **½ = 0.5**, **⅙ = 0.1666666666666** recurring.
Sometimes a group of digits is repeated.
Example: **³/₇ = 0.42857142857 142857142 . . .**

● **Golden ratio** Also called the golden section, the golden mean and the divine proportion, the golden ratio is an irrational number with the value of $^{(1 + \sqrt{5})}/_2$ or approximately **1.618034**.
It can be calculated using the Fibonacci sequence (see opposite). If each number in the Fibonacci sequence is divided by the number preceding it, it produces a ratio that eventually stabilises at around **1.618034**.

Number line The numbers on the line below are integers, used to count whole steps. The line of real numbers would be impossible to depict, since it would have to include the literally countless numbers that lie between integers.

-5 -4 -3 -2 -1 0 1 2 3 4 5

NUMBER PATTERNS

Number patterns – sometimes known as sequences – are ordered sets of successive numbers, which are governed by a rule.

A simple sequence is shown by the natural numbers: 1, 2, 3, 4, 5, 6, 7, 8, 9, 10, 11. These are connected by the rule 'add one to the previous number'.

Two common types of sequence are arithmetic progressions and geometric progressions.

● **Arithmetic progressions** In an arithmetic progression, the difference between successive numbers – the *common difference* – never varies.
Example: The sequence 4, 6.5, 9, 11.5, 13, 15.5, 18 is an increasing sequence with a common difference of 2.5.

The sequence 176, 150, 124, 98, 72, 46, 20 is a decreasing sequence with a common difference of 26.

If you know the common difference (d) and the first number (a) of an arithmetic progression, you can work out what any successive number in the sequence will be. To calculate the nth number (usually called a 'term') in the sequence, multiply d by n–1, then add a.
Formula: The value of the nth term
$= a + (n-1)d$.
Example: What is the value of the 11th term of this sequence:
6, 10, 14, 18, 22, 26 . . .?
a = 6 and d = 4
The value of the 11th term
$= 6 + (11-1) \times 4$
$= 6 + 10 \times 4 = 46$

● **Geometric progressions** Each number in a geometric progression is multiplied by a particular, fixed amount – the *common multiple* – to get the next number in the sequence.

Example: The sequence 2, 4, 8, 16, 32, 64, 128, 256 is a geometric progression where the common multiple is 2:
$2 \times 2 = 4, 2 \times 4 = 8, 2 \times 8 = 16$, and so on.

To work out the nth number, or term, in a geometric progression, calculate the value of the common multiple (m) to the power of n–1 (see Powers and roots on page 515), then multiply the result by a (the first number in the sequence).
Formula: The value of the nth term
$= am^{(n-1)}$.
Example: What is the value of the 8th term of this sequence:
3, 6, 12, 24, 48, 96 . . . ?
a = 3 and m = 2
The value of the 8th term
$= 3 \times 2^{(8-1)}$
$= 3 \times 2^7$ (that is, 2 multiplied by itself seven times)
$= 3 \times 128 = 384$

0   1   1   2   3   5   8   13   21   34   55

The Fibonacci sequence In the sequence above, each successive number, or term, is made by adding the previous two – $0 + 1 = 1, 1 + 1 = 2, 1 + 2 = 3, 2 + 3 = 5$, and so on.

The sequence was discovered by the mathematician Leonardo of Pisa or Leonardo Fibonacci (c.1170–1240). In the centuries since then, it has been found to have many interesting properties, related not only to mathematics but also to nature, art and architecture. It is also closely connected with the golden ratio (see opposite).

● **Rectangles and spirals** The Fibonacci sequence can be expressed not just as numbers, but also as a series of rectangles and as a spiral drawn using the rectangles. It is in this form that it most often occurs in nature and art.

Fibonacci rectangles are constructed as follows:
● Draw two small squares, each measuring 1 unit x 1 unit. Overall, they produce a rectangle measuring 1 x 2.
● Beneath this rectangle draw a square 2 x 2. Overall this produces a rectangle 2 x 3.
● Draw a new square 3 x 3, with one of its sides as the right-hand side of the previous rectangle. This produces a rectangle 3 x 5.
● Draw a new square 5 x 5, with one of its sides as the top side of the previous square. This produces a rectangle 5 x 8. (This process can be carried on indefinitely.)

To create the spiral, draw a quarter circle in each square, starting with the first. The resulting spiral is very similar to those found in the shells of certain molluscs, including snails and *Nautilus* shells.

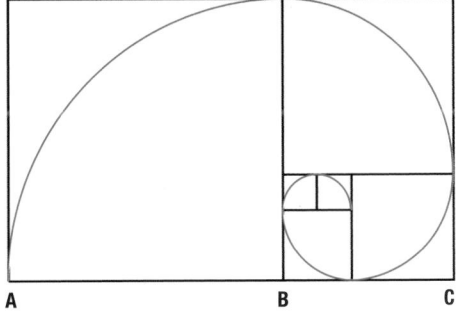

Fibonacci and the golden ratio Fibonacci rectangles have several curious properties. Each, for example, has sides that are two successive Fibonacci numbers long. The rectangles also involve the golden ratio. Take the rectangle measuring 5 x 8: 8 ÷ 5 = 1.6. The next rectangle after that would measure 8 x 13: 13 ÷ 8 = 1.625. The more rectangles are added, the closer the ratio comes to the golden ratio – roughly 1.618034.

These proportions are found in many of the things we find pleasing or beautiful. The ancient Greeks were aware of this, as is often revealed in their architecture. The front of the Parthenon in Athens, for example, is a Fibonacci rectangle, about 1.6 times wider than it is tall. Also, the dimensions of paintings frequently conform to the golden ratio, and have their focus of interest at the point where Fibonacci rectangles meet.

Fibonacci in nature and art
A *Nautilus* shell (above, left) forms a Fibonacci spiral. In the rectangles (below, left), the distance from A to C (13 units) divided by that from A to B (8 units) equals 1.625 – roughly the golden ratio. In the painting by J.M.W. Turner (above), the focal point, the locomotive, lies on the same axis.

see also
514-5 **Using numbers**
516-9 **Geometry**
520-1 **Statistics**
604-5 **Scales and measurements**

To transform numbers into useful tools for everyday life, it is necessary to acquire some basic skills in working with them. For example, a clear understanding of what *fractions, decimals and percentages are is essential for calculating the interest on money deposited in a bank account, or income tax, or even the tip in a restaurant.*

Fractions and decimals

In a fraction, the number above or before the dividing line is the numerator – the 'part of the whole'. The number below or after the dividing line is the denominator – the 'whole'.

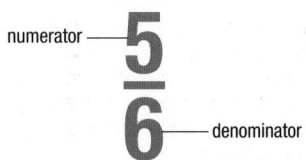

numerator — $\dfrac{5}{6}$ — denominator

⬤ **A proper (or vulgar) fraction**, such as $^3/_7$, has a numerator that is smaller than the denominator.
⬤ **An improper fraction**, such as $^{31}/_7$, is 'top heavy' because the numerator is larger than the denominator.

⬤ **Converting fractions to decimals**
Divide the numerator by the denominator.
Example: The fraction $^4/_5 = 4 ÷ 5 = 0.8$

⬤ **Converting decimals to fractions**
Make the number after the decimal point the numerator. For the denominator, raise

10 to the power (see opposite) of the number of decimal places.
Example: Convert 0.005 to a fraction.
Numerator = 5
There are three decimal places, so the denominator = $10^3 = 1000$
The fraction is $^5/_{1000} = ^1/_{200}$

⬤ **Equivalent fractions and cancelling**
If the numerator and denominator of a fraction are multiplied by the same number, this produces an equivalent fraction.
Example: $^1/_2 × 5 = ^5/_{10}$

Dividing the numerator and denominator by the same number also produces an equivalent fraction. This process is called cancelling.
Example: Reduce the fraction $^{44}/_{88}$ to its lowest form.
Cancel by 11: $^{44}/_{88} ÷ 11 = ^4/_8$
Cancel by 4: $^4/_8 ÷ 4 = ^1/_2$

⬤ **Adding and subtracting fractions**
If fractions have the same denominators, simply add or subtract the numerators.
Example: $^4/_7 – ^1/_7 = ^3/_7$

If fractions have different denominators, change them to equivalent fractions which have the same denominators.
Example: $^4/_7 + ^1/_3$
Multiply the first fraction by 3: $^4/_7 × 3 = ^{12}/_{21}$
Multiply the second by 7: $^1/_3 × 7 = ^7/_{21}$
Add the two equivalent fractions:
$^{12}/_{21} + ^7/_{21} = ^{19}/_{21}$
This is the final answer because $^{19}/_{21}$ cannot be reduced to a lower form.

⬤ **Multiplying fractions** Multiply the numerators together and multiply the denominators together. If possible, cancel 'opposite' numerators and denominators.
Example: $^{10}/_{11} × ^2/_{15}$
Cancel 'opposing' numerator and denominator 10 and 15 by 5:
$\dfrac{2}{11} × \dfrac{2}{15} = \dfrac{2×2}{11 × 3} = \dfrac{4}{33}$

⬤ **Dividing fractions** Change the sign from ÷ to x, and turn the second fraction 'upside-down'.
Example: $^4/_5 ÷ ^3/_4$
$= ^4/_5 × ^4/_3 = ^{16}/_{15} = 1^1/_{15}$

WORKING WITH PERCENTAGES

To calculate relative size as a percentage, divide the smaller quantity by the larger, and multiply the result by 100.
Formula: Percentage = (smaller quantity ÷ larger quantity) x 100
Example: An investor buys 52 000 of the 97 000 shares in a publicly quoted company. What percentage of the shares does he own?
(52 000 ÷ 97 000) x 100
= 0.536 x 100 = 53.6 per cent

⬤ **Percentage change** To express an increase or decrease in quantity as a percentage, first divide the change in quantity by the original quantity, then multiply by 100.
Formula: Percentage change = (change ÷ original amount) x 100
Example: A company's profits last year were £5.5 million; this year they are £6.6 million. What is the percentage increase in profits?
Change in profits
= 6.6 million – 5.5 million
= 1.1 million
Percentage increase
= (1.1 ÷ 5.5) x 100
= 0.2 x 100 = 20 per cent

⬤ **Reversing an increase or decrease**
If a quantity has increased or decreased,

and you know the percentage change, you can calculate the original quantity.
Example: If after 12 months of dieting a man has lost **20 per cent** of his body weight, and weighs **75 kilos**, what was his original weight?
100 per cent = his original weight
100 – 20 per cent = 80 per cent
= his current weight of 75 kilos
1 per cent of the original weight
= 75 ÷ 80 = 0.9375
The original weight
= 0.9375 x 100 = 93.75 kilos

⬤ **Increasing or decreasing an amount by a given percentage** This has many uses including calculating net amounts after tax has been deducted.
Example: A person's gross taxable salary is £25 000. If income tax at 22 per cent is deducted, what is the net annual sum received?
22 per cent of 25 000
= (22 x 25 000) ÷ 100
= 550 000 ÷ 100 = £5500.
The net income
= 25 000 – 5500 = £19 500

The calculation can also be made using a 'multiplier' as a shortcut.
Formula: The multiplier = ([+ or –] percentage change + 100) ÷ 100

Example: In the previous example, the multiplier
= (–22 + 100) ÷ 100
= 78 ÷ 100 = 0.78
0.78 x £25 000 = £19 500

Example: £10 000 is invested in a deposit account with an interest rate of **5.5 per cent**. How much money will be in the account after three years?
This involves calculating compound interest. The amount of interest earned in one year is based on the original sum invested plus the amount of interest earned in earlier years.

The multiplier
= (5.5 + 100) ÷ 100 = 1.055
End of year 1, sum in account =
£10 000 x 1.055 = £10 550
End of year 2, sum in account =
£10 550 x 1.055 = £11 130.25
End of year 3, sum in account =
£11 130.25 x 1.055 = £11 742.41

Alternatively, this short cut can be used:
Total amount = Original sum x (the multiplier)^n, where n = number of years

Total Amount = 10 000 x 1.055^3
= 10 000 x 1.1742413
= £11 742.41

NUMBER SYSTEMS

For most everyday purposes, we count using a number system based on ten – ultimately derived from the number of fingers or toes. This is the decimal system.

But any number can be the base for a number system. Also in common use are the
- **sexagesimal system (base 60)** for time: 60 seconds = 1 minute, 60 minutes = 1 hour.
- **duodecimal system (base 12)**: 12 in = 1 ft, 2 x 12 hours = 1 day, 12 old pence = 1 shilling.

Decimal system (base 10) Decimal numbers are constructed from the ten digits:

0 1 2 3 4 5 6 7 8 9

The value of any digit depends on its position.
Example: The number 23578 could be set out in columns, with each column representing increasing powers of ten:

10 000s	1000s	100s	10s	1s
10^4	10^3	10^2	10^1	10^0
2	3	5	7	8

Binary system (base 2) Binary numbers are constructed from just two digits:

0 1

The binary system is used to create the series of on-off signals in computer programs and digital communications.
Example: The binary number 11001 could be set out in columns, with each column representing increasing powers of two:

16s	8s	4s	2s	1s
2^4	2^3	2^2	2^1	2^0
1	1	0	0	1

To convert from binary to decimal, add the values of the columns that contain 1s.
Example: Convert 11001 into decimal.
Binary 11001
= decimal $2^4 + 2^3 + 2^0$
= 16 + 8 + 1 = 25

To convert from decimal to binary, find the largest power of two (p) that is less than the number to be converted (d). (See Powers and roots, below.) Put a 1 in that column and subtract p from the number to be converted. Find the largest power of two that is less than d − p and put a 1 in that column. Repeat the process until you reach the last column.
Example: Convert 22 into binary.
The largest power of two less than 22 is $2^4 = 16$
Put a 1 in the 2^4 column.
22 − 16 = 6
The largest power of two less than 6 is $2^2 = 4$
Put a 0 in the 2^3 column and a 1 in the 2^2 column.
6 − 4 = 2 = 2^1
Put a 1 in the 2^1 column and a 0 in the 2^0 column:

16s	8s	4s	2s	1s
2^4	2^3	2^2	2^1	2^0
1	0	1	1	0

Decimal 22 = binary 10110

Powers and roots The term power indicates how many times a number has been multiplied by itself. For example, 4 can be expressed as 2^2: 2 to the power of 2. Similarly, $8 = 2^3$: 2 to the power 3, that is 2 x 2 x 2.

The small raised number is called the **index** or **exponent**.

- Any number to the power 0 is 1. For example, $6^0 = 1$.
- Any number to the power 1 is itself. For example, $7^1 = 7$.
- Any number raised to the power of 2 is said to be squared.
- Any number raised to the power of 3 is said to be cubed.

Negative index A negative index shows how many times a number must be divided into the number 1.
Example: $8^{-2} = 1 \div 8^2 = 1 \div 64 = \frac{1}{64}$ or 0.0156
$10^{-1} = 1 \div 10^1 = \frac{1}{10}$ or 0.1
$10^{-2} = 1 \div 10^2 = 0.01$
$10^{-3} = 0.001$
$10^{-4} = 0.0001$
$10^{-5} = 0.00001$

Roots Where larger numbers are expressed as the power of smaller ones – for example, 8 as 2^3 – the smaller number is called the root of the larger one.
Example: 64 is 8^2: 8 is the **square root** of 64 or $\sqrt{64} = 8$
64 is also 4^3: 4 is the **cube root** of 64 or $\sqrt[3]{64} = 4$
64 is also 2^6: 2 is the **fourth root** of 64 or $\sqrt[4]{64} = 2$

Scientific notation Also called standard form, scientific notation is used in science and mathematics to express very large and very small numbers in a form that is easy to understand and manipulate, and that uses little space.
Example: The number 30 000 000 000 000 (30 trillion) can be represented more simply as 3×10^{13}.

Scientific notation makes it easier to compare large numbers. The number 6.1×10^9, for example, is about 10^3 or 1000 times bigger than 5.9×10^6.
Example: The number 0.000008 can be expressed in scientific notation as 8×10^{-6}.

Rounding up, rounding down

It is often convenient to round numbers off to a certain degree of accuracy – for example, to the nearest hundred, nearest ten, or a specified number of decimal places or significant numbers.

The convention is that 5 or more is rounded up; less than 5 is rounded down.
Example: If 1157 people attend a protest meeting, how many is that to the nearest hundred? The number after the 'hundreds' place is 5, so the number is rounded up to 1200.
Example: What is 376.246 correct to one decimal place? The second decimal place is 4, so the number is rounded down to 376.2.

Significant figures Significant figures are used to simplify both large and small numbers.
Example: What is 465 726 simplified to two significant figures? The significant figure in the third place is 5, so the number is rounded up to 470 000.
Example: What is 0.0003759 simplified to one significant figure? The first significant figure is 3, and the next place is 7, so the number is rounded up to 0.0004.

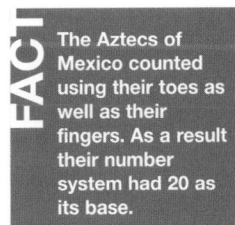

FACT The Aztecs of Mexico counted using their toes as well as their fingers. As a result their number system had 20 as its base.

Geometry is the branch of mathematics that studies the nature of lines, points, surfaces and solids. Fundamental to its understanding are definitions of the different kinds of angles and shapes, some of which were laid down by ancient Greek mathematicians as early as the sixth century BC. They established many principles that are still in use today. Until recently, most of the geometry taught in schools was that described by Euclid in the third century BC.

LINES

A **line** connects two or more points. It has only one dimension – length – and can be straight or curved.

A **point** is a position in space. It has no dimensions – neither length, width nor depth.

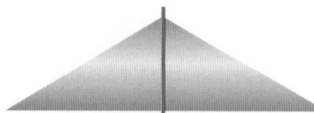

Axis or line of symmetry A line dividing a symmetrical shape (for example, an isosceles triangle) into two reflecting (mirror) halves is called a line of symmetry.

Perpendicular A straight line that meets a second straight line at a right angle (90°) is said to be perpendicular to the second line.

Parallel Two or more lines that are the same distances apart everywhere along their length are parallel. By convention, parallel lines are indicated by arrow-like marks.

Tangent A straight line that touches a curve at one point only, but does not cross it, is a tangent.

ANGLES

An angle is the space between two lines that meet or intersect. The point at which they meet is called a vertex. Angles are measured in degrees (°). There are six basic types of angle:

Acute angle An angle of less than 90°.

Right angle An angle of exactly 90° – indicated by a small square in diagrams.

Obtuse angle An angle of more than 90° and less than 180°.

Straight angle An angle of exactly 180°.

Reflex angle An angle of more than 180° and less than 360°.

Round angle An angle of exactly 360°.

TRIANGLES

A triangle has three vertices and three sides. The sum of the three internal angles in a triangle is always 180° (see diagram right). There are six basic types of triangle:

Sum of the angles As the internal angles of a triangle always add up to 180°, it is possible to work out the missing angle a: 180 – 80 – 40 = 60. The external angles (140 + 120 + 100) add up to 360°.

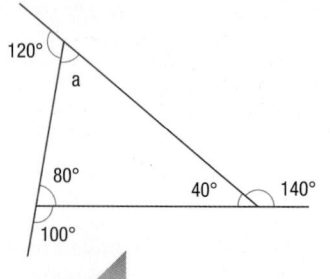

     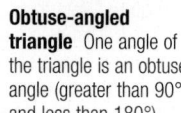

Equilateral triangle All three sides have the same length, and all three internal angles measure 60°. There are three axes of symmetry.

Isosceles triangle At least two sides have the same length, and at least two of the angles are the same. There is one axis of symmetry.

Scalene triangle All three sides are different lengths, and all three angles are different. There are no axes of symmetry.

Acute-angled triangle All three angles are acute (less than 90°).

Right-angled triangle One angle is exactly 90° – a right angle. The side opposite the right angle (the longest side) is called the hypotenuse.

Obtuse-angled triangle One angle of the triangle is an obtuse angle (greater than 90° and less than 180°).

QUADRILATERALS

A quadrilateral is a plane shape enclosed by four sides (also described as a four-sided polygon). The sum of the four internal angles of a quadrilateral is always 360°. There are six basic types of quadrilateral:

Rectangle All internal angles are right angles. Opposite sides are parallel and the same length.

Square An equal-sided rectangle. All four angles are right angles. All sides are the same length.

Parallelogram Opposite sides are parallel and equal in length. Opposite angles are equal.

Rhombus An equal-sided parallelogram. Opposite sides are parallel. Opposite angles are equal. All side are the same length.

Trapezium Two sides are parallel but have different lengths. If the other two, nonparallel sides have the same length, it is known as an isosceles trapezium.

Kite Two pairs of adjacent sides have the same length. Opposite angles are equal.

CIRCLES AND CURVES

Geometry is also concerned with curved lines and the shapes, both plane (for example, circles) and solid (for example, spheres), that are enclosed by them. The following terms describe curved shapes and their features:

 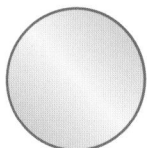    

Circle A flat shape enclosed by one curved line. All points on the curved line are equally distant from the circle's centre.

Circumference The line that marks the perimeter (boundary) of a circle. The term is also used to describe the distance around the perimeter.

Chord A straight line that joins any two points on the circumference.

Diameter A chord that passes through the centre of a circle. The term is also used to describe the length of that chord.

Radius A straight line joining the centre of a circle to any point on its circumference. It is also used to describe the length of that line.

Sphere A solid shape, enclosed by a single curved surface. All points on the curved surface are equally distant from the sphere's centre.

     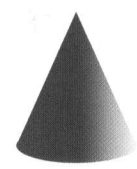

Ellipse Also known as an oval. Mathematically, an ellipse is a cross-section of a cone (see right) that does not pass through the base of the cone and is not parallel to it.

Major axis The long axis of an ellipse. A straight line that passes through the centre of an ellipse, divides it into two equal halves and joins the two opposite points on its circumference that are farthest apart.

Minor axis The short axis of an ellipse. A straight line that passes through the centre – at right angles to the major axis – and joins the two opposite points on the circumference that are closest to each other.

Ellipsoid Also known as an 'ovoid'. A solid shape whose cross-sections are all either ellipses or circles.

Cylinder A tubular solid shape that has straight sides and is circular in cross-section.

Cone A solid shape that has a circle for its base and curved sides that taper to a point at the apex (top).

Polygons

A polygon is any plane shape enclosed by three or more straight lines. A regular polygon, such as a square (regular quadrilateral), has sides of equal length and all its internal angles are the same size; an irregular polygon, such as a trapezium (irregular quadrilateral), has sides and angles of different sizes.

Polygons are named according to the number of sides they have. The more sides they have, the greater the sum of their internal angles. The sum of a polygon's external angles (see Triangles, opposite), however, is always 360°.

Name	Number of sides	Sum of internal angles
Triangle	Three	180°
Quadrilateral	Four	360°
Pentagon	Five	540°
Hexagon	Six	720°
Heptagon	Seven	900°
Octagon	Eight	1080°
Nonagon	Nine	1260°
Decagon	Ten	1440°

Practical geometry

518

Working with triangles, circles and spheres

The geometry of Euclid and his predecessors has many practical applications. Trigonometry, the science of measuring triangles, based on a 2500-year-old theorem by Pythagoras, has been used for centuries by engineers, surveyors and navigators to determine heights, angles and distances. In addition, there are numerous useful ancient Greek formulas for calculating the areas and volumes of, for example, circles and spheres.

PYTHAGORAS' THEOREM

Pythagoras (c.572–497 BC) famously formulated a theorem for calculating the length of the long side – known as the hypotenuse – of a right-angled triangle. It states that the square of the length of the hypotenuse is equal to the sum of the squares of the other two sides. This ability to establish the length of a third side by knowing the length of the other two is the basis for trigonometry (see below).

To do the calculations that are described here, you will need a calculator with a square root ($\sqrt{\ }$) key.

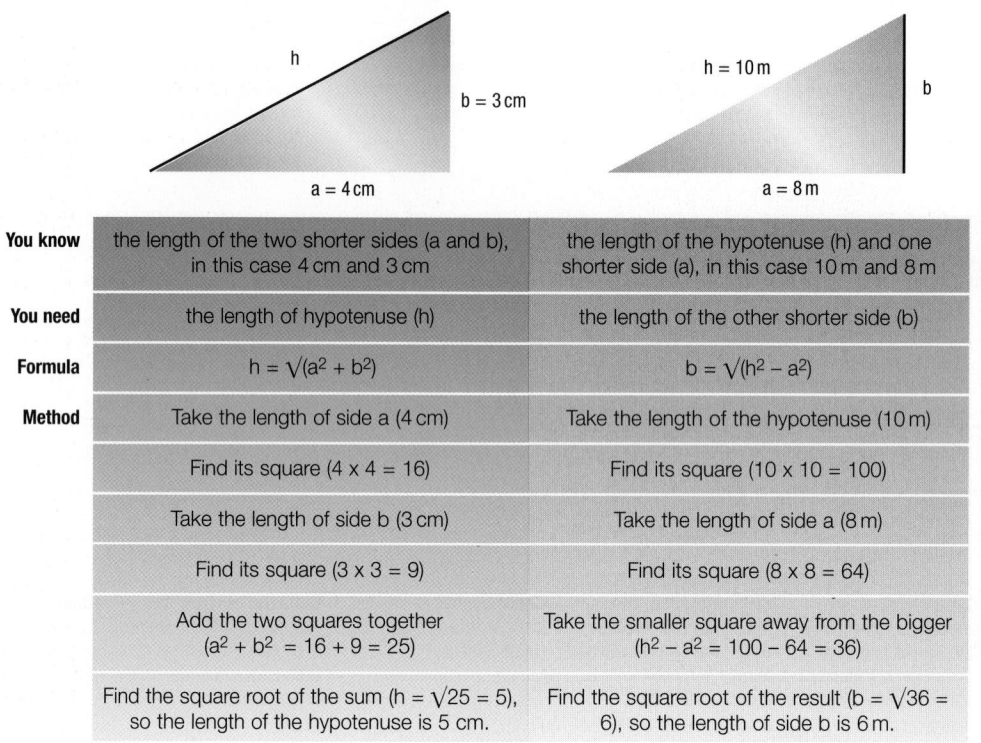

You know	the length of the two shorter sides (a and b), in this case 4 cm and 3 cm	the length of the hypotenuse (h) and one shorter side (a), in this case 10 m and 8 m
You need	the length of hypotenuse (h)	the length of the other shorter side (b)
Formula	$h = \sqrt{(a^2 + b^2)}$	$b = \sqrt{(h^2 - a^2)}$
Method	Take the length of side a (4 cm)	Take the length of the hypotenuse (10 m)
	Find its square (4 x 4 = 16)	Find its square (10 x 10 = 100)
	Take the length of side b (3 cm)	Take the length of side a (8 m)
	Find its square (3 x 3 = 9)	Find its square (8 x 8 = 64)
	Add the two squares together ($a^2 + b^2$ = 16 + 9 = 25)	Take the smaller square away from the bigger ($h^2 - a^2$ = 100 – 64 = 36)
	Find the square root of the sum (h = $\sqrt{25}$ = 5), so the length of the hypotenuse is 5 cm.	Find the square root of the result (b = $\sqrt{36}$ = 6), so the length of side b is 6 m.

THE USES OF TRIGONOMETRY

Tangent, sine and cosine – known as trigonometric ratios – relate to the proportions of right-angled triangles. If you know the length of one side of a right-angled triangle and the size of one of the two acute angles, you can use these ratios to work out the length of the other two sides and the size of the other acute angle.

Naming the sides In trigonometry, each side of a right-angled triangle is named in relation to the known acute angle x:
- the **hypotenuse** is the longest side, opposite the right angle.
- the **opposite** side is facing angle x.
- the **adjacent** side is the remaining side, next to angle x.

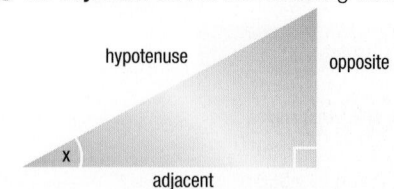

Tangent, sine and cosine Each of the three trigonometric ratios – known as tangent, sine and cosine – relates the size of angle x to the length of two of the sides.
 For example, the tangent (tan) of angle x is the ratio of the length of the opposite side to the length of adjacent side. Put mathematically, the tangent of angle x = the length of the opposite side ÷ the length of the adjacent side.

Or:
$$\tan x = \frac{opposite}{adjacent} \quad \sin x = \frac{opposite}{hypotenuse} \quad \cos x = \frac{adjacent}{hypotenuse}$$

Example A surveyor stands 450 m from the base of a tower and has to look upwards at an angle of 40° to the ground to see its top. How high is the tower? A scientific calculator provides values for tan, sin and cos.

Angle x = 40°
The length of the adjacent side = 450 m
The unknown is the opposite side.
If tan x = opposite ÷ adjacent
tan 40° = height ÷ 450
therefore,
height = 450 x tan 40°
= 450 x 0.839 = 377.6 m

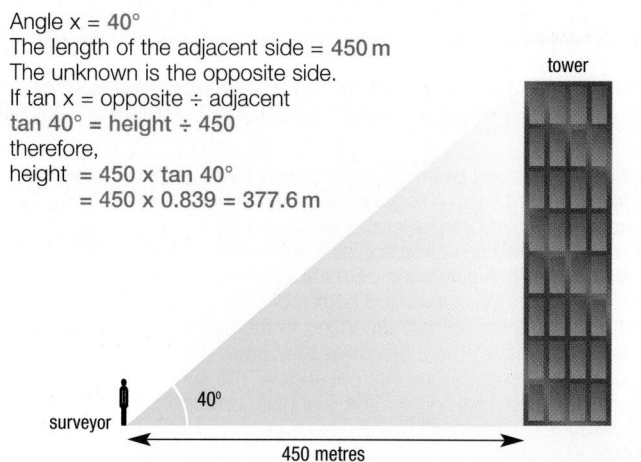

CALCULATING AREA AND VOLUME

The shapes described by geometry include plane (two-dimensional) shapes and solid (three-dimensional) shapes.

The formulas for calculating the area or volume of these different shapes are broken down here into a series of steps.

If your calculator does not have a pi (π) key, 3.14159 should be taken as the value of pi in these calculations.

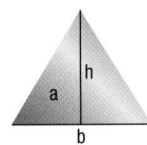 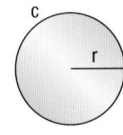 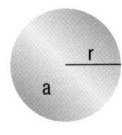 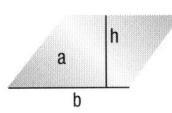  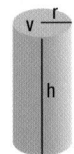

Shape	Triangle	Circle	Circle	Parallelogram	Cylinder	Cylinder
You know	length of base (b) and perpendicular height (h)	radius (r)	radius	length of base (b) and height (h)	radius (r) and height (h)	radius (r) and height (h)
You need	area (a)	circumference (c)	area (a)	area (a)	surface area (a)	volume (v)
Formula	$a = \dfrac{bh}{2}$	$c = 2\pi r$	$a = \pi r^2$	$a = bh$	$a = 2\pi r(r + h)$	$v = \pi r^2 h$
Method	Measure the length of the base (for example, 7 cm)	Measure the radius (for example, 6 cm)	Measure the radius (for example, 6 cm)	Measure the length of the base (for example, 9 cm)	Measure the radius (for example, 5 cm) and the height (for example, 9 cm)	Measure the radius (for example, 5 cm) and the height (for example, 9 cm)
	Measure the perpendicular height (for example, 12 cm)	Multiply by 2 (6 x 2 = 12)	Find its square (6 x 6 = 36)	Measure the height (for example, 5 cm)	Add the radius and the height together (5 + 9 = 14)	Find the square of the radius (5 x 5 = 25)
	Multiply the two together (7 x 12 = 84)				Multiply by 2 (14 x 2 = 28)	Multiply by the height (25 x 9 = 225)
					Multiply by the radius (28 x 5 = 140)	
	Divide by two (a = 84 ÷ 2 = 42 cm²),	Multiply by π (c = 12 x π = 37.7 cm)	Multiply by π (a = 36 x π = 113.1 cm²)	Multiply the two together (a = 9 x 5 = 45 cm²)	Multiply by π (a = 140 x π = 439.8 cm²)	Multiply by π (v = 225 x π = 706.9 cm³)

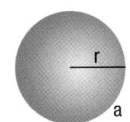 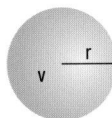 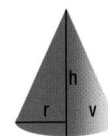

Shape	Sphere	Sphere	Cone
You know	radius (r)	radius (r)	height (h) and radius of base (r)
You need	surface area (a)	volume (v)	volume (v)
Formula	$a = 4\pi r^2$	$v = \dfrac{4\pi r^3}{3}$	$v = \dfrac{\pi r^2 h}{3}$
Method	Measure the radius (for example, 5 cm)	Measure the radius (for example 5 cm)	Measure the radius (for example, 3 cm) and the height (for example, 8 cm)
	Find its square (5 x 5 = 25)	Find its cube (5 x 5 x 5 = 125)	Find the square of the radius (3 x 3 = 9)
	Multiply by 4 (25 x 4 = 100)	Multiply by 4 (125 x 4 = 500)	Multiply by the height (9 x 8 = 72)
		Divide by 3 (500 ÷ 3 = 166.66)	Multiply by π (72 x π = 226.2)
	Multiply by π (a = 100 x π = 314.2 cm²)	Multiply by π (v = 166.66 x π = 523.6 cm³)	Divide by 3 (v = 226.2 ÷ 3 = 75.4)

see also

512-3 **Numbers and sequences**

514-5 **Using numbers**

520-1 **Statistics**

604-5 **Scales and measurements**

Statistics deals with the collecting, organising, presenting and interpreting of data. Statistical methods make it possible, among other things, to poll opinions and check the validity of experimental results. It is the branch of mathematics which aims by the use of scientific methods to quantify the probability of something happening.

Establishing the average

One of the jobs of statistics is to make sense of a jumble of data. For example, knowing how many runs a cricketer scored each match during a season may be interesting for the enthusiast, but knowing his average for the season as a whole is likely to be more useful. It enables us to compare his performance with that of other players. We can also judge his performance in individual matches – whether it was above or below his average.

When faced with many scores, measurements or other numbers, it is useful therefore to work out a 'typical value'. Statisticians look for three typical values: the mean, the median and the mode.

● **Mean** Statisticians call the average of a set of numbers, the 'mean' number of the set.
Calculating the mean To obtain the mean of a set of numbers, add the numbers together, then divide the total by the size of the set.
Example: Calculate the mean of these 11 Olympic scores:
7 4 5 4 1 9 6 10 6 7 4
The sum = 63
The mean = $\frac{63}{11}$ = 5.73 (approximately)

● **Median** The median is the central value in a set of numbers.
Calculating the median When the numbers are placed in order, starting with the smallest, the median is half way along the sorted list. If the set is even in size, the median is the mean of the middle two numbers.

Example: A sandwich shop records the sales of its sandwiches. The record over two weeks is as follows:

M	T	W	Th	F	S	M	T	W	Th	F	S
250	195	172	250	301	120	261	207	120	230	294	120

The owner wants to know the 'average' number of daily sales, without being unduly influenced by low sales on Saturdays and Wednesdays. Arranged in order, the sandwich sales are as follows:

120 120 120 172 195 | 207 230 | 250 250 261 294 301

The median of daily sandwich sales = $\frac{207 + 230}{2}$ = 218.5

● **Mode** This is the number that occurs most frequently. It is unrelated to either the mean or the median.
Example: A city council wants to tax car drivers according to how many passengers they carry during rush hours, so it organises a survey recording the number of occupants in cars passing a busy location between 8.30am and 9am.

Number of occupants	6	5	4	3	2	1
Number of cars	11	27	42	38	86	124

The mode is 1, as there are more cars with one occupant than with any other number.

Fair sampling

Data is the raw material of statistics. It comes from many sources, such as telephone polls, questionnaires and scientific experiments. It is vital to collect the right amount of data, and ensure it is accurate and unbiased.

Statisticians describe any group that they study and obtain data from as a 'population'. Some populations are too large to count, or measure, or question every member of. In such cases, data is taken from a representative sample, using a variety of techniques.

For opinion polls, 'random' sampling is often used. A computer generates random telephone numbers, and the owners of the numbers are contacted for their views. The point of this is that all members of the population have an equal chance of being selected.

Market researchers often use 'quota' sampling. For this the samples must include equal quotas, or agreed proportions of, say, men and women in certain age groups. This ensures that the views of these various groups are correctly identified. In 'stratified' sampling, the sizes of the different groups within the samples are weighted according to the size of each group in the population as a whole.

DISPLAYING AND ANALYSING

To aid interpretation and analysis, data is arranged in tables or is illustrated using a variety of diagrams

● **How many, how often** The commonest way of summarising data is as a table. Tables can record quantities, known as frequencies (f), of several groups that do not overlap.
Example: An entomologist sets up a moth trap one night and returns next morning to count her catch. Her tally is as follows:

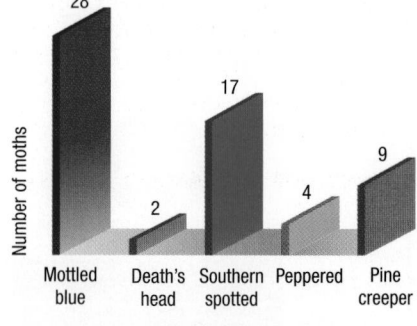

Species of moth (class)	Number of moths (frequency [f])
Mottled blue	28
Death's head	2
Southern spotted	17
Peppered	4
Pine creeper	9
Total	**60**

These figures can be represented diagrammatically as a bar chart (above right) or as a pie chart (right).

● **Gathered in groups** Sometimes it is useful to group data in various ways:
Example: The marks (per cent) for 50 students taking a French exam were as follows (arranged from lowest to highest):

4, 9, 18, 21, 21, 22, 27, 34, 39, 40, 40, 41, 42, 42, 44, 45, 45, 46, 47, 49, 49, 50, 50, 50, 51, 51, 52, 52, 52, 52, 53, 54, 54, 55, 55, 57, 59, 59, 59, 60, 63, 65, 65, 69, 70, 70, 75, 79, 81, 92

WHAT ARE THE CHANCES OF . . . ?

What is the probability of tossing a coin and getting heads? 50:50 What are the chances of throwing a dice and getting a three? One in six. In mathematics, the probability of an event happening (p) is represented by a number between 0 (impossible) and 1 (certain):

p = number of ways an event can occur (f)
        number of possible outcomes (n)

Example: In the case of throwing a dice and getting a three, f = 1 and n = 6.
Therefore p = $\frac{1}{6}$
This can also be expressed
● as a decimal: 0.167.
● as a percentage: 16.7 per cent.

Calculating probability The way you calculate probabilities for related events depends on whether they are mutually exclusive or independent:

⬤ **Mutually exclusive** If two events cannot happen at the same time, they are mutually exclusive – the one excludes the other. In this case, the probabilities are simply added.
Example: If a bag contains four red balls, six green balls and five blue balls, what is the probability of choosing either a green or blue ball?
Number of balls = 4 + 6 + 5 = 15
Probability of choosing a green ball = $\frac{6}{15}$

Probability of choosing a blue ball = $\frac{5}{15}$
Probability of choosing a green or a blue ball = $\frac{6 + 5}{15}$ = $\frac{11}{15}$ = 0.73 = 73 per cent.

⬤ **Independent** If the outcome of one event has no bearing on the outcome of another, they are independent. In this case, the probabilities are multiplied.
Example: You toss a coin twice. What are your chances of getting two heads?
Probability of one heads: $\frac{1}{2}$
Probability of two heads:
$\frac{1}{2}$ x $\frac{1}{2}$ = $\frac{1}{4}$ = 0.25
= 25 per cent
Calculations like this are made easier using tree diagrams (right):

All on the toss After two tosses of a coin, there are four possible outcomes: two heads, one heads and one tails, one tails and one heads, two tails (of course, the second and third are the same). From the diagram, it is easy to see that the probabilities at this stage are $\frac{1}{4}$ or 25 per cent for two heads, $\frac{2}{4}$ or $\frac{1}{2}$ or 50 per cent for one heads and one tails, $\frac{1}{4}$ or 25 per cent for two tails. The diagram can be extended indefinitely. The chances, for example, of six tails on the trot are $\frac{1}{64}$ or 1.56 per cent.

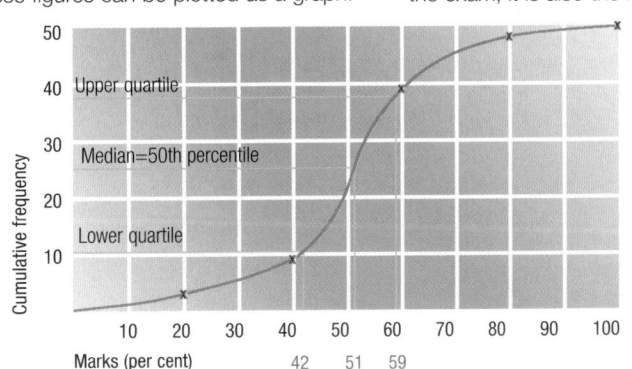

1 1H-0T	1 0H-1T				2 outcomes
1 2H-0T	2 1H-1T	1 0H-2T			4 outcomes
1 3H-0T	3 2H-1T	3 1H-2T	1 0H-3T		8 outcomes
1 4H-0T	4 3H-1T	6 2H-2T	4 1H-3T	1 0H-4T	16 outcomes
1 5H-0T	5 4H-1T	10 3H-2T	10 2H-3T	5 1H-4T	1 0H-5T 32 outcomes
1 6H-0T	6 5H-1T	15 4H-2T	20 3H-3T	15 2H-4T	6 1H-5T 1 0H-6T 64 outcomes

6 heads	5 heads 1 tail	4 heads 2 tails	3 heads 3 tails	2 heads 4 tails	1 head 5 tails	6 tails
1:64	6:64	15:64	20:64	15:64	6.64	1:64

All these unwieldy figures show is that the bottom mark was 4 per cent and the top was 92 per cent. The distribution of marks becomes clearer if the students are divided into five groups. This produces a 'grouped frequency distribution':

Marks (per cent)	Number of students (f)
0-19	3
20-39	6
40-59	30
60-79	9
80-99	2
Total	**50**

These figures can be show on a bar chart:

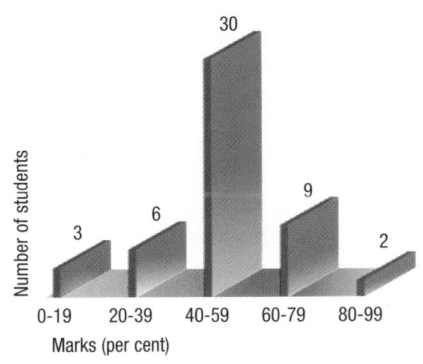

⬤ **Cumulative effect** Another way of showing how the marks are distributed is by using 'cumulative frequencies'.
Example: In the French exam 3 students gained marks of less than 20 per cent; 3 + 6 = 9 students gained marks of less than 40 per cent, and so on:

Marks (per cent)	Cumulative frequency
less than 20	3
less than 40	9
less than 60	39
less than 80	48
less than 100	50

These figures can be plotted as a graph:

⬤ **Percentiles and quartiles** Another useful tool for grouping and analysing results is to establish percentiles and quartiles.
To work out, for example, the 50th percentile, draw a line from the 50 per cent, or half-way, point of the Cumulative frequency axis of the graph (from 25 in the example below) to the curve. From this intersection, draw a vertical line to the Marks (per cent) or X-axis. This gives you the value of the 50th percentile: 51 in this example. Since the 50th percentile is the middle value of the overall marks gained in the exam, it is also the median mark.

The two most commonly used percentiles are the 25th, known as the lower quartile, and 75th, known as the upper quartile. In this example, the upper quartile is 59, and the lower quartile is 42.

The branch of physics that describes the effects of forces – pushes and pulls – on objects is called mechanics. It governs many aspects of life, from weighing a bag of potatoes to the trajectory of a space rocket. It is often divided into two fields: statics, dealing with mass, weight and gravity; and dynamics, dealing with moving, accelerating and colliding objects.

MASS, WEIGHT AND GRAVITY

The terms 'mass' and 'weight' are often used interchangeably for the same thing – how 'heavy' an object is. Yet each has its own distinct scientific meaning and units of measurement. The link between them is gravity.

● **Mass** is the amount of matter in an object – how much 'stuff' it contains. It is measured in grams (g), kilograms (kg) or tonnes (t) – or, in the Imperial system, ounces (oz), pounds (lb) and tons (t). The mass of an object remains the same wherever it is. A golfer, for example, would have the same mass on Earth and on the Moon – and so would his golf ball (see below).

● **Weight** is the force experienced by an object when gravity pulls it downwards. It is measured in newtons (N), and depends on both the mass of the object and the pull of gravity.
   Confusion arises because the weight of, for example, a supermarket bag of potatoes is quoted in kilograms (or pounds), not newtons. For everyday, nonscientific usage this does not matter because the weight of an object with a mass of 1 kg is the same at sea level everywhere on Earth. On the Moon, however, the pull of gravity is one-sixth that on Earth, so the object would have one-sixth its terrestrial weight.
   Weight is calculated by applying Newton's second law of motion (see right):

If the mass of an object   = 1 kg
Acceleration due to Earth's gravity = 9.8 m/s²
The weight of the object (that is, the force exerted by gravity) = mass x acceleration
= 1 kg x 9.8 m/s² = 9.8 N

● **Gravity** is generally thought of as the force that pulls on objects and makes them fall to the Earth's surface. For example, it keeps the feet of a juggler firmly on the ground and makes the skittles he has thrown into the air drop back to his hands. On Earth, gravity accelerates everything towards the ground at 9.8 m/s².
   In fact, a force of gravity exists between *all* objects – even between the juggler and his skittles – and depends on the mass of the objects and the distance between them. However, it is usually too weak to measure unless one or both objects has a large mass. The Earth's gravitational pull keeps the Moon in orbit around it. The Moon also exerts a gravitational pull on the Earth, although its mass – and, therefore, its gravitational pull – is only one-sixth that of Earth's mass. The theory of relativity explains gravity in terms of a curvature of space (see pages 534 and 535).

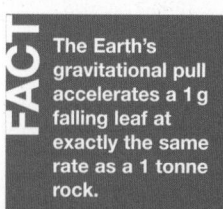

FACT The Earth's gravitational pull accelerates a 1 g falling leaf at exactly the same rate as a 1 tonne rock.

Newton's laws of motion

The English physicist and mathematician Isaac Newton (1642-1727) formulated his three laws of motion to describe how objects move when acted upon by forces.

1 First law of motion
An object will either stay still or keep moving in a straight line at a steady speed unless it is pushed or pulled by a force. This tendency to stay still or keep moving is referred to as the object's inertia (see opposite). A golf ball remains stationary unless hit by a club. Once in motion it continues, but is slowed by two forces – gravity and friction (air resistance).

2 Second law of motion
When a force acts on an object, the object will either start to move, speed up, slow down, stop or change direction. The size of a force, the acceleration it produces and the mass of the object are closely related.
   The force that accelerates the object (N) equals the mass of object (kg) multiplied by the acceleration produced (m/s²). (For units of acceleration, see box 'Measuring motion' opposite.) The greater the force, the greater the change of movement. A golf ball tapped with a putter will accelerate far less than one hit at full force with a driver.

3 Third law of motion
If one object exerts a force – a push or pull – on another, the second object will pull or push to an equal and opposite extent. This means that forces always act in pairs, called action and reaction. For example, the force that propels a shell out of a gun barrel (action) is accompanied by the equal and opposite force (reaction) of the gun recoiling or moving backwards.

Golf on Earth
Golfer's mass is 80 kg (176 lb).
Downward acceleration due to gravity is 9.8 m/s², so **golfer's weight** is 80 x 9.8 = 784 N.
Golf ball's mass is 0.045 kg; **ball's weight** is about 0.44N.

When the golfer hits the ball on Earth, he makes it travel about 100 m (109 yd). Gravity pulls the ball back to Earth, and air resistance also helps to slow down the ball.

Golf on the Moon
Golfer's mass is 80 kg (176 lb).
Downward acceleration due to gravity is 1.6 m/s², so **golfer's weight** is 80 x 1.6 = 128 N.
Golf ball's mass is 0.045 kg; **ball's weight** is about 0.072N.

On the Moon, the same swing would make the ball go about 600 m (656 yd) because the Moon's gravitational pull on the ball is one-sixth that on Earth. Also, there is no air resistance to slow the ball down.

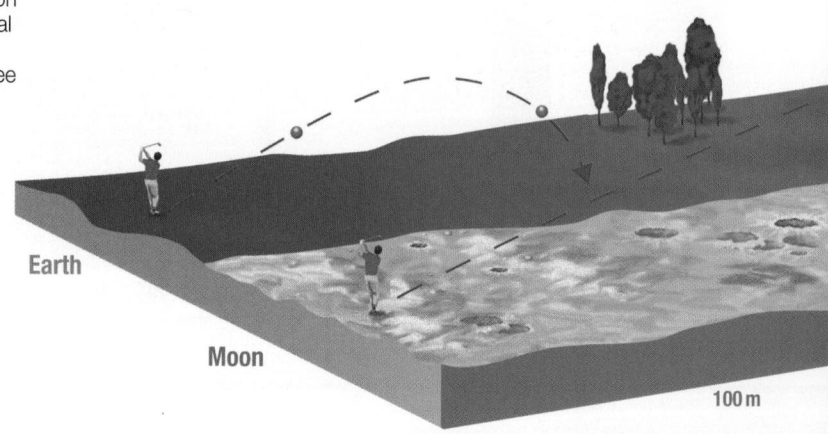

Earth

Moon

100 m

FORCE AND MOTION

A force is an invisible push or pull, the effects of which can be seen or felt. Forces cause objects that are free to move to start or stop moving, or change their direction or speed. They cause objects that are not free to move to stretch, bend, twist or change shape. A steadily moving or stationary object will continue in that state until and unless a force is applied to it.

Inertia

The tendency of an object to resist any change in its steady motion or stationary state is called inertia. Even assuming no friction, it takes a hard push to make a broken-down car roll forward because it resists any change in its state of motion. But once it moves, the car's inertia will try to keep it moving in a straight line. The greater the mass of the object, the greater its inertia.

Momentum

This is a measure of a moving object's tendency to keep moving, and the force needed to alter it. All moving objects have momentum, which is equal to mass multiplied by velocity; so the more massive and the faster the object, the greater its momentum. It is a vector quantity (see right).

When two objects collide, momentum is transferred. An important law of physics says that the total momentum of the objects is the same before and after the collision.

Friction

Friction is a force that opposes the motion of an object and reduces its momentum. It happens wherever the surfaces of two objects – however smooth they may appear – rub together. As they slide over each other, surface projections catch on each other and – however tiny these may be – slow down movement. That is why dragging a heavy object along the ground is such hard work. The rougher the surfaces, the greater the friction. Oil and other lubricants reduce friction by keeping the projections apart so that they do not catch.

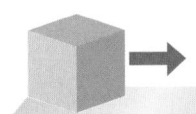

Friction between a sliding block and the surface soon slows the block down.

With a ball the area in contact with the surface is much less, and so much less friction is generated.

Air resistance is friction between moving objects and air molecules. Objects with a large surface area are usually in contact with more air than those with a small surface, so produce more air resistance.

MEASURING MOTION

As in all scientific fields, mechanical measurements are made in International System (SI) units, based on the metre (m) for distance, kilogram (kg) for mass and second (s) for time.

Distance and displacement Distance is simply the length of a straight line between two places. It can indicate how far apart two objects are, or how far an object has travelled from its starting point.

The displacement of an object moving from one point to another, on the other hand, includes direction of movement as well as the straight-line distance it moves. For example, a billiard ball might be displaced 2 m (7 ft) to the south-west.

Displacement is known as a **vector quantity** because it has both magnitude and direction; distance, which has magnitude but no particular direction, is a **scalar quantity**.

Speed and velocity Speed describes how fast an object is travelling by stating the distance it travels in a certain amount of time. For example, if a car travels 400 km (250 miles) in 5 hours, its average speed (allowing for variations during the journey) = 400 km ÷ 5 h = 80 km/h (50 mph).

Velocity is a measure of not only how fast an object is moving but also the direction of movement. So a car travelling 400 km north in 5 hours has a northward velocity of 80 km/h. The velocity of a moving object changes if either its speed or its direction alters. If the car travelling at 80 km/h turns a corner without changing its speed, its velocity still changes because it is changing direction. In other words, speed, like distance, is a scalar quantity, but velocity, like displacement, is a vector quantity.

Acceleration Acceleration measures the rate of change in the velocity of an object – that is, how quickly the object is speeding up in a particular direction. Acceleration equals the change in velocity (m/s) divided by the time taken for this change (s); it is measured in metres per second, per second (m/s/s or m/s^2). Acceleration is always a vector quantity.

Suppose this racing car accelerates from a standing start to a velocity of 180 km/h (50 m/s) in 5 seconds. Its acceleration = 50 m/s ÷ 5 s = 10 m/s^2. If the driver then applies the brakes and takes 4 seconds to stop, its acceleration = −50 m/s ÷ 4 s = −12.5 m/s^2.

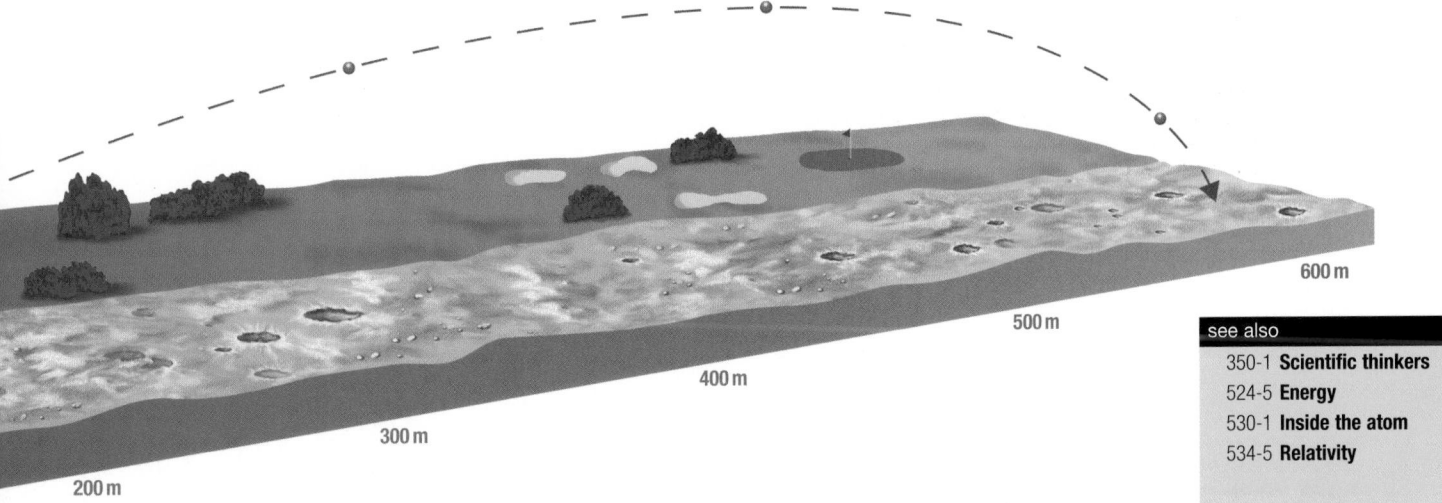

600 m
500 m
400 m
300 m
200 m

Every change in the Universe, from the whisper of a breeze to the explosion of a supernova, involves the expenditure or transfer of energy. The Universe itself was created in a huge burst of energy – the Big Bang – and 15 billion years later this energy still keeps the Universe in action. The meaning of the term in physics is more precise than in general usage: energy is the capacity to do work. Much of technology is concerned with changing energy from one form into another.

TYPES OF ENERGY

Energy exists in many different forms, and any physical change involves one form of energy changing into another. The process whereby an aircraft takes off, for example, illustrates almost every form of energy known to physics. Energy is never created or destroyed, but can only change its form. This principle is known as the conservation of energy (see box opposite).

Potential energy
This is stored energy that an object has because of its position or shape. An aircraft gains potential energy as it rises against the force of gravity; should it go into a dive, this potential energy is released and converted into kinetic energy. In a similar way, a squeezed ball or a stretched bowstring also holds potential energy which is unlocked when it is released.

Kinetic energy
This is the energy of movement. A moving aircraft, like every moving object, has kinetic energy, which returns to zero when it comes to rest. An important formula states that $E = mv^2$, where E is the kinetic energy of a moving object, m is its mass, and v its velocity, or speed. So, at the same speed, energy is proportional to mass, but doubling speed quadruples kinetic energy.

Nuclear energy
Nuclear energy is locked in the nuclei of atoms, in the forces that hold their component parts – subatomic particles – together. It is released as heat and electromagnetic energy by nuclear reactions, such as those in the Sun, and in nuclear reactors and explosions. Such reactions involve the annihilation of mass and its conversion into energy.

Chemical energy
This is the energy stored in chemical compounds, such as the fuel in an aircraft's tanks – which originated when sunlight produced sugars in fossil plants by photosynthesis. When an aircraft takes off, chemical energy is converted into heat by burning fuel, and that energy is converted into the kinetic energy of movement, the potential energy of height, plus sound energy.

Electrical energy
Electricity powers the lighting and runs many systems in an aircraft. Electrical energy, or electricity, is the movement of tiny charged subatomic particles called electrons. When electric current flows through a wire, electrons jump from atom to atom. Electricity is one of the most useful forms of energy, because it is easily transported and converted into other forms.

Light energy
Light, which can of course be detected by the eyes, is the best-known form of electromagnetic energy, which also includes infrared (the radiant form of heat). The Sun is Earth's primary source of light, but other sources of light energy include electricity (in light bulbs and fluorescent tubes) and burning (the conversion of chemical energy into heat and light energy).

Conservation of energy and mass

A basic principle of classical mechanics – the physics of the everyday world as set out by Newton (see page 522) – is the law of the conservation of energy. This states that energy is never created or destroyed, but only changes form. Similarly, physical and chemical activities always conserve mass (matter).

But the theory of relativity (page 534) showed that mass and energy are equivalents, linked by the equation $E = mc^2$. In ordinary mechanical systems, the mass change accompanying energy transfer cannot be measured, but it is significant in nuclear reactions. The new law of conservation of mass energy says that mass and energy together can never be created or destroyed.

Heat energy
This is the energy every object in the Universe possesses, due to the vibration or movement of the atoms and molecules that make it up. The faster these particles move, the more heat energy the object has and the hotter it is. Heat is generated in a jet engine by burning fuel, causing gases to expand and to shoot from the rear of the engine, propelling the aircraft.

Sound energy
Sound energy takes the form of pressure waves that pass through the air. They are produced by vibrations at the sound source, the gases shooting from an aircraft engine. When these sound waves reach the ear they are turned into electrical impulses by sensors, which travel to the brain where they are 'heard' as sounds.

HEAT

Heat represents the kinetic (movement) energy of an object's constantly moving atoms and molecules. If something warms up, 'fixed' molecules, such as those in a solid, vibrate more rapidly; those in a gas move around faster. It is possible to get close to absolute zero (–273.15°C), the temperature at which all atomic and molecular movement would cease, but impossible to actually reach it.

Temperature, measured using a thermometer, is not the same as heat. The more heat energy a particular object contains, the higher its temperature is, but different materials require different amounts of heat energy to raise their temperature by the same amount (measured in degrees). The heat needed to increase the temperature of 1 g of a substance by 1°C is called its specific heat.

Heat always flows from warmer places to cooler ones. It travels in three ways. **Conduction** is the transfer of heat through a substance, by hotter, faster-moving molecules colliding with their neighbours, so that they vibrate or move faster. **Convection** is the flow of heat in moving currents through a liquid or a gas. When part of a liquid or gas is heated, the molecules move farther apart, so it becomes less dense or lighter than any surrounding colder material. As a result, it rises, creating a circulating 'convection current' that transfers heat energy. **Radiation** is the flow of heat in the form of infrared rays from one object to another.

An important form of heat transfer takes place when a solid melts or a liquid evaporates: heat energy – called latent heat – is taken in without the substance changing temperature. Conversely, when a gas condenses to a liquid or a liquid freezes to a solid, latent heat is given out.

LIGHT

Light, like all forms of electromagnetic radiation (see page 528), travels through empty space at 299 792 km/s – the fastest anything can move. For light to travel from the Sun to the Earth takes just over 8 minutes. It moves more slowly in other transparent media – at about three-quarters its normal speed in water and two-thirds in glass.

Light rays travel in straight lines but bounce off most surfaces; this is called **reflection**. Light surfaces reflect more light than dark ones. Light rays are reflected from a polished surface, such as a mirror, at the same angle as they strike it, but rough surfaces scatter light in all directions.

When light rays enter glass or water from air, the slowing-down makes them bend towards the vertical. This bending is called **refraction**. Prisms refract light rays in this way, and lenses act by refracting rays so that they focus an image.

SOUND

Sound waves consist of waves of high pressure (compression) and low pressure (rarefaction) following each other and travelling outwards from the sound source. How loud a sound is depends on the difference between the high and low-pressure regions. The sound's pitch (low or high) depends on how quickly one wave follows another – the frequency. It is measured in hertz (Hz), or waves per second. People with good hearing can hear sounds from a lowest pitch of about 20 Hz to a high of 20 000 Hz (20 kHz).

Sound, unlike light, cannot travel through a vacuum. Its speed depends on the nature of the medium carrying it. Sound moves at about 340 m/s in air at sea level, more slowly at high altitudes; it travels five times faster in water.

Energy, work and power

● **Energy** is simply defined as the capacity to do work, or make things happen – moving something, heating it, or changing it in some way. It is measured in units called joules (J) and kilojoules (kJ; thousands of joules) – kJ are often used instead of calories to quantify the energy content of foods. Gas and electricity bills often use kilowatt-hours (kWh); 1 kWh = 3.6 million joules.

● **Work** is what energy 'makes happen'; it is the end result of energy being converted from one form into another. They are so closely related that, like energy, work is measured in joules.

In the case of movement, work is done when a force acts on an object, moving the object in the direction of the force. For example, a fork-lift truck does work by lifting crates against gravity, converting chemical energy (fuel) into potential energy (lift). If the crates have a mass of 300 kg, they weigh 2940 newtons (N). Suppose they are lifted vertically a distance of 2 m. Work done (J) = force (N) x distance moved (m) = 2940 N x 2 m = 5880 J (or 5.88 kJ).

● **Power** measures how quickly work is done – in other words, the rate at which energy is converted from one form to another. It is measured in watts (W); 1 W is the conversion of 1 J in one second. Suppose the fork-lift truck above lifts the crates in 6 seconds. Power (W) = work (J) ÷ time (s) = 5880 J ÷ 6 s = 980 W.

The power of an electrical appliance measures how quickly it 'consumes' electricity – that is, converts it into another form of energy. A 1000 W (1 kW) iron, for example, converts electricity into heat at a rate of 1000 J per second. In an hour, it uses 1 kWh of electricity.

Electricity and magnetism are closely linked, both caused by charged subatomic particles called electrons. Electricity can be generated using magnetism, and a magnetic field can be created with electricity. Their partnership results in one of the most useful inventions in history: the electric motor. In fact, the two forces are different aspects of the same fundamental force of nature: the electromagnetic force that helps to hold all matter together.

WHAT IS ELECTRICITY?

Electrons have a negative electrical charge. If a surplus of electrons builds up on an object – for example, by friction (rubbing) – it acquires an overall negative charge. An object with a deficit of electrons is positively charged. This kind of electricity is described as static – electricity that normally does not move, or flow. A high enough charge may cause a spark as electrons jump to a point of lower or opposite charge. Electrical charges have two other properties:

● **Attraction and repulsion** Objects with the same ('like') charges – both positive or both negative – repel each other, but opposite charges attract.

● **Induction** A charged object induces an opposite charge in another nearby object – positive induces negative, and vice versa.

Current electricity Atoms of some substances, such as metals, have loosely attached electrons that can easily be made to move from atom to atom. The moving electrons constitute an electric current. Because like charges repel, the movement of one negatively charged electron repels an electron in the next atom,

which knocks on the next electron in line, and so on. No single electron moves far, but the overall electrical disturbance travels along the conductor by a domino effect.

● **Current and voltage** The size of an electric current is a measure of how many electrons pass a given point each second. It is measured in ampères, or amps (A). One amp is equivalent to the flow of 6 million trillion electrons per second.

The force that pushes electrons along is called electromotive force. It may be created by a battery or a generator. Electromotive force is measured in volts (V), and is often referred to as voltage.

● **Resistance** How much any material opposes an electric current's flow is called resistance. It is caused by random collisions of atoms and electrons, which slows down electron flow, It is measured in ohms (Ω).

The relationship between voltage, current and resistance is given in Ohm's law. This states that voltage (V) equals current (I) multiplied by resistance (R):

$$V = I \times R$$

Or current equals voltage divided by resistance:

$$I = V \div R$$

Electrical circuits

There are two kinds of electrical circuit:

● **Series circuit** The components and electrical source are linked one after another in a series circuit. The same current flows through all of them in turn, but the increased resistance means the current is smaller. So, two light bulbs in series will glow less brightly than just one. A break in any part of a series circuit stops the whole current flowing

Two lamps in series
Resistance doubled; current halved

● **Parallel circuit** A circuit split into branches, with components side by side, is described as parallel. Each branch receives the full current because, in effect, each is connected directly to the source. This means that two bulbs in parallel glow brighter than the same two in series. Also, a break in one branch of a parallel circuit only stops current flow in that branch.

Lamps in parallel
Each lamp draws full current

Electrical conductivity

Materials differ in their ability to conduct an electric current – their conductivity. There are four groups:
● **Insulators** are materials such as plastics, rubber and ceramics that have a high resistance to the flow of electricity because they lack free electrons.
● **Conductors** have plenty of free electrons and conduct electricity well. They include most metals (silver and copper are best) and the nonmetal carbon.
● **Semiconductors**, such as silicon, have conductivity in between that of insulators and conductors.
● **Superconductors** offer no resistance at all to current flow. Most metals become superconductors near absolute zero (–273.16°C).

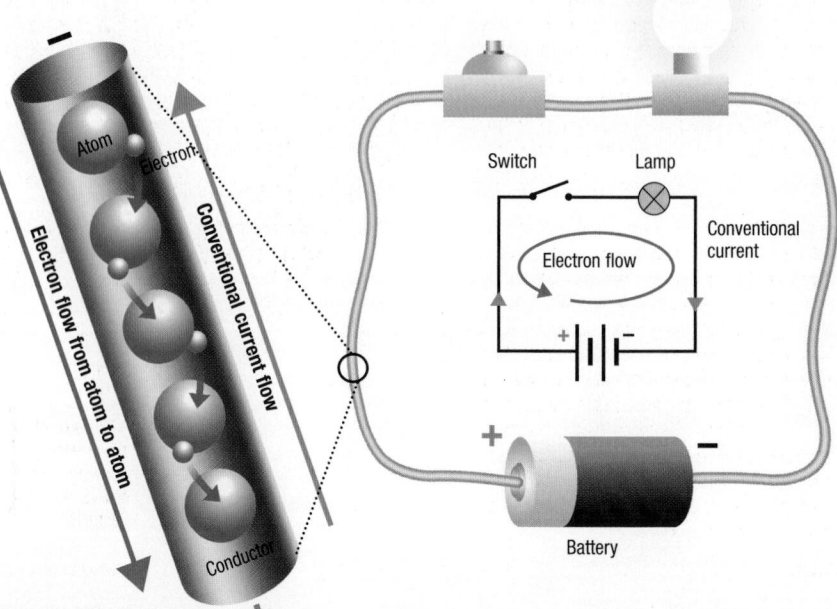

Current confusion
The basic laws governing electric charges and currents were worked out long before the electron was discovered. It was decided arbitrarily that electric current flowed from the positive pole of a battery to the negative. When the electron was discovered, it was realised that electron flow is actually in the opposite direction, but the direction of 'conventional' current flow was retained.

Atom
Electron
Electron flow from atom to atom
Conventional current flow
Conductor

Switch
Lamp
Conventional current
Electron flow
Battery

Showing circuits Electrical circuits are represented by circuit diagrams, that use internationally recognised symbols for the various components. The circuit on the left consists of a battery linked by wires to a switch and a light bulb. Chemical reactions inside the battery cause an electron build-up at its negative terminal. They travel along the wire to the positive terminal. On the way, they pass through a wire filament inside the light bulb. This heats the filament, causing it to glow, releasing light and heat energy. Opening the switch breaks the circuit, so that electrons can no longer flow.

WHAT IS MAGNETISM?

Like electricity, magnetism is a force produced by the movement of electrons inside atoms. All materials are magnetic, but some – notably iron, steel, cobalt, nickel and some ceramics – are far more strongly so than others; they are called ferromagnetic materials.

The spinning electrons inside atoms create minute magnetic fields – areas in which a magnetic force acts. In ferromagnetic materials, the fields of many atoms reinforce each other in small areas known as domains to form mini-magnets. Normally, the domains are arranged randomly, and their magnetic fields cancel out. But if the domains are all aligned in the same direction, a familiar bar magnet is created. This will attract – that is, exert a pulling force on – other ferromagnetic materials, and will attract or repel another magnet, depending on how they are aligned.

A permanent magnet, such as a bar magnet, is always magnetic. A temporary magnet, such as an electromagnet (see below), can gain and lose its magnetic force.

Magnetic poles Every magnet has two poles – north and south – at opposite ends. The Earth is magnetic, and a magnet's north pole is so called because it is attracted to the Earth's North Pole; its south pole is south-seeking. As with electrical charges, opposite magnetic poles attract each other, while like poles repel. If a magnet's north pole is near the south pole of another, the two snap together, but two north poles push each other apart.

Lines of force A magnetic field has direction; it acts along invisible lines called lines of force, or flux. These loop around a magnet from pole to pole, and can be seen if iron filings are sprinkled around a bar magnet. The filings cluster around the poles, where the flux lines are closest and the magnetic force is strongest.

Induction Just as an electric charge induces an opposite charge, a magnet induces magnetism in a nearby ferromagnetic material. A north pole induces a south pole and vice versa This is why magnets attract unmagnetised ferromagnetic materials, such as iron filings or a pin.

The magnetic compass

The Earth has a magnetic field, produced by the movement of molten iron in its core, and behaves like a giant bar magnet. A compass is a lightweight magnet that can swing freely to detect this field. The compass's north pole points to magnetic north, which is close to, but not the same as, geographic north. Confusingly, the compass's north pole is attracted northwards because what we call magnetic north pole is, in fact, the south pole of Earth's magnet.

Magnetic fields Iron filings sprinkled on a sheet of paper laid over magnets will show the direction and strength of the magnetic fields around them: (1) nearby north and south poles are attracted, and (2) two nearby south poles repel each other.

see also
30-31 **Structure of the Earth**
528-9 **Electromagnetic spectrum**
538-9 **The periodic table**

Electromagnetism

The relationship of electricity and magnetism – electromagnetism – is the basis of electric motors, and is exploited widely in industry.

Magnetism from electricity When electricity flows through a wire, it produces a weak magnetic field. The field is reinforced by winding the wire into a coil, so that fields produced by all the loops of wire add together. An iron core inside the coil concentrates the field even more. A coil like this is called an electromagnet; its magnetic field disappears as soon as the current is switched off.

Electric motors In its simplest form, an electric motor consists of a coil of wire pivoted in the magnetic field between the poles of a permanent magnet or an electromagnet. A current flowing through the coil creates its own magnetic field, with forces of attraction and repulsion between it and the magnetic field around it. These forces lead to movement: the coil spins, driving a shaft.

Current is fed to the coil through carbon rods called brushes. A device called a commutator links the brushes to the coil. It ensures that the direction of the current in the coil reverses every half-turn, so that the coil is always pushed upwards on one side and pulled down on the other. This creates a continuous rotary movement.

Electricity from magnetism Moving a wire or coil though a magnetic field generates an electric current inside the wire or coil. This is known as electromagnetic induction, and is how electricity is generated in a power station or – on a much smaller scale – a bicycle dynamo. If the turning coil of a dynamo has a commutator (as in an electric motor), the connection will be reversed each half-turn, so the current produced will always flow in the same direction; this is called direct current (DC). Without a commutator, the current reverses direction each half-turn; this is called alternating current (AC).

A transformer combines the electromagnetic effect with induction. AC electricity is fed to a coil, which creates a continually reversing magnetic field. This magnetic field, in turn, induces electricity, at a different voltage, in another coil on the same core.

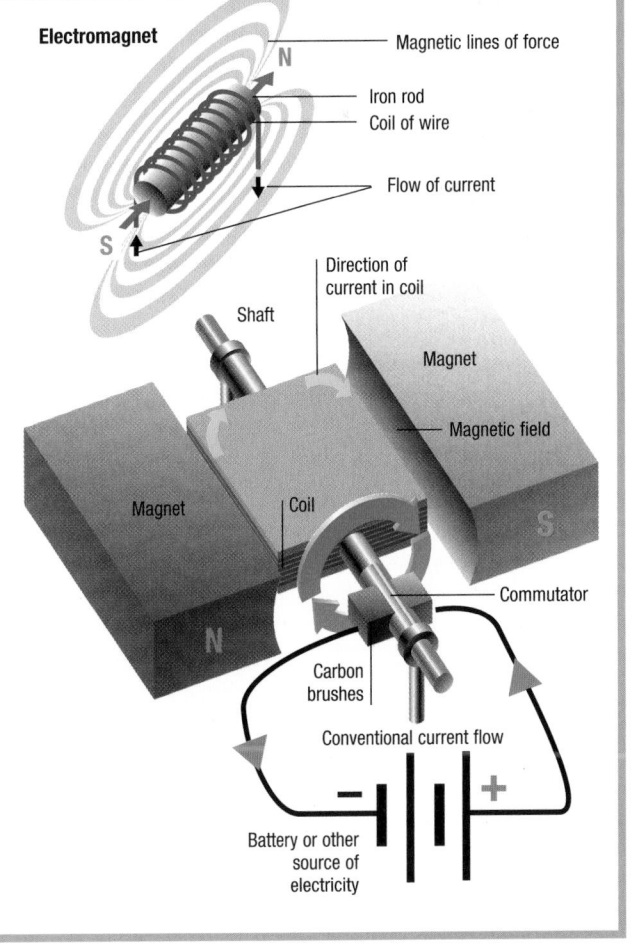

Electromagnet
Magnetic lines of force
Iron rod
Coil of wire
Flow of current
N
S

Direction of current in coil
Shaft
Magnet
Magnetic field
Magnet
Coil
Commutator
Carbon brushes
Conventional current flow
Battery or other source of electricity

The Universe is permeated with the energy of electromagnetic radiation. Of the many ways in which this radiation manifests itself, only visible light and infrared, or radiant heat, can be perceived by the senses. Other types range from radio waves to X-rays and the gamma rays produced by nuclear explosions. All, however, are made up of patterns of electrical and magnetic energy that move through the vacuum of space at the same constant speed – the speed of light.

WHAT ARE ELECTROMAGNETIC WAVES?

Any kind of electromagnetic radiation can be thought of as waves of energy, which are generated by oscillating electric and magnetic fields (see pages 526-27).

Radio waves, for example, are a form of electromagnetic radiation that can be created by oscillating electric currents in a wire. The negatively charged subatomic particles called electrons flowing along the wire create a zone (or field) of electrical influence around themselves; they also create a magnetic field. If the electrons are made to move rapidly backwards and forwards – that is, oscillate – the associated electric and magnetic fields change in unison, creating radio waves.

Frequency and wavelength
Differences in frequency and wavelength are largely what distinguish the various kinds of radiation.

● **Frequency** is the number of times each second the electrical and magnetic fields reach their maximum strength – that is, the number of complete oscillations or vibrations per second. It is measured in hertz (Hz).

● **Wavelength** is the distance a wave travels in the time it takes to complete one oscillation. It is measured in metres (m).

The higher the frequency, the shorter the wavelength, and vice versa. Mathematically, wavelength equals the speed of light divided by frequency. For example, a radio station broadcasting at 100 megahertz (100 000 000 Hz) has a wavelength (in metres) of 299 792 000 (m/s) ÷ 100 000 000 (Hz) = 2.99792 m.

The energy of electromagnetic waves depends on wavelength. Radio waves, microwaves and infrared have a longer wavelength (lower frequency) than visible light and carry less energy. Ultraviolet, X-rays and gamma rays have a shorter wavelength (higher frequency) than visible light and carry more energy. In fact, they carry sufficient energy to penetrate some solid material, such as flesh.

Waves or particles?

In most ways, electromagnetic radiation acts like waves, but sometimes it can be more like a stream of discrete particles. Particles of electromagnetic radiation are called quanta – or photons, in the case of light particles.

● **Wave effects** Radiation shows wave-like behaviour when it is reflected from certain surfaces. Light, for example, is reflected from a mirror, while radio waves bounce off aircraft to be detected on radar screens.

● **Particle effects** Radiation demonstrates particle-like properties, when it reacts with something to bring about physical or chemical change. For example, light particles or photons falling on a solar cell are converted into an electric current. This is called the photoelectric effect.

The way in which electromagnetic waves combine the properties of both waves and particles is known as wave-particle duality, and is the fundamental principle in quantum physics. This describes how the amount of energy in each quantum of electromagnetic radiation, depends on the frequency of the radiation.

TYPES OF RADIATION	Radio	Microwave
Frequency	Up to 3000 MHz	3000 MHz to 3000 GHz
Wavelength	More than 10^{-1} m (more than 10 cm)	10^{-1} to 10^{-4} m (10 cm to 0.1 mm)
Sources	Oscillating electric currents, sparks, cosmic sources	Magnetron, maser, cosmic sources
Detectors	Electronic circuits, including radio and television sets	Electronic circuits
General effects	Induces matching small oscillating electric currents in conductors	Induces matching small oscillating electric currents in conductors; heating effect if frequency matches natural vibration frequency of molecules
Applications	Radio and television broadcasting and telecommunications; also radio telescopes, 'cordless' phones, and 'wireless' computer network systems	Telephone and other telecommunications links; mobile telephones; radar; heating and cooking food; also microwave telescopes for astronomy
Uses in action	The use of radio frequencies is regulated by international and national bodies to avoid interference. Various 'bands' are reserved for particular uses, such as broadcasting, the police and emergency services, other mobile communications.	In a microwave oven, water molecules in food absorb the waves and get hot; plastic and ceramics absorb no microwaves. Radar works by sending out a narrow beam of microwaves and detecting the time it takes for their 'echo' to return from objects. Mobile phones use weak microwaves. Cosmic microwaves can indicate age of Universe.

Seeing colours

Light is detected by sensors in the retina, the inner lining of the eye. White light is a mixture of colours, with wavelengths ranging from red (longest) through orange, yellow, green and blue, to violet (shortest).

But our eyes cannot tell the difference between 'pure' colours of the true wavelengths and mixtures of certain other colours. For example, a mixture of red and green light looks yellow. This is because our eyes have only three types of colour sensors that respond to red, green and blue. Our brains interpret the signals from these sensors as all the subtle colours we perceive.

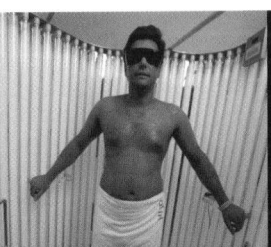
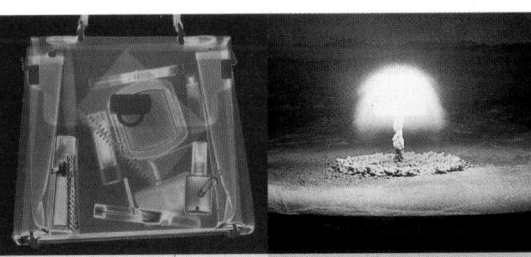

Infrared	Visible light	Ultraviolet	X-rays	Gamma rays
3000 GHz to 430 THz	430 to 750 THz	750 THz to 300 PHz	300 PHz to 30 EHz	More than 30 EHz
10^{-4} to 7×10^{-7} m (0.1 mm to 700 millionths of a millimetre)	7×10^{-7} to 4×10^{-7} m (700 to 400 millionths of a millimetre)	4×10^{-7} to 10^{-9} m (400 millionths to 1 millionth of a millimetre)	10^{-9} to 10^{-11} m (1 millionth to 10 billionths of a millimetre)	Less than 10^{-11} m (less than 10 billionths of a millimetre)
Warm and hot objects including light bulb with special filter; infrared laser	Hot or burning objects, including Sun and stars; fluorescent materials; electrical discharge; laser; some chemical reactions	Extremely hot objects, including Sun and stars; some fluorescent materials; electrical discharge; ultraviolet laser	Fast electron bombardment of metal target; Sun, stars and other cosmic sources	Nuclear reactions, including radioactive decay, nuclear reactor or explosion; stars and other cosmic sources
Thermopile (heat sensor); thermal imaging sensor; special photographic film	Eyes; photographic film; charge-coupled device; photoelectric cell	Fluorescent materials; photographic film; insects' eyes; electronic devices	Fluorescent materials; photographic film; indirectly, by detecting any ionisation they cause	Fluorescent materials; photographic film; indirectly, by detecting any ionisation they cause
Causes warming when radiation is absorbed	Triggers certain chemical reactions; triggers sensors in eyes of animals; when absorbed by chloroplasts in plant cells, powers photosynthesis	Tans, then burns skin, and may cause cancers; at high levels can cause blindness, kills bacteria and viruses, and damages or destroys plant life	Pass through many solid materials; can cause genetic mutations and cancers; can damage delicate electronic equipment	Pass through all but very thick or heavy solid materials; cause mutations and damage to cells, leading to 'radiation sickness' and often death
Radiant heaters; cookers and toasters; television remote controls; some night-vision devices and thermal-imaging cameras; infrared astronomy; aerial surveying	Vision; photography, cinematography and television; bleaching; power generation (using photocells); entertainment and communications (with lasers and fibre-optics)	Vision in insects (to detect some 'invisible' patterns on flowers); optical brighteners in washing powders; sterilisation in hospitals; some night-vision cameras	Observing bones and other internal body structures (densest parts are opaque to X-rays); checking metal joints and welds; destroying cancerous cells	Checking dense structures, such as aircraft bearings, for cracks and other flaws; destroying cancerous cells
Infrared aerial and satellite images can show crop ripening by detecting heat from crops; also used for spotting forest fires.	The many colours that we see consist of light of different wavelengths; red light has the longest wavelength, violet light has the shortest.	Many flowers have patterns, visible only in ultraviolet light. These patterns help insects to find nectar and pollen. Most of the Sun's intense ultraviolet rays are absorbed by the 'ozone layer', a thin zone, high in the stratosphere. This stops too much ultraviolet light reaching Earth, where it can harm living things.	Many stars produce X-rays; the Sun emits its most powerful X-rays during bursts of intense activity called 'solar flares'. These X-rays can damage satellite equipment in Earth orbit, and may also penetrate the Earth's atmosphere and damage delicate electrical equipment on the surface.	Gamma rays, although dangerous, do not cause as great tissue damage as some other types of nuclear radiation, such as alpha particles (see page 532). An extremely thick concrete shell is needed to shield people from gamma rays produced in nuclear reactors – or, in a fallout shelter, from a nuclear explosion.

One of the triumphs of 20th-century physics was the unravelling of the structure of matter in ever greater detail. Atoms – the smallest units of chemical elements – were found to be made up of even smaller, subatomic particles. By studying cosmic rays and using giant particle accelerators to collide particles together at very high speed, physicists found that these particles too were composed of yet smaller particles.

THE STRUCTURE OF AN ATOM

Atoms are the basic building blocks of chemical elements, such as carbon or oxygen – one atom of an element is the smallest part of it that is recognisable as that element. Despite their microscopic size – 10 million atoms placed side by side would extend just 1 mm – atoms can be split into smaller, subatomic particles. At the core of the atom is the nucleus, consisting of a bundle of protons and neutrons. Electrons spin around in the space surrounding the nucleus. So extensive is this space that most of an atom is in fact empty. If the protons and neutrons in the nucleus were the size of tennis balls, electrons would be smaller than pinheads, and the overall diameter of the atom would run to thousands of metres.

Particle physics has revealed the existence of more than 200 further types of subatomic particles, some of them components of particles such as protons and neutrons. Particles not made up of any known smaller particles are called fundamental or elementary particles. However, some modern physicists believe that even these are composed of line-like or loop-like units called superstrings that are billions of times smaller than the fundamental particles.

FORCES HOLDING MATTER TOGETHER

Four fundamental forces act on all matter and hold it together. Physicists believe that these forces are carried by particles called 'force carriers', or bosons, which move at the speed of light.

● **Gravity** is a force of attraction acting between any two objects that have mass. It is responsible for objects falling to the ground and for holding the planets in orbit around the Sun. It is weak, but acts over very long distances. It is probably carried by particles called gravitons, never yet detected.

● **Electromagnetic force** is much stronger than gravity. It causes attraction and repulsion between electrically charged particles, and is carried by photons – see page 528.

● **Weak nuclear force** (also known as weak interaction) is associated with radioactivity. It is carried by particles known as W and Z particles, or weakons. Billions of times weaker than the electromagnetic force, it acts only over distances of trillionths of a millimetre.

● **Strong nuclear force** (also known as strong interaction) holds quarks together inside protons and neutrons, and holds the protons and neutrons together inside atomic nuclei. It is carried by particles called gluons, and is a hundred times stronger than electromagnetic force. It only acts over extremely short distances.

The weak and strong nuclear forces are believed to be versions of the same force, called the **electroweak force**. A goal of modern physics is to show how these forces are related to the electromagnetic force through a so-called grand unified theory – and then, eventually, to unify these with gravity. A 'supergravity' theory might also enable physics at the particle scale to be combined with the theory of relativity.

Nucleus This is where almost all the mass of the atom is concentrated. It consists of protons and neutrons (or just a single proton in the case of hydrogen atoms). Each proton has a mass 1836 times that of an electron, each neutron a little more: 1839 electron masses. Protons have a positive electrical charge, and balance an equal number of negatively charged orbiting electrons to make the whole atom electrically neutral. Electromagnetic attraction between protons and electrons holds the atom together. Neutrons have no electrical charge.

Orbital shells Electrons travel around the nucleus in shells, or layers, called orbitals. They can travel anywhere in a shell. They can also move to an outer shell by taking in energy, or an inner shell by losing it. It is impossible to predict the exact position of an electron at any given time; they behave like a fuzzy cloud of negative charges around the nucleus.

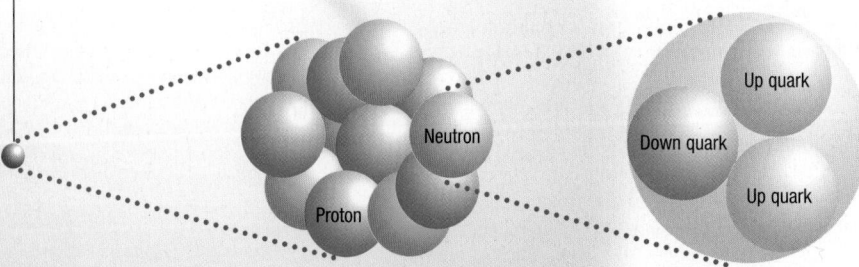

Quarks Each proton or neutron is, in its turn, made up of three particles called quarks. Two types of quark are found in protons and neutrons – 'up' quarks and 'down' quarks

Electrons Electrons are tiny particles with a negative electric charge that move at high speed around the nucleus. They are not solid 'balls', but packets of energy that move at the speed of light. Electrons seem to be fundamental particles that are not made up of smaller particles.

Cosmic rays

The Earth's atmosphere is constantly being bombarded by radiation from outer space. These cosmic rays consist of atomic nuclei – almost 90 per cent of them hydrogen nuclei, or protons, but also those of heavier elements. They are formed by stars and cosmic explosions, and accelerate for millions of years through space, acquiring huge amounts of energy. Few such 'primary' cosmic rays reach the Earth's surface. Most collide with other atoms in the upper atmosphere to create showers of 'secondary' cosmic rays, including every type of subatomic particle (see right). Each 100 cm^2 of the Earth's surface is hit by approximately 100 secondaries every minute.

Particle accelerators

Particle accelerators are vital for the study of particle physics. They are giant machines, commonly several kilometres long, that accelerate beams of charged particles, such as electrons, protons and atomic nuclei, almost to the speed of light. In this way, they mimic, on a small scale, the acceleration of cosmic rays in outer space. The fast-moving beams are made to strike other particles or nuclei – either stationary targets or beams of particles travelling the opposite way.

Every particle accelerator consists of four important elements:
- a source of charged particles.
- magnetic fields to guide the particles in a straight or circular path and focus them in a narrow beam.
- electric fields to accelerate the particles by giving them a 'kick' each time they pass by.
- detectors and computers to monitor the outcome of collisions.

Collisions inside accelerators smash particles apart, producing new particles that can be studied by particle physicists. Some of these new particles exist for no more than one billionth of a second.

The subatomic particle family

Subatomic particles are grouped according to their characteristics and properties. Some form parts of atoms, but others are created only in high-energy interactions, as in nuclear reactions or particle accelerator collisions. They are mostly very short-lived.

Composite particles Also known as hadrons, composite particles are all made up of quarks. They include protons and neutrons, both of which are types of baryons – hadrons that consists of three quarks.

Fundamental or elementary particles Particles with no known components are known as fundamental or elementary particles. They fall into three distinct groups: leptons (which include electrons), quarks, and the fundamental bosons or force-carriers, such as photons, weakons, gluons and probably the graviton – see box 'Forces holding matter together'.

Antiparticles The antimatter equivalents of normal particles are known collectively as antiparticles. They have the same mass as normal particles, but attributes such as electrical charge are the opposite. Examples include positrons (positively charged antielectrons), antineutrons, antiprotons, antiquarks and so on. Antiparticles, such as 'antihydrogen' atoms – positrons orbiting antiprotons – have been created in particle accelerators, but all have very short lives.

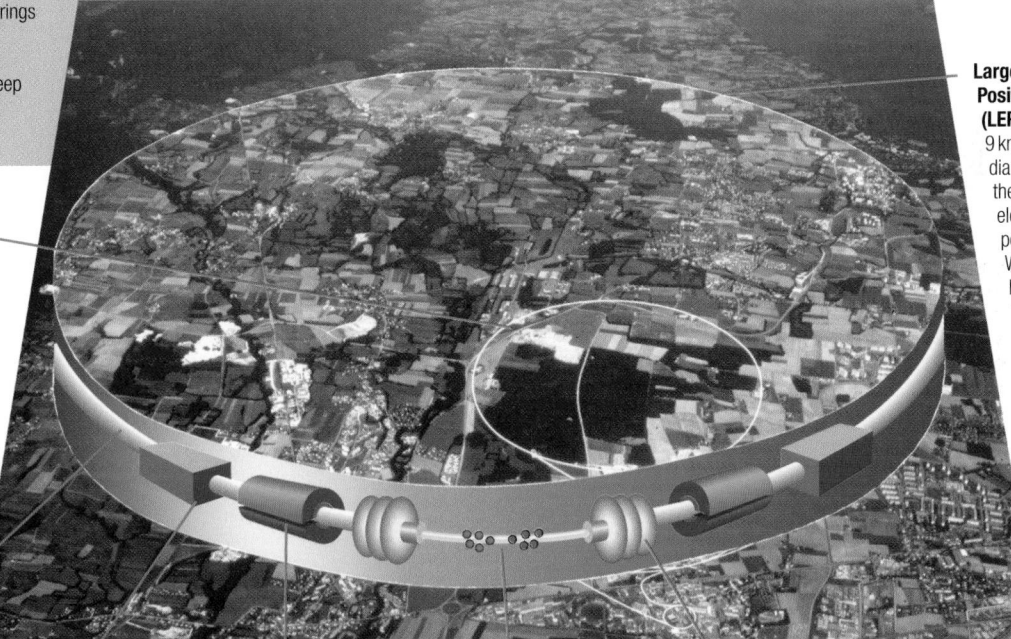

Big machine The rings of CERN's Geneva particle accelerator complex are built deep under the city's outskirts.

Large Electron Positron Collider (LEP) The LEP is 9 km (5½ miles) in diameter. It studies the collision of electrons and positrons to create W and Z particles. It is planned that the same tunnel will house the Large Hadron Collider (LHC), to study the high-energy, head-on collision of protons.

Super Proton Synchrotron (SPS) Measuring 2 km (1.2 miles) across, the SPS was built to accelerate protons to high speed. It was also used to accelerate heavy nuclei in order to mimic some of the events that took place soon after the Big Bang created the Universe.

Precision pipe The ring in which the particles accelerate contains a vacuum to prevent unwanted collision with air molecules. It is aligned to an accuracy of 0.1 mm.

Focusing magnets To keep the particles tightly packed together, strong focusing magnets, with four or six poles, are used. In the LEP, 100 billion particles are packed into a beam as thin as a hair.

Guiding magnets The particles are kept on a circular path by guiding magnets. The machine is so sensitive that even the movements of the Moon, the level of the nearby lake, and passing trains can affect the beam.

Colliding particles At four symmetrical points in the ring, the particles – groups of either electrons or positrons, orbiting in opposite directions – are focused down and made to collide. They split apart, with a huge outburst of energy.

Accelerating cavities On every orbit through the ring – more than 10 000 times a second – special accelerating cavities boost the particles' speed. They use electrical charges to attract and repel the charged particles.

Long before the structure of the atom was fully understood, mysterious radiation – some of which could pass through solid objects – was found to be emitted by certain natural elements. The phenomenon was termed radioactivity. The radiation was found to consist of three main types of ray, and the study of the rays helped to elucidate the structure of matter. It is now understood that radioactivity is a property of unstable atomic nuclei. It may occur naturally or be induced by bombarding unstable nuclei with subatomic particles from cosmic rays, from radioactive materials or from a nuclear reaction or explosion.

WHAT IS RADIOACTIVITY?

In radioactivity, unstable atomic nuclei emit high-energy subatomic particles or radiation. There are three types of radiation, each with different properties. Their discoverers called them alpha (α), beta (β) and gamma (γ) rays according to how far they could penetrate various materials.

Alpha and beta rays proved to be streams of subatomic particles – see page 531 – so they are now usually known as alpha and beta particles, rather than rays. Emission of either from a nucleus changes its structure and the structure of its atom, so that it becomes an

atom of a different element. This change is called decay or transformation. Gamma rays are like very powerful X-rays. Their emission does not involve nuclear decay but is simply the shedding of excess nuclear energy. They often accompany or follow the emission of alpha or beta particles, or both.

All three types of radiation can be harmful to the human body. In energy terms (and thus penetrating power), alpha particles are the weakest, gamma rays the strongest. However, the power of radiation to destroy cells can be harnessed to treat cancers.

Alpha particles

Each alpha particle consists of two protons and two neutrons packed together, and is in fact identical to the nucleus of a helium atom. Alpha particles have a positive charge. They are ejected as the nucleus of a radioactive atom decays. Alpha particles are too heavy to be knocked off course by the molecules in air, so they move in a straight path.

Penetration Alpha particles are stopped by a thin sheet of paper.

Effect Alpha particles cannot penetrate skin, and enter the body only if radioactive matter is consumed or inhaled. Inside the body, even a single alpha particle can cause harm by altering the make-up of a living cell, triggering cancer.

Example Uranium-238 emits alpha particles as it decays to form thorium-234.

Beta particles

A beta particle is a fast-moving electron emitted by a nucleus when an excess neutron (which is neutral) changes into a positively charged proton. This increases the atom's atomic number by one; the beta particle carries away the excess negative charge. Beta particles have very little mass, travel at around half the speed of light, and can be knocked off course by air molecules.

Penetration Beta particles are stopped by a 5 mm thick sheet of aluminium.

Effect Some beta particles can pass through the skin, but are most likely to cause damage if a beta-emitter is inhaled or eaten. If this contaminates the bones, for example, it may trigger leukaemia.

Example Strontium-90 emits beta particles when it decays to form yttrium-90.

Gamma rays

A form of electromagnetic radiation (see page 529), gamma rays are similar to X-rays but with a shorter wavelength. Like X-rays, they can penetrate most materials. Gamma rays have no mass, and travel in a straight path at the speed of light. They are produced when (or very shortly after) nuclei break down, along with any emissions of alpha or beta particles, or both.

Penetration A sheet of lead 4 cm thick reduces gamma ray intensity by about 90 per cent. Very thick concrete is needed to shield people completely.

Effect Gamma rays penetrate the body. They are dangerous mainly because they create ions (charged atoms), which damage living tissues.

Example Radium-226 emits gamma rays when it decays to form radon-222.

Differing versions of the same element

Almost all elements can exist in several chemically identical versions that have small physical differences at the atomic level; they are called isotopes. Their atoms share the same atomic number, but differ in atomic mass.
Atomic number The atoms that make up a particular element are defined by their atomic number – the number of protons in each nucleus (see page 530). For example, if an atom has six protons it must be carbon; if it has 92 protons, it is uranium.
Atomic mass The atomic mass of an atom, on the other hand, depends on the numbers of both protons and neutrons in its nucleus. Isotopes differ in atomic mass because they differ in the number of neutrons in their nuclei. Take the case of two isotopes of carbon, for example:

Carbon-12
Atomic number 6; atomic mass 12
Nucleus contains 6 protons and 6 neutrons

Carbon-14
Atomic number 6; atomic mass 14
Nucleus contains 6 protons and 8 neutrons

Radioisotopes
Isotopes with unstable nuclei (including carbon-14) are likely to decay. They are known as radioisotopes – that is, radioactive isotopes. About 1500 radioisotopes have been found. Sixty of them exist in nature; the rest have been made during nuclear reactions or particle physics experiments.

Chain of decay

Some radioactive isotopes decay in several steps (emitting various particles at each step) before they reach a stable state. The series of isotopes, often with widely differing half-lives, formed by the decay of one element into another is called a radioactive series. Thorium-232, for example, goes through ten transformations to become lead.

ALL IN HALF-LIVES

The half-life of an isotope is a measure of the rate at which it decays. The decay of any single nucleus is unpredictable, but in any collection of atoms, half will decay over a certain period; this is the half-life. Over the half-life period, radioactivity reduces by half. In the following same half-life period, half the remaining nuclei (not half the original number) decay, and the radioactivity falls to a quarter of the original level, and so on. The half-life of any given radioisotope can vary from a fraction of a second to many millions of years.

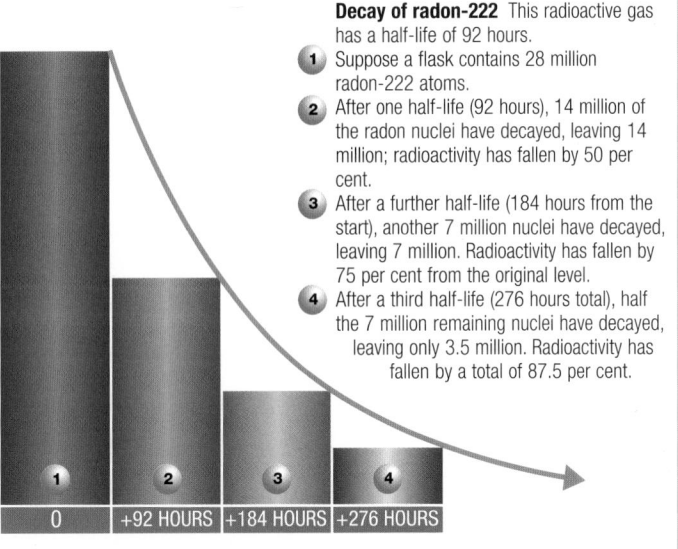

Decay of radon-222 This radioactive gas has a half-life of 92 hours.

1. Suppose a flask contains 28 million radon-222 atoms.
2. After one half-life (92 hours), 14 million of the radon nuclei have decayed, leaving 14 million; radioactivity has fallen by 50 per cent.
3. After a further half-life (184 hours from the start), another 7 million nuclei have decayed, leaving 7 million. Radioactivity has fallen by 75 per cent from the original level.
4. After a third half-life (276 hours total), half the 7 million remaining nuclei have decayed, leaving only 3.5 million. Radioactivity has fallen by a total of 87.5 per cent.

| 0 | +92 HOURS | +184 HOURS | +276 HOURS |

Natural radioactivity

Natural radioisotopes occur widely on Earth in rocks and minerals. They produce low levels of radioactivity known as 'background radiation'. In most places, this radiation is harmless, but in some areas radon gas leaks from rocks and can be harmful if it is trapped in cellars of houses. There are two groups of natural radioisotopes:

Primordial Created in the earliest days of the Universe, primordial radioisotopes are billions of years older than Earth itself. They have very long half-lives – about 4500 million years for uranium-238, for example.

Cosmogenic Created when cosmic rays (see page 530) bombard atoms in the upper atmosphere, cosmogenic radioisotopes have much shorter half-lives, but are constantly replenished. For example, carbon-14 has a half-life of 5730 years. It is taken up by living organisms, so its decay can be used to estimate when they died.

Nuclear fission and fusion

Nuclear reactors and nuclear weapons use the fact, established by the theory of relativity (see page 534), that mass and energy are two aspects of the same thing. Matter – mass – is annihilated and converted into energy, either by nuclear fission (the splitting of heavy nuclei) or by nuclear fusion (the joining of light nuclei). In either case, the mass of the fission or fusion products – including any subatomic particles emitted – is less than that of the initial nuclei. The 'lost' mass is turned into a burst of energy.

Fission Nuclear fission relies on the fact that the nuclei of some isotopes such as uranium-235 and plutonium-239 become highly unstable if they capture a neutron. They instantly split into two lighter nuclei plus further neutrons – which can then split more nuclei in a chain reaction (see right). Energy is released as gamma rays and other radiation, and as the kinetic energy of the fission products, creating a great deal of heat. In a bomb the chain reaction builds up in millionths of a second and the energy release is explosive. In a reactor, control rods ensure that there are just enough neutrons to maintain a steady reaction.

Fusion Nuclear fusion uses the heat of a fission reaction. This makes the nuclei of hydrogen or its isotopes deuterium and tritium fuse to form helium nuclei. Again there is a loss of mass and a huge release of energy. Fusion fuels the Sun, but no one has yet built a reliable fusion reactor for power generation.

Chain reaction Each time a neutron causes a uranium-235 (U-235) nucleus to split, surplus neutrons are produced. If there is a 'critical mass' of U-235 present, these neutrons cause more nuclei to split, and so on in a chain reaction. But if there is not enough U-235, too many neutrons escape and the reaction fizzles out.

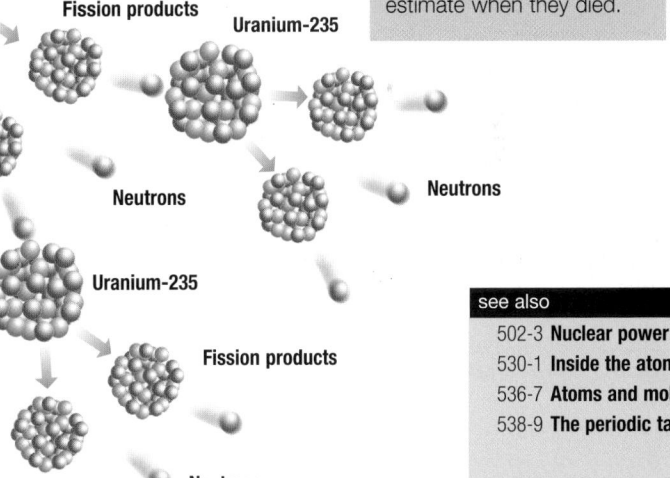

Neutron

Uranium-235

Fission products

Uranium-235

Neutrons

Neutrons

Uranium-235

Fission products

Neutrons

see also

502-3 **Nuclear power**
530-1 **Inside the atom**
536-7 **Atoms and molecules**
538-9 **The periodic table**

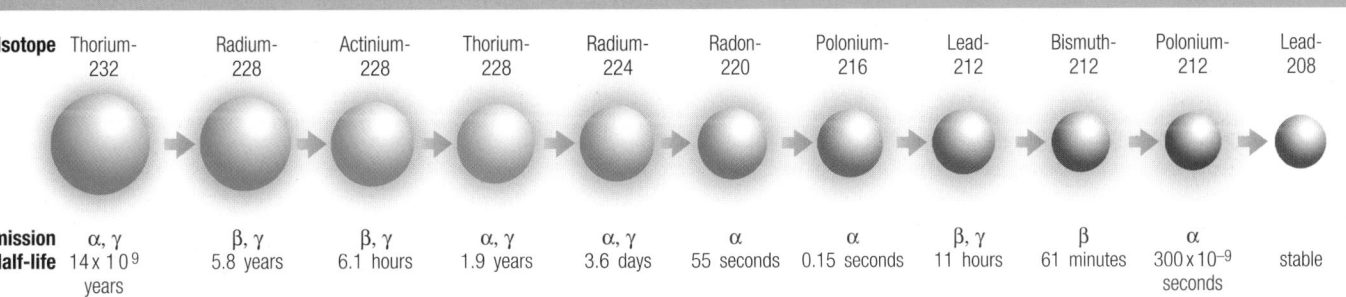

Isotope	Thorium-232	Radium-228	Actinium-228	Thorium-228	Radium-224	Radon-220	Polonium-216	Lead-212	Bismuth-212	Polonium-212	Lead-208
Emission	α, γ	β, γ	β, γ	α, γ	α, γ	α	α	β, γ	β	α	
Half-life	14 x 10⁹ years	5.8 years	6.1 hours	1.9 years	3.6 days	55 seconds	0.15 seconds	11 hours	61 minutes	300 x 10⁻⁹ seconds	stable

Albert Einstein's two theories of relativity are an attempt to explain the true nature of motion, mass, energy and gravity. His thinking superseded many of the concepts enshrined in the classical tradition of Newtonian physics. The General Theory deals with gravity; the Special Theory makes predictions about how objects behave at near-light speeds.

WHAT IS RELATIVITY?

At the heart of relativity lies an insight into how we measure space and time. Imagine a man sitting on a train reading a book. According to the man, his book is stationary – which, indeed, it is, within his particular **frame of reference**. Now imagine a woman standing on a railway platform seeing the man and his book through the window of the passing train. The train is travelling at 100 km/h so, for the woman, the book is moving forwards at 100 km/h.

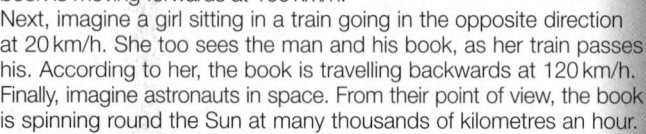

Next, imagine a girl sitting in a train going in the opposite direction at 20 km/h. She too sees the man and his book, as her train passes his. According to her, the book is travelling backwards at 120 km/h. Finally, imagine astronauts in space. From their point of view, the book is spinning round the Sun at many thousands of kilometres an hour.

No fixed point Everything depends on the frame of reference. Using different frames of reference, totally different measurements emerge, all legitimate in their different ways. Relativity, then, makes this key point: there is no such thing as an absolute measurement of space. No object is completely at rest in space. Consequently, no fixed point exists from which to make absolute measurements.

The speed of light But one absolute does exist: the speed of light. Imagine a car travelling towards you at 30 m/s (108 km/h). Common sense might tell you that because the car is moving towards you, light from the headlights is travelling at 30 m/s faster than the speed of light – that is, $c + 30$ m/s (where c is the speed of light). But common sense would be wrong. Regardless of how much or how fast an observer may move relative to a source of light, the speed of light remains the same. Unlike anything else in the Universe, the speed of light is independent of any frame of reference. But speed is distance over time. For the speed of light to be constant, distance and – crucially – time must be subject to change depending on the point of view of the observer. This is Einstein's greatest insight: time is not constant; it passes more quickly for some observers than others, depending on their circumstances.

A lot of energy from a little mass

Newtonian physics sees mass and energy as distinct. The Special Theory, however, removes the distinction: in relativity, mass is 'frozen' energy. And according to the equation $E = mc^2$, the energy locked up in mass is immense. Since c^2 – the square of the speed of light – is 90 000 000 000 000 000, for every unit of mass (m) the energy locked up in it is 90 000 000 000 000 000 that amount.

It was this insight that paved the way for the exploitation of energy from matter by the splitting of the atom (more precisely, the atomic nucleus). In a nuclear reactor, the amount of energy that can, in theory, be extracted from just 100 g (3½ oz) of fuel is enough to keep a million 100 watt lightbulbs lit for three years. A nuclear bomb can produce an equally large amount of energy from 100 g of fuel. This is why a warhead small enough to sit on a kitchen table can explode with enough force to destroy a city.

SPECIAL THEORY OF RELATIVITY

The Special Theory (published in 1905) deals with the behaviour of objects moving in the 'special', gravity-free environment of empty space.

Working from the basic insights about frame of reference and the speed of light, it makes a series of often startling predictions about mass, energy and time. Among other things, it states:
● that mass and energy are equivalent, and can be converted into one another. This leads to the famous equation, $E = mc^2$. In other words, the energy (E) of an object at rest equals its mass (m) multiplied by the speed of light (c) squared.
● that as a body accelerates, so its energy and mass increase and its length decreases in the direction of travel. Were an object able to reach the speed of light, it would have infinite mass and zero length. This means that the speed of light is the upper speed limit of the Universe.
● that when an object is moving, time seems to run more slowly to an 'outside' observer, although it seems to run 'normally' to the person moving. This discrepancy is noticeable only at near-light speeds. It means that measurements of time, like those of space, are relative, not absolute.

GENERAL THEORY OF RELATIVITY

Isaac Newton's law of gravitation published in 1687 states that gravity is a force that exists between two bodies of matter, and its size depends on their mass and the distance between them.

It suggests that the gravitational pull the Sun exerts on the planets of the Solar System, for example, takes place instantaneously over millions of kilometres. But this is incompatible with the concept, put forward in the Special Theory of Relativity, that nothing can travel faster than the speed of light.
● **Explaining gravity by relativity** In 1915, Einstein proposed a General Theory that explained gravity. According to the General Theory, gravity is a property of space, time and mass, and not a force of attraction between bodies. The presence of a gravitational field is the result of space-time (see opposite) becoming curved around a body, whereas the lack of a gravitational field leaves it flat.

This is easier to understand if space-time is imagined as a stretched rubber sheet. If a heavy ball is placed on the sheet, it creates a hollow. A smaller ball rolled across the sheet will be affected by the hollow and roll towards the heavy ball.
● **The Sun and planets** Newtonian physics explains the curved orbit of a planet around the Sun by saying that the planet is attracted by the force of gravity to the Sun. The General Theory says that the planet's path is curved because the Sun – with its great mass – distorts and curves space-time around it.

In the General Theory's distorted space, a curve is the shortest distance between two points, and is therefore the path followed by the planet. This also applies to light, which is 'bent' by the curve in space-time.

after 1 second

Time and relativity

How can it be that time passes at a different rate for one person than for another? Consider two spacecraft travelling through space at 99 per cent of the speed of light at a fixed distance of 300 000 000 m apart. A pulse of light is sent from one to the other. To astronauts on board, this pulse travels in a straight line, because the two craft are stationary relative to one another, and takes 1 second (see left).

An observer on Earth, however, viewing the spacecraft through a telescope, sees the light beam follow a diagonal path (see below). This path is obviously longer than the straight line observed by the astronauts, and the light takes longer, from this point of view, to travel from one craft to the other.

Both astronauts and Earth observer have witnessed the same event, but each from a different frame of reference. The Earth observer sees the beam taking seven times longer to travel between the spacecraft than the astronauts do. Yet the speed of light is constant – it is the only constant in the Universe. So the only explanation for the light seeming to take longer for the observer on Earth is that time itself was moving more slowly for him relative to the astronauts on the spacecraft. Time does not pass at the same rate for the astronauts and the observer. Time, like space, is related to the frame of reference in which it is being measured.

Spacecraft to spacecraft To the astronauts on board, the pulse of light travels in a straight line and takes 1 second, because it is travelling near the speed of light.

Seven-second beam With the spacecraft travelling at 99 per cent of the speed of light, the beam (watched from Earth) takes 7 seconds to pass from one craft to the other.

after 1 second

after 2 seconds

after 3 seconds

after 4 seconds

after 5 seconds

after 6 seconds

after 7 seconds

300 000 000 m/s

Seen from Earth For the observer on Earth, the beam takes a diagonal path because the second craft has moved on by the time the beam reaches it.

Space-time

The General Theory proposes a concept of space-time. In physics, space embodies the idea of distance, and has three dimensions, at right angles to each other. An object can move in three dimensions to reach a certain point: forwards or backwards, right or left, down or up.

Movement also, of course, involves a fourth dimension, namely time. Time and the three dimensions of space can be combined in a four-dimensional system of space-time, or a space-time continuum. According to the General Theory, space-time, mass and gravity are interdependent.

Relativity: the evidence

Since Einstein put forward his ideas of relativity, many of them have been tested experimentally and proved to be correct.

● Atomic clocks on spacecraft have been shown to be fractionally slower than atomic clocks left on Earth.
● Particle physics has shown that subatomic particles travelling at high speed gain mass by exactly the amount Einstein predicted.
● Light from stars has been shown to be 'bent' by the Sun, providing evidence for the distortion of space-time by a large mass.
● Particles in cosmic rays should only last a fraction of a second when they reach the Earth's atmosphere. But they exist significantly longer (long enough for detection) because they are travelling through space at the speed of light, and so time slows down for them.

What is gravity? If space-time is seen as a rubber sheet, it is easy to see how a larger object distorts it more than a smaller one. The smaller object then 'falls' towards the larger – the effect known as gravity.

Every substance on Earth is made up of the atoms of one or more elements. To understand why a substance appears as it does, and why it behaves in a certain way under particular circumstances, chemists study the properties of the atoms of the many different elements, and of the compounds the atoms combine to form. From their findings, they devise laws that help to describe the nature of matter.

WHAT IS AN ATOM?

An atom is the smallest particle of any element that can take part in a chemical reaction. It is composed of a positively charged central core – the nucleus (see below) – surrounded by orbiting, negatively charged electrons.

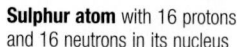

Carbon atom with 6 protons and 6 neutrons in its nucleus

Sulphur atom with 16 protons and 16 neutrons in its nucleus

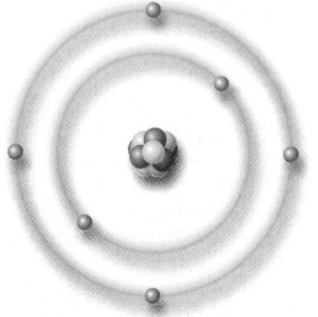
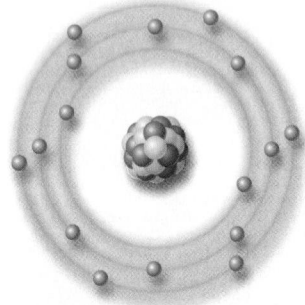

Orbiting electrons
2 in inner shell;
4 in outer shell

Orbiting electrons
2 in inner shell;
8 in middle shell
6 in outer shell

Electron shells   Electrons orbit the nucleus in layers or shells. The innermost shell can carry up to two electrons, the next shell can carry up to eight and the third shell can carry up to 18 electrons. The chemical characteristics of an atom are determined by the degree to which its outermost electron is filled.

● **The nucleus** Almost the entire mass of an atom resides in its nucleus, composed of protons and neutrons. Protons are positively charged; neutrons are electrically neutral. Any element is defined by the number of protons in the nucleus of each atom, known as its atomic number. Carbon, for example, contains six protons in the nucleus of each atom, so its atomic number is six.

● **The electrons** The nucleus is surrounded by orbiting electrons – tiny, negatively charged particles. For a neutral atom of any element, the number of orbiting electrons equals the number of protons. It is the orbiting electrons that determine the chemical behaviour of an atom, as atoms combine, or bond, by either sharing or transferring electrons (see page 540). The electrons are arranged in layers (shells) at different distances from the nucleus. Each shell can contain a certain maximum number of electrons.

● **Ions** An ion is an electrically charged atom or group of atoms. Normally the charge on an atom is neutral, but during chemical reactions electrons can swap from atom to atom, so that the atoms gain an overall positive or negative charge, producing positive or negative ions. Positively charged ions are known as cations, while negatively charged ions are called anions.

Branches of chemistry

The study of chemistry is divided into a number of distinct disciplines:
● **Analytical chemistry** develops and uses techniques to determine precisely what elements are present in a substance, and in what proportions.
● **Applied chemistry** is the practical application of chemical knowledge and techniques to agriculture, industry, medicine and other commercial areas.
● **Biochemistry** is the study of the chemical processes that take place in living organisms.
● **Inorganic chemistry** is the study of the properties of the elements and all their compounds, except for those of carbon.

● **Organic chemistry** is the study of the numerous compounds of carbon. All living organisms are based on carbon molecules – this is why the discipline is termed organic chemistry.
● **Physical chemistry** is concerned with the physical effects of chemical structures, particularly energy changes and reaction rates.
● **Polymer chemistry** is the study of compounds made from long repeating chains of molecules. Organic examples include DNA and proteins, while the majority of plastics are synthetic polymers.
● **Structural chemistry** is the study of how atoms are arranged in molecules and the types of bonds between them.

WHAT IS A MOLECULE?

Many substances are made up of molecules, which consist of two or more atoms – of the same or different elements – joined together. The bonds linking atoms in a molecule are formed by electrons being 'shared' (see page 540). A molecule is the smallest part of such a substance that can exist on its own.

A water molecule, for example, is made up of one oxygen atom bonded to two hydrogen atoms; if it were to be broken up into its constituent atoms, it would no longer have the properties we associate with water.

Any substance may be represented by its chemical formula. This shows the proportions of the atoms of the different elements in it. So the formula H_2O tells you that you need two hydrogen atoms to every oxygen atom to make water. Similarly the formula for sulphuric acid, H_2SO_4, tells you that sulphuric acid contains hydrogen, sulphur and oxygen in the ratio of 2:1:4.

Oxygen atom

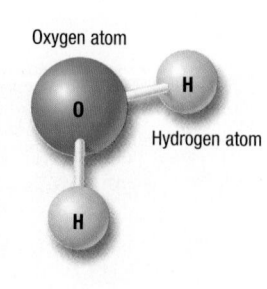

Hydrogen atom

Water molecule, H_2O

Sulphuric acid molecule, H_2SO_4

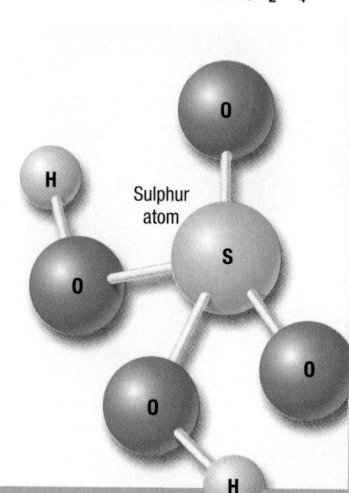

Sulphur atom

Naming an element

In chemistry, the basic substances are called elements. Any pure element consists of atoms that are chemically identical. A pure sample of the element gold, for example, will contain only gold atoms.

For convenience, chemists have given each element a specific name and symbol. The **symbol** for an element consists of one or two letters – usually a shortened version of its full name. These symbols have been agreed by scientists internationally.

The vast majority of the elements that are known today were discovered in the last two to three hundred years. Many of these have been given names that refer to their identifying characteristics, as perceived by their discoverer.

Oxygen, for example, means 'acid-former', from the 18th-century theory that all acids contain oxygen; while the name for chlorine – a greenish gas – is derived from the word *khloros*, a Greek term for yellow-green.

Some of the elements, however, have been known and used since antiquity. They usually have names which are derived from Latin or Ancient Greek:

Element	Latin	Symbol
Copper	Cuprum	Cu
Gold	Aurum	Au
Iron	Ferrum	Fe
Lead	Plumbum	Pb
Mercury	Hydrargyrum	Hg
Potassium	Kalium	K
Silver	Argentum	Ag

More recently, the convention has been to name elements in honour of famous scientists:

Curium (Marie Curie)
Nobelium (Alfred Nobel)
Fermium (Enrico Fermi)

This honour has also been extended to names of places:

Californium (California)
Americium (America)
Francium (France)
Polonium (Poland)

There is a new proposal to name the elements according to the Latin for their **atomic number** (see The nucleus, opposite). The transactinides (atomic numbers 104 and over) are already being named in this way – see the periodic table, pages 538-9.

EXISTING IN DIFFERENT FORMS

Some elements exist in more than one form of molecule or crystal. These different forms are called allotropes.

● **Allotropic gases** differ in their molecular structure. For example, a molecule of ordinary oxygen gas (O_2) is made of two oxygen atoms, while a molecule of the allotrope ozone (O_3) is made of three oxygen atoms. Their physical properties also differ: ordinary oxygen is odourless, while ozone has a sharp smell.
● **Solid allotropes** have different crystal structures. For example, carbon has three allotropes – diamond, graphite and fullerene – each of which has different physical properties. The different structures arise from the way the carbon atoms are linked together.

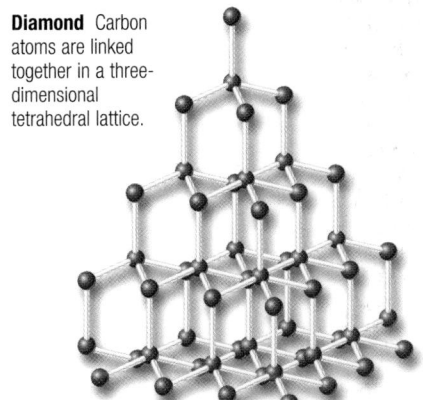

Diamond Carbon atoms are linked together in a three-dimensional tetrahedral lattice.

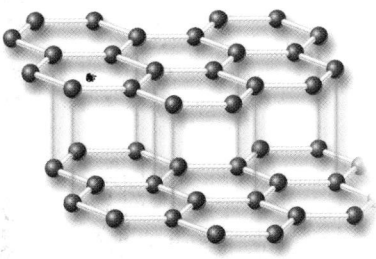

Graphite Sheets of strongly bonded carbon atoms are linked together by much weaker bonds, so can easily slide over each other.

● **Graphite** The weak bonds between the layers of atoms make graphite slippery and soft, and therefore a good lubricant. Being black, it is also used as a drawing medium.

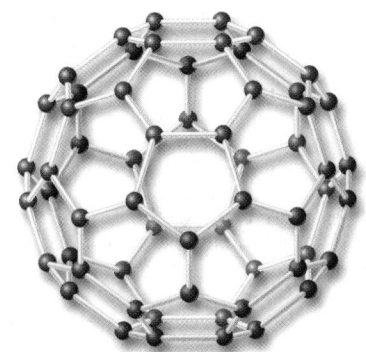

Fullerene Each molecule consists of a ball-shaped cluster of 60 carbon atoms.

● **Diamond** Strong bonds extend in all directions throughout the entire, transparent, diamond crystal, making it extremely inflexible and hard – it is the hardest known substance.

● **Fullerene** Soft, heat-resistant fullerene crystals were discovered in 1985, when a high-powered laser was aimed at graphite. It is sometimes known as buckminsterfullerene.

KEY TERMS

● **Atom** The smallest part of an element that can take part in a chemical reaction.
● **Atomic number** The number of protons in the nucleus of an atom. All atoms of the same element have the same atomic number.
● **Molecule** Two or more atoms that are chemically bonded together. With compounds, it is the smallest amount that can take part in a chemical reaction.
● **Ion** An atom or group of atoms that carry an electrical charge.
● **Element** A substance that consists entirely of chemically identical atoms.
● **Compound** A substance containing atoms of two or more different elements that are combined chemically.
● **Chemical reaction** A process involving two or more substances that results in a chemical change.
● **Catalyst** A substance that markedly alters the speed of a chemical reaction, without itself undergoing any permanent chemical change.
● **Combustion** A chemical reaction in which a substance reacts rapidly with oxygen, giving out heat and light in the form of a flame.
● **Oxidation** The addition of oxygen to an element or compound during a chemical reaction. Oxidation is also said to occur if hydrogen is removed.
● **Reduction** The addition of hydrogen to an element or compound during a chemical reaction. Reduction is also said to occur if oxygen is removed.
● **pH** A measure of acidity or alkalinity. A pH of 7 is neutral, while substances with lower pHs are acidic, and those with a higher number are alkaline.

see also

530-1 **Inside the atom**
538-9 **The periodic table**
540-1 **Chemistry of compounds**
542-3 **The processes of life**

The periodic table was constructed by the Russian chemist Dmitri Mendeleyev in 1869. He arranged all the elements according to their atomic number and the patterns he observed in their chemical properties. Though more elements are now known, the table remains basically the same, and is used by chemists to predict how elements might react together.

Groups

Eight vertical columns of elements, labelled I-VIII, are arranged down the left and right side of the periodic table. These are called groups. Each group contains elements that tend to react chemically in similar ways, because they all have atoms in which the arrangement of electrons around the nucleus is similar. As well as being numbered, each group of elements is given a name:

Group I	the alkali metals
Group II	the alkaline-earth metals
Group III	the boron elements
Group IV	the carbon elements
Group V	the nitrogen elements
Group VI	the oxygen elements
Group VII	the halogen elements
Group VIII	the noble gases

◒ The alkali metals (group I) each have just one electron in their outermost shell. This is easily lost, making these elements very reactive.
◒ Similarly, the halogen elements (group VII) are also very reactive, as they each lack just one electron to form a complete outer shell.
◒ By contrast, the noble gases (group VIII) have complete outer shells, so are unreactive.
◒ Moving down each group, certain features of the elements change: the diameter of their atoms increases; atoms lose their outermost electrons more easily; the density of the elements increases.

Periods

Each horizontal row in the table is called a 'period'. Reading across a period from left to right, the number of electrons in the outer shell or subshell of the elements increases. There are two other trends:
◒ The elements change from being metallic to nonmetallic in nature.
◒ The melting point of the elements gradually increases to a maximum in group IV (the carbon elements), decreasing again towards group VIII (the noble gases).

Transition elements

In the middle of the periodic table – from scandium to zinc, from yttrium to cadmium, and from hafnium to mercury – are the transition metals. These elements are similar in that their unfilled electron subshells are not in the outermost shell (unlike the elements in the left and right-hand blocks of the table). The subshells in the outer shells are filled while some of the 'places' in the inner shells are vacant. These elements are known for their high density, and are good conductors of heat and electricity.

Reading the periodic table

Each box in the periodic table gives four pieces of information:

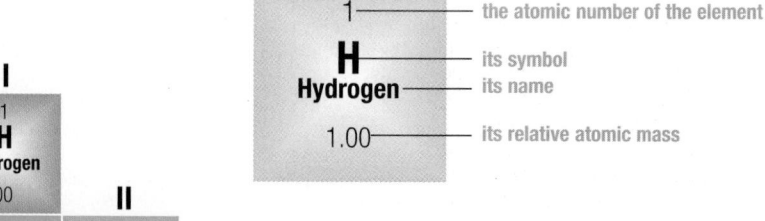

- 1 — the atomic number of the element
- **H** — its symbol
- Hydrogen — its name
- 1.00 — its relative atomic mass

I

1 **H** Hydrogen 1.00

II

3 **Li** Lithium 6.9	4 **Be** Beryllium 9.01
11 **Na** Sodium 23.0	12 **Mg** Magnesium 24.5

19 **K** Potassium 39.1	20 **Ca** Calcium 40.1	21 **Sc** Scandium 44.96	22 **Ti** Titanium 47.88	23 **V** Vanadium 50.94	24 **Cr** Chromium 51.00	25 **Mn** Manganese 54.94
37 **Rb** Rubidium 85.5	38 **Sr** Strontium 87.6	39 **Y** Yttrium 88.91	40 **Z** Zirconium 91.22	41 **Nb** Niobium 92.91	42 **Mo** Molybdenum 95.94	43 **Tc** Technetium 98
55 **Cs** Caesium 132.9	56 **Ba** Barium 137.4	57-71 Lanthanide series	72 **Hf** Hafnium 178.49	73 **Ta** Tantalum 180.95	74 **W** Tungsten 183.85	75 **Re** Rhenium 186.21
87 **Fr** Francium 223.0	88 **Ra** Radium 226.0	89-103 Actinide series	104 **Unq** Unnilquadium (261)	105 **Unp** Unnilpentium (262)	106 **Unh** Unnilhexium (263)	107 **Uns** Unnilseptium (264)

57 **La** Lanthanum 138.91	58 **Ce** Cerium 140.12	59 **Pr** Praseodymium 140.91	60 **Nd** Neodymium 144.24
89 **Ac** Actinium 227	90 **Th** Thorium 232.04	91 **Pa** Proctanium 231.04	92 **U** Uranium 238.03

Sheet copper Like many of the transition metals, copper is a good conductor of heat.

The sequence of transition metals is interrupted by the lanthanide (57–71) and actinide (89–103) series.

Since the 1960s, a number of extremely heavy elements – the transactinides (104 and above) have been created. These are all 'artificial', as they can be produced only in a nuclear reactor or particle accelerator, where atoms of lighter elements collide at high speed, merging briefly to form an atom of a new element.

Key:

- ◻ metals
- ◻ nonmetals
- ◻ metalloids
- ◻ transition elements

ATOMIC NUMBER AND MASS

Atomic number The number of protons in the nucleus (see page 536) of each atom of an element is known as the atomic number of that element.

Relative atomic mass How heavy an atom of a particular element is, relative to one atom of any other element, is expressed as relative atomic mass. Each proton and neutron is approximately equal to one atomic mass unit. So carbon, with six neutrons and six protons in the nucleus of its atoms, has a relative atomic mass of 12.

Sometimes an atom of a particular element contains extra neutrons in its nucleus, and is known as an isotope. An element may have several isotopes, with varying atomic masses, due to the extra neutrons. In this case, the atomic mass shown in the table is the average for the isotopes found in a typical sample of the element.

Native silver Like its periodic table neighbours copper and gold, silver conducts electricity well, so is widely used in electrical circuits.

					VIII
					2 **He** Helium 4
III	IV	V	VI	VII	
5 **B** Boron 10.81	6 **C** Carbon 12.00	7 **N** Nitrogen 14.01	8 **O** Oxygen 16.00	9 **F** Fluorine 19.00	10 **Ne** Neon 20.18
13 **Al** Aluminium 26.98	14 **Si** Silicon 28.09	15 **P** Phosphorus 30.97	16 **S** Sulphur 32.06	17 **Cl** Chlorine 35.45	18 **Ar** Argon 39.94

26 **Fe** Iron 55.85	27 **Co** Cobalt 58.93	28 **Ni** Nickel 58.69	29 **Cu** Copper 63.55	30 **Zn** Zinc 65.38	31 **Ga** Gallium 69.72	32 **Ge** Germanium 72.6	33 **As** Arsenic 74.92	34 **Se** Selenium 78.96	35 **Br** Bromine 79.90	36 **Kr** Krypton 83.80
44 **Ru** Ruthenium 101.07	45 **Rh** Rhodium 102.91	46 **Pd** Palladium 106.42	47 **Ag** Silver 107.87	48 **Cd** Cadmium 112.41	49 **In** Indium 114.82	50 **Sn** Tin 118.69	51 **Sb** Antimony 121.7	52 **Te** Tellurium 127.60	53 **I** Iodine 126.90	54 **Xe** Xenon 131.29
76 **Os** Osmium 190.2	77 **Ir** Iridium 192.22	78 **Pt** Platinum 195.08	79 **Au** Gold 196.97	80 **Hg** Mercury 200.59	81 **Tl** Thallium 204.38	82 **Pb** Lead 207.2	83 **Bi** Bismuth 208.98	84 **Po** Polonium 209	85 **At** Astatine 210	86 **Rn** Radon 222
108 **Uno** Unniloctium (265)	109 **Une** Unnilenium (266)	110 **Uun** Ununnilium (369)	111 **Uuu** Unununiun (266)							

61 **Pm** Promethium 145	62 **Sm** Samarium 150.36	63 **Eu** Europium 151.96	64 **Gd** Gadolinium 157	65 **Tb** Terbium 158.93	66 **Dy** Dysprosium 162.50	67 **Ho** Holmium 164.93	68 **Er** Erbium 167.26	69 **Tm** Thulium 168.93	70 **Yb** Ytterbium 173.04	71 **Lu** Lutetium 174.97
93 **Np** Neptunium 237.05	94 **Pu** Plutonium 244	95 **Am** Americium 243	96 **Cm** Curium 247	97 **Bk** Berkelium 247	98 **Cf** Californium 251	99 **Es** Einsteinium 252	100 **Fm** Fermium 257	101 **Md** Mendelevium 258	102 **No** Nobelium 259	103 **Lw** Lawrencium 260

Metals, nonmetals and metalloids

The periodic table is made up of metals, nonmetals, metalloids and transition elements.

Metals Most metals exhibit these properties:
- Solid at room temperature.
- Opaque, except in extremely thin films.
- Good conductors of heat and electricity.
- Exhibit a lustrous sheen when polished.
- Crystalline in structure when solid.

Nonmetals A typical nonmetallic element will be a gas at room temperature, and a poor conductor of heat and electricity.

Metalloids Metalloids, or semimetals, have some of the properties of metals and some of the properties of nonmetals.

Transition elements See opposite page.

When two or more atoms of different elements combine they form a compound. As there are many different elements, the potential for creating different compounds is enormous. The atoms in a compound are held together *by bonds, which can be very strong, such as metallic bonding, or relatively weak, as in covalent bonding. The type of bonds holding a compound together determine its physical properties, such as its melting and boiling points.*

How atoms bond Atoms of different elements bond with each other to form compounds. They do this by gaining, losing or sharing electrons in their outer electron shells (see page 536).

Ionic bonding Electrons are transferred between atoms, turning each into a positively or negatively charged ion (see page 536). An example of an ionic compound is common salt, sodium chloride (NaCl). Each sodium atom has lost an electron from its outer shell to form a positively charged sodium ion (Na^+); each chlorine atom has received an electron to form a negatively charged chloride ion (Cl^-).

With opposite charges, the ions are strongly attracted to one another. They arrange themselves in a lattice (see below), in which each ion is surrounded by as many as possible of the opposite charge. It takes a lot of energy to break the forces between them. As a result, most ionic compounds are solid at room temperature.

Ionic bonding in sodium chloride (NaCl)

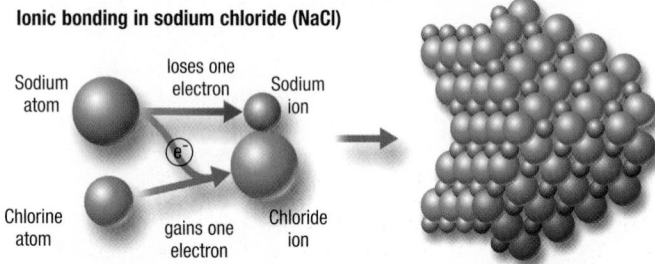

Covalent bonding A single covalent bond forms between two atoms when they share a pair of electrons between them, each contributing one of the electrons. Double and triple bonds can also form. Water (H_2O) is an example of a covalent compound, where one hydrogen atom shares electrons with two oxygen atoms.

Although each molecule in a covalent compound is held together by strong bonds, the electrostatic attraction between the molecules is weak. Consequently, the melting points of covalent compounds are usually lower than for ionic compounds: most are liquids and gases at room temperature.

Covalent bonding in water (H_2O)

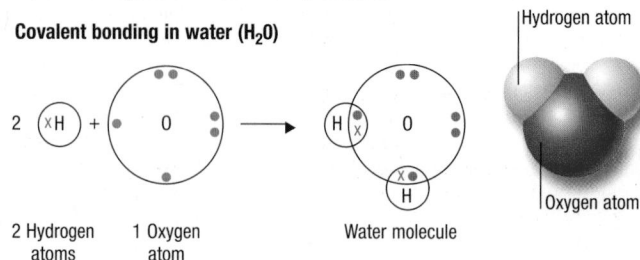

Metallic bonding In a metal, each atom has comparatively few electrons in its outer shell. As a result, the atoms readily lose their outer electrons, becoming positively charged ions. The 'lost' electrons then form a 'sea' of shared electrons flowing between the ions. This acts like a strong electrostatic 'glue', because of the powerful attraction between the oppositely charged ions and electrons. This is why metals are generally strong and have high melting points.

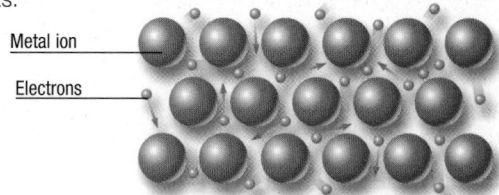

Understanding chemical reactions

Chemical reactions occur when elements or compounds react together to form different substances. The substances at the beginning of the reaction are called the reactants (or reagents), while those at the end are called the products.

Rates of reaction How fast a reaction occurs – or whether it occurs at all – depends not only on the reactants but also on prevailing conditions. For example, heating reactants together can speed up a reaction.

Catalysts are often used in industry to speed up chemical reactions or to help to make them take place. Metals and metal oxides, for example, can speed up a reaction between gases by providing a surface that absorbs the reactant molecules, bringing them closer together. A catalyst takes part in a reaction, but – unlike the reactants – remains unchanged and is not used up.

Changes in energy In any chemical reaction, energy is either given out or taken in. Energy is taken in to break bonds between atoms; it is given out when bonds are formed. A reaction in which energy is taken in is called an endothermic reaction; when energy is given out it is called an exothermic reaction.

Burning fuels is an exothermic reaction: energy is given out. Forming hydrogen and oxygen gas from water is an endothermic reaction: energy is taken in to break down the bonds between the hydrogen (H) and oxygen (O) atoms that water molecules (H_2O) are composed of.

Balanced equations

All chemical reactions can be described by means of an equation. For example, the reaction between sodium and water could be written as follows:

sodium + water ⟶ sodium hydroxide + hydrogen

However, this equation tells us only what substances are involved in the reaction. If it is written using their chemical formulas, it reveals what is happening to the atoms and molecules involved:

$Na + H_2O ⟶ NaOH + H_2$

But this equation is not balanced, because there are more hydrogen atoms on the right-hand side than on the left-hand side. All chemical reactions obey a simple law – the law of conservation of mass. This states that the total mass of all the products of a reaction equals the total mass of all the reactants. So, there must be the same number of atoms on either side of an equation for it to represent a reaction accurately:

$2Na + 2H_2O ⟶ 2NaOH + H_2$

It is now clear that when sodium reacts with water, two atoms of sodium combine with two molecules of water to produce two molecules of sodium hydroxide and one of hydrogen.

ACIDS AND ALKALIS

All substances are either acidic, alkaline or neutral. The exact degree can be measured using what is known as the pH (potential of hydrogen) scale. Neutral substances have a pH of 7, acids have a pH less than 7, and alkalis have a pH greater than 7.

Acids An acid dissolves in water to produce hydrogen ions. Hydrogen atoms in the molecules of the compound separate out from the other atoms to become positively charged ions (H^+), which move freely in solution.

For example, if the gas hydrogen chloride (HCl) is dissolved in water, the hydrogen and chlorine atoms separate out to become positively charged hydrogen ions (H^+) and negatively charged chlorine atoms (Cl^-) held in solution – hydrochloric acid.

The proportion of an acid's molecules that 'dissociate' in this way determines its strength. Common strong acids include nitric acid (HNO_3), used in fertilisers and explosives. Weak acids include ethanoic (or acetic) acid (CH_3CO_2H), found in vinegar, and citric acid ($C_6H_8O_7$), which gives lemons, grapefruits and other citrus fruit their distinctive taste.

Bases Bases can be seen as the 'opposite' of acids. They are a group of compounds, all of which react with the hydrogen ions produced by acids and neutralise them. If a base is water-soluble, it is called an alkali.

When an acid is neutralised by a base, the products are a salt (a type of ionic compound – see opposite) and water. For example, mixing hydrochloric acid (HCl) with potassium hydroxide (KOH) produces the salt potassium chloride plus water:

$$KOH + HCl \blacktriangleright KCl + H_2O$$

Alkalis An alkali is a base that will dissolve in water to produce hydroxide ions (OH^-). An example is sodium hydroxide (NaOH), or caustic soda, which is used in making soap and paper. When it is dissolved in water, its molecules break up to form positively charged sodium ions (Na^+) and negatively charged hydroxide ions (OH^-), which are held in solution. The strength of an alkali is determined by how many of its molecules 'dissociate' in this way to give off hydroxide ions.

One of the properties of alkalis is that they convert oil and grease into soluble soaps, that are easily washed away. They are therefore used in various cleaning agents. Ammonium hydroxide (NH_4OH), for example, is a common ingredient in household cleansers.

see also
500-1 **Fossil fuels**
530-1 **Inside the atom**
536-7 **Atoms and molecules**
538-9 **The periodic table**

ORGANIC COMPOUNDS

Carbon is unique in that its atoms can link up into long chains and rings. This often results in compounds with very large molecules. Many of these compounds were first discovered in living organisms, so their study is known as organic chemistry. But a number of industrial products – fuels, plastics, and man-made fibres – are also classified as organic, because they too have molecules that are based on a ring or chain of carbon atoms.

Hydrocarbons The most basic organic compounds are hydrocarbons, which contain only carbon and hydrogen atoms. They are largely used as fuels and as raw material for plastics, fibres, rubbers and industrial chemicals.

Aliphatic compounds Organic compounds whose carbon atoms are joined in a chain are called aliphatic. They are grouped into classes, according to the structure of their molecules:

Alkanes have single bonds between the carbon atoms. The simplest is methane (CH_4) – natural gas is 99 per cent methane. Others are also fuels: ethane (C_2H_6), propane (C_3H_8) and butane (C_4H_{10}).

Propane molecule

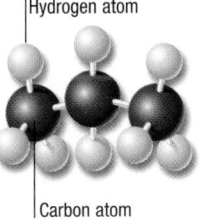
Hydrogen atom
Carbon atom

Alkenes have at least one double bond (see Covalent bonding, opposite) between the carbon atoms. They include ethene (C_2H_4), propene (C_3H_6) and butene (C_4H_8).

In a process known as polymerisation, the double bonds in alkene molecules can be broken. This allows a number of the molecules to link together as one huge molecule. Many plastics are made in this way. Polythene, for example, is a polymerised version of ethene.

Ethene molecule

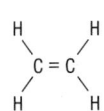

Alcohols contain one or more hydroxide group (OH^-). They include ethanol (C_2H_5OH), which is the alcohol in alcoholic drinks. It is produced when yeasts are fermented. It is also used as a solvent in products ranging from paints to glues and perfumes.

Ethanol molecule

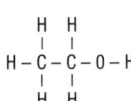 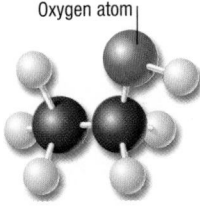
Oxygen atom

Aromatic compounds Organic compounds with molecules containing a group of six carbon atoms linked in a ring are termed 'aromatic'. This is because a group of these compounds, isolated from coal tar around 1860, had very strong and distinctive smells.

The simplest aromatic hydrocarbon is benzene; its molecular structure is known as the benzene ring (C_6H_6). In some aromatic compounds, other atoms or chemical groups replace the hydrogen atoms in the benzene ring. For example, phenol (C_6H_5OH) – also known as carbolic acid and used in disinfectants and plastics – is formed when a hydroxide group (OH^-) replaces one of the hydrogen atoms.

Benzene molecule

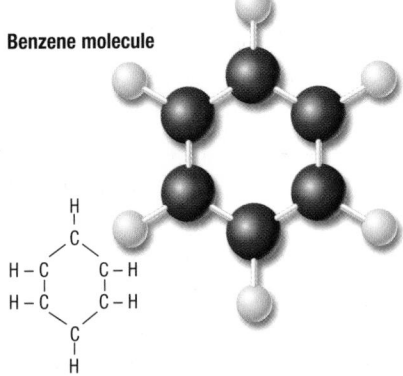

Cracking Long-chained hydrocarbon molecules are often converted into shorter ones – usually to create more useful compounds – using a process known as cracking. For example, crude oil obtained from oil fields contains many unusable hydrocarbons, such as decane. This is 'cracked' by heating to 500–900°C in the absence of oxygen, usually with a catalyst (see page 537), to produce octane – used in petrol – and ethene, another fuel.

All organisms share certain characteristics, which can be used to define them as living. One universal requirement among living things is for the chemical elements carbon and nitrogen. Carbon is involved in virtually all biological functions, including the generation of energy. Nitrogen is vital for the creation of proteins, which animals need in order to grow. All living things obtain their carbon and nitrogen from the environment, and eventually return it to their surroundings as part of a natural cycle.

CARBON CYCLE

Carbon exists in all biological molecules. It is a central component of the carbohydrates, proteins and fats of which all living things are made. The energy to power metabolic processes comes from 'burning' carbon-containing sugars with oxygen, releasing carbon dioxide as a waste product. Green plants use this carbon dioxide to make sugars in the process of photosynthesis; their 'waste product' is oxygen, which animals breathe.

The branches of biology

Traditionally, the study of biology has been divided according to the type of organism studied:
- Botany: the study of plants.
- Entomology: insects.
- Herpetology: amphibians and reptiles.
- Ichthyology: fishes.
- Microbiology: bacteria and other microorganisms.
- Mycology: fungi.
- Ornithology: birds.
- Physical anthropology: human beings.
- Zoology: animals generally.

In recent decades, biology has also been defined by the levels of life processes, from molecular interactions to the dynamics of whole populations.

Molecular biology deals with chemical and energy transformations among the billions of molecules that make up a living organism.
Cell biology is the study of cells, which are the basic structural and functional units of all living organisms. Cell biologists have adapted methods and theories from chemistry and physics to investigate cellular processes.
Population biology studies groups or populations of organisms inhabiting a given area, their interactions and the roles the different species play.
Ecology is the study of how living organisms interact with their environment.

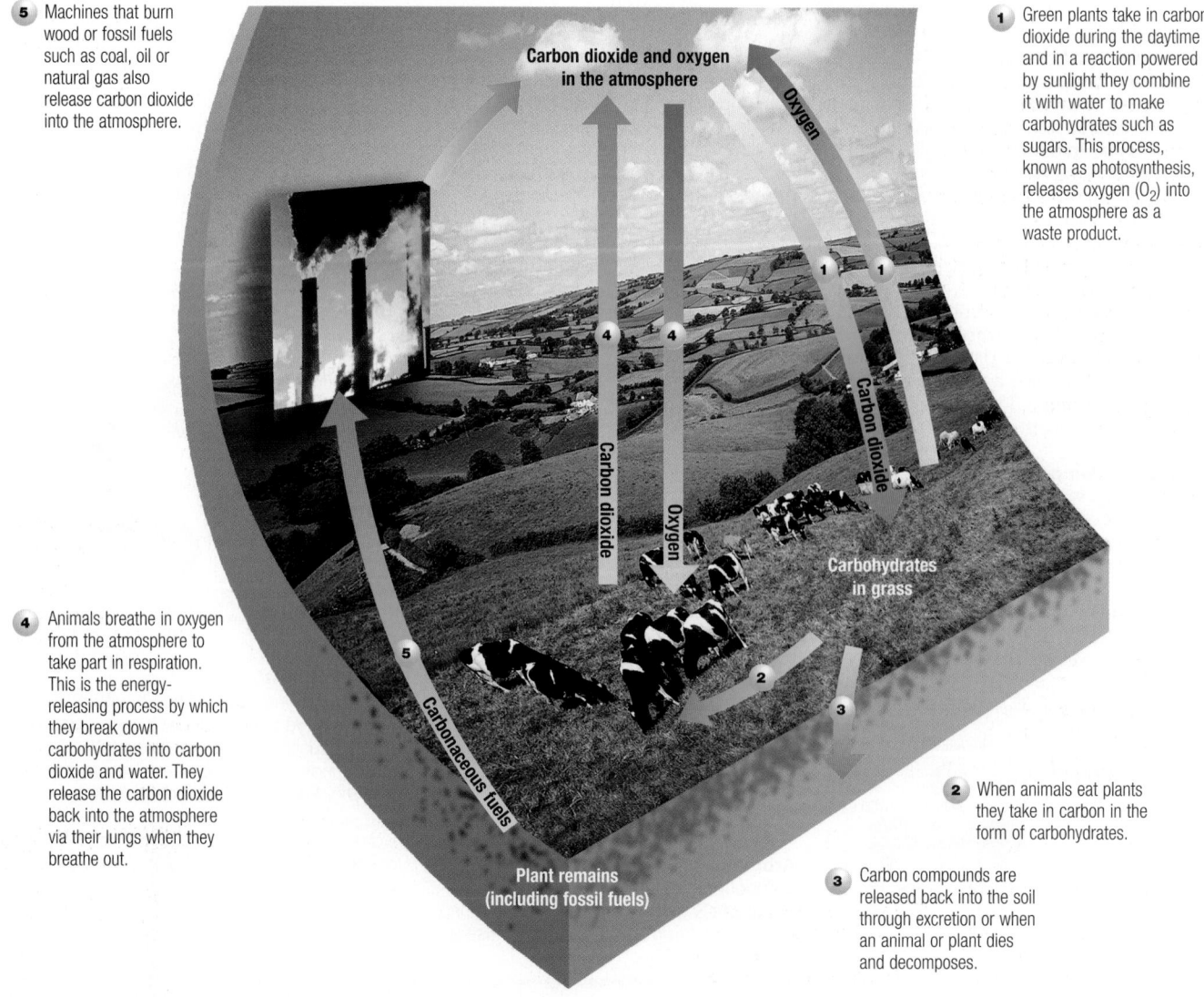

5 Machines that burn wood or fossil fuels such as coal, oil or natural gas also release carbon dioxide into the atmosphere.

1 Green plants take in carbon dioxide during the daytime and in a reaction powered by sunlight they combine it with water to make carbohydrates such as sugars. This process, known as photosynthesis, releases oxygen (O_2) into the atmosphere as a waste product.

4 Animals breathe in oxygen from the atmosphere to take part in respiration. This is the energy-releasing process by which they break down carbohydrates into carbon dioxide and water. They release the carbon dioxide back into the atmosphere via their lungs when they breathe out.

2 When animals eat plants they take in carbon in the form of carbohydrates.

3 Carbon compounds are released back into the soil through excretion or when an animal or plant dies and decomposes.

Carbon dioxide and oxygen in the atmosphere

Oxygen

Carbon dioxide

Oxygen

Carbon dioxide

Carbohydrates in grass

Carbonaceous fuels

Plant remains (including fossil fuels)

WHAT IS A LIVING THING?

There are six processes and characteristics common to all living organisms. Not every organism will exhibit every feature, but taken together they distinguish the living from the nonliving.

Adaptation In the short term, all living things adapt to changes in their environment – for example, by taking shelter or reducing their water loss in hot conditions. In the longer term, species become adapted through evolution.

Growth Organisms grow in an orderly, controlled manner; if nonliving things grow at all, it is by simple accretion (the addition of external layers). Plants grow throughout their lives, animals generally only until they reach maturity. Even after an animal stops growing, the cells it consists of are constantly renewed.

Metabolism A complex but controlled web of chemical processes takes place in every living organism, involving both the building up of simple substances into more complex ones – called *anabolism* – and the breaking down of complex materials into simpler substances – *catabolism*. An example of anabolism would be the creation of sugars in plants by *photosynthesis*. An example of catabolism would be the breaking down of sugars by *respiration* to release energy. The products of metabolism include unwanted and/or poisonous waste materials, which are got rid of by *excretion*.

Movement Most animals can freely move part or all of their body from one place to another. Plants do not have this freedom but they can move parts of their structure. For example, a plant's leaves move slowly towards sunlight and its roots grow downwards.

Reproduction Every living thing eventually dies, so it must reproduce itself if the species is to continue. Reproduction may involve the union of male and female cells of the same species (*sexual reproduction*), or an organism may produce more of its own kind on its own (*asexual* reproduction).

Responsiveness Living things respond to external changes, or *stimuli*, such as heat, light, sound and touch. Plants tend to respond much more slowly than animals, although exceptional examples such as the Venus's flytrap show that this is not always the case.

Snap The trap of a Venus's flytrap snaps shut when an insect disturbs hairs on its surface. Such plant movements are much simpler and more mechanical than most animal movements.

NITROGEN CYCLE

The atmosphere consists of 78 per cent nitrogen gas, but neither plants nor animals can use this. Plants need 'fixed' nitrogen in the form of chemical compounds called nitrates, which they convert into proteins and other substances. The nitrates they use are formed in two ways; by the effect of lightning on the atmosphere or by bacteria that live in the roots of plants or in the soil. Animals obtain their nitrogen from the proteins they ingest by eating.

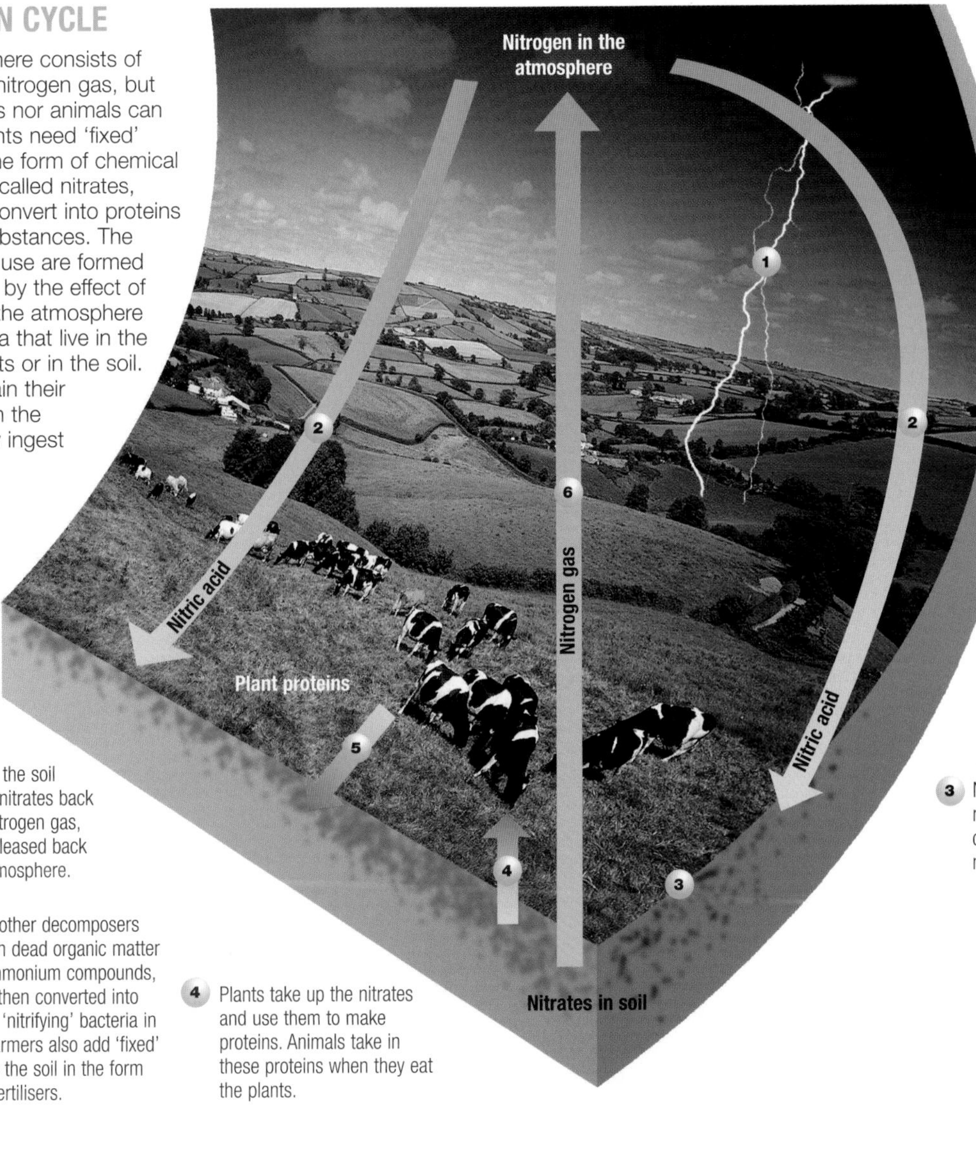

Nitrogen in the atmosphere

Nitric acid

Plant proteins

Nitrogen gas

Nitric acid

Nitrates in soil

1. Lightning 'fixes' some atmospheric nitrogen as nitrogen oxides.

2. Nitrogen oxides in the atmosphere dissolve in rain to form very dilute nitric acid, which in turn forms nitrates in the soil.

3. Nitrogen-fixing bacteria in the root nodules of plants such as clover, beans and peas convert nitrogen directly into nitrates.

6. Bacteria in the soil turn some nitrates back into free nitrogen gas, which is released back into the atmosphere.

5. Fungi and other decomposers break down dead organic matter to form ammonium compounds, which are then converted into nitrates by 'nitrifying' bacteria in the soil. Farmers also add 'fixed' nitrogen to the soil in the form of nitrate fertilisers.

4. Plants take up the nitrates and use them to make proteins. Animals take in these proteins when they eat the plants.

Living organisms come in myriad shapes and forms, yet at their most fundamental level they are all remarkably similar. The basic structural unit of every living thing is the cell. Cells with particular functions group together to form tissues, which in turn make up a plant's or animal's organs.

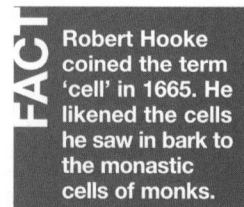

FACT Robert Hooke coined the term 'cell' in 1665. He likened the cells he saw in bark to the monastic cells of monks.

CELLS, TISSUES AND ORGANS

Cells are the tiny building blocks from which organisms are made. Most cells are invisible unless viewed under a microscope: as a rule only egg cells are large enough to be seen with the naked eye.

Many types of microscopic organism, such as bacteria and amoebae, are just a single cell. Larger organisms consist of many cells joined together. Simple multicellular organisms, such as sponges, are made of large numbers of just a few types of cell arranged randomly. But most plants and animals have specialised types of cell organised into tissues.

The cells in tissues are all of the same kind and have a particular function. Animal tissues include muscle – made of cells that have the ability to contract – and nervous tissue, which is formed from cells that can transmit electrical (nervous) impulses. The tissues of plants are less commonly known but include xylem and phloem (see page 76).

In most plants and animals, tissues are organised into organs. A few organs are composed almost entirely of one kind of tissue; the heart, for example, is made of cardiac muscle and very little else. However, most organs incorporate several tissue types. Organs may themselves be combined and work together in organ systems.

Cell structure All living cells have four features in common. They are:
- A cell membrane, which separates the contents of the cell from the outside world.
- Cytoplasm; a jelly-like substance that fills the cell.
- Protein-building bodies called ribosomes.
- DNA – the list of instructions that enables the cell to function and replicate itself.

Living organisms are divided into two groups by biologists – those that have cells with a nucleus and those that do not. The only organisms that lack cell nuclei are bacteria and cyanobacteria (commonly known as blue-green algae). They are the Earth's most primitive life forms and have their own kingdom in biological classification, the Monera.

All members of the other four kingdoms – Protista (which includes amoebae), Fungi, Plantae and Animalia – have a nucleus in their cells which contains their DNA. They also share a range of other internal cell structures called organelles, which (apart from ribosomes) are absent from bacteria and cyanobacteria. Organelles carry out various functions in the cell.

TYPES OF CELL

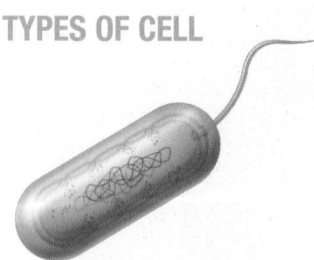

Bacterial cell Bacteria have no nucleus or other obvious internal structures; the genetic material is a simple DNA strand.

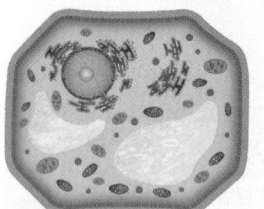

Plant cell Green plant cells are unique in having chloroplasts, tough cell walls and usually a fluid-filled central vacuole.

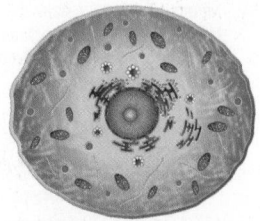

Animal cell With no rigid wall or vacuole, an animal cell has an irregular shape; no chloroplasts means it cannot make sugars.

Parts of a typical cell

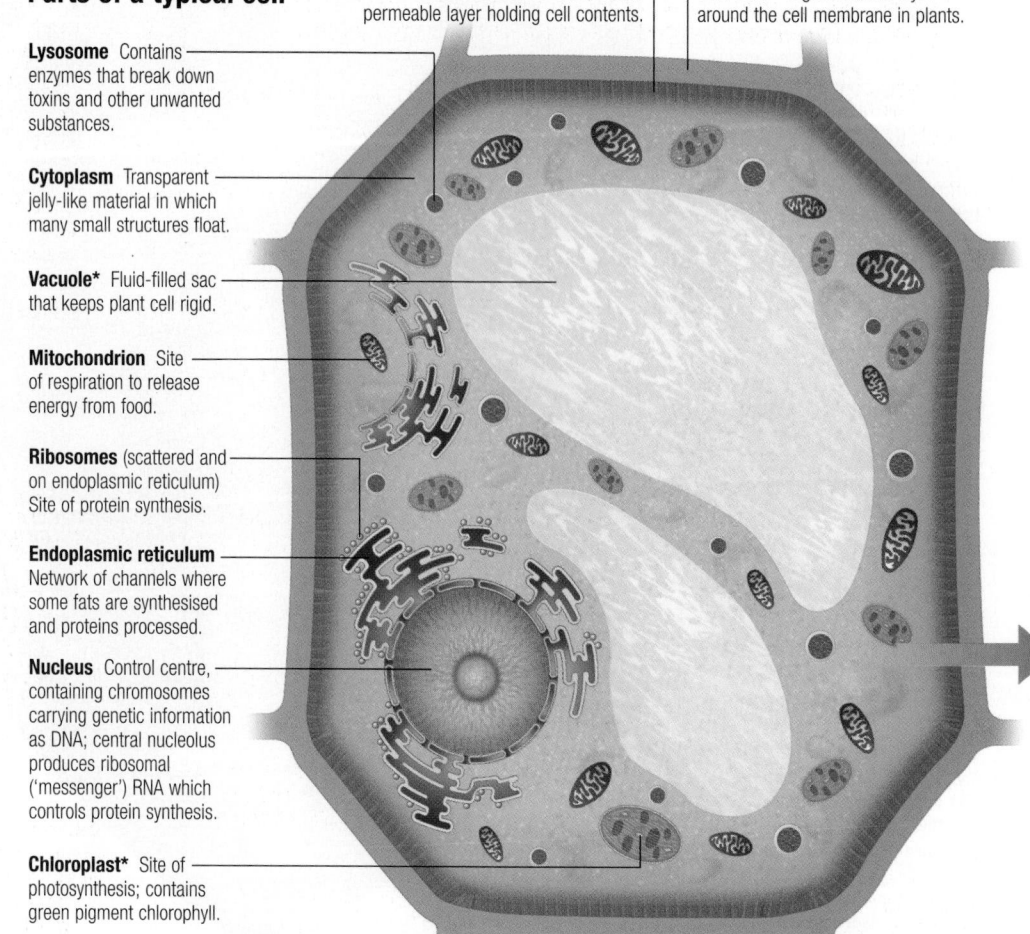

Cell membrane Thin, elastic permeable layer holding cell contents.

Cell wall* Rigid cellulose layer around the cell membrane in plants.

Lysosome Contains enzymes that break down toxins and other unwanted substances.

Cytoplasm Transparent jelly-like material in which many small structures float.

Vacuole* Fluid-filled sac that keeps plant cell rigid.

Mitochondrion Site of respiration to release energy from food.

Ribosomes (scattered and on endoplasmic reticulum) Site of protein synthesis.

Endoplasmic reticulum Network of channels where some fats are synthesised and proteins processed.

Nucleus Control centre, containing chromosomes carrying genetic information as DNA; central nucleolus produces ribosomal ('messenger') RNA which controls protein synthesis.

Chloroplast* Site of photosynthesis; contains green pigment chlorophyll.

*Structures found only in plant cells

THE CHEMICAL BASIS OF LIFE

A typical animal's body contains about 60 per cent water by weight; in a plant that figure may be higher. Apart from water, the main types of chemical found in all living things are nucleic acids (the components of DNA and RNA; see pages 150-1), proteins, carbohydrates and lipids.

● **Proteins** These form most of the structural materials in animals' bodies, and also make up the enzymes that control all biochemical activity in cells.

Proteins consist of chains of small molecules called amino acids. About 100 different amino acids exist in nature, but the proteins in animals' bodies are made out of just 20 types. Amino acids are classified as essential or non-essential. Non-essential amino acids can be synthesised from other proteins, but essential amino acids cannot, and must therefore be obtained through food.

Enzymes are specialised proteins made from between 100 and 1000 amino acids. The chain of amino acids in an enzyme folds into a unique shape which allows it to catalyse (speed up) a specific chemical reaction.

Every change that takes place inside every living cell is facilitated by enzymes. There are thousands of different types. A single-celled bacterium, for example, has about 1000 different enzymes floating around in its cytoplasm.

● **Carbohydrates** The principal role of carbohydrates in living organisms is the supply of energy. However, one type – cellulose – forms the cell walls of plants and is their main structural material.

All carbohydrate molecules are made up of carbon, hydrogen and oxygen atoms. Generally speaking, they contain twice as many hydrogen atoms as they do carbon or oxygen atoms.

Carbohydrates fall into three main groups: monosaccharides, disaccharides and polysaccharides.

Monosaccharides are simple sugars with up to ten carbon atoms in each molecule. Examples include glucose, which is involved in energy release in cells (see below).

Disaccharides, such as sucrose (cane sugar), consist of two monosaccharide molecules joined together. They must be broken down into monosaccharides before cells can release their energy.

Polysaccharides are also known as complex carbohydrates, and are made up of many monosaccharides joined together. The most important polysaccharides are starch and cellulose. Starch is the main food storage material of plants.

● **Lipids** Contain carbon, hydrogen and oxygen but have far fewer oxygen atoms than carbohydrates do. Lipids include fats, oils, waxes, phospholipids (which form cell membranes) and steroids (which include some hormones and other important substances). Lipids dissolve poorly in water, but store more than twice as much energy per gram as carbohydrates. Fats are animals' main energy storage materials.

ENERGY FROM RESPIRATION

Through the biochemical process known as respiration (not to be confused with breathing), cells combine oxygen with glucose to produce carbon dioxide, water and energy. The energy produced drives all life-sustaining processes.

$$C_6H_{12}O_6 + 6O_2 \rightarrow 6CO_2 + 6H_2O + energy$$

glucose + oxygen $\rightarrow$ carbon dioxide + water + energy

Respiration occurs in all living things. Where oxygen is available, it is an extremely efficient process, releasing 37 per cent of the total energy in glucose for use by the organism. Where oxygen is not available, respiration becomes less efficient. It may still occur in a simplified form, however, with glucose being split to produce two molecules of lactic or pyruvic acid.

Tissues (below) consist of groups of cells with a specific function.

The cell (left) is the basic unit that can display all the functions of a living thing – although that does not necessarily mean that it can survive on its own.

An organ (such as a leaf) is a functional unit made up of various tissues.

Dead cells and cell products

A living organism does not consist solely of living cells. Cells are constantly dying (and mostly being replaced as they do so) but many dead cells form important structures in their own right. An animal's skin, hair, feathers, scales, nails and claws are all formed from dead cells. So is the protective bark of a tree and the woody material of its trunk and branches (only the thin cambium layer beneath the bark is alive; see page 76). Many other important biological materials, including bone and shell, are inert matter secreted by the organism's cells.

Oak tree An entire organism may have many organs and specialised tissues, and consist of trillions of cells. Alternatively, it may be just one cell, as in the case of most microorganisms.

see also

74-5 **How plants live**

542-3 **The processes of life**

546-7 **Inherited characteristics**

The appearance of organisms is determined by their genes, which are passed down to them from their parents. The rules that govern this process were established in the second half of the 19th century and found to apply to all living things. This discovery marked the birth of a new discipline, genetics, which today is the fastest-growing branch of the biological sciences.

HOW TRAITS ARE PASSED ON

For thousands of years, farmers have encouraged desirable attributes in plants and animals by selective breeding. Yet it was a rather hit-and-miss process, since no one understood the mechanisms that govern heredity. Gregor Mendel (1822–84) was the first person to work out how characteristics are passed on from one generation to the next, from a series of experiments on peas in the 1860s.

Mendel wondered why peas have either purple flowers or white flowers, never shades in between. He noticed that when he crossed a pure-bred strain of purple-flowered peas with a white-flowered strain, the offspring (known as the f1 generation) always had purple flowers. But if he went on to fertilise one of the f1 plants with pollen from another, the second-generation (f2) offspring had some white-flowered plants and some purple, in a ratio of 1:3.

Mendel's peas This diagram shows the stages in Mendel's experiments in cross-breeding pea plants (see story above). Dominant forms of genes (alleles) are traditionally annotated with a capital letter, recessive ones with a letter in lower case. Here, the dominant allele is that for purple flowers (P) and the recessive one that for white flowers (w).

From these results he worked out that the inheritance of each characteristic is determined by paired factors (now called genes). Although an individual may inherit two different forms (alleles) of a gene – one from each parent – for a trait, only one of the forms will be expressed. Yet both can be passed on to the next generation.

The explanation is that some alleles are dominant – that is, they cause a visible characteristic even if another, so-called recessive, allele is also present. The f1 pea plants each carried a dominant allele for purple flowers (called P) and a recessive allele for white flowers (w); their genotype (genetic pattern) was Pw (see below). In the f2 generation, when Pw peas were self-pollinated, the result was peas with genotypes PP, Pw, wP and ww. Only the pea plants with two recessive alleles (ww) had white flowers; the rest were purple.

Mendel also crossed plants with yellow and green seeds, and ones with wrinkled and smooth seeds. He found that these characteristics follow the same rules. However, it is now known that some features (such as people's hair colour) are governed by a number of genes, and the pattern of heredity is not so clear-cut.

WHAT MAKES AN INDIVIDUAL?

Every cell in a living organism contains enough information to make a complete copy of that organism. The information is stored inside the nucleus of the cell in its chromosomes.

Chromosomes occur in pairs, usually of the same size and shape. In each pair, one chromosome came originally from the male parent, the other from the female. This fact is what makes people look similar to their parents but not exactly like either of them. Different organisms have different numbers of chromosomes in each cell. For example, humans have 23 pairs of chromosomes, chickens 18 pairs, peas seven pairs and fruit flies only four pairs.

Chromosomes are made up primarily of DNA (see pages 150-1), which is itself a combination of four chemical units called bases. Genes, which govern bodily characteristics, correspond to specific sections of the DNA – specific sequences of the bases. They are like instructions written in a four-letter chemical 'alphabet'. The genes in chromosomes are mixed up whenever new eggs or sperm are created (see opposite) and this is the reason that every one of us looks unique – except, of course, identical twins (see pages 150-1).

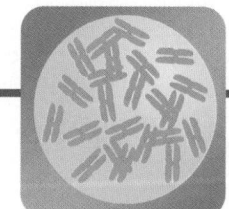

Male or female?

The gender of an organism is determined by its sex chromosomes. In most species there are two types of sex chromosome, X and Y. Females have two X chromosomes in each of their body cells, while the cells of males have an X and a Y. (In some insects, males have just one X and no Y; they are referred to as 'XO'.)

All eggs contain a single X chromosome (see How sex cells divide, opposite) while half a male's sperm carry an X chromosome and half a Y (or no sex chromosome at all in an XO insect). If an 'X' sperm fertilises an egg, the result is 'XX' – a female offspring. If a 'Y' (or 'O') sperm fertilises it, the result is 'XY' (or 'XO') – a male.

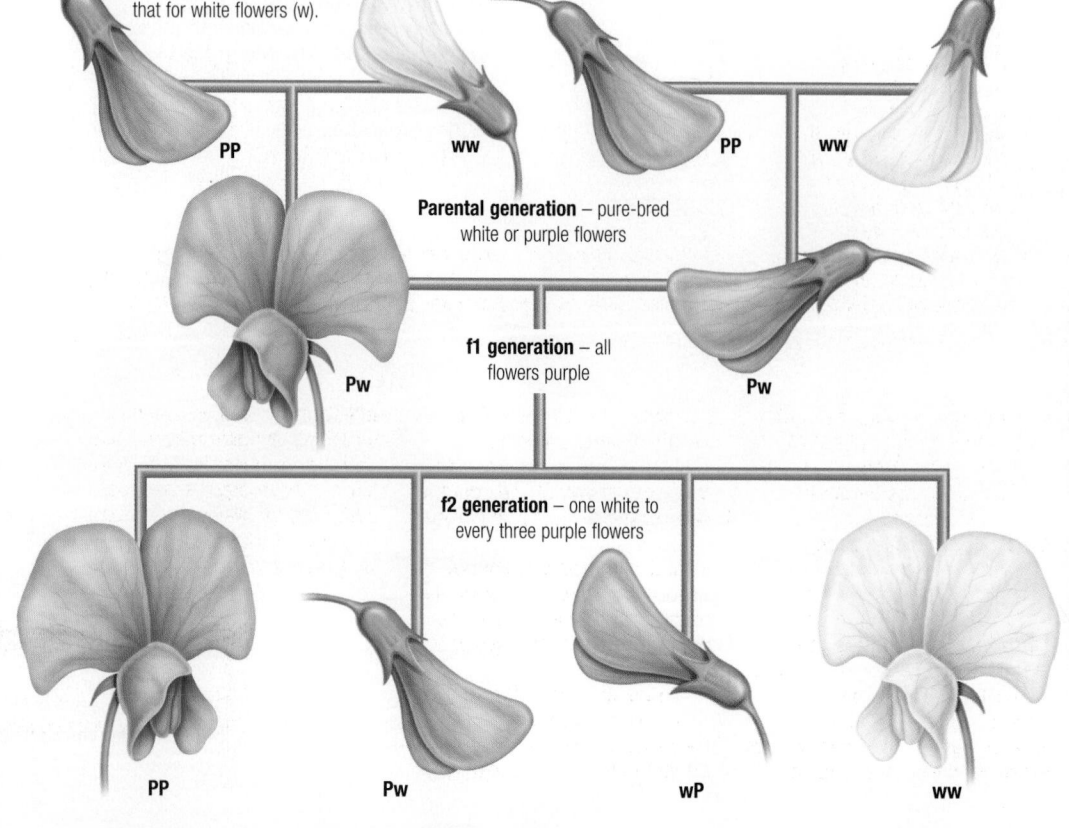

PP   ww   PP   ww

Parental generation – pure-bred white or purple flowers

f1 generation – all flowers purple

Pw   Pw

f2 generation – one white to every three purple flowers

PP   Pw   wP   ww

HOW CELLS DIVIDE FOR GROWTH

Growth involves an increase in the number of cells in an organism. The process by which cells divide to form new cells during growth is called mitosis. The parent cell divides into two daughter cells that are identical to each other and to the parent cell in every respect – including the number of chromosomes in the nucleus. In fact, every nonsex cell in an organism carries an identical genetic 'blueprint'. The nucleus always divides before the rest of the cell, after passing through a series of changes:

1 Just before cell division, the chromosomes in the nucleus get shorter and fatter, and can be seen with a microscope.

2 Each chromosome makes a copy of itself. The original chromosome and its copy are joined near the middle.

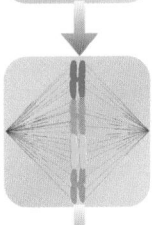

3 The joined chromosome copies arrange themselves near the centre of the cell. A structure called a spindle forms, with fibres spanning the length of the cell. The chromosome copies attach themselves to the spindle; it contracts, pulling the originals and copies to opposite ends of the cell.

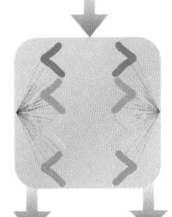

4 A new nuclear membrane begins to form around the two groups of chromosomes. A new cell membrane – known as the cell plate (not shown) – begins to form across the middle of the cell.

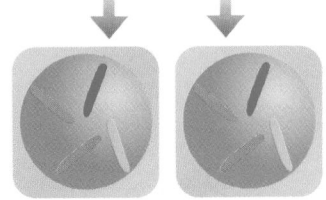

5 The cell plate eventually cuts the cell entirely in half to form two new cells. Once this has happened, the chromosomes begin to uncoil, becoming long and slender again until eventually they can no longer be seen.

The new cells are identical to each other and to the parent cell. The whole process of mitosis takes from about 15-20 minutes in bacteria to 18-20 hours in most animal and plant cells. The cells now grow to full size before dividing again.

HOW SEX CELLS DIVIDE

Genes are passed from parents to their offspring through their sex cells or gametes – sperm and eggs. These specialised cells contain only half the normal number of chromosomes, but they carry an assortment of characteristics inherited from the previous generation. They are produced by a special type of cell division called meiosis, which takes place in humans in the ovaries or testes.

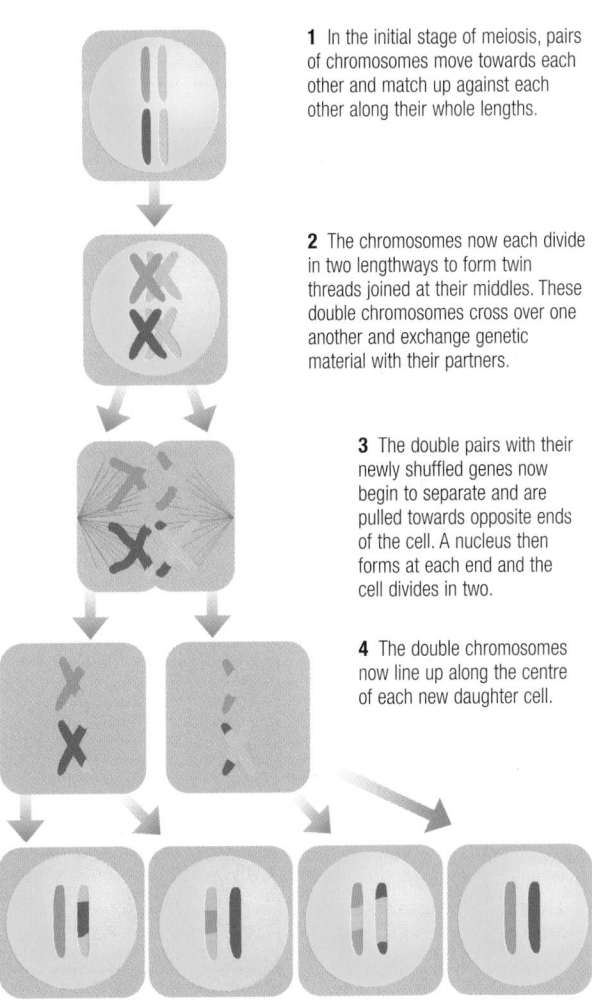

1 In the initial stage of meiosis, pairs of chromosomes move towards each other and match up against each other along their whole lengths.

2 The chromosomes now each divide in two lengthways to form twin threads joined at their middles. These double chromosomes cross over one another and exchange genetic material with their partners.

3 The double pairs with their newly shuffled genes now begin to separate and are pulled towards opposite ends of the cell. A nucleus then forms at each end and the cell divides in two.

4 The double chromosomes now line up along the centre of each new daughter cell.

5 Finally these double chromosomes separate and each daughter cell again divides in two, as in mitosis. This results in four daughter cells, each with half the number of chromosomes, with some genetic material from each original parent.

Key terms in genetics

Allele One of two or more alternative forms of a gene.
Base One of the chemical building blocks that make up DNA (see page 151).
Dominance An allele is said to be dominant with respect to an alternative allele if – when both alleles are present in an organism – the physical trait it encodes for is expressed and that which the other allele encodes for is not.

Genes The genetic material that determines all inherited characteristics. Genes operate by controlling the structure of particular proteins.
Genome The sequence of bases in all of the DNA, including the genes, of an organism's chromosomes.
Heterozygote An organism that received unlike alleles for a particular characteristic from each of its two parents.
Homozygote An organism that received similar alleles for a

particular characteristic from both of its two parents.
Meiosis The process of cell division that creates sex cells, in which the chromosome number is halved.
Mitosis The process of cell division for growth, in which the daughter cells have the same number of chromosomes as the parent cell.
Phenotype The visible effects of the expression of a gene.
Recessive An allele is said to be recessive if it produces an

effect only in individuals that inherit similar alleles from both parents. A recessive allele is not expressed in organisms that inherit unlike alleles from their two parents, but can be passed on to future generations.

see also

150-1 **Cells and DNA**
542-3 **Processes of life**
544-5 **Structure of living things**

The archaeologist's job is to piece together knowledge about vanished cultures from the material objects left behind – from buildings and boats to tools, clothes, weapons and household items. Many different sciences are involved in finding, interpreting and dating remains, and new techniques and technologies are continually advancing the discipline.

Archaeologists at work

Work on an archaeological site happens in a series of stages. First, the area is identified and surveyed. Then excavation begins. Buildings, temples and tombs are uncovered and their contents revealed. Finally, individual objects are taken away and analysed in detail. These two pages take you through the process at one of the great finds of recent times – the pyramids of Sipán in Peru, where excavations began in 1987.

1 Locating the site The pyramids of Sipán (above) were well known as an ancient site but remained unexcavated until recently. In 1987 looters found a royal tomb full of treasures from the 1st to 3rd century AD Moche civilisation. An informer told the police and as news leaked out excavations were hastily begun to protect the site from further raids.

2 Doing a survey A contour map of Sipán (above) helped to create a picture of how the site looked in ancient times. This was the start of the next stage of discovery – the survey. Surveying involves drawing an outline map, noting any relevant surrounding features such as rivers or ancient roads. A grid is placed on the map to enable points to be precisely located and finds accurately recorded. After the survey any artefacts on the surface of the site are recorded and removed so that excavation can begin.

3 Excavating the site Excavation is an extremely slow process – it took several years at Sipán. The exact location and nature of each item has to be recorded before it is removed for further analysis. Tiny fragments of, say, pottery may be recovered only by filtering soil through a sieve. The soil itself may be subjected to microscopic analysis. Tools range from a simple paintbrush, used to remove soil around the most delicate artefacts, to a mechanical digger for removing topsoil and cutting sections through a site.

Dating by tree rings

The science of dating wood from patterns of tree growth, known as dendrochronology, can often help archaeologists to determine the age of the site they are working on. Each year that a tree grows it adds a new ring to its girth. The thickness of the ring is determined by environmental conditions such as temperature and rainfall. Over time, patterns are formed among the rings that are common to all the trees of the same species in the same area. The rings can be counted to show the age of the tree at death; the pattern of the rings can also be compared with those of other trees of the same species to find out when the tree died.

To date an object made from a tree – a ship's mast, for instance – the pattern of rings is compared with those of wood from similar trees whose year of death is known, in order to search for matching growth patterns. By matching the patterns, it is possible to calculate the year in which the tree died or was cut down.

Because the growth rings and their patterns vary according to environmental conditions, wood can be used to date natural events such as droughts or glaciation, as well as man-made artefacts. Certain tree species are particularly useful to dendrochronologists because of their longevity. The American bristlecone pine, for example, lives for over 4500 years and can give clues to conditions long before recorded history.

Measuring decay

Radiocarbon dating
Radiocarbon dating (also known as carbon dating) has been used to date specimens as old as 35 000 years.

It is based on the principle that throughout life all living matter absorbs a radioactive form of carbon known as carbon-14. When a plant or animal dies it stops absorbing carbon-14 and the carbon-14 it contains gradually decays to form nitrogen-14.

Scientists can detect the presence of carbon-14 and know the rate at which it decays. They can measure the level of carbon-14 in the remains of a once-living object, say in the wooden mast of a ship. This can be compared with the carbon-14 in a living tree, revealing how long ago the tree died and giving a clue to the age of the mast.

Luminescence dating
For specimens that are more than 40 000 years old, archaeologists may resort to such techniques as luminescence dating. This can be used for specimens that contain minerals, such as quartz.

◖ As a result of exposure to natural radiation, in the form of heat or light, the mineral acquires a degree of latent 'luminescence'.

◖ When scientists re-expose an artefact containing minerals to heat or light, this luminescence is released and can be measured using a device known as a photomultiplier tube.

◖ From the amount of luminescence released, it is possible to work out when the object was last exposed to heat or light, and to estimate its approximate age.

Royal tomb, Sipán An artist's impression shows how this royal figure would have looked when buried. His ear ornaments were of gold and turquoise.

4 Analysis Special skills come into their own at this stage. A physical anthropologist examined a Sipán skeleton and was able to tell that the man had probably suffered from arthritis but since his teeth were in good condition, it is likely he had a healthy diet. He was between 35 and 45 when he died – a decent age for a Moche. Many complex techniques are used for such analysis, including powerful DNA testing. A procedure called the polymerase chain reaction (PCR) is carried out on tissue samples. This can amplify even the tiniest trace of DNA, helping to reveal details such as genetic defects and the cause of death.

FACT Clues from Homer's epic poem the *Iliad* helped Heinrich Schliemann to find the lost city of Troy in 1870.

Faithful unto death At the feet of the main figure the archaeologists found the coffin of a child, buried with his pet dog.

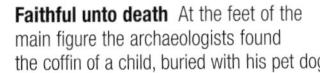
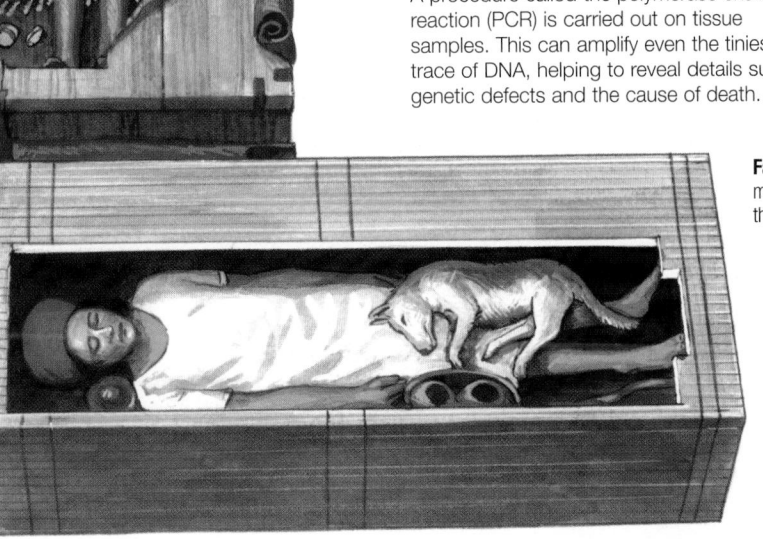

Great constructions such as Stonehenge and the pyramids of Egypt have always aroused wonder, speculation and myth-making. Only since the development of archaeology in the 19th century, however, have relics of the past been scientifically investigated. Allowed to speak for themselves, they give us vital clues to otherwise impenetrable worlds.

Archaeological sites of the world

Across the world a number of archaeological sites have played a key role in piecing together the history of different civilisations. Some have even rewritten history – like L'Anse-aux-Meadows in Newfoundland, Canada, which showed that the Vikings made the perilous sea journey to the Americas long before the Spanish conquistadors. This map shows 20 of the historically most important sites around the world.

Pioneer with a passion for Greece

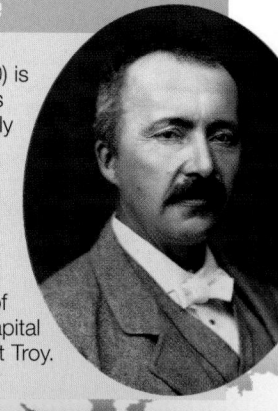

The German Heinrich Schliemann (1822–90) is often called the father of archaeology for his pioneering field work. His method of carefully preserving everything he discovered and accurately recording its position in the excavation became a basic principle of archaeology. He was also one of the first to value everyday objects as much as grand monuments. Fascinated since childhood by Greek legends, Schliemann found the site of Troy (in modern Turkey) and of Mycenae, capital of Agamemnon, who led the Greeks against Troy.

Self-taught scholar
Born into a poor family, Schliemann left school and went to work at 14. He made a fortune in business and retired at 41 to take up archaeology.

L'Anse-aux-Meadows **1**

2 Chaco Canyon

8 Hallstatt

9 Pompeii

Troy **11** **16** Çatal Hüyük

Knossos **12**

Alexandria **10** **15** **17** Babylon

Giza **13** Jericho

Valley of the Kings **14**

3 Teotihuacán

4 Tikal

Mayan warrior Images such as that on this plate from Tikal are a key source of visual information.

Face of history
French archaeologist Franck Goddio surveys a submerged sphinx at Alexandria.

7 Olduvai Gorge

Striking gold
Howard Carter found Tutankhamun's tomb sealed and intact. Hidden by rubble from a later tomb, it was never plundered.

5 Machu Picchu

6 Great Zimbabwe

The man who discovered Tutankhamun

In 1922, after more than 20 years of excavating, the British Egyptologist Howard Carter (1873–1939), with his patron the Earl of Carnarvon, unearthed the richest tomb ever found in the Valley of the Kings. It belonged to the boy-pharaoh Tutankhamun, who died c.1325 BC aged just 18. When the dazzling find was displayed in London in 1972 it attracted a record turnout of 1.7 million visitors.

1 L'Anse-aux-Meadows, Canada
Viking settlement
c.AD 1000
Norwegians Helge and Anne Ingstad excavated the site in the 1960s. It provides firm evidence that the Vikings sailed to North America long before Columbus in 1492.

2 Chaco Canyon, USA
Centre of Anasazi culture
c.100 BC–*c*.AD 1150
Multistorey communal houses, ceremonial chambers, pottery and trading goods show the sophistication of prehistoric Pueblo cultures.

3 Teotihuacán, Mexico
Mesoamerican city
c.AD 500–*c*.800
Excavations began in the late 19th century of this vast city, revealing such remarkable structures as the Pyramid of the Sun, the world's third-tallest pyramid at 75 m (246 ft).

19 Xian

aro

4 Tikal, Guatemala
Mayan city
AD 250–900
This once small village became the largest city of the Mayan Classic era. At its heart were funerary pyramids and a Great Plaza used for ceremonies.

5 Machu Picchu, Peru
Inca settlement
c.AD 1450
The complex of temples, baths and residences high in the Andes may have been a town or royal retreat. Abandoned after the Spanish Conquest, it was discovered in 1911 by Hiram Bingham.

6 Great Zimbabwe, Zimbabwe
Iron Age site
c.AD 300–*c*.1450
The site is a complex of Iron Age and later structures. The outer granite wall of the central Great Enclosure originally stood 9.8 m (32 ft) high and 244 m (800 ft) long.

7 Olduvai Gorge, Tanzania
Hominid fossils
c.2–3 million years old
In the 1930s Louis Leakey unearthed animal fossils and crude stone tools; in 1959 with his wife Mary he uncovered a fossil hominid *c*.1.75 million years old. These finds, and Mary's discovery of an even earlier footprint, located East Africa as the site of human evolution.

8 Hallstatt, Austria
Celtic mines and burial site
9th–5th centuries BC
The Bronze and Iron Age site was discovered by accident in 1846. Its treasury of human bones, clothing and tools was of such importance that phases of Celtic culture became known as Hallstatt A, B, C and D.

9 Pompeii, Italy
Roman town
AD 79
People and animals were found in 1748, buried in lava and ash from the sudden eruption of Mount Vesuvius in 79. The remains gave a vivid picture of daily life in a small Roman town.

10 Alexandria, Egypt
Graeco-Roman city
Founded 332 BC
A fifth of this great city had sunk into the sea by the 8th century AD. A statue of Cleopatra's son Caesarion was among the treasures recovered when the ruins were located in 1998.

11 Troy, Turkey
Ruined city
c.3000 BC–*c*.AD 300
Troy was built and rebuilt several times. The city besieged by the Greeks was probably the set of remains labelled Troy VIIa, which were destroyed around 1200 BC.

12 Knossos, Crete
Minoan city
c.3000–*c*.1400 BC
The thriving hub of the Minoan culture during the Bronze Age was mysteriously destroyed by fire. The fine palace has been extensively restored.

13 Giza, Egypt
Pyramids
c.2610–*c*.2495 BC
The three Great Pyramids at Giza – Khufu, Khafre and Menkaure – constitute one of the Seven Wonders of the World. The second pyramid was thought to be solid until excavations in 1818 revealed Pharaoh Khafre's burial chamber.

14 Valley of the Kings, Egypt
Royal burial site
16th–13th centuries BC
Since excavation started in 1919 this site has yielded more than 60 royal tombs, many with fine reliefs and decoration. New finds are still being made.

15 Jericho, Jordan Valley
Town
c.10 000 BC onwards
Probably the world's oldest-known settlement, Jericho has been continuously occupied since the times of the Natufian people. The Canaanite town was captured by the Israelites under Joshua *c*.1300 BC.

16 Çatal Hüyük, Turkey
Neolithic town
c.7000–*c*.5600 BC
Excavations in the 1960s by British archaeologist James Mellaart revealed the remains of a large Neolithic farming community. The site is one of the earliest from this period and has provided much valuable evidence about farming techniques in ancient times.

17 Babylon, Iraq
Ruined capital of Mesopotamia
2nd–1st millennium BC
Babylon was excavated by a German team in the early 20th century. The remains show a high point under Nebuchadnezzar in the 6th century BC, when the outer walls were about 18 km (11 miles) long.

18 Mohenjo-daro, Pakistan
Indus city
c.2500–*c*.1800 BC
In the 1920s excavations revealed what had once been a great city of the Indus, or Harappan, civilisation, measuring 5 km (3 miles) in circumference. Since the Indus script has never been deciphered, archaeology offers the only clues to this rich culture.

19 Xian, China
Tomb of Emperor Qin Shi Huangdi
c.215 BC
In 1974 peasants found an army of 6000 life-size terracotta warriors along with chariots and horses. The site turned out to be the grave of the emperor Shi Huangdi, founder of the Qin dynasty.

20 Lake Mungo, Australia
Aboriginal burial ground
c.30 000 years old
Lake Mungo, in New South Wales, has been dry for 15 000 years, but Aborigines once fished and hunted there. The discovery in 1969 of 30 000-year-old human bones at the lake pushed back the known date of Aboriginal occupation of Australia; since then, new evidence has established even earlier dates.

20 Lake Mungo

Underwater archaeology

Investigating sunken sites is a highly specialised branch of archaeology. Sophisticated tools are used, such as underwater robots, seabed metal detectors and side-scan sonar which builds up images of submerged objects from reflected sound waves.

The seabed can yield treasures every bit as exciting as the land: in 2000, French and Egyptian archaeologists discovered the underwater remains of Heracleion, an important port that once stood at the mouth of the Nile. Their finds included well-preserved statues, bronze vessels, gold coins and jewellery. Wrecked ships, of course, account for many underwater finds: divers found some 18 000 different objects aboard a single ship that sank in about 1300 BC off Turkey.

Raising a ship is a spectacular, if tricky, feat. Henry VIII's flagship, the *Mary Rose*, which sank in 1545, was located in 1971 using side-scan sonar. After 11 years of research, engineers devised a giant floating crane to hoist it in a vast cradle from the seabed.

Raising the *Mary Rose* A diving archaeologist working on the *Mary Rose* painted this scene of the historic wreck lying on the seabed.

see also
166-7 **The prehistoric world**
168-9 **Dawn of history**
548-9 **Archaeology**

The 70 years between 1850 and 1920 saw a revolution in devices for helping to make home life and some of its associated chores less tedious and more hygienic. Some inventions, such as the automatic washing machine, were electrically powered versions of older, hand-cranked models, while other inventions were brand-new household tools, from the toaster and vacuum cleaner to the food processor and refrigerator.

Mechanical clothes washer

In 1858, American inventor Hamilton Smith patented a hand-cranked mechanical washing machine – a wooden drum fitted with a dolly (a set of paddles fixed to a long handle). The drum had to be filled and emptied by hand. Automatic machines were not possible until hot and cold running water and domestic electricity became widely available in the early 20th century.

Sewing machine

Massachusetts factory worker Elias Howe provoked little public interest when he patented a hand-powered sewing machine in 1846. In 1851, while Howe searched for backers in England, another American, Isaac Singer, produced a foot-powered machine which violated the patent. Howe took legal action, re-established his patent in 1854, and began receiving royalties, but Singer's version became the earliest mass-produced domestic appliance.

Hand power
Hamilton Smith's mechanical washer did little to alleviate the physical effort involved in washing.

1870   **1876** Telephone

1860

1880 **1882** Electric iron

1850   **1888** Record player

1877 Phonograph   1890

1880
Food mincer,
perforated
toilet paper

Electric light

In 1878, British physicist Joseph Swan passed an electric current through a carbon filament sealed inside a glass tube, creating the first electric light, which burned for a few hours. Thomas Edison based his longer-lasting bulb of 1879 on Swan's idea.

1851 Gas oven

1889
Electric
oven

The world's most prolific inventor

When Ohio-born Thomas Alva Edison left school in 1859, the few electrical devices in existence ran on low-powered batteries. By the time of his death in 1931, as a result of his inventive genius and entrepreneurship, a network of generators and power cables supplied the electricity demands of every large city in the United States.

Edison's work as an inventor began in earnest in 1876, when he set up the world's first commercial laboratory in Menlo Park, New Jersey. During a lifetime of work on electricity and communications he took out patents on a record-breaking 1093 inventions, including:

1870 A high-speed stock ticker – a machine which recorded transactions at the stock exchange in Wall Street.

1872 The electric typewriter.
1874 The quadruplex telegraph, which sent four messages along a single telegraph line, simultaneously.
1877 The tinfoil phonograph, which reproduced sound using a stylus and foil cylinder.
1878 The carbon transmitter, for telephones and microphones.
1879 An electric light bulb with a carbon filament. Durability was increased by improving the vacuum inside the bulb.
1880 An electric tramway.
1891 The 'Kinetoscope', which projected the first moving pictures from celluloid film.
1900 The nickel-alkaline battery.

Artificial light
The carbon filament of Edison's early light bulb was replaced by the tungsten filament in 1911.

Ball and chain The 'Valveless water waste preventer', a design often credited to Englishman Thomas Crapper, was first patented by Albert Giblin.

Valveless water cistern

A toilet flushed by water from a cistern, invented by Thomas Brightfield, was first used in London in 1449. In 1775, Englishman Alexander Cummings introduced the S-bend pipe, which trapped water in the closet and reduced unpleasant smells. A domestic flush toilet remained impractical until the widespread installation of public sewerage in the 19th century. Thomas Twyford designed the first one-piece china toilet in 1885.

Vacuum flask
In 1892, Scottish physicist James Dewar developed a way of keeping liquid gases at low temperatures while in storage. He created a vacuum within the double walls of a glass bottle, which reduced heat transference to a minimum. The German Reinhold Burger marketed the technique for domestic use in 1902 as the Thermos flask.

Cold store The Kelvinator corporation produced some of the earliest electric refrigerators, such as this 1926 model.

Dewar flask James Dewar devised this flask to store liquid oxygen and nitrogen for experiments.

Refrigerator
German engineer Karl von Linde developed the first domestic refrigerator in 1879. His device used a steam pump to circulate ammonia, a coolant used in industrial refrigeration since the late 1850s. In 1923, Swedish engineers Carl Munters and Balzer von Platen created the first electric refrigerator, the Electrolux, using a motor instead of a steam pump. In the same decade, scientists developed synthetic refrigerants such as Freon to replace the toxic ammonia.

Formica
Americans Daniel O'Conor and Herbert Faber patented Formica as an insulation material for electric wiring in 1913. In the mid 1920s, they marketed it as a furniture laminate. The wipe-clean, heatproof qualities of Formica made it a popular material for cabinet surfaces in the new fitted kitchens of the following decade.

Food processors
The earliest electric whisk, produced in the USA in 1910, was low powered and unreliable. In 1919, Troy Metal Products launched the KitchenAid, the first mixer with a stand and bowl. In 1950, the Kenwood Chef appeared in Britain, with multiple attachments enabling everything from whisking to can-opening.

Vacuum cleaner
The first vacuum cleaner, operated from the street via a long hose, was invented in England in 1901 by Hubert Cecil Booth. Six years later American businessman William Hoover developed a lightweight, upright version for ease of use inside the home.

BABY DAISY VACUUM CLEANER

No 4

1890

1893 Spring-loaded clothes peg

1899 Electric hairdryer

1900

1900 Brownie box camera

1902 Air conditioning unit, espresso machine

1907 Electric washing machine

1909 Tumble dryer

1910

1913 Brillo pads

1915 Pyrex dishes

Toaster
The electric toaster has changed little since its introduction by the Essex-based Crompton company in 1893. Crompton's device – 'The Eclipse' – toasted bread one side at a time. The spring-loaded mechanism that ejects toasted bread originated in Minnesota, USA, in 1927. Three years later, thermostatic controls were added to trigger the spring when the toast was ready.

OXYGEN WASHING COMPOUND
Persil
REGISTERED
THE MODERN IDEAL WASHER
JOSEPH CROSFIELD & SONS LTD WARRINGTON

Washing powder
Babbitt's Best Soap, the earliest soap powder, went on sale in 1843. The arrival of the automatic washing machine in 1907 brought the first modern washing powder – Persil – produced by German company Henkel & Cie. The name of the powder came from its active ingredients, perborate and silicate, which release oxygen on contact with water, helping to lift dirt from clothes.

Suction sweeper With this pre-electric Baby Daisy cleaner, the person using it had to hand-pump the bellows that created the suction.

see also
554-5 **Everyday inventions**
556-7 **Telecommunications**
564-5 **Recorded sound**

In the 20th century, advances in electronics paved the way for the miniaturisation of items such as the radio and the introduction of the mobile phone. Man-made fibres and other synthetic products brought us nylon stockings, adhesive tape, nonstick cooking pans and magnetic tape for video recording.

Adhesive tape
Adhesive tape was a development of the waterproof Cellophane first produced by the DuPont company in 1927. This tape, adhesive only at the edges, was used in automobile spray-painting shops to guard windows and fittings. In 1934 fully coated adhesive tape became available and people started to use it in the home.

Can opener
It took nearly 130 years after the invention of the can for the can opener to come along in 1931. At first people had to open the cans with a hammer and chisel. Fixed openers appeared in the late 1850s and cutting wheels in the 1870s, but it was another 60 years before these developments were combined into a single device.

Microwave oven
During the Second World War, British physicists John Randall and Henry Boot were working on radar defences. There was anecdotal evidence that the microwaves generated by their radar system were killing birds. The microwaves were causing water molecules in the birds' bodies to rotate, which created friction, and the heat generated 'cooked' the birds. This is how all microwaved food is cooked and explains why an object without water molecules stays cool in a microwave oven. The microwave oven was patented in 1945, but did not feature in homes until the 1980s, when miniaturisation and economies of scale made it commercially viable.

ISBN 0-276-42434-4

9 780276 424342 >

Bar code
In 1949 American Bernard Silver and former fellow student Norman Woodland developed a code of thick and thin black stripes or bars. But it was not until the 1960s that two key advances – a laser beam to scan the bars and a microchip to process the information – made bar codes a practical possibility. The agreement by the US Department of Defense of an industry standard paved the way for the bar code to be widely adopted.

1921 Electric kettle

1922 Dishwasher

1920

1928 Television

1930

1934 Launderette

1935 Tape recorder

1938 Tupperware

1940

1948 Washing-up bowl

1950

1950 Rubber gloves

Portable valve radio
The first portable radio was portable in name only: it weighed about 4.5 kg (10 lb). It was designed by the American J. McWilliams Stone in 1922. At the time all radios were heavy, because of the large transformers needed to deliver the high voltages demanded by valve circuits. The small, lightweight, low-powered and more reliable transistor was invented in 1947, and by 1955 was being used in truly portable radios.

Big brown box Bulky valves and vacuum tubes meant bulky radios, even portable ones such as this Pye from 1929.

Nylon
Joseph Swan, the inventor of the light bulb, also developed the first man-made fibre in 1883. He was going to use it as a filament in his light bulb, but it proved unsuitable. Several other attempts were made to produce man-made fibres, but these met with little practical success. The American company DuPont produced the first successful synthetic fibre – nylon – in 1938. Originally used for toothbrush bristles, the new fibre was adapted for use in stockings in 1940. In the 1950s the principles involved in producing nylon were applied to make other synthetic materials, such as acrylic (1950), Dacron (1953) and Terylene (1954).

Alluring...Enduring...

Wolsey nylons

Seamed nylons Stretchable and yet tough, nylon was an ideal material for products ranging from bristles to stockings to parachutes.

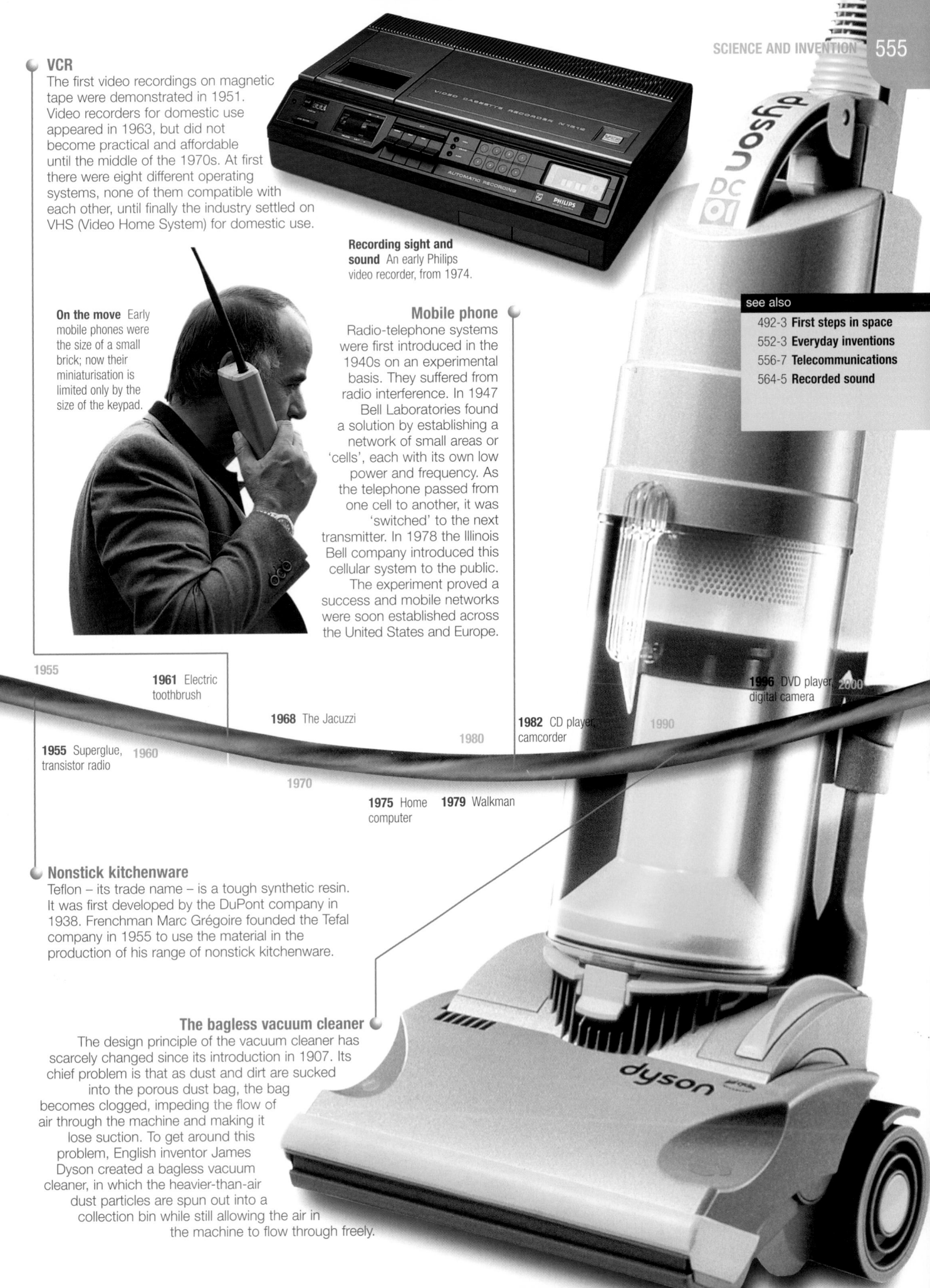

VCR

The first video recordings on magnetic tape were demonstrated in 1951. Video recorders for domestic use appeared in 1963, but did not become practical and affordable until the middle of the 1970s. At first there were eight different operating systems, none of them compatible with each other, until finally the industry settled on VHS (Video Home System) for domestic use.

Recording sight and sound An early Philips video recorder, from 1974.

On the move Early mobile phones were the size of a small brick; now their miniaturisation is limited only by the size of the keypad.

Mobile phone

Radio-telephone systems were first introduced in the 1940s on an experimental basis. They suffered from radio interference. In 1947 Bell Laboratories found a solution by establishing a network of small areas or 'cells', each with its own low power and frequency. As the telephone passed from one cell to another, it was 'switched' to the next transmitter. In 1978 the Illinois Bell company introduced this cellular system to the public. The experiment proved a success and mobile networks were soon established across the United States and Europe.

see also
492-3 **First steps in space**
552-3 **Everyday inventions**
556-7 **Telecommunications**
564-5 **Recorded sound**

1955
1961 Electric toothbrush
1968 The Jacuzzi
1980
1955 Superglue, transistor radio   1960
1970
1975 Home computer   **1979** Walkman
1982 CD player, camcorder   1990
1996 DVD player, digital camera   2000

Nonstick kitchenware

Teflon – its trade name – is a tough synthetic resin. It was first developed by the DuPont company in 1938. Frenchman Marc Grégoire founded the Tefal company in 1955 to use the material in the production of his range of nonstick kitchenware.

The bagless vacuum cleaner

The design principle of the vacuum cleaner has scarcely changed since its introduction in 1907. Its chief problem is that as dust and dirt are sucked into the porous dust bag, the bag becomes clogged, impeding the flow of air through the machine and making it lose suction. To get around this problem, English inventor James Dyson created a bagless vacuum cleaner, in which the heavier-than-air dust particles are spun out into a collection bin while still allowing the air in the machine to flow through freely.

Long-distance communication began in the 1840s, with telegraph messages sent by cable between cities, and later between continents. Then came telephones, which transmitted the human voice as a sound wave. Radio opened up 'wireless' communication, and microchips made instruments portable. With the advent of the modem it became possible to plug computers and other digital devices into a telephone line. New technologies cut costs and increased volume, but the demand for ever more communication continued to grow unabated.

1837 British scientists Charles Wheatstone and William Cooke patent an electromagnetic telegraph system.
1840 American inventor Samuel Morse patents his own electromagnetic telegraph.
1843 British clockmaker Alexander Bain invents a device for sending exact copies – the first facsimile (fax) machine.
1844 The first long-distance telegraph cable is laid, between Baltimore and Washington DC in the USA.

The first telegraph The message was converted into code on a strip of ticker tape.

● **Alexander Graham Bell** (1847–1922) Bell was a teacher of the deaf, and his work on the telephone grew out of attempts to create and transmit voice sounds electrically. He worked on his telephone apparatus with Thomas Watson in Boston, and the first words transmitted were, 'Mr Watson, come here – I want you.' Bell demonstrated his invention widely, and set up the Bell Telephone Company in 1877 to exploit it, but played little part in developing the business. Later in life he worked on other electrical inventions and for the welfare of the deaf.

Bell telephone, 1878 Queen Victoria used this instrument.

Exporting talent Bell was born in Scotland but moved to Canada for health reasons, and then to the USA. He did most of his work at Boston University where he was Professor of Vocal Physiology.

1830

1850–55 The first teleprinters are developed.
1861 In the United States, the Transcontinental Telegraph links California with Missouri and the east coast.
1866 The first permanent transatlantic telegraph cable links Ireland and Newfoundland.

1860

1869 American Thomas Edison invents the ticker-tape machine for transmitting Wall Street stock prices.
1872–6 Inventors including Thomas Edison devise systems for sending two, four, then five 'multiplexed' telegraph messages along one line simultaneously.

1870

1876 Scottish-born American inventor Alexander Graham Bell is granted the first patent for the electric telephone.
1878 Edison invents the carbon-granule telephone microphone, which gives much clearer speech.
1889 American Almon Strowger invents the automatic telephone exchange.
1895 Italian Guglielmo Marconi first demonstrates wireless (radio) telegraphy.

1900

1901 Marconi sends the first transatlantic wireless telegraph signal, from Cornwall to Newfoundland.
1902 German Arthur Korn invents the photoelectric scanning of images. By 1910 this is being used regularly to transmit newspaper pictures.
The first trans-pacific telegraph cable is laid between Canada and New Zealand.

Ordinary phone This sends and receives voice messages as analogue electrical signals.

Main exchange This routes calls as digital signals along various types of medium and long-distance cable or via radio links to other exchanges both in the same country and abroad.

THE TELEPHONE NETWORK

The telephone system was built to carry soundwaves – the human voice. Nowadays, fax machines, computers and mobile phones all link into the system, sending enormous quantities of data in digital form (as opposed to analogue – see page 562). To cope with the need for ever greater capacity most exchanges are now electronic and the links between them are generally digital, using fibre-optic, microwave and satellite technology. The weak point of the system is the connection to the user. For many businesses and homes the 'last mile' is still just a pair of copper wires – placing a severe limit on speed and capacity.

Fax machine A fax machine sends and receives signals via a modem that converts analogue signals into digital ones.

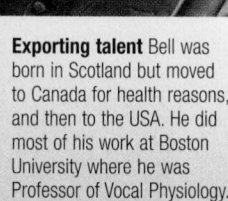

Digital phone Used in some offices, digital phones transmit digital signals directly to the exchange using an ISDN (Integrated Services Digital Network) link.

Local exchange The local exchange links local calls and converts analogue signals from ordinary phones into digital ones for long-distance transmission to a main exchange.

Biggest telephone users

Telephone mainlines Land lines per 100 people (1998)		Mobile phones Subscribers per 100 people (1998)	
1 Bermuda	84	1 Finland	57.1
2 Luxembourg	69.2	2 Hong Kong	47.5
3 Sweden	67.4	3 Norway	47.4
4 Switzerland	67.4	4 Sweden	46.4
5 United States	66.1	5 Japan	37.4
6 Denmark	66	6 Denmark	36.4
7 Norway	66	7 Israel	35.9
8 Iceland	64.7	8 Italy	35.7
9 Canada	63.5	9 Singapore	34.6
10 Netherlands	59.3	10 Iceland	33.1
11 France	57	11 United States	31.3
12 Germany	56.8	12 Portugal	30.9
13 Singapore	56.2	13 Luxembourg	30.8
14 Hong Kong	55.8	14 South Korea	30.2
15 United Kingdom	55.7	15 Australia	28.6

1960 The first communications satellite, Echo 1, is launched.
1962 PCM digital signals are used for the first time to make telephone transmissions.
1965 Early Bird (Intelsat 1) is the first geostationary commercial communications satellite. It can transmit 240 phone calls at any one time.

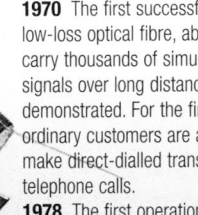

'Transportable' telephone, 1985 True portability did not come until the miniaturisation revolution of the 1990s.

1980s Cheap, compact and fast fax machines appear. They take off first in Japan, where pictographic writing makes telegraphy difficult.
1981 Europe's first cellular phone system is established in Scandinavia.
1988 The first transatlantic fibre-optic cable is laid. It can carry 40 000 simultaneous telephone calls.
1990s Digital cellular phone systems are introduced.
1999 Morse Code is abandoned for international signals with the growth of satellite communications.

1970 The first successful low-loss optical fibre, able to carry thousands of simultaneous signals over long distances, is demonstrated. For the first time, ordinary customers are able to make direct-dialled transatlantic telephone calls.
1978 The first operational cellular phone system is set up in Chicago.

1920s Glass rods suggested as a communications medium – the principle behind fibre optics.
1921 Detroit police introduce first two-way mobile radios.
1931 The first telex (public teleprinter) exchange is set up in London.

1947 Bell Laboratories devise a cellular mobile phone system.
1956 The first transatlantic telephone cable is laid.
1958 The modem is invented. Computers can communicate over telephone lines.

1920   1950   1960   1970   1980   2000

1937 American H.A. Reeves invents PCM (Pulse-Code Modulation), a radio wave that transmits in coded pulses as a way of sending signals digitally.

1958–9 The development of the first microchip leads to further miniaturisation, making digital communication possible.

Communications satellite Satellites relay signals where no cables exist (including to and from ships), or where cables are overloaded.

Network exchange This handles calls to and from subscribers' mobile cellphones.

Repeater This boosts signals at intervals along long-distance cables.

Terrestrial microwave link These are often used to link local and main exchanges. Dish aerials send and receive the microwave signals in a narrow beam along a line of sight.

Telephone

Fax machine

Telephone

Fibre-optic cable Many such cables cross land and sea, carrying thousands of simultaneous messages.

Telephone

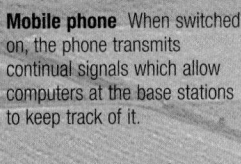

Mobile phone When switched on, the phone transmits continual signals which allow computers at the base stations to keep track of it.

How mobile phone networks work
Cellular networks divide the areas they cover into local 'cells', each with a transmitter-receiver base station. At the hub of every network is a network exchange, connected to the base stations by fibre-optic, microwave and other links.

As early as the 1830s there were machines – or plans for machines – that embodied many of the principles of modern computing. But their mechanism was too complex for 19th-century engineering, and the leap from theory to practice had to await the development of electronics – especially transistors and integrated circuits – over a century later.

Inventing the computer The first computer was Charles Babbage's design for an 'analytical engine' (see below). It was a true computer because it could be programmed not only to follow a series of logical steps, but also to take into account the results of previous steps in the program. Not until the Second World War, however, was it possible to build fully functioning electromechanical and finally electronic computers.

Electronic components work faster than mechanical ones and are relatively small. They can act as electronic switches, which represent the 0s and 1s of binary numbers, and be arranged in so-called logic circuits to carry out mathematical operations. Complex calculations, however, involve many such operations, and many components are needed. The first machines used valves that generated a lot of heat; these computers filled whole rooms and needed cooling. Transistors made smaller, more powerful computers possible. The final step was the integrated circuit that combined tiny components into a single unit and led to the development of the PC (personal computer).

Manchester's marvel The Mark 1 built at Manchester University achieved a record-breaking error-free run of nine hours on the night of June 16-17, 1949.

1642 French mathematician Blaise Pascal invents the first mechanical calculator.

1801 French engineer Joseph-Marie Jacquard builds a loom controlled by punched cards.

1888 The American Herman Hollerith invents a punched-card tabulating machine. His company becomes the International Business Machines (IBM) Corporation.

1943 'Colossus', a computer for breaking German codes, is built at Bletchley Park, England.

1946 ENIAC (Electronic Numerical Integrator and Computer) is unveiled at the University of Pennsylvania.

1947 John Bardeen, Walter H. Brattain and William B. Shockley invent the transistor while working at Bell Laboratories, USA.

1949 Manchester Mark I, the first stored-program computer, with random-access memory and magnetic drum storage, is built in Manchester.

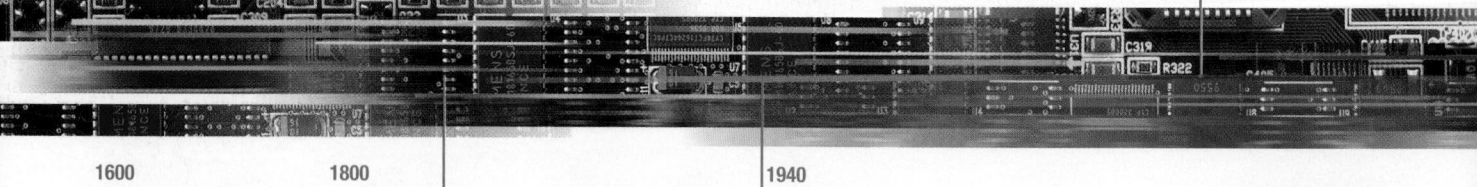

1600   1800   1940

Charles Babbage (1791–1871) English mathematician Charles Babbage designed calculating machines that contained many key elements of modern computers – but could not complete any of them. His 'difference engines' were intended to automate the calculation and printing of mathematical tables. His 'analytical engine' was designed to be programmed with punched cards to perform arithmetic operations in any order and even to follow programmed logic. It included separate 'mill' (processing) and 'store' (memory) units and other elements of modern computers. Babbage was hindered by engineering and financial problems, but London's Science Museum built a working difference engine in 1991.

Computing machine A section of the 'mill' (central processor) of Charles Babbage's 'analytical engine' was one of the few parts completed at the time of his death.

Alan Turing (1912–54) The British mathematician and logician Turing developed the logical processes by which computers operate. His paper *On Computable Numbers* (1937) described a theoretical 'universal machine' that could in principle carry out any calculation. Reading or scanning a tape, the machine would respond to sequential commands. Turing proved that this could, in theory, imitate logical human thought.

During the Second World War, Turing played an important part in cracking the German military 'Enigma' codes. He later contributed to the development of the Manchester Mark 1 and the Ferranti Mark 1. He was also a pioneer in artificial intelligence, predicting that computers would one day match human intelligence. His 'Turing test' was designed as an objective measure of what was to count as achieving this status.

Software: programming computers

Early computer programs were written in 'machine code' – a tedious and time-consuming process in which strings of binary numbers were generated to controll the mechanism directly. In 1952 the American scientist Grace Murray Hopper had the idea of writing programs in a higher-level, symbolic form, which would then be translated automatically into machine code. This was the start of the programming languages that revolutionised computing from the 1950s on. But programs still had to be custom-made for each computer and each new task; only with the arrival of program 'packages' – usable on a range of computers to handle standardised jobs such as accounting and word processing – did computers become simple enough for almost anyone to use.

Software pioneer Hopper was both a research scientist and a reserve naval officer.

The first personal computer The Altair 8800, from the New Mexico-based company MITS Inc, started the personal computer revolution. It was the first commercially available microcomputer, launched in kit form in 1975 for US$395. There was no software available for the machine, and users had to program it to perform calculations by flipping a row of switches; the output was read (in binary code) from a row of light-emitting diodes (LEDs). But now hobbyists could afford their own computer (at a time when commercial computers cost many thousands of dollars), and thousands bought one. Among them was the Harvard student Bill Gates, who saw an opportunity and wrote a version of the BASIC programming language for the 8800, making the machine much easier to program and launching a new software industry.

All in a box The Altair 8800 had no keyboard, no video screen, no tape or disk drive, and no more than 256 bytes of memory.

1951 The Ferranti Mark 1, the first commercially produced computer, is launched. Eight are eventually sold.

1958 Americans Jack Kilby of Texas Instruments and Robert Noyce of Fairchild make integrated circuits by placing two transistors on a single piece of silicon.

1958 The 'second generation' of computers, using transistors instead of valves, are produced. Computers start to become tools of business, not just of governments and universities.

1963 DEC (Digital Equipment Corporation) introduces the first minicomputer.

1964 BASIC (Beginner's All-purpose Symbolic Instruction Code) is invented, making programming easier.

1968 Alan Shugart of IBM launches the 8 in (20 cm) floppy magnetic disk.

1968 Doug Engelbart demonstrates the use of a computer mouse for the first time.

1969 Gary Starkweather of Xerox invents the laser printer.

1970 First computers using integrated circuit control chips are produced.

1971 Ted Hoff of Intel develops the first microprocessor – 'a computer on a chip' – the 4004.

1973 IBM launches the first hard disk drive.

1974 IBM produces the first super-fast computer, using parallel processing.

1979 The VisiCalc spreadsheet – the first major PC business program – is launched.

1980 Microsoft licenses QDOS from Seattle Computer Products, adapts it, and wins the contract to supply the operating system for IBM's new PC.

1980 The first miniature 5.25 in 'Winchester' hard-disk drive is launched.

1981 IBM introduces its first personal computer.

1950   1960   1970   1980

The transistor

Computers work by controlling the flow of electrical current so that it is sometimes on and sometimes off. At first they did this by means of valves, and were huge, costly, unreliable and power-hungry. After the Second World War transistors were developed. Their small size, reliability, low power needs and ability to function as an amplifier, oscillator and electronic switch were ideal in a wide range of electronic applications – but particularly computers, which use mainly the switching function. Integrated circuits (see page 561) with millions of tiny transistors have now largely replaced individual components.

Breakthrough The first transistor was developed in 1947 and stood 10 cm (4 in) high. Their modern descendants are far too small to be seen with the naked eye.

Steve Jobs (1955–)
Steve Wozniak (1950–)
Apple Computers' joint founders were Wozniak, an engineer, and Jobs, who had worked on video games and had a passion for technology. They built their first computer in the Jobs family garage in 1976. They sold 600 of this first Apple, then in 1977 launched the Apple II – a huge success thanks partly to its built-in colour graphics software. It appealed to businesses and schools alike, and for five years was the world's best-selling computer. In 1984, the Apple Macintosh was the first successful graphical computer (see *The gooey revolution*, page 560). However, management clashes led to both founders leaving the company in 1985. Jobs founded a new company, NeXT, but returned to lead Apple in 1997.

Apple growers Schoolfriends Jobs (right) and Wozniak joined forces to develop and market the Apple I, originally designed by Wozniak.

see also

350-1 **Scientific thinkers**
514-5 **Using numbers**
560-1 **The modern computer**
562-3 **Digital communications**

The 1980s and 90s were a revolutionary era in computing. Speed and power increased dramatically, while size and price diminished. Desktop machines appeared in offices, homes and schools, with new kinds of software for the new users. Powerful databases enabled organisations to store and process vast quantities of information, while network technology connected machines up, allowing data and software to be shared as never before.

Moore's Law in action

The speed at which microprocessors work, their 'clock speed', is measured in megahertz. The figures below are for processors at the time they were introduced.

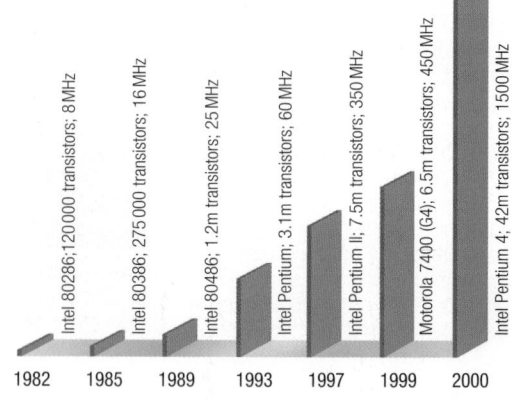

Intel 80286;120 000 transistors; 8MHz — 1982
Intel 80386; 275 000 transistors; 16 MHz — 1985
Intel 80486; 1.2m transistors; 25 MHz — 1989
Intel Pentium; 3.1m transistors; 60 MHz — 1993
Intel Pentium II; 7.5m transistors; 350 MHz — 1997
Motorola 7400 (G4); 6.5m transistors; 450 MHz — 1999
Intel Pentium 4; 42m transistors; 1500 MHz — 2000

Processing power The microprocessor is the 'brain' of the computer, the microchip that processes data at high speed according to programmed instructions – see opposite. Moore's Law, named after the Intel executive Gordon Moore, predicts a doubling in complexity and power of microprocessors every two years. So far, Moore's prediction has been easily met, at least for Intel processors. The Intel Pentium 4 microchip, for example, introduced in 2000, is more than 23 times faster than the first Pentium, introduced just seven years earlier in 1993.

1981 IBM launches its first personal computer. In the same year, the US$17 000 Xerox Star computer is equipped with the WIMP (Windows, Icons, Menus, Pointer) system – forerunner of the modern 'click and drag' GUI. The Star flops.

1982 Compaq launches the first IBM compatible computer.
1983 The Apple Lisa computer uses GUI.
1984 The Apple Macintosh, with extensive use of GUI, is the first successful graphical PC.

1985 The first desktop-publishing software is put on the market. In the same year, Microsoft launches the first version of Windows.
1989 NEC launches the first portable computer with a colour liquid-crystal diode (LCD) screen.

1990 Microsoft produces Windows 3, the first really successful version of Windows. The company's annual sales top US$1 billion.
1994 Apple launches its Power Macintosh.
1995 Microsoft comes out with the Macintosh-like Windows 95 GUI.

1998 Microsoft becomes world's most valuable company, valued on the US stock market at US$261 billion. Apple launches the iMac, a low-price version of the Power Macintosh with all-in-one case.

2000 The 'Lovebug' virus disables emails in the US Congress and British Parliament.

1980 — 1990 — 2000

The gooey revolution In the beginning, the only way to get a computer to do something was to type instructions in code or to press the 'function' keys. Programmers learned code like a foreign language and no one could use a computer without special training. The graphical user interface, or GUI (sometimes pronounced 'gooey') changed all that. The idea of the GUI was to use visual images (or 'icons') on the screen to represent commands – an approach that many users found more intuitive. Xerox developed the original GUI at its Palo Alto Research Center (PARC) in California in the 1960s. They spent more than US$100 million on the project, but never made a commercially successful product. Apple was the first to realise the true potential of GUI with the Macintosh computer, launched in 1984. The metaphor of the screen as a 'desktop' which could be controlled by a 'drag and drop' system proved hugely popular, and the following year Microsoft launched a similar system for IBM-compatible machines – Windows. Despite taking ten years to catch up with many features of the Apple system, Windows now runs on the great majority of the world's PCs.

Little Mac Apple's first attempt to introduce a personal computer using a GUI was the Lisa, introduced in 1983. It was slow and expensive, and flopped commercially. But the much cheaper Macintosh (left), launched the following year, had a profound impact, as Microsoft rushed to follow the trend with its GUI operating system Windows.

Bill Gates (1955–) Gates started programming at 13, and by the age of 32 was the world's richest man. As a schoolboy, he and a friend, Paul Allen, hacked into the security system of a local firm's computer, and were then asked to look for its weaknesses. At Harvard, he developed a version of the BASIC computer language for the Altair (see page 559), and then dropped out to form Micro-soft (the hyphen was later dropped) with Allen in 1975. They had a vision of computers as a useful tool for everyone. Their big break was a contract with IBM for an operating system for IBM's new personal computer. In the 1980s and 90s, Microsoft developed and made a huge success of its Windows GUI. But its business practices brought accusations of monopoly tactics.

WHAT IS SOFTWARE?

The instructions, or programs, that tell a computer what to do are known as software. Software is written in code, using languages such as BASIC, C or Pascal. These commands are then converted by other programs into simpler binary code (consisting of 1s and 0s) that directly operates the machine. In much modern software, users do not see the code or need to know how to program. Instead they issue commands by using graphic devices such as visual icons, 'buttons' or pull-down 'menus'.

There are four main types of software:
Operating system (OS) The OS controls the computer by performing everyday tasks such as receiving data from the keyboard, displaying information on screen, or storing it in memory or on a hard-disk drive. It works the whole time a computer is switched on. Users normally interact with the OS through a graphical user interface (GUI) and keyboard.
Applications Programs created to perform specific tasks are known as applications. They include word

processing (WP); database management (for storing details of a company's stock and customers, for example); desktop publishing (DTP) and spreadsheets for financial calculations such as budgets.
Peripherals software Scanners, digital cameras, printers and other devices all need software to connect to a computer.
Utilities 'Housekeeping' tasks such as screening data files for viruses, repairing damage to the hard disk and ensuring efficient data storage are handled by programs called utilities.

MAIN PARTS OF A MICROCOMPUTER

Most of the components in a computer fall into one of two categories: memory, or storage, components that hold data, and processing components that perform operations on the data.

RAM chips Microchips that store data and programs in use. Data in RAM is lost on switching off.

Floppy, CD-ROM and/or DVD-ROM drives Various types of data-storage devices that use removable disks – varying in capacity from 1.4 megabytes for a floppy disk to several thousand megabytes for a DVD-ROM.

Power-supply unit (PSU) It converts mains-voltage power to steady low-voltage direct current (DC) to power the various components.

Central processing unit (CPU) or microprocessor The microchip that processes data and coordinates input, output, storage devices. It generates a lot of heat, so usually has a cooling fan.

BIOS A chip that stores vital data even when the computer is switched off. It includes instructions for 'booting' (starting) up the computer.

Hard-disk drive The main permanent store of data and programs. It stores data as magnetic signals in binary code on metal disks. The data is 'read' from and 'written' to the disks, as they spin at high speed, by small magnetic heads like those of a tape recorder.

Motherboard The main circuit board – a printed circuit whose wires link the main components.

Expansion slots Connectors into which expansion cards adding special functions can be slotted.

Controller chips Specialised chips run functions such as graphics and control components such as hard-disk drives.

Microchips for everything

Microchips – also called silicon chips or simply 'chips' – consist of miniature electrical components connected together on a circuit board. They form part of all modern computers and most other electronic devices. Each chip has thousands or even millions of components such as tiny diodes and transistors etched on its surface by a photographic process. The components are linked by metal tracks less than a micron (one-thousandth of a millimetre) wide that carry electrical signals between them. At the core of a computer is the microprocessor chip, or central processing unit (CPU), which is responsible for most of the computational work. The smaller and more densely packed the components on a chip, the more complex and faster its operations. Scientists are now trying to develop yet faster microchips based on optical, chemical or 'quantum' (single-electron) activity rather than electric current.

KEY TERMS

Binary Number system based solely on 0s and 1s.
BIOS *Basic input-output system*. A chip that controls basic computer functions.
Bit *Binary digit*. The smallest unit of information.
Buffer Temporary memory that holds data ready for use.
Bus Main communicating wires on the motherboard.
Byte A group of eight bits; it represents – in binary – a number from 0 to 255 or a symbol.
CD-ROM *Compact disc read-only memory*. A CD that stores data or a program.
Clock speed The speed at which a processor works.
DVD *Digital versatile disc*. A very high-capacity disc for storing data or software.
File A piece of code or set of data kept together as a unit.
Hardware The physical components of a computer.
Modem *Modulator-demodulator*. A device linking a computer to a phone line.
Motherboard The printed circuit board that carries a computer's main microchips.
Network Two or more computers linked together.
RAM *Random-access memory*. Computer memory that can be changed by 'overwriting' it with new data.
ROM *Read-only memory*. Non-erasable memory.
Virus A damaging, self-replicating program.

Digital simply means numerical, and digital communications reduce everything – from the music of Beethoven to a Botticelli painting – to a series of numbers. The result is faster reproduction which is more easily stored and free from distortion. It was only with computer technology's ability to calculate and manipulate numbers that digital communications became possible.

Analogue and digital signals

In nature we get most of our information in the form of sound and light, which travel as waves of continuously varying quantities. Man-made communication systems, however, may use either continuous signals or discrete signals.

Systems that use continuous signals are known as analogue, since they construct fluctuating electrical currents or voltages that are analogues of the original continuous sound or light wave.

A microphone, for example, converts the air pressure fluctuations of sound waves into a continuously varying electrical current that mimics the shape of the original sound waves.

Digital communication systems, by contrast, measure the original waves and describe them as a series of discrete numbers. The numbers are converted into binary, a number system based on the digits 1 and 0 (see page 515). The binary numbers are used to generate a stream of electrical pulses, the digit 1 corresponding to 'on' and the digit 0 to 'off'. When the pulses are received, a digital-analogue converter (DAC) changes them back into sound or light, allowing us to hear a sound or see an image that was sent to us as nothing more than a long stream of 1s and 0s.

The benefits of digital

Digital transmission has many advantages over analogue. Because it is numerical, errors can be detected and corrected, and by identifying patterns in the numbers the information can be compressed for faster transmission. In addition, digital devices can communicate with one another since they all use information in the same, numerical form. This is why you can, for example, plug a digital camera into a computer, download music files from the Internet or send a photograph by email.

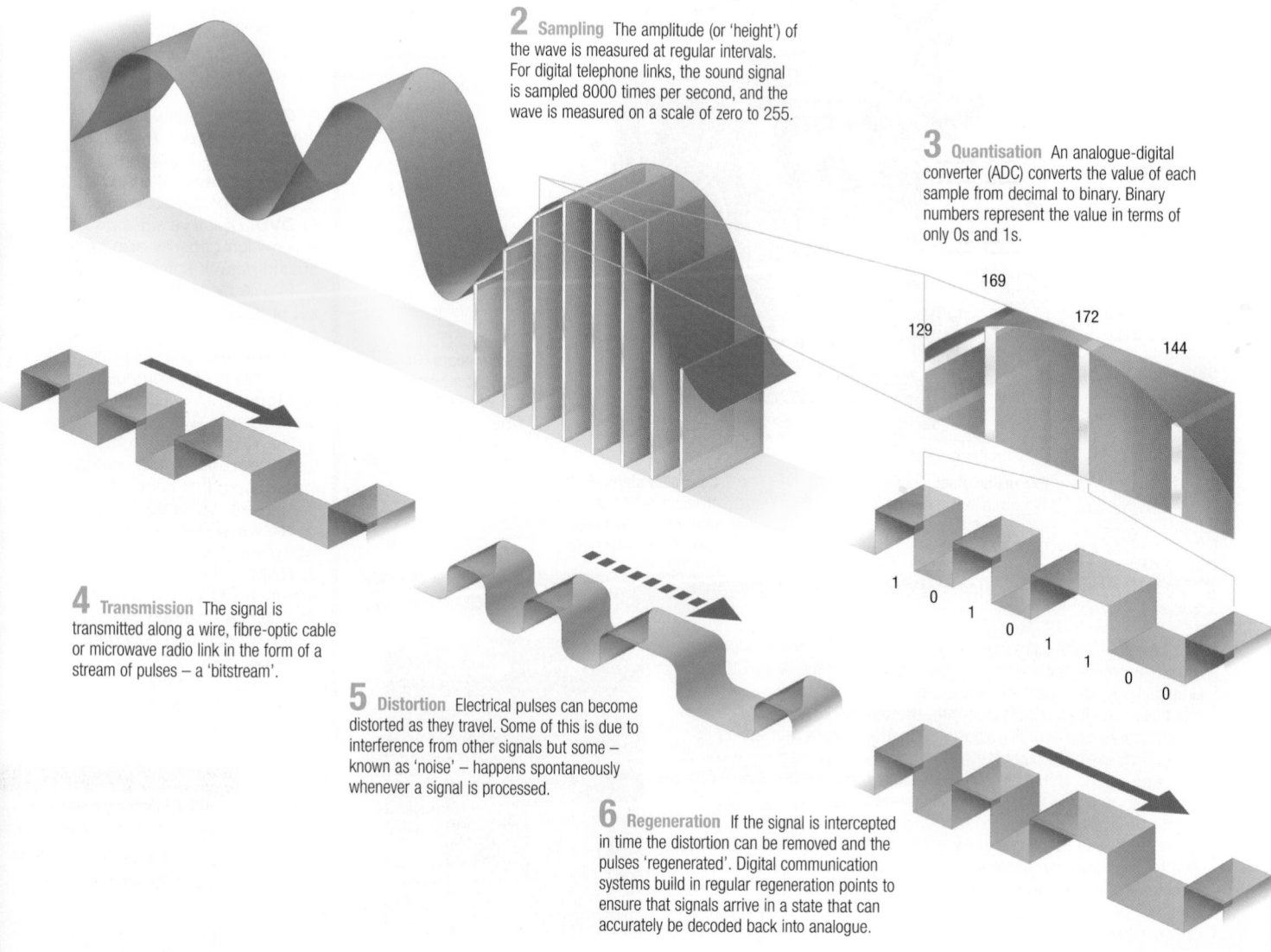

1 Analogue signal This consists of a varying electrical voltage or current. It may come, for example, from a microphone, representing a sound wave, or from a video camera, representing, say, the varying brightness of a scene.

2 Sampling The amplitude (or 'height') of the wave is measured at regular intervals. For digital telephone links, the sound signal is sampled 8000 times per second, and the wave is measured on a scale of zero to 255.

3 Quantisation An analogue-digital converter (ADC) converts the value of each sample from decimal to binary. Binary numbers represent the value in terms of only 0s and 1s.

169
172
129
144

1 0 1 0 1 1 0 0

4 Transmission The signal is transmitted along a wire, fibre-optic cable or microwave radio link in the form of a stream of pulses – a 'bitstream'.

5 Distortion Electrical pulses can become distorted as they travel. Some of this is due to interference from other signals but some – known as 'noise' – happens spontaneously whenever a signal is processed.

6 Regeneration If the signal is intercepted in time the distortion can be removed and the pulses 'regenerated'. Digital communication systems build in regular regeneration points to ensure that signals arrive in a state that can accurately be decoded back into analogue.

DIGITAL TYPE

All computers use binary numbers to represent letters, figures and written symbols. These computer 'codes' were first standardised with the American Standard Code for Information Interchange (ASCII), also known as the machine code, in 1963.

ASCII, now used by all personal computers in countries that use the Roman alphabet, employs a string of eight binary digits (or 'bits') to represent 128 characters. This is enough to encode small and capital letters, numerals, punctuation marks, and 32 special 'control

characters' to govern computer functions – with another 128 'extended' characters, such as accented and non-Latin letters and graphics symbols.

Examples of ASCII codes include:

Binary number	Decimal equivalent	Character encoded
00010010	36	$
01000001	65	A
01101011	107	k
10100100	164	ñ

The letter 'k', for example, is encoded by the number 107. When the 'k' key is pressed, this generates the machine code 107, which is then converted into the equivalnet binary number (01101011). The binary code signal can then be processed by the computer, and the letter 'k' will appear on the screen in front of you – and all this happens in microseconds.

Languages such as Chinese and Japanese have many more distinct characters, however, and have to be represented by 16 binary digits.

FACT A single CD-ROM can store 112 million words of digital text – about twice as much as the *Encyclopaedia Britannica*.

DIGITAL SOUND

The first use of digital sound was in transmitting telephone conversations. When a sound is converted from analogue to digital, it is measured ('sampled') at regular intervals. The quality of the signal that results depends both on the accuracy with which it is measured (the fineness of the scale) and the rate of sampling (the number of samples per second).

Two main types of sampling are used, 8-bit and 16-bit, though sampling technology is rapidly developing, allowing the development of higher and higher quality sound reproduction.

8-bit sampling Digital telephone links use 8-bit sampling, since the human voice does not have a very wide range of frequencies. In 8-bit sampling, sound wave frequencies are measured as an eight-digit binary number. Each sample is assigned one of 256 different values, 256 being the highest number that can be represented by eight digits in binary. This yields reasonably clear speech but is not suitable for music, for example. Digital telephones sample at a rate of 8000 times per second – or 8000 kHz. A rate of 10 000 samples per second – 10 000 kHz – is enough for speech recording.

16-bit sampling An audio CD uses 16-bit sampling – giving a scale with a possible 65 536 different levels – and samples are taken at the rate of 44 100 times per second (44 100 kHz) in each of two stereo channels. The result is much higher-fidelity sound than the low-frequency, 8-bit sampling used for the telephone. However, new systems such as DVD-Audio now offer 24-bit sampling (almost 17 million levels).

DIGITAL IMAGES

All electronic imaging systems work by scanning an image in narrow strips. Each strip is in turn divided into squares, called pixels ('picture elements'). For colour reproduction, each pixel is coded according to the levels of red, green and blue that it contains – the three primary colours of light.

The brightness of each colour is measured for each pixel, and, as with other digital systems, converted into a binary number. The result is a so-called 'bitmap' of the image that can be transmitted, recorded and reproduced on a TV screen, computer monitor or other digital device.

The clarity and accuracy of the image depends on several factors, including: the number of pixels in a given area, how frequently they are scanned and the

'colour depth' – the number of levels (as for sound) against which the brightness of each colour in each pixel is measured. High-quality colour images, such as those used in printing, are usually scanned at 12 bits per primary colour (4096 different levels of brightness) and 22 500 pixels per square inch, about eight times the number on a television or computer screen.

Patchwork picture The detail shows how each pixel interprets the colour values inside its own little square.

Life today would be unthinkable without recorded music, voice and sound. Yet the technology is little more than 100 years old. Sound recording began in the late 19th century with the cylinder phonograph. Film soundtracks, tape, stereo, the LP and the videocassette followed, joined in the digital era by a welter of high-tech devices, from the CD in 1982 to MiniDisc, DVD and MP3 in the 1990s.

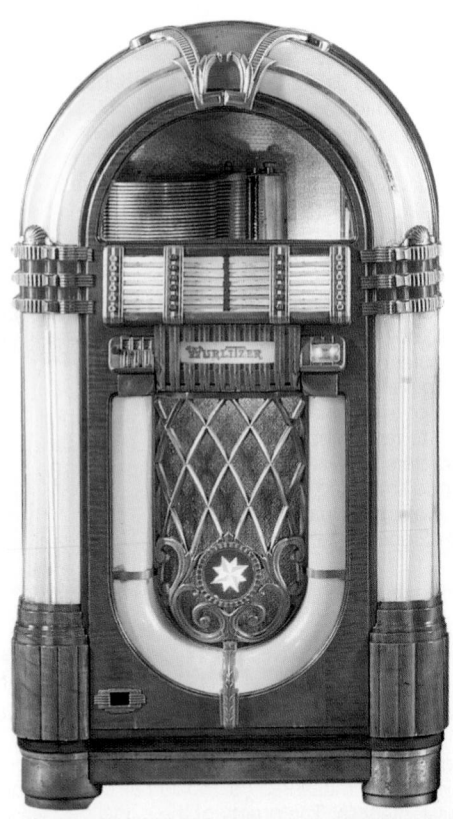

1877 American inventor Thomas Edison develops the cylinder phonograph for recording and playing back sound.
1887 German-American inventor Emile Berliner develops the gramophone.
1890 A coin-operated cylinder phonograph with four listening tubes is installed in a San Francisco saloon – an early forerunner of the jukebox.

1902 Double-sided discs are pioneered by a South American, Ademor Petit, who discovers that liquid shellac will spread more evenly if grooves are being impressed on both sides.
1927 The first successful sound films have sound-tracks recorded on 20 in (50 cm) discs, turning at 33⅓ rpm.
1927 The first all-electric jukebox is produced.
1927 British inventor John Logie Baird produces the first video recordings, capturing short TV programmes on discs made of wax and magnetic steel. He calls the technique Phonovision.

Music machine Jukeboxes arrived in the 1930s on a wave of enthusiasm for swing music.

1931 British inventor Alan Blumlein patents Binaural (stereo) recording.
1934 The Wurlitzer multiple-selection jukebox is introduced.

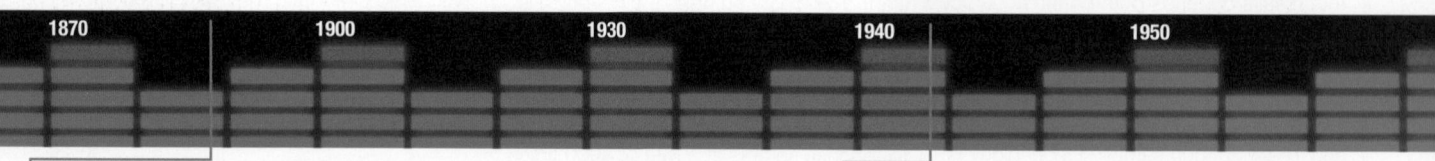

| 1870 | 1900 | 1930 | 1940 | 1950 |

From phonograph to gramophone Edison's phonograph used a rotating metal cylinder wrapped with tin foil; a stylus attached to a diaphragm vibrated according to the sound created and made indentations on the foil, recording the sounds. Later, he used wax-coated cardboard. The first words Edison recorded were 'Mary had a little lamb'. Although successful at first, Edison's phonograph was eventually displaced by Berliner's disc gramophone. This used hard rubber (later shellac) discs turning at 30 rpm, soon increased to 60 and later to 78 rpm (the increased speed gave better-quality sound). Berliner was also the first to mass-produce discs by pressing them from a metal master disc.

Edison phonograph, 1890s

1935 German engineers give a public demonstration of the Magnetophon tape recorder, manufactured by BASF and AEG.

1941 Stereo sound is used for the first time in the cinema.
1948 Birth of the LP: the 12 in (30 cm) long-playing 33⅓ rpm vinyl disc is launched. It is able to play for about 46 minutes.

1956 The first practicable professional videotape recorder is demonstrated in the United States.
1958 The first stereo LP discs are issued.

HOW A VINYL RECORD WORKS

A conventional gramophone disc carries sound information in the form of an oscillating spiral groove leading from the outside edge of the record almost to the centre. When the record turns, the pickup stylus (needle) follows the oscillations of the groove, which correspond to the peaks and troughs of the sound waves, converting them into a tiny electric current which is amplified and converted back into sound in the loudspeakers. In mono recordings, the stylus simply oscillates from side to side. In a stereo record, the left and right-hand channels are recorded as separate variations in the two walls of the groove.

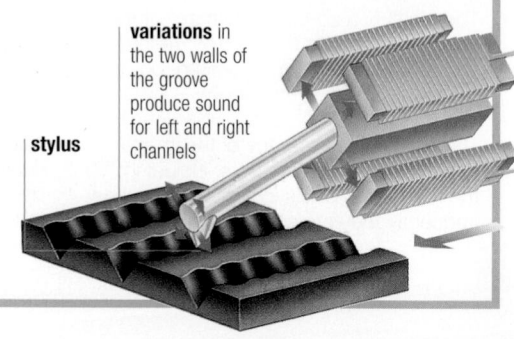

variations in the two walls of the groove produce sound for left and right channels

stylus

see also
378-81 **Popular music**
496-7 **Information economy**
562-3 **Digital communications**
582-3 **Cinema and music**

Dolby sound systems

The Dolby noise-reduction system involves boosting the recording level of high-pitched sound frequencies, then reducing their level on playback, which greatly reduces tape hiss. Dolby later developed digital and surround-sound systems for cinemas and home cinema systems. They record up to six channels of digital sound coded on one soundtrack, with normal stereo music speakers, a central front speaker for dialogue, and mono rear speakers for surround effects.

Akio Morita (1921–99) Akio Morita and the Japanese company he co-founded have been responsible for many of the most important innovations in home recording. It was Morita who pioneered the Walkman (originally Soundabout) personal cassette player – against the advice of many of his colleagues. By the time of his death, 100 million Walkmans had been sold in the United States alone. His company also pioneered the videocassette recorder, the camcorder, the MiniDisc and (jointly with Philips) the Compact Disc (CD) and Digital Audio Tape (DAT).

Sony Walkman, 1979 Akio Morita is said personally to have inspired the Walkman. He wanted a small, portable device to listen to music while on the golf course.

1992 The digital re-recordable MiniDisc (MD) is launched. It measures 6 cm (2½ in) across and can record up to 80 minutes.

1996 In Japan, Digital Versatile Discs (DVDs) are launched. They are the same size as CDs but can store 25 times the data.

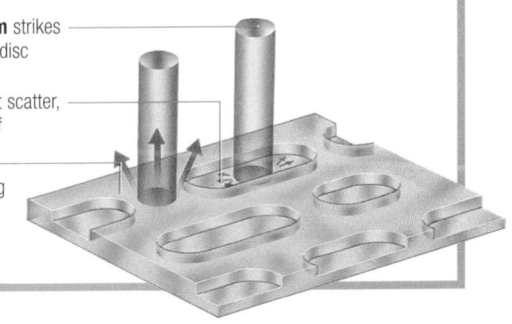

DVDs These discs can store the huge amount of data needed to display a full-length feature film. The digital picture quality is superior to that of video.

| 1960 | 1970 | 1980 | 1990 | 2000 |

1963 The compact tape cassette is introduced.
1965 Sony produces the first consumer videotape recorder.
1969 American electronics engineer Ray M. Dolby invents a system of noise-reduction for tape recordings.

1970 The first domestic videocassette recorders appear.
1975 Sony brings out the Betamax domestic videocassette.
1976 Sony launches the VHS (JVC) videocassette format, which overtakes its Betamax.

1980 The first domestic video camcorder is produced.
1982 The CD is launched. Measuring 12 cm (4½ in) across, it is able to record 74 minutes. It is the first commercially successful digital recording medium.

1997 The MP3 compressed digital recording system is launched, enabling high-quality sound transmission on the Internet.

2001 Domestic DVD-R (recordable DVD) video recorders are launched.

RECORDING ON MAGNETIC TAPE

Magnetic tape is a thin plastic ribbon coated on one side with a magnetic material. During recording the head magnetises the coating. The strength of the magnetisation corresponds to the amplitude of the sound input signal. During playback, the tape moving past the tape head causes a small varying electric signal which is amplified and fed to the loudspeakers. With video tape images the varying brightness of the three primary colours (red, green and blue) is recorded as variations in the strength of magnetisation.

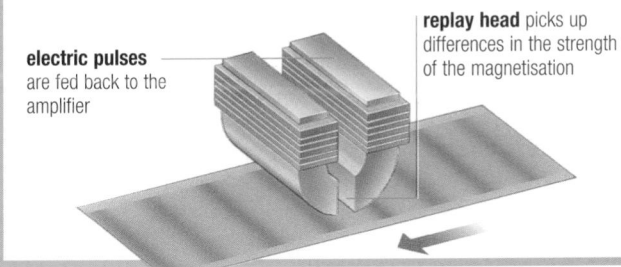

electric pulses are fed back to the amplifier

replay head picks up differences in the strength of the magnetisation

SOUND FROM A DIGITAL DISC

Digital data is stored on CDs, DVDs and MiniDiscs in the form of microscopically small 'pits' (which absorb light), separated by flat 'lands' (which reflect it). They are arranged in a spiral from the inside of the disc towards the outer edge. During playback, a laser beam shines on the spinning disc. A photocell responds to variations in the light reflected from the pits and lands, creating a succession of on/off electrical signals. A digital-analogue converter (DAC) decodes these digital signals to produce analogue electrical signals representing sounds or colours.

infrared laser beam strikes the underside of the disc

a pit makes the light scatter, registering a 0, or off

a land reflects the light back, registering a 1, or on

Computer networks began as a way of connecting massive mainframes in research laboratories and universities to increase their power and allow scientists to share data. Then came conventions called protocols that permitted exchanges across networks – literally internetwork communication. In the 1980s a system of unique addresses was developed, allowing any computer to contact any other – the Internet as we know it. As personal computing put machines into offices and homes across the world, applications such as the World Wide Web, e-commerce and email began to change the way we live, work and do business.

WHAT IS THE INTERNET?

The heart of the Internet consists of computers known as routers, connected by high-speed backbone links, using fibre-optic and other cable and satellite links. The routers are connected, in turn, with thousands of smaller networks and millions of individual computers.

Large companies and government and academic institutions often have direct Internet access via computers called Internet servers that are always connected. Other users dial in by telephone line from time to time, linking to a server at their Internet service provider.

Data is sent around the Internet by means of 'packet switching'. Whether it takes the form of email, web pages or computer files, the information is split up into small 'packets', each

Early 1960s In the United States, the Rand Corporation begins studies into secure military communications networks. The results of this research were later used in developing the Internet.

Early 1970s Email and newsgroup systems grow rapidly on the Arpanet. The network's controllers take the first steps to link separate networks in a network of networks – later known as the Internet. Key to this development is the transmission-control protocol (TCP) for communication between networks, devised by Californian computer scientist Vint Cerf.

1969 American military and academic researchers establish the Arpanet network, based on systems devised by Paul Baran. Initially, the Arpanet links just four mainframe computers – by 1971 there are 23 computers in the network.

● **Vint Cerf (1943–)**
Arpanet controllers take the first steps to link separate networks in a network of networks – later known as the Internet. Key to this development is the transmission-control protocol (TCP) for communication between networks, devised by Californian computer scientist Vint Cerf.

1982 The term 'Internet' is first used, by Vint Cerf and Bob Kahn.

1984 The system of domain names (Internet addresses) is introduced.

1960s

1970s

1980s

1965 Hypertext is invented. This is the system of clickable text later used to link web pages.

1974 Telnet, the first commercial version of Arpanet, is set up.

1975 Dial-up online bulletin boards and information services are established, including CompuServe and America OnLine (AOL).

1988 The number of 'host' computers on the Internet reaches 60 000. Host computers are permanently connected data-holding computers. They store vast amounts of data, but access is difficult.

● **Paul Baran (1926–)**
In 1962 Paul Baran at Rand proposes packet switching – a method of breaking messages into separate chunks that can travel across a network to the same destination but following different routes.

1973 The first transatlantic Arpanet links are established.

1984 The Canadian writer William Gibson coins the term 'cyberspace' in his novel *Neuromancer*.

1990 The original Arpanet is disbanded, leaving the Internet in its place.

THE LANGUAGE OF INTERNET ADDRESSES

Every computer connected to the Internet has to have a unique 'address' so that when information is requested other machines know where to send a response, and so that they in turn can request information from it. Most users on a personal computer do not have their own Internet address but connect through a service provider, using a temporarily assigned address.

Internet addresses take the form of four sets of numbers separated by dots – for example, 123.4567.89.1011. Often there is also a verbal name (called a domain name) associated with the numerical address to make it easier to remember. Powerful computers called domain-name servers (DNSs) store every address on the Internet and automatically translate domain names into numerical Internet addresses.

Computers that host websites generally have domain names that start 'www', followed by a dot, one or more words separated by dots, and a suffix such as '.com' or '.ac' identifying the type of organisation – commercial or academic in this case.

● **Uniform resource locators (URLs)** Web sites also have unique addresses, known as URLs. These start with 'http://', which identifies the protocol by which web information is transmitted. Then comes the domain name of the host computer on which the site is stored and, for particular pages or files within a website, a slash (/) and a file name, usually with a suffix such as .html.

Domain name

http://www.readersdigest.com

HyperText Transfer Protocol   Host name   Suffix

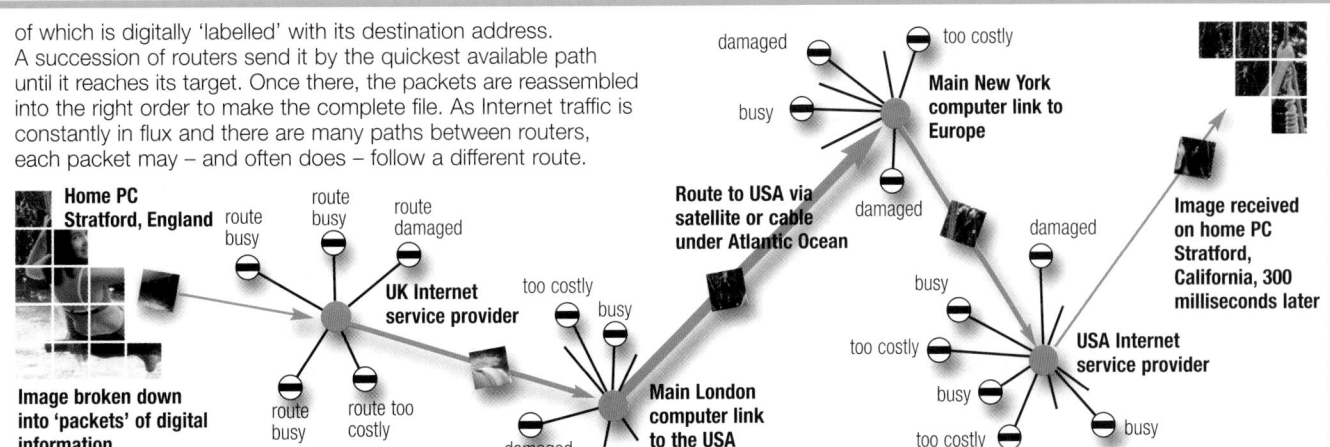

of which is digitally 'labelled' with its destination address. A succession of routers send it by the quickest available path until it reaches its target. Once there, the packets are reassembled into the right order to make the complete file. As Internet traffic is constantly in flux and there are many paths between routers, each packet may – and often does – follow a different route.

Home PC Stratford, England
route busy
route busy
route damaged

UK Internet service provider
too costly
busy

Image broken down into 'packets' of digital information
route busy
route too costly
damaged

Main London computer link to the USA

Route to USA via satellite or cable under Atlantic Ocean

damaged
too costly
busy
damaged

Main New York computer link to Europe
damaged

Image received on home PC Stratford, California, 300 milliseconds later

busy
damaged

USA Internet service provider
too costly
busy
too costly
busy

Tim Berners-Lee (1955–) an English scientist working at the European nuclear research centre in Geneva, develops the World Wide Web (WWW), and its URL, HTML and HTTP standards.

1994 Netscape Navigator is launched, a commercial version of Mosaic and the first mass-market web browser.

The first web radio stations and first online bank are established.

1995 The Java programming language enables more complex web pages.

The first search engines – online programs for finding information on the web – are created.

2000 The Internet has about 95 million host computers, about 25 million web sites and more than 1 billion web pages.

2000s

1990s

1991 The Internet is fully opened to commercial traffic.

The number of Internet host computers reaches 1 million.

The first Internet service providers (ISPs) offer inexpensive public Internet access via the telephone network.

Marc Andreessen (1971–) In 1993 Marc Andreessen and Eric Bina develop the Mosaic browser to display web pages.

1990s Web traffic multiplies by about 3500 annually.

1996 The number of host computers on the Internet reaches 10 million.

1999 Launch of Internet 2, or Abilene, a high-power research network.

see also

1995 Online bookseller Amazon.com is founded. It makes no money but leads the way for e-commerce.

KEY TERMS

Email – or electronic mail – uses the Internet to transmit messages between users with unique addresses. Messages are created and routed between computers with special software until they reach the correct address.

Newsgroups People with a common interest sign up and gain access to a dedicated Internet location. There they can post and read messages on an electronic 'bulletin board', make contact and enter into discussion.

GIF Graphic Interchange Format – a compressed format, used for the rapid transmission of graphics.

HTML HyperText Markup Language – the main programming language used to construct web pages.

HTTP HyperText Transfer Protocol – the system for moving hypertext files (that is, web pages) across the Internet.

ISP Internet Service Provider – an organisation through which subscribers connect to the Internet.

JPEG Joint Photographic Experts Group – a compressed format, used for the rapid transmission of graphics.

Log on/off Connect to (using a digital password) and disconnect from the Internet or a particular web server.

Modem Modulator-Demodulator – a device for converting digital data into analogue and back again, allowing a computer to use ordinary telephone lines.

MPEG Moving Pictures Experts Group – a compressed format, used for transmitting video files.

MP3 A compressed file format for music.

POP Point of Presence – a telephone number where a subscriber can dial in to an ISP's system and thus connect to the Internet.

Server Computer or program giving services (such as access or storage of web files or the forwarding of emails).

TCP/IP Transmission Control Protocol/Internet Protocol – the system that moves data around the Internet.

URL Uniform Resource Locator – the official name for a web page address.

WAP Wireless Application Protocol – method of accessing web pages on mobile phones; likely to be superseded by third generation (3G) mobile phones.

The foundations of medical science were laid early. Anatomy (the structure and form of the body) and physiology (the study of the body's functions) were taught in medical schools founded as early as 300 BC in Alexandria in Egypt. Over the next 2000 years, physicians gradually uncovered rational explanations for illnesses, and developed treatments for them.

Surgical pioneer The Indian surgeon Sushruta is credited with having written the first version of a medical textbook, called the *Sushruta-samhita*, in the 8th century BC. This outlines a number of surgical techniques and medicinal remedies. His Hindu religion forbade him to dissect dead bodies in order to learn more about human anatomy. Instead, he immersed the bodies in water for several days and then simply pulled them apart without the need for cutting. He administered alcohol as a sedative during operations, and a combination of hot oils and tar to staunch bleeding. As well as treating cataracts by the removal of the lens of the eye, he also pioneered the basic techniques of skin grafting and plastic surgery.

The spread of disease

In the second half of the 19th century it became apparent how infectious diseases spread. Until then, doctors believed that infection arose from noxious gases, or miasmas, produced by rotting matter and stagnant water.

The development of the microscope in the 17th century revealed the existence of microorganisms that were invisible to the naked eye. It was not until the 1860s that the French microbiologist Louis Pasteur (1822–95) demonstrated that some of these microorganisms caused disease. In 1882, a German doctor, Robert Koch (1843–1910), was the first to identify a germ responsible for a particular ailment: the tubercle bacillus that leads to tuberculosis.

c.AD 170 Greek physician Galen proves that arteries and veins carry blood, not air. He uses bloodletting to restore the body's fluids to 'perfect balance', and carries out some of the first scientific dissections.

1510 Ambroise Paré, 'father of modern surgery', is born. Rather than cauterising wounds, he applied soothing lotions, helping to cut death rates.
1543 Belgian anatomist Andreas Vesalius uses dissection to prove that many of Galen's ideas were wrong.

1604 Italian physician Hieronymus Fabricius publishes *De formato foetu*, a landmark in the study of embryology.
1628 English physician William Harvey outlines the circulation of blood in his *Anatomical Study of the Motion of the Heart and of the Blood in Animals*.

c.8000 BC Trepanning – the technique of boring a hole in the skull – is practised by Neolithic people, probably to release 'evil spirits'.

c.1000 BC *The Treatise of Medical Diagnosis and Prognosis*, describing symptoms for 3000 illnesses, is written on clay tablets in Babylon.

| 8000 BC | 1000 BC | 0 | AD 170 | 1500 | 1600 |

3000 BC The Chinese *Ne'i ching* makes the first reference to the circulation of blood. In Egypt, the physician Imhotep records his remedies.
2000 BC *The Vedas*, a sacred medical text on the treatment of diseases and the casting out of devils, is written in India.

384 BC The Greek philosopher Aristotle is born. His writings on biology, particularly on subjects such as comparative anatomy and embryology, were to have great influence on the science and practice of medicine for nearly 2000 years.

Father of medicine The Greek physician Hippocrates (c.460–c.370 BC) used observation and deductive reasoning to lay the foundation of a scientific approach to medicine. He also taught that diet, hygiene and environment can influence a person's health. No evidence exists that he formulated the Hippocratic oath of medical ethics, still taken by many medical school graduates.

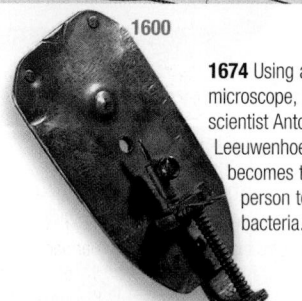

1674 Using a crude microscope, Dutch scientist Anton van Leeuwenhoek becomes the first person to observe bacteria.

Exploring a secret world Leeuwenhoek's pioneering microscope (above) could magnify up to 300 times.

HUMOURS AND BLOODLETTING

From the time of the ancient Greeks until the 18th century, it was believed that everything was made of four elements – air, water, fire and earth – and that these elements were mirrored in the body by four humours: blood, phlegm, choler (yellow bile) and black bile, respectively. Illness resulted when the natural balance of these humours was disturbed. Treatment involved drawing off excess or poisonous humours to restore the balance. This was usually done by bloodletting, either cutting open a vein or applying bloodsucking leeches. In the 19th century the humoral theory fell into disrepute.

Split personality The balance of the four humours was believed to affect mental as well as physical health. Each humour was linked with a distinct personality type (right): sanguine, melancholy, choleric or phlegmatic.

FLEGMAT   SANGVIN

ZAELANG   COLERIC

Antiseptics

Infection following surgery was a common cause of death until the late 19th century. Doctors routinely operated in blood-caked clothes, in dirty rooms with dirty hands and instruments.

In the 1840s, Hungarian obstetrician Ignaz Semmelweis demonstrated that if doctors just washed their hands the death rate of mothers after childbirth fell dramatically. But the main breakthrough came in 1865, when British surgeon Joseph Lister sprayed carbolic acid on wounds to kill bacteria, used antiseptic dressings and improved general hygiene.

HOSPITALS AND NURSING

Many public hospitals were founded in the 18th and 19th centuries, but the standard of care was often abysmal. In 1854, during the Crimean War, the Englishwoman Florence Nightingale (1820–1910) took 38 nurses to Scutari, where she turned a dirty, rat-infested hospital into a clean, bright area where wounded men could receive medical attention and adequate food. The death rate dropped from 40 to 2 per cent; Nightingale earned the nickname 'the lady of the lamp'. In 1860, she opened the first of many nurse training schools at St. Thomas' Hospital, London, which transformed the status of nursing.

Bestseller *Notes on Nursing* (1860) by Florence Nightingale (left) was published widely, in many languages.

Tribute On Nightingale's return from Crimea, £50 000 was raised to start her nursing school.

Inoculation Edward Jenner (1749–1823), a country doctor, noted that dairymaids who had contracted cowpox appeared to be immune to the deadlier smallpox. To test his theory, in 1796 Jenner deliberately infected an eight-year-old boy, James Phipps, with cowpox through two scratches on his arm. A few weeks later he inoculated him with smallpox, which proved harmless. He named the practice 'vaccination' after the Latin *vaccina* (cowpox). For his discovery, Parliament rewarded Jenner with grants totalling £30 000.

International recognition Napoleon had a medal struck to honour Edward Jenner (right).

1864 French scientist Louis Pasteur introduces the 'germ theory of disease'.
1865 Joseph Lister pioneers antiseptic surgery.
1866 Austrian monk Gregor Mendel experiments with crossbreeding pea plants. His results are the basis of genetics.
1867 Uncontrolled cell division is seen as the cause of cancer.

1892 Russian embryologist and immunologist Elie Metchnikoff identifies white blood cells.
1897 English physician Ronald Ross proves that mosquitoes are responsible for spreading the microscopic parasite that causes malaria.
1899 German chemists Felix Hoffman and Heinrich Dreser prepare aspirin from salicyclic acid found in willow bark.

1700	1800	1850	1860	1890

1753 Scottish naval surgeon James Lind records the benefits of citrus fruit in treating scurvy. Vitamins in food – in this case vitamin C – were not recognised as vital to life until 1906.
1816 French physician René Laënnec invents the stethoscope.

1847 Hungarian obstetrician Ignaz Semmelweis introduces the practice of cleansing the hands and instruments, with a solution of chloride of lime, before carrying out surgery.
1851 German physicist Hermann von Helmholtz invents the ophthalmoscope to observe the interior of the eye.

1853 French surgeon Charles Gabriel Pravaz and Scottish physician Alexander Wood independently invent the hypodermic syringe.
1854 British physician John Snow discovers that cholera is communicated by means of contaminated water.

X-rays While experimenting with electric current flow in a cathode ray tube, Wilhelm Röntgen (1845–1923) noticed that a nearby piece of the substance barium platinocyanide glowed whenever the tube was switched on, although he could see no light going towards it. He found that this 'new' form of light – actually a part of the electromagnetic spectrum that is invisible to the naked eye – was able to penetrate most materials and also leave an impression on a photographic plate. Armed with this information, he took the first X-ray (of his wife's hand) in 1895. In 1901 he was awarded the first Nobel prize for physics.

Visionary Wilhelm Röntgen's discovery of X-ray photography revolutionised medical diagnosis.

Anaesthetics

Until the mid 19th century, surgery was an agonising process. There were no satisfactory methods of numbing the pain, although various plant extracts and drugs such as opium and cocaine were used to reduce the effects. In many cases, terrified patients were held or tied down while the surgeon speedily wielded his scalpel. But in 1846, at Massachusetts General Hospital, dentist William Morgan successfully used inhaled ether vapour to render a patient unconscious, while surgeon John Warren painlessly removed a tumour from the patient's neck.

The following year, Edinburgh doctor James Young Simpson employed chloroform as an anaesthetic, and it soon replaced the more unpredictable ether. In 1853 Queen Victoria made anaesthetics publicly acceptable when she allowed her physician to give her chloroform during the birth of her eighth child.

Both ether and chloroform were superseded in the years that followed by safer, more controllable anaesthetics, some inhaled, others injected, that allowed surgeons the time to carry out longer and more complex operations.

see also
158-9 **Advances of medicine**
160-1 **Disorders and diseases**
528-9 **Electromagnetism**
570-1 **Modern medicine**

In the 20th century, the approach to the treatment of disease became increasingly scientific. Drugs were created to combat a wide range of complaints by manipulating the molecules of synthetic chemicals. Towards the end of the century a flourishing biotechnology industry was offering genetic engineering as a means of tackling disease even before it manifested itself. Technological advances made the successful replacement of body parts commonplace.

At the dentist

Modern technology has brought new, preventative and 'painless' techniques to dentistry.

● **Fluoride** Since the mid 1940s, when it was proved that fluoride helped to prevent tooth decay, it has been added to drinking water and toothpaste, and used to coat children's teeth.

● **Air abrasion** Rather than drilling out decay, dentists can now blow it away gently without the need for an anaesthetic. The resulting cavity is plugged with a safe, long-lasting filler, which is dried and cured (hardened) using ultraviolet light.

● **Ultrasound** Tartar build-up, often the cause of decay, was once removed by scraping. Now ultrasound can break down tartar without damaging the teeth.

● **Camera close-ups** The intra-oral camera, connected to a monitor, gives instant close-up detail of the mouth.

The Panorex camera produces panoramic views of the teeth and gums, providing information about existing dental work, supporting bone and any signs of infection.

● **Digital radiography** allows immediate X-rays, without the wait for X-ray plates to develop.

1901 Austrian physician Karl Landsteiner discovers and names the four blood groups – A, B, O and AB.
1903 Dutch physiologist Willem Einthoven develops the electrocardiograph (ECG). It records the heart's electrical impulses, allowing irregularities in heartbeat to be detected.
1906 German surgeon Eduard Zirm is first to transplant a cornea successfully.
1921 Johnson & Johnson start selling the Band-Aid (sticking plaster).

1931 German engineer Ernst Ruska designs the first electron microscope. The level of magnification and detail it allows make the observation of viruses possible.
1938 British surgeon John Wiles performs the first artificial hip replacement operation.

1943 Streptomycin, a cure for tuberculosis and meningitis, is discovered.
1944 American surgeon Alfred Blalock performs the first open-heart operation.

1953 American surgeon John H. Gibbon is the first to use a mechanical heart and blood purifier during surgery.
1953 Cambridge scientists James Watson and Francis Crick, with Rosalind Franklin and Maurice Wilkins, discover the double-spiral structure of DNA.

| 1900 | 1930 | 1940 | 1950 |

1924 German psychiatrist Hans Berger develops the electroencephalograph (EEG) for recording the electrical activity of the brain through the skull. It is helpful in diagnosing brain disorders.

● **Alexander Fleming (1881–1955)** In 1928, Fleming, a bacteriologist at St Mary's Hospital in London, noticed an unusual mould on a neglected culture dish in his laboratory. It appeared to be inhibiting the growth of bacteria, so he decided to investigate. He obtained a crude sample of the antibacterial agent in the mould, which he called penicillin.

Fleming's discovery, however, raised little interest. It was 1941 before two biochemists, Howard Florey and Ernst Chain, processed penicillin to create the first antibiotic drug. In 1945, they and Fleming shared the Nobel prize for medicine.

Lifesaver Alexander Fleming in his laboratory in St Mary's Hospital London.

1954 American physician Jonas Salk develops a polio vaccine.
1957 Scottish obstetrician Ian Donald uses ultrasound scanning to detect problems in an unborn child.

Replacement body parts

Artificial replacements for missing or damaged eyes and limbs have been in existence for at least 1000 years, but until the mid 20th century they were often cumbersome and of limited use. Sophisticated medical technology has brought a range of very effective, hi-tech devices.

It is now possible, for example, to restore eyesight using retinal implants. A microchip is placed in the retina and the patient issued with a pair of glasses fitted with a charge-coupled device (CCD), able to form images electronically.

Precision grip Touch sensors in the thumb and fingers of artificial hands can monitor how firmly an object is held.

Images collected by the CCD are fired, via a laser, to the microchip. The microchip interprets them, and converts them into a series of electrical pulses, which stimulate the nerve cells behind the retina.

Complex and lightweight artificial legs can mimic the movement characteristics of a real leg. This is achieved with the aid of motion detectors linked to pneumatic devices that act in place of the leg muscles to create a natural flowing movement.

Sensors in artificial arms and hands can pick up nerve impulses from the body and use them to trigger movement in the artificial limb.

DRUG DELIVERY SYSTEMS

Until recently, drugs were administered either through the mouth (orally) or by injection. Advances in the development of drug delivery systems mean that this need no longer be the case.

● **Slow-release patches** These consist of a thin membrane containing a dose of the drug – usually in the form of a gel – and a protective coating. They are held next to the skin by adhesive. The drug passes through the membrane at a steady rate, and is released into the patient's body through the skin. The rate of absorption is determined by the nature of the membrane.

● **Slow-release capsule** The capsule, which is sheathed in a thin, permeable membrane, is inserted under the skin. The drug, which is usually suspended in a gel, gradually passes through the membrane and into the bloodstream.

● **Injection gun** This uses a microcylinder of compressed helium to eject a drug at such a speed that it passes through the outer skin layers into the bloodstream, without puncturing. Unlike hypodermic needles, a single injection gun can be used on any number of people with no risk of transmitting disease.

Computer-designed drugs

Computers allow scientists to design a drug using a mathematical model of its molecular structure, and of the chemicals in the body it has to react with. The computer-designed molecules will 'fit' into the hollow receptor regions of the body's natural chemicals. Once a fit has been found, the drug is synthesised, then tested on living tissue before use.

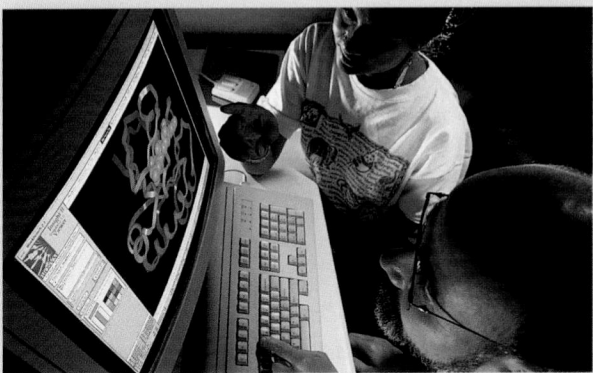

On-screen treatment By the end of the 20th century new drugs were being developed by scientists using complex computer software.

1961 American physician Albert Sabin develops a polio vaccine that can be administered orally.
1967 British electrical engineer Godfrey Hounsfield develops the computerised axial tomography (CAT) scanner.

1973 US biochemists Herbert Boyer and Stanley Cohen develop a technique for the cloning of DNA.
1974 US physician Raymond Damadian invents the MRI (magnetic resonance imaging) scanner.

1995 A patent is issued for a blood substitute that increases oxygen levels in the brain during cardiac surgery.

2000 Drugs are routinely designed by computer.

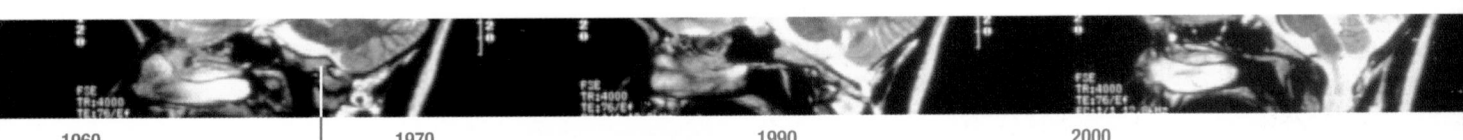

1960   1970   1990   2000

● **Christiaan Barnard (1922–)** The world's first human heart transplant took place at Cape Town's Groote Schuur Hospital on December 3, 1967. The cardiac surgeon Christiaan Barnard transferred the heart of a 25-year-old woman into the body of 55-year-old Louis Washkansky. The patient survived for 18 days.

Undeterred, Barnard carried out a second transplant on January 2, 1968. This time the recipient lived for 563 days after the operation.

New techniques have increased success rates dramatically. By 2000, there had been over 50 000 transplants, with patients leading active lives more than ten years after surgery.

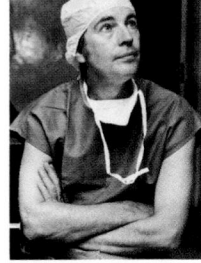

Pioneer The charismatic, good-looking Barnard won worldwide fame.

Minimal invasion

Some surgery can be performed without making large cuts into the body via a tube called an endoscope. It is inserted into a tiny 'keyhole' incision, or a natural orifice.

The endoscopic tube contains control wires and a set of optical fibres, which relay images to a monitor.

Surgery is carried out using specially adapted miniature tools that are passed down a central channel in the endoscope.

The bronchoscope (for chest and throat operations), arthroscope (for joints) and laparoscope (for abdomen), are all forms of endoscope.

LASER SURGERY

The laser is replacing the scalpel in many areas of surgery, and particularly in optical surgery, where absolute precision is required. Unlike a scalpel, which tears through flesh leaving blood vessels exposed and leaking, the laser acts to minimise bleeding.

● The laser cuts by generating heat in body tissues.
● This heat is sufficient to seal (cauterise) severed blood vessels, and so keeps bleeding to a minimum.
● In addition to acting as a scalpel, the heat from the laser can also be used to 'weld' delicate body parts, such as detached retinas, back together.

Painless Using a laser to perform eye surgery is quick and safe, and requires no anaesthetic.

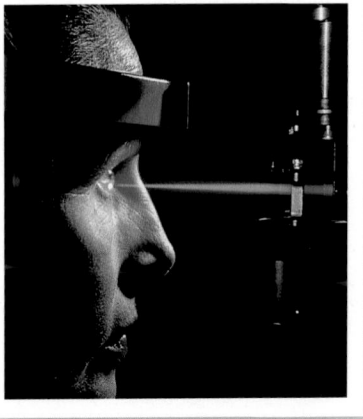

see also
158-9 **Advances of medicine**
160-1 **Disorders and diseases**
558-61 **Computers**
568-9 **Origins of medicine**

The earliest buildings used naturally occurring materials such as timber, mud and stone. But the introduction of man-made bricks, terracotta and – in Roman times – durable cement and concrete enabled builders to become far more inventive. Concrete was rediscovered less than 250 years ago, and was married with steel for strength in the 19th century. The development of high-tech materials in the 20th century allowed for ever taller and wider buildings.

SPANNING THE GAP

Architects have developed a range of building methods to produce wide interior spaces uncluttered by supports.

● **Cantilever** This is a concrete beam or girder, supported only at one end. It relies on the intrinsic rigidity of the reinforced or prestressed concrete.

● **Dome** A dome can be either hemispherical or pointed. If the base is not circular, triangular corner sections (pendentives) are needed.

● **Geodesic dome** This is a geometric framework of lightweight metal or plastic tubes forming a rigid structure.

● **Gothic arch** The pointed Gothic arch is able to span much wider spaces than the round arch. Its form is such that lateral (sideways) forces from the weight of the arch need to be braced, using

external buttresses. These buttresses were solid at first, but later flying (hollowed) buttresses were developed.

● **Post and lintel** A horizontal beam (lintel) rests on vertical columns (posts). Only a limited space can be spanned by this method without the need for intermediate columns. Timber and steel-framed construction are modern versions of the system.

● **Ridgepole and rafters** A ridgepole is the timber along the ridge of a roof to which the rafters are attached. Together they form a tent-like pitched roof.

● **Round arch** This was the earliest true arch. It is made of stone or concrete, built on a timber framework which is later removed. The load is transferred to the vertical columns.

---

c.6000 BC
Sun-dried bricks are used for building in the Middle East.

c.2650–2500 BC
In Egypt, the pyramids are built. The earliest is the Step Pyramid of Djoser (above) at Saqqara.

5th century BC The Royal Palace in Persepolis (Persia) and the Parthenon (Athens) are the world's largest post-and-lintel buildings.

3rd–2nd centuries BC
The Romans extend the round arch to form barrel vaulting.

c.250 BC The Pharos (lighthouse) of Alexandria, Egypt, is built. It may have stood over 122 m (400 ft) high.

121 BC The platform of the Roman temple of Concord is built using concrete. It survives to this day and is the oldest known Roman concrete structure.

| 7000 BC | 5000 BC | 3000 BC | 1000 BC | 550 BC | 450 BC | 350 BC | 250 BC | 150 BC | 50 BC | 50 AD | |
| 6000 BC | 4000 BC | 2000 BC | 600 BC | 500 BC | 400 BC | 300 BC | 100 BC | | 0 | 100 AD |

c.3500 BC Fired bricks are first used in the Middle East.

From c.1500 BC The post-and-lintel system is used for building huge Egyptian temples.

4th century BC The Romans first use the rounded masonry arch.

3rd century BC The Romans make hydraulic cement from volcanic silica dust (pozzolana) and lime.

118–28 AD Concrete is used to build the dome of the Pantheon in Rome, with a diameter of 43 m (141 ft).

TWO WAYS OF BUILDING HIGH

Along with the desire to build taller and taller buildings, architects have had to devise new methods of construction. Traditional load-bearing external walls have been replaced by metal frames and concrete cores.

● **Skeleton frame** The oldest and best-known structure for a tall building comprises a frame made from steel girders, reinforced concrete, or steel tubes. These support the floors and 'curtain' walling, which is hung around the frame. Sometimes diagonal cross-

bracing girders are used to strengthen the structure.

● **Cable-hung** This modern innovation comprises a concrete core (containing lifts and other services) and floor slabs. Each floor is supported by the core and by cables hanging from floor to floor around the perimeter. The slabs may be cast at ground level and hoisted into position.

● A hybrid version may use a **tubular steel frame** with triangular steel trusses placed at regular intervals, from which 'hangers' are suspended to support the floors.

The Pantheon
The dome of Rome's temple to the gods is based on a sphere: the height of the walls is equal to the radius of the dome.

Great Pyramid Giza's Great Pyramid stands 137 m (450 ft) high and contains about 2.3 million blocks of stone.

The Parthenon Athens' great temple was the supreme example of the simple Doric style in Greek architecture.

Hagia Sophia Istanbul's Hagia Sophia took just six years to build. The dome is 30 m (100 ft) in diameter.

On solid foundations

Foundations have to support a building's entire weight – which may run to many millions of tonnes. Their design depends on the size of the building and the nature of the ground.

Footings (slabs of reinforced concrete) are placed beyond the building's perimeter to spread the load. Cylindrical piers are used to transmit the load down to solid bedrock; in softer ground steel or concrete piles may be driven down to find firm soil or rock.

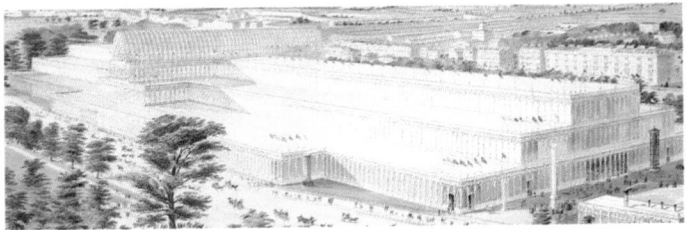

Palace of industry
Sir Joseph Paxton's Crystal Palace (1851) was the first example of prefabrication: the parts were factory-made and assembled on site.

Scaling new heights
Chicago's metal-framed Home Insurance building set the style for high-rise building.

1973 New York's World Trade Center, at 411 m (1349 ft), overtakes the Empire State.

1974 Chicago's Sears Roebuck Tower sets a new height record: 443 m (1454 ft).

1976 The 553 m (1815 ft) CN Tower in Toronto (above) tops the world's buildings. Glass-fronted lifts transport visitors to the viewing platforms.

532–7 Hagia Sophia in Constantinople (Istanbul) is built. The dome has a square base with triangular vaulted corners, known as pendentives.

1418–36 The Duomo – the dome of Florence Cathedral – is constructed.

1845 A reliable process is developed for producing Portland cement.

c.1850 French gardener Joseph Monier invents reinforced concrete with steel rods inserted for strength.

1885 The first steel-framed skyscraper, the ten-storey Home Insurance Building in Chicago, is constructed.

1889 The Eiffel Tower is erected in Paris. At 300 m (984 ft) it is the tallest structure in the world.

---

200 500 1000 1400 1600 1700 1750 1800 1825 1850 1875 1900 1910 1920 1930 1940 1950 1960 1970 1980 1990 2000

1144 In France, the abbey of Saint-Denis is the first building in the Gothic style, with pointed arches and buttresses.

c.1175 Flying buttresses are first used to support Gothic arches.

1653 The Taj Mahal is built in Agra, India.

1756 English engineer John Smeaton rediscovers hydraulic cement, first invented by the Romans.

1851 The vast Crystal Palace is built for the Great Exhibition in London using prefabricated iron and glass.

1852 In the USA, Elisha Otis invents the passenger lift, making skyscrapers feasible.

1855 The pneumatic Bessemer process dramatically increases steel production.

1922 German engineer Walter Bauersfeld invents the geodesic dome. It is later developed and popularised by Buckminster Fuller in the USA.

1931 The Empire State Building is constructed in New York. Rising to 381 m (1250 ft), it remained the world's tallest building for more than 40 years.

1996 The 452 m (1483 ft) twin Petronas Towers in Kuala Lumpur, Malaysia, overtake Sears Roebuck Tower as the world's tallest inhabited building.

1999 The Millennium Dome is completed in London. With a diameter of 320 m (1050 ft), it is the world's biggest dome.

2001 The World Financial Centre in Shanghai, China, is completed, standing 460 m (1509 ft) high. It becomes the world's tallest inhabited building.

Spreading the light

Large modern buildings are designed with systems that channel natural light into the interior. This saves energy as well as improving the quality of the environment within the building.

One method uses mirrored 'sun scoops' on the side walls, which reflect light inwards towards ceiling reflectors. A more sophisticated version uses a computer-controlled heliostat that tracks the Sun and reflects its light down a light guide in a central service shaft.

Mirrors and specially designed light extractors channel the light to where it is wanted. Light extractors are plastic tubes with a moulded 'microprism' on the outside, rather like the prismatic diffusers commonly used in fluorescent-tube lights.

Eden Project This geodesic conservatory, completed in 2001, was built in a former china clay pit in Cornwall, England. It is 200 m (650 ft) long and 45 m (145 ft) high.

see also

366-9 **Architecture**

574-5 **Civil engineering**

594-5 **Signs and wonders**

The Eiffel Tower The world-famous Parisian landmark was built from 7620 tonnes of iron.

CN Tower Built to transmit TV and radio signals, the CN Tower still outtops the world's highest inhabited buildings.

The Petronas Towers The record-breaking Malaysian towers were topped within just five years.

Technological advances and new materials have allowed ever more ambitious structures. These include Japan's Akashi-Kaikyo Bridge, the world's longest suspension bridge with a span of nearly 2 km (1¼ miles), and the Channel Tunnel, fulfilling a centuries-old dream of linking Britain with mainland Europe. They are two milestones along a road that began with the ancient Egyptians, the first people to show civil engineering skills with the building of a dam across the Nile in 3000 BC.

TUNNELLING

A fire lit against a tunnel face would be enough to crack any solid rock and allow progress in short stages. Later, holes were drilled and packed with explosives to break up the rock. A major advance for tunnelling through soft earth or rock came in 1815 with the invention of the tunnelling shield. It consisted of a protective tubular metal structure pushed forward by jacks. As it was moved, a tunnel lining – originally bricks or cast-iron sections, later reinforced concrete – was installed behind it.

The same basic system is used today, such as for the Channel Tunnel project (left), but the digging is done by a tunnel-boring machine, which looks like a giant drill with a rotating cutter head and hard tungsten carbide teeth. Other types of automatic equipment remove the spoil, and install lining segments.

c.3000 BC The ancient Egyptians build an earth dam across the Nile for flood control.

c.2200 BC The earliest known bridge is built in Babylon.

c.2000 BC The earliest known canals are built in Egypt and Mesopotamia.

3rd century BC The first major sections of the Great Wall of China are erected.

312 BC The Romans begin their first paved military highway, the Appian Way.

109 BC The Milvian Bridge is built in Rome. It consists of three semicircular stone arches.

c.AD 300 The Roman imperial road network extends for more than 80 000 km (50 000 miles).

15th century The Great Wall of China is rebuilt. Extending for around 6325 km (3930 miles), including branches, the new wall is the longest man-made structure on Earth.

13th-16th centuries The Incas of Peru build a network of 16 000 km (10 000 miles) of roads.

1779 The first iron-arch bridge is built at Ironbridge in England.

3000 BC | 1000 BC | 0 | AD 1000 | 1700

7th century BC The first Roman bridge, made from timber, is built across the River Tiber.

c.540 BC The Chinese start building the Grand Canal.

c.1st century BC The people of northern Luzon, Philippines, start a system of vast rice terraces, which today extend for around 22 500 km (14 000 miles).

c.1290 In China, the rebuilding and extending of the Grand Canal begins. When completed, it runs for 1780 km (1110 miles) from Beijing to Hangzhou.

17th century Gunpowder is used for the first time for blasting tunnels through rock.

1670s The first major transport tunnel is dug along the Canal du Midi, France.

Building materials

Concrete and steel are the materials that, above all others, have made possible large-scale modern civil engineering works. Concrete is strongest in compression, while steel is strongest under tension. Combining them in reinforced concrete achieves the advantages of both. In prestressed concrete, stretched steel cables embedded in the wet concrete are released after setting. Other materials used to reinforce concrete include glass or fibres embedded in it to add strength, or plastic reinforcing rods used in place of steel.

DAMS AND BARRIERS

Most big dams have a compacted core of stones or earth, usually faced with concrete and stabilised by their own great weight. Sometimes they are buttressed on the downstream side to help to withstand the weight of the water.

Smaller ones may be built of solid concrete with steel reinforcing rods or cables. In a narrow canyon, a dam is curved outwards on the upstream side, arched against the pressure of the water. The curvature pushes much of the water pressure away from the dam itself and onto the canyon walls.

A variation is the temporary dam, or barrier, such as the one across the Thames in London (below), which, at 520 m (1705 ft), is the world's longest movable tidal barrier. Underwater gates can be raised to deal with any sudden surges of water from the sea, then lowered again to allow ships to pass.

Road construction

Roman roads were built primarily for infantry and not vehicles, often using layers of rammed earth and gravel, with a top layer of flat stones to give the soldiers a firm footing.

The next major advance came 1500 years later with the French engineer Pierre Trésaguet and the Scottish engineers John McAdam and Thomas Telford. They used layers of compacted graded stones, with a camber to aid drainage. Telford preferred a surface of flat stones, but McAdam's compacted small broken stones proved best – particularly when he later bonded them with tar to make tarmacadam, or 'tarmac'.

asphalt sealing on compacted stones in bituminous material (for urban roads)

strong concrete mix (used on motorways)

compacted stones in bituminous material

natural ground

layer of chalk or limestone

Airport on water
Runway space is at a premium in a densely populated, mountainous country such as Japan. One solution is to build island airports, such as Nagasaki airport, opened in 1975 and built on an artificially enlarged island.

see also
476-91 **Transport**
504-7 **Renewable energy**
572-3 **Building**
594-5 **Signs and wonders**

*c.*1815 Scottish engineers John McAdam and Thomas Telford devise methods for building durable roads.

1826 Thomas Telford builds the first iron suspension bridge, across the Menai Straits in Wales.

1825–43 French-born engineer Marc Brunel invents the tunnelling shield, used to dig the first rail tunnel under the River Thames.

1869 The Suez Canal is opened. It is 190 km (118 miles) in length.

1874 The first steel-arch bridge is built, at St Louis, Missouri.

1883 Brooklyn Bridge, the first suspension bridge using steel cables, is built in New York.

1892 Frenchman François Hennebique invents prestressed concrete.

1906–32 The Dutch build a 32 km (20 mile) dyke as part of a scheme to drain the Zuider Zee.

1914 The Panama Canal is opened. It is 82 km (51 miles) long, and has 12 locks to traverse the mountains.

1932 The Sydney Harbour Bridge is built.

1936 The Hoover Dam on the border of Arizona and Nevada is built.

1937 The Golden Gate Bridge is built in San Francisco. Its main span is 1280 m (4200 ft).

1962 The Grand Dixence Dam is built in Switzerland. It becomes the world's highest concrete dam.

1964 The Volga-Baltic Canal is constructed in Russia; it is 850 km (528 miles) long.

1969 The second Lake Pontchartrain Causeway in Louisiana becomes the longest multispan bridge in the world, at 38 km (24 miles).

1984 The Thames Flood Barrier is built in London.

1988 The Seikan railway tunnel in Japan is completed. It is the world's longest at 54 km (34 miles).

1994 The Channel Tunnel between France and Britain is completed. It is the world's longest underwater tunnel at 50 km (31 miles).

1998 The Akashi-Kaikyo Bridge in Japan becomes the world's longest suspension bridge, with a main span of 1990 m (6529 ft).

2000 The Øresund Bridge, a double-decker road and rail link joining Denmark and Sweden, becomes the world's longest cable-stayed bridge, 1092 m (3583 ft) long.

1800 1850 1900 1950 2000

Bridge construction

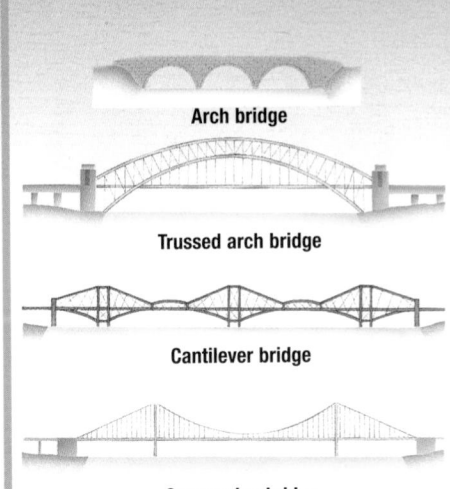

Arch bridge
Trussed arch bridge
Cantilever bridge
Suspension bridge

Bridge design has to take into account such factors as the gap to be spanned, the nature of the land underneath and on either side, and the type and amount of traffic it is intended to carry. There are seven main types:
Arch In an arch bridge, a deck formed of a rigid beam rests on a curved arch.
Beam This is the simplest of all bridge designs, in which the deck rests on piers at either end. Nowadays, the beam is made of reinforced concrete or steel girders.
Bowstring arch An arch, usually made of steel girders, rises above the deck beam, part or all of which is supported by hangers extending down from the arch.
Suspension This type of bridge can span longer distances than any other – up to 2000 m (7000 ft). The piers are extended upwards to form towers. Heavy, multistrand suspension cables, anchored firmly to the banks and passing over the top of the towers, support the deck via vertical hangers.
Cable-stayed This is similar to the suspension bridge, but regularly spaced individual steel cables run directly from the towers to the deck.
Trussed arch bridge In a trussed arch bridge, the deck beam is supported by a framework of bars that are arranged in a crisscross pattern for rigidity.
Cantilever This is a more complex version of a trussed bridge. There are usually two lozenge-shaped rigid trusses. Each is supported at its centre on a pier and anchored to the shore at one end. Their other ends are linked by a short beam.

The first weapons were implements designed for cutting wood or hunting, and adapted for use in combat. As civilisation advanced, however, weapons made solely for warfare began to appear. For more than 4000 years the emphasis was on hand-to-hand fighting and armour. Then, in the 16th century, everything changed as the development of firearms made killing from distance the most effective way of doing battle.

HISTORY OF ARMOUR

The earliest armour was made from padded leather, but the invention of the sword c.1500 BC created the need for greater protection. Ancient Greek warriors wore heavy bronze armour moulded to their body shape: at about the same time, bronze armour appeared in Egypt. The Iron Age brought chain mail – the oldest known piece is from Kiev, Ukraine, c.450 BC. Chain mail was standard issue for Roman soldiers until about the 1st century AD, when it was replaced with plate armour. This coped well with heavy blows, and remained in use for centuries.

30 000 BC The bow and arrow is already in use.
c.4000 BC Shields are first carried by Egyptian soldiers.
c.3000 BC Bronze axes appear in Mesopotamia.
c.2700 BC Warships with sails are used in the Mediterranean.
c.2500 BC Sumerians wear leather armour. They also invent the chariot.
c.1600 BC The Persians are the first soldiers known to use the war horse.

Roman helmet The Romans advanced both the technology and the art of war. Their legionary armies appeared around 100 BC.

c.900 In Europe, the first motte-and-bailey castles are built.
c.1000 The longbow appears in Wales.
c.1100 The trebuchet (siege catapult) is invented. The crossbow arrives in Europe.
1159 The Chinese develop the first rockets.
1200 The halberd and the pike (an extremely long-handled spear used by foot soldiers) are introduced.

Body shell Plate armour appeared in western Europe in the 1100s, and its design was perfected over the following four centuries. A full suit such as this (Germany c.1520) weighed around 32 kg (70 lb).

Visor

Gardbrace Deflected lance or pike thrusts away from the neck.

Pallette

Couter Covered the chain mailed elbow joint.

30 000 BC	AD 400	900	1200

c.1500 BC The Greeks invent bronze body armour.
c.1400 BC The first swords appear, also in Greece.
c.1200 BC Iron weapons appear in the Middle East.
c.500 BC The Persians invent a bow using animal tendons and horns, which stay elastic in hot weather.
c.400 BC The crossbow is invented in China.
c.250 BC Heavy artillery is mounted on Roman galleys.

AD 378 Gothic horsemen smash Roman legions at the Battle of Adrianople, bringing the age of cavalry to Europe.
475 The stirrup is invented in China, improving stability in the saddle for fighting.
c.800 The saddle arrives in Europe. European engineers develop mobile siege towers, called belfroys.
850 In China, a primitive gunpowder is described for the first time.

The halberd

An axe-cum-spear with a 2 m (6 ft) handle, the halberd allowed foot soldiers to do battle with men on horseback. The heavy axe blade cut cleanly through armour, while the long handle let the soldier keep his distance.

One disadvantage lay in the big swinging action needed to wield the halberd, which left the halberdier exposed. Cover was provided by men armed with swords and shields – the precursors of modern infantrymen.

Breastplate

Fauld Protected the hips and upper thighs while allowing them to move.

Gauntlet

Cuisse

Poleyn Hinged the cuisse and greave and covered the knee.

Greave

MOTTE AND BAILEY

Motte-and-bailey castles spread rapidly across Europe from the 10th century. Built originally of wood and later of stone, they consisted of a central tower (or keep) built on a mound (or motte); earthwork fortifications below the mound surrounded a courtyard (or bailey).

Returning Crusaders in the 12th century introduced refinements from the eastern Mediterranean, such as curtain walls with projecting towers. But by the 14th century castles were becoming outmoded in the face of a new weapon – the siege cannon.

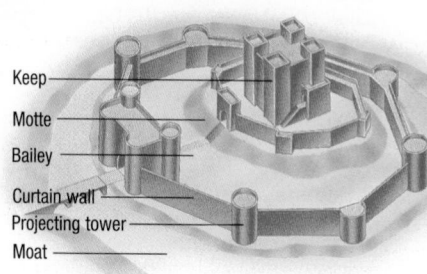

Keep
Motte
Bailey
Curtain wall
Projecting tower
Moat

Medieval fortress Castles changed over time. The moat was an early development, dating from the 900s.

THE BOW AND ARROW

The earliest bows were probably made from wood and strung with hide. A highly stressed wood/horn composite bow was introduced around 3000 BC – the horn strengthened the wood, increasing the bow's power and range.

Arrowheads were first fashioned from flint or obsidian, replaced later with bronze.

Preparing for battle A medieval warrior strings his longbow. The bow was capable of firing an arrow 180 m (600 ft) and could pierce armour at 60 m (200 ft).

Feather fletchings at the opposite end of the shaft improved the arrow's directional stability.

In the Middle Ages, the longbow transformed the battlefield. As tall as a man, it was capable of firing arrows with enough force to pierce chain mail. It could also shoot much farther than previous bows and, unlike the crossbow, was easy to load – a trained archer could easily fire 12 arrows a minute.

The longbow remained in use long after firearms were invented. It was finally superseded in the late 16th and early 17th centuries as musketry overtook it in power and accuracy.

1247 Firearms are used at the Siege of Seville – their first recorded appearance in battle.
1346 Cannons are introduced by English forces fighting the French at Crécy.
1370 The arbalest, a hand-cranked steel crossbow, is developed.
1385 Rockets are used in Europe for the first time.

1500 Rifling (grooving) is introduced in gun barrels. It produces a stabilising spin on the fired projectile.
1540 The first musket is made.
1650 The flintlock, designed to ignite the charge in small arms, is developed.

1740 The Dutch invent the short cannon, known as the howitzer.
1742 English mathematician and engineer Benjamin Robins establishes the science of ballistics, publishing his theories in *New Principles of Gunnery*.

Samuel Colt Colt (1814–62) patented his single-barrelled, five-shot revolver in 1836. Twenty years later he began manufacturing weapons using the production-line methods later adopted by Henry Ford for building cars. The six-shot, single-action .45-calibre Peacemaker, introduced 11 years after Colt's death, was to become the most popular hand gun in the American West.

Colt .45 This gun was the weapon of choice for most cowboys and used for years by the US Cavalry.

1240

1500

1700

1800

1860

1453 Sultan Muhammad II takes Constantinople with a cannon that can fire projectiles weighing up to 270 kg (600 lb).
1460 The matchlock, an early pistol, is developed.

The pistol The earliest pistols, dating from 1460, were called matchlocks – the gunpowder was ignited using a slow-burning match cord or wick. The next generation, flintlocks, had a flint mechanism instead. Both matchlocks and flintlocks fired balls of lead, which were loaded by being pushed down the muzzle.

1811 American John Hall patents the breech-loaded rifle.
1846 The first one-piece cartridge (charge, percussion cap and projectile in a single unit) is produced.
1849 The first modern bullet is made.
1858-9 The world's earliest iron-clad warship, *La Gloire*, is built for the French navy.

1862 American Richard Gatling invents the machine gun.
1863 TNT is invented.
1866 British engineer Robert Whitehead invents the torpedo.
1884 American Hiram Maxim develops the Maxim machine gun, capable of firing 600 rounds per minute.

Lethal weapon This deadly projectile, known as a quarrel or bolt, was fired from a crossbow.

FACT The shrapnel shell was invented by and named after British general Henry Shrapnel in 1784.

Flintlock pistol The successor to the matchlock used friction from a flint to ignite the charge.

FROM CATAPULT TO CANNON

The catapult and, later, the trebuchet were the first weapons designed to hurl heavy objects at the enemy. But it was not until the explosive power of gunpowder was harnessed that large weapons began to play a major role in warfare.

Originally made of bronze, then later of iron, the siege cannon led to the demise of the fortified city. By the end of the 1300s, siege cannons were capable of delivering stone cannonballs weighing 200 kg (450 lb). As foundry procedures improved in the 15th century, cannon capable of taking ever larger charges were cast. Stone cannonballs gave way to iron ones, which were denser and capable of causing greater damage.

Smaller cannon began to be adopted on warships, and by the 1500s were the main weapons of naval conflict.

Field gun The use of cannon in battle increased in the 18th and 19th centuries as guns became lighter and carriage design improved.

In the 20th century, two world wars greatly accelerated the development of weapons. Aircraft and armoured vehicles appeared, changing the way that campaigns were fought. As the Second World War ended, the nuclear era began and weapons of mass destruction proliferated. Today, computers play an increasingly important role, enabling smart weapons to hit targets with pinpoint accuracy.

NUCLEAR WEAPONS

The immense power of nuclear weapons is generated by the fission, or fusion, of atomic nuclei.

The first offensive nuclear weapon, used against Hiroshima, Japan, in 1945, delivered a 15 kiloton explosion from the fission of 60 kg (130 lb) of uranium. Later weapons were capable of delivering an explosive force four times greater than this

by using the energy from nuclear fission to drive an even more destructive fusion reaction.

During the postwar arms race, the USA and USSR amassed stockpiles of 32 000 and 33 000 warheads respectively. By 2001, seven countries were known for certain to have nuclear weapons: China, France, India, Pakistan, Russia, the UK and the USA.

1914 The Germans are the first to use submarines in war.
1915 A chlorine gas attack by German forces marks the beginning of modern chemical warfare. Zeppelin raids on Britain comprise the first strategic bombing offensive. Germany builds the first aeroplane with a machine gun that can fire between moving propeller blades.

1920 American John T. Thompson patents the submachine gun, also known as the tommy gun.
1922 For the first time a plane lands on an aircraft carrier, the USS *Langley*. Hitherto planes have only taken off from carriers.

1931 Soviet troops make the first parachute assault.
1935 The British develop a crude form of radar.
1936 The prototype of R.J. Mitchell's Spitfire makes its maiden flight.
1937 The British build a chain of radar defences along England's east coast.
1937 Wernher von Braun begins testing designs for the V-2 rocket.

◖ **Manhattan Project** In 1939 Albert Einstein brought to the attention of American President Roosevelt the destructive potential of nuclear fission – the principle behind the first atomic bomb. The USA had not at this point joined the Second World War; nonetheless, Roosevelt gave the go-ahead to what became code-named the Manhattan Project.

The project gathered pace after the USA entered the war in 1941. More than $2 billion had been spent on research by July 16, 1945, when the first atomic bomb was detonated at Alamogordo air base in New Mexico. The years of work culminated three weeks later when bombs detonated over the cities of Hiroshima and Nagasaki led to Japan's surrender.

| 1900 | 1920 | 1930 | 1940 |

1916 Tanks see action for the first time during the Battle of the Somme.
1918 The fully rotatable turret appears in tank design. atop the French Renault FT-17.

◖ **The tank** Tanks were developed to break the deadlock of trench warfare in the First World War. They could cross rough terrain, plough through barbed-wire defences and open the way for following infantry. Early models were capable of only 7 km/h (4 mph), but by the outbreak of the Second World War refinements had made tanks the principal weapons of land warfare.

Mark V This British tank was introduced in 1918.

1941 The US army takes delivery of its first Jeep.
1942 A controlled nuclear reaction takes place for the first time, at the University of Chicago.
1945 At 8.15 local time on August 6, a US plane drops the first atomic bomb, on Hiroshima, Japan.

1947 The US navy begins building nuclear-powered submarines.
1954 Britain develops the first vertical-take-off plane, nicknamed the 'flying bedstead'.
1957 Americans and Soviets both successfully develop intercontinental ballistic missiles.
1958 The US navy's nuclear submarine *Nautilus* travels under the North Pole.

THE MODERN FIREARM

The majority of soldiers today carry assault rifles. These are designed to combine the accuracy of a hunting rifle with the rapid firing capability of a machine gun. The world's most popular assault rifle is the Kalashnikov.

The original model, the AK47, was designed by the Soviet Army sergeant Mikhail Kalashnikov in 1947. In 1974, the gun was modified to fire smaller calibre bullets and renamed the AK74.

butt | trigger grip | gas piston | foresight

magazine | **AK47** Weighing just 3.15 kg (7 lb), the gas-operated AK47 is capable of firing 600 rounds a minute. It is estimated that as many as 50 million Kalashnikov assault rifles have been manufactured to date.

THE MODERN SOLDIER

Today's soldier is heavily armed but lightly armoured; survival in modern combat depends largely on not being seen. Camouflage was first used by soldiers in the First World War and now occurs in the uniforms of armies around the globe.

As well as weapons and uniform, today's soldiers carry everything they need to stay alive. This includes food, medical supplies and, in some cases, protective clothing for surviving attack with biological and chemical weapons.

Backpack Contains rations, ammunition, sleeping-bag, clothing, field dressings and entrenching tool.

US marine Dressed in full kit in standard woodland camouflage. During the Gulf War desert and night-time camouflage was developed, and used by the marines.

Helmet Made of Kevlar for lightness and strength.

M16 Fires up to 950 rounds per minute. Also used by Australian troops and the SAS.

Uniform Cotton or nylon but may include garments in modern fabrics such as Goretex for weather protection.

Biggest defence spenders	
	percentage of GDP, 1998
1 Eritrea	36.6
2 Saudi Arabia	15.7
3 Afghanistan	14.7
4 North Korea	14.3
5 Oman	12.7
6 Kuwait	12.6
7 Angola	11.8
8 Israel	11.7
9 Qatar	11.6
10 Croatia; Tajikistan	8.3

Largest armed forces	
	million service personnel, 1998
1 China	2.48[1]
2 United States	1.37
3 India	1.17
4 Russia	1.00[2]
5 South Korea	0.67[3]
6 Turkey	0.64[4]
7 Pakistan	0.59
8 Iran	0.55[5]
9 Vietnam	0.48
10 Egypt	0.45

[1] Including 51 per cent conscripts
[2] Including 33 per cent conscripts
[3] Including 24 per cent conscripts
[4] Including 83 per cent conscripts
[5] Including 46 per cent conscripts

1973 NASA launches Skylab 2, the first American space station.
1981 The space shuttle makes its first mission. A space transport plane, it was designed for use by the US military.

1983 The Lockheed F-117A, the first 'stealth' fighter (designed to be invisible to enemy radar), becomes operational.
1983 The USA takes the first steps towards a 'Star Wars' space-based defence system.

Disappearing act The F-117A was the first plane designed to elude radar.

Cruise control A harpoon missile heads for its target.

1980

1990

1984 First suspected use of nerve gas in war, by Iraqi forces fighting Iran.
1989 The United States Air Force introduces the stealth bomber.

1991 The Gulf War sees widespread use of smart weapons, such as the Tomahawk cruise missile.
2000 'Son of Star Wars' is proposed by the USA.

Star Wars In 1983 the USA announced its Strategic Defense Initiative. Nicknamed 'Star Wars', it was designed to defend the country from nuclear attack. Early-warning satellites would detect incoming missiles, which would in turn be shot down by space-based orbiting missile launchers. The US military invested around $2 billion in the project, but failed to devise a system that gave complete protection. 'Son of Star Wars', announced in 2000, was a simplified version: satellites would still help to detect incoming missiles, but these would be intercepted by land-based weapons.

SMART WEAPONS

A smart weapon is equipped with hi-tech systems designed to direct it with precision to its target. A laser-guided missile, for example, locks on to any target illuminated by a laser beam. The laser may be pointed at the target by a soldier on the ground (often special forces acting behind enemy lines) or aimed from an aircraft circling above.

Laser guided The GBU-16/B carries almost half a tonne of high explosive.

see also
208-9 **First World War**
214-5 **Second World War**
218-9 **The Cold War**
532 **Radioactivity**

Ready reference

Ready reference

The Oscars

The US Academy of Motion Picture Arts and Sciences made its first awards in 1929. Presentations take place in Los Angeles each March for films shown in US cinemas the previous year – in the lists of winners below the year is the one in which the film was first shown, not the year in which the award was given. There are various theories as to why the statuette received by winners was nicknamed 'Oscar'; one story relates that the academy's librarian joked that it looked like her uncle Oscar.

Best picture

Year	Film	Year	Film	Year	Film	Year	Film
1927-8	Wings	1940	Rebecca	1953	From Here to Eternity	1977	Annie Hall
1928-9	Broadway Melody	1941	How Green Was My Valley	1954	On the Waterfront	1978	The Deer Hunter
1929-30	All Quiet on the Western Front	1942	Mrs Miniver	1955	Marty	1979	Kramer vs Kramer
1930-1	Cimarron	1943	Casablanca	1956	Around the World in 80 Days	1980	Ordinary People
1931-2	Grand Hotel	1944	Going My Way	1957	The Bridge on the River Kwai	1981	Chariots of Fire
1932-3	Cavalcade	1945	The Lost Weekend	1958	Gigi	1982	Gandhi
1934	It Happened One Night	1946	The Best Years of Our Lives	1959	Ben Hur	1983	Terms of Endearment
1935	Mutiny on the Bounty	1947	Gentlemen's Agreement	1960	The Apartment	1984	Amadeus
1936	The Great Ziegfeld	1948	Hamlet	1961	West Side Story	1985	Out of Africa
1937	The Life of Emile Zola	1949	All the King's Men	1962	Lawrence of Arabia	1986	Platoon
1938	You Can't Take It With You	1950	All About Eve	1963	Tom Jones	1987	The Last Emperor
1939	Gone With the Wind	1951	An American in Paris	1964	My Fair Lady	1988	Rain Man
		1952	The Greatest Show on Earth	1965	The Sound of Music	1989	Driving Miss Daisy
				1966	A Man for All Seasons	1990	Dances With Wolves
				1967	In the Heat of the Night	1991	The Silence of the Lambs
				1968	Oliver!	1992	Unforgiven
				1969	Midnight Cowboy	1993	Schindler's List
				1970	Patton	1994	Forrest Gump
				1971	The French Connection	1995	Braveheart
				1972	The Godfather	1996	The English Patient
				1973	The Sting	1997	Titanic
				1974	The Godfather: Part II	1998	Shakespeare in Love
				1975	One Flew Over the Cuckoo's Nest	1999	American Beauty
				1976	Rocky	2000	Gladiator

Best actor

Year	Actor	Year	Actor	Year	Actor	Year	Actor
1927-8	Emil Jannings (The Last Command)	1943	Paul Lucas (Watch on the Rhine)	1963	Sydney Poitier (Lilies of the Field)	1984	F. Murray Abraham (Amadeus)
1928-9	Warner Baxter (In Old Arizona)	1944	Bing Crosby (Going My Way)	1964	Rex Harrison (My Fair Lady)	1985	William Hurt (Kiss of the Spider Woman)
1929-30	George Arliss (Disraeli)	1945	Ray Milland (The Lost Weekend)	1965	Lee Marvin (Cat Ballou)	1986	Paul Newman (The Color of Money)
1930-1	Lionel Barrymore (A Free Soul) Fredric March (The Royal Family of Broadway)	1946	Fredric March (The Best Years of Our Lives)	1966	Paul Scofield (A Man for All Seasons)	1987	Michael Douglas (Wall Street)
1931-2	Wallace Beery (The Champ) Fredric March (Dr Jekyll and Mr Hyde)	1947	Ronald Colman (A Double Life)	1967	Rod Steiger (In the Heat of the Night)	1988	Dustin Hoffman (Rain Man)
		1948	Laurence Olivier (Hamlet)	1968	Cliff Robertson (Charly)	1989	Daniel Day Lewis (My Left Foot)
1932-3	Charles Laughton (The Private Life of Henry VIII)	1949	Broderick Crawford (All the King's Men)	1969	John Wayne (True Grit)	1990	Jeremy Irons (Reversal of Fortune)
1934	Clark Gable (It Happened One Night)	1950	Jose Ferrer (Cyrano de Bergerac)	1970	George C. Scott (Patton)	1991	Anthony Hopkins (The Silence of the Lambs)
1935	Victor McLaglen (The Informer)	1951	Humphrey Bogart (The African Queen)	1971	Gene Hackman (The French Connection)	1992	Al Pacino (Scent of a Woman)
1936	Paul Muni (The Story of Louis Pasteur)	1952	Gary Cooper (High Noon)	1972	Marlon Brando (The Godfather)	1993	Tom Hanks (Philadelphia)
1937	Spencer Tracy (Captain Courageous)	1953	William Holden (Stalag 17)	1973	Jack Lemmon (Save the Tiger)	1994	Tom Hanks (Forrest Gump)
1938	Spencer Tracy (Boys' Town)	1954	Marlon Brando (On the Waterfront)	1974	Art Carney (Harry and Tonto)	1995	Nicholas Cage (Leaving Las Vegas)
1939	Robert Donat (Goodbye, Mr Chips)	1955	Ernest Borgnine (Marty)	1975	Jack Nicholson (One Flew Over the Cuckoo's Nest)	1996	Geoffrey Rush (Shine)
1940	James Stewart (The Philadelphia Story)	1956	Yul Brynner (The King and I)	1976	Peter Finch (Network)	1997	Jack Nicholson (As Good As It Gets)
1941	Gary Cooper (Sergeant York)	1957	Alec Guinness (The Bridge on the River Kwai)	1977	Richard Dreyfuss (The Goodbye Girl)	1998	Roberto Benigni (Life is Beautiful)
1942	James Cagney (Yankee Doodle Dandy)	1958	David Niven (Separate Tables)	1978	Jon Voight (Coming Home)	1999	Kevin Spacey (American Beauty)
		1959	Charlton Heston (Ben Hur)	1979	Dustin Hoffman (Kramer vs Kramer)	2000	Russell Crowe (Gladiator)
		1960	Burt Lancaster (Elmer Gantry)	1980	Robert De Niro (Raging Bull)		
		1961	Maximilian Schell (Judgment at Nuremberg)	1981	Henry Fonda (On Golden Pond)		
		1962	Gregory Peck (To Kill a Mockingbird)	1982	Ben Kingsley (Gandhi)		
				1983	Robert Duvall (Tender Mercies)		

Best actress

Year	Actress	Year	Actress	Year	Actress	Year	Actress
1927-8	Janet Gaynor (Seventh Heaven)	1938	Bette Davis (Jezebel)	1949	Olivia de Havilland (The Heiress)	1960	Elizabeth Taylor (Butterfield 8)
1928-9	Mary Pickford (Coquette)	1939	Vivien Leigh (Gone With the Wind)	1950	Judy Holliday (Born Yesterday)	1961	Sophia Loren (Two Women)
1929-30	Norma Shearer (The Divorcee)	1940	Ginger Rogers (Kitty Foyle)	1951	Vivien Leigh (A Streetcar Named Desire)	1962	Anne Bancroft (The Miracle Worker)
1930-1	Marie Dressler (Min and Bill)	1941	Joan Fontaine (Suspicion)	1952	Shirley Booth (Come Back, Little Sheba)	1963	Patricia Neal (Hud)
1931-2	Helen Hayes (The Sin of Madelon Claudet)	1942	Greer Garson (Mrs Miniver)	1953	Audrey Hepburn (Roman Holiday)	1964	Julie Andrews (Mary Poppins)
1932-3	Katharine Hepburn (Morning Glory)	1943	Jennifer Jones (The Song of Bernadette)	1954	Grace Kelly (The Country Girl)	1965	Julie Christie (Darling)
1934	Claudette Colbert (It Happened One Night)	1944	Ingrid Bergman (Gaslight)	1955	Anna Magnani (The Rose Tattoo)	1966	Elizabeth Taylor (Who's Afraid of Virginia Wolf?)
1935	Bette Davis (Dangerous)	1945	Joan Crawford (Mildred Pierce)	1956	Ingrid Bergman (Anastasia)	1967	Katharine Hepburn (Guess Who's Coming to Dinner)
1936	Luise Rainer (The Great Ziegfeld)	1946	Olivia de Havilland (To Each his Own)	1957	Joanne Woodward (The Three Faces of Eve)	1968	Katharine Hepburn (The Lion in Winter)
1937	Luise Rainer (The Good Earth)	1947	Loretta Young (The Farmer's Daughter)	1958	Susan Hayward (I Want to Live)	1969	Maggie Smith (The Prime of Miss Jean Brodie)
		1948	Jane Wyman (Johnny Belinda)	1959	Simone Signoret (Room at the Top)		

1970	Glenda Jackson (Women in Love)	1978	Jane Fonda (Coming Home)	1986	Marlee Matlin (Children of a Lesser God)	1994	Jessica Lange (Blue Sky)
1971	Jane Fonda (Klute)	1979	Sally Field (Norma Rae)	1987	Cher (Moonstruck)	1995	Susan Sarandon (Dead Man Walking)
1972	Liza Minnelli (Cabaret)	1980	Sissy Spacek (Coal Miner's Daughter)	1988	Jodie Foster (The Accused)	1996	Frances McDormand (Fargo)
1973	Glenda Jackson (A Touch of Class)	1981	Katharine Hepburn (On Golden Pond)	1989	Jessica Tandy (Driving Miss Daisy)	1997	Helen Hunt (As Good As It Gets)
1974	Ellen Burstyn (Alice Doesn't Live Here Anymore)	1982	Meryl Streep (Sophie's Choice)	1990	Kathy Bates (Misery)	1998	Gwyneth Paltrow (Shakespeare in Love)
1975	Louise Fletcher (One Flew Over the Cuckoo's Nest)	1983	Shirley MacLaine (Terms of Endearment)	1991	Jodie Foster (The Silence of the Lambs)	1999	Hilary Swank (Boys Don't Cry)
1976	Faye Dunaway (Network)	1984	Sally Field (Places in the Heart)	1992	Emma Thompson (Howard's End)	2000	Julia Roberts (Erin Brockovich)
1977	Diane Keaton (Annie Hall)	1985	Geraldine Page (The Trip to Bountiful)	1993	Holly Hunter (The Piano)		

Cannes Palme d'Or

The Cannes international film festival, which was first held in 1946, takes place in May each year. The award for best film, known as the Palme d'Or, has often been shared between two films.

1946	Battle of the Rails (La Bataille du Rail)	1974	The Conversation
1947	No award	1975	Chronicle of the Burning Years (Chronique des Années de Braise)
1948	No award		
1949	The Third Man	1976	Taxi Driver
1950	No award	1977	Padre Padrone
1951	Miracle in Milan (Miracolo a Milano)	1978	The Tree of Wooden Clogs (L'Albergo Degli Zoccoli)
	Miss Julie (Froken Julie)	1979	The Tin Drum (Die Blechtrommel)
1952	Two Pennyworth of Hope (Due Soldi di Speranza)		Apocalypse Now
	Othello	1980	Kagemusha
1953	The Wages of Fear (Le Salaire de la Peur)		All That Jazz
		1981	Man of Iron (L'Homme de Fer)
1954	Gate of Hell (Jigoku-Mon)	1982	Missing
1955	Marty		Yol
1956	The Silent World (Le Monde du Silence)	1983	The Ballad of Narayama (Narayama-Bushi-Ko)
1957	Friendly Persuasion	1984	Paris Texas
1958	The Cranes Are Flying (Letyat Zhuravli)	1985	When Father was Away on Business (Otac Na Sluzbenom Putu)
1959	Black Orpheus (Orfeu Negro)	1986	The Mission
1960	La Dolce Vita	1987	Under Satan's Sun (Sous le Soleil de Satan)
1961	Viridiana		
	The Long Absence (Une Aussi Longue Absence)	1988	Pelle the Conqueror (Pelle Erobreren)
1962	The Given Word (O Pagador de Promessas)	1989	Sex, Lies and Videotape
		1990	Wild at Heart
1963	The Leopard (Il Gattopardo)	1991	Barton Fink
1964	The Umbrellas of Cherbourg (Les Parapluies de Cherbourg)	1992	The Best Intentions (Den Goda Viljan)
1965	The Knack and How to Get It	1993	The Piano
1966	A Man and a Woman (Un Homme et une Femme)		Farewell my Concubine (Bawang Bieji)
	The Birds, the Bees, and the Italians (Signore e Signori)	1994	Pulp Fiction
		1995	Underground
1967	Blow Up	1996	Secrets and Lies
1968	No award	1997	The Eel (Unagi)
1969	If		The Taste of Cherry (Ta'm é Guilass)
1970	M*A*S*H		
1971	The Go-Between	1998	Eternity and a Day (Mia Eoniotita Ke Mia Mera)
1972	The Working Class Go to Heaven (La Classe Operaia Va in Paradiso)	1999	Rosetta
		2000	Dancer in the Dark
	The Mattei Affair (Il Caso Mattei)	2001	The Son's Room (La Stanza del Figlio)
1973	Scarecrow		
	The Hireling		

Eurovision Song Contest

The Eurovision Song Contest was first staged in Switzerland in 1956. The contest is organised by the European Broadcasting Union (EBU), which links Europe's leading TV broadcasters.

1956	'Refrain'	Lys Assia	Switzerland
1957	'Net Als Toen'	Corry Brokken	Netherlands
1958	'Dors Mon Amour'	André Claveau	France
1959	'Een Beetje'	Teddy Scholten	Netherlands
1960	'Tom Pillibi'	Jacqueline Boyer	France
1961	'Nous Les Amoureux'	Jean-Claude Pascal	Luxembourg
1962	'Un Premier Amour'	Isabelle Aubret	France
1963	'Dansevise'	Grethe and Jorgen Ingmann	Denmark
1964	'No Ho L'Eta'	Gigliola Cinquetti	Italy
1965	'Poupée de Cire, Poupée de Son'	France Gall	Luxembourg
1966	'Merci Chérie'	Udo Jurgens	Austria
1967	'Puppet On a String'	Sandie Shaw	UK
1968	'La La La'	Massiel	Spain
1969	'Boom Bang-A-Bang'	Lulu	UK
	'Un Jour, Un Enfant'	Frida Boccana	France
	'Vivo Cantando'	Salomé	Spain
	'De Troubadour'	Lennie Kuhr	Netherlands
1970	'All Kinds of Everything'	Dana	Ireland
1971	'Un Banc, Un Arbre, Une Rue'	Séverine	Monaco
1972	'Après Toi'	Vicky Leandros	Luxembourg
1973	'Tu Te Reconnaîtras'	Anne-Marie David	Luxembourg
1974	'Waterloo'	Abba	Sweden
1975	'Ding Dinge Dong'	Teach-In	Netherlands
1976	'Save Your Kisses For Me'	Brotherhood of Man	UK
1977	'L'Oiseau et L'Enfant'	Marie Myriam	France
1978	'A Ba Ni Bi'	Izhar Cohen and Alphabeta	Israel
1979	'Hallelujah'	Milk and Honey	Israel
1980	'What's Another Year'	Johnny Logan	Ireland
1981	'Making Your Mind Up'	Bucks Fizz	UK
1982	'Ein Bisschen Frieden'	Nicole	West Germany
1983	'Si La Vie Est Cadeau'	Corinne Hermès	Luxembourg
1984	'Diggi-Loo Diggi-Ley'	The Herreys	Sweden
1985	'La Det Swinge'	Bobbysocks	Norway
1986	'J'Aime La Vie'	Sandra Kim	Belgium
1987	'Hold Me Now'	Johnny Logan	Ireland
1988	'Ne Partez Pas Sans Moi'	Céline Dion	Switzerland
1989	'Rock Me'	Riva	Yugoslavia
1990	'Insieme: 1992'	Toto Cutugno	Italy
1991	'Fangad Av En Stormvind'	Carola	Sweden
1992	'Why Me?'	Linda Martin	Ireland
1993	'In Your Eyes'	Niamh Kavanagh	Ireland
1994	'Rock 'n Roll Kids'	Paul Harrington and Charlie McGettigan	Ireland
1995	'Nocturne'	Secret Garden	Norway
1996	'The Voice'	Eimear Quinn	Ireland
1997	'Love Shine a Light'	Katrina and the Waves	UK
1998	'Diva'	Dana International	Israel
1999	'Take Me to Your Heaven'	Charlotte Nilsson	Sweden
2000	'Fly on the Wings of Love'	The Olsen Brothers	Denmark
2001	'Everybody'	Tanel Padar and Dave Benton	Estonia

Nobel prizes

Alfred Bernhard Nobel, the Swedish inventor of dynamite and gelignite, left most of his fortune to found the Nobel prizes. These were to be awarded to those who have 'conferred the greatest benefit on mankind', and for a body of work rather than a single work. There are six categories: physics, chemistry, economics, physiology or medicine, literature and peace. Winners are announced each October. The awards are presented in December; the peace prize in Oslo, Norway, the rest in Stockholm, Sweden. The prizes are worth about £645 000 each.

Nobel prize for peace

1901	Jean Henri Dunant (Switzerland)
	Frederic Passy (France)
1902	Elie Ducommun (Switzerland)
	Charles Albert Gobat (Switzerland)
1903	Sir William Randal Cremer (UK)
1904	Institut de Droit International (Belgium)
1905	Baroness Bertha von Suttner (Austria)
1906	Theodore Roosevelt (USA)
1907	Ernesto Moneta (Italy)
	Louis Renault (France)
1908	Klas Arnoldson (Sweden)
	Fredrik Bajer (Denmark)
1909	Auguste Beernaert (Belgium)
	Paul d'Estournelles de Constant (France)
1910	Bureau International Permanent de la Paix (Switzerland)
1911	Tobias Asser (Netherlands)
	Alfred Fried (Austria)
1912	No award
1913	Elihu Root (USA)
	Henri la Fontaine (Belgium)
1914-16	No award
1917	Comité International de la Croix-Rouge (Red Cross) (Switzerland)
1918	No award
1919	Woodrow Wilson (USA)
1920	Leon Bourgeois (France)
1921	Karl Branting (Sweden)
	Christian Lange (Norway)
1922	Fridtjof Nansen (Norway)
1923-4	No award
1925	Joseph Chamberlain (UK)
	Charles Dawes (USA)
1926	Aristide Briand (France)
	Gustav Stresemann (Germany)
1927	Ferdinand Buisson (France)
	Ludwig Quidde (Germany)
1928	No award
1929	Frank Kellogg (USA)
1930	Lars Söderblom (Sweden)
1931	Jane Addams (USA)
	Nicholas Murray Butler (USA)
1932	No award
1933	Sir Norman Angell (UK)
1934	Arthur Henderson (UK)
1935	Carl von Ossietzky (Germany)
1936	Carlos Saavedra Lamas (Argentina)
1937	Viscount Cecil of Chelwood (UK)
1938	Office International Nansen pour les Refugiés (Switzerland)
1939-43	No award
1944	Comité International de la Croix-Rouge (Red Cross) (Switzerland)
1945	Cordell Hull (USA)
1946	Emily Greene Balch (USA)
	John Raleigh Mott (USA)
1947	The Friends Service Council (UK)
	The American Friends Service Committee (USA)
1948	No award
1949	Lord Boyd Orr of Brechin (UK)
1950	Ralph Bunche (USA)
1951	Léon Jouhaux (France)
1952	Albert Schweitzer (France)
1953	George Marshall (USA)
1954	Office of the United Nations High Commissioner for Refugees
1955-6	No award
1957	Lester Bowles Pearson (Canada)
1958	Georges Pire (Belgium)
1959	Philip Noel-Baker (UK)
1960	Albert Lutuli (South Africa)
1961	Dag Hammarskjöld (Sweden)
1962	Linus Pauling (USA)
1963	Comité International de la Croix-Rouge (Red Cross) (Switzerland)
	Ligue des Sociétés de la Croix-Rouge (Switzerland)
1964	Martin Luther King Jr (USA)
1965	United Nations Children's Fund (Unicef)
1966-7	No award
1968	René Cassin (France)
1969	International Labour Organisation (Switzerland)
1970	Norman Borlaug (USA)
1971	Willy Brandt (West Germany)
1972	No award
1973	Henry Kissinger (USA)
	Le Duc Tho (Vietnam, declined)
1974	Seán MacBride (Republic of Ireland)
	Sato Eisaku (Japan)
1975	Andrei Sakharov (USSR)
1976	Betty Williams (UK)
	Mairead Corrigan (UK)
1977	Amnesty International (UK)
1978	Anwar el Sadat (Egypt)
	Menachem Begin (Israel)
1979	Mother Teresa (Yugoslavia)
1980	Adolfo Perez Esquivel (Argentina)
1981	Office of the United Nations High Commissioner for Refugees
1982	Alva Myrdal (Sweden)
	Alfonso Garcia Robles (Mexico)
1983	Lech Walesa (Poland)
1984	Desmond Mpilo Tutu (South Africa)
1985	International Physicians for the Prevention of Nuclear War Inc (USA)
1986	Elie Wiesel (USA)
1987	Oscar Arias Sanchez (Costa Rica)
1988	UN Peace-keeping Forces
1989	Dalai Lama (Tenzin Gyatso) (Tibet)
1990	Mikhail Gorbachev (USSR)
1991	Aung San Suu Kyi (Myanmar)
1992	Rigoberta Menchú Tum (Guatemala)
1993	Nelson Mandela (South Africa)
	Frederik Willem de Klerk (South Africa)
1994	Yasser Arafat (PLO)
	Shimon Peres (Israel)
	Yitzhak Rabin (Israel)
1995	Joseph Rotblat (UK)
	Pugwash Conference on Science and World Affairs (Canada)
1996	Carlos Filipe Ximenese Belo (East Timor)
	José Ramos-Horta (East Timor)
1997	International Campaign to Ban Landmines (USA)
	Jody Williams (USA)
1998	John Hume (Northern Ireland)
	David Trimble (Northern Ireland)
1999	Médecins Sans Frontières (France)
2000	Kim Dae Jung (South Korea)

Nobel prize for literature

1901	Sully Prudhomme (France)
1902	Theodor Mommsen (Germany)
1903	Bjornstjerne Bjornson (Norway)
1904	Frederic Mistral (France)
	Jose Eizaguirre (Spain)
1905	Henryk Sienkiewicz (Poland)
1906	Giosue Carducci (Italy)
1907	Rudyard Kipling (UK)
1908	Rudolf Eucken (Germany)
1909	Selma Lagerlöf (Sweden)
1910	Paul von Heyse (Germany)
1911	Maurice Maeterlinck (Belgium)
1912	Gerhart Hauptmann (Germany)
1913	Rabindranath Tagore (India)
1914	No award
1915	Romain Rolland (France)
1916	Verner von Heidenstam (Sweden)
1917	Karl Gjellerup (Denmark)
	Henrik Pontoppidan (Denmark)
1918	No award
1919	Carl Spitteler (Switzerland)
1920	Knut Hamsun (Norway)
1921	Anatole France (France)
1922	Jacinto Martinez (Spain)
1923	W.B. Yeats (Ireland)
1924	Wladyslaw Stanislaw Reymont (Poland)
1925	George Bernard Shaw (UK)
1926	Grazia Deledda (Italy)
1927	Henri Louis Bergson (France)
1928	Sigrid Undset (Norway)
1929	Thomas Mann (Germany)
1930	Sinclair Lewis (USA)
1931	Erik Axel Karlfeldt (Sweden)
1932	John Galsworthy (UK)
1933	Ivan Bunin (Russian, domiciled France)
1934	Luigi Pirandello (Italy)
1935	No award
1936	Eugene O'Neill (USA)
1937	Roger Martin Du Gard (France)
1938	Pearl S. Buck (USA)
1939	Frans Eemil Sillanpaa (Finland)
1940-3	No award
1944	Johannes V. Jensen (Denmark)
1945	Gabriela Mistral (Chile)
1946	Hermann Hesse (Switzerland)
1947	André Gide (France)
1948	T.S. Eliot (UK)
1949	No award
1950	William Faulkner (USA)
	Bertrand Russell (UK)
1951	Pär Lagerkvist (Sweden)
1952	François Mauriac (France)
1953	Winston Churchill (UK)
1954	Ernest Hemingway (USA)
1955	Halldor Kiljan Laxness (Iceland)
1956	Juan Ramón Jiménez (Spain)
1957	Albert Camus (France)
1958	Boris Pasternak (USSR)
1959	Salvatore Quasimodo (Italy)
1960	Saint-John Perse (France)
1961	Ivo Andric (Yugoslavia)
1962	John Steinbeck (USA)
1963	George Seferis (Greece)
1964	Jean-Paul Sartre (France)
1965	Mikhail Sholokhov (USSR)
1966	S.Y. Agnon (Israel)
	Nelly Sachs (Sweden)
1967	Miguel Angel Asturias (Guatemala)
1968	Yasunari Kawabata (Japan)
1969	Samuel Beckett (Ireland)
1970	Alexander Solzhenitsyn (USSR)
1971	Pablo Neruda (Chile)
1972	Heinrich Böll (West Germany)
1973	Patrick White (Australia)
1974	Harry Martinson (Sweden)
	Eyind Johnson (Sweden)
1975	Eugenio Montale (Italy)
1976	Saul Bellow (USA)
1977	Vincente Aleixandre (Spain)
1978	Isaac Bashevis Singer (USA)
1979	Odysseus Elytis (Greece)
1980	Czeslaw Milosz (USA/Poland)
1981	Elias Canetti (UK)
1982	Gabriel García Márquez (Colombia)
1983	William Golding (UK)
1984	Jaroslav Seifert (Czechoslovakia)
1985	Claude Simon (France)
1986	Wole Soyinka (Nigeria)
1987	Joseph Brodsky (USA)
1988	Naguib Mahfouz (Egypt)
1989	Camilo José Cela (Spain)
1990	Octavio Paz (Mexico)
1991	Nadine Gordimer (South Africa)
1992	Derek Walcott (St Lucia)
1993	Toni Morrison (USA)
1994	Kenzaburo Oe (Japan)
1995	Seamus Heaney (Ireland)
1996	Wislawa Szymborska (Poland)
1997	Dario Fo (Italy)
1998	José Saramago (Portugal)
1999	Günter Grass (Germany)
2000	Gao Xingjian (China)

Pulitzer prizes

In his will, the US newpaper proprietor Joseph Pulitzer established the annual Pulitzer prizes for American journalism, music and letters. The prizes are awarded by the Columbia University School of Journalism, also founded by Pulitzer.

There are 14 categories for journalism, including investigative reporting and news photography, one category for music (composition), and six prizes for 'letters': novel, drama, poetry, biography, general non-fiction and general history. Winners in each category receive $7500.

Pulitzer prize: novel

1917	No award
1918	Ernest Poole, *His Family*
1919	Booth Tarkington, *The Magnificent Ambersons*
1920	No award
1921	Edith Wharton, *The Age of Innocence*
1922	Booth Tarkington, *Alice Adams*
1923	Willa Cather, *One of Ours*
1924	Margaret Wilson, *The Able McLaughlins*
1925	Edna Ferber, *So Big*
1926	Sinclair Lewis, *Arrowsmith*
1927	Louis Bromfield, *Early Autumn*
1928	Thornton Wilder, *The Bridge of San Luis*
1929	Julia Peterkin, *Scarlet Sister Mary*
1930	Oliver LaFarge, *Laughing Boy*
1931	Margaret Ayer Barnes, *Years of Grace*
1932	Pearl S. Buck, *The Good Earth*
1933	T.S. Stribling, *The Store*
1934	Caroline Miller, *Lamb in His Bosom*
1935	Josephine Winslow Johnson, *Now in November*
1936	Harold L. Davis, *Honey in the Horn*
1937	Margaret Mitchell, *Gone With the Wind*
1938	John Phillips Marquand, *The Late George*
1939	Marjorie Kinnan Rawlings, *The Yearling*
1940	John Steinbeck, *The Grapes of Wrath*
1941	No award
1942	Ellen Glasgow, *In This Our Life*
1943	Upton Sinclair, *Dragon's Teeth*
1944	Martin Flavin, *Journey in the Dark*
1945	John Hersey, *A Bell for Adano*
1946	No award
1947	Robert Penn Warren, *All The King's Men*
1948	James A. Michener, *Tales of the South Pacific*
1949	James Gould Cozzens, *Guard of Honor*
1950	A.B. Guthrie Jr, *The Way West*
1951	Conrad Richter, *The Town*
1952	Herman Wouk, *The Caine Mutiny*
1953	Ernest Hemingway, *The Old Man and the Sea*
1954	No award
1955	William Faulkner, *A Fable*
1956	MacKinlay Kantor, *Andersonville*
1957	No award
1958	James Agee, *A Death in the Family*
1959	Robert Lewis Taylor, *The Travels of Jaimie McPheeters*
1960	Allen Drury, *Advise and Consent*
1961	Harper Lee, *To Kill a Mockingbird*
1962	Edwin O'Connor, *The Edge of Sadness*
1963	William Faulkner, *The Reivers*
1964	No award
1965	Shirley Ann Grau, *The Keepers of the House*
1966	Katherine Anne Porter, *Collected Stories*
1967	Bernard Malamud, *The Fixer*
1968	William Styron, *The Confessions of Nat Turner*
1969	N. Scott Momaday, *House Made of Dawn*
1970	Jean Stafford, *Collected Stories*
1971	No award
1972	Wallace Stegner, *Angle of Repose*
1973	Eudora Welty, *The Optimist's Daughter*
1974	No award
1975	Michael Shaara, *The Killer Angels*
1976	Saul Bellow, *Humboldt's Gift*
1977	No award
1978	James Alan McPherson, *Elbow Room*
1979	John Cheever, *The Stories of John Cheever*
1980	Norman Mailer, *The Executioner's Song*
1981	John Kennedy Toole, *A Confederacy of Dunces*
1982	John Updike, *Rabbit is Rich*
1983	Alice Walker, *The Color Purple*
1984	William Kennedy, *Ironweed*
1985	Alison Lurie, *Foreign Affairs*
1986	Larry McMurty, *Lonesome Dove*
1987	Peter Taylor, *A Summons to Memphis*
1988	Toni Morrison, *Beloved*
1989	Anne Tyler, *Breathing Lessons*
1990	Oscar Hijuelos, *The Mambo Kings*
1991	John Updike, *Rabbit at Rest*
1992	Jane Smiley, *A Thousand Acres*
1993	Robert Olen Butler, *A Good Scent From a Strange Mountain*
1994	E. Annie Proulx, *The Shipping News*
1995	Carol Shields, *The Stone Diaries*
1996	Richard Ford, *Independence Day*
1997	Steven Millhauser, *Martin Dressler: The Tale of an American Dreamer*
1998	Philip Roth, *American Pastoral*
1999	Michael Cunningham, *The Hours*
2000	Jhumpa Lahiri, *Interpreter of Maladies*

Booker Prize

The Booker Prize, awarded to a novel written by a citizen of the United Kingdom, Republic of Ireland or the Commonwealth, was started in 1969 by food distributors Booker plc and the Publishers Association. Winners are announced each October in London. The original cash award was £5000; in 2000, the prize was £20 000, plus £1000 for each shortlisted author (normally six).

1969	P.H. Newby, *Something to Answer For*
1970	Bernice Rubens, *The Elected Member*
1971	V.S. Naipaul, *In a Free State*
1972	John Berger, *G*
1973	J.G. Farrell, *The Siege of Krishnapur*
1974	Nadine Gordimer, *The Conservationist* Stanley Middleton, *Holiday*
1975	Ruth Prawer Jhabvala, *Heat and Dust*
1976	David Storey, *Saville*
1977	Paul Scott, *Staying On*
1978	Iris Murdoch, *The Sea, The Sea*
1979	Penelope Fitzgerald, *Offshore*
1980	William Golding, *Rites of Passage*
1981	Salman Rushdie, *Midnight's Children*
1982	Thomas Keneally, *Schindler's Ark*
1983	J.M. Coetzee, *Life and Times of Michael K*
1984	Anita Brookner, *Hotel du Lac*
1985	Keri Hulme, *The Bone People*
1986	Kingsley Amis, *The Old Devils*
1987	Penelope Lively, *Moon Tiger*
1988	Peter Carey, *Oscar and Lucinda*
1989	Kazuo Ishiguro, *The Remains of the Day*
1990	A.S. Byatt, *Possession*
1991	Ben Okri, *The Famished Road*
1992	Michael Ondaatje, *The English Patient* Barry Unsworth, *Sacred Hunger*
1993	Roddy Doyle, *Paddy Clark Ha Ha Ha*
1994	James Kelman, *How Late it Was, How Late*
1995	Pat Barker, *The Ghost Road*
1996	Graham Swift, *Last Orders*
1997	Arundhati Roy, *The God of Small Things*
1998	Ian McEwan, *Amsterdam*
1999	J.M. Coetzee, *Disgrace*
2000	Margaret Atwood, *The Blind Assassin*

Whitbread literary awards

The Whitbread awards, sponsored by the hotel and leisure conglomerate Whitbread, are given to authors who have lived in the United Kingdom or Republic of Ireland for a minimum of three years. There are five categories – novel, first novel, biography, poetry and children's book; winners of these categories make up the shortlist for the Whitbread Book of the Year award (established in 1985). Each category winner receives £3500; in addition, the winner of the Book of the Year award receives £22 500.

Book of the Year award

1985	Douglas Dunn, *Elegies*
1986	Kazuo Ishiguro, *An Artist of the Floating World*
1987	Christopher Nolan, *Under the Eye of the Clock*
1988	Paul Sayer, *The Comforts of Madness*
1989	Richard Holmes, *Coleridge: Early Visions*
1990	Nicholas Mosley, *Hopeful Monsters*
1991	John Richardson, *A Life of Picasso*
1992	Jeff Torrington, *Swing Hammer Swing!*
1993	Joan Brady, *Theory of War*
1994	William Trevor, *Felicia's Journey*
1995	Kate Atkinson, *Behind the Scenes at the Museum*
1996	Seamus Heaney, *The Spirit Level*
1997	Ted Hughes, *Tales from Ovid*
1998	Ted Hughes, *Birthday Letters*
1999	Seamus Heaney, *Beowulf*
2000	Matthew Kneale, *English Passengers*

Turner arts prize

The Turner Prize, awarded each November to a British artist aged under 50, was established by the Tate Gallery Patrons of New Art. There have been up to six shortlisted artists in some years, but there are usually only four; the winner receives £20 000.

1984	Malcolm Morley	1990	(No prize)	1996	Douglas Gordon
1985	Howard Hodgkin	1991	Anish Kapoor	1997	Gillian Wearing
1986	Gilbert and George	1992	Grenville Davey	1998	Chris Ofili
1987	Richard Deacon	1993	Rachel Whiteread	1999	Steve McQueen
1988	Tony Cragg	1994	Antony Gormley	2000	Wolfgang Tillmans
1989	Richard Long	1995	Damien Hirst		

Greek

The Greek alphabet developed from the Phoenician system in the 9th century BC, but unlike the Phoenicians the Greeks created separate symbols for vowels and for upper case letters (capitals) and lower case. Until about 500 BC, it was written from right to left. Several variations existed until the Ionian form became the official Athenian alphabet in 403 BC. The modern Greek alphabet is used, almost unchanged, in the Greek-speaking world.

Letter	Name	Transliteration (sound)		Letter	Name	Transliteration (sound)
Α, α	alpha	a		Σ, σ	sigma	s
Β, β	beta	b		Τ, τ	tau	t
Γ, γ	gamma	g		Υ, υ	upsilon	y
Δ, δ	delta	d		Φ, φ	phi	f
Ε, ε	epsilon	e (short)		Χ, χ	chi	ch (as in *loch*)
Ζ, ζ	zeta	z		Ψ, ψ	psi	ps
Η, η	eta	e (long *ee*)		Ω, ω	omega	o (long *oh*)
Θ, θ	theta	th (soft)				
Ι, ι	iota	i				
Κ, κ	kappa	k				
Λ, λ	lambda	l				
Μ, μ	mu	m				
Ν, ν	nu	n				
Ξ, ξ	xi	x				
Ο, ο	omicron	o (short)				
Π, π	pi	p				
Ρ, ρ	rho	r				

Cyrillic

The Cyrillic alphabet, an offshoot of Greek, was created in the 9th century AD, reputedly by the Greek missionaries St Cyril and St Methodius. It became the script of the Russian, Ukrainian, Bulgarian, Serbian and Belorussian peoples. The alphabet originally had 43 letters, but modern versions have about 30, with national variations. There is no universally agreed transliteration system, but the equivalents shown here are widely used from Russian into English.

Letter	Transliteration (sound)		Letter	Transliteration (sound)
А, а	a		Р, р	r
Б, б	b		С, с	s
В, в	v		Т, т	t
Г, г	g		У, у	u
Д, д	d		Ф, ф	f
Е, е	ye		Х, х	kh
Ё, ё	yo		Ц, ц	ts
Ж, ж	zh		Ч, ч	ch
З, з	z		Ш, ш	sh
И, и	i		Щ, щ	shch
Й, й	i		Ъ, ъ	(hard sign)
К, к	k		Ы, ы	y
Л, л	l		Ь, ь	(soft sign)
М, м	m		Э, э	e
Н, н	n		Ю, ю	yu
О, о	o		Я, я	ya
П, п	p			

Hebrew

The Hebrew alphabet was standardised in about the 1st century AD and has remained almost unchanged. It is used to write the various forms of Hebrew, as well as Yiddish, a language derived from southern German dialects spoken by eastern European Jewish communities. It is written from right to left, and only the consonants are represented by letters. Vowels are indicated by marks placed below or to the left of a consonant; some marks, shown in the list below, also change the pronunciation of consonants. There is no universally agreed transliteration system for the Hebrew alphabet, but the one given here is widely used for transliterating into English.

Symbol		Name	Transliteration (sound)		Symbol		Name	Transliteration (sound)
א		alef	(silent)		ם	(as final letter)	mem	m
ב		bet	b, v		נ		nun	n
ג		gimmel	g, j		ן	(as final letter)	nun	n
ד		dalet	d		ס		samekh	s
ה		he	h (pronounced only with vowel marks)		ע		ayin	(silent)
ו		vav	v, w		פ		pe	p, f
ז		zayin	z		ף	(as final letter)	pe	p, f
ח		khet	strong *h* as in *loch*		צ		tzade	ts
ט		tet	t		ץ	(as final letter)	tzade	ts
י		yod	y		ק		qof	k
כ		kaf	kh		ר		resh	r
ך	(as final letter)	kaf	kh		ש		shin	sh, s
ל		lamed	l		ת		tav	t
מ		mem	m					

Arabic

The Arabic alphabet developed from around the 5th century AD. Today's alphabet is descended from the 10th-century Nashki form. It is written from right to left, and consists of consonant letters with vowels indicated by marks (vowel marks are usually omitted, except in children's books and the Koran). Letters are written differently according to whether they appear on their own (isolated), at the start of a word (initial), in the middle (medial) or at the end (final).

Name	Transliteration	Isolated	Final	Initial	Medial
alif	'	أ	ﻟ	أ	ﺎ
ba	b	ب	ﺐ	ﺑ	ﺒ
ta	t	ت	ﺖ	ﺗ	ﺘ
tha	th	ث	ﺚ	ﺛ	ﺜ
jim	j	ج	ﺞ	ﺟ	ﺠ
ha	h	ح	ﺢ	ﺣ	ﺤ
kha	kh	خ	ﺦ	ﺧ	ﺨ
dal	d	د	ﺪ	د	ﺪ
dha	dh	ذ	ﺬ	ذ	ﺬ
ra	r	ر	ﺮ	ر	ﺮ
za	z	ز	ﺰ	ز	ﺰ
sin	s	س	ﺲ	ﺳ	ﺴ
shin	sh	ش	ﺶ	ﺷ	ﺸ
sad	s	ص	ﺺ	ﺻ	ﺼ
dad	d	ض	ﺾ	ﺿ	ﻀ
ta	t	ط	ﻂ	ط	ﻂ
za	z	ظ	ﻆ	ظ	ﻆ
ain	'	ع	ﻊ	ﻋ	ﻌ
ghain	gh	غ	ﻎ	ﻏ	ﻐ
fa	f	ف	ﻒ	ﻓ	ﻔ
qaf	q	ق	ﻖ	ﻗ	ﻘ
kaf	k	ك	ﻚ	ﻛ	ﻜ
lam	l	ل	ﻞ	ﻟ	ﻠ
mim	m	م	ﻢ	ﻣ	ﻤ
nun	n	ن	ﻦ	ﻧ	ﻨ
ha	h	ﻩ	ﻪ	ﻫ	ﻬ
waw	w	و	ﻮ	و	ﻮ
ya	y	ى	ﻰ	ﻳ	ﻴ

Roman numerals

The Romans developed a numerical system based on seven letters representing seven numbers: I (1); V (5); X (10); L (50); C (100); D (500); and M (1000). All other numbers are derived by adding letters together (III represents 3) – except where a smaller letter is followed by a larger one, when the smaller is subtracted from the larger (IV represents 4). Calculations using Roman numerals were clumsy and difficult – which is why Arabic numerals triumphed.

I	1	LXVIII	68
II	2	LXIX	69
III	3	XC	90
IV	4	IC	99
V	5	C	100
VI	6	CIC	199
VII	7	CC	200
VIII	8	CD	400
IX	9	D	500
X	10	DC	600
XI	11	CM	900
XIV	14	M	1000
XV	15	MCMLXXXIX	1989
XVI	16		
XIX	19		
XX	20		
XXIX	29		
XXX	30		
XL	40		
IL	49		
L	50		
LIX	59		
LX	60		

Braille

In the Braille system of writing and printing for the blind, letters and numbers are represented by combinations of raised dots which are then read by touch. It was invented in France in 1829 by Louis Braille, who became blind at the age of three. Each character, or 'cell', consists of six dots, arranged vertically in two columns of three dots; there are two different sizes of dots, small and large. Both hands are used in reading: the right hand identifies the letters, while the left picks out the beginning of the next line.

Numbers: the 'cell' shown below indicates that a number follows. The numbers are indicated by the letters A–J.

Semaphore

In the semaphore visual signalling code, developed in the 1760s for long-distance communication, the positions of two movable pointers or hand-held flags represent different letters or numbers. At the start of a message, the signaller gives the alphabetic sign (the same as the letter J); the person receiving the message replies with the letter C. Before sending numbers, the signaller makes the numeral sign, then makes the alphabetic sign again when returning to ordinary letters.

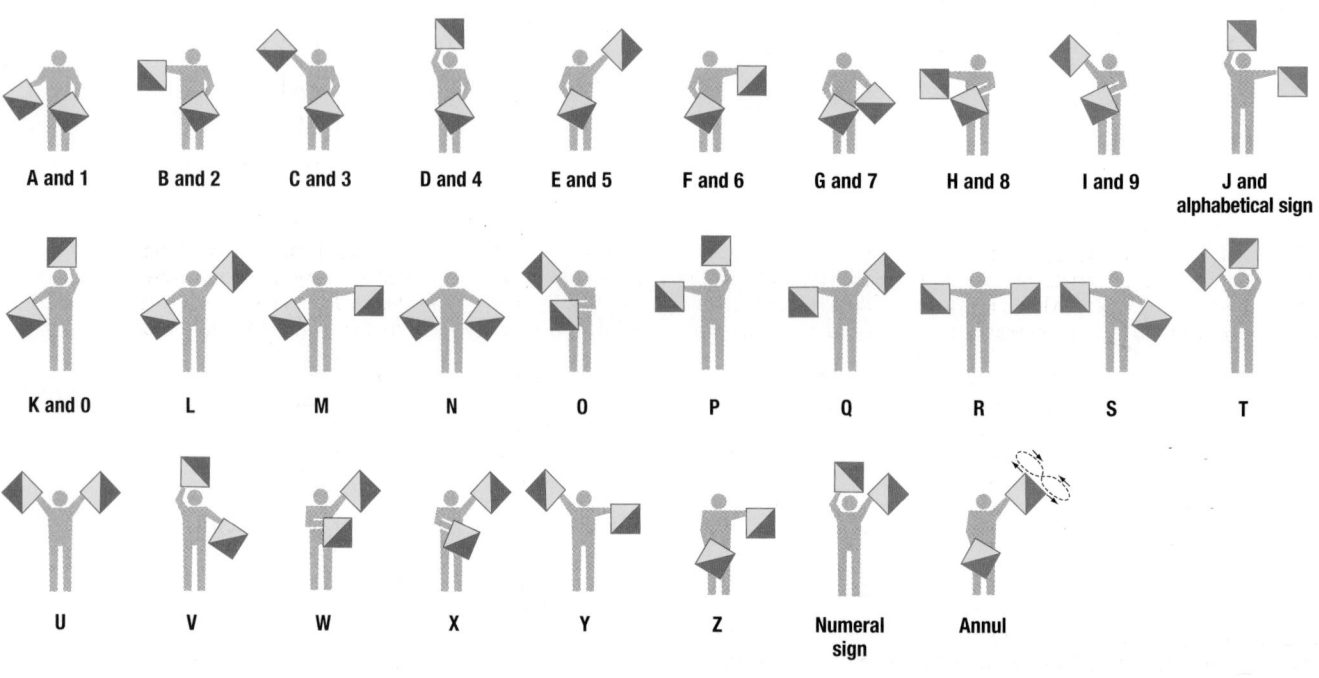

A and 1 · B and 2 · C and 3 · D and 4 · E and 5 · F and 6 · G and 7 · H and 8 · I and 9 · J and alphabetical sign

K and 0 · L · M · N · O · P · Q · R · S · T

U · V · W · X · Y · Z · Numeral sign · Annul

International code flags

Some symbols are universal – a white flag signals a truce, a yellow one the presence of infectious disease, while a flag flying at halfmast signifies mourning. An international code links letters of the alphabet and numbers to flags of various shapes and patterns, using the colours white, black, red, blue and yellow, so words and sentences can be communicated. In addition, a code book lists various combinations of letters which have special meanings. In the illustrations below, all the flags are shown with the roped edge on the left.

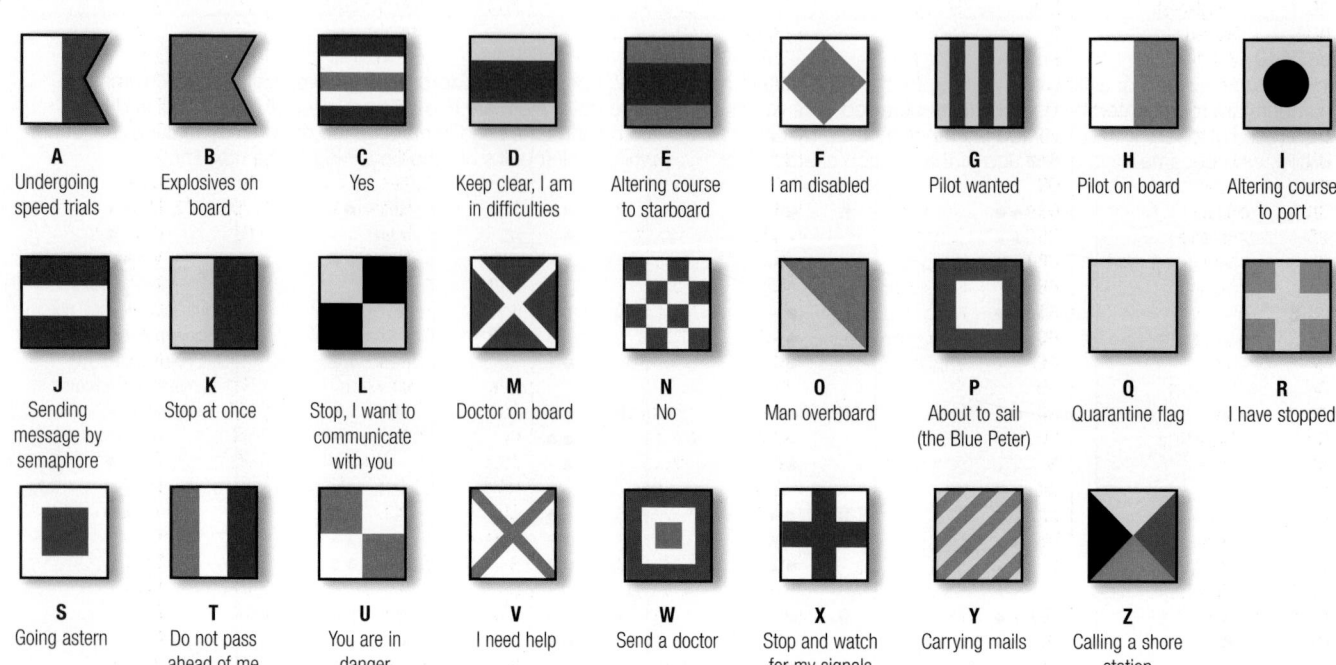

A – Undergoing speed trials
B – Explosives on board
C – Yes
D – Keep clear, I am in difficulties
E – Altering course to starboard
F – I am disabled
G – Pilot wanted
H – Pilot on board
I – Altering course to port

J – Sending message by semaphore
K – Stop at once
L – Stop, I want to communicate with you
M – Doctor on board
N – No
O – Man overboard
P – About to sail (the Blue Peter)
Q – Quarantine flag
R – I have stopped

S – Going astern
T – Do not pass ahead of me
U – You are in danger
V – I need help
W – Send a doctor
X – Stop and watch for my signals
Y – Carrying mails
Z – Calling a shore station

Phonetic alphabets

Various phonetic alphabets have developed as radio operators' codes for identifying letters of the alphabet. Listed here is the main phonetic alphabet used during the Second World War, and the NATO (North Atlantic Treaty Organisation) code now used by the USA, Canada, UK and other European countries. Many other versions are used in other languages.

	WW2	NATO												
A	Able	Alpha	G	George	Golf	N	Nan	November	U	Uncle	Uniform
B	Baker	Bravo	H	How	Hotel	O	Oboe	Oscar	V	Victor	Victor
C	Charlie	Charlie	I	Item	India	P	Peter	Papa	W	William	Whiskey
D	Dog	Delta	J	Jig	Juliet	Q	Queen	Quebec	X	X-ray	X-ray
E	Easy	Echo	K	King	Kilo	R	Roger	Romeo	Y	Yoke	Yankee
F	Fox	Foxtrot	L	Love	Lima	S	Sugar	Sierra	Z	Zebra	Zulu
			M	Mike	Mike	T	Tare	Tango			

Morse code

Samuel Morse developed his code in 1844. It was designed for sending long-distance messages over the electric telegraph that he had invented in 1837. The Morse code, in which letters of the alphabet and numbers are represented by signals of short duration (shown as dots) and long duration (dashes), soon became an international code for transmitting messages by wire or radio signals. The use of the international distress signal, 'S.O.S.' (three short signals, three long, three short), was discontinued in 1997.

A	•−	G	−−•	M	−−	S	•••	Y	−•−−
B	−•••	H	••••	N	−•	T	−	Z	−−••
C	−•−•	I	••	O	−−−	U	••−		
D	−••	J	•−−−	P	•−−•	V	•••−		
E	•	K	−•−	Q	−−•−	W	•−−		
F	••−•	L	•−••	R	•−•	X	−••−		

International distinguishing signs

A United Nations convention on road traffic regulates the sets of initials, known as international distinguishing signs, that identify a motor vehicle's country or territory of registration when driven abroad.

Code	Country	Code	Country	Code	Country	Code	Country	Code	Country
A	Austria	EAK	Kenya	IRQ	Iraq	PE	Peru	SME	Surinam
ADN	Yemen	EAT	Tanzania	IS	Iceland	PL	Poland	SN	Senegal
AFG	Afghanistan	EAU	Uganda	J	Japan	PNG	Papua New Guinea	SO	Somalia
AL	Albania	EAZ	Tanzania (Zanzibar)	JA	Jamaica	PY	Paraguay	SU	Former USSR
AND	Andorra	EC	Ecuador	K	Cambodia	QA	Qatar	SUD	Sudan
ARM	Armenia	ES	El Salvador	KS	Kyrgyzstan	RA	Argentina	SY	Seychelles
AUS	Australia	EST	Estonia	KWT	Kuwait	RB	Botswana	SYR	Syria
B	Belgium	ET	Egypt	KZ	Kazakhstan	RC	China	T	Thailand
BD	Bangladesh	ETH	Ethiopia	L	Luxembourg	RCA	Central African Republic	TG	Togo
BDS	Barbados	F	France	LAO	Laos			TJ	Tajikistan
BG	Bulgaria	FIN	Finland	LAR	Libya	RCB	Republic of the Congo	TM	Turkmenistan
BH	Belize	FJI	Fiji	LB	Liberia			TN	Tunisia
BIH	Bosnia-Herzegovina	FL	Liechtenstein	LV	Latvia	RCH	Chile	TR	Turkey
BOL	Bolivia	FO	Faroe Islands	LS	Lesotho	RG	Guinea	TT	Trinidad and Tobago
BR	Brazil	GAB	Gabon	LT	Lithuania	RH	Haiti		
BRN	Bahrain	GB	United Kingdom	M	Malta	RI	Indonesia	UA	Ukraine
BRU	Brunei	GBA	Alderney	MA	Morocco	RIM	Mauritania	USA	USA
BS	Bahamas	GBG	Guernsey	MAL	Malaysia	RL	Lebanon	UZ	Uzbekistan
BUR	Myanmar (Burma)	GBJ	Jersey	MC	Monaco	RM	Madagascar	V	Vatican City
CAM	Cameroon	GBM	Isle of Man	MD	Moldova	RMM	Mali	VN	Vietnam
CDN	Canada	GBZ	Gibraltar	MEX	Mexico	RN	Niger	WAG	Gambia
CH	Switzerland	GCA	Guatemala	MGL	Mongolia	RNR	Zambia	WAL	Sierra Leone
CI	Côte d'Ivoire	GE	Georgia	MK	Macedonia	RO	Romania	WAN	Nigeria
CL	Sri Lanka	GH	Ghana	MOC	Mozambique	ROK	South Korea	WD	Dominica
CO	Colombia	GR	Greece	MS	Mauritius	ROU	Uruguay	WG	Grenada
CR	Costa Rica	GUY	Guyana	MW	Malawi	RP	Philippines	WL	St Lucia
CU	Cuba	H	Hungary	N	Norway	RSM	San Marino	WV	St Vincent and the Grenadines
CZ	Czech Republic	HK	Hong Kong	NAM	Namibia	RU	Burundi		
CY	Cyprus	HKJ	Jordan	NEP	Nepal	RUS	Russia	YU	Yugoslavia
D	Germany	HR	Croatia	NIC	Nicaragua	RWA	Rwanda	YV	Venezuela
DK	Denmark	I	Italy	NL	Netherlands	S	Sweden	ZA	South Africa
DOM	Dominican Republic	IL	Israel	NZ	New Zealand	SD	Swaziland	ZRE	Democratic Republic of the Congo (Zaire)
DY	Benin	IND	India	P	Portugal	SGP	Singapore		
DZ	Algeria	IR	Iran	PA	Panama	SK	Slovakia		
E	Spain	IRL	Ireland	PK	Pakistan	SLO	Slovenia	ZW	Zimbabwe

Various calendars are used around the world. The following initials are used to identify the dating system used when referring to years.
AD Anno Domini, 'in the year of the Lord'. The Christian era is dated from the supposed year of Christ's birth. Also in common usage are CE ('Common Era') and BCE ('before the Common Era').
AM Anno Mundi, 'in the year of the world'. The Jewish era is computed from the supposed date of Creation – in 3761 BC, according to Christian reckoning.
AH Anno Hegirae, 'in the year of the Hegira'. The Muslim era is dated from the Hegira (emigration), when the Prophet Muhammad migrated from Mecca to Medina – in AD 622, according to Christian reckoning.

The Christian year: Principal fixed feasts and holy days

The Church year includes four special seasons:
Advent Advent Sunday to Christmas Eve
Christmas(tide) Christmas Day to the Sunday after Epiphany
Lent The 40 weekdays from Ash Wednesday to Easter Saturday
Easter(tide) Easter Sunday to Pentecost

8 Immaculate Conception of the Virgin Mary (Roman Catholic)
25 Nativity of the Lord (Christmas Day)

2 Presentation of the Lord in the Temple (Candlemas)
23 St George (patron saint of England)
29 St Peter and St Paul
29 St Michael and All Angels (Michaelmas)

| JANUARY | FEBRUARY | MARCH | APRIL | MAY | JUNE | JULY | AUGUST | SEPTEMBER | OCTOBER | NOVEMBER | DECEMBER |

1 Solemnity of Mary, Mother of God (Roman Catholic); **Circumcision of Christ** (Anglican)
6 Epiphany of the Lord
7 Christmas Day (Eastern Orthodox)[1]

1 St David (patron saint of Wales)
17 St Patrick (patron saint of Ireland)
19 St Joseph (husband of the Virgin Mary)
25 Annunciation of the Lord (Lady Day)

6 Transfiguration of the Lord
15 Assumption of the Virgin Mary (Roman Catholic, Eastern Orthodox)

1 All Saints
2 All Souls
30 St Andrew (patron saint of Scotland)

[1] Fixed feasts in the Eastern Orthodox Church generally follow the older Julian calendar, and most fall 13 days later than in the Western (Roman Catholic and Protestant) churches, which follow the Gregorian calendar.
[2] Advent Sunday is traditionally seen as the start of the Church year.
[3] In the Western churches, Easter is celebrated on the first Sunday after the full moon that follows the spring equinox (March 21): some time between March 22 and April 25. The calculation in the Eastern Orthodox Church is based on the Julian calendar.

Movable feasts and holy days

Advent Sunday[2]	Fourth Sunday before Christmas
Ash Wednesday	Seventh Wednesday before Easter
Palm (or Passion) Sunday	Sunday before Easter
Maundy Thursday	Thursday before Easter
Good Friday	Friday before Easter
Easter Day[3]	
Ascension Day	Fortieth day after Easter
Pentecost (Whit Sunday)	Seventh Sunday after Easter
Trinity Sunday	Sunday after Pentecost
Corpus Christi	Thursday after Trinity Sunday

The Jewish year: Festivals and fasts

1-2 Rosh Hashanah (New Year festival)
10 Yom Kippur (Day of Atonement)
15-21 Succoth (Feast of Tabernacles)

2-3 End of Hanukkah

14-15 Purim[3]

15-22 Pesach (Passover)

6-7 Shavuot (Festival of Weeks or Pentecost)

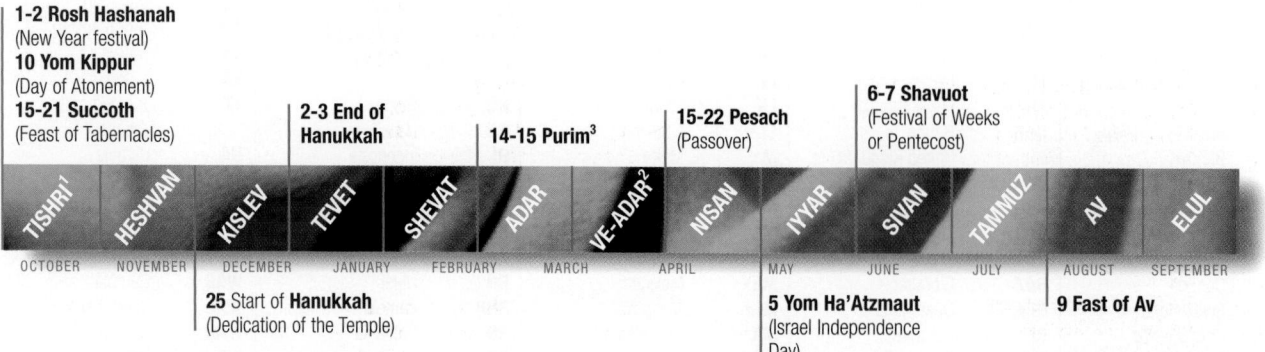

| TISHRI[1] | HESHVAN | KISLEV | TEVET | SHEVAT | ADAR | VE-ADAR[2] | NISAN | IYYAR | SIVAN | TAMMUZ | AV | ELUL |

| OCTOBER | NOVEMBER | DECEMBER | JANUARY | FEBRUARY | MARCH | APRIL | MAY | JUNE | JULY | AUGUST | SEPTEMBER |

25 Start of Hanukkah (Dedication of the Temple)

5 Yom Ha'Atzmaut (Israel Independence Day)

9 Fast of Av

[1] The Jewish New Year (Tishri 1) is variable, falling in late September or early October of the Western calendar. It is timed to coincide as nearly as possible with the moment in the lunar month when the Sun and Moon are closest in the sky.

[2] Jewish leap years occur in the 3rd, 6th, 8th, 11th, 14th, 17th and 19th years of a 19-year cycle. In leap years, a 13th month, known as Ve-Adar or Adar Sheni, is added after Adar.

[3] In leap years, Purim is held on Ve-Adar 14-15.

Jewish New Year

Year AM	Date AD	Year AM	Date AD
5761*	Sept 30, 2000	5767	Sept 23, 2006
5762	Sept 17, 2001	5768	Sept 13, 2007
5763	Sept 7, 2002	5769*	Sept 30, 2008
5764*	Sept 27, 2003	5770	Sept 19, 2009
5765	Sept 16, 2004	5771	Sept 9, 2010
5766*	Oct 4, 2005	* Leap year.	

Muslim year: Principal festivals

1 Hegira New Year

12 Birthday of the Prophet Muhammad

27 Laylat al-Miraj (Ascent of the Prophet Muhammad to Heaven)

Month of fasting during daylight hours
27 Laylat al-Qadir (Transmission of the Koran to the Prophet Muhammad)

8-13 Dhu 'l-Hijjah (annual pilgrimage to Mecca)

MUHARRAM · SAFAR · RABI I · RABI II · JUMAD I · JUMAD II · RAJAB · SHA'BAN · RAMADAN · SHAWWAL · DHU 'l-QADA · DHU 'l-HIJJAH

1 Id al-Fitr (celebration of end of fasting)

The Muslim year consists of 12 lunar months, making no allowance for the solar cycle and the seasons of the solar year, so a Muslim month will fall in turn in all of the seasons of the year over a 32½-year cycle.

[1] In accordance with the Koran, each month in the Islamic calendar begins when the crescent moon has first been seen by a human being. This results in some variation: for some Muslims, the month begins when the moon has been sighted locally; others go by a sighting by recognised authorities elsewhere in the Muslim world. This table for the Hegira New Year is based on estimates of when the crescent moon will be visible, but the real New Year may be a day earlier or later than predicted here.

Hegira New Year[1]

Year AH	Date AD	Year AH	Date AD
1421	April 6, 2000	1427	Jan 31, 2006
1422	March 26, 2001	1428	Jan 21, 2007
1423	March 15, 2002	1429	Jan 10, 2008
1424	March 4, 2003	1430	Dec 29, 2008
1425	Feb 22, 2004	1431	Dec 18, 2009
1426	Feb 10, 2005	1432	Dec 7, 2010

Hindu and Sikh year: Principal festivals

Baisakhi (Sikh New Year)

Rathayatra (Pilgrimage of the Chariot at Jagannath)

Janamashtami (Krishna's Birthday)

Guru Nanak Jayanti (Birthday of Nanak, founder of Sikhism)

Holi (spring festival)

VAISAKHA · ASADHA · BHADRAPADA · KARTTIKA · PAUSA · PHALGUNA

CAITRA · JYAISTHA · SRAVANA · ASVINA · MARGASIRSA · MAGHA

MARCH · APRIL · MAY · JUNE · JULY · AUGUST · SEPTEMBER · OCTOBER · NOVEMBER · DECEMBER · JANUARY · FEBRUARY · MARCH

Ramanavami (Rama's birthday)

Jhulanayatra (Swinging of Krishna)

Durga-puja (Festival of Durga)
Laksmipuja (Festival of Lakshmi)
Diwali (Strings of Lights)

Mahashivaratri (Great Night of Shiva)

Buddhist festivals

Myanmar (Burma)
April 16-17	New Year
May-June	The Buddha's Birth, Enlightenment and Death
July	The Buddha's First Sermon
July-Oct	Rains Retreat
Nov	Kathina Ceremony

Sri Lanka
April 13	New Year
May-June	The Buddha's Birth, Enlightenment and Death
June-July	Establishment of Buddhism in Sri Lanka
July	The Buddha's First Sermon
July-Aug	Procession of the Month of Asala
Sept	The Buddha's First Visit to Sri Lanka
Dec-Jan	Arrival of Sanghamitta

Thailand
April 13-16	New Year
May	The Buddha's Enlightenment
May-June	The Buddha's Cremation
July-Oct	Rains Retreat
Nov	Kathina Ceremony
	Festival of Lights
Feb	All Saints' Day

Tibet
Feb	New Year
May	The Buddha's Birth, Enlightenment and Death
June	Dzamling Chisang
June-July	The Buddha's First Sermon
Oct	The Buddha's Descent from Tushita
Nov	Death of Tsongkhapa
Jan	The conjunction of Nine Evils and the conjunction of Ten Virtues

Chinese festivals

Jan-Feb	Chinese New Year
Feb-March	Lantern Festival
March-April	Festival of Pure Brightness
May-June	Dragon Boat Festival
June-Aug	Summer Retreat
July-Aug	Herd Boy and Weaving Maid
Aug	All Souls' Festival
	Festival of Hungry Ghosts
	Gautama Buddha's Birth
	Kuan-yin
Sept	Mid-Autumn Festival
Sept-Oct	Double Ninth Festival
Nov-Dec	Winter Solstice

Japanese festivals

Jan 1-3	Oshogatsu (New Year)
March 3	Ohinamatsuri (Dolls' or Girls' Festival)
May 5	Tango no Sekku (Boys' Festival)
July 7	Hosh matsuri or Tanabata (Star Festival)
July 13-31	Obon (Buddhist All Souls' Festival)
Nov 15	Shichi-go-San (age celebrations for boys and girls)

Astronomers have divided the sky around the Earth into 88 areas, each of which contains a grouping of stars, or constellation. Many constellations were named after people and creatures in classical mythology, such as the flying horse Pegasus. Many constellations of the Southern Hemisphere were named in the 17th and 18th centuries after scientific instruments, such as the telescope.

The North Star

Polaris is the star closest to the north celestial pole; it lies at the end of the 'handle' of Ursa Minor. It is actually a triple star system made up of two stars in orbit around one another and a single star. Because the Earth wobbles on its axis, the North Star varies over time: in 12 000 years it will be Vega in the constellation Lyra.

The northern sky

Latin name	English name				
Andromeda	Andromeda	Cygnus	The Swan	Orion	The Hunter
Aquila	The Eagle	Delphinus	The Dolphin	Pegasus	The Flying Horse
Aries	The Ram	Draco	The Dragon	Perseus	Perseus
Auriga	The Charioteer	Equuleus	The Little Horse	Pisces	The Fishes
Boötes	The Herdsman		or Foal	Sagitta	The Arrow
Camelopardalis	The Giraffe	Gemini	The Twins	Serpens	The Serpent
Cancer	The Crab	Hercules	Hercules	Sextans	The Sextant
Canes Venatici	The Hunting Dogs	Hydra	The Water Snake	Taurus	The Bull
Canis Minor	The Little Dog	Lacerta	The Lizard	Triangulum	The Triangle
Cassiopeia	Cassiopeia	Leo	The Lion	Ursa Major	The Great Bear
Cepheus	Cepheus	Leo Minor	The Little Lion	Ursa Minor	The Little Bear
Cetus	The Whale	Lynx	The Lynx	Virgo	The Virgin
Coma Berenices	Berenice's Hair	Lyra	The Lyre	Vulpecula	The Fox
Corona Borealis	The Northern Crown	Ophiuchus	The Serpent Bearer		

Mapping the celestial sphere

From our vantage point on the Earth, the constellations appear to be laid out on the inside of a hollow sphere, which rotates around the Earth in an east–west direction once every 24 hours. Astronomers call this the celestial sphere, and the stars maps below are convenient ways of laying out the two halves of this sphere on paper.

The portion of the celestial sphere that is visible depends on the observer's position on the Earth's surface and the Earth's position in its orbit. For both maps, the stars on the edge are visible at certain seasons in the other hemisphere – Canis Major, for example, can be seen in the Northern Hemisphere in winter. Those in the centre are always invisible or very low in the sky in the other hemisphere.

The southern sky

Latin name	English name
Antlia	The Air Pump
Apus	The Bee
Aquarius	The Water Bearer
Ara	The Altar
Caelum	The Engraving Tool
Canis Major	The Great Dog
Capricornus	The Sea Goat
Carina	The Keel
Centaurus	The Centaur
Chamaeleon	The Chameleon
Circinus	The Pair of Compasses
Columba	The Dove
Corona Australis	The Southern Crown
Corvus	The Crow
Crater	The Cup
Crux Australis	The Southern Cross
Dorado	The Swordfish
Eridanus	The River
Fornax	The Furnace
Grus	The Crane
Horologium	The Clock
Hydrus	The Little Snake
Indus	The Indian
Lepus	The Hare
Libra	The Scales
Lupus	The Wolf
Mensa	The Table
Microscopium	The Microscope
Monoceros	The Unicorn
Musca	The Fly
Norma	The Rule
Octans	The Octant
Pavo	The Peacock
Phoenix	The Phoenix
Pictor	The Painter
Piscis Austrinus	The Southern Fish
Puppis	The Poop or Stern
Pyxis	The Mariner's Compass
Reticulum	The Net
Sagittarius	The Archer
Scorpius	The Scorpion
Sculptor	The Sculptor
Scutum	The Shield
Telescopium	The Telescope
Triangulum Australe	The Southern Triangle
Tucana	The Toucan
Vela	The Sail
Volans	The Flying Fish

Patron saints

Many Christian saints have been chosen as special protectors or guardians for countries, professional guilds and other groups. Angels can also be patrons saints. Patron saints are often selected because of a link between the patron and the object of patronage. For example, the faith of English Crusaders was strengthened by visions of St George, and he was chosen as England's patron saint.

Country/region	Patron saint	Feast day
The Americas	Our Lady of Guadalupe	Dec 12
Australia	Our Lady Help of Christians	May 24
Austria	St Joseph	March 19
Belgium	St Joseph	March 19
Canada	St Anne and St Joseph	July 26, March 19
Denmark	St Anskar	Feb 3
England	St George	April 23
Europe	St Benedict, Sts Cyril and Methodius	July 11, Feb 14
Finland	St Henry of Finland	Jan 19
France	St Joan of Arc	May 30
Germany	St Michael the Archangel	Sept 29
Greece	St Nicholas of Myra	Dec 6
Hungary	St Stephen of Hungary	Aug 16
Ireland	St Patrick	March 17
Italy	St Catherine of Sienna	April 29
Mexico	Our Lady of Guadalupe	Dec 12
Netherlands	St Willibrord	Nov 7
New Zealand	Our Lady Help of Christians	May 24
Norway	St Olaf	July 29
Portugal	St George	April 23
Russia	St Andrew	Nov 30
Scotland	St Andrew	Nov 30
Spain	St James the Great	July 25
Sweden	St Bridget of Sweden	July 23
Switzerland	St Nicholas of Flue	Sept 25
USA	Our Lady of the Immaculate Conception	Dec 8
Wales	St David	March 1

Occupation	Patron saint	Feast day
Accountants, bankers and tax collectors	St Matthew	Sept 21
Actors	St Genesius of Arles	June 3
Animals	St Francis of Assisi	Oct 4
Architects	St Thomas the Apostle	July 3
Astronauts	St Joseph of Copertino	Sept 18
Booksellers	St John of God	March 8
Carpenters	St Joseph	March 19
Cooks	St Laurence and St Martha	Aug 10, July 29
Dancers	St Vitus	June 15
Dentists	St Apollonia	Feb 9
Doctors	St Luke, Sts Cosmas and Damian	Oct 18, Sept 26
Engineers	St Ferdinand	May 30
Farmers	St Isidore the Farmer	May 15
Fishermen	St Andrew and St Peter	Nov 30, June 29
Librarians	St Jerome	Sept 30
Lost articles	St Antony of Padua	June 13
Lovers	St Valentine	Feb 14
Midwives	St Pantaleon and St Raymond Nonnatus	July 27, Aug 31
Mountaineers	St Bernard of Aosta	May 28
Musicians	St Cecilia, St Gregory the Great	Nov 22, Sept 3
Nurses	St Camillus de Lellis, St Elizabeth of Hungary and St John of God	July 14, Nov 17, March 8
Painters	St Luke	Oct 18
Priests	St John Vianney	Aug 4
Sailors	St Nicholas of Myra, St Francis of Paola and St Brendan the Navigator	Dec 6, April 2, May 16
Sick	St Michael the Archangel and St Camillus de Lellis	Sept 29, July 14
Students	St Catherine of Alexandria and St Thomas Aquinas	Nov 25, Jan 28
Taxi drivers	St Fiacre	Aug 30
Teachers	St John-Baptist de la Salle	April 7
Travellers	St Christopher	July 25
Vets	St Eloi (Eligius)	Dec 1
Winegrowers	St Vincent of Saragossa	Jan 22
Writers and journalists	St John the Evangelist and St Francis de Sales	Dec 27, Jan 24

Signs of the zodiac

The zodiac was the name given by the ancient Greeks to the band of the celestial sphere containing the paths of the Sun, the Moon and the principal planets. In Western astrology, this band is divided into 12 equal parts. Each part bears the name of a constellation for which it was originally named; but owing to the slow shift of the Earth on its axis, constellations do not now cover the same areas of sky as the zodiacal signs of the same name.

Constellation	English name	Symbol	Dates *
Aries	The Ram		March 21-April 19
Taurus	The Bull		April 20-May 20
Gemini	The Twins		May 21-June 21
Cancer	The Crab		June 22-July 22
Leo	The Lion		July 23-August 22
Virgo	The Virgin		August 23-September 22
Libra	The Scales		September 23-October 23
Scorpio	The Scorpion		October 24-November 21
Sagittarius	The Archer		November 22-December 21
Capricorn	The Sea Goat		December 22-January 19
Aquarius	The Water Bearer		January 20-February 18
Pisces	The Fishes		February 19-March 20

(* Dates may differ from year to year by one or two days)

Seven Wonders of the World

From the 2nd century BC, various lists record seven great monuments as wonders of human accomplishment:

The Pyramids at Giza, Egypt (the only one still standing).
The Hanging Gardens of Babylon (near modern-day Baghdad, in Iraq), stepped pyramids planted with trees and lush vegetation.
The tomb of King Mausolus at Halicarnassus (modern-day Bodrum, in Turkey); the magnificent monument is the origin of the word 'mausoleum'.
The Temple of Artemis at Ephesus, Turkey.
The Colossus of Rhodes, a huge bronze statue by the entrance to the harbour of the Greek island.
The statue of Zeus at Olympia, Greece, made of gold and ivory.
The Pharos of Alexandria, Egypt, a lighthouse.*

Some lists feature the walls of Babylon, or the palace of King Cyrus, instead of the Pharos of Alexandria.

Anniversaries

In many countries, wedding anniversaries and other commemorative celebrations are associated with particular materials. Traditionally, gifts should be made of the corresponding material.

1st anniversary	Cotton
2nd anniversary	Paper
3rd anniversary	Leather
4th anniversary	Fruit, flowers
5th anniversary	Wood
6th anniversary	Sugar
7th anniversary	Copper, wool
8th anniversary	Bronze, pottery
9th anniversary	Pottery, willow
10th anniversary	Tin
11th anniversary	Steel
12th anniversary	Silk, linen
13th anniversary	Lace
14th anniversary	Ivory
15th anniversary	Crystal
20th anniversary	China
25th anniversary	Silver
30th anniversary	Pearl
35th anniversary	Coral
40th anniversary	Ruby
50th anniversary	Gold
55th anniversary	Emerald
60th anniversary	Diamond
70th anniversary	Platinum

Birthstones

In folklore, gems are associated with a specific month. They are thought to bring good luck to a person born in that month.

January	Garnet
February	Amethyst
March	Bloodstone or aquamarine
April	Diamond
May	Agate or emerald
June	Pearl or moonstone
July	Ruby or onyx
August	Carnelian or peridot
September	Chrysolite or sapphire
October	Beryl, tourmaline or opal
November	Topaz
December	Turquoise or zircon

The world's longest tunnels

Name	Country	Year	Purpose	Length
1 Seikan	Japan	1985	Underwater, rail	53.9 km (33 miles)
2 Channel	England/France	1994	Underwater, rail	49.9 km (31 miles)
3 Moscow underground	Russia	1990	Railway	37.9 km (23 miles)
4 Chesapeake Bay	USA	1964	Road	28 km (17 miles)
5 Laerdal	Norway	2000	Road	24.5 km (15 miles)
6 Dai-shimizu	Japan	1979	Underwater, rail	22.5 km (14 miles)
7 Kanmon	Japan	1975	Railway	19.3 km (12 miles)
Simplon I	Switzerland	1906	Railway	19.3 km (12 miles)
Simplon II	Italy	1922	Railway	19.3 km (12 miles)
8 Apennine	Italy	1934	Railway	17.7 km (11 miles)
9 Rokko	Japan	1972	Railway	16 km (10 miles)
10 Mount MacDonald	Canada	1989	Railway	14.6 km (9 miles)

The world's tallest buildings

The world's tallest structures are telecommunications towers; the CN Tower, in Toronto, Canada, holds the record at 555 m (1821 ft). Below are the world's tallest habitable buildings.

Name	Location	Year	Height
Petronas Towers	Kuala Lumpur, Malaysia	1996	452 m (1482 ft)
Sears Tower (with spires)	Chicago, USA	1974	443 m (1454 ft) (520 m/1707 ft)
World Trade Center	New York, USA	1972	417 m (1368 ft)
World Finance Center	Hong Kong	2001	400 m (1312 ft)
Jin Mao Building (with spire)	Shanghai, China	1997	382 m (1255 ft) (420 m/1378 ft)
Empire State Building (with spire)	New York, USA	1931	381 m (1250 ft) (449 m/1472 ft)
T&C Tower	Kao-shiung, Taiwan	1997	348 m (1142 ft)
Amoco Building	Chicago, USA	1973	346 m (1136 ft)
John Hancock Center (with spires)	Chicago, USA	1969	343 m (1127 ft) (449 m/1470 ft)
Shun Hing Square (with spires)	Shenzen, China	1996	330 m (1082 ft) (384 m/1260 ft)

The world's longest bridges

Name	Country	Year	Length of main span
Suspension bridges			
1 Akashi-Kaikyo	Japan	1998	1990 m (6529 ft)
2 Great Belt East	Denmark	1997	1624 m (5328 ft)
3 Humber	England	1981	1410 m (4626 ft)
4 Jiangyin	China	1998	1385 m (4544 ft)
5 Tsing Ma	Hong Kong	1997	1377 m (4518 ft)
Cable-stayed bridges			
1 Øresund	Denmark/Sweden	2000	1092 m (3583 ft)
2 Tatara	Japan	1999	890 m (2920 ft)
3 Pont de Normandie	France	1994	856 m (2808 ft)
4 Qinghzhou Minjiang	China	1996	605 m (1985 ft)
5 Yang Pu	China	1993	602 m (1975 ft)
Cantilever bridges			
1 Pont de Québec	Canada	1917	549 m (1800 ft)
2 Forth Rail Bridge	Scotland	1890	521 m (1710 ft)
3 Minato	Japan	1974	510 m (1673 ft)
4 Commodore John Barry	USA	1974	494 m (1622 ft)
5 Greater New Orleans, 1 and 2	USA	1958, 1998	both 480 m (1575 ft)
Steel arch bridges			
1 New River Gorge	USA	1977	518 m (1700 ft)
2 Bayonne (Kill Van Kull)	USA	1931	504 m (1654 ft)
3 Sydney Harbour	Australia	1932	503 m (1650 ft)
4 Fremont	USA	1973	383 m (1257 ft)
5 Port Mann	Canada	1964	366 m (1200 ft)

Kings and queens of England and the United Kingdom

England started to emerge as a unified entity in the 9th century. Egbert, King of Wessex, also titled himself King of the English.

Saxon line

Egbert	802–39
Ethelwulf	839–55
Ethelbald	855–60
Ethelbert	860–6
Ethelred I	866–71
Alfred the Great	871–99
Edward the Elder	899–924
Athelstan	924–39
Edmund I	939–46
Eadred	946–55
Eadwig	955–9
Edgar	959–75
Edward the Martyr	975–8
Ethelred II the Unready	978–1016
Edmund II Ironside	1016 (Apr–Nov)

Danish line

Canute	1016–35
Harold I	1035–40
Hardicanute	1040–2

Saxon line

Edward the Confessor	1042–66
Harold II	1066 (Jan–Oct)

Norman line

William I the Conqueror	1066–87
William II Rufus	1087–1100
Henry I	1100–35
Stephen	1135–54

House of Plantagenet

Henry II	1154–89
Richard the Lionheart	1189–99
John	1199–1216
Henry III	1216–72
Edward I	1272–1307
Edward III	1327–77
Richard I	1377–99

House of Lancaster

Henry IV	1399–1413
Henry V	1413–22
Henry VI	1422–61, 1470–1

House of York

Edward IV	1461–70, 1471–83
Edward V	1483 (April–June)
Richard III	1483–85

House of Tudor

Henry VII	1485–1509
Henry VIII	1509–47
Edward VI	1547–53
Lady Jane Grey	1553 (10–19 July)
Mary I	1553–8
Elizabeth I	1558–1603

House of Stuart

James I	1603–25
(James VI of Scotland)	
Charles I	1625–49
Commonwealth	1649–60

Charles II	1660–85
James II	1685–8
William III and Mary II	1689–94
William III	1694–1702
Anne	1702–14

House of Hanover

George I	1714–27
George II	1727–60
George III	1760–1820
George IV	1820–30
William IV	1830–7
Victoria	1837–1901

House of Saxe-Coburg-Gotha

Edward VII	1901–10

House of Windsor

George V	1910–36
Edward VIII	1936
George VI	1936–52
Elizabeth II	1952–

Kings and queens of Scotland

Armed conflict between Scotland and England ceased after James VI inherited the English throne in 1603. The two kingdoms were united by the Act of Union of 1707.

Kenneth I Macalpin	843–58
Donald I	858–62
Constantine I	862–77
Aed	877–8
Giric and Eochaid	878–89
Donald II	889–900
Constantine II	900–43
Malcolm I	943–54

Indulf	954–62
Dubh	962–6
Culen	966–71
Kenneth II	971–95
Constantine III	995–7
Kenneth III	997–1005
Malcolm II	1005–34
Duncan I	1034–40
Macbeth	1040–57
Lulach	1057–8
Malcolm III	1058–93
Donald III	1093–4
Duncan II	1094
Donald III (restored)	1094–7

Edgar	1097–1107
Alexander I	1107–24
David I	1124–53
Malcolm IV	1153–65
William the Lion	1165–1214
Alexander II	1214–49
Alexander III	1249–86
Margaret Maid of Norway	1286–90
Interregnum	1290–2

House of Balliol

John Balliol	1292–6
Interregnum	1296–1306

House of Bruce

Robert Bruce	1306–29
David II	1329–71

House of Stewart (Stuart)

Robert II	1371–90
Robert III	1390–1406
James I	1406–37
James II	1437–60
James III	1460–88
James IV	1488–1513
James V	1513–42
Mary, Queen of Scots	1542–67
James VI	1567–1625
(King of England and Scotland from 1603)	

Sovereign princes of Wales

Edward I of England invaded Wales in 1277. In 1282, Edward proclaimed his son Prince of Wales, a title generally held by the English monarch's eldest son ever since. Wales was formally united with England in Henry VIII's Act of Union of 1536.

Rhodri Mawr	844–78
Anarawd	878–916
Hywel Dda	916–50
Iago ab Ieuaf	950–79
Hywel ab Ieuaf	979–85
Cadwallon	985–6
Maredudd	986–99

Cynan	999–1018
Llywelyn ap Seisyll	1018–23
Iago ab Idwal	1023–39
Gruffyd ap Llywelyn	1039–63
Bleddyn ap Cynfyn	1063–75
Trahaern ap Caradog	1075–81
Gruffyd ap Cynan	1081–1137

Owain Gwynedd	1137–70
Dafydd ab Owain	1170–94
Llywelyn Fawr	1194–1240
Dafyd ap Llywelyn	1240–6
Llywelyn ap Gruffydd	1246–82

British prime ministers

Name	Term	Party
Sir Robert Walpole	1721–42	Whig
Earl of Wilmington	1742–3	Whig
Henry Pelham	1743–54	Whig
Duke of Newcastle	1754–6	Whig
Duke of Devonshire	1756–7	Whig
Duke of Newcastle	1757–62	Whig
Earl of Bute	1762–3	Tory
George Grenville	1763–5	Whig
Marquess of Rockingham	1765–6	Whig
Earl of Chatham	1766–8	Whig
Duke of Grafton	1768–70	Whig
Lord North	1770–82	Tory
Marquess of Rockingham	1782	Whig
Earl of Shelburne	1782–3	Whig

Duke of Portland	1783	Coalition
William Pitt the Younger	1783–1801	Tory
Henry Addington	1801–4	Tory
William Pitt the Younger	1804–6	Tory
Lord Grenville	1806–7	Coalition
Duke of Portland	1807–9	Tory
Spencer Perceval	1809–12	Tory
Earl of Liverpool	1812–27	Tory
George Canning	1827	Coalition
Viscount Goderich	1827–8	Tory
Duke of Wellington	1828–30	Tory
Earl Grey	1830–4	Tory
Viscount Melbourne	1834	Whig
Sir Robert Peel	1834–5	Whig
Viscount Melbourne	1835–41	Whig

Sir Robert Peel	1841–6	Conservative
Lord John Russell	1846–52	Liberal
Earl of Derby	1852	Conservative
Lord Aberdeen	1852–5	Peelite
Viscount Palmerston	1855–8	Liberal
Earl of Derby	1858–9	Conservative
Viscount Palmerston	1859–65	Liberal
Lord John Russell	1865–6	Liberal
Early of Derby	1866–8	Conservative
Benjamin Disraeli	1868	Conservative
W.E. Gladstone	1868–74	Liberal
Benjamin Disraeli	1874–80	Conservative
W.E. Gladstone	1880–5	Liberal
Marquess of Salisbury	1885–6	Conservative
W.E. Gladstone	1886	Liberal

Marquess of Salisbury	1886–92	Conservative
W.E. Gladstone	1892–4	Liberal
Earl of Rosebery	1894–5	Liberal
Marquess of Salisbury	1895–1902	Conservative
Arthur James Balfour	1902–5	Conservative
Sir Henry Campbell-Bannerman		
	1905–8	Liberal
H.H. Asquith	1908–15	Liberal
	1915–6	Coalition
David Lloyd George	1916–22	Coalition
Andrew Bonar Law	1922–3	Conservative
Stanley Baldwin	1923–4	Conservative
Ramsay MacDonald	1924	Labour
Stanley Baldwin	1924–9	Conservative
Ramsay MacDonald	1929–31	Labour
	1931–5	National coalition
Stanley Baldwin	1935–7	National coalition
Neville Chamberlain	1937–40	National coalition

Winston Churchill	1940–5	Coalition
Clement Attlee	1945–51	Labour
Sir Winston Churchill	1951–5	Conservative
Sir Anthony Eden	1955–7	Conservative
Harold Macmillan	1957–63	Conservative
Sir Alec Douglas-Home	1963–4	Conservative
Harold Wilson	1964–70	Labour
Edward Heath	1970–4	Conservative
Harold Wilson	1974–6	Labour
James Callaghan	1976–9	Labour
Margaret Thatcher	1979–90	Conservative
John Major	1990–7	Conservative
Tony Blair	1997–	Labour

Scottish first ministers

Donald Dewar	1999–2000	Labour
Henry McLeish	2000–	Labour

Welsh first secretaries

Alun Michael	1999–2000	Labour
Rhodri Morgan	2000–	Labour

Northern Ireland prime and first ministers

Name	Term
James Craig (Viscount Craigavon)	1921–40
John Miller Andrews	1940–3
Sir Basil Brooke (Viscount Brookeborough)	1943–63
Terence O'Neill	1963–9
James Chichester-Clark	1969–71
Brian Faulkner	1971–2
Direct rule from Westminster	1972–99
David Trimble	1999–2001

The honours system

In Britain, many official honours are awarded for outstanding civilian or military service. They are awarded by the sovereign and are announced twice a year, at the New Year and on the occasion of the Queen's Official Birthday (the second Saturday in June). Within most orders there are several ranks.

Awards for bravery

Victoria Cross (VC) Established 1856. The highest award for military bravery.
George Cross (GC) Established 1940. Civilian: for acts of heroism or courage in dangerous circumstances.

Orders of chivalry (in order of precedence)

Order of the Garter Rank: KG (Knight). Established 1348. Consists of members of the Royal Family and 24 Knights Companion.

Order of the Thistle (Scottish) Rank: KT (Knight). Established around 1480. Consists of members of the Royal Family and 16 Knights.

Order of the Bath Ranks: GCB (Knight Grand Cross), KCB (Knight Commander), CB (Companion). Established 1725. Two divisions, military and civilian.

Order of Merit (OM) Established 1902. For outstanding merit in any form of endeavour. Limited to 24 members. Carries no title.

Order of St Michael and St George Ranks: GCMC (Knight Grand Cross), KCMG (Knight Commander), CMG (Companion). Established 1818. Mainly for diplomats.

Order of the British Empire Ranks: KBE (Knight Commander), DBE (Dame Commander), CBE (Commander), OBE (Officer), MBE (Member). Established 1917.

Order of the Companions of Honour (CH) Established 1917. Carries no title. Limited to 65 members.

Archbishops of Canterbury

Canterbury was established as the seat of England's first archbishopric after St Augustine founded an abbey there in AD 597. After Henry VIII's break with the Roman Catholic Church in 1534, the archbishop of Canterbury became the chief bishop of the Church of England and, later, of the worldwide Anglican Communion. Archbishops of Canterbury are appointed on ecclesiastical advice by the prime minister.

Name	Term as archbishop
Thomas Cranmer	1533–56
Reginald Pole	1556–8
Matthew Parker	1559–75
Edmund Grindal	1576–83
John Whitgift	1583–1604
Richard Bancroft	1604–10
George Abbot	1611–33
William Laud	1633–45*

After the beheading of Archbishop Laud during the Civil War, no new Archbishop of Canterbury was appointed until the restoration of Charles II in 1660.

William Juxon	1660–3
Gilbert Sheldon	1663–77
William Sancroft	1678–91
John Tillotson	1691–4

Thomas Tenison	1695–1715
William Wake	1716–37
John Potter	1737–47
Thomas Herring	1747–57
Matthew Hutton	1758
Thomas Secker	1758–68
Hon. Frederick Cornwallis	1768–83
John Moore	1783–1805
Charles Manners-Sutton	1805–28
William Howley	1828–48
John Bird Sumner	1848–62
Charles Longley	1862–68
Archibald Campbell Tait	1868–82
Edward White Benson	1883–96
Frederick Temple	1896–1902
Randall Thomas Davidson	1903–28
Cosmo Gordon Lang	1928–42
William Temple	1942–44
Geoffrey Fisher	1945–61
Arthur Ramsey	1961–74
Donald Coggan	1974–80
Robert Runcie	1980–91
George Carey	1991–

Archbishops of Westminster

After Henry VIII's break with Rome in the 16th century, there was no Catholic archbishop in England until the Pope appointed one in 1850, following the granting of full political and civil liberties to the country's Catholics in 1829. The Archbishop of Westminster is the leader of the Catholic Church in England and Wales.

Name	Term
Nicholas Wiseman	1850–65
Henry Edward Manning	1865–92
Herbert Vaughan	1892–1903
Francis Bourne	1903–35
Arthur Hinsley	1935–43
Bernard William Griffin	1943–56
William Godfrey	1956–63
John Carmel Heenan	1963–75
George Basil Hume	1976–99
Cormac Murphy O'Connor	2000–

Dynasties of ancient Egypt

Early period	First Dynasty	c.3100–2905 BC	Second Intermediate Period	Thirteenth to Seventeenth Dynasties	c.1786–1570 BC
	Second Dynasty	c.2905–2700 BC			
Old Kingdom	Third Dynasty	c.2700–2680 BC	New Kingdom	Eighteenth Dynasty	c.1570–1293 BC
	Fourth Dynasty	c.2680–2544 BC		Nineteenth Dynasty	c.1293–1185 BC
	Fifth Dynasty	c.2544–2407 BC		Twentieth Dynasty	c.1185–1100 BC
	Sixth Dynasty	c.2407–2200 BC	Third Intermediate Period	Twenty-first to Twenty-sixth Dynasties	c.1100–525 BC
First Intermediate Period	Seventh to Tenth Dynasties	c.2200–2100 BC			
Middle Kingdom	Eleventh Dynasty	c.2100–1991 BC	Late Dynastic Period	Twenty-seventh to Twenty-first Dynasties	c.525–332 BC
	Twelfth Dynasty	c.1991–1786 BC			

Roman emperors

The Julio-Claudian emperors
Augustus	27 BC–AD 14
Tiberius	14–37
Caligula	37–41
Claudius	41–54
Nero	54–68
Galba	68–69
Otho	69
Vitellius	69

The Flavian emperors
Vespasian	69–79
Titus	79–81
Domitian	81–96

The Antonine emperors
Nerva	97–98
Trajan	98–117
Hadrian	117–38
Antoninus Pius	138–61
Marcus Aurelius[1]	161–80
Lucius Verus[1]	161–9
Commodus	180–92
Pertinax	193
Didius Julianus	193

[1] Joint emperors.

The Severi
Septimius Severus	193–211
Caracalla[2]	211–17
Geta[2]	211–12
Macrinus	217–18
Elagabalus	218–22
Severus Alexander	222–35

[2] Joint emperors.

The soldier emperors
Maximinus the Thracian	235–38
Gordian I[3]	238
Gordian II[3]	238
Balbinus[4]	238
Pupienus[4]	238
Gordian III	238–44
Philip the Arabian	244–9
Decius	249–51
Trebonianus Gallus	251–3
Aemilianus	253
Valerian[5]	253–60
Gallienus[5]	253–68

[3] Joint emperors. [4] Joint emperors. [5] Joint emperors.

The Illyrian emperors
Claudius II Gothicus	268–70
Quintilus	270
Aurelian	270–75
Tacitus	275–76
Probus	276–82
Carus	282–3
Numerian[6]	283–4
Carinus[6]	283–4

[6] Joint emperors.

Diocletian and the Tetrarchy
Under the tetrarchy, four emperors ruled jointly, each with responsibility for a different sector of the empire.
Diocletian	284–305
Maximian	286–305
Constantius I Chlorus	293–306
Galerius	293–311
Severus	305–7
Maximinus	305–13
Maxentius	306–12
Licinius	308–24

Dynasty of Constantine
Constantine I the Great[7]	306–37
Constantine II[8]	337–40
Constans[8]	337–50
Constantius II[8]	337–61
Julian the Apostate	361–3
Jovian	363–4

[7] Sole emperor: 324–37.
[8] Joint emperors.

Western empire
Valentian split the empire into western and eastern halves, making his brother Valens ruler of the eastern empire.
Valentinian I	364–75
Gratian	375–83
Valentinian II	375–92
Maximus[9]	383–8
Eugenius[9]	392–4
Honorius	395–423
Constantine III[9]	409–11
Valentinian III	423–55
Petronius Maximus	455
Avitus	455–6
Majorian	457–61
Libius Severus	461–65
Anthemius	467–72
Olybrius	472
Glycerius	473–4
Julius Nepos	474–80
Romulus Augustulus	475–6[10]

[9] Usurpers.
[10] End of the Roman Empire in the west.

Eastern empire
Valens	364–78
Theodosius I the Great	379–95
Arcadius	395–408
Theodosius II	408–50
Marcian	450–57
Leo	457–74
Zeno	474–91

The eastern empire survived until the fall of its capital Constantinople (modern Istanbul) to the Ottoman Turks in 1453.

Caliphs

The caliph was the leader of the Muslim world. The title comes from the Arabic phrase for 'successor of the Messenger of God'. It was adopted by successors of the Prophet Muhammad's after his death in AD 632. The first caliph was Muhammad's father-in-law Abu Bakr, who set in motion the Arab conquests of Persia, Iraq and the Middle East. Abu Bakr and his three successors are known as the 'perfect' or 'rightly guided' (*al-rashidun*) caliphs.

Orthodox caliphate
Abu Bakr	632–34
Umar I	634–44
Uthman	644–56
Ali	656–61

Islam splits: the Shiites insist that only descendants of Ali should hold authority among Muslims, other Muslims accept the Umayyad dynasty of Damascus.

Umayyad caliphate
Mu'awiyah I	661–80
Yazid	680–3
Mu'awiyah II	683–4
Marwan	684–5
Abd al-Malik	685–705
al-Walid	705–15
Sulayman	715–17
'Umar II	717–20
Yazid II	720–4
Hisham	724–43
al-Walid II	743–4
Yazid III	744
Ibrahim	744
Marwan II	744–50

Abbasid caliphate
as-Saffah	749–54
al-Mansur	754–75
al-Mahdi	775–85
al-Hadi	785–6
Harun ar-Rashid	786–809
al-Amin	809–13
al-Ma'mun	813–33
al-Mutasim	833–42
al-Wathiq	842–47
al-Mutawwkkil	847–61
al-Muntasir	861–2
al-Mustain	862–6
al-Mu'tazz	866–9
al-Muhtadi	869–70
al-Mu'tamid	870–92
al-Mu'tazid	892–902
al-Muktafi	902–8
al-Muqtadir	908–32
al-Qahir	932–4
ar-Razi	934–40
al-Muttaqi	940–4
al-Mustagfi	944–5
al-Muti'	945–74
at-Tai	974–94
al-Qadir	994–1031
al-Qaim	1031–75
al-Muqtad	1075–94
al-Mustazhir	1094–1118
al-Mustarshid	1118–35
ar-Rashid	1135–6
al-Muqtafi	1136–60
al-Mustanjid	1160–70
al-Mustaz	1170–80
an-Nasir	1180–1225
az-Zahir	1225–6
al-Mustansir	1226–42
al-Musta'sim	1242–58

A puppet caliphate of Abbasid descent existed in Cairo until ousted in 1517 by the Ottomans. The title was then borne by Ottoman sultans until 1922 and was abolished by the Turkish republic in 1924.

Holy Roman Emperors

Beginning with the coronation of the Frankish king Charlemagne in AD 800, the Holy Roman Emperor was recognised by the Catholic Church as the secular ruler of Christendom. The empire was based in Germany, and the emperor was also usually the German king, elected by the leading German princes. Occasional clashes between Holy Roman Emperors and the papacy, and between claimants to the throne, led to periods where the title was claimed by more than one person. The title was abolished in 1806.

Carolingian House
Charles I the Great (Charlemagne)	800–14
Louis I the Pious	814–40
Lothair I	840–55
Louis II	855–75
Charles II the Bald	875–7
Charles III the Fat	877–87
Arnulf of Carinthia	887–98
Louis III the Child	899–911

House of Franconia
Conrad I	911–18

House of Saxony
Henry I the Fowler	919–36
Otto I the Great	936–73
Otto II	973–83
Otto III	983–1002
Henry II	1002–24

Salian House
Conrad II	1024–39
Henry III	1039–56
Henry IV	1056–1105
Henry V	1105–25

House of Supplinburg
Lothair II of Saxony	1125–37

House of Hohenstaufen
Conrad III	1138–52
Frederick I Barbarossa	1152–90
Henry VI	1190–97
Philip of Swabia	1198–1208

House of Welf
Otto IV of Brunswick[1]	1208–15

[1] German king: 1208–12. Emperor: 1209–15.

House of Hohenstaufen
Frederick II[2]	1212–50
Henry Raspe of Thuringia (rival)	1246–7
William of Holland (rival)	1247–56
Conrad IV[3]	1237–54

[2] German king: 1212–20. Emperor: 1220–50.
[3] German king only.

Interregnum 1254–73
Richard of Cornwall (rival)	
Alfonso X of Castile (rival)	

House of Habsburg
Rudolf I	1273–91

House of Nassau
Adolf	1292–8

House of Habsburg
Albert I of Austria	1298–1308

House of Luxembourg
Henry VII	1308–13

House of Wittelsbach
Louis IV of Bavaria	1314–46
Frederick of Austria (rival)	1314–30

House of Luxembourg
Charles IV	1346–78
Günther of Schwarzburg (rival)	1349
Wenceslas	1378–1400

House of Wittelsbach
Rupert of the Palatinate	1400–10

House of Luxembourg
Sigismund	1410–37
Jobst of Moravia (rival)	1410–11

House of Habsburg
Albert II of Austria	1438–9
Frederick III	1440–93
Maximilian I	1493–1519
Charles V	1519–56
Ferdinand I	1556–64
Maximilian II	1564–76
Rudolf II	1576–1612
Matthias	1612–19
Ferdinand II	1619–37
Ferdinand III	1637–57
Leopold I	1658–1705
Joseph I	1705–11
Charles VI	1711–40

House of Wittelsbach
Charles VII of Bavaria	1742–5

House of Habsburg-Lorraine
Francis I of Lorraine	1745–65
Joseph II	1765–90
Leopold II	1790–2
Francis II	1792–1806

Popes

The papacy traces itself back to St Peter. Listed here are the popes from 1417, when the papacy moved back to Rome after being based at Avignon in France for nearly 70 years.

Martin V (Oddone Colonna)	1417–31
Eugenius IV (Gabriele Condulmer)	1431–47
Nicholas V (Tommaso Parentucelli)	1447–55
Calixtus III (Alfonso de Borgia)	1455–58
Pius II (Aeneas Silvius Piccolomini)	1458–64
Paul II (Pietro Barbo)	1464–71
Sixtus IV (Francesco della Rovere)	1471–84
Innocent VIII (Giovanni Battista Cibo)	1484–92
Alexander VI (Rodrigo Borgia)	1492–1503
Pius III (Francesco Todeschini Piccolomini)	1503
Julius II (Giuliano della Rovere)	1503–13
Leo X (Giovanni de Medici)	1513–22
Adrian VI (Adrian Dedel)	1522–3
Clement VII (Giulio de Medici)	1523–34
Paul III (Alessandro Farnese)	1534–50
Julius III (Gianmaria del Monte)	1550–5
Marcellus II (Marcello Cervini)	1555
Paul IV (Giovanni Pietro Caraffa)	1555–9
Pius IV (Giovanni Angelo de Medici)	1559–66
Pius V (Michele Ghislieri)	1566–72
Gregory XIII (Ugo Buoncompagni)	1572–85
Sixtus V (Felice Peretti)	1585–90
Urban VII (Gianbattista Castagna)	1590
Gregory XIV (Niccolo Sfondrati)	1590–1
Innocent IX (Gian Antonio Facchinetti)	1591–2
Clement VIII (Ippolito Aldobrandini)	1592–1605
Leo XI (Alessandro de Medici-Ottaiano)	1605
Paul V (Camillo Borghese)	1605–21
Gregory XV (Alessandro Ludovisi)	1621–3
Urban VIII (Maffeo Barberini)	1623–44
Innocent X (Giambattista Pamfili)	1644–55
Alexander VII (Fabio Chigi)	1655–67
Clement IX (Giulio Rospigliosi)	1667–70
Clement X (Emilio Altieri)	1670–6
Innocent XI (Benedetto Odescalchi)	1676–89
Alexander VIII (Pietro Vito Ottoboni)	1689–91
Innocent XII (Antonio Pignatelli)	1691–1700
Clement XI (Gian Francesco Albani)	1700–21
Innocent XIII (Michelangelo dei Conti)	1721–24
Benedict XIII (Pietro Francesco Orsini)	1724–30
Clement XII (Lorenzo Corsini)	1730–40
Benedict XIV (Propero Lambertini)	1740–58
Clement XIII (Carlo Rezzonico)	1758–69
Clement XIV (Lorenzo Ganganelli)	1769–75
Pius VI (Giovani Angelo Braschi)	1775–1800
Pius VII (Barnaba Chiaramonti)	1800–23
Leo XII (Annibale della Genga)	1823–9
Pius VIII (Francesco Saveno Castiglioni)	1829–31
Gregory XVI (Bartolomeo Alberto Cappellari)	1831–46
Pius IX (Giovanni Maria Mastai Ferretti)	1846–78
Leo XIII (Vincenzo Gioacchino Pecci)	1878–1903
Pius X (Giuseppe Sarto)	1903–14
Benedict XV (Giacomo della Chiesa)	1914–22
Pius XI (Achille Ratti)	1922–39
Pius XII (Eugenio Pacelli)	1939–58
John XXIII (Angelo Giuseppe Roncali)	1958–63
Paul VI (Giovanni Battista Montini)	1963–78
John Paul I (Albino Luciani)	1978
John Paul II (Karol Jozef Wojtyla)	1978–

France

France emerged as a unified state at the end of the 15th century. The absolute rule of French kings came to an end with the French Revolution (1789–99).

Carolingian House

Pepin the Short	751–68
Carloman	768–71
Charles the Great (Charlemagne)	768–814
Louis I the Pious	814–40
Charles I the Bald	840–77
Louis II the Stammerer	877–9
Louis III	879–82
Carloman	882–4

Robertian House

Eudes	888–98

Carolingian House

Charles III the Simple	893–922

Robertian House

Robert I	922–3
Rudolf	923–36

Carolingian House

Louis IV d'Outremer	936–54
Lothair	954–86
Louis V the Sluggard	986–7

Capetian House

Hugh Capet	987–96
Robert II the Pious	996–1031
Henry I	1031–60
Philip I	1060–1108
Louis VI the Fat	1108–37
Louis VII the Younger	1137–80
Philip II Augustus	1180–1223
Louis VIII the Lion	1223–6
Louis IX	1226–70
Philip III the Bold	1270–85

Philip IV the Fair	1285–1314
Louis X the Stubborn	1314–16
John I	1316
Philip V the Tall	1316–22
Charles IV the Fair	1322–28

House of Valois

Philip VI	1328–50
John II the Good	1350–64
Charles V the Wise	1364–80
Charles VI the Mad	1380–1422
Charles VII the Victorious	1422–61
Louis XI	1461–83
Charles VIII	1483–98

Line of Orléans

Louis XII	1498–1515

Line of Angoulême

Francis I	1515–47
Henry II	1547–59
Francis II	1559–60
Charles IX	1560–74
Henry III	1574–89

House of Bourbon

Henry IV	1589–1610
Louis XIII	1610–43
Louis XIV	1643–1715
Louis XV	1715–74
Louis XVI	1774–92
Louis XVII	1793–5

First Republic

National Convention	1792–5
Directory	1795–9
Consulate:	
Napoleon Bonaparte, First Consul	1799–1804

House of Bonaparte, First Empire

Napoleon I	1804–14, 1815
Napoleon II	1815

House of Bourbon

Louis XVIII	1815–24
Charles X	1824–30

Line of Orléans

Louis Philippe I	1830–48

Second Republic

Louis Napoleon Bonaparte, President	1848–52

House of Bonaparte, Second Empire

Napoleon III	1852–70

Third Republic: presidents

Louis Adolphe Thiers	1871–3
Marie Edmé de MacMahon	1873–9
Jules Grévy	1879–87
Sadi Carnot	1887–94
Jean Paul Pierre Casimir-Périer	1894–5
François Félix Faure	1895–9
Émile Loubet	1899–1906
Armand Fallières	1906–13
Raymond Poincaré	1913–20
Paul Deschanel	1920
Alexandre Millerand	1920–4
Gaston Dourmergue	1924–31
Paul Doumer	1931–2
Albert Lebrun	1932–40

Fourth Republic: presidents

Vincent Auriol	1947–54
René Coty	1954–8

Fifth Republic: presidents

Charles de Gaulle	1958–69
Georges Pompidou	1969–74
Valéry Giscard d'Estaing	1974–81
François Mitterrand	1981–95
Jacques Chirac	1995–

Ireland

In 1921 the Anglo-Irish Treaty created the Irish Free State. A new constitution in 1937 established Ireland (Eire) as a sovereign state.

Presidents

Douglas Hyde	1938–45
Sean Thomas O'Kelly	1945–59
Eamon de Valera	1959–73
Erskine H. Childers	1973–74
Caroll Daly	1974–76
Patrick J. Hillery	1976–90
Mary Robinson	1990–7
Mary McAleese	1997–

Prime ministers (taoiseachs)

Eamon de Valera	1921
Arthur Griffith	1922
William Cosgrave	1922–32
Eamon de Valera	1932–48
John Aloysius Costello	1948–51
Eamon de Valera	1951–54
John Aloysius Costello	1954–57
Eamon de Valera	1957–59
Sean Lemass	1959–66
John Lynch	1966–73
Liam Cosgrave	1973–7
John Lynch	1977–9

Charles Haughey	1979–82
Garret Fitzgerald	1982–7
Charles Haughey	1987–92
Albert Reynolds	1992–4
John Bruton	1994–7
Bertie Ahern	1997–

Spain

Muslim Moors conquered most of Spain in the 8th century. Christian reconquest began in the 11th century; in 1492 Ferdinand II of Aragon and Isabella of Castile unified Spain.

House of Habsburg

Charles I*	1516–56
Philip II	1556–98
Philip III	1598–1621
Philip IV	1621–65
Charles II	1665–1700

*Charles I of Spain is better known to history as the Holy Roman Emperor Charles V – see page 599.

House of Bourbon

Philip V	1700–46

Ferdinand VI	1746–59
Charles III	1759–88
Charles IV	1788–1808
Ferdinand VII	1808

House of Bonaparte

Joseph Napoleon	1808–1813

House of Bourbon

Ferdinand VII	1813–33
Isabella II	1833–68

House of Savoy

Amadeus	1870–3

First Republic

Five presidents in just under two years.

House of Bourbon

Alfonso XII	1874–85

Alfonso XIII	1886–1931

Second Republic: presidents

Niceta Alcalá Zamora	1931–6
Manuel Azana	1936–9

Dictatorship: Caudillo (leader)

Francisco Franco y Bahamonde	1936–75

House of Bourbon

Juan Carlos I	1975–

Prime ministers since 1976

Adolfo Suárez González	1976–81
Leopoldo Calvo Sotelo y Bustelo	1981–82
Felipe González Marquez	1982–96
José Maria Aznar	1996–

Italy

In 1861, Vittorio Emanuele II of Piedmont became king of the newly united Italy. Benito Mussolini, prime minister from 1922 to 1943, held dictatorial powers from 1928.

House of Savoy

Vittorio Emanuele II	1861–78
Umberto I	1878–1900
Vittorio Emanuele III	1900–46
Umberto II	1946

Republic: presidents

Enrico da Nicola	1946–8
Luigi Einaudi	1948–55
Giovanni Gronchi	1955–62
Antonio Segni	1962–4
Giuseppe Saragat	1964–71
Giovanni Leone	1971–8
Sandro Pertini	1978–85
Francesco Cossiga	1985–92
Oscar Luigi Scalfaro	1992–9
Carlo Azeglio Ciampi	1999–

Prime ministers from 1945

Ferruccio Parri	1945
Alcide De Gasperi	1945–53
Giuseppe Pella	1953–4
Amintore Fanfani	1954
Mario Scelba	1954–5
Antonio Segni	1955–7
Adone Zoli	1957–8
Amintore Fanfani	1958–9
Antonio Segni	1959–60
Fernando Tambroni-Armaroli	1960
Amintore Fanfani	1960–3
Giovanni Leone	1963
Aldo Moro	1963–8
Giovanni Leone	1968
Mariano Rumor	1968–70
Emilio Colombo	1970–2
Giulio Andreotti	1972–3
Mariano Rumor	1973–4
Aldo Moro	1974–6
Giulio Andreotti	1976–9
Francesco Cossiga	1979–80
Arnaldo Forlani	1980–1
Giovanni Spadolini	1981–2
Amintore Fanfani	1982–3
Bettino Craxi	1983–7
Amintore Fanfani	1987
Giovanni Goria	1987–8
Ciriaco De Mita	1988–9
Giulio Andreotti	1989–92
Giuliano Amato	1992–3
Carlo Azeglio Ciampi	1993–4
Silvio Berlusconi	1994–5
Lamberto Dini	1995–6
Romano Prodi	1996–8
Massimo D'Alema	1998–2000
Giuliano Amato	2000–1
Silvio Berlusconi	2001–

Prussia and Germany

Kings of Prussia

Friedrich I	1701–13
Friedrich Wilhelm I the Soldier King	1713–40
Friedrich II the Great	1740–86
Friedrich Wilhelm II	1786–97
Friedrich Wilhelm III	1797–1840
Friedrich Wilhelm IV	1840–61
Wilhelm I	1861–71

Emperors (Kaisers) of Germany

Wilhelm I	1871–88
Friedrich III	1888
Wilhelm II	1888–1918

Weimar Republic: presidents

Friedrich Ebert	1919–25
Paul von Hindenburg	1925–34

Third Reich: Führer

Adolf Hitler	1934–45

Federal Republic: presidents

Theodore Heuss	1949–59
Heinrich Lübke	1959–69
Gustav Heinemann	1969–74
Walter Scheel	1974–9
Karl Carstens	1979–84
Richard von Weizsäcker	1984–94
Roman Herzog	1994–9
Johannes Rau	1999–

Chancellors

Otto von Bismarck	1871–90
Leo von Caprivi	1890–94
Chlodwig Karl Victor	1894–1900
Bernhard von Bülow	1900–9
Theobald von Bethmann-Holweg	1909–17
Georg Michaelis	1917
Georg von Hertling	1917
Max von Baden	1918
Friedrich Ebert	1918
Philipp Scheidemann	1919
Gustav Bauer	1919
Hermann Müller	1920
Konstantin Fehrenbach	1920
Karl Josef Wirth	1921
Wilhelm Cuno	1922
Gustaf Stresemann	1923
Wilhelm Marx	1923
Hans Luther	1925–6
Wilhelm Marx	1926–8
Heinrich Brüning	1929–32
Franz von Papen	1932
Kurt von Schleicher	1932–3
Adolf Hitler	1933–4*
Konrad Adenauer	1949–63

* In 1934, Hitler combined the posts of president and chancellor into the role of Führer (leader).

Ludwig Ehrhard	1963–6
Kurt Georg Kiesinger	1966–9
Willy Brandt	1969–74
Helmut Schmidt	1974–82
Helmut Kohl	1982–98
Gerhard Schröder	1998

German Democratic Republic (East Germany)

The GDR was created from the Soviet-occupied zone in post-war Germany. With German reunification in 1990 it was absorbed into the Federal Republic of Germany.

President

Wilhelm Pieck	1949–60

Chairmen of the Council of State

Walter Ulbricht	1960–73
Willi Stoph	1973–6
Erich Honecker	1976–89
Egon Krenz	1989
Gregor Gysi	1989–90

Russia

Rurik dynasty

Ivan III the Great	1472–1505
Vasily III	1505–33
Ivan IV the Terrible	1533–84
Boris Godunov	1598–1605

Romanov dynasty

Mikhail	1613–45
Alexei	1645–76
Fyodor III	1676–82
Peter I the Great	1682–1725
Catherine I	1725–27
Peter II	1727–30
Anna	1730–40
Ivan VI	1740–41
Elizabeth	1741–62
Peter III	1762
Catherine II the Great	1762–96

Paul I	1796–1800
Alexander I	1800–25
Nicholas I	1825–55
Alexander II	1855–81
Alexander III	1881–94
Nicholas II	1894–1917

Head of provisional government

Alexander Kerensky	March–October 1917

Soviet Union:
General secretaries of the Communist Party

Vladimir Lenin	1917–24
Joseph Stalin	1924–53
Nikita Khrushchev	1953–64
Leonid Brezhnev	1964–82
Yuri Andropov	1983–4
Konstantin Chernenko	1984–5
Mikhail Gorbachev	1985–91

Russian Federation: presidents

Boris Yeltsin	1991–9
Vladimir Putin	1999–

The Americas

The United States
Presidents

George Washington	1789–97	Federalist
John Adams	1797–1801	Federalist
Thomas Jefferson	1801–9	Democratic-Republican
James Madison	1809–17	Dem-Rep
James Monroe	1817–25	Dem-Rep
John Quincy Adams	1825–9	Independent
Andrew Jackson	1829–37	Democrat
Martin Van Buren	1837–41	Democrat
William H. Harrison	1841	Whig
John Tyler	1841–5	Whig, then Democrat
James K. Polk	1845–9	Democrat
Zachary Taylor	1849–50	Whig
Millard Fillmore	1850–3	Whig
Franklin Pierce	1853–7	Democrat
James Buchanan	1857–61	Democrat
Abraham Lincoln	1861–5	Republican
Andrew Johnson	1865–9	Democrat
Ulysses S. Grant	1869–77	Republican
Rutherford B. Hayes	1877–81	Republican
James A. Garfield	1881	Republican
Chester A. Arthur	1881–5	Republican
Grover Cleveland	1885–9	Democrat
Benjamin Harrison	1889–93	Republican
Grover Cleveland	1893–7	Democrat
William McKinley	1897–1901	Republican
Theodore Roosevelt	1901–9	Republican
William H. Taft	1909–13	Republican
Woodrow Wilson	1913–21	Democrat
Warren G. Harding	1921–3	Republican
Calvin Coolidge	1923–9	Republican
Herbert Hoover	1929–33	Republican
Franklin D. Roosevelt	1933–45	Democrat
Harry S Truman	1945–53	Democrat
Dwight D. Eisenhower	1953–61	Republican
John F. Kennedy	1961–3	Democrat
Lyndon B. Johnson	1963–9	Democrat
Richard M. Nixon	1969–74	Republican
Gerald R. Ford	1974–7	Republican
James Earl Carter	1977–81	Democrat
Ronald W. Reagan	1981–9	Republican
George H.W. Bush	1989–93	Republican
William J. Clinton	1993–2001	Democrat
George W. Bush	2001–	Republican

Canada
Prime ministers

John A. Macdonald	1867–73
Alexander Mackenzie	1873–8
John A. Macdonald	1878–91
John J.C. Abbott	1891–2
John S.D. Thompson	1892–4
Mackenzie Bowell	1894–6
Charles Tupper	1896
Wilfrid Laurier	1896–1911
Robert L. Borden	1911–20
Arthur Meighen	1920–1
W.L. Mackenzie King	1921–6
Arthur Meighen	1926
W.L. Mackenzie King	1926–30
Richard B. Bennett	1930–5
W.L. Mackenzie King	1935–48
Louis Stephen St Lauren	1948–57
John George Diefenbaker	1957–63
Lester B. Pearson	1963–8
Pierre Elliott Trudeau	1968–79
Joseph Clark	1979–80
Pierre Elliott Trudeau	1980–4
John Turner	1984
Brian Mulroney	1984–93
Jean Chrétien	1993–

Mexico
Presidents

Benito Juárez	1867–72
Sebastián Lerdo de Tejada y Corral	1872–6
Juan Méndez	1876–7
Porfirio Díaz	1877–80
Manuel González	1880–4
Porfirio Díaz	1884–1911
Francisco León de la Barra	1911
Francisco Indalecio Madero	1911–13
Victoriano Huerta	1913–14
Francisco Carvajal	1914
Venustiano Carranza	1914
Antonio Villarreal González	1914
Eulalio Martín Gutiérrez Ortiz	1914–15
Roque González Garza	1915
Francisco Lagos Cházaro	1915
Venustiano Carranza	1915–20
Adolfo de la Huerta	1920
Alvaro Obregón	1920–4
Plutarco Elías Calles	1924–8
Emilio Portes Gil	1928–30
Pascual Ortiz Rubio	1930–2
Abelardo Luján Rodríguez	1932–4
Lázaro Cárdenas	1934–40
Manuel Avila Camacho	1940–6
Miguel Alemán Valdés	1946–52
Adolfo Ruiz Cortines	1952–8
Adolfo López Mateos	1958–64
Gustavo Díaz Ordaz	1964–70
Luís Echeverría Alvarez	1970–6
José López Portillo y Pacheco	1976–82
Miguel de la Madrid Hurtado	1982–8
Carlos Salinas de Gortari	1988–94
Ernesto Zedillo Ponce de Leon	1994–2000
Vicente Fox Quesada	2000–

Africa and The Middle East

Israel
Prime ministers

David Ben-Gurion	1948–53
Moshe Sharett	1953–5
David Ben-Gurion	1955–63
Levi Eshkol	1963–9
Golda Meir	1969–74
Yitzhak Rabin	1974–7
Menachem Begin	1977–83
Yitzhak Shamir	1983–4
Shimon Peres	1984–6
Yitzhak Shamir	1986–92
Yitzhak Rabin	1992–5
Shimon Peres	1995–6
Binyamin Netanyahu	1996–9
Ehud Barak	1999–2001
Ariel Sharon	2001–

Turkey
Presidents

Mustafa Kemal Pasha (Atatürk from 1934)	1923–38
Ismet Inönü	1938–50
Celal Bayar	1950–60
Cemal Gürsel	1960–6
Cevdet Sunay	1966–73
Fahri Korutürk	1973–80
Kenan Evren	1980–9
Turgut Özal	1989–93
Süleyman Demirel	1993–2000
Ahmet Necdet Sezer	2000–

Egypt
Presidents

Gamal Abd al-Nasser	1953–70
Anwar Sadat	1970–81
Mohammed Hosni Mubarak	1981–

Saudi Arabia
Kings

Abdul Aziz (ibn Saud)	1932–53
Saud (ibn Abd al-Aziz)	1953–64
Faisal (ibn Abd al-Aziz)	1964–75
Khalid (ibn Abd Al-Aziz)	1975–82
Fahd (ibn Abd Al-Aziz)	1982–

South Africa
Prime ministers

Louis Botha	1910–19
Jan Smuts	1919–24
James Hertzog	1924–39
Jan Smuts	1939–48
Daniel Malan	1948–54
Johannes Strijdon	1954–8
Hendrik Verwoerd	1958–66
Balthazar Johannes Vorster	1966–78
Pieter Botha	1978–84*

Post abolished in 1984.

Presidents

Pieter Botha	1984–9
Frederick Willem de Klerk	1989–94
Nelson Mandela	1994–9
Thabo Mbeki	1999–

Asia and the Pacific

China
Dynasties and regimes

Five Emperors	2250–2140 BC
Xia	2140–1711 BC
Shang or Yin	1711–1066 BC
Zhou	1066–256 BC
Qin (Ch'in)	221–206 BC
Han	206 BC–AD 220
Three Kingdoms (San-kuo)	220–80
Tsin	265–420
South and North Dynasties	420–589
Sui	581–618
Tang	618–906
Five Dynasties	906–60
Song (Sung)	960–1279
Yuan	1279–1368
Ming	1368–1644
Qing (Ch'ing)	1644–1911
Republic	1912–49
People's Republic	1949–

People's Republic:
Chairmen or General Secretaries of the Communist Party

Mao Ze-dong	1949–76
Hua Guofeng	1976–81*
Hu Yaobang	1982–7
Zhao Ziyang	1987–9
Jiang Zemin	1989–

From 1978 to 1997, China's effective ruler, or 'Paramount leader', was Deng Xiaoping.

Presidents*

Li Xiannian	1983–8
Yang Shangkun	1988–93
Jiang Zemin	1993–

The post of president, abolished in the late 1960s, was re-created in 1982.

Japan
Emperors

According to tradition, Japan's first *tenno* or emperor was Jimmu (660–585 BC), a descendant of the sun goddess Amaterasu. He was the ancestor of all later emperors and empresses. Listed here are the emperors and empresses from the start of the Heian period.

Heian period

Kammu	781–806
Heizei	806–9
Saga	809–23
Junna	823–33
Nimmyo	833–50
Montoku	850–8
Seiwa	858–76
Yozei	877–84
Koko	884–7
Uda	887–97
Daigo	897–930
Suzaku	930–46
Murakami	946–67
Reizei	967–9
Enyu	969–84
Kazan	984–6
Ichijo	986–1011
Sanjo	1011–16
Ichijo II	1016–36
Suzaku II	1036–45
Reizei II	1045–68
Sanjo II	1068–72
Shirakawa	1072–86
Horikawa	1086–1107
Toba	1107–23
Sutoku	1123–41
Konoye	1141–55
Shirakawa II	1155–8
Nijo	1159–65
Rokujo	1166–8
Takakura	1169–80
Antoku	1181–3

Kamakura period

Toba II	1184–98
Tsuchimikado	1199–1210
Juntoku	1211–21
Chukyo	1221
Horikawa II	1222–32
Shijo	1233–42
Saga II	1243–6
Fukakusa II	1247–59
Kameyama	1260–74
Uda II	1275–87
Fushimi I	1288–98
Fushimi II	1299–1301
Nijo II	1302–8
Hanazono	1309–18
Daigo II	1319–38

Nambokucho period

For over 50 years from the 1330s, two different branches of the imperial family ruled at rival courts in the north and south.

Southern emperors

Murakami II	1339–68
Chokei	1369–72
Kameyama II	1373–92

Northern emperors

Kogon	1331–3
Komyo	1336–48
Suko	1349–52
Kogon II	1353–71
Enyu II	1372–82

Muromachi period

Komatsu II	1383–1412
Shoko	1413–28
Hanazono II	1429–64
Tsuchimikado II	1465–1500
Kashiwabara II	1501–26
Nara II	1527–57
Okimachi	1558–86

Azuchi-Momoyama period

Yozei II	1587–1611

Edo period

Mizunoo II	1611–29
Meisho	1630–43
Komyo II	1644–54
Saiin II	1655–62
Reigen	1663–86
Higashiyama	1687–1709
Nakamikado	1710–35
Sakuramachi	1736–46
Momozono	1746–62
Sakuramachi II	1763–70
Momozono II	1771–9
Kokaku	1780–1816
Ninko	1817–46
Komei	1847–66

Modern period

Mutsuhito	1866–1912
Yoshihito	1912–26
Hirohito	1926–89*
Akihito	1989–

* *Regent from 1921*

India
Emperors
Mughal dynasty

Babur	1526–30
Humayun	1530–40

Sur dynasty

Sher Shah	1540–5
Islam Shah	1545–53
Muhammad Adil	1554–5

Mughal dynasty

Humayun	1555–6
Akbar I the Great	1556–1605
Jahangir	1605–27
Shah Jahan I	1627–58
Aurangzeb Alamgir I	1658–1707
Bahadur Shah I	1707–12
Jahandar Shah	1712–13
Farrukhsiyar	1713–19
Rafi al-Darajat	1719
Shah Jahan II	1719
Muhammad Shah	1719–48
Ahmad Shah	1748–54
Alamgir II	1754–9
Shah Alam	1759–1806
Akbar II	1806–37
Bahadur Shah II	1837–58

After the British sent the last emperor into exile, Queen Victoria assumed the title of Empress of India.

Prime ministers since independence

Jawaharlal Nehru	1947–64
Lal Bahadur Shastri	1964–6
Indira Gandhi	1966–77
Marorji Desai	1977–9
Charan Singh	1979–80
Indira Gandhi	1980–4
Rajiv Gandhi	1984–9
Viswanath Pratap Singh	1989–90
Chandra Shekhar	1990–1
P.V. Narsimha Rao	1991–6
Atal Behari Vajpayee	1996
H.D. Deve Gowda	1996–7
Inder Kumar Gujral	1997–8
Atal Behari Vajpayee	1998–

Australia
Prime ministers

Edmund Barton	1901–3
Alfred Deakin	1903–4
John C. Watson	1904
George Houstoun Reid	1904–5
Alfred Deakin	1905–8
Andrew Fisher	1908–9
Alfred Deakin	1909–10
Andrew Fisher	1910–13
Joseph Cook	1913–14
Andrew Fisher	1914–15
William M. Hughes	1915–23
Stanley M. Bruce	1923–9
James H. Sculin	1929–31
Joseph A. Lyons	1932–9
Robert Gordon Menzies	1939–41
Arthur William Fadden	1941
John Curtin	1941–5
Joseph Benedict Chifley	1945–9
Robert Gordon Menzies	1949–66
Harold Edward Holt	1966–7
John Grey Gorton	1968–71
William McMahon	1971–2
Gough Whitlam	1972–5
J. Malcolm Fraser	1975–83
Robert J.L. Hawke	1983–91
Paul Keating	1991–6
John Howard	1996–

New Zealand
Prime ministers

Henry Sewell	1856
William Fox	1856
Edward William Stafford	1856–61
William Fox	1861–2
Alfred Domett	1862–3
Frederick Whitaker	1863–4
Frederick Aloysius Weld	1864–5
Edward William Stafford	1865–9
William Fox	1869–72
Edward William Stafford	1872
George M. Waterhouse	1872–3
William Fox	1873
Julius Vogel	1873–5
Daniel Pollen	1875–6
Julius Vogel	1876
Harry Albert Atkinson	1876–7
George Grey	1877–9
John Hall	1879–82
Frederick Whitaker	1882–3
Harry Albert Atkinson	1883–4
Robert Stout	1884
Harry Albert Atkinson	1884
Robert Stout	1884–7
Harry Albert Atkinson	1887–91
John Ballance	1891–3
Richard John Seddon	1893–1906
William Hall Jones	1906
Joseph George Ward	1906–12
Thomas Mackenzie	1912
William Ferguson Massey	1912–25
Francis Henry Dillion Bell	1925
Joseph Gordon Coates	1925–8
Joseph George Ward	1928–30
George William Forbes	1930–5
Michael J. Savage	1935–40
Peter Fraser	1940–9
Sidney J. Holland	1949–57
Keith J. Holyoake	1957
Walter Nash	1957–60
Keith J. Holyoake	1960–72
John R. Marshall	1972
Norman Kirk	1972–4
Wallace Rowling	1974–5
Robert D. Muldoon	1975–84
David Lange	1984–9
Geoffrey Palmer	1989–90
Michael Moore	1990
James Bolger	1990–7
Jenny Shipley	1997–9
Helen Clark	1999–

Metric system

The metric unit of length, the metre, was first defined in France in 1799, and all other lengths were derived from it in multiples of ten. This decimal system applies to all metric weights and measures.

Length

1 mm	1 millimetre (mm)
10 mm	1 centimetre (cm)
10 cm	1 decimetre (dm)
100 cm/10 dm	1 metre (m)
1000 m	1 kilometre (km)

Area

1 mm²	1 sq millimetre (mm²)
100 mm²	1 sq centimetre (cm²)
100 cm²	1 sq decimetre (dm²)
10 000 cm²	1 sq metre (m²)
10 000 m²	1 hectare (ha)
1 million m²/100 ha	1 sq kilometre (km²)

Weight

1 g	1 gram (g)
1000 g	1 kilogram (kg)
1000 kg	1 tonne (t)

Volume (solid)

1 cm³	1 cubic centimetre (cm³)
1000 cm³	1 cubic decimetre (dm³)
1000 dm³	1 cubic metre (m³)

Volume (liquid)

1 ml	1 millilitre (ml)
10 ml	1 centilitre (cl)
10 cl	1 decilitre (dl)
100 cl/10 dl	1 litre (l)
100 l	1 hectolitre (hl)

SI units

The Système International d'Unités (SI), or International System of Units, is a modernised form of the metric system, which was internationally agreed in 1960.

	SI unit	Symbol
absorbed radiation dose	gray	Gy
amount of substance	mole	mol
electric capacitance	farad	F
electric charge	coulomb	C
electric conductance	siemens	S
electric current	ampere	A
energy or work	joule	J
force	newton	N
frequency	hertz	Hz
illuminance	lux	lx
inductance	henry	H
length	metre	m
luminous flux	lumen	lm
luminous intensity	candela	cd
magnetic flux	weber	Wb
magnetic flux density	tesla	T
mass	kilogram	kg
plane angle	radian	rad
potential difference	volt	V
power	watt	W
pressure	pascal	Pa
radiation dose equivalent	sievert	Sv
radiation exposure	roentgen	r
radioactivity	becquerel	Bq
resistance	ohm	Ω
solid angle	steradian	sr
sound intensity	decibel	dB
temperature	degree Celsius	°C
temperature, thermodynamic	kelvin	K
time	second	s

SI prefixes

Multiples	Prefix	Symbol	Example
10	deca	da	darad (decaradian)
100 (10²)	hecto	h	hW (hectowatt)
1000 (10³)	kilo	k	km (kilometre)
1 000 000 (10⁶)	mega	M	MHz (megahertz)
1 000 000 000 (10⁹)	giga	G	GJ (gigajoule)
1 000 000 000 000 (10¹²)	tera	T	TV (teravolt)
1 000 000 000 000 000 (10¹⁵)	peta	P	PPa (petapascal)
1 000 000 000 000 000 000 (10¹⁸)	exa	E	Elx (exalux)
1/10 (10⁻¹)	deci	d	dSv (decisievert)
1/100 (10⁻²)	centi	c	cN (centinewton)
1/1000 (10⁻³)	milli	m	mA (milliampere)
1/1 000 000 (10⁻⁶)	micro	µ	µBq (microbecquerel)
1/1 000 000 000 (10⁻⁹)	nano	n	ns (nanosecond)
1/1 000 000 000 000 (10⁻¹²)	pico	p	pF (picofarad)
1/1 000 000 000 000 000 (10⁻¹⁵)	femto	f	fr (froentogen)
1/1 000 000 000 000 000 000 (10⁻¹⁸)	atto	a	aT (attotesla)

Imperial system

The Imperial system of weights and measures, used in Britain and the USA, evolved from a mix of Roman, old northern European and improvised units. The current length of the mile and weight of the pound were set in the late 1500s; the length of the inch, foot and yard in 1855.

Length

1 in	1 inch
12 in	1 foot (ft)
3 ft	1 yard (yd)
5½ yd	1 rod
22 yd/4 rods	1 chain
220 yd/10 chains	1 furlong
5280 ft/1760 yd/8 furlongs	1 mile

Length, nautical

6 ft	1 fathom
100 fathoms	1 cable length
6080 ft	1 nautical mile

Area

1 sq in	square inch
144 sq in	1 square foot (sq ft)
9 sq ft	1 square yard (sq yd)
304¼ sq yd	1 square rod
40 sq rods	1 rood
4840 sq yd/4 roods	1 acre
640 acres	1 square mile

Weight

1 oz	1 ounce
16 oz	1 pound (lb)
14 lb	1 stone
8 stones	1 hundred-weight (cwt)
2240 lb/20 cwt	1 ton

Volume (solid)

1 cu in	1 cubic inch
1728 cu in	1 cubic foot (cu ft)
27 cu ft	1 cubic yard (cu yd)

Volume (liquid)

1 fl oz (UK)	1 fluid ounce (=28.41 cm³)
20 fl oz	1 pint
2 pints	1 quart
4 quarts	1 gallon
1 fl oz (US)	(=29.6 cm³)
16 fl oz (US)	1 pint (US)

Temperature scales

The Celsius (or centigrade) temperature scale was devised by the 18th-century Swedish astronomer Anders Celsius. In the Celsius scale, water freezes at 0° and boils at 100°; each degree is one hundredth part of the range between the two.

The Fahrenheit temperature scale was also devised in the 18th century: by German instrument-maker Gabriel Fahrenheit. In it water freezes at 32° and boils at 212°.

A third scale is the Kelvin scale, whose zero point (0K) is absolute zero, approximately −273.15°C.

How to convert Fahrenheit to Celsius $F° = (C° \times 1.8) + 32$

How to convert Celsius to Fahrenheit $C° = (F° − 32) ÷ 1.8$

°C	°F	°C	°F
100	212	30	86
95	203	25	77
90	194	20	68
85	185	15	59
80	176	10	50
75	167	5	41
70	158	0	32
65	149	−5	23
60	140	−10	14
55	131	−15	5
50	122	−20	−4
45	113	−25	−13
40	104	−30	−22
35	95		

How to convert metric to Imperial

To convert	into	multiply by
Length		
millimetres	inches	0.0394
centimetres	inches	0.3937
metres	feet	3.2808
metres	yards	1.0936
kilometres	miles	0.6214
Area		
square centimetres	square inches	0.155
square metres	square feet	10.764
square metres	square yards	1.196
hectares	acres	2.471
square kilometres	square miles	0.386
Volume		
cubic centimetres	cubic inches	0.061
cubic metres	cubic feet	35.315
cubic metres	cubic yards	1.308
litres	pints	1.760
litres	gallons	0.220
Weight		
grams	ounces	0.0352
kilograms	pounds	2.2046
tonnes	tons	0.9842

How to convert Imperial to metric

To convert	into	multiply by
Length		
inches	millimetres	25.4
inches	centimetres	2.54
feet	metres	0.3048
yards	metres	0.9144
miles	kilometres	1.6093
Area		
square inches	square centimetres	6.4516
square feet	square metres	0.093
square yards	square metres	0.836
acres	hectares	0.405
square miles	square kilometres	2.58999
Volume		
cubic inches	cubic centimetres	16.387
cubic feet	cubic metres	0.0283
cubic yards	cubic metres	0.7646
fluid ounces	millilitres	28.41
pints	litres	0.568
gallons	litres	4.55
Weight		
ounces	grams	28.35
pounds	kilograms	0.45359
tons	tonnes	1.016

Decibel scale

The decibel (dB) is used to compare loudness or density of sound. An increase of ten decibels is equivalent to a ten-fold increase in the density of sound.

Decibels	Sound level
0	Faintest audible sound
10	Low whisper
20	Average whisper
20-50	Quiet conversation
50	Normal speech
50-65	Loud conversation
65-70	Traffic on busy street
65-90	Train
75-80	Factory (light to medium work)
90	Motorway traffic or other heavy traffic
90-100	Thunder
110-140	Jet aircraft taking off
130	Threshold of pain in the ear
140-190	Space rocket lifting off

Time zones

The Earth's surface is divided into 24 time zones. Each is 15 degrees of longitude wide, with local variations – for example, most of Western Europe keeps to time zone A, even though physically it straddles zones Z and A.

The zones begin at the Greenwich meridian (0° longitude). For every zone to the west of the Greenwich meridian, the clock time is one hour earlier; for every zone to the east, the time is one hour later. Some countries create daylight-saving hours by setting clocks one hour or more ahead of standard time for part of the year. The calendar date moves one day forward to the west of the International Date Line.

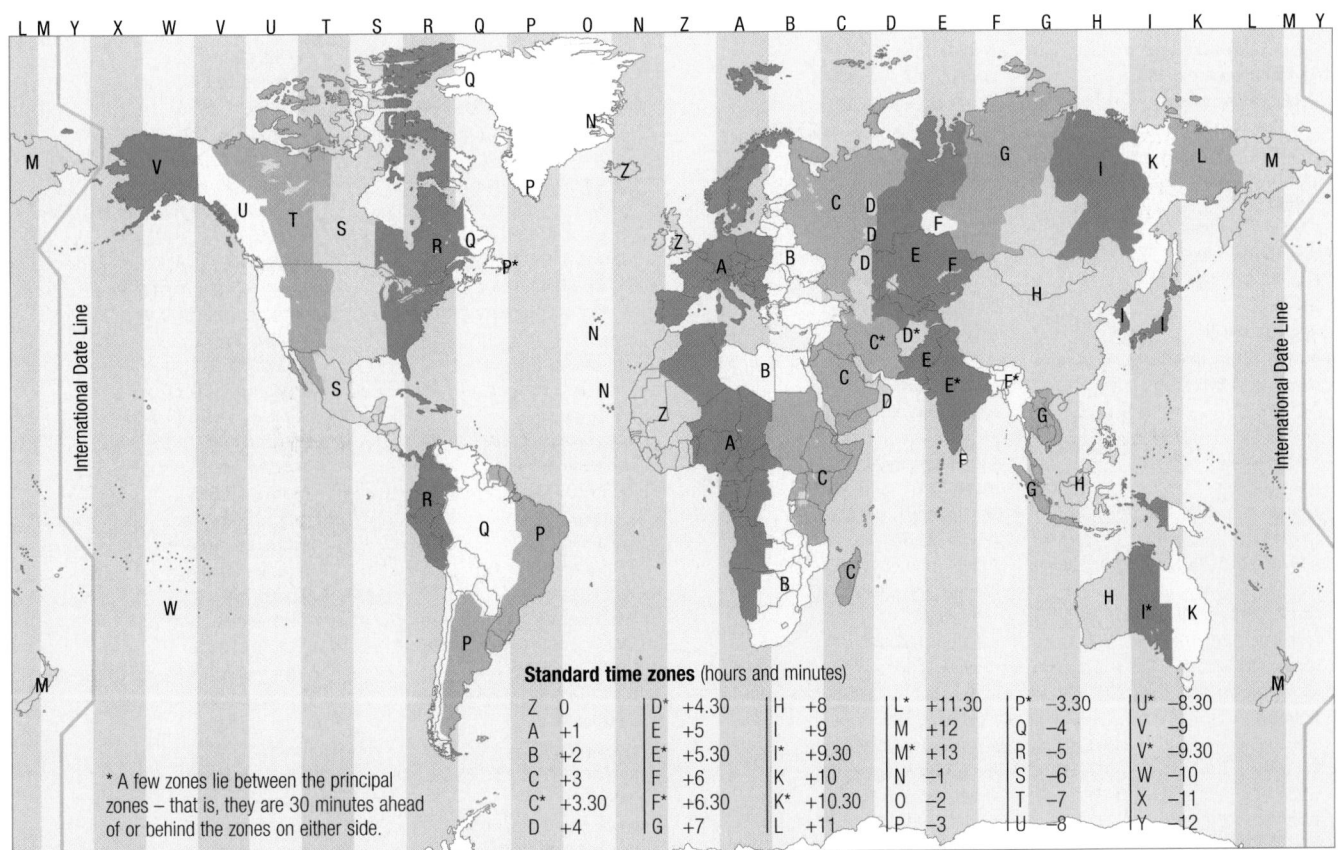

Standard time zones (hours and minutes)

Z	0	D*	+4.30	H	+8	L*	+11.30	P*	–3.30	U*	–8.30
A	+1	E	+5	I	+9	M	+12	Q	–4	V	–9
B	+2	E*	+5.30	I*	+9.30	M*	+13	R	–5	V*	–9.30
C	+3	F	+6	K	+10	N	–1	S	–6	W	–10
C*	+3.30	F*	+6.30	K*	+10.30	O	–2	T	–7	X	–11
D	+4	G	+7	L	+11	P	–3	U	–8	Y	–12

* A few zones lie between the principal zones – that is, they are 30 minutes ahead of or behind the zones on either side.

Page numbers in **bold** indicate main entries; those in *italics* indicate information in captions and/or illustrations only.

This index should be used in conjunction with the cross-referencing system in the text of the book.

A

E

J

S

U

X

Y

Z

636 Acknowledgments

Abbreviations:
T=Top; M=Middle; B=Bottom;
R=Right; L=Left

BBCNHU – BBC Natural History Unit Picture
   Library
DRK – DRK Photos
OSF – Oxford Scientific Films
SPL – Science Photo Library

Timelines: Bradbury & Williams.
2-11 © PhotoDisc Europe Ltd; ©
Digital Vision Ltd; Martin Woodward;
Image Quest 3-D; Mirashade.
13 Julian Baker Illustrations. **14**
Julian Baker Illustrations, TR; Michael
Robinson, B. **15** B. & C. Alexander, TR;
Julian Baker Illustrations, ML; SPL/PLI,
BR. **16-17** Julian Baker Illustrations.
18 Galaxy Picture Library/ESO, T;
SPL/Royal Observatory, Edinburgh, M;
SPL/T. & D. Hallas, B. **18-19** Tom
Stack & Associates/B. & S. Fletcher.
20-1 Julian Baker Illustrations.
22 SPL/NASA, ML; Julian Baker
Illustrations. **23** Galaxy Picture Library/
TRACE-1/Stanford-Lockheed Institute
for Space Research, T; Galaxy Picture
Library/KPNO/T.Rinmele, M.Hanna/
AURA/NOAO/NSF, B. **24** SPL/US
Geology Survey, TL; NASA/JPL, TM;
Genesis/NASA, TR; Artworks Ian
Atkinson. **25** NASA/JPL; Genesis/
NASA TM; SPL/STScI/NASA, TR;
Artworks Ian Atkinson. **26** Galaxy
Picture Library, ML; **26-7** SPL/NASA.
27 Michael Robinson, TR; DRK/S.
Nielsen, MR. **28** Julian Baker
Illustrations, ML; Michael Robinson, B.
29 Galaxy Picture Library/Roger
Lynds/AURA/NOAO/NSF, T; Auscape/
Jean-Paul Ferrero, B. **30** Julian Baker
Illustrations. **31** Michael Robinson;
map, Bradbury & Williams/Mountain
High. **32** Auscape/Jean-Paul Ferrero,
TR; DRK/Jeff Foott, BM; Michael
Robinson. **33** Robert Harding Picture
Library/Tony Gervis, TM; Natural
History Museum, London, BR;
Artworks Michael Robinson.
34-5 Artworks Michael Robinson;
Colorific/Greg Girard/Contact.
36 Minden/Frans Lanting, T; DRK/C.C.
Lockwood, ML; Ardea/D. Parer & E.
Parer-Cook, MM; Ardea/François
Gohier, MR; Artworks Michael
Robinson. **37** OSF/Hjalmar R.
Bardarson. **38** Michael Robinson, M;
Natural History Museum, London, BR.
39 Norman Brand, TR; Natural History
Museum, London, ML,BL.
40-1 Mountain High/Bradbury &
Williams. **41** Michael Robinson, BR.
42 SPL/Earth Satellite Corporation, TR;
Bradbury & Williams, MR; **42-3** DRK/
Kim Heacox. **43** Woodfall Wild Images/
David Woodfall, T. **44** Michael
Robinson, T; Katz Pictures/JD, BR.
45 FLPA/T. & P. Gardner, BL; John
Cleare Mountain Camera, BR.
46 Digital Vision, T; Hutchison
Library/Christina Dodwell, BL; NHPA/B.
Jones & M. Shimlock, BR. **47** SPL/
WorldSat International & J. Knighton/
Earth Satellite Corporation/WorldSat
Productions/NRSC/Tom Van Sant,
Geosphere Project/Planetary Visions.
48 Bradbury & Williams, T; Julian Baker

Illustrations, B. **48-9** Woodfall Wild
Images/David Woodfall. **50** Michael
Robinson, TR; Bradbury & Williams, M.
50-1 Woodfall Wild Images/David
Woodfall. **51** Bradbury & Williams/
Mountain High, TR; Woodfall Wild
Images/David Woodfall, ML; Ardea/
François Gohier, BL. **52** Julian Baker
Illustrations. **53** DRK/Johnny Johnson,
TR; Michael Robinson, MR; SPL/
NASA/Goddard Space Flight Centre,
BL. **54** Michael Robinson, ML.
54-5 SPL/Larry Miller. **55** Artwork
Michael Robinson; Woodfall Wild
Images/Ashley Cooper, T; DRK/Tom
Bean, ML; Tom Stack & Associates/
Mark Allen Stack, MM; Corbis/George
Lepp, ML; Corbis/Richard Hamilton
Smith, B. **56** Bradbury & Williams/
Mountain High, TR; DRK/Jeremy
Woodhouse, ML. **57** Bradbury &
Williams/Mountain High, TL; DRK/Tom
Bean, TR; Minden Pictures/Frans
Lanting, BL; Minden Pictures/Tui De
Roy, BR. **58, 59** Mountain High/Colin
Woodman, BR. **60** FLPA/S.
McCutcheon. **61** Mountain High/Colin
Woodman, BL. **63** Bruce Coleman/
Jorg & Petra Wegner; Wildlife Art Ltd.
64 SPL/PH. Plailly/Eurelios, TL; Wildlife
Art Ltd, TR; Bedrock Studios Ltd, BR.
65 SPL/Sinlair Stammers, TR; Wildlife
Art Ltd, TL, MM; Bedrock Studios Ltd,
BR. **66** Ardea/J.L. Mason, TM, TR;
WildLife Art, B. **67** Auscape/Nicholas
Birks, TR; DRK/Jeremy Woodhouse,
MR. **68-9** Wildlife Art Ltd. **69** SPL/
PH.Plailly/Eurelios, TL; Bradbury &
Williams, TR; BBCNHU/Bruce Davison,
BL. **70** SPL/Andrew Syred, TL;
OSF/Harold Taylor ABIPP, BL; Wildlife
Art, BR. **71** DRK/Tom Bean, TL;
OSF/David M. Dennis, TR, MR;
DRK/N.H. Cheatham, BL; Wildlife Art
Ltd, BR. **72** Wildlife Art Ltd.
73 Auscape/Mark Spencer, TL;
NHPA/Michael Tweedie, MM; OSF/Deni
Bown, BL; Ardea/François Gohier, MM;
DRK/Fred Bruemmer, BR. **74** Wildlife
Art Ltd, TR; Lee Peters, BL. **75** Wildlife
Art Ltd, TL, BL; SPL/Dr Jeremy
Burgess, MM; DRK/Jeff Foott, BR.
76 Bradbury & Williams. **77** NHPA/K.
Ghani, TL; NHPA/Joe Blossom,
MM; Still Pictures/Michel Viard,
TM; Ardea/Kenneth W. Fink, MR;
OSF/Edward Parker, B. **78** Wildlife
Art Ltd, MR. **79** SPL/Sinclair
Stammers, TM; Wildlife Art Ltd, ML;
Natural History Museum, London, MR.
80-1 Artworks Wildlife Art Ltd; SPL/D.
Roberts. **82** Tom Stack Associates/
David Young, TR; Reproduced by kind
permission of the Director, British
Geological Survey, NERC copyright
reserved, MM. **83** Wildlife Art Ltd, TL,
BR; Bradbury & Williams, BL. **84**
Ardea/François Gohier, TR; Bedrock
Studios Ltd/Bradbury & Williams, BM.
84-5 Bedrock Studios Ltd. **86** Tom
Stack & Associates/Tom & Therisa
Stack, TM. **86-7** Bedrock Studios Ltd.
88-9 Wildlife Art Ltd. **89** Bradbury &
Williams, TR. **90** Ardea/François
Gohier, TR; Wildlife Art Ltd, B. **91**
Digital Vision Ltd, BR. **92** NHPA J & M

Bain, MM; Artwork Wildlife Art Ltd,
MM; Digital Vision Ltd, BL.
93 Bradbury & Williams, T; Wildlife Art
Ltd, BM, BR. **94** Digital Vision Ltd, TL;
Bruce Coleman Collection/Kim Taylor,
MM; Artwork Wildlife Art Ltd, MM.
95 Bradbury & Williams, T; Wildlife Art
Ltd, BM. **96** Wildlife Art Ltd, TL, TM,
TR; Bruce Coleman Collection/Pacific
Stock, B. **97** Bradbury & Williams, T;
Wildlife Art Ltd, MM, BL; Minden
Pictures/Frans Lanting, BR.
98 Bradbury & Williams, T; Dorling
Kindersley Ltd/Frank Greenaway, BL;
Wildlife Art Ltd, MM, BR. **99** Bradbury
& Williams, T; Wildlife Art Ltd, ML, MR,
BL, BR. **100** Wildlife Art Ltd, TL; Bruce
Coleman Collection/Kim Taylor, MM;
Wildlife Art Ltd, MM; DRK/Michael
Fogden, BR. **101** Bradbury & Williams,
T; NHPA/Stephen Dalton, ML; Wildlife
Art Ltd, BR. **102** Minden Pictures/Frans
Lanting, MM; Wildlife Art Ltd, MM.
103 Bradbury & Williams, T; Wildlife Art
Ltd, MM, BR; NHPA/Stephen Dalton,
BL. **104** Wildlife Art Ltd, ML; Bruce
Coleman Collection/Kim Taylor, MM;
Wildlife Art Ltd, MM. **105** Bradbury &
Williams, T; Wildlife Art Ltd, MM, BR;
Ardea/Masahiro Iijima, BL.
106 Bradbury & Williams, T; Artworks
Wildlife Art Ltd. **107** Bradbury &
Williams, T; Wildlife Art Ltd, BL; Tom
Stack & Associates/Dave Watts, BR.
108 Bradbury & Williams, T; Wildlife Art
Ltd, ML, MR, BL. **109** Bradbury &
Williams, T; Wildlife Art Ltd, ML, MR;
DRK/Jeff Foott, BM. **110** Bradbury &
Williams, T; Wildlife Art Ltd, ML, MR;
Ardea/Zdenek Tunka, MM; DRK/Wayne
Lankinen, BL. **111** Wildlife Art Ltd.
112 DRK/Don & Pat Valenti, TR.
OSF/Robert Tyrell, BL. **113** Bruce
Coleman Collection/Jorg & Petra
Wegner. **114** DRK/Anup Shah.
115 Bradbury & Williams, T; Still
Pictures/Roland Seitre, ML; Wildlife Art
Ltd, MR; Minden Pictures/Mitsuaki
Iwago, BR. **116** Bradbury & Williams, T;
NHPA/Stephen Dalton, BL; DRK/M.
Harvey, BR. **117** Bradbury & Williams,
T; DRK/Michael Fogden, ML; Minden
Pictures/Frans Lanting, MM; Bradbury
& Williams, MR; DRK/Tom Brakefield,
BL; Wildlife Art Ltd, BR. **118** Bradbury
& Williams, T, ML; Wildlife Art Ltd, MR,
BR. **119** Bradbury & Williams, T, MR;
Wildlife Art Ltd, ML, MM, BR.
120 Wildlife Art Ltd, TL, TR, BR;
Digital Vision Ltd, TM; SPL/Eye of
Science, BL. **121** Image Quest 3-D, T;
Auscape/Lynn M.Stone, B. **122**
Gerald Cubitt, TR; Don Stephens &
Associates, ML; BBCNHU/Michael &
Patricia Fogden, BL; DRK/Marty
Cordano, BR. **123** Natural History
Museum, London, TL, TR; Mary Evans
Picture Library, TM; Doug Perrine/
Innerspace Visions, BL; NHPA/Stephen
Dalton, BR. **124** NHPA/Rod Planck,
BL; OSF/Zig Leszczynski, MM.
125 DRK/Tom Brakefield, MR; OSF/
David Haring, BL. **124-5** Bradbury &
Williams/Mountain High. **126** Bradbury
& Williams, TR, background, MM;
Wildlife Art Ltd, MM, BR. **127** Bradbury

& Williams, TR, background, MM;
Wildlife Art Ltd, MM. **128** Bradbury &
Williams, TR, background, MM, BL,
BM, BR; Wildlife Art Ltd, MM.
129 SPL/John Reader, TL; © Adrie &
Alfons Kennis, MM; Bottom left-right
DRK, Peter D. Pickford; Ardea/Jean-
Paul Ferrero; DRK/Stephen J.
Krasemann; DRK/Barbara Cushman
Rowell. **131** Mirashade. **132** Antbits,
BL; Mirashade, R. **133** Mirashade, L,
TR; Antbits, MM. **134** Mirashade, L;
Mirashade/Antbits, R. **135** Mirashade,
T; Martin Woodward, B.
136 Mirashade, L; Mirashade/Antbits,
R. **137** Antbits. **138** Mirashade.
139 Antbits, L; Mirashade/Antbits, R.
140 Martin Woodward, L; Mirashade,
R. **141** Martin Woodward, ML, MM,
BM; Mirashade, R. **142** Antbits, L;
SPL/Quest, R. **143** SPL/H. Raguet,
TM; SPL/John Burbidge, TR;
Bradbury & Williams, BR. **144** Martin
Woodward, TL; Mirashade/Martin
Woodward, R; Ishihara Plates/
Kanchara Shuppan Co Ltd, BL.
145 Martin Woodward, ML; Mirashade/
Antbits, R; Allsport USA/Mike Powell,
BL. **146** Martin Woodward. **147** Martin
Woodward, L; SPL/Prof. P. Motta, ML;
Mirashade, MR; NHPA/Stephen Dalton,
R. **148** SPL/Dr Yorgos Nikas, TR, BR.
149 Amanda Williams. SPL/James
Stevenson, BM. **150** SPL/Juergen
Berger, BL; SPL/Quest, BM; SPL/
CNRI, BR. **150-1** Martin Woodward.
151 SPL/J.C. Revy, TR. **152** Centre for
Brain & Cognitive Development,
Birkbeck College, T; Bradbury &
Williams/Kanizsa Square, BM;
background, photography Jane
Sackville West. **153** Bubbles/Angela
Hampton, TM; Katz Pictures/Karen
Kasmanski, BM; background,
photography John Meek. **154** Wildlife
Art Ltd/Bradbury & Williams.
155 Bradbury & Williams, BL;
Allsport/Tony Lewis. **156, 157** Martin
Woodward. **158** Science & Society
Picture Library, TR; Science & Society
Picture Library, ML; SPL/Custom
Medical, MR. **159** Hulton Getty, TL;
SPL/Salisbury District Hospital/Dr
Arthur Tucker/Simon Fraser/Mehau
Kulyk/Dr Monty Buchsbaum, T second
left to right; Corbis, ML; SPL/TEK
Image, MR; SPL/Dr Yorgos Nikas, BL.
163 AKG; Bradbury & Williams.
164 Maps Bradbury & Williams; Roger
Stewart, TM, MR; **165** Maps Bradbury
& Williams; Roger Stewart, TL, ML,
MR, BR. **166** Auscape/Ferrero-Labat,
TR; AKG/Erich Lessing/Natural History
Museum, Vienna, BL; AKG/Erich
Lessing/Natural History Museum,
Vienna, BR. **167** Museum of
Antiquities, University of Newcastle, TL;
British Museum, London, TR; Bradbury
& Williams/Mountain High, B.
168 Bradbury & Williams/Mountain
High, TR; Michael Holford/British
Museum, BL; AKG/Erich Lessing/
Department of Oriental Antiquities,
Louvre, Paris, BM. **169** Michael Holford/
British Museum, TL; The Art Archive/
Aleppo Museum, Syria/Dagli Orti, TM;

Bridgeman Art Library/Louvre, Paris, TR; map Bradbury & Williams/Mountain High. **170** Robert Harding/Simon Harris, TL; Michael Holford/British Museum, TR, BL. **170-1** Artwork Digital Wisdom. **171** AKG/Erich Lessing, BR. **172** Michael Holford, TR; Michael Holford/British Museum, BL; Bradbury & Williams/Mountain High, BR. **173** AKG/Erich Lessing/Musée Vivenel Compiégne, TL; AKG/Erich Lessing, TM; Michael Holford/British Museum, TR; AKG/Erich Lessing/National Museum of Archaeology, Naples, BL; Bradbury & Williams/Mountain High, BR. **174** Michael Holford, TL; Bridgeman Art Library, BR. **174-5** Map Bradbury & Williams/Mountain High. **176** Michael Holford/British Museum, TR; AKG/Erich Lessing/Louvre, Paris; Bradbury & Williams/Mountain High, BR. **177** Bradbury & Williams/Mountain High, TL; Werner Forman Archive/Viking Ship Museum, Bygdoy, TR; Bridgeman Art Library/Louvre, Paris, BL. **178-9** Map Bradbury & Williams/Mountain High. **179** Roger Stewart, TR. **180** Roy Williams, ML. **180-1** Map Bradbury & Williams/Mountain High. **181** The Art Archive/Dagli Orti, TR. **182-3** Map, Bradbury & Williams/Mountain High. **183** Werner Forman Archive/University Library, Prague, TM; Bridgeman Art Library/British Museum, London, BR. **184** Bradbury & Williams, TR, BL; AKG/Jean-Louis Nou, BM. **184-5** Corbis/© Ric Ergenbright. **185** Bridgeman Art Library/National Museum of India, New Delhi, TR; Bradbury & Williams, TL, BR; Michael Holford/Victoria & Albert Museum, London, BL. **186** Bridgeman Art Library, TR; The Art Archive/Victoria & Albert Museum, London, MR; Michael Holford/Victoria & Albert Museum, London, BL. **187** AKG/Erich Lessing/Musée Guimet, Paris, MR; The Art Archive/Gunshots, BL. **188** Werner Forman Archive/Courtesy Entwistle Gallery, London, BL. **188-9** Map Bradbury & Williams/Mountain High. **189** Michael Holford/ British Museum, TR; Werner Forman Archive/Private Collection, New York, MM. **190** Werner Forman Archive/Anthropology Museum, Veracruz University, Jalapa, TR; Werner Forman Archive, ML; Bradbury & Williams/Mountain High, MR; Werner Forman Archive/Museum für Volkerkunde, Vienna, BL; The Art Archive/Honduras Institute, Tegucigalpa/Dagli Orti, BM. **191** Map Bradbury & Williams/Mountain High; Werner Forman Archive/Musuem für Volkerkunde, Berlin, MM. **192** Jean-Loup Charmet, MM; Bildarchiv Preussischer Kulturbesitz, MR. **192-3** Map Bradbury & Williams/Mountain High. **193** Jean-Loup Charmet, TM; Bridgeman Art Library, BM. **194** *The Arnolfini Portrait*, 1434, oil on panel by Jan van Eyck, National Gallery, London/AKG/Erich Lessing, MM. **194-5** Michael Holford. **195** *The Flagellation*, c.1458, on panel

by Piero della Francesca, Galleria Nazionale delle Marche, Urbino/AKG. **196** Bildarchiv Preussischer Kulturbesitz/Kunstverein, Winterthur, TR; Bildarchiv Preussischer Kulturbesitz/Kubstmuseum, Basel, BL. **196-7** Background, *The St Bartholomew's Day Massacre*, 1572, 16th-century woodcut, German, Bibliotheque de Protestantisme, Paris/Bridgeman Art Library. **197** Corbis/© Elio Ciol, MR. **198** *Louis XIV*, 1701, oil on canvas by Hyacinthe Rigaud, Louvre, Paris/AKG/Erich Lessing; *Voltaire*, marble bust by Jean-Antoine Houdon, Louvre, Paris, BM. **199** The Art Archive/Musée de Versailles/Dagli Orti, TR; Bradbury & Williams/Mountain High, TM; Bildarchiv Preussischer Kulturbesitz/Uffizi Gallery, Florence, ML; AKG, MM; *Peter the Great*, 1717, oil on canvas by Jena-Marc Nattier, Hermitage, St Petersburg/Bridgeman Art Library, MR. **200** The Art Archive/Musée Carnavalet, Paris/Dagli Orti, BL; Bridgeman Art Library/Musée Carnavalet, Paris, BR. **200-1** Background, *The Battle of Austerlitz*, 1829, oil on canvas by François Gerard, Gallerie de Batailles, Versailles/AKG. **201** Bradbury & Williams/Mountain High. **202** Bridgeman Art Library/Private Collection, TR; Corbis/© Kevin Fleming, BL. **203** Bradbury & Williams/Mountain High, TR; Hulton Getty, BR. **204** Science & Society Picture Library, TL; Michael Holford/Science Museum, London, TR; Michael Holford/Science Museum, London, BR. **204-5** Background, Bildarchiv Preussischer Kulturbesitz. **205** State Library of New South Wales, Sydney, Australia, TL; Bridgeman Art Library/Stapleton Collection, TR; Corbis/Lewis Hine, BM. **206** The Art Archive/Richard Borough Council/Eileen Tweedy, MM; Corbis/© Paul Almasy, BL. **206-7** Map, Bradbury & Williams/Mountain High. **207** AKG/Archiv für Kunst & Geschichte, Berlin, TR. **208-9** Popperfoto, T; Maps, Bradbury & Williams/Mountain High. **210-11** David King Collection. **212** Bradbury & Williams/Mountain High, MM; Hulton Getty, BR; background, *Unemployed in the San Francisco Job Centre*, 1938, photograph by Dorothea Lange/AKG. **213** Hulton Getty, TR, BL; AKG, MM, BR. **214** Corbis, TM; The Art Archive/National Archives, BR. **214-15** AKG. **215** The Art Archive/Imperial War Museum, TM; © Magnum/Robert Capa, BL; Hulton Getty, BR. **216** ©Magnum/Nicolas Tikomiroff, ML. **216-17** Map, Bradbury & Williams/Mountain High. **217** Hulton Getty, BR. **218** Hulton Getty, BR. **218-19** © Bettmann/Corbis. **219** © Magnum/Susan Meiselas, ML; © Magnum/Philip Jones Griffiths, MR; AKG, BR. **220** © Bettmann/Corbis, TR; Corbis/© David & Peter Turnley, BR. **220-1** © Magnum/Jean Gaumy. **221** Corbis/David & Peter Turnley, TR; Frank Spooner Pictures/Patrick Piel, BL;

Corbis/© David & Peter Turnley, BR. **223** Esto/Tim Griffiths. **224-325** Maps © Readers Digest/revised and updated by Bradbury & Williams. **228** View/Dennis Gilbert. **230** Bradbury & Williams. **233** Scanpix. **235** Environmental Images/Martin Bond. **236** Bradbury & Williams, TL. **238** Esto © Ralph Richter. **241** Katz Pictures/Tommaso Bonaventura/Contrasto. **242** Bradbury & Williams, BR. **243** Katz Pictures/Jeremy Nicholl, TR; Corbis/© Layne Kennedy, BL. **244** Colin Woodman, BR. **245** Corbis/Reuters NewMedia Inc. **247** © Magnum/A. Venzago, MR. **248** Colin Woodman, BR. **250** Sonia Halliday Photographs, TL; The Art Archive/Archaeological Museum, Naples/Dagli Orti, TR. **252** Trip/M. Barlow. **254** Colin Woodman, TR. **255** Trip/T. Noorits, MM; Katz Pictures/Visum/Gerd Ludwig,BR. **258** Popperfoto. **260** Katz Pictures/Ben Gibson, BR. **261** Bradbury & Williams, MM. **263** © Magnum/Harry Gruyaert, BM. **264** Frank Spooner Pictures/Peterson, BL; Colin Woodman, BR. **269** Bradbury & Williams, TL. **270** Robert Harding Picture Library/James Green, MM. **272** Bradbury & Williams, MM; Esto/© Tim Griffiths, B. **275** Frank Spooner Pictures/Gamma, TR. **276** Bradbury & Williams, B. **277** © Magnum/Stuart Franklin, TR. **279** Popperfoto, BR. **280** Bradbury & Williams, ML; Popperfoto, BL. **281** Environmental Images/Mark Fallander, TR. **282** Bradbury & Williams, TR. **287** B. & C. Alexander, TR. **288** South American Pictures/Charlotte Lipson, ML. **290** Colin Woodman. **291** Katz Pictures/Tomasz Tomaszewski, BL. **298** Trip/Ben Belbin, B. **300** DRK/Jeff Footte, ML. **301** Trip/B. Gadsby, TR. **303** South American Pictures/© Tony Morrison, BL. **305** © Magnum/Stuart Franklin, BR. **310** OSF/Martyn Colbeck, BL. **326-7** The World Bank Group (WB): The International Bank for Reconstruction and Development (IBRD), International Development Association (IDA),International Finance Corporation (IFC), Multilateral Investment Guarantee Agency (MIGA); APEC; NATO; OECD. **328** Bradbury & Williams, BL. **331** Robert Harding Picture Library; Angelo Hornak Library; Arcaid/Richard Bryant. **332** Colin Woodman. **333, 334-5** Bradbury & Williams. **336** Bradbury & Williams, TR; Bridgeman Art Library/National Archaeological Museum, Athens, ML; Ronald Grant Archive, MM; Bridgeman Art Library, MR. **337** Ronald Grant Archive, TR; Bridgeman Art Library/Pergamon Museum, Berlin, BM. **338** Ronald Grant Archive, TR; Bridgeman Art Library/National Museum, Stockholm, BM. **339** Bridgeman Art Library/Bradford Art Galleries and Museums, TR; Werner Forman Archive/National Museum of Anthropology, Mexico, BL. **340** Colin Woodman. **341** Corbis/Richard T. Nowitz, TR; Bridgeman Art Library/

Koninklijk Museum voor Schone Kunsten, Antwerp, BR. **342** Bridgeman Art Library/Musée Condé, Chantilly, BR. **343** Michael Freeman, ML; © Magnum/Fred Mayer, BR. **344-7** Mirashade. **348** AKG, TL, TR; Bettmann/Corbis. **349** Left-right: Bettmann/Corbis; Topham Picturepoint; Corbis/Roger Messmeyer; Corbis/David Reed. **350** Bridgeman Art Library/Pinacoteca Capitolina Palazzo Conferratori, Rome, TR; Popperfoto, BM. **351** Bridgeman Art Library/British Library, London, TL; SPL/NASA, MR. **352** SCALA/Museo Nazionale, Napoli, TR; *The Visitation*, column statues from east portal of north trancept, c.1220, stone, Chartres Cathedral/Bridgeman Art Library/Peter Willi, MR; *The Apollo of Piombino*, Greek bronze, 1st century BC, Louvre, Paris/Bridgeman Art Library/Peter Willi, BL. **353** *The Wilton Diptych: Richard II presented to the Virgin and Child by his Patron Saint John the Baptist and Saints Edward and Edmund*, 1395-9, anonymous, tempera on panel, National Gallery, London, TR; *St Francis Honoured by a Simple Man*, 1296-7, fresco by Giotto di Bondone, San Francesco, Upper Church, Assisi/Bridgeman Art Library, BR. **354** *The Infanta Doña Margarita of Austria*, c.1660, oil on canvas by Diego Velázquez de Silva, Museo Nacional Del Prado, Madrid/Collection of Philip IV, TR; *David*, 1501-4, marble by Michelangelo Buonarroti, Galleria dell'Accademia, Florence/Bridgeman Art Library, ML; *The Supper At Emmaus*, 1601, oil and tempera on canvas by Michelangelo Merisi da Caravaggio, National Gallery, London, MR. **355** *The Death of Germanicus*, 1627, oil on canvas by Nicholas Poussin, The Minneapolis Institute of Arts/The William Hood Dunwoody Fund, TM; *The Avenue at Middelharnis*, 1689, oil on canvas by Meindert Hobbema, National Gallery, London, MM. **356** *Three Graces*, marble by Antonio Canova, V&A Picture Library, TR; *The Swing*, 1767, oil on canvas by Jean-Honoré Fragonard, Wallace Collection, London/Bridgeman Art Library, ML; *Rain, Steam, and Speed – The Great Western Railway*, oil on canvas by Joseph Mallord William Turner, National Gallery, London, MR. **357** *Burial at Ornans*, 1849-50, oil on canvas by Gustave Courbet, Musée d'Orsay, Paris/Bridgeman Art Library, TM; *Las Veneris*, 1873-5, oil and gold paint on canvas by Sir Edward Burne-Jones, Laing Art Gallery, Newcastle-upon-Tyne, Tyne & Wear/Bridgeman Art Gallery, ML. **358** *The Kiss*,1886, marble by Auguste Rodin, Musée Rodin, Paris/Bridgeman Art Library, TR; *The Waterlily Pond with the Japanese Bridge*, 1899, oil on canvas by Claude Monet, Private Collection/Bridgeman Art Library/Peter Willi, MM; *Guernica*, 1937, oil on canvas by Pablo Picasso, Museo Nacional Centro de Arte Reine Sofia, Madrid/Bridgeman Art Library/D.A.C.S., BR. **359** *The Fate of the*

Animals, 1913, oil on canvas by Franz Marc, Oeffentliche Kunstsammlung Basel, Kunstmuseum/Photography Martin Bühler, TL; *Metamorphosis of Narcissus*, 1937, oil on canvas by Salvador Dali, © Tate, London 2001, MR; *Velocity of Cars and Light*, 1913, oil on card by Giacomo Balla, Moderna Museet, Stockholm/Bridgeman Art Library/Peter Willi/D.A.C.S., BL. **360** *Blue Poles: Number II*, 1952, enamel and aluminium painted on glass by Jackson Pollock, Australian National Gallery, Camberra/Bridgeman Art Library/D.A.C.S., TR; *Mademoiselle Pogany III*, 1933, plaster by Constantine Brancusi, Musée National d'Art Moderne, Paris/Bridgeman Art Library/Peter Willi, TL; *Puppy*, 1992, by Jeff Koons, Guggenheim Museum, Bilbao/© Jeff Koons Productions, MM; *In the Car*, 1963, magna on canvas by Roy Lichtenstein, Scottish National Gallery of Modern Art, Edinburgh/Bridgeman Art Library/D.A.C.S., MR; *Cold Dark Matter: An Exploded View*, 1956, mixed media by Cornelia Parker, © Tate, London 2001/© Cornelia Parker, BL. **361** *American Collectors (Fred and Marcia Weisman)*, 1968, acrylic on canvas by David Hockney/© David Hockney, TM; *The Physical Impossibility of Death in the Mind of Someone Living*, 1991, tiger shark, glass, steel, 5% formaldehyde solution, by Damien Hirst, Saatchi Gallery, London/© Damien Hirst/photograph courtesy Science, MM; *Kangaroo Island, South Australia 26 February 1992* by Andy Goldsworthy/© Andy Goldsworthy, BL; **362** *Pastrycook, Cologne 1928* photograph by August Sander/© Die Photographische Sammlung/SK Stiftung Kultur-August Sander Archiv, Cologne, TL; *Grand Canyon from Point Imperial*, 1942, photograph by Ansel Adams/© Ansel Adams Publishing Rights Trust/Corbis, TR. **363** *Sunday on the Marne River*, 1938, photograph by Henri Cartier-Bresson/© Henri Cartier-Bresson Magnum, TL; *American Soldier, Leipzig, 18th April, 1945*, photograph by Robert Capa/© Robert Capa/Magnum, LR. **363-4** Background Bradbury & Williams. **364** Science & Society Picture Library. TM; Roy Williams, MR, BL, BR. **365** © Kodak/Weber Shandwick Worldwide, TM; Middle left-right: Michael Freeman, 1, 2, 3, 6; © Fuji, 4; © Kodak/Company Care, 5; Bottom left-right: Michael Freeman, 1, 2; Bradbury & Williams, 3, 4, 5, 6. **366-7** Middle left-right: Scala, 1, 2, 3, 5; Corbis/Ruggero Vanni, 5; Angelo Hornak, 6. **367** Martin Woodward, BM. **368-9** Middle left-right: Angelo Hornak, 1, 5, 7; View/© Andrew Holt, 2; View/© Nick Hulton, 3; Robert Harding Picture Library, 4; Arcaid/© Richard Bryant, 6; Arcaid/© John Edward Linden, BR. **370-1** Top left-right: V&A Picture Library, 1; Bridgeman Art Library/Private Collection, 2; Christie's Images, 3;

Bridgeman Art Library/Wallace Collection, London, 4; Bridgeman Art Library/Bethnal Green Museum, London, 5; Bridgeman Art Library/Fine Art Society, London, 6; Bottom left-right: Bridgeman Art Library, 1; Bridgeman Art Library/Private Collection, 2; Sotheby's Picture Library, 3, 4; V&A Picture Library, 5; © Philippe Starck, 6. **371** Silk Public Relations, TR. **372** Christie's Images. **373** Corbis/© James L. Amos, TR; Rex Features, BL; Crafts Council/© Jacqueline Mina 2000, BR. **374** The Art Archive/University of Heidelberg/Dagli Orti, TL; Christie's Images, TR; **375** V&A Picture Library, TL; AKG, TR; Bradbury & Williams, BM. **376** AKG/Breitkopf & Haertel Archive, Leipzig, TL; Lebrecht Collection, TR; Bradbury & Williams, BL; Lebrecht Collection/Robin Del Mar, BR. **377** AKG/Archiv für Kunst und Geschichte, Berlin, TL; Lebrecht Collection/George Newson, TR; Zoë Dominic Collection/© Catherine Ashmore, BL. **374-7** Timeline, *Prelude and Fugue in B minor for Organ*, handwritten score, Leipzig, c.1740 by J.S. Bach/Lebrecht Collection. **378** Brown Brothers, TL, BR. **379** © Bettmann/Corbis TR, ML; London Features. Redferns/© Michael Ochs Archives, TL, BR; © Bettmann/Corbis, TR. **381** Corbis/© Matthew Mendelsogn, TL; London Features, BR. **382** Redferns/David Redfern, TL; © Bill Cooper, ML; Redferns/Pankaj Shah, BR. **383** Rex Features, TR; Ronald Grant Archive, BL; Zoë Dominic, BR. **384** Bridgeman Art Library/Museo Archaelogico Nazionale, Naples, TL; Dante reading from the Divine Comedy, 1465 panel by Domenico di Michelino, Duomo, Florence, TM; *Portrait of Chaucer, from the Ellesmere Manuscript of Canterbury Tales by Chaucer* (facsimile edition), 1911/Bridgeman Art Library/Private Collection, TR; Mary Evans Picture Library, BL. **385** Bridgeman Art Library/British Library/Portrait engraving by Droeshurt, 1623, TM; *The Simoniac Pope*, pen, ink and watercolour, 1824-7 by William Blake, © Tate, London 2001, BL. **386** Bridgeman Art Library/Private Collection/Portrait by Nicholas de Largilliére, TL; Bridgeman Art Library/Private Collection, TR; Bridgeman Art Library/Private Collection/watercolour by John Nixon, BR; *John Milton's Signature*/Hulton Getty. **387** Bridgeman Art Library/Private Collection/Portrait engraving by C. Rolls, TL; Bridgeman Art Library/Neue Pinakothek, Munich/Portrait by Joseph Carl Stieler, TR; Mary Evans Picture Library/H. Richter, engraved by Staines, BR; *Pushkin's Signature*/© Novosti, London; *Goethe's Signature*/AKG. **388** © Novosti, London, TL; Bridgeman Art Library/Private Collection, TM; Hulton Getty, TR; Mary Evans Picture Library/Engraving by Marcus Stone, BL; © John

Glashan/from *Things*, edited by Tony & Carol Burgess (Ward Lock Educational), BR; *Tolstoy's Signature* and *Dostoevsky's Signature*/© Novosti, London. **389** © Bettmann/Corbis. **390** © Allan Titmuss/*The Oedipus Plays* by Sophocles, TL; Mander & Mitchenson Theatre Collection/*The York Cycle of Mystery Plays*, TR; © Catherine Ashmore/*Thyestes* by Seneca, MM; Martin Woodward, B. **391** © Simon Annand/*The Miser* by Moliere, TM; © Zoë Dominic/*King Lear* by William Shakespeare, ML; © Zoë Dominic/*The School For Scandal* by Richard Sheridan, MR. **392** © Mander & Mitchenson The, TM; © Haga Library Inc. Tokyo/© Toshiro Morita/Noh play *Othello*, ML; © Mark Drouet/Arena Images/*Uncle Vanya* by Chekhov, MR; © John Haynes/*Home* by David Storey, BR. **393** © John Haynes/ *Schweyk In The Second World War* by Bertolt Brecht, TL; © Zoë Dominic/ *Inadmissible Evidence* by John Osborne, TR; © Zoë Dominic/*Happy Days* by Samuel Beckett, MM. **394** Ronald Grant Archive, TR, ML; Joel Finler Collection, BM. **396** Joel Finler Collection, TR; Ronald Grant Archive, B. **397** Ronald Grant Archive, BL; Pictorial Press Limited, BR. **398** © Carolco/Kobal, TM; Rex Features, B. **399** © Lucas Film Ltd/Paramount/Kobal, ML; Ronald Grant Archive, BR. **394-8** Timeline, Ronald Grant Archive. **400** Rex Features/Denis Cameron. **401** © IMAX Corporation. **402-3** Timeline left-right: © BBC, 1; © Globe Photos Inc, 2; Culver Pictures, 3; SPL/NASA, 4; Rex Features, 5; © Sky News, 7; Popperfoto, 6, 8. **404** Topham Picturepoint, TL; Popperfoto, TR; Martin Woodward, BR. **405** Science & Society Picture Library, ML; © Magnum/Harry Gruyaert, MR; Martin Wooward, TR, BR. **406** Popperfoto, BM, BR. **407** Adrian Cronauer, BM; Katz Pictures/© Jason Bell, BR. **408** Science & Society Picture Library, TL, TR. **408-9** Backgound, SPL/NRSC Ltd/Artwork, Roger Stewart. **409** Hulton Getty, TM; Science & Society Picture Library, TR; SPL/Photo Library International, MM; Artwork, Bradbury & Williams, MM. **410** Paris Match Magazine, ML; John Frost Newspaper Collection, MR; Popperfoto, BL. **411** Hergé/Moulinsart 2001, BL; Printed by permission of the Norman Rockwell Family Trust Copyright © 1958 the Norman Rockwell Family Trust/AKG, BR. **412** Christine Vincent, MM; Bridgeman Art Library/British Library, BL. **413** Roy Williams, TL; Bradbury & Williams, BL, BM, BR. **414** John Meek, TL, BR; Advertising Archives/Trademarks reprinted by kind permission of Apple Computer, Inc. © 2001 Apple Computer, Inc. All rights reserved. Apple Mac and Macintosh are trademarks of Apple Computer, Inc, registered in the US and other

countries. iBook and iMac are trademarks of Apple Computer, Inc, TM; Marin 2001, TR; IKON Imaging, BL; FujiFilm Digital Imaging, MR. **415** IBM is a registered trademark of International Business Machines Corporation, TL; FedEx © Federal Express, TR; © Esso/Advertising Archives, MM; Lexis/Guinness, BR. **416** Corbis/© David & Peter Turnley, TR. **416-17** Timeline left-right: Mary Evans Picture Library, 1, 4; Bridgeman Art Library/Musée Carnavalet, Paris, 2; Hulton Getty, 3; Topham Picturepoint, 5; © Bettmann/Corbis, 6; Popperfoto, 7; Frank Spooner Picture Library/Gamma/Daniel Simon, 8; Rex Features/David Abian, 9; Rex Features, TR. **418-19** Middle left-right: Robert Harding Picture Library/© Roy Rainford, 1; Corbis/© Adam Woolfitt, 2; Corbis/© Jonathan Blair; Robert Harding Picture/© M. Joseph, 4; Corbis/© Richard T. Nowitz, 5; Corbis/© Catherine Karnow, 6; Corbis/© Diego Lezama Orezzoli, 7; Corbis/© Ted Spiegel, 8. **418** The Anthony Blake Photo Library/© RDL, BR. **419** Robert Opie Collection, TR. **420** Colin Woodman, T; Corbis/© Patrick Ward, BR. **421** Colin Woodman, T; Corbis/© Marc Geranger, MM. **422** Allsport, TM; Corbis/© Reuters NewMedia Inc, TR; Roger Stewart, BM. **423** Popperfoto, TR; Allsport/Hulton Collection, BL; www.sporting-heroes.net, BM; Colorsport/Olympia, BR. **424** Brown Brothers, TR; Allsport/Andy Lyone, MR; Colorsport, BL; Roger Stewart, BM. **425** Colorsport, TR; www.sporting-heroes.net, MR, BL; Roger Stewart, BM. **426** Hulton-Getty, TR; Allsport/Hulton-Getty, BL; Roger Stewart, BR. **427** Culver Pictures, MR,BR; Roger Stewart, BL. **428** © Bettmann/Corbis/David Tulis, ML; Allsport/Jonathan Daniel, BL; Roger Stewart, BR. **429** Colorsport, T; Allsport/Glenn Gratty, BR. **430** Colorsport, TR; www.sporting-heroes.net, B; **431** Allsport/David Cannon, T; Corbis/© Tony Roberts, ML; Corbis/© Tony Roberts, BR. **432** www.sporting-heroes.net, TM; Roger Stewart, BM. **433** Corbis/© Jerome Prevost, TL; www.sporting-heroes.net, BL; Roger Stewart, TR, BR. **434** Popperfoto, TR; © Bettmann/Corbis, BL; Roger Stewart, MM. **435** www.sporting-heroes.net, ML; SPL/Professor Harold Edgerton, BM; © Bettmann/Corbis, BR. **436** AKG/Albert Meyer, TL; Popperfoto, BL; Hulton-Getty, BR. **436-7** Background, Corbis/© Karl Weatherly. **437** Popperfoto, TM; Allsport/Gray Mortimore, ML; Allsport/Mike Hewitt, BR. **438** Corbis/© Jerry Cooke; Allsport, BM, BR. **439** Roger Stewart, T; Colorsport. **440** © Bettmann/Corbis, TR; Popperfoto, BL; Roger Stewart, MM. **441** Allsport/Hulton-Getty, TL; © Bettmann/Corbis, BL, BR. **442** Popperfoto, ML; LAT/© Peter Spinney, MR. **443** Allsport/Jon

Ferrey, TL; Allsport/Germano Gritti, TR; Allsport/Pascal Rondeau, MR. **442-3** Darren R. Awuah. **444** Colorsport, TR; © TempSport/ Corbis/Jean-Yves Ruszniewski, MM; Allsport/Mike Hewitt, BL; Roger Stewart, BR. **445** Popperfoto, background, BM; Roger Stewart, TR; Bradbury & Williams, BR. **446** Hulton-Getty, TR; Popperfoto, ML; Allsport/Adam Pretty, B. **447** SPL/ Professor Harold Edgerton, ML; Allsport/Shaun Boterill, MM; Roger Stewart, MR. **448** Corbis/© TempSport, TL; © Bettmann/ Corbis, MR; Roger Stewart, BL; © Bettmann/Corbis, BR. **449** Colorsport, TR; Corbis, BL; Popperfoto, BR. **450** Popperfoto, TL; www.sporting-heroes.net, TR; Sport.The Library, BL. **451** Popperfoto, TR; Roger Stewart, MM; Colorsport, BM. **453** Bradbury & Williams/Mountain High; Rex Features. **454-5** Bradbury & Williams/Mountain High. **456** Corbis/© Steve Raymer, BL; John Meek, BM; © The Economist Newspaper Ltd, 2001, BR. **456-7** Bradbury & Williams/Mountain High. **458** Diner's Club UK, TM; © Archivo Iconografico, S.A./Corbis, MM; Timeline, The Art Archive/Private Collection/Dagli Orti; Werner Forman Archive, BL; SCALA, BR. **459** © Archivo Iconografico, S.A./Corbis, MM; Timeline, Rex Features/Simon Walker; Corbis/© Charles O'Rear, BR. **460-1** Corbis/© Larry Lee. **462** Background, © Ford, BL; Artworks, Stefan Morris. **463** Top left-right: © Bettmann/Corbis, 2; Mary Evans Picture Library, 3; AKG, 4; © Hulton-Deutsch Collection/Corbis, 5; © Bettmann/Corbis, 6, 7; Corbis/© Roger Ressmeyer, 8; Artwork, Bradbury & Williams, T; Stefan Morris, BL **464** Panos Pictures/Duncan Simpson, MM; Corbis/Ted Spiegel, BM. **464-5** Map, Bradbury & Williams/Mountain High. **465** Background, Panos Pictures/Chris Sattlberger. **466** Martin Woodward, TR, BL. **466-7** Timeline, © Magnum/ Stuart Franklin. **467** Holt Studio International, TR; Panos Pictures/ Jeremy Horner, B. **468-9** Top-bottom, SPL/Astrid & Hanns-Friedler Michler, 1; SPL/Ed Young, 2; Still Pictures/Michel Breuil, 3; SPL/BSIP JOLYOT, 4; Still Pictures/Sophie Boussamba, 4. **470** SPL/Jeremy Walker. **471** SPL/Time David, TL; SPL/Cyril Ruosso, TR; Robert Harding Picture Library, BR. **472** Map, Bradbury & Williams/Mountain High. **473** Martin Woodward. **474-5** Map, Bradbury & Williams/Mountain High. **475** Still Pictures/Gil Mott, TL; Bradbury & Williams, TR; © Vic Sievey; Eye Ubiquitous/Corbis, BR. **476** Brown Brothers, TM; Science & Society Picture Library, BL, BM; © Volkswagen, BR. **477** Roger Stewart, TL; Science & Society Picture Library, TR; LAT, BL; Neill Bruce, BM; Alvey & Towers, BR. **478** Matthew White. **479** Bradbury & Williams. **480** © Bettmann/Corbis,TM; © Hulton-

Deutsch Collection/Corbis, MM; Science & Society Picture Library, BL, BR. **481** Background, Rex Features. SPL/Martin Bond, TM; © Hulton-Deutsch Collection, TR; SPL/François Sauze, BR. **482** Martin Franklin, T; The Art Archive/Dagli Orti, ML; Bradbury & Williams, B. **482-3** Background, The Art Archive/National Maritime Museum, London/Eileen Tweedy; Bradbury & Williams, BM; TRH Pictures, BR. **484** Stefan Morris, TR; Brown Brothers, ML. **484-5** Background, TRH Pictures; Artwork, Stefan Morris. **485** Mark Franklin, TL; TRH Pictures, TR; Bradbury & Williams, B. **486** SPL/ Jean-Loup Charmet, ML; SPL/David Parker, BL. **487** Bradbury & Williams, TR; © National Maritime Museum Picture Library, BL; Corbis/© The Military Picture Library/Peter Russell, MR. **488** Science & Society Picture Library, ML, MR; BR. **488-9** Background, The Flight Collection; Artwork, Mark Franklin. **489** The Flight Collection, TL; Aviation Photographs International, TR. **490-1** Matthew White. **491** Bradbury & Williams, MR. **492** SPL/Novosti, TL; NASA, BR. **492-3** Background, NASA. **493** Toucan Books, MR; SPL/US Geological Survey, BR. **494** Bradbury & Williams, ML; NASA, MM. **494-5** Background, SPL/NASA. **495** NASA. **496** Bradbury & Williams, TR; John Meek, BL. **497** Frank Spooner Pictures/Pace, ML; Allsport/Al Bello, MR; Kobal Collection/Miramax Films/Universal Pictures, BR. **498-9** Map, Bradbury & Williams/ Mountain High; Artwork, Bradbury & Williams; background, © Magnum/ Bruno Barbey. **500-1** Background, Corbis/© Bill Ross; Artwork, Mark Franklin; Timeline, Stefan Morris; Map, Bradbury & Williams/Mountain High. **502-3** Artwork, Matthew White; background, Corbis/© Charles E. Rotkin. **503** Corbis/© Roger Ressmeyer, BR. **504** Still Pictures/Julio Etchart, TR; Stefan Morris, BL; Matthew White, BR. **504-5** Background, Still Pictures/Julio Etchart; Timeline, Stefan Morris. **505** Matthew White, BL; Still Pictures/ Mike Jackson, BR. **506** Still Pictures/ Hartnut Schwarzbach, TR; Corbis/© Paul Almasy, BL. **506-7** Background, Corbis/© Roger Ressmeyer. **507** Bradbury & Williams, TL; Corbis/© Ecoscene, BL; Panos Pictures, BR. **508-9** Background, Panos Pictures/© Marc Schlossman. **509** SPL/Astrid & Hans Frieder Michler, TM; SPL/Russ Lapa, BL. **511** Martin Woodward; Bradbury & Williams. **513** Natural History Museum, London, MM; *Rain, Steam, and Speed – The Great Western Railway*, oil on canvas by Joseph Mallord William Turner, National Gallery, London, BR; Artwork, Bradbury & Williams, BM. **516-21** Artwork, Bradbury & Williams. **522** © Bettmann/Corbis, TR. **522-3** Artwork, Roger Stewart. **523** Bradbury & Williams, ML; Roy Williams, MR. **524-35** Background,

Corbis/© George Hall. **526** Bradbury & Williams. **527** Dorling Kindersley Ltd, TR; Roger Stewart, BR. **528-9** Top left-right: Rex Features, 1; John Meek, 2; SPL/NASA, 3; Woodfall Wild Images/Jeremy Moore, 4; Corbis/© Leif Skoogfors, 5; SPL/Hugh Turvey, 6; SPL/US Air Force, 7. **530** Bradbury & Williams. **531** © CERN, BM; Artwork, Bradbury & Williams, BM. **532-3** Bradbury & Williams, **534** AKG. **535** Matthew White, TL; MM; Bradbury & Williams, BL. **536-7** Martin Woodward. **538**, **539** Natural History Museum, London. **540-1** Martin Woodward. **542** Still Pictures/Klaus Andrews, ML; SPL/Tony Craddock, BM; Artwork, Bradbury & Williams, BM. **543** The Garden Picture Library/ Brigitte Thomas, TR; SPL/Tony Craddock, BM; Artwork, Bradbury & Williams, BM. **544** Martin Woodward. **545** Martin Wooward, BL; Woodfall Wild Images/Niel Hicks, BM; BBCNHU/Chris O'Reilly, BR. **546** Antbits, BL; Bradbury & Williams, MR. **547** Bradbury & Williams. **548** Bill Ballenberg/NGS Image Collection, TR; Painting, Alberto Gutiérrez/photograph Guillermo Hare, ML; Christopher Donnan/© Walter Ava/Bruning Museum, BR. **549** Artwork by Roger Stewart adapted from the painting of the Burial Chamber of Tomb 2 by Percy Fiestas, BL; Christopher Donnan/© Walter Ava/Bruning Museum, BR. **550** © Bettmann/Corbis, TR; The Art Archive/Francesco Venturi, MM; Courtesy Discovery Channel/UAD/ photo Jerome Delafosse, MR; Griffith Institute/Ashmolean Museum, Oxford, BL. **550-1** Map, Bradbury & Williams/ Mountain High. **551** Jon Adams, University of Southampton, MR. **552** Brown Brothers, TR; Michael Holford/Science Museum, BM; Science & Society Picture Library, BR. **553** Science & Society Picture Library, TM; Michael Holford/Royal Institution, London, ML; Robert Opie Collection, MR, BM. **554** © Reader's Digest, TR; Science & Society Picture Library, BL; Robert Opie Collection, BR. **555** Science & Society Picture Library, TM; SPL/ Adam Hart-Davis, ML; Trip/Dyson, R. **556** Rex Features, TL; Science & Society Picture Library, TM; SPL/Library of Congress, TR. **556-7** Background, Woodfall Wild Images/ David Woodfall; Artwork, Martin Woodward. **557** Science & Society Picture Library, TR; Science & Society Picture Library/NASA, MM. **558** Science & Society Picture Library, TR, BL; SPL, BR. **559** © Bettmann/ Corbis, TL; Science & Society Picture Library, TR, BL; Frank Spooner Pictures, BR. **560** Bradbury & Williams, TR; Science & Society Picture Library, BL. **561** © Steve McDonough, MM; Intel Corporation, BR. **562** Martin Woodward. **563** Digital Vision, BR. **564** Sotheby's Picture Library, TR; Robert Opie Collection, BL; Mark Franklin, BR. **565** © Sony, TL; Science & Society Picture Library, TM; Rex

Features/Adrian Denis; Mark Franklin, BL, BR. **566** Paul Baran, ML; © Vint Cerf, MR. **567** Bradbury & Williams, T; Frank Spooner Pictures/Carolina Salguero-FB, ML; Frank Spooner Pictures, MR. **568** Timeline, Science & Society Picture Library, MR; SPL/Jean-Loup Charmet, BM. **569** SPL/Stanley B. Burns, MD/The Burns Archive, New York, TL; SPL/George Bernard, TR; SPL, MM; Popperfoto, MR; Timeline, Science & Society Picture Library/ NMP/RMD. **570** Timeline, SPL/BSIP Boucharlet; SPL/St Mary's Hospital Medical School, MM; SPL/James King-Holmes, BL. **571** SPL/Geoff Tompkinson, TR; Timeline, SPL/James King-Holmes; AKG, MM; SPL/National Institutes of Health, BM. **572** The Art Archive/Dagli Orti, TL; © Magnum/ Fred Mayer, BR. **572-3** Background, Mark Franklin. **573** The Art Archive/ Eileen Tweedy, TL; Frank Spooner Pictures/ Gamma/Roger Viollet, TM; © Magnum/Stuart Franklin, BM. **574** Darren R. Awuah, TR; Trip/B. Gibbs, BR. **574-5** Background, Collections/B. Shuel. **575** Stefan Morris, TL; Corbis/ © Michael S. Yamashita, TR; Mark Franklin, BL. **576** AKG/Erich Lessing/ Israel Museum (IDAM), Jerusalem, TL; © The Board of Trustees of the Armouries (VII.1809), TM; © The Board of the Trustees of the Armouries (II.2), TR; Mark Franklin, BM. **577** British Library, London, TM; Chrysalis Images, TR; © The Board of the Trustees of the Armouries (Xii.5438), BL; Bridgeman Art Library/British Library, BM. **578** The Tank Museum, Bovington, MM; Chrysalis Images, BM. **579** TRH/DOD, ML; Timeline,TRH/McDonnell Douglas Missile Systems Company; TRH/Lockheed, MR; Chrysalis Images, BM. **581** Bradbury & Williams. **588** Stefan Morris. **592-3** Bradbury & Williams. **584** Bradbury & Williams. **605** Colin Woodman.

Section dividers: NASA. Bruce Coleman Collection/Kim Taylor; Wildlife Art Ltd. Martin Woodward. Michael Holford/British Museum. Corbis/© Ron Watts. Christie's Images. John Meek. Martin Woodward. Kobal Collection. © PhotoDisc Europe Ltd. © Digital Vision Ltd.

Covers: © PhotoDisc Europe Ltd. © Digital Vision Ltd.

Acknowledgments

Facts at your Fingertips was published by The Reader's Digest Association Limited, London

First edition Copyright © 2001 The Reader's Digest Association Limited, 11 Westferry Circus, Canary Wharf, London E14 4HE
www.readersdigest.co.uk

We are committed to both the quality of our products and the service we provide to our customers.
We value your comments, so please feel free to contact us on 08705 113366 or by email at:
cust_service@readersdigest.co.uk

If you have any comments or suggestions about the content of our books, email us at:
gbeditorial@readersdigest.co.uk

Copyright © 2001 Reader's Digest Association Far East Limited.
Philippines copyright © 2001 Reader's Digest Association Far East Limited

All rights reserved. No part of this book may be reproduced, stored in a retrieval system, or transmitted in any form or by any means, electronic, electrostatic, magnetic tape, mechanical, photocopying, recording or otherwise, without permission in writing from the publishers.

© Reader's Digest, The Digest and the Pegasus logo are registered trademarks of the Reader's Digest Association, Inc., of Pleasantville, New York, USA

Facts at your Fingertips was edited and produced by Toucan Books Ltd, London for the Reader's Digest Association Limited, London

Contributing authors
Sarah Angliss   Julia Bruce
Thomas Cussans   Mike Flynn
Richard German   Robin Hosie
Antony Mason   Nigel Rodgers
Carmine Ruggiero   Elizabeth Taylor
Helen Varley   Christine Vincent
John Wright   Michael Wright

Managing editors
Helen Douglas-Cooper
Andrew Kerr-Jarrett
Robert Sackville West

Editors
Alison Bravington   Liz Clasen
Celia Coyne   Finny Fox-Davies
Daniel Gilpin   Simon Hall
Jane Hutchings   Justine Johnstone
Cécile Landau   Marion Moisy
Alison Moss   Charlotte Rundall
Simon Tuite   Richard Walker
Susan Watt   Michael Wright

Researcher
Michael Paterson

Picture researchers
Sandra Assersohn   Christine Vincent
Caroline Wood

Consultants
Dominic Alexander   Sarah Angliss
Jock Boyd   David Burnie
Brian Candy   Joan Candy
Alison Ewington   Nigel Hawkes
David Kynaston   Frank Meddens
Colin Uttley

Proofreaders
Roy Butcher   Ken Vickery

Indexer
Laura Hicks

Design
Bradbury and Williams

Toucan Books would also like to thank the following for their assistance in the preparation of this book: Ian Barnett Central School of Ballet, London Janet Guggenheim   John Meek Alice Palmer   Stevie Williams

For Reader's Digest, London

Project Editor
Jonathan Bastable
Art Editor
Julie Bennett
Editorial assistants
Rachel Weaver   Liz Edwards
Proofreader
Barry Gage

Reader's Digest, General Books, London

Editorial Director
Cortina Butler
Art Director
Nick Clark
Executive Editor
Julian Browne
Publishing Projects Manager
Alastair Holmes
Development Editor
Ruth Binney
Picture Resource Manager
Martin Smith
Style Editor
Ron Pankhurst

Book production manager
Fiona McIntosh
Pre-press manager
Howard Reynolds
Senior production controller
Sarah Fox
Pre-press technical analyst
Martin Hendrick

Origination
Colour Systems Ltd

Printing and binding
Brepols, Belgium

ISBN 0 276 42498 0
BOOK CODE 040-961-01
CONCEPT CODE UK 1050/IC